International Business Law

Environments and Transactions

John H. Willes,
Business Affairs International

John A. Willes, Q.C.
Queen's University

McGraw-Hill Irwin

Boston   Burr Ridge, IL   Dubuque, IA   Madison, WI   New York   San Francisco   St. Louis
Bangkok   Bogotá   Caracas   Kuala Lumpur   Lisbon   London   Madrid   Mexico City
Milan   Montreal   New Delhi   Santiago   Seoul   Singapore   Sydney   Taipei   Toronto

 **McGraw-Hill Irwin**

INTERNATIONAL BUSINESS LAW: ENVIRONMENTS AND TRANSACTIONS
Published by McGraw-Hill/Irwin, a business unit of The McGraw-Hill Companies, Inc., 1221
Avenue of the Americas, New York, NY, 10020. Copyright © 2005 by The McGraw-Hill
Companies, Inc. All rights reserved. No part of this publication may be reproduced or distributed
in any form or by any means, or stored in a database or retrieval system, without the prior written
consent of The McGraw-Hill Companies, Inc., including, but not limited to, in any network or
other electronic storage or transmission, or broadcast for distance learning.
Some ancillaries, including electronic and print components, may not be available to customers
outside the United States.

Disclaimer: The wide range of topics in this text limit the treatment of the law to only the most general statements
of what are often complex, specialized and constantly changing areas of the law; consequently, the text content is not
intended nor should it in any way be considered as a substitute for the prompt and timely advice of competent legal
counsel in the jurisdictions concerned. No professional relationship is created, nor legal opinion rendered, between
the authors or publisher and any users of the text. The names and facts used in the discussion cases and examples are
entirely fictional, and any similarity to persons or corporations is entirely coincidental.

This book is printed on acid-free paper.

1 2 3 4 5 6 7 8 9 0 CCW/CCW 0 9 8 7 6 5 4

ISBN 0-07-282251-1

Vice president and editor-in-chief: *Robin J. Zwettler*
Editorial director: *John E. Biernat*
Senior sponsoring editor: *Andy Winston*
Marketing manager: *Lisa Nicks*
Project manager: *Marlena Pechan*
Manager, New book production: *Heather D. Burbridge*
Design Coordinator: *Mary E. Kazak*
Supplement producer: *Joyce J. Chappetto*
Senior digital content specialist: *Brian Nacik*
Cover design: *Eric Kass/Lodge Design*
Typeface: *10/12 Times Roman*
Compositor: *ElectraGraphics, Inc.*
Printer: *Courier Westford*

Library of Congress Cataloging-in-Publication Data

Willes, John H.
  International business law : environments and transactions / John H. Willes, John A. Willes.
    p. cm.
  Includes index.
  ISBN 0-07-282251-1 (alk. paper)
  1. Export sales contracts—Cases. 2. International business enterprises—Law and
legislation—Cases. 3. Foreign trade regulation—Cases. 4. Business law—Cases. I. Willes,
John A. II. Title.
K1030.W55 2005
343'.087—dc22   2003067174

www.mhhe.com

I dedicate my work to those who bore its greater weight in my absence: my family—my wife Carol and children Victoria, John, George, and Amelia. This book is an offering to any reader who has felt the flicker of wonder and a tinge of anticipation about discovering what lies over the next hill or in distant lands. JHW

This book, in a sense, is a family effort, but it would not have materialized had it not been for the encouragement and enthusiasm of my wife Fran. My special thanks go to her, and to her, this dedication. JAW

About the Authors

John H. Willes *BComm, LLB, MBA, LLM, CIM, FSALS, Barrister, Solicitor, Notary Public, Of the Bar of Ontario, Canada.*

John Henry Willes is an Ontario barrister and solicitor. For many years he taught at Queen's University in both the Faculty of Law and the School of Business in the MBA, Bachelor of Laws, and Bachelor of Commerce programs. He is the past coordinator and principal instructor of the Queen's University International Business and International Law Programme at Herstmonceux Castle International Study Centre in the United Kingdom.

He holds Bachelor of Commerce, Bachelor of Laws, and Master of Business Administration degrees from Queen's University, and a Master of International and Comparative Law from Vrije University, Brussels, Belgium. He also holds a Canadian Investment Manager designation from the Canadian Securities Institute. He has been elected as a Fellow of the Society for Advanced Legal Studies, in London, England, and was a Visiting Fellow at the University of London, England, in 2002.

In addition to serving clients in North America and western Europe, his business activities include advising on legislative transition in the republics of the former Soviet Union and enterprise restructuring and business management in the People's Republic of China. He is a member of the editorial advisory board of the *European Financial Law Review*. He is co-author of the seventh edition of *Contemporary Canadian Business Law* (McGraw-Hill Ryerson).

John A. Willes, Q.C. *BA, LLB, MBA, LLM; Barrister, Solicitor, Notary Public, Of the Bar of Ontario, Canada*

John A. Willes is a barrister and solicitor, and Emeritus Professor of Business Law and Labour Relations at the School of Business, Queen's University. He was called to the Bar of Ontario in 1960 and joined the faculty of Queen's University in 1969, where he assumed responsibility for the business law program. Throughout his teaching career, he carried on an extensive corporate/commercial law practice, and has acted as an arbitrator in hundreds of commercial and industrial disputes. During his long career as a lawyer, he has provided legal advice to many clients with extensive business interests in the United States, Canada, the Caribbean, and abroad. He was appointed as a Queen's Counsel by Her Majesty Queen Elizabeth II in 1984.

He holds a Bachelor of Arts degree from Queen's University; Bachelor of Laws and Master of Laws degrees from Osgoode Hall Law School, York University; and a Master of Business Administration degree from the University of Toronto. He completed the Program of Instruction for Lawyers at Harvard Law School in 1982. In addition to *Contemporary Canadian Business Law* (McGraw-Hill), he has authored numerous academic monographs and cases, and is the author of *Contemporary Canadian Labour Relations* (McGraw-Hill), *Canadian Labour Relations* (Prentice Hall), and *Out of the Clouds,* the official military history of the first Canadian Parachute Battalion in World War II.

Brief Contents

Contents

Chapter 14
Taxation of International Business Transactions 602

Foreword

Whether you are a business student or law student (and, undoubtedly, you recognize you are a bit of both), you are entering a demanding field that will challenge you in many ways—personally and professionally. This text will make those challenges plain to you. It also will equip you to deal with their foundations and to grow with them, as they become more complex.

Your interest in studying international business law and your later career will, with diligence, be highly rewarding. You will probably find, as we have, that the personal and emotional rewards will surprise you, motivate you, and even exceed the very significant financial rewards that are offered in this field.

If you are a law student now, your future may go well beyond merely domestic legal matters. If studying this course is any indication, you are interested in international affairs, and that preexisting interest will urge you to keep abreast of international developments, often ahead of both other lawyers and your clients. Sometimes these interests will lead you to new clients, and at other times your interests will attract clients to you. By ensuring that the senior members of your firm are aware of your interests, you may find yourself handed files or tasks that have international dimensions. In time, this field can become your specialty, or an adjunct to your domestic expertise.

If you are a business student now, your future will take on an international dimension even more easily. If your business does not seek out international business opportunities, then foreigners may seek you out, either as a competitor or as an ally. By studying this subject, you are making yourself more capable of dealing with the challenge. More so, you will be in a better position to get the most out of your relationship with an international lawyer. You will better understand the business options and transactions open to you. You will understand the reasons and risks that lie behind the strategies offered up by your lawyer. By being on the same wavelength, you and your lawyer can craft effective solutions together, to give your business the best possible chance of success in the international arena.

No matter who you are, by keeping yourself informed on international developments, and by being able to analyze their potential impact, you may, in the future, have the potential to make strategic offerings to the business at hand, in addition to making tactical offerings of legal or management services. In short, you may become a strategic advisor rather than just a line manager or service provider.

There are many employment options that provide exposure to international business transactions. Be it a law firm, business enterprise, or a multinational firm, many offer work abroad and many domestic firms engage in international transactions. Employment opportunities also exist in government or international organizations, or national or multinational corporations with established business interests abroad.

International training may give you the opportunity to travel the world, from days to years, to meet and work with people from as many backgrounds as you wish, and to engage in continuous personal and professional growth and learning. It is work in a dynamic world of changing environments and changing needs and responses, where powers of observation, knowledge, analysis, planning, and execution will be demanded, and the rewards will be limited only by your efforts.

The above is our point of departure in offering this text to you, the student. With them, we welcome you to the principles and practice of international business law.

Preface

Purpose of This Text and Learning Outcomes

The purpose of this text and its learning outcomes are

- To provide a clear, readable explanation of foundation topics in international business law for students in law and management studies.
- To create an understanding of how and why international business law affects business risks, opportunities, and the profitability of business ventures.
- To equip students with the knowledge and tools required to use international business law in creating effective corporate international business strategies and in executing international business transactions.
- To address the need for law students and future lawyers to understand more about their client's international business objectives.
- To address the need for business students and future businesspersons to understand their legal options and their lawyer's abilities and limitations to accommodate their international business objectives.
- To broaden student understanding of the divergent value systems and legal systems that will be encountered in the practice of international business and international business law.

Who Should Use This Text?

This text is written with two groups of students in mind: those enrolled at business schools and those at law schools. This dual focus strengthens this text, for it recognizes the reality that businesspersons need to know more about the law, and lawyers need to know more about business, in order to work more effectively together and to succeed in international business transactions.

This point deserves deliberate emphasis. Our experience as international lawyers, international businesspersons, and college and university instructors in both has made it plain that these disciplines have been held separately for too long. We are encouraged to see that this attitude has changed significantly in recent years, and this text is intended to reinforce that change.

Being a lawyer is being a businessperson. President Abraham Lincoln, also a lawyer, said, "Time and advice are a lawyer's stock in trade." He saw no distinction between a lawyer and a businessperson. To the extent that this text aids a law student, it increases in the future his or her ability to advise. To the extent that it aids a business student, it helps minimize his or her need to pay for that time and advice. Indeed, Lincoln would say advice, like time, is money.

Scope of This Text

This text is probably one of the first you have opened on the subject of international business law, and we thank you for the opportunity to share with you our knowledge and experience and the collected knowledge and experience of others.

As you might imagine, international business law is at work when any foreign element is introduced into an otherwise domestic business transaction. Also as you might imagine, like all other areas of the law, this subject can and does spawn entire libraries of books on the subject.

Our text provides an introduction to the most important and most frequently encountered aspects of international business law. These are the various environments of international business law (home country laws, host country laws, and international law and regulation), the primary relationships between players (business enterprises, service providers, and international bodies), and the principal transactions employed in international business (import–export, licensing, and investment).

As an introductory text, it is charged with a heavy responsibility. It cannot deal with all topics, nor can it deal in any detail on the topics it does cover. As a result, we have made many choices, including or excluding material. We have worked to include topics that will be of greatest value to ensure that you complete your course with a good map of the broad range of issues that await you in either advanced courses or later commerce or practice.

A number of good texts are available that cover broadly similar issues and facts. In writing this one, its readability has been uppermost in our minds. As a result, it is written in the plainest possible language, bearing in mind its professional subject. We hope you find it a pleasure to read.

As you might already know, law is a field of study where every rule or hard fact has its exceptions. Rather than deal with each exception in a dreary search that leaves no stone unturned, this text focuses on issues and situations that commonly occur. This does not, however, mean resorting to useless generalities. It means that the discussion of law and business found here does apply in the vast majority of situations, and we leave it to you to raise questions about the exceptions. When a "what if" question arises in your mind, you are probably on the right track toward an exception. Likewise, where a principle of law clearly fits with U.S. legal traditions, you shouldn't be surprised that it might not square with expectations in France, China, or Saudi Arabia.

We have aimed at including considerable detail in those areas where knowledge of fundamental building blocks is at stake. Less detail is offered on issues that change rapidly, so that you absorb key aspects and fill in what you need when you need it, without having to later "unlearn" the old. Equally, some areas appear only rarely in practice, and these are best served with a knowledge of the basics now, and further study as and when required.

Perspective

The text is written from a largely Anglo-American perspective, both in terms of the common law tradition and those aspects of business generally familiar to Anglo-American students. This is only a starting point, however, as emphasized in the "Themes" section below.

As this is an introductory text, we are aware that our own perceptions and biases will carry weight in setting or altering your own initial perceptions and biases in the subject. This creates the responsibility on us to confine our writing to views that are broadly held across the international business law community, or to note otherwise where divergent opinions exist. We have tried to fulfill this responsibility to the best of our ability, and to make clear that our opinions are our own when we are in the global minority.

Themes

Within the overall goal of a text blending legal and business considerations, there are a number of other critical themes. These go well beyond simply a statement of law and its relationship to international business. These are discussed in the following paragraphs.

Broadening the Individual Perspective

One of the central challenges of international business law is to understand and accept the different perspectives held by persons elsewhere in the world. This text accommodates that need to observe, analyze, understand, and incorporate differing perspectives by drawing on legal and business principles from around the world. Successful practitioners (in business or law) must look beyond their own borders, to the drivers that influence the behavior of foreign businesses and lawmakers. This exercise in personal growth requires examination, understanding, and acceptance of the history, geography, culture, economics, politics, and, finally, law of foreign lands. If this essential skill is not learned early on, your later business or practice will suffer. Lessons learned solely through experience often carry a very high price tag.

Dynamic and Proactive—Getting beyond the Empty Words

Businesspersons, lawyers, and politicians often speak of dynamic processes and proactive behavior, and then fail miserably at understanding the first and accomplishing the second. This is unacceptable, and this text aims to give you the tools to succeed where others may fail.

International business and law are dynamic processes, meaning that they change over time, often rapidly. Therefore, you cannot expect simple memorization of either law or business facts to turn you into a good professional in either arena. Storing facts costs only cents per megabyte these days, and such limited ability will get you no further than the back-office operation of a corporation or law firm. You must understand these dynamics or you will be left behind, frozen in time. Likewise, your textbook cannot be limited to facts, but must reveal these dynamics.

Something dynamic has a past, a present, and a future; it has come from somewhere, is somewhere, and is going somewhere else. To understand a dynamic such as the law obligates you to know more than just its present state. You must learn where it has come from, its history, and the possible direction that it is headed. A dot on a page is meaningless, while a vector is a dynamic: it has another dot, a line between theory that it has followed, and an arrow for its direction. From the point of view of our textbook, this means providing you with background, context, and history. It must not jump right into the current state of the law—that is territory for a practitioner's loose-leaf updated reference book.

As a student, you must learn where the law has come from to understand its state now, and to understand the direction in which it is going. Second, be aware that the line probably won't go straight ahead forever. All the forces bearing on the law must be understood, to get a more focused picture of what the future may look like. This represents a commitment to multidisciplinary study and the broadened individual perspective, coming to grips with the links that tie the law to business, economics, politics, history, and culture. Any law, anywhere, reflects a blend of local social demands, economic realities, political compromises, and historical experiences. These must be understood to grapple with the future.

It is this knowledge that opens the door to becoming proactive, to position yourself to take advantage of change. Being proactive requires you to anticipate changes in the coming future and adjust your strategies now, to be ready for those changes. This text sets out the dynamic and allows you to make proactive choices. You supply the initiative and courage to make them.

The Business Enterprise and Private Law Viewpoint

International business law has many stakeholders pushing their own interests. Governments desire economic growth; unions worry about jobs, and action groups are concerned about social conditions at home and abroad. Consumers demand goods from around the world at a fair price, while businesses focus on profits. That said, each of these stakeholders has a full slate of secondary interests, some shared and some not. A treatise on the law might canvass a wide range of these stakeholders, but our text is restricted to the factors that bear directly on business enterprise management. With the same intention, we address international public law (the law between nations) only to the extent that it affects private business transactions and the options and decisions of business enterprises.

Risk Management, Opportunity Identification, and International Business Strategy

No two societies on earth are identical. This simple fact breeds enormous opportunities in global commerce but at the same time creates a wide array of risk factors that require sound management responses. Many of these risks can be avoided or minimized by using and practicing the principles of international business law. These same principles also can be applied to capture or maximize the business opportunities afforded abroad. Going beyond just what the law is and where it is going, our text strives to make clear how and why international business law can be applied to transactions to create the best possible business outcomes.

Successful transactions are vital to international business success, but they must be aimed at a particular overall goal. A corporate international business strategy is required to determine that goal and to map out a pathway for achievement. International business law has an important role to play in setting that strategy, just as much as it provides the tools for tactical success. Our text sets out where legal considerations enter into the strategic decision making of the business enterprise.

Special Features

At many points throughout the text, special feature boxes appear. These are intended to challenge your thinking on the spot, to provide you with tips and tricks learned normally through experience, or to provide examples of international business law unfolding in domestic or international media.

The Old Wolf box will contain valuable tips, tricks, and strategies that you can add to your briefcase of tools—short illustrations of the text material as applied in practice, or the consequences of not doing so. They often illustrate the seeds of a problem being planted or the efforts made to avoid or resolve a thorny problem. All are drawn from the collective experience of the authors or other practitioners—sometimes at quite a price! This box also will contain statements intended to challenge conventional wisdom, or advance arguments that are often marginalized or ignored in mainstream discussion. Some can be effectively countered; others present irreconcilable differences or value judgments. They may be wise or foolish, practical or impossible, popular or unpopular, but each represents a sentiment that will be encountered by a practitioner or student.

The **Front Page Law** box will contain extracts from current news items that illustrate international business law principles at work, or situations that will soon require the intervention of international legal analysis or action.

Acknowledgments

We would particularly like to thank:

- Professor Don Macnamara of Queen's University, whose views on international issues were an early and important motivation for this text.
- Professor Barry Rider of the Institute of Advanced Legal Studies at the University of London, United Kingdom, home of one of the world's great libraries on international and comparative law, for his encouragement and the resources he placed at our disposal;
- The staff of Queen's University Law Library, whose attention to our inquiries was most appreciated;
- Our students over the years, who knowingly and unknowingly were the anvil upon which most of our teaching material was wrought;
- Our reviewers, for their time, effort, and expertise that was so clearly evident in their comments and suggestions, which we have tried to the greatest extent to incorporate, our omissions and inaccuracies being ours alone;
- Andy Winston, Sponsoring Editor and Marlena Pechan, Project Manager, of McGraw-Hill for their sponsorship, management, and support throughout, together with Betsy Blumenthal, Copyeditor, who took our manuscript and through their professionalism and skill turned it into a book; and
- Fran Willes, wife of one author and mother of the other, our liaison with our publisher and professional secretary of the Old School: part typist, editor, proofreader, project manager, whipcracker, and majordomo. In short, dear reader, but for her, none of this nor one of us would be here.

This text includes several important forms provided by the International Chamber of Commerce. Regarding these forms, we offer the following information:

- *ICC Uniform Customs and Practice for Documentary Credits–1993 Revision*
  ICC Publication No. 500—ISBN 92.842.1155.7
  Published in its official English version by the International Chamber of Commerce
  Copyright © 1993–International Chamber of Commerce (ICC), Paris
- *The ICC Model International Sale Contract*
  ICC Publication No. 556 E—ISBN 92.842.1210.3
  Published in its official English version by the International Chamber of Commerce
  Copyright © 1997–International Chamber of Commerce (ICC), Paris
- *Incoterms 2000^{TM} & ®**
  ICC Publication No. 560 (E)—ISBN 92.842.1199.9
  Published in its official English version by the International Chamber of Commerce, Paris
  Copyright © 1999–International Chamber of Commerce (ICC)

All available from ICC Publishing S.A., 38 Cours Albert ler, 75008 Paris, France; and www.iccbooks.com.

*Incoterms is a trademark of ICC, registered in the European Community and elsewhere.

The Environment of International Business and Law

Every profession has its technical skills, but these have little value without a good understanding of the context in which they are used, just as a handbook on desert survival is of no use to a sailor adrift in a lifeboat. The tools of international business law require context as well, and this is made up of its environments and relationships.

Therefore, the objectives of this part are to provide an understanding of

- International business and international business law environments, through an examination from a number of angles: the historical, geographical, sociocultural, political, and economic.
- The relevant elements of international law and international business law.

Chapters in this part are

1. The International Business Environment
2. The Foundations of the International Legal Environment
3. Principles of International Law
4. Public Organizations and International Agreements
5. Regional Integration

Chapter 1

The International Business Environment

Chapter Objectives

This textbook begins with a discussion of international business. While it is unusual to begin a legal textbook with something other than law, again context and perspective are important. You may already have completed a course on international business, in which case this chapter presents review material, or you may be new to the subject. Either way, this chapter is valuable, but even more importantly, this chapter gives you insight into the way the authors view the subject that is regulated by international business law. This viewpoint may be different than your instructor's view or your own. Here you will find

- A capsule outline of the business issues requiring legal responses that will be dealt with in the text.
- An introduction to the primary business players and interests who will become the shapers, negotiators, con-

  tractors, and litigants in international business law.
- The connection between international business law and the creation of international business strategy.

What Is International Business?

International business, in the minds of most people, is the image of heavy crates being loaded onto overseas freighters, or perhaps the well-dressed businessperson negotiating deals in distant capitals. These images are part of international business, but the definition is much broader. Simply, international business is any domestic business operation that includes an international element.

International elements create time and distance complications, which translate into increased transaction cost and risk. Factors such as differences in language, culture, expectations, economics, politics, laws, regulation, and international relations create their own barriers and costs. They also create opportunities. Goods, services, intellectual property, and investment funds in one country may find a ready market or more profitable opportunity elsewhere. These four categories are the principal markets of international business, and the degree of risk escalates as a business moves from goods to investments.

Principal Markets in International Business

- Goods
- Services
- Intellectual property
- Investment

2

Much has changed in the field of international business since the end of World War II. These changes can be collected under the headings of mobility, technology, and mindset. Mobility refers to the increased ability for goods, services, intellectual property, capital, and persons to move freely around the globe. This ability was achieved through technological advances (the practical means) and the more liberal mindset of governments (regulatory environment) surrounding these flows.

The first half of the 20th century was an unparalleled period of economic strife joined with the horror of global war. Nations of the world found that they must focus on the common interests that bound them together, rather than the issues that drove them apart.

The route adopted (consciously and unconsciously) has been to bind together the interests of the nations of the world, so as to make war unlikely, or, more hopefully, impossible. It has had its successes and failures, but on balance it has succeeded, certainly avoiding an all-out World War III.

This change in mindset has no parallel in the history of the world. It saw the creation of international organizations such as the United Nations, the World Bank and International Monetary Fund, and the World Trade Organization, which would have been unthinkable examples of international cooperation prior to the 1914–1918 First World War.[1]

Beyond international organizations, the practical opening of freer trade between nations has incrementally evolved. International negotiations have resulted in less protectionism through the lowering of tariffs on imports (border charges levied) and the lowering of nontariff barriers (such as customs inspection delays or unreasonable product standards). This openness allows nations, through their business enterprises, to take advantage of opportunities that might otherwise lie undeveloped in each other's territory. Such business activity creates bonds between nations—investments, supply and service relationships, and the movement of people. It takes away mistrust and suspicion and replaces them with shared interests and cooperation.

The change in mindsets applies to persons as well as government. Canada and the European Union have dramatically embraced the cultural diversity that has been the norm in the United States. Diversity in relationships also applies outside countries, and technology allows people from different backgrounds to have ever greater and easier access to one another and their respective businesses.

With this ease come more frequent cultural misunderstandings and their potential, if left unresolved, to damage business relationships even before they start. Significant parts of this text are devoted to these types of problems and those that will be encountered in international business law transactions.

This human and technological mobility was opened up through changes in governmental mindsets, but it was advances in technology that allowed business enterprises to capitalize on the shift, most importantly in all of the supporting industries that make business viable: banking, insurance, shipping, and communications. Quick and secure international financial links, more frequent and cheaper air travel, even more reliable and efficient containerized shipping, and widespread electronic communications have played their part to create mobility.

The individual business firm and its transactions lie at the heart of international business, but the commercial options open to the firm are shaped by its surrounding environments—the economic and political. These are among the primary drivers of international business law.

In the past, the political environment was the most powerful or superior environment. Arguably this has changed with the emergence of a global economy in the absence of a global government. Economic events have brought home the degree to which the world

---

[1] See www.un.org, www.worldbank.org, www.imf.org, and www.wto.org.

economy is integrated: the massive increase of oil prices in the 1970s, the default on debt payments of some Latin and South American countries in the 1980s, and the crisis in confidence in Asian currencies in the 1990s. Integration is felt in bad times as well as good.

While nations strive to protect their economy like the king in a game of chess, the most powerful single piece is the queen—the political environment. Through it, nations can take steps to advance their interests and those of their real international business players—their firms.

The Relationship between Primary Environments, the Firm, and Markets

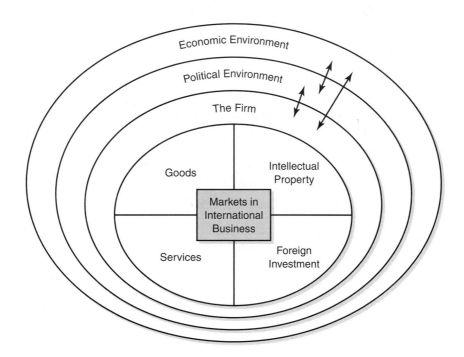

Each of the principal markets for international business firms—goods, services, intellectual property, and investments—has seen its share of changes described in the previous pages and we can examine each market in turn, from the perspective of its surrounding environments.

Trade in Goods

The Economic and Political Perspectives

Trade in goods is the natural starting point for the study and the practice of international business law, as its importance to the welfare of virtually all nations of the world cannot be underestimated. The term *goods* in international trade law includes all commodities, raw materials, and semifinished components and manufactured articles that leave or enter a particular territory. Examples include Saudi Arabian oil, U.S. lumber, Taiwanese microchips, and German automobiles, respectively. As these are tangible items, in the form of merchandise bought and sold, trade in goods is also known as *visible trade* or *merchandise trade*.

Consider an imaginary world of two nations, each making two products, milk and honey. It may well be that Country A is "better," or more efficient, at making both prod-

International trade does not create or entrench inequity in standards of living. In the extreme, nations that choose not to trade at all are left to continually reinvent the wheel, consuming vast quantities of national resources, when the answer to their needs may be purchased elsewhere much more cheaply, from someone who has already done the work. There are times when being self-sufficient and not relying on trade with others is important, such as to ensure basic food or energy supplies during times of war or emergency, but it is rarely prudent in the rational and coordinated development of nations, absent compelling reasons in national priorities.

ucts than Country B. In short, based on using the same inputs of labor and resources, Country A is capable of making more of both items. At first glance, then, international trade would seem impossible between these two countries, for why would the people of Country A ever consider swapping their milk for Country B's honey when they can do just as well or better themselves?

The answer lies in the principle of comparative advantage, and the relationship between the relative price of milk and honey in each country. Assume Country A produces milk and honey with equal ease. The price relationship in Country A will be 1:1, trading one unit for the other. Country B may be an inefficient producer of both, but assume it is even worse at making honey, say four times more inefficient. The price relationship in Country B will be 1:4, with a unit of milk priced at four units of honey. In isolation these economies will carry on with these prices, but what happens if they are allowed to trade with each other?

Looking across the border, the milk producers in Country A see that they can receive four units of honey for each unit of milk, where they received only one before. By the same token, the honey producers of Country B see a land abroad where only one unit of honey is needed to obtain a unit of milk, instead of giving up four. The resulting trade flows will set a price somewhere between the two extremes, but as long as the two nations specialize in the product where they have the greatest superiority *or* least inferiority, each will be able to consume more of both products.

The result is not without its drawbacks; it arises from the lower standard of living and wages originally existing in Country B, for initially honey producers in Country B only receive one-quarter of the milk received by their counterparts in Country A. In the end, Country A will say its suppliers are being undercut, and Country B will argue its workers are being exploited. Regardless, the income of both countries is rising as a result of trade. In the long term, the "winner" is the nation that prudently invests that income in productive tools, national infrastructure, and social development. The "loser" is the one that chooses to consume its increased income with no provision for the future.

Reality, of course, skews the economist's so-called perfect world. Some nations are endowed with more resources than others. All have different priorities, but even more suffer because of it. Defense and international relations impose unique one-time and ongoing costs. Corruption, waste, poor decisions, bad timing, and luck play a role, just as much as level playing fields and good decisions.

National governments are intensely interested in patterns of trade and its relationship to international affairs and domestic economic health. For statistical purposes and decision making, overall trade in goods is broken down into exports (goods sold and leaving a territory) and imports (goods bought and entering a territory). When these two amounts are totaled together, the result is an absolute measure of the international trade activity of a territory, known as its *two-way trade.*

U.S. Imports and Exports (Goods) 1980 to Forecast 2010 (Billions of Constant 1996 U.S. Dollars)

	1980	1990	2000	2010
Imports	260.6	497.9	1,315.6	2,954.5
Exports	238.9	393.2	836.1	1,821.2
Two-way trade	499.5	891.1	2,251.7	4,775.7

Source: U.S. Department of Commerce, Bureau of Economic Analysis, www.bea.doc.gov.

Two-way trade statistics are not as helpful a measure as they may seem, for they do not reveal the nature and balance of the underlying export–import activity. As a result, exports and imports are broken out separately, with exports given a positive dollar value and imports assigned a negative dollar value. Then, when added together, the result is a net balance between the two, and the measure makes up one component of a nation's *balance of payments.* Where a nation has a surplus of exports over imports, it is said to have a surplus in merchandise trade, or is a net exporter. Where the value of imports exceeds exports, the nation has a merchandise trade deficit, or is a net importer. Similar balances exist in true services, intellectual property, and investment payments, together making up a nation's *current account.*

U.S. Merchandise Trade Deficit 1980 to Forecast 2010 (Billions of Constant 1996 U.S. Dollars)

	1980	1990	2000	2010
Imports	−260.6	−497.9	−1,315.6	−2,954.5
Exports	238.9	393.2	836.1	1,821.2
Surplus (+)/ Deficit (−)	−21.7	−104.7	−479.5	−1,133.3

Source: Derived from previous table.

The significance of national accounting to international business law is that the economic performance of a nation today will become a major driver of its domestic business and foreign investment regulation tomorrow. By following trends and expectations in target market national accounts, the businessperson or lawyer can anticipate this regulation, rather than react to it.

Major shifts in current account items result in changes in currency exchange rates and interest rates, affecting international business profitability. Governments respond by either liberalizing or restricting market access through changes in tariff rates or export promotion activity. In the extreme, such shifts prompt direct government intervention in the marketplace.

The current account can be likened to the structure of a firm's income statement. For larger countries, these relative amounts would be in billions of dollars.

Current Account

Exports and Current Receipts[1]			Imports and Current Payments[2]		
Goods			Goods		
Merchandise or "visibles" trade		$ 800	Merchandise or "visibles" trade		$1,700
Services		1,500	Services		900
True services	$200		True services	$200	
Intellectual property	600		Intellectual property	100	
Payments from investments abroad	700		Payments from foreign investors	400	
Total		$2,300	Foreign aid	200	
			Total		$2,600
Current account deficit[3]		$ 300			

Equivalent to:

1. Revenue   2. Expenses   3. Loss or profit

on a corporate income statement.

This country is running a merchandise trade deficit of $900 ($800–$1,700), a balanced account in true services, and a surplus of $500 in intellectual property trade. Investment payments are in surplus, and the current account is in a $300 deficit overall, equivalent to a loss position for a business.

The final $300 current account deficit must be financed in some manner, and is reflected in the nation's "capital account" with the world, somewhat akin to a firm's balance sheet. Ignoring any changes in investment levels, government borrowing, or printing of money, the current account deficit is accounted for in changes to the Official Reserves account, the stock of a nation's foreign currency and gold.

Capital Account

Direct Investment—made abroad[1]	Foreign Investment—made at home[2]	
Opening: 10,000	Opening:	4,000	
Closing: 10,000 (no change over year)	Closing:	4,000	(no change over year)
	Liabilities to Foreign		
	Central Banks	+300	(increased over year)
	Total:	4,300	
	Official Reserves[3]		
	Opening: 6,000		
	Less: 300		(year's current account deficit)
	Closing Reserves: 5,700		
Total: 10,000	Total:	10,000	

Equivalent to

1. assets
2. liabilities
3. shareholder's equity

on a corporate balance sheet.

Major shifts in capital account items will cause governments to alter their policy toward foreign investment (either liberalizing it or prohibiting it), and may prompt a government to freeze the convertibility of its currency, or prohibit foreign currency from leaving its territory.

As far as governments and national accounts are concerned, exports are preferred to imports because they represent the end result of the fullest possible levels of national employment and utilization of resources.

A nation capable of exporting is usually fulfilling its own needs first (if it has such needs), with a surplus remaining that can be sold to other nations. Export profits enrich the seller, selling goods it could not use itself, or for which it could find a more profitable market abroad.

For example, in 2001, Denmark exported approximately $8 billion U.S. worth of agricultural produce, over and above its own consumption of its own produce. This performance is from a country of 16,000 square miles (only eight U.S. states are smaller than Denmark) and a population of 5.2 million persons. This figure represents revenue of $1,500 per person, in return for goods that the Danish population could not reasonably consume themselves. Denmark was thus in a position to purchase $1,500 per person worth of goods that it does not produce itself, or that it does not produce as efficiently, from other nations.

Not surprisingly then, exporters are the favorites of home governments around the world. Governments see importing as a drain on national resources, with money exiting the country to pay for those imports and no contribution to national employment being made. There are some rational limits to this thinking; all nations need imports, either to make their economy run in the first place (e.g., oil and energy supplies they do not have) or to enjoy the fruits of their labor (exotic imported foods, luxury goods not manufactured at home).

This is the first relationship that separates international business from domestic business—the attitude of the home government toward the economic activity. In domestic business, the government is not concerned whether you are a buyer or seller. On the international trade front, however, your government is far more willing to help and promote exporters than it is prepared to aid importers. Continuing with Denmark, consider the following report of the U.S. Department of Agriculture. The report itself is a U.S. government aid to U.S. exporters, monitoring the aid given to foreign exporters by their own governments. While the financial support offered by Denmark may seem limited, recall its total population is smaller than a large U.S. city.

Danish Promotion Activity

> Danish market promotion activities are funded primarily from producer levies and supplemented by partially rebated land and pesticide taxes, as well as a small appropriation from the legislature. These funds, which totaled about $89 million for 1998, are used primarily for domestic promotion. About $13 million is used for export promotion. Approximately $2 million of this amount is used to support activities of the Agricultural Marketing Board (AMB), which operates an office in Tokyo and coordinates Danish participation in international trade fairs. AMB is a private-sector organization that is a subdivision of the Danish Agricultural Council.
>
> Since 1995, the Danish Dairy Board has promoted exports only for Lurpak brand butter. Promotion activities are directed toward the United Kingdom, Germany, and the Middle East, which account for 85 percent of Denmark's butter exports. In the United Kingdom, television advertising dominates the budget. Other activities are brochures distributed to households and store promotions. In Germany, the activities are concentrated around Berlin and northern Germany, where the distribution is best organized. Television advertising, consumer promotions, and trade activities are dominant. In Japan, participation in FoodEx is financed by these promotion funds.
>
> The Danish Marketing Board, under the Agricultural Council, maintains an office in Japan to assist its members with sales promotions, especially for dairy and pork exports. The office helps pork exporters in their campaigns and cheese exporters in their price negotiations. The board also partly finances Danish national pavilions at major food fairs. The annual budget is $2.2 million.

Source: http://www.fas.usda.gov/cmp/com-study/1998/comp98-de.html.

A nation that runs a persistent trade deficit—as is the United States at present—will be closely watched by its international creditors (in light of its capital account) for any sign that it cannot repay the debts it is running up. On the other hand, a nation with a persistent trade surplus will be monitored for signs that it is unfairly supporting its own export sector in international trade. Japan was subject to this type of scrutiny through the 1980s. As a result, nations are both actors and targets in their relations with other countries, and must maintain active diplomatic and trade relations with others and within international organizations to protect their interests.

But in the relationship between the exporter-importer and the home government, are the interests identical? In 1952, General Motors Corporation President Charles E. Wilson testified to the U.S. Senate Armed Services Committee: "What is good for General Motors is good for the country, and what is good for the country is good for General Motors." That may have been true then, but only because, at that moment, the strategic interests of GM and the U.S. government were the same. The Korean War was raging and GM was producing the tanks and trucks the U.S. government was eagerly demanding.

The implicit warning contained within Wilson's remarks is that an exporter or importer may be either a winner or loser in a home government's international trade relations. The outcome depends on whether the business interests are sufficiently important to the government of the day.

Governments generally focus on the export welfare of entire industries, rather than the specific situation of a single company, but not exclusively so. Outside of general information and business contacts assistance offered to all individual exporters, there is the possibility of specific support, particularly where a trade dispute looms with another nation. If a particular company can exert some political influence over government, such as its corporate contribution to national employment, it may get assistance in the form of legislative action, diplomatic negotiation, or carriage of an action by the home government to an international dispute resolution forum.

The Business Enterprise Perspective
Motivations

The business enterprise is the primary force in international business and trade in goods, seeking to expand its profitability beyond its traditional home market, or to create advantages at home through sources of supply abroad. Given that it is generally easier to build a business at home than abroad, it is worth illustrating the most common motivations.

Unsatisfied needs or available sources abroad can be thought of as a prerequisite, as much as a motivation, for international trade. Constant observation of the economic, industrial, and consumer environments abroad will indicate foreign market opportunities that are within the ability of the home country trader to satisfy. These observations also may reveal alternative sources of supply of raw materials that generate cost savings in home country production operations.

Second, diversification of economic and business risk is a common motivator. Exporting finished goods or sourcing raw materials from a range of foreign countries may minimize the ups and downs of the home country economic cycle. Even if the impact of business cycle changes cannot be avoided, an international presence raises the possibility of early warning. A global network of agents, distributors, or foreign branch operations can sense these changes long before their impact arrives in the home country, and steps can be taken to attempt to insulate the firm from their effect.

Third, one of the most frequent motivations in goods trade is economy of scale. When additional production capacity is added, or a domestic economic downturn means there is available or idle capacity, addressing international markets can fill this slack. Hence, the search for new markets may take a firm into its first international sales, motivated primarily by domestic cost savings.

Finally, increased global competition is a motivation toward international trade, as a matter of both offense and defense. Advances in transport and communication allow much greater geographical range in business operations than ever before.

Motivations for International Trade in Goods

- Unsatisfied needs or available sources abroad.
- Diversification of economic and business risk.
- Lower per unit costs of production, capacity utilization.
- Increased global competition.

Through to the 1970s, Ford, General Motors, Chrysler, and American Motors had a stranglehold on the U.S. automobile market. Their dominance was first eroded with the arrival of inexpensive imported cars, later by new foreign entries into the U.S. luxury car market, and, today, by established foreign competitors with factories located within the United States. Half of the auto sales making up today's "Top 10 Models" list are a product of Japanese international business transactions and investments.

Top 10 Automobile Models Sold in the United States: Foreign Imports and U.S. Production by Foreign-Owned Manufacturers

	1971	2001
Manufacturers in Top 10 Models list	All U.S. firms	General Motors: 1,207,773 cars Honda: 1,083,657 Toyota: 954,588 Ford: 899,271
Japanese models in Top 10	None	Toyota Camry (#1), Corolla (#7) Honda Accord (#3), Civic (#4)
Units among Top 10	None	2,038,245 of a total of 4,145,289 cars
Share of "Top 10 Models" niche	0%	49%

Note: Beyond the Top 10 list of models, in 1971, *total* sales of *all* Japanese models was only 5 percent of sales of all U.S. models (according to the American Automobile Manufacturers Association).
Source: *Time Almanac 2003,* with data from Ward's AutoInfoBank, www.wardsauto.com.

International business has brought distant places closer, shrinking time to the point that the "virtual enterprise," a company without a unified physical location, is possible. Any shrinkage in time or distance represents a reduced risk factor in international operations. However, the same is true for all trade participants, and home markets increasingly come under siege by foreign competitors willing to stage a market entry. Mere presence abroad can be considered as another factor, making the home market player seem bigger (in truth or fiction) to its international competitors.

Methods of Trade in Goods

Importing   Three aspects of the international business environment shape the process of importing goods: regulatory compliance, transportation, and payment. The international business community has produced fairly standardized mechanisms to handle transportation and payment issues, but government regulation of imports is much more variable. Each is treated in a separate chapter in this text, and here we focus on broader issues in compliance.

Every country has an interest in knowing what is coming into its territory. As a result, some level of formality can be expected at every border crossing. The degree most often depends on the historical experience of the nation, its political system, and its economic orientation. Many countries, such as the United States, have a history of openness to trade that has led them to a much more informal system of import clearance than other countries whose political and economic systems are far more restrictive.

Import compliance requirements are a product of home country legislation,[2] and are in addition to any export requirements imposed by the source country. In addition, there may be home country requirements stemming from international agreements as a part of a global control regime. These may be as obvious as controls over trade in weapons or endangered animals, or less evident in commitments made to the World Trade Organization. A fuller discussion of this organization is a part of Chapter 4.

The regulation of imports goes beyond taxation and statistical monitoring by the home country of the importer. The home country has a genuine interest in the welfare of its citizens, and therefore imposes regulations aimed at preserving public safety, national security, consumer protection, health, the integrity of its agricultural environment, and the integrity of its own economic system. One example is the European Union's near-exclusion of genetically modified food products, a major cause of trade friction between it and the United States. As a result, the importer is required to comply with laws relating directly to

[2] See initially, for example, the U.S. Bureau of Customs and Border Protection, www.cbp.gov.

import practice but also with laws related to the use of the products. In many cases, these laws are complex and the importer requires expert help. These experts, known as customs brokers or freight forwarders, handle import compliance (documentation and transit) as their business and remain aware of any changes in applicable legislation. Of course, the importer itself can minimize costs on delays by keeping abreast of applicable legislation.

In addition to general regulatory compliance, some categories of goods require import licenses in virtually all countries of the world. Licenses are required for radioactive materials, weapons, drugs, and similar products. Other nations require import licenses for virtually all products that cross their borders.

Other private law matters require attention prior to importing. Often, a perspective importer must be certain of its right to market the proposed import, and that those rights have not been previously and exclusively given to someone else.

When the prospective import reaches its port of entry, compliance and taxation will be greatly affected by the type of entry desired. There are two types: entry for consumption and entry on an in-transit basis.

Entry for consumption is the most common type of import entry. Here, goods are destined for home country wholesale trade and later retail sale, or are arriving as raw materials for industrial use as commercial inputs. In either case, the goods will be consumed within the home country.

Where goods are cleared for import on an in-transit basis, no consumption will take place in the home country. The importing country merely serves as a way station as the goods progress to some further destination. For example, goods may arrive in North America by ocean freighter at a U.S. port of entry such as New York for onward shipment by truck or rail to central Canada. In this simplest form, other than for the collection of statistical data, the United States has no interest (either for taxation or control) in these goods.

Other situations also exist where the home country has little interest in bringing its full import clearance process to bear. Goods may arrive for the purposes of exhibition at a trade fair, as mere samples, or for periods of storage or warehousing against later transshipment.

Some countries also attempt to promote domestic economic activity by simplifying their import clearance process, particularly for goods that will be reworked or transformed and later exported. Special industrial areas are set aside in border regions allowing this kind of processing work with the relaxed clearance processes and, most often, duty-free transit. The United States maintains this type of localized administrative region—a foreign trade zone—along its borders with both Canada and Mexico. In other nations, particularly in the Caribbean, the vast majority of industrial production is subject to this type of regime, wherever it may be located in the country.

In entry for consumption, important parts of the import clearance process have been standardized globally. Most significant is the Harmonized Tariff System (HTS) of goods classification, establishing uniform categories of goods, similar to a catalog. National variations exist and the U.S. version comprises nearly 100 chapters, subdivided into thousands of different line items. Still, there is very little variance in goods classification across almost all other trading nations. The benefit of the system is its internationally recognized identification for a particular good.

The import clearance process is built on documentation and random or targeted inspection. Inspection of all imported goods is impossible in most nations; a timely flow of goods is critical for business operations and the system therefore relies primarily on documentation. This documentary requirement, at a minimum, includes an application for entry of goods, copies of related commercial invoices, and a bill of lading evidencing ownership of the goods. Additionally, a packing list for the shipment is usually required, as well as any certificates of origin or compliance related to the goods, and possibly a security bond for customs duties unpaid prior to release of the goods.

The import clearance process is a relationship confined to the buyer-importer and its home government. In commercial terms, however, the relationship between the buyer-importer and the seller-exporter also must be considered. Issues such as transportation insurance arrangements and payment must be settled between them. Trust, or lack of it, will play a major role. The parties will be a great distance from one another, and they may not know each other. The system of international trade has responded to this situation with tools and mechanisms necessary for dependable, trustworthy relationships. Industry standards have been established for contracts for sale and contracts of transport and insurance, as well as regimes for the inspection of goods. Standardized bank guarantees ensure payment for goods on fulfillment of delivery conditions, where the parties do not have a sufficient relationship to work on open credit account terms.

Importing is therefore a purchase transaction across a border, and differs very little in commercial terms from a domestic purchase. Both comprise a payment of a price in return for goods, based on a sales contract. It is the regulatory aspect that provides the real difference. As regulatory aspects have an attached cost in both time and money, a full knowledge of the process is critical to the profitability of any overseas opportunity.

Exporting Since every import represents a corresponding export from somewhere, an exporter must be aware of the obligations that will be faced by its buyer-importer. That realization alone goes a long way to creating stronger relationships. Equally, the exporter will face a range of issues that differ from conducting sales on a purely domestic basis.

The direct exporter is one who is dealing directly with the foreign buyer, a circumstance that gives the exporter more control (and more responsibility) for the export management process. A considerable amount of management thinking must go into the decision to become an exporter. There will be a significant research phase, large production and engineering questions to be addressed, as well as customer expectations to be managed.

For example, consider an American producer of consumer kitchen equipment. On return from an extended visit abroad, the president of the American firm may realize that there was a complete lack of toasters in a particular country. This might mean an opportunity exists, or it might not. Perhaps the people abroad do not eat toast—they take their starch from cooked rice (rather than from grain breads). A toaster would be useless to them. Even if toast is popular abroad, what issues exist in toaster engineering? Perhaps the foreign electrical system is based on 220 volts rather than the 110 volts found in the United States. Is the engineering redesign effort worth the size of the market opportunity? Maybe it isn't. Maybe it is worth it, to warn off other competitors who may sense a weakness or unwillingness in the firm to service or defend markets, including, perhaps, its own.

The potential exporter also must consider its customer's after-sale expectations. Who will do the warranty work on defective toasters? Will the American firm expect toasters to be returned to the United States for repairs? Such an approach would kill consumer interest in the product, so an overseas warranty repair facility must be considered. In short, exporters must make a commitment to their market, just as fully as they would at home. The potential liabilities of such commitment are part of the business law considerations in exporting.

If that commitment is made, marketing decisions follow regarding channel(s) of distribution in the export market. In the case of industrial goods, these are often best handled by a sales agent that searches for customers on the exporter's behalf. The agent never actually purchases or takes title to the goods, acting only as a salesperson. This usually arises when the agent could not possibly afford to purchase the goods or maintain an inventory, such as in the sale of aircraft or railroad cars.

On the other hand, the direct exporter may prefer to avoid catering to thousands of direct consumer purchasers, and therefore may maintain a single (or multiple) distributor in a foreign market. This eases the burden of administration in its supply, pricing, and warranty service. The foreign distributor purchases and takes title to the goods, completes the import formalities, and then services the market with the goods, all on its own account.

As a final step, the direct exporter may supply a foreign distribution company that it itself owns, keeping control over the entire operation. It is then acting as a multinational company, and is likely to make a significant foreign investment to do so. All choices made in distribution channels require application of principles of international business law to achieve commercial success.

The home country of the exporter will take an interest in export activity for data collection and monitoring the contribution to job creation and national well being. As it is in a nation's interest to export, there are very few instances of duties, charges, or taxes applied to exports by the exporting nation. To do so would make its exports less competitive in international markets, and would be counterproductive to the economic benefit such commercial activity generates.

Still, an export license may be required for some goods, where the nation sees its national security, cultural heritage, natural resources, international reputation, or health and safety issues at stake. Less obvious among these are controlling the export of software with military applications and preserving historical artifacts of national importance. Nations as young as Canada and as old as Egypt employ a process to evaluate the cultural significance of historical objects and retain the right to grant or withhold export licenses. The export of water through the diversion of a river, control of otherwise illegal substances, and monitoring of the movement of anything from hazardous waste through genetically modified foods also fall under export license regimes. As was the case with import permits, some national export license requirements are derived from international trade regulation agreements.

The commercial realities of the transaction facing the exporter are a mirror of the import transaction, with issues such as inspection, transport, insurance, transfer of title, and payment. Additionally, exporting creates costs that are not present or exceed the average found in domestic sales transactions. Relabeling of products for each separate export market is usually required, if not for consumer preference, then for import regulation compliance. Packing for transit is also usually more elaborate and costly, to protect the goods from rough handling conditions at sea and during unknown road and rail journeys.

Trade in Services

The Economic and Political Perspectives

Once the fact of the "invisible" nature of services is understood, there is little difference between trade in goods and trade in services. That said, governments around the world have been far slower to liberalize trade in services than in goods.

The difference lies in this invisible nature, and the control problem that it presents to governments. Services are exported and imported, but there is no box on the loading dock, no passage through government control for counting, monitoring, or taxation.

On the export side, the business enterprises of a home nation may provide transportation services with ships or trucks used by foreigners, even if these services do not begin or end in homeports of that nation. Insurance and banking services to foreign residents are also "exports." These often exist only in terms of their paper evidence, but translate into inbound cash flows to the service-providing nation. Somewhat more tangible are management or construction services, where home country enterprises act as consultants to foreign businesses or projects in return for a fee.

While trade in services has been greatly liberalized through international agreements, it still lags far behind the progress made in liberalizing trade in goods. While statistical monitoring and taxation of services are difficult, the historical unwillingness of governments to liberalize these have other roots. The economic sector of services in virtually all nations has grown rapidly in the last 50 years, and given the relatively slower development of government policy, this has bred caution in international relations.

As the United States supplies services that are in demand elsewhere (consistently running a surplus with the world, in contrast to its goods trade deficit), the United States is viewed with greater suspicion by foreign governments. They fear dependency on these services, and the mounting cost of their imports of U.S. services.

U.S. Trade in Services 1980 to Forecast 2010 (Billions of Constant 1996 U.S. Dollars)

	1980	1990	2000	2010
Imports	–65.6	–136.6	–218.7	–352.8
Exports	89.0	183.4	299.3	591.7
Surplus (+)/ Deficit (–)	23.4	46.8	80.6	238.9

Source: U.S. Bureau of Labor Statistics, *Monthly Labor Review,* November 2001.

Moreover, services that are related to trade infrastructure—for example, transportation and finance—can generate large follow-on problems in other economic sectors if they go wrong themselves. This is a sufficient reason for some governments to resist liberalization in trade or foreign investment rules.

As one example, governments are concerned that air transport liberalization would lead to the establishment of foreign-owned airlines in the country, targeting only the most profitable routes. If home country competitors were driven out, any later departure from the market by the foreign operator would leave a gaping hole in air service. It also would be impossible to fix the situation before it disrupted other areas of the economy. In the financial service example, bank deposits or insurance premiums are seen as leaving the home country to a financial institution essentially out of reach of the home country government. Thus, its citizens have no real guarantee of repayment or insurance coverage.

Liberalized trade in goods, comparing transaction versus transaction, simply does not have the potential to paralyze a nation to the degree that liberalized trade in services could. As such, it is not surprising that liberalization of service trade is taking a much slower path.

The Business Enterprise Perspective

Motivations

The distinction between goods and services that is so important to governments (control and economic security) vanishes at the business enterprise level. The motivations for international trade in services are essentially identical to the motivations that propel trade in goods. Some of the risks disappear as well, primarily those related to transportation and insurance against damage, due to the intangible nature of services. Having said that, trade in services is still risky.

Risks in payment for services rendered, and the risk of receiving poor quality services, remain. The foreign party is at a great distance, and taking legal action will incur greater time and cost than would be the case in enforcement against a home country party.

Methods of Trade in Services

Direct Commercial Services   In this case, the home country service provider treats the foreign party the same way it would treat a domestic client, be it in banking, insurance, transportation, accounting, or other similar market category.

Overseas Management Services   In the most elaborate case, a home country firm may undertake to completely build and initially operate a construction project abroad—for example, an airport—then transfer it to the host government or business operator. These are known as BOT (build, operate, transfer) or "turnkey" projects, and represent fee-based export earnings in the home country of the engineering or consulting firm.

Tourism   The services above are examples of foreign residents consuming, in their own country, the output of the providing country. This is not the only way that services are "exported," as the foreign party can consume services within the domestic territory of the "exporter." This makes little sense, until we consider tourism as an example. Foreign parties enter the home territory, consuming travel and hospitality services, creating export earnings in services. This "export" nature of tourism services is distinct from domestic consumption as the financial flow paying for them originates abroad, out of the foreign wealth of the traveler, and represents an inflow to the home country.

Intellectual Property

The Economic and Political Perspectives

Intellectual property—a patent, trademark, copyright, or undisclosed trade secret—is a valuable asset. It is that fact that makes intellectual property rights and their protection such a contentious issue between nations.

In the view of industrialized nations such as the United States, and those with a tradition of individual rights, intellectual property (IP) is an asset that belongs to the individual who created it. The creator of a process or a graphic or work of art should be entitled to exploit it, and should be offered the protective right to prosecute infringement. The right of society is a mere derivative: to enjoy the work on the accepted commercial terms that its creator negotiates. In the case of patents, society is entitled to access and use the IP only in certain cases where the creator refuses to put the work to any commercial purpose and its value would otherwise be wasted.

This need for protection of IP rights has always existed, but is particularly sensitive today, given the impact of technology. Technology is more valuable than ever before, but it has never been more vulnerable, given the ease by which it can be transmitted globally. Where a set of drawings or plans in the past could not be transmitted far without the knowledge of the owner, now email allows irretrievable global distribution of anything on a computer, within seconds. There are also plenty of possible abusers as well: since 2000, among the top 25 world economies, rates of computer ownership in almost all cases have exceeded automobile ownership rates.[3]

In the view of some nations, however, particularly those with a communitarian view of social ownership (historically, Communist nations), productive assets belong to the people. This viewpoint has held a traditional bias against exploitation and individual profit at the expense of society, and intellectual property protection has been absent, rare, or weakly enforced.

The third perspective falls somewhat nearer to the middle in developing and newly industrializing nations. There, intellectual property rights exist, largely dictated by their membership obligations in the World Trade Organization, and a desire for friendly trade relations with industrialized nations. This is the case for India, which also has a British colonial legacy incorporating IP rights. Still, IP rights protection creates a hardship for nations like India, as honoring that right by making payments of royalties to firms in industrialized nations is a financial drain. This takes advantage of such nation's great need for many technologies and pharmaceuticals. Accordingly, the policy of these nations is to minimize protection and maximize transition periods for the implementation of more stringent protection.

---

[3] "World in Figures 2000," *The Economist*.

India forcefully advanced this policy during the Uruguay Round negotiations that established the WTO. Her Minister of Commerce said at a GATT Ministerial meeting:

> In market access areas we have come on a quest for equity. In the areas in which we, like many other developing countries have comparative advantage namely, textiles and clothing, there is a long history of a highly restrictive and discriminatory international trade regime. It is time that this blot on the international trading system is wiped out. We often hear from our industrialized country trading partners exhortations for setting up level playing fields. . . . But the reality of the present world trade order is that the system is tilted against the developing countries. In trade-related aspects of intellectual property rights (TRIPs), the area of patents in general and scope of patentability in particular constitute our core concerns. The need for taking into account the technological, development and public interest objectives of developing countries is particularly important in this area. We have not been in favor of raising the levels of patent protection unduly, particularly in the area of pharmaceuticals, because of its adverse implications for the growth of indigenous industry as well as research and development efforts. Apart from the increase in foreign exchange outgoes, it is also likely to result in higher price of medicine for the common man. My Government is firm on this issue and unless a solution is found to our concerns, I do not envisage the possibility of an agreement.[4]

Some sympathy exists in industrialized nations for this view, and developing nations received long transition periods to implement increased patent protection. This sympathy is, however, limited. Industrialized nations like the United States possess a major competitive advantage in their firms' stocks of intellectual property. It is an extremely vulnerable asset, but it is difficult to police due to its intangible nature, and its value is easily lost if infringement or copying is widespread.

U.S. Competitive Advantage in Intellectual Property Trade (Billions of U.S. Dollars)

Royalties and License Fees					
	1980	**1985**	**1990**	**1995**	**2000**
Exports	7.1	6.6	17.1	30.3	39.6
Imports	0.7	1.2	3.2	6.9	16.1
Surplus trade balance	6.4	5.4	13.9	23.4	23.5

Source: U.S. Department of Commerce, Bureau of Economic Analysis, www.bea.doc.gov.

Intellectual property rights had become a fixture in commerce prior to the 1700s and were a matter of international agreement by the late 1800s. Still, as part of the WTO Agreement on Trade-Related Aspects of Intellectual Property, IP rights and protection are at the leading edge of issues evolving through negotiation between trading nations today.

The Business Enterprise Perspective

The broad heading of IP covers a wide range of international economic activities, which vary greatly between economic sectors. Essentially this is a grant of a right to use particular knowledge, a technology, or a business process in return for a payment. This payment can be a one-time or periodic financial flow (as a fee), or it can vary according to a formula based on the use of the property by the foreign party (in the form of a royalty).

Intellectual property transfers are usually governed by a licensing contract, setting out how the intellectual property may be employed, along with the basis of calculating the payment for it. A wide range of other terms will be prudently included to prevent abuse of the knowledge or technology. Most often, a license relates to the transfer of patented or trademarked processes or ideas of images, where the patent or trademark has been registered to

[4] Dr. Subramanian Swamy, Union Minister of Commerce, Law and Justice, Government of India, Uruguay Round GATT Ministerial Meeting, Brussels, December 3–7, 1990, reported in *A Commitment in Defence of Indian Patent Regime,* National Working Group on Patent Laws, New Delhi, 1991.

provide general legal protection against the world at large. Microsoft and Disney rank among the world's most profitable creators of patented and trademarked intellectual property.

A license also can be created for the transfer of unpatented know-how. This is simply a contract to supply advice in return for a royalty based on the activity of the business that receives that advice. It is common where an industrial firm has perfected a particular process (which may not even be patentable) and decides it can profitably share its secrets with others, but requires something more than a one-time fee.

At the other end of the spectrum, a business enterprise may wish to export its entire business process to another attractive market, but has no wish (or perhaps no ability) to exploit that market itself. In this case, licensing can be elevated to franchising, which goes well beyond the notions of a traditional license of a single technology. Coca-Cola and McDonald's are examples of international franchising, where direct export is not practical. Such businesses are concerned with product uniformity as well as maintaining a certain brand image. As a result, there are often very strict conditions imposed on the sources of supply, the raw materials used, product and delivery standards, and overall image. This may even include requirements that the overseas franchisee (licensee) source its raw materials and production equipment directly from the home market franchiser.

While a variable royalty based on sales or profits is the standard form of payment under a license agreement, there is no limit in flexibility in this regard. Accordingly, there may be a mixture of set fees just to establish the relationship, periodic payments for raw materials supplied, and tiers of escalating or declining royalty percentages based on profitability or sales.

Investment Trade

The Economic and Political Perspectives

Liberalization of conditions regarding international investment has proved even more elusive than achieving liberalization of trade in goods, services, or intellectual property. On reflection, this is not surprising, for an investment implies some form of ownership or control over assets located in one country by persons who are resident in another.

This represents a giving up of sovereignty by the host government, and no issue goes more to the center of the existence of a nation than its sense of sovereign control over its own affairs. It is an issue with implications for both economically strong and comparatively weaker nations. Wealthy nations are concerned that investments by its businesses will be confiscated or taken, with or without compensation, once those investments have been committed. Less-well-off nations fear economic dominance by stronger nations, if control over the assets they do possess passes into the hands of foreign investors. All nations lie somewhere on this spectrum, sometimes showing this concern in regard to particular investments only, and sometimes with respect to any investment made within its territory.

Concern is greatest among all nations where direct industrial investments (bricks and mortar) and portfolio investments (purchase of passive financial assets) threaten elements of national security and basic economic well-being. As a result, investments by foreigners in military production, energy supply infrastructure, critical agricultural supply, or land itself are often subject to host country prohibition or regulation. Generally, the fewest restrictions are found in nations that are well off, and comparatively more in those that are not, but every nation possesses a unique attitude. There are notable exceptions to this generality, as illustrated by many wealthy small island nations, where assets such as land are still subject to heavy regulation restricting ownership to citizens or legal residents. Even Australia, as a large and developed nation, places restrictions on foreign ownership of land.

While there are solid reasons for a nation to be wary of investment trade, there are strong reasons as well to permit and encourage it. Foreign investment represents an inflow of wealth into national accounts and the creation of jobs. It represents an increase in the technology base as well as the creation of potential exports. The value of the increased economic activity multiplies beyond the direct investment by stimulating other local industries engaged in supply and service to the new enterprise.

Foreign investment does not need to create new enterprises to be attractive to host governments. Passive investments, such as the purchase of bonds or securities issued by either the host government or its business enterprises, increases the stock of capital available for domestic investment and development.

U.S. Foreign Direct Investment, 2001   (Millions of U.S. Dollars)

	Canada	Europe	South and Central America	Asia–Pacific	Other Areas*	All
By U.S. firms abroad	139,031	725,793	163,975	216,501	136,374	1,381,674
By foreign investors into the United States	108,600	946,758	17,040	197,522	51,143	1,321,063
Surplus (+)/ Deficit (–)	30,431	–220,965	146,935	18,979	85,231	60,611

*Includes Middle East, Africa, Caribbean.
Source: U.S. Department of Commerce, Bureau of Economic Analysis, www.bea.doc.gov.

U.S. Portfolio Investment, 2001   (Millions of U.S. Dollars)

	Canada	Europe	South and Central America	Other Western Hemisphere	Asia–Pacific*	Other Areas**	All
U.S. holdings in	99,600	932,700	60,200	141,700	217,600	112,900	1,564,700

* Limited to Japan, Hong Kong, Singapore, and Australia.
** Middle East, Africa, other Asia–Pacific countries.
Source: U.S. Department of Commerce, Bureau of Economic Analysis, www.bea.doc.gov.

Finally, foreign investment allows a host nation to productively employ its savings elsewhere, removing the need to invent (and pay for) its own industrial base. As was the case with trade in goods, being relieved from reinventing the wheel by purchasing it from others only makes sense if those alternative investments are, in fact, wise investments.

The Business Enterprise Perspective

In making investments abroad, a business is committing funds in distant markets and is incurring a much greater degree of risk than it would if it was either investing at home (given similar economic conditions) or conducting trade through export or import of goods or services.

Often increased risk must simply be accepted if business is to be done. For example, at times nature will force the location of international business investment. An oil company such as Texaco must go where profitable oil reserves are located, regardless of how convenient (or not) they may be. Other businesses enjoy greater flexibility in location, but face the reality that their product is so large, heavy, unstable, perishable, fragile, or bulky that it must be produced very near to the place where it will be consumed. Diverse products such as sugar, dry cement, and glassware fit into this category.

Occasionally, an exporter will find itself forced into foreign investment where a host government has closed its markets to imports. The host government's intention is one step more liberal than closing itself off from the world. It intends to allow foreign business to supply its markets, but only if that foreign supplier will create the associated jobs, training, and factories within its borders. The resulting production is hardly foreign at all, but rather represents domestic production financed through foreign capital.

This type of protectionism can stem from a legal requirement to establish a joint venture, where the foreign investor is obliged to take on a domestic partner, possibly a majority partner. Host government restrictions such as these are most frequently found in nations with centrally planned economies, or ones with little free-market activity. Where such restrictions arise in otherwise free-market economies, the industries at issue are usually sensitive ones, such as military production or the manufacture and sale of legal drugs.

However, not all joint ventures are forced marriages due to government regulation. There are many instances where these are wise free-market business decisions. A home country manufacturer may see the opportunity and have the resources to produce inside a foreign market, but cannot do so alone, for it lacks the market savvy required to succeed. Without an existing reputation in the host market, it may be unable to access distribution channels without assistance. Alternatively, the home country investor may not have the cultural awareness to be able to create effective marketing campaigns without taking on a local partner.

Two options exist for a foreign direct investor to establish a presence in a foreign market. Subject to host government regulation, it may opt to establish either a subsidiary or a branch. The difference between the two is that a separate legal entity exists with a subsidiary, while a separate entity does not exist with a branch. In case of a subsidiary, the separate entity is usually a corporation, a creature of host country regulation. As a result of this host country creation, the subsidiary is almost always a resident of the host country. On the other hand, without the creation of the separate entity, a branch represents a nonresident conducting business in the host country. This distinction is more fully examined in Chapter 14, but as place of residence can greatly affect taxation, the two forms of business often differ significantly in final profitability. Where poorly informed establishment choices are made, double taxation can result, where both the host country and the home country have the right to tax the economic activity.

While investments in factories and distribution centers suggests that the foreign investor will take an active role in management, there are many other opportunities for passive portfolio investments. Surplus business profits can be parked in foreign jurisdictions and assets, possibly yielding superior returns than those available in the home country but still with acceptable levels of risk exposure.

Passive and liquid portfolio investments often are used as an element in the financial strategy accompanying international business operations. Where a foreign direct investment has been made—for example, a factory—retaining excess funds or profits in local currency investments ensures that working capital is available in the host country without exposure to risks associated with exchange rate fluctuations.

General Considerations in International Business

Each type and method of international business has its unique critical success factors, but some aspects cut across most situations. Financial and tax considerations will always be present, and trade in goods always generates questions about transportation and insurance.

Credit risk, or nonpayment risk, is a significant factor in international business, as the ability of the creditor to obtain credit information is usually far more limited than is possible at home. In addition, where a business accounts to its investors in its own currency but quotes its prices in the currency of its overseas customers, there is always the possibility of a drop in value of those other currencies in the period between quotation and payment. This currency risk gamble can also go in the exporter's favor, but most businesses seek to avoid such risks wherever possible. Strategies include payment in the home currency rather than in foreign currency, or the purchase of financial instruments that hedge (insure) against this risk for a fixed price. Currency risk cannot always be avoided, as some transactions (such as direct export consumer sales) must be denominated in local currency in order to attract customers, or in instances where the cost of hedging instruments is unreasonable given the transaction size.

Transportation and insurance pose costs and risks that must be absorbed by one or the other of the parties to international business transactions. These risks exist in domestic business as well, but not at as high a level as found in the international arena. A shipment across the United States from New York to Los Angeles may well be loaded and travel on a single truck from start to finish over the course of a few days, which is fairly secure in itself. Contrast this with a bulky shipment from Wuhan, China, to Maastricht in the Netherlands. Such a shipment will have at least two road legs, two long riverboat segments, and perhaps one or two rail segments, and could spend more than a month at sea, varying between hot and humid through cool and dry climates. Throughout the journey, risks abound including:

- Damage in loading and handling.
- Exposure to weather.
- Warehouse fires.
- Theft from containers.
- Loss to piracy (yes, you read that right, it still exists).
- Ships lost at sea and delays for repairs at sea.
- Misdirected shipments.
- Customs delays.

All of these are risks faced by parties who are otherwise trying to conduct their businesses on a "just-in-time" basis. Given all that can go wrong with international business, there is plenty of room for losses, and insurance against them. Insurance is a necessary expense; however, it is often not enough protection. Insurance on goods in transit will only cover the physical losses related to a shipment; it will not cover the consequential losses of a plant closure arising from a late shipment of raw materials, or the loss of clients and goodwill resulting from late deliveries.

Behind all international transactions lie the differing expectations of persons from different cultures. Ethical issues, often resulting from the meeting of two different value systems, are therefore constantly a part of international business law transactions. Bribery of a foreign official, for example, is an offense under U.S. laws but is a tax-deductible expense in other nations. Bribery may be an expected part of life in other places, or it may be a capital offense, as it is in the People's Republic of China.

The international trader will frequently meet these questions of ethical and unethical behavior. Certainly, he or she will be concerned as to whose law or what law applies to such situations, but the trader must remember that law identifies what is illegal, not what is unethical.

Sometimes the selection of an international market or the form of the overseas business entity will be dictated by conditions beyond the control of the prospective trader. Still, it is rare to find oneself totally without options, and the fact that these options exist requires a business and legal strategy to make appropriate choices.

All of these risks make international business a profitable field for lawyers, and serve as a clear warning to international businesspersons. This section began with a simple definition that international business is any domestic business operation that includes an international element. Do not be tempted by this simplicity to conclude that international business is merely an extension of domestic business to an "over there" place. The businessperson who can best employ international business law to minimize risks and maximize opportunities stands the best chance of long-term success.

The Relationship between International Business Strategy and Law

Defining International Business Strategy

Before tackling the definition of international business law, first consider the meaning of strategy, for law is an integral tool used to create business strategy.

The English word *strategy* is derived from the Greek word *strategos,* which describes the rank of a senior military commander—a general. Strategy is and remains the work of military generals, but the principle applies to anyone who must plan a course of action. A strategic plan must marshal available resources toward some overarching goal, balancing losses in one area against gains in another, all in the face of an adversary who is equally bent on success. The series of smaller steps resulting in incremental losses and gains represents tactical activity. Plotting the path to the overarching goal is creating strategy.

Winning any one tactical battle (or even a series of them) is not enough to succeed. As the saying goes, one can win all the battles and still lose the war. Winning one battle may cost such a high price that one is left with no resources to fight the next one. Just as often, the decision to fight can be a fatal one; negotiation, diplomacy, compromise, or the creation of alliances may be far more appropriate options. To achieve less is a failure of strategy, a failure in managing the balance of resources, or perhaps even a result of failing to select the appropriate goal.

A true strategist cannot afford to treat events purely in isolation, ignoring the impact one may have on the other. He or she must consider all factors in the matter at hand as well as developments occurring on other fronts. To make matters more difficult, changes occur during the course of events. Events that are going well turn for the worse, or good fortune intervenes. In short, a strategist is dealing with a dynamic, and so too are businesspersons and lawyers.

The common element for success in such strategic planning is to avoid obsession with the here-and-now, and to look toward the broader picture, to the future, in light of the past and in the context of surrounding events. Analysis and decisions on one subject cannot be made within a single box with clear boundaries. Searching for these outside factors and anticipating their future impact is what is really meant by "thinking outside the box."

Each time you read either a newspaper or a legal case, you are reading a fact situation—the thinking within the box. Turn these into a dynamic by asking yourself: "What actions of my own, or what series of events, governed by others would create a chain in which this event would impact on me?" That is the starting point of strategic planning and "thinking outside the box." It is spoken of by many, understood by less, and done by fewer still.

With that as a starting point, we can turn to the relationship between strategy and law. As your studies have progressed this far, you have realized that fitting a single subject into a box with clear boundaries is quite impossible. For example, setting aside international law, the study of U.S. law requires some knowledge of American society. Rights and wrongs are a reflection of the society that creates them, and law is our social expression of these. Also, every society is highly connected within itself, and dropping a stone into the pond in one place creates ripples everywhere else. Such an effect is fairly predictable, but as one ripple hits those of other stones, then the effect becomes much less predictable. To better understand U.S. society we require some knowledge of the ripples of U.S. history. In turn, that requires some knowledge of politics, which leads back to economics, and so it goes, all in a search to understand law. This is true no matter which nation is under study, and it takes strategic thinking to come up with a sense of the range of possible future results.

When we bump this up to the level of international law, the ripples are even less predictable. If law is a reflection of the society that creates it, then to deal with international law of any kind, we must know something about other societies and nations. This is one of the challenges making international business law an exciting and rewarding field, more than just dry law books filled with rules.

Combining your knowledge and understanding of business, politics, economics, history, geography, languages, culture, sociology, and psychology provides clues to understanding the implications of the law and where it is headed. These are the drivers that propel the developments and changes in law and business in every country, and will be the forces present in every transaction in international business law. The initial reaction of some people is to shy away, saying they do not have enough "background knowledge" for success. The short answer is that none of us have all of this "required" background knowledge. First, we all have some strengths and weaknesses (usually more of both than we realize), and second, we learn as we go, getting progressively more and more capable. The keys are the willingness to research and to analyze, to accept that others have ways and goals different than our own, and to have the courage to draw meaningful conclusions in our work. Oftentimes it is not easy, but it is always interesting.

International Business Law—A Working Definition

 Some scholars take the position that international law cannot exist, as there is no one "international" society or lawmaker. Others say that all our nation's international relations (and those of all other nations) fill this gap to create an effective body of international law. There are intermediate positions as well. One certainty is that international business law is a subset of this larger, and perhaps more general, law of nations.

For our purposes, we adopt the much less restrictive position, outlined below.

International Business Law

Where laws or rules of

1. my nation, my host nation, international organizations, or international relations
2. affect the choices made by me, my foreign business associates, my customers, or my clients
3. in taking business decisions, or the outcomes of those decisions,
4. where a foreign component exists,

I am working with international business law.

This definition will be further refined in later chapters on the international legal environment and business transactions, but its spirit will be retained throughout.

Impact of International Business Law on Decisions and Strategy

This general definition does not make it easy to put international business law into a small box when it comes to practical matters. Deciding to send a Houston oil-field worker across Texas is easy. It has no foreign component. But what of sending the same worker to Indonesia? Do the Indonesians have rules on that? Does the United States have rules on that? Suddenly, international business law has entered the picture.

I might open a sales office in Los Angeles, and a second one in Sacramento, but would a Korean company do the same thing? Would the effect of U.S. tax rules make it unwise for the Koreans to even enter the United States at all? Maybe the problem would lie in Korean tax rules or in some conflict between the joint application of U.S. and Korean tax rules. Getting taxed twice on the same income might sink the whole operation. You or I might be the local U.S. partner of the Korean firm, and we are the ones who lose out on a good business opportunity because the direct effect of those tax rules had a bearing on the choices made by the foreign business associate.

You may have a contract with a Boston distributor of your goods, which sets clear performance goals that will result in termination of the contract if those goals are not met, without any risk to you. That same contract with a distributor located in France may be subject to provisions of French law that make you liable to follow special procedures in order to terminate it. Your failure to know and follow this foreign law may expose you to serious financial penalties. While this is purely a matter of domestic French law, *you* are the foreign component, drawing the problem within the practical definition of international business law.

Sometimes just crossing the border with goods can be difficult. Where significant imbalances in bilateral trade exists, voluntary export restraints (VERs) are sometimes created by bilateral agreements between countries for the reduction of export–import trade between them. Though their use has diminished under World Trade Organization rules, they still exist. An exporter who runs into a VER will find that its only option for continued foreign market access is to give up exporting and become an investor, creating a factory inside the desired territory. It was VER agreements that resulted in the initial wave of Japanese automobile production inside the United States.

You may know the laws of the host country where your foreign factory is located. There is always the possibility of a change in that foreign government or social attitudes that leads to laws that make your factory a target. That factory may be taken away from you, with or without compensation. After all, you don't live there and you don't vote in their elections. Compensation offered to you may not be "enough," or might be paid or frozen in a useless currency that no one will accept. Back home, who will compensate you for your losses? Even if you can get a court judgment, it is not the type of job a collection agency will take on. Losses from expropriation are just one aspect of political risk, the vulnerability that comes with being exposed to the uncontrollable variables of a foreign political system. Political risk insurance can be purchased from home governments and insurance firms, but it represents only partial comfort in the wake of such business disruption.

The common thread in these scenarios is the increased business risk found in international business transactions. Clearly, no one can be an expert at all times in all aspects of every law and rule generated in every rule-making forum of the world. So how do we manage this increased risk? The answer is the same as in any area of business risk: we attempt to foresee it, reduce it generally, obtain protection by shifting it to others, and then accept or reject the remainder. Risk management is therefore the watchword of international business law. Success or failure in international business law will translate directly into bottom line business profitability every time, without exception, and is a critical business management skill.

When you know how to spot and handle risk, you are also capable of seizing situations where there is real opportunity for profit, without incurring excess risk. Simply being aware of this, being observant, and being honest with yourself in your assessments allow you to transform risk into opportunity.

For example, it can be taken for granted that doing business in a foreign country will expose your business to a foreign tax imposed by that host government. The level of taxation might render your business unprofitable. What may be less obvious is the existence of a tax treaty between the United States and that country, which credits all or part of the tax, making the impossible venture possible again. Or, if such a tax treaty does not exist, maybe another country that does have one will allow itself to serve as a base or conduit for such operations. Here, knowledge of your environments creates opportunities where none existed before.

You may identify a good sales opportunity abroad, but, without a previous relationship with the foreign buyer, you might pass it up for fear of not being paid. Here, knowledge of financing opportunities created through banks and subject to international business law comes into play. Your bank knows you, and the buyer's bank knows your buyer. As long as the banks trust each other, the field is set up for creation of a form of payment insurance. Knowledge of your options under international business law creates a business opportunity that would otherwise be lost.

Each step and outcome in risk management cannot be taken in isolation. Each factor in each step must be considered in terms of its effects on all other steps, just as we expect ripples in a pond to combine with each other. Each is linked to all the others, and they vary in importance from transaction to transaction.

Where an opportunity may exist, it should trigger a *systematic analysis* of the foreign business and legal environments in light of any prior lessons learned. Part of that analysis includes testing and narrowing a selection out of a range of possible transaction structures. Assuming a conclusion that the opportunity and remaining risk warrant carrying on, this must be followed up with *initial implementation* through effective negotiation and insurance. This process ends just before "signing on the dotted line," and if the opportunity and remaining risk still warrant carrying on, a *committed decision* toward the execution or avoidance of the transaction should be made, based on the corporate resources available to undertake action and absorb losses.

	Step	Through	By
Application of International Business Law in Opportunity and Risk Assessment	1. Identify opportunity	Observation	Using a systematic process of gathering data and tracking lessons learned.
	2. Identify objectives, assumptions, and critical success factors	Analysis of opportunity	Knowing your business goals, biases, business environment, and resources. Being objective, does the opportunity merit pursuit and is it achievable?
	3. Foresee risks	Analysis of the downside of each success factor, your competitors, foreign government, and the market	Knowing your business and legal environments.
	4. Assess risks	Analysis of type, probability, level, outcome, and impact of each risk	Knowing your business and legal environments.
	5. Reduce risks	Selection of structure of transaction	Knowing your options in international business transactions and law.
	6. Shift risks	Negotiation and insurance	Knowing your relationships and costs.
	7. Decide to —Accept risk —Reject risk	Execution Avoidance	Knowing your capabilities and limitations.

Using the earlier example in this chapter of the American toaster manufacturer, we can employ this process in its decision to pursue or forgo a foreign market.

As previously noted, the company president observed the "opportunity" for sales, but it was hardly done in a systematic way. Unfortunately, this is all too common. A better approach would be to assign traveling representatives, establish a presence at a foreign trade fair, or deliberately research the eating and cooking habits of this foreign country and its people.

If this observation and research do yield an opportunity to serve a market, step two requires assessment of the component parts of that opportunity: does it fit with corporate objectives, what assumptions have been made, and what are the critical factors for success in serving that market?

Simply to sell toasters is not a sufficient corporate objective, as moving into a new market generates its own new liabilities. The opportunity must be sufficiently large to pass the first hurdle of whether it is worth the trouble. Looking back into the United States, many foreign manufacturers forgo the lucrative American market simply because of its potential for litigation and liability. The same and similar rationale can be used in looking outward.

Also in step two, assumptions must be revisited, such as the operating voltage for electrical appliances and the general willingness of the market to accept this kind of appliance, even if they are a toast-eating people. The bias against "not invented here" must be combated in two directions: certainly to introduce the product to the new market but, more importantly, in our own minds. It may be that this foreign country already makes toast in a world-beating way and that the true opportunity lies not in exporting toasters, but in importing their product to America. Finally in step two, each critical success factor is reviewed to ensure the firm knows what standard it must reach to be successful and whether, initially, the reward is worth the cost.

In step three, each critical success factor suggests its own risk. Failure on a critical success factor, by definition, dooms the venture. Care must be exercised to look for risks beyond just immediate commercial factors. This must be broadened past obvious competitor moves to risks in the general economic, legal, and political environments. The foreign economy may turn sour, import regulations and nontariff barriers may be raised, and political decision making may turn a good opportunity into a poor one. This analytical process marks the point where your knowledge of international business law comes into play.

In step four of risk assessment (type, probability, level, and impact), international business law is a factor after the purely financial, actuarial and accounting considerations are made. International business law will be used to change the type of risk, reduce its probability of occurring, minimize its overall level, and cushion against its impact. It is not just the lawyer's job to see that this is done. In being responsible for a business, its managers have their own responsibility to be aware of what international business law can do, and see that it is used to best advantage.

Step five is to take those risk reduction steps by selecting a form for the international business transaction that satisfies the needs for proper execution while reducing (or at least not increasing) the risk level. In the case of toasters, this represents an analysis of whether it is better to simply export, to license production to a host country manufacturer, or to invest in the market with a subsidiary or branch in local production.

Step six, shifting risks, reminds the firm to seek ways to further reduce unnecessary exposure. This will turn largely on the transaction form selected, and can range from negotiations on rights and responsibilities with foreign governments and distributors, legal protection obtained through waivers from consumers, to insurance against cargoes lost or investments confiscated.

In step seven, the decision phase, only the toaster firm knows its capabilities and limitations, and it must assess these in light of the remaining risk that cannot be reduced or shifted. At that point, the decision is either a reasoned commitment to serving the foreign toaster market or abandonment of the opportunity.

Despite this step-by-step approach, an important message is that this is *not* a mechanical process with mechanical results. It is part science, part art, part research, and part experience. To be successful, you must find a concrete way to allow the knowledge and experience learned in one transaction to contribute to management decision making on international business risks and opportunities the next time around. Experience is a good teacher, but it is lost if the lessons are not recorded.

This process represents a corporate international business strategy where international business law considerations play a major role in creating that strategy, maximizing opportunities while minimizing risks, within acceptable limits. Further, this process is a high-level management function and should be part of the overall corporate strategy.

There is a warning lurking in this description. Too often, companies ease into international business slowly or almost by accident, and international commitments evolve on their own, without a strategy. Once corporate actions get ahead of strategy creation, there is trouble ahead, as is the case in any business area. The international business arena is one that must be entered with a strategy in hand, with an eye on future opportunities and risks, with the tools and knowledge to cope with rapid developments, and with the ability to take proactive as well as reactive decisions.

Your international business lawyer must work with you to create these outcomes. Understanding this fundamental relationship between international business and international business law will help the enterprise and the lawyer to create effective strategies and see them through to execution.

Chapter Summary

International business is any domestic business operation that includes an international element. It spans markets in the import and export of goods via agent or distributor, trade in services, the licensing of intellectual property, and foreign investment. Direct investment may take place through a joint venture or a wholly owned subsidiary, or as a branch operation. This international element creates opportunities, barriers, and costs, and the degree of risk escalates as a business moves from goods and services to investment.

Since 1945, increases in mobility and technology and changes in regulatory mindset have created an environment and the tools for rapid growth in international business. Governments have been concerned with the prevention of war and an increased standard of living, and binding together the interests of the nations has been a successful approach toward both. We have witnessed the creation of international organizations, standardized aspects of documentary customs control, a lowering of tariffs and nontariff barriers, and the freer movement of people and capital. Goods trade has been liberalized the most, as it is easily monitored by governments, while far less liberalization has occurred in IP and investment trade due to fears of loss of sovereignty.

Increased trade is in the best interests of nations, but global free trade has still not emerged, and with good reason. Nations maintain trade regulation as a result of home country legislation and international agreements aimed at promoting trade fairness while preserving national security, consumer protection, health, and the integrity of their economic systems.

Advances in technology (industrial, financial, communications, and transport) have allowed business to capitalize on this liberalization. Businesses are motivated to engage in international business as a result of unsatisfied needs or available input sources abroad, for diversification of economic and business risk, and for potentially lower per-unit costs of production. As well, they may be in search of greater capacity utilization, or acting as a result of increased global competition.

Each type and method of international business has its unique critical success factors, but some are common to most situations, particularly financial and tax considerations. Trade in goods generates further concerns about transportation and insurance, and many private companies exist solely to facilitate trade operations, including customs, transport, finance, and insurance.

Adopting and executing an international business strategy through the application of international business law is an important step toward business success abroad. Creation of a successful strategy requires systematic analysis of operating environments followed by selection from a range of possible transaction structures, and, if the risks are warranted, then implementation and commitment. It is a high-level management function and should be part of the overall corporate strategy.

For business and governments, the significant features of international markets and mechanisms can be summarized as shown in the table below:

Market Category	Business Activity	Related Financial Flow (Income)	Related Legal Mechanism Used in Transaction	National Accounts, Balance of Payments Category
Goods	Export–import trade	Price	Sales contracts with agents or distributors, some direct sales	Current account, merchandise (visibles) trade
Direct services	Services trade (including tourism)	Fee for service	Service agreement, no specific mechanism for tourism	Current account, invisibles trade
Intellectual property (services)	Intellectual property licensing	Royalty, may include a separate fee	License agreement, franchise agreement	Current account, invisibles trade
Investment	Foreign direct investment	Branch profits or subsidiary/joint venture dividend	Creation of branch, subsidiary, or joint venture business vehicle	In both cases: Capital account, for principal amounts of investments
	Portfolio investment	Interest or dividend or capital gain	Securities market purchase or private investment agreement	Current account, invisibles trade, for payments of dividends and interest

Chapter Questions

1. When a business enterprise sells goods domestically, in most jurisdictions it is obliged to charge sales tax. In most cases, the same firm does not have to charge sales tax when making export sales to foreigners. What policy reason lies behind the government action in this case?

2. If investing abroad is more risky than exporting abroad, presumably there is more to be lost, and hence more for foreign governments to gain. Why then do nations create roadblocks to stop foreign investment headed their way?

3. Explain the factors that drove nations to adopt a more liberal mindset toward trade in the second half of the 20th century.

4. Recently more corporations aim toward "offshore" operations, but not to trade with these jurisdictions; rather, they wish to relocate their corporate headquarters. What factors do businesses consider in making such a decision? Is this a strategic or tactical decision and what distinguishes one from the other?

5. Plastixtech Inc. is a U.S.-based manufacturer of very large, extremely light, one-piece hot tubs and shower enclosures. What might motivate Plastixtech to conduct international business, what business forms might be appropriate, and why?

BusinessWeek

The oil company has cut the fat that Armand Hammer was famous for, but now it must shift its focus overseas.

Led by Hammer's successor, Lebanon-born Ray R. Irani, 68, management is reaping the gains from a bold gamble Oxy made in the late '90s that it could squeeze profits from a collection of aging Texas and California gas and oil properties. Yet even Irani can't squeeze production out of his domestic oil fields forever. That's forcing him to reverse gears and shift the company's focus to overseas oil and gas production—precisely the sort of risky ventures that paid off big for Hammer, but that Irani had avoided. He is now counting on major new fields in Qatar and Ecuador to help boost oil and gas production by 5% annually over the next five years. At a time when other big oil companies are reducing their growth projections or eliminating them entirely, Irani is confident that Oxy's production will grow at twice the industry average. In fact, the Middle East and Latin America could account for 75% of the 85,000 bbl. per day in new production that the company predicts it will achieve by 2006. "People say, 'What are you doing in Qatar? It's so close to Iraq,'" Irani says. "I tell them the opportunity makes the extra effort worth it."

The most important change, however, was in realigning Occidental's oil and gas business. While most of the industry was shifting exploration efforts overseas because of the high cost and difficulty in finding new domestic reserves, Irani took a contrarian direction, piloting Oxy into two huge purchases in the U.S. He spent $3.5 billion in 1998 to gain control of the federal government's Elk Hills oil and gas field in California. Two years later, he spent $3.6 billion to buy Altura Energy, a joint venture of Royal Dutch/Shell Group (RD) and BP (BP). But now Occidental faces the depletion of those two big late-'90s purchases. The company's sophisticated recovery techniques should keep them active for another 12 years. To offset their eventual decline, Irani has ramped up development of big overseas oil fields. Although the political situation abroad is often risky, oil is both more plentiful abroad and cheaper to extract. This summer, with the completion of a new pipeline in Ecuador, Occidental expects to add another 30,000 bbl. of oil per day from the 150-million-bbl. Eden-Yuturi field there.

The company also has a promising new investment with its 25% stake in the $3.5 billion Dolphin Project, undertaken with the government of the United Arab Emirates and France's Total Fina Elf (TOT). Dolphin will transport 2 billion cubic feet per day of natural gas from Qatar to the U.A.E., where it will substitute for oil in electricity generation and water desalination starting in 2006. That, in turn, will allow the U.A.E. to take oil now used for its own domestic energy consumption and sell it in world markets.

Overseas expansion, however, is both risky and controversial. In Colombia, for example, guerrilla groups have long battled the government, with Occidental caught in the middle. The rebels have attacked the company's main pipeline more than 900 times in the past 17 years. The risks in the Middle East are even greater. In mid-March, three oil workers were murdered in Yemen, where Oxy has operations.

Occidental will also have to finesse objections from environmentalists if it wants to fully exploit its overseas projects. In Ecuador, eco-activists have targeted Occidental's expansion, saying it will add to political instability and environmental degradation in the region. Irani contends that Occidental has always operated internationally under the highest human-rights and environmental standards.

BusinessWeek

Sure, there's money to be made in exporting. But cracking the global market takes work.

Winnebago, a town of nearly 2,000 nestled in the fertile blue-earth plains of southern Minnesota, might not seem like an obvious place to look for globetrotters. But there sits Meter-Man Inc., where 25 employees make agricultural measuring devices. In 1989, the 35-year-old company began exploring the idea of exporting and three years later began shipping products to Europe. Today, a third of Meter-Man's sales are in 35 countries throughout Europe, South America, the Far East, South Africa, and Israel. The company expects international sales to account for about half its business by the turn of the century. "When you start exporting, you say to yourself, this will be icing on the cake," says James Neff, director of sales and marketing. "But now I say going international has become critical to our existence."

Meter-Man is far from alone. With the collapse of communism, the embrace of freer markets by much of the developing world, the completion of the North American Free Trade Agreement, and the conclusion of the Uruguay Round of the General Agreement on Tariffs & Trade, world trade in the 1990s is growing twice as fast as the overall world economy. These days, America's highly competitive manufacturers are grabbing a growing share of global merchandise trade. What's more, the U.S. is also the world's top service exporter. With the ranks of the middle class swelling around the world, governments everywhere deregulating their service industries, and the rapid spread of information technology, everyone from graphic designers to software developers to investment bankers is finding increasing opportunities abroad.

True, big companies still dominate international trade. Yet the share of small and midsize manufacturers that sold 10% or more of their products abroad rose from 27% in 1994 to 51% last year, according to a survey by Grant Thornton, the accounting and consulting firm. Ah, the joys of the global economy. A diversified stream of revenue. The promise of fatter profits. Dinner with customers in London and Buenos Aires. Research shows that U.S. exporters enjoy on average faster sales growth and employment gains than nonexporting companies, says Andrew Bernard, economist at Massachusetts Institute of Technology. And owners aren't the only ones who benefit: Wages for workers in jobs supported by exports are 13% to 16% higher than the national average. "Over time, you learn that the more people you can trade with, the more money you can make," says Abby Shapiro, head of International Strategies Inc., an electronic publisher of global business information.

Sounds terrific, doesn't it? But the risks from exporting are just as impressive. Fluctuating currencies. Impenetrable cultures. Faraway customers. Delayed payments. Byzantine business practices. "Small business sees the growth prospects outside the U.S., but the international market can burn and kill you in terms of cost," warns Browning Rockwell, president of Horizon Trading Co., an international trading company based in Washington. Adds Roger Prestwich, director of education at the Minnesota Trade Office: "Just because the U.S. is part of a global economy doesn't mean all—or any—of the 200-plus countries in the world are interested in your products."

How can a small-business owner succeed overseas? Consultants, financiers, and small-business owners with export experience cite several critical factors. Do lots of homework at the beginning. Plan on investing heavily in your overseas expansion. Tap into a network of professional consultants well versed in the quirks of international trade. And understand that going global is a long-term commitment. The typical small business should expect to spend anywhere from $10,000 to $20,000 just to do basic market research, take in a trade show, and fly overseas to visit a country or two. And it may take as long as three years to see any return on its investment.

The Internet offers an easy portal into the many export programs offered by the federal government, nonprofit organizations, and the private sector. Click on the Commerce Dept., the Small Business Administration, the Export-Import Bank, or the U.S. Business Advisor, and you can study the basics of exporting, learn how to apply for loan guarantees, get country and industry data, download customs and export-loan documents, and find links to trade resources elsewhere on the Net.

Many small-business exporters say trade shows are among the most valuable ways for a company to gain market intelligence, establish contacts, and swap global war stories with like-minded entrepreneurs. Meter-Man participated in a huge agricultural trade fair in Paris when it decided to expand into Europe. Over the course of five days, company executives held 21 meetings with potential customers and distributors. One contact from those meetings is now a major Parisian distributor of its measuring devices.

Which markets make the most sense to target? Obviously, it depends on what industry you're in and what your analysis of particular countries shows. Perhaps your software package or new drug will sell well in Spain but not in Italy, or flourish in Australia but fall flat in Southeast Asia. In general, trade experts say the bigger opportunities for small business probably lie in the rapidly expanding areas of Latin America and the Far East. And of course, with their proximity and market size, Canada and Mexico are popular export spots. But no matter how grand the market research suggests your prospects may be, keep your ambitions in check. "The big mistake we see is people taking a shotgun approach," warns one old hand at the small-business exporting game. "We take a rifle approach. We concentrate on one area before we move to another one."

Once you've done your homework, chosen your market, and developed a few contacts overseas, you'll need some professional help to navigate your way through unfamiliar business terrain, such as trade finance, international law, documentation, and local customs. Thanks to an alliance among the SBA, the Commerce Dept., and the federal bar association, new exporters can get a free consultation with an international attorney drawn from the Export Legal Assistance Network (ELAN). To get the name of the ELAN regional coordinator in your area, contact your local SBA district office, or call the Small Business Answer Desk at 800 8-ASK-SBA.

Service-sector firms, especially, seem to rely on joint ventures and other cooperative arrangements to smooth their way into a local market. The knowledge of local institutions is often invaluable in dealing with the bewildering maze of local rules and regulations that typically envelop banking, insurance, telecommunications, education, health care, and other service industries. "You can't just take a successful American practice or service overseas without making real adjustments for the local market," says Joseph Hartnett, director of international services for the central U.S. at Grant Thornton. "How you sell will be different."

Edaw Inc., a well-known landscape architecture firm in San Francisco, has built up an international business over the past 15 years. The 450-employee company first gained a strong reputation in the U.S. so that when an overseas company wanted to tap into American expertise and talent, Edaw was on the short list of contacts. It also had one or two people willing to take long flights, eat lousy food, and stay in hotel after hotel. In Europe, Australia, and Asia, the company has linked up with local partners, and it is buying a majority position in a Hong Kong company. "You have to go with local, recognized partners that are well-entrenched," says Jim Heid, partner and director of development at Edaw. "It's almost impossible to build up a business by sending a bunch of expatriates overseas."

It's also essential to line up enough financing to see you through the inevitable bumps in the export road. Taking on overseas customers brings with it the risk of political upheaval and currency fluctuations. What's more, it typically takes overseas companies longer to pay their bills, so new exporters often find their cash flow dwindling. The government offers a vast array of working-capital, loan-guarantee, and insurance programs for small-business exporters. The Ex-Im Bank, for instance, long criticized for being a banker solely for multinationals, is now eagerly wooing smaller companies. Its working-capital guarantees, with roughly 95% going to small exporters, reached $378 million last year, up from $181 million in 1994.

Bankers can help out in other ways, such as advising on the structure of overseas contracts and directing you to public or private insurance for transactions. "The biggest problem at many companies I see is a lack of coordination between sales and finance," says Jeanne Derderian, in charge of business development for exporting at Chicago-based LaSalle National Bank, a subsidiary of the Dutch banking behemoth ABN AMRO Group. "Salesmen are out there making promises on what the terms will be and later on the finance people say, we can't do that."

Better yet, take things slowly. When it comes to relying on an agent, a broker, or a joint-venture partner in overseas markets, a hasty choice can turn out to be ruinous. "I see it all the time," sighs Mark Levine, director of customs and duties practice at Coopers & Lybrand. "People think they are getting a reputable agent or broker, and they are just a fly-by-night operator."

Even with good planning and international savvy, going abroad is no cakewalk. Take the experience of California auto dealer Anthony A. Batarse Jr. In 1992, his four auto dealerships were pulling in about $17 million. He heard that the government of Cameroon was looking to spend $24 million on 500 customized vehicles and a service center. Batarse wasn't afraid of an international deal—the El Salvador native's father had been an exporter. Over two years, he got financing from the Ex-Im Bank and the State Dept.'s blessing. He even checked Cameroon's human rights record with Amnesty International. He took out his savings, refinanced his house, and mortgaged a couple of other buildings he owned. He sent engineers to Cameroon to start preliminary work on the service center and ordered the special cars from General Motors Corp. Then the State Dept. reversed itself, citing Cameroon's credit record and the risk that the vehicles would be used by abusive police. Batarse was forced to sell two of his dealerships to repay the $750,000 he had spent and is still in the red. "It almost put me out of business," he says.

Of course, luck knows no borders. When Meter-Man's Neff flew to a trade show in Barcelona a few years ago, he found himself sitting next to a man from Paraguay who was headed for the same show. The two struck up a relationship, and his travel companion ended up ordering about $200,000 of Meter-Man's product and is now a major South American distributor. "All the classes in the world don't get you sitting next to a guy interested in your product," says Neff. "I've tried drumming up business the same way another 50 times, but it hasn't worked again," he laughs. Whether doing business in Tuscaloosa or Timbuktu, success is a cross between hard work and good fortune.

Source: Christopher Farrell in St. Paul, Minn., with Edith Updike in New York. Copyright 1997, by The McGraw-Hill Companies Inc. All rights reserved.

Chapter 2

The Foundations of the International Legal Environment

Chapter Objectives

This chapter sets the stage for a closer look at international law (including international business law) by further examining the environments that combine to serve as its foundations. These new contributors are the geographical, historical, and sociocultural environments, in addition to the political, economic, and business environments discussed in Chapter 1. Every nation blends these elements differently, adding a measure of governmental power and the will to use that power. The result is the evolution of different national legal systems around the world. Taken as a whole, the national legal systems of the world, and the relationships formed between them and governments, establish the basis for international law of all kinds. Through this chapter you will understand

- The contribution of geography, history, and sociocultural experience to the formation of international law and international business law relationships.

- The role of governmental power and a government's will to use it.
- The resulting major legal systems of the world as the foundation for international law and international business law.

The Historical Perspective and Its Impact on the Future

No man is an island, entire of itself

John Donne, English poet (1573–1631)

Indeed, none of us are islands anymore. No longer are there maps with strange serpents at ☆ their unexplored margins, or notations that warn "here be monsters." Equally, few of us desire to be islands anymore, because none of our islands of society—our nations—provide us with all of what we want. We want goods and services, jobs for all, security, and good health. Many of these things, of course, we do truly need; however, a great many are simply wants, and they cannot be found in abundance on any given island. And so we trade, partly because we must, and partly because we just have "wants."

Consider the United States, indisputably an island of greatest abundance. Making and doing things for other people in other lands significantly fulfills its need for jobs and employment. American food and machinery exports create American jobs. Imports provide essential inputs to make that industry run and make life more enjoyable. An isolationist stance that cuts off relationships with other countries would result in many Americans' needs for employment and leisure going unfulfilled. Few of us, anywhere, are satisfied with just what we need to get by. In demanding fulfillment of our wants as well, we bind ourselves to the needs and wants of others.

 The expansion and fulfillment of needs and wants have forever been the hallmark of business in general, and, for our purposes, international business in particular. In the minds of many, chiefly capitalist societies, they are also the hallmarks of progress.

International business, since all but its earliest times, has not existed without some form of regulation or international business law, and certainly has not since the development of the city-state or nation-state. This is true partly by definition, as any concept of "international" must be founded upon the existence of nations, or some proxy such as a society. Coupled with the nation-state has been some form of governance and power structure, and with the exception of rare collectives of independent individuals, the power structures of nation-states have always been jealously guarded. It is not difficult, however, to recognize the permissive nod of a tribal chieftain to a clan member wanting to trade with another tribe as equivalent to a modern import license, or the marriage of a prince and princess of rival kingdoms as a modern bilateral economic or political treaty.

Every nation-state has since recognized international business and international business law as comprising both economic elements and political responsibilities. This mix has varied through history with the relative power and resources of the actors. Wars of conquest such as the expansion of the Roman Empire simply expanded the realm and reach of the domestic law and made the need for international law irrelevant. Only at the frontiers of ancient empires did any need arise for regulation of international business.

At these frontiers, in any of the world's early societies, the chief source of regulation came from the established conventions of the merchants themselves. Most early governmental proclamations were nothing more than making law out of that existing practice, with any added limitations being against elements that threatened governmental power.

Even today, international parties who desire to trade are largely left on their own to make their own rules in contract. A shipping container full of machinery is no problem, but if that same container is filled with arms or nuclear materials, the parties can expect considerable attention from government. This example is taken from two ends of the spectrum and the full relationship between law and international business spans between them.

To understand the present and predict the future in international business law, we can examine the experiences that have produced particular reactions from government and legislatures in the past. This is equivalent to reading case law to determine what a judge might rule in the future. Where similar situations have existed for governments in the past, we can expect similar responses from government today, leaving an allowance, however, for new options that did not exist in former times.

We will gain skill in understanding the present and forecasting the future through examining the past. It is a critical management skill for businesspersons and lawyers alike; said one way it is understanding the past and present so as to predict the future. Said another way, we describe such professionals as savvy, nimble and flexible managers who stay ahead of the competition by saying ahead of the curve. To make historical examination worthwhile, keep looking for the modern equivalents to these historical events and make note of the responses that resulted from them. Sometimes blatantly, and sometimes obscurely, history repeats itself.

International business and its regulation can be traced into ancient times, as the remains of Greek, Roman, and Phoenician trading ships readily show, but Europe's movement from the Dark Ages into the Middle Ages gave trade a quantum leap forward. This period saw the development of a merchant class. While still largely agrarian economies, nation-states in this period realized both the possibility of surplus rather than just subsistence farming and the emergence of industry in metalwork and weaponry. Now the foundations of a true merchant class, as well as a class of skilled labor, had been laid, with economic, social, and political repercussions. This development represented a power base within a nation but outside government, and initially posed a considerable threat to governance. No longer did a king worry only about neighboring kingdoms; now he had to be concerned with the increasing wealth (and perhaps ambitions) of his regional nobles. To retain power, government had to regulate in response to these social changes.

As for the skilled labor classes of metalworkers, masons, artisans, millers, and weavers, certain standards of skill and mercantile behavior began to emerge with the establishment of guilds for advancement of skill, training, trade, and, less admittedly, collective influence.

The merchant-nobles and the trade guilds produced an economic power shift in European nations, but not one that was wholly undesirable or unmanageable under royal authority. The total wealth of European kingdoms increased, thereby increasing domestic royal power through taxation and international power through trade. In fact, for a king having ultimate control of the appointment of the nobility and the armies and weapons to defend wealth, trade, and power, the results were a royally attractive outcome.

The legal consequence of these events was to entrench accepted domestic mercantile practice as law, either *de facto* (in fact and practice) or *de jure* (as recorded rules), often governed by the guilds themselves. The practice spread internationally as part of international trade. To the extent that this entrenched practice was identical or acceptable in other nations, trade flourished under common rules. To the extent that trade rules differed, either trade was stifled or merchants found other common ground, most particularly in dispute settlement, to make accommodations for their differences.

The course of European history beyond the Middle Ages through to the 1900s is littered, however, with examples of how economics and trade were triggering events in disputes where no accommodation could be reached and the final resort to arms was taken. One should remember that the foundation of the United States was built in part upon rebellion against British taxation of tea imports into its American colonies.

Over the last two hundred years, the epochs of the Industrial Revolution, the World Wars, and the Information Revolution have left their even more significant marks on the nature of international business and international business law.

The Industrial Revolution moved the world, certainly in obvious socioeconomic terms, but also importantly in terms of international business and law. At the time, international trade became a highly desirable means to convert an industrial surplus (that one nation had) into goods sourced abroad (which that nation did not have). In itself, that effect is elementary, but less obvious at the time were the seeds of interdependence that were sown. Former wants started to become needs as horizons broadened. Previously unknown wants became known, just as tea, tobacco, and spices had once been unknown. Colonization became a means of two-way trade (although almost always on unfair terms), where colonies that had once been simply sources of raw materials were now equally viewed as markets for goods produced at home.

Before the Industrial Revolution, most of Europe had ceded the responsibility for legal regulation to legislatures and had moved away from government by royal decree. These legislatures, in turn, had considerably intruded into the realm of what had once been the sole responsibility of the guilds. Regardless of governmental motive, it was legislatures that were now in a position to create the rules of trade, though most often only after the need or demand by business had shown itself.

It must be borne in mind that the presence of the European nobility could still be felt both in government and at the head of industry. Lord So-and-so, of a wealthy landholding family, often used that land as security to successfully finance trade, and also would wind up sitting in government as a hereditary consequence of being a noble. Similarly, in the United States, post–Industrial Revolution governments were dominated by the economic and industrial elite of the day.

This domination was not initially seen as a conflict of interest, but as an improvement. This governance by legislature produced far more sensible and effective regulation for business than what could ever be expected to result from direct royal decree or an imagined American equivalent. Whereas kings might view any concession to effect international trade as one that eroded sovereignty (and some governments to this day still do), legislators who are in fact industrialists can be depended upon to enact laws in the interest of business. This is, of course, self-interest, and did ignore (often horribly so) other competing and valid social interests, but it was certainly law in the interest of business.

Trade requires the movement of goods and the payment of the price; that in an international context can be a risky proposition, even today. As the Industrial Revolution created proportionally more overseas opportunities, the scope of risks to be faced also increased. How does one manage the risks of governments at war, pirates, ships in weather far beyond the horizon, and transporting of payment home in gold? Added to these problems was the increasing scale of transaction values. Industrial production translated into cargoes of great value and the rapidly increasing needs of both the New World and Old World meant many cargoes were at sea at the same time. The potential and effect of losses changed dramatically. Exploration and exploitation had ceased to be a royal prerogative and royal risk, becoming very personal and corporate risks.

Structures to mitigate risk had existed for centuries, even risks arising in the New World. The Hudson Bay Company, now a major Canadian department store, has traded since 1670 in what is now Canada, dividing risks and returns between its shareholders. The insurance market that is now Lloyd's of London began as a meeting of shipowners at Lloyds Coffee House in 1771. Great banking families such as the Medicis financed the trade and wars of European monarchs. Despite this, it was the circumstances of post–Industrial Revolution trade in which the first great wave of business service providers and their accompanying legal structures took place.

Syndication of business risk through use of corporations; through banking and payment systems, and insurance; and through formal bankruptcy rapidly became broader in scope and more frequent and deeper in application. In so doing, most New World jurisdictions borrowed heavily from the legal structures and provisions of the United Kingdom and France, either because they were colonies or dominions of those powers, had cultural affinities, or recognized the sensibility of conforming law and practice to that of the superpowers of those times. The United States and Canada were interesting hybrids that borrowed from both, using primarily British practice but reflecting the French Civil Code in Louisiana and Quebec, respectively.

The vast majority of modern international business law, despite its ancient roots, is a product of the World Wars and the Information Revolution, that is to say, of the 20th century to the present. The period from the beginning of the First World War in 1914 to the end of the Second World War in 1945 represents the single greatest upheaval the world has ever known, and was the largest determinant of the shape of the second half of the 20th century.

The First World War destroyed not only a European generation, but also a European form of social organization, which would never again fully trust a wholly birth-determined, class-dominated society. The joy that greeted the end of this war to end all wars, and that ran through the Roaring Twenties, also showed its transparency with the Great Depression that within a decade followed. Now the better part of a hundred years into economic mutual dependency, the Great Depression was quickly transported across borders and oceans as a global economic disaster of unemployment, deflation, and negative growth. Governments lost the confidence of their citizens due to the inability of legislatures to combat these phenomena. This inability to stimulate their economies was in large measure due to the international gold standard that fixed currency exchange rates proportionately to the amount of gold held by nations. In domestic terms, the gold standard meant that unless a nation could borrow, it could print no more paper currency than it had gold to later redeem against that currency. This effectively prevented government-led inflation when the system was working, but also prevented government from stimulating the economy by printing money, spending it, and creating employment when it truly needed to do so.

The gold standard was abandoned in stages, a slow death spanning from 1933 to 1971, but pressures between the World Wars, and the Second World War itself, sealed its fate. In an effort to make reparations payments demanded of it after the First World War, Germany simply printed money, ultimately causing hyperinflation as trillions of valueless new banknotes circulated. The United States first suspended gold convertibility in 1933, five months after creating the New Deal, in an effort to spend the United States out of the Depression. As for Britain, the capital requirements of fighting the Second World War, essentially alone from 1939 to late 1941, bled dry both the country and its civilian assets.

All of these events are reflected in trade regulation today, ending the traditional empire/colony political and trade relationship. These events also highlighted the interdependencies between national economies and the need for international cooperation. They gave rise to the truly international power of the United States (and later the Soviet Union), and drove Europe to the sensible desire to bind itself in an ever-closer union to prevent war and foster peaceful growth.

Immediately in the wake of the Second World War came the first of the effective international organizations. The end of the gold standard and the birth of the International Monetary Fund and the World Bank were the results of the 1944 Bretton Woods Conference, with the intent of stabilizing economies before a domino effect could trigger another global depression. The United Nations, founded in San Francisco in 1945, sought to achieve geopolitical stability through creation of not only a forum for discussion, but also member-state rights and responsibilities, which its predecessor, the League of Nations, had lacked.

In Europe, the European Coal and Steel Community Treaty of 1951 brought together management of both the French and German heavy industries with the goal of coordinating reconstruction of the continent while preventing allocation of those resources to weapons-building and warlike ends. In 1957, nuclear power was made the subject of the EURATOM treaty for similar reasons, and at the same time, the Treaty of Rome was signed. This treaty created the European Economic Community among its six original member states: Germany, France, Italy, Belgium, the Netherlands, and Luxembourg. It has evolved from free trade in goods across Europe through elimination of internal borders to include free movement of service, people, and capital. In its latest stage of expanded membership, now known as the European Union,[1] it shares a common currency in the Euro, a common fiscal policy, and a common supranational citizenship.

In international merchandise trade, the General Agreement on Tariffs and Trade (the predecessor of today's World Trade Organization[2]) was established in 1948. The need for the existence of this multilateral agreement was clear for four reasons, two economic and

---

[1]Including, as of early 2004, Austria, Belgium, Denmark, Ireland, Finland, France, Germany, Greece, Italy, Luxembourg, the Netherlands, Portugal, Spain, Sweden, and the United Kingdom. It is set to expand in 2004 and thereafter to include Bulgaria, the Czech Republic, Estonia, Cyprus, Latvia, Lithuania, Hungary, Malta, Poland, Romania, Slovenia, Slovakia, and Turkey. See www.europa.eu.int.

[2]See www.wto.org.

two geopolitical. First, experience had shown that high tariff barriers had intensified the effect of the Great Depression by stifling trade that could have been a major economic stimulus to national economies. Secondly, nations had discovered the power of income taxation during the First World War, and, with this alternative source of revenue, no longer needed to rely on import duties and tariffs to finance government.

Third, in geopolitical terms, the GATT was a response to the far larger number of national political actors at work in international trade. No longer could agreement of a superpower or empire ensure that its single government would carry along its colonies or allies. Through the 1950s and 60s, most colonial powers were in decline, giving birth to new states along the way. The 23 members in the GATT of 1948 had nearly tripled to 62 by 1964, while the United Nations' membership expanded from 51 to 115 in the same period. Each of these nations had its own interests and aspirations. Fourth, world powers sought influence among these states, and bringing them into agreements such as the GATT was one way of exercising that influence. Such agreements also worked well for these primarily smaller and poorer states, in that memberships in these agreements provided a forum in which they may be represented and heard and may exercise collective influence themselves.

The evolution of the GATT was marked by its expanding membership, successively lower tariff regimes, extension of a nation's lowest tariff to each of its member trading partners, and clearer rules for granting preferences and exceptions. The greatest shortcomings of the GATT, however, were that it was not a true organization (only an agreement), it ignored many aspects of international business beyond goods, and it lacked a truly effective dispute settlement provision. While GATT rulings could be obtained against acts contrary to its rules, the GATT did not provide for dispute resolution, sanction, or enforcement of its rules.

The mechanics of the GATT were successive sessions of negotiations known as rounds, taking place over the span of years. These included the early Geneva rounds (1947–56), the Dillon Round (1960–61), the Kennedy Round (1964–67), and the Tokyo Round (1973–79) and culminated in the Uruguay Round of 1986–94. At this point, the GATT had expanded to the greatest possible extent within its original "structure" (to 123 nations) and required significant changes to meet the needs of the future. It was rolled en bloc into a new organization on January 1, 1995, as the World Trade Organization, which was provided with dispute settlement procedures, enforcement mechanisms, and a mandate not limited to goods.

Economic interdependencies, positive or negative, have never known a period of decline; they simply keep binding nations closer. The root of these interdependencies is rarely attributable to the actions of governments; it is the result of the economic actions of individual people. Interdependencies can be forged through emigration. One leaves behind family in a homeland, but also creates a new link. Interdependencies may be forged through investment abroad, or forgoing a domestic contact for sales in favor of a new link overseas. Accordingly, government action is mostly reactive to the proactive behavior of people and corporations, as these people are the first to recognize opportunities and the benefits of such links. Normally then, international treaties such as free trade agreements are merely recognition of what links already exist. Canada and the United States first broached the notion of free trade in the mid-1800s. An agreement did not result until 1989, by which time the United States and Canada were each other's largest trading partner. In the case of Canada, 80 percent of its exports were already headed to the United States.

The 1989 Canada–United States Free Trade Agreement has since grown into the North American Free Trade Agreement[3] with the accession of Mexico (1994), and now has evolved into the Free Trade Agreement of the Americas negotiating process that began following the 1994 Summit of the Americas.[4]

[3]See www.nafta-sec-alena.org.
[4]See www.FTAA-ALCA.org.

Numerous other free-trade agreements exist in the world, most notably the borderless trade component of the even more encompassing European Union, as well as many more limited, goods-only bilateral agreements such as the 1985 United States–Israel Free Trade Agreement. These relationships have all developed under the umbrella of the Information Revolution, 1960 to the present. Rapidly expanding technologies continue to have their own contribution to the possibilities and problems in international business and international business law.

Consider the Cayman Islands, a dependent territory of the United Kingdom, lying in the Caribbean Sea. These islands of a mere 100 square miles possess virtually no natural re sources. Its 34,000 inhabitants create an annual income on the island of US$1 billion, or more than $29,000 per head. While sun-seeking tourists are a major resource, it is the local existence of 40,000 companies, 600 banks, and US$500 billion in banking assets that remain its most lucrative source of income. The lack of taxation in the Cayman Islands and the existence of its highly developed corporate law structures create an attraction to base business there, but it is computers and communication resources that provide the infrastructure for its continued existence. None of this would have been possible on such scale without the coming of the Information Revolution. Similar stories are played out in island states and geographically small nations around the world.

The Internet and e-commerce add new possibilities to the economic activity that can take place in these environments, beyond just money-management enterprises. By removing the requirement of physical presence as a component of management control, companies can effectively conduct any type of operation from small islands, or anywhere else. Granted, service industries not requiring a large labor force are best suited, but the range of future possibilities is only limited by imagination, which has proved to be enormously fertile.

These possibilities produce many problems in international business law and the regulation of international trade. In former times, questions of residency, location of commercial activity, applicable law, taxation, and liability were easily settled matters. What are we now to make of an Aruba company making offers for goods produced and shipped from China to an Australian buyer browsing and buying from a web page on a Belgian server with payment to be made in U.S. dollars to a Canadian bank branch in the Cayman Islands? Where is the "business" being done? Whose laws apply? Some legislative responses to these questions have been created, but again, if history is any measure, the business imagination of individuals will remain ahead of the legislative imagination of nations.

The desire for profit has fostered international enterprise, and has motivated governments to regulate international business in its own varied self-interests. Even in the new and unknown business areas, someone will always be willing to take risks and governments must prepare to regulate those activities in the best interest of all. One certainty is that there are no more islands, and that the events occurring in one place will soon be felt, in some measure, in all places. To a modern legal or business analyst, there are important lessons to be derived.

The historical tendency of government is to move in reaction to the actions of individuals, corporations, or groups, rather than to be proactive itself. By following patterns of individual or corporate international behavior, and then considering the effect of those actions on the power base or interests of government, the reactions of government in the arena of international business law can be reasonably forecasted.

The modern business and legal world is made up of much more than just trade in goods, and the scope of trade agreements now includes services, investment, movement of capital, and movement of people. To the extent that this can broaden or deepen, it will simply follow the patterns already set. Our interdependency grows through the movement of goods, people, and investment. It also grows through developments in computers and

History is a powerful force. How many times have you heard someone say: "Well, we've always done it that way." Thinking then freezes, history creates traditions, and traditions dictate practices. It can be overcome, but most often nations and people overcome their history through incremental change. The past is therefore likely to be a pretty good guide to at least the near future. Where rapid change occurs, a "paradigm shift," it is usually (a) difficult to predict and (b) pretty bumpy. The history of a host country will sweep along your business, in the current of a slow-moving river, or perhaps over a waterfall. Read the history of your host country and find out from where its rivers flow. That terrain will probably continue. Look ahead for the geography that will dictate its future course. You can hear waterfalls long before you see them.

communication. Given continued movement of the world's people, the further expansion of supranational governance, and with no rational end to the Information Revolution yet in sight, our interdependencies will only increase, not diminish. All this comes with the benefits and faults of interdependency. Left alone, the business cycles of the future could easily have lower lows and higher highs, and these tend to be unfairly borne. In periods of decline, the rich have more to cushion their fall than do the poor, be they individuals or nations. In prosperity, the rich have more at their ready disposal as tools for further wealth creation, while the poor start with nothing and have a tougher climb.

Interdependencies also transmit sudden shocks as well as ongoing longer-wave developments. We have seen the follow-on shocks of the events of September 11, 2001, into industries that seem far remote from air travel and tourism.

Interdependency will demand a buffering of these highs and lows, and in effect, in union there is strength. It has already been recognized that supporting faltering economies abroad is in our best interest in order to maintain foreign sources of supply and foreign markets for domestic goods. That imperative will only increase. A person who seeks only survival of the fittest will soon find himself or herself alone, a depressingly unprofitable situation for a businessperson. It may even be a painful process to critically review and rationalize our needs and wants, and prioritize them among us and against the needs and wants of people in other lands. At the highest level, we must measure our needs and wants against the ability of the earth to provide them. We will exceed the limits of the earth's sustainable development only once.

The international management of international business activity comes under the heading of international law, treaty, agreement, relations, and practice. With business at the fore of all international human activity, international business law is an immense component part of this body of international law. Based on our history, its application and effect will shape our business and legal environments for all the foreseeable future, giving ample reason for understanding where it has been, and where it is going.

The Sociogeographic Perspective: Taking a World View

Each of us perceives and makes judgments about the world around us only after its "true" state has passed through a complex range of human filters and lenses to become *our* reality. Perhaps only as infants do we have real clarity in that vision, giving rise to the phrase "from the mouths of babes" when they provide us with a refreshing and occasionally embarrassing reality check. The rest of our life is spent grinding our lens and changing our filters, consciously or unconsciously, for the better or the worse. We usually do this in only the smallest increments at a time, with great "awakenings" generally being rare.

**North American
World Wall Map**

Source: Reprinted with
permission from G. Challand,
J-P. Rageau, and C. Petit, *The
Strategic Atlas,* 3rd ed. (New
York: HarperPerennial, 1992).

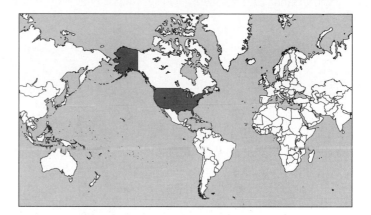

As schoolchildren, most North Americans will recall a large map hanging on the class-room wall, similar to that shown here. The United States lies in the center, with the attendant distortions of a sphere projected on a flat surface. After continuous exposure to this image, the mind is capable of concluding that this is the "correct" image, or the "best," or, most destructively, the "only" way of looking at the world. Even as this is happening, it is not doing so in isolation. The same thing happens all around the world. Schoolchildren in Europe view the world from a completely different geographical perspective, and, not surprisingly, it is from a geopolitical perspective with Europe in the central or dominant position.

**European World
Wall Map**

Source: Reproduced with
permission from G. Challand,
J-P. Rageau, and C. Petit, *The
Strategic Atlas,* 3rd ed. (New
York: HarperPerennial, 1992).

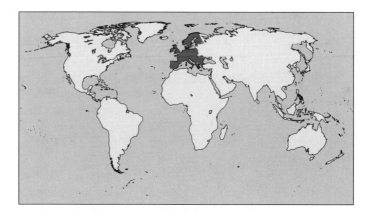

Consider the distortions between the two images. Greenland fades from continental proportions to an irrelevancy while Australia expands, better reflecting convergence of the poles. Asia becomes a solid mass rather than two disparate chunks. This is not to suggest that any particular perspective on the world is bad or invalid, or that one is more correct than the other, but only that we must recognize that even our most basic assumption about the shape of the world is unlikely to be shared by others.

Chinese World Map

Source: From the "Contemporary Atlas of the People's Republic of China," reproduced with permission from G. Challand, J-P. Rageau, and C. Petit, *The Strategic Atlas,* 3rd ed. (New York: HarperPerennial, 1992).

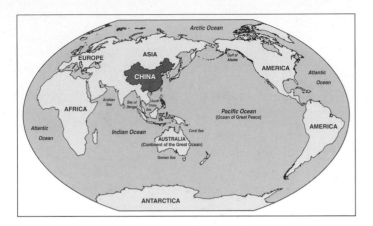

The view of the world portrayed on Chinese maps again plays tricks with the eye, making finding home a brief but unexpected challenge. With this kind of shaking, we should recognize the need for placing our other more cherished assumptions also into doubt, and to actively begin checking them. Experience shows that invalid assumptions about environments and perspectives are the single greatest cause of failure in international business. International business lawyers recognize this as one element of their bread-and-butter, and international businesspersons should work to keep out of such troubles rather than trying to resolve them later.

All law reflects the sum of national and personal values, aims, and objectives of a community, and those are the direct products of that community's geographical, historical, sociocultural, political, and economic uniqueness. These facts underpin the American reverence of the Constitution, the importance of the Civil Code to Louisianans and Quebecois-Canadians, and the strength of British parliamentary tradition.

These forces also make it very difficult to change the status quo of any set of laws, if not incrementally, then certainly on a wholesale basis. Economies in transition, namely those of the former Soviet Union and its satellite states, are a case in point. Despite mainstream and groundswell support for change, bringing it about is painful, even producing a desire in some for "the way that things were."

The World as a Product of Politics

Source: Reproduced with permission, www.worldatlas.com.

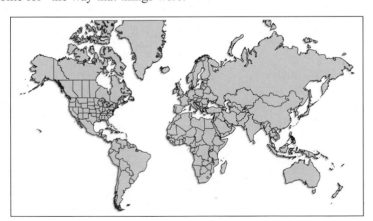

The world as a product of politics is a result of human actors battling against each other and nature. Their legal and practical compromises are reflected by the straight lines drawn by surveyors and treaties, and the irregular ones drawn by armies together with nature's natural boundaries of rivers, seas, and mountain ranges. The vast majority are politically recognized, though some significant ones are in dispute. Managing political borders is an es-

Americans in Europe and Europeans in America often complain about each other's restaurant staff being rude. Americans abroad often fume, waiting for their check that never comes. How dare they ignore us like that! Europeans in America are astonished when their check arrives without being requested. How dare they ask us to leave like that! Rudeness? No. Each is attempting to give the best service possible.

If such a small example of cross-cultural misunderstanding can cause so much ill feeling, can you imagine how culture can impact business negotiation?

tablished part of international law and international organizations such as the United Nations. More problematic are cultural boundaries, often confounded by the straight lines of surveyors and treaties. In almost every case, straight lines result in cutting a cultural group into majority and minority peoples on opposite sides of a political border. The international law problems begin at worst with questions of human rights and end at best with peaceful self-determination and the birth of new nations. The international businessperson is often one of the first to cross these borders, and he or she must be prepared to mitigate the risks through principles of international business law.

Our lenses of perception are constantly being ground, even as the environment we are viewing is also in transition. There will never be a shortage of differing viewpoints in international business and international business law. Businesspersons and lawyers must commit to accepting the inherent validity of viewpoints of other people, and the need to check their own assumptions, and should shoulder the obligation to seek common ground upon which good business and fair legal relations can take place.

The Cultural Perspective

The surest way to failure in international business law transactions is to ignore the role culture plays. The surest way toward success is to have a good sense of the basics of culture, and a detailed knowledge of the social, legal, and business culture of your host nation. That culture shapes the way business is done and the way it (and you) will be regulated.

The effect of culture is often invisible to those who live within it. When you speak to another person of your own culture, do you think about the distance between you before you speak? No. Does that distance vary according to the social situation? Yes, it varies depending on whether we are at a party, at a negotiation, with family, or with a member of the opposite sex. No one tells us these rules, and we do not actively consult them; we just do them, and expect others to respect them too. This aspect of culture, like so much else in culture, is invisible.

The rules are invisible to outsiders as well. They have their own rules, and instinctively they follow them. That is not a problem as long as the rules are the same, but when they are in conflict, our comfort level and trust drop rapidly. This is deadly in business and legal negotiations. Consider how your feelings would differ toward another person simply if he or she tried to speak to you nose to nose, or from across the room. This is just one example, and it is multiplied tens of thousands of times as culture invades and shapes the lives of all people. There is no getting around it, only coping with it.

The examples given here are purposely microlevel ones. They deal with such seemingly insignificant things as speech between two persons, restaurant checks, and people's conditioned reactions. But are such things truly insignificant, or are they critical foundations of behavior? They illustrate that cultural differences shape us long before governments, formal law, and international law get into the act.

The Old Wolf

Cross-cultural bonds come in many forms. Some years ago, I negotiated a Western investment in a Chinese factory. Other Western firms, with far deeper pockets, had failed before me, and I thought it was going to be a hopeless exercise. Like the others before me, time was at a premium as the factory was difficult to reach in a faraway province. The old civil engineer who ran the factory wanted to conduct a city tour prior to the negotiations, and I agreed. He was especially (and as an engineer, professionally) proud of his city's giant 500-year-old road archway, constructed without mortar. The interpreter refused to translate the claim to me, saying the old man was lying, but I could see for myself that the claim was true. I ignored the interpreter and indicated with my hands how the arch would fall but for the careful shaping of the stone. The engineer's eyes lit up, and within a day the factory deal was agreed. I later discovered I was the only negotiator ever to agree to take his city tour; the others wanted to "get down to business." The old man was giving up a part of what he considered to be "his" factory. He wanted an investor he liked, who would relate to what was important to him. His driving force was compatibility, not just money.

Culture acts at many levels, including at the macrolevel shaping of an entire society. Factors such as history and religion combine to mold attitudes toward everything, including business, law, and foreigners. To tell an Australian that one's bank is "an old established bank" is painting an instant picture of one that is, say, 50–75 years old, for modern Australia was only formed in 1901. To tell the same thing to a European can easily paint a picture of a financial institution founded when some people still thought the Earth was flat.

To complicate matters, not only does each of us possess our own culture that may be in conflict with foreign cultures, but also our understanding of each other's culture may be skewed. This distortion can be a result of active propaganda, poor information, stereotyping, good or bad previous experiences, or unrealistic impressions from movies or books. Even when we try to compensate for this by talking with people with experience in a particular culture, we may get dated answers about a land from which they emigrated decades ago. Their perceptions may still be true, or they may not.

Elevating this to legal or business negotiations requires the actor to check his or her assumptions about the national, regional, and local cultures, and, if possible, the specific culture of the person with whom he or she is negotiating. The more specific one's research is, the better. For example, Belgium is a country of three cultures, Flemish (a distinct derivative from the Netherlands), French, and German. Tensions within the country dictate that presentations and negotiations should be held with respect to the culture of the people involved. This may mean translation into all three languages, two, or one, depending on who is at the table. It is one of the few times when using English may be preferable to using the host language, if only to avoid a major mistake and to find common ground.

Every moment of time you spend in cross-cultural preparation for work in international business law transactions is, in reality, an investment in the possibilities for success. The failures, particularly overseas marketing gaffes in naming export products, are legendary. Witness the General Motors car, the Nova (Spanish, *no va* = doesn't go) or the whisky-cream liqueur "Irish Mist" (German, *mist* = horse manure). Their sales in Spanish- and German-speaking countries were predictably dismal.

Beyond sales, culture drives expectations of behavior in services and investments, such as the Chinese example above. Your effectiveness as an international business law negotiator will hinge on your awareness and preparation for these challenges and expectations, for they are reflected in both business and law.

Short-run stability in a nation through government oppression of its people does exist. The decision to trade with such a nation (or its people, which may be a different philosophical view) requires a more intense review of the trader's own values. Some people call this an ethical decision. Perhaps this is because the term "ethical decision" has taken on the commonplace meaning of a choice between right and wrong. An international businessperson will face many choices between right and wrong, particularly in relations with vulnerable persons in less developed countries or those governed by oppressive regimes. Having a clear understanding of your own values allows you to deal with the bulk of such challenges as clearly right or clearly wrong. An "ethical decision" is a label that might better be reserved for the tough choices between two things that are both *right*.

The Political and Economic Perspective: Governance and Prosperity

To some degree, the laws of every nation reflect the values and objectives of that nation's government. At best, the ruling body enjoys deep and widespread support for its policies among its population. At worst, it clings to power through military force.

Power is the ability to influence. Influence may be exercised through compelling reason, logic, and morality. It may be exercised by wielding an ability to hurt or heal, or by creation of conditions that advance or slow the ability of others to act. Effective power requires two conditions, being (a) some or all of these influential capabilities, coupled with (b) the will to employ them. A "paper tiger" neatly describes the situation of one condition in the absence of the other.

Assuming a government has both power and the will to use it, the final question is whether that government is stable, and whether it is legitimate. This is an important question for international business and law in a future-looking perspective, as it relates to the expected stability in business and legal environments.

We will focus on that forward-looking aspect, but it is important not to neglect consideration of unstable governments or the illegitimate exercise of power. Preferably, this consideration should take place before instability or illegitimacy arises. A missile launched by either an unstable or illegitimate government is just as destructive as one launched by a stable and legitimate state.

To understand the power structure of a nation, primarily its governance and laws, we must examine power, stability, and legitimacy in greater detail. Power within a nation can be either given by or taken from the population, and this means of acquisition by the government determines both the stability and legitimacy of its power. Legitimacy here does not refer to international recognition of a government by other states. There are many examples of highly illegitimate power grabs within states that are internationally recognized for the political expediency or necessity of accepting that control of a nation has changed, like it or not. From an American perspective these historically include the governments of the USSR, China, Vietnam, and Iran.

Legitimacy for our more general purpose means the valid transfer of power from a population to its governing body. This includes both the constitutional structure that creates the organs of government (a republic, a constitutional monarchy, and others) and the process of its functioning and maintenance: representation of the citizen and judicial process, for example. Long-run stability for our purposes means the ongoing confidence and willingness of the population to accept these structures and processes, without coercion.

Legitimacy and stability stem from the people as much as the government and an unmatched change in either group will erode legitimacy and stability. The question then

43

hinges on what makes a population first agree to the transfer of power and what creates confidence in the structures and processes in the exercise of power.

The answer lies within our existing definition of power. Aspects of reason, logic, and morality, or the limits of hurting and healing, or advancing or slowing an ability to act, are all value judgments. Each hinges on the values of the people who are governed. Not surprisingly then, governments that reflect the values of their people are both legitimate and stable. Those that ignore the values of their constituents run the risk of electoral defeat at best and revolution or civil war at worst.

Values can be divergent within society, and come to a head with opposing political parties to advance them, but even so, there is a large amount of common ground. To the extent that values are universally held within a society, for example, the democratic process, this compilation of values is termed a national ideology or philosophy. The process of translating national values, ideology, and philosophy into influential and practical power structures and outcomes is governance and law making.

As between societies, there are many differing values, ideologies, and philosophies. At times, people may migrate from one society to another to find national values that suit them, but most people do not. Nor would they, because their national values are a reflection of their culture and history. This reminds us of how deeply we are culturally programmed in our respective senses of appropriate philosophy, behavior, and other human values. The labels remain the same: justice, respect, progress, freedom; the means to achieve them can be radically different throughout the world, with no lack of people supporting one particular mechanism over another.

The international businessperson will recognize that examining the fundamental values and ideology of a nation will give great insight into its governance, legal structure, and business environment. All stable and legitimate national strategies will be aimed at the realization of national values and objectives. While the path may be full of compromises as other power is applied from outside or inside a nation, to know these national values and objectives is to know the future.

It is simple advice to suggest an examination of fundamental values and ideologies of a nation as a predictor of its objectives and strategies. In prospect it becomes more daunting as the questions of "how?" and "with what?" emerge.

Harvard Professors Lodge and Vogel best express the means in their 1987 book *Ideology and National Competitiveness.*[5] In it, they suggest the components of ideology exist along a spectrum from communitarianism to individualism and are made up of

1. The relationship between the human being and the community, the individual and the group, and the means to individual fulfillment and self-respect.
2. The institutional guarantees and manifestations of that relationship, for example, property rights.
3. The most appropriate means of controlling the production of goods and services.
4. The role of the state.
5. The prevailing perception of reality and conception of nature, for example, the role of science and the function of education.

Each of these five elements of ideology will be reflected in a society, driven by the sociocultural history and experience of that people (their values) and the political structures that govern them.

States that have communitarian values place importance upon the equality (or even a hierarchy) of results among its members, rather than the more individualistic desire for an equality of opportunity. Greater emphasis is placed on rights (to income, health, and pen-

[5]George C. Lodge and Ezra F. Vogel, ed., *Ideology and National Competitiveness: An Analysis of Nine Countries* (Boston: Harvard Business School Press, 1987).

sions) and duties (to the group) than in a more individualistic state that relies on contractual relationships to divide rights and responsibilities. It is the community itself that defines needs in communitarian states, rather than allowing the pluralism of a range of interest groups to define needs as is done in individualistic nations. Consequently, the spectrum reflects a range of government from the active, planning state to the more limited influence of the laissez-faire state that allows property rights and competition to meet consumer demands. Finally, communitarian states exhibit a greater sense of holism and interdependence among their members (the actions of one person affect all), in contrast to the cherished independence and scientific specialization of individualistic states.

Some nations jump instantly to mind as examples of both ends of the spectrum, notably Sweden and the United States among developed-world nations. Even when making generalizations as to placing a nation on this communitarian–individualistic spectrum, exceptions come to mind. Canada displays much of the United States' approach to property rights, contracts, and consumer needs, but veers much closer to Sweden in terms of equality of result in social welfare and health care. Again, the need to check assumptions and verify "facts" is clear.

Where can this evidence of values and ideology be found? It can be found, as above with Canada, by examining results, but these may not be wholly insightful into original national objectives. More broadly, research can examine values in ethnicity and culture, history, religion, language, art, literature, education, science, military experience, environmental realities, natural resources, and even the iconography of a nation.

In this latter case, consider an investigation of the values of the United States based solely on its coinage and banknotes. Admittedly, a sensible examination would cover many more dimensions, but even this casual survey reveals a great deal. The analyst would discover "E pluribus unum," meaning "out of many, one," and a nation's expression of unity among diverse and individual people. On the quarter-dollar is "Liberty," a timeless component of individual freedom. "In God We Trust" asserts that the highest governance does not belong to humankind. On banknotes is found: "This note is legal tender for all debts public and private," an irrelevancy if not for the existence of private contract and property rights. Perhaps most tellingly, the images of presidents and statesmen of the past, but not those of the present, speak to the integrity of its political process, and do not simply pay homage to the ruler of today, as is the practice in some other nations.

While politics mirrors the national values and objectives of nations, and indicates where any given nation lies on the spectrum from communitarianism to individualism, economics also plays a large part. At the end of the 20th century and start of the 21st century, we have been much less concerned (and perhaps unwarrantedly so) with the political alignment of nations. Economics has been much more relevant to business and international business law, more so than pure politics. We have found accommodations that allow trade with China, Russia, and Vietnam. Some political preconditions were necessary, but the preexisting desire for economic relations was the primary driver for the change in our interests.

The state of the national economy in large measure determines the international interests and objectives of nations. Where states are income-poor but asset-rich, such as Nigeria or Zambia, international companies knock at their door looking for rights to natural resources; in essence, international trade finds them. Some national economies, regardless of their wealth and sometimes because of it, have been outward-looking traders for centuries. Among these are the Netherlands, France, and, perhaps due to being an island nation in the first place, the United Kingdom. Other nations, such as the United States and Japan, have developed an economic structure built on importing missing key inputs and have been so productive as to preclude domestic consumption of all output.

These economic factors have created a rough division of interests between those of the "developed countries," those that are "newly industrialized countries" (NICs), and those

Prudence suggests engaging local counsel. They know their own political, economic, and legal systems far better than you ever will. Caution refers to checking your assumptions, and not taking important issues for granted, or as "givens." Deliberate preparation means being observant, and reading and digesting any material related to the politics, economics, and laws of the proposed host country. Often, your radar will pick up warning signals while reading about issues and transactions completely unrelated to your primary field of interest.

that are "lesser developed countries" (LDCs). With the extent of political change in Central and Eastern Europe and Asia through the 1990s to the present, a fourth grouping of nations can be termed as "economies in transition," an identifiable hybrid status that exists during these transitions.

It is not enough for the international businessperson or lawyer to conclude that a "green light" is given to business operations simply because the host country is a developed country or seemingly a free-market economy. The reverse is also true; LDCs should not be ruled out just because of their economic status. The business actor or advisor must be aware as to the point on the sociopolitical spectrum where the host country lies when forming strategic business plans.

For example, a U.S. firm may wish to set up a factory in Spain, and its lawyer is assisting it in this planning. By assuming that labor laws in Spain are broadly similar to those in the United States simply because Spain is a developed country (and a member of the G-8 Group of Nations), the firm and its lawyer would be making a grave mistake. It is very difficult to make adjustments to a labor force in Spain, be it in layoffs or eventual plant closures. To be aware of this as a strategic factor ahead of time is a critical advisory and business skill.

Now, it is quite forgivable that the business and the lawyer do not know the exact state of the law in Spain. What is *not* forgivable is *not* having the uneasy feeling that things might *not* be the same, *not* checking one's assumptions, and *not* engaging Spanish legal advisors for a briefing (even just for an overview).

Not being aware of the implications of politics and economics on local law is leading your business into a legal minefield. One mine will explode, and you will not know where the rest are, or you will run off in panic in random directions. Should you find yourself in this situation, the second-best strategy is just like in the movies: to freeze and feel your way out with guidance. Of course, the best way is to avoid the problem altogether by developing a sense for deliberate preparation, caution, and prudence in new encounters with foreign political and economic systems.

Bringing Perspectives Together

The importance of each perspective should be clear; however, it is worth underscoring the fact that each works in concert with all the others. History affects culture, culture affects politics, politics affects economics, economics affects law, and all of them independently bear on each other. As a result, your preparation for international business should be aimed at getting a cross-section of understanding on each of the environments, rather than focusing on one "most-important" environment to the exclusion of all the others. Work then toward achieving a greater depth of understanding across all, and only then devote extra time to the one environment that you feel will have the greatest single impact on your transactions.

As your transactions move from one country to another, so will the relative impact of each environment. Your pattern of analysis before conducting business transactions in Saudi Arabia will have much greater weight placed on culture (specifically religion) than say in the United Kingdom, where your understanding of the important historical influences on English business and law will be more relevant.

Major Legal Systems of the World

As an international businessperson, you must recognize that the majority of the world, regardless of whether measured by number of people, number of countries, or landmass, is governed in a radically different manner than that of the Anglo-American legal tradition.

We are all to be forgiven for being stopped in our tracks for a moment upon that discovery; our reaction is a product of human nature and our immersion in our own systems. The reality is, of course, that none of us—anywhere—are particularly special. We are just different.

The vast majority of trading nations of the world employ a variant of the European "civil code" system of law. Among the minority that do not, the Anglo-American "common law" is prevalent. Through the incorporation of social values into every system of law, religious values are often observable in the law. Historically, these religious values served a judicial purpose, and a number today still heavily influence the legal systems of some countries. This is particularly the case in Muslim states influenced or based on Shari'a, Islamic Law; in Israel as regards Jewish religious law; Hindu law contributions in India; and the Confucian tradition in China and the Far East. Finally, but much less significantly in trade terms, some regions remain influenced by customary or tribal law.

A student of international legal systems must conclude that these "other" systems of law must work just fine. Timeless values are universally held around the world, but find different expressions in different places. Business objectives are much the same around the world, within the constraints of local economics, though sometimes through different mechanisms. People move, ideas move, but rarely is something ineffective willingly maintained when other things work much better.

Why, then, do such alleged differences exist in legal systems? The first three parts of this section go a considerable distance toward explaining why, and reflection on them will bring the remaining part of the question into sharper focus. We are left to discover the contemporary sources of the differences, the major elements of the differences, and the dynamics of the situation. Our focus in the last element is to ask whether global law is coming into being, including an international law of business, or whether we will carry on with a patchwork of national laws and some amount of common ground called "international law."

The Traditions of the English Common Law

To begin understanding the legal traditions of others, we must first have some perspective on our own. The received tradition in the United States, Canada, Australia, Ireland, India, and virtually all members of the British Commonwealth originated in England.[6] As most of Britain was under Roman rule for such a short period of history, and for reasons discussed in the next section on the civil code tradition, the British approach to law differs markedly from that encountered elsewhere.

Before the Norman Conquest of 1066, Britain already had a tradition of strong central authority, resulting from the need to defend its island from Norse attacks. This resulted in feudal loyalty in return for the king's protection, and an administrative and taxation system of counties and townships known as shires and hundreds. Shire courts met infrequently and for significant matters, but the hundred met regularly to try breaches of the king's peace, witness transactions,

[6]A note on terminology: the "United Kingdom" refers informally to the United Kingdom of Great Britain and Northern Ireland. This unity is of the kingdoms of England and Scotland, the principality of Wales, and the province of Northern Ireland. Geographically speaking, England, Scotland, and Wales comprise the island known as Britain. At law, Scotland possesses a separate judicial system from that of the unified system of England and Wales.

and hear the king's word. If justice could be obtained in the hundred or shire court, an appeal to the king existed. In short, jurisdictions and rights of appeal predated the Norman invasion.

The Norman conqueror, William, swore to maintain the laws of England as they previously existed, and introduced trial by battle as a means to settle disputes.[7] While this certainly minimized the need for appeals, it formed the basis of today's adversarial process in litigation. William also inventoried his new territory, requiring traveling commissioners to make circuits and record oral statements made under oath, occasionally settling disputes to achieve an accurate record. This reinforced an earlier tradition, and firmly established circuit courts, sheriffs, and oaths as legal traditions.

The Saxon custom of having truthful men to "bear witness" in every suit was gradually formalized over two centuries into a grand (Norman French: large) jury, with the petty jury (a corruption of the French *petit,* or small) to weigh the merits of civil cases. The king eventually delegated authority to his chancellor and courts (consequently making them slightly more independent) as the monarch was more interested in true affairs of state rather than personally handling private disputes, even on appeal. Jurisdiction was thus subdivided into those matters of the king's interest (presumably the national interest, akin to a federal court) known as the Court of King's (or Queen's) Bench and the Court of Common Pleas, for private matters.

New lawyers were exclusively laypersons schooled through apprenticeships with experienced lawyers, who were themselves frequently appointed as judges in increasingly independent courts. This reinforced the legal profession as an independent guild. This is in contrast to the European practice of a judge as civil servant, university trained for such employment.

Trial by battle gave way to trial by jury as deciders of facts. Still, juries had to know what the law was; judges as deciders, or triers, of law provided this to them. The less the king was interested, or capable,[8] in private affairs, the more that judges created law. From the mid 1200s, judges created records to aid other judges; by the late 1600s, recorded judgments (precedents) took on real relevance. By the time of the American War of Independence, precedents were taking on a binding nature—the doctrine of stare decisis (Latin, to let the decision stand).

The binding and inflexible nature of precedent was felt early on, and the need for fairness in results gave rise to another body of law known as "equity." Its earliest source was the church, where clergy advised the king or chancellor when an appeal for mercy or fairness had been made. This led to the establishment of the chancery court that provided equitable remedies. By the late 1600s, equitable principles were an established part of the English court system and judge-made law, giving the common law the flexibility it needed for continuing evolution.

U.S. Legal Tradition

Beginning from these roots, the judicial structure of the United States accommodates a national system of federal courts operating alongside state courts. The U.S. Supreme Court is the only court created by the U.S. Constitution, with other federal courts being creatures of congressional enactment. Thus, other federal courts (district courts and courts of appeal) are limited in jurisdiction to matters within the scope of the federal government. This includes criminal breaches of federal law, cases in which the United States is a party, private disputes involving federal law, and cases between citizens of different states (including foreign states). As residual authority rests with the states themselves, state courts—first instance, appeal, and supreme—entertain both the broadest jurisdiction and the majority of civil litigation. Cases involving concurrent jurisdiction, such as application of a state law between parties from two different states, may be heard in state court if initiated there by the plaintiff, but are usually subject to removal to federal court on application of the defendant.

[7]O. Robinson, T. Fergus, and W. Gordon, *European Legal History,* 2nd ed. (London: Butterworths, 1994), pp. 129–30.

[8]The Magna Carta (or Charta) of 1215, reluctantly signed by King John, created one of the first practical Western expressions of civil rights and limits to royal prerogative.

The U.S. Supreme Court is a trial court only in disputes between states or states and the federal government, and it does not give advisory opinions to government. In appeal cases, access to the U.S. Supreme Court is not automatic. Appeal cases are screened for their judicial and social significance and the Court hears only a small proportion.

Canadian Legal Tradition

Canada also imported the full stock of British legal tradition *on its nationhood in 1867,* but as it stood and without the revolutionary desire for change in structure. The Canadian Constitution creates a federal government and provincial governments with enumerated powers, and grants residual power to the federal government, in a reverse of the American structure.

The Federal Court, Trial Division hears disputes between the provinces and the federal government, actions against the federal government, and matters within federal power such as admiralty, patents, trademarks, copyright, and taxation. An appeal lies to the Federal Court of Appeal, and with leave (screening review) to the Supreme Court of Canada.

The Supreme Court of Canada also hears appeals, on leave from the appeal courts of each province, and has the capacity to give opinions on the constitutionality of proposed government legislation.

Each province has a supreme court (covering both criminal and civil matters) and a court of appeal, but judges are appointed by the federal government. Provincial courts are also created and maintained by the provinces, without federal involvement, and have civil jurisdiction in only relatively small monetary amounts, conduct preliminary hearings, or try cases involving provincial offenses.

Characteristics of Anglo-American Common Law

1. Some form of constitutional separation and independence between the legislative and judicial branches of government.
2. An adversarial process of inquiry, presided over by an impartial judiciary.
3. The frequent use of a jury in the trial of facts.
4. The application of case-law precedent to facts under trial, *stare decisis.*
5. The principle that an understanding of law is derived after the fact through examination of past judgments, rather than existing before the fact in a statute book.

With the exception of number 1, much of this is different in civil code nations. The cause of our differences lies in the relative effect of ancient Roman practice on England in contrast to the effect Rome, and later Napoleon Bonaparte, had on the Continent. But for this, all of the Anglo-American world would likely also be made up of civil code jurisdictions.

The Civil Code Tradition

Civil code jurisdictions have legal ends similar to our own, but the means to those ends can be completely different. To set the stage for more elegant treatment, they can be contrasted to common law jurisdictions in very coarse terms. Civil code jurisdictions are ones in which law is found in statute books alone, where judges conduct examinations and are the main players in court, where precedent is purely secondary or tertiary, and where the adversarial system has little role.

Using a broad brush, modern civil code countries and regions include all of Europe (save the United Kingdom and Ireland), Russia, China, many Asian nations, Mexico, fragments of North America (Quebec, Louisiana, and Puerto Rico most notably), all of Central and South America, and parts of Africa. Those that received the civil code tradition did so primarily from one or the other branches of French or German tradition.

While the migration of the French civil code is a most frequently cited source of law, Germanic civil code has been surprisingly adept at migration. It was the law of the land to the east as far as modern Poland (then Prussia), and the model was adopted by Russia in turn. Before the People's Republic of China turned its back on the Soviet Union, it not only imported Communism, but it had also imported the USSR's German-inspired civil code system.

Civil code practice as found in South Asian and Southeast Asian nations today can be attributed to the French presence in Indochina, the Dutch in Indonesia, the Portuguese in Macao, or later Chinese export of Germanic-based doctrine. The Japanese legal system is very much a hybrid, with pre-war French and German influences mixed with American legal principles dating from the Occupation and post-war periods. Only Thailand, which remained free of colonial influence, and the former British colonies (notably India, Pakistan, Malaysia, Singapore, Australia, and New Zealand) of the common law tradition take a different approach within the region.

France exported its civil code through colonization in the New World, with the principal legacies today being found in Quebec and Louisiana. Spain and Portugal, being Romano-French derivatives as opposed to Germanic, account for the systems of Mexico and Central and South America, with the exception of those nations that are former French colonies.

It is quite a challenge for a common law lawyer to reconcile the systemic differences presented by the civil code tradition. On top of the systemic differences are the content of the law and its practice. Some very significant things exist in common law that are absent in civil code jurisdictions, and vice-versa, some things exist in both under different names, and some things that are right in one system are abjectly wrong in the other. Reconciling these differences comes from understanding their roots, and like so many of these roots of the Western world, all roads lead to Rome.

There were two golden periods of Roman law: that of the Eastern Roman Empire at the time of Emperor Justinian (527–560 CE[9]) and later in what is now northern Italy in the period 1100 to 1300 CE. All present-day civil code jurisdictions in some measure owe their law to these early influences, and all common law jurisdictions owe their uniqueness to their relative isolation from them.

Exported through conquest, Roman law took two forms, the *jus gentium* and the *jus civilus,* with the former applying to non-Roman citizens and the latter only to Romans. The *jus gentium* focused primarily on public law, and the great variety of local customary practice in farflung parts of the Empire was left on its own to continue a private law function. Thus, the average non-Roman was little affected by Rome in the private domain, while administrative affairs in all of Europe took on a distinctly Roman flavor. France can be cut into northern and southern halves and in northern France and Europe, Roman law held even less sway, and local custom prevailed.

As a result, Rome had the least comparative impact on Britain. There, the Romans arrived later and left earlier than anywhere else (55 BCE[10] to 75 CE), and little remained in their wake but Saxon customary law. The successful Norman Conquest, launched in 1066, brought with it Norman legal structures to supplant those of the Saxons. It imported little of the Roman tradition, however, for Normandy lies north of the line of Roman influence, and the Conquest took place before the second important "golden age" of Roman law. Thus, the laws of Britain developed on their own, on an island, subject to unique influences.

As stated above, the first of these "golden ages" is that of Justinian. This emperor embarked on collecting, organizing, and recording the laws of Rome, and the result was a series of books, the *Corpus Juris Civilus.* It was, and is, made up of four component parts. The first is the *Codex,* or organized record of imperial laws. The second is the *Digest,* made up of collected commentaries by legal thinkers of the age. The third, the *Institutes,* amounted to a legal textbook. The fourth is the *Novella,* which served as a citator, containing the updates, amendments, and new laws that followed the assembly of the *Codex* in 534 CE.

With the fall of Rome and the Dark Ages that followed, the *Corpus Juris Civilus* lay dormant, but was not lost. Over a half millennium after it was compiled, it was reborn through the efforts of scholars in northern Italy. The intervening centuries to 1100 CE and their own

---

[9]CE: Common Era, equivalent to the Christian designation A.D.
[10]BCE: Before Common Era, equivalent to the Christian designation B.C.

sociopolitical environment gave them perspectives of their own to add. Their marginal notes to the text, or glossaries, gave them the title of *The Glossators,* and their modern additions stand alone as an element of European legal influence. This second "golden age," which lasted through 1300 and the beginning of the Renaissance, missed being transmitted to Britain with the Conquest of 1066. It did, however, have a more northern influence, affecting areas that the Romans had not, such as the lands forming modern day Germany.

European law between 1300 and the late 1700s is a reflection of the history of feudalism and empire of those times. It is after the French Revolution and the Napoleonic Era when, for our purposes, two distinct branches of the civil code tradition are formed—the French and the German.

We must contrast the civil code jurisdictions and their single grand expressions of social order with common law jurisdictions whose legal system is centered on individual dispute resolution. The common law is a hodgepodge of court decisions, distinguished by discrete facts. To the extent that one fact situation mirrors another, the outcome of the case, or derived rights, will be similar. It can be a tough job to figure out what the common law is, even for a trained professional. The civil code citizen (except perhaps in Germany) does not need a lawyer to tell him or her what the law is; it is plain to anyone who can read. The law is what the legislature says it is, as found in the civil code. The role of the judge is increased from an arbitrator of the dispute to being the chief figure in interpreting the specific intent of the legislature.

A critic might say that judges play a similar role in common law jurisdictions. This is true when a judge interprets statute law in light of particular facts, but this ignores the fact that the vast majority of common law rights do not stem from the acts of legislatures—they come from case law. The judge is therefore, in effect, an arbitrator, comparing the relative merits of past events.

To the extent that this response is unsatisfactory, it is because common law jurisdictions are becoming more and more like their civil code counterparts with every passing year. More and more common law rights and privileges are being codified, where principles extracted from a body of case law are reduced to a single statute. The Uniform Commercial Code of the United States is an example, as are the Sale of Goods Acts found in British Commonwealth countries.

It is important to remember, however, that codification alone does not create a civil code jurisdiction. The piecemeal common law evolution in this direction still lacks the monolithic single-source approach of civil code jurisdictions, and the intent to organize all aspects of social order.

French Legal Tradition

In France, a few tentative steps had been taken through the centuries toward the codification of French law. The efficient administration of the state, despite regionally powerful dukes, indeed may have demanded it. Still, it is a mistake to assume that the landmark 1804 civil code, the Code Napoleon, was simply a latter-day Justinian Codex. Its drafters saw themselves on a higher mission.

The social period was the Age of Reason. The king and absolute monarchy were dead, as were feudalism and rights of the firstborn. Through revolution, the gutters ran with blood, but humanity stood tall, unchained from the past. For those of the times, the revolutionary ideals of "Liberty, Equality, Fraternity" were bounded only by the laws of nature. Thinkers of the day believed that the order of all human affairs could be investigated, rationalized, classified, and, being a product of the laws of nature, reduced to rules.

The mark of French philosophy of the Age of Reason is found throughout its Code Napoleon, and extends to this day, as the truly defining aspect of all classic civil code jurisdictions. The civil code is not merely a set of permissive and prohibitive rules, but to those jurists who created it, it represents a higher order of philosophy, a natural ordering of the affairs of humankind.

The methodology of the Code Civil, as the Code Napoleon was variously and eventually named, is essentially that of René Descartes (1596–1650), who significantly predated the Age of Reason, but whose thinking found fertile ground in post-revolution France. Descartes' *Discourse on the Method of Rightly Conducting the Reason, and Seeking Truth in the Sciences*[11] forms the basis of Cartesian thinking, not only within his discipline of mathematics, but in his extension of it to all matters of human affairs, including law.

It is worth the investment of time and energy to understand this thinking, as its result influences France and Europe today. Descartes reflected on architecture, observing:

> that there is seldom so much perfection in works composed of many separate parts, upon which different hands had been employed, as in those completed by a single master. Thus it is observable that the buildings which a single architect has planned and executed, are generally more elegant and commodious than those which several have attempted to improve.

In short, the fewer the cooks, the better the soup. He extended this to town planning, noting that the evolution of a large town usually leaves it "ill laid out compared with the regularity of constructed towns which a professional architect has freely planned on an open plain." In short, a professional cook makes an even better soup. He concludes that rational development of any undertaking must come from a centralized authority or planner, just as in the prevailing view of the times, that God has planned all human affairs. This aspect of social order and reason moved through an analysis of God, man, and thought, until he summarized what he believed to be the most rational methodology for analysis *and governance* on any subject, including the law. He reasoned that

> as a multitude of laws often only hampers justice, so that a state is best governed when, with few laws, these are rigidly administered; in like manner, instead of the great number of precepts of which logic is composed, I believed that the four following would prove perfectly sufficient for me, provided I took the firm and unwavering resolution never in a single instance to fail in observing them.
>
> The first was never to accept anything for true which I did not clearly know to be such; that is to say, carefully to avoid precipitancy and prejudice, and to comprise nothing more in my judgement than what was presented to my mind so clearly and distinctly as to exclude all ground of doubt.
>
> The second, to divide each of the difficulties under examination into as many parts as possible, and as might be necessary for its adequate solution.
>
> The third, to conduct my thoughts in such order that, by commencing with objects the simplest and easiest to know, I might ascend by little and little, and, as it were, step by step, to the knowledge of the more complex; assigning in thought a certain order even to those objects which in their own nature do not stand in a relation of antecedence and sequence.
>
> And the last, in every case to make enumerations so complete, and reviews so general, that I might be assured that nothing was omitted.

Here then is the basis for law that is comprehensive and unitary, logical and knowable, accessible and unchanging. It is a very different approach from that of the Anglo-American tradition. Civil code law must be comprehensive and unitary. For it to be "right," it must be an all-encompassing, single, new construction built from a master plan upon an empty plain and free from any poisonous legacy. It must proceed logically in order to be knowable and to achieve perfection. It must be readable by all, for possession of it is the right of citizens, and will be readable (accessible) as a result of its logic. It must be unchangeable, as it is to reflect God's intended ordering of the affairs of humankind, revealed by this careful and patient analysis.

---

[11]René Descartes, *Discours de la methode pour bien conduire sa raison, et chercher la verita dans les sciences,* Chapter 2 (1637).

There could be no legal methodology more attractive to an Age of Reason jurist. Examining the French civil code reveals three volumes dedicated in turn to Property, Family Relations, and Obligations. Each of these was a foundation stone of French society in the 1800s, and indeed of European society, satisfying the need for comprehensive social governance. It is unitary, in that one document was intended to cover all possible eventualities that may arise in each of these three spheres. It is a logical arrangement, following life from cradle to grave, with each new element proceeding from the one before it. It is knowable and accessible through this arrangement, like a database. Finally, it is rigid by virtue of the patience and logic invested in its creation, and that it reflects (to the European mind of the time) the greater order of the affairs of mankind. While it has grown since, it does not evolve through judge-made law, but rather through government legislation. These attitudes to law and central authority remain as strong in France today as they did in the time of Napoleon.

German Legal Tradition

The Germanic civil code tradition exhibits less influence of Roman roots, as most of Germany lies north of the line of Roman influence. While the revival of the *Corpus Juris Civilus* was felt, it was muted by the degree to which customary laws of local or regional application had already been codified.

German civil law also differs from the French in that the more modern German codification took place almost 100 years later, delayed by the necessity of creating Germany in the first place. The Germanic states existed as an empire until their dissolution in the Napoleonic era, and did not achieve union again until 1871 as the Second Empire, or Reich. Until that time, new legal influences came from France.

Twenty years of deliberate and almost scientific work resulted in a civil code by 1900. This code was (and is) highly technical, written by and for the legal specialist, and was focused far more on maintaining the fragile political union between states of the union than on reflecting social and economic concerns of citizens. As a result, the German civil code lacks the accessibility to the average person that is typical of the French civil code.

The German government was in an exceptionally influential position in the first half of the 20th century. Specialist courts divided jurisdiction, a clear requirement instructed judges to avoid law making, and law was primarily politically motivated. The First World War destroyed this government and those following were marked by crisis and instability as up to 35 political parties vied for power. Unfortunately, Article 48 of the Constitution in the early 1930s (of what had become the Weimar Republic) allowed the president "to take any step necessary to restore public order and security," serving only to erode democracy. It was the first step toward some of the darkest events in world history.[12]

Much of the post–World War II revision of the German civil code has centered on the institution and entrenchment of human rights and constitutional supremacy. Approximately one-third of the code has since been revised in an effort to make it less impenetrable, but it remains highly detailed and technical.[13]

Mexican Legal Tradition

Also using the French civil code system brought to it by Spain, Mexican law and its legal system reflects its revolutionary heritage. In its post-colonial period, a series of constitutions stemming from an 1814 model culminated in the present Constitution of 1917. As a revolutionary constitution, it echoes those of the United States and France. Further, Mexico's fear of exploitation led it to protect its patrimony by reserving natural resources to the state and limiting the rights of foreigners to own land and shoreline.

---

[12]N. Foster and S. Sule, *German Legal System and Laws*, 3rd ed. (Oxford: Oxford University Press, 2002), p. 30.
[13]Ibid., p. 33.

Supreme Court justices are appointed for life, and the Court in turn appoints lower court judges for a term of years, with rights of reappointment, essentially for life. Federal law and the Supreme Court and federal courts are the most important components of the Mexican legal system, as opposed to the more minor role of state courts.

Mexico goes further than most civil law countries in explicitly allowing for a form of precedent. The Supreme Court and federal courts, after a number of consecutive and consistent decisions are issued, may establish a precedent known as "jurisprudencia."[14] This precedent is binding on the issuing court and those below it in rank. A subsidiary form of guidance is the "tesis sobresalienties," decisions of note that are persuasive, but do not have binding effect on lower courts.

Chinese Legal Tradition

China can be described as a civil code country, but not as a result of any one received tradition, but rather because its legal system is statute based. Certainly China saw the codes of France and Germany, and its Nationalist government of 1911–1949 made efforts to copy them, but it never had the opportunity or the national unity to entrench this. More civil code structures were received initially from the Soviet Union by the Communist government of Mao, but his falling out with Moscow led China on its own path. Still, authoritarian governments are unlikely to appreciate judge-made law and power, and will steer more toward civil code judicial systems.

With this modern overlay thin as it is, China's legal traditions lie in its more distant past, with written records of law easily as old as those of Rome. Almost a millennium before Justinian (circa 500–200 BCE), China was publicly displaying written laws and codes. This was the time of the philosopher Confucius (551–479 BCE). His wisdom of harmony, balance, morality, social obligation, and social status was first rejected and then brutally repressed. Two centuries after his death, however, the more liberal Han Dynasty not only embraced Confucianism, but elevated it to the level of social ideology. Still, Chinese liberalism had no room for anything but absolute power in a heavenly emperor, no independent judicial branch, and no private law. Traditionally strong central authority and state supremacy over the interests of the individual and over traditional Confucian thinking still dominate the Chinese legal system today.[15]

As these traditional currents run deep, present-day changes to the Chinese legal system are more a government expedient toward achieving the economic and international trade and investment goals of the nation, rather than responding to a groundswell demand for individual rights.

Japanese Legal Tradition

Japanese law has its roots in traditional and religious law (Confucianism and Shintoism), and these existed inside a social order where the emperor was an omnipotent leader of both the state and religion. This prevailed through the latter part of the seventh century, where governance was effected through a series of penal and administrative codes, initially making Japan part of the civil code family.

The Empire was eventually toppled by warring clan-families, the Shogunates, who divided Japan and ruled personal feudal kingdoms for almost a millennium. The ancient codes remained with them, though these progressively became irrelevant, as written law became secondary to the dictates of the Shogun.

Japan remained isolated from the rest of the world, with very few exceptions, until the mid-1800s and the arrival of Commodore Perry of the U.S. Navy. This and later contacts with foreigners, trade, and weapons intensified rivalries. It created political turmoil and

---

[14]F. A. Avalos, *The Mexican Legal System,* 2nd ed. (Littleton, CO: Fred B. Rothman, 2000), p. 13.

[15]Wang Chenguang and Zhang Xianchu, *Introduction to Chinese Law* (Hong Kong: Sweet and Maxwell Asia, 1997), p. 15.

caused Japan to restore an emperor in 1868, with strong suspicion of foreign motives and a desire to modernize to avoid colonization. By 1870 Chinese legal codes had been imported, but as Europe was the economic model for modernization, Japan turned to European legal models as well.[16] As Germany also had an emperor in this period, while France did not, much of the Japanese inspiration was taken from Germany, and German legal advisors were consulted.

The emperor remained a divine figure, outside the constitution, perpetual and without restriction by government. This fact ultimately led to the rise of the military in the name of the emperor, and to Japanese ambitions of conquest.

In the aftermath of the Second World War, the United States occupied Japan and carried out reforms aimed at ensuring demilitarization, democracy, and the rule of law. As a result, the constitution and civil code of Japan today possess distinctively American roots. Socially however, distaste exists for the role of private law, litigation, and lawyers. This attitude stems from traditional aversion from disharmony and conflict, and toward a preference for indirect, nonconfrontational dispute settlement.

Theological Legal Systems

To differing degrees, theology and religion play a role in the legal systems of the world. This matter of degree varies from mere contributions to what are basically common law and civil code systems, to domination of the system itself. The application of modern law in world societies is a reflection of values and cultures, which in turn are based on deeply rooted sources of their own.

Even where theology has been largely divorced from secular administration of society, often described as a separation between church and state, civil administration still retains many fundamental values that are based on religious belief. In Western society, one need look no further than Moses' Ten Commandments to find the connection between religion and the prohibition against theft found in penal codes: "Thou shall not steal."

Islamic Law

Over one-fifth of the world population, representing more than a billion persons, include the religion of Islam in their lives. Islam (the self-surrender to the will of God) is reflected to varying degrees, in some instances completely, in the political and legal systems of many nations in Africa, the Middle East, and Asia.

The Middle East has richly endowed the world with religious tradition, as the geographical fountainhead of the Jewish, Christian, and Islamic faiths. Central to each of these faiths is that a prophet—Moses, Jesus, and Muhammad respectively—received the words of God, and lived a life in accordance with those received words. In each case, the prophet passed a body of words, deeds, and text to close followers and the whole of the faithful.

Among these prophets, Judaism accepts only Moses. Christianity embraces not only Moses and the Ten Commandments in the Old Testament, but also Jesus as the Son of God in the New Testament. Far from being fundamentally in conflict, Muslims (the self-surrendered) include both Moses and Jesus—though not as the Son of God—as prophetic historical figures. Muslims, however, believe that Muhammad, born in Mecca nearly 600 years after Jesus, is the third and final prophet.

No overarching institutional structure governs Islam, which in turn has particular consequences for the application of Islamic law in modern nations. Islam represents a personal relationship with God, accomplished through prayer. The clerical figure of "imam" is a prayer leader, and while he may serve to give theological interpretation to worshippers, an imam is no closer to God than the worshipper. Islam is therefore independent of an institutional hierarchy, and in that way bears no comparison to the Roman Catholic Church,

[16]Hiroshi Oda, *Japanese Law* (London: Butterworths, 1992), p. 26.

having no equivalent to a Pope or ecclesiastical organization. Separation of church and state is necessarily more difficult because there is no institution capable of being separated. Further, no separation of church and state is even desired under the tenets of Islam.

At the outset, one must note that while Arab states are Islamic nations, the reverse is not always true, and not all states with large Muslim populations are Islamic states. Half of all Islamic persons reside in the non-Arab states of Indonesia (170 million Muslims), Pakistan (120 million), Bangladesh (100 million), India (100 million), and Turkey (56 million). Indonesia, with a total population of over 230 million, and India, with over one billion, serve the point—the former is not Arab, and the latter is not Islamic.

Despite constitutions that may exclude or include Islam, an Islamic state or Islamic law exists in practice when Islam exists in the psyche of its citizens and governors, and is applied though its official organs. However, of most interest to international businesspersons are those that embrace Islamic legal traditions and are active in international business. These nations include Saudi Arabia, Iran, Pakistan, Indonesia, and Malaysia. Important distinctions should also be made for nations where Islamic law dominates on a regional basis (Nigeria), or can be applied to nationals who are Muslims (India).

Western business interests are extensive in these regions and where the Islamic law tradition exists, it possesses elements that are widely divergent from more familiar Western norms. An international businessperson or lawyer therefore must possess at least passing familiarity with the profile of this legal tradition.

Not only is the Islamic law tradition not monolithic, one quickly discovers that Islamic countries are not uniform, either vertically or horizontally within the tradition. This lack of uniformity arises from differences in legal thought between the two main branches of the Islamic faith (90 percent Sunni and 10 percent Shi'ite), and the fact that most Islamic nations were at one time subject to foreign domination. In this latter regard, present Islamic legal systems represent returns to, or revivals of, former legal practice. The process has varied in extent and desire, and in most cases a colonial or foreign legacy is found, ranging from small aspects to major or even dominant components.

Fundamental to any religion are its tenets of behavior and commands to its faithful. Like the Jewish Torah and the Christian Bible, the religious text of Islam is the Koran, preeminent to its adherents as being the word of God. The Koran was received by Muhammad in vision and orally given to close followers for transcription into text.

This text of more than 6,000 verses has a very broad scope, and no more than 10 percent can be considered to be laws. Therefore, while accepting the paramountcy of the Koran, Islamic law places much emphasis on the deeds of the prophet Muhammad, his sayings, and the interpretations of their meaning made by others. This inclusive process is similar to the interpretive exercises found both in Christian and Jewish practice.

This body of Islamic law that governs life is known as "Shari'a," or the "Road to Follow." The principal constituent parts of the Shari'a are the Koran itself, the Sunna, and Hudud. The Sunna is the way of the prophet, the behavior of Muhammad himself, obviously an important example set by the messenger of God. In a similar vein, the words of Muhammad, being his Hudud (singular, *haddith*), give important guidance to those who wish to follow the road of Islam.

Often, the average person was and is left in a quandary as to the proper interpretation of these instructions. In response to this, Islam provides *faqh,* or the science of Islam, which is the study and interpretation of the Shari'a—in other words, the choice of which particular *haddith*—performed by learned men known as *faqaha* (singular, *faqih*).

Just as denominations of Christians and Jews exist, so too are there different schools of the science of Islam. The four main Sunni schools of thought—the Hanafi, Maliki, Shafi'i, and Hanbali—are each named for the principal *faqih* whose tradition of interpretation is followed. Collectively, the schools of thought, or whole body of largely consensual interpretation, are termed the *ijima,* which is the fourth and last major source of Islamic law.

The personalities of Islamic law include not only the *faqih* (learned in theology) but also the *mujtahid* (one learned in the law) and the *mufti,* who is a *mujtahid* whose knowledge, experience, analysis, and opinion are so valued as to make him a "friend of the court." The *mufti* is free to independently advise the judge (*qadi*) in much the same way that civil code courts seek learned opinions from independent advisors.

To the extent that any judgment (*fatwa*) carries a legitimate weight, one must return to the notion of the Islamic faith as a personal relationship with God. The parties and actors in a legal case, the plaintiff and defendant (to use familiar adversarial terms), and the judge and advisors are highly active in the creation of the legal outcome. The application of Islamic law amounts to a collaborative effort between all the parties to first find the law from among the *haddith* and within the Shari'a. This is wholly unlike the mechanical application of a formal system of well-known and preexisting rules as would be the case (more so) in civil code jurisdictions or (less so) in common law jurisdictions.

When all parties have been participants in finding the law, the lack of stated and formal reasons for judgment are less relevant, for the parties should have every awareness of what they are, as they helped in their formulation. Moreover, Muslims who observe any *fatwa* are intellectually left to accept or reject the reasoning behind it in terms of their own relationship to God. If a *fatwa* is based on a patently faulty interpretation of *haddith* (the words of Muhammad), it is particularly open to criticism or rejection.

Deriving a modern system of commercial law on the basis of a few hundred Koranic verses may seem to be a difficult challenge, but perhaps not. Derived systems exist, based on the U.S. Constitution (which has seven articles), the Ten Commandments, and the English Magna Carta (which has 37 articles).

While Islam may have arguably closed its door to sources of law, it has not in terms of interpretation, and these interpretations are the basis of the modern legal systems of countries of the Islamic tradition. In some countries, this has allowed, in practical terms, the use of French or British-based institutional structures (Egypt and Pakistan as respective examples) to employ elements of Islamic jurisprudence.

It is in specific areas of Islamic law where difficulties arise, with the much-familiar example of the prohibition against charging interest (*riba*) frequently being cited. To some liberally minded Muslims, this means simply a prohibition against usury, just as usury (a criminally high interest rate) is prohibited in Western jurisdictions. To others, the prohibition stands against charging interest itself.

Set against this, the Koran urges the fruitful engagement in business in general and admonishes hoarding of wealth—it is to be worked for benefit. Thus, solutions both old and new are created in response to the debt–interest problem. The oldest is simply equity participation, for a lender to share in profits and losses as they arise. In modern fashion, a lease of an asset could replace a mortgage, with fixed monthly payments and a nominal purchase at the end of the term. Other aspects of business law are wholly unproblematic, such as contracts, bailment, and trusts, for Koranic provision can easily be found. As a result, the texts of judgments in many cases read with wholesale similarity to Western judgments.

Some Western concepts are difficult to fit within a closed system. A corporation with all the rights and duties of a natural person is a near impossibility within a religion that requires an active relationship with God. Resorting to trickery is also forbidden (unsurprisingly), and stricter adherents to Islam would question the legitimacy of the mortgage versus lease transaction noted above. Such are the challenges that await Western businesspersons and lawyers in an Islamic law environment, and such are the challenges Islamic legal systems find for themselves in interaction with the rest of the world.

The case below, edited from the 79-page original, illustrates that challenge.

LIAMCO v. Libya—Reconciling International and Theological Law

Libyan American Oil Company v. Government of the Libyan Arab Republic

Mahmassani, Sole Arbitrator; 12 April 1977

The Claimant Libyan American Oil Company (hereinafter called LIAMCO) stated: that under date of 12 December 1955, the United Kingdom of Libya, now the Libyan Arab Republic (the Respondent herein) . . . entered with the Claimant into three Petroleum Concessions . . . to the extraction of Petroleum from certain land areas in Libya over a period of fifty years . . .

The (Petroleum) Law (of 1955) is a modern enactment which established a framework for the exploration and production of petroleum within the Libyan Kingdom . . . This Law provided a concessionary system for the exploitation of petroleum products . . .

As a counterpart to the numerous obligations undertaken, the concessionaire received, pursuant to the terms of the Concessions as initially granted, the following protections:

(a) Security of Company's Rights (Clause 16). This provided, as above set forth, that the contractual rights expressly created by the concession shall not be altered except by mutual consent of the parties . . .

On 1 September 1969 a Revolutionary Command Council, headed by Colonel Muammar el Qadhafi, overthrew the Government of King Idriss, and announced the formation of the Libyan Arab Republic. The new regime, from the outset, assured foreign interests that there would be no specific changes in policy and that the obligations of the state would be respected.

In the summer of 1973, the Libyan Government asked the oil producers to accept a 51% participation by the state in the oil concessions. It set the end of August as a deadline for acceptance, under threat of taking "appropriate measures." As no acceptance was made . . . [the Claimant was nationalized].

[Clause 16] comes under what has been termed "stabilization" clauses, which have been considered as legally binding under international law. Moreover, Clause 16 is justified not only by the said Libyan Petroleum legislation, but also by the general principle of the sanctity of contracts recognized also in municipal [national] and international law . . . It is likewise consistent with the principle of non-retroactivity of laws . . . The principle of non-retroactivity of laws is also admitted by Islamic law, and is based on the following Coranic verse:

We never punish until We have sent a messenger (XVII, 15).

(Arabic translations omitted)

Concession agreements usually contain an explicit provision stating the intention of the parties as to the choice of the proper law to which they submit their contract. [The arbitrator then reviews the concession provisions and concludes the principal proper law of the contract] . . . is Libyan domestic law. But it is specified in the Agreements that this covers only "the principles of law of Libya common to the principles of international law" . . .

Article 1 para. 2 of the Libyan Civil Code . . . provides that . . . "If there is no legal text to be applied, the judge will adjudicate in accordance with the principles of Islamic law . . . [and] moreover, the Revolutionary Government underscored the importance of this source of law in its new legislation . . . [providing] that Islamic law shall be the principle source of Libyan legislation.

Islamic law considers custom as a source of law and as complementary to and explanatory of the contents of contracts, especially in commercial transactions. This is illustrated by many Islamic legal maxims, of which the following may be quoted:

- Custom is authoritative.
- Public usage is conclusive and action may be taken in accordance therewith.
- What is customary is deemed as if stipulated by agreement.
- What is customary amongst merchants is deemed as if agreed upon between them.
- A matter established by custom is like a matter established by law.

Thus it has been pointed out that Libyan law in general and Islamic law in particular have common rules and principles with international law and provide for the application of custom and equity as subsidiary sources. Consequently, these provisions are, in general, consistent and in harmony with the contents of the proper law of the contract chosen and agreed upon [in the] Concession Agreements . . .

[I]t is relevant to record that Islamic law recognized the inviolable character of the right of property, on the basis of the Holy Coranic Verse:

- And do not appropriate unlawfully each other's property (S II., 188) . . .

Treaties partake of the nature of contracts, and as such have the same contractual binding force. This is based on several Verses of the Holy Coran, particularly on the following:

- And fulfill the covenant (of God) if you have covenanted and do not violate the oaths after their confirmation (S XVI, 91).
- And fulfil the covenant, for the covenant entails responsibility (S XVII, 34).

From this basis, the Arbitrator goes on to conclude that Libya had no right to unilaterally nationalize the interests of LIAMCO, and that the firm was entitled to payment of restitution of almost $14 million for loss of its plant and equipment, $66 million for loss of its concession rights and $203,000 for its costs and expenses in arbitration.

Source: *LIAMCO v. Libya,* 62 I.L.R. 140 (1982).

A modern dispute on oilfield development and extraction, and yet the neutral arbitrator in judgment turns to ancient Koranic text to establish liability. Why was it appropriate and necessary for him to do so and what (concisely) were the major logical steps that he took?

Jewish and Israeli Law

Israeli constitutional practice is closer to that of Britain rather than the United States, in that no single constitutional document exists. In Israeli practice, it is a collection of nine Basic Laws (relating to the structure of government and the capital, lands, economics, military, finances, and the judiciary), supported by other documents and laws of constitutional significance (among them the 1948 Declaration of Independence and 1951 women's equal rights legislation).[17]

The Basic Law of the Judicature makes specific provision for the existence of secular courts (Supreme, district, and magistrate's) and religious courts (beit din, or rabbinical courts). However, not all Israeli law is Jewish law. Rabbinical courts apply Jewish law based on the Torah, the Jewish holy book. Broader Israeli law is, on the other hand, a complex mix of Jewish law, Ottoman law, English common law, European law, and independent Israeli statute law.[18] Indeed, Mr. Justice Aharon Barak has written: "We must not enslave ourselves to other legal families; but we also must not reinvent the wheel. We must draw interpretive inspiration from any proper source."[19]

[17]P. Lahav and P. Blaustein, *Constitutions of the Countries of the World, Israel* (Dobbs Ferry, NY: Oceana Publications, 1988); R. Hazan, *2001 Supplement* (Dobbs Ferry, NY: Oceana Publications, 2001).

[18]G. Shalev, "Review of 'The Law of the State of Israel: An Introduction,'" *Israel Law Review* 26, no. 2 (1992), p. 287.

[19]Aharon Barak, "The Israeli Legal System—Tradition and Culture," 40 *HaPraklit* 40 (1992), p. 197. In 1995, Mr. Justice Aharon Barak was appointed President (Chief Justice) of the Israeli Supreme Court.

As theology is a central aspect of Israel's existence, Israeli law reflects Jewish values and law. This is done through incorporation by deliberate reference and by implicit incorporation. In the latter case, this is achieved through the reflection of the legislator's religious values in the legislation.

Incorporation by reference exists in the grant of exclusive jurisdiction to rabbinical courts over matters such as marriage, divorce, and family law. The court acts regarding Jews and Jewish relationships and therefore the law applied stems from the Torah. Implicit incorporation is much less clear, but shows itself in the preamble and specific content of legislation. In other cases, the Jewish religious basis for law is in common with other religions, and it is difficult to say whether the source of the law is specifically Jewish law, or from one of the other sources of Israeli law. Examples include the philosophical basis behind laws on wage protection, bribery, civil wrongs, and severance pay.[20]

Considerable friction exists between secular courts and the fiercely independent rabbinical courts. The Israeli Supreme Court observed that it felt it "would give great weight to such [rabbinical] decisions and would, in general feel obliged to follow them."[21] However it also hoped that "Rabbinical courts would adopt the same respectful attitude and legally required obedience to the laws of the State or decisions of competent secular courts in matters arising before them."[22]

As Israel was created from the territory that was under British Mandate until 1948, it was last influenced by the British common law. As such it can be classified (in broad terms) as a common law jurisdiction with codification in various areas. Case law is used to guide judges and the doctrine of stare decisis exists, although jury trials are not employed.

Hindu Law

The title "Hindu Law" appeals to the Western desire to make categories and file information. But Hinduism does not readily lend itself to neat categories of law, religion, social order, and administration. Even the name Hindu is a creation of others. Muslim invaders of India and later British colonial administrators used it to refer to the people on the Indian side of the river Sindh (now the Indus).

Hinduism is a sweeping philosophy embracing ethics, religion and gods, culture, and societal interaction. It determines a person's future through their actions (karma): a cycle of birth, death, and rebirth until the doing of righteous deeds finally liberates the soul into perpetual peace, a union with the Supreme Being. This socioreligious philosophy is among the oldest, if not the oldest, on earth. No single holy book, single prophet, or founder exists—the origins of Hinduism are lost to time.

In ancient literature (the Vedas, the Upnishads, and the Gita), it is the gods who satisfy human wants. Thus, sacrifice, forbearance, and tolerance are the hallmarks of a nonmaterialistic philosophy. Hinduism draws on its ancient literature and rituals for its *dharma,* the closest word to a Western notion of law. These principles (the *dharma sastras*), together with custom, make up Hindu law. Today's judicial decisions and legislation further develop Hindu law, and collectively create the body of modern Indian law.

Hindu law is primarily applied, as was the case with Jewish law in Israel, to Indian family law matters (marriage, divorce, adoption) and succession law (inheritance). Still, one cannot ignore the way Hinduism underpins Indian society, and all Indian law will have a deep measure of respect for its principles.

---

[20]B. Lifshitz and E. Schochetman, "Israeli Law and Jewish Law—Interaction and Independence," *Israel Law Review* 24, no. 3 (1990), p. 513.

[21]Berinson J., speaking with the majority at (1970) 24(i) P.D. 792.

[22]Ibid., p. 813.

As it has been in most former British colonies, the common law influence has been retained in India. Procedure, case law, terminology, and judicial structures will be familiar to those businesspersons and lawyers with an Anglo-American background.

Other Legal Systems

Customary Law

The classification of the world's legal systems as common law, civil code, or theological is by no means exhaustive. Simply put, they are the ones that the international businessperson has the highest probability of encountering. Others do exist, one being the very broad category of "customary law."

Customary law must be approached carefully, for the argument for its existence takes two forms. First, as an objective category of legal systems, the term is often used to describe law in societies (such as some in Africa or the Pacific Ocean) that lack the more familiar rules and doctrine common in the Western world.

The label of customary law also has been in vogue in the 19th and 20th centuries, in the vocabulary of colonial administrators to distinguish the overlay of European judicial structures in colonies from whatever existed before European arrival. These customary law practices of indigenous peoples would often boil to the surface through the European practices, or were intentionally disregarded by colonial administration as matters in which the Mother Country did not wish to involve itself. As a result, subjects such as marriage, divorce, and inheritance rights were often left to "customary law" mechanisms—tribal elders and chiefs. The political and anthropological aspects of this type of law are best left to scientists in that field: is it a distinction convenient for colonial political expediency, or is it shorthand for any legal system that we do not trouble ourselves sufficiently to understand? Regardless, it is important for the international businessperson to know the term in that context, if only to distinguish it from its second, and related, use.

The second application of the term is more directly related to international relations between states, and other parties, and will be discussed in detail in the chapter that follows. At this juncture, it is sufficient to say that "customary law" is a field of international law between nations that exists outside any domestic law or formalized obligations between states. It is therefore likely not written or contractual, but it binds states nonetheless on the basis of long-standing historical practice. There are many debates about what customary law is, and many will not agree with the definition we have just provided, but it is sufficient for our purposes.

Socialist Law

From the Russian Revolution of 1917 until the closing years of the 20th century, the principles of socialist law constituted a major doctrinal branch among the legal systems of the world. While important socialist principles still remain in theory and practice among current and former Communist and socialist states, most have veered so sharply toward free-market economic practice that this distinction (as a doctrinal branch) bears little relevance to international business transactions today. Socialist legal principles of communal ownership and interest were readily adaptable to a civil code framework, and the civil code approach continues in these nations.

The former western European satellites of the Soviet Union are all in the process of becoming European Union members, requiring their ambitious incorporation of European Union law. In central Asia, as far as their international transactions are concerned, countries are engaged in a process of change to permit integration with Western business principles. A Western business enterprise will discover that surviving socialist legal principles are felt most strongly in the areas of employment and labor law, and in the ownership of real property.

Chapter Summary

The foundation of the international legal environment is comprised of its individual bricks, the legal systems of the nations of the world. These legal systems are, however, the products of the national experience of each country and its citizens: their history, culture, and economic and political environments, together with the country's traditions of government, the extent of government power, and the will to use it.

The tremendous liberalization and globalization of economic activity over the past 200 years, and most particularly in the last 50, have increased the interaction of societies. This interaction transmits both positive benefits and negative consequences. Intelligent analysis includes an appreciation of the effect that the past has had on shaping the present social and legal environment, and then prudently extending the impact of these drivers into the future, to permit proactive decision making on legal and business issues.

An international businessperson will find his or her transactions predominantly governed by either civil law, common law, or theological legal systems. These systems are doctrinally and procedurally different, and in every nation have been modified to account for local experience in history, geography, culture, politics, and economics.

Chapter Questions

1. "Unchecked growth in 'wants,' as opposed to the true 'needs' of humankind, is the root of most of the problems plaguing societies around the globe. Throughout history our wars, enslavement of entire peoples, imposition of religious values, contravention of human rights, and degradation of our natural environment can be traced directly to needs and wants. True 'progress' will not occur until humankind can learn the difference between its needs and its wants and exercise the restraint required for sustainable and peaceful development." Comment on this statement, providing your view of whether the time is right for global government over international business activities, or whether this is still best left to competing national governments and negotiation.

2. Contrast the characteristics and establish the difference between a legitimate but unstable nation, and an illegitimate but stable nation. Provide examples of each.

3. Describe the advantages that can flow from engaging local counsel to advise on an international business transaction.

4. Explain how culture and politics are reflected in the legal system of any given nation.

5. Describe the principal factors that distinguish a civil law jurisdiction from a common law jurisdiction. In the development of the world's legal systems, how did it come to pass that the common law system evolved independently, apart from the civil law tradition?

6. Goods, services, intellectual property, and investment trade have all been progressively liberalized, but each at a different pace. What factors have combined to result in these different rates of change?

7. Consult the CIA World Factbook at *www.odci.gov* and examine the descriptions of Norway, Belgium, and Canada. Compare one (or more) of these descriptions with the description of the United States. What aspects of these descriptions reveal the five "elements of ideology" as set out by Professors Lodge and Vogel?

BusinessWeek

Wolfgang Vogler wasn't exactly the only novice investor to get a black eye when shares of Munich media company EM.TV & Merchandising plunged late last year. The 41 year-old aluminum company executive lost $3,800, scuttling plans to take his four kids on a vacation. But rather than meekly accept his fate, Vogler did something daring by European standards: He called a lawyer, who on behalf of 450 EM.TV shareholders demanded on Mar. 6 that CEO Thomas Haffa pay $12 million in damages. Under German law, that's the first step toward a lawsuit charging Haffa—who denies wrongdoing—with deliberately misleading investors about the health of the company.

Are European punters finally getting tired of getting kicked around by arrogant managers? The signs are promising. Across Europe, shareholders are going to court, uniting to oppose company policies, and occasionally even forcing change. On Mar. 2, for example, the supervisory board of steel and auto parts giant ThyssenKrupp approved a management shakeup just minutes before the start of the company's annual meeting in Duisburg. The timing was no accident: The company faced more than 5,000 shareholders angry about top-level infighting at the company, which has struggled to boost results since a troubled merger two years ago. "People used to just take it," says Klaus Rotter, a lawyer based near Munich who is representing EM.TV shareholders. "Now they're refusing to be ripped off."

In the U.S., shareholder activism has been around for decades. But in Europe, mass stock ownership is a new phenomenon. Now, the choppy stock markets are exposing the flaws of the weakest companies. Individual shareholders, stung by steep price drops, are beginning to discover they have rights—and are taking action. "No company is immune," says Sophie L'Helias, a French-American lawyer based in Washington, who has advised minority shareholders in protests targeting such companies as Eurotunnel and investment bank Lazard Freres. Granted, the number of shareholder lawsuits is still small. But it's up from practically zero a year or two ago.

It's still an uphill battle for these new activists, especially when it comes to suing companies over shareholder rights. In Germany and France, plaintiffs in shareholder suits can't force a company to hand over documents. Germany doesn't allow class actions, which makes it tougher for ordinary shareholders to pool their resources and take on a rich corporation. And the burden of proof is so high in cases accusing managers of giving out false information that lawsuits have little chance of success unless the manager involved is first convicted of criminal charges.

Yet the shareholder-rights movement is getting another push from U.S. arbitrage specialists, who have been attracted to dealing in Europe by a surge in mergers and acquisitions. One is New York's Guy P. Wyser-Pratte, who buys stakes in companies he considers badly managed and then tries to force a turnaround. Last year, Wyser-Pratte rallied minority shareholders in Groupe Andre, a French retailer, to oust the company's top management and install a new team. "It was the first time in France that you had a board toppled by outsiders," says shareholder activist L'Helias. "People were stunned." Wyser-Pratte is eying Germany, and has already bought a stake in Rheinmetall, an engineering and defense company.

Pure economics should force the shareholder-rights movement to keep growing. Europeans, like Americans, need the superior returns stocks can provide to supplement the meager results of bonds and state pensions. In the long run, European shareholders cannot afford to give up on their activism. The region's shareholders have gotten a taste of their own potential power. Chances are they'll only want more.

Source: Jack Ewing in Frankfurt, with Carol Matlack in Paris and bureau reports. Copyright 2001, by The McGraw-Hill Companies Inc. All rights reserved.

Chapter 3

Principles of International Law

Chapter Objectives

We have thus far examined the effect of history and culture, geography, politics, and economics on the law of host nations and have come to the realization that many valid legal systems exist—common law, civil code, or theocratic—each colored by its own experiences. Welcome now to the arena where these national legal systems intersect and interact: the domain of international law. In this chapter we will explore

- The scope of international law and its effect on state sovereignty.
- The principal elements of private international law: jurisdiction, choice of applicable law, and the recognition and enforcement of judgments.

- The foundation this provides for international business law as created by the parties—their transactions.

The Scope of International Law

International law is a discipline littered with controversies. Many writers, including us, divide international law into two hemispheres: public and private. Some writers argue that such a division is impossible, for international law is law between nations and cannot have a private application. We find this too stilted in formal logic and labeling. In our view, international law is public when it works to define rights between nations, and it is private when it tries to sort out rights between persons who are separated by a border. This may be in part a determination on the public side between two nations as to which should have jurisdiction in a divorce matter or business contract, but it also has very significant private implications for the individual persons or companies involved. Little is gained by looking only at the label and not the substance and effect of the law.

The private sphere can be further divided into many subcategories: business law, family law, property law, and tort law, to name a few. Thus, our focus on private international business law is a subset of a much larger whole. We also are interested in the public sphere to the extent that the law of nations affects the business environment, this being the law of international economic relations. Here we will find the operation of international agreements and organizations such as the World Trade Organization and the International Monetary Fund.

Some private, as opposed to public, organizations have created contractual arrangements so universal that they amount to law making, though they are not acts of a legislature. Examples of this are the International Chamber of Commerce,[1] which has standardized the meaning of shipment terms in transport and the documentary credit processes in banking, and the International Air Transport Association, which has done the same in harmonizing and integrating transaction processing in air travel and cargo. The work of these organizations and others has become so important that their dictates are treated as quasi-law in many jurisdictions.

The relationship between the whole and the sum of its parts can be thought of in the following manner:

The Constituent Parts of International Law

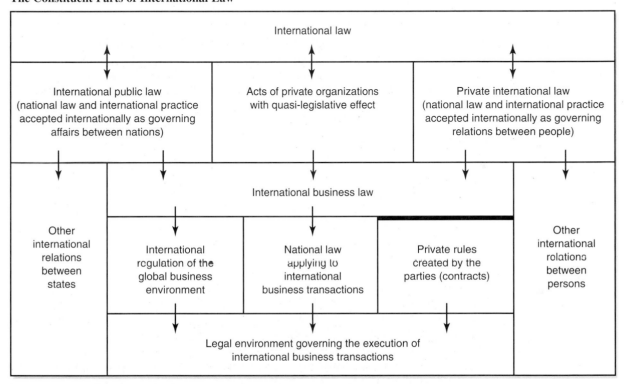

The heavy bar and lack of an arrow of influence to "Private rules" reflects the reservation held by most commentators and legal practitioners that private rules of contract should not be considered as a formal part of international law or international business law. However, as these self-made rules in contract will have a very immediate impact on the overall governance of international business transactions, businesspersons tend not to make this distinction.

International business law is a body of law, regulation, or practice affecting business interests that, while lacking clearly defined limits, can for various purposes and circumstances be taken to include

1. Arrangements, treaties, and agreements between nations, either bilaterally or multilaterally.

2. International organizations founded by governments, together with their charters, rules, and procedures.

3. International organizations founded privately, whose operations and rules have been judicially or legislatively recognized to have the force of law.

4. Amendments or exceptions made to domestic law to give effect to any of the above.

[1]See www.iccwbo.org.

5. Domestic law or regulation of any nation intended to have an effect beyond its territorial limits.

6. Domestic law or regulation affecting the international intentions or rights of any actor, be they national or alien, within its territorial limits.

7. General business practice that has become sufficiently universal as to merit judicial or legislative recognition as having the force of law.

8. Private business law arrangements (i.e., contractual relationships) involving international parties, subject matter, or performance (subject to the reservation noted in the chart on the previous page).

In the following sections and chapters, we will examine international law in general as it affects relations between states and international organizations and as it applies to private business transactions. A full discussion of the public aspects of international law is left to other books and courses devoted to the topic.

Private international law is national law operating where a material foreign element is present, and concerns itself with three major topics: civil jurisdiction, choices of forum and law, and the recognition and enforcement of foreign judgments. Every state has its own set of laws spanning the three topics of private international law, and the definition of state in this case extends to subunits of federal states.

Private International Law

- Civil jurisdiction
- Choices of forum and law
- Recognition and enforcement of foreign judgments

Sources of International Law

At the outset, be aware that "international law" can be a misleading term. In speaking of relationships between nations, we are referring to law that they have some mutual hand in creating—a treaty, for example. However, the term "international law" also can mean the domestic law of a nation that is intended to govern that nation's judicial behavior in cases with an international element. That is, its international law rules where its national rules may be in conflict with the national rules of other states. These make up the procedural framework that assists courts in determination of their jurisdiction, and their right to hear and decide any particular case. Therefore, there are as many sets of "international law" as there are nations in the world, with some of this international law being held in common and some of it in conflict.

As citizens of our respective countries, we receive the law of our lands from our government, and then we can obey the law or not. If we choose not to obey it, we face very personal consequences in receiving a penalty or jail. As citizens, we do not get to negotiate directly in the creation of law, nor do we get the opportunity to accept one law of our nation and opt out of another law. We have given up our personal sovereignty to make such choices to a political system that places our government above us, and gives it the right to punish us for failure to obey.

Nations, as opposed to individuals, have greater ability to maneuver. There is no global government to which all nations must submit. Nations themselves create the law of nations, or international law, and the result is far more like a contract between nations.

Two controversies surround international law, and we will not treat them in depth because they are of more interest to academics rather than practitioners of international business law. That said, a student should at least be aware that they exist.

The first is the question of whether "international law" is really "law." This debate stems from questions such as: "How do you 'arrest' a state?" and "Who and where is the international lawmaker?" Articles, books, and conferences abound on this topic, arguing in both directions. We are satisfied that international law exists, even if it does not take the form that we traditionally expect law to take. Even then, international law has its contractual relationships in treaties and conventions. It is accepted that states can commit torts such as genocide and that a breach of obligations will result in a penalty. This penalty may be a trade embargo that amounts to solitary confinement. Alternatively, an international war crimes tribunal looks like a court, and the waging of war against a nation resembles physical punishment.

Must we insist that every form of law look and operate like our own? If we did, there would be few lessons in the previous chapter of this book, and in the extreme, a common law jurist would dismiss civil law and theological law as not really being "law." We take the approach that an incomplete yet evolving and workable body of international law exists.

The second controversy is worth further investigation, for it helps expose the sources of international law. The debate is over whether preemptory norms *(jus cogens)* and customary law *(opinio juris,* custom with a sense of legal obligation) exist within the scope of international law and whether these bind nations. If these exist, they are norms of national behavior from which no derogation is permitted (e.g., prohibitions of slavery, genocide) and long-entrenched practice (custom) that has taken on the force of law through implied consent of states.

Another way of framing the debate is: where conflict exists between states, does natural law carry weight, and do principles of consent and implied consent have international law counterparts?

Absent world government, we know that there are only three mechanisms for conflict resolution in international affairs, and at times some or all are employed. They are war, diplomacy, and international law (having assumed that it exists). We can dispense with the first two quickly.

If a nation's vital interests are threatened, meaning those at the core of its existence, it is prepared to go to war. Usually this step follows the exhaustion of diplomacy—state-to-state negotiation of the problem—with settlement involving some form of compromise. Both of these eventualities leave a bad taste—a problem that could not sufficiently have been foreseen, such that it results in either brinkmanship or blood. Not all states are good at this type of forward thinking—many wars have been fought over trifles.

The forward-thinking option is preferable, and it lays bare the sources of international law, aided by diplomacy. International law is comprised of what nations have done historically and what nations commit to do in the future, through both customary law and treaties.

Treaties are the more straightforward source of international law. They are the written binding commitments of one nation toward one or more other nations to govern their own affairs in a particular way. The key is that they give rise to expectations of a binding nature on the affairs of state.[2] We go further yet to say that they are of a quasi-constitutional nature, a notion that finds support worldwide in practice, given that many nations (including the United States) place special conditions on their ratification.

---

[2]More formally, the Vienna Convention on the Law of Treaties defines *treaty* as meaning "an international agreement concluded between States in written form and governed by international law, whether embodied in a single instrument or in two or more related instruments and whatever its particular designation." Vienna Convention on the Law of Treaties, 1969, art 2(1)(a), 1155 U.N.T.S. 331, entered into force January 27, 1980, though not ratified by the United States. Despite its lack of ratification by the United States, American jurists regularly refer to its provisions with tacit approval. The full text may be found at www.un.org/law/ilc/texts/treaties.htm.

State practice is what gives rise to customary law, and the longer something has been practiced, all the greater is its claim to legitimacy. State practice is customary law to the extent that behavior is consistently exhibited by a nation, as though that nation is now compelled to observe that behavior.[3] The more nations that subscribe to the practice, the greater the claim to its position as part of customary law, somewhat like implied consent.

Of course, not all nations observe the same practices, though many are held in common. The result is that two bodies of state practice reside under a single umbrella of customary law: the ones virtually all nations always agree on and those in a gray area. Customary law based on state practice is a highly fluid definition, and if it cannot be pinned down within a set of formal lists, almost anything, with some imagination, can pass as customary law.

This is an explicit but only a partial criticism of customary law. It is partial because there is much in customary law that is so "right," or at least without debate, that it has become jus cogens. *Jus cogens* means a principle of behavior so fundamental to civilized states that no nation may ignore, avoid, or contract out of it. It is recognized among nations in the Vienna Convention in the following terms:

Vienna Convention: Article 53. Treaties Conflicting with a Peremptory Norm of General International Law (jus cogens)

A treaty is void if, at the time of its conclusion, it conflicts with a peremptory norm of general international law. For the purposes of the present Convention, a peremptory norm of general international law is a norm accepted and recognized by the international community of States as a whole as a norm from which no derogation is permitted and which can be modified only by a subsequent norm of general international law having the same character.

Source: Vienna Convention on the Law of Treaties, 1969, art. 53, 1155 U.N.T.S. 331.

Simple examples, as mentioned above, lie in international prohibitions against genocide and slavery. But jus cogens can still be criticized. As with customary law more generally, to the delight of politicians and the dismay of international lawyers, much can pass or try to be passed as jus cogens when governments try to justify state practices.[4]

Often nations (big and small) don't like the hand of cards that are dealt to them in the international arena. If the price of initiating war is too great, or the irritant insufficient, where diplomacy has failed in action or in time, where treaty has failed in foresight or in scope, there remains the final faint hope of international law: customary law based on either jus cogens or state practice. Whenever a country is down to its last card, it will say that jus cogens or state practice is on its side.

Treaties and conventions, customary law, and jus cogens are the primary sources of international law, and are recognized as such by the International Court of Justice of the United Nations, along with judicial decisions of domestic judges and legal writers. The Court is open to all members of the United Nations, but only about one-third of the members have accepted its compulsory jurisdiction. While the United States has not,[5] Great Britain, Japan, Canada, Mexico, Australia, Belgium, the Netherlands, Spain, and India are among those who have. The Statute of the Court clarifies its resources in deciding disputes as follows:

[3]American Law Institute, *Restatement (Third) of the Foreign Relations Law of the United States* (1987), § 102(2).

[4]See the aptly named "It's a Bird, It's a Plane, It's Jus Cogens," by Anthony D'Amato, *Connecticut Journal of International Law* 6 (1991), p. 1.

[5]The United States has grave concerns with the International Court of Justice and its newer sister, the International Criminal Court. While the general principles of behavior of civilized states are not in contention, the United States is concerned that in executing its international responsibilities as the preeminent world power, it would expose its citizens, military personnel, and political leaders to unfair and open-ended liability.

Statute of the International Court of Justice: Article 38

1. The Court, whose function is to decide in accordance with international law such disputes as are submitted to it, shall apply:
   a. international conventions, whether general or particular, establishing rules expressly recognized by the contesting states;
   b. international custom, as evidence of a general practice accepted as law;
   c. the general principles of law recognized by civilized nations;
   d. subject to the provisions of Article 59, judicial decisions and the teachings of the most highly qualified publicists of the various nations, as subsidiary means for the determination of rules of law.

This provision shall not prejudice the power of the Court to decide a case.

Source: Statute of the International Court of Justice, Chapter II, Article 38, annexed to the Charter of the United Nations, www.icj-cij.org/icjwww/ibasicdocuments/ibasictext/ibasicstatute.htm.

The International Court of Justice, and for that matter any national court, must actually interpret the meaning of these principles of law in order to apply them. All jurisdictions have statutory law in the form of "interpretation acts" to assist judges in this task. In the international context, the Vienna Convention again lends guidance for interpretation that has achieved international recognition through ratification of the Convention or with the implied consent of nations.

Vienna Convention: Articles 31 and 32

Article 31. General Rule of Interpretation

1. A treaty shall be interpreted in good faith in accordance with the ordinary meaning to be given to the terms of the treaty in their context and in the light of its object and purpose.
2. The context for the purpose of the interpretation of a treaty shall comprise, in addition to the text, including its preamble and annexes:
   (a) any agreement relating to the treaty which was made between all the parties in connexion with the conclusion of the treaty;
   (b) any instrument which was made by one or more parties in connexion with the conclusion of the treaty and accepted by the other parties as an instrument related to the treaty.
3. There shall be taken into account together with the context:
   (a) any subsequent agreement between the parties regarding the interpretation of the treaty or the application of its provisions;
   (b) any subsequent practice in the application of the treaty which establishes the agreement of the parties regarding its interpretation;
   (c) any relevant rules of international law applicable in the relations between the parties.
4. A special meaning shall be given to a term if it is established that the parties so intended.

Article 32. Supplementary Means of Interpretation

Recourse may be had to supplementary means of interpretation, including the preparatory work of the treaty and the circumstances of its conclusion, in order to confirm the meaning resulting from the application of article 31, or to determine the meaning when the interpretation according to article 31:

(a) leaves the meaning ambiguous or obscure; or
(b) leads to a result which is manifestly absurd or unreasonable.

Source: Vienna Convention on the Law of Treaties, 1969, arts. 31 and 32, 1155 U.N.T.S. 331.

Note that these principles of international law apply to the public sphere, that is, nations taking action against other nations, sometimes for harm done by nationals of one state doing business within the territory of the other state. It may be that the mistreatment of a business by a host nation is in violation of a trade or investment treaty between the home nation of the business and the host. Such a violation could be brought before the International Court

Recognize the fact that the two hemispheres of public and private international law join, but do not really intersect. If a domestic business operating internationally is harmed by a foreign state, the business may be able to take action on a private law basis in its home or foreign courts. Sometimes they can and do, but if that business asks its own government to take action, and it does, then that government acts in its own right, not in the name of the business. For example, where the Brazilian government harms a Mexican company, and the Mexican government takes action against Brazil, any settlement belongs to the Mexican government, not to the company. This is because Mexico itself was wronged as a result of ill treatment of one of its nationals. The Mexican firm can only hope that its own government will look favorably on its later claim for compensation.

of Justice, in an action between the states. However, only states are parties to international organs such as the ICJ, and therefore individuals and businesses cannot themselves bring a suit against a state in this Court or other similar international forum.

This scenario of a private actor in one nation harming nationals in another nation occurs often. It also may be the case that the damage is so widespread that the issue is taken up in diplomatic negotiation between the governments, and may lead to international arbitration, which can be considered as a final category of international lawmaking. This lawmaking is binding only as between the state parties, but well-reasoned arbitration awards have started, in recent decades, to become more and more persuasive in other arbitration cases and even in court proceedings.

One of the earlier and most significant arbitration proceedings was that established by the United States and Canada in 1935 to settle questions arising from damage caused to the U.S. state of Washington by sulfur and sulfur-dioxide emissions from a smelter located in Trail, British Columbia, Canada.[6] Canada did not dispute the fact that damage was occurring, and the fact that the Trail smelter was the cause. The subsequent arbitration on the amount of damages and commitment not to injure is an example of peaceful settlement of a dispute, but it required six years to reach a final settlement. Such time frames and even longer ones are, unfortunately, common.

The procedure was conducted in three parts: the initial establishment of an Arbitral Tribunal in 1935 that would accept a report from an already-existing Joint Commission, a first report of the Tribunal in 1938, and a final award of the Tribunal in 1941 that also disposed of a partial "appeal" of the 1938 findings.

The Trail Smelter Arbitration

The 1935 Convention Terms of Reference

Considering that the Government of the United States has complained to the Government of Canada that fumes discharged from the smelter of the Consolidated Mining and Smelting company at Trail, British Columbia, have been causing damage in the State of Washington, and . . . recognizing the desirability and necessity of effecting a permanent settlement, [the United States and Canada] have decided to conclude a convention for the purposes aforesaid . . . The Tribunal shall consist of a chairman and two national members. The chairman shall be a jurist of repute who is neither a British subject nor a citizen of the United States . . . The two national members shall be jurists of repute who have not been

[6]United Nations Reports of International Arbitral Awards 3 (1941), p. 1905.

associated, directly or indirectly, in the present controversy. One member shall be chosen by each of the Governments.

The Tribunal shall finally decide the questions . . .

1. Whether damage caused by the Trail Smelter in the State of Washington has occurred since the first day of January, 1932, and, if so, what indemnity should be paid therefor?
2. [W]hether the Trail Smelter should be required to refrain from causing damage in the State of Washington in the future and, if so, to what extent?
3. [W]hat measures or regime, if any, should be adopted or maintained by the Trail Smelter?

. . .

The Tribunal shall apply the law and practice followed in dealing with cognate question in the United States of America as well as international law and practice, and shall give consideration to the desire of the high-contracting parties to reach a solution just to all parties concerned . . . The Governments undertake to take such action as may be necessary in order to ensure due performance of the obligations undertaken hereunder, in compliance with the decision of the Tribunal.

. . .

The First Decision, April 1938

An earlier Commission analyzed the admitted cause and damage and assessed an indemnity of $350,000 in respect of damage up to 1932. Canada assumed this liability under the Convention an international responsibility. The U.S. protested the damage was an ongoing problem, and diplomatic negotiation gave rise to the arbitration convention. The Tribunal determined that post-1932 damage had been caused, and then considered the extent of the appropriate indemnity . . .

The United States presented claims for a total of $2,100,000 divided into damages to seven categories:

a. Cleared land and improvements
b. Uncleared land and improvements
c. Livestock
d. Property in the town of Northport
e. Wrong done the United States in violation of sovereignty, measured by cost of investigation from January 1, 1932 to June 30, 1936
f. Interest on $350,000 accepted in satisfaction of damage to January 1, 1932, but not paid on that date
g. Business enterprises.

The United States in its Statement claims (Item e) "damages in respect of the wrong done the United States in violation of sovereignty" . . . The Tribunal finds it unnecessary to decide whether the facts proven did or did not constitute an infringement or violation of sovereignty . . . In other cases of international arbitration cited by the United States, damages awarded for expenses were awarded, not as compensation for violation of national sovereignty, but as compensation for expenses incurred by individual claimants in prosecuting their claims for wrongful acts by the offending Government . . . The Tribunal is, therefore, of opinion that neither as a separable item of damage nor as an incident to other damages should any award be made for that which the United States terms "violation of sovereignty."

. . .

In conclusion, the Tribunal answers Question 1 in Article III, as follows: Damage [was] caused by the Trail Smelter . . . since the first day of January, 1932, and up to October 1, 1937, and the indemnity to be paid therefor is seventy-eight thousand dollars ($78,000), and is to be complete and final indemnity and compensation for all damage which occurred between such dates . . . This decision is not subject to alteration or modification by the Tribunal hereafter . . .

As to Question No. 2 . . . whether the Trail Smelter should be required to refrain from causing damage . . . The Tribunal decides that until the date of the final decision provided for in Part Four of this present decision, the Trail Smelter shall refrain from causing damage . . .

As to Question No. 3, what measures or regime, if any, should be adopted or maintained by the Trail Smelter . . . The Tribunal is unable at the present time, with the information that has been placed before it, to determine upon a permanent regime, for the operation of the Trail Smelter . . . To enable it to establish a permanent regime based on the more adequate and intensive study and knowledge referred to, the Tribunal establishes the following temporary regime . . .

The Second Decision, March 1941

This later decision was intended to establish a permanent control regime in place of the temporary one established in 1938, and as well heard a request by the United States for the Tribunal to reconsider its indemnity award with respect to damage to U.S. sovereignty.

. . .

The controversy is between two Governments involving damage occurring or having occurred, in the territory of one of them (the United States of America) and alleged to be due to an agency situated in the territory of the other (the Dominion of Canada). In this controversy, the Tribunal did not sit and is not sitting to pass upon claims presented by individuals . . . [It is] reflected in the provisions of the convention . . . that "the desire of the high-contracting parties" is "to reach a solution just to all parties concerned" . . . In arriving at its decisions, the Tribunal has had always to bear in mind that further fact that in the preamble to the Convention, it is stated that it is concluded with the recognition of "the desirability and necessity of effecting a permanent settlement" . . . The indemnity found by the Tribunal to be due for damage which had occurred since the first day of January, 1932 up to October 1, 1937, i.e. $78,000, was paid by the Dominion of Canada to the United States and received by the latter without reservations. . . . The decision of the Tribunal in respect of damage up to October 1, 1937, was thus complied with in conformity with Article XII of the convention. If it were not, in itself, final in this respect, the decision would have assumed a character of finality through this action of the parties. . . . There can be no doubt that the Tribunal intended to give a final answer to Question 1 for the period up to October 1, 1937. This is made abundantly clear by the passage quoted above, in particular by the words: "This decision is not subject to alteration or modification by the Tribunal hereafter."

As to the second question and the requirement to refrain from causing damage . . .

As Professor Eagleton puts it "A State owes at all times a duty to protect other States against injurious acts by individuals from within its jurisdiction." A great number of such general pronouncements by leading authorities concerning the duty of a State to respect other States and their territory have been presented to the Tribunal . . . This principle, as such, has not been questioned by Canada. But the real difficulty often arises rather when it comes to determine what . . . is deemed to constitute an injurious act . . . No case of air pollution dealt with by an international tribunal has been brought to the attention of the Tribunal nor does the Tribunal know of any such case. The nearest analogy is that of water pollution. But, here also, no decision of an international tribunal has been cited or has been found.

There are, however, as regards both air pollution and water pollution, certain decisions of the Supreme Court of the United States which may legitimately be taken as a guide in this field of international law, for it is reasonable to follow by analogy, in international cases, precedents established by that court in dealing with controversies between States of the Union or with other controversies concerning the quasi-sovereign rights of such States, where no contrary rule prevails in international law and no reason for rejecting such precedents can be adduced from the limitations of sovereignty inherent in the constitution of the United States.

. . .

Considering the circumstances of the case, the Tribunal holds that the Dominion of Canada is responsible in international law for the conduct of the Trail Smelter . . . It is, therefore, the duty of the government of the Dominion of Canada to see to it that this conduct should be in conformity with the obligation of the Dominion under international law as herein determined.

The Tribunal, therefore, answers [that] so long as the present conditions in the Columbia River Valley prevail, the Trail Smelter shall be required to refrain from causing any damage through fumes in the State of Washington . . . *and imposed a permanent regime for control of emissions from the Trail Smelter.*

Source: *United Nations Reports of International Arbitral Awards* 3 (1941), p. 1905.

Canada paid both the earlier-ordered $350,000 in damages and the later $78,000 indemnity, and was committed to the control of emissions. In this arbitration case, note particularly that

1. The composition of the arbitration tribunal is described.
2. The parties are committed to a permanent settlement, both for damage to date and control in the future.
3. The parties are willing to incorporate international law principles.
4. Damages for "violation of sovereignty" will not be entertained.
5. The Tribunal award cannot be appealed.
6. Claims of individuals are not at issue.
7. A state owes, under international law, at all times a duty to protect other states against injurious acts by individuals from within its jurisdiction.

This case and other post–World War I arbitration cases like it represent the turning of nations away from conflict and toward a committed process of building international law principles, not only in theory, but in practice.

Sovereignty

International businesspersons run into issues of sovereignty on a regular basis. Sovereignty is felt every time one presents a passport for inspection, every time a foreign tax is paid or forms are completed. It is felt when one submits to proceedings in a foreign jurisdiction or when foreign judgments are enforced at home.

Sovereignty is the entire bundle of attributes and rights that make a state a state. The U.S. *Restatement of Foreign Relations Law* defines a state as "an entity that has a defined territory and population under the control of a government and that engages in foreign relations."[7] State sovereignty represents the ultimate and all-encompassing authority within a defined territory, exercising legislative, administrative, and judicial competence under a system of governance that is to be respected and recognized by other equally sovereign states, with a reciprocal expectation of nonintervention.

The concept of sovereignty is so central to the integrity of states that it forms the first substantive obligation under the Charter of the United Nations:

UN Charter: Article 2 (excerpt only)

> The Organization and its Members, in pursuit of the Purposes stated in Article 1, shall act in accordance with the following Principles.
>
> 1. The Organization is based on the principle of the sovereign equality of all its Members.

Source: Charter of the United Nations, Article 2(1), www.un.org/Overview/Charter/chapter1.html.

Sovereignty, and particularly the issue of nonintervention in equally sovereign states, was born in ancient customary law, where the divine rights of kings dictated a certain impropriety in one deity interfering in the internal affairs of another deity. As a legal concept, it turned mere territory into something more substantial, giving states a body. The primary interest was obviously territorial, but it also created authority with an influence against the competing interests of outsiders.

This "body" is capable of dialog with other states. Power may be unequal in these exchanges, but the authority and communication are between peers, with a sense of equality between states. When exchanges of dialog do occur—speaking and listening—this recognition of sovereignty amounts to recognition of statehood.

These principles of sovereignty illustrate why one state will not blindly pursue the grievances of its own nationals that have been suffered at the hands of other states. The home state of the aggrieved must balance whether it is in its own national interest to pursue the matter at the expense of its friendly relations with others. To pursue every grievance is to invite other nations to do the same to it. The home nation does not want its international relations and the international order to descend into anarchy, or, worse yet, war. Political compromises in accordance with national interest, as opposed to business interests, can be expected to result.

Sovereign Immunity and the Act-of-State Doctrine

Sovereign Immunity

States are largely unwilling to expose themselves to lawsuits from individuals, and have been very reluctant to make commitments to international bodies that would allow such actions. Some liberalization has taken place in the field of human rights, but even then most international human rights tribunals can only act after there has been a clear exhaustion of the individual's rights at the national court level. It is in a nation's self-interest then to claim immunity from prosecution, and to extend that immunity to other sovereigns, hence the term *sovereign immunity*. Historically, these were absolute immunities, but now most nations limit this, and a principle of a more restricted sovereign immunity is usually applied.

In the case of the United States, near absolute immunity existed after Chief Justice Marshall ruled in 1812 that a sovereign was "bound by obligations of the highest character not to degrade the dignity of his nation, by placing himself or its sovereign rights within the jurisdiction of another."[8] In the Court's opinion, any exception to that could stem only from consent or waiver.[9]

[7]American Law Institute, *Restatement (Third) of the Foreign Relations Law of the United States* (1987), § 4.
[8]*Schooner Exchange v. M'Faddon,* 11 U.S. (7 Cranch) 116, 3 L.Ed. 287 (1812).
[9]Ibid., 11 U.S. (7 Cranch) at 136.

In the early 1950s, the U.S. Government and other world governments budged some, with the U.S. State Department willing to grant immunity to a sovereign where its acts were of a public act nature, but not with respect to its private acts.[10] Thus, a state may remain immune from private action when it refuses, say, to grant a travel visa, but may be sued for nonpayment if it ignores its accounts for grain that it purchases. Only in 1976 did the United States actually formalize this position with legislation,[11] and the range of exceptions to immunity has since expanded.

In particular, the Foreign Sovereign Immunities Act (28 U.S.C. § 1605) now provides that a foreign state shall not be immune from the jurisdiction (the right and authority to hear and rule on a case) of the courts of the United States or of the states in any case involving

Explicit or implicit waiver of immunity by the foreign state[12]
(for example, when a state agrees to submit to jurisdiction).

"[C]ommercial activity carried on in the United States . . . ; or . . . an act performed in the United States in connection with a commercial activity . . . elsewhere; or . . . an act outside the territory of the United States in connection with a commercial activity of the foreign state elsewhere . . . that . . . causes a direct effect in the United States[13]
(for example, lawsuits related to a foreign state-owned airline and the payment of its bills or damage that it causes).

"[P]roperty taken in violation of international law"[14]
(for example, a foreign government's expropriation of an American-owned factory abroad, without compensation).

"[R]ights in property in the United States acquired by succession or gift or rights in immovable property situated in the United States"[15]
(for example, a dispute over a building and land in the United States purchased by a foreign government).

"[M]oney damages . . . sought against a foreign state for personal injury or death, or damage to or loss of property, occurring in the United States and caused by the tortious act or omission of that foreign state"[16]
(for example, a lawsuit related to the crash in the United States of a foreign state-owned airliner).

An action brought "to enforce an agreement made by the foreign state with or for the benefit of a private party to submit to arbitration"[17]
(for example, an action to enforce the establishment of the LIAMCO v. Libya *arbitration tribunal discussed in Chapter 2).*

"[M]oney damages . . . sought against a foreign state for personal injury or death that was caused by an act of torture, extrajudicial killing, aircraft sabotage, hostage taking, or the provision of material support or resources . . . for such an act" if the foreign state is "designated as a state sponsor of terrorism under section 6(j) of the Export

---

[10]See the State Department position in *Alfred Dunhill of London, Inc. v. Republic of Cuba,* 425 U.S. 682 (1976).

[11]Foreign Sovereign Immunities Act of 1976, Pub. L. No. 94-583, codified at 28 U.S.C. § 1330, 1332(a), 1391(f), and 1601–1611.

[12]28 U.S.C. § 1605(a)(1).

[13]Ibid. § 1605(a)(2).

[14]Ibid. § 1605(a)(3).

[15]Ibid. § 1605(a)(4).

[16]Ibid. § 1605(a)(5).

[17]Ibid. § 1605(a)(6).

Flags are symbols of sovereignty. And a flag still hangs from the mast of every sunken and leaking oil tanker. So often these are "flags of convenience," a ship owned by wealthy businesses from a heavily regulated country but registered in another nation having little or no safety standards for seaworthiness of ships. Little or no inspections take place, only rudimentary crew training standards exist, and an "anything goes" attitude to granting registration prevails in these countries. Our oceans and seas pay the real price.

Administration Act of 1979 (50 U.S.C. App 2405(j)) or section 620A of the Foreign Assistance Act of 1961 (22 U.S.C. 2371)"[18]

(for example, at various times, Afghanistan, Libya, North Korea, among others).

"[A] suit in admiralty . . . brought to enforce a maritime lien against a vessel or cargo of the foreign state, which maritime lien is based upon a commercial activity of the foreign state"[19]

(for example, enforcement of rights against a ship containing grain purchased by a foreign state, where the ship has not paid its bills for fuel or provisions in a U.S. port).

Act-of-State Doctrine

The act-of-state doctrine works to provide foreign states an element of immunity from suit in domestic courts. It is best known as an American legal principle predating the Foreign Sovereign Immunities Act, but the doctrine is shared across a range of both common law and civil law jurisdictions. It removes from review by a domestic court any act performed by a foreign sovereign within the territory of that foreign state. It serves the interest of smoother foreign relations for a state that adopts this approach, making events abroad a matter for diplomacy and international relations by the executive branch, rather than a matter for the judiciary in domestic courts.

Unfortunately for individuals and businesses, it can work an injustice. Consider a business enterprise of the home country that faces expropriation of its assets abroad. It may well prefer to seek redress in its own courts, rather than those of the expropriating state, if only for the fact that it might receive a fairer accounting of its losses. Due to the act-of-state doctrine, however, it also may find that this avenue is closed, and its only option is to seek its damages in the foreign jurisdiction.

Historical expressions of the doctrine in American law read like definitions of sovereignty;[20] the contemporary statement is found in the case *Banco Nacional de Cuba v. Sabbatino.*[21] In this case, an American broker contracted for the purchase of sugar from a largely American-owned firm in Cuba, but before delivery, the Cuban government expropriated the assets of the American seller in response to U.S. government restrictions on sugar imports from Cuba. The broker was therefore ordered to pay for the sugar by making payment to a Cuban bank. Ultimately, the broker received the sugar but did not make payment. The Cuban bank brought action for payment, and while the District Court acknowledged the act-of-state doctrine, it nevertheless rendered judgment against the bank, on the basis that the doctrine was inapplicable when the act of state violated international

---

[18]Ibid. § 1605(a)(7).

[19]Ibid. § 1605(b).

[20]*Underhill v. Hernandez*, 168 U.S. 250 (1897). According to Justice Fuller: "Every sovereign state is bound to respect the independence of every other sovereign state, and the courts of one country will not sit in judgment on the acts of the government of another, done within its own territory."

[21]*Banco Nacional de Cuba v. Sabbatino*, 376 U.S. 398 (1964).

law. The court of appeals affirmed this judgment, further relying on State Department letters that it interpreted as a willingness of the executive branch to a judicial testing of the validity of the expropriation. The action then moved to the U.S. Supreme Court.

As you read the case, place yourself in the mindset of a lawmaker who will be faced with angry constituents as a result of the judgment. Be forewarned as you read it that the United States took steps to limit the act-of-state doctrine in the wake of the judgment. These limitations are discussed after the case.

Banco Nacional de Cuba v. Sabbatino

Supreme Court of the United States

March 23, 1964

Mr. Justice Harlan delivered the opinion of the Court:

Under principles of comity governing this country's relations with other nations, sovereign states are allowed to sue in the courts of the United States . . . This Court has called "comity" in the legal sense "neither a matter of absolute obligation, on the one hand, nor of mere courtesy and good will, upon the other." *Hilton v. Guyot,* 159 U.S. 113, 163–164 . . . [T]he privilege of suit has been denied only to governments at war with the United States . . .

We hold that this petitioner is not barred from access to the federal courts.
[*Quoting the case of* Oetjen v. Central Leather Co., *246 U.S. 297 (1918), Mr. Justice Harlan continued:*]

> "The principle that the conduct of one independent government cannot be successfully questioned in the courts of another is as applicable to a case involving the title to property brought within the custody of a court, such as we have here, as it was held to be to the cases cited, in which claims for damages were based upon acts done in a foreign country, for it rests at last upon the highest considerations of international comity and expediency. To permit the validity of the acts of one sovereign State to be reexamined and perhaps condemned by the courts of another would very certainly 'imperil the amicable relations between governments and vex the peace of nations.'"

. . .

The outcome of this case, therefore, turns upon whether any of the contentions urged by respondents against the application of the act of state doctrine in the premises is acceptable: (1) that the doctrine does not apply to acts of state which violate international law, as is claimed to be the case here; [*and*] (2) that the doctrine is inapplicable unless the Executive specifically interposes it in a particular case . . .

That international law does not require application of the doctrine is evidenced by the practice of nations. Most of the countries rendering decisions on the subject fail to follow the rule rigidly. No international arbitral or judicial decision discovered suggests that international law prescribes recognition of sovereign acts of foreign governments, see 1 Oppenheim's International Law, § 115aa (Lauterpacht, 8th ed. 1955), and apparently no claim has ever been raised before an international tribunal that failure to apply the act-of-state doctrine constitutes a breach of international obligation. If international law does not prescribe use of the doctrine, neither does it forbid application of the rule even if it is claimed that the act of state in question violated international law. The traditional view of international law is that it establishes substantive principles for determining whether one country has wronged another. Because of its peculiar nation-to-nation character the usual method for an individual to seek relief is to exhaust local remedies and then repair to the executive authorities of his own state to persuade them to champion his claim in diplomacy or before an international tribunal. See *United States v. Diekelman,* 92 U.S. 520, 524. Although it is, of course, true that United States courts apply international law as a part of our own in appropriate circumstances, *Ware v. Hylton,* 3 Dall. 199, 281; *The Nereide,* 9 Cranch 388, 423; *The Paquete Habana,* 175 U.S. 677, 700, the public law of nations can hardly dictate to a country which is in theory wronged how to treat that wrong within its domestic borders.

Despite the broad statement in *Oetjen* that "The conduct of the foreign relations of our Government is committed by the Constitution to the Executive and Legislative . . . Departments," 246 U.S., at 302, it cannot of course be thought that "every case or controversy which touches foreign relations lies beyond judicial cognizance." *Baker v. Carr,* 369 U.S. 186, 211. The text of the Constitution does not require the act-of-state doctrine; it does not irrevocably remove from the judiciary the capacity to review the validity of foreign acts-of-state.

 . . . We conclude that the scope of the act-of-state doctrine must be determined according to federal law . . .

If the act-of-state doctrine is a principle of decision binding on federal and state courts alike but compelled by neither international law nor the Constitution, its continuing vitality depends on its capacity to reflect the proper distribution of functions between the judicial and political branches of the Government on matters bearing upon foreign affairs. It should be apparent that the greater the degree of codification or consensus concerning a particular area of international law, the more appropriate it is for the judiciary to render decisions regarding it, since the courts can then focus on the application of an agreed principle to circumstances of fact rather than on the sensitive task of establishing a principle not inconsistent with the national interest or with international justice. It is also evident that some aspects of international law touch much more sharply on national nerves than do others; the less important the implications of an issue are for our foreign relations, the weaker the justification for exclusivity in the political branches. The balance of relevant considerations may also be shifted if the government which perpetrated the challenged act of state is no longer in existence . . . for the political interest of this country may, as a result, be measurably altered. Therefore, rather than laying down or reaffirming an inflexible and all-encompassing rule in this case, we decide only that the Judicial Branch will not examine the validity of a taking of property within its own territory by a foreign sovereign government, extant and recognized by this country at the time of suit, in the absence of a treaty or other unambiguous agreement regarding controlling legal principles, even if the complaint alleges that the taking violates customary international law.

 . . . Following an expropriation of any significance, the Executive engages in diplomacy aimed to assure that United States citizens who are harmed are compensated fairly. Representing all claimants of this country, it will often be able, either by bilateral or multilateral talks, by submission to the United Nations, or by the employment of economic and political sanctions, to achieve some degree of general redress. Judicial determinations of invalidity of title can, on the other hand, have only an occasional impact, since they depend on the fortuitous circumstance of the property in question being brought into this country. Such decisions would, if the acts involved were declared invalid, often be likely to give offense to the expropriating country; since the concept of territorial sovereignty is so deep seated, any state may resent the refusal of the courts of another sovereign to accord validity to acts within its territorial borders. Piecemeal dispositions of this sort involving the probability of affront to another state could seriously interfere with negotiations being carried on by the Executive Branch and might prevent or render less favorable the terms of an agreement that could otherwise be reached. Relations with third countries which have engaged in similar expropriations would not be immune from effect.

The dangers of such adjudication are present regardless of whether the State Department has, as it did in this case, asserted that the relevant act violated international law. If the Executive Branch has undertaken negotiations with an expropriating country, but has refrained from claims of violation of the law of nations, a determination to that effect by a court might be regarded as a serious insult, while a finding of compliance with international law, would greatly strengthen the bargaining hand of the other state with consequent detriment to American interests.

Even if the State Department has proclaimed the impropriety of the expropriation, the stamp of approval of its view by a judicial tribunal, however impartial, might increase any affront and the judicial decision might occur at a time, almost always well after the taking, when such an impact would be contrary to our national interest. Considerably more serious and far-reaching consequences would flow from a judicial finding that international law standards had been met if that determination flew in the face of a State Department proclamation to the contrary. When articulating principles of international law in its relations with other states, the Executive Branch speaks not only as an interpreter of generally accepted and traditional rules, as would the courts, but also as an advocate of standards it believes desirable for the community of nations and protective of national concerns. In short, whatever way the matter is cut, the possibility of conflict between the Judicial and Executive Branches could hardly be avoided.

Respondents contend that, even if there is not agreement regarding general standards for determining the validity of expropriations, the alleged combination of retaliation, discrimination, and inadequate compensation makes it patently clear that this particular expropriation was in violation of international law. If this view is accurate, it would still be unwise for the courts so to determine. Such a decision now would require the drawing of more difficult lines in subsequent cases and these would involve the possibility of conflict with the Executive view. Even if the courts avoided this course, either by presuming the validity of an act of state whenever the international law standard was thought unclear or by following the State Department declaration in such a situation, the very expression of judicial uncertainty might provide embarrassment to the Executive Branch.

. . .

Against the force of such considerations, we find respondents' countervailing arguments quite unpersuasive. Their basic contention is that United States courts could make a significant contribution to the growth of international law, a contribution whose importance, it is said, would be magnified by the relative paucity of decisional law by international bodies. But given the fluidity of present world conditions, the effectiveness of such a patchwork approach toward the formulation of an acceptable body of law concerning state responsibility for expropriations is, to say the least, highly conjectural. Moreover, it rests upon the sanguine presupposition that the decisions of the courts of the world's major capital exporting country and principal exponent of the free enterprise system would be accepted as disinterested expressions of sound legal principle by those adhering to widely different ideologies.

. . .

It is suggested that if the act-of-state doctrine is applicable to violations of international law, it should only be so when the Executive Branch expressly stipulates that it does not wish the courts to pass on the question of validity . . . It is highly questionable whether the examination of validity by the judiciary should depend on an educated guess by the Executive as to probable result and, at any rate, should a prediction be wrong, the Executive might be embarrassed in its dealings with other countries . . .

However offensive to the public policy of this country and its constituent States an expropriation of this kind may be, we conclude that both the national interest and progress toward the goal of establishing the rule of law among nations are best served by maintaining intact the act-of-state doctrine in this realm of its application.

Source: *Banco Nacional de Cuba v. Sabbatino*, 376 U.S. 398 (1964).

In short, the U.S. Supreme Court said that while the bank was an arm of the Communist Cuban government, it was under no disability as a result of the expropriations carried out by the Cuban government (the bank had a right to be heard by U.S. courts). Further, whether or not the act of expropriation was a violation of international law was a matter of politics for the executive branch, and the bank had the right not only to be heard, but to receive a district court decision based on the merits of its contract.

Having read the *Sabbatino* decision from the point of view of a lawmaker, what would you expect as your constituents' reaction to the decision? If your constituents include investors with interests abroad, would their reaction be in accord with the "national interest and progress toward the goal of establishing the rule of law among nations"? What would they want you to do? If your constituents are upset, is there still a good argument to be made that it is in an investor's best interest to align their views with the national interest? How would you explain that argument?

For substantially the same reasons given by the U.S. Supreme Court, this view of the act-of-state doctrine remains the case in many countries: courts don't interfere in political questions. In the United States, however, in response to the *Sabbatino* decision, the U.S. Congress then enacted the Second Hickenlooper Amendment, named after its sponsor, in an attempt to limit application of the act-of-state doctrine. The Foreign Sovereign Immunities Act is a further expression of that intention. Still, there is a great reluctance on the part of American courts to so involve themselves in foreign affairs, and such provisions have been strictly construed.

Second Hickenlooper Amendment (abridged)

> Notwithstanding any other provision of law, no court in the United States shall decline on the ground of the federal act of state doctrine to make a determination on the merits giving effect to the principles of international law in a case in which a claim of title or other right to property is asserted by any party including a foreign state (or a party claiming through such state) based upon (or traced through) a confiscation or other taking after January 1, 1959, by an act of that state in violation of the principles of international law, including the principles of compensation and the other standards set out in this subsection: Provided, That this subparagraph shall not be applicable
>
> (1) in any case in or other right to property acquired pursuant to an irrevocable letter of credit of not more than 180 days duration issued in good faith prior to the time of the confiscation or other taking, or
>
> (2) in any case with respect to which the President determines that application of the act of state doctrine is required in that particular case by the foreign policy interests of the United States and a suggestion to this effect is filed on his behalf in that case with the court.

Source: 22 U.S.C. § 2370(e)(2).

Jurisdiction Where No Immunity

The previous section provided the limits of sovereign immunity and, in consequence, where the outside limit of jurisdiction lies. Where there is no immunity, jurisdiction arises when a state or its organs possess one or more of judicial, legislative, or administrative competence over an event or place.[22] Nations set out their division of powers in their constitutions, and domestic statutes lay out the manner in which their national courts may or may not refuse to recognize the competence of foreign courts and their judgments.

[22]I. Brownlee, *Principles of Public International Law* (Oxford: Oxford University Press, 1973), p. 291.

Criminal Jurisdiction

Criminal jurisdiction will apply in cases of commercial crime in trade and investment; more generally, the internationalization of criminal law foresees five situations in which competing states may claim jurisdiction over an offender:

1. Territorial jurisdiction.
2. Effects doctrine and active personality.
3. Passive personality.
4. Universal jurisdiction.
5. State protection.

Territorial jurisdiction may be claimed by the state where the offense was committed, and it is a powerful claim, as the laws of that nation were broken and evidence is probably most easily obtained there.

Common law countries that allow extradition of their own nationals often employ the effects doctrine. The extradition of their own people to other prosecuting states occurs under conditions of reciprocity and formal extradition treaties. Being reciprocal, these nations request others to return an offender to them for prosecution when the effects of the criminal act were felt on their territory, even if the offense was not committed there. An example would be an extradition request for surrender of an offender arrested abroad who has run an investment fraud scheme from somewhere abroad, where the effects of it were felt in the requesting nation. In a similar vein, civil law countries that do not permit extradition of their own nationals by other nations seek the return of their own national offenders, committing them to prosecution in the name of active personality.

The doctrine of passive personality exists but is largely discredited. It seeks the surrender of an offender arrested abroad (of whatever nationality) simply because the victim was a national of the requesting state. It is discredited due to the implicit lack of trust it expresses about the system of justice that exists in foreign states.

The universal jurisdiction principle has gained authority in recent decades. This is the concept that some crimes (slavery or genocide) are so heinous that any country may assert jurisdiction over such offenders and stand ready to prosecute them if they are found inside their territory, regardless of where in the world the offense was committed. Some European countries, notably Belgium, have become active in asserting universal jurisdiction, launching prosecution against South American and African leaders for alleged war crimes or human rights abuses. Again, because of its active role in international affairs, the United States is especially wary of any national attempt or international movement to create universal jurisdiction. The fear is that U.S. citizens in hostile jurisdictions will face political persecution rather than proper judicial prosecution. Their treatment will not reflect their alleged crime, but will be a means for foreign regimes to strike at U.S. government policy.

The final basis for jurisdiction, state protection, is well recognized. A nation may call for the surrender of offenders of any nationality from any state having custody of them, where an offender has committed crimes that touch upon the integrity of the claiming state, such as counterfeiting its currency.

These claims of jurisdiction, born of national law, can easily be in conflict between claiming nations. Resolution is made in some cases through diplomatic negotiation and, in the majority of other cases, by preexisting extradition treaties. These extradition treaties usually contain exceptions, where an extradition request can be refused if

- The offense is not recognized as criminal in the requested state (e.g., tax evasion is an administrative offense but not a criminal offense in some countries).
- The offense is a "political" crime in the eyes of the requested state (e.g., protest or criticism of the state).

 • The possible punishment in the requesting state is against public policy in the requested state (e.g., mutilation in some countries, or the death penalty in others).

Jurisdictional claims beyond the borders of a state require some authority to make that claim, such as the latter four above. Until the creation of the Permanent Court of International Justice (PCIJ) under the 1919 League of Nations (the precursor of today's International Court of Justice founded under the UN Charter), no judicial forum existed in which these claims could be tested. One large question was whether a nation needed a permissive rule in international law to assert its jurisdiction, or whether merely the fact that none existed to forbid jurisdiction was sufficient. This question was finally considered in the now-famous *Lotus* case, heard in 1927 by the PCIJ.[23]

The facts concerned a charge of manslaughter against a French officer in a high-seas collision between French and Turkish vessels. The Turkish vessel sank and eight Turkish nationals died. The French vessel reached a Turkish port and the officer was arrested. But who should prosecute him: France or Turkey? Turkey went ahead and did so, and convicted the French officer. International law came immediately to bear, for the Convention of Lausanne, part of the World War I peace agreements, had limited Turkish jurisdiction. Upon diplomatic complaint by France, the two nations brought the question of whether Turkey had jurisdiction before the PCIJ.

The judgment is loaded with post–World War I political baggage, has been superceded by Law of the Sea Conventions, and has been dissected of certain meaning on other grounds, but one thread refuses to break. That thread is the conclusion of the court that, absent any clear international law or custom to the contrary, sovereign nations are free to exercise their sovereignty and jurisdiction as they see fit. A rule of permission is not required.

The *Lotus* Case

Permanent Court of International Justice, 1927

The Court recites that the event occurred on the high seas, and that it is the institution of criminal proceedings [against] Lieutenant Demons that precipitated the question of jurisdiction, not his guilt, conviction, or the proper or improper application of Turkish domestic law.

Having determined the position resulting from the terms of the special agreement, the Court must now ascertain which were the principles of international law that the prosecution of Lieutenant Demons could conceivably be said to contravene.

It is Article 15 of the Convention of Lausanne of July 24th, 1923, respecting conditions of residence and business and jurisdiction, which refers the contracting Parties to the principles of international law as regards the delimitation of their respective jurisdiction.

This clause is as follows: "Subject to the provisions of Article 16, all questions of jurisdiction shall, as between Turkey and the other contracting Powers, be decided in accordance with the principles of international law."

The French Government advances argument based on early drafts and working documents of the Convention. The Court rejects this, as the Convention is sufficiently clear on its face.

The Court, having to consider whether there are any rules of international law which may have been violated by the prosecution in pursuance of Turkish law of Lieutenant Demons, is confronted in the first place by a question of principle which, in the written and oral arguments of the two Parties, has proved to be a fundamental one. The French Government contends that the Turkish Courts, in order to have jurisdiction, should be able to

---

[23] *The Case of the S.S. "Lotus" (France v. Turkey), 1927 P.C.I.J. (ser. A) No. 10 (September 7).*

point to some title to jurisdiction recognized by international law in favour of Turkey. On the other hand, the Turkish Government takes the view that Article 15 allows Turkey jurisdiction whenever such jurisdiction does not come into conflict with a principle of international law.

The latter view seems to be in conformity with the special agreement itself, No. 1 of which asks the Court to say whether Turkey has acted contrary to the principles of international law and, if so, what principles. According to the special agreement, therefore, it is not a question of stating principles which would permit Turkey to take criminal proceedings, but of formulating the principles, if any, which might have been violated by such proceedings.

This way of stating the question is also dictated by the very nature and existing conditions of international law. International law governs relations between independent States. The rules of law binding upon States therefore emanate from their own free will as expressed in conventions or by usages generally accepted as expressing principles of law and established in order to regulate the relations between these co-existing independent communities or with a view to the achievement of common aims. Restrictions upon the independence of States cannot therefore be presumed.

Now the first and foremost restriction imposed by international law upon a State is that—failing the existence of a permissive rule to the contrary—it may not exercise its power in any form in the territory of another State. In this sense jurisdiction is certainly territorial; it cannot be exercised by a State outside its territory except by virtue of a permissive rule derived from international custom or from a convention.

It does not, however, follow that international law prohibits a State from exercising jurisdiction in its own territory, in respect of any case which relates to acts which have taken place abroad, and in which it cannot rely on some permissive rule of international law. Such a view would only be tenable if international law contained a general prohibition to States to extend the application of their laws and the jurisdiction of their courts to persons, property and acts outside their territory, and if, as an exception to this general prohibition, it allowed States to do so in certain specific cases. But this is certainly not the case under international law as it stands at present. Far from laying down a general prohibition to the effect that States may not extend the application of their laws and the jurisdiction of their courts to persons, property and acts outside their territory, it leaves them in this respect a wide measure of discretion, which is only limited in certain cases by prohibitive rules; as regards other cases, every State remains free to adopt the principles which it regards as best and most suitable . . .

In these circumstances all that can be required of a State is that it should not overstep the limits which international law places upon its jurisdiction; within these limits, its title to exercise jurisdiction rests in its sovereignty.

It follows from the foregoing that the contention of the French Government to the effect that Turkey must in each case be able to cite a rule of international law authorizing her to exercise jurisdiction, is opposed to the generally accepted international law to which Article 13 of the Convention of Lausanne refers . . .

The territoriality of criminal law, therefore, is not an absolute principle of international law and by no means coincides with territorial sovereignty.

The Court therefore must, in any event ascertain whether or not there exists a rule of international law limiting the freedom of States to extend the criminal jurisdiction of their courts to a situation uniting the circumstances of the present case.

The Court does not discover such a rule.

The Court will now proceed to ascertain whether general international law, to which Article 15 of the Convention of Lausanne refers, contains a rule prohibiting Turkey from prosecuting Lieutenant Demons. The arguments advanced by the French Government, other than those considered above, are, in substance . . .

1. International law does not allow a State to take proceedings with regard to offences committed by foreigners abroad, simply by reason of the nationality of the victim; and such is the situation in the present case because the offence must be regarded as having been committed on board the French vessel.

2. International law recognizes the exclusive jurisdiction of the State whose flag is flown as regards everything which occurs on board a ship on the high seas.

As regards the first argument, the Court feels obliged in the first place to recall that its examination is strictly confined to the specific situation in the present case, for it is only in regard to this situation that its decision is asked for.

As has already been observed, the characteristic features of the situation of fact are as follows: there has been a collision on the high seas between two vessels flying different flags, on one of which was one of the persons alleged to be guilty of the offence, whilst the victims were on board the other.

This being so, the Court does not think it necessary to consider the contention that a State cannot punish offences committed abroad by a foreigner simply by reason of the nationality of the victim. For this contention only relates to the case where the nationality of the victim is the only criterion on which the criminal jurisdiction of the State is based. Even if that argument were correct generally speaking—and in regard to this the Court reserves its opinion—it could only be used in the present case if international law forbade Turkey to take into consideration the fact that the offence produced its effects on the Turkish vessel and consequently in a place assimilated to Turkish territory in which the application of Turkish criminal law cannot be challenged, even in regard to offences committed there by foreigners. But no such rule of international law exists . . .

The second argument put forward by the French Government is the principle that the State whose flag is flown has exclusive jurisdiction over everything which occurs on board a merchant ship on the high seas. It is certainly true that—apart from certain special cases which are defined by international law—vessels on the high seas are subject to no authority except that of the State whose flag they fly. In virtue of the principle of the freedom of the seas, that is to say, the absence of any territorial sovereignty upon the high seas, no State may exercise any kind of jurisdiction over foreign vessels upon them . . .

But it by no means follows that a State can never in its own territory exercise jurisdiction over acts which have occurred on board a foreign ship on the high seas. A corollary of the principle of the freedom of the seas is that a ship on the high seas is assimilated to the territory of the State the flag of which it flies, for, just as in its own territory, that State exercises its authority, upon it, and no other State may do so . . .

If, therefore, a guilty act committed on the high seas produces its effects on a vessel flying another flag or in foreign territory, the same principles must be applied as if the territories of two different States were concerned, and the conclusion must therefore be drawn that there is no rule of international law prohibiting the State to which the ship on which the effects of the offence have taken place belongs, from regarding the offence as having been committed in its territory and prosecuting, accordingly, the delinquent.

This conclusion could only be overcome if it were shown that there was a rule of customary international law which, going further than the principle stated above, established the exclusive jurisdiction of the State whose flag was flown . . .

In the Court's opinion, the existence of such a rule has not been conclusively proved . . . The Court therefore has arrived at the conclusion that the second argument put forward by the French Government does not, any more than the first, establish the existence of a rule of international law prohibiting Turkey from prosecuting Lieutenant Demons.

FOR THESE REASONS, The Court, having heard both Parties, gives, by the President's casting vote—the votes being equally divided—judgment to the effect

1. that . . . Turkey, by instituting criminal proceedings in pursuance of Turkish law against Lieutenant Demons, officer of the watch on board the *Lotus* at the time of the collision, has not acted in conflict with the principles of international law, contrary to Article 15 of the Convention of Lausanne of July 24th, 1923, respecting conditions of residence and business and jurisdiction . . .

Source: *The Case of the S.S. "Lotus" (France v. Turkey),* 1927 P.C.I.J. (ser. A) No. 10 (September 7).

Do you approve of the wide discretion allowed to states that need only to be certain that there is not a prohibitive rule barring their actions? Would you prefer a system that required a permissive rule before states could act?

Now it was fortunate that these two states had access to a neutral arbitrator who could settle their jurisdictional dispute, but in private international disputes, businesspersons are not so fortunate. They are limited to using national courts that may easily come into conflict with the respective limits of their jurisdiction.

Both national courts may agree, under their own domestic rules, that one of them has jurisdiction, which would be a happy result if it happened every time. However, it does not happen that way every time, just as France and Turkey did not agree in the *Lotus* case. Domestic courts may each claim that it has jurisdiction to hear a case, or, in what is almost a worse result, each may rule that only the other has jurisdiction, and, therefore, it may refuse to hear the case.

Civil Jurisdiction

Civil jurisdiction may exist over persons, property (and the persons with an interest in that property), or a combination of both. These alternatives are referred to as *in personam, in rem,* and *quasi in rem,* respectively. Just being a person or a thing is not sufficient, however, to be subject to the jurisdiction of a court; there must be factors connecting the person or property to that jurisdiction. Without a sufficient connecting factor(s), the court cannot take jurisdiction.

Connecting Factors

Every nation (or federal subunit), under its own set of international law rules, defines the connecting factors that will be sufficient to enable its courts to take jurisdiction in civil matters. These encompass one or more of the following:

1. Transient physical presence in the forum state.
2. Residence (based on property ownership, or a presence greater than a transient period).
3. Domicile (habitual residence).
   a. Of origin (place that was your father's domicile of choice when you were born).
   b. Of choice (your habitual residence based on conduct, not words).
4. Nationality:
   a. By *jus loci* (place of birth).
   b. By *jus sanguinus* (nationality of parents).
   c. By naturalization (citizenship by operation of national law).
5. Long-arm statutes (statutes authorizing jurisdiction over persons outside a territory):
   a. Serving persons domiciled inside a territory when they are outside the territory.
   b. Jurisdiction over persons outside the territory for torts committed while inside it.
   c. Jurisdiction over contracts that were to have been performed inside the territory by persons outside it.

At any time, a person can exhibit one, some, or all of these connecting factors. The test is, however, whether the connection is appropriate or sufficient to trigger jurisdiction under the laws of the nation concerned, for the purpose concerned. Even within a single nation or federal subunit, the jurisdiction of its courts may vary on the basis of the subject matter, that is, whether the case is a tax case or a contract case.

For example, a woman was born in New York while her parents were working on a one-year contract for a Canadian company. Her parents were born in Prague, Czech Republic, then Czechoslovakia, and had emigrated to Canada. In later life, she moved to Switzerland, where she now lives and works in Geneva, paying Swiss tax and holding a Swiss driver's license and medical benefit entitlement. She owns a winter home in Marbella, Spain. She travels to New York for three months on behalf of a British company to represent their commercial products. While in New York, she fails to perform her contracted work and makes fraudulent promises to potential buyers. She returns to Geneva via London's Heathrow Airport, where the British company serves her with a claim for breach of that contract.

As we shall see, it is perfectly sensible (and valid) for a British court to take jurisdiction in this case. The plaintiff is British, the subject matter of the contract is British, and personal service on a person while he or she is in Britain on a transient basis constitutes valid service for British courts. This latter fact is enough of a connecting factor in itself, as far as British courts are concerned.

However, note how easy it is to encounter fact situations that create possible connecting factors to other jurisdictions. In the example above, six countries, one being a successor state of another, as well as one U.S. state, all have an interest in this woman.

It may not be enough of an interest to create jurisdiction in them for all matters, but it could. There is a possible conflict of laws facing American plaintiffs in tort, who may in this case wish to bring actions in New York. As the breach of contract and the tort of fraudulent misrepresentation are so closely related in this case, it may be advantageous to consolidate the actions. But where, and in whose courts should this take place?

Residence is a weak connecting factor, as it is easily changed (whereas domicile is not), and it and nationality are most often limited to use as one indicator of possible domicile of choice. Both arise more frequently in questions of liability for taxation and qualification for state benefits in a particular jurisdiction.

Nationality is central to questions of citizenship, which is governed by each state's national law. It is an essential prerequisite where an individual seeks diplomatic assistance from his or her government, or seeks to have that government advance his or her interests before an international organization. Students wishing to explore the implications of nationality and citizenship for international businesspersons should examine the *Nottebohm* case, another important case of the International Court of Justice.[24]

Jurisdiction over Natural and Legal Persons Present in the Forum

For the natural person, most common law jurisdictions require only mere or transient presence of the individual within the forum to make him or her subject to the jurisdiction of its courts. This is the case in the United Kingdom, as long as the person is personally served (subject to recent changes as a result of overarching European law). On occasion, this has seen travelers served while passing through ports and airports, in transit to other places, without any further personal link to the United Kingdom.[25] In the United States, a similar approach of mere presence and personal service has been held not to offend the Fourteenth Amendment requirement of Due Process, as it comports with traditional notions of fair play and substantial justice.[26]

---

[24]*Nottebohm Case (Liechtenstein v. Guatemala)*, [1955] I.C.J. Rep. 4.

[25]See *Maharanee of Baroda v. Wildenstein*, [1972] 2 QB 283, [1972] 2 All ER 689 (Court of Appeal).

[26]See *Burnham v. Superior Court of California*, 110 S. Ct. 2105 (1990).

On the other hand, civil law jurisdictions (those employing a civil code) around the world have no concept of transient presence, and compelling a person to submit to jurisdiction on that basis is held to offend the principles of substantial justice. Civil law jurisdictions require domicile within their territory of the person to be served (wherever the person may be at present), or, failing that, the effects doctrine is applied. In this latter situation, the forum court may take jurisdiction where the effect of the act or omission complained of is felt within the territory.

The predominantly civil law European Union[27] is an area of economic integration and political union whose citizens enjoy considerable rights of movement within it. With this mobility has come the need to harmonize and liberalize conflicting rules of jurisdiction between them and their nationals. Rules of jurisdiction in international cases between their nationals have been harmonized through a Council Regulation, the highest form of law known to the EU. Only Denmark is not participating, and specialized national quirks (such as Britain's common law jurisdiction through transient presence) have been restricted in their use as against persons domiciled in other member states of the Union. These national peculiarities still exist, but can only be used against national defendants in purely domestic cases, or against non-EU nationals.

Regarding legal persons (e.g., corporations and trusts), common law jurisdictions use the place of incorporation (or similar legal fiction) as the determinant of nationality and domicile for business organizations founded in those jurisdictions. In the United States, a corporation will be subject to the jurisdiction of both the place of its incorporation and the principal place of its business. In civil law jurisdictions (and in common law of the United Kingdom and Ireland, with respect to their treaty obligations toward the European Union), domicile is based on the corporation's "seat," or principal place of business. Using a test such as domicile or place of incorporation certainly confirms the right of a "home" or "creating" administrative jurisdiction to take judicial jurisdiction over its business enterprises.

The European Union approach, in contrast to the common law approach, is shown below. It is typical of the accommodation made to fit the principles of its two common-law members into the civil law process.

Council Regulation (EC) 44/2001, Article 60

1. For the purposes of this Regulation, a company or other legal person or association of natural or legal persons is domiciled at the place where it has its:
   (a) statutory seat, or
   (b) central administration, or
   (c) principal place of business.
2. For the purposes of the United Kingdom and Ireland "statutory seat" means the registered office or, where there is no such office anywhere, the place of incorporation or, where there is no such place anywhere, the place under the law of which the formation took place.
3. In order to determine whether a trust is domiciled in the Member State whose courts are seised of the matter, the court shall apply its rules of private international law.

Source: Council Regulation (EC) 44/2001, 2001 O.J. (L 012), 1.

Beyond the jurisdiction of its creation, and/or its principal place of business, a defendant corporation may have sufficient connecting factors as a result of its activities to bring it within the jurisdiction of a number of states or federal substates. In states of the United States, this is recognized in "general jurisdiction," stemming from a defendant's "continuous and systematic" contacts with a state. The presence of permanent offices or a factory

[27]Including as of early 2004, Austria, Belgium, Denmark, Ireland, Finland, France, Germany, Greece, Italy, Luxembourg, the Netherlands, Portugal, Spain, Sweden, and the United Kingdom. It is set to expand in 2004 and thereafter to include Bulgaria, the Czech Republic, Estonia, Cyprus, Latvia, Lithuania, Hungary, Malta, Poland, Romania, Slovenia, Slovakia, and Turkey. See www.europa.eu.int.

operation would allow a plaintiff to sue a defendant in that state even though the alleged tort or breach was not related to the defendant's activity in that state. For example, where a corporation has factories in five states, a plaintiff may choose any one of those five in which to bring an action, even if the activity complained of occurred elsewhere. While a factory operation would probably satisfy the need for a "continuous and systematic contact," many other businesses will fall far short of that. The question is what contact will be enough to create jurisdiction? This is examined in the following section.

Jurisdiction over Persons Absent and Nondomiciled Legal Persons

Where it is allowed, mere presence is a low standard of connection to the forum intending to take jurisdiction, but it still does not work unless the person is actually present. It may well be that a person who has breached a contract or committed a tort knows that he or she will fall within that forum's jurisdiction if he or she ever returns, and simply avoids ever traveling there again.

Long-arm statutes are laws that extend jurisdiction to these absent potential defendants. If a person is domiciled within the territory but is physically absent, then such statutes provide for service of notice of the action on that person outside the territory. If the action relates to the commission of a tort in the territory, then the long arm statute gives jurisdiction to the court (or forum) of that territory, whether the person is domiciled there or not. Similarly, if the action is in contract, and the contract was to have been performed in the territory, the forum can assert its jurisdiction. Actual service, or deemed service, will still be required under the procedural rules of the forum.

All states—federal substates and nations alike—face a more difficult question when enterprises arrive from abroad (being domiciled abroad) and begin conducting business. This may fall far short of having an office or factory as a connecting link to the forum state. It may be that the foreign corporation merely ships goods in response to orders, goods that are dangerous or defective that later cause injury in the forum state.

At what point (if ever) can it be said that a corporation has impliedly consented to the jurisdiction of another state by doing business in that state? Where conduct falls short of triggering general jurisdiction, common law states recognize "specific jurisdiction," which requires the application of a more complex series of tests.

In any state of the United States, since the mid 1940s,

- The civil action *must* be related to the nonresident defendant's activities within the forum state.
- The defendant must have "minimum contacts" with the forum state.[28]
- The defendant must have purposely availed itself of the privilege of doing business there and directed its actions toward that state.

Finally, it must be reasonable for that court to exercise its jurisdiction. The requirement of reasonableness was laid out by the U.S. Supreme Court in later jurisprudence[29] and includes a requirement of consideration of

- The state's interest in the outcome.
- The interests of justice in resolution of the matter.
- The interests of both the plaintiff and defendant.
- Whether the defendant could have ever reasonably expected to find itself before the courts of that forum.

---

[28]*International Shoe Co. v. Washington,* 326 U.S. 310 (1945).

[29]*Worldwide Volkswagen Corp. v. Woodson,* 444 U.S. 286 (1980).

The *Asahi* case quite separately presents the kind of oddities that international litigation can create. First, the claim of the motorcyclist was eventually settled out of court, but not until after the action had been launched. The court action then took on an air of the unreal. It left a Taiwanese tire firm and a Japanese valve firm locked in litigation over apportioning their liability in a California court, when neither of them had a presence in the state. If there was a dispute remaining between them, convenience alone would suggest that it would be better heard in an Asian court rather than in a North American one. The motorcycle tire could easily be shipped as evidence to a court abroad, where presumably all the technical evidence of manufacturing also would be located.

The test of reasonableness has found even more recent expression by the U.S. Supreme Court in *Asahi Metal Industry Co. v. Superior Court of California*.[30] In that case, Asahi (a Japanese tire valve maker) sold valves installed in a Taiwanese tire, which was further assembled into a Japanese motorcycle sold in the United States. The valve may have contributed to a later motorcycle accident in California. The U.S. Supreme Court ruled that "mere placement of a product (a valve or tire) 'into the stream of commerce' did not constitute a sufficient connection between a defendant manufacturer and the State." The Court found a lack of minimum contacts purposely directed toward the state, even with the awareness that the "stream of commerce" would sweep the product into the state.

As opposed to cases involving a simple import, there are contracts of service where little or no transport of goods across a border takes place. The next case, *Helicopteros Nacionales de Colombia v. Hall et al.,* illustrates this example of common law thinking in instances of services and supply.[31] The European Union relies on a traditional civil law approach, and its legislation appears after *Helicopteros Nacionales.*

Helicopteros Nacionales de Colombia v. Hall et al.

Supreme Court of the United States

April 24, 1984

Mr. Justice Blackmun delivered the opinion of the Court.

We granted [*review*] in this case, 460 U.S. 1021 (1983), to decide whether the Supreme Court of Texas correctly ruled that the contacts of a foreign corporation with the State of Texas were sufficient to allow a Texas state court to assert jurisdiction over the corporation in a cause of action not arising out of or related to the corporation's activities within the State.

Petitioner Helicopteros Nacionales de Colombia, S. A. (Helicol), is a Colombian corporation with its principal place of business in the city of Bogota in that country. It is engaged in the business of providing helicopter transportation for oil and construction companies in South America. On January 26, 1976, a helicopter owned by Helicol crashed in Peru. Four United States citizens were among those who lost their lives in the accident. Respondents are the survivors and representatives of the four decedents.

At the time of the crash, respondents' decedents were employed by Consorcio, a Peruvian consortium, and were working on a pipeline in Peru. Consorcio is the alter ego of a joint venture named Williams-Sedco-Horn (WSH). The venture had its headquarters in Houston, Tex. Consorcio had been formed to enable the venturers to enter into a contract

[30]480 U.S. 102 (1987).

[31]*Helicopteros Nacionales De Colombia, S. A. v. Hall et al.,* 466 U.S. 408 (1984).

with Petro Peru, the Peruvian state-owned oil company. Consorcio was to construct a pipeline for Petro Peru running from the interior of Peru westward to the Pacific Ocean. Peruvian law forbade construction of the pipeline by any non-Peruvian entity.

Consorcio/WSH needed helicopters to move personnel, materials, and equipment into and out of the construction area. In 1974, upon request of Consorcio/WSH, the chief executive officer of Helicol, Francisco Restrepo, flew to the United States and conferred in Houston with representatives of the three joint venturers. At that meeting, there was a discussion of prices, availability, working conditions, fuel, supplies, and housing. Restrepo represented that Helicol could have the first helicopter on the job in 15 days. The Consorcio/WSH representatives decided to accept the contract proposed by Restrepo. Helicol began performing before the agreement was formally signed in Peru on November 11, 1974. The contract was written in Spanish on official government stationery and provided that the residence of all the parties would be Lima, Peru. It further stated that controversies arising out of the contract would be submitted to the jurisdiction of Peruvian courts. In addition, it provided that Consorcio/WSH would make payments to Helicol's account with the Bank of America in New York City.

Aside from the negotiation session in Houston between Restrepo and the representatives of Consorcio/WSH, Helicol had other contacts with Texas. During the years 1970–1977, it purchased helicopters (approximately 80% of its fleet), spare parts, and accessories for more than $4 million from Bell Helicopter Company in Fort Worth. In that period, Helicol sent prospective pilots to Fort Worth for training and to ferry the aircraft to South America. It also sent management and maintenance personnel to visit Bell Helicopter in Fort Worth during the same period in order to receive "plant familiarization" and for technical consultation. Helicol received into its New York City and Panama City, Fla., bank accounts over $5 million in payments from Consorcio/WSH drawn upon First City National Bank of Houston.

Beyond the foregoing, there have been no other business contacts between Helicol and the State of Texas. Helicol never has been authorized to do business in Texas and never has had an agent for the service of process within the State. It never has performed helicopter operations in Texas or sold any product that reached Texas, never solicited business in Texas, never signed any contract in Texas, never had any employee based there, and never recruited an employee in Texas. In addition, Helicol never has owned real or personal property in Texas and never has maintained an office or establishment there. Helicol has maintained no records in Texas and has no shareholders in that State. None of the respondents or their decedents were domiciled in Texas, but all of the decedents were hired in Houston by Consorcio/WSH to work on the Petro Peru pipeline project.

Respondents instituted wrongful-death actions in the District Court of Harris County, Tex., against Consorcio/WSH, Bell Helicopter Company, and Helicol. Helicol filed special appearances and moved to dismiss the actions for lack of *in personam* jurisdiction over it. The motion was denied. After a consolidated jury trial, judgment was entered against Helicol on a jury verdict of $1,141,200 in favor of respondents.

The Texas Court of Civil Appeals, Houston, First District, reversed the judgment of the District Court, holding that *in personam* jurisdiction over Helicol was lacking. The Supreme Court of Texas, with three justices dissenting, initially affirmed the judgment of the Court of Civil Appeals. Seven months later, however, on motion for rehearing, the court withdrew its prior opinions and, again with three justices dissenting, reversed the judgment of the intermediate court. In ruling that the Texas courts had *in personam* jurisdiction, the Texas Supreme Court first held that the State's long-arm statute reaches as far as the Due Process Clause of the Fourteenth Amendment permits. Thus, the only question remaining for the court to decide was whether it was consistent with the Due Process Clause for Texas courts to assert *in personam* jurisdiction over Helicol.

The Due Process Clause of the Fourteenth Amendment operates to limit the power of a State to assert *in personam* jurisdiction over a nonresident defendant. *Pennoyer v. Neff,* 95 U.S. 714 (1878). Due process requirements are satisfied when *in personam* jurisdiction is asserted over a nonresident corporate defendant that has "certain minimum contacts with [the forum] such that the maintenance of the suit does not offend 'traditional notions of fair play and substantial justice.' " *International Shoe Co. v. Washington,* 326 U.S. 310, 316 (1945), quoting *Milliken v. Meyer,* 311 U.S. 457, 463 (1940). When a controversy is related to or "arises out of" a defendant's contacts with the forum, the Court has said that a "relationship among the defendant, the forum, and the litigation" is the essential foundation of in [sic] *in personam* jurisdiction. *Shaffer v. Heitner,* 433 U.S. 186, 204 (1977).

Even when the cause of action does not arise out of or relate to the foreign corporation's activities in the forum State, due process is not offended by a State's subjecting the corporation to its *in personam* jurisdiction when there are sufficient contacts between the State and the foreign corporation. *Perkins v. Benguet Consolidated Mining Co.,* 342 U.S. 437 (1952); see *Keeton v. Hustler Magazine, Inc.,* 465 U.S. 770, 779–780 (1984). In *Perkins,* the Court addressed a situation in which state courts had asserted general jurisdiction over a defendant foreign corporation. During the Japanese occupation of the Philippine Islands, the president and general manager of a Philippine mining corporation maintained an office in Ohio from which he conducted activities on behalf of the company. He kept company files and held directors' meetings in the office, carried on correspondence relating to the business, distributed salary checks drawn on two active Ohio bank accounts, engaged an Ohio bank to act as transfer agent, and supervised policies dealing with the rehabilitation of the corporation's properties in the Philippines. In short, the foreign corporation, through its president, "[had] been carrying on in Ohio a continuous and systematic, but limited, part of its general business," and the exercise of general jurisdiction over the Philippine corporation by an Ohio court was "reasonable and just." 342 U.S., at 438, 445.

All parties to the present case concede that respondents' claims against Helicol did not "arise out of," and are not related to, Helicol's activities within Texas. We thus must explore the nature of Helicol's contacts with the State of Texas to determine whether they constitute the kind of continuous and systematic general business contacts the Court found to exist in *Perkins.* We hold that they do not.

It is undisputed that Helicol does not have a place of business in Texas and never has been licensed to do business in the State. Basically, Helicol's contacts with Texas consisted of sending its chief executive officer to Houston for a contract-negotiation session; accepting into its New York bank account checks drawn on a Houston bank; purchasing helicopters, equipment, and training services from Bell Helicopter for substantial sums; and sending personnel to Bell's facilities in Fort Worth for training.

The one trip to Houston by Helicol's chief executive officer for the purpose of negotiating the transportation-services contract with Consorcio/WSH cannot be described or regarded as a contact of a "continuous and systematic" nature, as *Perkins* described it, see also *International Shoe Co. v. Washington,* 326 U.S., at 320, and thus cannot support an assertion of *in personam* jurisdiction over Helicol by a Texas court. Similarly, Helicol's acceptance from Consorcio/WSH of checks drawn on a Texas bank is of negligible significance for purposes of determining whether Helicol had sufficient contacts in Texas. There is no indication that Helicol ever requested that the checks be drawn on a Texas bank or that there was any negotiation between Helicol and Consorcio/WSH with respect to the location or identity of the bank on which checks would be drawn. Common sense and everyday experience suggest that, absent unusual circumstances, the bank on which a check is drawn is generally of little consequence to the payee and is a matter left to the discretion of the drawer. Such unilateral activity of another party or a third person is not an appropriate consideration when determining whether a defendant has sufficient contacts with a forum State to justify an assertion of jurisdiction.

The Texas Supreme Court focused on the purchases and the related training trips in finding contacts sufficient to support an assertion of jurisdiction. We do not agree with that assessment, for the Court's opinion in *Rosenberg Bros. & Co. v. Curtis Brown Co.,* 260 U.S. 516 (1923) (Brandeis, J., for a unanimous tribunal), makes clear that purchases and related trips, standing alone, are not a sufficient basis for a State's assertion of jurisdiction.

The defendant in *Rosenberg* was a small retailer in Tulsa, Okla., who dealt in men's clothing and furnishings. It never had applied for a license to do business in New York, nor had it at any time authorized suit to be brought against it there. It never had an established place of business in New York and never regularly carried on business in that State. Its only connection with New York was that it purchased from New York wholesalers a large portion of the merchandise sold in its Tulsa store. The purchases sometimes were made by correspondence and sometimes through visits to New York by an officer of the defendant. The Court concluded: "Visits on such business, even if occurring at regular intervals, would not warrant the inference that the corporation was present within the jurisdiction of [New York]."

This Court in *International Shoe* acknowledged and did not repudiate its holding in *Rosenberg.* In accordance with *Rosenberg,* we hold that mere purchases, even if occurring at regular intervals, are not enough to warrant a State's assertion of *in personam* jurisdiction over a nonresident corporation in a cause of action not related to those purchase transactions. Nor can we conclude that the fact that Helicol sent personnel into Texas for training in connection with the purchase of helicopters and equipment in that State in any way enhanced the nature of Helicol's contacts with Texas. The training was a part of the package of goods and services purchased by Helicol from Bell Helicopter. The brief presence of Helicol employees in Texas for the purpose of attending the training sessions is no more a significant contact than were the trips to New York made by the buyer for the retail store in *Rosenberg.* See also *Kulko v. California Superior Court,* 436 U.S., at 93 (basing California jurisdiction on 3-day and 1-day stopovers in that State "would make a mockery of" due process limitations on assertion of personal jurisdiction).

We hold that Helicol's contacts with the State of Texas were insufficient to satisfy the requirements of the Due Process Clause of the Fourteenth Amendment. Accordingly, we reverse the judgment of the Supreme Court of Texas.

(Accordingly, the surviving relatives of those killed could not sue the Colombian owner Helicol in Texas for the wrongful death of their family members.)

Source: *Helicopteros Nacionales de Colombia v. Hall et al.,* 466 U.S. 408 (1984).

The Supreme Court speaks quite clearly in this case, rapidly concluding that minimum contacts do not exist sufficient to establish Texas jurisdiction, with most of the facts not only uncontested, but agreed between the parties. The plaintiff-respondents clearly hoped the threshold for minimum contacts was much lower. What points this action toward Texas in the first place? What threshold of contacts would you expect to be sufficient?

Legal persons and their lack of physical form create this more difficult assessment of "presence" in a forum state. As can be seen above in the *Helicopteros* case, the U.S. Supreme Court is willing to accept "continuous and systematic contact" with a state that lies between the ends of the spectrum of no contact and having an office and being licensed to do business.

The range of connecting factors in cases of legal persons doing business in a particular forum can be summarized in the following table. These are reasonable indicators found in most common law jurisdictions, though the weight placed on any one of them will vary from forum to forum, depending on the circumstances of the case.

Do you think a court in Colombia or Peru would offer up $1,141,200 in damages, as did the Texas trial jury? Maybe yes, but given the tendencies among juries in the United States compared to elsewhere, likely no. In the 1981 case of *Reyno v. Piper Aircraft,* a Scottish aircraft accident resulted in a plaintiff filing suit in the United States for a variety of procedural reasons, not the least of which was that Scottish law would have made proceeding in Scotland highly disadvantageous. It required appeal to the U.S. Supreme Court to definitively settle that this entirely Scottish matter (save manufacture of the aircraft) should be heard in Scotland. A plaintiff's deliberate search for a favorable forum (in procedure, convenience, or probable damage awards) is known as "forum shopping." While courts are reluctant to disturb the plaintiff's choice of forum where available, no forum wishes to become a "flag of convenience" or judicial Las Vegas. Only the reasonable use of connecting factors can prevent this.

Connecting Factors beyond Domicile: U.S. and Other Common Law Jurisdictions

Valid Connecting Factors (though collectively insufficient in *Helicopteros*)	**Even Stronger Indices of Connection**
• Contract negotiations in forum state • Purchasing assets and ancillary equipment • Employee training in forum state • Accepting checks drawn on local bank	• Soliciting sales in forum state • Doing business in forum state • Maintaining an office or records in forum state • Executing contracts in forum state • Having local employees or an agent • Owning real or personal property in forum state • Being licensed to do business in that state • Recruiting in that state • Having shareholders in that state

   Civil jurisdiction among the member states of the European Union is legislated via a Council Regulation. The legislative process of the EU is considered in greater detail in Chapter 5; however, it is sufficient here to recognize that a Council Regulation is the highest order of legislation among the member states of the European Union. It is binding in its entirety and has direct effect and applicability in the Member States without requirement of any form of national enabling legislation. Any national law in conflict with a Council Regulation is, to the extent of the conflict, void. Be aware that the common law approach to jurisdiction in both Ireland and the United Kingdom, as members of the EU, is also modified by this legislation.

Council Regulation (EC) 44/2001 of 22 December 2000 on Jurisdiction and the Recognition and Enforcement of Judgments in Civil and Commercial Matters[32]

THE COUNCIL OF THE EUROPEAN UNION,
Having regard to the Treaty establishing the European Community . . .
Whereas:

[32]Of the member states, only Denmark is specifically exempt from this Regulation, as a result of rights reserved to it in accordance with Articles 1 and 2 of the Protocol on the Position of Denmark, annexed to the Treaty on European Union and to the Treaty Establishing the European Community.

1. The Community has set itself the objective of (establishing) . . . measures relating to judicial cooperation in civil matters which are necessary for the sound operation of the internal market.

2. Certain differences between national rules governing jurisdiction and recognition of judgments hamper the sound operation of the internal market . . .

Chapter II—Jurisdiction

Section 1—General Provisions

Article 2

1. Subject to this Regulation, persons domiciled in a Member State shall, whatever their nationality, be sued in the courts of that Member State.

2. Persons who are not nationals of the Member State in which they are domiciled shall be governed by the rules of jurisdiction applicable to nationals of that State.

Article 3

1. Persons domiciled in a Member State may be sued in the courts of another Member State only by virtue of the rules set out in Sections 2 to 7 of this Chapter.

2. In particular the rules of national jurisdiction set out in Annex I *(including Britain's transient presence rules)* shall not be applicable as against them.

Article 4

1. If the defendant is not domiciled in a Member State, the jurisdiction of the courts of each Member State shall, subject to Articles 22 and 23, be determined by the law of that Member State.

2. As against such a defendant, any person domiciled in a Member State may, whatever his nationality, avail himself in that State of the rules of jurisdiction there in force, and in particular those specified in Annex I *(including Britain's transient presence rules),* in the same way as the nationals of that State.

Section 2—Special Jurisdiction

Article 5

A person domiciled in a Member State may, in another Member State, be sued:

1. (a) in matters relating to a contract, in the courts for the place of performance of the obligation in question;
   (b) for the purpose of this provision and unless otherwise agreed, the place of performance of the obligation in question shall be:
   - in the case of the sale of goods, the place in a Member State where, under the contract, the goods were delivered or should have been delivered,
   - in the case of the provision of services, the place in a Member State where, under the contract, the services were provided or should have been provided,
   (c) if subparagraph (b) does not apply then subparagraph (a) applies;
2. in matters relating to maintenance, in the courts for the place where the maintenance creditor is domiciled or habitually resident or, if the matter is ancillary to proceedings concerning the status of a person, in the court which, according to its own law, has jurisdiction to entertain those proceedings, unless that jurisdiction is based solely on the nationality of one of the parties;
3. in matters relating to tort, delict or quasi-delict, in the courts for the place where the harmful event occurred or may occur;

4. as regards a civil claim for damages or restitution which is based on an act giving rise to criminal proceedings, in the court seised of those proceedings, to the extent that that court has jurisdiction under its own law to entertain civil proceedings;
5. as regards a dispute arising out of the operations of a branch, agency or other establishment, in the courts for the place in which the branch, agency or other establishment is situated;
6. as settlor, trustee or beneficiary of a trust created by the operation of a statute, or by a written instrument, or created orally and evidenced in writing, in the courts of the Member State in which the trust is domiciled;
7. as regards a dispute concerning the payment of remuneration claimed in respect of the salvage of a cargo or freight, in the court under the authority of which the cargo or freight in question:
    (a) has been arrested to secure such payment, or
    (b) could have been so arrested, but bail or other security has been given;
    provided that this provision shall apply only if it is claimed that the defendant has an interest in the cargo or freight or had such an interest at the time of salvage.

Article 6

A person domiciled in a Member State may also be sued:

1. where he is one of a number of defendants, in the courts for the place where any one of them is domiciled, provided the claims are so closely connected that it is expedient to hear and determine them together to avoid the risk of irreconcilable judgements resulting from separate proceedings;
2. as a third party in an action on a warranty or guarantee or in any other third party proceedings, in the court seised of the original proceedings, unless these were instituted solely with the object of removing him from the jurisdiction of the court which would be competent in his case;
3. on a counter-claim arising from the same contract or facts on which the original claim was based, in the court in which the original claim is pending;
4. in matters relating to a contract, if the action may be combined with an action against the same defendant in matters relating to rights in rem in immovable property, in the court of the Member State in which the property is situated.

Article 7

Where by virtue of this Regulation a court of a Member State has jurisdiction in actions relating to liability from the use or operation of a ship, that court, or any other court substituted for this purpose by the internal law of that Member State, shall also have jurisdiction over claims for limitation of such liability.

Sections 3, 4, and 5

Jurisdiction in matters relating to insurance, consumer contracts, and individual contracts of employment, giving greater freedom of forum selection to policyholders, consumers, and employees

Section 6—Exclusive Jurisdiction

Article 22

The following courts shall have exclusive jurisdiction, regardless of domicile:

1. in proceedings which have as their object rights in rem in immovable property or tenancies of immovable property, the courts of the Member State in which the property is situated. However, in proceedings which have as their object tenancies of immovable property concluded for temporary private use for a maximum period of six consecutive

months, the courts of the Member State in which the defendant is domiciled shall also have jurisdiction, provided that the tenant is a natural person and that the landlord and the tenant are domiciled in the same Member State;

2. in proceedings which have as their object the validity of the constitution, the nullity or the dissolution of companies or other legal persons or associations of natural or legal persons, or of the validity of the decisions of their organs, the courts of the Member State in which the company, legal person or association has its seat. In order to determine that seat, the court shall apply its rules of private international law;

3. in proceedings which have as their object the validity of entries in public registers, the courts of the Member State in which the register is kept;

4. in proceedings concerned with the registration or validity of patents, trade marks, designs, or other similar rights required to be deposited or registered, the courts of the Member State in which the deposit or registration has been applied for, has taken place or is under the terms of a Community instrument or an international convention deemed to have taken place. Without prejudice to the jurisdiction of the European Patent Office under the Convention on the Grant of European Patents, signed at Munich on 5 October 1973, the courts of each Member State shall have exclusive jurisdiction, regardless of domicile, in proceedings concerned with the registration or validity of any European patent granted for that State;

5. in proceedings concerned with the enforcement of judgements, the courts of the Member State in which the judgement has been or is to be enforced.

Section 7—Prorogation of Jurisdiction
Article 23

1. If the parties, one or more of whom is domiciled in a Member State, have agreed that a court or the courts of a Member State are to have jurisdiction to settle any disputes which have arisen or which may arise in connection with a particular legal relationship, that court or those courts shall have jurisdiction. Such jurisdiction shall be exclusive unless the parties have agreed otherwise. Such an agreement conferring jurisdiction shall be either:
   (a) in writing or evidenced in writing; or
   (b) in a form which accords with practices which the parties have established between themselves; or
   (c) in international trade or commerce, in a form which accords with a usage of which the parties are or ought to have been aware and which in such trade or commerce is widely known to, and regularly observed by, parties to contracts of the type involved in the particular trade or commerce concerned.

2. Any communication by electronic means which provides a durable record of the agreement shall be equivalent to "writing."

3. Where such an agreement is concluded by parties, none of whom is domiciled in a Member State, the courts of other Member States shall have no jurisdiction over their disputes unless the court or courts chosen have declined jurisdiction.

4. The court or courts of a Member State on which a trust instrument has conferred jurisdiction shall have exclusive jurisdiction in any proceedings brought against a settlor, trustee or beneficiary, if relations between these persons or their rights or obligations under the trust are involved.

5. Agreements or provisions of a trust instrument conferring jurisdiction shall have no legal force if they are contrary to Articles 13, 17 or 21, or if the courts whose jurisdiction they purport to exclude have exclusive jurisdiction by virtue of Article 22.

Article 24

Apart from jurisdiction derived from other provisions of this Regulation, a court of a
Member State before which a defendant enters an appearance shall have jurisdiction. This rule shall not apply where appearance was entered to contest the jurisdiction, or where another court has exclusive jurisdiction by virtue of Article 22 . . .

Source: Council Regulation (EC) 44/2001, 2001 O.J. (L 012) 1.

In analyzing the question of jurisdiction of a European forum, one must work through the application of the Regulation.

1. Does any court have exclusive jurisdiction over the matter? (Article 22)
2. If not, has the defendant submitted to jurisdiction through appearance? (Article 24)
3. If not, is the subject matter a contract of insurance, consumer rights, or employment? (Sections 3, 4, and 5, special provisions on selection clauses)
4. If not, is there a specific contractual choice of forum? (Article 23)
5. If not, does the matter relate to a contract with special jurisdiction? (Article 5)
6. If not, is the defendant domiciled in a Member State? If yes, then the appropriate forum is determined by the civil law rule of the Member State domicile of the defendant. (Articles 2 and 3)
7. If, having reached this point, the defendant is not domiciled in a member state, then each Member State applies its own rules. (Article 4)

Choices of Law and Forum

Choices of law and forum are the second of the three components of private international law.

At first it seems odd to think of a forum court applying law that is not its own law: a California court applying German law or a British applying French law. More naturally, one would presume that a court would stick to its own laws, which it obviously knows best.

Equally, having just condemned "forum shopping" by a plaintiff after an injury has occurred, it may seem odd to be all in favor of allowing parties to select their forum court in advance of their troubles. The preference for the parties to select their forum is the preferred route, and businesspersons should explore and understand why this is the case.

Choice of Law

Choice-of-law decisions must be made when connecting factors to another jurisdiction forces a judicial consideration of the types of rights that the parties had in mind when their relationship was formed. Consider, for example, a contractual relationship between two Swiss companies. It produces a product that causes harm to a person in Singapore. The injured Singaporean will seek redress. This is the same situation as in the Asahi Metal/motorcycle tire case (recall The Old Wolf on p. 89): parts of a tire caused an accident and harm to a California motorcyclist. The motorcyclist settled after the case began, leaving the two foreign manufacturers locked in a battle over who should indemnify the other, all in a California court.

In this Swiss-Singaporean example, the Swiss companies also will be concerned as to how their liability should be split between them. But what if they had been sufficiently concerned about their respective potential liability that they provided for it in an earlier contract between them, rather than leave it to the courts of the world to figure out?

Their contract would lie before the Singapore court, with all its rights, duties, and shared liabilities spelled out, as they would exist under Swiss law. Should the Singapore court apportion liability as it would do between two of its own companies or follow Swiss law as the parties originally contemplated in their dealings?

As far as the parties are concerned, the answer is clearly that the court should choose to apply Swiss law. Perhaps Singaporean liability laws are so different than Swiss that the parties would have made a vastly different deal had they known that they might wind up in a Singapore court. But how could they have known this in advance? The Swiss firms could not, so it is a vote in favor of applying Swiss law in a Singapore court.

There is a downside: the Singapore court is not an expert in Swiss law. Does that mean a bad decision will result? Of course not, for that is what lawyers are for, and working within the Singapore legal system, why would one think this to be so monumental a task? Another vote in favor of applying Swiss law in a Singapore court.

Now in the *Asahi* case, the Supreme Court of the United States ultimately decided that the California court had no jurisdiction over the foreign manufacturers for they lacked minimum contacts with the state. This would appear to be reversed thinking; in our example, the Singapore court not only should have refused to apply Swiss law, but it should have refused to hear the case at all as it was between the manufacturers.

To reconcile the Singaporean example with the *Asahi* case, recognize that the facts are different. In *Asahi,* the interest of the motorcyclist evaporated upon his settlement. There was then no liability for the California court to apportion between the manufacturers, and if the manufacturers wanted to fight about it anyway, they should be encouraged to head to a more appropriate venue. California had no further interest. In the Singaporean example, the forum does have an interest. It is looking to compensate its injured national. It is looking for the correct party to bear liability, with indemnity between the parties as they provided for among themselves. Provision for indemnity should be made under the law of the foreign state (Switzerland) within the manufacturers' contemplation at the time they made their agreement. And recognition should be given to such choices.

This is the path toward greater judicial certainty around the world, and, happily, most forum courts including those in the United States, acknowledge its sensibility. To do otherwise would place trading firms under all sorts of foreign laws that they could not possibly know. Applying local law in all cases would stifle international trade, and it is to be avoided.

Where the parties expressly state a choice of law to govern their business relationship, the forum court is greatly aided. Often, sadly, the choice is not explicit and must be inferred. Two Swiss companies must presumably intend to govern their relationship with Swiss law, even if they do not make this explicit choice. But what if one is French and the other is Swiss? Then the forum court must make a choice between the two.

If the forum court is of the civil law tradition, its choice will be spelled out in its national code, being the place of the law where the parties' underlying contractual rights had vested. Common law forum courts face the more difficult challenge of examining all the connecting factors to come up with the place that holds the most significant connection to the transaction. Often, the result is the same, but just as often, they can be at odds with one another.

One logical loop that must be avoided can occur in judicial analysis of choice-of-law matters—the concept of *renvoi*. This is relevant to international businesspersons because it creates great uncertainty as to the final outcome of the case, and will significantly delay getting to any kind of final resolution of a business dispute.

Renvoi[33] is a form of judicial ping-pong arising from a faulty choice-of-law examination. Assume a judge hearing a case in an initial forum (F1) finds that his or her own choice-of-law rules dictate the application of the law of another forum (F2). When the judge examines F2's law, he or she finds that it dictates the application of F1's law. This presumably could go on forever. It results from the F1 judge looking at the wrong F2 law.

[33]Correctly pronounced, due to its French origin, as "ron-vwah" (to send back); however, it is often encountered and pronounced as "renn-voy."

Common law courts, with their greater ability to put different weight on different connecting factors, have more flexibility in determining applicable law. As a result, some highly politically underlined judgments are given. Does any judge really want to apply the current law of a recent revolutionary government, when many of the connecting factors of a much earlier contract or the civil law statutes say that it must? No, the court puts heavier weight on the connecting factors that would draw it away from the suddenly messy legal system. It emphasizes those factors pulling toward a choice of laws that it can work with, and which may be more advantageous to all the parties.

The F1 judge, when sent elsewhere, should confine his or her examination to F2's substantive law, not its procedural choice-of-law rules. To look at procedural rules is to invite this kind of logical loop, and to delay settlement of business disputes.

Choice of Forum and Forum Non Conveniens

Common law forum courts can refuse jurisdiction over a case. This occurs when sufficient grounds to refuse exist, because of the court's flexibility in determining the sufficiency of connecting factors in jurisdiction and choice of law. This leads to consideration in common law courts of the doctrine of forum non conveniens. The doctrine amounts to a refusal of a forum court to take jurisdiction on the basis that it is inappropriate to do so. It is recognition of the sum of the interests of the parties, the interests of the forum state, and the need to preserve "comity"—the accommodations made between nations based on goodwill and respect.

Be aware that the doctrine of forum non conveniens does *not* exist in civil law jurisdictions. They must exercise their jurisdiction as dictated in their statutory civil codes.

For a debate to take place as to which court would be proper to hear a dispute, there must first be two or more possible forum courts with a claim to jurisdiction for the plaintiff to choose between. That may sound obvious, but it sometimes is not. Secondly, it introduces the right of choice by the plaintiff. Businesspersons sometimes attempt, through their lawyers, to harass their adversary or throw up obstacles by deliberately choosing courts that are inconvenient to the other party. Courts take a dim view of such selections (sometimes punishing such attempts), and these views form part of the judicial analysis that goes into determining the correct forum for hearing a dispute.

A line of U.S. cases[34] establish the doctrine of forum non conveniens in much the same way as is done in other common law countries. These cases traditionally consider the following factors in deciding which of two or more common law courts should hear a dispute:

Forum Non Conveniens Considerations

In the Interest of Parties	In the Public Interest
• Misuse of venue as harassment • Relative ease of access to sources of proof • Availability and cost of compulsory process for attendance of unwilling witnesses • Possibility of view of premises or the subject matter in dispute • Practical problems that make trial of a case easy, expeditious, and inexpensive	• Administrative difficulties • Contribution to congestion of forum's case list • Burden of jury duty should fall where the community interest lies • Trials should be held in the *view* of the interested public, so that they should not hear of it by report only • Local interests are better served by being heard at home • Preferably the forum of hearing should be the one most familiar with the governing law

[34]See *Canada Malting Co. Ltd. v. Paterson Steamships Ltd.,* 285 U.S. 413 (1932); *Gulf Oil v. Gilbert,* 330 U.S. 501 (1947).

As can be derived above, courts prefer not to let plaintiffs inflict expense or trouble on a defendant that is not necessary to the plaintiff's own right to pursue his remedy. On the other hand, unless the balance is strongly in favor of the defendant, the plaintiff's choice of forum should rarely be disturbed. Rights are, after all, rights.

But what if those rights to choose a forum court for the settlement of disputes are limited? What if the parties have agreed up-front—as a term in their business contract—that they will take their dispute to a particular court? Should a court recognize this explicit choice of forum? In the case below, *The Bremen v. Zapata Offshore,* the U.S. Supreme Court considers the effect to be given to explicit forum-selection clauses made by the parties in contract. Its view is widely shared by common law jurisdictions.

Unterweser, the German petitioner, entered into a contract to tow the American respondent's drilling rig from Louisiana to Italy. The parties included a forum-selection clause nominating the London Court of Justice as the forum to hear all disputes arising from the contract. While being towed, the rig was damaged in a storm and, at the direction of the respondent, Unterweser berthed the rig in the closest port, Tampa, Florida. Once there, the respondent brought an action against the petitioner. Unterweser sought dismissal for lack of jurisdiction, based on the forum-selection clause, and brought its own suit in London. The district court in Florida refused to recognize the forum-selection clause, and refused to decline jurisdiction, a decision that was affirmed on appeal. The case then moved to the U.S. Supreme Court.

The Bremen et al. v. Zapata Off-shore Co.

Supreme Court of the United States

Mr. Chief Justice Burger delivered the opinion of the Court.

We granted certiorari to review a judgment of the United States Court of Appeals for the Fifth Circuit declining to enforce a forum-selection clause governing disputes arising under an international towage contract between petitioners and respondent. The circuits have differed in their approach to such clauses. For the reasons stated hereafter, we vacate the judgment of the Court of Appeals.

In November 1967, respondent Zapata, a Houston-based American corporation, contracted with petitioner Unterweser, a German corporation, to tow Zapata's ocean-going, self-elevating drilling rig *Chaparral* from Louisiana to a point off Ravenna, Italy, in the Adriatic Sea, where Zapata had agreed to drill certain wells.

Zapata had solicited bids for the towage, and several companies including Unterweser had responded. Unterweser was the low bidder and Zapata requested it to submit a contract, which it did. The contract submitted by Unterweser contained the following provision, which is at issue in this case:

"Any dispute arising must be treated before the London Court of Justice."

In addition the contract contained two clauses purporting to exculpate Unterweser from liability for damages to the towed barge.

After reviewing the contract and making several changes, but without any alteration in the forum-selection or exculpatory clauses, a Zapata vice president executed the contract and forwarded it to Unterweser in Germany, where Unterweser accepted the changes, and the contract became effective.

On January 5, 1968, Unterweser's deep sea tug *Bremen* departed Venice, Louisiana, with the *Chaparral* in tow bound for Italy. On January 9, while the flotilla was in international waters in the middle of the Gulf of Mexico, a severe storm arose. The sharp roll of the *Chaparral* in Gulf waters caused its elevator legs, which had been raised for the voyage, to break off and fall into the sea, seriously damaging the *Chaparral.* In this emergency situation Zapata instructed the *Bremen* to tow its damaged rig to Tampa, Florida, the nearest port of refuge.

On January 12, Zapata, ignoring its contract promise to litigate "any dispute arising" in the English courts, commenced a suit in admiralty in the United States District Court at Tampa, seeking $3,500,000 damages against Unterweser *in personam* and the *Bremen in rem,* alleging negligent towage and breach of contract. Unterweser responded by invoking the forum clause of the towage contract, and moved to dismiss for lack of jurisdiction or on *forum non conveniens* grounds, or in the alternative to stay the action pending submission of the dispute to the "London Court of Justice." Shortly thereafter, in February, before the District Court had ruled on its motion to stay or dismiss the United States action, Unterweser commenced an action against Zapata seeking damages for breach of the towage contract in the High Court of Justice in London, as the contract provided. Zapata appeared in that court to contest jurisdiction, but its challenge was rejected, the English courts holding that the contractual forum provision conferred jurisdiction.

. . . [T]he District Court gave the forum-selection clause little, if any, weight. Instead, the court treated the motion to dismiss under normal *forum non conveniens* doctrine applicable in the absence of such a clause, citing *Gulf Oil Corp. v. Gilbert,* 330 U.S. 501 (1947). Under that doctrine "unless the balance is strongly in favor of the defendant, the plaintiff's choice of forum should rarely be disturbed." The District Court concluded: "The balance of conveniences here is not strongly in favor of [Unterweser] and [Zapata's] choice of forum should not be disturbed."

. . .

On appeal, a divided panel of the Court of Appeals affirmed. [The majority concluded] that "at the very least" that case stood for the proposition that a forum-selection clause "will not be enforced unless the selected state would provide a more convenient forum than the state in which suit is brought." From that premise the Court of Appeals proceeded to conclude that, apart from the forum-selection clause, the District Court did not abuse its discretion in refusing to decline jurisdiction on the basis of *forum non conveniens.* It noted that (1) the flotilla never "escaped the Fifth Circuit's mare nostrum, and the casualty occurred in close proximity to the district court"; (2) a considerable number of potential witnesses, including Zapata crewmen, resided in the Gulf Coast area; (3) preparation for the voyage and inspection and repair work had been performed in the Gulf area; (4) the testimony of the *Bremen* crew was available by way of deposition; (5) England had no interest in or contact with the controversy other than the forum-selection clause. . . .

We hold, with the six dissenting members of the Court of Appeals, that far too little weight and effect were given to the forum clause in resolving this controversy. For at least two decades we have witnessed an expansion of overseas commercial activities by business enterprises based in the United States. The barrier of distance that once tended to confine a business concern to a modest territory no longer does so. Here we see an American company with special expertise contracting with a foreign company to tow a complex machine thousands of miles across seas and oceans. The expansion of American business and industry will hardly be encouraged if, notwithstanding solemn contracts, we insist on a parochial concept that all disputes must be resolved under our laws and in our courts. Absent a contract forum, the considerations relied on by the Court of Appeals would be persuasive reasons for holding an American forum convenient in the traditional sense, but in an era of expanding world trade and commerce, the absolute aspects of the [traditional doctrine] have little place and would be a heavy hand indeed on the future development of international commercial dealings by Americans. We cannot have trade and commerce in world markets and international waters exclusively on our terms, governed by our laws, and resolved in our courts.

Forum-selection clauses have historically not been favored by American courts. Many courts, federal and state, have declined to enforce such clauses on the ground that they were "contrary to public policy," or that their effect was to "oust the jurisdiction" of the court. Although this view apparently still has considerable acceptance, other courts are tending to adopt a more hospitable attitude toward forum-selection clauses. This view, advanced in the well-reasoned dissenting opinion in the instant case, is that such clauses are prima facie valid and should be enforced unless enforcement is shown by the resisting party to be "unreasonable" under the circumstances. [Quoting an earlier case, the Chief Justice continued,] "It is settled . . . that parties to a contract may agree in advance to submit to the jurisdiction of a given court, to permit notice to be served by the opposing party, or even to waive notice altogether."

This approach is substantially that followed in other common-law countries including England. It is the view advanced by noted scholars and that adopted by the Restatement of the Conflict of Laws. It accords with ancient concepts of freedom of contract and reflects an appreciation of the expanding horizons of American contractors who seek business in all parts of the world. Not surprisingly, foreign businessmen prefer, as do we, to have disputes resolved in their own courts, but if that choice is not available, then in a neutral forum with expertise in the subject matter. Plainly, the courts of England meet the standards of neutrality and long experience in admiralty litigation. The choice of that forum was made in an arm's-length negotiation by experienced and sophisticated businessmen, and absent some compelling and countervailing reason it should be honored by the parties and enforced by the courts.

The argument that such clauses are improper because they tend to "oust" a court of jurisdiction is hardly more than a vestigial legal fiction. It appears to rest at core on historical judicial resistance to any attempt to reduce the power and business of a particular court and has little place in an era when all courts are overloaded and when businesses once essentially local now operate in world markets. It reflects something of a provincial attitude regarding the fairness of other tribunals. No one seriously contends in this case that the forum-selection clause "ousted" the District Court of jurisdiction over Zapata's action. The threshold question is whether that court should have exercised its jurisdiction to do more than give effect to the legitimate expectations of the parties, manifested in their freely negotiated agreement, by specifically enforcing the forum clause.

There are compelling reasons why a freely negotiated private international agreement, unaffected by fraud, undue influence, or overweening bargaining power, such as that involved here, should be given full effect. In this case, for example, we are concerned with a far from routine transaction between companies of two different nations contemplating the tow of an extremely costly piece of equipment from Louisiana across the Gulf of Mexico and the Atlantic Ocean, through the Mediterranean Sea to its final destination in the Adriatic Sea. In the course of its voyage, it was to traverse the waters of many jurisdictions. The *Chaparral* could have been damaged at any point along the route, and there were countless possible ports of refuge. That the accident occurred in the Gulf of Mexico and the barge was towed to Tampa in an emergency were mere fortuities. It cannot be doubted for a moment that the parties sought to provide for a neutral forum for the resolution of any disputes arising during the tow. Manifestly much uncertainty and possibly great inconvenience to both parties could arise if a suit could be maintained in any jurisdiction in which an accident might occur or if jurisdiction were left to any place where the *Bremen* or Unterweser might happen to be found. The elimination of all such uncertainties by agreeing in advance on a forum acceptable to both parties is an indispensable element in international trade, commerce, and contracting. There is strong evidence that the forum clause was a vital part of the agreement, and it would be unrealistic to think that the parties did not conduct their negotiations, including fixing the monetary terms, with the consequences of the forum clause figuring prominently in their calculations. Under these circumstances, as Justice Karminski reasoned in sustaining jurisdiction over Zapata in the [English] High Court of Justice, "the force of an agreement for litigation in this country, freely entered into between two competent parties, seems to me to be very powerful."

Thus, in the light of present-day commercial realities and expanding international trade we conclude that the forum clause should control absent a strong showing that it should be set aside. Although their opinions are not altogether explicit, it seems reasonably clear that the District Court and the Court of Appeals placed the burden on Unterweser to show that London would be a more convenient forum than Tampa, although the contract expressly resolved that issue. The correct approach would have been to enforce the forum clause specifically unless Zapata could clearly show that enforcement would be unreasonable and unjust, or that the clause was invalid for such reasons as fraud or overreaching . . .

Courts have also suggested that a forum clause, even though it is freely bargained for and contravenes no important public policy of the forum, may nevertheless be "unreasonable" and unenforceable if the chosen forum is seriously inconvenient for the trial of the action. Of course, where it can be said with reasonable assurance that at the time they entered the contract, the parties to a freely negotiated private international commercial agreement contemplated the claimed inconvenience, it is difficult to see why any such claim of inconvenience should be heard to render the forum clause unenforceable. We are not here dealing with an agreement between two Americans to resolve their essentially local disputes in a remote alien forum . . .

This case, however, involves a freely negotiated international commercial transaction between a German and an American corporation for towage of a vessel from the Gulf of Mexico to the Adriatic Sea. As noted, selection of a London forum was clearly a reasonable effort to bring vital certainty to this international transaction and to provide a neutral forum experienced and capable in the resolution of admiralty litigation. Whatever "inconvenience" Zapata would suffer by being forced to litigate in the contractual forum as it agreed to do was clearly foreseeable at the time of contracting. In such circumstances it should be incumbent on the party seeking to escape his contract to show that trial in the contractual forum will be so gravely difficult and inconvenient that he will for all practical purposes be deprived of his day in court. Absent that, there is no basis for concluding that it would be unfair, unjust, or unreasonable to hold that party to his bargain.

(The U.S. Supreme Court then ruled so as to allow the British courts, as nominated in the contract, to take control of the case and rule on the matter.)

Source: *The Bremen et al. v. Zapata Off-shore Co.,* 407 U.S. 1 (1972).

In the eyes of a court favored by a forum-selection clause (London, in this case), the clause is one of prorogation. Conversely, for the forum court that would take jurisdiction but for the existence of the clause (the U.S. courts), it is a derogation clause. Note the unwillingness of the U.S. Supreme Court to inject uncertainty into commercial affairs, and its preference to uphold such choice of law clauses where they are "unaffected by fraud, undue influence, or overweening bargaining power." It is up to the adverse party to meet a "heavy burden" that it would be "unfair, unjust, or unreasonable" to hold that party to its bargain.

The United Kingdom has arguably made the greatest contribution to the development of private international law over the past centuries. It has a richly developed body of case law, particularly in admiralty and transportation issues. As many of the problems in private international law stem from transportation mishaps, its long experience is a convincing aid to both the international businessperson and lawyers. Perhaps even more so, the fact that UK law touches on so many issues that have historically happened only infrequently, its case law is also a very good resource for specialized legal thinking and business strategy in foreseeing "unique" problems.

The following case is an example of English judicial wisdom on choice of forum, regarding a contract that selected the African nation of Angola as the forum. In reading it, note that as far as common law jurisdictions are concerned, a choice of forum is most often taken to mean a choice of law as well (where the agreement is otherwise nonindicative), and vice-versa. Here the English common law court saw itself as being asked to enforce not only a choice of Angola as the forum, but Angolan law as well.

Angola had achieved independence and undergone a dramatic Communist revolution between the time of execution of the contract and the time of dispute. This raised the question of whether a fair hearing could be expected in Angola (a public policy question under forum non conveniens) and whether the parties would have selected Angolan law had they been able to foresee the future.

This is an extremely rich case that illustrates strategic maneuvering in international business litigation. As you read it, consider why a Portuguese plaintiff wants to see the trial take place in England when all of the English defendant's assets rest in Angola, and the reverse, why the defendant wishes to invite action in the very place where its assets lie.

Carvalho v. Hull, Blyth (Angola) Ltd.

Court of Appeal

BROWNE L.J. This is an appeal by the defendants from a decision of Donaldson J. given on February 19, 1979, when he refused the defendants' application to stay the plaintiff's action, but gave leave to the appeal.

The defendants' application is based on clause 14 of the contract on which the plaintiff's action is based: I quote:

> "In the case of litigation arising the District Court of Luanda should be considered the sole court competent to adjudicate to the exclusion of all others."

The plaintiff formerly lived in Angola, but left in August 1975 and now lives in Portugal. The defendants are an English registered company, so there is no doubt that the English courts have jurisdiction, but we are told that the defendants have no assets here. They have carried on and still carry on business entirely in Angola. They have carried on business there for 100 years. Their present business is that of ships' agents, and they also carry on business as motor traders through subsidiary companies.

In 1970 their motor trading business was reorganized in such a way that there were five subsidiary companies known as the U.N.A.I.O. Group: in each of these companies the defendants owned 51 per cent of the share and the plaintiff owned 49 per cent. By a contract dated December 1973, the plaintiff agreed to sell and the defendants agreed to buy all his shares in the five subsidiary companies for a total price of 76 million escudos. Clause 6 of the contract provided for the payment of the price by four installments. The first three installments were paid. The fourth installment of 20 million escudos (of which the sterling equivalent is about £300,000)[35] should have been paid in January 1976 but has not been paid. On April 29, 1977, the plaintiff issued his writ in this action claiming that sum or its sterling equivalent. I have already quoted clause 14 of the contract.

Mr. Wood, for the defendants, submits that the proper law of the contract is Angolan law and tells us that the defence to the plaintiff's claim will be: (1) that, under Angolan law, the "economic hardship" suffered by the U.N.A.I.O. Group as a result of events in Angola from 1975 onwards would entitle them to a reduction or postponement of the payment claimed in action; (2) that, under the Angolan Exchange Control Regulations, the defendants are

[35]Approximately $450,000 U.S. Dollars.

precluded from making any payments otherwise than in Angola in the new currency, known as kwangas, which has superseded the escudo. Any judgement obtained by the plaintiff here could not be satisfied by the defendants without a breach of the Angolan Exchange Control Regulations which might expose them to criminal sanctions.

Until 1951 Angola was a colony of Portugal. In 1951 it became a province of Portugal. In January 1975, after a coup d'etat in Portugal in 1974 the new Portuguese government announced that Angola would become independent in November 1975. In 1975 civil war broke out in Angola, but on November 11 Angola did become independent and, in due course, a new constitution was promulgated to which I will refer to in a moment. A party or group known as M.P.L.A. assumed power—that being the Popular Movement for the Liberation of Angola—and Dr. Neto became President. Since then Angola has been recognised by her Majesty's Government, among a number of other states, and ambassadors have been exchanged between Angola and this country.

The plaintiff, as I have said, left Angola in August 1975. There was before Donaldson J. an affidavit by Mr. Englefield, the plaintiff's solicitor in these terms:

> "1. I have the carriage of this action on behalf of the plaintiff and have spoken to him on a number of occasions both in this country and in Portugal. The plaintiff has informed me that in August 1975 he was forced to leave Angola with his family and received threats against his life and the lives of his family. The plaintiff left behind in Angola his house, furniture, balance of his bank account and four farms belonging to him. The plaintiff's property and farms have now been taken over by officers of the Marxists's government. 2. The plaintiff is unwilling to return to Angola and believes that if he does so he will be liquidated."

Since the hearing before Donaldson J. an affidavit has been sworn by the plaintiff himself, verifying that affidavit and including a list of the property which he says he left behind in Angola and which has been confiscated. That affidavit was put before us without objection from Mr. Wood.

I should now refer to the Constitution, which is exhibited to Dr. de Almeida's affidavit of October 28, 1977. Article 1 provides:

> "The People's Republic of Angola is a sovereign, independent and democratic state, the foremost objective of which is the total liberation of the Angolan people from the vestiges of colonialism and from domination and aggression by Imperialism and the construction of a prosperous and democratic country, completely free from any form of exploitation of man by man, materialising, the inspirations of the popular masses."

Article 2:

> "All sovereignty is vested in the Angolan people. The political, economic and social guidance of the nation are vested in the M.P.L.A., its lawful representative, consisting of a wide front which includes all the patriotic forces engaged in the anti-Imperialist struggle."

Article 7:

> "The People's Republic of Angola is a lay state, there being complete separation between the state and religious Institutions. All religions will be respected and the state will grant protection for churches, places and objects of worship, provided that they comply with state laws."

Article 10:

> "The People's Republic of Angola recognises, protects, and guarantees private property and activities, even those foreigners, provided that they are useful to the economy of the country and the interests of the Angolan people."

Article 44:

> "The exercise of the jurisdictional function aimed at the realization of democratic justice is exclusively incumbent on the courts. The organization, composition and competence of the courts will be fixed by law."

Article 45:

"The judges will be independent, in the exercise of their duties."

Article 58:

"The laws and regulations currently in force will be applicable where not revoked or altered and provided that they do not conflict with the spirit of this Law and the Angolan Revolutionary Process."

We have an agreed note of the judgement of Donaldson J., approved by the judge. He said:

"Of course, I accept Brandon J.'s approach as set out in *The Eleftheria* [1970] P. 94, 99G; (dictum read). These are the sort of matters one would consider in the ordinary case where there has been no political change. However they are not necessarily applicable. I rely on the rule in Dicey; (rule 30 read).

"If I were to decide the matter at my discretion, I would note that the plaintiff left Angola in 1975 at the same time as some 300,000 other people who feared for the future, although they obviously had mixed motives. He left all his property there, and it has been seized. The recent affidavit of Mr. Englefield states that the plaintiff would be in fear of his life if he returned to Angola; and also that he might have difficulty in obtaining an entry visa, although, any such difficulty might be thought to be inconsistent with his life being at risk. It may be that litigation could proceed in his absence, but, in my view, if plaintiff is a party to an action he is entitled to attend the trial, and to consult with his legal advisers. "Mr Steyn"— who appeared for the plaintiff below—submits that there is some risk that the plaintiff may now be treated as an enemy of the Angolan people. Anyway, whether his reasons are good or bad, the plaintiff is not prepared to risk returning to Angola. Mr. Steyn submits that, as to the courts, there is some real doubt as to the quality of the legal representation that is now available. Certainly there has been a change in the judges in that now the appointees do not go up through the legal profession. It does seem to me that you are likely to have an entirely different type of judge; whether they are an improvement would be impertinent for me to say. At any rate, the court in contemplation when the contract was made is now different. A third important matter is the discontinuance of the final right of appeal to Lisbon. I take a broad and common sense view in saying that, at the time the contract was made, the courts in Angola operated under a colonial judicial system whereas now there is an entirely different system, a post-revolution court under a post-revolution constitution. I draw attention to article 2, article 54 and article 58 as to the laws. Surely part of the purpose of the revolution was to change the judicial system. Mr. Steyn says there has never been a case like this; the nearest similar case is perhaps a contract made in Imperial Russia, and the situation after the 1917 revolution, or, alternatively, a contract made during the Shah's regime in Iran, and being enforced in the present circumstances. I find strong grounds for refusing a stay either as a matter of construction of the clause, or because it would be just and proper to allow the plaintiff to continue. All the usual reasons for sending the matter back to Angola, including exchange control difficulties, are present, and all the elements here point to allowing the case to go ahead in Angola except the one thing that really matters, whether it is just and proper to remit the matter to Angola. I refuse a stay. Costs in cause. Leave to appeal."

In *The Eleftheria* [1970] P. 94–100 Brandon J. said—and this is the passage, as I understand it, quoted by Donaldson J.:

"The principles established by the authorities can, I think, be summarised as follows: (1) Where plaintiffs sue in England in breach of an agreement to refer disputes to a foreign court, and the defendants apply for a stay, the English court, assuming the claim to be otherwise within its jurisdiction, is not bound to grant a stay but has a discretion whether to do so or not. (2) The discretion should be exercised by granting a stay unless strong cause for not doing so is shown. (3) The burden of proving such strong cause is on the plaintiffs. (4) In exercising its discretion the court should take into account all the circumstances of the particular case. (5) In particular, but without prejudice to (4), the following matters, where they arise, may properly be regarded: (a) In what country the evidence on the issues of fact is situated, or more readily available, and the effect of that on the relative convenience and expense of trial as between the English and foreign courts. (b) Whether the law of the foreign court applies and, if so, whether it differs from English law in any material respects. (c) With what country either party is connected, and how closely. (d) Whether the defendants genuinely desire trial in the foreign country, or are only seeking procedural advantages. (e) Whether the plaintiffs would be prejudiced by having to sue in the foreign court because they would: (i) be deprived of security for their claim; (ii) be unable to enforce any judgement obtained; (iii) be faced with a time-bar not applicable in England; or (iv) for political, racial, religious or other reasons be unlikely to get a fair trial."

Rule 30 in *Dicey and Morris, The Conflict of Laws,* 9th ed. (1973), 222, on which the judge also relied, is in these terms:

"Where a contract provides that all disputes between the parties are to be referred to the exclusive jurisdiction of a foreign tribunal, the court will stay proceedings instituted in England in breach of such agreement, unless the plaintiff proves that it is just and proper to allow them to continue."

Mr. Wood for the defendants relied strongly on the passage from the judgement of Brandon J. which I have just quoted . . .

Mr. Siberry for the plaintiff says that there were two issues before Donaldson J.: (1) whether, as a matter of construction of the contract, the parties had agreed that litigation arising thereunder should [be] referred to the District Court of Luanda as now constituted (or, I suppose, strictly as constituted at the time of the commencement of this action) under the legal system as now prevailing in Angola; (2) whether the judge, in his discretion, should grant the stay, the question then being as he accepts, whether there are strong grounds for allowing the action to proceed here. Donaldson J. decided both issues in favour of the plaintiff, and Mr. Siberry submits that, the first issue having been decided in favour of the plaintiff, the second issue did not and does not arise.

Donaldson J.'s judgement was delivered extempore and is, perhaps, not as full and lucid as most judgements of that judge, but it is clear that he did consider and decide both issues. As to convenient to quote them again:

"At any rate, the court in contemplation when the contract was made is now different. . . . at the time the contract was made, the courts in Angola operated under a colonial judicial system whereas now there is an entirely different system, a post-revolution court under a post-revolution constitution . . . I find strong grounds for refusing a stay either as a matter of construction of the clause, or because it would be just and proper to allow the plaintiff to continue."

Mr. Siberry submits that the District Court of Luanda is a different court and Mr. Wood submits that it is not. He says that, although there are differences, they are not material.

It is clear from the affidavits filed on behalf of the plaintiff, and it is not disputed by the defendants, that, when the contract was made in December 1973, Angola was a province of Portugal. The law applied was Portuguese law and the legal system then in force was procedurally and substantively Portuguese. The judicial organization of Portuguese Angola was part of the judicial system of Portuguese Europe and was in every respect identical with it. The qualification of judges was the same as in Portugal: see the affidavits of Dr. de Almeida, and Dr. Carvalho, for the plaintiffs; and Dr. Oliveira for the defendants. Angola clearly then had no separate legal system and there was no such thing as Angolan law except, perhaps, in some native customary courts. Now Angola is an independent sovereign state with a new constitution. It is true that it seems, from the affidavits filed on behalf of the defendants that in general Portuguese law is still applied and that the previous structure of the courts still exists, except for the abolition of the right of appeal to the Supreme

Count in Lisbon. But it seems to me plain from the Constitution that this situation can be changed at any moment: see especially articles 44 and 58. It seems, from the proviso to article 58, that, without any formal change, the previous law will not be applied if it does "conflict with the spirit of this law and the Angolan revolutionary process."

One can perhaps test it in this way. If the parties had known in December 1973 what the situation would be in Angola now, would they have agreed to include clause 14 in the contract? I think it impossible to say that the answer must be "Yes." There is a complete conflict in the affidavit evidence about the present situation as to the administration of justice in Angola. This court cannot resolve this conflict but, in my view, it is unnecessary to do so to arrive at the conclusion that the present District Court of Luanda is a different court from that contemplated by the contract.

Mr. Wood's main criticisms of Donaldson J. and where he submits he went wrong in principle in exercising his discretion are (i) that he applied the wrong test, and (ii) that he relied on the political changes and changes in the structure of the legal system in Angola since the date of the contract. He submits that these changes . . .are irrelevant.

So far as the first point is concerned, Mr. Wood says that *Dicey* is wrong in saying that the test is "unless the plaintiff proves that it is just and proper to allow him to continue" . . .

The "just and proper test," it seems to me, is taken, among other places, from the judgment of Willmer J. in *The Fehmarn* [1957] 1 W.L.R. 815, 819 where he says:

> " . . . it is well established that, where there is a provision in a contract providing that disputes are to be referred to a foreign tribunal, then, prima facie, this court will stay proceedings instituted in this country in breach of such agreement, and will only allow them to proceed when satisfied that it is just and proper to do so. I think that fairly states the principle to be applied."

Mr. Wood's criticism of *Dicey*, as I understood it, was that it put the burden on the plaintiff too low and that it did not sufficiently emphasise the importance of holding people to their contracts. But, as I have already quoted from p. 223, *Dicey* does refer specifically to the importance of making people abide by their contracts and, in my judgement, there is no real difference between the two tests of "just and proper" and "strong cause."

In support of his other point that the judge attached undue importance to the political changes, Mr. Wood emphasizes that the judge did not find that the plaintiff could now get a fair trial in Angola . . . He submits that there is a presumption that there would be a fair trial in Angola . . .

It seems to me that, as I read the judgement, Donaldson J. did not hold that the political changes, as such, were enough to justify refusing a stay, and I am not convinced by this argument of Mr. Wood. Applying the established principle, I can find no sufficient ground for interfering with Donaldson J.'s exercise of his discretion . . . I would dismiss this appeal.

(Thus Donaldson J's refusal to stay the English action remains the case, and the trial continues in England, rather than being sent to Angola.)

Source: *Carvalho v. Hull, Blyth (Angola) Ltd.,* [1979] W.L.R. 1228.

> How does one go about reconciling a nation's willingness to accept the existence of an act-of-state doctrine with its unwillingness to send a particular case for hearing in the judicial system of another nation? Does this need or deserve to be reconciled? Is there a double standard at work? To behave ethically in our treatment of the political and judicial systems of other nations, must we be consistent, or does the ethical approach actually demand case-by-case treatment?

So the *Carvalho* trial was heard in the English courts of the United Kingdom. While not criticizing the underlying wisdom of this judgment, one important observation should be made. English courts (admittedly or not) see a continuance in their historical role as preeminent makers of law in international commercial relations. They do not shy from taking jurisdiction whenever there is a contribution to that body of law to be made.

Note as well the strategic posture of the parties in *Carvalho*. The plaintiff knows that he will not receive a judgment in Angola due to its revolutionary character, and that even if he did, it would likely be unsatisfactory and probably unenforceable. Even if all of those factors were miraculously overcome, a sum recovered in Angolan kwangas would be impossible to remove from the country and would be worthless outside Angola. None of this is lost on the defendant either, who wants to ensure that these roadblocks are thrown in the plaintiff's way.

Presumably, the defendant has no assets in Portugal, and even if there were, obtaining jurisdiction in a Portuguese court may be difficult, for the defendant is not Portuguese and the Angolan link to Portugal was severed with independence in 1975. This leaves England as the plaintiff's only sensible jurisdiction in which to bring suit, but while the defendant is English, there are no corporate assets there.

So why might the plaintiff proceed? The answer lies in the fact that while there are no assets in England now, there may be many in the near future, if only for short periods at a time. The defendant company is a ship's agent and a motor (automobile) broker. Undoubtedly, it has and will in future take an ownership interest in various cargoes headed to Angolan ports. Probably (considering its English roots) these cargoes will be purchased from English suppliers and will leave from English ports.

Armed with a judgment from an English court, the plaintiff will be able to choke off the defendant's source of supply, and will more likely be able to recover the debt owed. If the defendant does have assets in Portugal due to its colonial link, the plaintiff may find that he can more readily enforce his English judgment in Portugal, even though he could not have obtained jurisdiction for trial there. The subject of recognition and enforcement of foreign judgments is considered in the following section.

Recognition and Enforcement of Foreign Judgments

On the face of matters, obtaining a judgment in any forum is only worth as much as the defendant's assets that are present inside the forum that may be executed upon (seized). In the case of defective goods imported into a jurisdiction, the foreign exporter may well have *no* other assets in the forum of import where judgment is obtained against it. Unless the judgment of this forum is enforceable in a forum where the defendant does have assets (e.g., its factory), the aggrieved importer would have been engaged in a pointless exercise of its legal rights.

As a result, virtually all of the major trading nations of the world have realized that they must be willing to recognize and enforce foreign judgments, even though there may be conditions attached to that willingness. *Recognition* means the affirmation that a judicial act in an originating forum now has legal validity in the second forum. *Enforcement* means affording a recognized judgment the same access to the resources of the host state in execution that it would offer to judgments that issue from its own forum courts. These are important rights for international businesspersons.

The conditions of recognition vary widely. Some have harmonized rules, such as the European Union,[36] akin to the United States' offering of "full faith and credit" as to judgments originating in one U.S. state being recognized and enforced by other U.S. states. Some trading nations refuse to recognize foreign judgments unless there is reciprocity in recognition of their own judgments, and this arrangement is usually governed by a series

[36]Again, found in Council Regulation (EC) 44/2001, 2001 O.J. (L 012) 1, Chapter III, articles 32 et seq.

of treaties negotiated by governments. Mercifully, fewer and fewer nations require an examination on the merits of the judgment, as this would otherwise be a rejection of *res judicata*[37] and would strike at the very heart of the sensibility of recognition.

Most jurisdictions also distinguish between interlocutory[38] orders, final judgments, and judgments that are not capable of further appeal in the originating jurisdiction. Only when the possibility of an appeal has expired will other jurisdictions recognize the judgment as enforceable. This is because no state wishes to become meshed in the execution of a judgment of foreign origin only to find later that it has been overturned in the originating forum. Likewise, foreign judgments obtained by default will often not be recognized.

Aside from this question of timeliness, there are three preconditions for recognition of a foreign judgment. These represent valid defenses to recognition in almost all jurisdictions that do recognize foreign judgments, and the proceeding for recognition, regardless of how informal it may be, allows the judgment-defendant one last opportunity to evade execution.

First, if the originating forum court did not properly have jurisdiction, then the second forum will not recognize the judgment. For example, where the general trial court in the originating forum gives a judgment with respect to a ship, when the case should have been heard in an admiralty court, it will not be recognized by the second forum for want of jurisdiction in the originating court. Second, if the proceeding or judgment of the originating forum is contrary to the public policy of the second forum, the judgment will not be recognized. This may occur where due process is lacking in the originating forum, or the judgment is for relief that is unknown or offensive to the second forum. Equally, the refusal may result from the fact that the matter is already res judicata in the second forum, by virtue of a prior action. Lastly, the second forum will not involve itself in recognition of judgments with a penal component. To do so would place the apparatus of civil courts in too close proximity to matters that are more related to sovereignty, criminal law, and extradition.

The recognition and enforcement of foreign arbitration awards generally follow the practice of the state toward domestic arbitration awards. It is done in keeping with the consensual nature of arbitration and tends to be even easier. This ease comes from a more internationally uniform process applicable to arbitration awards than for obtaining recognition and enforcement of foreign judgments. The mechanics of arbitration and recognition and enforcement of its awards are described in Chapter 13, "International Alternative Dispute Resolution."

It may be the case that a forum is asked to recognize and enforce conflicting foreign judgments from two or more jurisdictions, each with respect to the same subject matter and parties, often seeking rights in the same property located in the forum of intended enforcement. This third forum then is faced with a choice of which judgment to recognize, to the exclusion of the other.

In some forums, such as the states of the United States, it is the most recent judgment that will be recognized. This is in the belief that the victor in the earlier judgment most certainly would have claimed (and clearly unsuccessfully) that the matter was res judicata in the second (later) forum. Other forum states take the opposite view, believing the interests of justice are best served by recognizing the earliest judgment as res judicata for all purposes. Each recognizing forum state's rules must be examined for its particular approach.

---

[37]The principle that cases that have been decided (after all appeals are complete) should not be reopened.
[38]Interim.

Chapter Summary

International law can be taken as any law that contains or relates to matters with a foreign element, and every state has international law rules of its own creation. In addition, customary law has evolved over centuries between nations, some of which has been formalized within treaties and conventions and through the formation of international organizations.

The three major branches of international law are international public law (as between nations), the body of private international law, and the quasi-legislative effect of private organizations. To the extent that aspects of these three areas touch on business affairs, it is international business law, and it is the body of law governing international business transactions.

This chapter focuses on the first two of the three, public and private international law. It covers the sources and scope of public international law, and the private issues of jurisdiction, choices of forum and law, and the recognition and enforcement of foreign judgments.

A determination of jurisdiction requires the presence of connecting factors between the defendant/transaction with the forum that intends to take jurisdiction. In determining its jurisdiction, all courts are aware of the limiting issue of sovereignty and internal acts of sovereign powers. Civil law courts will have reference to their statutory codes in determining jurisdiction, and common law courts must further wrestle with whether it is appropriate to exercise their jurisdiction over the case at bar due to the doctrine of forum non conveniens. Forum courts will apply the most appropriate law to the issue at bar, be it their own or that of another forum, as appropriate, and most jurisdictions are willing to recognize choices made by the parties. Once a judicial finding has been made and is beyond appeal in one jurisdiction, it is generally possible to seek recognition and enforcement of that judgment in other jurisdictions.

Chapter Questions

1. Describe the analytical process that results in a common law determination of forum non conveniens.

2. What factors do you consider the most persuasive in establishing that a nonresident corporation has sufficient "minimum contacts" to support jurisdiction of a forum court? What procedural safeguards are offered to defendants by requiring minimum contacts?

3. Distinguish between domicile, residence, and nationality of a natural person and a legal person.

4. In the *Asahi* case, in the first instance, the Superior Court in California stated: "Asahi (the valve maker) obviously does business on an international scale. It is not unreasonable that they defend claims of defect in their product on an international scale." What is appropriate and inappropriate about this line of reasoning?

5. Justify in your own words the legal doctrine within international law that dictates equality between the People's Republic of China (population approximately 1.3 billion) and the Republic of San Marino (population approximately 28,000).

6. "Where an 'act of state' registers an unseaworthy oil tanker, we should create state liability to clean up the mess that results from its sinking. We should seize these vessels when they enter our waters, and impound them until they are fixed. Better yet, we should just impose our rules on these countries to prevent them from registering such ships in the first place, and make sure they are enforcing a high standard. Global interest, global damage, global rules." Comment on this statement considering jus cogens (universal norms), the act-of-state doctrine, and sovereign independence of states.

7. When a local court is asked to recognize and enforce a foreign judgment, is it not sensible that the local court examine the merits of the case, to make sure that justice is being done? Since this examination does not routinely happen, why is it not done? What things are examinable when a request to recognize and enforce a foreign judgment comes before a local court?

Front Page Law: International Issues from Boardroom to Courtroom

BANKING'S GREAT WALL: NEWBRIDGE CAPITAL'S PLAN TO RUN A CHINESE BANK FALLS APART   *JUNE 2, 2003*

BusinessWeek

It was the deal that would change Chinese banking forever. When U.S.-based Newbridge Capital Inc. agreed last October to buy a controlling interest in Shenzhen Development Bank Co. (SDB), Chinese officials were so enthusiastic that they even allowed Newbridge to install its own management team before final details had been ironed out. At last, Chinese regulators and bankers seemed ready to allow a real commercial bank to flourish under foreign control.

Newbridge's managers came, but the deal never closed. And now the entire transaction appears to have blown up into a fight between U.S., Taiwanese, and Chinese interests. On May 12, officials at SDB dissolved the Newbridge-run management board at the bank. Two days later, Newbridge filed suit in a Texas court against one of Taiwan's leading banks, Chinatrust Commercial Bank Ltd., charging that it improperly plotted to gain control of SDB itself, thus undermining Newbridge's exclusive agreement with the Chinese bank. An amended complaint, filed on May 20, charges that the Shenzhen bank's president, Zhou Lin Fu, "conspired" with Chinatrust management to undercut the deal. SDB, however, is not a defendant in the suit. Despite repeated phone calls and faxes seeking comment, officials at Chinatrust and SDB had no comment on the lawsuit or on the allegations. Newbridge said it would have no comment either.

Newbridge Capital has been aggressively seeking opportunities in Asia since the 1997–98 financial crisis, and it counts some seasoned investors in its ranks. One principal is Texas Pacific Group, run by legendary buyout artist David Bonderman—the dealmaker best known for reviving Continental Airlines Inc. The other major investor in Newbridge is Blum Capital Partners L.P., a San Francisco boutique run by Richard C. Blum, the husband of U.S. Senator Dianne Feinstein (D-Calif.).

How could these pros find themselves in this fix? Even for the savviest players, acquiring control of financial assets in China is tricky. China's recent leadership shakeup may have played a part. When Zhu Rongji, China's former Premier and a key backer of the deal, retired in March, Newbridge lost a key backer. The replacement of top officials at China's central bank and securities agency added to the uncertainty.

Newbridge also finds itself squaring off against the Koo family, the powerful clan that runs Chinatrust. The Koos have long made it clear they wanted a deal with a mainland bank. In February, Newbridge wrote a strongly worded letter to Chinatrust Chairman Jeffrey L.S. Koo and Jeffrey J. L. Koo Jr., Koo's son and the bank's president. In the letter, which was filed with the court papers, Newbridge Managing Partner Daniel A. Carroll said the Koos had contacted a representative of Shenzhen shareholders with a potential buyout offer—in violation of Newbridge's arrangement to remain the exclusive outside investor (Newbridge had agreed to buy roughly 20% of SDB, a stake worth about $170 million). If Chinatrust didn't back off, Newbridge threatened legal action.

The dispute reached a new low on May 12, when SDB suddenly announced it was pulling the plug on the deal. Newbridge issued a statement saying: "We expect the Shenzhen government . . . to honor its obligations under this binding international contract with us." The only thing lacking was a signature, Newbridge said. The U.S. group also claimed that the deal was approved last August and September by the People's Bank of China and by the China Securities Regulatory Commission.

The next day, at a meeting of all the parties in Shenzhen, a negotiator for SDB told the group that the decision to dissolve the management committee was a "commercial" decision by the bank, rather than a government decision. The official also said that talks on Newbridge's deal would continue.

But Newbridge had waited long enough, and filed its suit. It's rare for even the most frustrated foreign investors in China to turn to the courts, for fear of jeopardizing future relationships. But Newbridge isn't a normal investor. The Chinese "didn't realize they were dealing with a nut case"—that is, a firm that wouldn't play by routine rules, says a knowledgeable source. If its claim is upheld, Newbridge may have some recourse, since Chinatrust has a U.S. subsidiary. Doing business in China is not for the fainthearted.

Source: Mark L. Clifford in Hong Kong. Copyright 2003, by The McGraw-Hill Companies Inc. All rights reserved.

Chapter 4

Public Organizations and International Agreements

Chapter Objectives

A variety of public organizations and international agreements provide an important framework for the operation of international business law. This framework dictates how national governments treat international businesses and how international businesses must conduct their transactions. Thus, political topics that seem very distant from the boardrooms of business have a very real impact on business operations. In this chapter we discuss

- The history and function of the United Nations, GATT, and the World Trade Organization.
- The fundamental principles of world trading norms: quantitative restrictions, most-favored-nation status, and national treatment, and their impact on business.

- The nature and effect of corporate dumping and government subsidies.
- The developing treatment of services and intellectual property.
- Dispute resolution between nations in international trade issues.

A Developing Institutional Framework

The overall legal environment in which commercial transactions take place is further shaped by international public organizations, driven by the interests of the home and foreign governments. The two foremost are the United Nations and the World Trade Organization.

Where intergovernmental relations take place outside public international organizations, it is done through bilateral and multilateral agreements, for example, the 1989 Canada–U.S. Free Trade Agreement (bilateral) and the 1947 General Agreement on Tariffs and Trade (multilateral). When a bilateral or multilateral agreement goes well beyond a limited economic sector and applies to a set of (usually) neighboring states, it is termed as "regional cooperation" or a "regional trading agreement." One example is the 1994 North American Free Trade Agreement. Even more ambitious is the movement toward political, social, and economic integration in the European Union.

The business transaction environment is further shaped by private organizations of interested parties where governments will not act (having no national interest or political will) or cannot act (a priority, but insufficient common ground for international agreement). Most private international organizations, such as the International Chamber of Commerce, find that it is a mixture of both of these drivers that propel their activities. For some private organizations, their initiatives are so successful in finding common ground (at least among businesspersons) that international governments leave them to it and back out to a considerable degree. This has been particularly true where the ICC has established common rules for documentary credit payments and legal terms defining the point at which delivery is complete in merchandise trade transactions.

The transportation of goods generates a number of critical relationships, some directly connected to the trade actors, but also establishing a string of relationships that the importer and exporter never fully see. In terms of direct links, each trade actor (the importer and exporter) will have a relationship with a bank, a freight forwarder and/or carrier, and an insurer. Subsidiary relationships beyond the sight of the actors will include commercial relations between the parties' banks in payment settlement, contracts between freight forwarders and carriers for different legs of the journey, assistance of customs brokers in handling border formalities, and relations between insurers in case of loss or liability. In almost every situation, these supporting players have a connection to a private international organization within their industry. These organizations draft rules, or at least guidelines, to prevent disputes or to help settle them after they occur.

Legal counsel at home and abroad will have their own relationships that range from meeting to negotiate the respective interests of the parties, to instances where home legal counsel engages foreign lawyers to act as their agent abroad, due to the latter's greater expertise in forum law.

All of these relationships and their effect shape the final transaction between the parties. Still, there is often a considerable distance between the home party and its foreign market or consumer. For example, the transaction relationship may commit the foreign party to act as an agent or distributor for the export seller, in which case there is a certain shared interest in the outcome of even further sales relationships in the foreign market.

With changes, where appropriate, these relationships as outlined above exist in not only goods trade, but in services and investment trade as well. At this point we have identified these organizations and relationships and see their importance in general terms. We can now examine each in greater detail.

The United Nations

The United Nations is widely known as a forum for the peaceful negotiation of international disputes, a supervisor in peacekeeping, and a key player in the establishment of widely held norms of human and political rights. Its organs include the Security Council, the General Assembly, and the Secretariat. Less well known is the work of other organs, UN Specialized Agencies, and related organizations, all existing or born under the UN umbrella. Together these have played a significant role in shaping the economic and business environments since 1945.

There have been setbacks as well as successes in the UN experience. While its success in peacemaking in places like the Mediterranean island of Cyprus (40 years in keeping Greek and Turkish factions from war) is largely unknown by the public, its failures in preventing Rwandan genocide and averting war in Iraq have been spectacular. Hopefully these failures will serve to reenergize the vital role that the chief international organization must play if it is to remain as relevant to the future as it has been to the past.

A lesser-known organ of the UN is the International Court of Justice, which provides a judicial forum between nations.[1] As we have seen earlier, its roots are found in the Perma-

[1]See www.icj-cij.org.

nent Court of International Justice, which was a creature of the predecessor in spirit of the UN, the 1919 League of Nations.

In addition to trying to provide forums in which to negotiate and litigate problems, the UN has tried to provide mechanisms to smooth the process of development and economic activity around the world, in order to prevent or minimize international problems in the first place. The United Nations Economic and Social Council (ECOSOC) is the vehicle. While it is also given the status of an "organ" of the UN, it is subordinate to, and reports to, the General Assembly.

ECOSOC has a very wide mandate—social as well as economic—and sponsors draft treaties and conventions that are open for adoption by UN member states. It ranges from the fundamental and universal (drafting conventions on human rights) to the technical and specialized (such as coordination with the International Civil Aviation Organization). Law-making is, however, between UN members, as neither ECOSOC nor the UN itself exercises any supranational legislative power. ECOSOC-inspired treaties and conventions become national law only after signature in the UN context and ratification under national constitutional processes.

Debate in 1961 within ECOSOC gave birth in 1964 to a new body, UNCTAD, the United Nations Conference on Trade and Development. At that time, the needs of the developing world in a post-war, post-colonial environment were growing, particularly as UN membership was increasing and set to increase further with new members who were predominantly in this category. Trade access to markets of developed nations was and is important to these developing nations. Also on the agenda were the worries of the developed world in security of foreign investment and preservation of their own national markets.

The term *conference* is misleading, for while there is an annual conference, UNCTAD has a structure of working parties and commissions working on an ongoing basis, as well as a secretary-general and a permanent physical presence in Geneva, Switzerland. UNCTAD has had a rocky existence. The issue of market access is not easy to negotiate, given the great gap in political and economic power between nations. UNCTAD, despite its challenges, has made important strides in creating market access and investment stability through the creation of acceptable compromises that have resulted in General Assembly resolutions on point.

In terms of the direct effect that UN initiatives have had on international business transactions, most significant is the work of UNCITRAL, the UN Commission on International Trade Law, established by the General Assembly in 1966.[2] The UN recognized the degree of disparity between the bodies of business law of nations and aimed at creating greater harmonization and eventual unification of law through cooperative drafting of international norms.

The 36 elected members of the Commission oversee six working groups covering most issues central to trade. The product of these working groups has been conventions and "model laws," available to be adopted into national law by UN members. Naturally, the more that member states accept the conventions and adopt the model laws as their own without amendment, the greater the international harmony and certainty. The most significant of these conventions and model laws relate to

1. International sale of goods.
2. International transport of goods.
3. International commercial arbitration.
4. International payments.
5. Electronic commerce.

[2]See www.uncitral.org.

One of these, the UN Convention on Contracts for the International Sale of Goods, entered into force in 1988. Since then (to early 2004), 62 nations are parties, including the United States and all other major trading nations. It establishes a code of legal rules governing the formation of contracts, the obligations of the buyer and seller, and remedies for breach of contract in the international sale of goods. The importance and effect of this convention is discussed in detail in Chapter 7.

The UN Convention on the Carriage of Goods by Sea, 1978 (the so-called Hamburg Rules), sets out rights and obligations of shippers, carriers, and consignees under a contract of carriage of goods by sea. Developing countries were spurred on by perceived injustices contained in the earlier Hague Rules, and urged the creation of this convention and have adopted it. While the Hamburg Rules are regionally important in dealing with developing countries, the Hague Rules (and another variant, Hague-Visby) prevail elsewhere. The Hamburg Rules are in force among 28 nations and offer greater protection to the owners of cargo against more powerful shipping companies. The differences between the Hague and Hamburg Rules are elaborated in Chapter 8.

UNCITRAL Arbitration Rules have achieved wide acceptance since their initial adoption in 1976. They provide procedural rules upon which parties may agree to conduct arbitration proceedings (informal private "courts") to settle their commercial disputes. These rules are chosen by the commercial parties and do not involve an adoption by nations. Also on the subject of arbitration is the Convention on the Recognition and Enforcement of Foreign Arbitral Awards (New York, 1958). This Convention was created prior to UNCITRAL, but furthering international application of these standardized rules is an important goal of the Commission. To early 2004, 132 nations (including all major trading nations) are parties to it.

To allow for smoother movement of payments, UNCITRAL authored common rules for financial instruments in 1988 with its Convention on International Bills of Exchange and International Promissory Notes, although it is yet to receive ratification by any state and is consequently not yet in force. The 1996 UNCITRAL Model Law on Electronic Commerce has fared better, but as a model law it is not adopted, per se, by states. It is a draft, or foundation, for creating national laws. National laws that incorporate or are based on the model law are developing rapidly, including in states of the United States.

The specialized agencies of the United Nations have made their own contribution to macroeconomic international order, primarily through the International Monetary Fund (IMF)[3] and the World Bank,[4] or, as it is more properly known, the International Bank for Reconstruction and Development.

Any time a nation has a temporary balance of payments problem, that is, a shortfall in making its payments, it is exporting its problems to creditor nations, causing difficulty with their own ability to pay their own accounts. The IMF provides liquidity to troubled economies (hopefully) before their lack of funds can trigger an international financial crisis through this domino effect. The World Bank initially was created to finance the postwar reconstruction of Europe, and with that challenge met, it has since provided funds and technical assistance to developing nations.

The GATT and WTO

Historical Foundations

In the world of international business transactions, most businesspersons have at least a passing awareness of the GATT (the General Agreement on Tariffs and Trade) and its suc-

---

[3]See www.imf.org.
[4]See www.worldbank.org.

cessor, the World Trade Organization.[5] The WTO incorporates the GATT and has a special relationship with the United Nations, though the WTO is not a UN Specialized Agency.

The GATT was the most successful multilateral initiative in economic liberalization that the world has ever known. That said, it seems odd that it was not more closely associated with the UN, which for the most part, has been its equal in achieving peaceful relations between states.

The fact is that the GATT was originally conceived to be more than an agreement, and was intended to be the "International Trade Organization," complementing the World Bank and IMF within the United Nations system. It was planned that three UN pillars would therefore prevent war through prosperity: development and reconstruction (the World Bank), financial liquidity in balance of payments (the IMF), and economic liberalization (the ITO). Unfortunately for the third pillar, this was not to be. The GATT was all that survived out of this U.S. "ITO" proposal, and, ironically, it was the United States that scuttled it.

The U.S. proposal was for a wide-ranging organization, covering trade, labor, and antitrust measures, and was sponsored within the UN system by ECOSOC in 1946. It had strong support among UN membership by 1948; then the process unraveled. For all governments, the pressures of war were truly gone (which lessened momentum), but, more profoundly, the U.S. president's executive authority to approve trade matters had expired, meaning that any proposed organization would be obliged to obtain ratification by two-thirds of the U.S. Senate. As this appeared politically unlikely, the idea of creating an actual organization had to be scrapped as far as the United States was concerned.

All that could then fit within the U.S. constitutional process and its political realities was an agreement on trade rules (the 1947 GATT being one chapter of what was to be the 1948 ITO Charter in Havana). As far as the rest of the world was concerned, an organization on trade that did not include the United States was simply a nonstarter. The lack of an organizational structure, lack of broad coverage, and lack of any real dispute settlement and enforcement procedure hamstrung the GATT for decades. There was, however, a silver lining: it made the GATT even easier for nations to accept. As is often said, you can do more to change people and nations by bringing them inside the club than by keeping them out.

Principles and Evolution

Short of closing one's borders to trade, customs duties (taxes charged against the value of property entering a territory) and excise taxes (taxes permitting the conduct of an act, such as the sale of alcohol) have been the surest way for nations to regulate trade volumes into their territory. Customs duties of a territory are listed in a published schedule known as a tariff, but the word *tariff* has come to mean "duty" in common language. High tariffs protected domestic producers by creating a barrier to trade, and while those producers therefore might not have much incentive to improve, such tariffs created employment in the home nation. But a nation cannot afford to insulate itself in this manner forever: inefficiencies have their own great cost (in reinventing the wheel), which eventually costs more than the value of the protection. Worse, this period of insulation can create isolation, and the international suspicion it breeds has led in the past to war.

The rationale behind the creation of the GATT was to lower tariff barriers to trade, but it has reduced nontariff barriers as well. Nontariff barriers to trade are government actions that restrict imports by means other than tariffs. This can include setting a limit or "quota" for particular imports (by volume or value, being a rather obvious barrier). Other examples are unnecessarily complex requirements for import permits or inspections of goods arriving, or unreasonable product-labeling requirements. The difficulty with nontariff barriers is recognizing between a legitimate interest of the host government (which is permitted under the

[5]See www.wto.org.

WTO rules) and a barrier created solely to render inbound goods noncompetitive through cost or administrative burden.

The three most fundamental liberalization principles of the GATT (and later the WTO) are the elimination of quantitative restrictions, the grant of most-favored-nation status, and the assurance of national treatment. In one sentence, these principles attempt to ensure that goods, in fact, can enter a territory, are charged no more duty than any other like imports, and, once inside the border, are treated no differently than domestically produced goods. Of course, there are exceptions to the rule, but that is the spirit of the GATT.

These provisions (quantitative restrictions, MFN, and national treatment) have existed since the GATT's foundation in 1947, but the process of liberalization in trade has deepened and widened over the decades. The deepening relates to "rounds" of negotiations, binding nations to a particular tariff for a particular good, then increasing the number of goods covered, and the further lowering of the duty rates to which nations are bound. The national tariff schedules (which are not found in the GATT, as they are products of national legislation) list rates on a product-by-product basis, and total more than 22,000 pages when summed together. However, goods and tariffs are only one dimension of the evolved GATT. The widening of GATT refers to the fact that it has expanded far beyond the original search for lower rates of duty across all goods. In its final evolution, GATT and its sister agreements inside the World Trade Organization touch on services, intellectual property, investment measures, and dispute settlement.

The trade negotiation rounds held under GATT lasted for years at a time, with eight being conducted between the GATT establishment in 1947 and 1994.[6] As tariffs fell, it became clear that governments were turning to nontariff barriers to frustrate imports and favor their national producers. Bear in mind that, despite their obligation to give national treatment, member governments will still favor domestic producers. It is these domestic businesses, not foreign producers, who contribute to their tax base and election expenses, and it is domestic workers who vote in elections in the expectation that their government will safeguard their jobs.

As a result, nontariff barriers can be quite creative. For example, a government may commit to treat all goods of like kind equally, but then try to tinker with product categories or regulation to the disadvantage of imports. The German government once instituted regulations limiting the noise level of lawn mowers, and the regulation applied to all lawn mowers sold in Germany—national treatment, as it were. However, it happened that all German lawn mowers were quiet machines and all foreign ones, perhaps with less attention to this aspect of design, were noisy. The result was a nontariff barrier: no foreign firm was prepared to completely redesign its lawn mower just so that it could sell lawn mowers in Germany. The regulation, while it lasted, kept out imports of foreign-made lawn mowers.

This type of government activity spurred later GATT rounds to deal with nontariff barriers and a host of other advanced issues. During the last round, the Uruguay Round of 1986–94, it became clear that the GATT had grown so large that it needed the status of a full-fledged organization to operate effectively. It also needed a dispute settlement mechanism that would allow it to enforce its rules. As a result, the World Trade Organization, in some ways less ambitious than its proposed 1948 Havana predecessor (it still does not deal with labor and antitrust issues), was born.

[6]Listed by date, name of round, subject matter, and number of members participating: 1947 Geneva (tariffs, 23), 1949 Annecy (tariffs, 13), 1951 Torquay (tariffs, 38), 1956 Geneva (tariffs, 26), 1960–1961 Dillon Round (tariffs, 26), 1964–1967 Kennedy Round (tariffs and antidumping, 62), 1973–1979 Tokyo Round (tariffs and nontariff measures, framework agreements, 102), 1986–1994 Uruguay Round (tariffs, nontariff measures, rules, services, intellectual property, dispute settlement, textiles, agriculture, creation of WTO, 123.)

Established on January 1, 1995, the World Trade Organization now has 144 members, as at early 2004. Of those territories that do not have membership, only Russia and Saudi Arabia are major trading nations. The word *territory* is important, for membership is open to separate customs territories, which may not be the same as "nations."[7] For example, a colony may not be self-governing in political matters, but it is a separate entity for GATT/WTO purposes if it maintains it own particular tariff schedule. In concrete terms, Hong Kong was a former Crown Colony of the United Kingdom, but as a separate customs territory, it had separate GATT membership. Even though Hong Kong has now become a Special Administrative Region of the People's Republic of China, it retains its WTO membership in its own right (for the same reason), alongside the membership of China.

The 1994 Agreement establishing the WTO[8] is fairly short, for the real substance lies in the annexes to it. Annex 1A is comprised of the Multilateral Agreements on Trade in Goods, Annex 1B is the General Agreement on Trade in Services (commonly known as GATS), and Annex 1C is the Agreement on Trade-Related Aspects of Intellectual Property Rights (TRIPs). Both GATS and TRIPs extend the application of goods-based GATT principles of fair treatment into the area of services and intellectual property rights. Annex 2 provides for the operation of the all-new Dispute Settlement Mechanism (DSU), while Annex 3 is a Trade Policy Review Mechanism that allows for examination of national measures to determine their compliance with the WTO agreements. Annex 4 contains the Plurilateral Trade Agreements (on trade in Civil Aircraft, Government Procurement, Dairy, and Bovine Meat), which only apply to WTO members who sign on to them separately.

The WTO is governed at the highest level by a Ministerial Conference of members meeting every two years. These are meetings of usually very senior members of national governments. Beneath the Ministerial Conference, the WTO operates under the supervision of a General Council of all members (appointees of member national governments). The General Council works on a standing basis and acts in its own right as the supervisory authority, as well as sitting as the Dispute Settlement Body for the Annex 2 DSU and as the Trade Policy Review Body for Annex 3. Reporting to the General Council is the Goods Council for Annex 1A matters, the GATS Council for Annex 1B, and the TRIPs Council for Annex 1C.

Annex 1A is complex, as it is the "primarily goods" umbrella for the GATT 1994 (which itself includes the bundle of the legally separate GATT 1947 and all its amendments, protocols, and decisions since 1947) as well as the

> Agreement on Agriculture
>
> Agreement on the Application of Sanitary and Phytosanitary Measures
>
> Agreement on Textiles and Clothing
>
> Agreement on Technical Barriers to Trade
>
> Agreement on Trade-Related Investment Measures[9]
>
> Agreement on Anti-dumping (Article VI, GATT 1994)
>
> Agreement on Customs Valuation (Article VII, GATT 1994)
>
> Agreement on Preshipment Inspection
>
> Agreement on Rules of Origin
>
> Agreement on Import Licensing Procedures
>
> Agreement on Subsidies and Countervailing Measures
>
> Agreement on Safeguards

[7]For sake of convenience and clarity in explanation, however, in this chapter we use the terms *nation, state, member,* and *contracting party* interchangeably to mean "separate customs territory," unless the contrary is indicated.

[8]Also available for examination at www.wto.org.

[9]Discussed in Chapter 12 on foreign direct investment.

WTO Organization

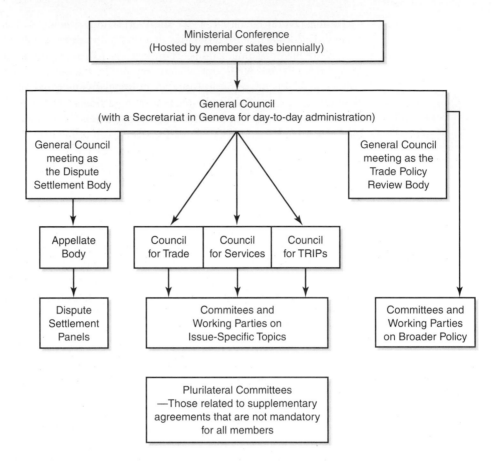

It should be no surprise that the WTO and its agreements do not create total uniformity. First, each customs territory within it is still setting its own rates of duty in its schedule of concessions to which it is binding itself. Further, there are limited grandfather rights to recognize special relationships and significant special concessions for developing countries.

This section has outlined in very general terms how the GATT, operating through the WTO, shapes the international business environment. As will be seen in the following sections, removal of quantitative restrictions and the benefits of most-favored-nation status allows fairer trade for all and lower costs for consumers, while national treatment attempts to prevent competitive distortions. Just as important are the expansions of the GATT principles into services, intellectual property, and investment trade. Other WTO provisions (within both the GATT 1947 and the Annex 1A Multilateral Agreements) relate to dumping and subsidies, both of which are market-distorting activities in themselves.

Dumping and subsidies can have a dramatic impact on individual trading firms because the problem originates from a "low price–quick sale" strategic decision made at the corporate level (in dumping cases), often made possible because the firm has received a government benefit (in the form of a subsidy). In the short run, the targeted market receives cheap goods; in the long run, it may face the ruin of its own industries that cannot compete. Under particular circumstances, these pricing decisions aimed at foreign markets and government support in the home market can attract the attention of GATT parties, and may result in proceedings under the WTO Dispute Settlement Understanding.

We turn now to a description of the WTO dispute settlement process, in order to understand its operation before seeing it act in determining the application of specificWTO rules.

Dispute Settlement

It is reality that nations will, on occasion, violate the commitments that they have made. As a result, any international system must have some method of attempting to right these wrongs. Three distinct phases of dispute management exist in terms of international trade disputes: pre-GATT, GATT, and the present WTO period.

Pre-GATT dispute settlement was simply the exercise of pure power politics—nations with power exercised it and the others were forced to follow. With the birth of the GATT, international trade graduated to a rule-based system. Despite its lack of a fully effective system and organization, do not underestimate the value of the move to the existence and recognition of rules. Just the existence of rules was a discipline it itself for nations, and was a valuable improvement toward more predictable outcomes in trade disputes.

In the first few years of the GATT, dispute settlement was via the "working party," a group of government representatives hammering out an essentially political and diplomatic solution to a trade problem. In the middle 1950s, this gave way to the establishment of panels staffed by experts with experience in the commodity and marketplace that was at issue in the dispute. This was certainly an improvement, for while the dispute remained political, at least the actors knew far more about the underlying economic situation at issue.

Throughout the GATT decades to 1995, the dispute settlement process remained hampered by the traditional GATT shortcoming of its lack of organizational status. Previously, there were no fixed timetables for dispute resolution. Decisions with respect to panel reports could only be taken where international political consensus existed, meaning unanimity among the contracting state parties. Clearly, no state on the losing end of a GATT panel report would back its adoption by the whole. Full consensus, therefore, would be blocked, and the process would end short of its goal. Only moral suasion and the usual good offices of mediation and consultation were available to bring contracting states and their behavior into line with their obligations under the Agreement.

With the creation of the WTO, a more courtlike and effective dispute settlement body now exists. While its organization and operation still must make concessions to the fact that it serves the interests of sovereign states (and is a creature of them), its decisions verge on becoming a body of jurisprudence, and a form of enforcement can follow more properly as a result of them.

The cases illustrated in following sections are representative of the WTO dispute settlement process, through to an Appellate Body report. The very word *Appellate,* with its judicial connotation, should be taken as a reflection of the type of changes in dispute settlement that have occurred with the evolution of the GATT into the WTO. The dispute settlement process (DSP) has taken its place as an integral part of a rule-driven organization, and membership in the organization now means accepting, without reservation, the disciplines of its adjudication in disputes.

The General Council of the WTO sits as the Dispute Settlement Body, carrying overall responsibility for the management of the settlement process, and is governed in its work by Annex 2 to the WTO Agreement, the Understanding on Rules and Procedures Governing the Settlement of Disputes. This agreement is more commonly termed as the "Dispute Settlement Understanding."

To suggest that the process is "adjudication" will cause some commentators to object, because it implies a court-type legal process, with all the other attributes that go along with courts: independence, interpretation, and the ability to set precedents. Indeed, the DSP still falls short of being such a "court," but it has enough of the attributes of justice to at least be thought of as a judicial process in informal terms.

First of these is the notion that a functioning judicial process should result in a certain decision in a certain time period. It is no longer possible to simply stonewall and delay a dispute into irrelevancy as was the case in the pre-WTO situation. Consultations on an issue between states now must take place unless consensus of the whole organization at the political level is such that they should not take place. This reverses the role that political consensus has previously played. If consultations fail, then a panel *will* be created by the Dispute Settlement Body, no later than upon a second request from a complaining state, unless there is a consensus within the DSB that it ought not create a panel. Fixed time limits exist for a dispute to move through each phase of investigation and reporting. If a panel report is not appealed, the Dispute Settlement Body will adopt it, unless there is a consensus at the political level to the contrary. That makes overturning an unappealed panel report quite a feat; the winner would have to agree to forgo adoption of the report. If the "loser" does not want to see the panel report adopted, then it must appeal, within time limits, to the Appellate Body, which will review the legal analysis of the report. The Appellate Body will not review or retry questions of fact, in line with the practice of most appellate jurisdictions of the world. Where an appeal is launched, again, time limits must be adhered to, and the Dispute Settlement Body will adopt the report of the Appellate Body unless there is political consensus to the contrary.

So politics is not wholly absent (in fact, it is alive and well), but its role has been essentially reversed to become consensus *against* action, rather than requiring consensus *for* action.

The following timetable is provided by the WTO as a guide to the timeline of a given dispute as it moves through the DSU stages, approximately 15 months from start to finish if an appeal is undertaken.[10]

How Long to Settle a Dispute?

These approximate periods for each stage of a dispute settlement procedure are target figures—the agreement is flexible. In addition, the countries can settle their dispute themselves at any stage. Totals are also approximate.

60 days	Consultations, mediation, etc.
45 days	Panel set up and panelists appointment
6 months	Final panel report to parties
3 weeks	Final panel report to WTO members
60 days	Dispute Settlement Body adopts report (if no appeal)
Total = 1 year	(without appeal)
60–90 days	Appeals report
30 days	Dispute Settlement Body adopts appeals report
Total = 1 year 3 months	(with appeal)

The consultation phase is mandatory, and the parties may seek the intervention of the WTO Director-General in mediation, if they desire. If this is not effective, the DSB will ultimately establish a panel. The panel will be composed of experts agreeable to the parties, but persons without government affiliation to the parties in the dispute. Therefore, while the panels are not a standing tribunal as courts would be in the domestic sense, they have the distance and independence that justice demands.

Cases are presented in writing, oral proceedings follow, and the panel will prepare and circulate a draft report as to facts and arguments, giving two weeks to allow for the comments of the parties. An interim report then follows, which contains the panel's findings and conclusions. Again, this is provided for the comments of the parties, with a three-week

[10]www.wto.org/english/thewto_e/whatis_e/tif_e/disp1_e.htm.

window (one for review and two for final meetings), which hopefully may lead to settlement before the final report is circulated to all WTO members.

Where the panel has concluded that a disputed measure is in breach of WTO obligations, it can only recommend that the measure be brought into conformity, but it generally offers up suggestions as to how the offending nation may accomplish this. The panel report ruling or recommendation becomes that of the Dispute Settlement Body after the expiration of the appeal period, unless it is rejected by consensus.

Either side or both are permitted to appeal a panel report. The appeal will be heard before three members of the permanent seven-member Appellate Body set up under the auspices of the Dispute Settlement Body. The members of the Appellate Body serve four-year terms, are individuals with recognized standing in the field of law and international trade, and must be independent of government influence.

As with most domestic legal systems, the appeal may uphold, modify, or reverse legal findings and conclusions. In contrast with most domestic legal systems, however, it is a rapid process, usually 60 days, with a cap at 90 days. After the appeal process is complete, the Dispute Settlement Body must act within a further 30 days to accept the report or, by consensus, reject it.

With regard to further differences between the WTO system and domestic court systems, it is important to understand the jurisprudential value of panel and Appellate reports and the extent to which they constitute precedent. As decisions, they are binding only between the parties to the dispute to which they relate. Article 3(2) of the Annex 2 Dispute Settlement Understanding makes clear that "[R]ecommendations and rulings of the DSB cannot add to or diminish the rights and obligations provided in the covered agreements." As such, it means that any one case cannot stand as an authoritative interpretation of the WTO rules. Despite this, however, the body of jurisprudence is building, and successive panels and appeals are following, relying on, citing, and distinguishing previous cases—a body of nonbinding, yet highly persuasive precedent.

Given a DSB determination that a nation is in the wrong, in the first instance the nation must bring its trade measure into "prompt compliance" with the ruling or recommendation and into conformity with its obligations under the Agreement. A "reasonable period of time" to effect change will be provided, but if the nation in default fails to correct its trade measure, then it must be prepared to offer acceptable compensation, or expect to face trade sanctions. Assuming no agreement on compensation can be reached, the DSB can be expected to grant permission to the complainant to "suspend concessions or obligations" (trade sanctions) against the defaulting party. This permission will be granted within 30 days after the expiration of the "reasonable period of time," unless there is a consensus against such a request.

Acceptable sanctions should mirror the default to the greatest degree possible, to prevent the scope of a dispute from widening. If Country A is found, for example, to be maintaining an improper subsidy in its steel industry that is causing prejudice to the steel industry of Country B, then Country B's trade sanctions should target its steel imports from Country A. If this is impossible or ineffective, then sanctions should first target related imports, then other goods generally, before branching out against trade in services or intellectual property or anything else other than goods.

We turn now to examination of the particular principles upon which the GATT and WTO are founded:

- Quantitative restrictions, MFN, and national treatment.
- Antidumping and subsidies.
- The General Agreement on Trade in Services.
- Trade Related Aspects of Intellectual Property.

Quantitative Restrictions

The founding members of the 1947 GATT reviewed their trading world and recognized that there were many ways nations used to block trade, both tariff and nontariff means. Each government tended to take action that gave it a short-run advantage, but in the long run, the collection of all governmental actions made the world less well off.

Those nations of the world that were not inclined toward trade liberalism simply remained outside the agreement. This catchall phrase, "not inclined," covers a lot of ground. Some countries such as the former Soviet Union were suspicious of capitalist organizations (a mutual feeling) and kept themselves apart. Even if they had been inclined toward membership, the Soviet Union and others such as China simply did not embrace comparable internal economic policies to become members. For others, such as Saudi Arabia, the easing of sovereign or religious control over their peoples and markets was unacceptable.

For nations that did become members of the GATT, it was recognized among them that outright prevention of trade through quotas or prohibition was the most destructive trade policy. Accordingly, the strategy was to adopt a mindset that trade was good and should not, as a matter of general principle, be restricted through quotas.

This is not to say that trade could not be managed or controlled. The advantage in eliminating quotas in principle meant that control would have to be exercised by governments by way of tariffs, rather than just closing the door on goods. With this as the accepted mindset, negotiation between governments in trade management would focus primarily on tariff levels, putting the entire international choir on the same page of the songbook.

The GATT focus on establishing tariff schedules, then reducing tariff rates and spreading the effects of reductions among all members, comes from this springboard of the general elimination of quantitative restrictions. Note, however, that the elimination is not complete, nor is it permanent. Many exceptions are permitted, as these are still sovereign nations who are quite unprepared to give up all their policy tools under all circumstances. The exceptions allow a nation to impose quantitative restrictions where circumstances are, in its own opinion, "essential," "critical," or "necessary." Considerable latitude also remains with respect to agriculture and fisheries products.

These two issues of agriculture and fisheries are dimensions of a bigger WTO/GATT stumbling block related to trade in foodstuffs. A nation does not want to grant any measure of control over its food supply to the international community, nor does it wish to give up any of its own rights related to feeding itself. For many years, Japan even went so far as to insist that its trade in rice was a matter of national security, and, therefore, not subject to trade negotiation; hence, Japan banned imports of rice into the country. When one considers that Japan is a small island, and that it is difficult to restore a rice paddy once it is paved over in building development, the Japanese government may have had a point in wishing to ensure it remained independent and self-sufficient in rice. In the years since, Japan has relented and now trades in rice, but as a nation it is more vulnerable to a trade embargo than ever before. Likewise, many European nations are fearful of future health effects of genetically modified foods. Access to European markets was previously prohibited for suppliers of GM foods, and now it is only granted where minute quantities are involved and under strict labeling requirements. Both of these issues—on rice and genetically modified foods—have been heard and debated in the WTO forum as questions of quantitative restrictions.

The general elimination of quantitative restrictions is now found in GATT 1947 Article XI, reproduced on page 125, and its operation is examined in the case following, concerning India's import restriction regime.

GATT 1947 Article XI *(excerpt)*[11]

Article XI

General Elimination of Quantitative Restrictions

1. No prohibitions or restrictions other than duties, taxes or other charges, whether made effective through quotas, import or export licences or other measures, shall be instituted or maintained by any contracting party on the importation of any product of the territory of any other contracting party or on the exportation or sale for export of any product destined for the territory of any other contracting party.

2. The provisions of paragraph 1 of this Article shall not extend to the following:

   (*a*) Export prohibitions or restrictions temporarily applied to prevent or relieve critical shortages of foodstuffs or other products essential to the exporting contracting party;

   (*b*) Import and export prohibitions or restrictions necessary to the application of standards or regulations for the classification, grading or marketing of commodities in international trade;

   (*c*) Import restrictions on any agricultural or fisheries product, imported in any form, necessary to the enforcement of governmental measures which operate:

      (i) to restrict the quantities of the like domestic product permitted to be marketed or produced, or, if there is no substantial domestic production of the like product, of a domestic product for which the imported product can be directly substituted; or

      (ii) to remove a temporary surplus of the like domestic product, or, if there is no substantial domestic production of the like product, of a domestic product for which the imported product can be directly substituted, by making the surplus available to certain groups of domestic consumers free of charge or at prices below the current market level; or

      (iii) to restrict the quantities permitted to be produced of any animal product the production of which is directly dependent, wholly or mainly, on the imported commodity, if the domestic production of that commodity is relatively negligible.

   Any contracting party applying restrictions on the importation of any product pursuant to subparagraph *(c)* of this paragraph shall give public notice of the total quantity or value of the product permitted to be imported during a specified future period and of any change in such quantity or value. Moreover, any restrictions applied under (i) above shall not be such as will reduce the total of imports relative to the total of domestic production, as compared with the proportion which might reasonably be expected to rule between the two in the absence of restrictions. In determining this proportion, the contracting party shall pay due regard to the proportion prevailing during a previous representative period and to any special factors which may have affected or may be affecting the trade in the product concerned.

The following WTO Dispute Settlement Panel Report applies the above Article XI principle of elimination of quantitative restrictions and highlights the policy and mechanics of exceptions.

While such restrictions are prohibited in general by Article XI, there are significant exceptions as shown above and in Article XVIII:B. Article XVIII:B is the true central issue

[11]Now incorporated with all amendments, protocols, accessions, understandings and decisions into GATT 1994. Full text is available at the WTO website; www.wto.org, indexed under "Documents."

in the case below. The Article recognizes that developing nations have limited reserves of foreign exchange (cash and gold equivalents), earned from exports and used in payment for imports. Without the right to control imports (and hence the outflow of payments for those imports), nations could find their foreign exchange cash reserves drained to zero. As a result, there would be no foreign exchange to pay (in the short run) for further, perhaps more critical, imports.

At that stage, the nation would face unhappy options. If it can, it could go deeper into debt through international borrowing. Alternatively or additionally, if foreigners are willing to accept its paper currency, it can print and spend more of its own currency, swapping one crisis for another. When currency is printed without any increase in national wealth, it only devalues all national currency that presently exist, and will eventually result in domestic price inflation.

To prevent these unfortunate outcomes as a result of compelling a nation to forgo quantitative restrictions, the exception exists, but only so far and as long as necessary. Paragraph 9 of Article XVIII:B permits the restrictions only so far as necessary to forestall, stop, and achieve a reasonable growth in reserves. Paragraph 11 requires removal of the restrictions when no longer necessary, while acknowledging that no country can be forced to alter its development priorities just to comply with this requirement. Paragraph 12 requires nations imposing restrictions to advise and consult with the GATT contracting parties as to the extent of the restrictions and the nature of their balance of payments difficulties.

WTO Panel Report, Article XI; *India—Quantitative Restrictions: India—Quantitative Restrictions on Imports of Agricultural, Textile and Industrial Products WT/DS90/R*[12]

Introduction

On 16 July 1997, the United States requested consultations with India, . . . concerning quantitative restrictions maintained by India on the importation of a number of agricultural, textile and industrial products. The United States considered that the quantitative restrictions maintained by India . . . appeared to be inconsistent with India's obligations under Article XI:1 and XVIII:11 of the GATT 1994, Article 4.2 of the Agreement on Agriculture and Article 3 of the Agreement on Import Licensing Procedures . . .

Claims and Main Arguments: Scope of the Complaint

3.2　At the request of the Panel, the United States clarified that it sought a ruling that India is not currently justified [in maintaining certain restrictions] under the balance-of-payments exception. If India asserted that these restrictions were justified under Article XVIII:B [the balance-of-payments exception] of GATT 1994, the United States requested the Panel to accept the findings and determinations made by the IMF. It also requested that the Panel find that the additional evidence presented by the United States corroborated the IMF's determination.

---

[12]All WTO dispute settlement cases can be found at www.wto.org/, specifically, www.wto.org/english/tratop_e/dispu_e/dispu_e.htm#disputes, after which cases are indexed and retrieved by any of the following: their case number, the countries party to it, or its subject matter. This particular case is numbered WT/DS90/R.

3.6 India requested the Panel to reject the US complaint. India claimed that it was clear from Article XVIII:12 and the 1994 Understanding that the conformity of import restrictions with Article XVIII:9 and 11 must be determined by the General Council and that the Member may maintain the import restrictions until it had been informed of their inconsistency with the criteria set out in Article XVIII:9 and 10 by the General Council. In the absence of such a determination by the General Council, India continued to have the right to maintain the remaining restrictions under Article XVIII:B. In India's view . . . [i]t would [otherwise] be a serious deviation from practices consistently followed under the GATT 1947 and result in transferring without any basis the authority to determine the legal status of import restrictions from the Committee and the General Council to the IMF and panels . . .

3.9 The United States contended that India maintained quantitative restrictions consisting of import licensing requirements on thousands of products. These were the items listed in the "Negative List of Imports" in India's official Export and Import Policy. Most imports into India remained subject to an arbitrary, non-transparent and discretionary import-licensing regime; formal quotas did not exist. Persons wishing to import an item on the Negative List had to apply for a license and explain their "justification for import": the authorities provided no explanation of the criteria for judging applications, and no advance notice of the volume or value of imports to be allowed. In fact, licenses were routinely refused on the basis that the import would compete with a domestic producer. The leading item on the Negative List was consumer goods (including many food items), and for many consumer goods inclusion on the Negative List had amounted to an import ban or close to it.

3.11 The United States noted that where an import license was granted for an item on the Negative List, it was only granted to an "Actual User." This "Actual User condition" ruled out any imports by wholesalers or other intermediaries, and itself was a further quantitative restriction on imports. Some of the restrictions on imports were made effective through "canalization": channelling of imports through state trading operations of authorized "canalizing agencies." Where canalizing agencies restricted imports, their operations were a quantitative restriction on imports. Some of the items on the Negative List could be imported by using "Special Import Licences (SILs)." However, these items too remained under restriction . . .

3.12 The United States requested the Panel to find that all four measures: (1) restriction of items through discretionary licensing (2) canalization; (3) restriction of items through special import licensing and (4) the "Actual User" condition, constituted quantitative restrictions within the meaning of Article XI:1.

5.76 India's basic argument is that it has a right to institute balance-of-payments measures without the prior approval of any WTO body and a right to maintain those measures until the BOP Committee or the General Council advises it to modify them under Article XVIII:12 or establishes a time-period for their removal under paragraph 13 of the 1994 Understanding. In the absence of such action by the Committee or General Council, India asserts that the issue of whether its measures are justified under Article XVIII:B cannot be raised in dispute settlement.

5.77 Under Article XVIII:B, it is clear that a Member has the right to institute balance-of-payments measures without the prior approval of any WTO body. India correctly notes that proposals in the past to require such approval were not adopted. [W]hen a Member institutes or intensifies balance-of-payments measures, it is required to consult with the BOP Committee . . .

5.78 We note at the outset that there is no explicit statement in Article XVIII:B or the 1994 Understanding that authorizes a Member to maintain its balance-of-payments measures in effect until the General Council or BOP Committee acts under one of the aforementioned provisions. Article XVIII:B, however, addresses the issue of the extent to which balance-of-payments measures may be maintained. Article XVIII:11 . . . specifies that a Member:

> "shall progressively relax any restrictions applied under this Section [i.e., Article XVIII:B] as conditions improve, maintaining them only to the extent necessary under the terms of paragraph 9 of this Article [XVIII] and shall eliminate them when conditions no longer justify their maintenance."

5.80   Moreover, the obligation in Article XVIII:11 requires action by the individual Member. It is qualified only by a proviso and Ad Note . . . and it is not made subject to the accomplishment of other procedures. In light of the unqualified nature of the Article XVIII:11 obligation, it would be inconsistent with the principle *pacta sunt servanda*[13] to conclude that a WTO Member has a right to maintain balance-of-payments measures, even if unjustified under Article XVIII:B, in the absence of a Committee or General Council decision in respect thereof. Thus, we find that India does not have a right to maintain its balance-of-payments measures until the General Council advises it to modify them under Article XVIII:12 or establishes a time-period for their removal under paragraph 13 of the 1994 Understanding.

5.127   Article XI contains one of the fundamental principles of the GATT/WTO legal system, the general prohibition of quantitative restrictions. Article XI:1 reads as follows:

> "No prohibitions or restrictions other than duties, taxes or other charges, whether made effective through quotas, import or export licences or other measures, shall be instituted or maintained by any [Member] on the importation of any product of the territory of any other [Member] or on the exportation or sale for export of any product of the territory of any other [Member]."

5.128   We note that the text of Article XI:1 is very broad in scope, providing for a general ban on import or export restrictions or prohibitions "other than duties, taxes or other charges." As was noted by the panel in *Japan—Trade in Semi-conductors,* the wording of Article XI:1 is comprehensive: it applies "to all measures instituted or maintained by a [Member] prohibiting or restricting the importation, exportation, or sale for export of products other than measures that take the form of duties, taxes or other charges." The scope of the term "restriction" is also broad, as seen in its ordinary meaning, which is "a limitation on action, a limiting condition or regulation."

5.129   Under the GATT 1947, panels have examined whether import and export licensing systems are restrictions under Article XI:1. . . . [D]iscretionary or non-automatic licensing systems by their very nature operate as limitations on action since certain imports may not be permitted. Thus, in light of the terms of Article XI:1, . . . we conclude that a discretionary or non-automatic import licensing requirement is a restriction prohibited by Article XI:1.

5.131   In light of these elements, we find that the import licensing system maintained by India for the products found in Annex II of the Negative List of Imports, to the extent that it applies to the products specified in WT/BOP/N/24, Annex I, Part B, operates as a restriction on imports within the meaning of Article XI:1.

A similar analysis leads to the same conclusion with respect to canalization, special import licences, and the actual user requirement.

5.145   Having determined that the measures at issue are quantitative restrictions within the meaning of Article XI:1 and therefore prohibited, we must examine the United States' second claim, i.e. violation of Article XVIII:11, and India's defence under the balance-of-payments provisions of GATT 1994 in order to determine whether India, by maintaining the measures at issue, violates Article XVIII:11.

[13]"Agreements are to be observed."

5.147   Under the terms of Article XVIII:9,

"the import restrictions instituted, maintained or intensified shall not exceed those necessary:

(a) to forestall the threat of, or to stop, a serious decline in monetary reserves, or

(b) in the case of a Member with inadequate monetary reserves, to achieve a reasonable rate of increase in its reserves"

due regard being paid to any special factors that may be affecting the reserves of the Member or its need for reserves.

5.148   The second sentence of Article XVIII:11 provides:

"[The Member concerned] shall progressively relax any restrictions applied under this section as conditions improve, maintaining them only to the extent necessary under the terms of paragraph 9 of this Article and shall eliminate them when conditions no longer justify such maintenance; Provided that no Member shall be required to withdraw or modify restrictions on the ground that a change in its development policy would render unnecessary the restrictions which it is applying under this section."

The Panel discussed the condition of India's monetary reserves, and . . .

5.184   We find that, as of the date of establishment of this Panel, India's balance-of-payments measures were not necessary to forestall the threat of, or to stop, a serious decline in its monetary reserves and that its reserves were not inadequate. As a result, its measures were not necessary and therefore "exceed those necessary" under the terms of Article XVIII:9 (a) or (b). Therefore, India would appear to be in violation of the requirements of Article XVIII:11 by maintaining its measures. However, a Note Ad Article XVIII:11 specifies that a Member need not remove its balance-of-payments measures, if such removal would thereupon produce conditions justifying their reinstitution. Moreover, a proviso to Article XVIII:11 states that a Member shall not be required to withdraw balance-of-payments measures on the grounds that a change in its development policy would render them unnecessary . . .

The Panel reviewed both the Ad Note and the proviso of Article XVIII:11, and found on the facts that India could not avail itself of either of them.

5.236   In conclusion, with regard to our examination of the United States' claim of violation by India of Article XVIII:11 and India's defence that its measures are justified under Article XVIII:B, we have found that India's balance-of-payments situation was not such as to allow the maintenance of measures for balance-of-payments purposes under the terms of Article XVIII:9, that India was not justified in maintaining its existing measures under the terms of Article XVIII:11, and that it does not have a right to maintain or phase-out these measures on the basis of other provisions of Article XVIII:B which it invoked in its defence. We therefore conclude that India's measures are not justified under the terms of Article XVIII:B.

5.237   It should be noted that our finding is without prejudice to any future developments in India's balance-of-payments situation which might justify India invoking the provisions Article XVIII:B and the Understanding, should one of the conditions contemplated in Article XVIII:9 be met. It is also without prejudice to the possible determination of a reasonable period of time under Article 21 of the DSU[14] for India to bring its measures into conformity with its obligations under the WTO Agreement.

---

[14]Dispute Settlement Understanding.

6.2   We therefore *recommend* that the DSB[15] request India to bring the measures at issue into conformity with its obligations under the WTO Agreement.

7.1   Article 19.1 of the DSU provides that in addition to its findings and recommendations, the Panel may suggest ways in which the Member concerned could implement the recommendations. In the light of this provision, we wish to highlight some factors which, in our considered opinion, are relevant to the manner in which India should bring its measures into conformity with its obligations under the WTO Agreement.

7.2   At the outset, we recall that the Preamble to the WTO Agreement recognizes both (i) the desirability of expanding international trade in goods and services and (ii) the need for positive efforts designed to ensure that developing countries secure a share in international trade commensurate with the needs of their economic development. In implementing these goals, WTO rules promote trade liberalization, but recognize the need for specific exceptions from the general rules to address special concerns, including those of developing countries.

7.3   The process of trade liberalisation is often fragile and can be interrupted by balance-of-payments problems, even when these problems are not attributable to trade liberalisation. Liberalisation is also fragile with respect to internal adjustment problems. This fragility suggests an implementation period which is attuned to sustaining support for liberalisation in the presence of external shocks, and to the internal adjustment process.

7.4   As reflected in our report, we have found that the balance-of-payments measures in question were inconsistent with India's obligations under Articles XI:1 and XVIII:11 of GATT 1994 and Article 4.2 of the Agreement on Agriculture, and therefore recommended that India bring those measures into conformity with its obligations under the WTO Agreement. India has claimed that it is entitled to a phase-out period in connection with the removal of those measures and that it should not be required to eliminate them immediately. We concluded that, under Article XVIII:B and in the circumstances of the case, India had no right to a phase-out of its balance-of-payments restrictions, which the dispute settlement system would have to "preserve" as provided by Article 3.2 of the DSU. However, we wish to stress that our findings and recommendations do not imply that the measures at issue must be removed instantly.

7.5   The DSU provides for "prompt compliance" with recommendations of the DSB, but it contemplates the possibility that it might be impractical for a Member to comply immediately, in which case "the Member shall have a reasonable period of time in which to do so" (Article 21.3). This panel suggests that a reasonable period of time be granted to India in order to remove the import restrictions which are not justified under Article XVIII:B. Normally, the reasonable period of time to implement a panel recommendation, when determined through arbitration, should not exceed fifteen months from the date of adoption of a panel or Appellate Body report. However, this 15-month period is "a "guideline for the arbitrator," not a rule," and as indicated in Article 21.3(c) of the DSU, "that time may be shorter or longer, depending upon the particular circumstances." In light of the factors mentioned above, the panel suggests that the "reasonable period" in this case could be longer than fifteen months . . .

7.6   The foregoing factors take an added importance in light of the principle of special and differential treatment. This principle should be highlighted, given that Article 21.2 of the DSU requires that "Particular attention should be paid to matters affecting the interests of developing country Members with respect to measures which have been subject to dispute settlement."

7.7   Accordingly, we suggest that the parties negotiate an implementation/phase-out period. Should it be impossible for them to do so, we suggest that the reasonable period of

---

[15]Dispute Settlement Body.

time, whether determined by arbitration (Article 21.3(c) of the DSU) or other means, be set in light of the above-listed factors.

Source:www.wto.org/english/tratop_e/dispu_e/dispu_e.htm#disputes, case WT/DS90/R, June 4, 1999.

> India has not adopted its policy and strategy simply to anger the United States. Recall the importance of recognizing strategy and national values when assessing an approach to a foreign market. What are the Indian government's policy objectives that it is attempting to achieve? Having considered what those objectives are, what can foreign businesspersons do that will satisfy their own profit motive and Indian policy objectives?

This panel report followed a period of consultations between the United States and India and was itself an intermediate step in the full dispute resolution process.

At this point, note that the panel at paragraph 6.2 above simply *recommends* that the Dispute Settlement Body (to which the panel is reporting) *request* India to bring its measures into conformity with India's obligations under the WTO Agreement.

The DSB still operates within an agreement between sovereign states, and "enforcement" in the WTO context still falls short of what is expected within the judicial system of a single sovereign state. Inside a single sovereign state, a party at fault can usually be compelled at law to make good for the wrongs it commits. As between sovereign states, the remedy is usually limited to allowing the aggrieved state to take retaliatory measures (tariff or nontariff) against the wrongdoer that would normally be forbidden under WTO trading rules.

Most-Favored-Nation Status (Normal Trade Relations)

MFN status has nothing to do with allowing one particular country preferential access to one's own national markets through a lower tariff. Quite the opposite, it is a mechanism that requires a member state, when it gives a preferential tariff rate to one country (even a non-WTO member), to offer that tariff rate to *all* other WTO members. In so doing, the requirement reflects the central WTO/GATT premise of nondiscrimination. Since 1998, MFN in American usage (but not globally) is known as Normal Trade Relations, or NTR.

The original GATT tariff negotiations were based on bilateral discussions between two members, each with its own primary interest in one commodity and a secondary interest in another. For example, Country A produces lumber but imports machine tools at a duty rate of 25 percent. Country B produces machine tools but imports lumber with a duty rate of 33 percent. Both are members of the GATT. If both countries lower their duty rates, each will be able to sell more and consume more of both products. There is not necessarily an equalization of the rates, but each country will decide what it is willing to give in return for what it can get. It may be that Country A is willing to reduce its machine tool duty to 10 percent if Country B lowers its duty on lumber to 16 percent. These new preferential rates bind the two countries, and then the MFN principle kicks in: Country A must charge no more than 10 percent on machine tools and Country B no more than 16 percent on lumber against all other like imports of machine tools and lumber from GATT member nations. A bilateral negotiation is made multilateral in application, and forms a schedule of concessions that must be granted to all members.

The process works, as it drives nations to negotiate with other nations that otherwise would be an economic threat. Canada may be willing to allow imports of Jamaican steel at zero duty, since Jamaica has no steel industry, but then it would be forced to allow all steel from GATT members into Canada on a duty-free basis, while Canada gets no meaningful market access or tariff reductions for products that it produces. Consequently, such a negotiation will not take place. It will be nations with true economic interests in each other's products that will form negotiating pairs, and all the other GATT nations will consequentially benefit from the negotiations of these nations that have a vested interest.

GATT 1947 Article I[16]

Article I

General Most-Favoured-Nation Treatment

1. With respect to customs duties and charges of any kind imposed on or in connection with importation or exportation or imposed on the international transfer of payments for imports or exports, and with respect to the method of levying such duties and charges, and with respect to all rules and formalities in connection with importation and exportation, and with respect to all matters referred to in paragraphs 2 and 4 of Article III, any advantage, favour, privilege or immunity granted by any contracting party to any product originating in or destined for any other country shall be accorded immediately and unconditionally to the like product originating in or destined for the territories of all other contracting parties.

The following case between Brazil and Spain predates the WTO, but at issue is the GATT obligation of most-favored-nation status that still continues today as Article I of GATT 1994. As Spain began liberalizing its markets in the late 1970s, it moved away from government purchasing of imported commodities for resale, allowing a greater role for private enterprise and private price setting. In so doing, where it had not previously applied duty to imports of coffee, it now set rates of duty for coffee imports. Spain differentiated between different types of coffee beans and applied either a 7 percent duty or a zero percent duty (duty-free), depending on the type.

Beans of the type primarily grown in Colombia (mild) were rated duty-free, while beans of the type primarily coming from Brazil (Arabica) were rated at the 7 percent duty. The effect was to place Brazilian coffee imports into Spain at a serious competitive disadvantage, and, according to Brazil, this was discriminatory. As far as Spain was concerned, it was not discriminatory; all mild beans, regardless of country of origin, were treated the same, and all Arabica beans were treated the same, regardless of country of origin.

The international businessperson must see past the international politics between nations and realize that these are business interests being affected, not the affairs of lawyers and politicians. These are *your* goals at issue, *your* costs in duty that will be charged, and *your* market access that is at stake.

The analysis of "like products" is a consideration and an eventual determination that must be regularly made in questions of a breach of MFN obligations. Is this discrimination in disguise, or should different types of coffee be distinguished, just as coffee itself might be distinguished from tea or cola beverages? Do history and culture and long-standing business relationships play a role in this tariff-setting regime? One can make guesses, but Colombia was once a Spanish colony and remains Spanish-speaking with a large presence of European Spanish business interests. Brazil, on the other hand, was formerly a colony of Portugal, remains Portuguese-speaking, and is home to business interests of Portugal, Spain's traditional Iberian Peninsula rival.

[16]Now incorporated with all amendments, protocols, accessions, understandings, and decisions into GATT 1994. Full text is available at the WTO website, www.wto.org, indexed under "Documents."

GATT Panel Report, Article I; Spain—Tariff Treatment of Unroasted Coffee (excerpts)

L/5135—28S/102
Report of the Panel, adopted 11 June 1981

I. Introduction

1.1   In a communication dated 13 September 1979 and circulated to contracting parties, Brazil informed that a new Spanish law had introduced certain modifications in the tariff treatment applied to imports of unroasted coffee, according to which imports into Spain of unroasted non-decaffeinated "unwashed Arabica" and Robusta coffees (tariff No. 09.01A) were now subject to a tariff treatment less favourable than that accorded to "mild" coffee. Prior to this new law there had been no differentiation in the tariff treatment applied by Spain to imports of unroasted coffee. As a main supplier of coffee to Spain, Brazil was concerned with the discriminatory character of the new tariff rates and had requested Article XXII:1 consultations with Spain.

1.2   At the meeting of the Council on 26 March 1980, the representative of Brazil informed the Council of Brazil's request to hold Article XXIII:1 consultations with Spain on this matter (L/4954). At the same meeting, the Council noted that consultations between the two contracting parties were getting under way.

1.3   At its meeting on 18 June 1980, the Council was informed that these consultations had not resulted in a satisfactory adjustment between the parties and that Brazil invoked the procedures of Article XXIII:2 requesting the examination of this matter by a panel.

1.4   The Council agreed to establish a panel with the following terms of reference:

"To examine, in the light of the relevant GATT provisions, the matter referred to the CONTRACTING PARTIES by Brazil, relating to the tariff treatment of imports of unroasted coffee into Spain, and to make such findings as will assist the CONTRACTING PARTIES in making recommendations or rulings as provided in Article XXIII."

1.7   In the course of its work the Panel heard statements by representatives of Brazil and Spain, Background documents and relevant information submitted by both parties, their replies to the questions put by the Panel as well as other information available to the Panel served as a basis for the examination of the matter subject to dispute.

II. Factual Aspects

2.1   The following is a brief description of factual aspects of the matter under dispute as the Panel understood them.

2.2   On 8 July 1979, the Spanish authorities enacted the Royal Decree No. 1764/79 (B.O.E. of 20 July) by which the tariff treatment and the sub-tariff classification applied to imports of unroasted, non-decaffeinated coffee (ex. CCCN 09.01) were modified and amended, effective by 1 March 1980. Imports of unroasted coffee, which prior to this last date entered Spain's customs territory under one and the same designation, was subdivided into five tariff lines to which duty rates applied as follows:

Spain's Present Tariff Treatment for Unroasted Non-decaffeinated Coffee Beans

Product Description	Duty Rate
1 Columbian mild	Free
2 Other mild	Free
3 Unwashed Arabica	7 per cent ad. val.
4 Robusta	7 per cent ad. val.
5 Other	7 per cent ad. val.

2.10 . . . While varying, the main suppliers always included both Brazil and Colombia, although neither was always the principal supplier.

2.11 Spain's imports of unroasted coffee from Brazil were constituted of almost entirely "unwashed Arabica" . . .

III. Main Arguments

Article I:1

3.1 *The representative of Brazil* argued that by introducing a 7 per cent tariff rate on imports of unroasted, non-decaffeinated coffee of the "unwashed Arabica" and Robusta groups, while affording duty-free treatment to coffee of other groups, the new Spanish tariff régime was discriminatory against Brazil, which exports mainly "unwashed Arabica," but also Robusta coffee, and therefore was in violation of Article I:1 of the General Agreement, according to which:

". . . any advantage, favour, privilege or immunity granted by any contracting party to any product originating in . . . any other country shall be accorded immediately and unconditionally to the like product originating in . . . the territories of all other contracting parties."

3.2 In this connection, he noted that, as did Spain herself under her previous tariff régime, no other contracting party discriminated in its customs tariff as between "types" or as among "groups" of coffee.

3.3 *The representative of Spain,* stressed that no contracting party was obliged to retain either its tariff structure, or its duties, applicable to the importation of products which have not been bound. He recalled that the Brussels nomenclature adopted by Spain did specify tariff headings but left it to each country to establish, if it is so wished, sub-headings within these headings. Accordingly, the Spanish authorities had the right to establish within a given heading the sub-divisions which were most suited to the characteristics of Spain's foreign trade, while respecting, as Spain has done on many occasions, the bound duties previously negotiated. The classification criterion adopted was based on classifications made by international organizations, specifically the International Coffee Organization (ICO).

3.4 In order to ascertain the coverage of Article I:1 it was necessary, in the view of the Spanish representative, to consider two aspects in detail: (a) meaning of the term "like products," and (b) existence of any preference or pretermission in respect of a country as a consequence of the new structure of heading No. 09.01.A.1 of the Spanish tariff. The Spanish authorities continued to hold that, in their judgement, the provisions of the Royal Decree 1764/79 were fully compatible with the obligations assumed by Spain under the General Agreement, and in particular Article I:1 thereof.

These authorities furnished photocopies of importing licences in Spain, issued after 1 March 1980, which evidenced that the new tariff classification was applied according to the nature of products, and completely independently of the country of origin. In particular, these licences evidenced that Brazilian "washed" coffee was imported into Spain free of duty.

"Like Products"

3.5   Recalling that in some past GATT cases it had been suggested that "like products" were all the products falling within the same tariff heading, *the representative of Spain* did not agree with that opinion. In his view, this interpretation could lead to serious mistakes, given that products falling within one and the same tariff heading could be unlike and clearly different, as for example: (i) in the case of all the residual tariff headings ("other products not specified"), covering a large number of heterogeneous products, and (ii) headings including homogeneous products where in many instances these were not "like products" (i.e. CCCN heading No. 15.07 including all kinds of vegetable oils; CCCN heading No. 22.05 including all wines, etc.).

3.6   The Spanish representative pointed out that qualitative differences did exist between various types of coffee considering both technico-agronomic, economic and commercial criteria. He argued that Robusta coffee bean was morphologically different from the Arabica coffee bean, having a different chemical composition and yielding a neutral beverage that was lacking in aroma and was richer in soluble solids than the beverage made from Arabica coffee.

3.7   Although both "mild" and "unwashed Arabica" coffees belonged to the group of Arabica, the Spanish representative further argued that differences in quality also existed between them, as a result of climatic and growing conditions as well as methods of cultivation and above all the preparation because aroma and taste, essential features in determining trade and consumption of these products, were completely different in "washed" and "unwashed" Arabica coffees. Different quotations in international trade and commodity markets were due to these factors.

3.8   As distinctive markets existed for the various types of unroasted coffee, the Spanish representative was of the view that such various types of coffee could not be regarded as "like products." This was particularly evident in the Spanish market where, for historical reasons, consumers' preference for the various types of coffee was well established, in contrast with other markets in which the use of blends was more generalized. When referring to the increasing market share of blends outside Spain, he argued that the existence of blends proved that the various types of coffee were not the same products.

3.9   For his part, *the representative of Brazil* argued that coffee was one single product and that, therefore, for the purpose of Article I:1 of the GATT, must be considered a "like product." He further argued that in the specific case of "mild" and "unwashed Arabica" coffees, both came from the same species of plant, and often from the same variety of tree. He also stated that, in such cases, the product could be extracted from the same individual tree, and the classification as "unwashed Arabica" or "mild" would depend exclusively on the treatment given to the berries.

3.10   He pointed out, therefore, that existing differences between "growths" or "groups" of coffee were essentially of an organoleptic nature (taste, aroma, body, etc.) resulting from geographical conditions and, principally, from the distinct methods of preparation of the beans.

3.11   He stated that the classification presently used by Spain for tariff purposes had been introduced by the International Coffee Organization in 1965/66, when the Council of the Organization decided to create groupings of coffee-producing countries as part of a system for the limited adjustment of export quotas in response to changes in an indicator price of "mild Arabicas," "unwashed Arabicas" and "Robustas." He further stated that the composition of each grouping depended upon political decisions taken yearly by the Council of the Organization, according to which each exporting country was placed in the group corresponding to the kind of coffee constituting the greater part of its production. He stressed that since 1972 these groupings had only served a statistical purpose.

3.12   He argued that, from the point of view of the consumer, virtually all coffee, either roasted or soluble, was sold today in the form of blends, combining in varying proportions coffee belonging to different groups. Moreover, in everyday language, the terms type, quality, and growth were used interchangeably to indicate specific grades of coffee, for instance Colombian Mams, El Salvador Central Standard, Paranà 4, Angola Ambriz 2AA, etc. In his view, this was the only characterization really meaningful for trading purposes, since no roaster did buy a "Colombian mild" or "unwashed Arabica" as such, but rather well-known grades, priced according to the beverage they could provide.

3.13   He further stated that with respect to its end use, coffee was a well determined and one single product, generally intended for drinking as a beverage.

Differentiation Made in the Spanish Tariff

3.14   Explaining the economic reasons beyond the differentiation introduced in the Spanish tariff by the Royal Decree No. 1764/79, *the representative of Spain* said that the lower customs duty applicable to "mild" coffee imported into Spain reflected the Spanish Government's deep concern over the possible impact on prices of measures to return coffee to the private sector and afford greater trade liberalization. In this connection, he noted that coffee accounted for more than 2 per cent in the Spanish consumer price index. He also said that in the previous trade system of State-trading in which a nil tariff duty existed since 1975, nevertheless the difference between import prices and selling prices to roasters ("precios de cesión") in practice constituted an implicit tariff affecting all imports of coffee. This implicit tariff was higher than the tariff duties effectively applied since March 1980.

3.15   Having recalled that a very high proportion of "mild" coffee was consumed in the Spanish market, he noted that this very high proportion of "mild" in Spanish consumption had been maintained by keeping artificially low the retail price of "mild" coffee through the operation of the previously existing system of authorized prices.

3.16   In view of the foregoing, he indicated that his authorities had considered that the only way of reconciling consumers' preference for "mild" coffee and the transfer of the coffee trade to the private sector was to establish different rates of custom duty, with a zero duty on the most expensive coffee, i.e. "mild" coffee. In so doing, his authorities had not at any time given any thought to which countries were producing the different types of coffee. In fact, different types or groups of coffee were often grown in one and the same country and more than thirty countries were producing both Robusta and "unwashed Arabica."

3.17   Finally, the Spanish representative stressed the transitional character of the coffee import régime actually applied by his country. He said that his authorities ultimately aimed, in the shortest possible time, at introducing in respect of coffee a system of automatic licensing and free domestic trade.

3.18   Referring to the stated anti-inflation objective of the Spanish measures, the representative of Brazil was of the view that such argument was not relevant to the case under dispute, since, whatever the motivation to introduce the new tariff régime for unroasted coffee, such motivation did not exempt Spain from complying with the provisions of Article I:1 of the GATT.

IV. Findings and Conclusions

4.1   The Panel has carried out its consideration of the matter referred to it for examination in the light of its terms of reference and on the basis of various factual information which was available to it, and of arguments presented to it by the parties to the dispute.

4.2   The Panel considered that it was called upon to examine whether the Spanish tariff régime for unroasted coffee introduced by Spain through the Royal Decree 1764/79 (ref. paragraph 2.2) was consistent with Spanish obligations under the GATT, and more precisely whether it was in conformity with the most-favoured-nation provision of Article I:1.

4.3   Having noted that Spain had not bound under the GATT its tariff rate on unroasted coffee, the Panel pointed out that Article I:1 equally applied to bound and unbound tariff items.

4.4   The Panel found that there was no obligation under the GATT to follow any particular system for classifying goods, and that a contracting party had the right to introduce in its customs tariff new positions or sub-positions as appropriate. The Panel considered, however, that, whatever the classification adopted, Article I:1 required that the same tariff treatment be applied to "like products."

4.5   The Panel, therefore, in accordance with its terms of reference, focused its examination on whether the various types of unroasted coffee listed in the Royal Decree 1764/79 should be regarded as "like products" within the meaning of Article I:1. Having reviewed how the concept of "like products" had been applied by the CONTRACTING PARTIES in previous cases involving, *inter alia,*[17] a recourse to Article I:1 the Panel noted that neither the General Agreement nor the settlement of previous cases gave any definition of such concept.

4.6   The Panel examined all arguments that had been advanced during the proceedings for the justification of a different tariff treatment for various groups and types of unroasted coffee. It noted that these arguments mainly related to organoleptic differences resulting from geographical factors, cultivation methods, the processing of the beans, and the genetic factor. The Panel did not consider that such differences were sufficient reason to allow for a different tariff treatment. It pointed out that it was not unusual in the case of agricultural products that the taste and aroma of the end-product would differ because of one or several of the above-mentioned factors.

4.7   The Panel furthermore found relevant to its examination of the matter that unroasted coffee was mainly, if not exclusively, sold in the form of blends, combining various types of coffee, and that coffee in its end-use, was universally regarded as a well-defined and single product intended for drinking.

4.8   The Panel noted that no other contracting party applied its tariff régime in respect of unroasted, non-decaffeinated coffee in such a way that different types of coffee were subject to different tariff rates.

4.9   In the light of the foregoing, the Panel *concluded* that unroasted, non-decaffeinated coffee beans listed in the Spanish Customs Tariffs under CCCN 09.01 A.1a, as amended by the Royal Decree 1764/79, should be considered as "like products" within the meaning of Article I:1.

4.10   The Panel further noted that Brazil exported to Spain mainly "unwashed Arabica" and also Robusta coffee which were both presently charged with higher duties than that applied to "mild" coffee. Since these were considered to be "like products," the Panel concluded that the tariff régime as presently applied by Spain was discriminatory vis-à-vis unroasted coffee originating in Brazil.

4.11   Having recalled that it had found the tariff régime for unroasted coffee introduced by Spain through the Royal Decree 1764/79 not to be in conformity with the provision of Article I:1, the Panel further concluded that this constituted *prima facie*[18] a case of impairment of benefits accruing to Brazil within the meaning of Article XXIII.

4.12   In the light of the above, the Panel suggest that the CONTRACTING PARTIES request Spain to take the necessary measures in order to make its tariff régime for unroasted coffee conform to Article I:1.

Source: www.wto.org/english/tratop_e/dispu_e/dispu_e.htm#disputes, indexed under "GATT Disputes" (predating the WTO itself), as L/5135—28S/102, June 11, 1981.

We now know what Spain did: it impaired the benefits owed to Brazil. What, in the specific terms of Article I, should Spain do now? What would this mean in economic and business terms?

[17]"Among other things."
[18]"Clear on its face."

Note that the panel does not venture into consideration of why Spain attempted to differentiate between types of coffee, for doing so would have only served to expose raw nerves in international relations. It was enough for it to conclude that

- The two types of coffee were "like products" as far as the GATT was concerned.
- Spain was in breach of its obligation to extend the most-favored-nation status it offered to Colombian coffee to include Brazilian coffee as well.

Still, not all coffee is automatically included; it would seem that the panel implicitly concludes that roasted or decaffeinated coffee beans would not be "like products" in comparison with unroasted beans.

Note further the terminology in paragraph 4.11, that the Spanish measure is an "impairment of the benefits accruing to Brazil" within the meaning of Article XXIII of the GATT. This article has an interesting effect on what constitutes harm as between trading nations within the GATT/WTO structure. Actual *damage* does not need to be proven by the aggrieved nation, only that a situation exists of nullification or impairment of its *benefits* under the Agreement.

The panel report reveals its age where the final paragraph shown (4.12) suggests that the Contracting Parties request Spain to bring its measures into conformity. In the 1947–1995 period when the GATT was "only an agreement," such actions could only be taken in the name of the parties to the GATT. Now as a formal organization, it is the WTO's Dispute Settlement Body that takes this final step.

National Treatment

A tariff reduction on imported goods (at the border) provides absolutely no benefit if the goods are later discriminated against in the market place (beyond the border) through actions of the host national government. Having exacted its tariff at the border, a government may still be tempted to introduce a differential sales tax that requires imported goods to be taxed at a higher rate than domestic production. Alternatively, it may impose other requirements of inspection, packaging, or standards that it does not apply to its national production. The concept of national treatment is intended to combat these possibilities, with a prohibition against negative discriminatory treatment of imports. Interestingly, national treatment does not insist on equality of treatment, just that imports shall be accorded treatment "no less favorable" than products of national origin. Thus, a nation can encourage imports when it is in its interest to do so, by treating them better than it does its own domestic production—perhaps through tax rebates or relaxed regulation.

GATT 1947 Article III *(excerpts)*[19]

Article III

National Treatment on Internal Taxation and Regulation

1. The contracting parties recognize that internal taxes and other internal charges, and laws, regulations and requirements affecting the internal sale, offering for sale, purchase, transportation, distribution or use of products, and internal quantitative regulations requiring the mixture, processing or use of products in specified amounts or proportions, should not be applied to imported or domestic products so as to afford protection to domestic production.*

[19]Now incorporated with all amendments, protocols, accessions, understandings, and decisions into GATT 1994. Full text is available at the WTO website, www.wto.org, indexed under "Documents."

2. The products of the territory of any contracting party imported into the territory of any other contracting party shall not be subject, directly or indirectly, to internal taxes or other internal charges of any kind in excess of those applied, directly or indirectly, to like domestic products. Moreover, no contracting party shall otherwise apply internal taxes or other internal charges to imported or domestic products in a manner contrary to the principles set forth in paragraph 1.*

*Ad Article III

Paragraph 2

A tax conforming to the requirements of the first sentence of paragraph 2 would be considered to be inconsistent with the provisions of the second sentence only in cases where competition was involved between, on the one hand, the taxed product and, on the other hand, a directly competitive or substitutable product which was not similarly taxed.

Again it is the principle of nondiscrimination that is at work, or, more properly in this Article, *nonnegative* discrimination against imports.

The key words to recognize with respect to national treatment in internal measures are that measures may not be applied

- *"so as to afford protection"* to domestic production

and of those that may be applied, they may not be

- *"in excess"* of those applied to
- *"like domestic products,"* or those that are
- *"directly competitive or substitutable product*(s)*"* and that are
- *"not similarly taxed"*

The following case sets out the meaning of these terms and the consequences that follow from those meanings. In addition, this case is a WTO Appeal Report, illustrating the process and results of appeal to the WTO Appellate Body from an original WTO panel report.

Keep in mind the central distinction between Articles I and III as you read the report. Article I (MFN) applies to both imports and exports, and seeks to ensure that no import receives better treatment than any other import into a territory. Article III (national treatment) applies to imports only and is focused on ensuring that imports are treated no worse than domestic production of that territory. Moreover, Article I relates to concessions; where they are given to one contracting party, they must be given to all others. Article III, on the other hand, applies whether concessions exist or not for a particular imported good, and even whether there is a tariff or not. It is a standard of fairness in the marketplace that is owed to all foreign goods properly landed inside a territory.

WTO Appeal Report, Article III; Japan—Taxes on Alcoholic Beverages

WT/DS8/AB/R, WT/DS10/AB/R, WT/DS11/AB/R, AB-1996-2
Report of the World Trade Organization Appellate Body

A. Introduction

Japan and the United States appeal from certain issues of law and legal interpretations in the Panel Report, *Japan—Taxes on Alcoholic Beverages* (the "Panel Report"). That Panel (the "Panel") was established to consider complaints by the European Communities, Canada and the United States against Japan relating to the Japanese Liquor Tax Law (Shuzeiho), Law No. 6 of 1953 as amended (the "Liquor Tax Law").

The Panel Report was circulated to the Members of the World Trade Organization (the "WTO") on 11 July 1996. It contains the following conclusions:

i. Shochu and vodka are like products and Japan, by taxing the latter in excess of the former, is in violation of its obligation under Article III:2, first sentence, of the General Agreement on Tariffs and Trade 1994.
ii. Shochu, whisky, brandy, rum, gin, genever, and liqueurs are "directly competitive or substitutable products" and Japan, by not taxing them similarly, is in violation of its obligation under Article III:2, second sentence, of the General Agreement on Tariffs and Trade 1994.

The Panel made the following recommendations:

> 7.2 The Panel recommends that the Dispute Settlement Body request Japan to bring the Liquor Tax Law into conformity with its obligations under the General Agreement on Tariffs and Trade 1994.

. . . then follows the Appellate Body analysis of submissions of the parties . . .

F. Interpretation of Article III

The *WTO Agreement* is a treaty—the international equivalent of a contract. It is self-evident that in an exercise of their sovereignty, and in pursuit of their own respective national interests, the Members of the WTO have made a bargain. In exchange for the benefits they expect to derive as Members of the WTO, they have agreed to exercise their sovereignty according to the commitments they have made in the *WTO Agreement.*

One of those commitments is Article III of the GATT 1994, which is entitled "National Treatment on Internal Taxation and Regulation." For the purpose of this appeal, the relevant parts of Article III read as follows:

Article III and Ad Article III, paragraph 2 are then recited . . .

The broad and fundamental purpose of Article III is to avoid protectionism in the application of internal tax and regulatory measures. More specifically, the purpose of Article III "is to ensure that internal measures 'not be applied to imported or domestic products so as to afford protection to domestic production.' " Toward this end, Article III obliges Members of the WTO to provide equality of competitive conditions for imported products in relation to domestic products. . . . Moreover, it is irrelevant that "the trade effects" of the tax differential between imported and domestic products, as reflected in the volumes of imports, are insignificant or even non-existent; Article III protects expectations not of any particular trade volume but rather of the equal competitive relationship between imported and domestic products. Members of the WTO are free to pursue their own domestic goals through internal taxation or regulation so long as they do not do so in a way that violates Article III or any of the other commitments they have made in the *WTO Agreement*.

. . .

G. Article III:1

The terms of Article III must be given their ordinary meaning—in their context and in the light of the overall object and purpose of the *WTO Agreement*. Thus, the words actually used in the Article provide the basis for an interpretation that must give meaning and effect to all its terms. The proper interpretation of the Article is, first of all, a textual interpretation. Consequently, the Panel is correct in seeing a distinction between Article III:1, which "contains general principles," and Article III:2, which "provides for specific obligations regarding internal taxes and internal charges." Article III:1 articulates a general principle that internal measures should not be applied so as to afford protection to domestic production. This general principle informs the rest of Article III . . . Any other reading of Article III would have the effect of rendering the words of Article III:1 meaningless, thereby violating the fundamental principle of effectiveness in treaty interpretation. Consistent with this principle of effectiveness, and with the textual differences in the two sentences, we believe that Article III:1 informs the first sentence and the second sentence of Article III:2 in different ways.

H. Article III:2

1. First Sentence

Article III:1 informs Article III:2, first sentence, by establishing that if imported products are taxed in excess of like domestic products, then that tax measure is inconsistent with Article III. Article III:2, first sentence does not refer specifically to Article III:1. There is no specific invocation in this first sentence of the general principle in Article III:1 that admonishes Members of the WTO not to apply measures "so as to afford protection." This omission must have some meaning. We believe the meaning is simply that the presence of a protective application need not be established separately from the specific requirements that are included in the first sentence in order to show that a tax measure is inconsistent with the general principle set out in the first sentence. However, this does not mean that the general principle of Article III:1 does not apply to this sentence. To the contrary, we believe the first sentence of Article III:2 is, in effect, an application of this general principle. The ordinary meaning of the words of Article III:2, first sentence leads inevitably to this conclusion. Read in their context and in the light of the overall object and purpose of the WTO Agreement, the words of the first sentence require an examination of the conformity of an internal tax measure with Article III by determining, first, whether the taxed imported and domestic products are "like" and, second, whether the taxes applied to the imported products are "in excess of" those applied to the like domestic products. If the imported and domestic products are "like products," and if the taxes applied to the imported products are "in excess of" those applied to the like domestic products, then the measure is inconsistent with Article III:2, first sentence.

. . .

(a) "Like Products"

Because the second sentence of Article III:2 provides for a separate and distinctive consideration of the protective aspect of a measure in examining its application to a broader category of products that are not "like products" as contemplated by the first sentence, we agree with the Panel that the first sentence of Article III:2 must be construed narrowly so as not to condemn measures that its strict terms are not meant to condemn. Consequently, we agree with the Panel also that the definition of "like products" in Article III:2, first sentence, should be construed narrowly.

How narrowly is a matter that should be determined separately for each tax measure in each case . . .

> Some criteria were suggested for determining, on a case-by-case basis, whether a product is "similar": the product's end-uses in a given market; consumers' tastes and habits, which change from country to country; the product's properties, nature and quality.

. . . [T]he accordion of "likeness" stretches and squeezes in different places as different provisions of the WTO Agreement are applied. We believe that, in Article III:2, first sentence of the GATT 1994, the accordion of "likeness" is meant to be narrowly squeezed.

The Panel determined in this case that shochu and vodka are "like products" for the purposes of Article III:2, first sentence. We note that the determination of whether vodka is a "like product" to shochu under Article III:2, first sentence, or a "directly competitive or substitutable product" to shochu under Article III:2, second sentence, does not materially affect the outcome of this case.

. . .

It is true that there are numerous tariff bindings which are in fact extremely precise with regard to product description and which, therefore, can provide significant guidance as to the identification of "like products" . . . However, tariff bindings that include a wide range of products are not a reliable criterion for determining or confirming product "likeness" under Article III:2.

With these modifications to the legal reasoning in the Panel Report, we affirm the legal conclusions and the findings of the Panel with respect to "like products" in all other respects.

(b) "In Excess Of"

The only remaining issue under Article III:2, first sentence, is whether the taxes on imported products are "in excess of" those on like domestic products. If so, then the Member that has imposed the tax is not in compliance with Article III. Even the smallest amount of "excess" is too much. "The prohibition of discriminatory taxes in Article III:2, first sentence, is not conditional on a 'trade effects test' nor is it qualified by a *de minimis* standard." We agree with the Panel's legal reasoning and with its conclusions on this aspect of the interpretation and application of Article III:2, first sentence.

2. Second Sentence

Article III:1 informs Article III:2, second sentence, through specific reference. Article III:2, second sentence, contains a general prohibition against "internal taxes or other internal charges" applied to "imported or domestic products in a manner contrary to the principles set forth in paragraph 1." As mentioned before, Article III:1 states that internal taxes and other internal charges "should not be applied to imported or domestic products so as to afford protection to domestic production" . . .

Article III:2, second sentence, and the accompanying *Ad* Article have equivalent legal status in that both are treaty language which was negotiated and agreed at the same time. The *Ad* Article does not replace or modify the language contained in Article III:2, second sentence, but, in fact, clarifies its meaning. Accordingly, the language of the second sentence and the Ad Article must be read together in order to give them their proper meaning.

. . . Giving full meaning to the text and to its context, three separate issues must be addressed to determine whether an internal tax measure is inconsistent with Article III:2, second sentence *[and the Ad Article]*. These three issues are whether:

1. the imported products and the domestic products *are "directly competitive or substitutable products" which are in competition with each other;*
2. the directly competitive or substitutable imported and domestic products *are "not similarly taxed";* and
3. the dissimilar taxation of the directly competitive or substitutable imported domestic products *is "applied . . . so as to afford protection to domestic production."*

. . . Each must be established separately by the complainant for a panel to find that a tax measure imposed by a Member of the WTO is inconsistent with Article III:2, second sentence.

(a) "Directly Competitive or Substitutable Products"

If imported and domestic products are not "like products" for the narrow purposes of Article III:2, first sentence, then they are not subject to the strictures of that sentence and there is no inconsistency with the requirements of that sentence. However, depending on their nature, and depending on the competitive conditions in the relevant market, those same products may well be among the broader category of "directly competitive or substitutable products" that fall within the domain of Article III:2, second sentence. How much broader that category of "directly competitive or substitutable products" may be in any given case is a matter for the panel to determine based on all the relevant facts in that case . . .

In this case, the Panel emphasized the need to look not only at such matters as physical characteristics, common end-uses, and tariff classifications, but also at the "market place." This seems appropriate. The GATT 1994 is a commercial agreement, and the WTO is concerned, after all, with markets. It does not seem inappropriate to look at competition in the relevant markets as one among a number of means of identifying the broader category of products that might be described as "directly competitive or substitutable."

Nor does it seem inappropriate to examine elasticity of substitution as one means of examining those relevant markets. The Panel did not say that cross-price elasticity of demand is "the decisive criterion" for determining whether products are "directly competitive or substitutable." The Panel stated the following:

> . . . the decisive criterion in order to determine whether two products are directly competitive or substitutable is whether they have common end-uses, *inter alia,* as shown by elasticity of substitution.

We agree. And, we find the Panel's legal analysis of whether the products are "directly competitive or substitutable products" . . . to be correct.

. . .

(b) "Not Similarly Taxed"

To give due meaning to the distinctions in the wording of Article III:2, first sentence, and Article III:2, second sentence, the phrase "not similarly taxed" in the *Ad* Article to the second sentence must not be construed so as to mean the same thing as the phrase "in excess of" in the first sentence. On its face, the phrase "in excess of" in the first sentence means any amount of tax on imported products "in excess of" the tax on domestic "like products." The phrase "not similarly taxed" in the *Ad* Article to the second sentence must therefore mean something else. It requires a different standard, just as "directly competitive or substitutable products" requires a different standard as compared to "like products" for these same interpretive purposes.

. . .

In this case, the Panel applied the correct legal reasoning in determining whether "directly competitive or substitutable" imported and domestic products were "not similarly taxed." However, the Panel erred in blurring the distinction between that issue and the entirely separate issue of whether the tax measure in question was applied "so as to afford protection." Again, these are separate issues that must be addressed individually. If "directly competitive or substitutable products" are *not* "not similarly taxed," then there is neither need nor justification under Article III:2, second sentence, for inquiring further as to whether the tax has been applied "so as to afford protection." But if such products are "not similarly taxed," a further inquiry must necessarily be made.

(c) "So As To Afford Protection"

This third inquiry under Article III:2, second sentence, must determine whether "directly competitive or substitutable products" are "not similarly taxed" in a way that affords protection. This is not an issue of intent. It is not necessary for a panel to sort through the many reasons legislators and regulators often have for what they do and weigh the relative significance of those reasons to establish legislative or regulatory intent . . . It is irrelevant that protectionism was not an intended objective if the particular tax measure in question is nevertheless, to echo Article III:1, *"applied* to imported or domestic products so as to afford protection to domestic production" . . .

. . .

Although it is true that the aim of a measure may not be easily ascertained, nevertheless its protective application can most often be discerned from the design, the architecture, and the revealing structure of a measure. The very magnitude of the dissimilar taxation in a particular case may be evidence of such a protective application, as the Panel rightly concluded in this case. Most often, there will be other factors to be considered as well. In conducting this inquiry, panels should give full consideration to all the relevant facts and all the relevant circumstances in any given case.

. . .

We have reviewed the Panel's reasoning in this case as well as its conclusions on the issue of "so as to afford protection" . . . *[and while it correctly concluded in law that]* . . .

> (ii) Shochu, whisky, brandy, rum, gin, genever, and liqueurs are "directly competitive or substitutable products" and Japan, by not taxing them similarly, is in violation of its obligation under Article III:2, second sentence, of the General Agreement on Tariffs and Trade 1994.

. . . *the Panel then* equated dissimilar taxation above a *de minimis* level with the separate and distinct requirement of demonstrating that the tax measure "affords protection to domestic production." As previously stated, a finding that "directly competitive or substitutable products" are "not similarly taxed" is necessary to find a violation of Article III:2, second sentence. Yet this is not enough. The dissimilar taxation must be more than *de minimis.* It may be so much more that it will be clear from that very differential that the dissimilar taxation was applied "so as to afford protection." In some cases, that may be enough to show a violation. In this case, the Panel concluded that it was enough. Yet in other cases, there may be other factors that will be just as relevant or more relevant to demonstrating that the dissimilar taxation at issue was applied "so as to afford protection." In any case, the three issues that must be addressed in determining whether there is such a violation must be addressed clearly and separately in each case and on a case-by-case basis. And, in every case, a careful, objective analysis, must be done of each and all relevant facts and all the relevant circumstances in order to determine "the existence of protective taxation." Although the Panel blurred its legal reasoning in this respect, nevertheless we conclude that it reasoned correctly that in this case, the Liquor Tax Law is not in compliance with Article III:2. As the Panel did, we note that:

> . . . the combination of customs duties and internal taxation in Japan has the following impact: on the one hand, it makes it difficult for foreign-produced shochu to penetrate the Japanese market and, on the other, it does not guarantee equality of competitive conditions between shochu and the rest of 'white' and 'brown' spirits. Thus, through a combination of high import duties and differentiated internal taxes, Japan manages to "isolate" domestically produced shochu from foreign competition, be it foreign produced shochu or any other of the mentioned white and brown spirits.

Our interpretation of Article III is faithful to the "customary rules of interpretation of public international law." WTO rules are reliable, comprehensible and enforceable. WTO rules are not so rigid or so inflexible as not to leave room for reasoned judgements in confronting the endless and ever-changing ebb and flow of real facts in real cases in the real world. They will serve the multilateral trading system best if they are interpreted with that in mind. In that way, we will achieve the "security and predictability" sought for the multilateral trading system by the Members of the WTO through the establishment of the dispute settlement system.

I. Conclusions and Recommendations

For the reasons set out in the preceding sections of this report, the Appellate Body has reached the following conclusions:

. . .

b. the Panel erred in law in failing to take into account Article III:1 in interpreting Article III:2, first and second sentences;

. . .

d. the Panel erred in law in failing to examine "so as to afford protection" in Article III:1 as a separate inquiry from "not similarly taxed" in the *Ad* Article to Article III:2, second sentence.

[In all other respects,] the Appellate Body affirms the Panel's conclusions that shochu and vodka are like products and that Japan, by taxing imported products in excess of like domestic products, is in violation of its obligations under Article III:2, first sentence, of the General Agreement on Tariffs and Trade 1994. Moreover, the Appellate Body concludes that shochu and other distilled spirits and liqueurs listed in HS 2208, except for vodka, are "directly competitive or substitutable products," and that Japan, in the application of the Liquor Tax Law, does not similarly tax imported and directly competitive or substitutable domestic products and affords protection to domestic production in violation of Article III:2, second sentence, of the General Agreement on Tariffs and Trade 1994.

The Appellate Body *recommends* that the Dispute Settlement Body request Japan to bring the Liquor Tax Law into conformity with its obligations under the General Agreement on Tariffs and Trade 1994.

Source: www.wto.org/english/tratop_e/dispu_e/dispu_e.htm#disputes, indexed as WT/DS8/AB/R, WT/DS10/AB/R, WT/DS11/AB/R, AB-1996-2, October 4, 1996.

Assume Japan taxes beer at a rate even lower than it presently taxes shochu. What argument might a foreign vodka-producing nation advance, and what would the natural (reasoned) Japanese rebuttal be?

It is easy to get overly focused on the issue of taxation, as much of Article III is devoted to that topic. However, bear in mind that the Article also relates to "laws, regulations and requirements affecting the internal sale, offering for sale, purchase, transportation, distribution or use of products." As a result, many anti-import discriminatory practices of host governments also can be attacked. For example, while it is not unreasonable for a host government to demand that product labels be printed in a language that most customers can read (e.g., French, in France), it is not reasonable that all labels in foreign languages be removed first. Such a measure as this latter requirement would cause considerable expense to an importer or manufacturer, and on many goods would be sufficiently discriminatory and expensive as to force the foreign seller to forgo sales in that market.

Antidumping

Dumping is a condemned (but not prohibited) activity by a foreign seller exporting into a host market. It stems from the seller's pricing decision, which is to price the goods for cheap and quick sale.

At first glance, one wonders why there could be anything wrong with pricing goods too low; surely, if the seller intends to supply at that price, then the foreign market will be all the better for it, getting goods today more cheaply than they would have cost yesterday. Since selling at too low a price and being upset about buying at too low a price both seem strange, it is necessary to consider the business drivers and macroeconomic effects of such a decision.

In setting a very low export price compared to prices in its home market, a firm may be intending to expand abroad and wants to become known, and is using a predatory pricing strategy to gain this market presence. Embarking on this route must be taken with care, for predatory pricing strategies may or may not be permitted in the host nation under its domestic law, thus creating liability even before any question of dumping is raised.

Alternatively, the firm may be trying to achieve economies of scale in large production runs, but is pursuing an export sales strategy really only as a sideline to its domestic market focus. In this second case, perhaps because of limited financial resources for expansion, it chooses to make as little commitment as possible to the foreign market. The firm therefore sells abroad at prices that are not much beyond its cost recovery and a minor profit, just so it can achieve these scale economies at home.

In either situation, the nature of the product is probably such that the company does not fear foreign entrepreneurs profitably reexporting the product back into its own home market. An example might be frozen foods produced in large runs (to achieve scale economies), but packaged with different branding or languages for different consumer markets. Whatever the economic reasons, the product is reaching foreign markets for sale at prices below the sale price in the home market, and is not expected to return to the home market.

A host government may conclude that this action is damaging to its own markets and producers. Certainly, every government likes to see its consumers enjoy a good deal, but if that "good deal" begins to threaten the existence of its own manufacturers, then the loss of national jobs and income outweighs the benefit.

The host government will question whether the pricing by the foreign firm is normal competitive activity (which will serve to make its own industry stronger in the long run) or a calculated move to clear out domestic competition, such that a later rise in prices can be extraordinarily high. Depending on how much this current difference is, why it exists, how long it is expected to prevail, and what the nature of the industry at risk is, the host government may conclude that the foreign business is dumping.

The host country only needs to discover a de minimus (minimal) level of dumping activity: a price differential of at least 2 percent, where the volume of dumped goods represent 3 percent of like imported goods. The host country is then in a position to carry on toward a conclusion that the foreign company is dumping its goods. The final threshold for action is that the dumping must "materially threaten" its industry. Nations make this determination completely independently from the WTO and its dispute settlement process. Whether it chooses to condemn this dumping will depend on the factors outlined above and the extent to which it is willing to create strain in its relations with its trading partner(s).

In reading Article VI of the GATT excerpted below, note that dumping is not prohibited; it is condemned only when material injury threatens, and by allowing countervailing duties, the GATT allows a nation to preserve the integrity of its national markets.

GATT 1947 Article VI *(excerpt only)*

Article VI

Anti-dumping and Countervailing Duties

1. The contracting parties recognize that dumping, by which products of one country are introduced into the commerce of another country at less than the normal value of the products, is to be condemned if it causes or threatens material injury to an established industry in the territory of a contracting party or materially retards the establishment of a domestic industry. For the purposes of this Article, a product is to be considered as being introduced into the commerce of an importing country at less than its normal value, if the price of the product exported from one country to another
   (a) is less than the comparable price, in the ordinary course of trade, for the like product when destined for consumption in the exporting country, or,
   (b) in the absence of such domestic price, is less than either
      (i) the highest comparable price for the like product for export to any third country in the ordinary course of trade, or
      (ii) the cost of production of the product in the country of origin plus a reasonable addition for selling cost and profit.
   Due allowance shall be made in each case for differences in conditions and terms of sale, for differences in taxation, and for other differences affecting price comparability.
2. In order to offset or prevent dumping, a contracting party may levy on any dumped product an anti-dumping duty not greater in amount than the margin of dumping in respect of such product. For the purposes of this Article, the margin of dumping is the price difference determined in accordance with the provisions of paragraph 1.
3. No countervailing duty shall be levied on any product of the territory of any contracting party imported into the territory of another contracting party in excess of an amount equal to the estimated bounty or subsidy determined to have been granted, directly or indirectly, on the manufacture, production or export of such product in the country of origin or exportation, including any special subsidy to the transportation of a particular product. The term "countervailing duty" shall be understood to mean a special duty levied for the purpose of offsetting any bounty or subsidy bestowed, directly, or indirectly, upon the manufacture, production or export of any merchandise.

. . .

6. (*a*) No contracting party shall levy any anti-dumping or countervailing duty on the importation of any product of the territory of another contracting party unless it

determines that the effect of the dumping or subsidization, as the case may be, is such as to cause or threaten material injury to an established domestic industry, or is such as to retard materially the establishment of a domestic industry.

Source: Full text is available at the WTO website, www.wto.org. Now incorporated with all amendments into GATT 1994.

Once a determination of dumping has been made, Article VI, paragraph 2, allows the host country to impose antidumping duties on the imported (dumped) product, thereby raising its price on the domestic market of the importing country. Note that the provisions on dumping are not punitive, but rather only to level the playing field between the imported and domestic product. Permitted antidumping duties cannot exceed the margin of dumping. These antidumping duties will be paid by the enterprise responsible for payment of regular customs duties owing. As a result, the exporting firm that wished to pursue a low-cost strategy to either penetrate the market or clear its inventory will be torpedoed just short of its goal.

The whole process of analysis must conform to the detailed rules in the separate Agreement on Implementation of Article VI (Anti-dumping), found in Annex 1A of the WTO Agreement. This separate Agreement amount is a full set of rules of procedure for the determination of dumping and determination of the injury suffered. It covers the process of initiation and investigation to be used by the importing country, the evidence to be used in appraisal, undertakings to change prices in search of a settlement, and the imposition and collection of antidumping duties.

With a full set of rules, the comparison of a domestic (home) selling price and an export price in foreign markets sounds simple, but it is not. Much controversy exists around how the two prices are derived so that they can be properly compared. Prices in either market may vary based on currency fluctuations, order quantity discounts, and taxation, among a range of other factors.

Beyond these direct factors, the manner in which the importing country selects examples of pricing to construct a weighted average representative price for the dumped goods may add its own distortion to reality. For example, where the proceeds from an importer's bankruptcy liquidation sale are included in calculating a representative average price (and hence depressing it), the margin of dumping will seem large, but will not reflect the fact that this was a one-time sale outside the normal course of trade.

As an example, consider the case of trade in softwood lumber that has plagued U.S.–Canada relations for many years. The dispute arises from many reasons, not the least of which is that Canadian foresters enjoy far greater access and rights to harvest trees from government lands than do their American counterparts. While that does not immediately imply that Canadian export prices will be any lower than Canadian domestic prices, it certainly creates the latitude for Canadian exporters to undercut their American rivals in the U.S. marketplace. When this occurs, there is every incentive for the U.S. industry (and government) to look for instances of dumping.

In the course of this dispute, the United States made a determination of dumping by calculating a weighted-average price for Canadian lumber in U.S. markets. The two countries undertook consultations (which failed), and Canada requested a WTO panel to examine the American determination. Among the Canadian objections was the U.S. use of "zeroing" negative dumping margins. In other words, where Canadian domestic prices for lumber were higher (i.e., no dumping), they were included in U.S. averages as just zero (for no dumping) rather than as a negative number, which would pull down the overall average margin of dumping. Had they been included as negative numbers (as an otherwise mathematical average would require), it might have revealed that no dumping, on average, took place at all.

What resources do less-advantaged nations have to devote to such investigations? If the bottom 20 countries in GDP per capita are summed up as one nation, together they don't even rate as one of the top 60 nations of the world. And what of the nature of goods that may be thought of as "dumped," or even just "fairly-traded"? Some drugs with side effects that bar their sale in the developed world are bought and sold in other countries on the basis that some medical protection is better than none at all.

Sure, there are many exceptions in the WTO and GATT intended to benefit developing nations, but what good do they do in the face of such gross economic imbalances? In the past 30 years, the price of bananas has doubled or tripled in U.S. dollars, from about 8–10 cents per pound at wholesale to 20–24 cents, while the price of the average car has risen nearly 10 times, from $2,500 to $24,000.

These economic imbalances place less developed nations on a playing field that is permanently slanted against them.

Where a nation disputes the finding of another nation that dumping is taking place, it typically focuses its criticism against the national tribunal, on the following grounds:

That the national tribunal:

1. did not include evidence reasonably available to it,

2. had insufficient evidence of dumping to justify initiation of the investigation,

3. failed to examine the accuracy and adequacy of information it did have,

4. erroneously determined there to be a single "like" product,

5. used methodologies based on improper and unfair comparisons between the export price and the normal value,

6. used "zeroing" for negative dumping margins,

7. failed to make due allowance for differences that affect price comparability, including differences in physical characteristics, and/or

8. failed to apply a reasonable method in calculating amounts for administrative, selling and general expenses,

any or all of which may result in artificial and/or inflated margins of dumping, and the levy of an anti-dumping duty greater than the margin of any dumping. Some or all of these grounds are regularly raised, with all of them appearing at one time or another during the U.S.–Canada softwood lumber dispute. See, for example, Canada's objections to U.S. practice in 2002, in WTO case WT/DS264/2.

Very few instances of dumping and antidumping duties reach the WTO dispute resolution process, for national investigations and tribunals established and operating within the Article VI Agreement resolve most disputes. These investigations are reported to the WTO, and typical six-month periods see 10–20 members initiating 100–150 antidumping investigations against exports from 40–50 different countries or customs territories. Developed countries tend to represent two-thirds of the countries initiating national investigations.

Subsidies and Countervailing Measures

GATT Article VI (Anti-dumping) introduces the notion of subsidies, which are payments of support or deferrals of charges by a government to the benefit of business enterprises. As with dumping, subsidies are treated in principle by the GATT 1994 (this time in Article XVI), and are supported by another Annex 1A Agreement, on Subsidies and Countervailing Measures (SCM).

The central problem with subsidies is that they can (and often do) distort trade flows through government underwriting of corporate costs and risks. A company in receipt of a subsidy is no longer making decisions based on market forces, for it knows that it is insulated from those market forces to the extent of the subsidy it receives. When that company sells abroad, it enjoys an unfair competitive advantage over domestic firms of the foreign market country. As the name of the SCM Agreement suggests, these distortions are remedied through "countervailing duties" imposed by the foreign market country, much in the same way that antidumping duties are applied.

Note, however, that subsidies can have a triangular effect that causes injury to a third country. When Country A subsidizes its national industry and its export production is headed for Country B, Country B may or may not be concerned, with goods imported at lower purchase prices than would otherwise be possible. Remember that the firms in Country A are freed of market pressures to the extent of the subsidy they receive. The real complaint about the Country A subsidy may come from a third country, Country C, and its firms, who are also trying to export into Country B. Lacking any national subsidy, their prices are likely higher, and their sales in Country B will suffer accordingly.

That said, to forbid a government from ever spending funds that wind up in the hands of its businesses is an obvious impossibility, and not even desirable. Governments make any number of wise expenditures to support their firms and economies, for example, funding medical and industrial research. Subsidies are not problematic where they are available to *all* applicant businesses, such as a general tax credit for performing research and development. This lacks the "specificity" required to fall within the scope of the SCM. Where there is specificity (a limiting of access to the subsidy), the subsidy may be prohibited, actionable, or nonactionable.[20]

Prohibited subsidies under the SCM Agreement are those granted based on the recipient's export performance or its use of domestic (as opposed to imported) inputs. This is the most trade-distorting of all subsidies. It represents direct government funding of exports and/or the suppression of import trade. If such subsidies are not prevented, other governments will respond in an escalating tit-for-tat exchange of granting subsidies that abandons free markets in favor of state financed production. Subsidies that *appear* to be prohibited are subject to an expedited timetable under the WTO's dispute settlement process.

Actionable subsidies under the SCM Agreement are those specific subsidies that cause adverse effects to the interests of other signatories, nullifying or impairing the benefits that those nations are entitled to under the WTO Agreements. For example, where a host nation binds itself to a reduced tariff of 12 percent on a particular good, down from 18 percent, then immediately gives its domestic producers a 6 percent subsidy, it has nullified all the benefit granted to other members of the GATT. It has ensured the competitive price differential between domestic and imported goods remains the same. An actionable subsidy of over 5 percent also reverses the burden of proof, forcing the subsidy-granting state to show that its subsidy does not do serious prejudice to the complaining member. A final determination on actionable subsidies is also made through the dispute settlement process, but not on an expedited basis.

Last are nonactionable subsidies under the SCM Agreement, exempt, either because they are not specific or because they apply to industrial research, regional development, or environmental protection. Still, these are a question of fact, and where another signatory nation believes it is suffering serious adverse effects, the subsidy may be reviewed.

The three levels of subsidies, if complaints are lodged with and move through the WTO dispute settlement process, can give rise to three broadly similar remedies.

[20]WTO Agreement Annex 1A, Agreement on Subsidies and Countervailing Measures, Article 2.

A nation aggrieved by the subsidies of another must take the economic hit, invoke the dispute settlement process, and bear the burden of proof of its claims. At least that's the way it's supposed to go, according to the rules. Remember, however, that these are sovereign states run by politicians keen on being reelected. So it should come as no surprise that an aggrieved nation sometimes imposes its own unilateral countervailing duty, equal to the foreign subsidy or adverse trade effect, and waits for the *other* country (suitably outraged) to invoke the DSP itself. The foreign party must then bear the burden of proof. As either route ends up in the DSP, the lesson is clear: if a nation is wronged, it might as well retaliate. The aggrieved government's message to its electorate is also clear: we intend to protect your jobs, even if it means breaching some of the niceties of our international obligations.

Agreement on Subsidies & Countervailing Measures—Select Remedy Articles

As regards prohibited subsidies:

4.10   In the event the recommendation of the DSB *[Dispute Settlement Body]* is not followed within the time-period specified by the panel, which shall commence from the date of adoption of the panel's report or the Appellate Body's report, the DSB shall grant authorization to the complaining Member to take appropriate countermeasures, unless the DSB decides by consensus to reject the request.

As regards actionable subsidies:

7.9   In the event the Member has not taken appropriate steps to remove the adverse effects of the subsidy or withdraw the subsidy within six months from the date when the DSB adopts the panel report or the Appellate Body report, and in the absence of agreement on compensation, the DSB shall grant authorization to the complaining Member to take countermeasures, commensurate with the degree and nature of the adverse effects determined to exist, unless the DSB decides by consensus to reject the request.

As regards non-actionable yet reviewed subsidies:

9.4   Where a matter is referred to the Committee *[on Subsidies and Countervailing Measures]*, the Committee shall immediately review the facts involved and the evidence of the effects referred to in paragraph 1. If the Committee determines that such effects exist, it may recommend to the subsidizing Member to modify this programme in such a way as to remove these effects. The Committee shall present its conclusions within 120 days from the date when the matter is referred to it under paragraph 3. In the event the recommendation is not followed within six months, the Committee shall authorize the requesting Member to take appropriate countermeasures commensurate with the nature and degree of the effects determined to exist.

Recall that the GATT is firmly focused on trade in goods. Over the past five decades, however, the marketplaces of the world (and most especially those of developed nations) have seen ever-increasing shares of gross domestic product being generated through the service sector and the employment of intellectual property. It is therefore not surprising that this evolution has sparked an interest in having the protections of the GATT expanded to include both of these areas.

GATS—General Agreement on Trade in Services[21]

While goods are extremely important to international business (a given), the fact that they represent a "mature" economic transaction has meant that it has been easier to reach agreement on concessions in trading rules for goods. International trade in services and intellectual property (as sectors) is comparatively new. Thus, negotiations over appropriate international rules is somewhat more jealously guarded, if only because the full effect of complete and sudden liberalization in all sectors has not yet been completely discovered. While it is the developed nations who most tend to favor liberalization in services, the "go fast—go slow" split is an odd mix. Lesser-developed nations have vulnerable infant service sectors, while some developed nations that are highly dependent on their service industries share their concerns. Accordingly, as a result of political compromise, there are more significant reservations available to member nations under the GATS than exist under the GATT.

Despite the reservations available, the GATS is part of the "single package" of the WTO Agreement, and, as such, WTO members cannot opt out of it. This is a departure from past practice of pre-WTO days, where codes and side agreements (outside of GATT 1947 itself) had to be individually accepted in order to be binding on contracting parties. Also, the "single package" means the Annex 2 Dispute Settlement Understanding applies where GATS issues between members arise.

All WTO members are bound to comply with the GATS Parts I, II, V, and VI (known informally as the Framework Agreement) and Annexes. The Framework Agreement contains the general rules of MFN treatment and requires transparent publication by members of all their domestic measures and international obligations affecting services. The Annexes create special rules for special issues, including movement of natural persons (allowing limitations on one's right to stay abroad), financial services (permitting regulation aimed at market integrity and stability), telecommunications (requiring nondiscriminatory network access), and air transport services (limited to coverage of rights other than traffic rights).

Beyond those, member nations submit Schedules of Specific Commitments, to which Parts III and IV of the GATS apply. These Schedules detail which domestic economic service sectors the member is prepared to expose to foreign service providers and what (WTO-acceptable) limitations it intends to apply to that foreign activity.

As opposed to all service *sectors* within a member nation, GATS applies to all service *types*. The four types of services are

1. Cross-border supply: services supplied from one country to another, such as insurance or international telephony.
2. Consumption abroad: where a consumer from one member state makes use of a service in another state, such as in tourism.
3. Commercial presence: where a foreign business wishes to set up a subsidiary or branch operation to provide a service in the other country, for example, an overseas bank branch.
4. Presence of natural persons: where individuals travel from their home country to supply services abroad, for example, performers and business consultants.

In all service sectors, the principle of most-favored-nation (MFN) status continues as it does in the case of goods, where treatment "no less favorable" than that extended to any other country's service providers must be extended to those of all WTO members. Provision is made in general terms (relating to all services trade) in Article I, and again in Article XVI with respect to market access in the sectors affected by Specific Commitments.

[21]Annex 1B to the WTO Agreement.

Article XVI has allowed members to invoke limitations to market access when submitting or expanding their Schedule of Specific Commitments. These are limitations on

1. The number of service suppliers,
2. The total value of service transactions or assets,
3. The total number of service operations or the total quantity of service output,
4. The total number of natural persons that may be employed in a particular service sector or that a service supplier may employ,

by way of quota (or equivalent measure) or economic needs test, as well as

5. Measures that restrict or require specific types of legal entity or joint venture through which a service supplier may supply a service and
6. Limitations on the participation of foreign capital in terms of the maximum percentage limit on foreign shareholding or the total value of individual or aggregate foreign investment.

As a result, MFN and market access are somewhat less effective in the GATS than in the GATT, even where members open up sectors to foreign service providers. Further, they are subject to exceptions (largely due to service agreements between trading partners that predate the GATS) that permit discriminatory treatment based on nationality. These one-time exceptions, under monitoring of the General Council sitting as the Council for Trade in Services, are to be phased out, hopefully by the end of 2005. National treatment exists in principle as well, but member obligations only arise where a sector has been committed to foreign participation under that member's Schedule of Specific Commitments and are subject to the limitations listed above.

The GATS aims at progressive liberalization through successive rounds of negotiations, and given the track record of the GATT, it will undoubtedly be successful in increasing the number and significance of service sectors liberalized through ever larger national Schedules of Specific Commitments.

TRIPs—Agreement on Trade Related Aspects of Intellectual Property[22]

The rule-based disciplines that are central to the GATT and GATS are brought to intellectual property with the TRIPs Agreement. This Agreement is also part of the single-package WTO and covers the full range of intellectual property, from copyright and trademarks, through geographic indications (appellations), to industrial designs, patents, integrated circuitry layouts, and trade secrets.

The importance and benefits of intellectual property rights are generally well known. Such private rights encourage inventors to invent and entrepreneurs and financiers to take risks. They underpin the profitable flow of technology from one place to another, secure in the knowledge that these rights and profits will be protected.

Many international conventions exist to preserve intellectual property rights, the most important of which predate not only the WTO but also the GATT itself by a wide margin. These include the 1883 Paris Convention (industrial property), the 1886 Berne Convention (literary and artistic works), the 1961 Rome Convention (performances, recording and broadcasting), and the 1989 Washington IPIC Treaty (integrated circuit design).[23]

[22]Annex 1C to the WTO Agreement.

[23]The 1883 Paris Convention for the Protection of Industrial Property (revised by the 1967 Stockholm Act, as amended 1979); the 1886 Berne Convention for the Protection of Literary and Artistic Works (revised by the 1971 Paris Act, as amended 1979); the 1961 Rome Convention being the International Convention for the Protection of Performers, Producers of Phonograms and Broadcasting Organizations; and the 1989 IPIC Treaty being the Treaty on Intellectual Property in Respect of Integrated Circuits, adopted at Washington.

The TRIPs Agreement does not permit any derogation from obligations that WTO members may have under these conventions, and, in fact, virtually all WTO members are also signatories to most of these conventions. Moreover, the World International Property Organization (WIPO)—a UN Specialized Agency—which supervises the Paris and Berne conventions, boasts an even larger membership than the WTO, meaning that the application of these conventions is even more widespread.[24] WIPO and its relationship to the WTO are further discussed in Chapter 11.

However, just because an intellectual property convention exists, it does not mean that there is not wide flexibility in how members may apply it, and one purpose of the TRIPs Agreement is to obtain a basis for uniformity in the application, creation, and enforcement of rights. As under the GATS, transparency requirements demand the publication of existing commitments toward intellectual property. The Agreement establishes minimum and standards of protection of intellectual property and standards for enforcement of intellectual property rights within domestic procedures and remedies, and requires WTO members to employ the WTO Dispute Settlement Understanding in resolution of disputes related to intellectual property measures.

For example, the 1883 Paris Convention provides for patent protection, but does not insist on a particular duration of a patent right. Now the TRIPs Agreement provides that patent protection must be of at least 20 years in duration (similarly, trademarks must be provided 7 years and industrial designs, 10 years). In addition to being a step toward harmonizing international practice, the TRIPs Agreement incorporates the WTO principles of national treatment and most-favored-nation status. While the former is commonly found in existing intellectual property conventions (to treat foreigners at least as well as one's own nationals), the latter is not. TRIPs therefore now requires any preferential relationship that a member has with any other country to be extended to all other WTO members, as is the case in goods and services.

Final Remarks on General Exceptions

Caution should be taken in thinking that the WTO is a system of absolute rules, regardless whether goods, services, or intellectual property is at issue. It is not.

Virtually all WTO rules are subject to exceptions for the pressing reasons of national security, balance of payments, morality and public order, public health, conservation of national resources and cultural property, and provisions favoring lesser developed nations. Lesser-developed nations still benefit from the Generalized System of Preferences (GSP), which are further tariff reductions applicable to their goods exported to developed nations. This exemption from MFN treatment means that this lower tariff rate is not further extended to other developed nations.

The Annex 4 Plurilateral Trade Agreements (on trade in civil aircraft, government procurement, dairy, and bovine meat) also can be considered as exceptions, as they only apply to WTO members who sign on to them separately.

Perhaps the largest single exception to the general WTO rules is its Article XXIV, which allows member states to create customs unions and free-trade areas. Such arrangements imply that all (or substantially all) trade between two or more nations will be conducted on a tariff-free basis. With MFN obligations, this preference would normally require extension to all other WTO members. An MFN exemption is given on the basis that the complete trade liberalization between states is really an even greater step toward achieving the goals of the WTO. The efforts of the states involved must be genuine, taken to mean a timetable of 10 years or less to full functionality of the contemplated agreement. These topics of customs unions and free-trade areas are a subset of regional integration, which is the subject of the next chapter.

[24]See www.wipo.int.

Chapter Summary

With a membership now encompassing the vast majority of nations of the world, the GATT and WTO are without parallel in the successful pursuit of liberalization in international business. The GATT founders intended an organization to govern trade within the UN system, but fell short of that goal and settled for an agreement creating progressively freer and fairer trade in goods.

Successive rounds of tariff reduction reinforced the fundamental principle of nondiscrimination. This principle found its voice in the general elimination of quantitative restrictions, most-favored-nation status (favor one, favor all), and national treatment: the commitment to treat foreigners as least as well as one's own nationals.

The negative aspects of dumping and government subsidies also are treated under GATT/WTO rules, creating greater transparency and fairness in international trade.

The 1995 WTO was born of the Uruguay Round of the GATT and addresses many of the long-running deficiencies of the GATT. Now a full-fledged organization, it offers a more predictable and effective dispute settlement mechanism and brings services and intellectual property (as well as trade-related investment measures) into its rule-based disciplines.

Chapter Questions

1. Country A imposes a tax on alcoholic beverages, regardless of the strength of alcohol, of $2.00 per 40 ounces (1.14 liters) of beverage. Domestic producers of whiskey pay their taxes when the alcohol is finished with the distillery process, still in the barrel at 80 percent alcohol. Once the tax is paid, the producers mix the strong whiskey with water, reducing its strength to 40 percent alcohol, before bottling and selling it. On the other hand, importers of whisky produced in Scotland pay their $2 tax on importation into Country A of each 40-ounce, 40-percent-strength bottle. They claim this system is unfair. It would be possible to import strong whisky from Scotland and dilute it locally in Country A, but then the bottle labels could not claim "Produced and Bottled in Scotland." Is this Country A tax system in violation of the WTO's GATT 1994 rules?

2. Do national obligations of WTO members arise differently through the operation of the GATT 1994 as opposed to the GATS? If so, how?

3. Succinctly explain the difference between *most-favored-nation status* and *national treatment.*

4. Explain the principal differences between the GATT 1947 and the WTO, and the contribution that these changes have made to a fairer and more complete regulation of conditions of international business.

5. Under the Agreement on Subsidies and Countervailing Measures, not all subsidies are created equal. Explain why this statement is true.

6. Outline the changes in international trade dispute settlement that have made the WTO dispute settlement procedure a more predictable and certain process than its predecessor(s).

7. What conditions must be met before a nation can take protective measures against dumping? Which protective measures will receive support from the WTO, and which will be condemned by it?

BusinessWeek

The trade body's judgments are arbitrary, secretive, and made by nonprofessionals. Here's how to fix all that.

Is Uncle Sam sporting a "kick me" sign on his back? It certainly seems so at the Geneva-based World Trade Organization. The 146-nation body, created in the mid-'90s as a forum for global trade expansion talks and a court to settle disputes, has handed the U.S. a string of costly losses. The latest: A July ruling overturning President George W. Bush's 2002 decision to give the beleaguered U.S. steel industry a breather by levying temporary tariffs on imports.

Altogether, the U.S. faces more than $6 billion in yearly trade sanctions from its losing streak. And with the WTO's negotiators set to reconvene in Cancun, Mexico, on Sept. 10, American lawmakers are losing patience. Some want to appoint a panel of U.S. judges to review the legal reasoning behind the WTO decisions. Others propose pulling out of the trade body altogether. The trend "is beginning to undermine a lot of U.S. confidence in international trade laws and support for international trade agreements," says Senator Max Baucus (D-Mont.), the ranking Democrat on the Senate Finance Committee who's pushing the commission idea.

No, the U.S. isn't likely to bolt the WTO. Its creation was an achievement of almost 20 years of trade liberalization. But as a July 30 report from Congress' General Accounting Office shows, something is definitely amiss in Geneva. The U.S., according to the GAO, has faced "substantially more challenges" in the world trade forum, is more likely to lose rulings than other countries, and is far more apt to face the highest penalties. WTO panels are particularly hostile toward any actions intended to counter foreign-export subsidies, illegal dumping, and sudden import surges, such as the U.S. steel tariffs, the GAO concluded. "There's a definite tilt against the U.S. in critical cases," says Representative Phil English (R-Pa.), "We're finding the WTO process to be very frustrating and the decisions to be extraordinarily arbitrary."

Of course, the U.S. deserves to lose some cases. Washington needs to scrap a $5 billion-a-year tax subsidy for U.S. exporters that the WTO has justifiably ruled illegal, for example. Yet, even if you agree with the findings of the organization's panels—and some legal experts do—the trade body's judicial process is so fraught with secrecy and conflicts of interest that it seems more like a kangaroo court than the impartial panel the WTO framers intended. To restore the WTO's credibility and to undercut critics who want the U.S. out, here's what should be done:

INTRODUCE MORE TRANSPARENCY

The panels hear testimony in secret. Filings are confidential. Interested parties—affected businesses, labor unions, or environmental groups—often can't file briefs on cases. Decisions aren't announced promptly, and the judges' reasoning may not be published for months. So let in the light. Webcast the sessions, allow amicus briefs, and release the pleadings.

GO PROFESSIONAL

Panelists, often trade officials or private lawyers from other nations, volunteer to serve, unpaid, as judges. Conflicts of interest abound, since panelists can be engaged in trade disputes with other countries on the same issues being adjudicated. The amateur judges often make up rules as they go along. Private meetings with one side in a dispute are not uncommon. The WTO should create a permanent, paid judiciary and set procedural rules.

SHOW SOME RESTRAINT

The WTO charter specifically allows for temporary measures to aid a domestic industry about to be overwhelmed by unfairly priced imports. Such relief raises public support for free and fair trade generally. Dispute panels should approve the so-called safeguard measures as long as the facts of the case are correct, just as the WTO charter requires them to do. "There are rogue panels substituting their own judgment for national authority, and that happens repeatedly," insists Alan Wolff, a former deputy U.S. Trade Representative who now represents U.S. steel companies.

FOLLOW PRECEDENT

WTO judges aren't legally bound by previous decisions. So rulings rarely are the basis for future actions. Case law, the foundation of most legal systems, can't work unless judges follow precedent. That's where professional trade jurists, trained in following precedents, could be crucial.

Under the legislation that prescribed U.S. participation in the WTO, Congress is to vote in 2005 on whether to stay in the organization. Meanwhile, discussions within the WTO on reforming the dispute-panel process have stalled. That has the Bush Administration worried. "We're not entirely pleased about how some WTO panels decided," says John Veroneau, legal counsel at the U.S. Trade Representative's office. "But let's not throw out the baby with bathwater."

Veroneau has a point. When the WTO's top negotiators meet in Mexico next week, reforming the WTO tribunals should be moved to the top of the agenda.

Source: Paul Magnusson, edited by Douglas Harbrecht.

BusinessWeek

With the WTO talks in Mexico ending early in acrimony and recriminations, a global agreement by January 2005 looks doomed.

The World Trade Organization's two-year attempt to create a new global trade pact collapsed on Sept. 14 in Cancun, Mexico, as talks involving 148 nations deadlocked. The negotiations stalled over contentious issues ranging from eliminating farm subsidies for rich nations to lowering trade barriers among poor nations to international rules protecting foreign investments. As ministers prepared to head home, proponents of trade liberalization vowed to continue negotiations at the WTO headquarters in Geneva at a much lower level, but even they admitted it could be years before the effort is revived with the same intensity.

The breakup struck a serious blow to the Bush Administration's efforts at opening markets worldwide for U.S. exports and shrinking America's massive $500 billion trade deficit with the rest of the world. It will also complicate the parallel effort to fashion a hemispheric free trade area in the Americas. The WTO's critics, who had been demonstrating in the streets and the convention center against the trade talks, danced and shouted in glee as news of the deadlock spread. "We are elated that our voice has now been heard," says Philippine Trade Minister Manuel Roxas. The U.S. agenda ignored poor nations in favor of "the large corporations bankrolling President Bush's reelection effort," says Lori Wallach, director of the Washington (D.C.)-based Global Trade Watch.

African nations, led by Kenya, walked out of the talks on Sept. 14 in frustration at what they said was the lack of concessions from U.S. and Europe. "The differences were very wide, and it was impossible to close the gap," said George Odour Ong'wen, Kenya's representative. A group of 23 developing nations led by Brazil had been pushing for a quick end to the subsidies given to farmers in the U.S., the EU, and Japan, which total about $300 billion a year, according to estimates from the Paris-based Organization for Economic Cooperation & Development. Developing nations said the rich-nation farm subsidies are impoverishing their farmers and damaging their economies. Yet, the effort ended unsuccessfully in Cancun.

U.S. Trade Representative Robert B. Zoellick blamed "won't-do countries." Said Zoellick: "The larger lesson of Cancun is that useful compromise among 148 countries requires a serious willingness to focus on work, not rhetoric." Asked about the damage to the talks, Zoellick replied:

"It's hard to imagine how we'll finish on time" by the WTO's self-imposed January, 2005 deadline.

The Cancun summit marks the second time in four years that a WTO ministerial collapsed in acrimony and disagreement. It tried to begin a new round of global talks in 1999 in Seattle but developing nations refused to go along with the agenda written by wealthier nations. Two years later, a subsequent meeting in Doha, Qatar, barely managed to initiate a new round of trade talks, called the "Doha Development Round," by promising that they would focus on issues of interest to poorer nations, which now dominate the membership of the WTO. The World Bank has estimated that a successful Doha Round would raise 144 million people out of poverty—many of them in sub-Sahara Africa—and increase the global economy by $520 billion yearly by 2015.

It now appears that expectations among the developing nations may have been raised too high. Too few of the developing nations at the Cancun trade talks were willing to offer anything in return for promised concessions from the rich nations, U.S. trade negotiators complained. They blamed the collapse on the unwillingness of Europe and the developing nations to compromise on the inclusion of four issues in the talks, known as the "Singapore issues." They included rules on foreign investment, government procurement, antitrust issues, and customs procedures. Poorer nations steadfastly refused even to talk about adopting rules protecting investment from government overregulation and about antitrust issues. Europe insisted that it couldn't make concessions on agriculture without a deal on the four issues.

The developing nations blamed the stalemate on rich nations ignoring their demands and on attempts to divide them. "We are a group of developing countries united under no political banner but by issues," says Brazil's Foreign Minister Celso Amorim. "This was not an ideological debate, but a concentration on issues of great interest to our countries and a large part of the developing world as well." A split between the U.S. and Brazil may have additional consequences. The two nations are to chair the effort to achieve a hemispheric trade deal, called the Free Trade Area of the Americas, also by January, 2005. Acrimony in Cancun doesn't bode well for progress this year.

5

Regional Integration

Chapter Objectives

Increasingly, nations are building ever closer relationships with their trading partners, for a variety of reasons. Some of these efforts are more formal and more extensive than others, but all have a significant impact on the strategic goals and individual transactions of international businesspersons.

In this chapter we will explore:

- The spectrum and effect of regional integration efforts.
- Specific examples of regional integration in action in major markets.

- The strategic challenges and options these create for international business.

Introduction

A moment spent on definition is a worthwhile thing, because the title of this chapter can mean different things to different persons. To "integrate a region" implies many things. First, integration can be the combination of parts into a whole, the completion of an imperfect thing, or a coming together in equal participation and membership in a society.[1] Secondly, a region suggests an area of land having definable boundaries or characteristics.[2] Taken together, the term implies a form of union (or at least a process of union) between nations of a particular area of the world. While some attempts at regional integration do look like this, a full range of international relationships in varying degrees of significance also fall under this heading, sometimes between nations that are not in the same geographic region of the world.

Regional integration, as it concerns us in international business law, starts with attempts to create free trade between two or more nations, progressing through efforts to harmonize tariff rates (make them uniform), to creating full freedom of movement of any or all goods, services, persons, and capital. Going further, it can mean the economic erasing of national borders all the way to any or all of economic, social, military, and political union. From free trade to the creation of what amounts to a superstate, "regional integration" can have a broad definition.

Some motivations for regional integration are ancient, and remain today: economic prosperity, political influence, and regional military security. The newest motivation is the creation and maintenance of peace, for historical regional integration has meant little more than bloody conquest, empire, and colonialism. These themes will be explored in context, in later sections below.

[1] *Oxford English Reference Dictionary,* 2nd ed. (Oxford: Oxford University Press, 1996), p. 731.
[2] Ibid., p. 1214.

Political power and giant markets through integration? Maybe not. Member states in any trade arrangement jealously guard their turf, and regional lawmaking results in lumbering political compromises. Huge markets can be meaningless: it will always be harder to sell air-conditioning units in the Arctic than in the Tropics. Moreover, all consumers want to be served in their native language, so a different battalion of salespersons is necessary in each linguistic area.

Regional integration holds special importance for the international businessperson and the international business lawyer. Often it is discussed in terms of its political and economic impact: the creation of a new political entity with greater muscle on the world stage and the creation of a larger economic block with hundreds of millions of consumers where fragmented millions existed before.

The North American Free Trade Agreement of 1994 (the United States, Canada, and Mexico) is one example of initial integration, the free trade agreement. A good example of advanced integration is the European Union, spanning most European nations from Spain and Portugal in the southwest to Finland in the northeast, with new members on its eastern borders. While politics and economics are important, this type of regional integration creates another higher level of law and regulation.

Businesspersons beware: when conducting foreign operations in an integrated region, it is easy to forget (at first) that this higher level of law exists. After all, when operating in, say, France, wouldn't French law be supreme? Not so: European law is supreme in France, as France is a member of the European Union. This can be learned quite inexpensively right now, but becomes an expensive (and unforgettable) mistake for businesses if learned through experience.

Forms of Regional Integration

For ready reference in the sections that follow, the chart appearing on page 160 summarizes the principal differences and degrees between the various forms of regional integration.

Free Trade Area

Aside from arrangements between adjacent nations for frontier traffic and sectoral liberalization, the first real level of meaningful integration is the *free trade area*. As noted, one example is the 1994 North American Free Trade Agreement between the United States, Canada, and Mexico.

At the outset, a free trade area should be distinguished from the unfortunately similar terms of *foreign trade zone* or *free trade zone*. A foreign or free trade zone (FTZ) refers to a place, often a seaport, where import formalities and taxation are relaxed on goods inbound for processing, on the basis that the goods will almost immediately depart for other foreign markets once the processing is completed. Only goods passing into the domestic territory beyond the FTZ are dutiable. Not only does such an arrangement encourage establishment of processing facilities inside the FTZ, it dispenses with paperwork that, for re-exported goods, would have been pointless other than for statistical purposes.

"Free trade" refers to the elimination of tariff and nontariff barriers between two or more nations. The economic case for trade (and by implication, free trade) is made throughout Chapters 1 through 4, but the social implications of free trade are significant as well, for they translate into legal consequences for the international businessperson.

159

Progressive Levels of Regional Integration

Feature	Free Trade Area	Customs Union	Common Market	Economic Union	Economic and Monetary Union	Political Union
Unitary government policy						X
Tax harmonization						X
Monetary policy harmonization and single monetary unit					X	X
Full economic policy harmonization				X	X	X
Free movement of labor			May be present in degrees	X	X	X
Free movement of capital, payments, and establishment			X	X	X	X
Some economic policy harmonization			X	X	X	X
Free movement of all goods		X	X	X	X	X
Common external tariff		X	X	X	X	X
Customs policy harmonization		X	X	X	X	X
Free trade in goods originating inside area	X	X	X	X	X	X

Free trade will result in increased net national income for each participant nation. Each participant will be free to focus on economic sectors to which it is best suited, and can freely trade its surpluses in exchange for its needs. While that is a happy outcome, this <u>net</u> growth in national income will not be felt equally among workers: many jobs will be created, but others will be lost as structural economic change occurs. Unless the participant nations are identical in all sociopolitical-economic respects (which is never the case), there will be structural changes and costs in all of these environments as free trade is implemented. The more that the participant nations are dissimilar (particularly economically), the more these economic and social costs will be. However, critics of free trade often exaggerate this cost.

Job gains and losses and other economic structural changes occur on the opening of free trade as a result of loss of tariff and nontariff protection of markets. In economic terms, this is a good thing for developed nations. When a worker in a developed nation can perform any activity, it is a waste for that worker to produce below his or her potential. A developed nation that aspires to maintain its first-class infrastructure and social conditions will have trouble finding the tax revenue to do so if its workers are producing low-value added goods, easily duplicated by others willing to work for less. Not surprisingly then, these are the jobs that migrate, and these are the goods that will be imported when free trade is implemented.

For lesser-developed nations, free trade means forgoing the strategy of import substitution. This economic development strategy is to close one's border to imports in order to force local production of desired products, and it is incompatible with free trade. As a result, the concern is often raised that free trade may lead to exploitation of a low-priced labor force without any associated development benefit. Initially this is true, but something suddenly in demand (labor) does not stay cheaply priced for long, unless other factors (chiefly political and social) come into play to keep its price down.

For both developed and lesser-developed nations, therefore, free trade does not create or avoid these outcomes on its own; it is the government response to this new and changed trading environment that will dictate the future course of events. The real measure of the desirability of free trade is how a participant nation intends to use its gains from free trade to offset its losses. Will it retrain workers in vulnerable industries? Will it provide a social safety net for older workers who are not likely to be trainable for new vocations? Will it ensure that the growth and gains from trade are accessible to and enjoyed by all citizens, or will it perpetuate an economy dominated by a tiny and elite segment of society?

A sensibly undertaken free trade area (FTA) is generally in the economic best interest of those nations that participate in it. It is an undertaking requiring considerable political maturity, as it represents a loss of sovereign ability to exclude foreigners from internal markets, at least with respect to nationals of the other participant nations. With good governance (admittedly a leap of faith in some cases), it is also generally in the social and political best interest of those nations.

An international businessperson therefore should expect that this good governance obligation would result in a flurry of legislative activity prior to and after the establishment of an FTA, as governments respond to the changing reality of their internal markets. These may include provisional or transitional implementation of the free trade agreement itself, as well as significant national regulation on matters such as labor conditions, natural resources, and environmental protection.

For its own part, a free trade agreement will create its own institutions (a political management secretariat between member governments), sectoral oversight committees, its own administrative procedures, and some form of an arbitral tribunal or dispute settlement mechanism. In the fullness of time, any dispute settlement mechanism will develop a body of quasi-jurisprudence (nonbinding but persuasive), much as is the case in the WTO DSU.

The free trade area, as defined in Article XXIV of the GATT 1947, represents a group of two or more customs territories in which the duties and other restrictive regulations of commerce are eliminated on substantially all the trade between them in products originating in those territories. As may be recalled from the previous chapter, conforming to the GATT definition is critical, for otherwise the free trade area members would be obliged through MFN to extend the free-trading privilege to all other WTO members.

A second important GATT rule applying to a proposed FTA agreement is that it must move from an interim agreement (one or two sectors) to a fully functional regime (all sectors) within "a reasonable time." This is taken to mean 10 years or less. The provision exists to prevent a WTO member from creating a private preference with another nation (and still avoid MFN obligations) by saying that the preferred sector is just the first in the creation of an FTA on a 100-year time horizon. If this type of sham were allowed without a sensible maximum time limit, it would not be surprising that no second sector would ever be negotiated for inclusion into the proposed "deal," and MFN would cease to be a meaningful part of international economics.

Further, the GATT forbids any FTA from raising barriers to trade by its members with other WTO members, and the "duties and other regulations of commerce" that result from the formation of an FTA cannot be higher or more restrictive than those that existed before its formation.

While tariffs and nontariff barriers are removed in FTAs between the members of the area, each member remains free to set its own external tariffs, which it applies to inbound goods *not* originating in one of the FTA member states. Equally, foreign goods that have been landed in one of the member nations do *not*, in principle, enjoy duty-free re-export into the territory of other member states. The internal borders between member states continue to exist, waving through goods originating in member states (with a certificate of origin as proof), but levying duty on those that originate outside the FTA.

The diagram below illustrates the trading relationships between FTA members (X and Y, both WTO members) and the remainder of their trading partners (A and B) in a world consisting of a single good.

The following observations may be made:

1. Goods originating inside either X or Y (white arrows) cross their internal border on a duty-free basis.
2. Each of X and Y maintains its own external tariff regime toward nonmembers of the FTA. (X uses a 12 percent tariff and Y uses a 7 percent tariff.)
3. X is more protectionist than Y. (The tariffs of X are significantly higher (12 percent) than those of Y (7 percent), toward both A and B.)
4. MFN obligations are satisfied in both X and Y. (X treats A and B equally, and Y treats A and B equally.)
5. Goods originating in B arrive in X
   a. Net 12 percent: Flat rate of duty on direct export to X.

Trading Relationships in a Free Trade Area

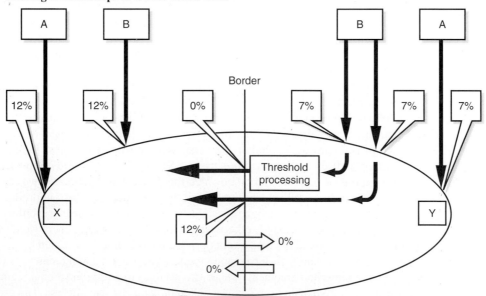

Where an exporter *into* an FTA also intends to perform value-added work inside the area (such as an exporter of machine parts to a subsidiary assembly plant located in the FTA abroad), there will almost always be a preferred point of entry into the FTA. Find the member with the lowest external tariff and export (parts) for assembly in that country. As long as the value added inside the FTA (assembly) is significant enough to meet a threshold (often 50 to 60 percent of total final export value), the final assembled goods will qualify as "originating" in that FTA member state. The goods may then be exported on a duty-free basis to any other FTA member.

  b. *Net 12 percent:* A gross rate of 19 percent duty charged for landing first in Y then proceeding to X (7 percent on entering Y, then 12 percent on entering X), subject to a "duty drawback" (refund) of 7 percent from Y when re-export to X is proved, for a net 12 percent (7+12–7=12).
  c. *Net 0 percent:*
    i. A gross rate of 7 percent duty charged where goods are landed and value is added in Y (7 percent on entering Y, then duty-free entering X), subject to a duty drawback of 7 percent from Y upon re-export to X, making net 0 percent. Duty-free entry into X occurs only when the value added to the goods while in Y meets a prescribed threshold.
    ii. Failure to meet this threshold will result in a duty of 12 percent charged at the border of X (an example of case 5b above). The right to receive the duty drawback from Y is not affected by a failure to meet this threshold; the duty drawback refund is contingent only on re-exporting from Y what was previously imported from B.
6. Note that the gross rates are important. Even if they are ultimately refunded, they are a hidden cost of doing international business. A company in Y that is continually cycling $5,000,000 in imported parts through processing and re-export to X will have $350,000 in cash flow (7 percent) permanently on deposit and tied up in the hands of Government Y. Assuming the company faces a cost of capital of 10 percent, this will result in an additional direct cost to the company of $35,000 per year.

Customs Union

The customs union is an extension of the free trade area concept, with an additional degree of integration in that

1. A common external tariff schedule is adopted toward nonmember countries.
2. All goods (regardless of origin) cross internal frontiers on a duty-free basis.

The fact that a common external tariff is *used* may be an "integrating" factor as far as traders exporting into the customs union are concerned, but that is not the most significant factor. More important is that a common tariff could even be *created*. The common tariff cannot be plucked from thin air; it is the result of intergovernmental negotiation and compromise, joint policy creation, and harmonization of regulation. This is the true substance of regional integration.

  The European Union (EU) is frequently and somewhat incorrectly cited (even by the WTO) as an example of a customs union. While it does incorporate a customs union (initiated in 1957 and fully operative since 1968), and is perhaps historically best known for that achievement, it has evolved through further steps of regional integration. More classical is the South American regional trading arrangement of MERCOSUR, an arrangement between Argentina, Brazil, Paraguay, and Uruguay. While MERCOSUR terms itself as a common market, this more advanced objective has been largely suspended in favor of completion of a workable customs union.

The political, administrative, and arbitral structures associated with a free trade area remain present in a customs union, but the greater degree of integration in the latter demands greater depth in policy coordination.

The common external tariff rate may vary from one type of goods to another, but whatever the rate, each member of a customs union will levy the same rate on each type of imported good. The GATT, also in Article XXIV, requires that this new replacement tariff schedule not represent an increase in the general incidence of duty charged or a greater restriction on commerce.

In the single-commodity example above, if Countries X and Y are to form a customs union, they must come to an agreement on the single tariff that will be levied on the imported good. If Country X imports a total of 100 units annually at a tariff of 12 percent and Country Y imports a total of 200 units at 7 percent, the GATT expects the customs union between X and Y to impose a duty no more than their trade-weighted average. This would be

$$([100 \times 12\%] + [200 \times 7\%]) \div 300 = 8.67\%$$

The trading partners of Country X will be delighted, for they will see a drop in rates that are charged against their exports, from 12 percent to 8.67 percent, while those trading into Country Y will be dismayed to see an increase in their rates from 7 percent to 8.67 percent.

As the customs union employs this common external tariff, the member states do not need to concern themselves for tariff purposes with the origin of goods crossing their internal borders. All customs duties are collected on first entry into a member state of the customs union. Bear in mind that there is no effective change for those who previously traded in the same weighted average measure with both Countries X and Y. Those traders paid a weighted average of 8.67 percent, and now will continue to do so, with the added freedom to ship to anywhere inside the customs union. If a nonmember nation is particularly hard done by, perhaps, having previously conducted all its trade in that good with Country Y, it may request a "compensatory adjustment."

Such an adjustment is a payment or a concession equivalent to its impairment of its GATT benefit. In coming to a settlement, the GATT requires that account be taken of the fact that this complaining nation now receives access to other markets at more attractive rates of duty than before. In the example above, the complaining nation now receives access to all demand in Country X, which it chose to ignore previously, now at a rate of duty reduced by almost one-third (8.67 percent versus 12 percent).

Bearing in mind that both classical free trade areas and customs unions focus on goods only, regional integration increases when this scope increases to cover all other factors of production, as in the common market, described below.

Common Market

As regional integration most often is an evolutionary process, a common market does not tend to be a spontaneous development, but rather is usually a product of further integration within a customs union. A common market includes the elimination of tariff and nontariff barriers between members just as in a free trade agreement or customs union. It also includes the common external tariff of a customs union and the free passage between member states of all goods regardless of origin, as well as the policy coordination that goes along with that level of integration.

What differentiates a common market from a customs union is the additional integration of national economies and policies to also accommodate free passage of services, business establishment, capital, and payments. Thus, it represents a level of integration well beyond goods, but one still driven by goods.

The rationale for this step is quite straightforward, assuming that a reasonable level of success has been achieved between member states in a previous customs union stage. Starting from the free passage of goods across internal frontiers, it soon becomes apparent that, regardless of this wonderful economic advance, the real prize of economic liberalization is still just beyond reach. Bluntly, what is the benefit of free passage of goods if a trader cannot receive payments owing and located in other member states, due to member state currency export controls? What is the benefit of selling in another member state market if one cannot establish a local warranty service center, due to restrictions on investment? These are not explicitly restrictions on the passage of goods, and therefore they can exist in either an FTA or a customs union, but they certainly throw a bucket of cold water on the potential for great success in integration.

To address these problems, a customs union may evolve into a common market. These national restrictions are removed or harmonized by member governments so that all traders may *effectively* treat the collected member state markets as a single market. All factors of production (with the exception of workers, in some cases) are thus liberalized to allow their movement and unrestricted employment in each member state.

Obviously it is not a requirement that customs unions make this evolutionary step. For some, this may be seen as handing over just too much sovereign control of their national economies to their trading partners.

Beware that some writers use "customs union" and "common market" as interchangeable terms, which is imprecise. Other writers will refer to "*the* Common Market" when meaning what was once the European Economic Community, now the European Union. Just to complicate matters, the term *common market* was in vogue when the EEC was in fact a customs union, and fell into disuse after the EEC actually achieved true common market status (and more) in 1992. The European Union still possesses its common market, but again, it has evolved beyond even this stage. As far as the WTO is concerned, a common market *does* fall under the heading of a customs union for the purpose of Article XXIV oversight of its common external tariff arrangements.

Economic Union/Economic and Monetary Union

Even though it is the most advanced form of regional integration, the supposed unity of an economic union or an economic and monetary union is unlikely to reduce the levels of governance and administration faced by the international businessperson. An economic union provides for harmonized regulation, and an economic and monetary union additionally creates a single monetary unit, all over and above the attributes of a common market. However, the sovereign nature of member states will still prevail, ensuring that economic union (in either form) adds a federal or supranational level of governance, rather than actually dissolving national governments.

To the collected attributes of a common market, both types of economic union add full labor mobility, if not previously permitted in a predecessor common market. In addition, there will be economic policy harmonization between governments, as well as considerable harmonization of social benefits. Social benefits harmonization is necessary in order to make workers fully free to move and not lose their accumulated pension and other similar benefits. Economic and monetary union goes one step further than economic union and ties the monetary policies of the member nations together through the creation of a central bank and common currency unit.

As the last and most significant national policy lever, common taxation is the final step in harmonization, and one that has not been achieved by any modern economic and monetary union composed of sovereign nations. Even within historically federal states such as the United States (or other similar forms of political union), state sales taxes vary, creating tolerated economic distortion rather than complete union.

Economic union or economic and monetary union, therefore, does not immediately equate to political union, although such are preconditions. Political union requires the merging of much more, including large portions of the civil service, everything from the post office to the armed forces. Political union further requires the subordination of once fully sovereign nations to a greater sovereign authority, albeit under a constitutional arrangement.

To its advantage, the United States (a political union, but still not unitary) was created in much simpler economic times with the common driver of independence from a higher power. Thus, it has been able to grow organically as a single federal unit, as opposed to being forged with greater compromise in a more complex political and economic environment out of more widely varying states.

In the 20th century, examples of union include the 1921 Belgium-Luxembourg Economic Union (BLEU), which has lasted to the present day, and the set-to-expand 15-member European Union. The EU has deliberately followed a path toward economic union since the 1950s, progressing through the stages of a customs union and a common market. It can be said to have finally arrived at economic and monetary union with the advent of its common monetary policy and common currency, the euro (€).

Regional Integration in the Americas—FTA to Common Markets

North and South America effectively illustrate the initial steps involved in regional integration in international business, the free trade area moving toward a customs union and common markets. These arrangements have a direct impact on the costs and procedures used to conduct international business in the region.

North American Free Trade Agreement

Perspective

The 10 years between the 1985 opening of negotiations on the U.S.–Canada Free Trade Agreement and the 1994 entry into force of the North American Free Trade Agreement (U.S.–Canada–Mexico) was the coming of age of "globalization." Neither of these triggered globalization, but they were policies that were suitable for the political and economic times that surrounded them.

This period saw the collapse of Communism and the end of the Cold War, releasing nations in both the East and West to chart their course more independently of both the Soviet Union and the United States. New nations were rapidly constituted as artificial political constructs of the Cold War unwound. In Asia, greater economic liberalism in China created emerging opportunities for Western business, with widespread growth diverting attention and investment to that region—the so-called Asian Tiger economies. In western Europe, the single market was completed and economic and monetary union was becoming a reality.

As old political and economic arrangements dissolved, others were beginning to form. Commentators saw a political success in Europe that might lead to an economic powerhouse, and an economic powerhouse emerging in Asia that might one day lead to a political success. What then could be done in North America or, in the longer run, for all of the Americas? The NAFTA was a response to this question.

Most often, free trade agreements are examined in light of the tariff-free exchange of goods. This was not the critical factor, however, that propelled the Canadians toward free trade with the United States in the 1980s. As GATT members, both Canada and the United States had already reduced their tariffs considerably in previous multilateral rounds. As matters then stood, 70 percent of U.S. merchandise exports to Canada were duty-free, as were 85 percent of Canadian merchandise exports to the United States. More importantly, in a world of three emerging trade blocks, Canada sought to guarantee its access to its most critical export market, the United States. It was a market that Canada needed far more than the United States needed Canada.

That said, the standard reasons for free trade (market economies of scale, reduced tariffs, healthy competition, reduced transaction costs) were good ones for both the United States and Canada, given the high degree of similarity between their economies. Therefore, despite the social debate and political furor that accompanied the treaty negotiations, the conclusion of the U.S.–Canada treaty and its eventual success for both nations is, frankly, unsurprising.

The U.S.–Canada agreement was signed in January 1988; six months later, Carlos Salinas de Gortari was elected as Mexican president. He had served from 1982 to 1987 as Minister of Planning and Budget in his predecessor's cabinet, orchestrating Mexico's entry into the GATT in 1986. That alone was a major step for Mexico, historically dominated by state enterprise and import controls, and famous for its 1938 nationalization of foreign ownership in its oil industry. Salinas was decidedly in favor of liberalizing the Mexican economy. For Mexico too, the rationale for free trade was not primarily focused on tariffs. In bringing the Mexican economy out of crisis, Salinas sought to convince the international business community that Mexico possessed the stability, maturity, and potential for foreign investment and growth. To prove that and to institutionalize change, he engaged the United States in discussion on a separate free trade arrangement for Mexico.

This development could have been disastrous for Canada; foreign investment seeking lower wages would locate in Mexico, while foreign investment seeking trade access to the entire continent would locate in the United States. As a result, Canada braved an even worse domestic political storm and insisted on being included in what would become the North American Free Trade Agreement.

Reductions in tariff barriers had always been of greater interest to the United States than either Canada or Mexico. Market access, reductions in nontariff barriers, and improved conditions for investment further acted as reasons for U.S. participation in NAFTA. Moreover, the United States had another interest regarding Mexico: the stability of America's southern neighbor.

A neighbor in crisis is never a good thing; its problems eventually become its principal export. In the 1980s, the United States had been concerned with Soviet and Cuban threats to Latin America. The region's corrosive and prolonged financial crisis prompted U.S. debt refinancing through the Brady Plan, supplemented with the 1990 "Enterprise of the Americas Initiative" for debt management and the promotion of free trade. While the Soviet threat soon passed from sight, Mexico's continuing financial problems did not. Taking all reasonable steps to promote stability, growth, and prosperity in Mexico remained in the best interest of the United States, with NAFTA becoming the key vehicle.

The differential between the countries is shown in the table below, after the agreement had been in force eight years. Not only had Mexico made considerable economic process in that time, it had done well to manage through further economic and currency problems at the same time. Had NAFTA not been in place, those difficult times would have been considerably worse without the international credibility that NAFTA has given to the Mexican economy.

International Business Performance under NAFTA— The Results

One prominent NAFTA doomsayer was then–U.S. presidential candidate H. Ross Perot, who in a 1992 statement forecasted "a giant sucking sound" as jobs would move to Mexico

Comparison of Economic Factors among NAFTA Nations

Factor (Year 2001 unless noted otherwise)	Canada	United States	Mexico
Area (total; sq. km.)	9,976,140	9,629,091	1,972,550
Population (July 2002)	31,902,268	280,562,489	103,400,165
GDP	$875 billion	$10.082 trillion	$920 billion
GDP real growth rate	1.9%	0.3% (2001 est.)	–0.3%
GDP per capita	$27,700	$36,300	$9,000
GDP composition by sector:			
Agriculture	2%	2%	5%
Industry	29%	18%	26%
Services	69%	80%	69%
Household income or consumption by percentage share:			
Lowest 10%	2.8%	1.8%	1.6%
Highest 10%	23.8% (1994)	30.5% (1997)	41.1%
Inflation rate (consumer prices)	2.8%	2.8%	6.5%
Labor force	16.4 million	141.8 million (includes unemployed)	39.8 million (2000)
Labor force by occupation	Services 74%, manufacturing 15%, construction 5%, agriculture 3%, other 3% (2000)	Managerial and professional 31%; technical, sales, and administrative support 28.9%; services 13.6%; manufacturing, mining, transportation, and crafts 24.1%; farming, forestry, and fishing 2.4%	Agriculture 20%, industry 24%, services 56% (1998)
Unemployment rate	7.2%	5%	Urban 3%, plus considerable underemployment
Budget:			
Revenues	$178.6 billion	$1.828 trillion	$136 billion
Expenditures	$161.4 billion	$1.703 trillion	$140 billion
Industrial production growth rate	0.5%	–3.7%	–3.4%
Exports (f.o.b.)	$273.8 billion	$723 billion	$159 billion
Exports partners	United States 86%, Japan 3%, United Kingdom, Germany, South Korea, Netherlands, China (1999)	Canada 22.4%, Mexico 13.9%, Japan 7.9%, United Kingdom 5.6%, Germany 4.1%, France, Netherlands	United States 88.4%, Canada 2%, Germany 0.9%, Spain 0.8%, Netherlands Antilles 0.6%, Japan 0.4%, United Kingdom 0.4%, Venezuela 0.4%
Imports (f.o.b.)	$238.3 billion	$1.148 trillion	$168 billion
Import partners	United States 74%, European Union 9%, Japan 3% (2000)	Canada 19%, Mexico 11.5%, Japan 11.1%, China 8.9%, Germany 5.2%, United Kingdom, Taiwan	United States 68.4%, Japan 4.7%, Germany 3.6%, Canada 2.5%, China 2.2%, South Korea 2.1%, Taiwan 1.6%, Italy 1.3%, Brazil 1.1%

Source: *Central Intelligence Agency World Factbook 2002* (edited compilation).

under the North American Free Trade Agreement.[3] This has not happened on any such scale, largely because of relative labor efficiencies (and inefficiencies) between the United States, Canada, and Mexico. Cheaper labor is not cheap at all if its lack of capital and tools make it inefficient as well. Empirical evidence collected in the 10 years after the establishment of NAFTA shows that job migration (movement of jobs but not workers) from one nation to another does occur, but not at a rate anywhere near that which critics feared and forecasted.

In fact, the economic gains from free trade are well borne out with experience: growth in two-way trade between Mexico, the United States, and Canada has far outpaced growth in their trade with the rest of the world. Their respective GDP figures also have grown faster than both their peers and the rest of the world in the same period. We should expect that the United States and Canada would perform on the high side of average, as they are among the nations best able to do so; however, their trade improvements speak for themselves and their GDP performance has been twice that of their developed peers. Mexico, too, has seen similar performance. Not only has its trade skyrocketed since NAFTA, its GDP performance (a measure across all sectors) has been nearly twice that of the balance of Latin America.

Growth in Two-Way NAFTA Trade, 1994–2001

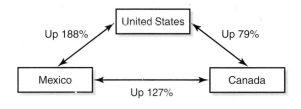

In same period, trade growth with rest of world:

United States	Up 67%
Canada	Up 52%
Mexico (est.)	Up 100%

GDP growth (annual average)

United States	5.0%
Canada	4.3%
Mexico	7.1%

Versus average annual GDP growth in:

Rest of world	3.5%
Developed nations	2.3%
Latin America	3.7%

Source: Derived from national accounts, inflation adjusted, merchandise trade balances.

And what of the forecasted job losses in the United States and Canada? Certainly some have occurred, but not on the scale envisioned by candidate Perot. Still, we must remember that we are all in the North American lifeboat together, and what job losses have occurred are Mexico's gain, floating the lifeboat a little higher in the water for all of us.

Moreover, to whatever extent jobs have migrated to Mexico, it is because Mexico's present level of development is appropriate to support them. For exactly that reason, it was not appropriate for the U.S. and Canadian economies to continue to support these jobs. Nations hoping to maintain and pay for some of the highest living standards in the world cannot hope to do so while working at low-value-added jobs.

[3]"Debating Our Destiny: The Third Presidential Debate," *NewsHour,* PBS, October 19, 1992, www.pbs.org/newshour/debatingourdestiny/92debates/3prez2.html.

Of course, Mexico does not want to take on this role forever, and it will not take forever. Development is an evolutionary process that took two centuries in Northern America with chief export markets across an ocean. Mexico will advance rapidly with readily available technologies and services, and the world's most consumer-oriented markets on its doorstep.

Structure and Substance

NAFTA is more than the classical economist's definition of a free trade area for goods. For the international businessperson, NAFTA includes provisions on services, investment, intellectual property, and dispute settlement (both state versus state and investor versus state).

As all three members of NAFTA are also members of the GATT/WTO, it should come as no surprise that NAFTA conformed to the GATT Article XXIV requirements for formation of a free trade area. Moreover, NAFTA adopted a very similar structure, even incorporating GATT principles by reference, in some cases allowing for future evolution of the GATT to automatically become part of NAFTA. For businesspersons and lawyers, the implication is that a good understanding of the GATT and WTO will go a long way to understanding how NAFTA works.

In grand terms, and always subject to listed exceptions, NAFTA has progressively reduced all tariffs (all to zero in 2008); it applies to both national and subordinate governments, and those governments must accord national treatment to goods that fall under the umbrella of the agreement. The listed exceptions and reservations of Mexico are much more extensive than those of either the United States or Canada, which is neither surprising nor concerning given its level of economic development and its much more recent entry into the rigors of GATT/WTO membership.

NAFTA is a large and detailed agreement, but it can be seen as having three main themes:

1. Administration.
2. Rules.
3. Problem solving.

Administrative measures provide for institutions (a supervisory Free Trade Commission assisted by a management Secretariat) and the exchange of information between governments, as well as a common customs procedure and rules of origin for traders.

General rules are created to govern trade in goods and services, and aspects of intellectual property and investment. Special rules apply to sensitive sectors, representing reservations and compromise important to the parties. Provisions on regulatory measures prevent technical standards, sanitary measures, and competition policy from becoming nontariff barriers.

Problem solving takes two forms: protective measures and dispute settlement. For protective measures, where a crisis in trade arises causing injury, the use of emergency measures is permitted. All governments reserve the right to act in the interest and preservation of their national security, taxation, balance of payments, and culture. Problems are avoided in some sectors through the use of reservations and exceptions, by taking them outside NAFTA application. Dispute settlement measures allow arbitral review of government decisions in dumping cases or the application of countervailing duties, as well as in general intergovernmental dispute settlement, and in cases of investor–state disputes on investment matters.

Operation of the Agreement
Goods

 NAFTA establishes a free trade area for goods between the state parties through obligations of national treatment, tariff elimination, and prohibition of trade restrictions. Note the use of GATT principles through incorporation by reference.

Structure of the North American Free Trade Agreement

NAFTA Topic	Found in Articles
1. Administration	
Between governments	
Institutional arrangements	2001–2002
Information exchange	1801–1806
For traders	
Rules of origin	400–415 + Annexes
Customs administration	500–514
2. Rules	
General market rules	
Trade in goods	300–318
Cross-border trade in services	1201–1213 + Annexes
Intellectual property	1701–1721 + Annexes
Investment	1101–1114, 1139 (see also further dispute settlement procedures, below)
Temporary entry for business persons	1601–1608 + Annexes
Government procurement	1001–1025 + Annexes
Special and sensitive sector rules	
Textiles and apparel	Annex 300-B
Automotive goods	Annex 300-A
Energy and basic petrochemicals	601–609 + Annexes
Agriculture	701–708 + Annexes
Telecommunications	1301–1310 + Annex
Financial services	1401–1416 + Annexes (see also further dispute settlement procedures, below)
Land transportation	Annex 1212
Environmental provisions	North American Agreement on Environmental Cooperation*
Labor provisions	North American Agreement on Labor Cooperation**
Regulatory standards	
Technical standards	901–915 + Annexes
Sanitary and phytosanitary measures	709–724
Competition policy, monopolies, and state enterprises	1501–1505 + Annex
3. Problem Solving	
Protective measures	
Emergency action	801–805 + Annexes
Exceptions	2101–2107 + Annexes
National lists of reservations & exceptions (investment, cross-border trade in services, and financial services)	Annexes I through VII
Conflict resolution	
Review of antidumping and CVD matters	1901–1911 + Annexes
Further dispute settlement procedures	
State versus state, generally	2003–2022 + Annexes
Investor versus state	1115–1138 + Annexes
Financial services	1415

*Side agreement signed August 1993, entered into force with NAFTA, January 1, 1994.
**Side agreement signed September 1993, entered into force with NAFTA, January 1, 1994.

Select Articles, Part 2—Trade in Goods, Chapter 3

Article 301: National Treatment

1. Each Party shall accord national treatment to the goods of another Party in accordance with Article III of the *General Agreement on Tariffs and Trade* (GATT), including its interpretative notes, and to this end Article III of the GATT and its interpretative notes, or any equivalent provision of a successor agreement to which all Parties are party, are incorporated into and made part of this Agreement.

2. The provisions of paragraph 1 regarding national treatment shall mean, with respect to a state or province, treatment no less favorable than the most favorable treatment accorded by such state or province to any like, directly competitive or substitutable goods, as the case may be, of the Party of which it forms a part.

3. Paragraphs 1 and 2 do not apply to the measures set out in Annex 301.3.

Article 302: Tariff Elimination

1. Except as otherwise provided in this Agreement, no Party may increase any existing customs duty, or adopt any customs duty, on an originating good.

2. Except as otherwise provided in this Agreement, each Party shall progressively eliminate its customs duties on originating goods in accordance with its Schedule to Annex 302.2.

Article 309: Import and Export Restrictions

1. Except as otherwise provided in this Agreement, no Party may adopt or maintain any prohibition or restriction on the importation of any good of another Party or on the exportation or sale for export of any good destined for the territory of another Party, except in accordance with Article XI of the GATT, including its interpretative notes, and to this end Article XI of the GATT and its interpretative notes, or any equivalent provision of a successor agreement to which all Parties are party, are incorporated into and made a part of this Agreement.

Source: Reproduced with permission of NAFTA Secretariat. Full text (subject to disclaimer) is available in English at http://www.nafta-sec-alena.org/english/nafta/nafta.htm, or in Spanish at http://www.nafta-sec-alena.org/spanish/nafta/nafta.htm.

In order to gain the benefits of the agreement, goods must be as the agreement puts it, "goods of another Party" or "originating goods." Those goods that are not "originating" remain liable for assessment of duty under the national tariff and restrictions of the importing country.

To establish whether the goods originate inside the FTA, NAFTA provides for rules of origin. Naturally, if "goods" are North American in every respect of their content and manufacture, they are "originating goods." Other goods, however, may contain nonregional raw materials, but if they are sufficiently "worked on" so as to sufficiently change their tariff classification, they will also be considered as North American. The key lies in this transformation of the raw materials; repackaging alone will not be sufficient, and, in some instances, goods must pass a threshold of North American content in addition to the transformation requirement. Where, subject to some exceptions, nonoriginating goods are imported as parts and are assembled within North America, the final assembly is classed

Where there is no doubt as to meeting the threshold, many firms use the transaction value method, if permitted. Record keeping is minimal as the commercial invoice proves the value. The net cost method should be used where the result will be close to the threshold, and every penny and peso count. It requires much more accounting documentation to be kept on file and more complex calculation, but gives a lower threshold in the bargain.

as originating goods as long as a regional value content of either 60 percent transaction value or 50 percent net cost is met.[4] Special rules can apply; in the case of automotive products, North American content must be 60 percent by net cost (62.5 percent for passenger cars and light trucks).

The transaction value method is based on the f.o.b.[5] sale price of the goods, and 60 percent of that becomes the regional content threshold. The net cost method starts from total cost in the hands of the would-be exporter, with deductions for freight, sales promotion, allowable interest, and royalties, to arrive at the net cost, 50 percent of which is the threshold.

The rules of origin require the exporter to produce a NAFTA standard form Certificate of Origin in order to claim preferential treatment, but the requirements are not onerous.[6] If the exporter is not the producer, the exporter can either obtain one from the producer voluntarily or make the declaration based on its own knowledge or reliance on the producer's written representation that the good qualifies as an originating good. A single certificate can be valid for multiple shipments.

Investment

NAFTA investors and their investments in one of the other member nations must be accorded national treatment (no less favorable than that accorded to that states's own investors and investments) in all aspects of the creation, operation, or disposition of investments.[7] If one of the states offers an even better preference to another non-NAFTA state, then a supplemental most-favored-nation requirement demands that the preference also be extended to NAFTA members.[8]

Of particular interest to the United States and its investment security objectives was the inclusion of Article 1105, addressing a minimum standard of treatment for foreign investment. The article requires that

1. Each Party shall accord to investments of investors of another Party treatment in accordance with international law, including fair and equitable treatment and full protection and security.
2. Without prejudice to paragraph 1 and notwithstanding Article 1108(7)(b), each Party shall accord to investors of another Party, and to investments of investors of another Party, non-discriminatory treatment with respect to measures it adopts or maintains relating to losses suffered by investments in its territory owing to armed conflict or civil strife.

The motivations for this article are both old and new. Mexican-American relations were badly scarred in the late 1930s with Mexican nationalization of oil assets that were, in the main, U.S. owned. The dispute raised the question of what, if anything, international law

---

[4]NAFTA Article 402.

[5]Free on board, followed by place of delivery to onward carrier. The sale price includes the cost of transport and loading at the named place; for example, f.o.b. New York, f.o.b. Halifax, or f.o.b. Veracruz.

[6]NAFTA Article 501.

[7]NAFTA Article 1102.

[8]NAFTA Articles 1103 and 1104.

prescribed in terms of compensation for such state takings. While the United States took the position (and maintains it today) that international law requires "prompt, adequate and effective" compensation, this position has been historically rejected in Latin America, particularly in the context of major economic reform. The provisions of Article 1105(1) indicate just how far Mexico and the United States have come in reconstituting their relationship. The new motivations behind Article 1105(2) include more modern U.S. concerns with civil conflict that has occurred in Mexico's Chiapas region, and conflict that could occur in the Canadian province of Quebec.

Cross-Border Trade in Services

NAFTA Chapter 12 (a modest chapter with considerable scope for exceptions) applies to all aspects of service provision across borders, except the important sectors of telecommunications and financial services (covered separately in NAFTA Chapters 13 and 14), air services, and government procurement. The exceptions exist largely as a reflection of the fact that services are simply at an earlier stage of liberalization (compared to goods) on the greater world trade agenda. Bear in mind that NAFTA was being negotiated at the same time as the WTO and its GATS services agreement were under negotiation, so it is not surprising that NAFTA Chapter 12 and GATS represent similar (more limited) progress in liberalization.

As was the case with investment, the better of national treatment or MFN applies as the operative standard of treatment to which service providers are entitled, and service providers are not to be required to establish a local office or representation as a condition of providing their cross-border service. While services *procurement* by governments is not subject to NAFTA provisions, governments are bound to recognize their NAFTA commitments in the way in which they *regulate* services, according the better of national treatment of MFN.

It is important for international businesspersons to realize that the right to provide services does not come with attached rights of permanent entry into another member nation. Temporary access for professionals is provided for in the agreement, but otherwise, each nation's immigration rules continue to apply.

The sensitive nature of service liberalization already has been referred to NAFTA Dispute Resolution Panels for consideration and interpretation. In the example below, the question in transport services was whether the entire Mexican regime of trucking control had to reach the U.S. regulatory standard before Mexican truckers could offer cross-border services. In contrast to this U.S. view, Mexico asserted that it was only necessary for individual Mexican carriers to meet U.S. standards on their merits in order to receive the right to operate.

NAFTA Final Report on Cross-Border Trucking Services

February 6, 2001
Final Report of the Panel

A. The Dispute

1. The Panel in this proceeding must decide whether the United States is in breach of Articles 1202 (national treatment for cross-border services) and/or 1203 (most-favored-nation treatment for cross-border services) of NAFTA by failing to lift its moratorium on the processing of applications by Mexican-owned trucking firms for

authority to operate in the U.S. border states. Similarly, the Panel must decide whether the United States breached Articles 1102 (national treatment) and/or 1103 (most-favored-nation treatment) by refusing to permit Mexican investment in companies in the United States that provide transportation of international cargo. Given the expiration on December 17, 1995 of the Annex I reservation that the United States took to allowing cross-border trucking services and investment, the maintenance of the moratorium must be justified either under the language of Articles 1202 or 1203, or by some other provision of NAFTA, such as those found in Chapter Nine (standards) or by Article 2101 (general exceptions).

The Parties' views are summarized as follows:

2. **Mexico** contends that the United States has violated NAFTA by failing to phase out U.S. restrictions on cross-border trucking services and on Mexican investment in the U.S. trucking industry, as is required by the U.S. commitments in Annex I, despite affording Canada national treatment. Mexico believes such failure is a violation of the national treatment and most-favored-nation provisions found in Articles 1202 and 1203 (cross-border services) and Articles 1102 and 1103 (investment).

3. Mexico also contests the U.S. interpretation of Articles 1202 and 1203, without arguing that the Mexican regulatory system is equivalent to those of the United States and Canada. According to Mexico, Mexican trucking firms are entitled to the same rights as U.S. carriers under U.S. law, that is "(i) consideration on their individual merits and (ii) a full opportunity to contest the denial of operating authority." Any other approach is a violation of Articles 1202 and 1203. During the NAFTA negotiations, both governments understood that "motor carriers would have to comply fully with the standards *of the country in which they were providing service.*" However, the obligations of the Parties were "not made contingent upon completion of the standards-capability work program" or the adoption of an identical regulatory system in Mexico.

4. Mexico asserts that the U.S. conduct must be reviewed in light of Article 102(2) of NAFTA, which requires that the "Parties shall interpret and apply the provisions of the [NAFTA] Agreement in the light of its objectives set out in paragraph 1." Among others, the objectives include eliminating barriers to trade in services and increasing investment opportunities "in accordance with applicable rules of international law." Mexico contends that the U.S. conduct does not further these objectives.

5. According to Mexico, "There are no exceptions to the relevant NAFTA provisions that could even potentially be applicable." Mexico contends that the U.S. failure to implement its cross-border trucking services and investment obligations is not justified by the standards provisions contained in Chapter Nine (standards) nor by Article 2101 (general exceptions), particularly in light of the fact that when NAFTA was negotiated the United States was well aware that Mexico's regulatory system was significantly different from those operating in the United States and Canada.

6. Mexico charges that the U.S. inaction is motivated not by safety concerns but by political considerations relating to opposition by organized labor in the United States to the implementation of NAFTA's cross-border trucking obligations.

7. The **United States** argues that because Mexico does not maintain the same rigorous standards as the regulatory systems in the United States and Canada, "the in like circumstances" language in Article 1202 means that service providers [from Mexico] may be treated differently in order to address a legitimate regulatory objective. Further, since the Canadian regulatory system is "equivalent" to that of the United States, it is not a violation of the most-favored-nation treatment under Article 1203

for the United States to treat Canadian trucking firms which are "in like circumstances" vis-a-vis U.S. trucking firms in a more favorable manner than Mexican trucking firms.

8. According to the United States, the inclusion in NAFTA Articles 1202 and 1203 of the phrase "in like circumstances" limits the national treatment and most-favored-nation obligations to circumstances with regard to trucking operations which are like, and that because "adequate procedures are not yet in place [in Mexico] to ensure U.S. highway safety," NAFTA permits "Parties to accord differential, and even less favorable, treatment where appropriate to meet legitimate regulatory objectives."

9. The United States believes its interpretation is confirmed by Article 2101, which provides that:

> nothing in . . . Chapter Twelve (Cross-Border Trade in Services) . . . shall be construed to prevent the adoption or enforcement by any Party of measures necessary to secure compliance with laws or regulations that are not inconsistent with the provisions of this Agreement, including those relating to health and safety and consumer protection.

10. The United States also rejects Mexico's contention that the U.S. failure to implement Annex I with regard to cross-border trucking services and investment was politically motivated. At best, the United States contends, political motivation is "only of marginal relevance" to this case in the sense that highway safety has generated controversy in the United States. Moreover, the United States asserts that WTO practice is to avoid inquiring into the intent of parties accused of WTO violations. The issue, rather, is "whether Mexico has met its burden of proving a violation by the United States of its NAFTA obligations."

The Panel then conducted an exhaustive analysis over 285 paragraphs, and made the following:

Findings, Determinations and Recommendations

A. Findings and Determinations

295. On the basis of the analysis set out above, the Panel unanimously determines that the U.S. blanket refusal to review and consider for approval any Mexican-owned carrier applications for authority to provide cross-border trucking services was and remains a breach of the U.S. obligations under Annex I (reservations for existing measures and liberalization commitments), Article 1202 (national treatment for cross-border services), and Article 1203 (most-favored-nation treatment for cross-border services) of NAFTA. An exception to these obligations is not authorized by the "in like circumstances" language in Articles 1202 and 1203, or by the exceptions set out in Chapter Nine or under Article 2101.

296. The Panel unanimously determines that the inadequacies of the Mexican regulatory system provide an insufficient legal basis for the United States to maintain a moratorium on the consideration of applications for U.S. operating authority from Mexican-owned and/or domiciled trucking service providers.

297. The Panel further unanimously determines that the United States was and remains in breach of its obligations under Annex I (reservations for existing measures and liberalization commitments), Article 1102 (national treatment), and Article 1103 (most-favored-nation treatment) to permit Mexican nationals to invest in enterprises in the United States that provide transportation of international cargo within the United States.

298. It is important to note what the Panel is not determining. It is not making a determination that the Parties to NAFTA may not set the level of protection that they consider appropriate in pursuit of legitimate regulatory objectives. It is not disagreeing that the safety of trucking services is a legitimate regulatory objective. Nor is the Panel imposing a limitation on the application of safety standards properly established and applied pursuant to the applicable obligations of the Parties under NAFTA. Furthermore, since the issue before the Panel concerns the so-called "blanket" ban, the Panel expresses neither approval nor disapproval of past determinations by appropriate regulatory authorities relating to the safety of any individual truck operators, drivers or vehicles, as to which the Panel did not receive any submissions or evidence.

B. Recommendations

299. The Panel recommends that the United States take appropriate steps to bring its practices with respect to cross-border trucking services and investment into compliance with its obligations under the applicable provisions of NAFTA.

300. The Panel notes that compliance by the United States with its NAFTA obligations would not necessarily require providing favorable consideration to all or to any specific number of applications from Mexican-owned trucking firms, when it is evident that a particular applicant or applicants may be unable to comply with U.S. trucking regulations when operating in the United States. Nor does it require that all Mexican-domiciled firms currently providing trucking services in the United States be allowed to continue to do so, if and when they fail to comply with U.S. safety regulations. The United States may not be required to treat applications from Mexican trucking firms in exactly the same manner as applications from U.S. or Canadian firms, as long as they are reviewed on a case by case basis. U.S. authorities are responsible for the safe operation of trucks within U.S. territory, whether ownership is U.S., Canadian or Mexican.

301. Similarly, it may not be unreasonable for a NAFTA Party to conclude that to ensure compliance with its own local standards by service providers from another NAFTA country, it may be necessary to implement different procedures with respect to such service providers. Thus, to the extent that the inspection and licensing requirements for Mexican trucks and drivers wishing to operate in the United States may not be "like" those in place in the United States, different methods of ensuring compliance with the U.S. regulatory regime may be justifiable. However, if in order to satisfy its own legitimate safety concerns the United States decides, exceptionally, to impose requirements on Mexican carriers that differ from those imposed on U.S. or Canadian carriers, then any such decision must (a) be made in good faith with respect to a legitimate safety concern and (b) implement differing requirements that fully conform with all relevant NAFTA provisions.

302. These considerations are inapplicable with regard to the U.S. refusal to permit Mexican nationals to invest in enterprises in the United States that provide transportation of international cargo within the United States, since both Mexico and the United States have agreed that such investment does not raise issues of safety.

Source: North American Free Trade Agreement Arbitral Panel Established Pursuant to Chapter Twenty, In the Matter of Cross-Border Trucking Services (Secretariat File No. USA-MEX-98-2008-01), www.nafta-sec-alena.org/app/DocRepository/1/Dispute/english/NAFTA_Chapter_20/USA/ub98010e.pdf.

Dispute Settlement and Review Procedures

The ministerial Trade Commission and the administrative Secretariat are responsible for implementation of the agreement, and manage its structure and process in dispute settlement.

   As with many international organizations, the first stage is consultation, in the hope of an early and amicable settlement between governments. If this fails, any member may call a meeting of the Trade Commission with all three governments represented. If the countries at issue cannot resolve their dispute through the Commission and no other mechanism can be agreed upon (mediation, arbitration, etc.), then proceedings may be initiated. In many cases, this could be under either GATT or NAFTA, given their overlapping coverage. Once one forum is selected, the other is then closed for that dispute. If no agreement on forum can be reached, then the NAFTA forum prevails.

A NAFTA arbitral panel is comprised of five members, charged with making findings of fact, determining whether a party is acting inconsistently with its NAFTA obligations, and may make recommendations to resolve the complaint. The third country may choose to join in the complaint, make submissions, or remain apart. These five experts are chosen by agreement from a roster and may be from non-NAFTA states.

The time limits for hearing and disposition are fixed, and within 90 days of selection, the panel is to render a confidential initial report, in the hope of spurring settlement. Thirty days after that, the report becomes final and is published by the Commission. Once the report is received, the parties to it are to mutually decide on a final resolution, which normally would be a course of action in line with the panel recommendation. If a mutually satisfactory resolution cannot be reached, then the aggrieved party may suspend benefits extended to the other in equal measure.

Since the member nations retain their right to make antidumping and countervailing duty determinations, these national measures are subject to panel review in an effort to prevent them from becoming used as barriers to trade. The panel review takes the place of what would have been judicial review in the country applying the measure. The decision of the panel is binding, and may uphold the determination or return it to the national authority for reconsideration not inconsistent with the panel opinion.

In the case of private investment, arbitration is permitted in disputes between investors and NAFTA governments, with recognition and enforcement of awards carried out under national law.

 Mercosur

The Mercado Común del Sur Treaty (Mercosur),[9] or the Common Market of the Southern Cone, was established by the Treaty of Asunción on January 1, 1995, between Brazil, Argentina, Paraguay, and Uruguay. Together, their economies represent two-thirds of South American GDP. While outside the operation of the treaty, Bolivia and Chile have associate member status.

Mercosur aspires to one day become a common market, but these plans have been deferred on an indefinite basis so that members may first achieve closer approximation of their economic policies. As such, Mercosur is a customs union with a common external tariff ranging over 85 percent of all traded goods. Even this has been under pressure, due to Brazilian and Argentinean economic instability, which in 2001 threatened to reduce Mercosur to a free trade agreement. The objectives, however, have been reaffirmed, primarily to maintain investor confidence in the arrangement. Those objectives are, per Article 1 of the treaty,[10]

> The free movement of goods, services and factors of production between countries through, inter alia, the elimination of customs duties and non-tariff restrictions on the movement of goods, and any other equivalent measures;

[9]Or Mercosul, in Portuguese, bearing in mind that it is the official language of Brazil.

[10]Treaty of Asunción, the Mercosur authoritative text, available in Spanish at http://www.mercosur.org.uy/espanol/snor/normativa/asuncion.htm with English translation by the Organization of American States at http://www.sice.oas.org/trade/mrcsr/mrcsrtoc.asp.

The establishment of a common external tariff and the adoption of a common trade policy in relation to third States or groups of States, and the co-ordination of positions in regional and international economic and commercial forums;

The co-ordination of macroeconomic and sectoral policies between the States Parties in the areas of foreign trade, agriculture, industry, fiscal and monetary matters, foreign exchange and capital, services, customs, transport and communications and any other areas that may be agreed upon, in order to ensure proper competition between the States Parties;

The commitment by States Parties to harmonize their legislation in the relevant areas in order to strengthen the integration process.

It is an ambitious agenda, following the global trend, and while it has had its problems due to economic conditions within member states, it has also achieved significant success in freer trade. The lists of exceptions maintained by members remain long, but the encouragement for their continued reduction lies in the rapid increases since 1995 in both value and volume of intramember trade.

Like NAFTA, rules of origin are in place to qualify trade for preferential tariffs, based on any of exclusive origin, a 60 percent Mercosur content rule based on final value, or transformation in tariff classification.

The Treaty does not provide for supranational institutions as in the case of the European Union, nor does it possess an independent court. As a result, disputes are a matter for direct negotiation between parties, with the good offices of its Common Market Group and the Council of the Common Market providing conciliation, mediation, and recommendations to the parties.

Free Trade Area of the Americas

Leaders of the 34 democracies in the Americas agreed in December of 1994 to pursue the creation of a single free trade agreement in the Americas, with a target date for completion in 2005. A series of ministerial meetings took place during the preparatory phase of the FTAA process, culminating in the formal launch of negotiations in April 1998, which produced its first draft text in April 2001.

National trade ministers from each government continue to meet on an 18-month basis, to guide a Trade Negotiations Committee comprised of deputy ministers for trade of the parties. This latter committee directly manages the progress of negotiations conducted by nine negotiating groups. Each negotiating group has a specific mandate, which indicates the priorities within this future free trade area. These are market access; investment; services; government procurement; dispute settlement; agriculture; intellectual property rights; subsidies, antidumping, and countervailing duties; and competition policy.

Regional Integration in Europe—From Common Market to Union

The European Union is the largest and most successful experiment in regional integration in the world.[11] It is also not easy to understand the EU today, or forecast its future actions, without a solid understanding of the forces and history behind it. Certainly there are larger and more important U.S. trading partners when comparing individual EU members on a state-by-state basis (Canada, Mexico, and Japan being examples), but

[11]The European Union includes as of early 2004, Austria, Belgium, Denmark, Ireland, Finland, France, Germany, Greece, Italy, Luxembourg, the Netherlands, Portugal, Spain, Sweden, and the United Kingdom. It is set to expand in 2004 and beyond to include Bulgaria, the Czech Republic, Estonia, Cyprus, Latvia, Lithuania, Hungary, Malta, Poland, Romania, Slovenia, Slovakia, and Turkey. See www.europa.eu.int.

- When the EU is viewed collectively, no other market matches it in international business opportunities.
- It is the largest single market in the world save for China and India.

- Its wealth and overall purchasing power are second to no other foreign market.
- Its regulation of business can affect millions of U.S. trading relationships at a single stroke.
- It is an active regulator and frequently takes approaches different than the United States.

As a result, it is vital that international businesspersons understand the EU and its business regulation in considerable detail.

The European Economic Community and European Union

Origin and History

The origins and history of the European Union are important to the international businessperson for these are the means toward understanding the reality of supranational governance of a marketplace with a population of 375 million persons, presently one-third larger than the United States. Further, the EU is set to expand to 440 million persons with its new applicant member countries. The present members are developed markets with established demand for imported products and services. The applicant members are actively seeking foreign investment and are increasingly in a position to demand imports.

Some commentators believe this large union, moving from 15 members to 28, will be too awkward to be workable. While it may perhaps outgrow its clothes, it is not going to go away. The European Union will continue to be the dominant governor of Europe's internal market and its trade with the world, regardless of what political form it may adopt in the future. Despite its evolution, the European Union has never been, and will never be, far from its historical roots. Just as U.S. leaders repeat the wisdom of "founding fathers," or invoke names such as Washington, Jefferson, Lincoln, and Kennedy, their European counterparts cast an even more recent shadow over affairs on the Continent.

Immediately after the Second World War (1939–45), Europe was again a smoking ruin, having stuck to its historical timetable of two or three major wars per century. On this landscape lay the full unhappy history of European nationalism and militarism, and the dark future of U.S.–Soviet confrontation. Yet amidst the despair of having repeated the "War to end all Wars" of 1914–1918, there was no shortage of philosophers, a breed with which Europe is also traditionally well endowed.

The question then was whether their words would be turned into action, and whether a second European Renaissance would see the creation of "something" that would ensure peace. Three names stand out earlier and taller than the rest in conveying what that "something" should be:

- Winston Churchill, Britain's wartime prime minister.
- Altiero Spinelli, an Italian antifascist turned Federalist.
- Jean Monnet, a French government planner and former Deputy Secretary-General of the League of Nations.

Winston Churchill spoke of the need for a European regional family as a "United States of Europe."[12] Spinelli called for a "movement for a free and united Europe."[13] Monnet, in-

---

[12]Winston Churchill, *Speech at Zurich University,* September 19, 1946, http://www.eurplace.org/federal/churdisco.html.

[13]Altiero Spinelli, *The Ventotene Manifesto* (1941), http://www.eurplace.org/federal/spinelen.html.

strumental in drafting the Schuman Declaration,[14] asserted that war was the consequence of failing to achieve a "united Europe."

These and similar sentiments propelled France to do the nearly unthinkable: to actually build peace (as opposed to just the absence of war) with Germany, still the enemy in the minds of many. The plan was modest and immense at the same time: to bring control over coal and steel production in both France and Germany under a single supervisory body. It only represented two industries, but it was the geographic region (Alsace-Lorraine–Ruhr) over which the two nations had warred previously, and the one economic sector key to both reconstruction and making armaments. The proposal was made to Germany in May 1950 by the then–Foreign Minister of France, Robert Schuman, and led to the creation of the 1951 European Coal and Steel Community (ECSC) Treaty.[15] In addition to France and Germany, Italy, Belgium, the Netherlands, and Luxembourg joined as equal founding members, and are termed "The Six."

Political union between The Six was raised soon thereafter, but was stillborn. "Union" then, as now, did not mean unification or fusion or a State of Europe, but rather meant joined in joint action and policy coordination, a plurality with distinctive parts.

From the success of the ECSC Treaty, the European Atomic Energy Community (EURATOM) Treaty[16] and the Treaty Establishing the European Economic Community[17] followed rapidly. All are advances toward the goal of an "ever closer union"[18] "among peoples long divided by bloody conflicts . . . to lay the foundations for institutions which will give direction to a destiny henceforward shared."[19]

The Treaty Establishing the European Community (the TEC, formerly and formally styled "the European Economic Community") demanded the approximation of economic polices and the establishment of the common market,[20] including both a common external tariff and common commercial policy, as well as closer relations between the member states.[21] It continues to be the most powerful treaty in terms of dictating the shape of the European internal market, as amended by treaties that followed it in time.

The "common market" refers to the basic freedoms enjoyed under this essentially constitutional guarantee: freedom of movement of goods, establishment, services, workers (as distinct from persons), and capital and payments.

Member states retain their identities and those powers falling outside the treaty. However, in what is known as "competence creep," more and more policy matters are taken to be within the scope of the treaty, and thus national government competence has been continually eroded.

While the three Communities remained legally separate (the ECSC having expired in 2002), their three sets of governing institutions were merged into one set of institutions in 1965, and thereafter the European (Economic) Community eclipsed both the ECSC and EURATOM.

[14]Robert B. Schuman, *Declaration on Behalf of the Government of France,* May 9, 1950, http://www.robert-schuman.org/anglais/robert-schuman/declaration.htm.

[15]"Treaty Establishing the European Coal and Steel Community," April 18, 1951, Paris, http://europa.eu.int/abc/obj/treaties/en/entoc29.htm [herein after ECSC].

[16]"Treaty Establishing the European Atomic Energy Community," March 25, 1957, Rome, http://europa.eu.int/abc/obj/treaties/en/entoc38.htm.

[17]"Treaty Establishing the European Economic Community," March 25, 1957, Rome, http://www.europa.eu.int/eur-lex/en/treaties/selected/livre2_c.html [herein after TEC].

[18]"Treaty on European Union," February 7, 1992, Maastricht, http://europa.eu.int/eur-lex/en/treaties/dat/eu_cons_treaty_en.pdf [herein after TEC], Title I, Article A.

[19]ECSC, Preamble.

[20]TEC, Articles 2, 3, 4, 5, and 6.

[21]Ibid., Article 2.

The European Community has legal personality[22] and a supranational character, the latter illustrated by its power to compel action (or inaction) of member states.[23] Beyond simply compelling action, it may impose itself directly upon the legal systems of the member states through the direct applicability of its regulations[24] (taking precedence over national legislation) and their direct effect in conferring rights upon those subject to Community law.[25] Additionally, the Community may exercise powers not provided for by the treaty[26] where such powers are necessary to achieve one of the objectives of the treaty in the course of operation of the common market. The total of these (personality, power over sovereign nations, and discretionary power) makes for a truly supranational body.

Denmark, Ireland, and the United Kingdom (acknowledged as the most reluctant member) joined the Community in 1973, as did Greece in 1981, and Spain and Portugal in 1986, then making a total of 12.

The period from the mid 1970s to the mid 1980s was one of stagnation for the European Community, as members focused on the economic troubles of the international oil crisis, inflation, and their domestic economies. The 1986 Single European Act helped end this period, focusing on integration commitments geared to completing the internal market (a TEC objective), and it also broached policy issues in the area of monetary union and foreign policy.[27]

This was moved forward with the 1992 Treaty on European Union (TEU).[28] In it, as its name implies, the world is first introduced to a European political expression of "Union." The Union is not given a legal personality, and it remains even today a state of mind, but it is one that now confers citizenship and passports. It does not create new institutions of its own; rather, it relies on the single institutional framework of the Communities.[29]

The TEU sought to combat the negative distorting effect on the common market of variances in exchange rates and interest rates among member states by setting conditions for future economic and monetary union, with the intention of creating a single currency to replace national currencies. It also created what are now habitually known as the "Three Pillars" (illustrated below), adding new Community fields of action and matters for further cooperation on an intergovernmental basis.

The first pillar is that of the European Communities, consisting of matters solely within the competence (and control) of Community institutions. The second pillar consists of the common foreign and security policy, which is managed essentially on an intergovernmental basis (i.e., not subject to full Community control) and therefore with the potential for member state veto. The third pillar was justice and home affairs, now termed Police and Judicial Cooperation in Criminal Matters, which is also administered on an intergovernmental basis.

Austria, Finland, and Sweden joined the Union in 1995 (creating 15 members) and the Schengen Agreement, allowing free internal passage of all persons (whether EU citizens or not), came into force, although the United Kingdom and Ireland remain outside this arrangement.

In 1997 the "Consolidated" Treaty of Amsterdam was signed rendering the TEC and its amendments more readable, and providing clarification as to civil rights, personal mobil-

---

[22]Ibid., Article 281.

[23]Ibid., Article 10.

[24]Ibid., Article 249.

[25]P. S. R. F. Mathijsen, *A Guide to European Union Law,* 7th ed. (London: Sweet & Maxwell, 1999), p. 27. Direct effect allows individuals to invoke principles of Community law before national tribunals.

[26]TEC, Article 308.

[27]"Single European Act of February 17 and 28, 1986," entered into force July 1, 1987, http://www.europa.eu.int/eur-lex/en/treaties/selected/livre509.html.

[28]See footnote 18.

[29]TEU, Articles 1 and 3.

ity, and citizenship; extending aspects of the common foreign and security policy; and setting preconditions for further enlargement of the union.[30] It came into force in 1999. In 2002, the final stage of monetary union was reached with the introduction of euro coins and notes into circulation and the withdrawal of national currency.

The Treaty of Nice, which came into force in 2003, provided for more instances of decision making based on qualified majority voting and institutional change to further accommodate impending enlargement.[31] This enlargement will see 13 more nations join,[32] in two or more groups, likely before 2010, and sooner, rather than later.

The Three Pillars of the European Union and the Distribution of Principal Responsibilities

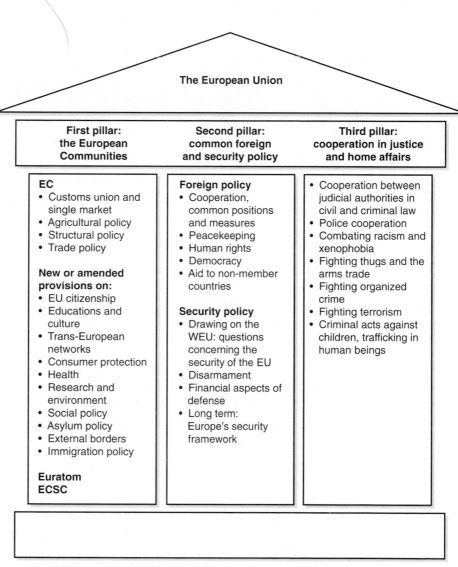

The European Union

First pillar: the European Communities	Second pillar: common foreign and security policy	Third pillar: cooperation in justice and home affairs
EC • Customs union and single market • Agricultural policy • Structural policy • Trade policy **New or amended provisions on:** • EU citizenship • Educations and culture • Trans-European networks • Consumer protection • Health • Research and environment • Social policy • Asylum policy • External borders • Immigration policy **Euratom** **ECSC**	**Foreign policy** • Cooperation, common positions and measures • Peacekeeping • Human rights • Democracy • Aid to non-member countries **Security policy** • Drawing on the WEU: questions concerning the security of the EU • Disarmament • Financial aspects of defense • Long term: Europe's security framework	• Cooperation between judicial authorities in civil and criminal law • Police cooperation • Combating racism and xenophobia • Fighting thugs and the arms trade • Fighting organized crime • Fighting terrorism • Criminal acts against children, trafficking in human beings

Source: © European Communities, 1998–2003. Reproduced without charge and through the kind permission of the European Communities. http://europa.eu.int/eur-lex/en/about/abc/abc_12.html.

[30]"Treaty of Amsterdam," October 2, 1997, Amsterdam, http://www.europa.eu.int/eur-lex/en/treaties/selected/livre545.html.

[31]"Treaty of Nice," February 26, 2001, Nice, http://www.europa.eu.int/eur-lex/en/treaties/dat/nice_treaty_en.pdf.

[32]Bulgaria, Cyprus, the Czech Republic, Estonia, Latvia, Lithuania, Hungary, Malta, Poland, Romania, Slovenia, Slovakia, and Turkey are current applicants under active negotiation.

Institutions of the European Union

Having no institutions of its own, the Union operates through the European Council (heads of state or government of the member states) and the five official institutions of the European Community.

Simplified Organization Chart of the European Union

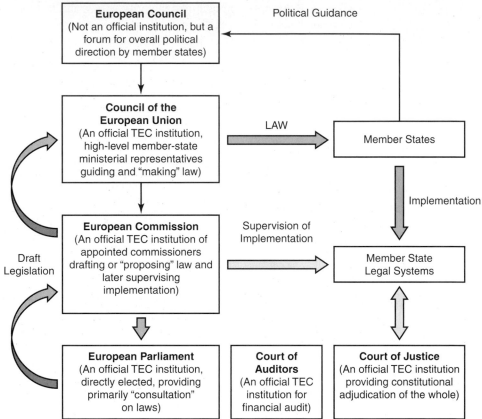

The six institutions of the Union (the first unofficial and the five official) are

European Council (heads of state and government)

Council of the European Union (ministerial representatives)

European Commission (appointees)

European Parliament (elected)

Court of Justice (appointed judiciary)

Court of Auditors (financial auditors)

European Council

The European Council (not to be confused with the Council of the European Union, but born from it) gives the high-level political guidance required for setting policy objectives of the Union. It meets twice per year with the president of the Commission and receives an address from the president of the Parliament. As it is primarily comprised of national politicians, it is therefore an intergovernmental forum, and while it does not create law, it shapes it. The European Council projects a common position representing the member states in international issues through the development of the Union's common foreign and security policy.

Council of the European Union

Universally known as simply "the Council," this is the decision maker in European Union affairs, and as such acts as the Union legislature, despite the existence of a Parliament. With a rotating six-month presidency under successive member states, it is composed of cabinet ministers of the member states, who meet according to their functional responsibility. Finance ministers meet as "the Council" on finance issues, agriculture ministers meet as "the Council" on agricultural issues, and so on. Their routine work is prepared by COREPER. This is a body of permanent ambassadorial representatives from each member state together with bureaucrats from national ministries and a permanent General Secretariat.

The Council is therefore an intergovernmental body that intersects with the affairs of the Union and Community. Given its national political composition, Council direction is a product of domestic political pressures while attempting to create compromises and advances that will be workable Community-wide.

The function of the Council is to ensure that treaty objectives are met through its legislation and to ensure the coordination of the general economic policies of the member states.[33] It adopts international agreements within the Community sphere on behalf of EU members. The measures enacted by the Council (of all kinds) are customarily delegated to the Commission for implementation.

While the Council takes such decisions, it lacks the right of initiative to create draft laws itself, which is a function reserved to the Commission. The Council, however, does have the power to require the Commission to present such "proposals" for consideration, so that a legislative void cannot be created. Depending on the type of legislative proposal, Council decisions may be made by simple majority, qualified majority, or unanimity. Unanimity requirements apply to issues on a constitutional scale (e.g., treaty amendments) or sensitive issues such as taxation, while a qualified majority (62 out of 87 votes)[34] is becoming more and more the norm; otherwise, a simple majority from among the 15 nations is sufficient.[35]

To legally take a decision, the Council will also require input from the Parliament. This may be actual assent, agreement, or codecision (and happily for democrats, increasingly so), but in many instances it is just mere consultation of parliamentary opinion.

European Commission

The European Commission is the most powerful Community institution. As noted above, it possesses the right of initiative for legislative proposals and is charged with implementing the decisions enacted by the Council on those proposals. A civil service made up of 25 Directorates-General (each responsible for one or more of the functional areas related to Community policies) conducts this implementation.

Moreover, the Commission is the guardian of the treaty itself, monitoring the activities of member states and taking action against them (or other institutions) in cases of noncompliance with treaty provisions or Community law.[36] The Commission has not been shy in exercising this power, bringing member states and institutions before the Court of Justice.

To do this effectively, the Commission has been granted independence in its operation from national interests. The Commission as an institution and Commissioners individually must act in the interests of the Community at all times, neither seeking nor taking national

---

[33]TEC, Article 202.

[34]When weighted for a qualified majority vote, the 15 nations have the following number of votes: France, Germany, Italy, and the United Kingdom, 10 votes each; Spain, 8; Belgium, Greece, the Netherlands, and Portugal, 5; Austria and Sweden, 4; Denmark, Finland, and Ireland, 3; and Luxembourg, 2.

[35]TEC, Article 205.

[36]TEC, Article 211.

instructions from the member states. The Commission president and 20 commissioners are nominated for a five-year term by the member states in a two-stage process subject to parliamentary approval.[37]

European Parliament

The European Parliament is not a legislature in the way that the term is known in the traditions of the United States or the British Commonwealth. It is a forum for discussion that has input into decision-making processes dominated by the Commission and the Council.

The Parliament has no right of initiative, this despite being able to provide suggested amendments to Commission proposals. Even where it possesses a right of joint decision with the Council, it cannot force its position on the Council. It can only slow and stop the legislative process, but even then it is subject to a conciliation process intended to bring the two institutions into agreement on an amended text.

The Parliament is not completely without power, for it has the right to reject nominees for president of the Commission and commissioners, as well as the right to reject the Community budget, neither of which are insubstantial powers. It may pose questions and has the right to answers from both the Council and Commission. Subsequent enlargements of the Union also will be subject to approval of the Parliament. The role of the Parliament is slowly expanding and is being given greater constitutional power toward ensuring representative democracy. Direct control of the EU through general election is still, however, a long time off in the future.

Elections for the 626-seat[38] Parliament are held by direct vote of the people every five years. Plenary sessions are held in Strasbourg, France, while committees meet in Brussels, Belgium, moving in a continual monthly shuttle between these cities, while the Parliament's Secretariat is based in Luxembourg. Such historical oddities as these are the product of original political compromises and are lightning rods for critics who charge that the Union is unworkable. What was national pride in the 1950s is now seen as wasted expenditure in the 21st century, and will likely be soon brought to an end.

Court of Justice

The Court of Justice, with its seat in Luxembourg, is made up of 15 judges and 8 advocates-general. It acts as a constitutional court to ensure uniform interpretation and application of the treaties and Community law.[39] It may hear actions brought by member states or institutions for annulment of Community law based on incompatibility with the treaties, or the reverse, actions against an institution or member states for failure to act.[40]

Also in its constitutional interpretation role, it serves as a supreme court for national courts, which are obliged to apply Community law in the course of justice. These national courts may, and courts from which there is no national right of appeal must, refer questions of interpretation of Community law to the Court of Justice as a preliminary reference case.[41] The results of such preliminary references are binding on all courts in all member states.

The judicial office of an advocate-general is one that is largely unfamiliar to lawyers of the common law tradition. He or she acts in an independent and impartial capacity as what

---

[37]France, Germany, Italy, Spain, and the United Kingdom appoint two nominees each, with one each from each of the remaining members.

[38]A 700-seat maximum has been established in light of impending enlargement. As at early 2004, Germany has 99 seats; France, Italy, and the United Kingdom each has 87 seats; Spain 64; the Netherlands 31; Belgium, Greece, and Portugal 25 each; Sweden 22; Austria 21; Denmark and Finland 16 each; Ireland 15; and Luxembourg 6.

[39]TEC, Article 220.

[40]Ibid., Articles 226–33.

[41]Ibid., Article 234; for that reason, it is commonly known as an Article 234 Reference.

may be described a "friend of the court." An advocate-general prepares a reasoned submission as to law and recommended disposition of the case, delivering it in open court, for consideration by the court when it retires to consider its own judgment. Advocates-general of the court are selected on same basis as its judges; namely, qualifications sufficient to make them candidates for the highest court of their respective countries.

The Court of Justice also acts as an appellate court, on matters of law only, from the Court of First Instance, which is a separate judicial chamber attached to the Court of Justice. The Court of First Instance has jurisdiction in principle to hear any Community case except a preliminary reference,[42] but in practice hears

1. Actions for annulment or failure to act brought against Community institutions by legal or natural persons.
2. Actions brought by legal or natural persons in response to Community measures directed at or concerning them.
3. Internal disputes between the Community and its staff.

The Court of First Instance was created in 1989 as a means to cope with case backlog and to allow the Court of Justice to concentrate on cases of broader legal significance, either in original hearing, by reference, or on appeal.

Court of Auditors

This 15-member institution is charged with conducting the audit under the Treaty Establishing the European Community.[43] It is to examine whether all revenue has been received and all expenditures have been incurred in a lawful and regular manner, and whether the financial management has been sound.[44] Its annual reports are forwarded to the other institutions and are published in the *Official Journal of the European Communities.*

Chlef Legal Implications for International Traders

The centerpiece of the Treaty Establishing the European Community (TEC) is comprised of the common market and an economic and monetary union, as required by the tasks and activities set out in Articles 2 through 4 of the TEC. These articles provide the international trader (located anywhere in the world) the right to treat the EU member states as a single market.

Articles 2 through 4, Treaty Establishing the European Community

Article 2 (ex Article 2)

The Community shall have as its task, by establishing a common market and an economic and monetary union and by implementing common policies or activities referred to in Articles 3 and 4, to promote throughout the Community a harmonious, balanced and sustainable development of economic activities, a high level of employment and of social protection, equality between men and women, sustainable and non-inflationary growth, a high degree of competitiveness and convergence of economic performance, a high level of protection and improvement of the quality of the environment, the raising of the standard of

---

[42]Ibid., Article 225.
[43]Ibid., Article 246.
[44]Ibid., Article 248.

living and quality of life, and economic and social cohesion and solidarity among Member States.

Article 3 (ex Article 3)

1. For the purposes set out in Article 2, the activities of the Community shall include, as provided in this Treaty and in accordance with the timetable set out therein:
   a. the prohibition, as between Member States, of customs duties and quantitative restrictions on the import and export of goods, and of all other measures having equivalent effect;
   b. a common commercial policy;
   c. an internal market characterised by the abolition, as between Member States, of obstacles to the free movement of goods, persons, services and capital;
   d. measures concerning the entry and movement of persons as provided for in Title IV;
   e. a common policy in the sphere of agriculture and fisheries;
   f. a common policy in the sphere of transport;
   g. a system ensuring that competition in the internal market is not distorted;
   h. the approximation of the laws of Member States to the extent required for the functioning of the common market;
   i. the promotion of coordination between employment policies of the Member States with a view to enhancing their effectiveness by developing a coordinated strategy for employment;
   j. a policy in the social sphere comprising a European Social Fund;
   k. the strengthening of economic and social cohesion;
   l. a policy in the sphere of the environment;
   m. the strengthening of the competitiveness of Community industry;
   n. the promotion of research and technological development;
   o. encouragement for the establishment and development of trans-European networks;
   p. a contribution to the attainment of a high level of health protection;
   q. a contribution to education and training of quality and to the flowering of the cultures of the Member States;
   r. a policy in the sphere of development cooperation;
   s. the association of the overseas countries and territories in order to increase trade and promote jointly economic and social development;
   t. a contribution to the strengthening of consumer protection;
   u. measures in the spheres of energy, civil protection and tourism.
2. In all the activities referred to in this Article, the Community shall aim to eliminate inequalities, and to promote equality, between men and women.

Article 4 (ex Article 3a)

1. For the purposes set out in Article 2, the activities of the Member States and the Community shall include, as provided in this Treaty and in accordance with the timetable set out therein, the adoption of an economic policy which is based on the close coordination of Member States' economic policies, on the internal market and on the definition of common objectives, and conducted in accordance with the principle of an open market economy with free competition.
2. Concurrently with the foregoing, and as provided in this Treaty and in accordance with the timetable and the procedures set out therein, these activities shall include the irre-

vocable fixing of exchange rates leading to the introduction of a single currency, the ECU,[45] and the definition and conduct of a single monetary policy and exchange-rate policy the primary objective of both of which shall be to maintain price stability and, without prejudice to this objective, to support the general economic policies in the Community, in accordance with the principle of an open market economy with free competition.

3. These activities of the Member States and the Community shall entail compliance with the following guiding principles: stable prices, sound public finances and monetary conditions and a sustainable balance of payments.

Source: http://europa.eu.int/eur-lex/en/treaties/dat/ec_cons_treaty_en.pdf.

The competence of the Community to make law, and particularly whether any such competence is exclusive to the Community or shared with the member states, is not always clear-cut. An evolving body of Court of Justice case law addresses that issue pending future treaty clarification. However, of importance to international businesspersons and lawyers, where there has been harmonization or common policy created by the Community, the Community competence is exclusive. Most importantly to these international traders is the exclusive Community competence in matters covered by Article 3(1)(a) through (h).

Community law can take the form of regulations, directives, decisions, recommendations, or opinions.[46] They are differentiated as follows:

European Community Legislative Measures

Community Measure	Breadth of Application	Binding Nature	Applicability	Creation of Legal Rights
Regulation (most powerful)	Communitywide	Binding in entirety	Yes, directly applicable	Yes, direct effect
Directive (powerful)	Addressed to one or more member states	Binding as to result member state is to achieve	No, requires transposition through national legislation	Most often with direct effect
Decision (very significant)	Addressed to member state or individual or legal person	Binding in entirety	Directly applicable	Yes, direct effect
Recommendation or opinion (weak)	Application clear from context	Not binding	Little more than moral suasion	No creation of rights

Regulations and directives are very powerful legislative instruments that must be respected by national legislatures of member states. While the focus of these instruments is to create a harmonized internal market, the resulting form of harmony may be completely different than the results expected by international traders.

For example, the requirements for safeguarding of personal data gathered in the course of commercial business differ very greatly from North American practice. European Union directives[47] enshrine confidentiality and the requirement of consent in dealing with personal data, even to the extent of forbidding transmission to third countries, unless adequate confidentiality safeguards are in place in those countries. While Canada's statutory safeguards

[45]Originally the European currency unit, now the euro.

[46]TEC, Article 249.

[47]Particularly Directive 95/46 of 24 October 1995 on protection of personal data and Directive 2002/58/EC on protection of privacy in the electronic communications sector.

have received approval by the European Commission, those of the United States have not. This considerably complicates international transfer of customer data, for example, between a European subsidiary company and an American parent corporation.

Internal Market Freedom for Goods

The common market, with no definition other than a reference in Article 2 of the TEC, is made up of the Community's common policies together with its "internal market," which is an "area without internal frontiers where the free movement of goods, persons,[48] services and capital is ensured."[49] The importance of free movement of business elements should be instantly apparent to international businesspersons.

The free movement of goods objectives of Article 3(1)(a), (b), and (c), reproduced in the treaty extract above, are amplified in Articles 23 to 30. In those articles, customs duties and quantitative restrictions on the import and export of goods between members, as well as "all other measures having equivalent effect," are prohibited. Removal of customs duties and quantitative restrictions is an objective matter, but "all other measures having equivalent effect" immediately raises the legal question of: what is "equivalent"? As Article 30 contains restrictions that member states *may* place on the free movement of goods, it is equally important to understand the constitutional limit on this freedom.

Articles 23 through 30, Treaty Establishing the European Community

Article 23 (ex Article 9)

1. The Community shall be based upon a customs union which shall cover all trade in goods and which shall involve the prohibition between Member States of customs duties on imports and exports and of all charges having equivalent effect, and the adoption of a common customs tariff in their relations with third countries.

2. The provisions of Article 25 and of Chapter 2 of this Title shall apply to products originating in Member States and to products coming from third countries which are in free circulation in Member States.

Article 24 (ex Article 10)

Products coming from a third country shall be considered to be in free circulation in a Member State if the import formalities have been complied with and any customs duties or charges having equivalent effect which are payable have been levied in that Member State, and if they have not benefited from a total or partial drawback of such duties or charges.

Article 25 (ex Article 12)

Customs duties on imports and exports and charges having equivalent effect shall be prohibited between Member States. This prohibition shall also apply to customs duties of a fiscal nature.

---

[48]Freedom of movement of "persons," more generally, arises from Title IV of the TEC (Visas, Asylum, Immigration and Other Policies Related to the Free Movement of Persons), rather than being part of the internal market provisions, which are limited to workers' rights.

[49]TEC, Article 14.

Article 26 (ex Article 28)

Common Customs Tariff duties shall be fixed by the Council acting by a qualified majority on a proposal from the Commission.

Article 27 (ex Article 29)

In carrying out the tasks entrusted to it under this Chapter the Commission shall be guided by:

A. the need to promote trade between Member States and third countries;

B. developments in conditions of competition within the Community insofar as they lead to an improvement in the competitive capacity of undertakings;

C. the requirements of the Community as regards the supply of raw materials and semi-finished goods; in this connection the Commission shall take care to avoid distorting conditions of competition between Member States in respect of finished goods;

D. the need to avoid serious disturbances in the economies of Member States and to ensure rational development of production and an expansion of consumption within the Community.

Article 28 (ex Article 30)

Quantitative restrictions on imports and all measures having equivalent effect shall be prohibited between Member States.

Article 29 (ex Article 34)

Quantitative restrictions on exports, and all measures having equivalent effect, shall be prohibited between Member States.

Article 30 (ex Article 36)

The provisions of Articles 28 and 29 shall not preclude prohibitions or restrictions on imports, exports or goods in transit justified on grounds of public morality, public policy or public security; the protection of health and life of humans, animals or plants; the protection of national treasures possessing artistic, historic or archaeological value; or the protection of industrial and commercial property. Such prohibitions or restrictions shall not, however, constitute a means of arbitrary discrimination or a disguised restriction on trade between Member States.

Source: http://europa.eu.int/eur-lex/en/treaties/dat/ec_cons_treaty_en.pdf.

The following case represents interpretation by the European Court of Justice on the meaning of free movement of goods and measures having an equivalent effect to quantitative restrictions, and it is one of the cornerstones of Community jurisprudence.

In it, a Belgian firm—Dassonville—purchased scotch whisky produced in the United Kingdom (specifically Scotland) from a distributor located in France. At the time, 1970, the United Kingdom was not a member of the Community, and thus its exports did not benefit from direct right of free movement.

France and Belgium had different requirements when an imported good carried a regional designation like "Scotch." Belgian law required that the import bear a certificate of authenticity label issued by the United Kingdom, but France merely required a bond guarantee to be lodged with the French government. Not needing a label, the French importer had not obtained one, but did comply with the French law by lodging a bond. On purchasing the whisky from the French distributor, Dassonville therefore lacked the certificate labels required under Belgian law even though the goods were in legal circulation in France. The only way Dassonville could get such a certificate label would be to return the whisky to the UK authorities for inspection and labeling. As that would have been prohibitively expensive, he made his own labels, quoting the French bond registration number, relying on his right to import into Belgium what had been properly imported into France.

Dassonville had Belgian competitors, Fourcroy and Breuval, who themselves were importing directly from the United Kingdom (and thus in possession of certificate labels), acting as exclusive distributors in Belgium for the Scottish distillery. Fourcroy and Breuval did not appreciate Dassonville's commercial presence. Their exclusive dealing agreement with the distillery meant that the distillery could not sell to other Belgian distributors, but as Dassonville had purchased from the French, there was little that Fourcroy or Breuval could do about it. They did, however, complain that Dassonville should be prevented from importing into Belgium, as he lacked the correct certificate labels.

When brought before the national courts of Belgium for importing (from France) without proper certificates, the national court judge requested an Article 234 preliminary reference ruling (then Article 177) from the European Court of Justice. The first question was whether the Belgian requirement of a certificate must be considered as a quantitative restriction or as a measure having equivalent effect. The second question queried the exclusive deal of the Belgian competitors. Was it void on antitrust grounds (then Article 85, now Article 81) because, when coupled with the label requirement, no one except someone dealing directly with the distillery could legally import whisky into Belgium? This prevention of legal "parallel imports" was of serious concern to the Community. The reasoning of the court in the reference case in regard to both questions is laid out below. We shall return to the question of anticompetitive behavior and the effect of Article 81 provisions on international traders later in Chapter 12.

Case 8/74: *Procureur du Roi v. Dassonville*

In Case 8/74

Reference to the Court under Article 177 of the EEC Treaty[50] by the Tribunal de première instance of Brussels for a preliminary ruling in the criminal proceedings pending before that Court . . .

On the interpretation of Articles 30 to 33, 36 and 85 of the EEC Treaty,[51]

1. By judgment of 11 January 1974, received at the registry of the court on 8 February 1974, the Tribunal de première instance of Brussels referred, under Article 177 of the EEC Treaty, two questions on the interpretation of Articles 30, 31, 32, 33, 36 and 85 of the EEC Treaty, relating to the requirement of an official document issued by the government of the exporting country for products bearing a designation of origin.

2. By the first question it is asked whether a national provision prohibiting the import of goods bearing a designation of origin where such goods are not accompanied by an official document issued by the government of the exporting country certifying their right to such designation constitutes a measure having an effect equivalent to a quantitative restriction within the meaning of Article 30 of the Treaty.

---

[50]Article 177 is now Article 234.

[51]Article 30 is now Article 28; Article 36 is now Article 30; Article 85 is now Article 81.

3. This question was raised within the context of criminal proceedings instituted in Belgium against traders who duly acquired a consignment of scotch whisky in free circulation in France and imported it into Belgium without being in possession of a certificate of origin from the British customs authorities, thereby infringing Belgian rules.

4. It emerges from the file and from the oral proceedings that a trader, wishing to import into Belgium scotch whisky which is already in free circulation in France, can obtain such a certificate only with great difficulty, unlike the importer who imports directly from the producer country.

5. All trading rules enacted by member states which are capable of hindering, directly or indirectly, actually or potentially, intra-community trade are to be considered as measures having an effect equivalent to quantitative restrictions.

6. In the absence of a community system guaranteeing for consumers the authenticity of a product's designation of origin, if a member state takes measures to prevent unfair practices in this connexion, it is however subject to the condition that these measures should be reasonable and that the means of proof required should not act as a hindrance to trade between member states and should, in consequence, be accessible to all community nationals.

7. Even without having to examine whether or not such measures are covered by Article 36, they must not, in any case, by virtue of the principle expressed in the second sentence of that Article, constitute a means of arbitrary discrimination or a disguised restriction on trade between member states.

8. That may be the case with formalities, required by a member state for the purpose of proving the origin of a product, which only direct importers are really in a position to satisfy without facing serious difficulties.

9. Consequently, the requirement by a member state of a certificate of authenticity which is less easily obtainable by importers of an authentic product which has been put into free circulation in a regular manner in another member state than by importers of the same product coming directly from the country of origin constitutes a measure having an effect equivalent to a quantitative restriction as prohibited by the Treaty.

10. By the second question it is asked whether an agreement the effect of which is to restrict competition and adversely to affect trade between member states when taken in conjunction with a national rule with regard to certificates of origin is void when that agreement merely authorizes the exclusive importer to exploit that rule for the purpose of preventing parallel imports or does not prohibit him from doing so.

11. An exclusive dealing agreement falls within the prohibition of Article 85 when it impedes, in law or in fact, the importation of the products in question from other member states into the protected territory by persons other than the exclusive importer.

12. More particularly, an exclusive dealing agreement may adversely affect trade between member states and can have the effect of hindering competition if the concessionaire is able to prevent parallel imports from other member states into the territory covered by the concession by means of the combined effects of the agreement and a national law requiring the exclusive use of a certain means of proof of authenticity.

13. For the purpose of judging whether this is the case, account must be taken not only of the rights and obligations flowing from the provisions of the agreement, but also of the legal and economic context in which it is situated and, in particular, the possible existence of similar agreements concluded between the same producer and concessionaires established in other member states.

14. In this connexion, the maintenance within a member state of prices appreciably higher than those in force in another member state may prompt an examination as to whether

the exclusive dealing agreement is being used for the purpose of preventing importers from obtaining the means of proof of authenticity of the product in question, required by national rules of the type envisaged by the question.

15. However, the fact that an agreement merely authorizes the concessionaire to exploit such a national rule or does not prohibit him from doing so, does not suffice, in itself, to render the agreement null and void . . .

On those grounds, the Court, in answer to the questions referred to it by the Tribunal de première instance of Brussels by judgment of 11 January 1974, hereby rules:

1. The requirement of a member state of a certificate of authenticity which is less easily obtainable by importers of an authentic product which has been put into free circulation in a regular manner in another member state than by importers of the same product coming directly from the country of origin constitutes a measure having an effect equivalent to a quantitative restriction as prohibited by the Treaty.

2. The fact that an agreement merely authorizes the concessionaire to exploit such a national rule or does not prohibit him from doing so does not suffice, in itself, to render the agreement null and void.

Source: This case, as with all other ECJ cases, may be reviewed at http://curia.eu.int/en/content/juris/index.htm, where it is indexed by case number and year, here case #8 of 1974, indexed as Case 8/74.

The interest of this case to foreign (i.e., non–member state) international businesspersons is that all trading rules enacted by member states that are capable of hindering, directly or indirectly, actually or potentially, intra-Community trade are to be considered as measures having an effect equivalent to quantitative restrictions, and are therefore prohibited. Encouragingly, there was no de minimus test, no actual harm test, and the case involved goods originally produced in what was then a non–member state (a true foreign import).

These Community laws apply to situations that involve some form of cross-border element. Where there is no cross-border element, member states are free to impose their own limitations on selling and marketing arrangements, and they do. For example, it is illegal to resell goods at a loss in France, but not illegal to do so in the United Kingdom. While this may create some competitive market distortion in frontier areas, it has been held to be a "selling arrangement" rather than a "trading rule."

In the *Dassonville* case, the commodity was scotch whisky, a product whose attributes were well understood by both France and Belgium, despite the Belgian desire to "protect" its consumers by demanding a certificate as to its authenticity. Indeed, scotch whisky competes with other alcohol, but in the end, scotch whisky only comes from Scotland. What about machinery or clothing, or food that can come from anywhere, which may induce member nations to become more clever in an attempt to protect their domestic industries? What about other cases where foreign traders wish to sell goods in the European Community that may not be so unique? Can a foreign supplier really treat the European single market as a single market?

The European Court of Justice supplied the answer in a case involving a French producer, though the lesson applies, by extension, to foreign producers as well. In this case, a French producer of Cassis de Dijon (a liqueur extracted from black currants), attempted to sell its product in Germany, where a similar product is produced. German law prohibited marketing such liqueur where it contained less than 25 percent alcohol. German producers met this threshold, but the traditional French product, produced at its birthplace, ranged only as high as 20 percent.

The German government argued that its measure was nondiscriminatory (true, in that it applied to all producers) and that it had been enacted, among other reasons, to safeguard public health (strong drinks discourage consumption!). One does not envy the government lawyer who was forced to advance this line of argument with a straight face. The court then took its turn.

Case 120/78: *Cassis de Dijon* (Formally *Rewe-Zentral AG v. Bundesmonopolverwaltung für Branntwein*)

In Case 120/78

Reference to the Court under Article 177[52] of the EEC Treaty by the Hessisches Finanzgericht for a preliminary ruling in the action pending before that Court between

REWE-ZENTRAL AG, having its registered office in Cologne, and

BUNDESMONOPOLVERWALTUNG FÜR BRANNTWEIN (Federal Monopoly Administration for Spirits),

on the interpretation of Articles 30 and 37 of the EEC Treaty[53] in relation to Article 100(3) of the German law on the monopoly in spirits,

1. By order of 28 April 1978, which was received at the Court on 22 May, the Hessisches Finanzgericht referred two questions to the Court under Article 177 of the EEC Treaty for a preliminary ruling on the interpretation of Articles 30 and 37 of the EEC Treaty, for the purpose of assessing the compatibility with Community law of a provision of the German rules relating to the marketing of alcoholic beverages fixing a minimum alcoholic strength for various categories of alcoholic products.

2. It appears from the order making the reference that the plaintiff in the main action intends to import a consignment of "Cassis de Dijon" originating in France for the purpose of marketing it in the Federal Republic of Germany.

    The plaintiff applied to the Bundesmonopolverwaltung (Federal Monopoly Administration for Spirits) for authorization to import the product in question and the Monopoly Administration informed it that because of its insufficient alcoholic strength the said product does not have the characteristics required in order to be marketed within the Federal Republic of Germany.

3. The Monopoly Administration's attitude is based on Article 100 of the Branntweinmonopolgesetz and on the rules drawn up by the Monopoly Administration pursuant to that provision, the effect of which is to fix the minimum alcohol content of specified categories of liqueurs and other potable spirits (Verordnung über den mindestweingeistgehalt von trinkbranntweinen of 28 February 1958, Bundesanzeiger no. 48 of 11 March 1958).

    Those provisions lay down that the marketing of fruit liqueurs, such as "Cassis de Dijon," is conditional upon a minimum alcohol content of 25%, whereas the alcohol content of the product in question, which is freely marketed as such in France, is between 15 and 20%.

4. The plaintiff takes the view that the fixing by the German rules of a minimum alcohol content leads to the result that well-known spirits products from other member states of the Community cannot be sold in the Federal Republic of Germany and that the said provision therefore constitutes a restriction on the free movement of goods between member states which exceeds the bounds of the trade rules reserved to the latter.

---

[52]Article 177 is now Article 234.

[53]Article 30 is now Article 28 and Article 37 is now Article 31 (regarding behavior of state monopolies).

In its view it is a measure having an effect equivalent to a quantitative restriction on imports contrary to Article 30 of the EEC Treaty.

Since, furthermore, it is a measure adopted within the context of the management of the spirits monopoly, the plaintiff considers that there is also an infringement of Article 37, according to which the member states shall progressively adjust any state monopolies of a commercial character so as to ensure that when the transitional period has ended no discrimination regarding the conditions under which goods are procured or marketed exists between nationals of member states.

5. In order to reach a decision on this dispute the Hessisches Finanzgericht has referred two questions to the Court, worded as follows:

> 1. Must the concept of measures having an effect equivalent to quantitative restrictions on imports contained in Article 30 of the EEC Treaty be understood as meaning that the fixing of a minimum wine-spirit content for potable spirits laid down in the German Branntweinmonopolgesetz, the result of which is that traditional products of other member states whose wine-spirit content is below the fixed limit cannot be put into circulation in the Federal Republic of Germany, also comes within this concept?

> 2. May the fixing of such a minimum wine-spirit content come within the concept of "discrimination regarding the conditions under which goods are procured and marketed . . . between nationals of member states" contained in Article 37 of the EEC Treaty?

6. The national Court is thereby asking for assistance in the matter of interpretation in order to enable it to assess whether the requirement of a minimum alcohol content may be covered either by the prohibition on all measures having an effect equivalent to quantitative restrictions in trade between member states contained in Article 30 of the Treaty or by the prohibition on all discrimination regarding the conditions under which goods are procured and marketed between nationals of member states within the meaning of Article 37.

7. It should be noted in this connexion that Article 37 relates specifically to state monopolies of a commercial character.

That provision is therefore irrelevant with regard to national provisions which do not concern the exercise by a public monopoly of its specific function—namely, its exclusive right—but apply in a general manner to the production and marketing of alcoholic beverages, whether or not the latter are covered by the monopoly in question.

That being the case, the effect on intra-Community trade of the measure referred to by the national Court must be examined solely in relation to the requirements under Article 30, as referred to by the first question.

8. In the absence of common rules relating to the production and marketing of alcohol— a proposal for a regulation submitted to the Council by the Commission on 7 December 1976 (Official Journal C 309, p. 2) not yet having received the Council's approval—it is for the member states to regulate all matters relating to the production and marketing of alcohol and alcoholic beverages on their own territory.

Obstacles to movement within the Community resulting from disparities between the national laws relating to the marketing of the products in question must be accepted in so far as those provisions may be recognized as being necessary in order to satisfy mandatory requirements relating in particular to the effectiveness of fiscal supervision, the protection of public health, the fairness of commercial transactions and the defence of the consumer.

9. The government of the Federal Republic of Germany, intervening in the proceedings, put forward various arguments which, in its view, justify the application of provisions relating to the minimum alcohol content of alcoholic beverages, adducing considerations relating on the one hand to the protection of public health and on the other to the protection of the consumer against unfair commercial practices.

10. As regards the protection of public health the German government states that the purpose of the fixing of minimum alcohol contents by national legislation is to avoid the proliferation of alcoholic beverages on the national market, in particular alcoholic beverages with a low alcohol content, since, in its view, such products may more easily induce a tolerance towards alcohol than more highly alcoholic beverages.

11. Such considerations are not decisive since the consumer can obtain on the market an extremely wide range of weakly or moderately alcoholic products and furthermore a large proportion of alcoholic beverages with a high alcohol content freely sold on the German market is generally consumed in a diluted form.

12. The German government also claims that the fixing of a lower limit for the alcohol content of certain liqueurs is designed to protect the consumer against unfair practices on the part of producers and distributors of alcoholic beverages.

    This argument is based on the consideration that the lowering of the alcohol content secures a competitive advantage in relation to beverages with a higher alcohol content, since alcohol constitutes by far the most expensive constituent of beverages by reason of the high rate of tax to which it is subject.

    Furthermore, according to the German government, to allow alcoholic products into free circulation wherever, as regards their alcohol content, they comply with the rules laid down in the country of production would have the effect of imposing as a common standard within the Community the lowest alcohol content permitted in any of the member states, and even of rendering any requirements in this field inoperative since a lower limit of this nature is foreign to the rules of several member states.

13. As the Commission rightly observed, the fixing of limits in relation to the alcohol content of beverages may lead to the standardization of products placed on the market and of their designations, in the interests of a greater transparency of commercial transactions and offers for sale to the public.

    However, this line of argument cannot be taken so far as to regard the mandatory fixing of minimum alcohol contents as being an essential guarantee of the fairness of commercial transactions, since it is a simple matter to ensure that suitable information is conveyed to the purchaser by requiring the display of an indication of origin and of the alcohol content on the packaging of products.

14. It is clear from the foregoing that the requirements relating to the minimum alcohol content of alcoholic beverages do not serve a purpose which is in the general interest and such as to take precedence over the requirements of the free movement of goods, which constitutes one of the fundamental rules of the Community.

    In practice, the principle effect of requirements of this nature is to promote alcoholic beverages having a high alcohol content by excluding from the national market products of other member states which do not answer that description.

    It therefore appears that the unilateral requirement imposed by the rules of a member state of a minimum alcohol content for the purposes of the sale of alcoholic beverages constitutes an obstacle to trade which is incompatible with the provisions of Article 30 of the Treaty.

    There is therefore no valid reason why, provided that they have been lawfully produced and marketed in one of the member states, alcoholic beverages should not be introduced into any other member state; the sale of such products may not be subject to a legal prohibition on the marketing of beverages with an alcohol content lower than the limit set by the national rules.

15. Consequently, the first question should be answered to the effect that the concept of "measures having an effect equivalent to quantitative restrictions on imports" contained in Article 30 of the Treaty is to be understood to mean that the fixing of a minimum alcohol content for alcoholic beverages intended for human consumption by the

legislation of a member state also falls within the prohibition laid down in that provision where the importation of alcoholic beverages lawfully produced and marketed in another member state is concerned.

On those grounds, the Court, in answer to the questions referred to it by the Hessisches Finanzgericht by order of 28 April 1978, hereby rules:

> the concept of "measures having an effect equivalent to quantitative restrictions on imports" contained in Article 30 of the EEC Treaty is to be understood to mean that the fixing of a minimum alcohol content for alcoholic beverages intended for human consumption by the legislation of a member state also falls within the prohibition laid down in that provision where the importation of alcoholic beverages lawfully produced and marketed in another member state is concerned.

Source: http://curia.eu.int/en/content/juris/index.htm, Case 120/78.

The lesson to be drawn from *Cassis de Dijon* is the requirement of mutual recognition between member states. It is not true harmonization. If goods have been lawfully produced and marketed in one member state (including imports from outside the Community, by operation of Article 23) and therefore are in free circulation, then they may be introduced into any other member state. International traders can therefore realistically create distribution strategies based on serving the entire Community from a single member state.

In terms of a limitation to this right of free movement, three factors arise:

1. Common rules relating to production and marketing, where the Community acts.
2. Member state regulation to satisfy "mandatory requirements" (see *Cassis de Dijon* at paragraph 9) relating to the effectiveness of fiscal supervision, the protection of public health, the fairness of commercial transactions, and the defense of the consumer.
3. The general exceptions found in Article 30.

It bears repeating that Community measures will be felt where the Community has undertaken harmonization or approximation of member state measures through either Article 249 regulations or directives. In the case of directives, national implementing legislation that is to bring about the result desired by the Community will evidence these. While national laws therefore will vary in form, they should not vary as to the result. One should recall that the direct applicability of Article 249 regulations into national legal systems means that no national implementing legislation is required.

Where matters have not been subject to Community legislation, and where no issue of mutual recognition between member states arises (as would be the case where no cross-border element is present), national laws may remain different from one another on internal matters. In such cases, there can be no call for a member state to change its laws just because another member state has a different law with different provisions. For example, an Italian law may require shops to be closed on Sundays. There may be no such law in France, but an Italian may not use that difference in national legal systems to demand that his or her own government must change its law. Without a cross-border element, there can be no challenge. Even then, while a French trader wishing to have the freedom to do business in Italy on a Sunday may allege a cross-border effect on trade, such a measure is one regulating selling (affecting both domestic goods and Community imports), rather than cross-border trade.[54]

Internal Market Freedom of Establishment and Services

International businesspersons located outside the European Union are interested as to the extent that they may establish businesses inside the territory of the Union, under both national laws and Community law.

---

[54]A modified example based on Joined Case 418/93 (and 15 others), *Semeraro Casa Uno Srl.*

The notion of establishment is something more than the movement of goods. In an abstract sense, it entails people going somewhere to "set up" or "do something," and thus for each member state of the Community, it touches deeper into issues of national sovereignty and control than the movement of mere inanimate goods ever could. This is reflected in the TEC. Natural and legal persons who are nationals of states outside the Community do not enjoy any immediate freedom as a result of the relevant Community measures on services or establishment. These freedoms are, in principle, reserved for the enjoyment of Community nationals only.

In terms of companies or firms, the situation is more liberal. Formation of a company inside one member state is first a matter of member state regulation; therefore, bear in mind that each member state may well have specific rules applicable to companies owned by persons or corporations who are not Community nationals.[55] That said, once a company[56] is formed in accordance with the law of a member state and has its registered office, central administration, or principal place of business in the Community, then it is to be treated in the same way as natural persons who are nationals of member states.[57] The international businessperson also should keep in mind that this applies to the provision of services as well.[58] In short, while having the nationality of a member state is critical for individuals to enjoy the freedom of establishment and to provide services, an "equivalent-to-national" status can be obtained through the vehicle of a legal person. This is entirely in harmony with the practice in most jurisdictions of the world, which consider legal persons to be nationals of the jurisdiction that created them.

For the international businessperson interested in setting up a web of corporate subsidiaries in member states of the Community, such as national or regional sales offices, there are two options available. The first entails setting up a holding company in one member state with corporate operating subsidiaries in each targeted member state. This must be done in compliance with the laws of each state, accepting the fact that each subsidiary will face different requirements and limitations in reporting, operating, administration, and worker participation requirements, to name a few.

The second option is the formation of a European company, or "Societas Europaea," giving rise to its corporate designation suffix of "SE." The legislation enabling the creation of this type of corporation enters into force in October of 2004.[59]

This corporate form is suitable for even medium-sized companies, as it requires only €120,000 in subscribed capital.[60] Being established as an SE allows a firm to operate in multiple member states as a single company under Community law, under one set of rules, with a unified management and reporting system, rather than under the different national laws of each member state where subsidiaries would otherwise exist.

The main advantages envisioned for these pan-European corporations are

---

[55]See in Chapter 12 the section "Forms of Business Associations" for specific types of national European corporations.

[56]TEC, Article 48, paragraph 2: "Companies or firms constituted under civil or commercial law, including cooperative societies, and other legal persons governed by public or private law, save for those which are non-profit-making."

[57]TEC, Article 48, paragraph 1: "Companies or firms formed in accordance with the law of a Member State and having their registered office, central administration or principal place of business within the Community shall, for the purposes of this Chapter, be treated in the same way as natural persons who are nationals of Member States."

[58]TEC, Article 55.

[59]Council Regulation (EC) No. 2157/2001, on the Statute for a European Company (SE), and Council Directive 2001/86/EC, supplementing the Statute for a European Company with regard to the involvement of employees.

[60]Approximately US$138,000 in early 2004.

1. Single legal structure, requiring no network of subsidiaries.
2. Reduced administrative costs through uniform procedure.
3. Considerably greater ease in future mergers.
4. Possible tax savings (may be able to offset profits in one member state against losses in another).
5. Potentially greater ease in raising capital as a larger, unified corporation.
6. A move of registered office to another member state does not require winding up the firm.

An SE may be formed through a true merger, as a joint holding or subsidiary company, or in transformation of an existing firm, as follows:

1. Merger of two or more existing public limited companies from at least two different EU member states.
2. As a holding company promoted by public or private limited companies from at least two different member states.
3. As a subsidiary of companies from at least two different member states.
4. By transformation of a public limited company that, for at least two years, has had a subsidiary in another member state.

European labor relations have long included worker participation in corporate governance, though in varying degrees from state to state. This ranges under national legislation from mere information requirements right through to worker representation and voting at the board of directors level. All existing European labor representation models remain available for adoption by SEs under the directive, and labor–management negotiation is mandated as a means to settle what degree of representation will prevail in any given SE. If negotiation fails, then a default set of provisions will apply, which, by North American standards, make for significant worker participation.

Internal Market Freedom of Capital and Payments

Compared to any other freedom created by the Treaty Establishing the European Community, none has more fully completed either its evolutionary process or its objectives than that of free movement of capital and payments. Since 1992 and the TEC amending provisions of the Treaty on European Union, that freedom has been a legal reality,[61] and since 2002 and the introduction of euro notes and coins, that reality has become irrevocable for all practical purposes.

This freedom has some limitations and the international trader must always envision the possibility of capital controls on outflows to third countries imposed by the Community in the same manner that could be imposed by any unitary sovereign state. Community law provides for this possibility in Article 57 of the TEC.

As far as individual member states are concerned, the right of taxation by sovereign states over nonresidents remains untouched by the treaty. Powers of prudential supervision over financial institutions remain, as well as member state rights to compel declarations[62] of capital movements for statistical purposes or other measures justified on grounds of public policy or public security.

---

[61]Article 56 (ex Article 73b):
1. Within the framework of the provisions set out in this Chapter, all restrictions on the movement of capital between Member States and between Member States and third countries shall be prohibited.
2. Within the framework of the provisions set out in this Chapter, all restrictions on payments between Member States and between Member States and third countries shall be prohibited.

[62]But not requiring prior authorizations. See Joined Cases C-358/93 and C-416/93 at paragraph 31.

Regional Integration Initiatives outside North America and Europe

With varying degrees of success, longevity, and future potential, a short list of other discussion groups, free trade areas, customs unions, and common markets would include

Andean Community

Arab Cooperation Council

Asia-Pacific Economic Cooperation (APEC)

Association of Southeast Asian Nations (ASEAN)

Black Sea Economic Cooperation Zone

Caribbean Community and Common Market (Caricom)

Central American Common Market

Economic Community of West African States

European Free Trade Association (EFTA)

Latin American Integration Association

Southern African Customs Union

West African Economic and Monetary Union

Of these, among the most promising are in Asia: ASEAN (free trade)[63] and APEC (policy coordination leading to free trade).[64] They are Asian counterweights to both the EU and NAFTA, to resist protectionism and maintain the pace of trade liberalization in the region. The APEC goal is to achieve free trade between the members by 2020, with an earlier target date between the industrialized members.

In addition to multilateral arrangements, the number of bilateral free trade agreements continues to grow. For example, outside the NAFTA agreement, Mexico is a party to over a dozen other free trade agreements, from Bolivia, Chile, and Costa Rica, to EFTA, the EU, and Israel.

Regional integration (of sorts) also can take place for specific purposes. Among the more familiar is OPEC, the Organization of Petroleum Exporting Countries.[65] It is an invitation-only producer's cartel designed to control oil production and export levels among members and to influence world oil prices. Accounting for approximately 40 percent of the world oil supply, its production agreements insulate oil-exporting nations from price swings due to oversupply. If permitted, such swings would create instability, as members are largely dependent on oil as their chief income-earner. For nations largely dependent on oil imports, the view is reversed; they see OPEC as an oligopoly intent on maintaining high prices for oil.

Finally, integration can take the form of mutual defense commitments, as is the case in NATO, the North Atlantic Treaty Organization.[66] While NATO is properly seen as a military

---

[63]Formed in 1967, members now include Brunei, Cambodia, Indonesia, Laos, Malaysia, Myanmar, Philippines, Singapore, Thailand, and Vietnam. Papua New Guinea holds observer status, while Russia and China are "consultative partners." Tariff reduction toward eventual free trade among members began in 1993.

[64]Formed in 1989 between members of ASEAN and NAFTA and Australia, New Zealand, and Chile.

[65]Members are Algeria, Indonesia, Iran, Iraq, Kuwait, Libya, Nigeria, Qatar, Saudi Arabia, United Arab Emirates, and Venezuela.

[66]NATO has 19 members as at 2004: Belgium, Canada, the Czech Republic, Denmark, France, Germany, Greece, Hungary, Iceland, Italy, Luxembourg, the Netherlands, Norway, Poland, Portugal, Spain, Turkey, the United Kingdom, and the United States.

alliance against external threats, it has a significant role in managing political and economic relations between its member states. The NATO forum was used to defuse tension between Spain and Canada on North Atlantic overfishing of cod and for many years has contributed heavily to stable relations between Greece and Turkey, at odds over the Mediterranean island Cyprus. NATO standards for defense equipment contribute to greater uniformity and development in defense production and lead to sharing of research and development in the defense industry.

Perhaps most significant to its future is its integration of former Communist states. NATO has played a large role in conversion of defense industries to civilian production and ensuring democratic control over armed forces of these nations. Collectively, this helps establish stable markets for civilian international business development.

Chapter Summary

Perhaps the greatest success of regional integration is also one that does not appear in trade statistics: peace. Nations that trade together and become progressively more interdependent have ever-growing reasons not to allow their politicians to fan the embers of war. The range of this increasing interdependence runs from free trade through customs unions to economic and monetary union, each tying nations and their region closer together.

Many nations have found that rapid trade and economic gains can be realized from deepening and widening these relationships with their neighbors. This is in contrast to the great deal of political capital a nation must spend to win even the smallest gains from an organization as large as the WTO. It is worth questioning whether trade blocs are the new fortresses in economic warfare. It is worth considering whether the original intention of GATT authorization of integration measures has been, or could be, stretched too far. Even with that thought in mind, still the result of integration and freer trade is an economic positive. More importantly, however, it is in nations where social justice prevails that those results will be shared as a social positive.

Chapter Questions

1. What specific business and social advantages can be expected from regional integration?
2. Describe the chief political and economic features of the European Union that distinguish it from the North American Free Trade Agreement for the purposes of international businesspersons.
3. Why is closer approximation of economic and social policy an important step to be completed prior to the establishment of a common market?
4. Briefly state, in your own words, the two rules resulting from the *Dassonville* and *Cassis de Dijon* cases that create a single market in Europe for international businesspersons.
5. Explain why certificates of origin are irrelevant within a customs union. Why should anyone care, other than the parties, how long it takes to fully implement a free trade agreement or customs union?

BusinessWeek

I have my own test of European sincerity on the fiery issue of genetically modified food. When members of the European Parliament are at Capitol Hill luncheons, I make a point of asking if they're afraid of the meals they're eating. Invariably, they answer no. But they add sheepishly that they would risk unemployment if they publicly defended the genetically modified American imports that send protesters into the streets of the Continent.

Now, however, the Europeans appear to be putting their irrational fear of "Frankenfood" aside. Faced with an American President angry over the bad-mouthing of U.S. products, regulators in Brussels on Oct. 17 will issue new guidelines for licensing genetically modified food. That will seemingly end an ad hoc, three-year moratorium on new American biotech food products.

But rather than opening its market, the European Union is simply playing games. To comply with the new regs, U.S. farmers and food processors would have to completely change the way they grow, store, produce, and transport their goods. This sham compromise still pits prejudice against science and sets misinformed consumers and protectionist farmers in Europe against producers in America. That's why the Bush Administration needs to act quickly to take the case to the World Trade Organization. There, science and the law may finally prevail.

For the U.S. agriculture industry, the world leader in food technology, the stakes are huge. Farmers are 2.5 times more dependent on exports than the rest of the economy. One out of every three acres in America is planted for export. And much of that crop has been genetically modified to produce strains that are more productive and pest-resistant. Nearly three-quarters of soybeans and a third of all corn grown in the U.S. have been altered by introducing new genes.

Beyond the threat to the U.S. farm sector, there's a more important reason for swift action. The panic over genetically modified food is spreading around the globe. In famine-stricken southern Africa, 14 million people face starvation while their confused leaders follow the Europeans and their junk science. Zimbabwe and Zambia, for example, have rejected U.S. food aid, complaining that the grain is "contaminated" with ingredients that Europeans won't eat. "They watched carefully what the Europeans actually did," says Alan P. Larson, Assistant Secretary of State for agricultural affairs. Although China is itself developing a biotech food industry, it, too, has held up purchases of modified U.S. soybeans. And New Zealand and Japan show signs of following Europe's Chicken Littles.

The new European rules aren't just strict, they're unworkable. The labeling requirements, for example, are more a warning than an attempt to inform consumers. European supermarket chains, such as Carrefour of France and Britain's Tesco, have already vowed to exclude any products containing genetically modified food from their shelves. Oddly, European wines and cheeses, developed with genetically modified enzymes, would be exempt from the labeling regs.

The traceability standards are particularly onerous, requiring the U.S. industry to track genetically modified ingredients "from farm to fork," even if they contained just 1% of transgenic food. That would require separate harvesting equipment, silos, shipping containers—even factory production lines—and extensive testing at each step of the process. As for the question of human health, science has already decided. Numerous studies, including those by the National Academies of Science, say genetically modified food is safe. So does the World Health Organization. Even EU Health Commissioner David Byrne conceded to African leaders that the U.S. food aid quarantined in Zambian warehouses was safe to eat.

None of this is meant to imply that rigorous scientific testing of genetically modified foods shouldn't go on or that other concerns might not eventually rule out some biotech foods. The technology has to be regulated to ensure it doesn't replicate allergens or harm wild plant and animal species. But science—not suspicion—should decide each case.

Come Oct. 17, U.S. food producers should be prepared with their license applications. And the Administration should be ready at the courthouse door in Geneva.

Source: Paul Magnusson. Copyright 2002, by The McGraw-Hill Companies Inc. All rights reserved.

BusinessWeek

Chile's chief trade negotiator Osvaldo Rosales talks about the many positive effects of finally getting a deal with the U.S.

Osvaldo Rosales, director of international economic relations at Chile's Foreign Relations Ministry, has spent the last two years hammering out a free trade agreement with the U.S.—as well as accords with the European Union and South Korea. The U.S.-Chile deal, which is expected to be approved by both countries' congresses this fall, is described as a "third-generation" accord because it covers not only tariffs and quotas but also regulates fast-growing trade in electronic services, intellectual property, and government contract bidding.

Rosales met in his Santiago office with Geri Smith, *BusinessWeek*'s Latin America correspondent, on May 27, and during their chat his office phone, cell phone, and computer instant messenger all started beeping: He learned that Washington had finally scheduled a signing of the Chile-U.S. free trade agreement on June 6 after the Bush Administration, "disappointed" over Chile's refusal to back the U.S.-led war in Iraq, had postponed it for several months. Following are edited excerpts from their interview:

Q: Why is the Chile-U.S. free trade agreement so important for Chile? After all, Chile over the years has diversified its trade so that it's almost evenly split among Europe, Asia, Latin America, and the U.S.
A: We've adopted a strategy of international participation. We've reached agreements with the European Union and with Korea, and it was a natural step to reach a free trade agreement with the largest market in the world. By reaching this agreement, we hope to have three kinds of benefits: commercial, investment, and a favorable impact on our macroeconomic regime.

Under the Generalized System of Preferences (GSP), many Chilean products [already] entered the U.S. with zero tariff, but GSP is a voluntary, unilateral mechanism that can be revoked. Under this new trade agreement, all of those products will have permanent zero tariffs. That permanence changes our investment panorama radically. We expect to diversify our exports and think they'll grow 20% or more in just three years. That's a conservative estimate. One pleasant surprise we've had with our new free trade agreement with the European Union, which has just been in effect for around three months: Our noncopper exports to the EU already have grown 27%.

Q: Are you expecting a boom in foreign direct investment?
A: We believe the main impact of the free trade agreement will be on investment. When a country establishes a free trade agreement with the U.S., that has an immediate favorable repercussion on the country's [image] and makes it easier for major multinational companies to make decisions [to invest].

Q: Chile already had a very good reputation as a country with disciplined macroeconomic policies and a wide-open trade policy. The country unilaterally reduced its overall import tariffs over the years, recently dropping them to 6% across the board.
A: Yes, but this will reinforce that [reputation]. Let me give you one small example: About five months ago, a millionaire Greek investor came to Chile to look into some possible casino investments, and his comment was that he wanted to come to Chile to learn more about the country that had reached free trade agreements with the European Union and with the U.S. Chile had appeared on investors' agendas because of that. We'll be able to capture a larger flow of foreign direct investment.

Q: Chile already has a number of free trade agreements, starting with one signed with Mexico in 1992, followed by one with Canada, the European Union, even Korea. What does that mean for Chile?
A: It makes it interesting for foreign investors, because if they locate in Chile, they can have zero-tariff access to a large market potentially of 1.2 billion people [in Europe and the Americas]. We've even heard from some Brazilian investors who are exploring business opportunities here in textiles and leather and footwear because textiles from Chile won zero tariffs not only for the U.S. but for the European Union. This could help us in the short term with a strengthening of the Chilean industrial park. As President [Ricardo] Lagos has said, in 10 years we want to transform Chile into a bridge of trade and investment between South America and [other regions such as] the Asian-Pacific.

Q: Chile has been rated investment-grade since the mid-1990s. That has helped it borrow internationally at decent rates.
A: Yes, but now we expect capital flows to be more stable. When an economy has trade agreements with the European Union and the U.S., this means the establishment of discipline in relations with investors, it offers dispute-resolution mechanisms. It offers a climate of certainty. And most important, economic policy cannot be changed simply because the government in power has changed. It offers an institutional anchor of sorts for economic policy. That's good news not only for international investors but

for Chilean investors. When we finished negotiating the pact at the end of 2002, the Chilean stock market rose and the currency strengthened in anticipation even though we knew it would be another year before the agreement would be translated and approved by both congresses.

Q: Some opponents of the Chile-U.S. agreement here say they're concerned that the "anchor" of certainty that the accord offers might act more like a straitjacket. For example, Chile doesn't charge royalties for mining companies. What if the country decides it needs to charge royalties, as many countries do, for nonrenewable resources? Will these agreements make it difficult for Chile to change policies that may affect foreign investors?

A: Strictly speaking, the free trade agreements don't limit the possibility [of changing that policy] because taxation policy isn't part of the agreement. Countries maintain the ability to change their taxes. The only requirement is that [any policy change] can't be discriminatory. The tax change would have to apply for everyone, not just for foreign investors but also for domestic investors. And if any investor believes that his rights have been violated, there is room for disputes to be resolved. These agreements tie our hands, but in the good sense: The public sector keeps its ability to regulate different aspects of economic policy, including balance of payments, environmental issues, taxation, and so on.

Q: How important to Chile is the Free Trade Area of the Americas?

A: It's important for three reasons: We already have agreements with almost all of the FTAA countries, except the Caribbean. So in terms of market access, the FTAA won't mean that much. But it will allow us to negotiate issues such as services and investment. And we think Chile has developed competitive advantages in services and overseas investment [in the region]. Second, it will allow the region to have uniform rules on safeguards, customs, technical norms, and sanitary issues. One might have low tariffs, but there's always a temptation, if a country is having difficulty in one economic sector, to be "creative" with customs rules, permits, export licenses, or other bureaucratic procedures. The FTAA will change that. Finally and most important, when the FTAA is operating the whole region will have an export mentality, a business mentality. It's not enough to just have low tariffs—we must maintain policies that keep our commitment to free trade.

Q: So it requires a complete change in mentality?

A: It's more than lowering tariffs, it requires a complete mind shift. Our private sector in Chile already has an export vision . . . which involves not only selling a product but establishing alliances with investors from other countries, with Brazilians, Argentines, Colombians.

Q: Is Chile's business community prepared for the difficulties that may arise with this latest market opening?

A: Fortunately, our private sector was closely involved in the trade negotiations. It already has an open-markets mentality. So we knew when we made certain offers to the North Americans that we had the backing of the private sector because we had discussed it with them. If you don't do that, then you run the risk of a very intense internal debate [after the fact]. And that's not good.

Source: Patricia O'Connell. Copyright 2003, by The McGraw-Hill Companies Inc. All rights reserved.

International Business Law Transactions

Part

2

To this point, we have identified and described the impact of international law, national governments, and public organizations in shaping the legal environment in which international business transactions are conducted. This shaping has defined the boundaries and the range of options open to any particular international business transaction.

Within these boundaries, any selected business option will, of course, involve the immediate parties who wish to do business together. Less obvious are the secondary relationships required to bring the transaction to a successful conclusion. Depending on the subject matter of the transaction, these can include lawyers, shippers, customs brokers, bankers, insurers, or arbitrators.

The objectives of this part are to

- Investigate and understand the application of the primary forms of international business transactions and the law that governs them.
- Investigate and understand the impact of secondary relationships in the structure and execution of international business law transactions.

Chapters in this part are

International Business Law Transactions— An Introduction

Linking Part 1 with Parts 2 and 3

Part 1 of this text was devoted to the description, analysis, and conclusions on the environment surrounding the conduct of international business and international business law.

Parts 2 and 3 of this text outline the strategy and tactics, the skills and techniques, the dealing and decisions, and the tricks and traps of international business law transactions.

If you are opening this book for the first time, go back and read Part 1. People are often in a hurry to reach the "hands-on" material, whether it is in international business law or in playing computer games. The problem is the same with both: No one ever reads the manual or the "read-me" file until they get in trouble for not having done so in the first place. In international business and international business law, a good knowledge of Part 1 issues often makes the difference between success and failure, and it often sets the extraordinary players apart from the average traders.

Having read and understood Part 1 on international environments, it is important at the outset of Part 2 to understand why and how they are linked together. Understanding either one in a vacuum really doesn't do much good. In the initial international business decision stage, canvasing the environments allows you to find business opportunities and threats abroad. When you look for a lawyer, knowing your business environment well allows you to assess whether your lawyer understands what is motivating your interest abroad and shares your understanding of the general types of threats you might encounter. Such preparation also allows you to meet the lawyer on equal terms at the initial client meeting, avoiding that "deer in the headlights" look on both sides.

That, however, is just the first stage. In the second stage, you want to discuss your intentions on the basis of reasonably well-formed but flexible plans, with clear goals setting out what you wish to accomplish in the international arena. Flexible plans (and knowledge of options) are a better scenario for your lawyer to work with, as they allow the lawyer to provide input into the plan based on his or her knowledge of the associated risks and opportunities attached to your ideas. Fully formed ideas (ones cast in stone) are tougher for your lawyer. The lawyer who identifies real risks applicable to your ideas often will have a tougher job of convincing you to see the dangers (with you having become the guardian of your brainchild).

208

Your knowledge of international business and international law environments is your contribution toward ensuring that you get good value-added service from your lawyer. While you cannot dictate what set of options is open to you, your knowledge of the potential options (and your experience) should be leveraged to your benefit. The international businessperson should be looking for legal counsel who has a similar (or even greater) level of initial knowledge and contribution to make. If you feel you must first educate your lawyer on the transaction options, you have the wrong lawyer.

In the third stage, where a developed relationship between you and your lawyer exists, you have the opportunity to advance that relationship by ensuring that your lawyer is an integral part of your planning team for international operations. Having counsel with a portfolio of added-value services to offer, which is deeply integrated early on in the strategic planning process, means enjoying a great competitive advantage. Time and resources will not be wasted on business options that seem workable, but are nonfeasible options from the legal standpoint. Minefields of problems can be identified early on that must be worked into both the strategy and tactics. More accurate pricing decisions and more reliable profit forecasts result from better knowledge and appreciation of the costs of strategic and tactical decisions. Keeping your lawyer "up-to-speed" and part of the ongoing planning process means never having to take time out to brief counsel on decisions already taken, with the possibility of overlooking critical dimensions in the summary or in a hasty recap of events.

The paragraphs above explain *why* the connection is important between Part 1 environments and Parts 2 and 3 on transactions. Between the lines, it sheds some light on *how* this is done, but until it becomes second nature through practice, it is worth reviewing Part 1 and expanding on the skill.

First, the net of observation must be widely cast across all relevant geographical and topical environments; these are the target country and region; its historical and cultural context; and its political, military, economic, social, and legal environments. Your first task is to read all you can on these subjects, from current sources as well as historical ones. In the beginning, you will rely on secondary analysis (the analysis of other people: authors, editors, commentators), but with time and experience, you will read and observe first hand accounts and draw your own conclusions.

Next, whether your data consist of conclusions of others or your own (and probably both), you will create a synthesis from these, an overall emerging picture about what is happening in that business and legal environment. As the factors contribute to each other and to the creation of the whole picture, significant risks and opportunities will begin to present themselves. Perhaps your target market is a lesser developed country with a history of good relations with your own; its politics are stable and its economy is growing. In such a case, a more ambitious business plan can be considered, for example, establishing a distributorship or even local investment. If, on the other hand, its political environment is unstable and its economy is shaky, then while it may be a market with local demand, it should be served by direct export with cash payment for each shipment. Both alternatives demand different business law transaction vehicles to accomplish the desired results.

The factors will almost always be contradictory, which is where and why judgment comes into play. Where all the factors are positive, it rarely represents a ground-floor opportunity, unless you are the fastest mover in the industry.

The judgment required in the final stages is to balance risk and opportunity factors in light of the resources and strategic goals of the international business enterprise. Recall from Chapter 1 the following table:

Application of International Business Law in Opportunity and Risk Assessment

Step	Through	By
1. Identify opportunity.	Observation.	Using a systematic process of gathering data and tracking lessons learned.
2. Identify objectives, assumptions, and critical success factors.	Analysis of opportunity.	Knowing your business goals, biases, business environment and resources. Being objective, does the opportunity merit pursuit and is it achievable?
3. Foresee risks.	Analysis of downside of each success factor, your competitors, foreign government, and market.	Knowing your business and legal environments.
4. Assess risks.	Analysis of type, probability, level, outcome, and impact of each risk.	Knowing your business and legal environments.
5. Reduce risks.	Selection of structure of transaction	Knowing your options in international business transactions and law.
6. Shift risks.	Negotiation and insurance.	Your relationships and costs.
7. Decide to		
• Accept risk	Execution	Knowing your capabilities
• Reject risk	Avoidance	and limitations.

Risk can be reduced and opportunity can be enhanced through the selection of appropriate strategies and tactics. With that word *tactics,* we are introducing for the first time the possibility of selecting a transaction. Where the business strategy is to enter a foreign market and supply it with goods, the tactics cover a spectrum from direct sale to establishing an overseas factory. Each transaction option will have its own inherent risks and rewards. A direct sale may not be as profitable as local manufacture, but it cannot be expropriated or nationalized by the foreign government, as is possible where a factory is built.

Even when the transaction is selected—for example, the direct sale—each transaction still has elements of risk that can be managed inside it through negotiation or insurance. A sale requires a buyer; a second party; and where there is a second party, the opportunity to offload risk to that party through negotiation. As long as each party believes that the risk accepted or forgone is less than the concession extracted or received in return, a deal is possible.

Even in a transaction as simple as a sale, there is plenty of risk that may be negotiated. Who is paying for the shipping: the buyer or seller? What is the resulting price for the goods in light of that? Is the price on cash terms, or will credit be granted? Where does title (and risk to the goods) pass from one party to the other?

When all is laid out, the final step is to obtain insurance against those risks that are inherent in the environment, those that are inherent in the transaction structure, and those that could not be negotiated away on acceptable terms.

Each of these elements will be revisited in the chapters on transactions that follow, and these elements of risk management are the true link between Parts 1 and the balance of this text.

The Parties in International Transactions

In every transaction, there are the real actors, the business enterprises that wish to establish a relationship with one another. Even in cases of direct overseas investment, there is the relationship between the parent firm at home and its wholly owned subsidiary or branch in the host country. This primary relationship is between the actors (the home and foreign businesses) and their supporting relationships, shown below:

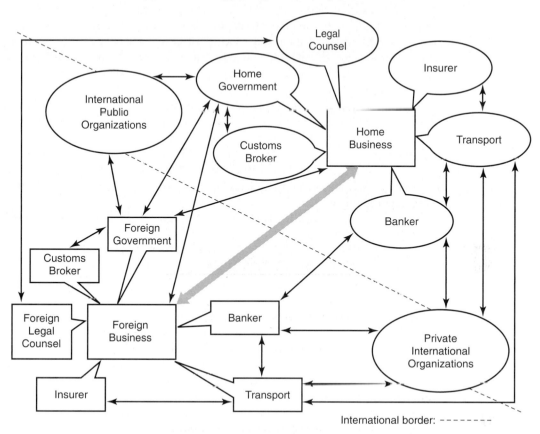

International border: --------

We have already considered some of these relationships in terms of general host and home government regulation of international business, as well as intergovernmental relationships, both bilateral (U.S.–Canada Free Trade Agreement) and multilateral (NAFTA and EU), and through multilateral international public organizations (GATT, WTO, UN). Some further international public organizations will be discussed in particular sections.

To this we must add all the other secondary actors who shape the international business environment for particular transactions. These include international private organizations, banks and financial institutions, the transportation industry, insurers, and legal counsel. While the function of each of these is generally self-explanatory and will be explored further as they arise in turn, international private organizations benefit from some explanation at the outset.

These organizations are private, meaning that they are composed primarily of members of industry and private business. They may have governments as observers, but their function is to organize the international affairs of interested business.[1] This function of organization among some businesses can result in the setting of legally recognized standards for all businesses, essentially creating an international lex mercatoria ("law merchant," or commercial law) standard.

[1]In addition to the ICC discussed at length below, these include IATA, the International Air Transport Association (www.iata.org); SWIFT, the Society for Worldwide Interbank Financial Telecommunication (www.swift.com); the ISF, the International Shipping Federation (www.marisec.org); and, for stock and commodity exchanges, the WFE, the World Federation of Exchanges (www.fibv.com); among a wide range of others.

One of the most important examples is the International Chamber of Commerce, headquartered in Paris, France. To those who have not heard of it before, its name may suggest the image of a social club or Better Business Bureau, but it is something very much more significant. It has established trade terms for use worldwide in commercial contracts that serve to establish many of the responsibilities of buyers and sellers. It has drafted model contracts for the international sale of goods, available for use by traders. It has established arbitration processes for the private and expeditious settlement of commercial international trade disputes.

One may ask why governments have not done this. Sometimes they have, but the measures created by private organizations stand as alternatives for use by the private sector (most governments provide for some recognition and opting out of national measures—think of choice-of-forum clauses). Sometimes governments have tried and failed for lack of international governmental consensus. Private firms under commercial pressure, seeking certainty rather than sovereignty, have been able to create international standards where governments could not.

A Short Primer on the Domestic Law of Contract

The need for knowledge of international business law spans a diverse group of persons, and this diversity is reflected in the users of this textbook. While some users will be quite familiar with the domestic forms of law and contract discussed in the remaining chapters, for other users, this will be their first (and often only) course in law.

Many laws apply to international business matters, but of these laws, the law of contract is perhaps the most important.

Contracts are an integral part of all the chapters that follow, as contracts, for the most part, define the rights between private business parties (and sometimes between them and governments). A failure in understanding the operation of contracts will doom all later understanding of contractual rights between international parties.

Accordingly, the section that follows is intended to familiarize business students with the essential elements of the private law of contract in the Anglo-American tradition. It applies, for the most part, to the domestic law of the United States, United Kingdom, Canada, Australia and New Zealand, Ireland, Hong Kong, Singapore, and virtually all former colonies of Great Britain. The domestic law discussed below is usually found in each country at the state or provincial level, rather than as federal or national law. The rules outlined are "bare bones" common law rules of contract, subject to many exceptions and statute amendments depending upon jurisdiction, but should be adequate for an understanding of the basic concepts.

Law students and other users who have previously undertaken legal studies may safely omit the section that follows, or use it for review. From them, we ask their indulgence in including this section and offer an observation. When they enter legal practice, they will find it refreshing to have clients who are well-informed on fundamental legal issues. Time is money for everyone involved in international business transactions.

Essential Elements in Contract

In the Anglo-American common law tradition, shared in principle by civil law systems, contracts require the existence of seven essential elements:

1. There is an **intention** to create a legal relationship.
2. An **offer** must be made (as opposed to an invitation to do business).
3. There must be **acceptance** of that offer, prior to the lapse or revocation of the offer.
4. Some exchange of mutual promises or value, known as **consideration,** must exist.

5. The parties must have **capacity** to contract, which is the ability at law to make contracts.

6. Requirements of **form** and **writing** must be met, if any.

7. The contract must have **legality** of object (must not involve illegal acts).

You will frequently have cause to check whether all of these elements are present, for if any are missing, the contract may not be valid, or, if valid, may not be enforceable. If there is no validity or no enforceability, then the party on the other side of the "contract" can carry on doing (or not doing) whatever it likes.

Intention   While this is a relatively simple element, its importance should not be ignored. Courts distinguish between cases where intention to contract is considered present (such as an agreement between strangers in a business setting) and those where it is not (for example, a family agreement of a casual nature). The test applied in these cases is generally that of the "reasonable person" and whether such a person would regard the agreement as one intended to create a legal relationship. It is an essential element for validity of a contract.

Offer   An offer sets forth the complete conditions upon which the offeror intends to be bound upon acceptance. An offer, however, must be distinguished from a mere invitation to do business, which often, for example, is a general advertisement to the public at large. In responding to advertisements, a member of the public actually becomes the offeror and the advertising seller can choose to accept or decline such offers. For instance, a seller advertising in a trade magazine is merely advising of its existence, and buyers are the ones who will make offers to purchase goods.

In some cases, an invitation or advertisement may be treated as an offer (and hence open for acceptance by the public, becoming a contract) if it spells out the conditions that the public must perform to accept the offer and bind the advertising seller. In a simple example, if a product advertisement offers a reward or contains a guarantee, the purchaser can bind that seller to that promise by simply doing the required act or buying the product. The purchaser does not need to first make its own demand to benefit from the promise.

An offer to a specific person ends when the specific person receives notice of the offer being revoked before the offer has been accepted. An offer also may end by lapse, which is the expiration of a previously fixed time period, or after a "reasonable time" if no date had been specified in the offer, or if the offeror dies or becomes bankrupt. An offer is an essential element for validity of a contract.

Acceptance   An offer is therefore open for acceptance until it is revoked or lapses. In the traditional common law approach, acceptance must be unconditional and in accordance with the terms of the offer; otherwise, the attempt to accept becomes a counteroffer. Acceptance cannot precede the offer, and silence cannot constitute acceptance unless the parties have previously agreed this would be the case. All this said, some exceptions exist to accommodate situations like a battle between preprinted offer and acceptance forms.

If the offeror specifies the means to be used for acceptance (letter, e-mail), then the person accepting must use that form, and acceptance is effective when the person has done all he or she could to transmit the acceptance. If the person accepting uses another form, then acceptance is only effective when it is actually received, and runs the risk of lapse or revocation in the meantime. An acceptance is an essential element for validity of a contract.

Consideration   This concept represents the "something" that a party receives under a contract in return for his or her own promise; for example, a promise to supply 100 tons of steel offered in return for a promise to pay a sum of money. The twin promises must exist, but they do not need to be equal. Courts will only, with greatest rarity, investigate the adequacy of consideration, and even then, usually only when supported by consumer protection law. In short, courts do not regulate good deals or bad bargains. In cases where there is only one promise flowing in one direction, it is a gratuitous promise and is not a valid contract, unless made under "seal." A seal (usually a small red sticker) is placed at the point of signature indicating that the promisor intends to be bound by its gratuitous promise. For example, at common law this may arise when a creditor agrees to unilaterally reduce the debt of a debtor. It is not obligated to make the reduction, and it receives nothing in return for its promise to accept less money on the preexisting debt. The fact that the creditor agrees under seal binds the creditor to its new promise to accept less.

At any time that a gratuitous promise arises (for example, where a seller grants a potential buyer an option to purchase, open for a fixed period of time), such an agreement should be made under seal to be enforceable. Alternatively, something or anything—just one dollar or a peppercorn—should be given in exchange for that promise, in order to make it binding.

There are exceptions to this, the most important known as "promissory estoppel," which allows a person who has relied on a gratuitous promise to his or her detriment to enforce that promise. However, for our purposes, the existence of consideration is an essential element for a valid contract.

Capacity   For an otherwise valid contract to be enforced against a party, that party must have had the capacity to create a contract at the time it was made. Contracts (except for "necessaries") cannot be enforced against persons under the age of majority, or those intoxicated or insane (unless ratified by them once they have overcome their incapacity). More important, in large-scale business transactions, some corporations by operation of statute law may lack capacity to make particular contracts (e.g., a bank may be forbidden from engaging in the insurance trade). Undischarged commercial bankrupts usually lack all meaningful capacity to contract business in their own name. Therefore, it is important to review the records of the competent authorities of a jurisdiction to ensure that potential business partners have the required capacity at law to make contracts.

Form and Writing   Most jurisdictions impose certain requirements of form and writing for particular contracts to be valid in the first place, or, if valid, to be enforceable. Typically, gratuitous promises must be in writing and under seal to be valid and enforceable. Usually contracts concerning land must be in writing in order to enforceable, even if they are otherwise valid. The same is usually true of guarantees for the indebtedness of another, or in some jurisdictions, contracts that cannot be performed in less than a year or period of years.

These requirements in Anglo-American jurisdictions are spelled out in legislation often called a "statute of frauds" and frequently translated into commercial codes and sale-of-goods acts. Statute of frauds is a modern use of a term used centuries ago in England, with the "fraud" being the worry that certain agreements were open to abuse if they were not properly recorded. Failure to comply with a statute of frauds requirement results in the unenforceability of the otherwise valid contract.

Written contracts are usually subject to the "parol evidence rule," meaning that no evidence (oral or written) can be raised to add to, change, or contradict the terms of a written agreement intended to be a final record that is otherwise clear on its face. The major exceptions to this rule are the admissibility of a collateral agreement (a second separate agreement with separate consideration modifying the first) or the application of the doctrine of implied term. The doctrine of implied term is the willingness of courts to recognize certain terms as being a part of the agreement even if they are not included, if the terms are those that by custom or practice the parties normally include, and the terms were omitted due to an oversight.

Legality   Contracts that have an illegal object are both not valid and unenforceable. The possible range of illegal contracts is very broad, with an obvious business example being an agreement between firms that violates antitrust statute provisions. Any violation of law by a business firm, including administrative law (such as operating without meeting licensing requirements), can result in illegality of the firm's contracts and may rob that party of the ability to launch or defend a court action.

Where a contract term contains an element that is against public policy in a jurisdiction, the term will fail the legality test, and may even doom the entire contract as void and unenforceable. For example, if a supplier's distribution contract provides that after its expiration the local distributor may never again engage in commercial distribution business for anyone else, anywhere, such a term would be against public policy and would be void and unenforceable.

Avoiding Enforceability in Valid Contracts

Despite being an otherwise valid contract, some contracts may suffer from defects arising in the course of negotiation that may render them unenforceable. These are contracts that have been created through

1. Undue influence (a dominant party in a special position of influence coercing a weaker party).
2. Duress (through threats of physical violence or similar action).
3. Mistake (of material facts or law).
4. Misrepresentation (innocent or fraudulent material statements inducing a party into a contract).

Undue Influence   Undue influence has difficulty arising in international commercial affairs, as it requires a special relationship of trust or dependence between the parties, such as that of parent–child, doctor–patient, or, perhaps more plausibly, lawyer–client. It is conceivable that a businessperson operating abroad, relying on foreign legal counsel of the other party (an unwise state of affairs), could be deliberately tricked. If the disadvantaged party was depending on translation of documents and was misled as to the true nature of a particular document, a defense to later enforcement may lie in "non est factum"—it is not my doing. Carelessness, however, will not permit the use of the non est factum defense.

Duress   While infrequent, the possibility can and does exist that a businessperson abroad may "get in over his or her head" and face physical threats to enter a contract. Instances do exist of such treatment of foreign businesspersons by hostile regimes, with signing a contract on dictated terms being the only way to be allowed to leave the country. Such a contract would be unenforceable, but as in the case of undue influence, these contracts must be repudiated at the first available opportunity lest they be seen as "ratified."

Mistake   Mistake occurs where the parties have formed an untrue view of the agreement that they have made. It does not mean a simple "oversight." If, unknown to the parties, the subject matter of their contract has been destroyed, say a ship at sea having sunk, the parties are operating under a mistake of fact. A mistake of law occurs where the parties create an agreement thinking that a law applies to them, but it does not (or vice-versa). Many jurisdictions treat mistakes of law as simply mistakes of fact. Mistake renders the agreement voidable or void depending upon the nature of the mistake.

Misrepresentation   Misrepresentation is a statement of a material fact by one party that induces the other party to enter into the agreement, and may be *innocent* or *fraudulent*. Innocent misrepresentation is a statement of a material fact that the person who makes the statement believes to be true, but that is later discovered to be false. Fraudulent misrepresentation is a statement of a material fact that the person knows is false (or is made recklessly) and is made with the intention to deceive. It is an actionable civil wrong in itself. In both cases, the other party must be induced to enter into the agreement on the basis of the statement. The victim of the misrepresentation may treat the contract as voidable and take steps to end the contract, but is deemed to ratify it if the party continues to accept benefits under the agreement.

Transfer of Contractual Rights and Responsibilities

Parties who create a contract between them are said to have privity—the right and duty to enforce the contract and accept its liabilities. Third parties do not enjoy these rights (unless the contact has been made for their benefit) and are exempt from its liabilities. That said, there are many instances where the participation of third parties is desirable or necessary.

Third parties may enter into an existing contract by way of

Novation. This occurs when one party wishes to leave the contract on the consent of the other, to be substituted by another acceptable and willing party. Novation can be established by a formal agreement, or be inferred from an exchange of letters or even from the conduct of the parties. It is essentially a new agreement that arises between the new parties that releases the old contracting party.

Vicarious performance. This occurs when actual performance of a contract is done by a person other than the contracting party, but in this case, the original contracting party remains liable for the performance if it is done improperly. The most common situation is where an employee of a contracting party actually performs the work required under the agreement. If the employee does the work negligently, the employer as contractor is liable.

Assignment. Assignments are the transfer of some, but not necessarily all, rights and duties of one party to a contract to a third party. Commonly, this occurs in debt situations, where the right to collect an account is assigned to a bank or financial institution. Once notice of the assignment is made to the debtor, the debtor is liable to make future payments to the assignee, rather than the original creditor. The assignee gets no more rights than the original creditor and is subject to all the defenses to payment that the debtor could have raised against the original creditor.

Discharge

Once a valid and enforceable contract exists between parties, they are obligated to satisfy or "perform" their contractual obligations. Once this is done, the contract is "discharged." Unfortunately, contracts are often discharged by means other than performance: by law, through termination as a right, by creation of a substitute agreement, by material alteration of the terms, through waiver, by frustration, or by breach of contract.

Performance. Performance means the action or payment required of a party to carry out a contract obligation. A failure or refusal to perform a contract in accordance with its terms at the time required for performance constitutes a breach of the contract and entitles the injured party to seek redress through the courts. In some, but by no means all, cases, the injured party may exempt him- or herself from performance.

While proper performance is the most desirable outcome, contracts can be discharged by

Law. Where the contract was once legal, subsequent new legislation can make it illegal, thus discharging the parties from performance.

Termination. Here, the parties have expressly agreed in their contract that one party or both may declare the contract is at an end.

Substitution. Where the parties are mutually unsatisfied with their bargain, they may expressly choose to terminate a first agreement and substitute it (completely) with another.

Alteration. Where the parties stop short of ending their existing contract, but sufficiently alter material terms such that the true character of the first agreement is lost, the amended terms constitute discharge of the former terms.

Waiver. Where one party "forgives" (either express or implied) a breach of obligation by the other, the other party is discharged of his or her responsibility to perform to that extent.

The Old Wolf

The Old Wolf finds no shame in using memory aids when millions of dollars can be lost on simple oversight. Use these to avoid a whole new world of hurt.

Summary of Contract Law

Essential Elements	Memory Aid
Intention, Offer, Acceptance, Consideration, Capacity, Form, Writing, Legality	I Only Accept Cold Cash For Working Late.
Avoiding Enforceability	
Undue Influence, Duress, Mistake, Misrepresentation	Usually I Do Make Money
Transfer of Contractual Rights and Responsibilities	
Novation, Vicarious Performance, Assignment	New Ventures Propose Adventure.
Discharge	
Performance, Law, Termination, Substitution, Alteration, Waiver, Frustration	Perseverance & Luck: These Sustain All Work & Fortune.
Breach of Contract and Remedies	
Breach: Conditions, Warranties, Mitigation	Business Creates Wealth & Money.
Remedies: Nominal, Restitution, Punitive, Specific Performance	Risks, Not Rewards, Plainly Sink Plans.

Frustration. Where an unanticipated event renders performance of a contract impossible (such as an act of God—force majeure—or some other event completely outside the control of the parties), the contract is at an end at common law, and the parties are discharged from further performance. Frustrated contract legislation exists in many jurisdictions to guide courts in apportioning losses in an equitable manner.

Breach of Contract and Remedies

If a party expressly says that it will not perform its obligations, the other party may treat the contract as at an end, and immediately sue for resulting damages on the basis of the statement. Alternatively, the injured party may wait for the date of performance and then sue for nonperformance, but accept the risk that frustration may discharge the contract in the meantime.

Where a party performs its contractual obligations only partially, a right to maintain an action for redress arises. The **breach** may be a failure to honor a **condition** (serious aspect) of the contract or a **warranty** of the contract (a lesser term). Sadly for sellers, failure in delivery is usually taken as a breach of condition, while failure of payment is taken as a breach of warranty. A breach of warranty does not entitle the injured party to treat the contract as ended, and that party must still perform. Where there is a breach of condition, more latitude exists for the injured party to withhold its own performance. In cases where a party's performance is so substandard as to mean that the injured party has received nothing, the breach is known as a fundamental breach. Not only can the injured party treat the contract as ended, but any exemption or escape clause relied on by the party in breach may have no effect. The injured party is not entitled to simply let the damages mount if he or she is in any position to mitigate the losses. A failure in **mitigation** of losses where that was possible may result in a reduced award of damages, to those that were an unavoidable consequence of the breach.

217

Remedies for breach include the following:

Nominal damages. If there has been no real damage, then the remedy is only "nominal" ($1), in recognition of the wrong.

Restitution damages. Where more substantial damage results from the breach, the general remedy is "restitutio in integrum," or to be restored to the position one would have been in but for the breach. This is the usual type of damages awarded by courts.

Punitive damages. Where a breach has occurred that is particularly offensive to the law, even greater punitive damages may be assessed as a penalty, in addition to damages in restitution.

Specific performance. Where the subject matter of the contract is unique (parcels of land, for example, are taken to be unique), the remedy given may require the party in breach to offer up the unique article or subject matter, rather than a monetary "equivalent."

Chapter 6

Importing

Chapter Objectives

International sale transactions consist of exporting and importing, technically, the shipment of goods or provision of services, and their reception, from one customs territory to another. The separate phases are subject to the public law of the two customs territories involved and we begin with the import phase of a sale of goods transaction, focusing on the public law and regulatory requirements. The private law of contract considerations surrounding imports should also be noted, as these considerations are factors that cause expense or trouble for importers, and must be negotiated during the creation of the sales contract itself.

In this chapter we will explore:

- The entry clearance process and documentary requirements
- Classification of goods for customs purposes

- Business implications, strategy and tactics associated with importing

Entry Clearance and Documentation

All trading nations impose some form of order on the process of entering goods into their territory, and virtually all impose some form of tax on those goods. The United States' administration and taxation of imports are fairly typical of most developed trading nations.

Both the process and the taxation must be kept in mind when potential importers search for sources of supply abroad. What seems to be a cheap price for goods sourced abroad may not be cheap at all: administration costs, duty, transportation, and insurance must all be factored into the cost structure. At bare minimum, importing traders must use extra diligence in their purchase price negotiations to ensure that they will still be able to meet their profit targets on resale.

One of the first supporting business parties will be encountered at this point: the customs broker. Customs brokers are licensed individuals and firms whose expertise lies in assisting importers (and exporters), for a fee, to comply with customs administration, documentation, and the payment of duties owing. This private sector business is engaged in all aspects of the clearance process and has the technical skill to remain abreast of the myriad of regulations that apply to specific transactions and types of goods. Equally important, customs brokers maintain a financial surety bond with the Customs Service. Such security for duty to be paid is technically a requirement for all imports, and by using a broker, the importer benefits by not having to supply its own bond. The importer ultimately remains responsible for duty owing, and a lien for unpaid duty attaches to the goods, but this feature of the customs broker is attractive in its own right. A power of attorney is required to authorize the customs broker to act on behalf of the consignee[1] or owner of the goods.

[1]Person or organization receiving the shipment.

The U.S. Customs Service,[2] an arm of the Border and Transportation Security Directorate of the Department of Homeland Security, administers customs clearance in the United States. The Customs Service is responsible for upholding major elements of nearly 400 different laws where border measures are relevant. As an example of this diversity, this responsibility extends from the Honeybee Act[3] (agriculture) and the Flammable Fabrics Act[4] (consumer protection) through the Currency and Foreign Transactions Reporting Act[5] (revenue and criminal law) to the North American Free Trade Agreement (trade promotion, tariffs, and customs clearance).

Following the terrorist acts of September 11, 2001, the entire regime of border protection and control has received increased attention and funding. While it cannot be described as ever having been lax, many informal practices aimed at business efficiency have been tightened to ensure compliance and control.

Of the Customs Service responsibilities, however, the Tariff Act of 1930, as amended,[6] and the Trade Act of 1974[7] are the most broadly applicable to the import clearance process.

The Tariff Act of 1930 authorizes the Customs Service to enforce laws relating to assessment and collection of duty and the exclusion of prohibited goods, as well as regulation of vessels and customs brokers. Under the act, all goods entering the United States must clear customs and are subject to customs duties, unless exempted by law. The Trade Act of 1974 extends Customs Service responsibilities to include antidumping and countervailing duties, as well as administration of the Generalized System of Preferences, which will be discussed below.

The U.S. import clearance process consists of six stages, with the same or similar process and terminology used in most other nations. These stages are

1. Arrival
2. Entry
3. Inspection
4. Classification
5. Appraisement
6. Liquidation

Arrival is just that—goods unloaded from a carrier within a port of entry—and is a defined term to distinguish it from entry itself. Entry is the presentation of goods and their related documentation to the Customs Service, again at a port of entry. Entry must follow arrival within 15 calendar days, or the goods may be sold as unclaimed by the Customs Service. An informal and streamlined entry process (including postal entry) does exist for shipments valued under $2,000. However, these smaller transactions are not within the scope of this text.

Inspection is the process of verification by the Customs Service that the shipment and the goods conform to their documentation, and that the goods are not otherwise prohibited

---

[2]The U.S. Customs Service was renamed the Bureau of Customs and Border Protection of the Department of Homeland Security, effective March 1, 2003. See H.R. Doc. No. 108–32 (2003). Having been named "the Customs Service" for more than 200 years, we retain this term for convenience and brevity until common usage dictates otherwise.

[3]7 U.S.C. §§ 281–286: prohibition on the importation of honeybees unless the country of origin is free of harmful diseases or parasites, or undesirable species or subspecies.

[4]15 U.S.C. §§ 1191–1204: prohibits the importation of any product that fails to conform to flammability standards.

[5]31 U.S.C. §§ 5301–5326: requires report of export and import of monetary instruments in excess of $10,000.

[6]19 U.S.C. §§ 1202–1677.

[7]19 U.S.C. §§ 2101–2119.

Even if a firm is more interested in exporting than importing, it must be aware of these steps, processes, and documentation. This is the system that will be faced by the exporter's customers, and the exporter will want to ensure that it does everything possible at its own end to ensure trouble-free customs clearance for its buyers. Exporters providing "customs-friendly" assistance in goods labeling, packing, shipment marking, and documentation will enjoy repeat business. Those that do not make this effort can look forward to confining their business to their domestic market.

from entry. After the goods have been inspected, or more often based on the importer's declaration, classification is the process of the exact identification of the goods and the rate of duty that applies to goods of that class. Once an appropriate duty rate has been determined, the value of the goods must be ascertained, which is the process of appraisement. Liquidation refers to the assessment and settlement of the resultant duty payable.

There are two types of formal entry of goods: the most common is "entry for consumption," while the second (and also widely used) is "in-bond" entry. In the first case, the goods immediately enter the domestic market and its stream of commerce, without restriction, with duty liquidated (paid).

In cases of entry "in bond," the goods are either in transit to another port of entry or are to be stored in a bonded warehouse. In such cases, the importer will not pay the duty owing until he or she intends to bring out the goods and put them into the stream of commerce.

At first glance, this may seem an odd arrangement, but it is highly appropriate for large-volume or high-value shipments. A manufacturer may wish to buy in bulk and import a year's worth of component parts in one shipment, but would otherwise be faced with a gigantic one-time charge for the import duty. The bonded warehouse concept (privately owned, having posted a bond) allows the goods to trickle out as needed, with duty gradually paid to the Customs authority. The bonded warehouse therefore creates a neutral zone, with the goods "in country" but not "in commerce." A storage fee is paid directly to the warehouse operator, representing the transaction cost of selecting this entry and storage option.

Consumption entries require, at minimum, the following documents:[8]

1. Entry application
   a. Entry/Immediate Delivery (Customs Form 3461) for any goods.
   b. Entry Manifest (Customs Form 7533) for goods imported from contiguous countries (Canada and Mexico).
2. Bill of lading, airway bill, or carrier's certificate (as a document of title, it represents evidence of the consignee's right to make entry).
3. Seller's commercial invoice (indicating value and description of the goods, and thus serving as evidence supporting the appropriate duty calculation).
4. Packing list (itemization of contents of crates and cartons).
5. Certificate of origin (if claiming preferential tariff).
6. Other declarations for particular types of goods, as required under federal, state, or local law.
7. Within 10 days of entry, an Entry Summary (Customs Form 7501). If this form is filed at the time of entry, then it serves in place of either Form 3461 or 7533, which would not be required.

[8]Pursuant to 19 C.F.R. §142.

Entry Application and Inspection

The Entry/Immediate Delivery Form 3461 (shown on page 223) triggers the full entry clearance process, unless a Form 7501 is submitted at the time of application. Form 3461 is an application for release of the goods from customs control, and as such it lists the particulars of the consignee, the carrier, and the merchandise. It recites that a bond has been posted and that it is sufficient to cover the duty owed.

The starting point for the determination of that duty is the importer's declaration as to the nature of the goods and their value; thus, the most essential elements of the application are the value declaration at Box 19 and the Harmonized System number, or H.S. Number, at Box 24. The significance of the Harmonized System number is the subject of the following section, but, in short, it is a universal identifier for individual commodities that will lead to a particular tariff rate to be applied to such goods.

The Entry/Immediate Delivery Form 3461 is completed with the primary information for the import into the United States of 250 electrical ceiling fans. The fans have been imported by US Global Imports Inc. (the buyer and consignee), at a value of US$16,000, from a source in the United Kingdom. They have arrived at the port of New York on December 14, 2004, aboard the ocean vessel *Ocean Starlight.*

Not all commercial shipments are physically inspected. However, proportions are closely examined to discourage smuggling, and this proportion has increased as an antiterrorist measure. The term *inspection,* in most cases, is a documentary review to verify that the described merchandise

- Fits under the nominated H.S. number.
- Is not prohibited.
- Is not in excess of any quota limit then in force.
- Meets admissibility standards for origin markings.
- Is accompanied by relevant government agency permits (if any are required).

The accompanying commercial invoice will be examined for completeness and accuracy, comparing it to the goods it lists to ensure neither a shortage nor overage would result in an incorrect assessment of duty.

The enforcement role on behalf of other interested government agencies is not an incidental part of Customs Service operations; it is central to its chief obligation of public security. Enforcement of the Honeybee Act may seem trivial at first glance. On reflection, it is the vigilant enforcement of such acts through Customs inspection that prevents contamination by prohibited items from causing widespread illness or destruction of agricultural resources.

Other aspects of public security (more tangibly, consumer protection) are served with inspection for compliance with intellectual property regimes (combating counterfeit goods); hazardous, toxic, or flammable materials; electrical products standards; and toy safety standards. It should go without saying, but sadly it needs repeating: an attempt to falsify documentation or otherwise mislead the course of inspection or the entry clearance process is a serious offense.

Penalties can be levied in addition to lawful duties in cases of fraud, gross negligence, and simple negligence in compliance.[9] If the violation did not affect the assessment of duties, then gross negligence attracts a penalty of 40 percent of the dutiable value of the merchandise, and 20 percent in the case of simple negligence. Some clemency is available in reduced penalties for those that come forward and disclose their fraud or negligence.

---

[9] 19 U.S.C. §1592.

Entry/Immediate Delivery Customs Form 3461 (pending amendment to Department of Homeland Security)

DEPARTMENT OF THE TREASURY

UNITED STATES CUSTOMS SERVICE

ENTRY/IMMEDIATE DELIVERY

19 CFR 142.3, 142.16, 142.22, 142.24

1.Arrival Date 14-12-2004		2.Elected Entry Date 14-12-2004	3.Entry Type Code/Name		4.Entry Number
5.Port New York		6.Single Trans. Bond	7.Broker/Importer File Number		
		8.Consignee Number			9.Importer Number
10.Ultimate Consignee Name US Global Imports Inc., 123 Commercial Avenue Bridgetown, New York, USA 13601					
12.Carrier Code		13.Voyage/Flight/Trip	14.Location of Goods-Codes(s)/Name(s)		
15.Vessel Code/Name M/V Ocean Starlight					
16.US Port of Unloading New York		17.Manifest Number	18.G.O. Number		19.Total Value $16,000
20.Description of Merchandise Ceiling Fans, 100 Watts					

21. IT/BL/AWB Code	22. IT/BL/AWB No.	23.Manifest Quantity	24.H.S.Number	25.Country of Origin	26.Manufacturer ID.
		250	8414.51.00.30	United Kingdom	

27. CERTIFICATION	28. CUSTOMS USE ONLY
I hereby make application for entry/immediate delivery. I certify that the above information is accurate, the bond is sufficient, valid, and current, and that all requirements of 19 CFR Part 142 have been met.	☐ Other agency action required, namely:
Signature of Applicant X *Doug Smith* per US Global Imports Inc.	☐ Customs Examination Required.
Phone No. (212) 605 1212	Date 14-12-2004
29.BROKER OR OTHER GOVT. AGENCY USE	☐ Entry Rejected, because:
	Delivery Authorized: Signature Date

Other "penalties" also exist. Customs violations are logged, and a violator can expect that its next series of import transactions will receive additional "attention." In some cases, "Do Not Ship" advisories are issued to shipping lines, and the importer may find it impossible to find a shipper willing to bring its goods to U.S. ports.

Where the payment of proper duty is in question, the maximum penalty for fraud is equivalent to the domestic value of the merchandise. For gross negligence, the penalty is the lesser of the value of the merchandise or four times the duty, and for negligence, the penalty is the lesser of the value of the goods or two times the duty. The following case illustrates how easy it is to attract more than a million dollars in penalties, even when the business partners thought they had paid the correct amount.

United States v. Hitachi America, Ltd.

United States of America, Plaintiff v. Hitachi America, Ltd. and Hitachi, Ltd., Defendant

United States Court of International Trade

November 5, 1999

Musgrave, Judge

[On remand from a decision of Court of Appeals for the Federal Circuit, assessment of civil penalty against Hitachi America, Ltd.]

Memorandum Opinion

Previously, this Court found Hitachi America Ltd. ("HAL") and Hitachi, Ltd. ("Hitachi Japan") negligent with respect to the declared dutiable value(s) of 41 entries of 120 subway cars and parts imported between June 16, 1984 and May 27, 1987 for use by the Metropolitan Atlanta Rapid Transit Authority ("MARTA"). The decision was appealed. The Court of Appeals for the Federal Circuit reversed judgment on Hitachi Japan and affirmed that HAL was negligent in declaring the dutiable transaction in US dollars rather than yen, but noted that the penalty had been assessed on "domestic transaction value (based on dollars) rather than on . . . import transaction value (based on yen)" . . . This memorandum addresses the amount of the civil penalty against HAL.

19 U.S.C. § 1592(c)("Maximum penalties") states that negligence is punishable by the lesser of the domestic value of the merchandise or twice the "lawful duties." Either case requires a proper determination of the "price actually paid or payable" for imported merchandise. The Court's prior opinion described MARTA's public contract ("CQ-311") with the importing joint venture, consisting of HAL (the importer of record) and C.Itoh America ("CIA") . . .

Under CQ-311's terms, MARTA could choose to pay foreign labor and material costs in US dollars or in yen at the rate of ¥269.7:$1.00. The invoices to MARTA itemized those payment obligations as required. MARTA chose to make all foreign-source payments to HAL/CIA in US dollars and in accordance with the invoices received. CIA, acting as a banker, exchanged an amount equivalent to these dollars for yen at the rate of ¥269.7:$1.00 . . . and remitted yen corresponding to MARTA's payments to its parent, C. Itoh Japan ("CIJ"). Separately, Hitachi Japan, the manufacturer, invoiced CIJ for payment in yen corresponding to the contract amounts MARTA was obligated to pay HAL/CIA . . .

. . .

The government viewed . . . MARTA's dollar payments . . . as indicative of the lawful transaction value of the merchandise. The defendants urged acceptance of the HAL/CIA-to-CIJ duty figure. The prior opinion of this Court did not regard the CIJ "sale" to HAL/CIA as at "arm's length" and therefore found the government's proffered methodology acceptable . . . The [Court of Appeals for the Federal Circuit] disagreed, finding

> [t]he sole dispute [to be] over which sales transaction must be used as a basis for calculating the penalty. The three available transactions are (1) the sale from Hitachi Japan to CIJ in Japan; (2) the sale from CIJ in Japan to the HAL/CIA joint venture in the U.S.; and (3) the sale between the joint venture and MARTA within the U.S. The value of the second sale, the import transaction value, was $632,102 (based on yen). The value of the third sale, the domestic transaction value, was $947,854 (based on dollars).

The first sale was not found applicable since there was observed agreement among the parties "that the correct transaction for penalty calculation purposes is the sale from CIJ to HAL/CIA." The [Court of Appeals for the Federal Circuit] therefore instructed use of that import transaction value in assessing the penalty . . . [T]he penalty is therefore assessed in accordance with 19 U.S.C. § 1592(c)(3)(A)(ii) at twice the import transaction value of the result of the government's alternative methodology, or $1,264,204.46 [two times $632,102].

Judgment will enter accordingly.

Source: Slip Op. 99–121, Court No. 93-06-00373, available at http://www.cit.uscourts.gov.

Why would the government advocate "MARTA's dollar payments as indicative of the lawful transaction value" in this case? Why would the CIJ to HAL/CIA be the most appropriate transaction value?

Classification and the Harmonized System

The effective management of a tariff system of duties requires some means of cataloging all possible imports and then assigning them a particular rate of duty. This system of cataloging is known as the Harmonized System (H.S.) and is used by virtually all countries to reach uniform descriptions of goods.

The H.S. number refers, globally, to the Harmonized Commodity Description and Coding System in each nation employing a tariff schedule based on that system, and in the United States, to the Harmonized Tariff Schedule of the United States.[10] The Harmonized System is a global standard listing of approximately 5,000 commodity groups developed by the World Customs Organization (WCO).[11] Each of the commodity groups is identified by a six-digit code, arranged in a legal and logical structure through negotiation between the over 175 members of the WCO. The numbered commodity groups make up more than 98 percent of world merchandise trade.

The H.S. system is vital to ensure that governments and traders are talking about the same items in their negotiations, taxation, and transactions. For example, if a government imposes a countervailing duty on "imported wood products," does it mean it intends to tax only rough-cut logs, or will artificial fire logs made partially of wood by-products be taxed as well? It is a completely unglamorous question of absolutely no significance to anyone

[10]http://dataweb.usitc.gov/SCRIPTS/tariff/toc.html.
[11]http://wcoomd.org.

except importers of artificial fire logs, for which it may mean the difference between life and death for their business.

For effective international trade, a universal nomenclature for goods contributes certainty as to the identity of particular goods in any given issue. A small slice of the U.S. Harmonized Tariff Schedule (HTSUS) is shown below, for logs and artificial fire logs. With the universal H.S. six-digit number (the first two being the chapter number), U.S. subheadings (two digits), and U.S. statistical suffixes (two digits), the full numeric identifier of a commodity, unless speaking of the class generally, is 10 digits. Thus, artificial logs are classified as 4401.30.20.00 and rough Ponderosa pine logs are classified as 4403.20.00.25 for trade purposes.

Harmonized Tariff Schedule of the United States (2003) (Rev. 1)
Annotated for Statistical Reporting Purposes
CHAPTER 44
WOOD AND ARTICLES OF WOOD; WOOD CHARCOAL

Heading/ Subheading	Stat. Suf-fix	Article Description	Unit of Quantity	Rates of Duty 1 General	Rates of Duty 1 Special	2
4401		Fuel Wood				
4401.30.20	00	**Artificial fire logs**, composed of wax and sawdust, with or without added materials . . .	kg	0.2%	Free	20%
4403		Wood in the rough, whether or not stripped of bark or sapwood, or roughly squared:				
4403.20.00		Other, coniferous		Free		Free
		Pulpwood:				
	04	Balsam, fir or spruce...................	m3			
	08	Other	m3			
		Logs and timber:				
	50	Pine (Pinus spp.): Southern yellow pine (Loblolly pine (Pinus taeda), long leaf pine (Pinus palustris), pitch pine (Pinus rigida), short leaf pine (Pinus echinada), slash pine (Pinus elliottii) and Virginia pine (Pinus virginiana)	m3			
	25	Ponderosa pine (Pinus ponderosa)	m3			

The importer enters what he or she believes to be the correct H.S. number for the commodity being imported onto Customs Form 3461, the Entry/Immediate Release document. Associated with each H.S. number in the Harmonized Tariff Schedule (HTS) will be a corresponding rate of duty.

The Customs Service is by no means bound by the importer's classification of the goods, and in the course of its own inspection will make a final determination of classification. Where necessary, in cases representing significant government revenue, possible fraud, or public safety, the inspection can turn into a laboratory analysis. For these reasons, it may be necessary to distinguish between Ponderosa pine and endangered tropical woods, or artificial fire logs made of petroleum by-products rather than those made of wood.

Some rules of thumb on the HS:

1. First, seek out and test the narrowest classification for the goods. If the goods will qualify for a preference, it is more likely to be under a narrow classification.
2. A corollary of the first: If your goods are in a category marked "Other," ensure you belong there, and that it has *not* been selected because someone (employee, broker, Customs officer) could not be bothered to work through the rules to find the correct category. In many countries, the "Other" (or "Misc.") category carries heavy rates of duty as a deterrent for just that reason.
3. If the duty will be assessed at a heavy rate, try changing the classification of the goods. Can the goods properly be interpreted as falling under another, better H.S. number (one with a lower rate of duty)? Can the goods be imported in another form (and therefore another H.S. number, e.g., as subassemblies or as components) that attracts a lower rate of duty?
4. If the duty is heavy and you can't change the classification, try changing the country of origin. Can originating goods be obtained from another country that is a free-trade partner?
5. An import manager who really knows how to use the HTS and rules is worth his or her "weight in gold," and perhaps more.

General rules of interpretation are available, as well as notes to each chapter of the HTS, in an effort to ensure that importers can determine H.S. numbers on their own. In addition, while nonbinding oral rulings may be obtained from ports of entry, binding advance classification rulings may be obtained in writing from the Customs Service.

The application of the HTS and classification rules is an exercise in legal interpretation. As such, there may be interpretations that benefit a particular good, transaction, or client, and others that do not. International traders can create or erase a profit based on their appreciation of different classifications of the HTS and the corresponding rates of duty.

Consider the Old Wolf's rules of thumb in the example below:

This is a fabric flower glued to a clip. Is it

1. A comb, hairslide, and the like, including a curling grip?
2. An artificial rose made of nylon, assembled with glue, with incidental clip?
3. A piece of imitation jewelry, excluding haircombs, not metal, not a necklace, over 20 U.S. cents per dozen, not made of plastic?

Perhaps it is something else again, but assuming it is fairly described as one of the above, one of the following duty rates will apply under the HTSUS. The particular rate that does apply depends on the country of origin of the goods.

The significance of the rate of duty categories is explained in detail in the notes below, but can be summarized as the nonpreferential MFN rate (General), the preferential rate for free trade partners and lesser-developed partners (Special), and an essentially punitive rate to discourage trade with hostile regimes (Category 2).

Selected HTS Lines—Combs, Roses, and Jewelry

Harmonized Tariff Schedule of the United States (2003) (Rev. 1)

Heading/ Subheading	Stat. Suf-fix	Article Description	Unit of Quantity	Rates of Duty		
				1		2
				General (Note 1)	Special (Note 2)	(Note 3)
9615.1130	00	Comb, hairslide and the like, including a curling grip	gross	28.8¢ per gross plus 4.6%	Free, except Jordan at 7.2¢ per gross plus 1.1%	$2.88 per gross plus 35%
6702.10.20	20	Artificial rose	unit	8.4%	Free	60%
7177.90.90	00	Imitation jewelry, excluding haircombs, not metal, not a necklace, over 20 US cents per dozen, not made of plastic	unit	17.0%	Free except Jordan at 6.8%	90%

Therefore, a $3,600 shipment of 14,400 such items would attract duty in the amounts shown below.

Duty, in Dollars, Resulting from HTSUS Application

Article Description	Rates of Duty		
	1		2
	General (Note 1) eg: goods originating in European Union	Special (Note 2) eg: goods originating in Canada or Mexico	(Note 3) eg: goods originating in North Korea
Comb, hairslide and the like, including a curling grip	$453.60	$0.00, or if from Jordan: $111.60	$4,140.00
Artificial rose	$302.00	$0.00	$2,160.00
Imitation jewelry, excluding haircombs, not metal, not a necklace, over 20 US cents per dozen, not made of plastic	$612.00	$0.00, or if from Jordan: $244.80	$3,240.00

Note 1: Category 1 General Rate

- The general, or normal trade relations (NTR), rate applicable to products of those countries that are not entitled to special tariff treatment. Normal trade relations is the U.S. substitute term for most-favored nation (MFN) status.

Note 2: Category 1 Special Rate

- Rate applicable where products originate from a territory where a special tariff treatment programs is in effect; see Remarks below.

Note 3: Category 2

- Rate applicable to products from countries that do not legally qualify under U.S. law for MFN status (policy sanctions against Communist non-market-economy nations and those who do not allow free emigration of their peoples), pursuant to
  - Section 401 of the Tariff Classification Act of 1962.
  - Section 231 or 257(e)(2) of the Trade Expansion Act of 1962.
  - Section 404(a) of the Trade Act of 1974.
  - Any other applicable section of law or action taken by the president.

  As of 2003, the list includes Cuba, Laos, and North Korea.

If the goods originate in Mexico, there will be no duty owing, no matter what the classification. If the goods originate in Europe, the duty can run from $302, if classified as an artificial rose, to more than twice that, if classified as jewelry. The foolishness of doing business with North Korea is evident. The overseas buyers for this company interested in importing flowers on clips may have no idea how the U.S. Harmonized Tariff will treat goods originating abroad; it is the import manager for the company who is really in the position to create or destroy profits. Clearly, a skilled import manager with input into decision making on sources of supply is vital to the success of an importing firm.

Remarks

- Beneficiary countries are chiefly those trade partners under
  - NAFTA (Canada, Mexico).
  - U.S.–Jordan and U.S.–Israel Free Trade Agreements.
  - Generalized System of Preferences.
  - Andean Trade Promotion and Drug Eradication Act.[12]
  - African Growth and Opportunity Act.
  - Caribbean Basin Economic Recovery Act.[13]
  - United States–Caribbean Basin Trade Partnership Act.

---

[12]Bolivia, Colombia, Ecuador, and Peru.

[13]As at early 2004, Antigua and Barbuda, Aruba, Bahamas, Barbados, Belize, British Virgin Islands, Costa Rica, Dominica, Dominican Republic, El Salvador, Grenada, Guatemala, Guyana, Haiti, Honduras, Jamaica, Montserrat, Netherlands Antilles, Nicaragua, Panama, Saint Kitts and Nevis, Saint Lucia, Saint Vincent and the Grenadines, and Trinidad and Tobago.

The Generalized System of Preferences (GSP) is a schedule of tariffs applicable to goods originating in developing countries.[14] It is akin to similar tariff schedules maintained by other developed countries, allowing for duty-free access to developed markets, subject to some significant limitations.[15]

Country of Origin and Certification

Effective regulation of international trade requires rules with respect to identification and certification of the country of origin of goods. Note that two separate principles are at work: identification and certification.

Virtually all customs territories of the world require the country of origin of goods to be physically marked on all imported goods.[16] Where it is impossible or impractical to mark the goods themselves (e.g., crude oil or necklace beads, respectively), it is their containers that must be marked. Other exemptions exist where it is simply undesirable to mark the goods, such as in the case of artworks. Foreign products that were not made for export but are imported by returning travelers for personal use are also exempt.

The requirement of marking, while helpful for determination of duty status, exists regardless of whether the goods are subject to duty or are duty-free. In every case where markings are required, they must be conspicuous to the ultimate purchaser, not just the Customs Service or the importer. The requirement speaks more to consumer protection, or, less delicately, nationalism and integrity of domestic markets. Perhaps these reasons are less significant in today's global economy, but a government at minimum wants its consumers to be informed when their purchases are supporting foreign jobs, and at best wants to encourage purchases from domestic production.

Where marking and certification of origin of goods intersect with actual border measures is in the qualification of certain goods for entry at all, or embargo, quarantine, quotas, tariff preferences, or punitive tariffs in the form of antidumping or countervailing duties.

Without such rules, governments have little hope for exercising any kind of effective trade policy. If an importing (destination) territory offers a preference to goods of Country A, but not

[14]As at early 2004, there are 144 customs territories: Afghanistan (since January 2003), Albania, Angola, Anguilla, Antigua and Barbuda, Argentina, Armenia, Bahrain, Bangladesh, Barbados, Belize, Benin, Bhutan, Bolivia, Bosnia and Herçegovina, Botswana, Brazil, British Indian Ocean Territory, British Virgin Islands, Bulgaria, Burkina Faso, Burundi, Cambodia, Cameroon, Cape Verde, Central African Republic, Chad, Chile, Christmas Island (Australia), Cocos (Keeling) Islands, Colombia, Comoros, Congo (Brazzaville), Congo (Kinshasa), Cook Islands, Costa Rica, Côte d'Ivoire, Croatia, the Czech Republic, Djibouti, Dominica, Dominican Republic, Ecuador, Egypt, El Salvador, Equatorial Guinea, Eritrea, Estonia, Ethiopia, Falkland Islands (Islas Malvinas), Fiji, Gabon, The Gambia, Georgia, Ghana, Gibraltar, Grenada, Guatemala, Guinea, Guinea-Bissau, Guyana, Haiti, Heard Island and McDonald Islands, Honduras, Hungary, India, Indonesia, Jamaica, Jordan, Kazakhstan, Kenya, Kiribati, Kyrgyzstan, Latvia, Lebanon, Lesotho, Lithuania, Former Yugoslav Republic of Macedonia, Madagascar, Malawi, Mali, Mauritania, Mauritius, Moldova, Mongolia, Montserrat, Morocco, Mozambique, Namibia, Nepal, Niger, Nigeria, Niue, Norfolk Island, Oman, Pakistan, Panama, Papua New Guinea, Paraguay, Peru, Philippines, Pitcairn Islands, Poland, Romania, Russia, Rwanda, Saint Helena, St. Kitts and Nevis, Saint Lucia, Saint Vincent and the Grenadines, Samoa, São Tomé and Príncipe, Senegal, Seychelles, Sierra Leone, Slovakia, Solomon Islands, Somalia, South Africa, Sri Lanka, Suriname, Swaziland, Tanzania, Thailand, Togo, Tokelau, Tonga, Trinidad and Tobago, Tunisia, Turkey, Turks and Caicos Islands, Tuvalu, Uganda, Uruguay, Uzbekistan, Vanuatu, Venezuela, Wallis and Futuna, West Bank and Gaza Strip, Western Sahara, Republic of Yemen, Zambia, and Zimbabwe.

[15]Be aware that specialized rules of origin apply, and no preference is extended to textiles and apparel; watches; import-sensitive electronics, steel, and glass; certain footwear, handbags, luggage, flat goods, work gloves, and leather wearing apparel; agricultural product in excess of quota; and any other articles that the president determines to be import-sensitive in the context of the GSP.

[16]In the United States, this is required by the Tariff Act of 1930 (19 U.S.C. §1304) and implemented by 19 C.F.R. 134.11.

DEPARTMENT OF THE TREASURY
UNITED STATES CUSTOMS SERVICE

**NORTH AMERICAN FREE TRADE AGREEMENT
CERTIFICATE OF ORIGIN**

OMB No. 1651-0098

Please print or type   19 CFR 181.11, 181.22

1. EXPORTER NAME AND ADDRESS	2. BLANKET PERIOD (DD/MM/YY)
TAX IDENTIFICATION NUMBER:	FROM TO
3. PRODUCER NAME AND ADDRESS	4. IMPORTER NAME AND ADDRESS
TAX IDENTIFICATION NUMBER:	TAX IDENTIFICATION NUMBER:

5. DESCRIPTION OF GOOD(S)	6. HS TARIFF CLASSIFICATION NUMBER	7. PREFERENCE CRITERION	8. PRODUCER	9. NET COST	10. COUNTRY OF ORIGIN

I CERTIFY THAT:

- THE INFORMATION ON THIS DOCUMENT IS TRUE AND ACCURATE AND I ASSUME THE RESPONSIBILITY FOR PROVING SUCH REPRESENTATIONS. I UNDERSTAND THAT I AM LIABLE FOR ANY FALSE STATEMENTS OR MATERIAL OMISSIONS MADE ON OR IN CONNECTION WITH THIS DOCUMENT;

- I AGREE TO MAINTAIN AND PRESENT UPON REQUEST, DOCUMENTATION NECESSARY TO SUPPORT THIS CERTIFICATE, AND TO INFORM, IN WRITING, ALL PERSONS TO WHOM THE CERTIFICATE WAS GIVEN OF ANY CHANGES THAT COULD AFFECT THE ACCURACY OR VALIDITY OF THIS CERTIFICATE;

- THE GOODS ORIGINATED IN THE TERRITORY OF ONE OR MORE OF THE PARTIES, AND COMPLY WITH THE ORIGIN REQUIREMENTS SPECIFIED FOR THOSE GOODS IN THE NORTH AMERICAN FREE TRADE AGREEMENT, AND UNLESS SPECIFICALLY EXEMPTED IN ARTICLE 411 OR ANNEX 401, THERE HAS BEEN NO FURTHER PRODUCTION OR ANY OTHER OPERATION OUTSIDE THE TERRITORIES OF THE PARTIES; AND,

- THIS CERTIFICATE CONSISTS OF   PAGES, INCLUDING ALL ATTACHMENTS.

11.	11a. AUTHORIZED SIGNATURE		11b. COMPANY	
	11c. NAME		11d. TITLE	
	11e. DATE (MM/DD/YYYY)	11f. TELEPHONE NUMBER >	(Voice)	(Facsimile)

Customs Form 434 (040397)

those produced by Country B, then without marking and certification of origin rules, the goods of Country B will anonymously migrate to Country A. They will do so with the intention of fraudulently entering the destination territory from Country A, at the preferred rate of duty.

A claim for a preferential tariff such as normal trade relations (MFN), NAFTA, or GSP cannot be maintained without compliance with marking requirements and, additionally, an accompanying certificate of origin. Each trading nation employs a general certificate of origin of its own for general purposes and special documents typically for special trading relationships. In the case of NAFTA, the certificate of origin shown on page 231 is a trilaterally agreed document, which gives rise to the importer's claim for duty-free treatment of the goods.

Where all aspects of the origin of goods are confined to one nation (be it a NAFTA nation or otherwise), the completion of any certificate of origin is not a problem. Trouble arises when the goods, or parts of them, originate in one place and are assembled with other components or transformed in another place. The question arises as to where the assembled good, or the new good, should be properly described as originating. The particular NAFTA treatment of this situation is described in Chapter 5 in this text and is provided for in law in NAFTA Articles 400–415 together with their annexes. Globally, the key is usually one of substantial transformation of the component goods into some other goods, where the former identity is lost and a new one is assumed. For example, black-and-white Italian Carrera marble blocks may be imported into Mexico. There, some are sliced into small squares and bonded to form stone chessboards, while other blocks are carved into the chess pieces. This transformation from stone blocks into gaming sets is a major alteration in the name, character, and use of the component material. It would justify not only a change in the tariff classification from stone to game, but also the view that the chess sets originated in Mexico. An example of a more contentious situation forms the basis of the case below.

Bestfoods v. United States

United States Court of Appeals for the Federal Circuit

BESTFOODS (formerly known as CPC International, Inc.), Plaintiff-Appellee
v. UNITED STATES, Defendant-Appellant.

July 26, 2001

ARCHER, Senior Circuit Judge.

The United States appeals from the judgment of the Court of International Trade holding that 19 C.F.R. § 102.13(b) is arbitrary, capricious, an abuse of discretion, and otherwise contrary to law. This regulation withholds de minimis[17] treatment under the federal marking statute from most agricultural products. Concluding that 19 C.F.R. § 102.13(b) is a valid exercise of discretion by the United States Customs Service ("Customs"), we reverse.

Background

Bestfoods makes Skippy peanut butter in Little Rock, Arkansas. The peanut butter is manufactured from peanut slurry, a gritty, peanut-based paste. Most of the peanut slurry in Bestfood's peanut butter is made in the United States, but 10–40% of the peanut slurry is made in Canada from peanuts grown elsewhere.

In January 1993, Bestfoods sought an administrative ruling from the United States Customs Service ("Customs") that it was not required to indicate under the federal marking

---

[17]Author's note: In short, where only a tiny amount or technical violation exists, the law should not apply.

statute, 19 U.S.C. § 1304(a), that its peanut butter was partially of Canadian origin. The federal marking statute requires "article[s] of foreign origin . . . imported into the United States [to] be marked in a conspicuous manner . . . to indicate to an ultimate purchaser the English name of the country of origin of the article." However, where foreign materials or raw ingredients are included as components in a product manufactured in the United States, the marking statute may not be triggered if the foreign ingredient is substantially transformed in the manufacture of the final product. In arguing that it was not required to mark its peanut butter as a product of Canada, Bestfoods initially contended that the Canadian peanut slurry was substantially transformed in the manufacture of the peanut butter.

Customs determined, however, that Bestfoods was required to mark its product to indicate the Canadian origin of the peanut slurry. In reaching this conclusion, Customs applied regulations promulgated pursuant to the North American Free Trade Agreement ("NAFTA"). Those regulations replaced the traditional case-by-case substantial transformation test with a "tariff shift" method. Under this tariff shift method, a good, or component of a good, is considered of United States origin if the subsequent manufacturing processes in the United States are sufficient to change that good or component's tariff classification. Peanut slurry and peanut butter are classified under the same tariff classification, HTSUS 2008.11.10. Therefore, because the peanut slurry does not undergo a tariff shift in the processing, Customs determined that the peanut butter containing this Canadian slurry must be marked to indicate the Canadian origin of the slurry.

Bestfoods appealed to the Court of International Trade, arguing that Customs had improperly replaced the traditional case-by-case substantial transformation test set forth in *United States v. Gibson-Thomsen Co.,* 27 C.C.P.A. 267, 1940 WL 4085 (1940) ("the Gibson-Thomsen test"). The court agreed with Bestfoods, and remanded to Customs to determine substantial transformation under the Gibson-Thomsen test. On remand, Customs again concluded that the peanut slurry did not undergo substantial transformation, and Bestfoods again appealed to the Court of International Trade. The court affirmed Customs' determination [*but*] . . . Bestfoods raised the new argument that 19 C.F.R. § 102.13(b) (2000) is arbitrary and capricious. This provision is a subsection of 19 C.F.R. § 102.13, and sets forth a de minimis rule that excepts from the marking requirement incorporated foreign material making up less than 7 percent of the overall value of the good (or 10 percent of the value for a good of Chapter 22, Harmonized System).[18] This de minimis exception is not applicable, however, to most agricultural products, as set forth in 19 C.F.R. § 102.13(b). Bestfoods argued [*before the Court of International Trade*] that the exclusion of agricultural products, such as its peanut butter, from the de minimis exception was arbitrary and capricious and, therefore, invalid. The Court of International Trade agreed with Bestfoods and entered judgment invalidating 19 C.F.R. § 102.13(b), effectively extending the de minimis rule of 19 C.F.R. § 102.13 to agricultural products such as Bestfoods' peanut butter.

The United States now appeals that judgment, arguing that 19 C.F.R. § 102.13(b) is a valid exercise of Customs' discretion and was improperly invalidated.

---

[18]In pertinent part, this regulation reads as follows:

§ 102.13 De Minimis

I. I. (a) Except as otherwise provided in paragraphs (b) and (c) of this section, foreign materials that do not undergo the applicable change in tariff classification set out in § 102.20 or satisfy the other applicable requirements of that section when incorporated into a good shall be disregarded in determining the country of origin of that good if the value of those materials is no more than 7% of the value of the good or 10% of the value of a good of Chapter 22, Harmonized System.

(b) Paragraph (a) of this section does not apply to a foreign material incorporated in a good provided for in Chapter 1, 2, 3, 4, 7, 8, 11, 12, 15, 17, or 20 of the Harmonized System.

19 C.F.R. § 102.13.

Discussion

We review the Court of International Trade's consideration of Customs' regulations . . . The federal marking statute expressly delegates to the Secretary of the Treasury the authority to promulgate regulations implementing the marking statute, in general, and as it specifically applies to goods imported from a NAFTA country.[19] In reviewing the regulations promulgated pursuant to this grant of authority, we must defer to the administrative agency and, under the APA standard of judicial review, we must uphold these regulations unless they are "arbitrary, capricious, an abuse of discretion, or otherwise not in accordance with law."

The United States argues that 19 C.F.R. § 102.13(b) is a valid exercise of Customs' discretion in promulgating regulations to implement the federal marking statute and the NAFTA marking rules. It notes that the federal marking statute does not require any de minimis exceptions. Moreover, the limited de minimis exception in the regulations corresponds with Customs' past practice and harmonizes the marking regulations with similar country of origin rules associated with the NAFTA Tariff Preference Rules. Accordingly, the United States asserts that the Court of International Trade improperly invalidated 19 C.F.R. § 102.13(b). We agree.

The regulation at issue, 19 C.F.R. § 102.13(b), is not arbitrary, capricious, an abuse of discretion, or otherwise not in accordance with law. Neither the federal marking statute, 19 U.S.C. § 1304(a), nor the NAFTA marking rules, set out in Annex 311 of the NAFTA, requires a de minimis exception for agricultural products. Indeed, the federal marking statute does not provide specifically for any such de minimis exceptions. In general, it requires that "*every* article of foreign origin . . . be marked." The marking statute then sets out certain circumstances where a foreign product need not be marked. For example, no marking is required when the article cannot be marked or the article was produced more than 20 years before its import or where marking of the article in question would be economically prohibitive. In view of the broad statutory language requiring marking of all articles, except for the listed exceptions, we cannot conclude that Customs was required to allow further exceptions from the marking requirement.

As the United States points out, Customs' treatment of agricultural products under the NAFTA marking rules codifies its past practice of strictly enforcing the marking statute with respect to such articles. For example, in 1985, Customs determined that orange juice manufacturers were required to mark their products to identify every source of foreign concentrate included in their juice.[20]

In addition, withholding the de minimis exception from agricultural products tends to harmonize the country of origin rules for marking purposes with the country of origin rules for preferential tariff treatment under the NAFTA. The country of origin rules for preferential tariff treatment, while providing a de minimis exception for components comprising less than 7% of the value of the overall good, withhold this treatment from agricultural products.[21] Customs' action in establishing a de minimis rule, for purposes of the NAFTA marking rules, that closely tracks the de minimis rule for preferential tariff treatment under the NAFTA is not arbitrary.

---

[19]The United States Customs Service is within the Department of the Treasury and promulgated the regulations in question. It also has responsibility for enforcing the federal marking statute.

[20]Customs subsequently relaxed this requirement, following a showing by the juice manufacturers that the marking was economically prohibitive. Treas. Dec. 89–66 (1989), reprinted in 54 Fed. Reg. 29,540 (July 13, 1989). Bestfoods argues that this subsequent decision indicates that Customs' past practice was not to enforce strictly the marking requirement. We disagree. Customs' decision to relax the marking requirement for juice manufacturers was based on a specific showing of economic harm, which is an enumerated exception to the general rule set out in the statute. *See* 19 U.S.C. § 1304(a)(3)(K) (1994).

[21]These rules withhold de minimis treatment from various other products as well.

We also reject Bestfoods' contention that the regulations, which do not apply the principle of *de minimis non curat lex*[22] to the marking of agricultural products, are inconsistent with our decision in *Alcan Aluminum, Inc. v. United States,* 165 F.3d 898 (Fed. Cir. 1999). The present case is readily distinguishable from *Alcan*. In *Alcan*, [*the aluminum ingots at issue were only 1 percent Canadian in origin, and*] in light of the general principle of *de minimis non curat lex,* over 99% transformation was sufficient to meet the requirements of the properly-construed tariff classification.

In the present case, however, we are not confronted with foreign components on the order of one percent. Rather, Bestfoods seeks to take advantage of the relatively generous de minimis standard articulated in the marking regulations—7% of the value of the final product. Therefore, the question presented by this case is whether the regulations arbitrarily withhold the 7% exception from agricultural products. For the reasons stated above, we conclude that they do not.

We also reject Bestfoods' arguments that the regulations at issue are based on inappropriate health and safety concerns and lead to absurd results. Pointing to published comments concerning the regulation at issue, Bestfoods contends that Customs improperly withheld the de minimis exception from agricultural products out of a misplaced concern for consumer safety. Bestfoods argues that it is not the role of Customs to address food safety issues and, therefore, this was an inappropriate justification for Customs' regulation. We do not agree. Customs has the discretion to promulgate regulations to implement the federal marking statute, 19 U.S.C. § 1304(a), as further directed by the NAFTA marking rules, for products from NAFTA countries. As noted above, the purpose of marking products under the marking statute is to inform consumers of the origin of foreign goods. It was surely within Customs' discretion to determine that consumers might be more concerned about foreign materials in agricultural products, including foods. Thus, Customs' reference to "health and food safety concerns" does not necessarily indicate that Customs has improperly taken on a role assigned to other federal agencies that are directly responsible for ensuring food safety. Rather, Customs was merely exercising its discretion to craft rules that would best inform consumers.

We similarly reject Bestfoods' arguments that the regulation leads to absurd results. Bestfoods points out that under the marking regulations consumers are not informed about any quantity of foreign ingredients, if such ingredients are substantially transformed (so as to undergo a shift in tariff classification) during manufacturing of the final product. Further, Bestfoods argues that potentially toxic foreign non-agricultural additives are subject to the de minimis exceptions, and the foreign origins of such additives need not be indicated if less than 7%. Again, we do not find Bestfoods' contentions persuasive. Although the marking regulations will not always indicate to consumers the foreign origin of certain components, we cannot conclude that it was arbitrary or capricious for Customs to consider substantially-transformed ingredients to be products of the country of manufacture, even if the raw materials come from some foreign location. Indeed, this was exactly the conclusion that the NAFTA Marking Rules required. As for Bestfoods' contention concerning non-agricultural additives, it is simply incorrect. The de minimis exception is withheld for foreign material incorporated into any agricultural product identified in § 102.13(b), no matter whether the incorporated foreign material is an agricultural product or non-agricultural food additive.

Finally, in its briefing and at oral argument, Bestfoods contended that Customs' marking regulations lead to absurd results in that products that are otherwise of domestic origin must be labeled as foreign products even if only minute quantities of foreign materials are added. We have carefully considered Bestfoods' arguments and we have carefully reviewed the additional briefing by both parties on this issue. We conclude that the regulations, when properly interpreted, do not lead to any absurd results.

---

[22]Author's note: "the court does not concern itself with trifles."

Conclusion

For the reasons stated above, 19 C.F.R. § 102.13(b) is not arbitrary, capricious, an abuse of discretion, or otherwise contrary to law. Accordingly, the judgment of the Court of International Trade invalidating this regulation is reversed.

Source: Available at http://www.ll.georgetown.edu/federal/judicial/fed/opinions/00opinions/00-1547.html.

Having considered the *Bestfoods* case:

1. What merit or rationale exists for de minimis tests?
2. Should agricultural products face a different standard than industrial products?
3. Do marking requirements stand as nontariff barriers to trade?
4. What consideration should be given to the views of the American consumer?
5. Is Bestfoods denied some form of competitive "benefit" or "advantage" in this case?

Bestfoods' concerns are in marking, not in cost; it enjoys the duty free movement of its goods under NAFTA. A cost reduction—an equally important competitive advantage—is being sought in the next case, which also seeks a classification review. In this case, *Drexel,* the company's entire strategy of sourcing abroad is at risk.

Drexel v. U.S.

Drexel Chemical Company, Plaintiff, v. The United States, Defendant
United States Court of International Trade
June 5, 2003
Musgrave, Judge

This action concerns the proper classification of certain entries of Diuron Technical and Diuron 80-WP herbicides imported from Malaysia by Plaintiff Drexel Chemical Company ("Drexel"). The United States Customs Service . . . classified the entries of Diuron Technical under subheading 2924.21.1500 of the Harmonized Tariff Schedule of the United States ("HTSUS"), which specifies a duty rate of 13.5% *ad valorem,* and Diuron 80-WP under HTSUS subheading 3808.30.1000 which specifies a duty rate of $0.18/kg plus 9.7%. Drexel asserts that the Diuron Technical should have been classified under A2924.21.1500 and the Diuron 80-WP under A3808.30.1000, the "A" prefix indicating that the merchandise is eligible for duty-free entry pursuant to the Generalized System of Preferences ("GSP"), as the product of a beneficiary developing country. Resolution of this dispute turns on whether chemicals imported into Malaysia and used in the production of the Diuron Technical and Diuron 80-WP underwent a dual substantial transformation . . .

Standard of Review

. . . [T]he burden of proof is on the party challenging the classification. Nevertheless, it is the Court's role to "consider whether the government's classification is correct, both independently and in comparison with the importer's alternative."
   . . . The term "produced in the beneficiary developing country" is defined to mean that "the constituent materials of which the eligible article is composed . . . are either (1) [w]holly the growth, product, or manufacture of the beneficiary developing country; or (2) [s]ubstantially transformed in the beneficiary developing country into a new and different article of commerce." 19 C.F.R. § 10.177(a) (1993 & 1994). A substantial transformation occurs when material undergoes "a processing that results in a new article having a distinctive name, character, or use." *Torrington Co. v. United States,* 8 CIT 150, 154, 596 F.

Supp. 1083, 1086 (1984), *aff'd* 764 F.2d 1563 (Fed. Cir. 1985). "All three of these elements need not be met before a court may find a substantial transformation."

Background

. . . Diuron and DCU are common names for dichloro diphenyl dimethyl urea, which acts as an herbicide by inhibiting the Hill Reaction in plants. Diuron Technical is used to formulate other herbicides such as . . . Diuron 80-WP. Diuron 80-WP is a dry, powdered herbicide that the end-user mixes and applies with a spray tank. The merchandise at issue was purchased from Ancom, a Malaysian company not affiliated with Drexel.

. . . The first step in [*Ancom*] production involves the reaction of imported [*into Malaysia*] dichlorophenyl isocynate and dimethylamine along with solvents to produce DCU [*cake*] . . .

. . . The DCU cake is then put through a "sugar mill" to grind it into smaller particles to make it easier to handle. During this initial grinding process silica and clay are added to the DCU to coat the surface of the particles and prevent them from agglomerating . . . After this, the DCU is in a powder form . . . If Diuron 80-WP is being produced a dry surfactant is added during the blending in addition to the silica and clay. After blending, the mixture is air milled in an impact mill . . . The milling process is the final step in the production of Diuron Technical and Diuron 80-WP, and once this is complete the ground material is bagged and placed on pallets.

Arguments

In the present case, there is no dispute that the initial reaction of imported [*into Malaysia*] dichlorophenyl isocynate ("DCPI") and dimethylamine ("DMA") to produce the DCU cake was a substantial transformation. Nevertheless, since the DCPI and DMA were not from a beneficiary developing country, the DCU cake [*would not be*] entitled to duty-free import [*into the United States*] under the GSP. The issue is whether the subsequent air milling [*in Malaysia*] of the DCU into fine particles, five microns or less in size, effected a second substantial transformation, thus enabling the value of the DCU cake to be counted toward the requirement . . . that 35 percent of the appraised value of the merchandise be derived from materials produced or processing operations performed in the beneficiary developing country.

. . .

Customs argues that there is not a second substantial transformation . . . , but that the DCU cake is merely an intermediate product. Customs places great emphasis on the fact that the grinding processes do not change the structure of the Diuron molecule, which is present in the initial DCU cake, and argues that this molecule is the essence of [*the final products*].

. . .

Analysis

Prior decisions by this court in *Torrington Co. v. United States,* 8 CIT 150, 596 F. Supp. 1083 (1984), *aff'd* 764 F.2d 1563 (Fed. Cir. 1985), [and] *Azteca Milling Co. v. United States,* 12 CIT 1153, 703 F. Supp. 949 (1988), *aff'd* 890 F.2d 1150 (Fed. Cir. 1989) are relevant to the present action. In *Torrington* the court held that there was a dual substantial transformation where wire from a non-beneficiary developing country was processed first into sewing machine needle blanks and then into finished needles in Portugal. The court found that the character of the wire changed in its processing into the needle blanks, noting that it "has been cut to a specific length, beveled to meet specifications, and its circumference has been altered." The court also found that the needle blanks were a "new and different article of commerce" based on two sales of the needle blanks by the plaintiff to a related company and instances where other companies imported similar merchandise. Furthermore, the court found that a second substantial transformation took place when the needle blanks were processed into industrial sewing machine needles by having an eye pressed into them, being mill flashed to remove excess material around the eye, and having a point placed on the needle along with identifying information regarding the size, type, and brand.

In *Azteca* the plaintiff alleged that three distinct intermediate products were formed during the production of tortilla and taco shell flour in Mexico. First, corn from the United States was cooked to form a product called nixtamal, which was then ground to form a second product called masa. The masa was then dried to form a third product referred to as tamale flour, which was finally sifted to form the tortilla and taco shell flour. The court found that

> [t]he products resulting at certain steps in plaintiff's patented process may be more refined than the constituent material of corn, but, nevertheless, are clearly recognizable as processed corn . . . . each product has not "lost the identifying characteristics of its constituent material."

Significantly, the court also found that the products formed at each stage of the production process were not "distinct 'articles of commerce' " because the plaintiff had not shown any commercial transactions or a market for them. Thus the court held that there had not been a dual substantial transformation.

. . .

In the present action the Court finds the processing of the DCU into the Diuron Technical and 80-WP similar to the processing of the needle blanks into the finished needles in *Torrington*. Customs argues that the present case is more analogous to *Azteca* . . . in that the identifying characteristic, namely the Diuron molecule, is equally present in the DCU cake and the final products. Nevertheless, the Court finds that in this instance the final product has gained new identifying characteristics in addition to the diuron molecule. The Court finds that the air milling process causes not only a physical change in the size of the particle, but also a chemical change . . . Moreover, while the Diuron molecule is equally present both before and after the air milling process, the DCU "is useless as a herbicide," but "[t]he final product that comes out is a herbicide." Based on these findings, the Court concludes that there was a change in the character of the DCU in its processing into Diuron Technical and Diuron 80-WP.

The Court also finds that Drexel has demonstrated that the DCU is an article of commerce . . . DCU is ultimately sold to a manufacturer for further processing and ultimate use as an herbicide, [*but*] it is nevertheless an article of commerce with a different character than the finished product.

Finally, the *Torrington* court noted that "the GSP was enacted to promote 'economic diversification, and export development' in less developed countries." Based on the technical nature of the manufacturing operations performed . . . in Malaysia and the value of the machinery required, which was at least 1.5 million dollars, the Court finds that the goals of the GSP have been satisfied in this instance.

Conclusion

Taking the record as a whole, . . . the Court finds that a dual substantial transformation occurred in the manufacture of Diuron Technical and Diuron 80-WP. Customs shall therefore reliquidate the entries at issue duty-free under HTSUS subheading A2924.21.1500 or A3808.30.1000.

Source: Slip Op. 03–60, Court No. 98-02-00295-S, available at http://www.cit.uscourts.gov.

In *Drexel,*

1. What are the "dual transformations" the court is looking for?
2. Why is it important that DCU *fail* as a herbicide?
3. In its dealings with the Customs Service, there is a chance that Drexel could have avoided this court action. At least, it could have had its day in court long before it imported its first pallet of Diuron. How might it have done so?

Appraisement

Once a final determination is made as to what the goods are, and their resulting H.S. classification, one can make an informed judgment as to the value of the goods. Most often this is self evident from the seller's commercial invoice, where an arm's-length transaction has set a fair market value in the truest sense of the words.

Below is a sample British seller's commercial invoice for the sale of ceiling fans to a U.S. importer, related to the transaction example used in the Entry/Immediate Release Form 3461. For the purposes of duty calculation, the fair market value can be taken to be 10,000 UK pounds sterling (abbreviated GBP), which will be converted to U.S. dollars ($16,000) by the Customs Service at the official rate prevailing at the time of entry. As the invoice is "ex works," the U.S. importer has itself arranged and paid for shipping the goods, and thus there is no transportation charge imbedded in the price. Where there is a transportation charge within the price, the importer is entitled to deduct such charges in appraisement, so that the duty charged reflects only that which is payable on the goods themselves. Note that the exporter has indicated the universal six-digit H.S. heading and subheading number on the invoice, although this must be verified by the importer and must be expanded to the 8 or 10 digits required under the HTSUS for the specific item within the subheading.

In this case, a scan of the HTSUS reveals that the classification in the United States for ceiling fans not exceeding 125 watts is HS 8414.51.00.30, with a normal trade relations (MFN) duty rate of 4.7 percent applicable to fans of United Kingdom origin.

The appraisement for duty for these ceiling fans, assuming an exchange rate of $1.60 to each UK pound sterling, is $16,000.00. The duty levied follows at 4.7 percent of that amount, or $752.00. A further Customs merchandise processing fee of $33.60 is also payable, levied at a rate of 0.21 percent of the appraisement, with a $25.00 minimum and a $485 maximum.

In passing, note that the goods were exempt from UK domestic sales tax, known there as value-added tax, or VAT; domestic consumption taxes are not levied on merchandise for export in any jurisdiction. Any nation that did so would be placing its export production at a competitive disadvantage against the produce of other nations.

In the majority of cases, duty is assessed, as it was here, at ad valorem rates: a percentage of the dutiable value of the imported goods. Some items, however, are dutiable at a specific rate per piece or unit of weight, and yet others are assessed a compound rate that combines both ad valorem and specific rates. The previous example of the fabric flower employed all three methods in calculation, with the use of each dependent on the place of origin of the goods.

In some cases, an ad valorem rate is impossible to calculate, or would be inaccurate, based on a particular invoice. The invoice may not exist at all or may have a zero transaction value, in the case of imported goods that are free warranty replacements. Similarly, an invoice may not correctly reflect the value of the goods when the sale is not at arm's length, such as transfers of goods between related corporations. In such cases as these, the value of the imported goods under appraisement is the transaction value of identical merchandise. If merchandise identical to the imported goods cannot be found, then the value is the transaction value of

Sample Seller's Commercial Invoice

Hydroaire PLC

Ship To:

As per Billing
Address

Bill To:

US Global Imports Ltd
123 Commercial Avenue
Bridgetown, New York
USA 13601

Invoice # 4604
Date: 12/3/2004
Cust#: 1406

Date	Your Order #	Our Order #	Terms	Shipping Instructions
2/12/2004	412-03	X4935677	Ex Works	Export packing, Purchaser's Carrier, PU from our loading bay

Quantity	Item #	Description	Price per Unit	Total
250	40-2	Ceiling fans, 100 Watt	40.00 GBP	10,000.00 GBP
		Memo HS: 8414.51		

Subtotal	10,000.00 GBP
Tax	<exempt>
Shipping	Nil
Other	Nil
Balance Due	10,000.00 GBP

1411 Coast Road, Dover, Kent, United Kingdom
Phone: (41323) 833233   Fax: (41323) 18332447
orders@hydroaire.co.uk
www.hydroaire.co.uk

similar merchandise. To qualify as similar, the merchandise used in the comparison would have to be recently imported and commercially interchangeable with the merchandise being appraised.

Do not be tempted to agree to "double invoicing." Here, the exporter offers to save you money on duty (in the hope of sweetening the deal or getting your business) by providing a false invoice showing a lower value. This lower value would become the value for duty, resulting in a lower assessment.

The dangers are many in this common but foolish and illegal practice. Obviously, if the Customs Service finds out, there will be penalties, and your supplier may later blackmail you with the threat of disclosure. If the goods are damaged in transit, your insurance company will only pay out on the basis of the declared value shown on the commercial invoice and Customs documents. Being known to engage in fraud will complicate all future relations with shippers, insurers, and the Customs Service, who won't care whether "you've learned your lesson."

Liquidation

All steps in the formal entry clearance process are summarized on the Entry Summary Customs Form 7501. If the Form 7501 is filed at the time the Entry/Immediate Delivery Form 3461 would have been filed, then Form 3461 is not required. If the Form 7501 follows later, it must be filed no later than 10 days after entry of the goods. Continuing with the example of the British export of ceiling fans to a U.S. importer, the primary fields in Form 7501 would appear as shown in the example on page 242.

The Customs Service will make an estimated assessment of duty owing based on the inspection and classification steps, and this will be entered on the entry summary. Where the entry has been handled by a customs broker with a bond in place, the goods will be released on that basis with a bill for duty to follow. Otherwise, the importer must post a bond of its own prior to release of the goods.

The estimated duty therefore becomes due and payable, but the file remains open until it is liquidated. Liquidation means the final computation or ascertainment of the duty accruing on an entry and closure of the assessment process. This may be achieved through a Customs audit (which may alter the duty payable) or by operation of the law. In the case of operation by law, which is essentially a limitation period placed on the audit, liquidation is deemed to be in accordance with the importer's filings one year after entry. Alternatively, the estimation and liquidation regime can be seen as giving the Customs Service an automatic right to re-assessment for one year based on the premise that the transaction is not closed before then.

Protest

An importer has 90 days after the date of an entry clearance decision or liquidation to protest such a decision or assessment. A protest and request for administrative review must be lodged with the port director of the port where the decision was made. This mechanism is intended to provide local dispute resolution, where most complaints will have arisen from administrative error, are easily recognized, and are easily corrected.

Where matters are more contentious, and as long as a request for further review was made at the time of protest, there is an automatic right of review of the port director's decision by the Customs Service Center. Any protest denied may be contested in a civil action before the U.S. Court of International Trade.

DEPARTMENT OF THE TREASURY
UNITED STATES CUSTOMS SERVICE

ENTRY SUMMARY

Importer's Broker's Name And Address CustomsHelp Inc, 4402 Port Street, New York, NY	1. Entry No.		2. Entry Type Code	3. Entry Summary Date 14-12-2004
	4. Entry Date 14-12-2004		5. Port Code	
	6. Bond No. A61393		7. Bond Type Code	8. Broker/Importer File No.

9. Ultimate Consignee Name and Address	10. Consignee No.	11. Importer of Record Name and Address Consignee		12. Importer No.
US Global Imports Inc, 123 Commercial Avenue, Bridgetown, New York, USA 13601		13. Exporting Country United Kingdom		14. Export Date
		15. Country of Origin United Kingdom		16. Missing Documents
		17. I.T. No.		18. I.T. Date

19. B/L or AWB No.	20. Mode of Transportation Ocean	21. Manufacturer I.D.	22. Reference No.
23. Importing Carrier Starlight Lines - M/V Ocean Starlight	24. Foreign Port of Lading Dover, UK	25. Location of Goods / G.O. No.	
26. U.S. Port of Unlading New York	27. Import Date 14-12-2004		

28. Line No.	29. Description of Merchandise			33.	34.	35. Duty and I.R. Tax	
	30. A. T.S.U.S.A No. B. ADA / CVD Case No.	31. A. Gross Weight B. Manifest Qty.	32. Net Quantity in T.S.U.S.A. Units	A. Entered Value B. CHGS C. Relationship	A. T.S.U.S.A. Rate B. ADA/CVD Rate C. I.R.C. Rate D. Visa No.	Dollars	Cents
1	A. HS 8414.51.00.30	B. 250 units	250 units	A. $16,000.00	A. 4.7%	752	00

36. Declaration of Importer of Record (Owner or Purchaser) or Authorized Agent	U.S. CUSTOMS USE		TOTALS	
I declare that I am the ☐ importer of record and that the actual OR ☒ owner or purchaser or agent thereof. owner purchaser, or consignee for customs purposes is shown above.	A. Liq. Code	B. Ascertained Duty	37. Duty	752 00
I further declare that the merchandise ☒ was obtained pursuant to a purchase OR ☐ was not obtained pursuant to a purchase or agreement to purchase and that the prices set forth in the invoices are true. or agreement to purchase and the statements in the invoices as to value or price are true to the best of my knowledge and belief.		C. Ascertained Tax	38. Tax	
I also declare that the statements in the documents herein filed fully disclose to the best of my knowledge and belief the true prices, values, quantities, rebates, drawbacks, fees, commissions, and royalties and are true and correct, and that all goods or services provided to the seller of the merchandise either free or at reduced cost are fully disclosed. I will immediately furnish to the appropriate customs officer any information showing a different state of facts.		D. Ascertained Other	39. Other	33 61
		E. Ascertained Total	40. Total	785 61

Notice required by Paperwork Reduction Act of 1980. This information is needed to ensure that importers / exporters are complying with U.S. Customs laws, to allow us to compute and collect the right amount of money, to enforce other agency requirements, and to collect accurate statistical information on imports. Your response is mandatory.	41. Signature of Declarant, Title, and Date *Doug Smith*, Import Manager, US Global Imports 14-12-2004

Canadian Regulatory Requirements for Imports

Canada requires similar documentation to that of the United States and follows a substantially similar process for clearance. In Canada, border control authority rests with the Canada Customs and Revenue Agency (CCRA). It derives the most part of its authority in border measures from three Canadian federal acts: the Customs Act, the Customs Tariff Act, and the Special Import Measures Act.

The Customs Act is an administrative law setting out the powers and duties of Customs officers, the procedures for the importation of goods, and the rules for the collection of customs duties. The Customs Act also provides appeal procedures that may be taken by importers who disagree with alleged customs violations or duty rate decisions, as well as penalties imposed for violation or for attempts to avoid proper payment of duty. The Customs Tariff Act sets out the rates of duty, both general and preferential, that will be charged on goods brought into Canada. It also contains a list of prohibited goods (such as weapons and drugs) that may not be imported into Canada or require special permission. The Special Import Measures Act addresses the dumping of foreign goods into Canada and countervailing duties.

Canada Customs and Revenue Agency—Cargo Control Document (CCD)

Canada Customs and Revenue Agency	Agence des douanes et du revenu du Canada	Acquittal No. - N° de l'acquittement
IN BOND EN DOUANE	**CUSTOMS CARGO CONTROL DOCUMENT DOCUMENT DE CONTRÔLE DU FRET DES DOUANES**	

U.S. port of exit - Bureau de sortie des É.-U.	In transit - En transit	
Manifest from - Manifeste de	To - À	

Carrier code - Code du transporteur   Cargo control No. - N° de contrôle du fret

Consignee name and address - Nom et adresse du destinataire

Shipper name and address - Nom et adresse de l'expéditeur

Previous cargo control No. - N° de contrôle du fret antérieur

No. of pkgs. Nombre de colis	Description and marks Désignation et marques	Weight Poids	Rate Taux	Advances Avances	Prepaid Port payé	Collect Port dû

Foreign point of lading - Port de chargement étranger   Location of goods - Emplacement des marchandises

Name of carrier - Nom du transporteur   Conveyance identification - Identification du moyen de transport

A8A(B)

MAIL COPY - EXEMPLAIRE DE LA POSTE

Canada Customs and Revenue Agency—Customs Coding Form B-3

Canada Customs and Revenue Agency | Agence des douanes et du revenu du Canada

CANADA CUSTOMS CODING FORM
DOUANES CANADA - FORMULE DE CODAGE

PROTECTED (WHEN COMPLETED) PROTÉGÉ (UNE FOIS REMPLI)

1 IMPORTER NAME AND ADDRESS NOM ET ADRESSE DE L'IMPORTATEUR	NO. - N°
2 TRANSACTION NO. - N° DE TRANSACTION	
3 TYPE	4 OFFICE NO. N° DE BUREAU
5 GST REGISTRATION NO. N° DE TPS	6 PAYMENT CODE CODE DE PAIEMENT
7 MODE OF TRANS. MODE DE TRANS.	8 PORT OF UNLADING PORT DE DÉBARQ.
9 TOTAL VFD - TOTAL DE LA VD	
10 SUB HDR NO. N° DE SOUS-EN-TÊTE	11 VENDOR NAME - NOM DU VENDEUR
NO. - N°	12 COUNTRY OF ORIGIN PAYS D'ORIGINE
13 PLACE OF EXPORT LIEU D'EXPORTATION	14 TARIFF TREATMENT TRAITEMENT TARIFAIRE
15 U.S. PORT OF EXIT BUREAU DE SORTIE DES É.-U.	16 DIRECT SHIPMENT DATE DATE D'EXPÉDITION DIRECTE M D/J
17 CRCY. CODE CODE DEVISE	18 TIME LIMIT - DÉLAI
19 FREIGHT - FRET	20 RELEASE DATE - DATE DE LA MAINLEVÉE

21 LINE LIGNE	22 DESCRIPTION DÉSIGNATION	23 WEIGHT / KGM POIDS / KGM	PREVIOUS TRANSACTION - TRANSACTION ANTÉRIEURE 24 NUMBER - NUMÉRO	25 LINE-LIGNE	26 SPECIAL AUTHORITY AUTORISATION SPÉCIALE	
27 CLASSIFICATION NO. N° DE CLASSEMENT	28 TARIFF CODE TARIFAIRE	29 QUANTITY QUANTITÉ	30 U - M	31 VFD CODE CODE VD	32 SIMA CODE CODE DE LMSI	33 RATE OF CUSTOMS DUTY TAUX DE DROIT DE DOUANE
34 E.T. RATE TAUX T.A.	35 RATE OF GST TAUX DE TPS	36 VALUE FOR CURRENCY CONVERSION CONVERSION VALEUR POUR CHANGE				
37 VALUE FOR DUTY VALEUR EN DOUANE	38 CUSTOMS DUTIES DROITS DE DOUANE	39 SIMA ASSESSMENT COTISATION DE LMSI	40 EXCISE TAX TAXE D'ACCISE	41 VALUE FOR TAX VALEUR POUR TAXE	42 GST TPS	
21 LINE LIGNE	22 DESCRIPTION DÉSIGNATION	23 WEIGHT / KGM POIDS / KGM	PREVIOUS TRANSACTION - TRANSACTION ANTÉRIEURE 24 NUMBER - NUMÉRO	25 LINE-LIGNE	26 SPECIAL AUTHORITY AUTORISATION SPÉCIALE	
27 CLASSIFICATION NO. N° DE CLASSEMENT	28 TARIFF CODE TARIFAIRE	29 QUANTITY QUANTITÉ	30 U - M	31 VFD CODE CODE VD	32 SIMA CODE CODE DE LMSI	33 RATE OF CUSTOMS DUTY TAUX DE DROIT DE DOUANE
34 E.T. RATE TAUX T.A.	35 RATE OF GST TAUX DE TPS	36 VALUE FOR CURRENCY CONVERSION CONVERSION VALEUR POUR CHANGE				
37 VALUE FOR DUTY VALEUR EN DOUANE	38 CUSTOMS DUTIES DROITS DE DOUANE	39 SIMA ASSESSMENT COTISATION DE LMSI	40 EXCISE TAX TAXE D'ACCISE	41 VALUE FOR TAX VALEUR POUR TAXE	42 GST TPS	
21 LINE LIGNE	22 DESCRIPTION DÉSIGNATION	23 WEIGHT / KGM POIDS / KGM	PREVIOUS TRANSACTION - TRANSACTION ANTÉRIEURE 24 NUMBER - NUMÉRO	25 LINE-LIGNE	26 SPECIAL AUTHORITY AUTORISATION SPÉCIALE	
27 CLASSIFICATION NO. N° DE CLASSEMENT	28 TARIFF CODE TARIFAIRE	29 QUANTITY QUANTITÉ	30 U - M	31 VFD CODE CODE VD	32 SIMA CODE CODE DE LMSI	33 RATE OF CUSTOMS DUTY TAUX DE DROIT DE DOUANE
34 E.T. RATE TAUX T.A.	35 RATE OF GST TAUX DE TPS	36 VALUE FOR CURRENCY CONVERSION CONVERSION VALEUR POUR CHANGE				
37 VALUE FOR DUTY VALEUR EN DOUANE	38 CUSTOMS DUTIES DROITS DE DOUANE	39 SIMA ASSESSMENT COTISATION DE LMSI	40 EXCISE TAX TAXE D'ACCISE	41 VALUE FOR TAX VALEUR POUR TAXE	42 GST TPS	
21 LINE LIGNE	22 DESCRIPTION DÉSIGNATION	23 WEIGHT / KGM POIDS / KGM	PREVIOUS TRANSACTION - TRANSACTION ANTÉRIEURE 24 NUMBER - NUMÉRO	25 LINE-LIGNE	26 SPECIAL AUTHORITY AUTORISATION SPÉCIALE	
27 CLASSIFICATION NO. N° DE CLASSEMENT	28 TARIFF CODE TARIFAIRE	29 QUANTITY QUANTITÉ	30 U - M	31 VFD CODE CODE VD	32 SIMA CODE CODE DE LMSI	33 RATE OF CUSTOMS DUTY TAUX DE DROIT DE DOUANE
34 E.T. RATE TAUX T.A.	35 RATE OF GST TAUX DE TPS	36 VALUE FOR CURRENCY CONVERSION CONVERSION VALEUR POUR CHANGE				
37 VALUE FOR DUTY VALEUR EN DOUANE	38 CUSTOMS DUTIES DROITS DE DOUANE	39 SIMA ASSESSMENT COTISATION DE LMSI	40 EXCISE TAX TAXE D'ACCISE	41 VALUE FOR TAX VALEUR POUR TAXE	42 GST TPS	
21 LINE LIGNE	22 DESCRIPTION DÉSIGNATION	23 WEIGHT / KGM POIDS / KGM	PREVIOUS TRANSACTION - TRANSACTION ANTÉRIEURE 24 NUMBER - NUMÉRO	25 LINE-LIGNE	26 SPECIAL AUTHORITY AUTORISATION SPÉCIALE	
27 CLASSIFICATION NO. N° DE CLASSEMENT	28 TARIFF CODE TARIFAIRE	29 QUANTITY QUANTITÉ	30 U - M	31 VFD CODE CODE VD	32 SIMA CODE CODE DE LMSI	33 RATE OF CUSTOMS DUTY TAUX DE DROIT DE DOUANE
34 E.T. RATE TAUX T.A.	35 RATE OF GST TAUX DE TPS	36 VALUE FOR CURRENCY CONVERSION CONVERSION VALEUR POUR CHANGE				
37 VALUE FOR DUTY VALEUR EN DOUANE	38 CUSTOMS DUTIES DROITS DE DOUANE	39 SIMA ASSESSMENT COTISATION DE LMSI	40 EXCISE TAX TAXE D'ACCISE	41 VALUE FOR TAX VALEUR POUR TAXE	42 GST TPS	

DECLARATION - DÉCLARATION

I / JE ____________________
PLEASE PRINT NAME - LETTRES MOULÉES S.V.P.

OF / DE ____________________
IMPORTER / AGENT - IMPORTATEUR / AGENT

DECLARE THE PARTICULARS OF THIS DOCUMENT TO BE TRUE, ACCURATE AND COMPLETE.
DÉCLARE QUE LES RENSEIGNEMENTS CI-DESSUS SONT VRAIS ET COMPLETS.

DATE ____________ SIGNATURE ____________

43 DEPOSIT - DÉPÔT

44 WAREHOUSE NO. - N° D'ENTREPÔT

45 CARGO CONTROL NO. - N° DE CONTRÔLE DU FRET

46 CARRIER CODE AT IMPORTATION CODE DE TRANSPORTEUR À L'IMPORTATION

47 CUSTOMS DUTIES DROITS DE DOUANE	
48 SIMA ASSESSMENT COTISATION DE LMSI	
49 EXCISE TAX TAXE D'ACCISE	
50 GST TPS	
51 TOTAL	

B3-3
Printed in Canada - Imprimé au Canada

Canada

Source: http://www.cbsa-asfc.gc.ca/formspubs/menu-e.html © Canada Customs and Revenue Agency, reproduced with permission of the Minister of Public Works and Government Services Canada, 2004.

Canada Customs and Revenue Agency—Canada Customs Invoice

◆✦◆ Canada Customs and Revenue Agency	Agence des douanes et du revenu du Canada	**CANADA CUSTOMS INVOICE** **FACTURE DES DOUANES CANADIENNES**

Page ___ of / de ___

1. Vendor (name and address) - Vendeur (nom et adresse)

2. Date of direct shipment to Canada - Date d'expédition directe vers le Canada

3. Other references (include purchaser's order No.)
   Autres références (inclure le n° de commande de l'acheteur)

4. Consignee (name and address) - Destinataire (nom et adresse)

5. Purchaser's name and address (if other than consignee)
   Nom et adresse de l'acheteur (s'il diffère du destinataire)

6. Country of transhipment - Pays de transbordement

7. Country of origin of goods
   Pays d'origine des marchandises

   IF SHIPMENT INCLUDES GOODS OF DIFFERENT ORIGINS ENTER ORIGINS AGAINST ITEMS IN 12.
   SI L'EXPÉDITION COMPREND DES MARCHANDISES D'ORIGINES DIFFÉRENTES, PRÉCISEZ LEUR PROVENANCE EN 12.

8. Transportation: Give mode and place of direct shipment to Canada
   Transport : Précisez mode et point d'expédition directe vers le Canada

9. Conditions of sale and terms of payment
   (i.e. sale, consignment shipment, leased goods, etc.)
   Conditions de vente et modalités de paiement
   (p. ex. vente, expédition en consignation, location de marchandises, etc.)

10. Currency of settlement - Devises du paiement

11. Number of packages Nombre de colis	12. Specification of commodities (kind of packages, marks and numbers, general description and characteristics, i.e., grade, quality) Désignation des articles (nature des colis, marques et numéros, description générale et caractéristiques, p. ex. classe, qualité)	13. Quantity (state unit) Quantité (précisez l'unité)	Selling price - Prix de vente	
			14. Unit price Prix unitaire	15. Total

18. If any of fields 1 to 17 are included on an attached commercial invoice, check this box
    Si tout renseignement relativement aux zones 1 à 17 figure sur une ou des factures commerciales ci-attachées, cochez cette case ☐
    Commercial Invoice No. / N° de la facture commerciale _____

16. Total weight - Poids total
    Net ___ Gross - Brut ___

17. Invoice total
    Total de la facture

19. Exporter's name and address (if other than vendor)
    Nom et adresse de l'exportateur (s'il diffère du vendeur)

20. Originator (name and address) - Expéditeur d'origine (nom et adresse)

21. CCRA ruling (if applicable) - Décision de l'Agence (s'il y a lieu)

22. If fields 23 to 25 are not applicable, check this box
    Si les zones 23 à 25 sont sans objet, cochez cette case ☐

23. If included in field 17 indicate amount:
    Si compris dans le total à la zone 17, précisez :

    (i) Transportation charges, expenses and insurance from the place of direct shipment to Canada
    Les frais de transport, dépenses et assurances à partir du point d'expédition directe vers le Canada _____

    (ii) Costs for construction, erection and assembly incurred after importation into Canada
    Les coûts de construction, d'érection et d'assemblage après importation au Canada _____

    (iii) Export packing
    Le coût de l'emballage d'exportation _____

24. If not included in field 17 indicate amount:
    Si non compris dans le total à la zone 17, précisez :

    (i) Transportation charges, expenses and insurance to the place of direct shipment to Canada
    Les frais de transport, dépenses et assurances jusqu'au point d'expédition directe vers le Canada _____

    (ii) Amounts for commissions other than buying commissions
    Les commissions autres que celles versées pour l'achat _____

    (iii) Export packing
    Le coût de l'emballage d'exportation _____

25. Check (if applicable):
    Cochez (s'il y a lieu) :

    (i) Royalty payments or subsequent proceeds are paid or payable by the purchaser
    Des redevances ou produits ont été ou seront versés par l'acheteur ☐

    (ii) The purchaser has supplied goods or services for use in the production of these goods
    L'acheteur a fourni des marchandises ou des services pour la production de ces marchandises ☐

Dans ce formulaire, toutes les expressions désignant des personnes visent à la fois les hommes et les femmes.

CI1 (00) Printed in Canada - Imprimé au Canada

A466

As in the United States, goods entry into Canada relies heavily on documentation, including

- Two copies of a completed Cargo Control Document (CCD).
- Two copies of a completed Form B3, Canada Customs Coding Form.
- Form A—Certificate of Origin (when necessary).
- Two copies of the customs invoice.
- Any import permits, health certificates, or forms required by other Canadian government departments.

The Form A—Certificate of Origin is substantially similar to its U.S. counterpart (with a common NAFTA form used by all three member nations); CCD, Form B-3, and a customs invoice are reproduced below.

The importer is further required to calculate and declare the value for duty of the imported goods according to the valuation provisions of the Customs Act, must ensure that the goods are properly marked with their country of origin, and must make payment of resulting duties.

Chapter Summary

International sale transactions consist of the exportation and importation of goods (or in some case, services) from one customs territory to another. These sales must take into consideration not only the process imposed by the importing nation, but the tax that may be imposed on the goods as well, as both of these factors affect the profit potential of the sales.

The U.S. import clearance process, which is typical of most trading nations, may be divided into six stages, consisting of arrival, entry, inspection, classification, appraisement, and liquidation.

The arrival stage is the unloading of the goods at the port of entry, and the entry stage is the presentation of the goods and their related documentation to the Customs Service at the port of entry. The inspection stage is the verification process by the Customs Service to ensure that the shipment of goods conforms to the documentation and does not represent prohibited goods. The classification stage that follows is the process of identification of the goods for the assessment of duty. The appraisement stage is the determination of the value of the goods for taxation purposes, and the liquidation stage is the process whereby the duty on the goods is calculated and paid.

In some cases, goods are imported "in bond," whereby the goods are imported and stored under controlled or bonded warehouse conditions in the importing country and the duty is paid only when the goods are removed from the bonded warehouse. This process permits the importation of large quantities of goods, allowing importers to take advantage of economies of scale in the shipment of goods, but postpones the payment of duty until the goods are placed in commerce.

Because the importation of goods is complex (the classification and appraisement processes in particular), importers frequently use the services of customs brokers to facilitate the import process. Customs brokers are skilled in all aspects of the clearance process and are familiar with the myriad of regulations imposed on the importation of goods by the importing nation. Customs brokers also maintain a financial security bond with the Customs Service, which relieves importers of the responsibility of supplying their own bonds to the Customs Service. The importers, nevertheless, are ultimately responsible for the payment of the duty.

If an importer does not agree with the assessment of the goods made by the Customs Service, a protest and request for administrative review may be lodged with the port director of the port where the initial decision was made. At this point, administrative errors may be quickly corrected, but if the matter is not resolved at this level, using the U.S. Customs Service as an example, a review process is available to the Customs Service Center. Any protest denied may then be taken as a civil action to the U.S. Court of International Trade.

Chapter Questions

1. Consider all of the reasons for the following statement: "A knowledge of the import process is of equal importance to both the seller and the buyer of goods in an international trade contract." Why is a knowledge of the process and the various steps of the process important to the seller as well as the buyer of the goods?

2. Briefly outline the Customs clearance process, using the U.S. Customs Service as an example.

3. How does a certificate of origin support the policy objectives of an importing nation?

4. Spirits and Wines Inc. imports alcoholic beverages from Europe. Rather than pay each of its 40 European suppliers to ship a small amount (100 cases) monthly, it consolidates its purchases into single large ocean shipments of approximately 24,000 cases per shipment. These bulk shipments, leaving once every six months from Rotterdam, the Netherlands, create large cost savings in transportation. Explain what aspects of the import process will be of great interest to Spirits and Wines Inc. and why and how it can use these to its financial advantage.

5. Outline the role of the customs broker in an import transaction. How does a customs broker facilitate matters for an importer? How does a customs broker acquire authority to deal with the goods?

6. If an importer does not agree with the classification or appraisement of the goods imported, how might the dispute be resolved?

7. What is the Generalized System of Preferences? How could a domestic importer use the GSP to its advantage in formulating its business strategy? What advantage is received by the exporter? What national policy goals are being achieved for the governments of both the exporter's and importer's nations? Recalling the content of Chapter 4, how do you suppose GSP might be reconciled with the WTO/GATT requirements of most-favored-nation status (normal trade relations)?

8. You are the manager with a U.S.-based electrical goods company. A Japanese firm offers to sell and export clock-radios to you for U.S. distribution. You may opt to buy output from its factory in Mexico at $16.00 per unit (delivered) or from its factory in North Korea at $13.00 per unit (delivered). Your customs broker suggests that the clock-radios could enter the United States under the HTSUS heading of "Electrical Goods, Other, Not Included Elsewhere." What are your opinions and observations on this transaction?

Front Page Law: International Issues from Boardroom to Courtroom

SHIPPERS GET CAUGHT IN CUSTOMS' NET: NEW SECURITY RULES ARE COSTING PLENTY—AND COULD SLOW TRADE   MARCH 24, 2003

BusinessWeek

Officials at the U.S. Customs Service are casting a virtual safety net around the country. And they're ensnaring people they never meant to inconvenience. Freight forwarder Jose Aguirre, for one, has been forced to upgrade the software his Miami-based shipping company uses to track merchandise. The new program must be able to notify U.S. Customs officials 24 hours before goods arrive from overseas via cargo ship. The upgrade cost his company $25,000, which he can ill afford when margins are shrinking. "We just had to eat it," says Aguirre, senior vice-president of Miami International Forwarders. "Our customers won't let us pass this cost onto them."

Aguirre isn't suffering alone. Everyone from air-express giant United Parcel Service Inc. (UPS) to mom-and-pop trucking outfits has been notified that they may soon face the same regimen. Customs, which is part of the Dept. of Homeland Security, believes that by taking a long, hard look at data accompanying every shipment into the U.S., it'll be able to spot inconsistencies, which can be red flags for smuggled bombs or biological weapons. "In effect, we're creating a much-needed virtual border," says Charles W. Winwood, senior vice-president of industry consultant Sandler & Travis Trade Advisory Services and a former deputy Customs commissioner.

The first steps toward creating this net have disrupted legitimate business. In just one month of operation, Customs issued at least 167 no-load orders, delaying U.S.-bound shiploads on docks worldwide. To meet the new reporting requirements, some of the biggest ocean carriers have privately stated they've spent $600,000 and more to upgrade computerized tracking systems. The program could eventually hit air shippers even harder. Customs is considering requirements that might make the international overnight air delivery of cargo all but impossible. "It would put air-express carriers out of business," says Norman Schenk, a vice-president at UPS Supply Chain Solutions.

Nobody is confused about the intentions of the new shipping requirements. They were implemented as part of the Trade Act of 2002, when shock waves from the September 11 World Trade Center and Pentagon attacks were rippling through every branch of government and industry. The Act mandated advance notice for all cargo entering the U.S. The idea was to push the country's line of defense back to the point of origin for all incoming goods. Such vigilance "should prove a deterrent to terrorists trying to use the maritime system," says Brian C. Goebel, a border protection adviser in the Homeland Security Dept.

In February, Customs began requiring every ocean carrier to electronically file a detailed list of its cargo 24 hours before departing for U.S. ports. Armed with sophisticated software, Customs officials analyze those manifests for telltale signs, such as a clothing retailer suddenly shipping electronic parts. They can order any load held over. And the agency has inspectors in the world's 20 largest ports, equipped with machines that can scrutinize even 40-foot metal containers using X-rays.

Although this program hasn't yet netted any terror suspects, Customs is confident that the 24-hour notice will make a difference. In the past, merchants rushed to load goods up to the last hour before departure. On the U.S. side, the total that was unloaded came to 915 million short tons in 2001, the latest figure available. For this flood of goods, merchants provided only the vaguest accounting—such as "clothing" or "general cargo"—and the shipment information often arrived after the goods had already been unloaded.

The new regs will rectify that situation. And so far, they have hardly derailed trade. Indeed, not one big shipment has been stranded at sea. And all 167 no-load orders have been resolved to Customs' satisfaction and shipped on. "Customs has tried very hard not to disrupt trade," says Christopher L. Coch, president and CEO of the World Shipping Council, a trade group representing ocean carriers.

Still, industry execs say the measures have turned their process upside down, forcing exporters and their shippers to catalogue shipped merchandise first rather than last. "It has thrown a real monkey wrench in exporters' plans," says Miami International's Aguirre. And more intrusive changes are coming. By October, truck, rail, and air carriers will have to provide advance electronic notice of their cargo, too. In January, Customs proposed eight-hour advance notice of air freight. FedEx Corp. (FDX) and UPS said such a requirement was unworkable, since freight continues to be loaded up to the final hour before takeoff. Instead, air-express carriers have proposed filing an electronic manifest in-flight, reaching Customs at least an hour before arrival, with some exceptions. UPS' Schenk is confident that the carriers can strike a reasonable deal with Customs.

All sides agree that, no matter what the final regulations are, transportation here and overseas is on the brink of a massive, irreversible change. "The U.S. is the model for the rest of the world, and everyone will adopt [the safety measures] in the name of maintaining world trade," predicts Paul Bingham, a principal at industry consultant Global Insights Inc. The whole world, in short, will have to learn to function in the confines of electronic security fences.

7

Direct Sale
of Goods Exports

Chapter Objectives

Every import demands a corresponding export, from somewhere. In this chapter, we examine exports, the sale activity as an international business transaction. This chapter is confined to direct sales of goods to foreign buyers, followed by the mechanics of delivery and payment in Chapters 8 and 9 respectively. Issues related to more complex systems and strategies in goods exports appear in Chapter 10 on distribution. The export of services is a subject within the broader topics of intellectual property and foreign investment, and is covered in Chapters 11 and 12.

In this chapter, we will explore the international sale transaction and

- The strategic considerations of business in developing export markets.
- How and why international law modifies domestic regulation of the sale contract.
- What business must do to respond to these changes.

The Significance of the Export Transaction

Exporting is usually the first step in "taking the business abroad," compared to importing, where the firm's market for sales remains at home. The first question—why to export—has been discussed previously: market diversification, market expansion, or the meeting of foreign competition in its own markets. The strategic business questions now faced by the firm are

1. *How*   should export sales be structured? (In what form: directly or indirectly?)
2. *Where*   are the markets where sensible opportunities exist within workable commercial and legal environments? (What are the relevant markets?)
3. *What*   channels should be used? (Home office control or marketing through a distribution network?)
4. *Who*   specifically, if anyone in addition to the exporting firm or distributors, will undertake foreign marketing of its exports? (Agents or representatives?)
5. *What*   rules will govern our choices?

Each of these business-specific strategic choices has a large element of international commercial law and private law that will apply to its analysis, and we examine each in turn.

Direct versus Indirect Exports

Exporting can be conducted on either a direct or indirect basis, and these words are commonly used in a number of contexts, giving rise to confusion.

Direct exports can mean

1. Direct sale to a foreign *buyer,* possibly a reseller (a direct export in the eyes of the seller).
2. Direct sale to a foreign *end user* (a direct export in relation to the foreign market).
3. Direct shipment to the *territory* of end use without first formally landing in another customs territory (an important distinction for governments).

For many exporting firms, the distinction between the first two definitions (buyers versus end users) is irrelevant. For other exporters, developing a close relationship with the end user of their goods is either absolutely necessary (aircraft manufacturers with airlines) or something totally avoided (coffee growers with drinkers). Thus, the distinction is important for all firms because it effectively creates two different international business transaction mindsets: the traders (who don't normally concern themselves with end users) and the merchants (who do). Just knowing which one you are—the labels being our own creation—will help you identify critical rules that apply to your business and deserve attention: Are you just a supplier or are you a server? Does this rule govern transfers, or does it govern relationships?

In the third use of the words *direct exports,* the relevance is to governments in avoiding double counting in national trade statistics. For example, a large proportion of Hong Kong's "exports" (as it is a separate customs territory) are goods in transit from China bound for the rest of the world. The distinction between those goods passing through and those actually originating in Hong Kong is important for the accuracy of the national accounts of each of Hong Kong, China, and their trading partners.

Indirect exports can mean the reverse of the three cases above and are

1. Direct domestic sales to a domestic buyer whose business is finding and serving foreign markets on its own account through its own direct export sales.
2. Domestic goods sold to domestic buyers as component parts of other domestic goods that are themselves ultimately exported (e.g., domestic tires sold to a domestic buyer that are fitted to an aircraft built for export).

Unless the context implies otherwise, we use *direct exports* to mean sales to a foreign buyer and *indirect exports* to mean sales to a domestic buyer who exports on its own account rather than using the goods as components. Some of these buyers may be closely related to export sellers, for many export sales are intrafirm exports rather than interfirm. For example, DaimlerChrysler of Canada may export components and fittings from its plant in Windsor, Ontario, to its German-American parent firm for use in assembly factories located in the United States. Some large firms with a web of global factories go as far as setting up a subsidiary corporation to act as purchasing agent and internal export manager for raw material and supplies for the whole firm.

Relevant Markets

At times, identifying relevant markets is easy, for the market has presented itself to the attention of the firm that has become interested in international trade. Starting from a clean slate is, however, a different question: where in the entire world should we go in search of attractive opportunities?

Not only must the commercial opportunity exist, but the foreign market also must present itself as a place where legal rights exist so as to create certainty in commercial transactions. Those rights and rules may be different than one's own, but they must lead to fair and certain results for business to flourish. We cannot ignore the possibility that territories exist that are undiscovered gems, but investigating markets where business already does flourish is one approach to identify places with commercial law (and respect for international law) that can be relied on.

Still, this is a large task. Rather than try to become an expert on the business and law of all markets, concentrating on the main markets for international transactions is more useful. The table below shows the structure of U.S. international merchandise trade, and many useful conclusions can be drawn from it. Begin by considering the significance of the first three lines. NAFTA and the top EU traders represent half of all U.S. trade. Having a solid understanding of the legal systems and trade law of these nations and the international law between them will cover many eventualities.

The United States, as a market, imports more than it exports; it runs a merchandise trade deficit with the world, and with 18 of its 25 largest partners. For the economist, this represents a net outflow of payments that must be financed one way or another. For the businessperson, this means more import transactions than export work, based on a dollar volume. It also means that government will keenly support exporters, to the fullest extent it can under WTO rules.

U.S. Trade Partners Data (Millions of U.S. Dollars)

Trade Partner, 2001	Rank as Overall U.S. Trade Partner	Total U.S. Two-Way Trade with	Share of Total U.S. Two-Way Trade	U.S. Exports to	Rank as U.S. Export Destination	U.S. Imports from	Rank as Source of U.S. Imports	U.S. Trade Surplus or Deficit
Canada	1	379,692	20%	163,424	1	216,268	1	−52,844
*Top EU members	2	333,438	18%	140,621	2	192,816	2	−52,195
Mexico	2	232,634	12%	101,297	2	131,338	2	−30,041
Japan	3	183,925	10%	57,452	3	126,473	3	−69,021
China	4	121,461	6%	19,182	9	102,278	4	−83,096
Germany*	5	89,072	5%	29,995	5	59,077	5	−29,082
United Kingdom*	6	82,083	4%	40,714	4	41,369	6	−655
Korea	7	57,362	3%	22,181	6	35,181	7	−13,000
Taiwan	8	51,496	3%	18,122	10	33,375	8	−15,253
France*	9	50,273	3%	19,865	7	30,408	9	−10,543
Italy*	10	33,706	2%	9,916	16	23,790	10	−13,874
Singapore	11	32,652	2%	17,652	11	15,000	14	2,652
Malaysia	12	31,698	2%	9,358	18	22,340	11	−12,982
Brazil	13	30,346	2%	15,880	12	14,466	16	1,414
Netherlands*	14	29,000	2%	19,485	8	9,515	25	9,970
Ireland*	15	25,643	1%	7,144	21	18,499	12	−11,355
Hong Kong	16	23,674	1%	14,028	13	9,646	23	4,382
Belgium*	17	23,661	1%	13,502	14	10,158	20	3,344
Venezuela	18	20,893	1%	5,642	25	15,251	13	−9,609
Thailand	19	20717	1%	5,989	22	14,727	15	−8,738
Israel	20	19,434	1%	7,475	20	11,959	18	−4,484
Switzerland	21	19,477	1%	9,807	17	9,670	24	137
Saudi Arabia	22	19,230	1%	5,958	23	13,272	17	−7,314
Philippines	23	18,985	1%	7,660	19	11,325	19	−3,665
Australia	24	17,408	1%	10,931	15	6,478	28	4,453
India	25	13,494	1%	3,757	29	9,737	22	−5,980

Source: Office of Trade and Economic Analysis, U.S. Department of Commerce, 2003. Compilation of extracts from Tables 6–9 and 55–58, available at http://www.ita.doc.gov/td/industry/otea/usfth/tabcon.html.

This next chart represents an enormous volume of U.S. exports, and successful exporting to foreign markets depends much more heavily on understanding foreign legal systems than does importing from those markets. It is not difficult to prioritize on which markets U.S. business law students should focus their studies.

Priority of U.S. Export Trading Relationships (Millions of U.S. Dollars)

Major Partners	Total U.S. Two-Way Trade with	Share of Total U.S. Two-Way Trade	U.S. Exports to	Share of U.S. Exports to World (rounded)	U.S. Imports from	Share of U.S. Imports from	U.S. Surplus or Deficit	Share
World (256 partners)	1,872,985	100%	731,026	100%	1,141,959	100%	–410,933	100%
Canada	379,692	20%	163,424	22%	216,268	19%	–52,844	13%
NAFTA partners	612,327	33%	264,721	36%	347,606	30%	–82,885	20%
Top 5 export markets	967,406	52%	392,882	54%	574,525	50%	–181,643	44%
Top 5 trade partners	1,006,784	54%	371,350	51%	635,434	56%	–264,084	64%
EU members in top 25	333,438	18%	140,621	19%	192,816	17%	–52,195	13%
Top 10 trade partners	1,281,705	68%	491,717	67%	799,557	70%	–317,409	77%
Top 25 trade partners	1,628,016	87%	636,416	87%	991,600	87%	–355,184	86%

Source: Derived from previous table.

By devoting study to the business environment and legal systems of Canada, Mexico, the United Kingdom, Germany, and Japan, the businessperson and lawyer will have some understanding of markets that consume over half of U.S. exports. When this study is expanded to include the other top EU traders as well as China, Korea, and Taiwan, almost three-quarters of all U.S. merchandise trade is covered.

In each of these markets, the rule of law governs international business transactions, most quite firmly entrenched, and developing well in others. Their growth as economies depends heavily on their consistent and increasing respect for international transaction law and private rules of contract. Each market, including the United States and excluding the United Kingdom and Japan, also recognizes the 1980 United Nations Convention on Contracts for the International Sale of Goods. A discussion of this convention and the extent to which it modifies the more familiar domestic contract law of its members appears later in this chapter.

The empirical evidence of successful economies and convention membership (or a long history of commercial and legal certainty) is an important guide to selecting where international business transactions should be directed.

Strategic Market Entry Options for Exporters

Having selected a foreign market(s), every international export transaction represents some type of adventure into international business, and selecting an entry vehicle should be part of a conscious entry strategy into foreign markets. Granted, it can be as simple a strategy as letting foreign buyers search out the domestic supplier, or it can be involved and complex, with wholly owned subsidiaries of the domestic producer handling distribution in foreign territories.

The spectrum of strategic market entry options is found in the diagram below, with each option varying in risk, complexity, and cost to the foreign exporter:

**Strategic Market
Entry Options
for Exporters**

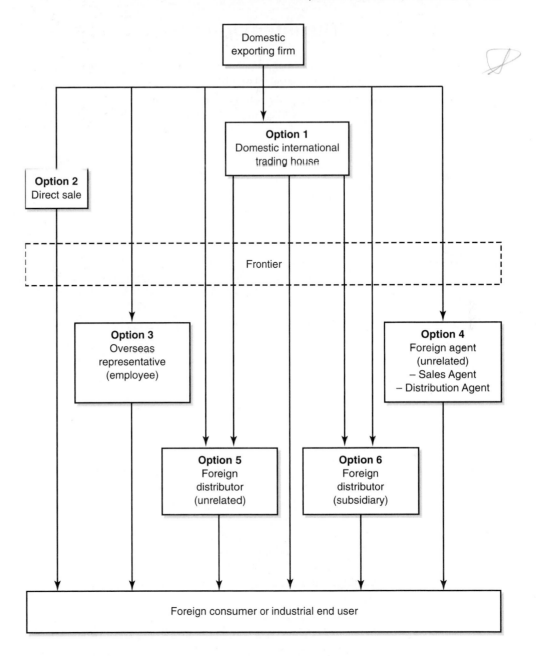

It is difficult to make general statements in comparing each option, other than to say that as the control that may be exercised by the domestic firm decreases, its overall business risk tends to increase. "Control" in this sense means the firm's ability to manage the variables of business—to set standards and maintain its reputation for quality and service, to receive feedback on market developments, to set prices for end users. As business functions are transferred to representatives, agents, and foreign distributors, this ability to control decreases.

As a result, the appropriateness of any export strategy depends heavily on the characteristics of the product to be exported, the resources and capabilities of the exporter, and the unique characteristics of the target market and its consumers. The first four export strategy options are detailed in turn in the next sections in this chapter, with distribution options 5 and 6 the subject of Chapter 10.

Export Option 1: The International Trading House

Indirect exporting through an international trading house really does not qualify as exporting in the technical sense, unless the trading house acts merely as an agent, as the sale is made and executed on the domestic side of the frontier. That said, such a domestic sale transaction does have an export dimension, as the final destination of the goods is abroad. An international trading house takes the form of either an export management company (EMC) or an export trading company (ETC), private firms engaged in export trade but who are not producers of goods.

In the case of the export management company, the EMC fulfills the role of an export department for smaller firms that lack either the ability or interest to handle their own export business. This "outsourced" expertise may locate foreign buyers for either a fixed retainer fee or a commission or both (an agency relationship, in any event), or may buy and sell on its own account (owning the goods). In either case, this represents an expensive option, has the disadvantage of distancing the producer from the eventual consumer (no feedback of market intelligence), and is rarely appropriate where an ongoing relationship with the consumer is desired (as in warranty and repair services). Where this method of actual export is executed through an agency relationship, it is additionally subject to the reservations described below in the agency section later in this chapter.

Export management companies exist around the world, as do export trading companies, and these businesses, despite their similar names, are distinct from one another. There is also a difference between U.S. ETCs and those of other nations. ETCs established outside the United States are ventures acting as brokers or principals in international trade that have grown and evolved organically, meaning that they are often products of the historical trade routes of the great trading nations of the United Kingdom and the Netherlands, and, more recently, Japan.

Most ETCs are large buyers and sellers of a wide range of finished goods and raw materials, consumer and industrial. Some are originally offshoots of financial institutions, others of colonial trading companies, and still others represent a consortium of exporters in the same industry. Other foreign trading houses might include a number of industrial exporters, a financial institution to provide capital, and domestic buyers standing ready to import back other goods from the export target market, as a "sweetener" to make the export deal "happen" in the first place. Such houses are therefore not geared to providing an export management service for small firms, although this may be an incidental result of their existence; they are classic entrepreneurs, making markets, buying anything low, and selling it high.

Lacking the organic growth of a privileged position supervising colonial trade, U.S. exporters envied the ability of foreign firms to group together to achieve economies of scale in export trade. Hobbled by U.S. antitrust laws and/or the threat of civil suits by the public, U.S. exporters could not create such structures until the passage of the Export Trading Company Act of 1982. This act represents a significant relaxation in U.S. antitrust laws to permit direct collaboration between firms, marketers, financiers, and banks to advance export trade. It creates what is as close as may be imagined to immunity from antitrust public prosecution (by government) or civil action (by consumers or competitors) for planning or executing such collaborative action, through the grant of a certificate of review by the Secretary of Commerce. Knowing in advance that reviewed activities will be virtually immune from suit allows much greater confidence in export operations. Unfortunately, this powerful tool is simply neither widely known nor utilized to its fullest extent by potential U.S.-resident beneficiaries. An application for a certificate of review is at all times confidential and has a 90-day scrutiny period; if rejected, such a determination is subject to judicial review, and no aspect of the process is admissible as evidence in any later antitrust proceeding.

Where a domestic manufacturer utilizes an export management company or export trading company as an agent, the domestic manufacturer remains the true exporter, and all further sections of this text, except direct sales, still remain as business strategy considerations. Moreover, where the EMC or ETC acts as principal, buying and selling on its own account, all further sections including direct sales still remain as strategic considerations. In this latter case, the EMC or ETC has simply stepped into the shoes of the domestic firm as the true exporter.

Export Option 2: Direct Sales

Nature and Suitability of the Transaction

Direct sales may arise as a result of an express business export strategy in which the export seller pursues foreign customers, or as a result of the reverse, where the foreign customer has sought out the domestic seller. In the first case, the exporter will likely be (or should be) well prepared to execute a direct sale transaction. In the latter case, particularly if the seller is new to international business, it may not be familiar with the situation at all.

It is tempting to say that the international direct sale transaction does not vary much from its domestic counterpart, and while many commentators do say that, it is because their considerable experience has desensitized them to the importance of critical differences at the business level. Certainly both the domestic and international sale transactions are contracts for the purchase and sale of goods. That is similar. Other legal elements have a surface similarity, such as the process of negotiation, the similarity of legal terminology, the use of a carrier in transportation, or the acquisition of insurance against loss. The surface similarity ends when particular risks and the nature of the international business relationships are examined:

1. Buyers and sellers from different nations (and cultures) may have little experience with
   - The cultural norms and expected behavior in contract negotiation with the other party,
   - Understanding of the economic reality of the other party's business environment (costs, consumer tastes, profitability, pricing, labor constraints, etc.),
   - The relative importance that the other party places on detailed paper contracts,
   - The relative importance of time (including differences in meaning for words like *now, soon,* or *later*), and
   - The relative importance of short-term profits versus long-term relationships,

   all of which create a veil of unease that can rapidly spiral into mistrust and unwarranted second-guessing of the motives of the other party, either right from the beginning of the relationship or bubbling to the surface at a later time. These are corrosive and represent gaps to be bridged through cultural research and understanding.
2. While goods are also in the hands of carriers and are insured in the course of domestic transactions, the nature of these relationships is different in international sales, and their effect on the sale parties is different.
   - The goods are out of sight for longer periods in international sales, replaced by documents as evidence of title.
   - More opportunities for loss are present in international shipment (loadings, unloadings, changes in mode of transport, rougher all-weather environments at sea and in

Many legal battles in direct sales can be traced to the seller's carelessness in export pricing. The pattern is this: an inexperienced exporter is asked for a price quotation, and one is hastily given, perhaps orally. Negotiations follow. When a request for a firm written quote is received, there is pressure to at least keep it in line with the earlier quotation, to maintain trust. The exporter then underestimates the costs of export packaging, customs documentation, and paperwork administration. To its horror, the exporter realizes that some aspect of the product must be modified for the foreign market (translation of instruction sheets, even design elements). The contract is still made at the quoted price even though there is no longer much of a profit for the exporter, but there is the hope of repeat business on better terms. As this first contract progresses toward completion, other costs arise; shipping or insurance costs come in higher than expected. At this point, the exporter begins to cut corners to avoid taking a loss: inadequate insurance or the bare minimum for packaging. In the meantime, the foreign buyer is becoming increasingly reliant on the contract (arranging financing, buying inventory or equipment complementary to its plans for using the imported goods, setting up distribution channels). The goods wind up on a dock and their shoddy crates and packaging allow weather damage to occur. The insurer refuses to indemnify the exporter's own negligence in packaging. Scapegoats are sought: the carrier should have taken better care; the buyer should have requested particular packaging, and so it goes. The legal battle is on. Lesson? Take time and care in making the price quotation, and half the legal battles will disappear.

ports) and more actual losses occur. Damaged goods lead to inconvenience (at best), lost profits, and mistrust (at worst) between the sale parties.

- Ocean carriers are larger, more distant (or out of legal reach in practical terms), and more commercially powerful than smaller domestic trucking firms, greatly diminishing the shipper's ability to exert influence over it.

3. Uncertainties exist that are not found in domestic transactions, such as unfamiliar payment vehicles (e.g., documentary credits), exchange rate risks of foreign currency fluctuation, import duty assessment, time required for customs clearance, and increased dependence on third-party service providers (customs brokers, freight forwarders, bankers).

4. Familiar domestic regulation of trade is replaced by international regulation (such as the UN CISG Convention) that uses similar terms with different meanings for contracts or has unexpected provisions.

5. Some goods that may be traded without regulation in the domestic market are subject to export control. In the United States, some types of computer software, communications and data encryption devices, and goods and technology with military applications are subject to either prohibition on export, export only to allied nations, or case-by-case approval.

These are five broad categories of differences between domestic and international sale transactions that translate into very real differences in the legal protection needed and sought, despite the fact there is surface similarity in the contractual nature of the relationship.

The direct sale transaction is not suitable for all types of international goods trade situations. It contemplates sale to the foreign end user, which is a relationship the exporter may or may not be willing to create for the long run. For the distribution of consumer goods, the exporter will have no wish to deal with each foreign end-user (the consumer) individually, as the transaction costs alone would be far too high. At the other end of the spectrum, in the case of high-value industrial goods such as ships or aircraft, direct sale may be an

Good for long term relations @ aircraft

absolute necessity, where the buyer and seller have so many unique concerns (customization, options, payment plans) that must be dealt with in face-to-face negotiations. Other firms may find themselves in direct sale situations where the relationship is a "one-time deal," perhaps as a result of a trade show encounter. This typically is not a consumer sale. It can represent an export sale for distribution in a small market that represents no ongoing priority for the exporter, or where the single sale of durable products will supply the needs of that market for years to come. For example, the sale of 2,000 sets of mechanics' wrenches to a distributor in the Caribbean islands of Trinidad and Tobago (population under 1.5 million) is not likely to be followed by a repeat order in the near future, nor is this order creating a true, full-blown, supplier–distributor relationship. It is simply a form of direct sale, although one made to a reseller.

Reaching a Deal: Establishing the Terms of an Export Contract of Sale

Both the import buyer and export seller must be fully aware of what is contained in the export price, and recognize that costly matters not negotiated or otherwise provided for must still be arranged and paid if the transaction is to be completed.

Contracts of sale can be written up with great formality as long and detailed agreements (hopefully) touching on all eventualities. While lawyers undoubtedly appreciate that, still the vast majority of international contracts of sale result from an exchange of communication (letters, faxes, or emails). The contract offer is usually the seller's offer to sell (as opposed to a buyer's offer to buy), and the seller's offer usually takes the form of a *pro forma invoice.*

The pro forma invoice is often misunderstood; it is not an invoice for payment. It is an offer, open for acceptance, that may lead to a contract. As an offer, it is saying: "if you and I ever got so far as actually creating a contract, these would be the terms, and if you took delivery of the goods, this is what the invoice would look like that you would have to pay."

Under international law, which will be discussed next, an offer is a proposal for concluding a contract addressed to one or more specific persons that is sufficiently definite and indicates the intention of the offeror to be bound in case of acceptance. Such a proposal is sufficiently definite if it indicates the goods and expressly or implicitly fixes or makes provision for determining the quantity and the price. As pro forma invoices (properly constructed) fit this definition, they are offers open for acceptance and not merely invitations to do business with the import purchaser, unless such a contrary intention is clearly indicated. An export price list, which is not addressed to a specific person, would not normally be considered to be an offer.

As an export seller creating a pro forma invoice, it is important to include all relevant contractual terms, for two different and important reasons. First, as an offer, it is defining the terms of the contractual relationship that will exist when it is accepted by the purchaser. This alone is sufficient reason for care in drafting, for amendments later will always carry a price attached. Second is the fact that the purchaser may well be paying via a letter of credit (discussed in detail in Chapter 9).

The letter of credit will be prepared by the buyer and executed by bankers in accordance with the pro forma invoice. While any aspect of the contract that may have been overlooked in creating the pro forma invoice can be easily rectified later by the parties (as between themselves), it is *not* easy to later rectify or amend the letter of credit. For practical purposes and to serve as an incentive to get things right the first time, the parties should consider that the terms of the letter of credit are cast in stone once it is created. This is because the bankers to a transaction involving a letter of credit have the power, and will use it to refuse, to release payment (or trigger delivery of the goods) on any terms that are not in *precise* accordance with the letter of credit. Operating in exact accordance with the letter of credit is the bank's commitment to the parties, regardless of what the parties may later informally wish or plead or hope, and the bank is not going to expose itself to liability for acting incorrectly. Therefore, the parties, whatever their amended intention may have been, can find themselves trapped by the terms of the original pro forma invoice, as the information contained in it is transferred and imported into the terms of the letter of credit.

As indicated in The Old Wolf, attention must be given to the hidden costs of exporting on direct sales to derive a sensible export price. If any of these factors are overlooked in creating the pro forma invoice (the offer), then there are unanswered questions as to who does what and who pays for what. These are expensive legal battles just waiting to happen. The list of easily overlooked factors includes

- Cost of communications and courier.
- Market development, promotion, and travel costs.
- Translation of documents, instructions, and labeling.
- Export packing and marking requirements.
- Cost of freight and insurance to the destination including inland local transport in both the exporter's and importer's countries (if contractually agreed to be the exporter's responsibility).
- Exporter's own insurance to the point and time of transfer of title.
- Export documentation for customs.
- Inspection and certification fees.
- Stevedoring, loading, and unloading costs.
- Warehouse expenses at any point in shipment.
- Bank and finance charges.
- Customs brokerage charges (if contractually agreed to be the exporter's responsibility).
- Import duties (if contractually agreed to be the exporter's responsibility).

The pro forma invoice should be in a regular form, on a corporate letterhead, identifying itself as a pro forma invoice. It should bear complete contact information and the addresses of both parties and place of delivery, with the federal states and countries spelled out in full and complete telephone numbers including not only area code but international dialing codes as well (+1 for the United States, Canada, and the Caribbean). A unique file number, order number, or serial number should be created to avoid confusion between orders, and dates should be spelled out in full (when is 06-04-05?) or a legend such as YYMMDD should be provided in the alternative.

The pro forma invoice should clearly indicate specific goods, in terms of

- Quantity, description, gross weight (per item, per shipping unit, and overall).
- Price per unit and total order price.
- Shipment labeling and marking.
- Terms of payment, including currency.
- Terms of sale and place of delivery.[1]

[1]This will be largely achieved through use of INCOTERMS, internationally accepted trade terms developed by the International Chamber of Commerce. These trade terms summarize, by convention and through a simple abbreviation, which party is responsible for carriage of the goods, to and from what point, as well as which party is responsible for export and import clearance, and the division of risks and costs between them. Commonly recognized INCOTERMS include FOB and CIF, but 11 others are in common use. These are discussed in full detail in Chapter 8, "Transportation and Logistics." Note that the meaning of INCOTERMS trade terms used internationally differs from the meaning of the same terms as used domestically under the Uniform Commercial Code of states of the United States.

- Period of validity of the offer in which it is open for acceptance, and the manner in which it may be accepted.

- Governing law of any resulting contract.

- Proposed date of overseas shipment leg, measured in terms of days following receipt of the buyer's acceptance via a purchase order or letter of credit.

- Accounting of separate charges in addition to price of the goods (freight, insurance, packing).

Assuming that the buyer has advised the seller of its documentation needs, reference in the pro forma invoice should be made to the packing slips and certificates of inspection, insurance, or origin that will be provided or otherwise included with the shipment.

A sample of a pro forma invoice conforming to these criteria is shown on page 260. When matched by acceptance in the form of an irrevocable letter of credit (or certified funds) as contemplated by the pro forma invoice offer, a basic international sale contract will exist.

Electronic Contracts and International Law

As international parties increasingly rely on electronic communication by email and Internet, these forms of contracting have begun to take their place in the international legal order. Some commentators see this as revolutionary, while others do not. Perhaps better said, they are evolutionary steps. They will be accommodated by the law in much the same way as the telegraph, telephone, telex, and fax machine that have preceded them.

The United Nations Commission on International Trade (UNCITRAL) has drafted working documents that nations may use to create their own laws governing electronic commercial transactions. These are its Model Law on Electronic Commerce (adopted in 1996) and its Model Law on Electronic Signatures.[2]

National laws based on the Model Law on Electronic Commerce would extend the scope of e-commerce regulation to any kind of information in the form of a data message used in the context of commercial activities, with national exceptions permitted. It has been highly influential in creating a base level of uniformity in the approaches used by nations and states to regulate e-commerce, with its effect felt in all of the United States, Canada, and the European Union.

The object of most national e-commerce laws (in line with the UNICTRAL model) has been to create functional equivalency between electronic data messages and written documents. In the United States at the federal level, this was accomplished in 2000 through the Electronic Signatures in Global and National Commerce Act, also known as the E-Sign Act.[3] The Canadian equivalent is the Personal Information Protection and Electronic Documents Act[4] (with subsequent provincial acts), and in the EU, the Electronic Commerce Directive and the Electronic Signatures Directive.[5]

Typical of these, the E-Sign Act gives electronic contracts the same legal validity as written ones, as the electronic form may not be used as the sole basis for denying validity of a document or signature. Due to the federal nature of the United States, the E-Sign Act preempts U.S. state laws to the contrary until such time as uniform legislation is adopted across the states of the United States. In large measure, this has been achieved, with over 40 states having enacted close versions of the Uniform Electronic Transactions Act (UETA), a product of the National Conference of Commissioners on Uniform State Laws.[6] UETA deems that electronic documents and signatures are, in commercial transactions, in full satisfaction of requirements of writing and signature.

[2] General Assembly Resolution 51/162, December 16, 1996. Both may be viewed at www.uncitral.org.
[3] 15 U.S.C. § 7001 et seq.
[4] S.C. 2000, c. C-6.
[5] Council Directives 2000/31/EC [2000] and 1999/93/EC [2000]. May be viewed at www.europa.eu.int.
[6] The Model UETA may be viewed at www.law.upenn.edu/bll/ulc/ulc_frame.htm, the official NCCUSL site.

PRO FORMA INVOICE

12345-04

FROM:
E&M Machine Equipment Ltd.
123 Thousand Island Boulevard,
Watertown, New York, USA
13601
Telephone: +1 (123) 456-7890

SOLD TO:
General Tool and Machine Co.
412 Sussex Lane,
Herstmonceux, East Sussex,
United Kingdom
BN27 1RP
Telephone: +44 (81323) 633-033

Date of Invoice: 27 January 2005
Expiration Date: 27 February 2005
Our Reference No.: 39245
Your Reference No.: File 22-05

FORWARDING AGENT
Ocean Container Co.
Suite 2205, 22nd Floor
26 Harbor Square,
New York, New York,
USA 10039
Telephone: +1 (212) 555-1212

PACKING AND MARKS
Ocean going export packing, wooden crate
THIS END UP
STOW BELOW DECK ONLY
USE NO HOOKS

MERCHANDISE:

QUANTITY	DESCRIPTION	UNIT PRICE	SUBTOTAL
12	Stamping Press, Model 221	$3,000.00	$36,000.00

Quotation Basis

Number of Crates, Cubic Meters per Crate	Estimated Gross Weight per Crate	Total Gross Weight of Shipment	Total Shipping Volume	Port of Embarkation
				New York, USA
12 crates, 1.70 cubic meters each	900 kilograms, gross	10,800 kilograms	102 cubic meters	Port of Discharge
				Dover, UK

(√) FOB   (   ) CIF   (   ) C & F

Delivered on board purchaser's nominated vessel, no less than 60, not more than 90, days after receipt of irrevocable confirmed letter of credit, or certified funds drawn in U.S. dollars on a U.S. bank. All letters of credit must be payable upon presentation of shipping documents and must specify that all related charges incurred are applicant's liability. Seller will provide three copies of certificate of origin and packing slips. Application of the 1980 Convention on Contracts for International Sale of Goods is expressly excluded and this transaction will be governed under the Uniform Commercial Code as adopted under the law of the State of New York.

Ex Works Price (subtotal above) ……………………….............................. $36,000.00 USD
Export Crating fee.. 720.00
Inland Freight via Highway Transport to Port of New York……………….. 1,500.00
Freight Forwarder Charges.. 380.00
Ocean Freight to   via   …………………………….   Purchaser to Arrange and Pay
Insurance..   Purchaser to Arrange and Pay
Consular Fees and Import Duties………………………………….....   Purchaser Responsible
Total $38,600.00 U.S. dollars

I certify the above to be true and correct.

E&M Machine Equipment Ltd.
Per: *Kim Martin*

Authorized Officer

Case law also has emerged with respect to electronic contracts. Like U.S. domestic cases on accepting terms by breaking the shrink-wrap on software,[7] so too has the click-wrap acceptance of terms (the "I Agree" button) been determined as binding, and as between international parties. In a Canadian case, *Rudder v. Microsoft Corp.*, the failure of a Canadian party to read the scrolling terms of a U.S. software license acceptance dialog box was held against the party.[8] In failing to scroll and read the terms, the court drew the analogy with someone who carelessly signs a paper contract without first reading it.

Jurisdiction of the courts and the minimum contacts requirement do pose the potential for difficulty in international electronic contracts of sale. While merely using an international medium such as the Internet would not be sufficient to meet a minimum contacts requirement, that plus repeated contacts and performance probably would. While again domestic cases exist, this has yet to have been extensively litigated across national boundaries. One case involving U.S. and Canadian parties has noted, however, that there is considerable danger in courts taking jurisdiction solely on the basis of electronic contact.[9] Speaking on the posting of a Canadian on a Texas investment bulletin board, the Court of Appeal of the Canadian province of British Columbia noted: "It would create a crippling effect on freedom of expression if, in every jurisdiction the world over in which access to the internet could be achieved, a person who posts fair comment on a bulletin board could be hauled before the courts of each of those countries where access to this bulletin could be obtained."

UN Convention on Contracts for the International Sale of Goods (CISG)

International law governing the international sale of goods has been incorporated into the legal systems of many trading nations, including the law of the states of the United States. Foremost among these legal provisions is the 1980 United Nations Convention on Contracts for the International Sale of Goods. This convention, also known as the Vienna Sales Convention or CISG, entered into force in 1988, and 62 countries (including most senior trading nations and the United States) have signed and ratified it.[10]

The traditional common law rules of contract are summarized in the primer on domestic law opening Part 2 of this text. Among common law nations, these rules vary to a degree, with each jurisdiction consolidating its common law (case law) rules into statutory codes or laws. This has been done primarily at the state or provincial level, except in the United Kingdom, which uses a single national law. These laws are the Uniform Commercial Code (particularly Article 2 on sales) in U.S. states and the Sale of Goods Acts of British Commonwealth jurisdictions. The CISG covers much of the same ground as these.[11] To the extent that domestic jurisdictions differ with each other or with the CISG, the CISG puts everyone on common ground for rules in international contracts of sale.

[7]See *ProCD, Inc. v. Zeidenburg and Silken Mountain Web Services,* 86 F.3d 1447 (7th Cir. 1996).

[8]See *Rudder v. Microsoft Corp.,* (1999) 47 C.C.L.T. (2d) 168 (Ontario Superior Court of Justice).

[9]See Goldie, JA in *Braintech, Inc. v. Kostiuk,* (1999) 171 D.L.R. (4th) 46 (B.C.C.A.). Leave to appeal to the Supreme Court of Canada refused, March 9, 2000.

[10]As at early 2004, Argentina, Australia, Austria, Belarus, Belgium, Bosnia and Herzegovina, Bulgaria, Burundi, Canada, Chile, China, Colombia, Croatia, Cuba, the Czech Republic, Denmark, Ecuador, Egypt, Estonia, Finland, France, Georgia, Germany, Ghana (signature only), Greece, Guinea, Honduras, Hungary, Iceland, Iraq, Israel, Italy, Kyrgyzstan, Latvia, Lesotho, Lithuania, Luxembourg, Mauritania, Mexico, Mongolia, the Netherlands, New Zealand, Norway, Peru, Poland, Republic of Moldova, Romania, the Russian Federation, Saint Vincent and the Grenadines, Serbia and Montenegro, Singapore, Slovakia, Slovenia, Spain, Sweden, Switzerland, Syrian Arab Republic, Uganda, Ukraine, United States of America, Uruguay, Uzbekistan, Venezuela (signature only), and Zambia. The significant absentees are the United Kingdom and Japan.

[11]A superb CISG resource exists in the Pace Law School website at www.cisg.law.pace.edu/cisg.

The CISG governs the formation of the contract of sale itself and the procedural rights and obligations of the seller and the buyer (for example, timing of revocation of an offer, or place and timing of payment or delivery, if the contract is silent).[12] It applies automatically to transactions whenever and wherever the places of business of the parties to the sale are located in different member states.[13] It can even apply when neither party is located in a member state, when choice of laws rules lead to the application of the law of a state that *is* a party to the CISG. Some nations have taken a permitted exception to this (the United States being one) that excludes this possibility.[14]

As such, the CISG does not need to be invoked by the parties; it governs because it ousts local laws in member states (state or national or both, as the case may be) due to the supremacy rules attached to treaties and conventions that have been ratified by nations. Although it applies by default, the CISG rules can still be avoided in three ways.

First, the CISG does not apply to certain classes of contracts. Contracts dealing with goods sold for personal use (consumer contracts) are excluded from the CISG, as are contracts for stocks, securities, ships, aircraft, and electricity.[15] Local law prevails on these matters.

Second, as the CISG represents only in-filling of contract gaps, the parties should provide for the essential terms of the contract themselves; clear, mutually agreed provisions will supersede the provisions of the CISG. For example, if the parties expressly state when and where payment and delivery are to occur, then those statements will govern. The CISG only dictates where the parties have been silent.

Third, the entire CISG can be ousted from application by making a specific exclusion to that effect.[16] It would be insufficient, however, to merely use a choice-of-law clause (choosing local law) to try to accomplish this. This is insufficient because a contract provision stating that the laws of Delaware or Mexico or Ontario are to prevail fails to recognize that the CISG *is* the law of those places as part of the supreme law of the United States, Mexico, and Canada. The parties may wish to exclude application of the CISG simply because they are unfamiliar with its provisions. They may be more familiar with local law, or find themselves in a business or industry that has developed its own, more appropriate customs and rules (although customs and trade practice are accommodated by the CISG).

Also operating as a final type of exclusion, the CISG does not concern itself with general matters of validity of contracts—some of the previously discussed "essential elements" of consideration, capacity, undue influence, duress, mistake, and misrepresentation. Local law continues to apply to these matters as well.

In summary, where a business firm located in a CISG country (such as the United States) enters into a commercial international business contract with a firm located in another CISG country, the CISG will likely apply. In the case of a U.S. firm, where the Uniform Commercial Code ousts inconsistent rules of traditional state common law, the CISG in turn ousts inconsistent rules of the UCC. All of this is subject to express opt-out (total) and the right to make one's own private rules of contract, just as the UCC itself allows for autonomy in contract.

[12]The CISG is supported by a second convention, the 1980 UN Convention on the Limitation Period in the International Sale of Goods. This convention sets limitation periods for the commencement of claims under the CISG in national court actions, unifying the diverse limitation periods under national law. Application of this convention is not automatic with CISG membership. The United States implemented the Limitation Convention in 1994.

[13]Article 1.

[14]As at early 2004, China, the Czech Republic, Germany, Saint Vincent and the Grenadines, Singapore, and Slovakia have done so as well.

[15]A broader scope of norms (but not rules) spans goods, services, and investments in the 1994 UNIDROIT Principles of International Commercial Contracts. While private parties may *choose* to use these as rules within their contracts, it does not represent uniform law with automatic applicability.

[16]Article 6.

In substance, there is not a great deal of incompatibility in the first place between the CISG and U.S. state law, nor with that of Canadian provinces or other common law signatories such as Australia. In fact, to be considered successful, an international trade agreement must involve and accommodate the principal trading nations. With the United States in the original handful of contracting parties when the CISG came into force, it should come as no surprise that the CISG was geared toward compatibility with U.S. interests.

There are, however, some notably different aspects of the CISG that are at odds with both the traditional common law approach to contracts and state law codification. These relate to the formation of contracts, their substantive provisions, and remedies for breach. The full text of the CISG, with a concordance between it and the major provisions of both the Uniform Commercial Code (U.S. states, New York being representative) and the French Civil Code appears as Appendix 1 to this chapter. As the European Union is presently drafting a uniform set of rules for contract law, an index to the important terms of that draft is included in the concordance.

Chief Differences between the CISG, UCC, and Traditional Common Law

Formation of Contracts

1. Firm offers (Article 16). An offer said to be irrevocable remains so, even if there is no consideration for the promise to hold it open.
2. Time of acceptance (Articles 18 and 24). Acceptance is complete when it is received, rather than when it is sent.
3. Acceptance inconsistent with offer, also known as "The Battle of the Preprinted Forms" (Article 19).
   a. *Traditional common law* (British Commonwealth) requires acceptance to be a mirror image of the offer, additions or changes are a rejection and a counteroffer. The "last shot" that results in acceptance indicated by subsequent conduct (performance) will govern.
   b. With the *Uniform Commercial Code* (U.S. states), a definite acceptance but with additional or different terms makes a contract (between merchants) and the additional terms become part of the contract if
      i. They are expressly accepted by the offeror, or
      ii. The offer does not expressly limit acceptance to the terms of the offer, AND the additional terms do not materially alter the contract, AND the offeror does not object to the additional terms, or
      iii. having failed to make a contract as above, there is a contract only on the terms held in common, with the UCC filling required gaps.
   c. CISG uses the mirror image rule but allows additional or different terms that are neither material nor objected to by the first offeror. So much is considered material, however, that one should expect application of the mirror image rule.

Substantive Provisions

4. No requirement of a written contract (Article 11). This applies unless the contract specifies so, or unless a state has made a permitted CISG reservation to that effect (neither the United States nor Canada has taken this reservation[17]).
5. No "parol evidence" rule (Article 8). Any evidence may be introduced to prove terms of the contract, including witnesses, oral evidence, or other documents.

Remedies for Breach

6. Specific performance is available in principle (Article 28). Specific performance is more easily available (to both buyer and seller) than under either the traditional common law

---

[17]Argentina, Belarus, Chile, China, Estonia, Latvia, Lithuania, the Russian Federation, Ukraine, and Hungary, however, have reimposed the requirement of writing through this reservation.

or UCC, which restrict it to cases where money damages are insufficient. However, courts are not required to grant specific performance awards unless they would do so in similar domestic cases.

7. No "perfect tender" rule (Articles 25 and 49).

   a. Under traditional common law, the obligation of a party to perform is not released by a nonmaterial breach by the other party. Perfect tender of performance is not required.

   b. Under the Uniform Commercial Code, a buyer may reject delivery if they "fail in *any* respect to conform to the contract." Perfect tender is required.

   c. Under the *CISG,* a party may only avoid a contract where the failure to perform by the other party "results in such detriment to the other party as substantially to deprive him of what he is entitled to expect under the contract." Perfect tender is not required.

8. Remoteness of recoverable damages (Article 74).

   a. Under the traditional common law, recoverable damages are those reasonably *foreseeable* at the time of contract formation as the *probable* result of breach (a strict standard).

   b. Under the Uniform Commercial Code, recoverable damages are *any* loss resulting from requirements and needs of which the seller at the time of contract formation had reason to know and *that could not reasonably be prevented* (a less strict standard).

   c. Under the CISG, recoverable damages are *any* losses not exceeding those that were foreseen (or ought to have been) at the time of contract formation, as a *possible* consequence of the breach of contract (an even less strict standard).

Cases on Application of the CISG

As many as 2,000 cases have emerged from the judicial systems of CISG contracting states since its entry into force in 1988. Given the limited language skills found in most of the English-speaking world, practical access exists to only half of the jurisprudence available to guide businesspersons. Of this, less than 100 cases from the United States attract the attention of U.S. courts, lawyers, and businesspersons. Indeed, the U.S. Court of Appeals for the Fourth Circuit concluded as recently as 2002 that "Both parties agree that this case is governed by the CISG, but there is some disagreement concerning how this court should interpret that treaty. Case law interpreting the CISG is rather sparse."[18]

U.S. case law interpreting the CISG may be sparse, but elsewhere it is rich. Considering also that the convention is uniform law and not foreign law, the requirements of CISG Article 7 remind courts of the need to interpret the convention with regard to its international character and to the need to promote uniformity in its application. The following case illustrates some of the more interesting aspects of the CISG: application of the Convention itself, an oral contract, nonconforming goods, and notice requirements.

---

[18]*Schmitz-Werke v. Rockland,* 2002 U.S. App. LEXIS 12336 (4th Cir. June 21, 2002), also available at http://cisgw3.law.pace.edu/cases/020621u1.html.

Oral Contracts and Nonconforming Goods:
La San Giuseppe v. Forti Moulding Ltd.

Ontario Superior Court of Justice
August 31, 1999
Swinton, J.

Reasons for Judgment

(1) La San Giuseppe ("LSG") brought an action claiming damages for breach of contract against the defendant, Forti Moulding Ltd. LSG is a company situated in Venice, Italy, which manufactures picture frame mouldings. It supplied mouldings to the defendant, a distributor of mouldings and picture frames located in Toronto, from 1989 to 1996.

(2) Generally, Forti Moulding placed orders by fax, specifying whether shipments were to be by sea or air. The mouldings were sold according to code numbers assigned to a particular profile, colour and wood finish. Samples corresponding to the code numbers were kept by the factory to ensure that new orders matched earlier production. Some products had been created to meet Forti's specifications.

. . .

(4) The parties never had a written agreement. When they began dealing in 1989, there was no commitment as to the volume of product to be supplied by LSG or prices. While Mr. Forti claimed that LSG promised an "exclusive" contract, it was not clear what he meant by that term. Representatives of LSG denied that they promised to make Forti the exclusive Canadian distributor. I find, on the evidence, that there was no agreement that LSG would make Forti Moulding its exclusive Canadian distributor, meaning that LSG would supply only to Forti Moulding for the Canadian Market.

(5) At first, shipments were sent on a C.O.D. basis, followed by a requirement that payment be made within 30 days. Over the years, payments were not necessarily made within the 30 day period, but were made more or less currently until 1995. When an order was placed, it was understood by both parties that the amount shipped might vary above or below the ordered amount by up to 10%. There was no requirement that a specified quantity need by [*sic*] purchased at any time, except with respect to certain items made specially for Forti Moulding, where there were some minimum amounts that had to be ordered at one time.

(6) By January, 1996, Giovanni Moschini, the individual then in charge of foreign sales for LSG, had become concerned about the long delay in payment by Forti Moulding. Therefore, he wrote on January 18, 1996, complaining that the delays had reached six months and requesting that the defendant pay the outstanding balance within 60 days. Mr. Moschini testified that while Nelson Forti promised to do his best to shorten the time for payment, there was no immediate payment. Nevertheless, LSG filled a further order dated March 5, 1996 in April of that year. These goods, the last shipped by LSG to Forti Moulding arrived by June, according to Mr. Forti.

(7) After a further request for payment, LSG received a letter from Carolina Forti, Mr. Forti's wife, dated May 6, 1996. The evidence is clear that she wrote this letter with Mr. Forti's authority. In it, she indicated that the defendant was about to send a payment, stating that they had been unable to send the money earlier as a few of their customers had been late with their payments. Forti Moulding then sent 15 million Italian Lira. Mr. Moschini wrote in reply, indicating that he had been expecting 20 million Lira.

. . .

(9) Negotiations continued on the terms of payment of the outstanding account, which had reached 64,216,671 Lira by the end of June, 1966. On July 15, for example, Mr. Forti's letter proposed the following: to pay 5 million Lira a month for 13 months, to sell the product at 40% off his cost, or to return the merchandise to Italy at LSG's cost. Again, no mention was made of defects in the product supplied.

(10) . . . After further unsuccessful demands for payment, the plaintiff commenced this action, seeking the outstanding balance of 48,707,460 Lira plus interest.

(11) There is no dispute that the defendant received product priced at this amount for which it did not pay, and so it owes the plaintiff that amount. However, the defendant has counterclaimed for damages and setoff, alleging that some of the mouldings received from LSG over the years were defective. The defendant claimed damages for defective LSG stock which it claims to have in storage in the amount of $32,251.38, damages for repairs to mouldings ($13,117.90), storage costs of $7,864.50, labour and travel costs, and credits for overshipments of $13,906.50. As well, LSG sold Forti Moulding a double mitre saw in 1994, which Forti Moulding claimed was deficient. Therefore, the defendant has asked for the difference between the purchase price and sale price, plus the cost of a replacement saw. Overall, the defendant counterclaimed for $94,341.12 plus the return of the 15 million Lira paid, to be credited against the plaintiff's claim.

The Complaints

. . .

(13) Essentially, the complaints were about poor quality in production, as allegedly demonstrated by the presence of cross-grain and curly grain in some mouldings, dents under the finish, improper colour that did not match the sample or varied within a shipment . . . Numerous sample[s] of moulding were made exhibits, generally in the form of pieces under a metre in length, which were identified by Mr. Forti as having come from LSG. He then linked them to shipments recorded in invoices from 1993, 1994, 1995, and January and April, 1996.

. . . *[A review of the evidence supporting the existence of nonconforming goods was conducted, and]* . . .

(25) Mr. Forti complained that the saw sent was not the one ordered, because it was not computerized. However, the saw was paid for without written complaint. Mr. Ganss remembered no complaints about its performance when he was dealing with Forti. Mr. Moschini testified that there were no complaints about the performance of the saw until these legal proceedings commenced.

(26) Alex Hurrutia, who works as a framer for Forti Moulding, testified that the saw did not work properly, because it did not clamp the wood tightly, with the result that corners were not properly cut and needed further hand finishing. While there were attempt[s] to correct this problem, they were unsuccessful. This complaint appears to have nothing to do with the fact that the saw was not computerized.

(27) Forti Moulding used the saw for four years on a daily basis, and then sold it in 1998 for $5,350.00. The original price was 13,400,000 Lira or $11,751.80. The defendant purchased a new saw for $1,650.00, and claims the difference in value between the purchase and selling prices of the old saw, plus the value of the new saw.

The Law

(28) Counsel for the plaintiff relies on the *International Sale of Goods Contracts Convention Act,* S.C. 1991, c. 13, which has been in effect in Ontario since 1992 because of the

International Sale of Goods Act, R.S.O. 1990, c.1.10. These two acts brought into effect in Canada the United Nations *Convention on Contracts for the International Sale of Goods.* While the plaintiff failed to provide documentation that Italy is a signatory, it is a matter of public record that Italy ratified the convention in 1986. Moreover, pursuant to Article 1, the Convention applies both because the contracting parties have places of business in contracting states, and because the rules of private international law lead to the application of the law of a contracting state—namely, Ontario.

(29) The defendant argued that the Convention does not apply because the contract between the parties was made before the Convention came into effect in Ontario—namely, in 1989. Having considered the evidence, I do not find that the parties made a contract in 1989, which continued through to 1996. In their 1989 dealings, the parties began to establish a business relationship that would last several years, but they did not make a contract that set out the terms of their relationship, since they did not set out the key terms of their agreement—for example, price, volume, term, or payment arrangements. In effect, they had an agreement to agree, and each time an order was made by Forti Moulding and accepted by LSG, a contract was created for the shipment of goods. Therefore, the parties had a series of contracts for the supply of goods over the years. The complaints here all arise with respect to shipments in and after 1993, so the Convention does apply.

(30) Moreover, this is a contract for the sale of commercial goods, not a contract for the supply of personal or domestic goods. Therefore, Article 2(a), which provides that the Convention does not apply to goods bought for personal, family or household use, does not exclude these contracts between parties.

(31) Article 39(1) of the Convention requires that notice of a lack of conformity of the goods must be given to the seller within a reasonable time after the buyer discovers or ought to have discovered it, and not later than two years after actual delivery. The seller cannot rely on this limitation period if the seller knew or ought reasonably to have been aware of the lack of conformity and did not disclose it to the buyer (Article 40). At the outset of the trial, leave was given to the plaintiff to amend its Defense to Counterclaim to plead this limitation period, as I determined that there was no prejudice to the defendant. The trial was then adjourned briefly to allow discovery of Mr. Ganss.

(32) The plaintiff claimed that there were no complaints about quality or overshipment until the Statement of Defense and Counterclaim was issued in April, 1998, and so the claims are barred. However, Mr. Forti claimed to have raised his complaints orally with LSG on many occasions. Therefore, the defendant argued that the complaints are not barred, and the serious defects in the goods, as well as overshipments, entitle it to remedies in accordance with the *Sale of Goods Act,* R.S.O. 1990, c.S.1.

Findings

Quality of the Goods

(33) There was a great deal of evidence led on the quality of the mouldings provided by LSG. There is no question that there were some dents, gold leaf defects and grain problems in some of the pieces of mouldings introduced as exhibits. Mr. Van Zyl *[expert evidence on behalf of Forti]* also found defects when he investigated four to five boxes of unopened mouldings in the warehouse. I accept that some of the exhibits may have come from LSG. It is less clear, however, that all the mouldings seen by Mr. Zyl were from LSG, given that he saw no identifying marks on the boxes. But even accepting that there were some defective pieces of LSG moulding, I do not find that the quality problems with LSG products were as serious as Mr. Forti would have had me believe, nor [*sic*] that he made frequent and timely complaints to LSG. Where his evidence is in conflict with that of Mr. Moschini or Mr. Ganss, I prefer their evidence. I reach those conclusions for the following reasons.

(34) Most important is the fact that Mr. Forti made no written complaints about the quality of the mouldings throughout his negotiations over payment with Mr. Moschini in the first half of 1996. The only written complaints in evidence respecting quality or amounts shipped were dated in August and October, 1994. The existence of his letter of August 10, 1994 dealing with damaged goods demonstrates that he had, in the past, made complaints about defects in writing. Moreover, he gave evidence that he visited the LSG factory several times between 1989 and 1992 to discuss quality problems. Mr. Van Zyl testified that he found Mr. Forti to be a demanding customer when he had done work for Forti Moulding. Yet in the letters written to LSG in 1996, the only message from Forti Moulding was that the company needed time to pay, because of financial problems. Nowhere was defective merchandise mentioned, even though the defendant now alleges that there was some $32,000.00 worth of defective product from years back sitting in the warehouse. Instead, payments were promised, and several were made.

(35) Mr. Forti testified that he did not mention the defects, as he needed time to calculate how much defective product was on hand, so that he could calculate the amount to be set off. Having heard his evidence, and that of his family members, I do not accept this version of events . . . Had there been serious quality problems over the years, one would have expected Mr. Forti to react—for example, by complaining, or by withholding payments to LSG . . .

(36) Mr. Forti tried to portray his company as a victim, subject to pressure from LSG to accept defective products because of the lack of available credit from other suppliers. However, the evidence showed that Forti Moulding was able to obtain some credit from other suppliers several years before terminating the relationship with LSG. The fact that Mr. Forti chose not to change suppliers earlier because the financial arrangements were better with LSG demonstrates, again, that he found the arrangement with LSG a satisfactory one, and he was content with the general quality of the merchandise.

(37) I note that Mr. Forti conceded that there were defects in the products supplied by any supplier in the range of five to eight per cent, and his current supplier, Abitare, also supplies defective product at times. Therefore, some level of tolerance for defects is to be expected, and Mr. Van Zyl indicated this to be the case, as well. The exhibits filed were mostly small lengths of moulding, often with small defects. There was no way of knowing for certain that these were all from LSG, but even if they were, I do not know whether they came within a range of tolerance in a larger shipment without defects. Moreover, it was not clear, with respect to the exhibits with colour variations, whether these sticks were all from the same shipment. Mr. Van Zyl indicated that some colour variation over shipments was to be expected.

(38) The fact that Mr. Forti was able to provide replacement product to Mr. Snyder, his customer, when there were problems indicates that the LSG products were not all defective. Finally, I note that Mr. Forti has overreached in his claims for damages—for example, by presenting invoices from C & B Guilders and Frame Craft that date from a period well after LSG product was being supplied. This is a further reason why I do not accept his version of events that there were extensive defects between 1993 and 1996, and why Forti's statement said that LSG's product was generally not that bad rings true.

(39) Therefore, I reject the claim that the defendant should receive damages for defective merchandise from LSG. I find that he failed to make timely complaints prior to the Statement of Defense, and this is a bar under Article 39 of the International Convention. The evidence does not support a conclusion that the seller was aware of the defects or should have been aware of the defects and, thus, is barred from relying on the limitation period because of Article 40. Moreover, the lack of complaint is also telling evidence that the material shipped was not defective. I find that there is no basis for the claims that the goods were not of merchantable quality nor in compliance with their description under ss. 14

through 16 of the *Sale of Goods Act.* Therefore, the claims for credits, storage costs, and value of goods in the warehouse, labour costs, and repair costs are dismissed. While I note that many of these claims were poorly documented, there is no need to examine in detail the overreaching nature of these claims.

The Saw

(40) There is no merit to this claim for damages. LSG gave no warranty in selling the saw to the defendant, and none should be implied. The model was Mr. Forti's choice, and I am not satisfied that the saw received was different from what he ordered in any significant way, especially given the fact that he paid for it and made no written complaints about it. There was no evidence that the lack of computerization affected performance.

(41) While Mr. Forti claimed that the saw did not work properly, his company used it for several years, and sold it for a significant amount. Given the facts, I find that LSG bears no responsibility for the saw's performance, and there is no basis for this claim for damages.

Overshipments

(42) Mr. Forti admitted that it was a term of the contract that he could be shipped 10% more or less of the product ordered. While he complained about overshipments in his testimony, he could point to a written complaint about a short shipment only once in 1994, for which he sought a credit of 54 metres. He claimed that there were overshipments in 1994, as well, pointing to a particular invoice, yet he did not make a written complaint. Given that he made a complaint in writing about the quality of some of the goods in the same shipment in which he claimed an overshipment, I do not believe his claim with respect to overshipments in 1994.

(43) In any event, even if there had been overshipments, I find that the defendant accepted those goods and, in fact, paid for them. In accordance with Article 52(2) of the Convention and s.29(2) of the *Sale of Goods Act,* there can be no complaint several years later.

(44) The only other overshipment alleged was in April, 1996, the last shipment. While there were complaints at trial about this, a careful reading of the invoice indicates that several of the items allegedly overshipped were within the 10% tolerance. As to the other items, given Mr. Forti's lack of forthrightness in his evidence generally and again, the lack of a complaint and a promise to pay, I do not accept that there was a problem of overshipment, and I find that the defendant accepted the quantity shipped. This claim is rejected as well.

Conclusion

(45) For these reasons, there shall be judgements for the plaintiff in the amount of Canadian dollars sufficient to purchase the sum owing of 48,707,460 Italian Lira, which shall be determined by the rate of exchange quoted by a bank in Ontario listed in Schedule I of the *Bank Act* (Can.) as of the day that this judgment is released, in accordance with s. 121(1) of the *Courts of Justice Act.* There shall be pre-judgment interest in accordance with s. 128 of the *Courts of Justice Act* from the date the cause of action arose, which I find to be from the date of the final invoice of April 16, 1996, as well as post-judgment interest. The counterclaim is dismissed. If the parties are unable to agree with respect to costs, they may make an appointment through my secretary.

Source: 90 A.C.W.S. 3d 871; may be reviewed at http://cisgw3.law.pace.edu/cases/990831c4.html.

- Why, specifically, does the CISG apply in this case?
- What specific steps could Forti Moulding have taken, while the business relationship developed, that would have bolstered its defense at trial?

The Italian firm in the case above traveled to Canada to collect its account in a Canadian court. Undoubtedly it would have been a less expensive option to submit this to arbitration, had this been possible. It would appear that the defendant would not be moved by anything less than a court judgment, and arbitration can be ruled out, for it is impossible to set up an arbitration panel on an oral contract unless it is based on mutual consent. The defendant's consent under facts such as those provided in the case above would seem unlikely, and such are the dangers of oral contracts.

Most parties want to avoid outcomes such as this and, therefore, reduce their sales contracts to writing, if only for sensible management, accounting, and record keeping. The evidentiary dilemma associated with oral agreements does not entirely disappear just because contracts are made in writing. Amendments of written contracts are made orally far too frequently (permitted by CISG Article 29) and are never properly recorded. One does hope that the ease and lack of expense in email communication might work to reduce such problems in the future. The CISG willingness to recognize oral contracts stems from the civil law tradition, but requesting and obtaining a commitment to writing should not be problematic. Documentation is the "stuff" of international trade, and an absolute necessity where bank financing, insurance, and customs clearance are at issue.

Writing does become problematic when both parties are advancing written terms (often on preprinted forms—a "battle of the forms") that are in conflict with one another. In the end, the acceptance is therefore inconsistent with the offer. In the usual situation where this conflict occurs, the seller sends the pro forma invoice (with preprinted conditions incorporated) to the buyer. The buyer responds with a purchase order containing different preprinted conditions. The seller then answers with a confirmation of receipt of the purchase order, reaffirming its own conditions, and ships the goods. The buyer (having been silent in the face of the reaffirmed conditions) then is left with the decision to either receive or reject the goods.

In strict common law terms (for example, in the United Kingdom, not being a contracting party to the CISG), the "last shot" will prevail, meaning that a faulty attempt to accept becomes a counteroffer. This continues until there is at last acceptance by conduct when, in this example, the buyer accepts the goods (and hence only then a contract) on the seller's terms.[19]

Among U.S. states, the Uniform Commercial Code approach is to take an expression of acceptance as actual acceptance (a purchase order accepting the contents of a pro forma invoice) and treat its additional or different terms as proposals for addition. A contract

---

[19]See also *Butler Machine Tool Co. Ltd. v. Ex-Cell-O Corp. (England) Ltd.,* [1979] 1 W.L.R. 401. Butler offered to sell to Ex-Cell-O, with the printed offer containing Butler's standard terms and this included a clause allowing Butler to vary its price to that prevailing on the date of delivery. The form also stated that Butler's terms and conditions were to prevail over any terms of the buyer. Ex-Cell-O placed its order on its own standard form, which included a tear-off slip for acknowledgment of acceptance of the order on the buyer's terms and conditions. Butler executed and returned the slip. When the order was delivered, Butler claimed a higher price under its variation clause. Lord Denning, MR, held Butler could not alter the price. The buyer's conditions amounted to a counteroffer, rejecting Butler's own original offer. Butler accepted the counteroffer when the acknowledgment slip was returned.

therefore exists at this earlier point, and whether the additional terms join the contract is a matter of rather mechanical determination.[20]

The CISG provides that an acceptance containing additions or modifications is a rejection of the offer and constitutes a counteroffer.[21] An acceptance containing additions or modifications that *do not materially alter* the terms of the offer will still constitute an acceptance, unless the offeror objects without undue delay (orally or in writing). Where the offeror fails to object in a timely manner, these nonmaterial modifications will be incorporated in the contract. The important question is then one of materiality,[22] and this does not move the CISG much closer to the UCC approach. Very few aspects of an international sale are not material. Therefore, the CISG can be considered to be following the stricter common law approach, with an extra dash of sensibility that prevents nonmaterial matters from delaying formation of the contract until delivery and receipt of the goods.

In the following case, Filanto attempted to avoid an arbitration clause imposed by an offer. Filanto said that it previously had objected to arbitration, and on the litigated occasion, its rejection of the terms made for a counteroffer under the CISG. That should be true, but the court ultimately found against Filanto that an agreement to arbitration did exist. As you go through this case, ask yourself: is the court getting this wrong, or is it getting it right for different reasons? The Old Wolf can't get into the judge's mind, but perhaps there is a clue in the comment that "the State Department undertook to fix something that was not broken" in the Uniform Commercial Code.

---

[20]For example, the West Virginia Code, at Chapter 46 provides:

§2-207. Additional terms in acceptance or confirmation.

(1) A definite and seasonable expression of acceptance or a written confirmation which is sent within a reasonable time operates as an acceptance even though it states terms additional to or different from those offered or agreed upon, unless acceptance is expressly made conditional on assent to the additional or different terms.

(2) The additional terms are to be construed as proposals for addition to the contract. Between merchants such terms become part of the contract unless:
   (a) The offer expressly limits acceptance to the terms of the offer;
   (b) they materially alter it; or
   (c) notification of objection to them has already been given or is given within a reasonable time after notice of them is received.

(3) Conduct by both parties which recognizes the existence of a contract is sufficient to establish a contract for sale although the writings of the parties do not otherwise establish a contract. In such case the terms of the particular contract consist of those terms on which the writings of the parties agree, together with any supplementary terms incorporated under any other provisions of this chapter.

[21]CISG, Article 19(1).

[22]CISG, Article 19(3) acknowledges the materiality of, inter alia, price, payment, quality and quantity of the goods, place and time of delivery, extent of one party's liability to the other, and the settlement of disputes.

Acceptance Inconsistent with Offer—The Battle of the Forms: *Filanto, S.p.A. v. Chilewich International Corp.*

United States District Court for the Southern District of New York
April 14, 1992
Opinion by Chief Judge Brieant

By motion fully submitted on December 11, 1991, defendant Chilewich International Corp. moves to stay this action pending arbitration in Moscow. Plaintiff Filanto has moved to enjoin arbitration or to order arbitration in this federal district.

This case is a striking example of how a lawsuit involving a relatively straightforward international commercial transaction can raise an array of complex questions. Accordingly, the Court will recount the factual background of the case, derived from both parties, memoranda of law and supporting affidavits in some detail.

Plaintiff Filanto is an Italian corporation engaged in the manufacture and sale of footwear. Defendant Chilewich is an export-import firm incorporated in the state of New York with its principal place of business in White Plains. On February 28, 1989, Chilewich's agent in the United Kingdom, Byerly Johnson, Ltd., signed a contract with Raznoexport, the Soviet Foreign Economic Association, which obligated Byerly Johnson to supply footwear to Raznoexport. Section 10 of this contract—the "Russian Contract"—is an arbitration clause, which reads in pertinent part as follows:

> "All disputes or differencies [sic] which may arise out of or in connection with the present Contract are to be settled, jurisdiction of ordinary courts being excluded, by the Arbitration at the USSR Chamber of Commerce and Industry, Moscow, in accordance with the Regulations of the said Arbitration." [sic]

This contract was signed by Byerly Johnson and by Raznoexport, and is sometimes referred to as "Contract No. 32-03/93085."

The first exchange of correspondence between the parties to this lawsuit is a letter dated July 27, 1989 from Mr. Melvin Chilewich of Chilewich International to Mr. Antonio Filograna, chief executive officer of Filanto. This letter refers to a recent visit by Chilewich and Byerly Johnson personnel to Filanto's factories in Italy, presumably to negotiate a purchase to fulfill the Russian Contract, and then states as follows:

> "Attached please find our contract to cover our purchase from you. Same is governed by the conditions which are enumerated in the standard contract in effect with the Soviet buyers [the Russian contract], copy of which is also enclosed."

The next item in the record is a letter from Filanto to Chilewich dated September 2, 1989 . . . The last paragraph . . . states as follows:

> "Returning back the enclosed contracts n 10001-10002-10003 signed for acceptance, we communicate, if we do not misunderstood, the Soviet's contract that you sent us together with your above mentioned contract, that of this contract we have to respect only the following points of it:
>
> -n 5 Packing and marking
>
> -n 6 Way of Shipment
>
> -n 7 Delivery—Acceptance of Goods
>
> "We ask for your acceptance by return of post." [sic]

The intent of this paragraph, clearly, was to exclude from incorporation by reference *inter alia* section 10 of the Russian contract, which provides for arbitration. Chilewich, for its part, claims never to have received this September 2 letter. In any event, it relates only to prior course of conduct.

It is apparent from the record that further negotiations occurred in early 1990, but the content of those negotiations is unclear; it is, however, clear that deliveries of boots from Filanto to Chilewich were occurring at this time, pursuant to other contracts, since there is a reference to a shipment occurring between April 23, 1990 and June 11, 1990.

The next document in this case, and the focal point of the parties' dispute regarding whether an arbitration agreement exists, is a Memorandum Agreement dated March 13, 1990. This Memorandum Agreement, number 9003002, is a standard merchant's memo prepared by Chilewich for signature by both parties confirming that Filanto will deliver 100,000 pairs of boots to Chilewich at the Italian/Yugoslav border on September 15, 1990, with the balance of 150,000 pairs to be delivered on November 1, 1990. Chilewich's obligations were to open a Letter of Credit in Filanto's favor prior to the September 15 delivery, and another letter prior to the November delivery. This Memorandum includes the following provision:

> "It is understood between Buyer and Seller that USSR Contract No. 32-03/93085 [the Russian Contract] is hereby incorporated in this contract as far as practicable, and specifically that any arbitration shall be in accordance with that Contract."

Chilewich signed this Memorandum Agreement, and sent it to Filanto. Filanto at that time did not sign or return the document. Nevertheless, on May 7, 1990, Chilewich opened a Letter of Credit in Filanto's favor in the sum of $ 2,595,600.00. The Letter of Credit itself mentions the Russian Contract, but only insofar as concerns packing and labeling.

Again, on July 23, 1990, Filanto sent another letter to Chilewich, which reads in relevant parts as follows:

> "We refer to Point 3, Special Conditions, to point out that: returning back the above-mentioned contract, signed for acceptance, from Soviet Contract 32-03/93085 we have to respect only the following points of it:
> - No. 5—Packing and Marking
> - No. 6—Way of Shipment
> - No. 7—Delivery Acceptance of Goods."

. . .

This letter caused some concern on the part of Chilewich and its agents: a July 30, 1990 fax from Byerly Johnson, Chilewich's agent, to Chilewich, mentions Filanto's July 23 letter, asserts that it "very neatly dodges" certain issues, other than arbitration, covered by the Russian Contract, and states that Johnson would "take it up" with Filanto during a visit to Filanto's offices the next week.

Then, on August 7, 1990, Filanto returned the Memorandum Agreement, sued on here, that Chilewich had signed and sent to it in March; though Filanto had signed the Memorandum Agreement, it once again appended a covering letter, purporting to exclude all but three sections of the Russian Contract.

There is also in the record an August 7, 1990 telex from Chilewich to Byerly Johnson, stating that Chilewich would not open the second Letter of Credit unless it received from Filanto a signed copy of the contract without any exclusions. In order to resolve this issue, Byerly Johnson on August 29, 1990 sent a fax to Italian Trading SRL, an intermediary, reading in relevant part:

> "We have checked back through our records for last year, and can find no exclusions by Filanto from the Soviet Master Contract and, in the event, we do not believe that this has caused any difficulties between us.

"We would, therefore, ask you to amend your letters of the 23rd July 1990 and the 7th August 1990, so that you accept all points of the Soviet Master Contract No. 32-03/93085 as far as practicable. You will note that this is specified in our Special Condition No. 3 of our contracts Nos. 9003001 and 9003 [illegible]."

Filanto later confirmed to Italian Trading that it received this fax.

As the date specified in the Memorandum Agreement for delivery of the first shipment of boots—September 15, 1990—was approaching, the parties evidently decided to make further efforts to resolve this issue: what actually happened, though, is a matter of some dispute.

. . .

On September 27, 1990, Mr. Filograna faxed a letter to Chilewich. This letter refers to "assurances during our meeting in Paris," and complains that Chilewich had not yet opened the second Letter of Credit for the second delivery, which it had supposedly promised to do by September 25. Mr. Chilewich responded by fax on the same day; his fax states that he is "totally cognizant of the contractual obligations which exist," but goes on to say that Chilewich had encountered difficulties with the Russian buyers, that Chilewich needed to "reduce the rate of shipments," and denies that Chilewich promised to open the Letter of Credit by September 25.

According to the Complaint, what ultimately happened was that Chilewich bought and paid for 60,000 pairs of boots in January 1991, but never purchased the 90,000 pairs of boots that comprise the balance of Chilewich's original order. It is Chilewich's failure to do so that forms the basis of this lawsuit, commenced by Filanto on May 14, 1991.

There is in the record, however, one document that post-dates the filing of the Complaint: a letter from Filanto to Chilewich dated June 21, 1991. This letter is in response to claims by Byerly Johnson that some of the boots that had been supplied by Filanto were defective. The letter expressly relies on a section of the Russian contract which Filanto had earlier purported to exclude—Section 9 regarding claims procedures—and states that "The April Shipment and the September Shipment are governed by the Master Purchase Contract of February 28, 1989, n 32-03/93085 (the "Master Purchase Contract")."

This letter must be regarded as an admission in law by Filanto, the party to be charged. A litigant may not blow hot and cold in a lawsuit. The letter of June 21, 1991 clearly shows that when Filanto thought it desirable to do so, it recognized that it was bound by the incorporation by reference of portions of the Russian Contract, which, prior to the Paris meeting, it had purported to exclude. This letter shows that Filanto regarded itself as the beneficiary of the claims adjustment provisions of the Russian Contract. This legal position is entirely inconsistent with the position which Filanto had professed prior to the Paris meeting, and is inconsistent with its present position. Consistent with the position of the defendant in this action, Filanto admits that the other relevant clauses of the Russian Contract were incorporated by agreement of the parties, and made a part of the bargain. Of necessity, this must include the agreement to arbitrate in Moscow . . .

. . .

However, the focus of this dispute, apparent from the parties' submissions, is not on the scope of the arbitration provision included in the Russian contract; rather, the threshold question is whether these parties actually agreed to arbitrate their disputes at all . . .

However, as plaintiff correctly notes, the "general principles of contract law" relevant to this action, do not include the Uniform Commercial Code; rather, the "federal law of contracts" to be applied in this case is found in the United Nations Convention on Contracts for the International Sale of Goods . . .

Not surprisingly, the parties offer varying interpretations of the numerous letters and documents exchanged between them. The Court will briefly summarize their respective contentions.

Defendant Chilewich contends that the Memorandum Agreement dated March 13 which it signed and sent to Filanto was an offer. It then argues that Filanto's retention of the letter, along with its subsequent acceptance of Chilewich's performance under the Agreement—the furnishing of the May 11 letter of credit—estops it from denying its acceptance of the contract. Although phrased as an estoppel argument, this contention is better viewed as an acceptance by conduct argument, e.g., that in light of the parties' course of dealing, Filanto had a duty timely to inform Chilewich that it objected to the incorporation by reference of all the terms of the Russian contract. Under this view, the return of the Memorandum Agreement, signed by Filanto, on August 7, 1990, along with the covering letter purporting to exclude parts of the Russian Contract, was ineffective as a matter of law as a rejection of the March 13 offer, because this occurred some five months after Filanto received the Memorandum Agreement and two months after Chilewich furnished the Letter of Credit. Instead, in Chilewich's view, this action was a proposal for modification of the March 13 Agreement. Chilewich rejected this proposal, by its letter of August 7 to Byerly Johnson, and the August 9 fax by Johnson to Italian Trading SRL, which communication Filanto acknowledges receiving. Accordingly, Filanto under this interpretation is bound by the written terms of the March 13 Memorandum Agreement; since that agreement incorporates by reference the Russian Contract containing the arbitration provision, Filanto is bound to arbitrate.

Plaintiff Filanto's interpretation of the evidence is rather different. While Filanto apparently agrees that the March 13 Memorandum Agreement was indeed an offer, it characterizes its August 7 return of the signed Memorandum Agreement with the covering letter as a counteroffer. While defendant contends that under Uniform Commercial Code § 2-207 this action would be viewed as an acceptance with a proposal for a material modification, the Uniform Commercial Code, as previously noted does not apply to this case, because the State Department undertook to fix something that was not broken by helping to create the Sale of Goods Convention which varies from the Uniform Commercial Code in many significant ways. Instead, under this analysis, Article 19(1) of the Sale of Goods Convention would apply. That section, as the Commentary to the Sale of Goods Convention notes, reverses the rule of Uniform Commercial Code § 2-207, and reverts to the common law rule that "A reply to an offer which purports to be an acceptance but contains additions, limitations or other modifications is a rejection of the offer and constitutes a counter-offer." Sale of Goods Convention Article 19(1). Although the Convention, like the Uniform Commercial Code, does state that non-material terms do become part of the contract unless objected to, Sale of Goods Convention Article 19(2), the Convention treats inclusion (or deletion) of an arbitration provision as "material," Sale of Goods Convention Article 19(3). The August 7 letter, therefore, was a counteroffer which, according to Filanto, Chilewich accepted by its letter dated September 27, 1990. Though that letter refers to and acknowledges the "contractual obligations" between the parties, it is doubtful whether it can be characterized as an acceptance.

. . .

The Court is satisfied on this record that there *was* indeed an agreement to arbitrate between these parties.

There is simply no satisfactory explanation as to why Filanto failed to object to the incorporation by reference of the Russian Contract in a timely fashion. As noted above, Chilewich had in the meantime commenced its performance under the Agreement, and the Letter of Credit it furnished Filanto on May 11 itself mentioned the Russian Contract. An offeree who, knowing that the offeror has commenced performance, fails to notify the offeror of its objection to the terms of the contract within a reasonable time will, under certain circumstances, be deemed to have assented to those terms . . . The Sale of Goods Convention itself recognizes this rule: Article 18(1), provides that "A statement made by or other conduct of the offeree indicating assent to an offer is an acceptance." Although mere "silence or inactivity" does not constitute acceptance, Sale of Goods Convention Article 18(l), the Court may consider previous relations between the parties in assessing whether a party's conduct constituted acceptance, Sale of Goods Convention Article 8(3). In this case, in light of the extensive course of prior dealing between these parties, Filanto was certainly under a duty to alert Chilewich in timely fashion to its objections to the terms of the March 13 Memorandum Agreement—particularly since Chilewich had repeatedly referred it to the Russian Contract and Filanto had had a copy of that document for some time.

There are three other convincing manifestations of Filanto's true understanding of the terms of this agreement. First, Filanto's Complaint in this action, as well as affidavits subsequently submitted to the Court by Mr. Filograna, refer to the March 13 contract: the Complaint, for example, states that "On or about March 13, 1990, Filanto entered into a contract with Chilewich. . . ." Indeed, Filanto finds itself in an awkward position: it has sued on a contract whose terms it must now question, in light of the defendant's assertion that the contract contains an arbitration provision . . . ("In short, the plaintiffs cannot have it both ways. They cannot rely on the contract, when it works to their advantage, and repudiate it when it works to their disadvantage").

Second, Filanto did sign the March 13 Memorandum Agreement. That Agreement, as noted above, specifically referred to the incorporation by reference of the arbitration provision in the Russian Contract; although Filanto, in its August 7 letter, did purport to "have to respect" only a small part of the Russian Contract, Filanto in that very letter noted that it was returning the March 13 Memorandum Agreement "signed for acceptance." In light of Filanto's knowledge that Chilewich had already performed its part of the bargain by furnishing it the Letter of Credit, Filanto's characterization of this action as a rejection and a counteroffer is almost frivolous.

Third, and most important, Filanto, in a letter to Byerly Johnson dated June 21, 1991, explicitly stated that "the April Shipment and the September shipment are governed by the Master Purchase Contract of February 28, 1989 [the Russian Contract]." Furthermore, the letter, which responds to claims by Johnson that some of the boots that were supplied were defective, expressly relies on section 9 of the Russian Contract—another section which Filanto had in its earlier correspondence purported to exclude. The Sale of Goods Convention specifically directs that "in determining the intent of a party . . . due consideration is to be given to . . . any subsequent conduct of the parties," Sale of Goods Convention Article 8(3). In this case, as the letter post-dates the partial performance of the contract, it is particularly strong evidence that Filanto recognized itself to be bound by all the terms of the Russian Contract.

In light of these factors, and heeding the presumption in favor of arbitration, which is even stronger in the context of international commercial transactions, the Court holds that Filanto is bound by the terms of the March 13 Memorandum Agreement, and so must arbitrate its dispute in Moscow; . . . the chosen forum in this case does have a reasonable relation to the contract at issue, as the ultimate purchaser of the boots was a Russian concern and the Russian Contract was incorporated by reference into Filanto's Memorandum Agreement with Chilewich. Furthermore, though conditions in the Republic of Russia are unsettled, they continue to improve and there is no reason to believe that the Chamber of Commerce in Moscow cannot provide fair and impartial justice to these litigants.

Source: 91 Civ. 3253 (CLB), available at cisgw3.law.pace.edu/cases/92041u1.html.

As international businesspersons who also will face this situation, two questions should come to mind as lessons from this case:

- What *should* Filanto have done in setting up its acceptance to ensure it avoided the arbitration provision that it did not want?

- Going on the basis of the court's reasoning, what *did* Filanto *do* that sunk its chances of avoiding the arbitration term that it did not want?

The CISG offers an interesting balance in terms of buyers' and sellers' rights where the goods at the time of delivery are not in conformity with the terms of the contract. To strengthen the hand of the seller, the buyer may not treat the contract as at an end, or avoid it, unless the nonconformity can be considered to amount to a fundamental breach,[23] meaning a substantial deprivation, foreseeable to the seller, of what the buyer was entitled to expect from the contract.[24] Balancing this protection of the seller is the buyer's unilateral remedy, born of the civil law tradition, of a price reduction to the extent of any nonconformity. Such a price reduction is available to the buyer where the seller will not, or cannot, remedy the nonconformity of the goods.[25] Specific performance is a qualified right of the buyer and seller,[26] rather than an exception, or if it is not unreasonable in the circumstances, the buyer may demand repair of the goods if they are not in conformity with the contract.[27]

The case below, *Delchi,* explores the appropriate remedies where goods are not in conformance with the contract of sale and the standard of foreseeability to create liability. When the court in *Delchi* mentions *Hadley v. Baxendale,* it is referring to the traditional common law standard of foreseeability and liability for damages. The traditional common law standard refers to *probable* damages as recoverable for a breach, and the CISG concerns itself with *possible* damages. Probable and possible are not the same standard, but the court equates the two as if they are. Once again, ask yourself whether the court is getting this right, even if the court comes to a likely fair conclusion in the end. Judges are not perfect creatures, the CISG is relatively new law, and, as international businesspersons, you must be prepared to work in an uncertain environment.

Remedies—Avoidance, Damages, and Fundamental Breach: *Delchi Carrier S.p.A. v. Rotorex Corp.*

United States Court of Appeals for the Second Circuit
Decided: December 6, 1995
Winter, Circuit Judge:

Rotorex Corporation, a New York corporation, appeals from a judgment of $1,785,772.44 in damages for lost profits and other consequential damages awarded to Delchi Carrier SpA . . .

Background

In January 1988, Rotorex agreed to sell 10,800 compressors to Delchi for use in Delchi's "Ariele" line of portable room air conditioners. The air conditioners were scheduled to go on sale in the spring and summer of 1988. Prior to executing the contract, Rotorex sent

[23]CISG, Articles 49(1) and 51(2).
[24]Article 25.
[25]Article 50.
[26]Article 46 (buyer's right) and Article 62 (seller's right). Note, however, that Article 28 may limit the right to specific performance.
[27]Article 46(3).

Delchi a sample compressor and accompanying written performance specifications. The compressors were scheduled to be delivered in three shipments before May 15, 1988.

Rotorex sent the first shipment by sea on March 26. Delchi paid for this shipment, which arrived at its Italian factory on April 20, by letter of credit. Rotorex sent a second shipment of compressors on or about May 9. Delchi also remitted payment for this shipment by letter of credit. While the second shipment was en route, Delchi discovered that the first lot of compressors did not conform to the sample model and accompanying specifications. On May 13, after a Rotorex representative visited the Delchi factory in Italy, Delchi informed Rotorex that 93 percent of the compressors were rejected in quality control checks because they had lower cooling capacity and consumed more power than the sample model and specifications. After several unsuccessful attempts to cure the defects in the compressors, Delchi asked Rotorex to supply new compressors conforming to the original sample and specifications. Rotorex refused, claiming that the performance specifications were "inadvertently communicated" to Delchi.

In a faxed letter dated May 23, 1988, Delchi cancelled the contract. Although it was able to expedite a previously planned order of suitable compressors from Sanyo, another supplier, Delchi was unable to obtain in a timely fashion substitute compressors from other sources and thus suffered a loss in its sales volume of Arieles during the 1988 selling season. Delchi filed the instant action under the United Nations Convention on Contracts for the International Sale of Goods ("CISG" or "the Convention") for breach of contract and failure to deliver conforming goods. On January 10, 1991, Judge Cholakis granted Delchi's motion for partial summary judgment, holding Rotorex liable for breach of contract.

After three years of discovery and a bench trial on the issue of damages, Judge Munson, to whom the case had been transferred, held Rotorex liable to Delchi for $1,248,331.87. This amount included consequential damages for: (i) lost profits resulting from a diminished sales level of Ariele units, (ii) expenses that Delchi incurred in attempting to remedy the nonconformity of the compressors, (iii) the cost of expediting shipment of previously ordered Sanyo compressors after Delchi rejected the Rotorex compressors, and (iv) costs of handling and storing the rejected compressors. The district court also awarded prejudgment interest under CISG art. 78.

. . .

On appeal, Rotorex argues that it did not breach the agreement, that Delchi is not entitled to lost profits because it maintained inventory levels in excess of the maximum number of possible lost sales, that the calculation of the number of lost sales was improper, and that the district court improperly excluded fixed costs and depreciation from the manufacturing cost in calculating lost profits. Delchi cross-appeals, claiming that it is entitled to the additional out-of-pocket expenses and the lost profits on additional sales denied by Judge Munson.

Discussion

The district court held, and the parties agree, that the instant matter is governed by the CISG, reprinted at 15 U.S.C.A. Appendix (West Supp. 1995), a self-executing agreement between the United States and other signatories, including Italy. Because there is virtually no case law under the Convention, we look to its language and to "the general principles" upon which it is based. See CISG art. 7(2). The Convention directs that its interpretation be informed by its "international character and . . . the need to promote uniformity in its application and the observance of good faith in international trade." See CISG art. 7(1); see generally John Honnold, Uniform Law for International Sales Under the 1980 United Nations Convention 60–62 (2d ed. 1991). Case law interpreting analogous provisions of

Article 2 of the Uniform Commercial Code ("UCC"), may also inform a court where the language of the relevant CISG provisions tracks that of the UCC. However, UCC case law "is not per se applicable." *Orbisphere Corp. v. United States.*

We first address the liability issue. . .

Under the CISG, "[t]he seller must deliver goods which are of the quantity, quality and description required by the contract," and "the goods do not conform with the contract unless they . . . [p]ossess the qualities of goods which the seller has held out to the buyer as a sample or model." CISG art. 35. The CISG further states that "[t]he seller is liable in accordance with the contract and this Convention for any lack of conformity." CISG art. 36.

Judge Cholakis held that "there is no question that [Rotorex's] compressors did not conform to the terms of the contract between the parties" and noted that "[t]here are ample admissions [by Rotorex] to that effect." We agree. The agreement between Delchi and Rotorex was based upon a sample compressor supplied by Rotorex and upon written specifications regarding cooling capacity and power consumption. After the problems were discovered, Rotorex's engineering representative, Ernest Gamache, admitted in a May 13, 1988 letter that the specification sheet was "in error" and that the compressors would actually generate less cooling power and consume more energy than the specifications indicated . . . There was thus no genuine issue of material fact regarding liability, and summary judgment was proper.

Under the CISG, if the breach is "fundamental" the buyer may either require delivery of substitute goods, CISG art. 46, or declare the contract void, CISG art. 49, and seek damages. With regard to what kind of breach is fundamental, Article 25 provides:

> A breach of contract committed by one of the parties is fundamental if it results in such detriment to the other party as substantially to deprive him of what he is entitled to expect under the contract, unless the party in breach did not foresee and a reasonable person of the same kind in the same circumstances would not have foreseen such a result.

CISG art. 25. In granting summary judgment, the district court held that "[t]here appears to be no question that [Delchi] did not substantially receive that which [it] was entitled to expect" and that "any reasonable person could foresee that shipping non-conforming goods to a buyer would result in the buyer not receiving that which he expected and was entitled to receive." Because the cooling power and energy consumption of an air conditioner compressor are important determinants of the product's value, the district court's conclusion that Rotorex was liable for a fundamental breach of contract under the Convention was proper.

We turn now to the district court's award of damages following the bench trial. A reviewing court must defer to the trial judge's findings of fact unless they are clearly erroneous. However, we review questions of law, including "the measure of damages upon which the factual computation is based," de novo.[28] The CISG provides:

> Damages for breach of contract by one party consist of a sum equal to the loss, including loss of profit, suffered by the other party as a consequence of the breach. Such damages may not exceed the loss which the party in breach foresaw or ought to have foreseen at the time of the conclusion of the contract, in the light of the facts and matters of which he then knew or ought to have known, as a possible consequence of the breach of contract.

CISG art. 74. This provision is "designed to place the aggrieved party in as good a position as if the other party had properly performed the contract." Honnold, *supra,* at 503.

Rotorex argues that Delchi is not entitled to lost profits because it was able to maintain inventory levels of Ariele air conditioning units in excess of the maximum number of possible lost sales. In Rotorex's view, therefore, there was no actual shortfall of Ariele units available for sale because of Rotorex's delivery of nonconforming compressors. Rotorex's

[28]Anew.

argument goes as follows. The end of the air conditioner selling season is August 1. If one totals the number of units available to Delchi from March to August 1, the sum is enough to fill all sales. We may assume that the evidence in the record supports the factual premise. Nevertheless, the argument is fallacious. Because of Rotorex's breach, Delchi had to shut down its manufacturing operation for a few days in May, and the date on which particular units were available for sale was substantially delayed. For example, units available in late July could not be used to meet orders in the spring. As a result, Delchi lost sales in the spring and early summer. We therefore conclude that the district court's findings regarding lost sales are not clearly erroneous. A detailed discussion of the precise number of lost sales is unnecessary because the district court's findings were, if anything, conservative.

Rotorex contends, in the alternative, that the district court improperly awarded lost profits for unfilled orders from Delchi affiliates in Europe and from sales agents within Italy. We disagree. The CISG requires that damages be limited by the familiar principle of foreseeability established[29] in *Hadley v. Baxendale,* 156 Eng. Rep. 145 (1854). CISG art. 74. However, it was objectively foreseeable that Delchi would take orders for Ariele sales based on the number of compressors it had ordered and expected to have ready for the season. The district court was entitled to rely upon the documents and testimony regarding these lost sales and was well within its authority in deciding which orders were proven with sufficient certainty.

. . .

In its cross-appeal, Delchi challenges the district court's denial of various consequential and incidental damages, including reimbursement for: (i) shipping, customs, and incidentals relating to the first and second shipments—rejected and returned—of Rotorex compressors; (ii) obsolete insulation materials and tubing purchased for use only with Rotorex compressors; (iii) obsolete tooling purchased exclusively for production of units with Rotorex compressors; and (iv) labor costs for the period of May 16–19, 1988, when the Delchi production line was idle due to a lack of compressors to install in Ariele air conditioning units. The district court denied damages for these items on the ground that they "are accounted for in Delchi's recovery on its lost profits claim," and, therefore, an award would constitute a double recovery for Delchi. We disagree.

The Convention provides that a contract plaintiff may collect damages to compensate for the full loss. This includes, but is not limited to, lost profits, subject only to the familiar limitation that the breaching party must have foreseen, or should have foreseen, the loss as a probable consequence. CISG art. 74; see *Hadley v. Baxendale, supra.*

An award for lost profits will not compensate Delchi for the expenses in question. Delchi's lost profits are determined by calculating the hypothetical revenues to be derived from unmade sales less the hypothetical variable costs that would have been, but were not, incurred. This figure, however, does not compensate for costs actually incurred that led to no sales. Thus, to award damages for costs actually incurred in no way creates a double recovery and instead furthers the purpose of giving the injured party damages "equal to the loss." CISG art. 74.

The only remaining inquiries, therefore, are whether the expenses were reasonably foreseeable and legitimate incidental or consequential damages. The expenses incurred by Delchi for shipping, customs, and related matters for the two returned shipments of Rotorex compressors, including storage expenses for the second shipment at Genoa, were clearly foreseeable and recoverable incidental expenses. These are up-front expenses that had to be paid to get the goods to the manufacturing plant for inspection and were thus incurred largely before the nonconformities were detected. To deny reimbursement to Delchi for these inciden-

---

[29]Text author's note: Hmmm . . . Hadley says recoverable damages are those reasonably *foreseeable* at the time of contract formation as the *probable* result of breach. CISG at Article 74 says losses not exceeding those that were foreseen (or ought to have been foreseen) at the time of contract formation as a *possible* consequence of the breach of contract. Are these really the same?

You can foul up your business transaction and create legal problems for yourself:

- By not failing to take any steps to protect yourself *(La San Giuseppe)*. You might get lucky; then again, you might not.
- When you do take steps to protect yourself, but do not make a complete job of it *(Filanto)*. You might get lucky; then again, you might not.
- When you do virtually everything right to protect yourself *(Delchi)*, but the court misapplies the law. You *still* may get lucky; then again, you might not.

The best way to avoid relying on courts and luck is to try and ensure that your contract documents are as clear and complete a statement of your terms as they can possibly be. This is your evidence of your deal. If your evidence is overwhelmingly clear in support of your position, little is left to chance, and it acts as a real deterrent to the other side from commencing a legal action. Further, it makes any action *you* launch much less likely to rely on luck, and much more likely to succeed on *your* terms.

tal damages would effectively cut into the lost profits award. The same is true of unreimbursed tooling expenses and the cost of the useless insulation and tubing materials. These are legitimate consequential damages that in no way duplicate lost profits damages.

The labor expense incurred as a result of the production line shutdown of May 16–19, 1988 is also a reasonably foreseeable result of delivering nonconforming compressors for installation in air conditioners. However, Rotorex argues that the labor costs in question were fixed costs that would have been incurred whether or not there was a breach . . . We therefore remand to the district court on this issue.

. . .

Conclusion

We affirm the award of damages. We reverse in part the denial of incidental and consequential damages. We remand for further proceedings in accord with this opinion.

Source: Docket Nos. 95-7182, 95-7186, available at cisgw3.law.pace.edu/cases/951206u1.html.

Aside from illustrating an application of the CISG in damages, and despite the fact that both parties get what they deserve even though there is some questionable logic in the analysis, this case carries another important lesson for international businesspersons. Please see The Old Wolf above.

Naturally the question arises then: how should international businesspersons record their deal?

Recording the Deal: The ICC Model International Sale Contract

When the parties seek to reduce their agreement to writing, in a situation that will be governed by the CISG, perhaps the most suitable basis to begin drafting an agreement is the Model International Sale Contract, drafted by the International Chamber of Commerce in Paris. The ICC Model International Sale Contract is tailored for compatibility with both the CISG and the ICC trade terms, *INCOTERMS 2000*. At the outset, then, the parties are minimizing the potential conflicts that can arise between their own constructs, the CISG, and national law that may otherwise be applicable. The ICC model contract shown below is further tailored for the manufactured goods intended for resale and for a "one-off" sale, rather than a recurring sale or distributorship arrangement. The INCOTERMS are further divided into "recommended" for multimodal (combinations of road, rail, and sea transport) and container shipping and "other" for ocean shipment of bulk commodities.

In the sample ICC model contract on page 283, the specific conditions of Part A make reference to article numbers. These references are to the articles comprising the general conditions found in Part B of the model. The model is a starting point, with the intention that the parties will adapt it to their specific needs, but remains generally fair to both parties. Where one party has greater bargaining power over the other, the modifications that result will likely reflect this, as is generally the case in contract negotiation and drafting.

International Sale Contract (Manufactured Goods Intended for Resale)

A. SPECIFIC CONDITIONS

SELLER name and address	CONTACT PERSON name and address	BUYER name and address	CONTACT PERSON name and address
_____	_____	_____	_____
_____	_____	_____	_____

A-1 GOODS SOLD
DESCRIPTION OF THE GOODS

If there is insufficient space parties may use an annex

A-2 CONTRACT PRICE (ART. 4)

Currency: _____

amount in numbers: _____   amount in letters: _____

A-3 DELIVERY TERMS

Recommended terms (according to Incoterms 2000):

_____	**EXW**	Ex Works	named place: _____
_____	**FCA**	Free Carrier	named place: _____
_____	**CPT**	Carriage Paid To	named place of destination: _____
_____	**CIP**	Carriage and Insurance Paid To	named place of destination: _____
_____	**DAF**	Delivered At Frontier	named place: _____
_____	**DDU**	Delivered Duty Unpaid	named place of destination: _____
_____	**DDP**	Delivered Duty Paid	named place of destination: _____

Other terms (according to Incoterms 2000):

_____	**FAS**	Free Alongside Ship	named port of shipment: _____
_____	**FOB**	Free On Board	named port of shipment: _____
_____	**CFR**	Cost and Freight	named port of destination: _____
_____	**CIF**	Cost Insurance and Freight	named port of destination: _____
_____	**DES**	Delivered Ex Ship	named port of destination: _____
_____	**DEQ**	Delivered Ex Quay (duty paid)	named port of destination: _____

Other delivery terms

CARRIER (where applicable)

NAME AND ADDRESS	CONTACT PERSON
_____	_____
_____	_____

The present contract of sale will be governed by these Specific Conditions (to the extent that the relevant boxes have been completed) and by the ICC General Conditions of Sale (Manufactured Goods Intended for Resale) which constitute part B of this document.

SELLER signature	BUYER signature
_____	_____

place _____ date _____   place _____ date _____

A-4 TIME OF DELIVERY

Indicate here the date or period (e.g., week or month) at which or within which the Seller must perform his delivery obligations according to clause A.4 of the respective Incoterm.

_____

_____

A-5 INSPECTION OF THE GOODS BY BUYER (ART. 3)

_____ Before shipment   place of inspection: _____

_____ Other: _____

A-6 RETENTION OF TITLE (ART. 7)

_____ YES

_____ NO

A-7 PAYMENT CONDITIONS (ART. 5)

_____ **Payment on open account (art. 5.1)**
        Time for payment (if different from art. 5.1) _____ days from date of invoice. Other: _____
        __ Open account backed by demand guarantee or standby letter of credit (art. 5.5)

_____ **Payment in advance (art. 5.2)**
        Date (if different from art. 5.2): _____   _____ Total price _____% of the price

_____ **Documentary Collection (art. 5.5)**
        ___ D/P Documents against payment   ___ D/A Documents against acceptance

_____ **Irrevocable documentary credit (art. 5.3)**   ___Confirmed   ___ Unconfirmed
        Place of issue (if applicable): _____   Place of confirmation (if applicable): _____

        Credit available: *Partial shipments:*   *Transhipment:*
        __ By payment at sight   __ Allowed   __ Allowed
        __ By deferred payment at: ___ days   __ Not allowed   __ Not allowed
        __ By acceptance of drafts at: ___ days
        __ By negotiation

        Date on which the documentary credit must be notified to seller (if different from art. 5.3)
        _____ days before date of delivery   __ other: _____

_____ **Other:** _____
        (e.g. cheque, bank draft, electronic funds transfer to designated bank account of seller)

A-8 DOCUMENTS

Indicate here documents to be provided by Seller. Parties are advised to check the Incoterm they have selected under A-3 of these Specific Conditions. (As concerns transport documents, see also Introduction, § 8)

__ **Transport documents:** indicate type of transport document required _____
__ **Commercial Invoice**   __ **Certificate of origin**
__ **Packing list**   __ **Certificate of inspection**
__ **Insurance document**   __ **Other:** _____

A-9 CANCELLATION DATE

TO BE COMPLETED ONLY IF THE PARTIES WISH TO MODIFY ARTICLE 10.3
If the goods are not delivered for any reason whatsoever (including force majeure) by (date) _____ the Buyer will be
entitled to CANCEL THE CONTRACT IMMEDIATELY BY NOTIFICATION TO THE SELLER

A-10 LIABILITY FOR DELAY (art. 10.1, 10.4 AND 11.3)

TO BE COMPLETED ONLY IF THE PARTIES WISH TO MODIFY ART. 10.1, 10.4 OR 11.3
Liquidated damages for delay in delivery shall be:
__   _____ % (of price of delayed goods) per week, with a maximum of _____ % (of price of delayed goods)

or:

__   _____ (specify amount)

In case of termination for delay, Seller's liability for damages for delay is limited to _____ % of the price of the non-delivered goods

A-11 LIMITATION OF LIABILITY FOR LACK OF CONFORMITY **(ART. 11.5)**
TO BE COMPLETED ONLY IF THE PARTIES WISH TO MODIFY ART. 11.5.

Seller's liability for damages arising from lack of conformity of the goods shall be:
___   limited to proven loss (including consequential loss, loss of profit, etc.) not exceeding ___ % of the contract price;
or:
___   as follows (specify):

_____

A-12 LIMITATION OF LIABILITY WHERE NON-CONFORMING GOODS ARE RETAINED BY THE BUYER **(ART. 11.6)**
TO BE COMPLETED ONLY IF THE PARTIES WISH TO MODIFY ART. 11.6

The price abatement for retained non-conforming goods shall not exceed:

___   ___% of the price of such goods

or:

___   _____ (specify amount)

A-13 TIME-BAR (Art.11.8)
TO BE COMPLETED ONLY IF THE PARTIES WISH TO MODIFY ART. 11.8.

Any action for non-conformity of the goods (as defined in article 11.8) must be taken by the Buyer not later than _____ from the date of arrival of the goods at destination

A-14(a), A-14(b) APPLICABLE LAW (Art.1.2)
TO BE COMPLETED ONLY IF THE PARTIES WISH TO SUBMIT THE SALE CONTRACT TO A NATIONAL LAW INSTEAD OF **CISG**. The solution hereunder is not recommended (see Introduction, § 3)

(a) This sales contract is governed by the domestic law of _____ (country)

To be completed if the parties wish to choose a law other than that of the seller for questions not covered by CISG

(b) Any questions not covered by CISG will be governed by the law of _____ (country)

A-15 RESOLUTION OF DISPUTES (Art.14)
The two solutions hereunder (arbitration or litigation before ordinary courts) are alternatives: parties cannot choose both of them. If no choice is made, ICC arbitration will apply, according to art. 14.

__ **ARBITRATION**	__ **LITIGATION (ordinary courts)**
__ ICC (according to art. 14.1)	In case of dispute the courts of
Place of arbitration _____	_____ (place)
__ Other _____ (specify)	shall have jurisdiction

A-16 OTHER

International Sale Contract (Manufactured Goods Intended for Resale)

B.   **GENERAL CONDITIONS**

Art. 1 GENERAL

1.1   These General Conditions are intended to be applied together with the Specific Conditions (part A) of the International Sale Contract (Manufactured Goods Intended for Resale), but they may also be incorporated on their own into any sale contract. Where these General Conditions (Part B) are used independently of the said Specific Conditions (Part A), any reference in Part B to Part A will be interpreted as a reference to any relevant specific conditions agreed by the parties. In case of contradiction between these General Conditions and any specific conditions agreed upon between the parties, the specific conditions shall prevail.

1.2   Any questions relating to this Contract which are not expressly or implicitly settled by the provisions contained in the Contract itself (i.e., these General Conditions and any specific conditions agreed upon by the parties) shall be governed:

A. by the United Nations Convention on Contracts for the International Sale of Goods (Vienna Convention of 1980, hereafter referred to as CISG), and

B. to the extent that such questions are not covered by CISG, by reference to the law of the country where the Seller has his place of business.

1.3   Any reference made to trade terms (such as EXW, FCA, etc.) is deemed to be made to the relevant term of Incoterms published by the International Chamber of Commerce.

1.4   Any reference made to a publication of the International Chamber of Commerce is deemed to be made to the version current at the date of conclusion of the Contract.

1.5   No modification of the Contract is valid unless agreed or evidenced in writing. However, a party may be precluded by his conduct from asserting this provision to the extent that the other party has relied on that conduct.

ART. 2 CHARACTERISTICS OF THE GOODS

2.1   It is agreed that any information relating to the goods and their use, such as weights, dimensions, capacities, prices, colours and other data contained in catalogues, prospectuses, circulars, advertisements, illustrations, price-lists of the Seller, shall not take effect as terms of the Contract unless expressly referred to in the Contract.

2.2   Unless otherwise agreed, the Buyer does not acquire any property rights in software, drawings, etc. which may have been made available to him. The Seller also remains the exclusive owner of any intellectual or industrial property rights relating to the goods.

ART. 3   INSPECTION OF THE GOODS BEFORE SHIPMENT

If the parties have agreed that the Buyer is entitled to inspect the goods before shipment, the Seller must notify the Buyer within a reasonable time before the shipment that the goods are ready for inspection at the agreed place.

ART. 4   PRICE

4.1   If no price has been agreed, the Seller's current list price at the time of the conclusion of the Contract shall apply. In the absence of such a current list price, the price generally charged for such goods at the time of the conclusion of the Contract shall apply.

4.2   Unless otherwise agreed in writing, the price does not include VAT, and is not subject to price adjustment.

4.3   The price indicated under A-2 (contract price) includes any costs which are at the Seller's charge according to this Contract. However, should the Seller bear any costs which, according to this Contract, are for the Buyer's account (e.g. for transportation or insurance under EXW or FCA), such sums shall not be considered as having been included in the price under A-2 and shall be reimbursed by the Buyer.

ART. 5   PAYMENT CONDITIONS

5.1   Unless otherwise agreed in writing, or implied from a prior course of dealing between the parties, payment of the price and of any other sums due by the Buyer to the Seller shall be on open account and time of payment shall be 30 days from the date of invoice. The amounts due shall be transferred, unless otherwise agreed, by teletransmission to the Seller's bank in the Seller's country for the account of the Seller and the Buyer shall be deemed to have performed his payment obligations when the respective sums due have been received by the Seller's bank in immediately available funds.

5.2   If the parties have agreed on payment in advance, without further indication, it will be assumed that such advance payment, unless otherwise agreed, refers to the full price, and that the advance payment must be received by the Seller's bank in immediately available funds at least 30 days before the agreed date of delivery or the earliest date within the agreed delivery period. If advance payment has been agreed only for a part of the contract price, the payment conditions of the remaining amount will be determined according to the rules set forth in this article.

5.3   If the parties have agreed on payment by documentary credit, then, unless otherwise agreed, the Buyer must arrange for a documentary credit in favour of the Seller to be issued by a reputable bank, subject to the Uniform Customs and Practice for Documentary Credits published by the International Chamber of Commerce, and to be notified at least 30 days before the agreed date of delivery or at least 30 days before the earliest date within the agreed delivery period. Unless otherwise agreed, the documentary credit shall be payable at sight and allow partial shipments and transhipments.

5.4   If the parties have agreed on payment by documentary collection, then, unless otherwise agreed, documents will be tendered against payment (D/P) and the tender will in any case be subject to the Uniform Rules for Collections published by the International Chamber of Commerce.

5.5   To the extent that the parties have agreed that payment is to be backed by a bank guarantee, the Buyer is to provide, at least 30 days before the agreed date of delivery or at least 30 days before the earliest date within the agreed delivery period, a first demand bank guarantee subject to the Uniform Rules for Demand Guarantees published by the International Chamber of Commerce, or a standby letter of credit subject either to such Rules or to the Uniform Customs and Practice for Documentary Credits published by the International Chamber of Commerce, in either case issued by a reputable bank.

ART. 6 INTEREST IN CASE OF DELAYED PAYMENT

6.1   If a party does not pay a sum of money when it falls due, the other party is entitled to interest upon that sum from the time when payment is due to the time of payment.

6.2   Unless otherwise agreed, the rate of interest shall be 2% above the average bank short-term lending rate to prime borrowers prevailing for the currency of payment at the place of payment, or where no such rate exists at that place, then the same rate in the State of the currency of payment. In the absence of such a rate at either place the rate of interest shall be the appropriate rate fixed by the law of the State of the currency of payment.

ART. 7 RETENTION OF TITLE

If the parties have validly agreed on retention of title, the goods shall remain the property of the Seller until the complete payment of the price, or as otherwise agreed.

ART. 8 CONTRACTUAL TERM OF DELIVERY

Unless otherwise agreed, delivery shall be "Ex Works" (EXW).

ART. 9 DOCUMENTS

Unless otherwise agreed, the Seller must provide the documents (if any) indicated in the applicable Incoterm or, if no Incoterm is applicable, according to any previous course of dealing.

ART. 10 LATE-DELIVERY, NON-DELIVERY AND REMEDIES THEREFOR

10.1 When there is delay in delivery of any goods, the Buyer is entitled to claim liquidated damages equal to 0.5% or such other percentage as may be agreed of the price of those goods for each complete week of delay, provided the Buyer notifies the Seller of the delay. Where the Buyer so notifies the Seller within 15 days from the agreed date of delivery, damages will run from the agreed date of delivery or from the last day within the agreed period of delivery. Where the Buyer so notifies the Seller after 15 days of the agreed date of delivery, damages will run from the date of the notice. Liquidated damages for delay shall not exceed 5% of the price of the delayed goods or such other maximum amount as may be agreed.

10.2 If the parties have agreed upon a cancellation date in Box A-9, the Buyer may terminate the Contract by notification to the Seller as regards goods which have not been delivered by such cancellation date for any reason whatsoever (including a force majeure event).

10.3 When article 10.2 does not apply and the Seller has not delivered the goods by the date on which the Buyer has become entitled to the maximum amount of liquidated damages under article 10.1, the Buyer may give notice in writing to terminate the Contract as regards such goods, if they have not been delivered to the Buyer within 5 days of receipt of such notice by the Seller.

10.4 In case of termination of the Contract under article 10.2 or 10.3 then in addition to any amount paid or payable under article 10.1, the Buyer is entitled to claim damages for any additional loss not exceeding 10% of the price of the non-delivered goods.

10.5 The remedies under this article are exclusive of any other remedy for delay in delivery or non-delivery.

ART. 11 NON-CONFORMITY OF THE GOODS

11.1 The Buyer shall examine the goods as soon as possible after their arrival at destination and shall notify the Seller in writing of any lack of conformity of the goods within 15 days from the date when the Buyer discovers or ought to have discovered the lack of conformity. In any case the Buyer shall have no remedy for lack of conformity if he fails to notify the Seller thereof within 12 months from the date of arrival of the goods at the agreed destination.

11.2 Goods will be deemed to conform to the Contract despite minor discrepancies which are usual in the particular trade or through course of dealing between the parties but the Buyer will be entitled to any abatement of the price usual in the trade or through course of dealing for such discrepancies.

11.3 Where goods are non-conforming (and provided the Buyer, having given notice of the lack of conformity in compliance with article 11.1, does not elect in the notice to retain them), the Seller shall at his option:

(a)   replace the goods with conforming goods, without any additional expense to the Buyer, or

(b)   repair the goods, without any additional expense to the Buyer, or

(c)   reimburse to the Buyer the price paid for the non-conforming goods and thereby terminate the Contract as regards those goods.

The Buyer will be entitled to liquidated damages as quantified under article 10.1 for each complete week of delay between the date of notification of the non-conformity according to article 11.1 and the supply of substitute goods under article 11.3(a) or repair under article 11.3(b) above. Such damages may be accumulated with damages (if any) payable under article 10.1, but can in no case exceed in the aggregate 5% of the price of those goods.

11.4   If the Seller has failed to perform his duties under article 11.3 by the date on which the Buyer becomes entitled to the maximum amount of liquidated damages according to that article, the Buyer may give notice in writing to terminate the Contract as regards the non-conforming goods unless the supply of replacement goods or the repair is effected within 5 days of receipt of such notice by the Seller.

11.5   Where the Contract is terminated under article 11.3(c) or article 11.4, then in addition to any amount paid or payable under article 11.3 as reimbursement of the price and damages for any delay, the Buyer is entitled to damages for any additional loss not exceeding 10% of the price of the non-conforming goods.

11.6   Where the Buyer elects to retain non-conforming goods, he shall be entitled to a sum equal to the difference between the value of the goods at the agreed place of destination if they had conformed with the Contract and their value at the same place as delivered, such sum not to exceed 15% of the price of those goods.

11.7   Unless otherwise agreed in writing, the remedies under this article 11 are exclusive of any other remedy for non-conformity.

11.8   Unless otherwise agreed in writing, no action for lack of conformity can be taken by the Buyer, whether before judicial or arbitral tribunals, after 2 years from the date of arrival of the goods. It is expressly agreed that after the expiry of such term, the Buyer will not plead non-conformity of the goods, or make a counter-claim thereon, in defence to any action taken by the Seller against the Buyer for non-performance of this Contract.

ART. 12 COOPERATION BETWEEN THE PARTIES

12.1   The Buyer shall promptly inform the Seller of any claim made against the Buyer by his customers or third parties concerning the goods delivered or intellectual property rights related thereto.

12.2   The Seller will promptly inform the Buyer of any claim which may involve the product liability of the Buyer.

ART. 13 FORCE MAJEURE

13.1   A party is not liable for a failure to perform any of his obligations in so far as he proves:

(a)   that the failure was due to an impediment beyond his control, and

(b)   that he could not reasonably be expected to have taken into account the impediment and its effects upon his ability to perform at the time of the conclusion of the Contract, and

(c)   that he could not reasonably have avoided or overcome it or its effects.

13.2   A party seeking relief shall, as soon as practicable after the impediment and its effects upon his ability to perform become known to him, give notice to the other party of such impediment and its effects on his ability to perform. Notice shall also be given when the ground of relief ceases.

Failure to give either notice makes the party thus failing liable in damages for loss which otherwise could have been avoided.

13.3   Without prejudice to article 10.2, a ground of relief under this clause relieves the party failing to perform from liability in damages, from penalties and other contractual sanctions, except from the duty to pay interest on money owing as long as and to the extent that the ground subsists.

13.4   If the grounds of relief subsist for more than six months, either party shall be entitled to terminate the Contract with notice.

ART. 14 RESOLUTION OF DISPUTES

14.1   Unless otherwise agreed in writing, all disputes arising in connection with the present Contract shall be finally settled under the Rules of Arbitration of the International Chamber of Commerce by one or more arbitrators appointed in accordance with the said Rules.

14.2   An arbitration clause does not prevent any party from requesting interim or conservatory measures from the courts.

Negotiation of a direct sale contract may be conducted by principals meeting in person, but just as often, negotiations will be handled by either agents or overseas representatives in the home market of the buyer. These relationships between an international business firm and its agents or representatives are the subject of the next section.

Export Options 3 and 4: Overseas Representative versus Sales Agent

As opposed to direct dealings between a seller and its buyers, direct exporters also can choose market entry strategies based on intermediaries: agents or representatives. Use of these options allows the exporter to carry on with its domestic affairs without distraction and leave its affairs to others who are "in country."

Business and Legal Considerations of Agents and Representatives

International agency and representation are not particularly different in their legal mechanics from their domestic counterparts. The international agent is a contractual fiduciary relationship with the domestic exporter,[30] and the overseas representative is an employee of the domestic exporter. The business implications of these choices are, however, generally more significant than in the domestic business environment.

As with the option of direct sale itself, any choice between agency and representation may be influenced by the nature of the goods and long-standing industrial practice, neither of which the exporter can hope to change. Despite this, on a case-by-case basis, there can be strong reasons to prefer one type of relationship to the other.

General Factors: Agents versus Representatives

Factor	Agent	Employee Representative
Cost	Cheapest—meets own expenses from commissions earned.	Costly—must be supported, both personally (apartment or home) and professionally (office).
Authority	Usually has express authority to contract.	Usually must send proposals "back to head office."
Payment	No performance, no pay (on commission).	Paid regardless of performance (salary).
Will exporter be bound if authority is exceeded?	Often—if agent had "apparent authority."	Only rarely, as long as employment relationship was known to third party.
Third-party expectations in industry?	Where expected, use of agents is essential. Use of a representative is unproductive.	Agents can usually do everything representatives do, and more.
Ease	Easy to obtain, often a foreign resident who knows the territory well.	Often an expatriate sent abroad; can be difficult to find a "volunteer." Less knowledge of foreign territory.
Small market?	Cost-effective.	Large expense for small return.

In the general commercial law of agency in most jurisdictions of the world, a principal is bound in contract and liable in tort for actions of its agent within the scope of his or her employment. This allows for very useful, full-function, low-cost, rapidly deployed representation in international markets. However, the exporter employing an agent must recognize that these same features give the agent considerable power and autonomy to create liability in his or her principal. Regarding representatives, as employees they have much less scope of au-

[30]Where the "principal" (the one who engages the agent) is entitled to behavior in utmost good faith from the agent.

thority to create binding legal liability. Given that the agent and the representative operate "beyond the horizon," the exporter must be certain that it can control what the agent or representative is doing in the name of the exporter. Unfortunately, also in the general law of agency of most of the world, "apparent authority" of an agent is recognized; where the agent holds him- or herself out as having authority, the principal will be liable for it.

As mentioned above, custom of the trade may leave the exporter no choice; it is agency or nothing at all. In such situations, agency is probably a good choice on its own merits; otherwise, it would not have become the custom of the trade. Alternatively, the exporter may find that agents are required under local law, and that these agents be citizens or nationals of the country concerned. This gives the local authorities some measure of control over the business conducted in their territory by foreigners, and such requirements are frequently encountered in the Middle East.

Despite the advantages of agents and over and above generally higher liability, there are other concerns that must be addressed in choosing agency as an entry into foreign markets. Foreign agents also may be beneficiaries of local law that protects their relationship, making it very expensive to dismiss the agent once the relationship is created. These dimensions also apply to distributors and are treated in some depth in Chapter 10. Liability of the principal also may be expanded under local foreign law, with expanded remedies available to foreign consumers. Perhaps the expectations of the foreign purchaser and its degree of reliance and faith given to statements of the agent will differ greatly from those of purchasers located in the seller's domestic market. Thus, the threshold for an allegation of misrepresentation or fraud may be reached earlier under foreign legal systems, again with the principal liable.

Such situations speak to business concerns that cannot simply be papered over with a contractual term through which the agent indemnifies its principal. First, the agent is unlikely to possess sufficient substantial wealth to make such security meaningful. Secondly, an actionable indemnity from an agent is worthless to the principal where the real harm is the incalculable damage to its commercial reputation caused by an allegation of fraud, particularly in a new market.

It is quite appropriate to observe that an overseas employee may make the same mistakes that an agent might, and that there is no greater recourse (and perhaps less) against an employee than exists against an agent. That may be true, but the degree of control that can be placed on and exercised over an employee is greater at all times and places. Moreover, employees with some previous length of employment as insiders tend to have a greater sense and understanding of the overall strategy, objectives, and values of the exporting firm. The employee-representative also will not be distracted by competing opportunities (to represent competing goods or, in fact, be working for your competitors) that might otherwise lure away the attention of an agent. This translates into business decisions made by employee-representatives that are matched more closely to corporate objectives than decisions made by agents in similar situations.

Naturally, there is some balance that must be interjected here. An agent with 25 years' experience in selling an exporter's product line is probably going to make better decisions on behalf of his or her principal than a recent university graduate, newly employed, having just transferred to sales from the finance department.

The overseas employee-representative may have other drawbacks as well. One is that overseas representatives tend not to be local hires in the foreign market. Thus, they often lack sufficient local understanding, cultural sensitivity, language ability, or local business expertise to be as effective as they might otherwise be. As agents do tend to be local to the markets they serve, this usually is a point in their favor.

Overseas employee-representatives are usually not local hires, but expatriate managers sent abroad. They tend to be more expensive to maintain in foreign markets. Such employees must be transferred and moved abroad, which is a cost in itself (and an expensive

Criminals looking to exploit exporters are not the only ones who use intermediaries as "cut-outs." Exporters who are also criminals frequently do so as well. Exporters willing to engage in the illegal and unethical activity of bribery often make payments for the services of an intermediary in arranging foreign sales, and knowingly or unknowingly, some of these payments become bribes to foreign government officials for entering contracts with the exporter, or inbound import clearance. The U.S. Foreign Corrupt Practices Act and similar legislation in many other nations make this an illegal practice, with heavy sanctions.

Such doings are also grave unethical obstacles to the dignified development of nations. Often, the targets and proponents of bribery are officials in developing nations, nations that can least afford (if any can) to have the rule of law corroded. Each time a nation falls deeper into cronyism or dictatorship, international businesspersons from the developed world can consider their role in having brought about or avoiding such a state of affairs.

one), and the cost of enhanced employee benefits (travel for visits home, tuition for children at private or boarding schools, and the like) can escalate rapidly. Again, the locally engaged agent (or employee, for that matter) does not present these concerns.

Dangers of Intermediaries between the Seller and Buyer

A number of concerns exist when anyone is placed between the seller and the buyer, and these two parties find themselves without direct contact. This can certainly create the potential for carelessness, but also fraud and criminal activity.

An exporter must be particularly on guard where, rather than looking for an agent or representative, one comes looking for an exporter. Either one may be looking for an exporter to exploit or cheat. Hard-working agents looking for business, of course, will approach the exporter, and only a tiny fraction of solicited business has criminal motives; still, the exporter must be vigilant. The concern applies to all exporters, for shipments of all kinds easily run into tens and hundreds of thousands of dollars, and it is far easier and profitable to defraud an exporter than it is to rob a bank. Every scam ever invented by con artists is easier and safer for criminals to perform in the international environment. This is due to increased distance and time for communications and transit, difficulty in verifying facts about "buyers," and, perhaps most importantly, the sad lack of truly efficient global police cooperation.

Fraudsters are frequently employed as a "front" by criminal gangs and pirate organizations. True piracy remains alive and, unfortunately, well on the high seas. It still comes complete with boarding, theft, murder, and the scuttling of vessels. Agents act as cut-outs, masking the fact that no true purchaser exists for the exporter's goods, thereby lulling the exporter into a false sense of security, and often coming up with soothing reasons why a transaction should be handled in an unorthodox manner. In these situations, the agent often survives the "sting" and continues to operate openly as he or she is above suspicion, and, by all appearances, it is the phantom foreign buyer who is the criminal.

Intermediary parties (of any kind, including intermediate buyers) also give rise to business and legal concerns where the goods are subject to export licensing. An export license requirement represents government monitoring, control, and even prohibition of certain transactions of certain commodities with certain persons or countries. This is discussed further in the next section of this chapter. All governments exercise licensing requirements to some extent, if only with respect to dangerous or highly regulated items such as weapons, radioactive materials, and alcohol, and naturally there is criminal interest in these items.

Where there is an intermediary between the exporter and importer buyer in a licensed transaction, the exporter must remember that as seller, it remains liable to the government for actions and declarations taken in its name. Thus, if an agent obtains an export license through fraudulent statements, or if the end-user or purchaser of the goods is not as has been declared, it will be the exporter who is liable in the first instance. Where it is discovered that licensed goods are not headed to an approved destination, but rather to prohibited persons or unfriendly regimes, the government assumption will be that this illegal action is a conspiracy, not that the exporter has simply been duped.

A final risk of using intermediaries, particularly representatives, is the question of liability for tax. An export shipment to a foreign land certainly does not suggest that the exporter has any type of permanent establishment abroad and is consequently exempt from local taxation. The presence of an overseas representative employee in the foreign territory, however, does raise the question of whether the exporter's firm is "carrying on business" in the foreign territory. Where the representative's role is purely informational or to facilitate orders, and sales are booked offshore, this is generally not problematic. What is concerning is the dividing line between mere presence and being an active part of the foreign economy, which can trigger a variety of national measures. These range from simple requirements to register that presence with the authorities, to qualification for local industrial benefits, or the opposite, liability for local taxation.

This is an irrelevancy in the case of representation via an agent, for it is the agent who must comply with local legislation and regulation, whereas the exporter is completely offshore and dealing with the market only on an invoiced sale basis.

Making the Decision

In summary, the decision to use an intermediary in the first place is driven far more by the business considerations than questions of potential legal liability. Once that decision has been made, either for the firm by its industry practice or given the smaller priority the market presents, the choice becomes one of agent versus representative. If control and potential liability are serious issues, then agency should be avoided, but otherwise it remains the simpler, lower-cost approach.

Export Licensing and Documentation

While every nation wishes to encourage exports, and therefore wishes to create as few barriers to exporting as possible, there are exceptions to this general rule, the foremost being a requirement of licensing and export documentation.

Different nations take different approaches. Some require licensing as a means of controlling the departure of goods or commodities that otherwise may be in short supply in the domestic economy, while other nations insist on licensing in order to maintain strict control over their economies. The United States has the capability of exercising this type of strict control through its system of general and validated licenses. Most exports are subject to general licensing, which does not require any documentation but is rather recognition at law that the exporter is not acting as a matter of right, but as a matter of privilege only. The government can translate this general license to a requirement of "validated" license at any time, which it has done with a range of commodities.

A validated license for export is not obtained from the Customs Service. Rather, the Customs Service is charged with ensuring that the correct documentation is presented with export shipments, and licenses are issued to exporters by the relevant government agency responsible for the commodity being exported. In the main, export licenses are issued through the U.S. Department of Commerce, Bureau of Industry and Security; the Department of State, Office of Defense Trade Controls; the Bureau of Alcohol, Tobacco and Firearms; the Drug Enforcement Administration; the Nuclear Regulatory Commission; and the Office of Foreign Assets Control. To name the principal product types and categories, validated licenses are required for export of computer encryption software,

Shipper's Export Declaration

U.S. DEPARTMENT OF COMMERCE — U.S. CENSUS BUREAU – Economics and Statistics Administration — BUREAU OF EXPORT ADMINISTRATION

FORM **7525-V**   **SHIPPER'S EXPORT DECLARATION**

1a. U.S. PRINCIPAL PARTY IN INTEREST (USPPI) *(Complete name and address)*			
	ZIP CODE	2. DATE OF EXPORTATION	3. TRANSPORTATION REFERENCE NO.
b. USPPI EIN (IRS) OR ID NO.	c. PARTIES TO TRANSACTION Related Non-related		
4a. ULTIMATE CONSIGNEE *(Complete name and address)*			
b. INTERMEDIATE CONSIGNEE *(Complete name and address)*			
5. FORWARDING AGENT *(Complete name and address)*			
		6. POINT (STATE) OF ORIGIN or FTZ NO.	7. COUNTRY OF ULTIMATE DESTINATION
8. LOADING PIER *(Vessel only)*	9. METHOD OF TRANSPORTATION *(Specify)*	14. CARRIER IDENTIFICATION CODE	15. SHIPMENT REFERENCE NO.
10. EXPORTING CARRIER	11. PORT OF EXPORT	16. ENTRY NUMBER	17. HAZARDOUS MATERIALS Yes No
12. PORT OF UNLOADING *(Vessel and air only)*	13. CONTAINERIZED *(Vessel only)* Yes No	18. IN BOND CODE	19. ROUTED EXPORT TRANSACTION Yes No

20. SCHEDULE B DESCRIPTION OF COMMODITIES *(Use columns 22–24)*

D/F or M (21)	SCHEDULE B NUMBER (22)	QUANTITY – SCHEDULE B UNIT(S) (23)	SHIPPING WEIGHT *(Kilograms)* (24)	VIN/PRODUCT NUMBER/ VEHICLE TITLE NUMBER (25)	VALUE (U.S. dollars, omit cents) *(Selling price or cost if not sold)* (26)

27. LICENSE NO./LICENSE EXCEPTION SYMBOL/AUTHORIZATION	28. ECCN *(When required)*	
29. Duly authorized officer or employee	The USPPI authorizes the forwarder named above to act as forwarding agent for export control and customs purposes.	
30. I certify that all statements made and all information contained herein are true and correct and that I have read and understand the instructions for preparation of this document, set forth in the **"Correct Way to Fill Out the Shipper's Export Declaration."** I understand that civil and criminal penalties, including forfeiture and sale, may be imposed for making false or fraudulent statements herein, failing to provide the requested information or for violation of U.S. laws on exportation (13 U.S.C. Sec. 305; 22 U.S.C. Sec. 401; 18 U.S.C. Sec. 1001; 50 U.S.C. App. 2410).		
Signature	Confidential – For use solely for official purposes authorized by the Secretary of Commerce (13 U.S.C. 301 (g)).	
Title	*Export shipments are subject to inspection by U.S. Customs Service and/or Office of Export Enforcement.*	
Date	31. AUTHENTICATION (When required)	
Telephone No. *(Include Area Code)*	E-mail address	

weapons and munitions, listed chemicals, *any* trade with listed persons, nuclear material, natural gas and electricity, defense-related technology, endangered wildlife, drugs, and toxic waste.

Most of these requirements represent matters of U.S. policy, but others represent commitments under international agreements. For example, the Wassenaar Arrangement on Export Controls for Conventional Arms and Dual-Use Goods and Technologies was established in July 1996; the United States is one of the 33 participating states. Its intention is to control on a multilateral basis the traffic in arms and weapons, or technologies that may be used as such. Other examples arise from international agreements on endangered species or international covenants prohibiting shipment of toxic waste to lesser-developed nations.

While validated licenses are not required for the vast majority of U.S. exports, many *do* require export documentation in the form of a Shipper's Export Declaration (SED), or "Ex Dec," as it is known to those in the trade. An export shipment requiring a validated license also requires a SED. However, exports to Canada do not require a SED, nor do any export shipments under $2,500 in value.

A sample SED appears on page 296. Box 20 refers to a "Schedule B" description of the goods, which is the U.S. Census Bureau index equivalent to the Harmonized Tariff System (HTS) import codes administered by the U.S. International Trade Commission. In fact, the Schedule B export codes are the same as the HTS codes down to the six-digit level, but may vary through the 10-digit level of specificity.

Chapter Summary

Direct sale exporting places the exporter in direct contact with the final consumer or a buyer for resale, as opposed to creating an ongoing distributorship arrangement. Most often this buyer is abroad, but it may take the form of an international trading house in the exporter's own country. Thus, the goods are destined for export, but the sale is not a true export.

Domestic and international sale transactions are similar, but international business relationships generate different and increased risks to the seller, with the goods in the hands of carriers longer and with different currency, credit, and collection risks. Most often, one-off transactions are conducted through an exchange of letters, primarily a pro forma invoice as an offer followed by the buyer's acceptance via a purchase order.

These contracts will be governed by the UN Convention on Contracts for the International Sale of Goods (CISG), where the sale parties have their place of business located in different contracting states. While the CISG does not constrain the substantive aspects of sale contracts, it is effective in providing harmonized procedural rules for the formation and operation of contracts by generating rights and responsibilities for both the seller and buyer where they have failed to make their own provisions. The International Chamber of Commerce has created a model contract that is in concord with the CISG and is well suited to the international nature of export–import sales.

Agents or overseas employee representatives may be utilized to conduct negotiations or otherwise facilitate direct sale exports. While each type of assistance may be particularly appropriate in certain situations, the employee-representative presents less potential liability for the exporter, although is a more costly option.

Export licensing is a requirement that is common in most trading nations, even among those most interested in free trade. In the United States, this comprises general licensing and a more restrictive regime of validated licenses issued by competent branches of government. Export documentation is primarily statistical in nature, with export declarations required for most shipments, other than those to Canada.

Chapter Questions

1. What advantages can an export management company offer, and how is it different from an export trading company?
2. What role does the pro forma invoice play in a sale transaction, and what aspects of the transaction should it record?
3. Where a contract can be easily amended on consent, why is it so important to get the pro forma invoice correct in the first instance, where a letter of credit is contemplated for payment?
4. How can commercial parties avoid application of the CISG, and why might they want to do so?

5. A commercial exporter in the United States attempts to contract with a Mexican buyer for the sale of a container load of house wares. The exporter's pro forma invoice is dated and sent August 20th. The Mexican acceptance is mailed on August 30th and received by the exporter on September 9th. The exporter, however, mailed a revocation of its offer on September 3rd, which was received by the Mexican party on September 10th. Is this transaction subject to the CISG? Is there a contract? Why or why not, and when was it either formed or terminated?

6. Describe the effect of an acceptance that is not a mirror image of the offer, where the contract would be governed by the CISG.

7. Describe the remedies available to a buyer who has received delivery of nonconforming goods in a contract subject to application of the CISG.

8. Illustrate, with examples, your understanding of the different standard of remoteness of damages that are recoverable in contracts where the traditional common law applies, compared to instances where the Uniform Commercial Code or the CISG applies.

9. Contrast the relative merits of using agents versus overseas employee representation for small commercial exporters. Is there likely to be a preference? Do you reach different conclusions where the exporter is a large enterprise?

10. What tax implications can result from a choice between an agent and an employee-representative in international marketing abroad?

Appendix 1

Table of Concordance

UN Convention on the International Sale of Goods (Multilateral)*	Uniform Commerical Code (U.S. states represented here as enacted by New York State)	Civil Code (France)	Draft Principles of European Contract Law (EU)
PART I: GENERAL PROVISIONS			
Chapter 1. Sphere of Application			
Article 1 Applicability (1) This Convention applies to contracts of sale of goods between parties whose places of business are in different States: (a) when the States are Contracting States; or (b) when the rules of private international law lead to the application of the law of a Contracting State. (2) The fact that the parties have their places of business in different States is to be disregarded whenever this fact does not appear either from the contract or from any dealings between, or from information disclosed by, the	**§ 2-102. Scope; Certain Security and Other Transactions Excluded From This Article.** Unless the context otherwise requires, this Article applies to transactions in goods; it does not apply to any transaction which although in the form of an unconditional contract to sell or present sale is intended to operate only as a security transaction nor does this Article impair or repeal any statute regulating sales to consumers, farmers or other specified classes of buyers.	**Art. 1101** A contract is an agreement by which one or several persons bind themselves, towards one or several others, to transfer, to do or not to do something. **Art. 1582** A sale is an agreement by which one person binds himself to deliver a thing, and another to pay for it. It may be made by an authentic instrument or by an instrument under private signature. **Art. 1589** A promise of sale is the same as a sale, where there is reciprocal consent of both parties as to the thing and the price.	

UN Convention on the International Sale of Goods (Multilateral)*	Uniform Commerical Code (U.S. states represented here as enacted by New York State)	Civil Code (France)	Draft Principles of European Contract Law (EU)
parties at any time before or at the conclusion of the contract. (3) Neither the nationality of the parties nor the civil or commercial character of the parties or of the contract is to be taken into consideration in determining the application of this Convention.			
Article 2 General exclusions This Convention does not apply to sales: (a) of goods bought for personal, family or household use, unless the seller, at any time before or at the conclusion of the contract, neither knew nor ought to have known that the goods were bought for any such use; (b) by auction; (c) on execution or otherwise by authority of law; (d) of stocks, shares, investment securities, negotiable instruments or money; (e) of ships, vessels, hovercraft or aircraft; (f) of electricity.		**Art. 1598** Everything which may be the subject of legal transactions between private individuals may be sold, where special statutes do not prohibit their alienation.	
Article 3 Goods to be manufactured; services (1) Contracts for the supply of goods to be manufactured or produced are to be considered sales unless the party who orders the goods undertakes to supply a substantial part of the materials necessary for such manufacture or production. (2) This Convention does not apply to contracts in which the preponderant part of the obligations of the party who furnishes the goods consists in the supply of labour or other services.	**§ 2-105. Definitions:** (1) "Goods" means all things (including specially manufactured goods) which are movable at the time of identification to the contract for sale other than the money in which the price is to be paid, investment securities (Article 8) and things in action. "Goods" also includes the unborn young of animals and growing crops and other identified things attached to realty as described in the section on goods to be severed from realty (Section 2-107). (2) Goods must be both existing and identified before any interest in them can pass. Goods which are not both existing and identified are "future" goods. A purported present sale of future goods or of any interest therein operates as a contract to sell. (3) There may be a sale of a part interest in existing identified goods.	**Art. 1129** An obligation must have for its object a thing determined at least as to its kind. The quantity of the thing may be uncertain, provided it can be determined. **Art. 1130** Future things may be the object of an obligation. One may not however renounce a succession which is not open, or make any stipulation with respect to such succession, even with the consent of him whose succession is concerned.	
Article 4 Formation of contract; exclusions This Convention governs only the formation of the contract of sale and the rights and obligations of the seller and the buyer arising from such a contract. In particular, except as otherwise expressly provided in this Convention, it is not concerned with:			

UN Convention on the International Sale of Goods (Multilateral)*	Uniform Commerical Code (U.S. states represented here as enacted by New York State)	Civil Code (France)	Draft Principles of European Contract Law (EU)

(a) the validity of the contract or of any of its provisions or of any usage;
(b) the effect which the contract may have on the property in the goods sold.

Article 5 Exclusion as to liability for injury
This Convention does not apply to the liability of the seller for death or personal injury caused by the goods to any person.

Art. 1386-1
A producer is liable for damages caused by a defect in his product, whether he was bound by a contract with the injured person or not.

Article 6 Exclusion, derogation by parties
The parties may exclude the application of this Convention or, subject to article 12, derogate from or vary the effect of any of its provisions.

Articles 1:102 [Freedom of Contract] and 1:103 [Mandatory Law]

Chapter II. General Provisions

Article 7 Interpretation of Convention
(1) In the interpretation of this Convention, regard is to be had to its international character and to the need to promote uniformity in its application and the observance of good faith in international trade.
(2) Questions concerning matters governed by this Convention which are not expressly settled in it are to be settled in conformity with the general principles on which it is based or, in the absence of such principles, in conformity with the law applicable by virtue of the rules of private international law.

Articles 1:106 [Interpreting and Supplementation], 1:107 [Application of the Principles by Way of Analogy], 1:201 [Good Faith and Fair Dealing], 1:202 [Duty to Co-operate]

Article 8 Interpretation of statements or conduct
(1) For the purposes of this Convention statements made by and other conduct of a party are to be interpreted according to his intent where the other party knew or could not have been unaware what that intent was.
(2) If the preceding paragraph is not applicable, statements made by and other conduct of a party are to be interpreted according to the understanding that a reasonable person of the same kind as the other party

§ § 2-103–2-106 Other Specific Definitions.

Art. 1156
One must in agreements seek what the common intention of the contracting parties was, rather than pay attention to the literal meaning of the terms.
Art. 1158
Terms which admit of two meanings shall be taken in the meaning which best suits the subject matter of the contract.

Articles 2:102 [Intention], 5:101 [General Rules of Interpretation], 5:102 [Relevant Circumstances], 5:103 [Contra Proferentem Rule], 5:104 [Preference to Negotiated Terms], 5:105 [Reference to Contract as a Whole], 5:106 [Terms to be Given Effect], 5:107 [Linguistic Discrepancies]

UN Convention on the International Sale of Goods (Multilateral)*	Uniform Commerical Code (U.S. states represented here as enacted by New York State)	Civil Code (France)	Draft Principles of European Contract Law (EU)
would have had in the same circumstances. (3) In determining the intent of a party or the understanding a reasonable person would have had, due consideration is to be given to all relevant circumstances of the case including the negotiations, any practices which the parties have established between themselves, usages and any subsequent conduct of the parties.			
Article 9 Parties bound by usage (1) The parties are bound by any usage to which they have agreed and by any practices which they have established between themselves. (2) The parties are considered, unless otherwise agreed, to have impliedly made applicable to their contract or its formation a usage of which the parties knew or ought to have known and which in international trade is widely known to, and regularly observed by, parties to contracts of the type involved in the particular trade concerned.		**Art. 1160** Terms which are customary shall be supplemented in the contract, even though they are not expressed there. **Art. 1162** In case of doubt, an agreement shall be interpreted against the one who has stipulated, and in favour of the one who has contracted the obligation.	Article 1:105 [Usages and Practices]
Article 9 Place of business; meaning of For the purposes of this Convention: (a) if a party has more than one place of business, the place of business is that which has the closest relationship to the contract and its performance, having regard to the circumstances known to or contemplated by the parties at any time before or at the conclusion of the contract; (b) if a party does not have a place of business, reference is to be made to his habitual residence.			Article 7:101(2) and (3) [Place of Business]
Article 11 No requirement of writing A contract of sale need not be concluded in or evidenced by writing and is not subject to any other requirement as to	**§ 2-201. Formal Requirements; Statute of Frauds.** (1) Except as otherwise provided in this section a contract for the sale of goods	**Art. 1341** An instrument before *notaires* or under private signature must be executed in all matters exceeding a sum or value fixed by decree,* even for voluntary	Article 2:101(2) [No Formal Requirement]

UN Convention on the International Sale of Goods (Multilateral)*	Uniform Commerical Code (U.S. states represented here as enacted by New York State)	Civil Code (France)	Draft Principles of European Contract Law (EU)
form. It may be proved by any means, including witnesses. **Article 12 Declarations by Contracting States preserving requirement as to form** Any provision of article 11, article 29 or Part II of this Convention that allows a contract of sale or its modification or termination by agreement or any offer, acceptance or other indication of intention to be made in any form other than in writing does not apply where any party has his place of business in a Contracting State which has made a declaration under article 96 of this Convention. The parties may not derogate from or vary the effect of this article. **Article 13 Writing includes telegram and telex** For the purposes of this Convention "writing" includes telegram and telex.	for the price of $500 or more is not enforceable by way of action or defense unless there is some writing sufficient to indicate that a contract for sale has been made between the parties and signed by the party against whom enforcement is sought or by his authorized agent or broker. A writing is not insufficient because it omits or incorrectly states a term agreed upon but the contract is not enforceable under this paragraph beyond the quantity of goods shown in such writing. (2) Between merchants if within a reasonable time a writing in confirmation of the contract and sufficient against the sender is received and the party receiving it has reason to know its contents, it satisfies the requirements of subsection (1) against such party unless written notice of objection to its contents is given within 10 days after it is received. (3) A contract which does not satisfy the requirements of subsection (1) but which is valid in other respects is enforceable (a) if the goods are to be specially manufactured for the buyer and are not suitable for sale to others in the ordinary course of the seller's business and the seller, before notice of repudiation is received and under circumstances which reasonably indicate that the goods are for the buyer, has made either a substantial beginning of their manufacture or commitments for their procurement; or (b) if the party against whom enforcement is sought admits in his pleading, testimony or otherwise in court that a contract for sale was made, but the contract is not enforceable under this provision beyond the quantity of goods admitted; or (c) with respect to goods for which payment has been made and accepted or which have been received and accepted (Sec. 2-606).	deposits, and no proof by witness is allowed against or beyond the contents of instruments, or as to what is alleged to have been said before, at the time of, or after the instruments, although it is a question of a lesser sum or value. All of which without prejudice to what is prescribed in the statutes relating to commerce. *D. n° 80-533 of 15 July 1980 : 5 000 F (800 €)* **Art. 1316-3** An electronic-based document has the same probative value as a paper-based document.	Article 1:301(6) [Definition: Written Statements]

UN Convention on the International Sale of Goods (Multilateral)*	Uniform Commerical Code (U.S. states represented here as enacted by New York State)	Civil Code (France)	Draft Principles of European Contract Law (EU)
	§ 2-202. Final Written Expression: Parol or Extrinsic Evidence. Terms with respect to which the confirmatory memoranda of the parties agree or which are otherwise set forth in a writing intended by the parties as a final expression of their agreement with respect to such terms as are included therein may not be contradicted by evidence of any prior agreement or of a contemporaneous oral agreement but may be explained or supplemented (a) by course of dealing or usage of trade (Section 1-205) or by course of performance (Section 2-208); and (b) by evidence of consistent additional terms unless the court finds the writing to have been intended also as a complete and exclusive statement of the terms of the agreement.		
Article 14 Nature of offer (1) A proposal for concluding a contract addressed to one or more specific persons constitutes an offer if it is sufficiently definite and indicates the intention of the offeror to be bound in case of acceptance. A proposal is sufficiently definite if it indicates the goods and expressly or implicitly fixes or makes provision for determining the quantity and the price. (2) A proposal other than one addressed to one or more specific persons is to be considered merely as an invitation to make offers, unless the contrary is clearly indicated by the person making the proposal. **Article 15 When offer effective** (1) An offer becomes effective when it reaches the offeree.	**§ 2-204. Formation in General.** (1) A contract for sale of goods may be made in any manner sufficient to show agreement, including conduct by both parties which recognizes the existence of such a contract. (2) An agreement sufficient to constitute a contract for sale may be found even though the moment of its making is undetermined. (3) Even though one or more terms are left open a contract for sale does not fail for indefiniteness if the parties have intended to make a contract and there is a reasonably certain basis for giving an appropriate remedy. **§ 2-205. Firm Offers.** An offer by a merchant to buy or sell goods in a signed writing which by its terms gives assurance that it will be held open is not revocable, for lack		Articles 2:201 [Offer], 2:101 [Conditions for the Conclusion of a Contract], 2:102 [Intention], 2:103 [Sufficient Agreement], 2:104 [Terms Not Individually Negotiated], 2:211 [Contracts Not Concluded through Offer and Acceptance]

UN Convention on the International Sale of Goods (Multilateral)*

(2) An offer, even if it is irrevocable, may be withdrawn if the withdrawal reaches the offeree before or at the same time as the offer.

Article 16 Revocation of offer

(1) Until a contract is concluded an offer may be revoked if the revocation reaches the offeree before he has dispatched an acceptance.

(2) However, an offer cannot be revoked:

(a) if it indicates, whether by stating a fixed time for acceptance or otherwise, that it is irrevocable; or

(b) if it was reasonable for the offeree to rely on the offer as being irrevocable and the offeree has acted in reliance on the offer.

Article 17 When rejection effective

An offer, even if it is irrevocable, is terminated when a rejection reaches the offeror.

Article 18 Nature of acceptance

(1) A statement made by or other conduct of the offeree indicating assent to an offer is an acceptance. Silence or inactivity does not in itself amount to acceptance.

(2) An acceptance of an offer becomes effective at the moment the indication of assent reaches the offeror. An acceptance is not effective if the indication of assent does

Uniform Commerical Code (U.S. states represented here as enacted by New York State)

of consideration, during the time stated or if no time is stated for a reasonable time, but in no event may such period of irrevocability exceed three months; but any such term of assurance on a form supplied by the offeree must be separately signed by the offeror.

§ 2-206. Offer and acceptance in formation of contract.

(1) Unless otherwise unambiguously indicated by the language or circumstances

(a) an offer to make a contract shall be construed as inviting acceptance in any manner and by any medium reasonable in the circumstances;

(b) an order or other offer to buy goods for prompt or current shipment shall be construed as inviting acceptance either by a prompt promise to ship or by the prompt or current shipment of conforming or non-conforming goods, but such a shipment of non-conforming goods does not constitute an acceptance if the seller seasonably notifies the buyer that the shipment is offered only as an accommodation to the buyer.

(2) Where the beginning of a requested performance is a reasonable mode of acceptance an offeror who is not notified of acceptance within a reasonable time may treat the offer as having lapsed before acceptance.

§ 2-207. Additional Terms in Acceptance or Confirmation.

(1) A definite and seasonable expression of acceptance or a written confirmation which is sent within a reasonable time operates as an acceptance even though it states terms additional to or different from those offered or agreed upon, unless acceptance is expressly made conditional on assent to the additional or different terms.

Civil Code (France)

Art. 1590

Where a promise to sell was made with an earnest, each contracting party is at liberty to withdraw. The one who has given it, by losing it. And the one who has received it, by returning twice the amount.

Draft Principles of European Contract Law (EU)

Article 2:202 [Revocation of Offer]

Article 2:203 [Rejection of Offer]

Articles 2:204 [Acceptance of Offer], 2:206 [Time Limit for Acceptance], 2:211 [Contracts Not Concluded through Offer and Acceptance]

UN Convention on the International Sale of Goods (Multilateral)*	Uniform Commerical Code (U.S. states represented here as enacted by New York State)	Civil Code (France)	Draft Principles of European Contract Law (EU)

UN Convention on the International Sale of Goods (Multilateral)*

not reach the offeror within the time he has fixed or, if no time is fixed, within a reasonable time, due account being taken of the circumstances of the transaction, including the rapidity of the means of communication employed by the offeror. An oral offer must be accepted immediately unless the circumstances indicate otherwise.

(3) However, if, by virtue of the offer or as a result of practices which the parties have established between themselves or of usage, the offeree may indicate assent by performing an act, such as one relating to the dispatch of the goods or payment of the price, without notice to the offeror, the acceptance is effective at the moment the act is performed, provided that the act is performed within the period of time laid down in the preceding paragraph.

Article 19 Acceptance, material alteration, and counteroffer
(1) A reply to an offer which purports to be an acceptance but contains additions, limitations or other modifications is a rejection of the offer and constitutes a counteroffer.
(2) However, a reply to an offer which purports to be an acceptance but contains additional or different terms which do not materially alter the terms of the offer constitutes an acceptance, unless the offeror, without undue delay, objects orally to the discrepancy or dispatches a notice to that effect. If he does not so object, the terms of the contract are the terms of the offer with the modifications contained in the acceptance.
(3) Additional or different terms relating, among other things, to the price, payment, quality and quantity of the

Uniform Commerical Code (U.S. states represented here as enacted by New York State)

(2) The additional terms are to be construed as proposals for addition to the contract. Between merchants such terms become part of the contract unless:
(a) the offer expressly limits acceptance to the terms of the offer;
(b) they materially alter it; or
(c) notification of objection to them has already been given or is given within a reasonable time after notice of them is received.
(3) Conduct by both parties which recognizes the existence of a contract is sufficient to establish a contract for sale although the writings of the parties do not otherwise establish a contract. In such case the terms of the particular contract consist of those terms on which the writings of the parties agree, together with any supplementary terms incorporated under any other provisions of this Act.

Draft Principles of European Contract Law (EU)

Articles 2:208 [Modified Acceptance], 2:209 [Conflicting General Conditions], 2:210 [Professional's Written Confirmation], 2:211 [Contracts Not Concluded through Offer and Acceptance]

UN Convention on the International Sale of Goods (Multilateral)*	Uniform Commerical Code (U.S. states represented here as enacted by New York State)	Civil Code (France)	Draft Principles of European Contract Law (EU)
goods, place and time of delivery, extent of one party's liability to the other or the settlement of disputes are considered to alter the terms of the offer materially.			
Article 20 Time limits			Article 1:304 [Computation of Time]
(1) A period of time of acceptance fixed by the offeror in a telegram or a letter begins to run from the moment the telegram is handed in for dispatch or from the date shown on the letter or, if no such date is shown, from the date shown on the envelope. A period of time for acceptance fixed by the offeror by telephone, telex or other means of instantaneous communication, begins to run from the moment that the offer reaches the offeree.			
(2) Official holidays or non-business days occurring during the period for acceptance are included in calculating the period. However, if a notice of acceptance cannot be delivered at the address of the offeror on the last day of the period because that day falls on an official holiday or a non-business day at the place of business of the offeror, the period is extended until the first business day which follows.			
Article 21 Late acceptance			Article 2:207 [Late Acceptance]
(1) A late acceptance is nevertheless effective as an acceptance if without delay the offeror orally so informs the offeree or dispatches a notice to that effect.			
(2) If a letter or other writing containing a late acceptance shows that it has been sent in such circumstances that if its transmission had been normal it would have reached the offeror in due time, the late acceptance is effective as an acceptance unless, without delay, the offeror orally informs the offeree that he considers his offer as having lapsed or dispatches a notice to that effect.			

UN Convention on the International Sale of Goods (Multilateral)*	Uniform Commerical Code (U.S. states represented here as enacted by New York State)	Civil Code (France)	Draft Principles of European Contract Law (EU)
Article 22 Withdrawal of acceptance An acceptance may be withdrawn if the withdrawal reaches the offeror before or at the same time as the acceptance would have become effective.			Article 2:205 [Time of Conclusion of the Contract]
Article 23 Conclusion of contract A contract is concluded at the moment when an acceptance of an offer becomes effective in accordance with the provisions of this Convention.			
Article 24 "Reaches"; meaning of For the purposes of this Part of the Convention, an offer, declaration of acceptance or any other indication of intention "reaches" the addressee when it is made orally to him or delivered by any other means to him personally, to his place of business or mailing address or, if he does not have a place of business or mailing address, to his habitual residence.			

PART III: SALE OF GOODS

Chapter I. General Provisions

Article 25 Fundamental breach A breach of contract committed by one of the parties is fundamental if it results in such detriment to the other party as substantially to deprive him of what he is entitled to expect under the contract, unless the party in breach did not foresee and a reasonable person of the same kind in the same circumstances would not have foreseen such a result.			Article 8:103 [Fundamental Non-Performance]
Article 26 Avoidance A declaration of avoidance of the contract is effective only if made by notice to the other party.			Article 9:303 [Notice of Termination]
Article 27 Delay in communication Unless otherwise expressly provided in this Part of the Convention, if any notice,			Article 1:303 [Notice]

UN Convention on the International Sale of Goods (Multilateral)*	Uniform Commerical Code (U.S. states represented here as enacted by New York State)	Civil Code (France)	Draft Principles of European Contract Law (EU)
request or other communication is given or made by a party in accordance with this Part and by means appropriate in the circumstances, a delay or error in the transmission of the communication or its failure to arrive does not deprive that party of the right to rely on the communication.			
Article 28 Specific performance If, in accordance with the provisions of this Convention, one party is entitled to require performance of any obligation by the other party, a court is not bound to enter a judgement for specific performance unless the court would do so under its own law in respect of similar contracts of sale not governed by this Convention.	**§ 2-716. Buyer's Right to Specific Performance or Replevin.** (1) Specific performance may be decreed where the goods are unique or in other proper circumstances. (2) The decree for specific performance may include such terms and conditions as to payment of the price, damages, or other relief as the court may deem just. (3) The buyer has a right of replevin for goods identified to the contract if after reasonable effort he is unable to effect cover for such goods or the circumstances reasonably indicate that such effort will be unavailing or if the goods have been shipped under reservation and satisfaction of the security interest in them has been made or tendered. In the case of goods bought for personal, family, or household purposes, the buyer's right of replevin vests upon acquisition of a special property, even if the seller had not then repudiated or failed to deliver.		Articles 9:101 [Right to Performance of Monetary Obligations] and 9:102 [Right to Performance of Non-Monetary Obligations]
Article 29 Modification by agreement; where requirement of writing (1) A contract may be modified or terminated by the mere agreement of the parties. (2) A contract in writing which contains a provision requiring any modification or termination by agreement to be in writing may not be otherwise modified or terminated by agreement. However, a party may be	**§ 2-209. Modification, Rescission and Waiver.** (1) An agreement modifying a contract within this Article needs no consideration to be binding. (2) A signed agreement which excludes modification or rescission except by a signed writing cannot be otherwise modified or rescinded, but except as between merchants such a requirement on a form supplied by the merchant must		Articles 2:105 [Merger Clause], 2:106 [Written Modification Only], 2:107 [Promises Binding without Acceptance]

UN Convention on the International Sale of Goods (Multilateral)*	Uniform Commerical Code (U.S. states represented here as enacted by New York State)	Civil Code (France)	Draft Principles of European Contract Law (EU)
precluded by his conduct from asserting such a provision to the extent that the other party has relied on that conduct.	be separately signed by the other party. (3) The requirements of the statute of frauds section of this Article (Section 2-201) must be satisfied if the contract as modified is within its provisions. (4) Although an attempt at modification or rescission does not satisfy the requirements of subsection (2) or (3) it can operate as a waiver. (5) A party who has made a waiver affecting an executory portion of the contract may retract the waiver by reasonable notification received by the other party that strict performance will be required of any term waived, unless the retraction would be unjust in view of a material change of position in reliance on the waiver.		

Chapter II. Obligations of the Seller

| **Article 30 Seller's transfer obligation** The seller must deliver the goods, hand over any documents relating to them and transfer the property in the goods, as required by the contract and this Convention. | **§ 2-301. General Obligations of Parties.** The obligation of the seller is to transfer and deliver and that of the buyer is to accept and pay in accordance with the contract. **§ 2-306. Output, Requirements and Exclusive Dealings.** (1) A term which measures the quantity by the output of the seller or the requirements of the buyer means such actual output or requirements as may occur in good faith, except that no quantity unreasonably disproportionate to any stated estimate or in the absence of a stated estimate to any normal or otherwise comparable prior output or requirements may be tendered or demanded. (2) A lawful agreement by either the seller or the buyer for exclusive dealing in the kind of goods concerned imposes unless otherwise agreed an obligation by the seller to use best efforts to supply the goods and by the buyer to use best efforts to promote their sale. | **Art. 1602** The seller is obliged to explain clearly what he binds himself to. Any obscure or ambiguous agreement shall be interpreted against the seller. **Art. 1603** He has two main obligations, that to deliver and that to warrant the thing which he sells. **Art. 1604** Delivery is the transfer of the thing sold into the power and possession of the buyer. **Art. 1607** Delivery of intangible rights is made either by handing over the instruments of title, or by the use which the purchaser makes of them with the consent of the seller. | |

UN Convention on the International Sale of Goods (Multilateral)*	Uniform Commerical Code (U.S. states represented here as enacted by New York State)	Civil Code (France)	Draft Principles of European Contract Law (EU)
	§ 2-307. Delivery in Single Lot or Several Lots. Unless otherwise agreed all goods called for by a contract for sale must be tendered in a single delivery and payment is due only on such tender but where the circumstances give either party the right to make or demand delivery in lots the price if it can be apportioned may be demanded for each lot. **§ 2-503. Manner of Seller's Tender of Delivery.** (1) Tender of delivery requires that the seller put and hold conforming goods at the buyer's disposition and give the buyer any notification reasonably necessary to enable him to take delivery. The manner, time and place for tender are determined by the agreement and this Article, and in particular (a) tender must be at a reasonable hour, and if it is of goods they must be kept available for the period reasonably necessary to enable the buyer to take possession; but (b) unless otherwise agreed the buyer must furnish facilities reasonably suited to the receipt of the goods. (2) Where the case is within the next section respecting shipment tender requires that the seller comply with its provisions. (3) Where the seller is required to deliver at a particular destination tender requires that he comply with subsection (1) and also in any appropriate case tender documents as described in subsections (4) and (5) of this section. (4) Where goods are in the possession of a bailee and are to be delivered without being moved (a) tender requires that the seller either tender a negotiable document of title covering such goods or procure acknowledgment by the bailee of the buyer's right to		

UN Convention on the International Sale of Goods (Multilateral)*	Uniform Commerical Code (U.S. states represented here as enacted by New York State)	Civil Code (France)	Draft Principles of European Contract Law (EU)
	possession of the goods; but (b) tender to the buyer of a non-negotiable document of title or of a written direction to the bailee to deliver is sufficient tender unless the buyer seasonably objects, and receipt by the bailee of notification of the buyer's rights fixes those rights as against the bailee and all third persons; but risk of loss of the goods and of any failure by the bailee to honor the non-negotiable document of title or to obey the direction remains on the seller until the buyer has had a reasonable time to present the document or direction, and a refusal by the bailee to honor the document or to obey the direction defeats the tender. (5) Where the contract requires the seller to deliver documents (a) he must tender all such documents in correct form, except as provided in this Article with respect to bills of lading in a set (subsection (2) of Section 2-323); and (b) tender through customary banking channels is sufficient and dishonor of a draft accompanying the documents constitutes non-acceptance or rejection.		

Section I. Delivery of the goods and handing over of documents

Article 31 Place of delivery If the seller is not bound to deliver the goods at any other particular place, his obligation to deliver consists: (a) if the contract of sale involves carriage of the goods—in handing the goods over to the first carrier for transmission to the buyer; (b) if, in cases not within the preceding subparagraph, the contract relates to specific goods, or unidentified goods to be drawn from a specific stock or to be manufactured or	**§ 2-308. Absence of Specified Place for Delivery.** Unless otherwise agreed (a) the place for delivery of goods is the seller's place of business or if he has none his residence; but (b) in a contract for sale of identified goods which to the knowledge of the parties at the time of contracting are in some other place, that place is the place for their delivery; and (c) documents of title may be delivered through customary banking channels.	**Art. 1609** Delivery shall be made at the place where the thing sold was at the time of the sale, unless otherwise agreed.	Article 7:101 [Place of Performance]

UN Convention on the International Sale of Goods (Multilateral)*	Uniform Commercial Code (U.S. states represented here as enacted by New York State)	Civil Code (France)	Draft Principles of European Contract Law (EU)
produced, and at the time of the conclusion of the contract the parties knew that the goods were at, or were to be manufactured or produced at, a particular place—in placing the goods at the buyer's disposal at that place; (c) in other cases—in placing the goods at the buyer's disposal at the place where the seller had his place of business at the time of the conclusion of the contract.			
Article 32 Shipping arrangements; notice to buyer (1) If the seller, in accordance with the contract or this Convention, hands the goods over to a carrier and if the goods are not dearly identified to the contract by markings on the goods, by shipping documents or otherwise, the seller must give the buyer notice of the consignment specifying the goods. (2) If the seller is bound to arrange for carriage of the goods, he must make such contracts as are necessary for carriage to the place fixed by means of transportation appropriate in the circumstances and according to the usual terms for such transportation. (3) If the seller is not bound to effect insurance in respect of the carriage of the goods, he must, at the buyer's request, provide him with all available information necessary to enable him to effect such insurance.	**§ 2-504. Shipment by Seller.** Where the seller is required or authorized to send the goods to the buyer and the contract does not require him to deliver them at a particular destination, then unless otherwise agreed he must (a) put the goods in the possession of such a carrier and make such a contract for their transportation as may be reasonable having regard to the nature of the goods and other circumstances of the case; and (b) obtain and promptly deliver or tender in due form any document necessary to enable the buyer to obtain possession of the goods or otherwise required by the agreement or by usage of trade; and (c) promptly notify the buyer of the shipment. Failure to notify the buyer under paragraph (c) or to make a proper contract under paragraph (a) is a ground for rejection only if material delay or loss ensues.		
Article 33 Timing of delivery The seller must deliver the goods: (a) if a date is fixed by or determinable from the contract, on that date; (b) if a period of time is fixed by or determinable from the contract, at any time within that period unless circumstances indicate that the	**§ 2-309. Absence of Specific Time Provisions; Notice of Termination.** (1) The time for shipment or delivery or any other action under a contract if not provided in this Article or agreed upon shall be a reasonable time. (2) Where the contract provides for successive		Article 7:102 [Time of Performance]

UN Convention on the International Sale of Goods (Multilateral)*	Uniform Commerical Code (U.S. states represented here as enacted by New York State)	Civil Code (France)	Draft Principles of European Contract Law (EU)

buyer is to choose a date; or (c) in any other case, within a reasonable time after the conclusion of the contract.

performances but is indefinite in duration it is valid for a reasonable time but unless otherwise agreed may be terminated at any time by either party.
(3) Termination of a contract by one party except on the happening of an agreed event requires that reasonable notification be received by the other party and an agreement dispensing with notification is invalid if its operation would be unconscionable.

Article 34 Delivery of documentation
If the seller is bound to hand over documents relating to the goods, he must hand them over at the time and place and in the form required by the contract. If the seller has handed over documents before that time, he may, up to that time, cure any lack of conformity in the documents, if the exercise of this right does not cause the buyer unreasonable inconvenience or unreasonable expense. However, the buyer retains any right to claim damages as provided for in this Convention.

Section II. Conformity of the goods and third party claims

Article 35 Conformity of goods with contract
(1) The seller must deliver goods which are of the quantity, quality and description required by the contract and which are contained or packaged in the manner required by the contract.
(2) Except where the parties have agreed otherwise, the goods do not conform with the contract unless they:
(a) are fit for the purposes for which goods of the same description would ordinarily be used;

§ 2-313. Express Warranties by Affirmation, Promise, Description, Sample.
(1) Express warranties by the seller are created as follows:
(a) Any affirmation of fact or promise made by the seller to the buyer which relates to the goods and becomes part of the basis of the bargain creates an express warranty that the goods shall conform to the affirmation or promise.
(b) Any description of the goods which is made part of the basis of the bargain creates

Art. 1614
The thing must be delivered in the condition in which it is at the time of the sale. From that day, all the fruits belong to the purchaser.
Art. 1615
The obligation to deliver the thing includes its accessories and all that was designed for its perpetual use.
Art. 1616
The seller is obliged to deliver the capacity such as it is specified in the contract, subject to the modifications hereinafter expressed.

UN Convention on the International Sale of Goods (Multilateral)*

(b) are fit for any particular purpose expressly or impliedly made known to the seller at the time of the conclusion of the contract, except where the circumstances show that the buyer did not rely, or that it was unreasonable for him to rely, on the seller's skill and judgement;

(c) possess the qualities of goods which the seller has held out to the buyer as a sample or model;

(d) are contained or packaged in the manner usual for such goods or, where there is no such manner, in a manner adequate to preserve and protect the goods.

(3) The seller is not liable under subparagraphs (a) to (d) of the preceding paragraph for any lack of conformity of the goods if at the time of the conclusion of the contract the buyer knew or could not have been unaware of such lack of conformity.

Article 36 Lack of conformity

(1) The seller is liable in accordance with the contract and this Convention for any lack of conformity which exists at the time when the risk passes to the buyer, even though the lack of conformity becomes apparent only after that time.

(2) The seller is also liable for any lack of conformitywhich occurs after the time indicated in the preceding paragraph and which is due to a breach of any of his obligations, including a breach of any guarantee that for a period of time the goods will remain fit for their ordinary purpose or for some particular purpose or will retain specified qualities or characteristics.

Article 37 Right to remedy non-conformity

If the seller has delivered goods before the date for delivery, he may, up to that date, deliver

Uniform Commerical Code (U.S. states represented here as enacted by New York State)

an express warranty that the goods shall conform to the description.

(c) Any sample or model which is made part of the basis of the bargain creates an express warranty that the whole of the goods shall conform to the sample or model.

(2) It is not necessary to the creation of an express warranty that the seller use formal words such as "warrant" or "guarantee" or that he have a specific intention to make a warranty, but an affirmation merely of the value of the goods or a statement purporting to be merely the seller's opinion or commendation of the goods does not create a warranty.

§ 2-314. Implied Warranty: Merchantability; Usage of Trade.

§ 2-315. Implied Warranty: Fitness for Particular Purpose. Where the seller at the time of contracting has reason to know any particular purpose for which the goods are required and that the buyer is relying on the seller's skill or judgment to select or furnish suitable goods, there is unless excluded or modified under the next section an implied warranty that the goods shall be fit for such purpose.

§ 2-316. Exclusion or Modification of Warranties.

§ 2-317. Cumulation and Conflict of Warranties Express or Implied.

§ 2-318. Third Party Beneficiaries of Warranties Express or Implied.

§ 2-508. Cure by Seller of Improper Tender or Delivery; Replacement.

(1) Where any tender or delivery by the seller is rejected

Civil Code (France)

Art. 1641

A seller is bound to a warranty on account of the latent defects of the thing sold which render it unfit for the use for which it was intended, or which so impair that use that the buyer would not have acquired it, or would only have given a lesser price for it, had he known of them.

Art. 1642

A seller is not liable for defects which are patent and which the buyer could ascertain for himself.

Draft Principles of European Contract Law (EU)

UN Convention on the International Sale of Goods (Multilateral)*	Uniform Commerical Code (U.S. states represented here as enacted by New York State)	Civil Code (France)	Draft Principles of European Contract Law (EU)

any missing part or make up any deficiency in the quantity of the goods delivered, or deliver goods in replacement of any non-conforming goods delivered or remedy any lack of conformity in the goods delivered, provided that the exercise of this right does not cause the buyer unreasonable inconvenience or unreasonable expense. However, the buyer retains any right to claim damages as provided for in this Convention.

Article 38 Time for examination
(1) The buyer must examine the goods, or cause them to be examined, within as short a period as is practicable in the circumstances.
(2) If the contract involves carriage of the goods, examination may be deferred until after the goods have arrived at their destination.
(3) If the goods are redirected in transit or redispatched by the buyer without a reasonable opportunity for examination by him and at the time of the conclusion of the contract the seller knew or ought to have known of the possibility of such redirection or redispatch, examination may be deferred until after the goods have arrived at the new destination.

because non-conforming and the time for performance has not yet expired, the seller may seasonably notify the buyer of his intention to cure and may then within the contract time make a conforming delivery.
(2) Where the buyer rejects a non-conforming tender which the seller had reasonable grounds to believe would be acceptable with or without money allowance the seller may if he seasonably notifies the buyer have a further reasonable time to substitute a conforming tender.

§ 2-513. Buyer's Right to Inspection of Goods.
(1) Unless otherwise agreed and subject to subsection (3), where goods are tendered or delivered or identified to the contract for sale, the buyer has a right before payment or acceptance to inspect them at any reasonable place and time and in any reasonable manner. When the seller is required or authorized to send the goods to the buyer, the inspection may be after their arrival.
(2) Expenses of inspection must be borne by the buyer but may be recovered from the seller if the goods do not conform and are rejected.
(3) Unless otherwise agreed and subject to the provisions of this Article on C.I.F. contracts (subsection (3) of Section 2-321), the buyer is not entitled to inspect the goods before payment of the price when the contract provides
(a) for delivery "C.O.D." or on other like terms; or
(b) for payment against documents of title, except where such payment is due only after the goods are to become available for inspection.
(4) A place or method of inspection fixed by the parties is presumed to be exclusive but unless otherwise expressly

Art. 1588
A sale made upon trial shall always be deemed made under a condition precedent.

UN Convention on the International Sale of Goods (Multilateral)*	Uniform Commerical Code (U.S. states represented here as enacted by New York State)	Civil Code (France)	Draft Principles of European Contract Law (EU)
	agreed it does not postpone identification or shift the place for delivery or for passing the risk of loss. If compliance becomes impossible, inspection shall be as provided in this section unless the place or method fixed was clearly intended as an indispensable condition failure of which avoids the contract.		

Article 39 Notice of non-conformity

(1) The buyer loses the right to rely on a lack of conformity of the goods if he does not give notice to the seller specifying the nature of the lack of conformity within a reasonable time after he has discovered it or ought to have discovered it.

(2) In any event, the buyer loses the right to rely on a lack of conformity of the goods if he does not give the seller notice thereof at the latest within a period of two years from the date on which the goods were actually handed over to the buyer, unless this time-limit is inconsistent with a contractual period of guarantee.

Article 40 Seller aware of non-conformity

The seller is not entitled to rely on the provisions of articles 38 and 39 if the lack of conformity relates to facts of which he knew or could not have been unaware and which he did not disclose to the buyer.

Article 41 Third-party claims in goods

The seller must deliver goods which are free from any right or claim of a third party, unless the buyer agreed to take the goods subject to that right or claim. However, if such right or claim is based on industrial property or other intellectual property, the seller's obligation is governed by article 42.

§ 2-312. Warranty of Title and Against Infringement; Buyer's Obligation Against Infringement.

(1) Subject to subsection (2) there is in a contract for sale a warranty by the seller that

(a) the title conveyed shall be good, and its transfer rightful; and

(b) the goods shall be delivered free from any security interest or other lien or encumbrance of which the buyer at the time of contracting has no knowledge.

Art. 1625

The warranty which the seller owes to the purchaser has two objects: the first is the peaceful possession of the thing sold; the second, the latent defects of that thing, or redhibitory vices.

Art. 1626

Although no stipulation as to warranty has been made at the time of the sale, the seller is obliged as of right to warrant the purchaser against a dispossession of the thing sold which he may suffer in whole

UN Convention on the International Sale of Goods (Multilateral)*	Uniform Commerical Code (U.S. states represented here as enacted by New York State)	Civil Code (France)	Draft Principles of European Contract Law (EU)

UN Convention on the International Sale of Goods (Multilateral)*

Article 42 Third-party claims based on intellectual property

(1) The seller must deliver goods which are free from any right or claim of a third party based on industrial property or other intellectual property, of which at the time of the conclusion of the contract the seller knew or could not have been unaware, provided that the right or claim is based on industrial property or other intellectual property:

(a) under the law of the State where the goods will be resold or otherwise used, if it was contemplated by the parties at the time of the conclusion of the contract that the goods would be resold or otherwise used in that State; or

(b) in any other case, under the law of the State where the buyer has his place of business.

(2) The obligation of the seller under the preceding paragraph does not extend to cases where:

(a) at the time of the conclusion of the contract the buyer knew or could not have been unaware of the right or claim; or

(b) the right or claim results from the seller's compliance with technical drawings, designs, formulae or other such specifications furnished by the buyer.

Article 43 Notice of third-party claim

(1) The buyer loses the right to rely on the provisions of article 41 or article 42 if he does not give notice to the seller specifying the nature of the right or claim of the third party within a reasonable time after he has become aware or ought to have become aware of the right or claim.

Uniform Commerical Code (U.S. states represented here as enacted by New York State)

(2) A warranty under subsection (1) will be excluded or modified only by specific language or by circumstances which give the buyer reason to know that the person selling does not claim title in himself or that he is purporting to sell only such right or title as he or a third person may have.

(3) Unless otherwise agreed a seller who is a merchant regularly dealing in goods of the kind warrants that the goods shall be delivered free of the rightful claim of any third person by way of infringement or the like but a buyer who furnishes specifications to the seller must hold the seller harmless against any such claim which arises out of compliance with the specifications.

Civil Code (France)

or in part, or against encumbrances alleged on that thing, and not declared at the time of the sale.

UN Convention on the International Sale of Goods (Multilateral)*	Uniform Commerical Code (U.S. states represented here as enacted by New York State)	Civil Code (France)	Draft Principles of European Contract Law (EU)
(2) The seller is not entitled to rely on the provisions of the preceding paragraph if he knew of the right or claim of the third party and the nature of it. **Article 44 Failure to notify; excuse** Notwithstanding the provisions of paragraph (1) of article 39 and paragraph (1) of article 43, the buyer may reduce the price in accordance with article 50 or claim damages, except for loss of profit, if he has a reasonable excuse for his failure to give the required notice.			

Section III. Remedies for breach of contract by the seller

Article 45 Buyer's remedies (1) If the seller fails to perform any of his obligations under the contract or this Convention, the buyer may: (a) exercise the rights provided in articles 46 to 52; (b) claim damages as provided in articles 74 to 77. (2) The buyer is not deprived of any right he may have to claim damages by exercising his right to other remedies. (3) No period of grace may be granted to the seller by a court or arbitral tribunal when the buyer resorts to a remedy for breach of contract.	**§ 2-601. Buyer's Rights on Improper Delivery.** Subject to the provisions of this Article on breach in installment contracts (Section 2-612) and unless otherwise agreed under the sections on contractual limitations of remedy (Sections 2-718 and 2-719), if the goods or the tender of delivery fail in any respect to conform to the contract , the buyer may (a) reject the whole; or (b) accept the whole; or (c) accept any commercial unit or units and reject the rest. **§ 2-602. Manner and Effect of Rightful Rejection.** **§ 2-603. Merchant Buyer's Duties as to Rightfully Rejected Goods.** **§ 2-604. Buyer's Options as to Salvage of Rightfully Rejected Goods.** **§ 2-605. Waiver of Buyer's Objections by Failure to Particularize.** **§ 2-711. Buyer's Remedies in General; Buyer's Security Interest in Rejected Goods.** (1) Where the seller fails to make delivery or repudiates or the buyer rightfully rejects or justifiably revokes acceptance then with respect to any goods involved, and with respect to	**Art. 1610** Where the seller fails to make delivery within the time agreed upon between the parties, the purchaser may, at his choice, apply for avoidance of the sale, or for his being vested with possession, if the delay results only from an act of the seller. **Art. 1611** In all cases, the seller shall be ordered to pay damages, where the purchaser has suffered a loss because of the failure to deliver at the agreed time. **Art. 1612** The seller is not obliged to deliver the thing where the buyer does not pay the price of it unless the seller has granted him time for the payment. **Art. 1613** Nor is he obliged to deliver, even if he has allowed time for the payment, where, since the sale, the buyer [is under a judicial arrangement] or insolvent, so that the seller is in imminent danger of losing the price; unless the buyer gives him security to pay at the time-limit.	Articles 8:101 [Remedies Available], 8:102 [Cumulation of Remedies]

UN Convention on the International Sale of Goods (Multilateral)*	Uniform Commerical Code (U.S. states represented here as enacted by New York State)	Civil Code (France)	Draft Principles of European Contract Law (EU)
	the whole if the breach goes to the whole contract (Section 2-612), the buyer may cancel and whether or not he has done so may in addition to recovering so much of the price as has been paid (a) "cover" and have damages under the next section as to all the goods affected whether or not they have been identified to the contract; or (b) recover damages for non-delivery as provided in this Article (Section 2-713). (2) Where the seller fails to deliver or repudiates the buyer may also (a) if the goods have been identified recover them as provided in this Article (Section 2-502); or (b) in a proper case obtain specific performance or replevy the goods as provided in this Article (Section 2-716). (3) On rightful rejection or justifiable revocation of acceptance a buyer has a security interest in goods in his possession or control for any payments made on their price and any expenses reasonably incurred in their inspection, receipt , transportation, care and custody and may hold such goods and resell them in like manner as an aggrieved seller (Section 2-706). **§ 2-712. "Cover"; Buyer's Procurement of Substitute Goods.** **§ 2-713. Buyer's Damages for Non-delivery or Repudiation.** **§ 2-714. Buyer's Damages for Breach in Regard to Accepted Goods.** **§ 2-715. Buyer's Incidental and Consequential Damages.** **§ 2-716. Buyer's Right to Specific Performance or Replevin.**		
Article 46 May require performance (1) The buyer may require performance by the seller of his obligations unless the buyer			Articles 9:102 [Right to Performance: Non-Monetary Obligations], 9:101 [Right to Performance: Monetary Obligations], 9:103 [Right to

UN Convention on the International Sale of Goods (Multilateral)*	Uniform Commerical Code (U.S. states represented here as enacted by New York State)	Civil Code (France)	Draft Principles of European Contract Law (EU)
has resorted to a remedy which is inconsistent with this requirement.			Performance: Damages Not Precluded]
(2) If the goods do not conform with the contract, the buyer may require delivery of substitute goods only if the lack of conformity constitutes a fundamental breach of contract and a request for substitute goods is made either in conjunction with notice given under article 39 or within a reasonable time thereafter.			
(3) If the goods do not conform with the contract, the buyer may require the seller to remedy the lack of conformity by repair, unless this is unreasonable having regard to all the circumstances. A request for repair must be made either in conjunction with notice given under article 39 or within a reasonable time thereafter.			
Article 47 Additional period for performance			Article 8:106 [Notice Fixing Additional Period for Performance]
(1) The buyer may fix an additional period of time of reasonable length for performance by the seller of his obligations.			
(2) Unless the buyer has received notice from the seller that he will not perform within the period so fixed, the buyer may not, during that period, resort to any remedy for breach of contract. However, the buyer is not deprived thereby of any right he may have to claim damages for delay in performance.			
Article 48 Seller may remedy failure; requests and notice	**§ 2-508. Cure by Seller of Improper Tender or Delivery; Replacement.**		Article 8:104 [Cure by Non-Performing Party]
(1) Subject to article 49, the seller may, even after the date for delivery, remedy at his own expense any failure to perform his obligations, if he can do so without unreasonable delay and without causing the buyer unreasonable inconvenience or uncertainty of reimbursement by the seller of expenses advanced by the buyer. However, the buyer retains any	(1) Where any tender or delivery by the seller is rejected because non-conforming and the time for performance has not yet expired, the seller may seasonably notify the buyer of his intention to cure and may then within the contract time make a conforming delivery.		
	(2) Where the buyer rejects a		

UN Convention on the International Sale of Goods (Multilateral)*	Uniform Commerical Code (U.S. states represented here as enacted by New York State)	Civil Code (France)	Draft Principles of European Contract Law (EU)

UN Convention on the International Sale of Goods (Multilateral)*

right to claim damages as provided for in this Convention.

(2) If the seller requests the buyer to make known whether he will accept performance and the buyer does not comply with the request within a reasonable time, the seller may perform within the time indicated in his request. The buyer may not, during that period of time, resort to any remedy which is inconsistent with performance by the seller.

(3) A notice by the seller that he will perform within a specified period of time is assumed to include a request, under the preceding paragraph, that the buyer make known his decision.

(4) A request or notice by the seller under paragraph (2) or (3) of this article is not effective unless received by the buyer.

Article 49 Buyer's right to avoid contract

(1) The buyer may declare the contract avoided:

(a) if the failure by the seller to perform any of his obligations under the contract or this Convention amounts to a fundamental breach of contract; or

(b) in case of non-delivery, if the seller does not deliver the goods within the additional period of time fixed by the buyer in accordance with paragraph (1) of article 47 or declares that he will not deliver within the period so fixed.

(2) However, in cases where the seller has delivered the goods, the buyer loses the right to declare the contract avoided unless he does so:

(a) in respect of late delivery, within a reasonable time after he has become aware that delivery has been made;

(b) in respect of any breach other than late delivery, within a reasonable time:

(i) after he knew or ought to

Uniform Commerical Code (U.S. states represented here as enacted by New York State)

non-conforming tender which the seller had reasonable grounds to believe would be acceptable with or without money allowance the seller may if he seasonably notifies the buyer have a further reasonable time to substitute a conforming tender.

Draft Principles of European Contract Law (EU)

Articles 9:301 [Right to Terminate the Contract], 9:303 [Notice of Termination]

UN Convention on the International Sale of Goods (Multilateral)*	Uniform Commerical Code (U.S. states represented here as enacted by New York State)	Civil Code (France)	Draft Principles of European Contract Law (EU)
have known of the breach; (ii) after the expiration of any additional period of time fixed by the buyer in accordance with paragraph (1) of article 47, or after the seller has declared that he will not perform his obligations within such an additional period; or (iii) after the expiration of any additional period of time indicated by the seller in accordance with paragraph (2) of article 48, or after the buyer has declared that he will not accept performances.			
Article 50 Reduction in price where non-conformity If the goods do not conform with the contract and whether or not the price has already been paid, the buyer may reduce the price in the same proportion as the value that the goods actually delivered had at the time of the delivery bears to the value that conforming goods would have had at that time. However, if the seller remedies any failure to perform his obligations in accordance with article 37 or article 48 or if the buyer refuses to accept performance by the seller in accordance with those articles, the buyer may not reduce the price.	**§ 2-717. Deduction of Damages From the Price.** The buyer on notifying the seller of his intention to do so may deduct all or any part of the damages resulting from any breach of the contract from any part of the price still due under the same contract.	**Art. 1644** In the cases of Articles 1641 and 1643, the buyer has the choice either of returning the thing and having the price repaid to him or of keeping the thing and having a part of the price repaid to him, as appraised by experts. **Art. 1645** Where the seller knew of the defects of the thing, he is liable, in addition to restitution of the price which he received from him, for all damages towards the buyer. **Art. 1646** Where the seller did not know of the defects of the thing, he is only liable for restitution of the price and for reimbursing the buyer for the costs occasioned by the sale.	Article 9:401 [Right to Reduce Price]
Article 51 Part delivery; part non-conformity (1) If the seller delivers only a part of the goods or if only a part of the goods delivered is in conformity with the contract, articles 46 to 50 apply in respect of the part which is missing or which does not conform. (2) The buyer may declare the contract avoided in its entirety only if the failure to make delivery completely or in conformity with the contract amounts to a fundamental breach of the contract.			Articles 9:302 [Contract to be Performed in Parts], 9:306 [Property Reduced in Value]

UN Convention on the International Sale of Goods (Multilateral)*	Uniform Commerical Code (U.S. states represented here as enacted by New York State)	Civil Code (France)	Draft Principles of European Contract Law (EU)
Article 52 Early or excess delivery (1) If the seller delivers the goods before the date fixed, the buyer may take delivery or refuse to take delivery. (2) If the seller delivers a quantity of goods greater than that provided for in the contract, the buyer may take delivery or refuse to take delivery of the excess quantity. If the buyer takes delivery of all or part of the excess quantity, he must pay for it at the contract rate.		**Art. 1618** Where [*an amount supplied*] is greater than the one stated in the contract, the purchaser has the choice to provide the surplus of the price, or to repudiate the contract, if the excess is one-twentieth above the capacity declared. **Art. 1619** In all other cases, Whether the sale is made of a definite and limited thing, Whether it has as its object distinct and separate tenements, Whether it begins with the measure, or by the designation of the property sold followed by the measure, The expression of that measure does not give rise to any increase of price, in favour of the seller for the excess of measure, or in favour of the purchaser, to any diminution in price for lesser measure, unless the difference between the actual measure and the one expressed in the contract is of one-twentieth more or less, with regard to the value of all the things sold, unless otherwise stipulated.	Article 7:103 [Early Performance]

Chapter III. Obligations of the Buyer

Article 53 Buyer to pay and take delivery The buyer must pay the price for the goods and take delivery of them as required by the contract and this Convention.	**§ 2-301. General Obligations of Parties.** The obligation of the seller is to transfer and deliver and that of the buyer is to accept and pay in accordance with the contract.	**Art. 1650** The main obligation of the buyer is to pay the price on the day and at the place fixed by the sale.	

Section I. Payment of the price

Article 54 Where steps to effect payment required The buyer's obligation to pay the price includes taking such steps and complying with such formalities as may be required under the contract or any laws and regulations to enable payment to be made.	**§ 2-304. Price Payable in Money, Goods, Realty, or Otherwise.** (1) The price can be made payable in money or otherwise. If it is payable in whole or in part in goods each party is a seller of the goods which he is to transfer. (2) Even though all or part of the price is payable in an interest in realty the transfer of the goods and the seller's		

UN Convention on the International Sale of Goods (Multilateral)*	Uniform Commerical Code (U.S. states represented here as enacted by New York State)	Civil Code (France)	Draft Principles of European Contract Law (EU)
	obligations with reference to them are subject to this Article, but not the transfer of the interest in realty or the transferor's obligations in connection therewith.		
Article 55 Where price not explict Where a contract has been validly concluded but does not expressly or implicitly fix or make provision for determining the price, the parties are considered, in the absence of any indication to the contrary, to have impliedly made reference to the price generally charged at the time of the conclusion of the contract for such goods sold under comparable circumstances in the trade concerned.	**§ 2-305. Open Price Term.** (1) The parties if they so intend can conclude a contract for sale even though the price is not settled. In such a case the price is a reasonable price at the time for delivery if (a) nothing is said as to price; or (b) the price is left to be agreed by the parties and they fail to agree; or (c) the price is to be fixed in terms of some agreed market or other standard as set or recorded by a third person or agency and it is not so set or recorded. (2) A price to be fixed by the seller or by the buyer means a price for him to fix in good faith. (3) When a price left to be fixed otherwise than by agreement of the parties fails to be fixed through fault of one party the other may at his option treat the contract as cancelled or himself fix a reasonable price. (4) Where, however, the parties intend not to be bound unless the price be fixed or agreed and it is not fixed or agreed there is no contract . In such a case the buyer must return any goods already received or if unable so to do must pay their reasonable value at the time of delivery and the seller must return any portion of the price paid on account.	**Art. 1591** The price of a sale must be determined and stated by the parties. **Art. 1592** It may however [be] left to the estimation of a third person; where that person is unwilling or unable to make an estimate, there is no sale.	Articles 6:104 [Determination of Price], 6:105 [Unilateral Determination by a Party], 6:106 [Determination by a Third Person], 6:107 [Reference to a Non-Existent Factor]
Article 56 Net weight If the price is fixed according to the weight of the goods, in case of doubt it is to be determined by the net weight.			
Article 57 Place of payment (1) If the buyer is not bound to pay the price at any other particular place, he must pay it to the seller: (a) at the seller's place of business; or	**§ 2-310. Open Time for Payment or Running of Credit; Authority to Ship Under Reservation.** Unless otherwise agreed (a) payment is due at the time and place at which the buyer is	**Art. 1247** Payment must be made in the place designated by the agreement. Where a place is not designated, payment, if it is for a thing certain and determined, must be made at	Article 7:101 [Place of Performance]

UN Convention on the International Sale of Goods (Multilateral)*	Uniform Commerical Code (U.S. states represented here as enacted by New York State)	Civil Code (France)	Draft Principles of European Contract Law (EU)

(b) if the payment is to be made against the handing over of the goods or of documents, at the place where the handing over takes place.

(2) The seller must bear any increase in the expenses incidental to payment which is caused by a change in his place of business subsequent to the conclusion of the contract.

to receive the goods even though the place of shipment is the place of delivery; and (b) if the seller is authorized to send the goods he may ship them under reservation, and may tender the documents of title, but the buyer may inspect the goods after their arrival before payment is due unless such inspection is inconsistent with the terms of the contract (Section 2-513); and (c) if delivery is authorized and made by way of documents of title otherwise than by subsection (b) then payment is due at the time and place at which the buyer is to receive the documents regardless of where the goods are to be received; and (d) where the seller is required or authorized to ship the goods on credit the credit period runs from the time of shipment but post-dating the invoice or delaying its dispatch will correspondingly delay the starting of the credit period.

the place where the thing forming the object of the obligation was at the time of that obligation.
Apart from those cases, payment must be made at the domicile of the debtor.

Art. 1651
Where nothing has been fixed in this regard at the time of the sale, the buyer must pay at the place and at the time where and when delivery is to be made.

Article 58 Time for payment and inspection
(1) If the buyer is not bound to pay the price at any other specific time he must pay it when the seller places either the goods or documents controlling their disposition at the buyer's disposal in accordance with the contract and this Convention. The seller may make such payment a condition for handing over the goods or documents.
(2) If the contract involves carriage of the goods, the seller may dispatch the goods on terms whereby the goods, or documents controlling their disposition, will not be handed over to the buyer except against payment of the price.
(3) The buyer is not bound to pay the price until he has had an opportunity to examine the goods, unless the procedures for delivery or payment agreed upon by the parties are inconsistent with his having such an opportunity.

§ 2-511. Tender of Payment by Buyer; Payment by Check.
(1) Unless otherwise agreed tender of payment is a condition to the seller's duty to tender and complete any delivery.
(2) Tender of payment is sufficient when made by any means or in any manner current in the ordinary course of business unless the seller demands payment in legal tender and gives any extension of time reasonably necessary to procure it.
(3) Subject to the provisions of this Act on the effect of an instrument on an obligation (Section 3-802), payment by check is conditional and is defeated as between the parties by dishonor of the check on due presentment.
§ 2-512. Payment by Buyer Before Inspection.
(1) Where the contract requires payment before inspection non-conformity of the goods

Articles 7:102 [Time of Performance], 7:104 [Order of Performance], 7:106 [Performance by a Third Person], 7:107 [Form of Payment], 7:108 [Currency of Payment], 7:109 [Appropriation of Performance]

UN Convention on the International Sale of Goods (Multilateral)*	Uniform Commerical Code (U.S. states represented here as enacted by New York State)	Civil Code (France)	Draft Principles of European Contract Law (EU)
	does not excuse the buyer from so making payment unless (a) the non-conformity appears without inspection; or (b) despite tender of the required documents the circumstances would justify injunction against honor under this Act (Section 5-109(b)). (2) Payment pursuant to subsection (1) does not constitute an acceptance of goods or impair the buyer's right to inspect or any of his remedies.		

Article 59 No request for payment required
The buyer must pay the price on the date fixed by or determinable from the contract and this Convention without the need for any request or compliance with any formality on the part of the seller.

Section II. Taking delivery

| **Article 60 Buyer to take delivery**
The buyer's obligation to take delivery consists:
(a) in doing all the acts which could reasonably be expected of him in order to enable the seller to make delivery; and
(b) in taking over the goods. | **§ 2-507. Effect of Seller's Tender; Delivery on Condition.**
(1) Tender of delivery is a condition to the buyer's duty to accept the goods and, unless otherwise agreed, to his duty to pay for them. Tender entitles the seller to acceptance of the goods and to payment according to the contract.
(2) Where payment is due and demanded on the delivery to the buyer of goods or documents of title, his right as against the seller to retain or dispose of them is conditional upon his making the payment due. | | |

Section III. Remedies for breach of contract by the buyer

| **Article 61 Seller's remedies**
(1) If the buyer fails to perform any of his obligations under the contract or this Convention, the seller may:
(a) exercise the rights provided in articles 62 to 65;
(b) claim damages as provided in articles 74 to 77. | **§ 2-703. Seller's Remedies in General.**
Where the buyer wrongfully rejects or revokes acceptance of goods or fails to make a payment due on or before delivery or repudiates with respect to a part or the whole, then with respect to any goods | **Art. 1142**
Any obligation to do or not to do resolves itself into damages, in case of non-performance on the part of the debtor.
Art. 1654
Where the buyer does not pay the price, the seller may apply for avoidance of the sale. | Articles 8:101 [Remedies Available], 8:102 [Cumulation of Remedies] |

UN Convention on the International Sale of Goods (Multilateral)*	Uniform Commerical Code (U.S. states represented here as enacted by New York State)	Civil Code (France)	Draft Principles of European Contract Law (EU)
(2) The seller is not deprived of any right he may have to claim damages by exercising his right to other remedies. (3) No period of grace may be granted to the buyer by a court or arbitral tribunal when the seller resorts to a remedy for breach of contract.	directly affected and, if the breach is of the whole contract (Section 2-612), then also with respect to the whole undelivered balance, the aggrieved seller may (a) withhold delivery of such goods; (b) stop delivery by any bailee as hereafter provided (Section 2-705); (c) proceed under the next section respecting goods still unidentified to the contract; (d) resell and recover damages as hereafter provided (Section 2-706); (e) recover damages for non-acceptance (Section 2-708) or in a proper case the price (Section 2-709); (f) cancel.	**Art. 1657** In matters of sale of commodities and movable effects, the avoidance of the sale takes place by operation of law, and without any demand, for the benefit of the seller, after the expiry of the period agreed upon for the removal.	
Article 62 May require performance The seller may require the buyer to pay the price, take delivery or perform his other obligations, unless the seller has resorted to a remedy which is inconsistent with this requirement. **Article 63 Additional period for performance** (1) The seller may fix an additional period of time of reasonable length for performance by the buyer of his obligations. (2) Unless the seller has received notice from the buyer that he will not perform within the period so fixed, the seller may not, during that period, resort to any remedy for breach of contract. However, the seller is not deprived thereby of any right he may have to claim damages for delay in performance.	**§ 2-704. Seller's Right to Identify Goods to the Contract Notwithstanding Breach or to Salvage Unfinished Goods.** **§ 2-705. Seller's Stoppage of Delivery in Transit or Otherwise.** **§ 2-706. Seller's Resale Including Contract for Resale.** **§ 2-707. "Person in the Position of a Seller".** **§ 2-708. Seller's Damages for Non-acceptance or Repudiation.** **§ 2-709. Action for the Price.** (1) When the buyer fails to pay the price as it becomes due the seller may recover, together with any incidental damages under the next section, the price (a) of goods accepted or of conforming goods lost or damaged within a commercially reasonable time after risk of their loss has passed to the buyer; and (b) of goods identified to the contract if the seller is unable after reasonable effort to resell them at a reasonable price or the circumstances reasonably indicate that such effort will be unavailing. (2) Where the seller sues for the price he must hold for the	**Art. 1146** Damages are due only where a debtor is given notice to fulfil his obligation, except nevertheless where the thing which the debtor has bound himself to transfer or to do could be transferred or done only within a certain time which he has allowed to elapse. "Notice of default may follow from a letter missive where a sufficient requisition results from it" *(Act n° 91-650 of 9 July 1991).* **Art. 1147** A debtor shall be ordered to pay damages, if there is occasion, either by reason of the non-performance of the obligation, or by reason of delay in performing, whenever he does not prove that the non-performance comes from an external cause which may not be ascribed to him, although there is no bad faith on his part.	Articles 9:101 [Right to Performance: Monetary Obligations], 9:102 [Right to Performance: Non-Monetary Obligations], 9:103 [Right to Performance: Damages Not Precluded] Article 8:106 [Notice Fixing Additional Period for Performance]

UN Convention on the International Sale of Goods (Multilateral)*	Uniform Commerical Code (U.S. states represented here as enacted by New York State)	Civil Code (France)	Draft Principles of European Contract Law (EU)
	buyer any goods which have been identified to the contract and are still in his control except that if resale becomes possible he may resell them at any time prior to the collection of the judgment. The net proceeds of any such resale must be credited to the buyer and payment of the judgment entitles him to any goods not resold. (3) After the buyer has wrongfully rejected or revoked acceptance of the goods or has failed to make a payment due or has repudiated (Section 2-610), a seller who is held not entitled to the price under this section shall nevertheless be awarded damages for non-acceptance under the preceding section. **§ 2-710. Seller's Incidental Damages.**		
Article 64 Seller's right to avoid contract (1) The seller may declare the contract avoided: (a) if the failure by the buyer to perform any of his obligations under the contract or this Convention amounts to a fundamental breach of contract; or (b) if the buyer does not, within the additional period of time fixed by the seller in accordance with paragraph (1) of article 63, perform his obligation to pay the price or take delivery of the goods, or if he declares that he will not do so within the period so fixed; (2) However, in cases where the buyer has paid the price, the seller loses the right to declare the contract avoided unless he does so: (a) in respect of late performance by the buyer, before the seller has become aware that performance has been rendered; or (b) in respect of any breach other than late performance by the buyer, within a reasonable time: (i) after the seller knew or ought to have known of the breach; or			Articles 9:301 [Right to Terminate the Contract], 9:303 [Notice of Termination]

UN Convention on the International Sale of Goods (Multilateral)*	Uniform Commerical Code (U.S. states represented here as enacted by New York State)	Civil Code (France)	Draft Principles of European Contract Law (EU)

(ii) after the expiration of any additional period of time fixed by the seller in accordance with paragraph (1) of article 63, or after the buyer has declared that he will not perform his obligations within such an additional period.

Article 65 Seller may make specifications; notice of
(1) If under the contract the buyer is to specify the form, measurement or other features of the goods and he fails to make such specification either on the date agreed upon or within a reasonable time after receipt of a request from the seller, the seller may, without prejudice to any other rights he may have, make the specification himself in accordance with the requirements of the buyer that may be known to him.
(2) If the seller makes the specification himself, he must inform the buyer of the details thereof and must fix a reasonable time within which the buyer may make a different specification. If, after receipt of such a communication, the buyer fails to do so within the time so fixed, the specification made by the seller is binding.

Article 7:105 [Alternative Performance]

CHAPTER IV. PASSING OF RISK

Article 66 Loss; no discharge of payment obligation
Loss of or damage to the goods after the risk has passed to the buyer does not discharge him from his obligation to pay the price, unless the loss or damage is due to an act or omission of the seller.

Article 67 Passage of risk; where contract involves carriage
(1) If the contract of sale involves carriage of the goods and the seller is not bound to hand them over at a particular place, the risk passes to the buyer when the goods are

§ 2-509. Risk of Loss in the Absence of Breach.
(1) Where the contract requires or authorizes the seller to ship the goods by carrier
(a) if it does not require him to deliver them at a particular destination, the risk of loss passes to the buyer when the goods are duly delivered to the carrier even though the shipment is under reservation (Section 2-505); but
(b) if it does require him to deliver them at a particular destination and the goods are there duly tendered while in the possession of the carrier, the risk of loss passes to the

UN Convention on the International Sale of Goods (Multilateral)*

handed over to the first carrier for transmission to the buyer in accordance with the contract of sale. If the seller is bound to hand the goods over to a carrier at a particular place, the risk does not pass to the buyer until the goods are handed over to the carrier at that place. The fact that the seller is authorized to retain documents controlling the disposition of the goods does not affect the passage of the risk.
(2) Nevertheless, the risk does not pass to the buyer until the goods are clearly identified to the contract, whether by markings on the goods, by shipping documents, by notice given to the buyer or otherwise.

Article 68 Goods sold in transit

The risk in respect of goods sold in transit passes to the buyer from the time of the conclusion of the contract. However, if the circumstances so indicate, the risk is assumed by the buyer from the time the goods were handed over to the carrier who issued the documents embodying the contract of carriage. Nevertheless, if at the time of the conclusion of the contract of sale the seller knew or ought to have known that the goods had been lost or damaged and did not disclose this to the buyer, the loss or damage is at the risk of the seller.

Article 69 Passage of risk; further rules

(1) In cases not within articles 67 and 68, the risk passes to the buyer when he takes over the goods or, if he does not do so in due time, from the time when the goods are placed at his disposal and he commits a breach of contract by failing to take delivery.
(2) However, if the buyer is bound to take over the goods at a place other than a place of

Uniform Commerical Code (U.S. states represented here as enacted by New York State)

buyer when the goods are there duly so tendered as to enable the buyer to take delivery.
(2) Where the goods are held by a bailee to be delivered without being moved, the risk of loss passes to the buyer
(a) on his receipt of a negotiable document of title covering the goods; or
(b) on acknowledgment by the bailee of the buyer's right to possession of the goods; or
(c) after his receipt of a non-negotiable document of title or other written direction to deliver, as provided in subsection (4)(b) of Section 2-503.
(3) In any case not within subsection (1) or (2), the risk of loss passes to the buyer on his receipt of the goods if the seller is a merchant; otherwise the risk passes to the buyer on tender of delivery.
(4) The provisions of this section are subject to contrary agreement of the parties and to the provisions of this Article on sale on approval (Section 2-327) and on effect of breach on risk of loss (Section 2-510).

§ 2-510. Effect of Breach on Risk of Loss.

(1) Where a tender or delivery of goods so fails to conform to the contract as to give a right of rejection the risk of their loss remains on the seller until cure or acceptance.
(2) Where the buyer rightfully revokes acceptance he may to the extent of any deficiency in his effective insurance coverage treat the risk of loss as having rested on the seller from the beginning.

Civil Code (France)

Art. 1583
It is complete between the parties, and ownership is acquired as of right by the buyer with respect to the seller, as soon as the thing and the price have been agreed upon, although the thing has not yet been delivered or the price paid.

Art. 1585
Where goods are not sold in bulk but by weight, number or measure, a sale is not

Draft Principles of European Contract Law (EU)

UN Convention on the International Sale of Goods (Multilateral)*	Uniform Commerical Code (U.S. states represented here as enacted by New York State)	Civil Code (France)	Draft Principles of European Contract Law (EU)
business of the seller, the risk passes when delivery is due and the buyer is aware of the fact that the goods are placed at his disposal at that place. (3) It the contract relates to goods not then identified, the goods are considered not to be placed at the disposal of the buyer until they are clearly identified to the contract.	(3) Where the buyer as to conforming goods already identified to the contract for sale repudiates or is otherwise in breach before risk of their loss has passed to him, the seller may to the extent of any deficiency in his effective insurance coverage treat the risk of loss as resting on the buyer for a commercially reasonable time.	complete, in that the things sold are at the risk of the seller until they have been weighed, counted or measured; but the buyer may claim either the delivery or damages, if there is occasion, in case of non-performance of the undertaking. **Art. 1586** Where, on the contrary, the goods have been sold in bulk, the sale is complete although the goods have not yet been weighed, counted or measured.	

Article 70 Where seller in fundamental breach

If the seller has committed a fundamental breach of contract, articles 67, 68 and 69 do not impair the remedies available to the buyer on account of the breach.

CHAPTER V. PROVISIONS COMMON TO THE OBLIGATIONS OF THE SELLER AND OF THE BUYER

Section I. Anticipatory breach and instalment contracts

Article 71 Suspension of performance (1) A party may suspend the performance of his obligations if, after the conclusion of the contract, it becomes apparent that the other party will not perform a substantial part of his obligations as a result of: (a) a serious deficiency in his ability to perform or in his creditworthiness; or (b) his conduct in preparing to perform or in performing the contract. (2) If the seller has already dispatched the goods before the grounds described in the preceding paragraph become evident, he may prevent the handing over of the goods to the buyer even though the buyer holds a document which entitles him to obtain them. The present paragraph relates only to the rights in the goods as between the buyer and the seller.	**§ 2-610. Anticipatory Repudiation.** When either party repudiates the contract with respect to a performance not yet due the loss of which will substantially impair the value of the contract to the other, the aggrieved party may (a) for a commercially reasonable time await performance by the repudiating party; or (b) resort to any remedy for breach (Section 2-703 or Section 2-711), even though he has notified the repudiating party that he would await the latter's performance and has urged retraction; and (c) in either case suspend his own performance or proceed in accordance with the provisions of this Article on the seller's right to identify goods to the contract notwithstanding breach or to salvage unfinished goods (Section 2-704).

UN Convention on the International Sale of Goods (Multilateral)*	Uniform Commerical Code (U.S. states represented here as enacted by New York State)	Civil Code (France)	Draft Principles of European Contract Law (EU)
(3) A party suspending performance, whether before or after dispatch of the goods, must immediately give notice of the suspension to the other party and must continue with performance if the other party provides adequate assurance of his performance. **Article 72 Avoidance in anticipation of breach** (1) If prior to the date for performance of the contract it is clear that one of the parties will commit a fundamental breach of contract, the other party may declare the contract avoided. (2) If time allows, the party intending to declare the contract avoided must give reasonable notice to the other party in order to permit him to provide adequate assurance of his performance. (3) The requirements of the preceding paragraph do not apply if the other party has declared that he will not perform his obligations. **Article 73 Instalment contracts; avoidance** (1) In the case of a contract for delivery of goods by instalments, if the failure of one party to perform any of his obligations in respect of any instalment constitutes a fundamental breach of contract with respect to that instalment, the other party may declare the contract avoided with respect to that instalment. (2) If one party's failure to perform any of his obligations in respect of any instalment gives the other party good grounds to conclude that a fundamental breach of contract will occur with			Article 9:304 [Anticipatory Non-Performance]
	§ 2-612. "Installment contract"; Breach. (1) An "installment contract" is one which requires or authorizes the delivery of goods in separate lots to be separately accepted, even though the contract contains a clause "each delivery is a separate contract" or its equivalent. (2) The buyer may reject any installment which is non-conforming if the non-conformity substantially impairs the value of that installment and cannot be cured or if the non-conformity is a defect in the required documents; but if the non-conformity does not fall within subsection (3) and the seller gives adequate assurance of its cure the buyer		Articles 9:302 [Contract to be Performed in Parts], 9:306 [Property to be Reduced in Value]

UN Convention on the International Sale of Goods (Multilateral)*	Uniform Commerical Code (U.S. states represented here as enacted by New York State)	Civil Code (France)	Draft Principles of European Contract Law (EU)
respect to future installments, he may declare the contract avoided for the future, provided that he does so within a reasonable time. (3) A buyer who declares the contract avoided in respect of any delivery may, at the same time, declare it avoided in respect of deliveries already made or of future deliveries if, by reason of their interdependence, those deliveries could not be used for the purpose contemplated by the parties at the time of the conclusion of the contract.	must accept that installment. (3) Whenever non-conformity or default with respect to one or more installments substantially impairs the value of the whole contract there is a breach of the whole. But the aggrieved party reinstates the contract if he accepts a non-conforming installment without seasonably notifying of cancellation or if he brings an action with respect only to past installments or demands performance as to future installments.		

Section II. Damages

Article 74 Damages; quantum Damages for breach of contract by one party consist of a sum equal to the loss, including loss of profit, suffered by the other party as a consequence of the breach. Such damages may not exceed the loss which the party in breach foresaw or ought to have foreseen at the time of the conclusion of the contract, in the light of the facts and matters of which he then knew or ought to have known, as a possible consequence of the breach of contract.		**Art. 1149** Damages due to a creditor are, as a rule, for the loss which he has suffered and the profit which he has been deprived of, subject to the exceptions and modifications below. **Art. 1150** A debtor is liable only for damages which were foreseen or which could have been foreseen at the time of the contract, where it is not through his own intentional breach that the obligation is not fulfilled.	Articles 9:501 [Right to Damages], 9:502 [General Measure of Damages], 9:503 [Foreseeability], 9:504 [Loss Attributable to Third Party], 9:509 [Agreed Payment for Non-Performance], 9:510 [Currency by which Damages to be Measured]
Article 75 Where contract avoided If the contract is avoided and if, in a reasonable manner and within a reasonable time after avoidance, the buyer has bought goods in replacement or the seller has resold the goods, the party claiming damages may recover the difference between the contract price and the price in the substitute transaction as well as any further damages recoverable under article 74.			Article 9:506 [Damages: Substitute Transaction]
Article 76 Where contract avoided; further (1) If the contract is avoided and there is a current price for the goods, the party claiming damages may, if he has not made a purchase or resale under article 75, recover the difference			Article 9:507 [Damages: Current Price where No Substitute Transaction]

UN Convention on the International Sale of Goods (Multilateral)*	Uniform Commerical Code (U.S. states represented here as enacted by New York State)	Civil Code (France)	Draft Principles of European Contract Law (EU)

between the price fixed by the contract and the current price at the time of avoidance as well as any further damages recoverable under article 74. If, however, the party claiming damages has avoided the contract after taking over the goods, the current price at the time of such taking over shall be applied instead of the current price at the time of avoidance. (2) For the purposes of the preceding paragraph, the current price is the price prevailing at the place where delivery of the goods should have been made or, if there is no current price at that place, the price at such other place as serves as a reasonable substitute, making due allowance for differences in the cost of transporting the goods.

Article 77 Requirement of mitigation
A party who relies on a breach of contract must take such measures as are reasonable in the circumstances to mitigate the loss, including loss of profit, resulting from the breach. If he fails to take such measures, the party in breach may claim a reduction in the damages in the amount by which the loss should have been mitigated.

Article 9:505 [Mitigation: Reduction of Loss]

Section III. Interest

Article 78 Entitlement
If a party fails to pay the price or any other sum that is in arrears, the other party is entitled to interest on it, without prejudice to any claim for damages recoverable under article 74.

Art. 1652
The buyer owes interest on the price of the sale up to the time of the payment, in the three following cases:
Where it has been so agreed at the time of the sale;
Where the thing sold and delivered produces fruits or other incomes;
Where the buyer is under notice to pay.
In that last case, interest runs only from the notice

Article 9:508 [Interest: Delay in Payment of Money]

UN Convention on the International Sale of Goods (Multilateral)*

Uniform Commerical Code (U.S. states represented here as enacted by New York State)

Civil Code (France)

Draft Principles of European Contract Law (EU)

Section IV. Exemption

Article 79 Impediment; exemption from liability; notice

(1) A party is not liable for a failure to perform any of his obligations if he proves that the failure was due to an impediment beyond his control and that he could not reasonably be expected to have taken the impediment into account at the time of the conclusion of the contract or to have avoided or overcome it or its consequences.

(2) If the party's failure is due to the failure by a third person whom he has engaged to perform the whole or a part of the contract, that party is exempt from liability only if:

(a) he is exempt under the preceding paragraph; and

(b) the person whom he has so engaged would he so exempt if the provisions of that paragraph were applied to him.

(3) The exemption provided by this article has effect for the period during which the impediment exists.

(4) The party who fails to perform must give notice to the other party of the impediment and its effect on his ability to perform. If the notice is not received by the other party within a reasonable time after the party who fails to perform knew or ought to have known of the impediment, he is liable for damages resulting from such nonreceipt.

(5) Nothing in this article prevents either party from exercising any right other than to claim damages under this Convention.

Article 80 Where failure induced by other party

A party may not rely on a failure of the other party to perform, to the extent that such failure was caused by the first party's act or omission.

Art. 1601
Where, at the time of the sale, the thing sold has wholly perished, the sale is void. Where only a part of the thing has perished, the buyer has the choice to waive the sale or to claim the part saved, by having the price determined proportionally.

Art. 1599
The sale of a thing belonging to another is void: it may give rise to damages where the buyer did not know that the thing belonged to another.

Art. 1148
There is no occasion for any damages where a debtor was prevented from transferring or from doing that to which he was bound, or did what was forbidden to him, by reason of *force majeure* or of a fortuitous event.

Articles 8:108 [Excuse Due to an Impediment], 8:107 [Performance Entrusted to Another], 6:111 [Hardship]

Articles 8:101(3) [Own Act Causing Other Party Non-Performance], 1:301(1) [Meaning of Terms: Definition of "act"], 9:504 [Loss Attributable to Aggrieved Party]

UN Convention on the International Sale of Goods (Multilateral)*	Uniform Commerical Code (U.S. states represented here as enacted by New York State)	Civil Code (France)	Draft Principles of European Contract Law (EU)

Section V. Effects of avoidance

Article 81 Effect; restitution where performance

(1) Avoidance of the contract releases both parties from their obligations under it, subject to any damages which may be due. Avoidance does not affect any provision of the contract for the settlement of disputes or any other provision of the contract governing the rights and obligations of the parties consequent upon the avoidance of the contract.

(2) A party who has performed the contract either wholly or in part may claim restitution from the other party of whatever the first party has supplied or paid under the contract. If both parties are bound to make restitution, they must do so concurrently.

Articles 9:305 [Effects of Termination in General], 9:306 [Property Reduced in Value], 9:307 [Recovery of Money Paid], 9:308 [Recovery of Property], 9:309 [Recovery for Performance that Cannot be Returned]

Article 82 Where buyer's restitution impossible

(1) The buyer loses the right to declare the contract avoided or to require the seller to deliver substitute goods if it is impossible for him to make restitution of the goods substantially in the condition in which he received them.

(2) The preceding paragraph does not apply:

(a) if the impossibility of making restitution of the goods or of making restitution of the goods substantially in the condition in which the buyer received them is not due to his act or omission;

(b) the goods or part of the goods have perished or deteriorated as a result of the examination provided for in article 38; or

(c) if the goods or part of the goods have been sold in the normal course of business or have been consumed or transformed by the buyer in the course of normal use before he discovered or ought to have discovered the lack of conformity.

Article 9:309 [Recovery for Performance that Cannot be Returned]

UN Convention on the International Sale of Goods (Multilateral)*	Uniform Commerical Code (U.S. states represented here as enacted by New York State)	Civil Code (France)	Draft Principles of European Contract Law (EU)

Article 83 Buyer's other remedies retained
A buyer who has lost the right to declare the contract avoided or to require the seller to deliver substitute goods in accordance with article 82 retains all other remedies under the contract and this Convention.

Article 84 Effect; further
(1) If the seller is bound to refund the price, he must also pay interest on it, from the date on which the price was paid.
(2) The buyer must account to the seller for all benefits which he has derived from the goods or part of them:
(a) if he must make restitution of the goods or part of them; or
(b) if it is impossible for him to make restitution of all or part of the goods or to make restitution of all or part of the goods substantially in the condition in which he received them, but he has nevertheless declared the contract avoided or required the seller to deliver substitute goods.

Article 9:508 [Interest: Delay in Payment of Money]

Section VI. Preservation of the goods

Article 85 Seller's duty to preserve
If the buyer is in delay in taking delivery of the goods or, where payment of the price and delivery of the goods are to be made concurrently, if he fails to pay the price, and the seller is either in possession of the goods or otherwise able to control their disposition, the seller must take such steps as are reasonable in the circumstances to preserve them. He is entitled to retain them until he has been reimbursed his reasonable expenses by the buyer.

Article 86 Buyer's duty to preserve
(1) If the buyer has received the goods and intends to exercise any right under the contract or this Convention to

Art. 1624
The question of ascertaining upon whom, between the seller and the purchaser, falls the loss or deterioration of the thing sold before its delivery, shall be decided according to the rules prescribed in the Title *Of Contracts or of Conventional Obligations in General.*

Articles 7:110 [Property Not Accepted], 7:111 [Money Not Accepted], 7:112 [Costs of Performance]

UN Convention on the International Sale of Goods (Multilateral)*	Uniform Commerical Code (U.S. states represented here as enacted by New York State)	Civil Code (France)	Draft Principles of European Contract Law (EU)

UN Convention on the International Sale of Goods (Multilateral)*

reject them, he must take such steps to preserve them as are reasonable in the circumstances. He is entitled to retain them until he has been reimbursed his reasonable expenses by the seller.

(2) If goods dispatched to the buyer have been placed at his disposal at their destination and he exercises the right to reject them, he must take possession of them on behalf of the seller, provided that this can be done without payment of the price and without unreasonable inconvenience or unreasonable expense. This provision does not apply if the seller or a person authorized to take charge of the goods on his behalf is present at the destination. If the buyer takes possession of the goods under this paragraph, his rights and obligations are governed by the preceding paragraph.

Article 87 Warehouse preservation

A party who is bound to take steps to preserve the goods may deposit them in a warehouse of a third person at the expense of the other party provided that the expense incurred is not unreasonable.

Article 88 Sale where delay, deterioration; notice

(1) A party who is bound to preserve the goods in accordance with article 85 or 86 may sell them by any appropriate means if there has been an unreasonable delay by the other party in taking possession of the goods or in taking them back or in paying the price or the cost of preservation, provided that reasonable notice of the intention to sell has been given to the other party.

(2) If the goods are subject to rapid deterioration or their preservation would involve unreasonable expense, a party who is bound to preserve the goods in accordance with

**UN Convention on
the International Sale
of Goods
(Multilateral)***

article 85 or 86 must take
reasonable measures to sell
them. To the extent possible he
must give notice to the other
party of his intention to sell.
(3) A party selling the goods
has the right to retain out of
the proceeds of sale an amount
equal to the reasonable
expenses of preserving the
goods and of selling them. He
must account to the other
party for the balance.

PART IV: FINAL PROVISIONS OF CONVENTION ON THE INTERNATIONAL SALE OF GOODS.

Article 89
The Secretary-General of the United Nations is hereby designated as the depositary for this Convention.

Article 90
This Convention does not prevail over any international agreement which has already been or may be entered into and which contains provisions concerning the matters governed by this Convention, provided that the parties have their places of business in States parties, to such agreement.

Article 91
(1) This Convention is open for signature at the concluding meeting of the United Nations Conference on Contracts for the International Sale of Goods and will remain open for signature by all States at the Headquarters of the United Nations, New York until 30 September 1981.
(2) This Convention is subject to ratification, acceptance or approval by the signatory States.
(3) This Convention is open for accession by all States which are not signatory States as from the date it is open for signature.
(4) Instruments of ratification, acceptance, approval and accession are to be deposited with the Secretary-General of the United Nations.

Article 92
(1) A Contracting State may declare at the time of signature, ratification, acceptance, approval or accession that it will not be bound by Part II of this Convention or that it will not be bound by Part III of this Convention.
(2) A Contracting State which makes a declaration in accordance with the preceding paragraph in respect of Part II or Part III of this Convention is not to be considered a Contracting State within paragraph (1) of article 1 of this Convention in respect of matters governed by the Part to which the declaration applies.

Article 93
(1) If a Contracting State has two or more territorial units in which, according to its constitution, different systems of law are applicable in relation to the matters dealt with in this Convention, it may, at the time of signature, ratification, acceptance, approval or accession, declare that this Convention is to extend to all its territorial units or only to one or more of them, and may amend its declaration by submitting another declaration at any time.
(2) These declarations are to be notified to the depositary and are to state expressly the territorial units to which the Convention extends.
(3) If, by virtue of a declaration under this article, this Convention extends to one or more but not all of the territorial units of a Contracting State, and if the place of business of a party is located in that State, this place of business, for the purposes of this Convention, is considered not to be in a Contracting State, unless it is in a territorial unit to which the Convention extends.
(4) If a Contracting State makes no declaration under paragraph (1) of this article, the Convention is to extend to all territorial units of that State.

Article 94
(1) Two or more Contracting States which have the same or closely related legal rules on matters governed by this Convention may at any time declare that the Convention is not to apply to contracts of sale or to their formation where the parties have their places of business in those States. Such declarations may be made jointly or by reciprocal unilateral declarations.
(2) A Contracting State which has the same or closely related legal rules on matters governed by this Convention as one or more non-Contracting States may at any time declare that the Convention is not to apply to contracts of sale or to their formation where the parties have their places of business in those States.
(3) If a State which is the object of a declaration under the preceding paragraph subsequently becomes a Contracting State, the declaration made will, as from the date on which the Convention enters into force in respect of the new Contracting State, have the effect of a declaration made under paragraph (1), provided that the new Contracting State joins in such declaration or makes a reciprocal unilateral declaration.

UN Convention on the International Sale of Goods (Multilateral)*

Article 95

Any State may declare at the time of the deposit of its instrument of ratification, acceptance, approval or accession that it will not be bound by subparagraph (1)(b) of article 1 of this Convention.

Article 96

A Contracting State whose legislation requires contracts of sale to be concluded in or evidenced by writing may at any time make a declaration in accordance with article 12 that any provision of article 11, article 29, or Part II of this Convention, that allows a contract of sale or its modification or termination by agreement or any offer, acceptance, or other indication of intention to be made in any form other than in writing, does not apply where any party has his place of business in that State.

Article 97

(1) Declarations made under this Convention at the time of signature are subject to confirmation upon ratification, acceptance or approval.

(2) Declarations and confirmations of declarations are to be in writing and be formally notified to the depositary.

(3) A declaration takes effect simultaneously with the entry into force of this Convention in respect of the State concerned. However, a declaration of which the depositary receives formal notification after such entry into force takes effect on the first day of the month following the expiration of six months after the date of its receipt by the depositary. Reciprocal unilateral declarations under article 94 take effect on the first day of the month following the expiration of six months after the receipt of the latest declaration by the depositary.

(4) Any State which makes a declaration under this Convention may withdraw it at any time by a formal notification in writing addressed to the depositary. Such withdrawal is to take effect on the first day of the month following the expiration of six months after the date of the receipt of the notification by the depositary.

(5) A withdrawal of a declaration made under article 94 renders inoperative, as from the date on which the withdrawal takes effect, any reciprocal declaration made by another State under that article.

Article 98

No reservations are permitted except those expressly authorized in this Convention.

Article 99

(1) This Convention enters into force, subject to the provisions of paragraph (6) of this article, on the first day of the month following the expiration of twelve months after the date of deposit of the tenth instrument of ratification, acceptance, approval or accession, including an instrument which contains a declaration made under article 92.

(2) When a State ratifies, accepts, approves or accedes to this Convention after the deposit of the tenth instrument of ratification, acceptance, approval or accession, this Convention, with the exception of the Part excluded, enters into force in respect of that State, subject to the provisions of paragraph (6) of this article, on the first day of the month following the expiration of twelve months after the date of the deposit of its instrument of ratification, acceptance, approval or accession.

(3) A State which ratifies, accepts, approves or accedes to this Convention and is a party to either or both the Convention relating to a Uniform Law on the Formation of Contracts for the International Sale of Goods done at The Hague on 1 July 1964 (1964 Hague Formation Convention) and the Convention relating to a Uniform Law on the International Sale of Goods done at The Hague on 1 July 1964 (1964 Hague Sales Convention) shall at the same time denounce, as the case may be, either or both the 1964 Hague Sales Convention and the 1964 Hague Formation Convention by notifying the Government of the Netherlands to that effect.

(4) A State party to the 1964 Hague Sales Convention which ratifies, accepts, approves or accedes to the present Convention and declares or has declared under article 92 that it will not be bound by Part II of this Convention shall at the time of ratification, acceptance, approval or accession denounce the 1964 Hague Sales Convention by notifying the Government of the Netherlands to that effect.

(5) A State party to the 1964 Hague Formation Convention which ratifies, accepts, approves or accedes to the present Convention and declares or has declared under article 92 that it will not be bound by Part III of this Convention shall at the time of ratification, acceptance, approval or accession denounce the 1964 Hague Formation Convention by notifying the Government of the Netherlands to that effect.

(6) For the purpose of this article, ratifications, acceptances, approvals and accessions in respect of this Convention by States parties to the 1964 Hague Formation Convention or to the 1964 Hague Sales Convention shall not be effective until such denunciations as may be required on the part of those States in respect of the latter two Conventions have themselves become effective. The depositary of this Convention shall consult with the Government of the Netherlands, as the depositary of the 1964 Conventions, so as to ensure necessary co-ordination in this respect.

Article 100

(1) This Convention applies to the formation of a contract only when the proposal for concluding the contract is made on or after the date when the Convention enters into force in respect of the Contracting States referred to in subparagraph (1)(a) or the Contracting State referred to in subparagraph (1)(b) of article 1.

(2) This Convention applies only to contracts concluded on or after the date when the Convention enters into force in respect of the Contracting States referred to in subparagraph (1)(a) or the Contracting State referred to in subparagraph (1)(b) of article 1.

Article 101

(1) A Contracting State may denounce this Convention, or Part II or Part III of the Convention, by a formal notification in writing addressed to the depositary.

UN Convention on the International Sale of Goods (Multilateral)*

(2) The denunciation takes effect on the first day of the month following the expiration of twelve months after the notification is received by the depositary. Where a longer period for the denunciation to take effect is specified in the notification, the denunciation takes effect upon the expiration of such longer period after the notification is received by the depositary.

DONE at Vienna, this day of eleventh day of April, one thousand nine hundred and eighty, in a single original, of which the Arabic, Chinese, English, French, Russian and Spanish texts are equally authentic.

IN WITNESS WHEREOF the undersigned plenipotentiaries, being duly authorized by their respective Governments, have signed this Convention.

*The CISG does not provide summary titles for each CISG article. Those that are shown for ease of reference are the text author's creation.

Source: 1980 UN Convention on Contracts for the International Sale of Goods (CISG), available at www.cisg.law.pace.edu/cisg; Uniform Commercial Code (New York State), Sales, chief provisions available at http://assembly.state.ny.us; Civil Code (France), chief provisions, available in English and Spanish at www.legifrance.gouv.fr/html/codes_traduits/liste.htm; Draft Principles of European Contract Law (EU) (index to headings created by the Lando Commission on European Contract Law), available (with commentary) at www.cbs.dk/departments/law/staff/ol/commission_on_ecl/survey_pecl.htm.

BusinessWeek

Technology and a declining dollar are making it much easier for small outfits to export their wares, as sailmaker Tim Yourieff explains.

With a weak dollar turning U.S. goods into bargains overseas and prompting greater growth in export markets than domestic ones, many small companies are opening or expanding their export divisions. And now that international freight-and-delivery services have tech solutions in place to smooth the way through customs, selling abroad is not as complicated or costly as it once was, says Tim Yourieff, of Neil Pryde Sails. The Milford (Conn.) sailmaker brings in about $3 million in annual revenue and regards the Web as a godsend that, as Yourieff puts it, keeps making the global marketplace "smaller and smaller."

Yourieff spoke recently to Smart Answers columnist Karen E. Klein about his outfit's global perspective and its recent expansion into Denmark. Edited excerpts of their conversation follow:

Q: Your headquarters is in Connecticut, but your company is really an international presence in the yachting world, isn't it?
A: Yes. My partner, Bob Pattison, and our designer are the only three people who work in the U.S. All our sail manufacturing is done in a factory in Shenzhen, China. And we have sales reps all over the world selling our products, which range from tiny Sunfish sails that retail for $170 each, to huge sails for 100-foot yachts that might cost $3,000 each. We recently established a distributorship in Denmark, and from there we hope to expand our sales all over Western Europe and into Eastern Europe.

Q: How has the decline of the dollar affected your sales in the U.S. market and overseas?
A: We've always had sales worldwide but the U.S. has represented the lion's share of our business, particularly since the tariffs here on goods coming from China are low compared to those in Europe. But in the last few years, business in the U.S. has fallen off considerably. During that time, however, the dollar has declined 25% against the Euro, so that has made up for a lot of the disadvantage we had in Europe on the tariff issue. It lowered the cost of our product to Europeans and increased our sales to existing European distributors.

Q: How much of a difference have you seen?
A: In the past several years, our European sales have almost doubled. We used to do 90% of our sales in the U.S., 8% in Europe, and 2% in Asia. Last year, U.S. sales accounted for about 83%, Europe was up to 15% and we're still at 2% in Asia. Overall, business is down, although sailboat owners

tend to be wealthier people, who are a bit more "recessionproof" than the general population. But while our sales are considerably down domestically, the increase in international sales helps smooth out the downturn.

Q: Between the language differences, the currency fluctuations and the delivery logistics, selling overseas sounds like a headache to many small-business owners. How do you wade through all the complexities?
A: It is tough, particularly since there are a lot of tiers in our business model—the sales reps, the distributors' agents, us, the manufacturers. Being price competitive is not easy when there are so many layers. We have to maintain a very slim overhead and we do it by having all our systems automated, from placing orders to designing, processing, and shipping. Nothing is entered manually because we don't have the time or the personnel to do that. Because each boat is slightly different and each application is unique in terms of finishing details and technical specs, sailmakers used to take hand measurements, write up orders, and then go into the back of the shop [to] cut the cloth. We actually were one of the earliest sailmakers to centralize manufacturing operations and we've been leaders in making custom sails on economies of scale.

Q: How does the automation work?
A: Over the years, we've developed pretty sophisticated software. Distributors take orders from all over the world and send them to us online, we process them here, our designer figures out the specs for each custom sail and sends them over the Internet to our factory in China. Within literally a few hours, the manufacturing plant is cutting and assembling the sails for drop-shipment back to the distributors. Because of this, and our excellent shipping contract, we can promise delivery to our customers within three weeks and we're able to stay very close to that, even during spring rush.

Q: Everything's so highly automated in your company. Do you still find that you have to travel quite a bit?
A: Oh sure. This is still a personal business, and we have to see our sales reps all over the world on a regular basis. They attend all the local boat shows and trade exhibits in their area, and we try to make sure that one of us is always there to help them out. One of our largest boatbuilders organizes rendezvous for us with their customers so that we can make presentations in person, get feedback from them, and educate them on how to use the sails.

8

Transportation and Logistics

Chapter Objectives

The vast majority of international business transactions—certainly all goods and a fair proportion of services—involve some dimension of transportation and logistics. These create further business relationships in contract that support the original contract between the principal trading parties. These "secondary" contracts between the business party and the service provider undertaking transport or logistics, are not secondary at all; they are critical relationships that must be properly executed in accordance with their terms if the original trade contract is to be honored. Put more bluntly, failure to correctly execute these supporting transactions has an instant negative impact on one's ability to perform the obligations of the trade contract.

In this chapter, we discuss transportation and logistics transactions and

- Legal and business issues related to the international carriage of goods by sea, air, and land.
- The impact of international law on these issues and contractual relationships.

- The negotiations and responsibilities between seller-exporters and buyer-importers.

Introduction

Shipping and payment issues (this latter topic being the subject of Chapter 9) are the largest transactional elements that separate international trade from discrete domestic sales made at much closer range or even face-to-face. They also represent the most fertile ground for the growth of disputes between traders. Consequently, a thorough knowledge of shipping contracts and terms of trade is essential to properly understand finance and payment issues, and to deal with the problems they create.

Two truths go along with the conduct and study of these elements. First, they are generally inseparable topics; failures in satisfactory shipping tend to create failures in satisfactory payment, for the simple fact that buyers do not wish to pay for goods that do not arrive, or arrive but in damaged condition. Second, the parties have the ability to sow the seeds of success or failure in these elements at an early stage of their transaction, often without knowing it.

In both situations, compounding the actions of the traders, third parties such as bankers, carriers, and insurers enter the picture. These participants produce three alternative endings for the transaction:

1. A successful conclusion.
2. Failure due to *proper* conduct of the third parties that reveals the errors made by the traders.
3. Failure of the transaction resulting from *improper* conduct of the third parties.

The successful conclusion, result 1, is the natural result of the absence of the other two failures. A failure resulting from errors of the traders, result 2, might be a refusal of the carrier (acting properly) to deliver goods to an intended party due to the seller's mistakes made in creating the shipping contract. The carrier will deliver in accordance with its instructions; incorrect instructions resulting from a lack of understanding of the law of shipping is a problem for the traders, not for the carrier. The third situation reflects the fact that the carrier, banker, or insurer may make mistakes of its own, resulting in improper payment or delivery. These may be corrected with time, effort, or money, but the underlying business relationship of the traders is the first to suffer. As an international businessperson, it is your obligation to understand your rights and liabilities in transportation and logistics contracts, and to ensure you avoid these negative outcomes.

This chapter relies heavily on "learning the law," particularly case law. It is tempting to say that this is the job of lawyers, and while that is true, it is important for international businesspersons to have some familiarity with the operation of the law. Frequently, transportation issues are negotiated or firm price quotations are issued before the lawyer is consulted on the transaction. If this happens (and it shouldn't, but it does), the trader should have a clear understanding of what he or she is getting into.

Logistics and Lex Mercatoria

Questions of logistics and shipment (and payment) are as old as trade itself, and even with the advent of pinpoint navigation of ships and instant electronic funds transfer, the risks of doing business at great distance have not gone away. Ships still sink, damage and theft occurs in transit, currency fluctuates in value, banks fail, and long-distance trust is hard to build and easy to lose. In what may be unbelievable to the modern reader, boarding and piracy remain in full bloom worldwide, with the Straits of Malacca in Southeast Asia[1] being particularly notorious waters.

The early Mediterranean traders of Rome, Greece, and Rhodes knew these risks and were forced to make provision against them for themselves. Trade benefited their kingdoms and empires, but common rules were left to the traders to develop. Such sensibilities also were known in Northern Europe, among the later Hanseatic towns of the Baltic Sea region. The body of rules that emerged from the conduct of merchants was and is known as the "law merchant" or "lex mercatoria."

Such rules were separate from the local law of the homeport states of the trading parties. These rules applied to a limited set of facts (trade) and that trade that was conducted on an international basis. Just as they created their rules, the merchants themselves initially adjudicated their own disputes. This did not represent any particular power held by international traders, but rather the benign neglect of sovereigns, who rarely concerned their crowned heads with the private problems of their citizens, especially those occurring beyond their shores.

For example, the contemporary Law of General Average can trace its roots to ancient Rhodes. When ships from Rhodes found themselves in trouble at sea, the captain's first action was to toss some of the cargo overboard in the hope of staying afloat. The goods of many traders were likely on board, and by convention, all chipped in to cover the loss of

---

[1]Between Malaysia and the island of Sumatra; this is the main sea route linking the Indian Ocean with the Pacific Ocean, and offshore from Singapore, one of the world's busiest ports.

the one trader whose goods had gone over the rail. This customary provision remains in shipping law today, as do many more that share similar roots.

The later great historical traders of the sea-lanes have all left a mark on maritime commercial law. These include the British, Dutch, Italians, Spanish, Portuguese, and, more recently, the Americans. Of these, however, it was England's rise as a sea power, and its dominance over the maritime cargo trade through the 18th and 19th centuries, that produced a legal legacy that remains to this day.

To the extent that Britain did rule the waves, it established the rules regarding cargo carried on British ships and those entering and leaving British-controlled ports. Naturally, this legacy can, therefore, be found not only in international conventions established while Britain's influence was high, but also in the local law of countries that were once British colonies, including the United States and Canada, India, Singapore, Australia, and South Africa. The centuries of experience and jurisprudence of the English courts is still given great deference in many jurisdictions, even those with no connection to Britain.

Even though much of the lex mercatoria has since been absorbed into the local law of trading nations, recall that its roots are the privately created solutions of international traders. This tradition remains vibrant. Privately created rules are unquestionably more flexible and are a faster response to problems created by rapid advances in transportation and communication than any legislature can hope to achieve.

Uniformity of rules is, however, another matter when traders are free to establish them themselves. Accordingly, private organizations of businesspersons have stepped forward in a search for both flexibility and uniformity. Perhaps the most important of these is one introduced in previous chapters, the International Chamber of Commerce, or ICC, based in Paris, France.

The ICC was founded in 1919 and has been granted consultative status at the highest level with the United Nations and its specialized agencies. It is made up of business members and associations from virtually all sectors of the world economy, represented by national committees from over 130 countries. It considers issues across the entire international business spectrum from financial services to marketing ethics and intellectual property, making recommendations to nations and international bodies on policy and law. For traders, whether members or not, it drafts model agreements (such as the model sale contract discussed in the previous chapter), provides dispute resolution services, and establishes conventional terminology and terms of trade.

The ICC is best known for its three wide-ranging successes:

1. INCOTERMS terms of trade (discussed below in this chapter).
2. Documentary credits (an important payment system, discussed in Chapter 9).
3. The ICC Court of Arbitration (one of the subjects of Chapter 13).

Each of these areas of work is dedicated to a search for common ground, to define terms and processes that allow business to be conducted with all parties "singing from the same song sheet." When all parties know the rules that they have agreed to in their contract negotiations, then problem avoidance is maximized and problem solving is minimized.

Terms of Trade and INCOTERMS

Most nations recognize some variety of "terms of trade." These are shorthand references to some of the expected rights and responsibilities in contracts. By incorporating by reference one of these shorthand terms in their contract of sale, the parties are automatically covering well-defined contractual responsibilities. A single term can define responsibilities between the parties for delivery, clearing export and import customs, payment of costs of loading and discharge, risk of loss, and arrangement of insurance.

Traders *must* identify *what* trade terms (by naming the jurisdiction or international organization) they intend to incorporate into their contracts. There is also a strong preference for *not* allowing a default position that will result in national interpretations. The internationally recognized ICC trade terms (INCOTERMS) are sufficiently clear and fair, and access to their meaning is universally open to all traders. Thus, a firm needs only to understand its rights and obligations once, and then it is well prepared to work in any world market, with any customer. An example of explicit and express incorporation is to state "FOB (named port of shipment) INCOTERMS 2000" in the pro forma invoice, making it part of the offer; for example, "FOB New York INCOTERMS 2000." The use of a trade term requires the naming of a place or port (as the case may be), or the term loses all meaning. The reference to 2000 is the current version of INCOTERMS at the time of writing.

Allocations of responsibility using INCOTERMS can be seen as a low-cost form of arbitration in themselves, when the parties, as is rather frequently done, do not understand the full impact of the terms. Of course, this is no substitute for knowing the meaning of the terms and their allocation of responsibilities in the first place.

A few of these terms, such as FOB and CIF, may be familiar to many readers. Unfortunately, familiarity is not enough, and the meaning of these terms can and does vary, leading to differing expectations of sellers and buyers as to the nature of their rights and duties. When problems of differing expectations come before either local courts or arbitrators, the judicial task becomes one of contractual interpretation to determine the intention of the parties as to the allocation of those rights and responsibilities. International businesspersons may even find that lawyers are not as well versed in the impact of these terms as they should be.

Bear in mind that most countries embody confusingly similar or identical trade terms into their own national law, but with their own national interpretation. Beyond being national rules in some jurisdictions, this, of course, is on a state-by-state basis in the United States, given the nature of its Uniform Commercial Code.[2] Traders also should recognize that the UN's Sales Convention (the CISG) makes no provision for defining trade terms. This is not a deficiency of the CISG; rather, it is a strength, for it allows maximum flexibility for traders to make their own choices.

Drafted under the auspices of the International Chamber of Commerce, INCOTERMS (short for International Commercial Terms) have existed since 1936. These terms represent an international common alternative to national definitions. With periodic revisions, they now comprise 13 different terms, fitting different situations, depending on how the parties wish to divide their responsibilities.

When prices for goods are quoted and the offer is accepted, the inclusion of these trade terms represents an allocation of responsibilities by the parties themselves, but they do not represent the whole contract, and there are many more issues that must be settled between the parties. For example, while allocation of risk of loss or damage to the goods is an element of trade terms, the trade term itself does not define the point of transfer of title to the goods. This, among other things, must be defined separately by international businesspersons in their contract of sale.

If there is any need to attempt to modify a recognized trade term, or express some contrary intention, it is a signal that the wrong trade term is being used in the first place, and the correct one should be sought out. Consequently, trade terms must not be used carelessly, or their unintended consequences will become a matter of dispute.

---

[2] A typical example is the California Commercial Code, Sections 2-319 and 2-320, defining FOB and CIF trade terms, respectively.

Before turning to the INCOTERMS themselves, it is useful to understand the critical places associated with the international transfer of goods, for these are vital in the correct selection of trade terms. In practical terms, these points are critical in transportation and logistics contracts for the reason that they represent places where your goods in transit are at greatest risk of loss, damage, or delay.

Critical Points in Transportation and Logistics

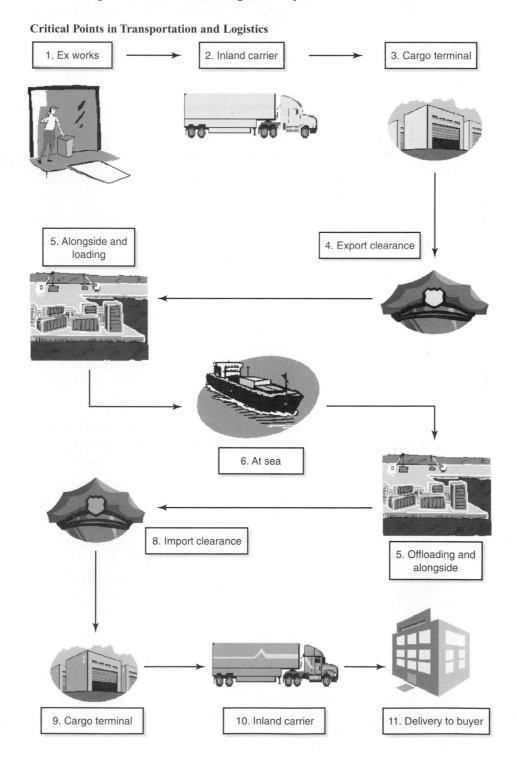

Consequently, INCOTERMS use and require precision in locations. A specification of delivery "alongside ship" means exactly that, and does not include delivery "on board," which involves incurring and paying the cost of loading, as well as bearing the very real risk of damage to the goods in the course of loading.

It is worth emphasizing as well (with frequent reminders) that delivery of the goods and transfer of title are not the same thing. These may well occur at different times, and very often do. Sellers may make express reservations of title in the sales contract (preventing passage of title to the goods), in order to preserve their interest in the goods (and a right to reclaim them) right up to the point where full payment is made, if payment is to follow delivery.

The 13 Trade Terms of INCOTERMS 2000

Term	Required Abbreviation	Qualifier
Ex Works	EXW	Named place
Free Carrier	FCA	Named place
Free Alongside Ship	FAS	Named port of shipment
Free on Board	FOB	Named port of shipment
Cost and Freight	CFR	Named port of destination
Cost, Insurance and Freight	CIF	Named port of destination
Carriage Paid to	CPT	Named place of destination
Carriage and Insurance Paid to	CIP	Named place of destination
Delivered at Frontier	DAF	Named place
Delivered Ex Ship	DES	Named port of destination
Delivered Ex Quay (Duty Paid)	DEQ	Named port of destination
Delivered Duty Unpaid	DDU	Named place of destination
Delivered Duty Paid	DDP	Named place of destination

As one proceeds down this list, INCOTERMS place increasing responsibilities on the seller, and should the seller be willing to accept those responsibilities, the seller must adjust its price accordingly. These are business decisions with respect to price that lead to legal implications in performance. Thus, the buyer's delivery, insurance, and risk preferences must be known to the seller before a firm quotation can be made, or otherwise a set of price quotations must be made. In the case of use of the EXW term, the seller simply makes the goods available to the buyer at the seller's loading dock. At the other end of the spectrum, DDP, the seller can be responsible for all aspects of carriage, insurance, documentation, payment of duty, and delivery, right to the buyer's loading dock.

The terms can be classified, save Ex Works, into "F-Terms," "C-Terms," and "D-Terms." F- and C-Terms are shipment terms and D-Terms are arrival terms, which, with a number of important qualifiers, summarize the seller's responsibility under them.

Also speaking broadly, F-Terms require delivery of the goods to a nominated carrier free of risk and expense to the buyer; the main carriage cost is *unpaid* by the seller. C-Terms require the seller to bear particular costs *past* the point of division where risk of loss and damage to the goods passes to the buyer; the main carriage is *paid* by the seller. D-Terms require specified destination delivery by the seller and payment of *all* carriage to that point. It should be possible for the seller to rule out using some INCOTERMS on this basis alone.

If the seller is new to international trade and lacks the experience to properly price for export, then Ex Works may be the only option; it is also appropriate for those businesses whose products are in such demand that they can entirely offload the logistics responsibility to their customers.

If the seller is unwilling or unable (on either a cost or administrative efficiency basis) to deliver overseas to the buyer's country, then D-Terms can be eliminated from contractual consideration. This is usually the case at opposite ends of the commercial spectrum, where

In domestic industrial trade, FOB is widely used in practice and has a defined domestic meaning under the Uniform Commercial Code. When using INCOTERMS, however, the meaning changes. FOB and FAS only have meaning where there is a ship involved, a vessel for the goods to be "on board" or "alongside," making for proper delivery. In most cases of improper use of these terms—where road, air, or rail are concerned—the parties should have preserved their intention by agreeing on Free Carrier (FCA), meaning delivery to the custody of the carrier.

the smallest firms lack the expertise and financial leverage and the largest do not wish to incur the administrative burden.

As most exporters fall between these extremes, F- and C-Terms will be the most frequently encountered, with the principal question being whether the seller wishes to involve itself (for a price) in the arrangement and payment for carriage. It may be that it is a competitive advantage for the seller to do so, as it can enjoy economies of scale in logistics that its buyers cannot achieve, thus resulting in an attractive landed price for the buyer at its door.

If the seller *cannot* create a competitive advantage either through cost savings or by desiring to make life easier for its customers, then F-Terms (FCA, FAS, FOB) are an appropriate contractual choice for the seller. As between the F-Terms, there is escalating risk and cost to the seller, progressing from mere delivery of the goods to the carrier, to placing them alongside the ship, to loading them across the ship's rail. Again, this is a compensated risk, for each degree means a higher export price to the buyer. They are, however, worthwhile services that the customer is often willing to pay for within the price, as these steps are generally easier for the seller to arrange than the buyer.

C-Terms (CFR, CIF, CPT, CIP) are in order where the seller feels that making arrangements and paying for shipping *are* a competitive service advantage. Then the seller must consider whether it also wishes to arrange insurance for the voyage, either for reasons of control (sufficiency, breadth of coverage) or cost advantage. If so, then CIF or CIP is appropriate, while C-Terms avoiding insurance responsibilities are represented by CFR and CPT. The final determinant is whether it is more appropriate for the seller to end its delivery responsibility upon turning the goods over to the carrier or only when the goods go over the ship's rail in the course of loading. The buyer will have an opinion on this, one way or the other, or it may be impossible for the seller to exercise control over the goods at any time after handing over the goods to the carrier. CIF and CFR delivery responsibilities (and hence risk of loss or damage) end over the ship's rail, while CIP and CPT risks end with delivery to the carrier's premises. It is worth underscoring the potential for confusion for the buyer in C-Terms. C-Terms name a port of arrival as the point to which carriage is paid; buyers often mistake this as the point where risk will be transferred, but they are wrong. The risk will have been transferred long before, on delivery to the carrier's premises (CIP and CPT) or over the ship's rail (CIF and CFR).

The seller's decision making within C-Terms can be displayed as follows:

	Seller's Delivery at Carrier's Premises (end of delivery and risk responsibility)	Seller's Delivery over Ship's Rail (end of delivery and risk responsibility)
Seller arranges and pays insurance	CIP	CIF
Buyer arranges and pays insurance	CPT	CFR

Note that CIF and CFR may only be used for sea transport, whereas CIP and CPT may be used for any form of transport. In trade usage, CFR is frequently written, incorrectly, as C&F.

There is no substitute for consulting the authoritative works of the ICC on the provision of INCOTERMS. International businesspersons must ensure that they and their attorneys are working from the most current set, which can be reviewed and purchased from the ICC website.[3]

INCOTERMS Provisions

INCOTERMS 2000 Summary

EXW

Ex Works (. . . named place)

"Ex works" means that the seller delivers when he places the goods at the disposal of the buyer at the seller's premises or another named place (i.e. works, factory, warehouse, etc.) not cleared for export and not loaded on any collecting vehicle.

This term thus represents the minimum obligation for the seller, and the buyer has to bear all costs and risks involved in taking the goods from the seller's premises.

However, if the parties wish the seller to be responsible for the loading of the goods on departure and to bear the risks and all the costs of such loading, this should be made clear by adding explicit wording to this effect in the contract of sale. This term should not be used when the buyer cannot carry out the export formalities directly or indirectly. In such circumstances, the FCA term should be used, provided the seller agrees that he will load at his cost and risk.

FCA

Free Carrier (. . . named place)

"Free Carrier" means that the seller delivers the goods, cleared for export, to the carrier nominated by the buyer at the named place. It should be noted that the chosen place of delivery has an impact on the obligations of loading and unloading the goods at that place. If delivery occurs at the seller's premises, the seller is responsible for loading. If delivery occurs at any other place, the seller is not responsible for unloading.

This term may be used irrespective of the mode of transport, including multimodal transport.

"Carrier" means any person who, in a contract of carriage, undertakes to perform or to procure the performance of transport by rail, road, air, sea, inland waterway or by a combination of such modes.

If the buyer nominates a person other than a carrier to receive the goods, the seller is deemed to have fulfilled his obligation to deliver the goods when they are delivered to that person.

FAS

Free Alongside Ship (. . . named port of shipment)

"Free Alongside Ship" means that the seller delivers when the goods are placed alongside the vessel at the named port of shipment. This means that the buyer has to bear all costs and risks of loss of or damage to the goods from that moment.

The FAS term requires the seller to clear the goods for export.

[3]www.iccwbo.org.

THIS IS A REVERSAL FROM PREVIOUS INCOTERMS VERSIONS WHICH RE-QUIRED THE BUYER TO ARRANGE FOR EXPORT CLEARANCE.

However, if the parties wish the buyer to clear the goods for export, this should be made clear by adding explicit wording to this effect in the contract of sale.

This term can be used only for sea or inland waterway transport.

FOB

Free on Board (. . . named port of shipment)

"Free on Board" means that the seller delivers when the goods pass the ship's rail at the named port of shipment. This means that the buyer has to bear all costs and risks of loss of or damage to the goods from that point. The FOB term requires the seller to clear the goods for export. This term can be used only for sea or inland waterway transport. If the parties do not intend to deliver the goods across the ship's rail, the FCA term should be used.

CFR

Cost and Freight (. . . named port of destination)

"Cost and Freight" means that the seller delivers when the goods pass the ship's rail in the port of shipment. The seller must pay the costs and freight necessary to bring the goods to the named port of destination BUT the risk of loss of or damage to the goods, as well as any additional costs due to events occurring after the time of delivery, are transferred from the seller to the buyer.

The CFR term requires the seller to clear the goods for export.

This term can be used only for sea and inland waterway transport. If the parties do not intend to deliver the goods across the ship's rail, the CPT term should be used.

CIF

Cost, Insurance, and Freight (. . . named port of destination)

"Cost, Insurance and Freight" means that the seller delivers when the goods pass the ship's rail in the port of shipment.

The seller must pay the costs and freight necessary to bring the goods to the named port of destination BUT the risk of loss of or damage to the goods, as well as any additional costs due to events occurring after the time of delivery, are transferred from the seller to the buyer. However, in CIF the seller also has to procure marine insurance against the buyer's risk of loss of or damage to the goods during the carriage.

Consequently, the seller contracts for insurance and pays the insurance premium. The buyer should note that under the CIF term the seller is required to obtain insurance only on minimum cover. Should the buyer wish to have the protection of greater cover, he would either need to agree as much expressly with the seller or to make his own extra insurance arrangements.

The CIF term requires the seller to clear the goods for export.

This term can be used only for sea and inland waterway transport. If the parties do not intend to deliver the goods across the ship's rail, the CIP term should be used.

CPT

Carriage Paid to (. . . named place of destination)

"Carriage paid to . . ." means that the seller delivers the goods to the carrier nominated by him but the seller must in addition pay the cost of carriage necessary to bring the goods to the named destination. This means that the buyer bears all risks and any other costs occurring after the goods have been so delivered.

"Carrier" means any person who, in a contract of carriage, undertakes to perform or to procure the performance of transport, by rail, road, air, sea, inland waterway or by a combination of such modes.

If subsequent carriers are used for the carriage to the agreed destination, the risk passes when the goods have been delivered to the first carrier.

The CPT term requires the seller to clear the goods for export.

This term may be used irrespective of the mode of transport including multimodal transport.

CIP

Carriage and Insurance Paid to (. . . named place of destination)

"Carriage and Insurance paid to . . ." means that the seller delivers the goods to the carrier nominated by him but the seller must in addition pay the cost of carriage necessary to bring the goods to the named destination. This means that the buyer bears all risks and any additional costs occurring after the goods have been so delivered. However, in CIP the seller also has to procure insurance against the buyer's risk of loss of or damage to the goods during the carriage.

Consequently, the seller contracts for insurance and pays the insurance premium.

The buyer should note that under the CIP term the seller is required to obtain insurance only on minimum cover. Should the buyer wish to have the protection of greater cover, he would either need to agree as much expressly with the seller or to make his own extra insurance arrangements.

"Carrier" means any person who, in a contract of carriage, undertakes to perform or to procure the performance of transport, by rail, road, air, sea, inland waterway or by a combination of such modes.

If subsequent carriers are used for the carriage to the agreed destination, the risk passes when the goods have been delivered to the first carrier.

The CIP term requires the seller to clear the goods for export.

This term may be used irrespective of the mode of transport including multimodal transport.

DAF

Delivered at Frontier (. . . named place)

"Delivered at Frontier" means that the seller delivers when the goods are placed at the disposal of the buyer on the arriving means of transport not unloaded, cleared for export, but not cleared for import at the named point and place at the frontier, but before the customs border of the adjoining country. The term "frontier" may be used for any frontier including that of the country of export. Therefore, it is of vital importance that the frontier in question be defined precisely by always naming the point and place in the term.

However, if the parties wish the seller to be responsible for the unloading of the goods from the arriving means of transport and to bear the risks and costs of unloading, this should be made clear by adding explicit wording to this effect in the contract of sale.

This term may be used irrespective of the mode of transport when goods are to be delivered at a land frontier. When delivery is to take place in the port of destination, on board a vessel or on the quay (wharf), the DES or DEQ terms should be used.

DES

Delivered Ex Ship (. . . named port of destination)

"Delivered Ex Ship" means that the seller delivers when the goods are placed at the disposal of the buyer on board the ship not cleared for import at the named port of destination. The seller has to bear all the costs and risks involved in bringing the goods to the named port of destination before discharging. If the parties wish the seller to bear the costs and risks of discharging the goods, then the DEQ term should be used.

This term can be used only when the goods are to be delivered by sea or inland waterway or multimodal transport on a vessel in the port of destination.

DEQ

Delivered Ex Quay (. . . named port of destination)

"Delivered Ex Quay" means that the seller delivers when the goods are placed at the disposal of the buyer, not cleared for import on the quay (wharf) at the named port of destination. The seller has to bear costs and risks involved in bringing the goods to the named port of destination and discharging the goods on the quay (wharf). The DEQ term requires the buyer to clear the goods for import and to pay for all formalities, duties, taxes and other charges upon import.

THIS IS A REVERSAL FROM PREVIOUS INCOTERMS VERSIONS WHICH REQUIRED THE SELLER TO ARRANGE FOR IMPORT CLEARANCE.

If the parties wish to include in the seller's obligations all or part of the costs payable upon import of the goods, this should be made clear by adding explicit wording to this effect in the contract of sale.

This term can be used only when the goods are to be delivered by sea or inland waterway or multimodal transport on discharge from a vessel onto the quay (wharf) in the port of destination. However, if the parties wish to include in the seller's obligations the risks and costs of the handling of the goods from the quay to another place (warehouse, terminal, transport station, etc.) in or outside the port, the DDU or DDP terms should be used.

DDU

Delivered Duty Unpaid (. . . named place of destination)

"Delivered duty unpaid" means that the seller delivers the goods to the buyer, not cleared for import, and not unloaded from any arriving means of transport at the named place of destination. The seller has to bear the costs and risks involved in bringing the goods thereto, other than, where applicable, any "duty" (which term includes the responsibility for and the risks of the carrying out of customs formalities, and the payment of formalities, customs duties, taxes and other charges) for import in the country of destination. Such "duty" has to be borne by the buyer as well as any costs and risks caused by his failure to clear the goods for import in time.

However, if the parties wish the seller to carry out customs formalities and bear the costs and risks resulting therefrom, as well as some of the costs payable upon import of the goods, this should be made clear by adding explicit wording to this effect in the contract of sale.

This term may be used irrespective of the mode of transport but when delivery is to take place in the port of destination on board the vessel or on the quay (wharf), the DES or DEQ terms should be used.

DDP

Delivered Duty Paid (. . . named place of destination)

"Delivered duty paid" means that the seller delivers the goods to the buyer, cleared for import, and not unloaded from any arriving means of transport at the named place of destination. The seller has to bear all the costs and risks involved in bringing the goods thereto, including, where applicable, any "duty" (which term includes the responsibility for and the risk of the carrying out of customs formalities and the payment of formalities, customs duties, taxes and other charges) for import in the country of destination.

Whilst the EXW term represents the minimum obligation for the seller, DDP represents the maximum obligation.

This term should not be used if the seller is unable directly or indirectly to obtain the import license.

However, if the parties wish to exclude from the seller's obligations some of the costs payable upon import of the goods (such as value-added tax: VAT), this should be made clear by adding explicit wording to this effect in the contract of sale.

If the parties wish the buyer to bear all risks and costs of the import, the DDU term should be used.

This term may be used irrespective of the mode of transport, but when delivery is to take place in the port of destination on board the vessel or on the quay (wharf), the DES or DEQ terms should be used.

Source: International Chamber of Commerce Publication #560. Reproduced with kind permission. These summaries do not replace the authoritative text and greater detail found in Publication #560.

The table on page 355 illustrates the critical places in a transaction and the effect of each INCOTERM in a typical transaction, involving carriage by an independent inland carrier and warehousing at an independent cargo terminal, pending the handover of the goods to a maritime carrier, with the process reversed on arrival.

INCOTERMS and Issues of Risk and Title

Experience shows that traders often confuse making and taking delivery of the goods, and consequential shift in risk of loss or damage, with the transfer of title to the goods. The answer is that INCOTERMS do not determine the transfer of title to the goods; they simply specify where delivery takes place. Once the seller makes delivery in accordance with the term, all further risks and expenses not included in the term become the responsibility of the buyer, but this should not be equated with transfer of title. Recall that the CISG also has provisions for the passage of risk,[4] and these are entirely compatible with INCOTERMS, but neither do they affect passage of title.

On reflection, it should be clear to traders that defining passage of risk need not be synonymous with passage of ownership and title. The INCOTERMS define a division of costs and risks of damage and delay. It is the parties who have the freedom and responsibility to set the time, place, and conditions of transfer of title in their contract. Indeed, the seller may wish to transfer title only when paid in full (a retention of title clause in the sale contract), or the buyer may wish to resell good title to the goods at some point before delivery.

[4]CISG, Chapter IV, Articles 66 through 70. Article 67(1) provides: "If the seller is bound to hand the goods over to a carrier at a particular place, the risk does not pass to the buyer until the goods are handed over to the carrier at that place."

	STAGE / TERM	EXW	FCA	FAS	FOB	CFR	CIF	CPT	CIP	DAF	DES	DEQ	DDU	DDP
1	Goods available on the factory platform	X												
2	Inland carrier loading													
3	Goods into custody of inland carrier													
4	Transport to cargo terminal													
5	Terminal charges													
6	Documentation and export clearance									X2				
7	Into custody of maritime carrier		X1					X	X					
8	Goods alongside ship			X										
9	Arrange and pay loading													
10	Goods over ship's rail				X	X	X							
11	Arrange and pay maritime carriage													
12	Arrange and pay maritime insurance													
	Arrival of ship in port of destination										X		X	
13	Arrange and pay unloading					●	●	●	●					
14	Goods alongside ship											X		
15	Documentation and import clearance													
16	Payment of duty													
17	Arrival into cargo terminal													
18	Cargo terminal charges													
19	Inland transport to buyer's premises													X3
20	Offloading at buyer's premises													

Responsibility of:				
Seller		●	Seller arranges and pays if included as part of its contract with carrier	
Buyer		X	Seller's risk of loss or damage to the goods ends with this point, unless otherwise provided for in the sale contract (retention of title clause)	

Notes

X1: Under FCA, the seller's responsibility, by agreement, may end at delivery of the goods to custody of the first inland carrier (stage 3). In such case, the seller will still remain responsible for export documentation and clearance (stage 6).

X2: Delivered at Frontier, DAF, is shown in this case as delivered only to the seller's frontier. While it may be used with any mode of transport, it is primarily confined to road or rail transport between adjoining countries. For maritime transport, it also may arise where the seaport of destination is *not* in the buyer's country, but an adjoining one, and thus the seller would be responsible for cost, risk, and delivery to a point before the inland frontier of the buyer's country. For example, goods shipped from New York as DAF, Basel, Switzerland INCOTERMS 2000, may be carried by sea to Hamburg, Germany, with the seller responsible for all aspects of carriage including road transport across Germany and through transit export clearance on the German–Swiss frontier.

X3: The example shown indicates that the seller has agreed to deliver to the buyer's premises.

The trial and appeal reports of the following case illustrate the type of problems that arise when a full understanding of INCOTERMS (and trade terms, generally) is lacking. On appeal, the judgment was affirmed for "substantially similar reasons," the significance of which will be seen below.

Here, a German seller wishes to avoid responsibility in a CIF contract for a magnetic resonance imaging (MRI) machine that arrived in the United States in damaged condition. The contract specifies CIF but fails to invoke the INCOTERMS interpretation. Nevertheless, the court accepts the INCOTERMS interpretation based on the totality of custom, the governing CISG, and German law. The parties authored their own difficulty through this failure to specify a basis of interpretation (such as CIF New York INCOTERMS 1990 [the version then in force]), obliging the court to work through the interpretive exercise.

Somewhat horrifyingly, the plaintiff's own complaint stated that the MRI was loaded undamaged, and in good working order, aboard ship in the port of Antwerp, in the Netherlands. As CIF passes risk of damage from seller to buyer once the goods go over the ship's rail, this is ultimately fatal to the plaintiff's claim.

The trial court (correctly) concludes that the INCOTERMS interpretation of CIF must apply, which should mean that passing the ship's rail is the defining point for transfer of risk. The court then (incorrectly) proceeds *in the same paragraph* to back up the point of transfer of risk to the buyer to the seller's delivery at the port of shipment. Presumably this is based on the court's reading of the CISG, and the seller's contention that this is the meaning of CIF. This confusion appears to be the substance of the appeal; such a conclusion ignores the possibility that the goods were damaged between delivery to Antwerp and the time that the goods went over the ship's rail, a period in which the risk still belonged to the seller. Despite the momentary hope this would offer to the plaintiff in launching its appeal, it is sunk by its own assertion that the goods were loaded aboard without damage.

The plaintiff's alternate line of argument at trial was to suggest that delayed transfer of title also delayed transfer of risk, but this was fully (and properly) answered by a reasonable reading of the CISG, INCOTERMS, and German law, each of which fails to support such a conclusion.

St. Paul Guardian Insurance Company v. Neuromed Medical Systems & Support—Trial

United States District Court for the Southern District of New York
March 26, 2002
Opinion by: Sidney H. Stein, U.S. District Judge.

Plaintiffs St. Paul Guardian Insurance Company and Travelers Property Casualty Insurance Company have brought this action as subrogrees [*sic*] of Shared Imaging, Inc., to recover $285,000 they paid to Shared Imaging for damage to a mobile magnetic resonance imaging system ("MRI") purchased by Shared Imaging from defendant Neuromed Medical Systems & Support GmbH ("Neuromed").

[*For purposes of this case presentation, Plaintiffs St. Paul Guardian Insurance Company and Travelers Property Casualty Insurance Company and their subrogor Shared Imaging Inc. are hereinafter collectively referred to as* [buyer]; *Defendant Neuromed Medical Systems & Support GmbH ("Neuromed") is referred to as* [seller].]

[Seller] has moved to dismiss the complaint on two grounds, namely that (1) the forum selection clause of the underlying contract requires the litigation to take place in Germany and (2) pursuant to Fed. R. Civ. P. 12(b)(6), the complaint fails to state a claim for relief.

In an Order dated December 3, 2001, this Court first found that the contractual forum selection clause did not mandate that the action proceed in Germany and second, held the rest of the motion in abeyance pending submissions by the parties on German law, which, pursuant to the underlying contract, is the applicable law. The parties have now submitted affidavits from German legal experts.

The crux of [seller's] argument is that it had no further obligations regarding the risk of loss once it delivered the MRI to the vessel at the port of shipment due to a "CIF" clause included in the underlying contract. [Buyer] respond[s] that (1) the generally understood definition of the "CIF" term as defined by the International Chamber of Commerce's publication, Incoterms 1990, is inapplicable here and (2) the "CIF" term was effectively superceded by other contract terms such that the risk of loss remained on [seller].

Pursuant to the applicable German law—the UN Convention on Contracts for the International Sale of Goods—the "CIF" term in the contract operated to pass the risk of loss to [buyer] at the port of shipment, at which time, the parties agree, the MRI was undamaged and in good working order. Accordingly, [seller's] motion to dismiss the complaint should be granted and the complaint dismissed.

Background

[Buyer], an American corporation, and [seller], a German corporation, entered into a contract of sale for a Siemens Harmony 1.0 Tesla mobile MRI. Thereafter, both parties engaged various entities to transport, insure and provide customs entry service for the MRI. [Buyer] originally named those entities as defendants, but the action has been discontinued against them by agreement of the parties. [Seller] is the sole remaining defendant.

According to the complaint, the MRI was loaded aboard the vessel "Atlantic Carrier" undamaged and in good working order. When it reached its destination of [Calumet] City, Illinois, it had been damaged and was in need of extensive repair, which led [buyer] to conclude that the MRI had been damaged in transit.

The one page contract of sale contains nine headings, including: "Product;" "Delivery Terms;" "Payment Terms;" "Disclaimer;" and "Applicable Law." Under "Product" the contract provides, the "system will be delivered cold and fully functional." Under "Delivery Terms" it provides, "CIF New York Seaport, the buyer will arrange and pay for customs clearance as well as transport to Calmut City."

Under "Payment Terms" it states, "By money transfer to one of our accounts, with following payment terms: US $93,000—down payment to secure the system; US $744,000—prior to shipping; US $93,000—upon acceptance by Siemens of the MRI system within 3 business days after arrival in Calmut City." In addition, under "Disclaimer" it states, "system including all accessories and options remain the property of [seller] till complete payment has been received." Preceding this clause is a handwritten note, allegedly initialed by Raymond Stachowiak of [buyer], stating, "Acceptance subject to Inspection."

Discussion

[Seller] contends that because the delivery terms were "CIF New York Seaport," its contractual obligation, with regard to risk of loss or damage, ended when it delivered the MRI to the vessel at the port of shipment and therefore the action must be dismissed because [buyer] ha[s] failed to state a claim for which relief can be granted. [Buyer] respond[s] that the generally accepted definition of the "CIF" term as defined in Incoterms 1990, is inapplicable. Moreover, [buyer] suggest[s] that other provisions of the contract are inconsistent with the "CIF" term because [seller], pursuant to the contract, retained title subsequent to delivery to the vessel at the port of shipment and thus, [buyer] manifestly retained the risk of loss.

A. Legal Standards

In reviewing a motion to dismiss pursuant to Fed. R. Civ. P. 12(b)(6), a district court's role is to assess the legal feasibility of the complaint; it is not to weigh the evidence which might be offered at trial. A motion to dismiss should not be granted unless "it appears beyond doubt that the plaintiff [the buyer in the instant case] can prove no set of facts in support of the claim which would entitle him to relief."

B. Applicable Law

1. Rule 44.1

Pursuant to Fed. R. Civ. P. 44.1, determinations of foreign law are questions of law. The Court "may consider any relevant material or source" to determine foreign law, whether or not submitted by a party or admissible under the Federal Rules of Evidence." Fed. R. Civ. P. 44.1. In short, under Rule 44.1, the court may "consider any material that is relevant to a foreign law issue, whether submitted by counsel or unearthed by the court's own research."

The parties have each submitted relevant opinions of German legal experts (Werkmeister *Op.;* Strube *Op.;* Werkmeister Reply *Op.*) and the Court has independently researched the applicable foreign law. On the basis of those submissions and analysis, the Court finds the expert opinion of Karl-Ulrich Werkmeister for the [seller] to be an accurate statement of German law.

2. Applicable German Law

The parties concede that pursuant to German law, the UN Convention on Contracts for the International Sale of Goods ("CISG") governs this transaction because (1) both the U.S. and Germany are Contracting States to that Convention, and (2) neither party chose, by express provision in the contract, to opt out of the application of the CISG. (Strube *Op.* at 2; Werkmeister *Op.* at 2.); *See* CISG, art. 1(1)(a), reprinted in 15 U.S.C.A. App.; Larry A. DiMatteo, The Law of International Contracting, 206 (2000) (hereinafter Contracting).

The CISG aims to bring uniformity to international business transactions, using simple, non–nation specific language. To that end, it is comprised of rules applicable to the conclusion of contracts of sale of international goods. In its application regard is to be paid to comity and interpretations grounded in its underlying principles rather than in specific national conventions. *See* CISG art. 7(1), (2); *see* also *Delchi Carrier S.p.A. v. Rotorex Corp.,* 71 F.3d 1024, 1028 (2d Cir. 1995) [<http://cisgw3.law.pace.edu/cases/951206u1.html>].

Germany has been a Contracting State since 1991, and the CISG is an integral part of German law. Where parties, as here, designate a choice of law clause in their contract—selecting the law of a Contracting State without expressly excluding application of the CISG—German courts uphold application of the Convention as the law of the designated Contracting state. To hold otherwise would undermine the objectives of the Convention which Germany has agreed to uphold.

C. CISG, INCOTERMS and "CIF"

"CIF," which stands for "cost, insurance and freight," is a commercial trade term that is defined in Incoterms 1990, published by the International Chamber of Commerce ("ICC"). The aim of INCOTERMS, which stands for international commercial terms, is "to provide a set of international rules for the interpretation of the most commonly used trade terms in foreign trade." (Werkmeister *Op.* Ex. Incoterms 1990, at 106.) These "trade terms are used to allocate the costs of freight and insurance" in addition to designating the point in time when the risk of loss passes to the purchaser. DiMatteo, *supra,* Contracting at 188. INCOTERMS are incorporated into the CISG through Article 9(2) which provides that,

> "The parties are considered, unless otherwise agreed, to have impliedly made applicable to their contract or its formation a usage of which the parties knew or ought to have known

and which in international trade is widely known to, and regularly observed by, parties to contracts of the type involved in the particular trade concerned." CISG, art. 9(2), reprinted in 15 U.S.C.A. App.

At the time the contract was entered into, Incoterms 1990 was applicable. (Werkmeister Reply at 2). INCOTERMS define "CIF" (named port of destination) to mean the seller delivers when the goods pass "the ship's rail in the port of shipment." (Werkmeister *Op.* Ex. Incoterms 1990 at 152.) The seller is responsible for paying the cost, freight and insurance coverage necessary to bring the goods to the named port of destination, but the risk of loss or damage to the goods passes from seller to buyer upon delivery to the port of shipment. Further, "CIF" requires the seller to obtain insurance only on minimum cover.

[Buyer's] legal expert contends that INCOTERMS are inapplicable here because the contract fails to specifically incorporate them. (Strube *Op.* at 9.) Nonetheless, he cites and acknowledges that the German Supreme Court (*Bundesgerichtshof* [BGH])—the court of last resort in the Federal Republic of Germany for civil matters—concluded that a clause "fob" without specific reference to INCOTERMS was to be interpreted according to INCOTERMS "simply because the [INCOTERMS] include a clause 'fob'."

Conceding that commercial practice attains the force of law under section 346 of the German Commercial Code (Handelsgesetzbuch [HGB]), [buyer's] expert concludes that the opinion of the BGH "amounts to saying that the [INCOTERMS] definitions in Germany have the force of law as trade custom." As encapsulated by [seller's] legal expert, "It is accepted under German law that in case a contract refers to CIF-delivery, the parties refer to the INCOTERMS rules. . . ." (Werkmeister *Op.* at 7.)

The use of the "CIF" term in the contract demonstrates that the parties "agreed to the detailed oriented [INCOTERMS] in order to enhance the Convention." Thus, pursuant to CISG art. 9(2), INCOTERMS definitions should be applied to the contract despite the lack of an explicit INCOTERMS reference in the contract.

D. INCOTERMS, the CISG, and the Passage of Risk of Loss and Title

[Buyer] argue[s] that [seller's] explicit retention of title in the contract to the MRI machine modified the "CIF" term, such that [seller] retained title and assumed the risk of loss. INCOTERMS, however, only address passage of risk, not transfer of title. Under the CISG, the passage of risk is likewise independent of the transfer of title. See CISG art. 67(1). [Buyer's] legal expert mistakenly asserts that the moment of "passing of risk" has not been defined in the CISG. (Strube *Op.* at 4.) Chapter IV of that Convention, entitled "Passing of Risk," explicitly defines the time at which risk passes from seller to buyer pursuant to Article 67(1),

> "If the contract of sale involves carriage of the goods and seller is not bound to hand them over at a particular place, the risk passes to the buyer when the goods are handed over to the first carrier for transmission to the buyer in accordance with the contract of sale. If the seller is bound to hand the goods over to a carrier at a particular place, the risk does not pass to the buyer until the goods are handed over to the carrier at that place." CISG, art 67(1), reprinted in 15 U.S.C.A. App.

Pursuant to the CISG, the risk passes without taking into account who owns the goods. The passing of ownership is not regulated by the CISG according to art. 4(b). Article 4(b) provides that the Convention is not concerned with "the effect which the contract may have on the property in the goods sold." CISG art. 4(b). Moreover, according to Article 67(1), the passage of risk and transfer of title need not occur at the same time, as the seller's retention of "documents controlling the disposition of the goods does not affect the passage of risk." CISG art. 67(1).

Had the CISG been silent, as [buyer's] expert claimed, the Court would have been required to turn to German law as a "gap filler." (Werkmeister *Op.* at 2; Strube *Op.* at 4.) There again, [buyer's] assertions falter. German law also recognizes passage of risk and transfer of title as two independent legal acts. (Werkmeister Reply *Op.* at 3.) In fact, it is standard "practice under German law to agree that the transfer of title will only occur upon payment of the entire purchase price, well after the date of passing of risk and after receipt of the goods by the buyer." Support for this proposition of German law is cited by both experts. They each refer to section 447 of the German Civil Code (*Bürgerliches Gesetzbuch* [BGB]), a provision dealing with long distance sales, providing in part—as translated by [buyer's] expert—that "the risk of loss passes to the buyer at the moment when the seller has handed the matter to the forwarder, the carrier or to the otherwise determined person or institution for the transport." (Strube *Op.* at 5; see also Werkmeister *Op.* at 7.)

Accordingly, pursuant to INCOTERMS, the CISG, and specific German law, [seller's] retention of title did not thereby implicate retention of the risk of loss or damage.

E. The Contract Terms

[Buyer] next contend[s] that even if the "CIF" term did not mandate that title and risk of loss pass together, the other terms in the contract are evidence that the parties' intention to supercede and replace the "CIF" term such that [seller] retained title and the risk of loss. That is incorrect.

1. "Delivery Terms"

Citing the "Delivery Terms" clause in the contract, [buyer] posit[s] that had the parties intended to abide by the strictures of INCOTERMS there would have been no need to define the buyer's obligations to pay customs and arrange further transport. (Strube *Op.* at 13 P 2.23(a–b).) [Buyer's] argument, however, is undermined by Incoterms 1990, which provides that "it is normally desirable that customs clearance is arranged by the party domiciled in the country where such clearance should take place." (*See* Werkmeister *Op.* Ex. Incoterms 1990 at 109.) The "CIF" term as defined by INCOTERMS only requires the seller to "clear the goods for export" and is silent as to which party bears the obligation to arrange for customs clearance. (*Id.* at 151.) The parties are therefore left to negotiate these obligations. As such, a clause defining the terms of customs clearance neither alters nor affects the "CIF" clause in the contract.

2. "Payment Terms"

[Buyer] also cite[s] to the "Payment Terms" clause of the contract, which specified that final payment was not to be made upon seller's delivery of the machine to the port of shipment, but rather, upon buyer's acceptance of the machine in Calumet City. These terms speak to the final disposition of the property, not to the risk for loss or damage. INCOTERMS do not mandate a payment structure, but rather simply establish that the buyer bears an obligation to "pay the price as provided in the contract of sale." Inclusion of the terms of payment in the contract does not modify the "CIF" clause.

3. The Handwritten Note

Finally, [buyer] emphasize[s] the handwritten note, "Acceptance upon inspection." Based upon its placement within the contract and express terms, the note must serve to qualify the final clauses of the "Payment Terms," obliging buyer to effect final payment upon acceptance of the machine. As [seller's] expert correctly depicts, "A reasonable recipient, acting in good faith, would understand that the buyer wanted to make sure that receipt of the good should not be construed as the acceptance of the buyer that the good is free of defects of design or workmanship and that the good is performing as specified. This addition does not relate to the place of delivery." (Werkmeister Reply *Op.* at 3.) Accordingly, despite [buyer's] arguments to the contrary, the handwritten note does not modify the "CIF" clause; it instead serves to qualify the terms of the transfer of title.

The terms of the contract do not modify the "CIF" clause in the contract such that the risk of loss remained with [seller]. The fact remains that the CISG, INCOTERMS, and German law all distinguish between the passage of the risk of loss and the transfer of title. Thus, because (1) [seller's] risk of loss of, or damage to, the MRI machine under the contract passed to [buyer] upon delivery of the machine to the carrier at the port of shipment and (2) it is undisputed that the MRI machine was delivered to the carrier undamaged and in good working order, [seller's] motion to dismiss for failure to state a claim is hereby granted.

Conclusion

For the foregoing reasons, [seller's] motion to dismiss for failure to state a claim is granted and the complaint is dismissed.

Source: Indexed as 00 Civ. 934 (SHS), available at http://www.cisg.law.pace.edu/cases/020326u1. html.

Note court's error in the final paragraph above the "Conclusion." While the result of the case would be the same, transfer of risk in CIF contracts occurs when the goods pass the ship's rail, not when they are delivered to the carrier. Many bad things can happen to goods between these two very distinct points in time. This explains why the appeal court, whose reasons appear below, affirms the dismissal of the complaint "for *substantially* the reasons set forth in the district court's opinion."

St. Paul Guardian Insurance Company v. Neuromed Medical Systems & Support—Appeal

United States Court of Appeals for the Second District

The Court, unanimous:

UPON DUE CONSIDERATION, IT IS HEREBY ORDERED, ADJUDGED, AND DECREED that the judgment of the district court be, and it hereby is, affirmed.

The plaintiffs appeal from an April 2, 2002, judgment granting the defendant's Rule 12(b)(6) motion to dismiss their complaint claiming breach of contract and negligence. Fed. R. Civ. P. 12(b)(6). The subject of the dispute is a mobile magnetic resonance imaging ("MRI") system, which was damaged due to cold weather after the defendant delivered it to the port of shipment in Antwerp. Applying German law under the contract's choice-of-law provision, the district court concluded that the contract's risk-of-loss provision precluded recovery by the plaintiffs. The court also concluded that the contract's "CIF" term relieved the defendant of responsibility for damage that occurred after the MRI system passed the ship's rail at the port of shipment, at which point the MRI was fully functional, according to the complaint. For substantially the reasons set forth in the district court's opinion, we affirm the dismissal of the complaint.

The defendant cross-appeals from the district court's denial of its alternative ground for dismissal under Rule 12(b)(6): that the contract at issue required this dispute to be brought in the court of justice in Castrop-Rauxel, Germany. The defendant agreed at oral argument, however, that we need reach its cross-appeal only if we reverse the district court's dismissal of the complaint on the basis of the risk-of-loss provision. Since we agree with the district court on that issue, we need not and do not reach the arguments raised by the defendant in the cross-appeal.

For the foregoing reasons, the judgment of the district court is hereby AFFIRMED.

Source: 2002 U.S. App. LEXIS 26787 (2d Cir. 2002). Summary Orders are expedient dispositions issued by U.S. Courts of Appeals where the judgment is unanimous and all judges believe that no jurisprudential purpose would be served by a written opinion. Summary Orders are not published in the Federal Reporter and may not be cited as precedent.

Comments on the substantive issues of this case appear in the introduction to it and in the text above, but they do not address the primary tactical approach of the buyer's insurer. The tactical approach for the buyer's insurer is to claim that title and risk had not passed; thus, the problem belongs to the seller, as well as the responsibility to reimburse the subrogated insurer. Had that been established, the case would have ended quite neatly for the insurer; as no real evidence of how the damage occurred, or by whom, this would become the seller's problem to seek out and prove. As a result of its failure to avoid transfer of risk, the buyer's insurer must now prove a case in damages against the carrier and/or its agents, which will be distinctly more difficult, as shall be seen. The involvement and liability of a carrier is therefore the subject of the next section.

Carriage of Goods by Sea

Rules between the individual parties to a shipping contract, the carrier versus the "cargo interest" (persons having an insurable interest in the cargo), must be seen in the light of their relative bargaining power. Carriers (sea, air, road, and rail) have always held a great deal of bargaining power, compared to their clients. In fact, any shipper that can match their bargaining power (by having a continuously large quantity of goods to ship) might well think about managing or owning its own shipping business on an in-house basis. It should come as no surprise, therefore, that shipping contracts have been (and, in many respects, continue to be) quite one-sided contracts in favor of the carrier.

On the other hand, this one-sided nature is not without a counterbalance. The carrier of the goods has no first-hand knowledge of what is in the boxes being shipped. For all it knows, save for weighing the boxes, the boxes could be empty or contain something very different than what is claimed by the shipper.

In the majority of cases of smaller export sellers, where the seller must arrange carriage, it will do so through a freight forwarder. A freight forwarder is a specialist in determining availability and timing of shipping space, price quotations for carriage and insurance, and bookings for both. A freight forwarder is usually ready to assist, for a fee, with export formalities and preparation of required export documentation.

Following are some terms to assist with understanding this text and in future dealing with attorneys and the shipping industry:

Bill of lading is a document issued by a carrier, among other things, evidencing a contract of carriage.

Booking note is the contract of carriage. Booking note terms supercede any terms contained in the bill of lading to the extent they conflict.

Carrier is a general term, refined at law to **common carrier,** where a person or corporation is in the business of carrying goods for any member of the public that chooses to engage its services. In this text, reference to a carrier refers to a common carrier, unless otherwise specified.

Contract of carriage is a contract between the shipper and the carrier for carriage of a cargo. It is separate from the contract of sale that exists between the buyer and seller, with independent rights and responsibilities. A contract of carriage may also be called a **contract of affreightment.**

Consignor, or, in the case of maritime carriage, a **shipper,** refers to the person delivering up the cargo into the hands of the carrier, and, bearing in mind the provisions of INCOTERMS, this could be either the buyer or the seller. The same party may be both consignor and consignee.

Consignee refers to the person entitled to delivery of the shipment.

Freight refers to the fee payable for carriage, rather than the cargo itself.

Charterparty is the hire of an entire ship; **by demise** is a lease of the entire vessel; **voyage** charterparty is a hire of the entire cargo space for a particular voyage; and **time** charterparty is a hire of the entire cargo space for a fixed period.

In rem is a court action against property. While ships are property of their owners, ships are juridical entities and are sued *in rem.* They also may be arrested (seized) and liens may be attached to a ship or its cargo for nonpayment of debts it incurs.

Bills of Lading

General

A bill of lading is an ancient and highly flexible document, and while indeed evidencing a contract of carriage (usually incorporating those terms on its reverse), it also serves as a receipt for the delivery of the goods to the carrier for shipment. It is prima facie evidence of ownership of the goods (a document of title), and it plays a major role in financing international trade (as will be seen in the next chapter).

A bill of lading is issued by a carrier to a shipper when the goods are received into the carrier's custody or when the goods are alongside or stowed, as the case may be. The shipper, presumably having performed in accordance with its sale agreement, then forwards the bill of lading (either by fast mail or electronically) to the consignee, again presumably against some guarantee of payment. The consignee receives the bill of lading, and is thus fully armed to surrender it back to the carrier on arrival of the goods. Multiple original bills of lading are usually produced, some of which can be required for financing the transaction, but as soon as one original is produced, the carrier may hand over the goods and the other originals are void.

Traveling with the bill of lading will be all other documentation that the consignee will require (other than those that it must create itself) in order to clear the goods through (import) customs, or that are necessary to trigger payment by the buyer's bank to the seller. These are the documents that have been discussed in Chapters 6 and 7: the commercial invoice, certificate of origin, any export licenses, inspection certificates, and insurance policies.

In practice, you will not likely have the chance or desire to meet with a lawyer prior to dealing with every bill of lading that you encounter. That said, as a company moves into the international trade field, where risks warrant (transaction size or volume), it should continue to seek advice until such time as it is comfortable dealing with the documentation on its own. Of course, as new wrinkles appear in familiar business transactions, advice should be sought against unintentional liabilities that may arise.

Ocean Bills

The ocean bill of lading, evidence of the contract of carriage used in sea transport, can take on a range of attributes. These vary on the basis of the desires of the shipper, the condition of the cargo on delivery to the carrier, and the conditions of onward carriage (if any). These attributes (and restrictions) possess their own customary terminology recognized at law and any one bill may have any number of them. A sample bill of lading is shown on page 364, and the features of the bill are discussed following it.

Ocean Bill of Lading

Shipper US Global Exports Ltd, 123 Evans Road, Watertown, New York, USA 13601	**Ocean Bill of Lading** Serial Nº: *ORIGINAL* C-**26491**
Consignee To Order DeutscheKredit Bank, Wolfburg Branch, Heinrichstrasse 110, Dortmund, Germany Tel: +49 5294-68373	Number of Original Bs/L: **3** **American Oceanic**
Notify Address: (carrier not to be responsible for failure to notify) Schmitt & Sohn GmBh, Dieselstrasse, 42, Dortmund, Germany Tel: +49 4623-98334	**Shipping Lines Company**

Local Vessel*	From*	
—	—	

Ocean Vessel	Port of Loading	Voyage #	Port of Discharge	Final Destination: (if on-carriage)*
M/V Polar Fire	New York	AT-64	Hamburg	—

Marks & Nos	Number and kind of packages; description of the goods	Gross Weight (kg)	
	67 Crates Milled End Tubular Torsion Bars 16.502 kg/crate 0.25m³ /crate 1105.634 kg SHIPPING MARKS: SCHMITT & SOHN GERMANY *AOSL New York* *CLEAN ON BOARD* *SHIPPED*		Particulars Furnished by Shipper of Goods

Total Volume	Rate/kg GW	Ocean Freight	Quay Charges	Total	Prepaid	Collect
16.75 m³	$3.16	$3493.80	$225.00	$3718.80	0.00	$3718.80

Shipper's Ref: 03-4612	**Freight Payable at:** Destination	SHIPPED in apparent good order and condition unless otherwise specified on board the aforementioned vessel the goods described above (the particulars given being supplied by the Shipper and the measurement, weight quantity, brand, contents, marks, numbers, quality, and value being unknown to the carrier) for the carriage to the port of discharge or so near thereunto as she may safely go subject to the terms, conditions and exemptions of this Bill of Lading. In accepting this Bill of Lading the Owners of the goods expressly accept and agree to all its stipulations on both pages, whether written, printed, stamped, or otherwise incorporated, as fully as if they were all signed by the Owners of the goods. In witness whereof the Master, Purser or Agent of the said vessel has signed the number of original Bills of Lading stated above, all of this tenor and date, one of which being accomplished, the others stand void. One of the Bills of Lading must be given up, fully endorsed in exchange for the goods.
* Applicable only when document used as a Through Bill of Lading		
Place and Date of Issue: New York 14-07-2005	for the Master: *William Jones Master*	

SEE TERMS AND CONDITIONS ON REVERSE

While there are other forms of a bill of lading used for particular purposes, the most common bills of lading for maritime carriage are

1. **Straight** versus **order** versus **bearer** bill,

being marked as

2. **Received** or **Alongside** versus **Shipped** or **On Board** or **Laden on Board,**

which must be either

3. **Clean** versus **claused** or **foul,**

and it is either

4. **Prepaid** or **collect,**

and it also may be a

5. **Through** bill, **combined transport bill,** or **container** bill.

Bearing in mind that every bill of lading represents title to the goods, a **straight** bill of lading is **nonnegotiable.** The bill names a shipper (consignor) and a recipient of the goods, the consignee, and only the person named as consignee is entitled to claim the goods under a straight bill of lading. This prevents misdirection but creates inflexibility in the delivery.

In indicating the consignee, an **order** bill of lading is marked **TO ORDER OF** <named party>. The bill is thus **negotiable,** for that named party may endorse the bill on its reverse, and a subsequent holder can recover possession of the goods at the other end of the voyage. This is often a requirement of the financial institution of the buyer of the cargo. The buyer's bank, for example, will be forwarding payment to the seller of the goods, and thus may require a bill to its order for security, so that it controls the title to goods until the buyer settles its debt to the bank. Once repaid for what it has already paid the seller, the bank will endorse away its rights in favor of the buyer, who will recover the goods from the carrier.

Such an arrangement also creates security for the seller that does not exist with a straight bill. With a straight bill, unless the buyer's payment has been received in advance of shipment, the seller is taking the risk that the buyer will claim the goods and disappear.

A **bearer** bill of lading is a special form of an order bill where the consignee is marked as **TO ORDER BLANK ENDORSED.** Here, the shipper retains title until it endorses the bill, and, after it does so, the bill becomes a bearer instrument of title. Any person in possession of the bill may then claim the goods on their delivery to the port of discharge. While this creates complete flexibility in transferring title where markets for the cargo are fluid and the shipper knows the goods will be sold (or even resold) in transit without knowing who its final buyer will be, it is enormously risky.

As a bill of lading is a document of title, the bearer of an endorsed order bill may obtain delivery from the carrier even as against the true owner. In the United Kingdom, under common law, the transfer of a bill of lading from one party to another party transfers the same rights as those of the original holder. Thus, if a shipper ships 97 units under a bill of lading issued by the carrier that states 100 units, a subsequent holder may only claim 97 units. In Europe, under civil law, the subsequent holder can improve upon the rights of the shipper. The subsequent holder may claim 100 units from the carrier, who will be left to chase the buyer for reimbursement. The latter approach is taken in the United States for a subsequent holder without notice.

The contract evidenced by a bill of lading does not simply create liabilities for the carrier. Rather obviously, a liability falls upon the shipper to pay the freight charges. Less obvious is the extent of other liability of the shipper, and whether the shipper's liabilities extend to others to whom the shipper subsequently transfers the bill of lading. This is explored in the following case, as a matter of traditional common law.

Effort Shipping Co. Ltd. V. Linden Management S.A.

House of Lords
January 22, 1998

Lord Lloyd of Berwick:

What is the nature and scope of any implied obligation at common law as to the shipment of dangerous goods? [I]t seems desirable for us to express an opinion. Even though that opinion will not form part of the ratio decidendi,[5] it may at least help to resolve a long-standing controversy.

The relevant facts are all agreed. On 18 November 1990 the appellant shipped a cargo of ground-nut extractions at Dakar, Senegal, for carriage to Rio Haina in the Dominican Republic. The ground-nut cargo was loaded in number 4 hold of the respondents' vessel "Giannis N.K." under a bill of lading. It is agreed that the groundnut cargo was infested with khapra beetle at the time of shipment. But this was unknown to the appellant shippers as well as the respondent carriers.

The vessel had previously loaded a cargo of wheat pellets in numbers 2 and 3 holds for carriage to San Juan, Puerto Rico and Rio Haina. There was no danger of the beetle infestation spreading from the ground-nut cargo in number 4 hold to the wheat cargo in numbers 2 and 3 holds. But the beetle infestation in number 4 hold nevertheless rendered the vessel and its cargo (including the wheat cargo) subject to exclusion from the countries where the cargo was to be discharged.

After discharging part of the wheat cargo at San Juan, the vessel proceeded to Rio Haina where she was placed in quarantine after the discovery of insects in number 4 hold. It was thought that the insects might be khapra beetles. The vessel was fumigated twice. But it did not eradicate the insects. Accordingly on 21 December the vessel was ordered to leave port with all her remaining cargo.

She returned to San Juan, in an attempt to find a purchaser for the cargo, [b]ut when she arrived at San Juan, the U.S. authorities identified a khapra beetle and a khapra beetle larva, both dead, in number 4 hold. On 31 January 1991 the U.S. authorities issued a notice requiring the carrier to return the cargo to its country of origin, or to dump it at sea, but at all events to leave U.S. ports. It is common ground that in those circumstances the carrier had no practical alternative but to dump the whole of the cargo at sea, including the wheat cargo. The vessel sailed on 3 February, and the cargo was dumped between 4 and 12 February.

When the vessel returned to San Juan after dumping her cargo there was a further inspection. Eighteen live khapra beetles and khapra beetle larvae were found in number 4 hold. There was a further fumigation. The vessel was eventually cleared to load under her next charter, at Wilmington, North Carolina after a delay of two-and-a-half months. The question is who is to pay for the delay?

Assuming against himself that the shippers were otherwise liable to the carrier for the shipment of the infested groundnuts, that liability was, says Mr. Johnson (appearing for the shippers), divested when the property in the groundnuts passed to the receivers by endorsement of the bill of lading. In order to understand the argument it is necessary to set out verbatim the preamble and sections 1 and 2 of the Bills of Lading Act 1855.

---

[5]Reasons for judgment with binding effect.

"Whereas by the custom of merchants a bill of lading of goods being transferable by endorsement the property in the goods may thereby pass to the endorsee, but nevertheless all rights in respect of the contract contained in the bill of lading continue in the original shipper or owner, and it is expedient that such rights should pass with the property . . .

1. Every consignee of goods named in a bill of lading, and every endorsee of a bill of lading to whom the property in the goods therein mentioned shall pass, upon or by reason of such consignment or endorsement, shall have transferred to and vested in him all rights of suit, and be subject to the same liabilities in respect of such goods as if the contract contained in the bill of lading had been made with himself.

2. Nothing herein contained shall prejudice or affect any right of stoppage in transitu, or any right to claim freight against the original shipper or owner, or any liability of the consignee or endorsee by reason or in consequence of his being such consignee or endorsee, or of his receipt of the goods by reason or in consequence of such consignment or endorsement."

It will be noticed that whereas the preamble refers, as one would expect, to the passing of rights under the contract, it says nothing about the passing of liabilities. One finds the same contrast in section 1. It provides for all rights of suit to be "transferred to and vested in" the holder of the bill of lading; it does not provide for the transfer of liabilities. Instead it provides for the holder of the bill of lading to be subject to the same liabilities as the shipper. It seems clear that this difference of language was intentional. Whereas a statutory assignment of rights under the bill of lading contract would represent but a modest step forward in pursuit of commercial convenience, a statutory novation, depriving the carriers of their rights against the shippers, and substituting rights against an unknown receiver, would have represented a much more radical change in the established course of business.

The legislative solution was ingenious. Whereas the rights under the contract of carriage were to be transferred, the liabilities were not. The shippers were to remain liable, but the holder of the bill of lading was to come under the same liability as the shippers. His liability was to be by way of addition, not substitution.

Mr. Johnson advanced a number of more wide ranging arguments, that to hold the shippers strictly liable for shipping dangerous goods would be impracticable and unreasonable, and create an anomalous imbalance between the rights and liabilities of shippers and carriers. But equally strong arguments of a general nature can be advanced on the other side.

The dispute between the shippers and the carriers on this point is a dispute which has been rumbling on for well over a century. It is time for your Lordships to make a decision one way or the other. [I] would hold that the liability of a shipper for shipping dangerous goods at common law, when it arises, does not depend on his knowledge or means of knowledge that the goods are dangerous.

Source: [1998] H.L.J. No. 1.

While this case addresses the particular question of dangerous goods, it has more general importance. A subsequent endorsee receives the same rights and is subject to the same liabilities as the original shipper. On endorsement, the original shipper assigns its rights, but is not relieved of its liabilities under the contract of carriage.

From the businessperson's perspective, what are your views on adding parties to the liability, but not releasing those who have given up their right to benefits? Moreover, what reasoning would you give to support either the civil or common law approach over the other when it comes to a consignee being able to improve (or not) on the rights of the consignor?

The bill of lading shown in this chapter is an example of an order bill. The "Notify Address" is that of US Global Export's true purchaser, Schmitt & Sohn, who, on settlement with the consignee bank, will receive the right to collect the goods in Hamburg.

Anything less than a clean and shipped bill of lading is likely to create serious problems for the seller in receiving payment if the buyer is paying through a letter of credit. Banks will not involve themselves in ready-made lawsuits over damaged goods, and it will likely insist on a clean and shipped bill as a condition of the credit.

A bill marked **Received** or **Alongside** means that the cargo has been received by the carrier in its terminal for shipping, or set on the quay alongside the ship. This is appropriate for FCA, CIF, or CIP (Received) or FAS (Alongside) INCOTERMS. If this was the shipper's contractual INCOTERM obligation to the buyer (and to any other consignee through him), then contractual delivery under the sale agreement has been made. A bill of lading given in receipt and so marked satisfies that requirement. If the bill is endorsed **Shipped** or **On Board** or **Laden on Board,** it evidences that the cargo has passed the ship's rail as per FOB, CFR, or CIF contracts and is stowed. The bill of lading shown above is an example of a Shipped bill. It is stamped as much, though a redundancy over the master's written words "Clean on Board," which has further meaning.

Where a bill is marked **Clean,** it means that the goods in the hands of the carrier are in apparent good order. This does not mean that the carrier has physically examined the contents of packages or containers, but only that the cartons and crating are in good order, that all are present and accounted for, and that there are no stains or other signs that would give concern as to the condition of the contents inside them. A bill is **claused** or **foul** if it records particulars to that effect. Such particulars put the shipper on notice that the carrier will not entertain liability for damage related to that part of the cargo (as long as the carrier itself is not responsible for the damage) and gives notice to any other person with a later interest in the bill that the cargo is defective. Typical clausing notations might include "insufficient packaging," "three boxes short," or "broken security seal." The bill of lading shown above is a clean bill, evidenced by the master's notation to that effect.

Prepaid versus **collect** is a reference to whether the freight has been paid, again putting future holders of the bill on notice of both compliance with terms of the contract of sale and the potential for a carrier's lien for unpaid freight, if this is otherwise unexpected by the consignee. The bill above is collect.

As the bill above is a simple ocean bill, it is neither a through bill a combined transport bill, nor a container bill. **Through** bills contemplate two or more legs of carriage conducted by different carriers, and allow the shipper to contract only with the issuer of the bill, who will be responsible for execution of the other legs of carriage. A **combined transport** bill extends the through bill beyond an ocean bill to one that covers two or more different forms of transport to the point of delivery (i.e., road or rail).

Electronic Bills of Lading

Although paper bills of lading are the historical norm, the trading world is on the verge of conversion to electronic standards. This has been greatly facilitated by the UNCITRAL Model Law on Electronic Commerce (discussed in Chapter 7) and national laws that have followed it. In 1990 the CMI[6] adopted its Rules for Electronic Bills of Lading, for use when parties elect to use electronic data interchange (EDI) in shipping contracts. These rules establish a functional equivalency between EDI and written paper documents, although the need to agree on this is rapidly falling away with national adoptions of e-commerce laws based on the UN Model. More importantly then, the CMI Rules deal with means of authenticating EDI messages, by means of a "private key," a code to ensure the integrity of messages and the identity of the sender.

[6]Comité Maritime International, or International Maritime Committee.

This code is generated by the carrier (as would the paper bill of lading) and is placed in a receipt message given to the shipper, in the same manner that a paper bill of lading would be given to the shipper. At this point, not only does the code ensure integrity and identity, it serves as the negotiable aspect of the bill of lading. When the private key is passed to the consignee (or anyone else becoming entitled to delivery of the goods), the consignee uses that electronic key as its demand for delivery of the goods from the carrier.

International Conventions Applicable to Shipping

The business of common carriage is one of the oldest professions in international trade. As a result, contracts of carriage have had plenty of time to evolve differently in different jurisdictions. At the very least, every common carrier historically wrote its own rules, leading to great uncertainty for shippers.

At the same time, there have been forces to drive contracts of carriage towards similarity. First, unequal bargaining power led earlier carriers to exclude all risks, to the point that shippers could do nothing more than pray that goods reached their destination safely; while that was hardly good news for shippers, it did create some predictability.[7] The second force, though again a modest one, was that all carriers faced similar risks of weather, fire, and navigation, and thus they provided for substantially similar risks in their contracts, one-sided as they were.

As every international contract of carriage involves a beginning and an end in different jurisdictions, nations differently imposed their will on contracts of carriage in an effort to mitigate the inequity between shipper and carrier.

For example, the United States enacted the Harter Act in 1893, which remains in force today, in an attempt to correct the inequities then found in bills of lading.[8] It was not until the early part of the 20th century that an international response was formed. The process

[7]Predictably bad news. For example, see the English case of *Dakin v. Oxley,* [1864] 10 L.T. 268. Willes, Chief Justice of the Court of Common Pleas, gave judgment in favor of a ship owner for payment of the freight charges where the ship's master had succeeded, through "unskillful navigation," in completely destroying the cargo while in transit. Such would be only stuff of family legend but for the perpetual record of the common law. By 1896, this had changed (for the better). A shipment of fruit from the Persian Gulf to London became contaminated with sewage and was unfit for human consumption. Indignant that its customer refused to pay the freight charge, the carrier still contended that the now-fermenting pulpy muck could be distilled into "something" merchantable. Thus, the carrier believed it was owed its freight charge for having delivered the "goods." The court held an actual total insurance loss occurs when the goods shipped have, for business purposes, become "something else." Freight charges were not payable. See *Asfar & Co. v. Blundell,* [1896] 1 Q.B. 123.

[8]46 U.S.C. App. §§ 190–195, which provide in part:

> **§ 190. Stipulations relieving from liability for negligence**   It shall not be lawful for the manager, agent, master, or owner of any vessel transporting merchandise or property from or between ports of the United States and foreign ports to insert in any bill of lading or shipping document any clause, covenant, or agreement whereby it, he, or they shall be relieved from liability for loss or damage arising from negligence, fault, or failure in proper loading, stowage, custody, care, or proper delivery of any and all lawful merchandise or property committed to its or their charge. Any and all words or clauses of such import inserted in bills of lading or shipping receipts shall be null and void and of no effect.

> **§ 191. Stipulations relieving from exercise of due diligence in equipping vessels**   It shall not be lawful for any vessel transporting merchandise or property from or between ports of the United States of America and foreign ports, her owner, master, agent, or manager, to insert in any bill of lading or shipping document any covenant or agreement whereby the obligations of the owner or owners of said vessel to exercise due diligence [to] properly equip, man, provision, and outfit said vessel, and to make said vessel seaworthy and capable of performing her intended voyage, or whereby the obligations of the master, officers, agents, or servants to carefully handle and stow her cargo and to care for and properly deliver same, shall in any wise be lessened, weakened, or avoided.

was begun in 1921 at The Hague, Netherlands, and completed at Brussels, Belgium, in 1924 with the creation of the International Convention for the Unification of Certain Rules of Law Relating to Bills of Lading. This mouthful of a title is universally referred to simply as "the Hague Rules 1924," despite coming into force in 1931 and being referred to in French as the "Convention de Bruxelles."

The Hague Rules 1924 governing sea carriage are presently in force in many trading nations[9] (including, with reservation, the United States) and since 1968 countries have been free to accept a block of amendments to the Rules known as the Brussels Protocol, or, more commonly, "the Hague-Visby Rules." These are in force in a number of important trading nations.[10] Finally, a 1978 initiative of the United Nations, its Convention on the Carriage of Goods at Sea, came into force in 1992, but the contracting parties do not represent a large segment of the shipping community.[11] These conventions are brought into local law by enabling legislation, most often under the title of Carriage of Goods at Sea (or Water) Acts.[12]

The remaining nations not accounted for under these conventions rely on local law to make provision for the rights and responsibilities of shippers and carriers.[13] Each of these conventions sets out minimum due diligence standards for carriers. To determine if the carrier can be held liable for damage or loss of a cargo, the cargo interest must embark on a four-step process. The first is to determine which rules apply to the contract.

The Hague Rules have mandatory application where the bill of lading is issued in a contracting state, or a clause of express incorporation is inserted, known as a *clause paramount*. As enacted in the United States, however, the Hague Rules apply through the Carriage of Goods at Sea Act to all maritime bills of lading *regardless* whether they are issued in the United States for exports or issued elsewhere with a U.S. destination port.[14] While the Hague and Hague-Visby Rules do not apply to charterparties with respect to liability, they do apply to the content of bills of lading.

The Hague-Visby Rules have mandatory application where a bill of lading is issued in a contracting state, the carriage is from a port in a contracting state, or a clause paramount or the legislation of any state gives them effect to govern the contract.

The Hamburg Rules apply to both exports and imports of a contracting state (like the U.S. Hague Rules), but also to all its contracts of carriage, not just bills of lading for sea carriage. The Hamburg Rules do not apply to charterparties.

---

[9]**Hague Rules,** as of early 2004: Algeria, Angola, Antigua and Barbuda, Argentina, Bahamas, Barbados, Belize, Bolivia, Botswana, Bosnia, Congo, Croatia, Cuba, Cyprus, Fiji, Gambia, Ghana, Grenada, Guyana, Iran, Ireland, Israel, Ivory Coast, Jamaica, Kenya, Kiribati, Kuwait, Macedonia, Madagascar, Mauritius, Monaco, Nauru, The Netherlands, Nigeria, Papua New Guinea, Paraguay, Peru, Portugal, Saint Kitts & Nevis, Saint Lucia, Saint Vincent, Solomon Islands, Seychelles, Slovenia, Somalia, Trinidad & Tobago, Turkey, Tuvalu, the United States, and Yugoslavia.

[10]**Hague-Visby Rules,** as of early 2004: Australia, Belgium, Canada, Denmark, Ecuador, Finland, France, Greece, Italy, Japan, Latvia, Luxembourg, the Netherlands, New Zealand, Norway, Poland, Singapore, Spain, Sri Lanka, Sweden, Switzerland, Syria, Tonga, and the United Kingdom.

[11]**Hamburg Rules,** as of early 2004: Austria, Barbados, Botswana, Burkina Faso, Chile, Egypt, Guinea, Kenya, Lebanon, Lesotho, Malawi, Mexico, Morocco, Romania, Senegal, Sierra Leone, Tanzania, Tunisia, Uganda, and Zambia.

[12]See, for example, in the United States, 46 U.S.C. App. §§ 1305–1315; in the United Kingdom, the Carriage of Goods at Sea Act 1992, Chapter c.50 (Bills of Lading), and the Carriage of Goods at Sea Act 1971, Chapter c.19 (Hague-Visby Rules). Canada remains committed to the Hague-Visby Rules; however, the Marine Liability Act, 2001, Chapter C-6, provides for the eventual accession to the Hamburg Rules and has replaced the former Carriage of Goods by Water Act, 1993, Chapter C-21.

[13]For example, the Maritime Code of the People's Republic of China, 1993, is essentially a hybrid of the Hague-Visby and Hamburg Rules.

[14]46 U.S.C. App. § 1312.

Carrier's Liability under the Hague and Hague-Visby Rules

Having determined which set of rules applies, the cargo interest who has suffered a loss must next find a breach of the carrier's primary responsibilities under the rules. The provisions of both the Hague and Hague-Visby Rules are identical in content and numbering in respect of these primary responsibilities:

Hague and Hague-Visby Rules

Article III

1. The carrier shall be bound before and at the beginning of the voyage to exercise due diligence to:
   a. Make the ship seaworthy;
   b. Properly man, equip and supply the ship;
   c. Make the holds, refrigerating and cool chambers, and all other parts of the ship in which goods are carried, fit and safe for their reception, carriage and preservation.
2. Subject to the provisions of Article IV, the carrier shall properly and carefully load, handle, stow, carry, keep, care for, and discharge the goods carried.

Source: Enacted in the United States as 46 U.S.C. App. § 1303(1) and (2). See the Hague-Visby Rules at www.jus.uio.no/lm/sea.carriage.hague.visby.rules.1968/doc.html.

The period of the carrier's responsibility extends from the commencement of loading to the completion of unloading, or "tackle to tackle," and this duty of due diligence cannot be delegated under either set of rules. A claim for breach against a carrier may be initiated anytime up to one year after delivery or intended delivery of the cargo. The cargo interest bears the burden of proving that the goods were undamaged prior to the point of tackle, and if this is borne out, the burden shifts to the carrier. Assuming there is a breach of the carrier's duty, the cargo interest's third hurdle toward (some) recovery is whether or not one of the carrier's exceptions to liability is present. Again, the rules are the same under both the Hague and Hague-Visby Rules, as follows:

Hague and Hague-Visby Rules

Article IV

1. Neither the carrier nor the ship shall be liable for loss or damage arising or resulting from unseaworthiness unless caused by want of due diligence on the part of the carrier to make the ship seaworthy, and to secure that the ship is properly manned, equipped and supplied, and to make the holds, refrigerating and cool chambers and all other parts of the ship in which goods are carried fit and safe for their reception, carriage and preservation in accordance with the provisions of paragraph 1 of Article III. Whenever loss or damage has resulted from unseaworthiness the burden of proving the exercise of due diligence shall be on the carrier or other person claiming exemption under this article.
2. Neither the carrier nor the ship shall be responsible for loss or damage arising or resulting from:
   a. Act, neglect, or default of the master, mariner, pilot, or the servants of the carrier in the navigation or in the management of the ship.
   b. Fire, unless caused by the actual fault or privity of the carrier.
   c. Perils, dangers and accidents of the sea or other navigable waters.

d. Act of God.

e. Act of war.

f. Act of public enemies.

g. Arrest or restraint of princes, rulers or people, or seizure under legal process.

h. Quarantine restrictions.

i. Act or omission of the shipper or owner of the goods, his agent or representative.

j. Strikes or lockouts or stoppage or restraint of labour from whatever cause, whether partial or general.

k. Riots and civil commotions.

l. Saving or attempting to save life or property at sea.

m. Wastage in bulk or weight or any other loss or damage arising from inherent defect, quality or vice of the goods.

n. Insufficiency of packing.

o. Insufficiency or inadequacy of marks.

p. Latent defects not discoverable by due diligence.

q. Any other cause arising without the actual fault or privity of the carrier, or without the actual fault or neglect of the agents or servants of the carrier, but the burden of proof shall be on the person claiming the benefit of this exception to show that neither the actual fault or privity of the carrier nor the fault or neglect of the agents or servants of the carrier contributed to the loss or damage.

Source: Enacted in the United States as 46 U.S.C. App. § 1304(1) and (2). See the Hague-Visby Rules at www.jus.ui.no/lm/sea.carriage.hague.visby.rules.1968/doc.html.

These are very onerous exceptions, to the benefit of the carrier and to the detriment of the cargo interest. If this hurdle is cleared, the cargo interest faces final bars to full recovery, which are the monetary limitations on liability.

Under the Hague Rules, this limitation is set at 100 British pounds (or equivalent; US$500 at 1924 exchange rates) per package or customary freight unit. While this might have been generous compensation in 1924, it has been ravaged by inflation, and as a result has led to frequent litigation as to the "customary freight unit" for any particular cargo.

The Hague-Visby Rules are more generous. They first established a limit expressed in terms of the Poincaire franc, then in 1979 switched to the International Monetary Fund's Special Drawing Right, currently equivalent to approximately US$1.36. This limit of the carrier's liability is now set at the greater of two Special Drawing Rights per kilogram of the goods lost or damaged or 666.67 SDRs per package (approximately US$2.72 and US$906.67, respectively).

As a final note, neither the Hague nor the Hague-Visby Rules apply to cargo carried on deck, nor to the carriage of live animals or noncommercial goods (such as personal and household effects). The following case illustrates the desperate attempt of an insurer of a cargo interest to invoke the weight-based liability limits of the Hague-Visby Rules in the face of the Hague Rules' limit of $500 per package. In this case, the difference between the two runs to over $1,000,000.

Nippon Fire & Marine Insurance v. M.V. Tourcoing, et al.

United States Court of Appeals for the Second Circuit

Decided: February 2, 1999

For the Court:

Plaintiff Nippon Fire & Marine Insurance Company ("Nippon") appeals from a final judgment of the United States District Court for the Southern District of New York (Miriam

The Hague-Visby kilogram limit works in favor of the cargo interest where the package weight is greater than 333 kilograms, or 732 pounds. Where each package weighs less than this figure, the per package limit is more favorable to the cargo interest. Of course, the successful claimant receives the greater of the two figures, but while weight is fixed, the claimant should not rely on its own opinion of what constitutes a "customary freight unit." The court might not agree.

Goldman Cedarbaum, *Judge*) dismissing defendant vessel, which had been named but not "arrested," and ordering recovery of $3,750 by Nippon—for damage to cargo shipped by Nippon's insured—from a cargo carrier, defendant Wilhelmsen Lines A.S. ("Wilhelmsen"), and a stevedore, defendant Maher Terminals, Inc. ("Maher"). Nippon contends that the District Court erred by applying the $500 per package limitation on liability contained in the Carriage of Goods by Sea Act ("COGSA"), 46 U.S.C. App. §1300 *et seq.*, and in Clause 11 of the bill of lading. We conclude that COGSA compulsorily applies to this case, that the parties did not agree to a higher liability limit, and that the shipper had a "fair opportunity" to declare a higher value and pay an excess charge in exchange for greater liability. Accordingly, we affirm the District Court's judgment.

I.

Wilhelmsen carried a printing press aboard the M.V. Tourcoing from Japan to the United States for Nippon's insured, Komori America Corp. During the course of unloading by Maher, several parts of the printing press (which had been disassembled into thirteen containers) were damaged. In this action, Nippon seeks recovery of $1,186,467.87 that it paid Komori pursuant to a marine cargo insurance policy.

Because Wilhelmsen and Maher admitted liability, the only issue presented by the parties' cross-motions for summary judgment was whether Wilhelmsen, Maher, or both were entitled to the $500 per package limitation on liability contained in COGSA and in Clause 11 of the bill of lading. The District Court concluded that the bill of lading's Clause 7 (the "clause paramount") did not create any ambiguity concerning application of the $500 per package limit in this case; nor did it otherwise deprive the shipper of a fair opportunity to pay a higher rate for a higher liability limit. The District Court therefore held that the $500 per package liability limit applied to Wilhelmsen. For reasons not relevant to this appeal, the District Court ultimately found that this limit extended to Maher's liability as well.

The District Court entered judgment dismissing the defendant vessel and ordering recovery of $3,750 by Nippon from Wilhelmsen and Maher. This timely appeal followed.

II.

COGSA, which is based upon the International Convention for the Unification of Certain Rules of Law Relating to Bills of Lading (the "Hague Rules"), applies *ex proprio vigore* to all contracts for carriage of goods by sea between the ports of the United States and the ports of foreign countries. 46 U.S.C. App. §§ 1300, 1312. Accordingly, because in this case the cargo was shipped from Japan to the United States, COGSA applies.

The statute provides that the carrier's liability is limited to $500 per package unless a higher value is declared by the shipper and inserted in the bill of lading, or the parties agree to a higher limit. Under the "fair opportunity" doctrine, however, the COGSA limit is inapplicable if the shipper does not have a fair opportunity to declare higher value and pay an excess charge for additional protection.

In addition to the applicable terms of COGSA, Clause 11 of the bill of lading in this case expressly limits liability to $500 per package. In addition, Box 16 on the front of the bill of lading is labeled "DECLARED VALUE (SEE CLAUSE 11 RE: $500 LIMIT)" and provides a space for the shipper to insert a higher value; no such higher value was declared. Clause 11 and Box 16 demonstrate that the parties did not contract to avoid the COGSA liability limit. Furthermore, Clause 11 and Box 16 demonstrate that the shipper had a fair opportunity to declare higher value in order to increase the carrier's liability. *See [General Elec. Co. v. M. V. Nedlloyd,* 817 F.2d 1022, 1029 (2d Cir. 1987)] ("[T]he language on the back of the [bill of lading] incorporating COGSA's provisions and the space for declaring excess value on the front are sufficient notice of the limitation of liability and the means of avoiding it."); *Binladen BSB Landscaping v. M.V. Nedlloyd Rotterdam,* 759 F.2d 1006, 1017 n.12 (2d Cir. 1985).

Nippon's arguments on appeal are based entirely upon the bill of lading's Clause 7, the "clause paramount," which states in relevant part:

> With respect to water transportation, this Bill of Lading shall be subject to the provisions of the Carriage of Goods by Sea Act of the United States, approved April 16, 1936, which Act is incorporated herein, or to any law similar to the 1924 Hague Rules or Hague-Visby Rules if such Law is compulsorily applicable to this Bill of Lading in the country where suit is brought. . . .

As noted above, an international effort to unify the rules of law relating to bills of lading resulted in the 1924 Hague Rules, which the United States has adopted and implemented through COGSA. Many of the countries that adopted the Hague Rules, but not the United States, also have adopted a 1968 amending protocol (the "Visby Rules") and a 1979 amending protocol (the "S.D.R. Protocol") imposing standard per-package or per-kilogram limitations which generally are higher than the $500 per package limitation of COGSA.

Nippon relies upon several cases from the Southern District of New York which involve paramount clauses referring to the Hague-Visby Rules. In general, these cases stand for the proposition that if the bill of lading makes the Hague-Visby Rules applicable to the shipment at issue, then the parties have agreed to the higher liability limitations contained in those rules. The judges in some of these cases held that the incorporation of the Hague-Visby Rules does not conflict with a specific provision—such as Clause 11 here—tracking the $500 per package language of COGSA, because the latter type of provision is meant to apply only when COGSA applies. Moreover, in cases where it was unclear from the bill of lading whether the Hague-Visby Rules were meant to apply, several of these judges resolved the ambiguity against the carrier and adopted the higher liability limit.

In this case, however, the references in Clause 7 to the Hague-Visby Rules create no ambiguity. Clause 7 expressly incorporates COGSA, and it simply acknowledges that suit might be brought in a country where rules other than COGSA compulsorily apply. As noted previously, COGSA—and its $500 per package liability limit—unquestionably governs this case, and thus the holdings noted above are inapposite.

Finally, we emphatically reject Nippon's argument that Clause 7 is an allegedly invalid "floating choice of law" clause incorporating the varying liability limits of approximately 100 different Hague and Hague-Visby countries. In particular, Nippon contends that the shipper could not have been certain, at the time the bill of lading was issued, where suit would be brought and which rules would apply. Such uncertainty, however, is inherent to international shipping, and it in fact explains the longstanding efforts, embodied in the various multilateral conventions discussed above, to create greater uniformity in liability limits and other rules relating to bills of lading. Contrary to Nippon's strained interpretation, Clause 7 does not increase this uncertainty by somehow incorporating otherwise inapplicable rules; as noted above, Clause 7 merely recognizes the potential for application of differing rules depending upon where suit is brought. Therefore, many shippers face the same asserted uncertainties faced by Nippon's insured, but the COGSA limitation routinely applies nonetheless.

In any event, we agree with the District Court that on a shipment from Japan to the United States, the shipper could hardly avoid recognition of the United States as a likely forum for suit. More importantly, the very fact that the shipper insured its cargo through Nippon demonstrates that it appreciated the substantial likelihood of a relatively low limit on the carrier's liability. *See, e.g., Vision Air Flight Serv., Inc. v. M/V National Pride,* 155 F.3d 1165, 1169 (9th Cir. 1998) (shipper "cannot contend that it was not given a 'fair opportunity' to opt for higher coverage precisely because [the shipper] *did* opt for higher coverage when it insured the [cargo] through an independent entity").

In sum, the shipper had a "fair opportunity" to contract for greater protection, and thus the District Court did not err when it gave effect to the $500 per package liability limit which both COGSA and the bill of lading unambiguously require.

The judgment of the District Court is affirmed.

Source: 167 F.3d 99.

This case serves to illustrate the importance to a shipper of obtaining sufficient insurance cover (from whatever source). It also underscores the importance of fully understanding the limitations that may be imposed as a result of applicable conventions for the carriage of goods at sea. Who had the "fair opportunity" to contract for greater protection? How did Nippon Fire get involved in the first place? How much was Nippon Fire seeking and how much did it get? How might this affect the way Nippon Fire does business in the future?

Carrier's Liability under the Hamburg Rules

The Hamburg Rules are generally unpopular with carriers, as they remove much of the protection carriers enjoy under the other two regimes. Recall that relatively few trading nations have adopted the Hamburg Rules and that the rules apply to all voyages to or from a Hamburg Rules port, governing all contracts of carriage by sea regardless whether a bill of lading (or other document) is issued or not.

This leads directly to a conflict of application of rules when the cargo, for example, departs a Hague port (such as Los Angeles, United States) or a Hague-Visby port (Southampton, United Kingdom), bound for a Hamburg Rules port, such as Valparaiso, Chile. In case of dispute, in practice, the governing rules will be those in force where proceedings for damage or loss are commenced, assuming that the forum court is properly seized of the matter.

The first major difference from Hague and Hague-Visby is the Hamburg presumption of carrier liability. The carrier is liable for loss and damage, as well as from delay in delivery, if the occurrence that caused the loss or delay took place while the goods were in its charge, unless it can prove that it or its agents took all measures that could reasonably be required to avoid the occurrence and its consequences. Note that this is a reversal of the burden of proof, and there is also no exception for negligent navigation. Only in cases of loss, damage, or delay due to fire does the burden shift to the cargo interest to show that the loss was occasioned through the carrier's fault. Unlike "tackle to tackle" under the other two sets of rules, "in its charge" means the entire period from taking custody of the cargo at the port of loading to the time when it delivers the cargo to the consignee, or places it at the disposal of the consignee.

Delay is defined as anytime after the agreed day of delivery if there is an express agreement, or a time reasonable to require of a diligent carrier, if there is no express agreement. The cargo interest may treat cargo as lost if it is not delivered 60 days after either date.

The carrier's liability for loss under the above circumstances is the greater of 835 SDRs per package or other shipping unit or 2.5 SDRs per kilogram (US$1,135 or

US$3.40, respectively). Liability for delay is the lesser of the total freight or two and a half times the freight payable for the goods delayed. The sum of liability for loss and delay cannot exceed the limit of liability for total loss.

A claim against a carrier may be initiated anytime up to two years after delivery or intended delivery. Court proceedings may be commenced by the cargo interest in the jurisdiction of the principal place of business of the carrier or the place where the contract of carriage was made (provided the carrier had a place of business there through which the contract was made). Further, proceedings may be commenced in the jurisdiction of the port of loading or discharge, or the place named in the contract of carriage. Finally, proceedings may be brought in any contracting state where the carrier's vessel or any other vessel owned by the carrier can be arrested. Through a clause paramount requirement, for documents that evidence contracts of carriage made in a contracting state, the Hamburg Rules attempt to secure their application in courts of noncontracting states. This element is likely to be successful, as the Hamburg Rules place a greater burden on carriers, and the other regimes do permit carriers to surrender their rights.

The Hamburg Rules apply to deck cargo and live animals; however, the carrier may only carry cargo on deck with the agreement of the shipper, or if it is in the usage of the trade or by statutory requirement. If the carrier proceeds without color of right, and as long as there was no express agreement forbidding deck carriage, it will be liable for loss, damage, and delay for deck carriage, saved only by its liability limit.

Marine Insurance

As the preceding sections make abundantly clear, marine cargo insurance is a necessity for all persons with an interest in the cargo. Recalling the ancient Rhodes law of average, communal underwriting of risk at sea traces its roots to the earliest times. Somewhat more modern is the commercial practice of Lloyd's of London, forming syndicates to underwrite marine risk from groups of shipowners and merchants since at least 1688. In contemporary times, new risks emerge. Terrorism and more inherently dangerous cargoes (chemicals and fuels) create more potential for loss (and delay), as do generally larger ships carrying hundreds of containers with tens of thousands of potentially dangerous and hazardous goods. Goods at sea or in warehouses may not be lost through any particular vice of their own, as the culprit may be a fire or other mishap resulting from goods stored or shipped alongside them.

The choice of trade term dictates whether the seller or the buyer will be obligated to purchase the marine insurance covering the goods represented by the sale contract. As in the contract of carriage, this will be a separate contract, apart from the sale.

Since risks at sea can range from uncontrollable Acts of God through willful damage by the crew of a ship, an agreement to underwrite risks requires some particular definition of those risks.

Many of these risks (both covered and excluded) have been distilled into sets of "Institute Clauses" that are incorporated by reference into contracts of marine insurance. Two principal sets of Institute Clauses exist: those of the Institute of London Underwriters and the American Institute of Marine Underwriters. These clauses, the London clauses or American clauses, are, unfortunately, often simply referred to as Institute Clauses, giving rise to the need to accurately specify which are intended by the parties.

The American Institute clauses, known individually as Institute Cargo Clause A, B, or C, can be summarized as follows. First, each embodies a number of identical exclusions, which are loss, damage, or expense stemming from

- Willful conduct by the assured.
- Ordinary leakage or ordinary loss in weight or volume of the cargo.

Even if the seller has fulfilled all its responsibilities, it is in the seller's interest to maintain insurance coverage against loss, for unforeseen difficulties may arise in the sale transaction. If the goods are lost, and a defect in the seller's performance leads to a conclusion that title has not passed, or if the buyer becomes bankrupt, the protection will seem cheap. The seller's obligation in CIF and CIP contracts is only to obtain minimum coverage; thus, if the buyer has any doubts as to the sufficiency of coverage, it should act in its own right, either to obtain its own coverage or to negotiate for greater protection.

- Ordinary wear and tear.
- Insufficiency or unsuitability of packing or preparation of the cargo.
- Inherent vice or nature of the cargo.
- Delay, even though the delay is caused by a risk insured against.
- Insolvency or financial default of the owners, managers, charterers, or operators of the vessel.
- Atomic weapons.
- Unseaworthiness of vessels or containers.
- War, revolution, or belligerent powers.
- Capture or seizure.
- Derelict weapons of war.
- Strikes, labor disturbances, and riots.
- Terrorism or political crimes.

If the shipper has taken out insurance conforming to Institute Cargo Clause **C,** then coverage is provided for loss or damage to the cargo reasonably attributable to

1. Fire.
2. Explosion.
3. Vessel or craft being stranded, grounded, sunk, or capsized.
4. Overturning or derailment of land conveyance.
5. Collision or contact of vessel, craft, or conveyance with any external object other than water.
6. Discharge of cargo at a port of distress.
7. General average sacrifice.
8. Jettison.

If the shipper has taken out insurance, at an increased cost, conforming to Institute Cargo Clause **B,** then coverage is provided for all the risks covered in Clause C *plus* loss or damage to the cargo reasonably attributable to

9. Being washed overboard.
10. Earthquakes, volcanic eruption, or lightning.
11. Water entry into vessel or hold, container, or place of storage.
12. Total loss of any package lost overboard or dropped in loading or unloading.

If the shipper has taken out even more expensive insurance conforming to Institute Cargo Clause **A,** then coverage is provided for all the risks covered in Clauses B and C *plus* loss or damage to the cargo reasonably attributable to

13. All risks, meaning accidental or malicious damage.

Increased coverage for declared values beyond those described in international rules conventions, on-deck carriage, and wars or strikes is generally available under riders or separate policies. Again, if the buyer of goods feels that the minimum coverage supplied by the shipper (if so agreed in the first place) is insufficient for the risks faced, the buyer is at liberty to purchase its own increased coverage, either in dollar amount or against otherwise uninsured risks. This may be arranged to cover from the seller's warehouse to the buyer's warehouse, if need be, against all risks. One should be first warned that even if goods can be shipped, some may not be insurable or only insurable with low limits or extremely high premiums. This can be due to the hazardous nature, perishability, inherent instability, or high value of the goods, which must be declared upon application for insurance. Examples of such might include explosives, fresh foods, and jewelry, and for some insurers, any cargo to be shipped on deck.

Third-Party Beneficiaries

While the shipper deals directly with the carrier, there may be any number of other independent contractors and servants who may be involved with the loading and transit of the goods, including stevedoring (loading and unloading) companies, their employees, crew, and port employees, to name a few. Stevedoring companies will have contractual relationships with carriers under which they perform their work, but no such contractual relationship exists between these dockworkers and the shipper. This gives rise to a traditional common law problem caused by lack of privity of contract and the questionable existence of third-party benefits.

Negligence law gives a right of action to the shipper for loss or damage to its goods, and the Hague/Hague-Visby/Hamburg Rules create exceptions and limitations limits for bills of lading issued by carriers, but what of the stevedores?

The response under the Hamburg Rules is quite straightforward; these Rules extend the carrier's liability from port to port, not just tackle to tackle. Coupled with the expansive definition of carrier, dockworkers and the like would be brought within the liability limits of the rules.

The more commonly encountered Hague and Hague-Visby Rules present a different matter, for there is no such broad definition of carrier, and the rules apply only from tackle to tackle. Thus, a specific clause, the Himalaya clause,[15] inserted in the bill of lading is required to extend protection and benefit to third parties.

A Himalaya clause is not usually identified as such in the contract of carriage or bill of lading, but may be recognized by words to the effect of

> The conditions of this contract apply whenever claims relating to the performance of the contract are made against any servant, agent or other person (including any independent contractor) whose services have been used by the Carrier in order to perform the contract. In entering into this contract as evidenced by this Bill of Lading, the Carrier, to the extent of these provisions, does not only act on his own behalf, but also as agent or trustee for such persons, who to this extent will be deemed to be parties to this contract.

Such a clause extends the terms of the contract to third parties on one hand, and makes them a party to the contract, to the extent of their involvement. In the United Kingdom, a jurisdiction traditionally hostile to third-party rights, Himalaya clauses are now provided for by statute.[16]

In the United States, Himalaya clauses are acceptable; however, a contract must exist between the carrier and specific classes of parties who perform services of a "maritime na-

---

[15]Arising in the English case of *Adler v. Dickson (The Himalaya)*, [1954] 2 Lloyd's Rep. 267, [1955] 1 Q.B. 158. A passenger on the vessel *Himalaya* was injured when a gangway fell, which pitched her to the quay below. The carrier relied on an exemption, but the exemption was not extended to its servants. Clauses in response to this are thus known as Himalaya Clauses.

[16]Contracts (Rights of Third Parties) Act, (U.K.) 1999, c. 31.

ture."[17] The shipper also must be given a fair chance to negotiate a higher liability limit in light of the broader risk.

Multimodal Container Transport

Standardized steel containers either 20 or 40 feet long by 8 feet wide by 8.5 feet high now play an important part in international trade, and have significantly reduced handling costs and the potential for theft or damage to goods. They also have altered the structure of trade transactions, as they are often loaded at the premises of the shipper and are transported by road to the port of departure. As the carriage is by both road and water, the bill of lading is termed as a combined transport bill or a multimodal bill, and will be so titled on its face. Where damage occurs to the goods in container traffic, the applicable rules for liability may be dependent upon the type of transport that was being used at the time of damage.

One concern of the cargo interest should be the interpretation of a standard container versus a "customary freight unit" for the calculation of liability limits. In containerized traffic, it is important to enumerate on the bill of lading the number of packages inside the container. In the face of failure to do this, the entire container will be accepted as a single package or customary freight unit, explicitly so under the Hamburg Rules and in practice under the Hague and Hague-Visby Rules. This would lead to an overall Hague liability limit of £100 or US$500 (or a limit in the order of $906 or $1,135 under Hague-Visby and Hamburg Rules), if the goods are comparatively light.

While the UN has taken action to create uniform rules for multimodal carriage liability, the result has not received the blessing of the major trading nations. Only a handful of nations[18] (among them Chile and Mexico) have ratified the 1980 United Nations Convention on International Multimodal Transport of Goods, out of the 30-nation ratification requirement for it to enter into force.

Filling this regulatory void are the 1992 UNCTAD-ICC Rules for Multimodal Transport Documents.[19] These rules do not have mandatory application and must be specifically invoked by the contract of carriage. Once invoked, any contractual terms inconsistent with the rules are null and void, unless the contractual terms serve to increase the liability of the multimodal transport operator (MTO).

Where the rules have been invoked, the multimodal transport document serves as prima facie evidence of the contract of carriage, and the MTO's liability extends from the point where the goods are taken in charge to the point of delivery to the consignee. As a result, the FCA INCOTERM is the most appropriate trade term to insert in contracts of sale contemplating multimodal shipments.

The MTO is liable for loss (or damage or delay in delivery) of the goods, if the occurrence that caused the loss took place while the goods were in its charge. The onus then shifts to the MTO to prove that no fault or neglect of its own, its servants or agents, or any other person it engaged, caused or contributed to the loss.

The MTO is allowed the exception of liability for goods carried at sea where the loss was caused by neglect in navigation or management of the ship, or fire, unless caused by the actual fault or privity of the carrier. If the loss results from unseaworthiness of the ship, the onus is on the MTO to prove that it exercised due diligence to make the ship seaworthy at the commencement of the voyage.

The general limit for MTO liability is the equivalent of 666.67 SDR (US$906) per package or unit or 2 SDR (US$2.72) per kilogram of gross weight of the goods lost or damaged,

---

[17]*Caterpillar Overseas, S.A. v. Marine Transport, Inc.,* 900 F.2d 714, 724 (4th Cir. 1990).

[18]As of early 2004, Chile, Mexico, Morocco, and Senegal have ratified the convention, while Malawi and Rwanda have acceded. There have been no ratifications in the last 10 years.

[19]UNCTAD is the United Nations Conference on Trade and Development. ICC is the ubiquitous and influential International Chamber of Commerce.

whichever is the higher, and if there is no sea leg, the package limit is raised to 8.33 SDR ($11.33) per kilogram. Third parties engaged by the MTO have the benefit of a Himalaya Clause that is an integral part of the rules, and where a claim for damage does arise, in contract or in tort, notice of damage must be lodged with the MTO within six days of delivery, and an action must be commenced within nine months.

Carriage of Goods by Land

International conventions exist for land transport (road and rail), governing terms of carriage, liability, and documentation for land transport.[20] As far as North America is concerned, however, neither the United States, Canada, nor Mexico is a party to these conventions, save Mexico's participation in the not-yet-in-force Multimodal Convention.

As a result, in the case of multimodal land transport (rail *and* road) in North America, the 1992 UNCTAD-ICC Rules for Multimodal Transport Documents apply, but only if the parties have invoked the rules to govern their contract of carriage. If they have not made this provision, or if unimodal transport (either road *or* rail) is the subject of the contract, then local law will govern the contract of carriage.

The application of international conventions in road and rail transport is much more advanced in Europe, where international connections in these networks are extensive. The membership of the COTIF and CMR conventions comprises the EU nations, and some located in North Africa and the Middle East.

These conventions are still significant for North American exporters, for if any shipment to Europe also contains a road leg in delivery, the CMR (or COTIF) may apply.

Quantum Corp. v. Plane Trucking Ltd.

England and Wales Court of Appeal (Civil Division)
March 27, 2002

Lord Justice Mance:

This appeal raises a point of principle regarding the applicability of the CMR Convention ("CMR"), scheduled to the Carriage of Goods by Road Act 1965, in circumstances where a contract embraces more than one type of carriage. Tomlinson J concluded that the correct approach was to characterise the contract as a whole, and that, unless the contract as a whole could be said to be for carriage by road internationally, any road carriage which it embraced fell outside the terms of the Convention. He gave permission to appeal, because of the general importance of the point.

The dispute arises between the four claimants/appellants and the second defendants, Air France. The four claimants are Quantum Corporation Inc., a Californian corporation, Quantum Peripheral Products (Ireland) Ltd. of Eire ("Quantum Ireland"), Expeditors (S) Pte Ltd. of Singapore ("Expeditors Singapore") and Expeditors Sea Sky (Dublin) Ltd. of Eire ("Expeditors Ireland"). The last two companies were freight forwarders. The claim relates to the loss in transit between Singapore and Dublin of a consignment of 11,520 hard disks. Expeditors Singapore on 21st September 1998 issued its own house air waybill no. 4710119916 naming Quantum Asia Pacific Pte Ltd. as consignor and Quantum Ireland as consignee. For

[20]Convention concerning International Carriage by Rail, 1980 (the COTIF—Convention des Transports Internationaux Ferrovaires); the Convention on the Contract for International Carriage by Road, 1956, (the CMR—Convention relative au contrat de transport international de Marchandises par Route); and, as discussed above in the section on multimodal transport, the 1980 United Nations Convention on International Multimodal Transport of Goods. For further information, see the website of the Central Office for International Carriage by Rail at www.unece.org/trade/cotif.

the purposes of the actual carriage, it consolidated the consignment with another (apparently also consisting of computer parts originating with one or other Quantum company), and, as agent for Air France, also issued a master air waybill no. 057-52326621 on 21st September 1998 naming itself as consignor and Expeditors Ireland as consignee.

Air France had no direct flight from Singapore to Dublin. The master air waybill thus recorded that the goods were to be carried in two stages. The first was to be from Singapore to Charles de Gaulle airport, Roissy, Paris by Air France, and the second (from there) to Dublin by Air France. Two corresponding entries appeared in a further box, each under a heading "Flight/Date," namely "AF6753/22" and "AF9408/22." It is common ground that these identify, firstly, an Air France flight from Singapore to Charles de Gaulle in France, and secondly a trucking service used by Air France to carry goods from Charles de Gaulle to Dublin airport. Its carriage by road on a roll-on, roll-off basis from Charles de Gaulle to Dublin was sub-contracted by Air France to the first defendant, Plane Trucking, now insolvent. The consignment of hard disks (alleged to have been worth some US $1.5 million) was lost in North Wales by a pretended "hi-jack" in which the truck driver and one of Plane Trucking's supervisors were involved as conspirators—each pleaded guilty and each has been sentenced to three years and nine months imprisonment.

Counsel's statements before the judge went on to identify as fundamental issues (a) whether the CMR Convention applied to the trucking leg from Charles de Gaulle to Dublin and (b) if so, whether the circumstances of the theft were such as to amount to wilful default within the meaning of CMR (cf article 29). We are only concerned with the former issue. If the second arises, it has been agreed to refer it back to the Commercial Court for resolution.

Chapter I of the Convention, consisting of articles 1 and 2, is entitled "Scope of Application." It provides as follows:

> Article 1(1): This Convention shall apply to every contract for the carriage of goods by road in vehicles for reward, when the place of taking over of the goods and the place designated for delivery, as specified in the contract, are situated in two different countries, of which at least one is a Contracting country, irrespective of the place of residence and the nationality of the parties.

Under article 17 of CMR, a carrier is liable for total or partial loss occurring between the time he takes over the goods and the time of delivery, the only relevant exception for present purposes being if the loss was caused "through circumstances which the carrier could not avoid and the consequences of which he was unable to prevent." Article 23(3) limits compensation to 8.33 units of account per kilogram of gross weight short. But, if the damage was caused by wilful default—by the international road carrier or by its servants or agents or any other persons of whose services it makes use for the performance of the carriage—article 29 prevents the carrier from limiting its liability.

Taking the first question, attention can for a moment be confined to a simple contract for carriage from A to B, without any unloading from the trailer. There is a range of possibilities, each of which may actually lead to goods being carried by road internationally: Thus: (a) the carrier may have promised unconditionally to carry by road and on the trailer, (b) the carrier may have promised this, but reserved either a general or a limited option to elect for some other means of carriage for all or part of the way, (c) the carrier may have left the means of transport open, either entirely or as between a number of possibilities at least one of them being carriage by road, or (d) the carrier may have undertaken to carry by some other means, but reserved either a general or a limited option to carry by road.

The First Question—Summary

The European authority on the first question can be summarised as follows. The Belgian, Dutch and German courts have all held that CMR can apply to carriage by road internationally in case (d), as well as necessarily in cases (a), (b) and (c). The present case falls, I have concluded, within case (b). So all such European authority as has been produced suggests that CMR should be applied to the carriage by road from Paris to Dublin, subject to the answer to the second question.

The weight of the European authority is thus firmly in favour of a conclusion that CMR is applicable to an international road leg of a larger contract in cases (a), (b) and (c) . . . my own inclination, apart from authority, would have been in the same sense. As it is, and with the benefit of such authority, I have no real hesitation about adopting the conclusion which other European countries have reached.

I would therefore conclude that the present contract was for carriage by road within article 1(1) of CMR in relation to the roll-on, roll-off leg from Charles de Gaulle, Paris to Dublin, and that Air France's own conditions are to the extent that they would limit Air France's liability overridden accordingly. It is thus open to the claimants to seek to show under article 29 of CMR that there was wilful misconduct or equivalent default, disentitling Air France to limit its liability for the loss which occurred during the road transit. It has been however agreed between counsel that this issue should be remitted to the Commercial Court to be dealt with there.

Source: [2002] E.W.J. No. 1437

Why was it so important for Quantum Corp. to ensure that both the convention applied and that Air France was made a defendant when it had been wronged by Plane Trucking?

Carriage of Goods by Air

The *international* commercial carriage of goods by air has been regulated by international convention since 1929, almost as long as the Hague Convention has for sea carriage, but with far more widespread ratification.

The Convention for the Unification of Certain Rules Relating to International Carriage by Air (the Warsaw Convention) has two amendments in force and available for separate ratification: the Hague Protocol of 1955 and the Montreal Protocol No. 4 of 1975. Virtually all major trading nations have ratified the convention and both of these protocols.[21] In the conceptual sense, the Warsaw Convention does for air what the Hague, Hague-Visby, and Hamburg Rules do for sea carriage. The Warsaw Convention also applies to passengers and their luggage, with specific terms in that regard. The remarks below are confined to cargo only, and may or may not apply to passengers and luggage.

The principal legal document in air carriage of cargo is the air waybill (under the Montreal Protocol) or an air consignment note (under the original convention). The chief legal difference between principal documents related to contracts of air carriage versus sea carriage is that the air waybill is not a document of title. An air waybill serves as a receipt for the goods, evidences the existence of a contract for air carriage, and gives the consignee the right to take delivery of the goods on arrival, on payment of the airfreight and charges. Under the Montreal Protocol, an air waybill may be in electronic form.

Despite that an air waybill is not a document of title, it is not impossible for the right to claim the cargo to be made transferable from the consignee to a third party, making it, in effect, a negotiable air waybill. In practice this does not happen, for the high expense of air carriage is balanced by the very few hours involved in transit, and negotiability would serve no useful purpose. This is because the air waybill, unlike the ocean bill, travels between the consignor and consignee with the shipment itself. Since the consignee must ap-

[21]As of early 2004, this includes all NAFTA and EU members; in South America: Argentina, Brazil, and Chile, among most others; in Asia: Australia, Singapore, Japan, China, and India, among most others. Taiwan is most significant of the very few nations with no relationship to the convention.

pear at the airport to acknowledge the carrier's delivery of the cargo (equivalent to presenting an earlier-arrived ocean bill), the consignee might as well take physical delivery of the cargo to which the bill is attached and make its own arrangements for transfer of the cargo to another.

While the convention (with or without the ratification of the protocols) makes the carrier responsible from the point at which it accepts the cargo until delivery (airport to airport, but not beyond), it also adopts the traditional exceptions to liability:

1. Inherent defect, quality, or vice of the cargo.
2. Defective packing.
3. Acts of war or an armed conflict.
4. Acts of public authority.

The carrier may rely on principles of contributory negligence regardless of the forum in which claims are initiated, and the Montreal Protocol establishes a maximum liability limitation for cargo of 17 SDRs per kilogram, or approximately US$23.00.

The consignor is responsible for the correctness of particulars of the cargo on the air waybill and for any loss or damage that an irregularity causes to the carrier or another (such as failure to indicate dangerous goods). Particulars noting quantity, volume, and condition of the cargo do not constitute prima facie evidence against the carrier unless they are stated in the air waybill and have been checked by the carrier in the presence of the consignor.

Chapter Summary

Transportation law today finds its roots in lex mercatoria, historic practice as conducted between merchants. This has been absorbed into the local law of trading nations, but the tradition of privately created solutions remains vibrant. One of the most important private rule-making bodies in international trade is the International Chamber of Commerce, based in Paris, France.

The ICC has developed standardized trade terms to make expectations and rights and responsibilities more uniform in international sale transactions. These 13 terms, known as INCOTERMS, are Ex Works; Free Carrier; Free Alongside Ship; Free on Board; Cost and Freight; Cost, Insurance and Freight; Carriage Paid to; Carriage and Insurance Paid to; Delivered at Frontier; Delivered Ex Ship; Delivered Ex Quay (Duty Paid); Delivered Duty Unpaid; and Delivered Duty Paid.

F-Terms require the seller to deliver the goods to a nominated carrier free of risk and expense to the buyer; the main carriage cost is *unpaid* by the seller. C-Terms require the seller to bear particular costs *past* the point of division where risk of loss and damage to the goods passes to the buyer; the main carriage is *paid* by the seller. D-Terms require specified destination delivery by the seller and payment of *all* carriage to that point.

When the shipper (often the seller) enters into a contract for carriage of the goods at sea, a bill of lading serves as evidence of that contract. These are ancient and highly flexible documents, serving as a receipt for the goods and also are prima facie evidence of title. Most often, bills are straight versus order (negotiable), received versus shipped (the goods are on board), and clean versus foul (cargo with apparent defects).

As carriers tend to be more powerful than shippers, abuses were once rife, which led to both local law and international conventions on the rights and liabilities of carriers. The main conventions in this area are the Hague Rules, the Hague-Visby Rules, and the Hamburg Rules, though the latter arise infrequently among major trading nations. These conventions are brought into local law by enabling legislation, most often under the title of Carriage of Goods at Sea (or Water) Acts.

Under these conventions and local law, the carrier may have specific responsibilities, but it is primarily bound to exercise due diligence in caring for matters that affect the shipper's cargo. Breaches of the carrier's duty of care are still subject to a range of exceptions and internationally agreed limits of financial liability.

As the shipper remains exposed to many risks from accidental loss to deliberate terrorism, insurance of the cargo is extremely important. Insurance also has been subject to private measures, through which standardized clauses have been created by associations of insurers. These clauses offer the shipper increasing levels of protection against particular risks, each progressively more expensive.

Third parties frequently are called in to assist the carrier, particularly in storage, loading, and discharge. As they are not parties to the contract of carriage, a clause (known as a Himalaya clause) extending liability protection to these service providers is inserted into the contract of carriage.

Multimodal transport lacks a broadly accepted international convention to establish rights and liabilities. The transport trade has therefore turned to UNCTAD and the ICC to establish nonmandatory rules, which are capable of being incorporated by reference into multimodal contracts of carriage. The international carriage of goods by air has been regulated since 1929 under the Warsaw Convention. This convention, like those applicable to sea carriers, establishes rights and liabilities of air carriers. The general construction of sea carriage conventions inspired the Warsaw Convention, but many aspects differ, responding to the more unique aspects of air transit.

Chapter Questions

1. Describe the differing responsibilities that fall to an ocean shipper when the term "FOB New York INCOTERMS 2000" is used, versus "CIF Rotterdam INCOTERMS 2000," for a cargo being sent between those two ports. Which direction is the cargo going across the Atlantic, east or west?

2. Explain, in a business context, how a large business operation might be ideally suited to the two extremes of INCOTERMS, Ex Works and DDP.

3. Distinguish between transfer of title and transfer of risk with respect to INCOTERMS.

4. Outline the critical differences in the responsibilities and liabilities of buyers and sellers among the C-Terms: CIF, CFR, CIP, and CPT.

5. What are the attributes of a bill of lading that make it particularly well suited to ocean transport of cargo? Which bill of lading offers greater flexibility: a straight bill or an order bill?

6. Explain both the business significance and the legal significance of a bill of lading marked "Clean on Board" in an FOB INCOTERMS 2000 transaction.

7. Explain the role being played by a bank when it is named as consignee to a bill of lading.

8. Under the Hague Rules, what carrier's liability limit would apply to the total loss of a standard container filled with 40 wooden crates of machine parts, each containing 5 inner cardboard boxes, with a total weight of 2,000 kilograms and a value of $40,000, where the bill of lading indicates "1 container said to contain 40 crates machine parts"? Would the shipper be any more or less happy, or indifferent, if the Hague-Visby Rules applied?

9. Explain why and how a Himalaya clause is of particular interest to those firms engaged in the loading and unloading of ships. How does it affect the rights of the cargo interest?

10. Regardless of any particular INCOTERM selection, what advice on cargo insurance would you offer to buyers of goods in international sale transactions?

Front Page Law: International Issues from Boardroom to Courtroom

THE JOLLY ROGER FLIES HIGH . . . MAY 24, 1999

BusinessWeek

At 2 A.M. on Mar. 17, a bright moon hung over the Strait of Malacca. A twin-motor speedboat sped along the narrow body of water between Malaysia and Indonesia in pursuit of its target, the 5,590-ton Marine Master, registered in Panama and hauling soda ash. About 20 men clad in army fatigues, automatic rifles slung over their shoulders, scrambled up a rope ladder onto the stern and caught the 21-member crew by surprise. On Mar. 21, the pirates put the crew in nine inflatable life rafts and set them adrift; six days later they were picked up by a Thai vessel. As for the Marine Master, "by now she would have had a makeover—new name, flag, paint, and crew. The soda ash would have been sold and the ship chartered out," says Noel Chong, Kuala Lumpur manager of the London-based international Maritime Bureau (IMB), part of the International Chamber of Commerce.

At least no one died. Piracy has long been a scourge in Asia, but the economic crisis has turned it even more vicious and costly for shippers. "In the last quarter of 1998, we saw ships hijacked and whole crews murdered in cold blood," says Pottengal Mukundan, an IMB director. Of the 192 reported pirate attacks worldwide last year, 95 took place in the waters of the Far East and Southeast Asia, down from 110 the year before. But last year, 162 crew members were assaulted, maimed, or killed worldwide, up from 105 in 1997—and all but one of the 67 reported murders occurred around the South China Sea and the Strait of Malacca. Ship hijackings shot up 50% last year, to 15 ships from around 10 in '97.

Besides its cost in life and millions of dollars in cargo, piracy poses a grave threat to the environment. Experts fear a disaster like the Exxon Valdez oil spill in Alaska. "A similar incident in the Strait of Malacca could prove catastrophic," says Jayant Abhayankar, deputy director of the International Maritime Organization in London. Pirates have concentrated their attacks on a crowded 30-kilometer stretch of the Philip Channel, the southern half of the Strait of Malacca, through which pass eastbound supertankers. During one incident in the Philip Channel, the bridge of a large tanker was left unmanned for 70 minutes. Fortunately, no accident occurred.

And many incidents are not reported at all because of concerns that an inquiry would disrupt schedules. "We make money when a ship is sailing, not when it's grounded," says an official from Bangkok-based Great Eastern Shipping.

Unfortunately, there's not much shippers can do to ward off attacks. Many nations won't allow firearms on commercial ships flying their flags, and others won't accept armed vessels at their ports. "All we have are water cannons on deck to douse the pirates and instructions to stay clear of small islands around Indonesia," says Lars D. Nielsen, chartering manager at Norden Tankers & Bulkers in Singapore.

The IMB's Mukundan says there are indications that pirates are shifting their targets from general cargo vessels to tankers carrying marine fuel oil. "In these waters, with all the small vessels and fishing boats, there's always a ready market for fuel at bargain prices," he says. And much of the pirated oil has been sold openly in China, say oil traders. As long as such opportunity beckons, the disciples of Blackbeard will ply their trade.

Source: Sethuraman Dinakar in Singapore. Copyright 1999, The McGraw-Hill Companies, Inc. All rights reserved.

9

Trade Payment and Finance

Chapter Objectives

Payment and finance are central obligations and concerns of both buyers and sellers in international transactions. Sellers are concerned that they will receive certainty for payment for goods shipped beyond the horizon, and receive that payment in a timely manner. Buyers want to know that they will receive the goods they have committed to pay for, and further want to ensure that a secure payment process is neither cumbersome nor additionally expensive.

The objectives of this chapter are to

- Lay out the range of options in payment and finance, both informal and formal, that may be considered by buyers and sellers.
- Consider the impact of international law and practice on payment and finance.

- Learn how these financial mechanisms may be used appropriately in business and law.
- Discover how risks beyond payment, in exchange and repatriation, can be hedged against loss.

Introduction

This chapter focuses on the international flow of payments in international business. While we will primarily treat the example of an international sale of goods, most of the forms of payment described below are equally applicable to the flow of funds under a services, licensing, or investment contract.

Much as was the case in international contracts of sale, the rules and law of international payments are a blend of historical commercial practice, the rules of private organizations (such as, again, the International Chamber of Commerce), and local law. In the absence of a unifying body of international law, the law of international payments is a collection of the local laws of nations. This body of local law is a combination of long-standing law of domestic payments, with further domestic modifications accommodating international commercial practice.

The chief difficulty in international payments is the distance between the parties. This manufactures problems of its own that do not exist in the domestic commercial situation. Even if two domestic parties are far apart geographically, either they are still usually members of the same local law jurisdiction (one large state) or they reside in separate jurisdictions that give full faith and credit to judgments of each other (different states of a federal state). This ensures that the leverage of the law remains directly over the heads of both parties, encouraging them to fulfill their contractual responsibilities.

Once the transaction becomes truly international, that leverage is lost. Of course, this is a statement that can be applied to every area of international business, not just payments, and total leverage is not gone due to the international recognition of judgments. Despite that, however, international enforcement is expensive and time consuming. Collection of funds (and delivery of goods) becomes more difficult, as some parties seem to take their contractual responsibilities less seriously once that direct judicial threat is removed. It would not be correct to say that this is universally true, but it is sufficiently true that international traders take the issue of security in payment and delivery much more seriously.

Reflecting this, the desire for greater security in both delivery and payment is not cheap, and it is certainly much more formal in its structure. Banks and common carriers have their role to play in ensuring the operation of transactions, and as they are liable for the correctness of their actions (paying the correct person, delivering to the right party), they insist on formal adherence to rules that the parties might waive if they were in full control of the logistics and payment steps themselves.

International payments are further complicated by the fact that international parties are, in all likelihood, operating behind the transaction (in general business operations) in two different domestic currencies. The transaction—the underlying contract of sale or investment—will probably refer to only one currency, and that will not be the national currency of at least one of the parties.

It is a luxury for a trader to operate with contractual amounts denominated in their home currency. U.S. traders are perhaps the most fortunate in this regard, as many foreign traders abroad are willing to do business in U.S. dollars. Additionally, some commodities are quoted almost universally in U.S. dollars. Despite this, even U.S. international businesspersons must be aware of currency fluctuation and its effect on the party opposite in a transaction.

A fluctuation in the exchange rate between one's domestic currency and the currency in which the transaction is denominated, in the interim between the time of contract offer and the time of payment, may result in that party becoming either a financial winner (receiving more or paying less) or a financial loser (receiving less or paying more) when the foreign transaction currency is converted into a domestic amount. Such currency fluctuations, therefore, for any trader, can easily propel a party on the downside of the risk toward breach of contract. The chance of a lawsuit for payment or delivery may be the lesser evil compared to the certainty of financial ruin in extreme currency fluctuations.

Aside from currency risk, a seller must be concerned about credit risk (the creditworthiness) of its buyer, and a buyer will be deeply concerned about the risk of nondelivery of the goods by its seller. Not surprisingly then, trustworthy mechanisms have been developed to relieve these concerns, and once again they find their roots in ancient times.

There are numerous methods used by buyers and sellers to pay for the goods that are the subject of their dealings. These methods range from the simple payment by check to a complex letter of credit often involving two or more banks. Importers and exporters will choose that method that satisfies their mutual needs. They will weigh the methods on such factors as the speed of payment needed to feed cash flow, security and assurance of payment, and ease of claiming the goods. Much will depend on how well the parties know and trust each other, the size of an order, the ongoing nature of their business relationship, and their respective relationship and creditworthiness with their banks. Most of this examination will focus on the more complex methods of payment—documentary collections and letters of credit, which have taken prominence in the international trade scene and for which practices are standardized around the world.

Chief Types of Financial Payment Mechanisms

Informal—Cheap, quick, riskier (for one party), useful in established relationships or for low transaction values		
	Payment in advance	
	Open account	
Formal—Costlier, slower, less risky, useful in establishing relationships or for high transaction values		
	Drafts and bills of exchange	
	Documentary collections	
		Documents against payment
		Documents against acceptance
	Documentary credits	
		Revocable letter of credit
		Irrevocable letter of credit
		Other types of letters of credit
Combination—A middle ground in all factors		
	Open account backed by stand-by documentary credit	
Special transactions—For special circumstances		
	Factoring	
	Leasing	

Informal Payment Mechanisms

As will be seen, formal payment systems are both more cumbersome and more expensive than other methods of payment. They have their uses, but frequently the parties desire a more informal system. This arises when the parties

- Are related companies.
- Have a long history of doing business together.
- Are in an industry known for its informality or a premium is placed on speed or a handshake and honor (the international diamond trade being a particularly interesting example of this latter case).
- Are located in developed areas of the world with high degrees of integration, communication, and reliable legal infrastructure for promise enforcement (the United States and Canada, or Belgium, the Netherlands, and Luxembourg, for example, and an increasing trend generally).
- At the other extreme, are located in less-developed areas of the world with a less reliable legal infrastructure for promise enforcement, making informal relationships the norm, based on honor. (The hawala banking system found in India and among Indian expatriates is an interesting example of this case. A depositor leaves payment with a

trusted individual in one country, who telephones instructions to an associate in another country, to release payment to a named party in settlement.)

Payment in Advance

Payment in advance, as the term plainly suggests, requires the buyer-importer to remit payment in full before receiving the goods it orders from the seller-exporter. This alternative works wholly to the seller-exporter's advantage and leaves the buyer-importer with essentially no recourse but to the courts if it is unsatisfied with the goods if and when they arrive. Where this method is used, there is usually a large power differential between the seller and the buyer, and orders tend to be smaller.

In a world where sellers often grant credit, this method is much less common, but it is indeed the safest alternative for the exporter. The seller is relieved of collection problems and additionally it receives immediate use of the funds. For the buyer, unless the order is relatively insignificant, it may resist such terms due to the extent to which its capital will be tied up without goods in its hands. The question of whether the goods will ever arrive also looms large for the buyer unless there is a strong relationship, which would beg the question as to why payment in advance would be required in the first place.

Some sellers require the buyer to make payment of a percentage of the total price before shipping the goods, often where the seller must specially underwrite the cost of its production of the goods out of its own cash or actually incurs specific debt. In other cases, seen from the buyer's perspective, an initial partial payment allows for a balance to be retained until such time as the goods are received in merchantable condition.

Payment in advance is usually effected through a check or a bank transfer by wire, directly from the account of the buyer to the account of the seller.

Open Account

In an open account arrangement, the exporter ships the goods "on account" and the importer pays agreed amounts (the entire balance or installments) at particular times, for example, monthly or at month ends. In this case, the importer will receive the bill(s) of lading in advance, either accompanying or in advance of the arrival of the goods, as delivery is not linked to the payment itself.

This is the flip-side of the payment in advance situation, as now maximum risk lies with the seller-exporter, and it is only appropriate where the seller is certain of the integrity of the buyer, possibly through either investigation, reputation, or prior experience. Here, the seller becomes a creditor of the buyer and assumes the consequential risks attached to that role, as well as the obligation to finance production without being in receipt of cash flow from the buyer.

Open account payments are also usually effected through a check or a bank transfer by wire, directly from the account of the buyer to the account of the seller.

Formal Payment Mechanisms

Where so much in shipping and delivery revolved around the bill of lading, its counterpart and centerpiece in international payments is the bill of exchange, or draft.

Drafts and Bills of Exchange

Drafts, or bills of exchange, as they are also known, are the primary payment instrument in international trade. While there are important differences between a draft and a check, since the use of a check is widely understood, it is not a bad memory aid to launch a discussion of drafts. We are therefore discussing a paper document (moving towards an electronic system), a negotiable instrument that links parties in a payment obligation. In large

The Old Wolf

The terms *bill of exchange* and *draft* suffer from a combination of partial interchangeability, local law distinctions, and trade usage. What the U.S. Uniform Commercial Code terms as a draft is known as a bill of exchange in Britain and Commonwealth common law countries. Elsewhere in the world, both terms are used, but draft commonly refers to domestic payments only and bill of exchange is used for international transactions. In most European countries, bill of exchange is the appropriate term, but the formal requirements constituting a bill are greater than in either the British or American practice. The ICC uses both terms as interchangeable with a preference for draft. With that warning, in the remainder of this text, we use the word *draft* universally, and bill of exchange is used only in the historical commentary and when particular reference is being made to other jurisdictions.

probability, a financial institution may be present, facilitating or even committing itself to payment on the instrument.

At the dawn of human commerce, a draft, a bill of exchange, or other negotiable instrument would have been meaningless. Traders simply met over short distances and bartered their surplus goods in exchange for goods they desired, on a face-to-face basis. Rapidly, the need for a medium of exchange presented itself, and gold and silver became the universal standard.

Traders kept their gold in their pockets, and in the event of a buyer's promise to pay a seller at a future date, a note was made to record it—what we might recognize today as a promissory note. As trading distances grew, traveling traders found themselves and their gold prey to thieves. The answer was to travel without gold, and thus perhaps as much as 2,000 years ago, and certainly as early as the eighth century, the root of the modern bill of exchange was planted.

By depositing gold in one fortified place and taking a bill or receipt for the same, the trader could redeem his gold at a later time—essentially, then, a deposit account. Better yet, by making the bill exchangeable, the trader could deposit his profits from trade in one market town and redeem them later in his hometown, from a similar depository. The depositories could be left to settle among themselves with the aid of armed caravans. The result was the birth of a banking system and a rudimentary bill of exchange.

While this created security for travelers, it did little to assist buyers and sellers in actually conducting their transactions. To step beyond the personal *promise* to pay contained in a promissory note, it was necessary for a buyer (or a seller with the buyer's acceptance) to be able to draft an *order*, compelling the buyer's third-party depository (or another party) to pay the seller—a much more useful bill of exchange.

Where a buyer wished to pay a seller at a future time, one party would draft an order to that effect. The seller might draft the order to set out its expectations of the terms of payment, to be accepted by the buyer. Alternatively, knowing the terms of payment, the buyer might draft its own order committing its bank or another party to pay on its behalf.

Of course, the system was not without its problems, such as lost instruments, fraud, discrepancies, and misinterpretations of the provisions of the instrument. *Lex mercatoria*, the law as between and made by merchant custom, also therefore made provision for rules relating to bills of exchange, and this survived until almost the 20th century.

In 1882, the United Kingdom codified the law merchant jurisprudence then existing in Britain with its Bills of Exchange Act.[1] Canada and the now-former colonies of the British Empire followed suit,[2] as did the United States in the first two decades of the 20th century.

[1] 45 & 46 Vict., (U.K.) c.61.
[2] Bills of Exchange Act, 1890, 53 Vict., c.33, now R.S.C. 1985, c.B-4, as amended.

The codification of the law relating to bills of exchange in U.S. states is now found as part of the Uniform Commercial Code,[3] where the term *draft* has been embedded.

Both promises (promissory notes) and orders are negotiable instruments (if they meet formal requirements at law), but only orders can be considered as drafts in the United States or as bills of exchange in the United Kingdom and Commonwealth. Checks, being orders drawn on a bank *and* payable on demand, are distinguished from drafts in the United States on this basis by the UCC, while the British tradition, using the same features, treats them as a separate type of bill of exchange. In Europe, as the names of the multiple conventions below suggest, checks are regulated separately from bills of exchange.

The European experience in the harmonization of rules related to bills of exchange dates from the early 1930s with the Geneva Convention Providing a Uniform Law for Bills of Exchange and Promissory Notes and the Geneva Convention Providing a Uniform Law for Cheques. Both of these were created under the auspices of the League of Nations at Geneva and entered into force on January 1, 1934. Nations well beyond Europe are also members[4] (although with widespread reservations) and the membership reflects those nations that follow the civil law tradition as opposed to the Anglo-American common law. These conventions are incorporated into the legal systems of the state parties and continue to regulate their bills of exchange, promissory notes, and checks in those nations.

As between governments and local law systems, there has been an effort made to create international harmonization of the law applicable to international drafts; however, it has not seen much success. The result to date has been the United Nations Convention on International Bills of Exchange and International Promissory Notes, done at New York in 1988. The convention has been signed but not ratified by Canada, Russia, and the United States, and acceded to only by Mexico, Honduras, and Guinea, and, consequently, has not yet entered into force.

In principle, most negotiable instruments today would be recognizable to 17th century traders, if not their earlier predecessors. The terminology associated with the parties to a draft or bill of exchange is also a product of long financial and legal practice. They are shown in the following table.

Drawer	The party who issues the draft or bill of exchange
Drawee	The party who is ordered to pay the funds contemplated by the instrument
Acceptor	A drawee who has accepted the responsibility to pay*
Payee	The party who, on the face of the bill, is to receive payment
Endorser	A person, initially the payee, who transfers the draft or bill by signature endorsement and delivery to another person, that person becoming an endorsee; any endorsee may then, subject to any preceding restrictive endorsement, become an endorser as well

*In the United States, the drawee need only sign the face of the draft. In Britain and the British Commonwealth, the drawee becomes an acceptor by signing the bill and writing "accepted," together with the date and place of payment.

[3]While the Code is of general application in all states save Louisiana, in regard to shipping and payments Louisiana has adopted UCC Article 1, General Provisions; Article 3, Commercial Paper; Article 4, Bank Deposits and Collections; Article 5, Letters of Credit; and Article 7, Warehouse Receipts, Bills of Lading and Other Documents of Title, harmonizing its shipping and payments legislation with that of other U.S. states.

[4]**Members of the Geneva Convention on Bills of Exchange and Promissory Notes,** as of early 2004, are Austria, Belarus, Belgium, Brazil, Denmark, Finland, France, Germany, Greece, Hungary, Italy, Japan, Kazakhstan, Lithuania, Luxembourg, Monaco, the Netherlands, Norway, Poland, Portugal, Russia, Sweden, Switzerland, and Ukraine. **Members of the Geneva Convention on Cheques,** as of early 2004 are Austria, Belgium, Brazil, Denmark, Finland, France, Germany, Greece, Hungary, Indonesia, Italy, Japan, Lithuania, Luxembourg, Malawi, Monaco, the Netherlands, Nicaragua, Norway, Poland, Portugal, Sweden, and Switzerland. Supplemental conventions exist for both Bills of Exchange/Promissory Notes and Cheques aimed at resolving conflicts of laws, as well as a Convention on Stamp Laws applicable to Bills of Exchange and Promissory Notes. The full text of each may be reviewed at www.jus.uio.no/lm/treaties.and.organisations/lm.chronological.html#1930's.

Note that a drawee may become an acceptor of a draft, but this is not necessary in the case of the demand or "sight" draft, as the drawee (usually a bank) will not see the draft until it is presented for payment. At that time, the drawee will either pay or dishonor the draft, so acceptance is moot. Acceptance of the draft by the drawee comes into play when the draft is payable at a fixed or determinable time in the future, and is thus a time draft (or time or "term" bill). In this latter case, the drawee's act of acceptance crystallizes its obligation to pay at the future date.

Other parties such as holders, holders in due course, bearers, and "avals"[5] may be present in a transaction related to drafts and bills of exchange. As every nation regulates international bills of exchange according to its own local law, the same local law that governs the draft or bill of exchange itself will govern the rights and responsibilities of all parties.

It is worth warning that the Geneva Convention nations, largely due to their different regard for equitable remedies, differ from the Anglo-American common law practice in many small but significant rules. For example, there is no distinction drawn between holders and holders in due course as is done with common law negotiable instruments. Even within the common law tradition there exist procedural differences, for while three days' grace is given for payment in the United Kingdom and Commonwealth jurisdictions, grace is not contemplated by the UCC in U.S. states and is forbidden in the Geneva Convention.

The treatment of the formal requirements of drafts in both the Anglo-American tradition and the Geneva Convention regime is shown below, with the more evident lack of formal requirements in the common law system.

The Essentials of Negotiability of a Draft

Anglo-American Tradition	Geneva Convention
1. Unconditional **order**	1. Unconditional order
2. In writing	2. In writing
3. Signed by drawer	3. Signed by drawer
4. a. Addressed to drawee	4. a. Addressed to drawee
b. Often a bank	b. Often a bank
5. To pay a sum certain in money	5. To pay a sum certain in money
6. a. On demand (sight draft or sight bill) or	6. a. On demand or
b. At a fixed or determinable time	b. At a fixed or determinable time
(time draft or term/time bill)	
7. To the order of a specified person or bearer (payee)	7. To the order of a specified person or bearer (payee)
	8. Must contain the words "bill of exchange"
	9. Must state the place where payment is to be made
	10. Must state the date and place where the bill is issued

Note: A combination of 4b and 6a makes the instrument a check in the United States (the same thing as a "cheque" in the United Kingdom and Commonwealth). Combining 4b and 6a with the substitution of the word "cheque" for "bill of exchange" in 8 creates a cheque in Geneva Convention nations.

Source: A summation of both the U.S. Uniform Commercial Code, Article 3, § 3-104 (also reflecting the UK Bills of Exchange Act), and the Geneva Convention Providing a Uniform Law for Bills of Exchange and Promissory Notes, Articles 1, 2, and 14.

The following exhibits illustrate types of drafts that may be used in a transaction between a U.S. export seller and a British import buyer. Be aware that no universal format exists for drafts, but rather the structure of individual drafts may vary, although all required information must be present for them to be valid and negotiable.

Here, the promise of the British buyer contained in the underlying sale is formalized into a negotiable instrument. This may be done in order that the American seller might use it as collateral for borrowed money or to sell the instrument before its maturity, at a discount, for immediate cash. As the draft is payable at a fixed or determinable future time

[5]A form of guarantor provided for under the Geneva conventions, likely recognizable in U.S. states under UCC § 3-416, and not recognized under UK law; see *G+H Montage GmBh v. Irvani,* [1990] 1 Lloyd's Rep. 14 C.A. 1989.

(90 days after October 16, 2005), it is a time draft (to the American seller) and a term draft in the mind of the British buyer.

As the trade buyer itself is the drawee and acceptor, such drafts are known as *trade acceptances.*

Trade Acceptance

$10,000 United States Dollars	October 16, 2005
Ninety days after date of this FIRST of Exchange (second unpaid) For value received PAY TO THE ORDER OF: GLOBAL AMERICAN EXPORTS INC	*"Accepted" 21 Oct 2005* *British Import Ltd* *per John Myers* *Payable at London UK*
To: British Import Ltd, London UK	GLOBAL AMERICAN EXPORTS INC Los Angeles California USA Per: *Karen Grant* Authorized Officer

The words "FIRST of Exchange (second unpaid)" are an indication that this draft has been made up with two original copies sent in two different letters or courier packages to the offices of British Imports for acceptance and later return to Global American to hold to maturity. The second original will read "SECOND of Exchange (first unpaid)." The idea is to ensure that at least one of the two copies makes it to its destination and back, and when either one is presented for payment, the other original becomes void. The notion is similar to the multiple originals found in bills of lading.

Note that in this case, the British buyer has complied with the British requirements for acceptance, which exceed the simple signature requirement under the Uniform Commercial Code found in U.S. states.

It may, however, be the case that the slight increase in security enjoyed by Global American Exports really does not do it much good in attempting to raise money through the sale of the draft. British Import Ltd.'s creditworthiness may simply be unknown to finance sources that Global American Exports might approach. As a result, Global American might have suggested using a "banker's acceptance" under similar terms. In this case, the draft will not be drawn on or accepted by British Import Ltd., but rather by its banker, Eastminster Bank.

Banker's Acceptance

$10,000 United States Dollars	October 16, 2005
Ninety days after date of this FIRST of Exchange (second unpaid) For value received PAY TO THE ORDER OF: GLOBAL AMERICAN EXPORTS INC Charge same to account of: British Imports Ltd	Accepted 21 Oct 2005 Eastminster Bank per O.L. Threadneedle, Manager Payable at London UK
To: Eastminster Bank London UK	GLOBAL AMERICAN EXPORTS INC Los Angeles California USA Per: *Karen Grant* Authorized Officer

Now Global American knows that it has a guarantee of payment backed by the creditworthiness of the Eastminster Bank. Usually the bank will have taken steps to protect itself for its own later repayment from British Imports. It may do so (1) by knowing its customers and granting this type of facility to only the better ones or (2) by taking security from British Imports, and/or (3) charging a fee for the service itself.

Through these two examples, however, we have not considered the position of British Imports. It has a vested interest in seeing that the goods it has ordered actually arrive from Los Angeles to London, United Kingdom. The drafts above simply confirm that Global American Exports will receive payment, from either British Imports itself or Eastminster Bank.

Perhaps British Imports has received its assurance of receipt of the goods by virtue of the fact that it has already received the clean, on-board bill of lading from Global American Exports. In such a case, British Imports does not mind committing itself to eventual payment. If, however, the goods have not already been sent, or if British Imports has no means to claim them from the carrier on their arrival (i.e., no bill of lading in hand), it will be much less enthusiastic about committing itself to payment. The payment mechanisms that offer this delivery protection to the buyer-importer (as well as more secure payment protection to the seller) are the subject of the following sections.

Collections

In the last example draft in the section above, the draft was payable at the Eastminister Bank in London, United Kingdom. This represents a hardship for the seller-export; Global American Exports Inc., located in Los Angeles, California, in the United States. In response, Global American will be interested in using the services of its own bank to collect this draft on its behalf. Global American's bank (for the purposes of the examples below, the Bank of Western America) will have either an office of its own in London or a correspondent relationship with another bank to make the link. The service package offered by the bank makes it far more convenient for the bank to collect on the draft than for Global American to do it itself in person. This is the essence of the collection process.

At no time in a collection is Global American's bank, the Bank of Western America, taking on liability under the draft itself or the underlying sales contract; it is merely acting as an agent for the seller-exporter, and all credit and exchange rate risk remains with the seller.

The banks involved in a collection have no way of knowing if the goods are properly described, or if insurance was required, or what forms and documents were required for import entry. It is therefore up to the parties to ensure that the documents they are giving and receiving are all present, complete, correct, and endorsed. The banks will do nothing more than examine to ensure that the package of documents conforms to the collection order itself.

Collections come in three forms. The first, a clean collection, occurs where the Bank of Western America (the remitting bank) presents the draft (either for acceptance or, if already accepted, at maturity for payment, or if a demand draft, then for payment) to the drawee/acceptor and no other documents accompany the draft. This presumes the buyer has already received the shipping documents, for the mechanism offers the buyer no delivery guarantee. It is merely a straight collection vehicle for the seller.

The other two forms of collection, both of which are documentary collections, offer the desired delivery guarantees to the buyer. These are "documents against payment" and "documents against acceptance."

Steps in a Collection with Delivery Guarantee— Documents against Either Payment or Acceptance

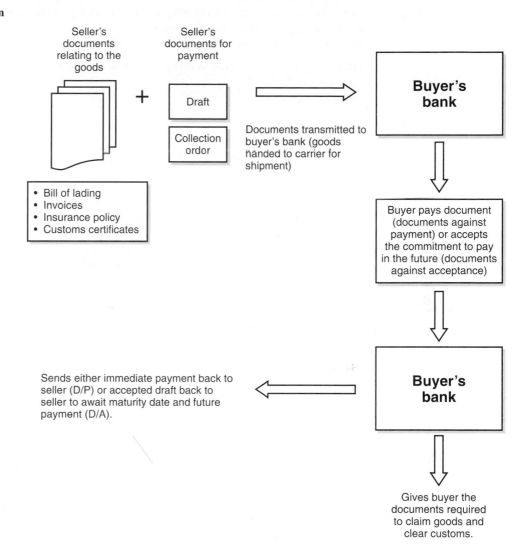

Seller's documents relating to the goods

+

Seller's documents for payment

Draft

Collection ordor

- Bill of lading
- Invoices
- Insurance policy
- Customs certificates

Documents transmitted to buyer's bank (goods handed to carrier for shipment)

Buyer's bank

Buyer pays document (documents against payment) or accepts the commitment to pay in the future (documents against acceptance)

Buyer's bank

Sends either immediate payment back to seller (D/P) or accepted draft back to seller to await maturity date and future payment (D/A).

Gives buyer the documents required to claim goods and clear customs.

Documents against Payment

As the international banking community is intensely interested in uniform rules, it has been quick to adopt such measures as developed by the International Chamber of Commerce. With respect to collections, these are the ICC Uniform Rules of Collection (URC522), last revised effective January 1, 1996, to which virtually all banks engaged in international operations adhere.[6]

Despite near universal observation of these rules, they remain private rules, and therefore must be specifically invoked by express incorporation into the collection order that will accompany the draft and the shipping documents in their travel.

A documents against payment (D/P) collection does as its name implies: the buyer will be given the shipping documents in return for payment against the draft. This forms a delivery guarantee for the buyer, as there can be no clean, on-board bill of lading unless the goods are already in transit.

[6]ICC Publication No. 522.

The seller prepares a collection order, essentially an application form containing the instructions for the collection, incorporating the ICC URC522 rules, and attaches to this collection order all documents relevant to the shipment, principally being the

1. Draft sought to be collected (a demand or sight draft, as the seller is expecting immediate payment).
2. Bill of lading.
3. Commercial invoice.
4. Customs invoice.
5. Insurance documentation (if required).
6. Inspection certificates (if required).

The documentary package is provided to the seller's bank (the remitting bank, Bank of Western America), which forwards the documents to the collecting bank (often the buyer's own bank, in this example the Eastminster Bank) in the buyer's country. On arrival, the collecting bank, Eastminster, presents the collection to the buyer, British Imports Ltd., who then pays the draft to the collecting bank and receives the documents. The collecting bank, Eastminster Bank, then sends the payment to the original remitting bank, Bank of Western America, which then advises and pays its customer, the seller, Global American Exports Inc.

Documents against Acceptance

This documentary collection works in exactly the same manner as documents against payment but relates to time drafts and term bills, for the draft is yet to be accepted by the drawee and will have a fixed or determinable future maturity date. Here the documents (and therefore, the goods) are released to the buyer once the draft has been accepted. Instead of payment returning after the draft is accepted, it will be the accepted draft that is returned to the seller to await maturity. The risk for the seller lies in the fact that it is depending upon the creditworthiness of the drawee, as the goods will be gone if the draft, on maturity, is dishonored by the drawee. Naturally, it is far superior (where possible) for the seller-exporter to have the draft drawn against the buyer's bank (and gain its creditworthiness as a guarantee), rather than on just the buyer-importer itself.

Letters of Credit/Documentary Credits

When one reflects on the previous section on collections, it must be remembered that the seller's certainty of payment only begins to arise when the draft is accepted, and, thereafter, only solidifies when the maturity date arrives and the draft is paid without dishonor. None of this is particularly helpful to the seller-exporter that needs cash up front as working capital in order to finance the actual production of the goods, and this is the situation in the vast bulk of international commercial sale transactions. The seller might approach its bank, with the buyer's order in hand, to seek working capital, but when a bank learns that goods may be produced for a buyer who might not pay, it is rarely interested in shouldering that risk on behalf of the seller, even at a price.

Thus, a mechanism is required that will allow the seller to have the confidence to produce the goods and proceed with the transaction, knowing that if it complies with the order and delivery instructions, it will receive its contractual amounts then due. When this kind of payment guarantee is given by a major financial institution (presumably that of the buyer), that is a guarantee upon whose strength the seller *can* raise working capital from its own bank. The key reason that this works is because the bank that finances the seller's production, while it does not trust the creditworthiness of the buyer, will trust the creditworthiness of the buyer's bank, whom it is in a much better position to know something about. The mechanism that creates this type of certainty, not only in payment but also in delivery, is the letter of credit.

The term *letter of credit* is also referred to more generally as an L/C, a credit, a documentary credit, a documentary letter of credit, or a commercial letter of credit, all meaning the same type of financial payment transaction. It is founded on an undertaking by a bank to honor the seller's draft once the seller has complied with those conditions contained in the terms of the credit. As it is issued after the sale contract has been agreed, the use of an L/C for payment must be one of the negotiated matters between the sale parties, and provision for it must be made in the sale contract itself. This being the case, the buyer will apply to its bank for an L/C to be opened in favor of the seller. Its terms will, in effect, state the following:

> If the seller sends complete shipping documents to *us* [meaning the buyer's bank and the bill of lading—confirming that the goods are in transit—and other documents required by the buyer in the L/C application], then *we* commit to pay the accompanying draft in accordance with the credit.

Unlike the collection process, this is the buyer's bank's commitment to pay the seller, not the buyer's commitment to pay the seller. How the buyer's bank intends to retrieve payment from its own customer is the bank's business, not the concern of the seller. Presumably, the buyer's bank will not release the shipping documents until it is satisfied that its customer *will* pay up.

The L/C will describe only those items that must be reflected on the shipping, insurance, and customs documents to be forwarded by the seller. As a result, the bank will be unaware of large aspects of the sale contract, and usually never sees the sale contract. Nor does the bank want to involve itself in the sale contract. In fact, to the contrary, it will specifically disclaim that type of liability. The bank is in the business of facilitating payments, not refereeing trade disputes nor inspecting shipments.

As was the case in collections, then, the banks involved are removed from and have no part in the underlying sale contract, and their connection to the parties is under the independent contract that is the letter of credit. Usually, the seller will dictate the terms of payment and the buyer will dictate the terms of delivery, and once this is done, the banks will release payment when documentary delivery is complete on its face. The crates may be empty, or filled with defective goods, but that is of no concern of the banks involved: that is a matter between the parties to the sale, and one best addressed by pre-shipment inspection.[7] As long as the buyer makes the right payment (or makes complete acceptance of the draft, etc., as the case may be), it will receive the shipping documents, and thereby the right to claim the goods from the dock.

The process is best illustrated with a diagram, continuing with the relationship between Global American Exports Inc. (the seller) and British Imports Ltd. (the buyer), as shown on page 398.

---

[7]The buyer need not travel to do this in person. Survey and inspection companies will perform this service for a price, under a separate contract.

Operation of a Documentary Letter of Credit

L/C Letter of Credit
B/L Bill of Lading

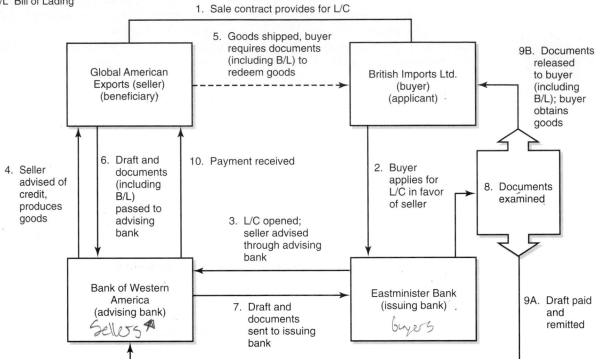

Parties to a Letter of Credit

The following are the parties to a letter of credit:

- Advising bank—a bank in the beneficiary country, named in the credit by the issuing bank (usually having been initially nominated by the seller), to which the credit is forwarded. The advising bank advises the beneficiary of the existence of the credit but attracts no liability unless it becomes a confirming bank.
- Applicant—the buyer-importer who requested that the credit be issued.
- Beneficiary—the seller-exporter to whom the credit is addressed.
- Confirming bank—a bank (often that of the seller-exporter) that adds its creditworthiness to that of the issuing bank, thereby enhancing the beneficiary's guarantee of payment once that beneficiary has complied with the terms of the credit.
- Issuing bank—the bank (generally that of the buyer-importer) that issues the credit and in so doing undertakes to honor the later claim for payment by the beneficiary once that beneficiary has complied with the terms of the credit.

Types and Conditions of Letters of Credit

Types of Letters of Credit   The general workings of a letter of credit as shown above can be further classified by other criteria. Most frequently, the L/C is documentary or standby, irrevocable or revocable, confirmed or unconfirmed, and payable via sight or time draft. The vast majority of letters of credit used in international trade are documentary, irrevocable, and confirmed.

Documentary versus Standby   The *documentary* letter of credit is used to ensure payment against shipment of goods (as was shown above) or for the provision of services. A

A revocable credit is nearly useless for arm's-length trade between strangers. First, it can be canceled at the buyer's will, leaving unclaimed goods stranded abroad. Such goods have a habit of disappearing. Second, it cannot be turned into a confirmed credit. Third, no bank will provide working capital based on such a shaky payment promise. Finally, if such a credit is the best the buyer can muster, absent other reasons, it's not a particularly good reflection on what the buyer's bank thinks of its own customer.

Revocable credits are cheaper (they represent less risk to the bank, as the bank can terminate its promise), but because of their higher risk, they should only be used in transactions between parties with the greatest of faith in one another, as an example, between related firms who have the same parent company. Even so, as revocable credits offer little more security than open account terms, one is right to question their worth in trouble or expense. Beware of strangers offering revocable credits in payment; they may be fraud artists.

standby letter of credit, in contrast, is not intended as a means of payment, but rather as a seller's guarantee or security for performance. The seller's right to demand payment from the bank that issues the standby credit arises only when the buyer fails to make payment in accordance with its contractual responsibility. Most often, (irrevocable) standby letters of credit are offered as a backup to an open account arrangement where bills are expected to be paid in cash on timely basis, with the standby L/C in the background. Note, however, the Old Wolf's comments above on open account guarantees through revocable L/Cs of any kind.

Irrevocable versus Revocable   An *irrevocable* credit is an issuing bank's undertaking that it will make payment, provided the terms and conditions contained in the credit are satisfied, and this undertaking cannot be amended or canceled without the consent of all parties, including the beneficiary. This comfort is also extended to any subsequent endorsers of drafts drawn under the credit. A *revocable* credit, on the other hand, may be either canceled or amended by the issuing bank, either of its own initiative or that of the applicant.

Confirmed versus Unconfirmed   Where another bank has added its guarantee of payment to the letter of credit, through a request made to it by the issuing bank and stemming from an initial request of the seller, that letter of credit is *confirmed*. A confirmation can only be added to an irrevocable credit. Often, the advising bank will become a confirming bank, but it is not so obligated. If there is a confirming bank, it may very well be another bank involved, one that is not the advising bank. Where there is no confirming bank, the letter of credit is described as *unconfirmed,* and only the issuing bank has the responsibility to honor drafts presented to it for payment.

The drafts by which the credit will be paid may be at sight (on demand) or at a fixed or determinable future date (time or terms drafts), as previously defined.

Transferable Credit   A transferable credit is one under which the beneficiary (usually the seller) is expressly permitted to transfer the letter of credit in favor of another person. The credit must be set up as transferable when initially created, and is usually employed where the seller is only an intermediary, buying goods and reselling them, thus having its own payment obligation to its own suppliers. A transferable credit must be distinguished from an assignment of proceeds where, being entitled under the credit, the seller assigns its rights to the proceeds. In this latter case, the letter of credit itself is not actually being transferred between the parties, only the right to payment.

Back-to-Back Credit Where the seller-beneficiary of a confirmed credit uses it as security to open its own new credit with its own bank in favor of its own suppliers (in order to finance its own end of the deal before payment), this second credit is said to be a back-to-back credit. The first is known as the *overriding credit.*

General Conditions The bank issuing the L/C (under contract with the buyer, in favor of the seller) will take certain legal steps in contract to protect its own interests, while disclaiming any liability under the underlying sales contract. Typically, these steps will include

1. Not holding the bank responsible for the goods or their condition at any time, or for any delay resulting from the sale contract or the credit (save the bank's own direct negligence).
2. Taking security in, or holding title to, the goods in transit (usually through possession of the bill of lading until the buyer repays the credit, or other payment arrangements are made).
3. Requiring, in its own right, that the goods are and remain insured.
4. Requiring the buyer to clear the goods promptly through customs (whether the buyer is responsible under the sale contract or not) and indemnifying the bank in that regard.

Law and Practice in Letters of Credit

Local law (in one form or another) does exist to some extent in most jurisdictions to govern letters of credit, even if it is a matter of straight contract law. Specific legislation does exist, for example, in the United States under the Uniform Commercial Code, Article 5.[8]

In most jurisdictions, banking practice has been coupled with the law related to bills of exchange and negotiable instruments to produce effective governance, and once again the singular contributions of the International Chamber of Commerce have formed the harmonizing element in the international treatment of letters of credit.

The ICC Uniform Customs and Practice of Documentary Credits, last revised in 1993 and known as UCP500,[9] is adhered to by essentially every major and most minor banking institutions of the world, and accommodation exists in most local legal systems (including the UCC of U.S. states) for incorporation of these rules into letters of credit. UCP500 is now further supplemented by eUCP, which establishes standards for electronic presentation. Moreover, the Opinions of the ICC Banking Commission constitute the private equivalent of jurisprudence on the interpretation and application of the rules.[10]

Due to this adherence of banks and accommodation of national systems, the UCP500 rules can be considered virtually universal, but they still must be deliberately invoked in contract.[11] This is not problematic, as banking forms are prepared by the banks themselves for use in letters of credit, and therefore contain the appropriate words of invocation.

Since the objective of letters of credit is to confine bank participation to ensuring that payment is remitted when documents of title arrive, and in consequence remove banks from any consideration of the underlying sale contract, the overall transaction is therefore broken into two parts: the sale and the payment.

This creates a universe of four true contractual relationships, which cannot be better stated than has been done by Lord Diplock of the United Kingdom:

---

[8]With revised UCC Article 5 having been adopted by all states except Georgia, Kentucky, and Wisconsin, however, and including the District of Columbia and the Virgin Islands.

[9]Publication no. 500.

[10]See, for example, ICC Banking Commission Collected Opinions 1995-2001, ICC Publication 632, available through www.iccwbo.org.

[11]They remain the product guidelines of private rule makers, not lawmakers, and Article 1 of UCP500 requires specific reference to the rules for them to apply.

. . . [T]here are four independent, although inter-connected, contracts. They are:

1. the contract for the sale of goods between the buyer and seller;
2. the contract between the buyer and his bank whereby the latter issues the credit and agrees to pay the seller (or to accept or negotiate bills of exchange drawn by the seller) either through an advising or a confirming bank upon receipt of specified documents;
3. if payment is to be made through an advising bank, then the arrangement by that bank to accept the documents for transmittal. If payment is to be made through a confirming bank, then the inter-bank contract whereby the confirming bank agrees to pay to the beneficiary upon receipt of the stipulated documents and the issuing bank agrees to reimburse the confirming bank upon receipt thereof; and
4. the arrangement whereby the seller's bank undertakes either to receive and transmit documents (unconfirmed) or to pay, without recourse, to the seller upon receipt of the appropriate documents (confirmed).[12]

What is often termed the "independence doctrine" of the letter of credit as apart from the underlying sale contract is echoed in the United States within the Uniform Commercial Code at Article 5, Sections 5-108 (e–g) of the 1995 revision:

e. An issuer shall observe standard practice of financial institutions that regularly issue letters of credit. Determination of the issuer's observance of the standard practice is a matter of interpretation for the court. The court shall offer the parties a reasonable opportunity to present evidence of the standard practice.
f. An issuer is not responsible for:
1. the performance or nonperformance of the underlying contract, arrangement, or transaction,
2. an act or omission of others, or
3. observance or knowledge of the usage of a particular trade other than the standard practice referred to in subsection (e).
g. If an undertaking constituting a letter of credit under Section 5-102(a)(10) contains nondocumentary conditions, an issuer shall disregard the nondocumentary conditions and treat them as if they were not stated.

This autonomy or independence doctrine is found in the UCP500 at Article 4, with liability of issuing and confirming banks in the form and notification of credits at Article 9, a standard for examination of documents at Article 13, and discrepant documents and notice treated at Article 14.

[12]*United City Merchants (Investment) Limited and Glass Fibres and Equipment Ltd. v. Royal Bank of Canada, Vitrorefuerzos S.A. and Banco Continental S.A.,* [1982] 2 W.L.R. 1039 at 1045, affirmed [1983] A.C. 168 (House of Lords).

ICC UCP500—Selected Articles and Excerpts Only

Article 4 (complete)

Documents v. Goods/Services/Performances

In Credit operations all parties concerned deal with documents, and not with goods, services and/or other performances to which the documents may relate.

Article 9 (excerpt)

Liability of Issuing and Confirming Banks

a. An irrevocable Credit constitutes a definite undertaking of the Issuing Bank, provided that the stipulated documents are presented to the Nominated Bank or to the Issuing Bank and that the terms and conditions of the Credit are complied with: . . .

b. A confirmation of an irrevocable Credit by another bank (the "Confirming Bank") upon the authorisation or request of the Issuing Bank, constitutes a definite undertaking of the Confirming Bank, in addition to that of the Issuing Bank, provided that the stipulated documents are presented to the Confirming Bank or to any other Nominated Bank and that the terms and conditions of the Credit are complied with: . . .

Article 13 (complete)

Standard for Examination of Documents

a. Banks must examine all documents stipulated in the Credit with reasonable care, to ascertain whether or not they appear, on their face, to be in compliance with the terms and conditions of the Credit. Compliance of the stipulated documents on their face with the terms and conditions of the Credit shall be determined by international standard banking practice as reflected in these Articles. Documents which appear on their face to be inconsistent with one another will be considered as not appearing on their face to be in compliance with the terms and conditions of the Credit.

   Documents not stipulated in the Credit will not be examined by banks. If they receive such documents, they shall return them to the presenter or pass them on without responsibility.

b. The Issuing Bank, the Confirming Bank, if any, or a Nominated Bank acting on their behalf, shall each have a reasonable time, not to exceed seven banking days following the day of receipt of the documents, to examine the documents and determine whether to take up or refuse the documents and to inform the party from which it received the documents accordingly.

c. If a credit contains conditions without stating the document(s) to be presented in compliance therewith, banks will deem such conditions as not stated and will disregard them.

Article 14 (complete)

Discrepant Documents and Notice

a. When the Issuing Bank authorises another bank to pay, incur a deferred payment undertaking, accept Draft(s), or negotiate against documents which appear on their face to be in compliance with the terms and conditions of the Credit, the Issuing Bank and the Confirming Bank, if any, are bound:
   i. to reimburse the Nominated Bank which has paid, incurred a deferred payment undertaking, accepted Draft(s), or negotiated,
   ii. to take up the documents.

b. Upon receipt of the documents the Issuing Bank and/or Confirming Bank, if any, or a Nominated Bank acting on their behalf, must determine on the basis of the documents alone whether or not they appear on their face to be in compliance with the terms and conditions of the Credit. If the documents appear on their face not to be in compliance with the terms and conditions of the Credit, such banks may refuse to take up the documents.

c. If the Issuing bank determines that the documents appear on their face not to be in compliance with the terms and conditions of the Credit, it may in its sole judgement approach the Applicant for a waiver of the discrepancy(ies). This does not, however, extend the period mentioned in sub-Article 13 (b).

d. i. If the Issuing Bank and/or the Confirming Bank, if any, or a Nominated bank acting on their behalf, decides to refuse the documents, it must give notice to that effect by telecommunication or, if that is not possible, by other expeditious means, without delay but no later than the close of the seventh banking day following the day of receipt of the documents. Such notice shall be given to the bank from which it received the documents, or to the Beneficiary, if it received the documents directly from him.

   ii. Such notice must state all discrepancies in respect of which the bank refuses the documents and must also state whether it is holding the documents at the disposal of, or is returning them to, the presenter.

   iii. The Issuing Bank and/or Confirming Bank, if, any, shall then be entitled to claim from the remitting bank refund, with interest, of any reimbursement which has been made to that bank.

e. If the Issuing Bank and/or Confirming Bank, if any, fails to act in accordance with the provisions of this Article and/or fails to hold the documents at the disposal of, or return them to the presenter, the Issuing bank and/or Confirming Bank, if any, shall be precluded from claiming that the documents are not in compliance with the terms and conditions of the Credit.

f. If the remitting bank draws the attention of the Issuing Bank and/or Confirming Bank, if any, to any discrepancy(ies) in the document(s) or advises such banks that it has paid, incurred a deferred payment undertaking, accepted Draft(s) or negotiated under reserve or against an indemnity in respect of such discrepancy(ies), the Issuing Bank and/or Confirming Bank, if any, shall not be thereby relieved from any of their obligations under any provision of this Article. Such reserve or indemnity concerns only the relations between the remitting bank and the party towards whom the reserve was made, or from whom, or on whose behalf, the indemnity was obtained.

As can be seen from the rules excerpted above, the concerns of the banking industry need only, properly, be focused on the payment relationship created through the letter of credit. The bank is not obliged to look beyond the credit into the underlying sale contract. Still, the banks involved must act with speed and precision, or they will have no recourse but to pay in accordance with the credit. The real issues then become whether the documents conform to the requirements as laid out in the credit transaction and, in some cases, whether the transaction or documents are fraudulent.

In the first instance, where documents must conform strictly to requirements, the question is "how strict" is "sufficiently strict" to say that compliance has been achieved? If the test of compliance fails, the bank may refuse payment. It refuses payment because it owes its duty under the credit contract to its customer (the applicant), not the beneficiary of the payment. If the bank goes ahead and makes a payment where a discrepancy has not been waived by the bank's customer-applicant, then the bank faces a defense to reimbursement by its customer, as it has acted on its own account.

An example serves the point:

- U.S. customer A approaches U.S. bank C to apply for a letter of credit in payment to European seller-beneficiary D for 10,000 industry-standard bags of walnuts. When D presents the evidence of shipment and requests payment from C, the bill of lading issued by the carrier E indicates that "10,000 20-kilogram bags" were loaded and shipped, clean on board. Who says a 20-kilogram (44-pound) bag is "industry standard"? What if an industry-standard bag is 50 pounds for U.S. industry and a 20-kilogram bag is standard in Europe? Bank C will
  1. Not want to pay in principle (which is its right to do in case of discrepancies).
  2. Not want to get into a dispute over the A–D sales contract (questions of intentions of the parties).
  3. Not want to find that it has paid D the full amount for a shipment that is 60,000 pounds light ((50–44) × 10,000 bags). In such a case, bank C's customer A, the applicant, will want to pay only for what it has received and will refuse to compensate the bank for the loss caused by the bank.
- When bank C examines the documents and compares them to the L/C, it should notice the difference between "industry-standard" and "20-kilogram" bags. The proper response by the bank should then be to contact its customer A, ask if this is correct, and, if so, ask it to provide the bank with a waiver to go ahead and release payment. If the customer refuses to waive the discrepancy, the bank should refuse to pay.

Many cases have litigated this point, without benefit of a clear rule, but the standard is a strict one. International businesspersons (buyers or sellers) should expect and aim for this strict standard of compliance in their documents, and not take any leeway for granted. Consider this review by Judge Powell of the U.S. Court of Appeals for the 11th Circuit:

Kerr-McGee Chem. Corp. v. FDIC

Under Florida law, letters of credit are subject to a rule of "strict compliance." Documents presented for payment must precisely meet the requirements set forth in the credit. Any discrepancy entitles the bank to refuse payment, and the bank bases its decision on the documents alone. See, e.g., *Fidelity National Bank v. Dade County,* 371 So. 2d 545, 548 (Fla. Dist. Ct. App. 3d Dist. 1979). If the documents do not on their face meet the requirements of the credit, the fact that a defect is a mere "technicality" does not matter. See, e.g., *Id.; Beyene v. Irving Trust Co.,* 762 F.2d 4 (2d Cir. 1985) (misspelling on bill of lading was grounds for dishonor); *Courtaulds North America, Inc. v. North Carolina National Bank,* 528 F.2d 802 (4th Cir. 1975) (discrepancy between terms "100% acrylic yarn" and "imported acrylic yarn" grounds for dishonor). As expressed by the Florida Court of Appeals: "Compliance with the terms of a letter of credit is not like pitching horseshoes. No points are awarded for being close." *Fidelity National Bank,* 371 So. 2d at 546."[13]

Most jurisdictions show an attitude that tends toward, not away from, the attitudes found in the State of Florida. While a doctrine of "substantial performance" does exist in the United States—that is, does an intelligent reading of the shipping documents lead to a conclusion that they are in compliance with the terms of the credit?—Florida shows that this is a risky approach to doing business. It would be pleasing if the discussion could be left at that, but there are examples of both liberal interpretations of "strict" compliance, and just as many or more of very strict requirements. This lack of consistency is present in the United States, and encountered just as frequently in the rest of the world. Some British and Commonwealth cases are typical:

Equitable Trust v. Dawson

[Viscount Sumner:] The accepting bank can only claim indemnity if the conditions on which it is authorised to accept are in the matter of the accompanying documents strictly observed. There is no room for documents which are almost the same, or which will do just as well.[14]

[13]872 F.2d 971, 973 (11th Cir. 1989).
[14][1926] 27 Lloyd's List L. Rep. 49.

Discrepancies are depressingly frequent, opening the door to a bank refusing payment. Banks report that 50 percent of presentations of documents for payment routinely contain discrepancies, although most are waived or the L/C is amended, indicating the commitment of banks in making the system work. International businesspersons should not become dependent on these acts of charity, however, and should do their part in understanding the process to ensure that their applications and documents are free of discrepancies. Most can be avoided with attention and care in the application stage.

Bank de L'Indochine v. Rayner

[Parker J:] I have no doubt that so long as the documents can be plainly seen to be linked with each other, are not inconsistent with each other or with the terms of the credit, do not call for enquiry and between them state all that is required in the credit to be stated, the beneficiary is entitled to be paid . . . some margin must and can be allowed, but it is slight, and banks will be at risk in most cases where there is less than strict compliance.[15]

Hing Yip Hing Fat Co. Ltd. v. Daiwa Bank

[Kaplan J, where the buyer, Cheergoal Industries Ltd., was described in the documents as Cheergoal "Industrial" Ltd. and an "inspection certificate of quality/quantity" was offered where a "certificate of quality/quantity" was called for:] It is clear that a printed inspection certificate has been adapted to meet the facts of this case. I therefore find that this certificate is in conformity with the terms of this credit. [Further he writes the] use of the word "Industrial" was an obvious typographical error for the word "Industries" [and] not a discrepancy on which Daiwa can rely."[16]

The clear implication is that the more complications that are inserted in a letter of credit, the greater the probability of discrepancies, and the greater chance of effective dishonor. Second, fraud at any stage of the L/C process creates an exception to the independence doctrine and the bank also may refuse payment.

The following British case is very rich. It illustrates

- The entire operation of the L/C issue and presentation process.
- Discrepancies.
- Avoidance of payment by an issuing bank.
- The difficulty experienced by a confirming bank in recovery where it had missed discrepancies and waived its rights.
- Ethical issues surrounding letters of credit and their abuse.
- The liability of shipowners and a beneficiary for fraud.

Standard Chartered Bank v. Pakistan National Shipping Corp.

House of Lords
November 6, 2002
Lord Hoffmann:

My Lords,

Mr Mehra was the managing director of Oakprime Ltd, the beneficiary under a letter of credit which had been issued by Incombank, a Vietnamese bank, and confirmed by Standard

[15][1983] 2 W.L.R. 841.
[16][1991] 1 H.K.C. 383.

Chartered Bank, London ("SCB"). The credit was issued in connection with a cif sale of Iranian bitumen by Oakprime to Vietranscimex, a Vietnamese organisation. A condition of the credit was "Shipment must be effected not later than 25 October 1993." The last date for negotiation was 10 November 1993.

Loading was delayed and Oakprime was unable to ship the goods before 25 October 1993. But the shipping agents and shipowners (Pakistan National Shipping Corporation ("PNSC")) agreed with Mr Mehra to issue bills of lading dated 25 October 1993 and did so on 8 November 1993, before the goods had been shipped. On 9 November 1993 Oakprime presented the bill of lading and other documents to SCB under cover of a letter signed by Mr Mehra stating that (with one omission) the documents were all those required by the credit. This statement was false to the knowledge of Mr Mehra because he had himself arranged for the backdating of the bill of lading. The false statement was made to obtain payment under the letter of credit and it is agreed that if there had been no bill of lading or SCB had known that it was falsely dated, payment would not have been made. The omitted document was presented a few days later and certain other documents which had shown discrepancies from the terms of the credit were resubmitted after the final date for negotiation of the credit had passed. Notwithstanding that SCB knew that these documents had been presented late, it decided to waive late presentation. It authorised payment of US$1,155,772.77 on 15 November 1993.

SCB then sought reimbursement from Incombank. It sent a standard form letter that included a statement that the documents had been presented before the expiry date. This statement was known by a relevant employee of SCB to be false. Incombank, although unaware of both Mr Mehra's false dating of the bill of lading and SCB's false dating of the presentation of the documents, rejected the documents on account of other discrepancies which SCB had not noticed. Despite further requests, SCB was unable to obtain reimbursement.

SCB then sued the shipowners (PNSC), the shipping agents, Oakprime and Mr Mehra for deceit. They had all joined in issuing a false bill of lading intending it to be used to obtain payment from SCB under the credit. Cresswell J held that they were all liable for damages to be assessed.

PNSC appealed on the ground that the loss suffered by SCB had been partly the result of its own "fault" within the meaning of section 1(1) of the Law Reform (Contributory Negligence) Act 1945 and that its damages should therefore be reduced to such extent as the court thought just and equitable. Sir Anthony Evans would have accepted this argument and reduced the damages by 25%. But the majority of the court (Aldous and Ward LJJ) ([2001] QB 167) held that SCB's conduct was not "fault" as defined in the Act because it was not at common law a defence to an action in deceit: see the definition in section 4 of the Act.

Mr Mehra appealed on the ground that he had made the fraudulent representation on behalf of Oakprime and not personally. The court unanimously upheld this ground of appeal. It ordered SCB to pay Mr Mehra's costs before that court and three-quarters of his costs at trial.

PNSC appealed to your Lordships' House against the decision that the damages could not be reduced and SCB appealed against the decision that Mr Mehra was not personally liable. Shortly before the hearing, PNSC agreed to pay SCB US$1.7m in full and final settlement of its claims to damages, interest and costs. There was no apportionment between these heads of claim and the settlement agreement expressly preserved SCB's claims against other parties. Your Lordships have allowed the petition of PNSC for leave to withdraw its appeal.

At the commencement of the hearing, Mr Cherryman QC submitted on behalf of Mr Mehra that the settlement gave SCB the whole of any damages to which it could be entitled against PNSC and Mr Mehra as joint tortfeasors. It would therefore be an abuse of the process of the court to pursue the appeal against Mr Mehra. The appeal should be stayed. He did not however propose that any change should be made to the Court of Appeal's order for costs in favour of Mr Mehra. Your Lordships refused the application for a stay on the ground that, quite apart from the question of whether the settlement moneys discharged the whole of SCB's claim, it was entitled to proceed so as to have the order for costs set aside and to obtain an order in its favour.

Before your Lordships Mr Mehra argued that not only was he not liable at all, for the reasons given by the Court of Appeal, but that if he was liable, the damages should be reduced on account of the contributory negligence of SCB.

My Lords, I shall consider first the defence of contributory negligence . . .

[His Lordship then reviews the British law of contributory negligence . . . setting the question as] whether at common law SCB's conduct would be a defence to its claim for deceit . . . It would be more accurate to say that it was careless in making payment against documents which, as it knew or ought to have known, did not comply with the terms of the credit, on the assumption that it could successfully conceal these matters from Incombank. In respect of the loss suffered, SCB was in my opinion negligent.

Be that as it may, the real question is whether the conduct of SCB would at common law be a defence to a claim in deceit . . . In the case of fraudulent misrepresentation, however, I agree with Mummery J in *Alliance & Leicester Building Society v Edgestop Ltd* [1993] 1 WLR 1462 that there is no common law defence of contributory negligence. It follows that, in agreement with the majority in the Court of Appeal, I think that no apportionment under the 1945 Act is possible.

[Having concluded that SCB's negligence does not provide Mehra with a defence to a claim in deceit . . .]

My Lords, I come next to the question of whether Mr Mehra was liable for his deceit. To put the question in this way may seem tendentious but I do not think that it is unfair. Mr Mehra says, and the Court of Appeal accepted, that he committed no deceit because he made the representation on behalf of Oakprime and it was relied upon as a representation by Oakprime. That is true but seems to me irrelevant. Mr Mehra made a fraudulent misrepresentation intending SCB to rely upon it and SCB did rely upon it. The fact that by virtue of the law of agency his representation and the knowledge with which he made it would also be attributed to Oakprime would be of interest in an action against Oakprime. But that cannot detract from the fact that they were his representation and his knowledge. He was the only human being involved in making the representation to SCB (apart from administrative assistance like someone to type the letter and carry the papers round to the bank). It is true that SCB relied upon Mr Mehra's representation being attributable to Oakprime because it was the beneficiary under the credit. But they also relied upon it being Mr Mehra's representation, because otherwise there could have been no representation and no attribution.

The Court of Appeal appear to have based their conclusion upon the decision of your Lordships' House in *Williams v Natural Life Health Foods Ltd* [1998] 1 WLR 830. That was an action for damages for negligent misrepresentation. My noble and learned friend, Lord Steyn, pointed out that in such a case liability depended upon an assumption of responsibility by the defendant. As Lord Devlin said in *Hedley Byrne & Co Ltd v Heller & Partners* [1964] AC 465, 530, the basis of liability is analogous to contract. And just as an agent can contract on behalf of another without incurring personal liability, so an agent can assume responsibility on behalf of another for the purposes of the *Hedley Byrne* rule without assuming personal responsibility. Their Lordships decided that on the facts of the case, the agent had not assumed any personal responsibility.

This reasoning cannot in my opinion apply to liability for fraud. No one can escape liability for his fraud by saying "I wish to make it clear that I am committing this fraud on behalf of someone else and I am not to be personally liable." Sir Anthony Evans framed the question ([2000] 1 Lloyd's Rep 218, 230) as being "whether the director may be held liable for the company's tort." But Mr Mehra was not being sued for the company's tort. He was being sued for his own tort and all the elements of that tort were proved against him. Having put the question in the way he did, Sir Anthony answered it by saying that the fact that Mr Mehra was a director did not in itself make him liable. That of course is true. He is liable not because he was a director but because he committed a fraud.

Both Sir Anthony Evans and Aldous LJ treated the *Williams* case [1998] 1 WLR 830 as being based upon the separate legal personality of a company. Aldous LJ referred ([2000] Lloyd's Rep 218, 233) to *Salomon v A Salomon & Co Ltd* [1897] AC 22. But my noble and learned friend, Lord Steyn, made it clear (at p 835) that the decision had nothing to do with company law. It was an application of the law of principal and agent to the requirement of assumption of responsibility under the *Hedley Byrne* principle. Lord Steyn said it would have made no difference if Mr Williams's principal had been a natural person. So one may test the matter by asking whether, if Mr Mehra had been acting as manager for the owner of the business who lived in the south of France and had made a fraudulent representation within the scope of his employment, he could escape personal liability by saying that it must have been perfectly clear that he was not being fraudulent on his own behalf but exclusively on behalf of his employer.

I would therefore allow the appeal against Mr Mehra and restore the order which Cresswell J made against him. In enforcing this order, SCB will of course have to give credit for the money it has received from PNSC but how this sum should be apportioned is not a matter which your Lordships have been asked to consider.

Source: [2002] U.K.H.L. 43.

- What serious breaches of proper and ethical behavior occurred here?
- What and why did Incombank do what it did, and how was it protecting both • itself and its customer, Vietranscimex?
- If you can ignore that it had to wage a 10-year legal battle, then SCB could be said to have been "lucky." How was SCB "lucky," and what could have happened to make things much worse? What should SCB have done in the first place?

An equally interesting U.S. example of a transferable L/C case follows below, where a bank was barred from claiming fraud and from relying on discrepancies to reject a payment demand.

Hamilton Bank, N.A. v. Kookmin Bank

United States Court of Appeals for the Second Circuit
March 15, 2001
Pooler, Circuit Judge

Plaintiff Hamilton Bank, N.A. ("Hamilton") issued a $1.5 million letter of credit on behalf of Sky Industries Corporation ("Sky") for the benefit of Sung-Jin Trading Co. ("SungJin"). The letter of credit contained several conditions including a requirement that the entity negotiating it provide an authenticated telex from Hamilton. Sung-Jin, a Korean company, negotiated the letter of credit to Kookmin Bank ("Kookmin"), a Korean financial institution, without the required telex and with certain other documents that may have been altered or forged. When Kookmin presented the letter of credit to Hamilton for payment, Hamilton refused, claiming that the documents presented did not meet the requirements of the letter of credit but failing to specify the particular deficiencies. Hamilton later issued a second but untimely disclaimer specifying the missing telex—and other deficiencies no longer at issue—as the reasons for its refusal to pay. Hamilton argues that Kookmin's negligence and/or its fraudulent collusion with Sung-Jin in initially accepting the documents precludes Kookmin from relying on the untimeliness of Hamilton's disclaimer. Hamilton also contends that Kookmin defamed Hamilton in a letter Kookmin sent to the Office of the Comptroller of the Currency ("OCC").

Background

. . .

On June 11, 1996, Hamilton issued a $1.5 million letter of credit on behalf of Sky and for the benefit of Sung-Jin in connection with Sky's planned purchase of leather sport shoes from Sung-Jin. The letter provided that drafts could be negotiated "at 180 days after transport document date" upon presentation of the letter along with a bill of lading, an original and three copies of a commercial invoice and packing list, and a "copy of authenticated (sic) telex from issuing bank to advising bank, indicating quantity to be shipped, destination, and nominating transporting company." The letter also specified that it was issued pursuant to the Uniform Customs and Practice for Documentary Credits ("UCP") (1993 revision) ICC Pub. No. 500. Hamilton amended the letter of credit three times. The only change relevant to this litigation was made in the third amendment and provided:

> "no further amendments of this l/c will be issued by applicant, any other condition should
> be in accordance with 'option contract.' signed by applicant and beneficiary dated May 31,
> 1986. ALL OTHER TERMS AND CONDITIONS REMAIN UNCHANGED. SUBJECT
> TO UCP 500."

Kookmin Negotiates the Letter of Credit

In June 1996, Sung-Jin's principal, Jin Kon Kim attempted to negotiate the letter of credit to Kookmin. Taek Su Jun, an employee of Kookmin, repeatedly told Kim that Kookmin would not accept the letter of credit without an authenticated telex, and Kim responded that he would take care of this problem. However, on July 13, 1996, Kim returned to Kookmin and again presented the amended letter of credit along with a purported option contract between Sky and Sung-Jin and special instructions allegedly signed by Sky but without the authenticated telex . . .

The special instructions allowed Sung-Jin to choose the transportation company and provided that the shoes must be shipped to New York. In addition, Kim gave Jun a bill of lading representing that 40,000 pairs of sport shoes had been loaded on board the Hanjin Savannah on July 12, 1996.

Jun testified that Kim persuaded him that the option contract—with its reference to special instructions—eliminated the authenticated telex requirement. Although Jun never had heard of Sung-Jin prior to that company's attempts to negotiate the letter of credit, he accepted it. Jun first asked for security but later decided to rely on insurance through the Korean Export Insurance Authority. On the day he negotiated the letter, Jun contacted Hamilton's advising bank in Korea, Dongnam Bank, to determine whether the letter of credit and amendments were authentic but did not ask whether the option contract and special instructions replaced the authenticated telex as a basis for negotiating the letter.

Hamilton's Rejection

On July 22, 1996, Kookmin presented the letter of credit, draft, and shipping documents to Hamilton in order to obtain payment. Hamilton returned the documents to Kookmin via

DHL courier on July 24, 1996, along with a letter stating that Hamilton would not honor the letter because presentment was "not in compliance with the terms and conditions of the credit." Kookmin received the documents on July 27, 1996, and presented them again on August 2, 1996. On August 6, 1996, Hamilton rejected the presentation a second time. On that date, Kookmin also received a "SWIFT," which we assume to be a telecommunication, from Hamilton explaining that Hamilton rejected the presentation because it lacked an authenticated telex.

. . .

. . . Kookmin . . . unsuccessfully attempted to call Kim several times. In August 1996, Jun went to Sung-Jin's office and found it empty and unlocked . . .

. . . Kookmin's insurance carrier disclaimed coverage based on Kookmin's "serious negligence" in accepting the letter of credit. Fifteen months later, Kookmin disciplined Jun for his failure to follow appropriate procedures.

No-one ever retrieved the goods covered by the letter of credit, and ultimately, U.S. customs officials sold them at a public auction which realized $25,000.

. . .

The Korean Action

In December 1997, Kookmin filed a lawsuit in Korea to recover damages for Hamilton's refusal to honor its letter of credit.

The District Court Action

On March 25, 1998, Hamilton sued Kookmin in the United States District Court for the Southern District of New York. Hamilton sought an order enjoining the Korean lawsuit, a judgment declaring that it was not liable on the letter of credit, damages for libel, an award of lost profits, and punitive damages. Hamilton also named Sky as a defendant, requesting indemnification in the event that it had to pay Kookmin. Kookmin counterclaimed for breach of the letter of credit. After the district court (Kaplan, J.) denied Hamilton's request for injunctive relief, the Korean court ruled in Kookmin's favor. In November 1998, Kookmin moved for summary judgment, arguing principally that (1) because Hamilton failed to make a timely and specific disclaimer, Article 14 of the UCP precluded it from disclaiming and (2) the letter to the comptroller was a privileged statement of opinion. In response, Hamilton argued that Kookmin itself violated the duty of due care imposed on it by Article 13 of the UCP; Kookmin may have accepted the letter of credit with culpable knowledge, thus vitiating its status as a holder in due course; Kookmin failed to mitigate its damages; and Kookmin's malice destroyed any privilege it might have enjoyed.

The district court ruled in Kookmin's favor on both the letter of credit and libel claims. In pertinent part, the court found that (1) Hamilton's disclaimer was untimely and insufficiently specific; (2) any fraudulent documentation alleged by Hamilton was immaterial because it did not gull Hamilton into accepting the obviously insufficient documentation; (3) fraud in the transaction was not available to Hamilton as a defense because the bank alleged documentary fraud rather than the complete worthlessness of the goods shipped; (4) Kookmin's failure to comply with Article 13 of the UCP did not excuse Hamilton's failure to make a timely and specific disclaimer; (5) Hamilton's mitigation of damages defense lacked merit; and (6) Kookmin's letter to OCC enjoyed a qualified privilege that it did not abuse. Subsequently, the court entered a judgment submitted by Hamilton and dismissed without prejudice all claims against Sky.

This appeal followed.

Discussion

. . .

A. Choice of Law

The district court determined that Florida law governed the parties' dispute over the letter of credit . . . In addition, Hamilton specified that its letter of credit would be governed by the UCP (1993 revision) ICC Publication No. 500. Therefore, the parties' claims also are subject to the International Chamber of Commerce Uniform Customs and Practice for Documentary Credits, 1993 revision.

B. The Merits

Article 14 of the UCP allows an issuing bank to refuse to pay on a letter of credit if it "determines that the documents appear on their face not to be in compliance with the terms and conditions of the Credit." UCP Art. 14(c). However, the issuing bank "must give notice [of its refusal] by telecommunication or, if that is not possible, by other expeditious means, without delay but no later than the close of the seventh banking day following the day of receipt of the documents," and its "notice must state all discrepancies in respect of which the bank refuses the documents." UCP Art. 14(d)(i), (ii). Failure to comply with Article 14's notice provisions, "preclude[s the issuing bank] from claiming that the documents are not in compliance with the terms and conditions of the Credit." UCP Art. 14(e).

Hamilton did not comply with Article 14 in two respects: its first and only timely disclaimer was not sent by telecommunication and did not specify the grounds for disclaimer. Nevertheless, the bank seeks to avoid preclusion by arguing that (1) fraud tainted both the underlying transaction and the documents presented to Hamilton and (2) Kookmin knowingly forwarded non-conforming documents in violation of Article 13 of the UCP.

1. Fraud

Hamilton bases its fraud defense on evidence that the option contract and special instructions proffered to Kookmin were fakes and differed in substantive ways from the signed originals. Most significantly, the copy of the option contract Kim gave to Kookmin, but not the alleged original, contained a reference to "special instructions" upon which Kookmin allegedly relied in disregarding the absence of an authenticated telex. However, the option contract also referred to the need for an authenticated telex, and the special instructions did not address that requirement at all.

As it must, Hamilton concedes that the UCP does not explicitly provide for belated dishonor based on fraud but claims that a Florida Uniform Commercial Code provision permitted it to refuse to negotiate the letter of credit after the UCP Art. 14(d)(i) period expired. At the time the letter of credit was negotiated, Section 675.114 of the Florida Statutes Annotated provided:

> (2) Unless otherwise agreed when documents appear on their face to comply with the terms of a credit but a required document does not in fact conform to the warranties made on negotiation or transfer of a document of title (§ 677.507) or of a certificated security (§ 678.1081) or is forged or fraudulent or there is fraud in the transaction:
>
> (a) The issuer must honor the draft or demand for payment if honor is demanded by a negotiating bank or other holder of the draft or demand which has taken the draft or demand under the credit and under circumstances which would make it a holder in due course (§ 677.3021).

Fla. Stat. Ann. § 675.114 (West 1998). Moreover, an Eleventh Circuit case involving a Florida Bank confirms that fraud in the transaction and fraudulent documentation are defenses even in cases governed by the UCP. *See Harris,* 691 F.2d at 1355 n.19.

However, Section 675.114 and Harris leave open two important questions. First, former section 675.114 does not address the time period in which an issuing bank must make an objection based on forged or fraudulent documents. Must these objections, too, be made within seven business days? Second, Hamilton's letter of credit did not demand that the negotiating bank furnish either the special instructions or the option contract to Hamilton. Under these circumstances, can Hamilton refuse to pay because those documents are false or fraudulent?

Based on a comparison of the language of the UCP with Section 675.114(2) and examination of relevant cases, we believe that an issuing bank can disclaim based on latent fraud more than seven days after receipt of a negotiating bank's presentation. Article 14 indicates that it applies only to "documents [that] appear on their face" not to conform with the letter of credit. UCP Art. 14(c). On the other hand, Section 675.114(2) applies only where a defect in the documentation cannot be discerned from the face of the document itself (indicating that fraud exception applies "when documents appear on their face to comply with the terms of a credit" but documents are fraudulent or there is fraud in the transaction). Thus, according a defrauded bank more than seven days to reject a fraudulent presentation would not undermine the purposes of Article 14(e) of the UCP because latent fraud is not covered by Article 14. Case law that would assist in assessing the interplay between UCP Art. 14(d)'s seven-day limitations period for disclaiming based on defects in documentation required by a letter of credit and Section 675.114(2) is sparse. However, the cases that exist support allowing an issuing bank to disclaim based on latent but not patent fraud in documents or in the transaction after the Article 14(d)(i) period has passed. *See, e.g., Boston Hides & Furs, Ltd. v. Sumitomo Bank, Ltd.,* 870 F. Supp. 1153, 1162–63 (D. Mass. 1994) (allowing fraudulent document defense despite earlier disclaimer based on different grounds); *Semetex Corp. v. UBAF Arab Am. Bank,* 853 F. Supp. 759, 772 (S.D.N.Y. 1994) (stating that UCP governs only "facial discrepancies"), *aff'd,* 51 F.3d 13 (2d Cir. 1995). The *Boston Hides* court well articulated the policy reason for treating latent frauds differently from frauds evident from the face of the document. It said:

> Preclusion under Article 16 [Article 14's predecessor] is designed to both balance the beneficiary's obligation of strict compliance under a letter of credit and give the beneficiary prompt notice of defects so it can cure them. It is, in a sense, punishment for an issuer's failure to timely meet its obligations under the letter of credit. Where a beneficiary submits false documents, however, the defect is latent, not apparent from the face of the material presented. To preclude the [issuing banks] for failure to assert such an intentional "discrepancy" which they could not have discovered "without delay" would improperly punish them for [the beneficiary's] wrongful conduct and not for their own error.

See Boston Hides, 870 F. Supp. at 1163. We find this distinction to be persuasive and believe that the Florida courts would also find that an issuing bank can disclaim based on latent fraud after the Article 14(d)(i) period has expired as long as the negotiating bank is not a holder in due course.

However, Section 675.114 applies only to documents required by a letter of credit. The letter of credit here did not require that the negotiating bank furnish either an option contract or special instructions. Therefore, fraud in these two documents did not entitle Hamilton to disclaim pursuant to Section 675.114. The documents are also immaterial. Because the documents, on their face, do not eliminate the authenticated telex requirement and Hamilton, which dictated the terms of the letter of credit, could not have been fooled into thinking that they did, Hamilton cannot disclaim based on fraud. If the forged option contract or special instructions had purported to eliminate any requirement under the letter of credit, arguably they would have been material, but in the absence of any connection to the requirements of the letter of credit, they cannot justify Hamilton's disclaimer.

The letter of credit did require a bill of lading. However, Hamilton did not argue below that false statements in the bill of lading permitted it to refuse payment. Therefore, we will not consider the impact of the allegedly false statements in the bill of lading. *See, e.g., Baldwin,* 223 F.3d at 102.

2. Knowing Submission of Non-Conforming Documents

In addition to arguing that Kookmin was complicit in Sung-Jin's submission of fraudulent documents, Hamilton also argues that, at a minimum, there is an issue of fact as to whether Kookmin negligently or knowingly forwarded non-complying documents by submitting the letter of credit without the required authenticated telex. We agree that a reasonable juror could find that Kookmin knew or should have known an authenticated telex was required, but we find that this issue of fact is not material.

Hamilton relies on Article 13(a) of the UCP, which states that "banks must examine all documents stipulated in the Credit with reasonable care, to ascertain whether or not they appear on their face, to be in compliance with the terms and conditions of the credit." Hamilton contends that Kookmin's failure to comply with Article 13(a) prevents it from relying on Article 14 . . . Nothing in Article 14 requires that the negotiating bank comply with Article 13 . . .

3. Damages

Hamilton also argues that Kookmin cannot recover the full amount due under the letter of credit because it failed to mitigate its damages and because it retained a commission of $50,421 and received an additional $31,319 from Sung-Jin.

Hamilton's mitigation argument rests on Kookmin's failure to seize and sell the shoes referred to in the letter of credit or to notify Hamilton that the U.S. Customs Service intended to sell them as well as its less than vigorous attempts to pursue recovery from Sung-Jin. Preliminarily, Kookmin responds that Hamilton waived this defense by failing to assert it in response to Kookmin's counterclaim. We disagree. The pretrial order deemed the pleadings amended to include an assertion that Kookmin should have mitigated its damages. In addition, the district court considered the mitigation defense on the merits. *See Hamilton,* 44 F. Supp. 2d at 664. However, Kookmin correctly argues that it had no duty to mitigate its damages. *See Chrysler Motors Corp. v. Florida Nat'l Bank at Gainesville,* 382 So. 2d 32, 38 (Fla. Dist. Ct. App. 1979) (holding that in light of the "sanctity . . . attached to a letter of credit," beneficiary had no duty to issuing bank to mitigate damages by self-help repossession even though contract between beneficiary and its vendee authorized this remedy). We also note that representatives of the shippers who held the shoes testified that they would not have released the goods to Kookmin without an original bill of lading endorsed by Hamilton, and Hamilton conceded that it made no efforts to exercise its own rights under the bill of lading.

Hamilton argued to the district court in a footnote only that Kookmin's judgment should be reduced by the commission it charged Sung Jin and the additional money it recovered. Given the scanty attention Hamilton paid to this issue, the district court understandably did not address it. We believe it appropriate that the district court consider this issue in the first instance and therefore vacate the judgment insofar as it sets the amount of damages and remand so that the court can consider the parties' arguments concerning Kookmin's commission and Sung-Jin's payment.

. . .

Conclusion

For the reasons we have discussed, we affirm the judgment of the district court insofar as it determined the liabilities of the parties but vacate and remand for further proceedings consistent with this opinion insofar as the judgment determines the amount of damages.

Source: 245 F.3d 82.

- Had it done things right, what should Hamilton have done, and when?
- Since it was out of time under the UCP 500, on what did Hamilton base its right to refuse payment?
- Despite being able to refuse payment after the seven-day deadline, Hamilton's defense to payment still did not work. Why? What would Hamilton have had to show in order to disclaim payment after the seven-day limit?

Assuming that a seller is acting legitimately rather than fraudulently, avoiding dishonor is therefore largely a matter of ensuring that there are no discrepancies between the instruction of the credit and the documents that will be presented along with the draft, and the bank assuring itself of that fact.

Under the letter of credit (sample) displayed on page 415, Global American Exports Inc. (the seller/exporter/beneficiary) can anticipate dishonor of its draft by Eastminster Bank (the issuing bank under UCP500), or by any later confirming bank, if Global American Exports Inc., among other things:

1. Describes merchandise in the documents that does not match terms of the L/C; for example, if it describes "Bar-B-Q" as "barbeque" in the British custom of the word in any document.
2. Does not send all documents required under the L/C; for example, it sends only two copies of the commercial invoice, not three, or misses a document altogether.
3. Fails to obtain clean, on-board bills of lading.
4. Fails to prepay freight, such that this is not shown on the bill of lading.
5. Fails to mark the draft and other documents correctly; for example, omitting "Documentary Credit No. 472956" on any document or failing to mark the draft "Drawn under Eastminster Bank Credit No. 472956 dated October 23, 2005."
6. Fails to insure goods in accordance with the L/C; for example, it omits to obtain war coverage.
7. Presents documents after the L/C has expired; for example, after December 18, 2005 (see also item 8 below, where December 1 is the more restrictive date regarding presentment).
8. Presents documents after the final date for presentment; for example, after December 1, 2005 (see also item 7 above).
9. Ships goods (i.e., bill of lading dated) after the date specified in the L/C; for example, after November 21, 2005.
10. Sends invoice/draft with documents that exceeds limit of the L/C; for example, for an amount greater than US$145,000.
11. Makes a partial shipment where forbidden under the terms of the L/C; for example, fewer than 900 units shipped.
12. Fails to obtain insurance coverage soon enough; for example, insurance coverage begins after bill of lading date.

For all the foregoing analysis, formal documentary payment mechanisms are the importer's best assurance of receiving the goods at the time of payment, and represent the exporter's

Sample Letter of Credit

Eastminster Bank
Irrevocable Documentary Credit

Eastminster Bank	**Date of Issue**
174 Threadneedle Street,	October 23, 2005
London W1 UK	**No.** 472956
Beneficiary	**Applicant**
Global American Exports Inc	British Imports Ltd
1440 Palm Boulevard	4402 Alderney Lane
Los Angeles California USA	London W1 UK
Advising Bank	**Amount**
Bank of Western America	US$ 145,000
2390 Grove Road	ONE HUNDRED AND
Los Angeles California	FORTY FIVE THOUSAND
USA	UNITED STATES DOLLARS
Credit Available by:	**Expiry Date**
Payment	December 18, 2005

Dear Sir or Madam:

We hereby issue in your favour this documentary credit available by your draft at sight drawn on Eastminster Bank, London, England, accompanied by the following documents:

1. Signed commercial invoice in triplicate
2. Full set (3 of 3) clean on board ocean bills of lading made to order of Eastminster Bank, marked "freight prepaid" and "notify the applicant," dated no later than November 21, 2005
3. Certificate of origin
4. Packing list
5. Insurance certificate covering all risks and war

Covering

900 units propane "Bar-B-Q" cookers at US$150 per set CIF LONDON

SHIP FROM ANY US PORT–PARTIAL SHIPMENTS NOT PERMITTED–TRANSHIPMENT NOT PERMITTED

Special Instructions: Documents must be presented within 10 days of bill of lading date but within validity of credit. All banking charges outside England are for the beneficiary's account. All documents must show Documentary Credit No. 472956. All drafts must be marked "Drawn under Eastminster Bank Credit No. 472956 dated October 23, 2005"

Authorized Signature

Margaret Bentley

D/C Manager

EXCEPT AS OTHERWISE EXPRESSLY STATED, THIS CREDIT IS SUBJECT TO UNIFORM CUSTOMS AND PRACTICE FOR DOCUMENTARY CREDITS (1993 REVISION) INTERNATIONAL CHAMBER OF COMMERCE PUBLICATION NO. 500

> The seller is the one in the best position to protect itself, beginning at the time of negotiation of the contract of sale. The seller should only describe the goods offered in precisely the manner to which they will be later referred in the commercial invoice and in the customs documentation. By starting off the buyer with the correct understanding of the description of the merchandise, the higher probability exists that the buyer will apply for the L/C using the same terms. The same goes for anything else—shipping dates, insurance, and the like. Once the credit advice arrives, the seller must check it thoroughly for any requirement that is a discrepancy "in the making."

best security for payment without loss of its goods. If the exporter is being paid in its own national currency, then exchange rate risk is eliminated on its part, but if it is selling in other currencies, then this remaining financial risk must be addressed.

Electronic Letters of Credit

As the international sale transaction is so largely document-based, one imagines it as an ideal candidate for conversion to an electronic system. By the same token, shippers, carriers, and banks have been so heavily dependent on paper documents that it is difficult to coordinate simultaneous change. Moreover, as the law tends to be slower to change than business practice, there has been a regulatory gap that has inhibited rapid evolution.

That frozen scenario is beginning to change. Starting from UNCITRAL electronic commerce model law, *transport* documents benefit from the provisions of both the U.S. E-SIGN and Uniform Electronic Transactions Acts, but *letters of credit* are still specifically exempted from the application of this legislation. This is partially due to the document dependence of the current system; blanket recognition of electronic L/Cs would create an "anything goes" environment without integrated rule systems and industry standards being firmly rooted in place. Additionally, accommodation has already been made for electronic L/Cs, insofar as the United States is concerned, in the Uniform Commercial Code, Article 5.

Article 5 of the UCC allows issuance of L/Cs in any form that is a "record" (not specifying paper), with the express provision that a record may be electronic.[17] Presentation of these records also may be made electronically,[18] unless the parties agree to the contrary, with authentication procedures (signature substitutes) left to agreement of the parties or industry practice.[19]

The industry practice in the widest sense is the application of the ICC's UCP500, with its supplement on electronic presentation of documents, eUCP, in effect since 2002. The eUCP sets the requirements for effective presentation, examination of the presentation by the paying bank, and giving notice of refusal of presentation.[20] If there should be any doubt as to message integrity (a virus or other corruption), the rules provide for representation. The UCP500 continues to apply, but in the case of partially or completely electronic transactions, the eUCP rules prevail over the UCP to the extent of any conflict.

Other private ventures also have responded to the desire for electronic letters of credit and have been filling the void in their own way. Some financial institutions have created software to automate the credit application process and to ensure data integrity in the transfer of those data to the actual L/C issued.

[17]L/Cs may be issued as "records" (UCC § 5-104), which are anything inscribed or stored in "electronic or other medium" (UCC § 5-102(a)(14)), and the term "documents" includes records (UCC § 5-102(a)(6)).

[18]Also UCC § 5-102(a)(6).

[19]UCC §§ 5-104 and 5-106(e).

[20]See ICC Publications 500/2 and 500/3, Supplement to UCP 500 for Electronic Presentation (eUCP).

Other projects have been even more ambitious. BOLERO is a 1998 initiative, originally between the most important international banking communications cooperative, SWIFT, and TT Club, a preeminent shipping insurance firm.[21] BOLERO provides a platform for secure electronic document transfers, identification, and payment, using SWIFT's messaging and payment network. To provide for the bills of lading side of the transaction, BOLERO uses a "title registry" so that title can be transferred electronically from party to party. The mechanics of BOLERO are contained in its Rule Book, which most importantly represents a contractual agreement between users that an electronic message is equivalent to the paper document it intends to replace.

Foreign Exchange Risks

The rate of exchange of a currency is simply the value of one unit of that currency expressed in terms of another currency, or, in other words, the price of foreign currency. For example, *spot* rates (current rates for immediate settlement) may be quoted in financial newspapers:

One of These ↓	Buys the Amount of These Shown →	U.S. Dollar	Canadian Dollar	Mexican Peso	British Pound	European Euro
U.S. Dollar		1.0	1.47	10.5	0.63	0.91
Canadian Dollar		0.68	1.0	7.14	0.43	0.60
Mexican Peso		0.095	0.14	1.0	0.06	0.09
British Pound		1.58	2.33	16.63	1.0	1.44
European Euro		1.09	1.59	11.35	0.69	1.0

As noted in the chapter introduction, both international business lawyers and international businesspersons must have at least a passing familiarity with the financial and legal mechanisms used to control exchange rate risk, even if the transaction currency is in that party's own currency. This is a truth from two angles. First, this is true because exchange rate risk management tools are founded in contract, which is just another of the full portfolio of legal relationships that bear on international trade. Second, this is true because the trader dealing in its own currency is dealing with another trader that is not. One must be ever mindful of the contractual relationships of the party on the other side in order to be prepared for the indirect effects such contracts may have on one's own interests.

Risk Situation 1 You as a U.S. seller are owed $145,000 to be paid to you by your British buyer six months from now. If the U.S. dollar rises in value against British pounds, the cost of the sale contract rises for the British buyer as it must obtain US$145,000 that is

[21] Society for Worldwide Interbank Financial Telecommunication (www.swift.com) and TT Club (www.ttclub.com), with other alliance members as BOLERO (www.bolero.net).

becoming progressively more expensive to buy with pounds. Your British buyer might be tempted to default in payment or back out of the deal. Neither option is good for you.

Risk Situation 2 You as a U.S. seller are owed £ 91,772 (British pounds) (currently worth $145,000) to be paid to you by your British buyer six months from now. If the U.S. dollar rises in value against British pounds, the value of the sale contract falls for you, as on conversion you will obtain fewer U.S. dollars, as they are becoming progressively more expensive to buy with pounds. You might be tempted to default in delivery or back out of the deal. Neither option is good for you and your firm's trading reputation in the long run.

Two more situations exist on these facts in the circumstances where the U.S. dollar falls in value during the period. As a U.S. seller, neither of these two further situations presents an increase in risk. Can you determine what the situations are and why your risk does not increase?

Exchange Rate Risk Management Tools

Five major financial tools exist to control, or at least manage, exchange rate risk, each of which involves a contract with a financial institution:

1. Foreign currency account.
2. Foreign currency loan agreement.
3. Forward contracts.
4. Foreign currency option contracts.
5. Foreign currency futures contracts.

We shall consider each in turn below, using the existing example of the Global American Exports seller and the British Imports buyer, but translating the payment obligation from US$145,000 into £91,772 (British pounds, or GBP) at the spot rate (from the table above) of US$1.58 buying 1 GBP.

Where a U.S. seller is to receive pounds in the future, the U.S. seller will be a winner and the British buyer will be unaffected if, between the time of contract and the time of payment, the U.S. dollar falls in value against the pound. Why? As the U.S. dollar falls in value, one British pound will buy more of them, thus meaning that the U.S. seller will receive more U.S. dollars than it otherwise expected. The British buyer will be unaffected, as the obligation upon it to deliver £91,772 is the same at time of payment as it was at the time of contract.

On the other hand, if the U.S. dollar *rises* in the same interim against the British pound, the U.S. seller will be a *loser* and the British buyer will still be unaffected. Now it is becoming progressively more expensive for British pounds to purchase U.S. dollars, and, consequently, a fixed number of pounds will buy fewer dollars. The British buyer still will be unaffected, as the obligation upon it is again to deliver £91,772, unchanged between the time of contract and the time of payment.

Had the sale contract been denominated in U.S. dollars, it would be the British party facing these windfalls and risks, on exactly the same terms. While this is an ideal casino for risk takers, international businesspersons are in the business of reducing risk rather than going out and looking for it, thus, resort is made to the following tools.

Foreign Currency Account

As the name suggests, this is simply an account held by the seller (or any party expecting to receive funds) that is denominated in a currency that is not its own. Such an account may be maintained in the United States (denominated in pounds), where it will be a true foreign currency account to both Global American Exports Inc. and its bank. Alternatively, it may be maintained overseas, perhaps in the United Kingdom itself in a UK bank, where it will only be a foreign currency account in the eyes of Global American—it will just be a regular bank account to Eastminster Bank, but one with a non–UK resident owner.

The usefulness of such an account to the U.S. seller is dependent on the nature of its business operations. By depositing £91,772 into this account when its export payment is received, it will be insulated from exchange rate movements (it will have "hedged") to the extent that it has £91,772 worth of expenses in the United Kingdom. This may be the cost of operation of a London office, or the amount of goods it wishes to export back to the United States. Global American will know that whatever goods or services US$145,000 would have bought in the United Kingdom today will always and forever be purchasable there, in exchange rate terms anyway, with the £91,772 it has on deposit either in London or Los Angeles.

Where the account is maintained in London, a foreign accountholder will be subject to UK taxation on the interest it earns, and may be subject to taxation on that same income in its home jurisdiction, perhaps subject to both withholding tax abroad and credits at home for foreign tax paid. The subject of taxation is explored in greater detail in Chapter 14.

At law, the account will operate through a standard bank operating agreement, one whose terms are likely not unfamiliar to most readers, but subject to the banking law of the jurisdiction in which the account is maintained.

This type of arrangement is perfect for the international trader who expects to incur liabilities in foreign currency in approximately the same frequency and amount that it generates assets in that same foreign currency. If that is not the case, or if the exporter simply wishes to be able to bring its profits home with some certainty as to the amount, then further options must be explored.

Foreign Currency Loan Agreement

Where an asset is expected to arrive in the future, denominated in foreign currency (the compliance with the L/C and the presentment of the £91,772 draft in this case), to be assured of a particular number of U.S. dollars now, the seller need only incur a future liability of the same date and amount, with proceeds in U.S. dollars available now. This is a foreign currency loan agreement.

A firm such as Global American Exports Inc., assuming it is sufficiently creditworthy, may borrow from a bank (its own, or perhaps Eastminster Bank) £91,772 now (October 23, 2005) and convert that into U.S. dollars now. Then, on December 1, 2005, when it receives payment of its £91,772 draft, it may use those proceeds to liquidate the British pound loan that it has incurred.

In the meantime, it will have received a sum certain in U.S. dollars and will be secure in the knowledge that, whatever may happen to the dollar–pound exchange rate, it is fully hedged. The only cost to Global American is the interest paid on the loan, charged in pounds. If it wished to be hedged against this as well, it could have deducted the amount of interest known to be payable in the future from the proceeds of the £91,772 loan and only converted the balance of this into dollars. As a result, it would have the exact amount required in pounds, in hand in cash, on the date of liquidation to cover its interest cost as well. The interest cost of this 39-day loan will, at, say, 5 percent simple interest, be £490, in other words, the cost of its insurance against unfavorable currency swings in that period.

As was the case with foreign currency accounts, the foreign currency loan agreement will operate at law like any other loan contract in the local law jurisdiction where it is made.

Forward Contracts

A forward contract bears some passing similarity to the loan arrangement, in that a forward contract made between Global American and a financial institution compels Global American to deliver its foreign currency amount to its counterparty at an agreed date in the future (presumably December 1, 2005). In exchange, the counterparty financial institution, at that future time, will deliver to Global American a sum of U.S. dollars at an exchange rate agreed upon at the time the contract was entered into. This exchange rate will be the *forward rate* for settlements 39 days hence that the financial institution was offering to its customers on the date that the contract was entered into. While forward contracts can be entered into for any period with a willing party, they are customarily quoted and published as 30-day, 90-day, or 180-day rates (or rates extending a year or more). The security against exchange rate changes for the counterparty lies in the fact that it self-hedges parties wishing to sell currencies (such as Global's desire to sell pounds forward) with parties wishing to buy that same currency forward on the same term. Its profit lies in the fact that the rates that it is willing to offer are favorable to itself, and it may charge a set-up fee for the transaction.

The local law of the jurisdiction where the contract is formed will, once again, govern the contract.

Foreign Currency Option Contracts

An interest cost of £490, in what may be called a *hedge premium* for this loan protection, or the cost of a forward contract, should be compared to the cost of an option. While the previous mechanisms hedged against the downside risk of an unfavorable swing in exchange rates, an option contract not only hedges the downside but also allows the party to take any profit available in the favorable movement of exchange rates.

In this case the option will be purchased through a financial institution, more commonly through a securities brokerage house, as options are exchange-traded. It provides for the right of the purchaser of the option at a future date to buy (call) or sell (put) one currency for another at a fixed price (the strike price). In this case, it would be a contractual right of Global American Exports to sell on December 1, 2005, the £91,772 it will have received on December 1, 2005, at the rate previously determined on October 23, 2005. This would be a put option as opposed to a call option.

American options, by convention, allow the purchaser of the option to exercise its option at the strike price any time during the life of the option. European-style options only allow exercise of the option, if desired, on its expiry date. The commentary below assumes that Global American makes its choice to act on the final date of December 1.

It is, however, only a right, not an obligation, for Global American Exports to sell pounds at the previously agreed strike price. If the pound has fallen against the dollar in that interval, then it will wish to exercise this right, for its £91,772 would generate more dollars from the option contract than if Global American Exports simply sells at the lower spot, or market, price then prevailing on December 1. Global American would not exercise its option if the value of the pound has climbed against the dollar, for the pounds in it hands would generate more dollars on December 1 at the spot market price than they would under the terms of the contract and the strike price.

In our example, assume that on October 23, when the then-prevailing spot price of dollars is $1.58 for each pound, a financial institution is willing to offer Global American the right to put (sell) £91,772 on December 1 (or earlier) at a strike price of US$1.57 per pound. This guarantees that Global American, if it exercises its option, will receive a yield of US$144,082 on December 1 (or as earlier may be exercised).

Assume then that the actual market spot exchange rate of pounds to dollars on December 1 is US$1.44 per pound. The pound, therefore, in the interim from October 23 to December 1, has fallen against the dollar, for one pound now buys only US$1.44 rather than the $1.58 spot value of October 23, or the strike price contractually agreed on October 23 of $1.57. Global American therefore *will* exercise its option on December 1 to sell pounds under its contract at $1.57 per pound, rather than sell its pounds on the open market of December 1. If it chose not to exercise its option and to sell its pounds in the spot market, each pound would bring only the $1.44 spot price.

On the other hand, assume that the actual market spot exchange rate of pounds to dollars on December 1 is US$1.66 per pound. The pound, therefore, in the interim, has gained against the dollar, for one pound now buys US$1.66 rather than the $1.58 spot value of October 23, or the strike price contractually agreed on October 23 of $1.57. Global American *will not* exercise its option on December 1 to sell pounds under its contract at $1.57 per pound; instead, it would sell its pounds on the open market of December 1, where each pound will bring a premium rate of $1.66.

In this second case, the option is allowed to lapse without being exercised, and while the cost of the option will thus be notionally wasted, the option will have done its protective job and turned a windfall profit in the bargain.

Spot Value, October 23, of £ in US$	Rate Contractually Available on October 23 for December 1 Pound Put Options	Spot Value of £ Discovered on December 1	Exercise Option?	Value of £ 91,772 in US$ under Each Alternative on December 1
1.58	1.57	1.44 (pound fell, dollar rose)	Yes, sell pounds under contract at US$1.57 per pound	$144,082
		1.66 (pound rose, dollar fell)	No, sell pounds to market at $1.66 per pound spot price	$152,341

Whether spot rates on December 1 turn out to be higher or lower than the strike price of $1.57, Global American will generate at least US$144,082. It has known since October 23 that it would do so and has been able to take that minimum figure into its financial planning.

The cost of the option will be a fixed sum charged by the financial institution on the other side of the option contract, and the governing law will be that of the jurisdiction in which the option was contracted.

Foreign Currency Futures Contracts

Futures contracts are also exchange-traded, and are obtained primarily through securities brokerage houses, but are denominated in standardized amounts, with fixed settlement dates. They operate in essentially the same manner as forward contracts, where the obligation is to purchase or sell a specific currency at a specific date. As a result of these standardized amounts (such as $100,000), futures are more appropriate for speculators, rather than for parties truly interested in taking physical delivery of a particular amount of the underlying commodity (the dollars or pounds). Unlike a forward contract with a bank, where the holder depends on the creditworthiness of the financial institution to deliver its funds on the agreed date, the clearinghouse of the exchange on which futures contracts are traded guarantees their payment. Futures contracts are also subject to margin calls over their life, making them further unwieldy for international business finance, meaning that if the exchange rate drifts too far against the holder, security against what appears to be a future losing position must be maintained. The fact that the holder will receive the full amount of the foreign currency sufficient to liquidate its position on the closing date (by receiving its trade payment) will be irrelevant during the life of the contract. This may cause cash flow difficulties for the holder who is subject to any margin call in that period.

Changing Attributes of the Cash Flow

Depending on the circumstance of the international transaction, it may be desirable to change attributes of the cash flow coming back to the seller.

Factoring: Changing the Immediate Payer

For sellers holding an account receivable from a foreign buyer (payer), but also having a need for immediate cash, *factoring* may be the answer. Factoring at law is a contract of assignment, where the right to collect an account is assigned to another party, a third party. A third party (in effect a collection agency for accounts not yet due) may be found that is willing to take up the right to collect $145,000 or £91,772 from British Imports Ltd. at a future date. In exchange for getting that future right, that third party—the factor—may be willing to pay anything between 70 and 90 percent of that sum to Global American today. The factor might be an American collection firm, or it may be either of the banks of the parties to the sale, but it will most likely be a collection firm located in the jurisdiction of the buyer who is to make payment. This is because such a firm is usually best placed to gather credit information about the payer, to come up with a decision regarding what percentage to offer to the account holder.

In the case of assignments in the nature of factoring, they may be done on a recourse or nonrecourse basis. In recourse, the factor has the right to claim against the assignor if the account debtor does not pay up. In nonrecourse factoring, there is no such right, and the factor will succeed or fail on its own. Naturally, the percentage offered to account holders is lower for nonrecourse business than is offered for recourse business, as the factor's risk is higher in the former case.

Leasing: Changing the Nature of the Flow

Instances may arise in international transactions where a payment of a price is simply not the best outcome; better outcomes may be created. One instance, which is a function of national income tax legislation (this can be any nation), is the tax treatment of leases.

In some countries (including most Western nations), amounts paid under certain leases for capital goods are fully tax deductible in the year in which the expense is incurred. If the same transaction was for capital goods that were purchased rather than leased, then a fixed amount of that sum is tax deductible as depreciation. The two sums are not likely to be the same; thus, the potential tax deductions will not be the same.

If, and this requires detailed reading of the appropriate national tax legislation of the countries concerned, it is legal to structure the transaction as a lease or a purchase, there will likely be one structure over the other that is preferable to the buyer. The seller also may have a preference, if lease payments are granted any tax advantage over simple income from sales. Presumably, to structure a sale as a lease with some commercial sense, the lease payments would have to amount to the equivalent of the payment of a sales price. At the end of the lease, the party leasing the goods would be afforded the option to return the goods or buy them, with the latter option being at a highly attractive, perhaps nominal price.

It must be noted however, that structuring a transaction to disguise its true nature and to evade taxes is a tax offense in most jurisdictions. This does not mean that some structuring cannot be undertaken, just that it must be properly done within the confines of the tax laws of the nations concerned. This topic is considered further in Chapter 14.

Repatriation Rights for Finances and Profits

The example used thus far of a U.S. seller and a British buyer has placed them within two nations that do not presently engage in exchange controls, or other limitations placed upon the quantities and nature of funds crossing their borders. This is not always true for other nations of the world. Admittedly, nations are moving toward the free flow of capital and payments; however, it can be recalled from the text material on the WTO that many powers are reserved to governments to protect their national economies as they see fit through such controls.

International traders intending to be active in a particular nation must be aware of whether

1. Total exchange prohibition exists in that nation (funds, particularly foreign currencies, cannot be taken outside that nation for any reason).
2. Partial exchange restriction exists (funds may be removed from a nation only for specified purposes; for example, the repatriation of capital but not profits).
3. Limits or caps are imposed on withdrawals of foreign currency, either in general or for particular purposes or transactions.
4. Unrealistic government-imposed exchange rates are placed upon funds leaving that nation.
5. Similar requirements of mandatory conversions at unrealistic rates of exchange are imposed on foreign currencies entering that nation.
6. Bank accounts or borrowing in foreign currencies by persons or corporations resident in that nation are permitted.

Such local law regulation of international exchange may create serious problems for traders, or, for that matter, their counterparty purchasers. It is quite possible that a foreign exporter may deliver goods to a party in another nation, receive payment in that nation in either local or foreign currency, and then only discover that such currency or currencies cannot be repatriated to its home country. In such cases, the only resolution may be to leave that currency in place and use it for in-country expenses, or to purchase goods that may be exported back to the original exporter's or service provider's home country. Transactions of this latter nature are known as *countertrade.* If they make up part of a planned contractual sequence of an export and an offsetting import in payment, they are known as *counterpurchase* transactions.

The best defense for an exporter against unwittingly running into this type of situation is for it to clarify with its bankers its understanding of the economic policy and exchange policy of its target nation, or approach the central banking authorities of that nation. In some cases of businesses particularly attractive to some nations, it may be possible to obtain or negotiate exemptions (whole or partial) from capital and payments controls for particular purposes or transactions.

International traders and lawyers should be wary at the best of times of any nation that has either a track record or an inclination toward capital or payments control, and should deeply question the probable profitability of operations in such environments.

Governmental Financial Support for International Business

In general, governments would like to support export industries. As has been discussed previously in Chapter 4, exports are a net benefit to a nation but financial support by government can distort global trade flows.

The WTO Agreement, specifically GATT 1994 and the Agreement on Subsidies and Countervailing Measures, has concerns with these distortions and prohibits trade-damaging subsidies. However, there are exceptions to the rule, which is a search to find a balance between the good and the bad aspects of government financial support.

There is internationally agreed policy behind these exceptions. First, using a broad brush, is the general assumption that government support (whatever form it takes) of international business should never crowd out the private sector. If the private sector can make loans to exporters or offer guarantees of compensation should a buyer fail to pay, then the private sector should do that business, and governments should not.

Second is the recognition that there are some transactions that are too risky for private sector risk managers to underwrite. If a German firm wants to sell shoes in Cuba, it is accepting the risk that its buyer may not pay. Beyond the reasons why buyers anywhere may not pay, there is the further risk that the condition of the Cuban economy means that there is not enough foreign currency in Cuba to pay the German account, or perhaps the Cuban government may forbid payment. The German firm may find that this kind of risk is unacceptable to its lenders or insurers (and to itself), and as a result the transaction must be aborted before it begins.

If governments are allowed to provide payment guarantees to their exporters in these situations, then they are not crowding out the private sector. The private sector risk managers were never in in the first place. The transaction will occur, an export sale will be made, and payment will be forthcoming. If payment is not forthcoming from the importer, then the exporter may look to its own government for payment. Any disputes can then be settled between governments if need be. Thus, a transaction that never would have occurred does occur, but only because of the intervention of government financial support.

As a matter of practice, government export assistance is available in most industrialized nations through special-purpose publicly owned financial institutions,[22] and a growing number of developing nations and countries in transition have done likewise.[23] The product lineup in most cases includes exporter's working capital and insurance, loan guarantees, and direct loans to purchasers of exports.

Now it is easy to say (and rightly so) that some nations are more capable of supporting their exporters than others, and that allowing them to do so is unfair to those who cannot afford to support their own. One also can ask that, surely, somewhere there is someone willing to underwrite such risk as long as the price is high enough. These two criticisms are valid, but are outweighed by the fact that the export business was worthwhile not only to the exporter, but to the importer as well. Germany benefited, as did Cuba, clearly receiving something that it wanted. Second, the lone private insurer willing to take such risks has an increased premium not only because of the nature of that risk, but because there is no apparent competition to insure that risk. It can charge whatever the market will bear.

Thus, there is room for government support for international business, as a limited exception to the principle that fair trading should occur without subsidies. We can now use a finer brush for the details.

The Organization for Economic Cooperation and Development (OECD),[24] as a club of wealthy nations, has developed a set of guidelines[25] for government financing of the export trade of its members.[26] Be aware that these guidelines are (1) self-regulatory and thus bounded by self-interest and (2) not binding in law as they establish only commercial terms to guide government financing.

[22]In the United States, for example, the Export-Import Bank (www.exim.gov), or in Canada, the Export Development Corporation (www.edc.ca).

[23]For example, the Export-Import Bank of India, www.eximbankindia.com.

[24]www.oecd.org. Membership as of early 2004 is Australia, Canada, the Czech Republic, all 15 EU members, Hungary, Iceland, Japan, Korea, Mexico, New Zealand, Norway, Poland, the Slovak Republic, Switzerland, Turkey, and the United States.

[25]The Arrangement on Guidelines for Officially Supported Export Credits, 1978, may be reviewed at www.oecd.org/dataoecd.

[26]All OECD members except, as of early 2004, Hungary, Iceland, Mexico, Poland, the Slovak Republic, and Turkey.

These set the terms for government financing behavior, relaxing the requirement of non–crowding out, with appropriate minimum and maximum terms, in assisting both foreign purchasers and domestic exporters. These establish minimum levels for premiums for risk coverage, required minimums for down payments by purchasers of goods, and maximum payment periods for sales. For loans, maximum maturity dates are established, with minimum levels for setting interest rates and maximum repayment periods. Without minimums and maximums set with reference to market rates, governments could both undercut private financial institutions and accept all risks on behalf of their exporters, which would be a clear case of distorting subsidy.

While this may be the OECD's self-described "gentlemen's agreement," it still would be in contravention of WTO rules but for the WTO exceptions. The specific exception permitting this type of export financing activity is found in Annex 1 to the WTO Subsidies and Countervailing Measures Agreement. It allows financial concessions where the "signatory is a party to an international undertaking on official export credits" to which at least 12 original members of the Subsidies Agreement are parties "as of 1 January 1979." Clearly then, this contemplated approval of the 1978 OECD guidelines, but whether a "gentlemen's agreement" is truly an "undertaking" is another matter.

Chapter Summary	The international flow of payments is the lifeblood of international business, just as much as the flow of goods, services, or investments. The law of international payments is made up of historical rules of commerce, presently advanced largely by private organizations such as the International Chamber of Commerce, and is embodied in local law. Unfortunately, no unifying body of truly international law exists in this sphere.

The geographical distance between the parties and their removal from a single local law system create a problem of compliance, in ensuring both delivery and payment. Parties who are comfortable with their relationship have an easier time through the use of informal payment systems at either extreme from open account to payment in advance, but others are not so fortunate. These relationships rely on formal payment and delivery mechanisms through the use of drafts.

The draft is an old and reliable vehicle in international payments, and its documentary nature allows an intermediary to ensure that delivery is in order and payment is in hand before releasing either the documents of title to the goods or the payment for them.

As a documentary transaction is separate from the underlying sale transaction, it is critical that all formalities of documentary delivery be present for the payment demand to be honored. This responsibility for compliance rests first upon the seller (in making the application) and next upon the buyer in presentation of conforming documents, with responsibility for examination and assessment of compliance made by the bank issuing the credit calling for that compliance. Failure to comply exposes the seller to the possibility of not receiving payment, although not losing its goods. Failure of the buyer to comply means that it will be unable to take delivery of its goods. Failure of banks to properly assess that compliance may result in improper payment by an issuing or confirming bank.

Aside from credit and delivery risks, the parties to a sale and payment transaction also face exchange rate risk in the interim between the time of contract formation and the time of payment. A variety of mechanisms exist to hedge against exchange rate risk, all of them effective, but none without cost. This protection is a cost of doing international business, but it generates financial certainty as to the amount that will eventually be paid or received, which is a valuable commodity in itself.

Chapter Questions

1. What risks does a seller face in receiving its payment? What can be done to reduce each of those risks?

2. List and describe the elements of negotiability required of a draft or bill of exchange in the Anglo-American tradition. Indicate what additional characteristics are required under the Geneva conventions for European bills of exchange.

3. How do documents against acceptance and documents against payments collections function, and what differentiates the two?

4. Explain the responsibilities and liability of a bank issuing a letter of credit under UCP500.

5. Explain how the liability of a confirming bank in a letter of credit transaction differs from that of a remitting bank in a documentary collection.

6. Why is it, when the payment function is so essential to the conduct of a sale transaction, that the bank engaged via a letter of credit has no interest in the underlying sales contract and is not a party to it? Explain why this is so.

7. What remedies exist where presentation of documents is nonconforming to the L/C, but the parties want the transaction to go forward?

8. Differentiate between the features of a put option and a forward contract for the sale of foreign currency.

9. What is the risk faced by a seller who has engaged in factoring with recourse?

10. What are the hallmarks of capital and payments controls in a foreign nation, and how may a trader best address them?

Front Page Law: International Issues from Boardroom to Courtroom

MEXICO: SAY ADIOS TO THE SUPER PESO   JUNE 17, 2002

BusinessWeek

Mexico's exporters are breathing easier after the peso's 5.1% devaluation since April. The peso, which hovered around 11 cents (U.S.) for much of the past year, closed at 10.27 cents on June 5.

The weakening was due partly to Mexican companies raising money at low peso interest rates and buying greenbacks to pay down dollar-denominated loans. Rates on 28-day Cetes were 7% on June 5, but had recently touched an historic low of 5.28%. The Central Bank's recent modest easing of monetary policy signaled that a slightly weaker peso would not aggravate inflation, now at 4.4%.

The decline relieved worries that an overly strong peso might eventually face an abrupt correction, spooking investors. The "super peso" was clobbering the export-driven economy: Over the past year, Mexico lost 350 factories and 240,000 jobs in the maquiladora assembly industry, which produced half of its $158.5 billion in exports last year.

Economic recovery hinges on a U.S. rebound. The U.S. takes 88% of Mexico's exports. After shrinking 1.4% last year, Mexico is expected to grow 1.8% in 2002. While the economy shrank 2% in the first quarter, April brought promising signs: Exports and imports both rose above year-ago levels for the first time in 11 months.

The cheaper peso could kick-start foreign direct investment, which last quarter was down $300 million from a year ago. Investors are waiting for Mexico's divided Congress to decide on opening the electricity sector to private investment and on new loan-collection rules to encourage bank lending, which has slumped badly since the 1995 peso crisis.

Buyers may also trickle back to stocks. Foreigners invested $150 million in stocks and bonds through March, compared with more than $550 million in the first quarter of 2001. The Mexican bolsa gained 10% in dollar terms in 2001. It is up 4.1% this year, and a correction may be inevitable. Mexican equities would then look very attractive to investors with dollars to spend.

Altius and Fortius: Transactions with Higher and Stronger Foreign Market Commitments

Part 3

To this point, we have discussed the international business law environment and initial transactions of import and export, along with the central elements of transportation and payment. Firms that confine their business to simple variations of these *are* international traders, but a further class consists of firms making higher and stronger commitments to foreign markets.

These are firms that are integrating their business with foreign economies and industries (higher commitments), in the sense that it is much harder to pull out of the foreign market should apparent risks increase significantly. The transactions can more honestly be described as relationships (stronger commitments), without depreciating the effort that basic importers and exporters invest in their own.

These relationship transactions include international distribution, licensing, and foreign investment, together with the supporting concerns of dispute resolution and taxation taking on more significance than they did in previously discussed transactions.

To emphasize—higher and stronger commitments are much more difficult and expensive to back out of later. Therefore, they require more analysis and thoughtful decision making while under strategic consideration.

Chapters in this part are

Chapter 10

International Distribution

Chapter Objectives

Where doing "good business" in the export trade of goods or services requires a greater market presence abroad, effective distribution strategies are required to capture market opportunities. As an international business strategy, international distribution has legal dimensions that must be brought into the strategic decision-making process, and thereafter must be considered in the development, management, and termination of the resulting relationship.

In this chapter, we discuss international distribution and

- Strategic business considerations requiring responses in law.
- National and multinational law touching on issues in international distribution.

- Private law rights and responsibilities in contract between agents and principals and between supplier-exporters and distributor-importers.

Introduction

Some seller-exporters have the luxury of limited involvement with foreign markets, with customers searching them out as a supplier and beating a path to their door. As readers can guess, however, this does not happen very often. Even if foreign consumers are willing to travel to make purchases, they will prefer to do business with the firm (domestic or foreign) that makes the effort to come to them. Thus, among international exporters, the vast majority either want or are forced to develop their international sales relationships into something more complex.

A more complex relationship might be required for expanding and developing the foreign market for the exported products or services, providing after-sales service, or maintaining a presence to develop goodwill or brand loyalty or to obtain market feedback on sales or the product attributes as perceived by that market.

In consequence, these more complex relationships are also closer relationships with the foreign market, requiring higher and stronger commitment to market service. They bring other foreign business parties into the picture and increase the range and scope of strategic and tactical decisions that must be made. All of these relationships and decisions also bring the seller-exporter into closer contact with the local legal system of the target country. These considerations must form part of both the strategic business planning function in international business and the strategic and tactical business law responses to that plan.

All of our previous coverage of importing and exporting continues to apply, with the twist that foreigners acting within their own markets will perform the international marketing function. The seller-exporter's leverage to control this activity at a distance can only be derived by the commercial relationship and the legal relationship between the parties.

The commercial relationship between the seller-exporter and the foreign party must make commercial sense for both (or it won't work); it must provide a fair chance for profit and be based on value for service and on other sound commercial principles. The legal relationship must respect the rights and duties of both parties that flow from the commercial relationship so that the contract reflects their commercial reality; this too is simply good business practice. Further, the legal relationship must properly exist within the confines of contract law and the general local law of both the jurisdiction of the seller *and* that of the foreign party.

When the strategic business environment demands that a close relationship be established with a foreign market, the equally strategic question arises of how this should be accomplished. Recall the diagram and strategic options laid out in Chapter 7, "Direct Sale of Goods Exports":

Strategic Market Entry Options for Exporters

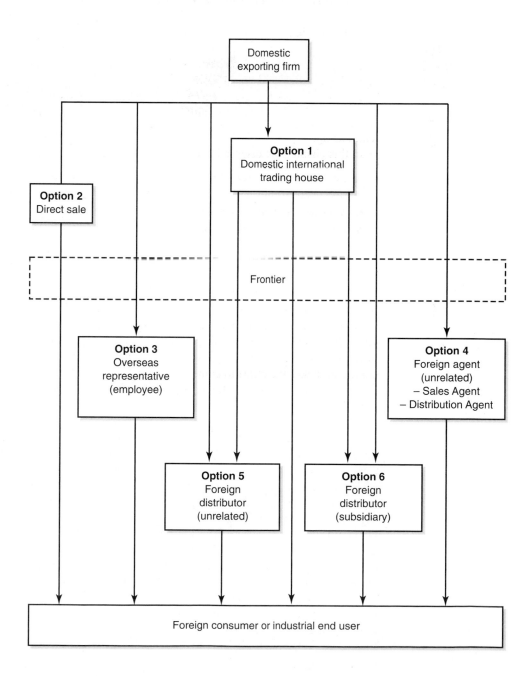

In relationship-based international distribution, we are firmly fixed among Options 4, 5, and 6. Option 4, agency, has arisen before (in Chapter 7) but in circumstances where there was much greater direct control by the exporter: a fairly dependent agent, which had to be distinguished from an employee representative. Now the difference may be subtle, but the shoe is on the other foot. The exporter is very much more dependent on the agent, or on a distributor or network of distributors.

Agency versus Distributorship

By exporting through its own efforts or those of closely controlled agents, the domestic exporter often gets the sense that there is "something big" somewhere "out there." This sense of the market is often only hazy. The exporter's buyer is a foreign commercial reseller of the goods; there is little or no feedback as to how the goods are being used by the end-user consumer, or what after-sale service would help grow the market, and what overseas market potential actually exists.

In searching for this ability to "grow the market," the domestic seller-exporter discovers it must transfer more control over transactions and the market to international marketers working on its behalf, unless it is prepared to build overseas establishments and make foreign investments itself. These international marketers are agents and distributors.

Agents are bound by a contract of agency with a principal (the exporter) to represent him or her, and to speak and make contracts with others in the name of the principal. Distributors are bound to a supplier (the exporter) by a contract of sale with further contract terms on how the process will be managed to properly service the market and end-user demand. In both cases, international businesspersons should not let their commitments get ahead of them, before their attorney has had an opportunity to provide input on the factors to be considered in choosing between the two options.

While agents and distributors can be differentiated in fact and law on the basis of a number of criteria, two factors are of chief importance:

1. Agents are empowered to make contracts binding the principal to those terms, and for this reason owe a legal duty to their principal to act with *utmost* good faith (known as a *fiduciary duty*). Neither of these circumstances applies to distributors, who need only act in general good faith.

2. Distributors actually buy and take title to goods, then resell them on their own account. Agents do not; the principal retains title to the goods until such time as it is transferred directly to the purchaser.

Features of Agents and Distributors

Factor	Agent	Distributor
Nature of relationship	Behavior in utmost good faith owed by agent; the principal is responsible for acts of the agent.	No duty owed to supplier other than an absence of deceit (to act in good faith), plus to execute contractual responsibilities.
Cost	Cheapest—meets own expenses from commissions earned. Support and promotion costs can be met by principal, but tend generally to be lower, reflecting a more modest approach to market.	Can be costly—must be supported with specialized advertising and promotion materials, service and support technology, training programs for distributor and employees.
Authority	Usually has express authority to contract with others in the name of the principal.	Never has authority to contract in name of supplier-exporter. Contracts in own name with others.
Payment	No performance, no pay (on commission).	Paid from its own gross profit margin between revenue on goods sold to consumers and cost of goods purchased from supplier-exporter.
Will exporter be bound if authority exceeded?	Often—if agent had "apparent authority."	Not applicable.
Transfer of title to distributed goods	Does not take title at any time.	Always takes title and resells title to end-users.
Third-party expectations in industry?	Where expected, use of agents is essential, particularly where orders and options must be placed and selected with overseas supplier.	Particularly suitable where consumer has no expectation or desire to have contact with supplier-exporter located abroad.
Ease	Easy to obtain, often a foreign resident who knows the territory well. Usually minor regulatory compliance (e.g., registration).	Hard to obtain good ones. Even when wholly owned subsidiary of the supplier-exporter, usually is staffed with local hires. Knows foreign market very well. Compliance requirements may escalate, particularly if foreign-owned.
Small market?	More cost-effective.	Such elaborate step may not be justified, unless cost recognized as an element of a "being seen everywhere" strategy.

Different industries have different preferences of agents over distributors, as do consumers. While every case varies, some generalities often hold up. Agents tend to travel, bringing the name of the principal-exporter to the customer, while distributors act as a fixed point where customers can come to access all items and services the supplier-exporter is offering to that market. Agents are found more predominantly representing high cost or made-to-order goods (custom industrial machinery, for example) where end-user/supplier contact is still essential, even if through an intermediary. Distributors tend to be more the opposite, where managing the continued smooth flow of standardized goods through channels of supply to waiting customers is the priority (for example, toothpaste, beer, and gasoline).

Export Option 4: Agents in Distribution

The agency relationship, seen from a liberal free-market perspective, casts the agent in the role of a market finder and order taker on behalf of the seller-exporter. It would be pleasant if the legal reality was this simple, but it is not. Unfortunately, despite whatever contractual

Many exporters speak of their "agent" abroad, collectively meaning almost any kind of trade representation. Aside from being imprecise, this is dangerous practice, particularly when the representative is not a true agent. Doing so may create serious and unintended legal liability. If third parties believe a person is an agent, one who apparently possesses the authority of an agent because he or she is described as such, then the parties making that description of their "agent" will be held to their word. You will be bound by contracts that third parties believe to exist, as they rely on innocent statements made by an "agent" who had no real authority at all.

relationship the parties may devise,[1] foreign legal systems may impose significant liability on the seller-exporter as principal within an agent–principal relationship. This is in addition to liabilities imposed under the domestic law of the seller-exporter's own jurisdiction.

General Legal and Business Risks and Considerations

There are legal and business dangers associated with allowing agency relationships to flower without planning and control, and these traps are deceptively easy to fall into because agency is such an inexpensive relationship. Initially, prospective agents, sensing an opportunity for profit, approach the seller-exporter, willing to represent the seller's goods. Note that subtle distinction: the seller's goods. In fact, as agents in law, they will be representing the seller itself, not its goods. Glossing over that, the seller is delighted, as this offers a zero-cost option to gain exposure in foreign markets. All too often, the relationship carries on informally, with nothing more than the seller providing the agent with a package of promotional material and its best wishes for success. From that point on, the legal troubles truly begin. For example, the agent of the seller:

- In Country A bribes a government official to obtain a contract approval.
- In Country B hits a pedestrian while en route to a sales call.
- In Country C makes wild claims as to product performance.
- In Country D commits the principal to unreasonably low price quotations.
- In Country E accomplishes nothing, prompting the principal to terminate the relationship.
- In Country F styles himself as a permanent commercial outpost of the principal.

In short order, the seller-exporter-principal may wind up facing a series of public and private court actions, with the merits of the investigations or suits not being relevant at all. The damage is done simply by being accused in the public arena of wrongdoing, which may undo years of hard work in building a good international reputation. For example, the seller-exporter-principal might become, on the basis of the situations above:

- In Country A: A named party to an investigation and prosecution abroad for corrupt practices, as well as possible investigation and prosecution at home on like charges (in the United States, under the Foreign Corrupt Practices Act).
- In Country B: Named as a defendant in a foreign court action for committing a civil wrong (a *tort*) and may become a prime target for the assessment of damages where an eye to the deepest pockets is cast.
- In Country C: Named as a defendant in an action for breach of contract condition or warranty for fitness (at best), or a product liability suit (at worst).

[1]A good starting point is the ICC Model Commercial Agency Contract, 2nd ed., ICC Publication No. 646, www.iccwbo.org.

- In Country D: Named in a suit for breach of contract or for misrepresentation, in the probable event of nondelivery on those terms.
- In Country E: Named in a private or public prosecution for damages for loss of income or for failure to terminate in accordance with foreign local law provisions.
- In Country F: Liable for income tax on revenues generated in the foreign jurisdiction.

All of these are unintended consequences from the informal naming of foreign agents. They can still arise even when the appointment of an agent is a deliberate strategy, but these potential outcomes should be foremost in mind when agent–principal relations are contemplated. Agents are valuable; just do not cavalierly name them as an uncontrolled army of salespersons.

Lest it be thought that the principal is running all the risk in using an agent, recognize that being an agent is risky business as well. Once agents have devoted themselves to the interests of the principal, they can easily find that the principal is ignoring their work or maltreating potential prospects that they have brought to the door of the principal. Worse, the agent can find that the principal is attempting to cut side deals with clients arranged by the agent in an effort to reduce or avoid paying a commission to the agent. Usually such schemes are based on "don't tell my agent you are buying from me, and I'll reduce the price by half of the commission I would have paid." It should not be surprising, then, that many jurisdictions have enacted laws to protect the interests of the agent from its almost-always-stronger principal.

Often practice and custom of the trade dictate the use of commercial agents, and no other means of selling will do. The example of where contact and information flow between supplier and end-user has been mentioned, but the need for agents exists at the other extreme as well. An example is the sales of heavy industrial machines that are useful across many industries. While these are fairly standard products, say, lathes, drills, or presses, the customer still needs large amounts of information about the machine, but the supplier cannot field all incoming queries from global markets. Still, the market in any one place is small and orders are infrequent, making a permanent distribution operation impossible in every market. The answer is the agent, who may fill the remainder of his or her time with other business, when not actively seeking out customers for the supplier. Often in these cases, different agents will take on different niche markets for the same product. One agent will focus on selling the machinery to aircraft manufacturers; another will represent the same machinery for use in the auto industry, and one agent will never cross the path of the other. The agent in these cases usually has specialized knowledge of not only the product, but also the industry in which it will be used, perhaps having formerly worked in that industry as a user of goods of a similar type.

Where an "agency" relationship is intended only to create markets and solicit orders (in which the seller-exporter will step forward to form contracts), a clearly defined contract must establish this fact. If the only function of the "agent" is to make a market, and he or she has no authority to bind the principal in contract, then the "agent" is in reality just a representative. Such limitations also must be made clear to third-party buyers. The principal must resist using the agent as a means of convenient communication with customers, such that it begins to cloak the agent with unintended authority.

Commissionaires

This is an intermediary in distribution and a term that has long-standing meaning in civil law jurisdictions and, more recently, in common law jurisdictions as well. The commissionaire is an agent who distributes goods on behalf of a foreign firm, but does not disclose that he or she is merely an agent. The commissionaire, for all appearances, is trading on his or her own account, buying and selling the goods. While this may appear shady, it is legal and has a legitimate purpose.

A determination of a "permanent establishment" can have quite an impact on profitability of the firm, particularly if the export sales in a high-tax jurisdiction were being purposely made from a low-tax jurisdiction where manufacturing was taking place. The firm would like to avoid having its careful plan undone, and avoid the jurisdiction of sale totaling up the firm's (high) sales, subtracting its (low) offshore costs, and taxing the (big) difference at its (high) tax rate. Also of note, the use of a commmissionaire—properly structured, and both a tax lawyer and accountants would be required here—also may avoid application of certain U.S. tax rules. Of particular interest are the U.S. provisions aimed at imputing the profits (for tax purposes) of U.S.-controlled foreign corporations back to their U.S. parent firms—known as "Subpart F" income tax (26 U.S.C. § 952). See also Chapter 14 in this text.

In common law jurisdictions, such an arrangement creates rights for third parties. If the third-party buyer discovers the undisclosed principal, the third party may enforce its rights against either the agent (the commissionaire in this case) or the previously undisclosed principal. This is not the case in civil law jurisdictions, where no rights are created against the now-revealed principal—the transaction remains between the third-party buyer and the agent (selling in its own name but for the account and risk of a principal).

An observation is important. As agent, the commissionaire is not taking title to the goods; appearances aside, title passes directly from the principal to the buyer. Therefore, the nature of the principal's activity remains purely as an export-seller, without risking the accusation that it is "carrying on business" or has a "permanent establishment" in the commissionaire's local market.

The accusation has potential to stick, particularly if the "agent" of the exporter is looking more and more like a dependent entity, perhaps maintaining an inventory or honoring warranty claims. With the commissionaire, it is he or she who has a permanent establishment, not the export-seller. Otherwise, if such a finding could be supported that the export-seller was carrying on business (i.e., distribution), the export-seller would find itself becoming a taxpayer of the foreign jurisdiction.

Responsibility of the Principal

If the agent becomes in practice a dependent contractor, or essentially an employee of the seller-exporter, then the seller-exporter will attract the type of vicarious liability associated with employees: in tort, in contract, or under civil legislation such as antibribery statutes. In concrete terms, this means keeping the agent on commission rather than salary, providing the agent with autonomy to conduct its own affairs without direction, and not insisting that the agent represent only the products of the seller-exporter. The more that the agent becomes closely tied to the seller-exporter, the greater the probability that the "commercial agent" (as it is meant in the trade) is either an agent at law with the capability to bind the principal or an employee for whom the seller is vicariously liable.[2]

Where a seller-exporter does choose to employ a true agent (one capable of binding the principal in contract), the seller-exporter must be ever mindful of the responsibilities of a principal not only under its own local law, but also under that of foreign jurisdictions. Many foreign jurisdictions, and notably the member states of the European Union, impose significant liability on principals, even ones not resident in the European Union.

Certain responsibilities imposed by law override any provision contained in the agency agreement that is otherwise to the detriment of the commercial agent, making those contractual provisions void as against the agent. Moreover European Union law, applicable in

---

[2]Being responsible in law for the acts of another person.

all member states, provides for automatic renewal of fixed term agency contracts, fixed notice periods for termination, and indemnity and payment for commissions or other earnings beyond the end of the agency contract where the agent has been instrumental in generating the business. This is in addition to a right of the agent to seek damages, or any member state national provision that further extends protection to the agent. Further, no noncompete clause is valid for more than two years after the termination of an agency agreement. Some of the salient aspects of this overarching law are reproduced below.

Council Directive 86/653/EEC

of 18 December 1986 on the coordination of the laws of the Member States relating to self-employed commercial agents

Article 1

2. For the purposes of this Directive, 'commercial agent' shall mean a self-employed intermediary who has continuing authority to negotiate the sale or the purchase of goods on behalf of another person, hereinafter called the 'principal,' or to negotiate and conclude such transactions on behalf of and in the name of that principal.

Article 7

1. A commercial agent shall be entitled to commission on commercial transactions concluded during the period covered by the agency contract:
   a. where the transaction has been concluded as a result of his action; or
   b. where the transaction is concluded with a third party whom he has previously acquired as a customer for transactions of the same kind.
2. A commercial agent shall also be entitled to commission on transactions concluded during the period covered by the agency contract:
   —either where he is entrusted with a specific geographical area or group of customers,
   —or where he has an exclusive right to a specific geographical area or group of customers,

and where the transaction has been entered into with a customer belonging to that area or group.
   Member States shall include in their legislation one of the possibilities referred to in the above two indents.

Article 8

A commercial agent shall be entitled to commission on commercial transactions concluded after the agency contract has terminated:
   a. if the transaction is mainly attributable to the commercial agent's efforts during the period covered by the agency contract and if the transaction was entered into within a reasonable period after that contract terminated; or
   b. if, in accordance with the conditions mentioned in Article 7, the order of the third party reached the principal or the commercial agent before the agency contract terminated.

Article 14

An agency contract for a fixed period which continues to be performed by both parties after that period has expired shall be deemed to be converted into an agency contract for an indefinite period.

Article 15

1. Where an agency contract is concluded for an indefinite period either party may terminate it by notice.
2. The period of notice shall be one month for the first year of the contract, two months for the second year commenced, and three months for the third year commenced and subsequent years. The parties may not agree on shorter periods of notice.
3. Member States may fix the period of notice at four months for the fourth year of the contract, five months for the fifth year and six months for the sixth and subsequent years. They may decide that the parties may not agree to shorter periods.

Article 17

1. Member States shall take the measures necessary to ensure that the commercial agent is, after termination of the agency contract, indemnified in accordance with paragraph 2 or compensated for damage in accordance with paragraph 3.
2. *a.* The commercial agent shall be entitled to an indemnity if and to the extent that:
   —he has brought the principal new customers or has significantly increased the volume of business with existing customers and the principal continues to derive substantial benefits from the business with such customers, and
   —the payment of this indemnity is equitable having regard to all the circumstances and, in particular, the commission lost by the commercial agent on the business transacted with such customers.
   Member States may provide for such circumstances also to include the application or otherwise of a restraint of trade clause, within the meaning of Article 20;
   b. The amount of the indemnity may not exceed a figure equivalent to an indemnity for one year calculated from the commercial agent's average annual remuneration over the preceding five years and if the contract goes back less than five years the indemnity shall be calculated on the average for the period in question;
   c. The grant of such an indemnity shall not prevent the commercial agent from seeking damages.
3. The commercial agent shall be entitled to compensation for the damage he suffers as a result of the termination of his relations with the principal.
   Such damage shall be deemed to occur particularly when the termination takes place in circumstances:
   —depriving the commercial agent of the commission which proper performance of the agency contract would have procured him whilst providing the principal with substantial benefits linked to the commercial agent's activities,
   —and/or which have not enabled the commercial agent to amortize the costs and expenses that he had incurred for the performance of the agency contract on the principal's advice.
4. Entitlement to the indemnity as provided for in paragraph 2 or to compensation for damage as provided for under paragraph 3, shall also arise where the agency contract is terminated as a result of the commercial agent's death.

Article 20

1. For the purposes of this Directive an agreement restricting the business activities of a commercial agent following termination of the agency contract is hereinafter referred to as a restraint of trade clause.
2. A restraint of trade clause shall be valid only if and to the extent that:

    a. it is concluded in writing; and

    b. it relates to the geographical area or the group of customers and the geographical area entrusted to the commercial agent and to the kind of goods covered by his agency under the contract.

3. A restraint of trade clause shall be valid for not more than two years after termination of the agency contract.

4. This Article shall not affect provisions of national law which impose other restrictions on the validity or enforceability of restraint of trade clauses or which enable the courts to reduce the obligations on the parties resulting from such an agreement.

Source: May be viewed in full at www.europa.eu.int/eur-lex/en/index.html, under Legislation (in force), Year 1986, Document Number 653 (Directive).

These provisions, reproduced only in part above, serve to protect European agents, but give rise to the question whether they are binding on non-EU principals to the agency agreement. This was the question faced by a British court, where a U.S. principal terminated an agency contract with its UK/European agent and sought to avoid indemnifying that agent. In this case, the agency contract made the express provision that California law would govern the contract.

Recall that a choice-of-law clause is a statement by the parties of which rules they want to govern their relationship. Should nations have the ability to override that to achieve particular public policy goals? To inject some enforced "fairness" as a nation sees fit, where a party did not or could not?

The British court in the *Ingmar* case seeks an interpretation of the effect of the EU Council Directive, and to do so applied to its highest authority on EU law, the European Court of Justice, for a ruling on this set of questions.

Case C-381/98, *Ingmar v. Eaton Technologies*

Indexed as Case C-381/98, *Ingmar GB Ltd v. Eaton Leonard Technologies Inc.*
European Court of Justice, Reference re: Council Directive 86/653
November 9, 2000

REFERENCE to the Court under Article 177 of the EC Treaty (now Article 234 EC) by the Court of Appeal of England and Wales (Civil Division), United Kingdom, for a preliminary ruling in the proceedings pending before that court between Ingmar GB Ltd and Eaton Leonard Technologies Inc.

Judgment

1. By order of 31 July 1998, received at the Court on 26 October 1998, the Court of Appeal of England and Wales (Civil Division) referred to the Court for a preliminary ruling under Article 177 of the EC Treaty (now Article 234 EC) a question on the interpretation of Council Directive 86/653/EEC of 18 December 1986 on the coordination of the laws of the Member States relating to self-employed commercial agents (OJ 1986 L 382, p. 17; 'the Directive').

2. That question has been raised in proceedings between Ingmar GB Ltd ('Ingmar'), a company established in the United Kingdom, and Eaton Leonard Technologies Inc. ('Eaton'), a company established in California, concerning the payment of sums claimed to be due on account, in particular, of the termination of an agency contract.

Legal Framework

Community Legislation

3. In the second recital in its preamble it is stated that the Directive was adopted in the light of the fact that the differences in national laws concerning commercial representation substantially affect the conditions of competition and the carrying-on of that activity within the Community and are detrimental both to the protection available to commercial agents *vis-à-vis* their principals and to the security of commercial transactions.

4. Articles 17 and 18 of the Directive specify the circumstances in which the commercial agent is entitled, on termination of the contract, to an indemnity or to compensation for the damage he suffers as a result of the termination of his relations with the principal.

5. Article 17(1) of the Directive provides:

> [M]ember States shall take the measures necessary to ensure that the commercial agent is, after termination of the agency contract, indemnified in accordance with paragraph 2 or compensated for damage in accordance with paragraph 3.

6. Article 19 of the Directive provides:

> [T]he parties may not derogate from Articles 17 and 18 to the detriment of the commercial agent before the agency contract expires.

7. Under Article 22(1) and (3) thereof, the Directive was to be implemented before 1 January 1990 and, with regard to the United Kingdom, before 1 January 1994. Under Article 22(1), the national provisions implementing the Directive must apply at least to contracts concluded after their entry into force and, in any event, to contracts in operation by 1 January 1994 at the latest.

National Legislation

8. In the United Kingdom, the Directive was implemented by the Commercial Agents (Council Directive) Regulations 1993, which entered into force on 1 January 1994 ('the Regulations').

9. Regulation 1(2) and (3) provides:

> 2. These Regulations govern the relations between commercial agents and their principals and, subject to paragraph 3, apply in relation to the activities of commercial agents in Great Britain.
>
> 3. Regulations 3 to 22 do not apply where the parties have agreed that the agency contract is to be governed by the law of another Member State.

The Main Proceedings

10. In 1989, Ingmar and Eaton concluded a contract under which Ingmar was appointed as Eaton's commercial agent in the United Kingdom. A clause of the contract stipulated that the contract was governed by the law of the State of California.

11. The contract was terminated in 1996. Ingmar instituted proceedings before the High Court of Justice of England and Wales, Queen's Bench Division, seeking payment of commission and, pursuant to Regulation 17, compensation for damage suffered as a result of the termination of its relations with Eaton.

12. By judgment of 23 October 1997, the High Court held that the Regulations did not apply, since the contract was governed by the law of the State of California.

13. Ingmar appealed against that judgment to the Court of Appeal of England and Wales (Civil Division), which decided to stay proceedings and to refer the following question to the Court for a preliminary ruling:

> Under English law, effect will be given to the applicable law as chosen by the parties, unless there is a public policy reason, such as an overriding provision, for not so doing. In such circumstances, are the provisions of Council Directive 86/653/EEC, as implemented in the laws of the Member States, and in particular those provisions relating to the payment of compensation to agents on termination of their agreements with their principals, applicable when:
>
> a. a principal appoints an exclusive agent in the United Kingdom and the Republic of Ireland for the sale of its products therein; and
>
> b. in so far as sales of the products in the United Kingdom are concerned, the agent carries out its activities in the United Kingdom; and
>
> c. the principal is a company incorporated in a non-EU State, and in particular in the State of California, USA, and situated there; and
>
> d. the express applicable law of the contract between the parties is that of the State of California, USA?

The Question Referred for Preliminary Ruling

14. By its question, the national court seeks to ascertain, essentially, whether Articles 17 and 18 of the Directive, which guarantee certain rights to commercial agents after termination of agency contracts, must be applied where the commercial agent carried on his activity in a Member State although the principal is established in a non-member country and a clause of the contract stipulates that the contract is to be governed by the law of that country.

15. The parties to the main proceedings, the United Kingdom and German Governments and the Commission agree that the freedom of contracting parties to choose the system of law by which they wish their contractual relations to be governed is a basic tenet of private international law and that that freedom is removed only by rules that are mandatory.

16. However, their submissions differ as to the conditions which a legal rule must satisfy in order to be classified as a mandatory rule for the purposes of private international law.

17. Eaton contends that such mandatory rules can arise only in extremely limited circumstances and that, in the present case, there is no reason to apply the Directive, which is intended to harmonise the domestic laws of the Member States, to parties established outside the European Union.

18. Ingmar, the United Kingdom Government and the Commission submit that the question of the territorial scope of the Directive is a question of Community law. In their submission, the objectives pursued by the Directive require that its provisions be applied to all commercial agents established in a Member State, irrespective of the nationality or the place of establishment of their principal.

19. According to the German Government, in the absence of any express provision in the Directive as regards its territorial scope, it is for the court of a Member State seised of a dispute concerning a commercial agent's entitlement to indemnity or compensation to examine the question whether the applicable national rules are to be regarded as mandatory rules for the purposes of private international law.

20. In that respect, it should be borne in mind, first, that the Directive is designed to protect commercial agents, as defined in the Directive (Case C-215/97 *Bellone* v *Yokohama* [1998] ECR I-2191, paragraph 13).

21. The purpose of Articles 17 to 19 of the Directive, in particular, is to protect the commercial agent after termination of the contract. The regime established by the Directive for that purpose is mandatory in nature. Article 17 requires Member States to put in place a mechanism for providing reparation to the commercial agent after termination of the contract. Admittedly, that article allows the Member States to choose between indemnification and compensation for damage. However, Articles 17 and 18 prescribe a precise framework within which the Member States may exercise their discretion as to the choice of methods for calculating the indemnity or compensation to be granted.

22. The mandatory nature of those articles is confirmed by the fact that, under Article 19 of the Directive, the parties may not derogate from them to the detriment of the commercial agent before the contract expires. It is also borne out by the fact that, with regard to the United Kingdom, Article 22 of the Directive provides for the immediate application of the national provisions implementing the Directive to contracts in operation.

23. Second, it should be borne in mind that, as is apparent from the second recital in the preamble to the Directive, the harmonising measures laid down by the Directive are intended, *inter alia,* to eliminate restrictions on the carrying-on of the activities of commercial agents, to make the conditions of competition within the Community uniform and to increase the security of commercial transactions (see, to that effect, *Bellone,* paragraph 17).

24. The purpose of the regime established in Articles 17 to 19 of the Directive is thus to protect, for all commercial agents, freedom of establishment and the operation of undistorted competition in the internal market. Those provisions must therefore be observed throughout the Community if those Treaty objectives are to be attained.

25. It must therefore be held that it is essential for the Community legal order that a principal established in a non-member country, whose commercial agent carries on his activity within the Community, cannot evade those provisions by the simple expedient of a choice-of-law clause. The purpose served by the provisions in question requires that they be applied where the situation is closely connected with the Community, in particular where the commercial agent carries on his activity in the territory of a Member State, irrespective of the law by which the parties intended the contract to be governed.

26. In the light of those considerations, the answer to the question must be that Articles 17 and 18 of the Directive, which guarantee certain rights to commercial agents after termination of agency contracts, must be applied where the commercial agent carried on his activity in a Member State although the principal is established in a non-member country and a clause of the contract stipulates that the contract is to be governed by the law of that country.

. . .

On those grounds, THE COURT (Fifth Chamber), in answer to the question referred to it by the Court of Appeal of England and Wales (Civil Division) by order of 31 July 1998, hereby rules:

Articles 17 and 18 of Council Directive 86/653/EEC of 18 December 1986 on the coordination of the laws of the Member States relating to self-employed commercial agents, which guarantee certain rights to commercial agents after termination of agency contracts, must be applied where the commercial agent carried on his activity in a Member State although the principal is established in a non-member country and a clause of the contract stipulates that the contract is to be governed by the law of that country.

Source: May be viewed at the European Court of Justice website, located at http://curia.eu.int/en/content/juris/index.htm.

Will European Union law of agency automatically apply to non-EU principals contracting with EU agents? Can a choice of law clause effectively opt-out of application of the law where it does apply? Do member states have broad or narrow discretion in the application of nation rules to protect agents?

Export Options 5 and 6: Foreign Distributors

Where the end-user or consumer of goods needs a permanent or at least fixed point of contact for sales and service of the goods, the distributor and distributor network relationships fit the requirement. Examples can be found in everything from car dealerships to "big-box" stores. Sometimes these are supplier-owned shops, but most often are owned by the foreign distributor itself. Some distributors carry goods and perform services for a number of suppliers; for example, an audiovisual store may import and carry a range of models from a dozen manufacturers. In others, particularly those that are supplier-owned, distributors may confine themselves to products of only one supplier ("The Sony Store," for example).

While the distributor holds a great degree of power, as it controls the meaningful contact with the consuming public, there is also great variability in this power. An automobile supplier, for example, Volkswagen or Ford, knows that it can replace its distributors quite quickly if the distributor does not live up to the terms of its distribution agreement. The distributor knows this too. On the other hand, suppliers to retail giants such as Wal-Mart have little power over the policies that this distributor may impose on them as suppliers.

Distributors who lack power can find themselves targeted for abuse if they fail to follow directives or "suggestions" from their suppliers. These efforts to keep distributors "in line" are actions in bad faith, such as delaying shipments and withholding information and marketing support. Of course, the reasonable businessperson should look at such behavior and see the supplier cutting its own throat, but such counterproductive activities take place. The distributor with little power does little to complain, as it is dependent on the continued relationship, sometimes no matter how badly it is treated. To that end, national laws exist in many jurisdictions to give distributors power that they would otherwise lack, particularly where termination of the distributorship is a threat.

Recall that distributors do not owe a fiduciary (utmost good faith) duty to the supplier, as they do not act in the name of the supplier. They buy, sell, and contract in their own name and account, and hold title to the goods prior to their resale to end-users. These facts make it easier to differentiate between distributors and agents, but remember the dangers of a seller-exporter habitually referring to its distributor as "agent." It may well find at a future time that a foreign plaintiff will try to hold it to that characterization of its relationship, so that it can sue the wealthier supplier, rather than the perhaps-poorer distributor.

This can be problematic for seller-exporters (who are often, though not necessarily, manufacturers) because they truly desire a close relationship with their distributors who purchase goods from them, and wish to benefit from the distributor's intimate knowledge of the target market. It is simply essential that the seller-exporter not allow the cloak of apparent authority to be worn by the distributor.

In every case, the closer relationship between the seller-exporter (supplier) and the distributor will be founded in contract.[3] The closer relationship reflects the desire of the supplier to have the distributor not only handle sales, but also a range of other tasks. These include local after-sale service, warranty repair, and accessory items, or being a foreign point of contact for information, either for incoming requests or for outgoing information such as product catalogs or recall notices.

[3]A good starting point being the ICC Model Distributorship Contract, ICC Publication #644, www.iccwbo.org.

Choosing a good distributor for international markets requires the same assessments as would be made in choosing a domestic one, and then some. Not only must the distributor have the incentive, ability, and financial resources to build markets, but also it must be someone who can cope with the international dimension. This dimension includes coping with cross-cultural expectations and negotiations, time zones, language barriers, and the built-in delays of transport, communication, customs clearance, and payment that make international business so different than doing business "around the corner." It is worth remembering that the seller and the seller's lawyer must measure up to this test as well!

On the operational side, in the day to day management of the relationship, constant contact and clear communication will be keys to success. Option 5 (unrelated distributor) and Option 6 (subsidiary) have all the same contracts, agreements, duties, and responsibilities to be settled. The fact that under one option the distributor is unrelated and under the other it is wholly owed by the supplier only means that disputes and control are less contentious under Option 6. Where a firm opts to create or purchase a wholly owned distribution operation overseas, it will find that not only the management and legal issues discussed here apply, but also those in Chapter 12, "Foreign Investment."

Obligations of the Distributor

Registration

More commonly in Europe, the Middle East, and South America, distributors (and agents) must be registered with the national government of the jurisdiction in which they operate. Failure to do so can render the distributorship agreement void for illegality, and may have a consequential effect on other contracts with end-users.

Action in Best Interest of Supplier

The foreign seller–local distributor relationship expects something beyond a simple sale contract. While it is not a relationship of utmost good faith (a fiduciary relationship, as would be the case with agency), it still should expect, through its contract language, a dedication to the task of developing the market in the interest of the supplier as well as that of the distributor.

It is precisely because there is no preexisting fiduciary duty in a distributorship that these responsibilities must be created through drafting contract terms that compel equivalent behavior. The agreement should commit the distributor to definite and measurable sales targets (particularly in the case of exclusive distributorships), or at least a "best efforts clause," preferably also measurable in one manner or another. These are required in order to justify later termination or, in happier thinking, to justify increased supplier support or price reductions for volume of trade.

A supplier must be mindful of the fact that distributors may carry competing lines or brands of goods, although in most jurisdictions it is possible to create a noncompete clause prohibiting the distributor from carrying the competing products of other suppliers. Where such clauses are permitted, a further prohibition on the distributor from carrying anything from other suppliers (i.e., noncompeting goods of other suppliers) may be held to be a violation of competition rules. Tying a distributor to selling only those goods of the foreign supplier may therefore be impossible under local law or in commercial reality, and thus it will be the strength and quality of the commercial relationship that will cause a distributor to promote one competing product over another. Resorting to contract law alone to shore up a fundamentally weak commercial relationship is hardly a recipe for success.

Going beyond sales effort, the agreement should expect information exchange as to local market attitudes toward product attributes and pricing (from the distributor) and advance warning of plans, product attribute/volume/price changes, or advertising campaigns (on the part of the supplier).

Finally, the distributor must be contractually bound to observe confidentiality with respect to all trade secrets related to the goods and information not in the public domain. While this falls generally under the heading of action in the best interest of the supplier, its critical nature as an ongoing obligation should be emphasized. Trade secrets may be nonadvertised features of the goods about which the supplier has instructed the distributor not to reveal details—anything from the recipe for secret sauces divulged to a distributor who must make up the product locally, to technical details of mechanical goods that give a performance edge. The need for this to be enshrined as a term of the contract again is due to the lack of a fiduciary relationship between the supplier and distributor, which otherwise does exist between an agent and principal. Between suppliers and distributors "acting in the best interest" is still a lower duty of responsible behavior compared to acting "in utmost good faith," and thus particular duties and desired behavior by the distributor should appear as particular terms in the distributorship contract.

Inventory, Orders, and Service

As part of the commitment to serve the local market properly, the distributor should be committed in contract to maintaining sufficient inventory of the goods to meet trade demands, as well as a stock of parts and accessories, as may be required.

For commercial certainty, economy, and control, it can be useful to establish minimum order quantities and/or frequency in the contract. This contributes to the achievement of contractual minimum sales by recommitting the distributor to periodic and significant purchases, and provides it with the incentive to live up to its promotion and sale obligations.

It may be further necessary to establish warranty and repair services in the local jurisdiction, and this requires contractual commitment not only by the distributor, but also by the supplier for the provision of necessary training, tools, and support for repairs and service.

Use of Trademark and Branding

One of the most appealing aspects of the relationship for distributors is the opportunity to offer name-brand goods for sale. To some degree, recognized name brands sell themselves on the basis of their reputation, prior consumer exposure, or advertising support. In its own efforts, the distributor will want to make use of this brand recognition through display or media advertising bearing the trademarks, logos, or other trade dress of the goods.

Provision should be made for the licensing of this right to the distributor from the supplier, for the life of the distributorship agreement. This is assuming, of course, that the supplier, perhaps as a manufacturer, has the right to create such a license as this in the first place. The distributor, of course, will require contractual assurance of that fact.

It is also open to the supplier to place restrictions in the contract on the use of trade dress, including the requirement of individual use approval. This topic will be considered further in Chapter 11, on the licensing of intellectual property.

Obligations of the Seller-Exporter-Supplier

Delivery and Support

The supplier will be obligated to honor orders from the distributor, subject to force majeure conditions, and foresight should be given to any limitations the supplier may wish to place in advance on order quantities. It may be a prudent policy to combat poaching on the territory of other distributors by limiting orders to an assessed level of demand that can be expected within the distributor's own territory. It is worth noting that some jurisdictions, notably France,[4] place severe penalties on a supplier's refusal to sell to the distributor, where this is equated to abuse of a dominant position.

---

[4]Article L-420-2 of the French Commercial Code.

Supplier abuse of distributors often follows a pattern. A seller-exporter that is anxious to develop and supply a foreign market makes a contract with a distributor in that nation, requiring the local party to develop a distribution network. As part of its recitals, the contract provides for optimistic sales expectations, and as part of its terms, provides for large minimum order quantities, or commits the distributor to accepting a large inventory of the goods at a future date. In default of such sales, the supplier-exporter may terminate the relationship, or may not renew it upon expiration of the first year, or the contract may simply provide for its termination on notice by the supplier as a matter of right. The distributor then puts every effort into developing the market through widespread information and advertising; it visits trade shows and travels the territory visiting prospective customers. Not surprisingly, sales begin slowly and then show signs of significant potential. At this moment, the supplier terminates the agreement either as is its apparent right to do, or by invoking any one of the minimum clauses then being in default, but to which no attention has been previously paid. The distributor is then ejected from the picture, having developed the market at its own expense and with nothing to show for it, and the foreign supplier moves in to capture the whole, at zero expense to itself.

From your perspective, is this just the dog-eat-dog nature of business, or is something fundamentally wrong with such a market capture strategy?

The distributor also may seek the aid of the supplier on a range of other issues immediately connected to the goods, such as in technical matters or advertising and promotion. The former could be to serve as a resource for response to questions and the provision of training (which the supplier may well be willing to do), and the latter may include financial contributions, visits, and materials (which the supplier may be less willing to do). These should be provided for or excluded by the contract, with appropriate limits as the case may be.

Protection

Once beyond the goods themselves, the distributor may seek the help of the supplier in a range of protection issues. These can include assistance and indemnity in the case of suit for patent or trademark infringement, or while on the offensive in defending the territory and sales from the anticompetitive practices of other suppliers and their distribution networks. It can be in the best interest of the supplier to defend alongside its distributors, if only for the protection of its brand name, and more so where a particular suit may lead to either a precedent set or to other suits of greater magnitude. Often, the fact that the distributor has limited financial resources sets in motion the possibility of a default judgment against it or both it and the supplier unless the supplier steps forward to carry the action. The extent to which the supplier is willing to provide this type of protection also should be set out in the distributorship agreement.

Application of Local Law to Distribution

The relationship between the seller-exporter and the distributor should always be founded upon a written contract, and unless the power relationship is heavily skewed to the distributor's favor, that contract will likely be created under the local law of the seller, with a choice-of-law clause to that effect.

Despite such choice-of-law clauses, however, the contract will not escape the attention of the local law of the distributor's jurisdiction, as was the case for agents, where that local law contains statutes governing the content and terms of any distribution agreement that is intended to operate in that foreign jurisdiction. Many jurisdictions have such statutes similar to that of some European, Caribbean, and South American nations, which protect local distributors from abuse by their suppliers.

V. Suarez & Co., Inc. v. Dow Brands, Inc.

United States Court of Appeals for the First Circuit
July 21, 2003
Lynch, Circuit Judge

This case involves the circumstances under which Puerto Rico Act 75 is intended to protect local dealers from termination of their distribution agreement in market withdrawal situations.

A manufacturer of household cleaning supplies, Dow Brands, sold a product line to another company and, as a result, terminated its relationship with Suarez, the local dealer/distributor of those products in Puerto Rico. The dealer sued, claiming a violation of Act 75, the Puerto Rico distributorship protection statute. We hold that the manufacturer's termination of the dealer relationship was with just cause, and we affirm the summary judgment dismissal of the case.

I.

A. Factual History

The following facts are uncontested by the parties. V. Suarez & Company, Inc. was a distributor of many household products in Puerto Rico, including over twenty products manufactured by Dow Brands, Inc., such as Fantastik, Glass Plus, Spray 'N Wash, Pine Magic, Janitor in a Drum, Spray 'N Starch, and Wood Plus. By 1990, its annual sales of Dow products exceeded $4 million.

For whatever reasons, Suarez's sales of Dow products have decreased every year since 1992. In May 1995, a consulting company hired by Suarez recommended that it divest itself of several Dow products, and Suarez incorporated this concept into its corporate strategy for 1995 and 1996. In August 1996, Suarez stopped distributing a number of Dow products. By early 1998, Suarez distributed only three Dow products, all household cleaners: Fantastik, Glass Plus, and Spray 'N Wash. At that time, its annual sales of these products were less than $1.1 million, out of total annual sales of more than $312 million. The Dow products Suarez distributed constituted only 0.35% of Suarez's total business. In the spring of 1997, Suarez was at least contemplating the idea of divesting itself of the remaining Dow products. In February 1997, it hired another consulting firm to perform a valuation of the Dow product line in order to "estimate the fair market value of the distribution rights . . . for their possible sale."

On October 27, 1997, Dow entered into an agreement to sell its worldwide consumer products business to S. C. Johnson & Son, Inc. The sale included the trademarks to, and the rights to produce and sell, the three Dow products Suarez was still distributing in Puerto Rico. S. C. Johnson did not agree to assume any distributorship agreements, including the one with Suarez. During the negotiations, Dow entered into a confidentiality agreement, as is common, which prevented it from disclosing its negotiations with S. C. Johnson until the sale was completed. The sale closed on January 23, 1998. That same day, Dow informed Suarez that it would no longer be able to provide products to Suarez for distribution because Johnson now owned the product line.

B. Procedural History

On April 7, 1999, Suarez filed suit against Dow in a Puerto Rico court. It alleged that Dow violated Act 75, the Puerto Rico distributor protection statute. Dow removed the case to the federal district court on diversity grounds.

On August 30, 2001, after discovery, Dow filed a motion for summary judgment. Dow argued that the sale of its product line to S. C. Johnson constituted just cause for the termination of the distribution relationship with Suarez. On October 23, Suarez responded and filed its own summary judgment motion. On April 22, 2002, the district court granted Dow's motion and dismissed the lawsuit. Suarez timely appealed.

II.

. . .

B. Act 75

Act 75 protects distributor contracts:

> [N]o principal or grantor may directly or indirectly perform any act detrimental to the established relationship or refuse to renew said contract on its normal expiration, except for just cause.

10 P.R. Laws. Ann. § 278a. "Just cause" is defined in the statute as "nonperformance of any of the essential obligations of the dealer's contract, on the part of the dealer, or any action or omission on his part that adversely and substantially affects the interests of the principal or grantor in promoting the marketing or distribution of the merchandise or service." 10 P.R. Laws. Ann. § 278(d).

From a plain reading of the statute, it may appear that only action or inaction on the part of the dealer would provide just cause to allow a principal to terminate the relationship. But a plain reading of Act 75 would produce, in some situations, absurd and constitutionally suspect results. As a consequence, the courts have filled in other readings.

In *Medina & Medina v. Country Pride Foods, Ltd.,* 825 F.2d 1, 2–3 (1st Cir. 1987) (Breyer, J.), this court addressed a related question about market withdrawal and certified the question to the Puerto Rico Supreme Court. In doing so, we recognized a primary intention of the act. "Law 75 was intended to protect dealers who built up a market, from suppliers who wish to appropriate their established clientele."

. . .

The Puerto Rico Supreme Court responded by explaining that "market withdrawal" may constitute just cause:

> Act No. 75 of June 24, 1964, does not bar the principal from totally withdrawing from the Puerto Rican market when his action is not aimed at reaping the good will or clientele established by the dealer, and when such withdrawal—which constitutes just cause for terminating the relationship—is due to the fact that the parties have bargained in good faith but have not been able to reach an agreement as to price, credit, or some other essential element of the dealership. In any case, said withdrawal must be preceded by a previous notice term which shall depend on the nature of the franchise, the characteristics of the dealer, and the nature of the pre-termination negotiations.

. . .

In a more recent and more pertinent case, the Puerto Rico Supreme Court further clarified when a market withdrawal constitutes just cause. In *Borg Warner International Corp. v. Quasar Co.,* 138 P.R. Dec. 60 (1995), the defendant principal, Quasar, stopped selling products to distributors; that business was transferred to a different division as part of a corporate reorganization by the parent company. The other division continued to distribute its goods in Puerto Rico through a chain of retailers and attempted to negotiate in good faith an agreement with plaintiff, but was unable to do so.

In this context, the Puerto Rico Supreme Court made two pertinent rulings. First, it held that a market withdrawal constitutes just cause if the defendant has withdrawn from the market and there was a breakdown in the negotiations over time; it matters not if others continue to sell the product in question. "The issue here is whether any of the defendants, taking advantage of the market created by [the plaintiff], has continued to sell [the product] in Puerto Rico . . ." The court looked only to the *"defendants'* business activity" and ignored allegations that the product at issue was still being sold in Puerto Rico through other channels . . .

Second, the court in *Borg Warner* excused lack of prior notice in some circumstances. The court explained that the "cardinal purpose of the previous notice term is to allow the dealer to . . . prepare for the effects said withdrawal could have on his business operations." In *Borg Warner,* no notice had been given because the principal did not plan to terminate the relationship; it was the distributor who walked away from negotiations.

. . . But *Borg Warner* also extended the just cause definition in two senses: it found just cause even when the product line continued to be distributed in Puerto Rico, and it dispensed with prior notice in circumstances where the principal's legitimate corporate reasons, totally independent of the plaintiff dealer, made giving notice to the dealer unreasonable.

. . .

C. Analysis

It is uncontested that Suarez had a dealership arrangement with Dow. Once Suarez has shown that the contract was terminated, Dow has the burden of persuasion to show just cause.

Dow says it has just cause because it has withdrawn from the market and no longer sells the products at all. Suarez has three primary arguments against Dow's showing of just cause. First, Suarez argues, this is not a market withdrawal because the products continue to be sold in Puerto Rico, albeit not by Dow. Second, there was no negotiation in good faith. Third, there was no advance notice to Suarez. We consider these in turn and find none persuasive.

Suarez first argues that it is within the scope of statutory protection that this court identified in *Medina:* protection of dealers from the appropriation of their established clientele by suppliers. Suarez says that Dow appropriated its good will and established clientele when it sold its household product line to S. C. Johnson. Because of its efforts in distributing these products in Puerto Rico, plaintiff argues, Dow was able to fetch a higher price for the product line. The district court correctly found that Suarez had not presented evidence that Dow was attempting to take advantage of or profited from the good will and clientele Suarez had developed. Importantly, Suarez does not allege that Dow at any time acted in bad faith.

From *Borg Warner,* we know that mere continuation of distribution of the product in the market does not mean that the defendant principal did not have just cause. To put it differently, the statute is not necessarily violated if there is an *opportunity* to trade on the good will built up by the plaintiff . . .

Further, the opportunity to trade on good will in this situation is limited. As in *Borg Warner,* the new principal supplier, here S. C. Johnson, presumably already has a set of dealers in its distribution network for its products and wishes to use those dealers. Suarez may have the opportunity to negotiate a distributorship agreement with S. C. Johnson. Importantly, this is not an instance in which the defendant, here Dow, benefits by substituting itself for its dealer which has built up the brands in the Puerto Rico market. There is none of the unfairness, caused by a principal and from which the principal benefits, that Act 75 was meant to prevent . . .

A more significant question is raised by Suarez's second argument. Both *Medina* and *Borg Warner* involve "market withdrawals" occasioned by the failure of plaintiff dealers and the principal (or substituted principal) to come to terms after good faith negotiations . . .

Here, Dow never negotiated with Suarez because there was nothing to negotiate; Dow wished to remove itself from the business of manufacturing and selling these products entirely, including in Puerto Rico. The Puerto Rico Supreme Court has not made explicit whether the negotiation requirement applies in these circumstances. Our conclusion is that the Puerto Rico Supreme Court would not require such prior negotiation . . .

Primarily, a requirement of negotiation with the plaintiff dealer in these circumstances would not serve the statute's main interest: prevention of unfair usurpation by the principal of the distributor's hard-won clientele and good will . . .

Here, either negotiation would be meaningless or the plaintiff dealer would acquire leverage it would not otherwise possess. This latter effect would create a new imbalance of power, making the entirely legitimate and unrelated corporate interests of the principal in divesting itself of a product line subject to the interests of dealers. To read the Act to require such a result could discourage national and multinational companies from entering into distributorship agreements subject to Act 75 in Puerto Rico.

Further, the Puerto Rico Supreme Court has indicated that it would agree with our reasoning. The *Borg Warner* court cited with approval the law review article by Antonetti-Zequeira that took the position that Act 75 would not require compensation if a company sold off the ability to manufacture a product as part of a corporate reorganization. Puerto Rico is a civil law jurisdiction and follows the rule of such jurisdictions of heavier reliance on learned commentators than common law jurisdictions. *See* J. H. Merryman, *The Civil Law Tradition* 56–57 (2d ed. 1985) ("The civil law is a law of the professors. . . . The common law is still a law of the judges.").

Third, Suarez argues that Dow's withdrawal from the market did not constitute "just cause" because no notice was given. *Borg Warner* made clear that in some circumstances, notice could be excused. In that case, notice was excused because the principal had no intention of terminating the relationship until the negotiations fell through. Here, Dow knew well in advance that it would be ending the distributorship arrangement with Suarez if it consummated the deal with S. C. Johnson, but due to a confidentiality clause in the purchase agreement it was bound to silence.

We are doubtful that Puerto Rico law would impose any notice requirement at all for the same reasons there can be market withdrawal in these circumstances without negotiation . . .

The purpose of the notice requirement "is to allow the dealer to find out well in advance about the principal's intention to withdraw from the market so that he can prepare for the effects said withdrawal could have on his business operations." *Borg Warner, supra.* The importance of the notice requirement depends on the relationship between the dealer and the principal:

> The less lines a dealer represents, the greater his reliance on each line he sells, and thus the greater the importance of the previous notice. . . . [T]he termination of a contract that only represents a small fraction of the dealer's business will not seriously throw his business off-balance, hence the importance of the previous notice shall be less.

Also to be considered are "the age of the ties broken by the dealer, the market conditions of the specific commercial sector, and his relationship with other suppliers and with the clientele of the withdrawing product." *Medina, supra.*

On the facts here, Suarez cannot establish a notice requirement. When Dow terminated the dealer contract, Suarez's annual sales for the three products were less than $1.1 million, out of total annual sales of $312 million; the Dow products constituted about 0.35% of Suarez's total business. Suarez was at one time contemplating abandoning the Dow products altogether. Thus, there was little reliance by Suarez on this line of business, and there was little Suarez could have done to prepare for this termination had it received advance notice from Dow. We find that on these facts, advance notice was not required, and Dow's failure to notify Suarez is not a bar to a finding of just cause for the contract termination.

Suarez's counsel have ably argued their client's cause. Nonetheless, Dow's termination of the dealership relationship with Suarez, precipitated by Dow's sale of the product line, constituted just cause.

III.

The district court's grant of summary judgment to the defendant is *affirmed*. Costs are awarded to Dow.

Source: 337 F.3d 1.

- Simply stated, what is the policy objective behind Act 75?
- Having said that the burden of persuasion lies on Dow, the court merely notes that "Dow says it has just cause." The court never returns to anything that Dow has to say or might want to prove, and carries on methodically setting up and knocking down Suarez's arguments. What's going on?
- Undoubtedly the case was ably argued, but do you think that Suarez really wanted to litigate this action?

Local law provisions that combat this type of behavior may result in courts willing to interpret contract language (particularly "boilerplate"[5]) in a manner that gives the greatest fairness (equity) to the distributor. Consider this Canadian common law case below, in which the Canadian subsidiary of a multinational American parent firm terminated the distributorship of a Canadian representative.

Hillis Oil v. Wynn's Canada

Indexed as *Hillis Oil & Sales Ltd. v. Wynn's Canada Ltd.*
Supreme Court of Canada
February 28, 1986
LE DAIN J.:

This appeal raises a rather narrow issue concerning the interpretation of a termination clause in a distributorship agreement. The issue is whether a clause providing for termination of the agreement by the manufacturer or the distributor "at any time" with or without cause should be construed as impliedly requiring reasonable notice of termination because another clause of the agreement providing for termination by the manufacturer in certain events, including any breach of the agreement by the distributor, stipulates that termination in such case shall take effect upon the giving of the notice of termination.

The appeal is by leave of this Court from the judgment of the Supreme Court of Nova Scotia, Appeal Division, on February 14, 1983, allowing the appeal from the judgment of Richard J. in the Trial Division on August 26, 1982, which awarded the appellant damages for breach of contract because of the respondent's failure to give the appellant reasonable notice of termination of the agreements under which the appellant was an exclusive distributor of certain of the respondent's products in Nova Scotia, New Brunswick and Prince Edward Island.

[5]Reams of contract terms that go unread and not negotiated, granting all sorts of (unreasonable) protection to the powerful side who has drafted the contract.

I

During the relevant period the respondent Wynn's Canada, Ltd. (hereinafter referred to as "Wynn's") was the subsidiary of Wynn Oil Company of Los Angeles, California, and part of a multinational business organization with distributor networks in some eighty countries. It was engaged in the manufacture and sale of automotive engine and cooling system additives as well as industrial lubricants and coolants, among other products. It distributed its products through wholesale distributors with exclusive sales territories. The standard terms of the form of distributorship agreement (or "distributor's agreement," as it is entitled) offered by Wynn's and its parent to prospective distributors were not subject to negotiation or modification. As the president of Wynn's acknowledged in his testimony, it was a case of sign the standard form or not be a distributor.

The appellant Hillis Oil and Sales Limited (hereinafter referred to as "Hillis") was incorporated as a distributorship company in Nova Scotia in 1959. Its relationship with Wynn's, which began in 1969, is reflected in a series of agreements which may be briefly identified. By a distributor's agreement of October 1, 1969 Hillis was appointed as the exclusive distributor in Nova Scotia of a line of products in the marketing division of Wynn's designated as "Automotive." That agreement was replaced by a distributor's agreement of July 18, 1972, which made Hillis the exclusive distributor in Nova Scotia and Prince Edward Island of certain "XTEND" products in the marketing division of Wynn's designated as "Automotive & Fleet." A modification agreement of July 17, 1974 added "X-TEND GUARANTEE KITS" (sometimes referred to as "warranty sales") to the products covered by the agreement of July 18, 1972. A modification agreement of February 23, 1976 extended the exclusive territory covered by the agreement of July 18, 1972 to include New Brunswick and Newfoundland. A modification agreement of February 4, 1977 deleted the word "Fleet" from the designation of the marketing division covered by the agreement of July 18, 1972. A distributor's agreement of February 11, 1977 made Hillis the exclusive distributor in the four Atlantic Provinces of certain lines of products in the marketing division of Wynn's designated as "INDUSTRIAL/FLEET." By agreement effective July 1, 1979 Newfoundland was withdrawn from the Hillis territory. The action in damages is based on the termination of the distributor's agreements of July 18, 1972 and February 11, 1977, as modified from time to time, but the agreement of July 18, 1972 is the one that is generally referred to, being the more important of the two.

From 1959 to 1969, when the Wynn's distributorship began, the business of Hillis was chiefly dependent on the sale of one product, Quaker State Motor Oil. By 1978 the sale of Wynn's products was accounting for about 90 percent of the company's profit. Hillis made a considerable investment in time and money to develop the potential of the Wynn's distributorship. In particular, it hired a sales manager and increased its sales staff from an average of two to an average of eight or nine. It also enlarged its warehousing facilities and stocked inventory at various locations for its salesmen. A high proportion of its development costs were incurred in connection with the introduction in 1976 of the "flush unit program" for cleaning radiators and promoting the sale of Wynn's radiator additives and with the difficulties experienced with that program in the following year or two. The president of Hillis estimated that it would have taken three or four years to recover the company's investment or development costs but that was made impossible by the termination of the distributor's agreements in early 1980. It should perhaps be observed that while the standard distributor's agreement did not expressly prohibit Hillis from handling products that would be competitive with those of Wynn's, there was a clear understanding from Wynn's that Hillis should not do so.

The distributor's agreements of July 18, 1972 and February 11, 1977 contain the following clauses 20 and 23 providing for termination, the terms of which give rise to the issue in the appeal:

20. In the event that Distributor shall breach, or shall have breached, any of the terms, provisions or conditions of this Agreement, or in the event there be filed proceedings in bankruptcy, voluntary or involuntary, by or against Distributor, or that Distributor becomes insolvent or determined, voluntarily or involuntarily, to be bankrupt, or in the event of any dissolution of, or change in, partnership, if Distributor is a partnership, then, in any of such events, Manufacturer may, at its option, by notice in writing to Distributor by mail to Distributor's last known address, terminate and cancel this Agreement; and upon the giving of such notice, this Agreement shall be cancelled, terminated and at an end.

23. That Distributor acknowledges the receipt of a duplicate of this Agreement and accepts such appointment as a distributor subject to, and conditioned upon, Distributor's keeping, observing and performing all of the terms, provisions and conditions in this Agreement set forth all to the full satisfaction of Manufacturer.

   That this Agreement may be terminated and ended, wholly or as to any Marketing Division designated in this Agreement, and/or as to any "XTEND Products" specified in this Agreement, at any time, with or without cause, by either party hereto, by written notice given to the other of them by mail addressed to the last known address of the party to whom said notice is directed. And upon any termination of this Agreement by either party, the Distributor shall remain liable for all sums due to Manufacturer for purchases made by Distributor and unpaid for up to the time of such termination.

Clause 24 of the standard distributor's agreement provides that "in the event of, and upon, termination of this Agreement at any time by either party with or without cause under any circumstances whatsoever" the manufacturer shall have the option to repurchase products from the distributor at a defined price and that notice of the intention to exercise such option shall be given "at the time of the effective date of such termination or at any time within ten days after said effective date of such termination."

By letter dated February 11, 1980 Wynn's gave Hillis notice of termination of the distributor's agreement of July 18, 1972 as follows:

By the terms of the Distributor's Agreement between you and Wynn's Canada Ltd., dated July 18th, 1972, it is provided, among other things:

"That this Agreement may be terminated and ended, wholly or as to any Marketing Division designated in this Agreement, and/or as to any product specified in this Agreement, at any time, with or without cause, by either party hereto, by written notice given to the party to whom said notice is directed. And upon any termination of this Agreement by either party, the Distributor shall remain liable for all sums due to Manufacturer for purchases made by Distributor and unpaid for up to the time of such termination."

In accordance with the foregoing provision, this company does hereby give you written notice that said Distributor's Agreement, dated July 18th, 1972, shall be and hereby is terminated and ended wholly and as to all Marketing Divisions and all products specified in said Agreement.

By letter dated April 22, 1980 Wynn's gave Hillis notice of termination of the distributor's agreement of February 11, 1977 as follows:

Notice is hereby given that the Distributor's Agreement between you and Wynn's Canada Ltd., dated February 11, 1977, is hereby terminated and ended wholly as to all marketing divisions and all products specified in the said Agreement, effective immediately pursuant to the provisions of the said Agreement.

Following the termination of the agreements Wynn's established four new distributorships with former employees of Hillis in the territory covered by the Hillis distributorship. Hillis sued the new distributors as well as Wynn's but the claim against the new distributors was settled before trial.

It was agreed at a pre-trial conference that the termination of the distributor's agreements of July 18, 1972 and February 11, 1977 purported to be made pursuant to clause 23 of the agreements rather than clause 20, as indeed is clear from the terms of the notice of February 11, 1980. Considerable evidence was adduced at the trial concerning the performance of Hillis and the reasons for the termination, but the trial judge held that it was irrelevant, in so far as the interpretation and application of clause 23 were concerned, since that clause provided for termination with or without cause. He did not make a finding as to whether Wynn's had cause.

In maintaining the action of Hillis against Wynn's for breach of contract Richard J. held that one year would have been reasonable notice of termination of the distributor's agreements and fixed the damages at $91,846. From this amount was to be deducted the sum of $18,924.72, which was agreed by the parties to be owing by Hillis to Wynn's, for a net award of $72,921.28, with interest at the rate of 15 percent from August 11, 1980. The length of notice required and the amount to which Hillis is entitled if Wynn's is liable for breach of contract are not in dispute. The sole issue in this Court, as in the Court of Appeal, is whether, in terminating the distributor's agreements pursuant to clause 23, Wynn's was obliged to give Hillis reasonable notice of termination.

The reasoning of the trial judge on this issue is contained in the following passages of his reasons for judgment:

> There is no question the Distribution Agreement is prepared by Wynn's and is totally non-negotiable as to variations. The agreement is the same used by Wynn's throughout the world—albeit in the appropriate language. Kenneth M. Lovett, President of Wynn's Canada said the Distributor Agreement is the only one used by Wynn's—"sign that form or not be a distributor." Mr. Lovett indicated it was normal practice for Wynn's not to give prior notice of cancellation of an agreement because of the impossibility of a continuing relationship after notice had been given.
>
> I am satisfied that the *contra proferentem*[6] rule applies here and any ambiguity must be interpreted against the author—in this case Wynn's.
>
> The difference in the wording of the two termination clauses—20 and 23—bears some comment. Under clause 20 notice must be given "in writing" and "upon the giving of such notice, *this Agreement shall be cancelled, terminated and at an end."* It is clear from this that a notice given pursuant to clause 20 is effective on the giving—by mail—of the written notice.
>
> In the case of a notice of termination under clause 23 it is not expressly stated when the notice is to take effect. Standing alone, clause 23 could be interpreted as making the termination effective as of the time of delivery of the written notice to the other party. However, when read in conjunction with clause 20 it appears clause 23 lacks the specificity of the earlier clause. If both clauses resulted in immediate termination without notice, then the final phrase of clause 20 ("this Agreement shall be cancelled, terminated and at an end.") would be redundant. In my view, the court ought to assume that words in a contract mean something, and, that when two phrases differ, the author meant the result or effect to be different.
>
> With respect to clause 20, it is obvious the notice was meant to be immediately effective. One must conclude, therefore, that the author of clause 23 meant its effect to be something other than clause 20. The only reasonable conclusion is that a termination under clause 23 would take place upon notice rather than immediately.

In the Court of Appeal Hart J.A., delivering the unanimous judgment of the Court, held that there was no ambiguity arising from the terms of clauses 20 and 23 as to whether the agreement could be terminated with immediate effect pursuant to clause 23. He said:

> I am persuaded by the arguments of counsel for the appellant that we have here a case where the terms of the contract are perfectly clear. I can see no ambiguity relating to the termination provisions, and, in my opinion, the trial judge was in error when he implied an additional agreement between the parties which was not necessary to the interpretation of the written contract between them. Either party had the right to terminate the distributor's agree-

[6]That an ambiguity in a contract's terms will be held against the person who has constructed it.

ment without cause at any time they chose, and Wynn's chose February 11, 1980 the date upon which they delivered the notice of termination to Hillis.

II

If it stood alone as the only termination clause in the distributorship agreements clause 23 would have to be construed, I think, as permitting termination with or without cause by either party with immediate effect. But clause 23 cannot be regarded as standing alone; it must be construed in the light of the agreement as a whole, and in particular in the light of the other termination provision in clause 20. The general principle was stated by Estey J. in *Consolidated-Bathurst Export Ltd. v. Mutual Boiler and Machinery Insurance Co.,* [1980] 1 S.C.R. 888, at p. 901, where he said that "the normal rules of construction lead a court to search for an interpretation which, from the whole of the contract, would appear to promote or advance the true intent of the parties at the time of entry into the contract." Also particularly apposite are the words of Dickson J. (as he then was) in *McClelland and Stewart Ltd. v. Mutual Life Assurance Co. of Canada,* [1981] 2 S.C.R. 6, at p. 19, where he said:

> Taken alone and read without consideration of the scheme of the policy the kindred language of the self-destruction clause and the Declaration undoubtedly create a formidable argument in support of the case of the assurance company. It is plain however these cannot be read in an isolated and disjunctive way. The question before us is not to be determined on a mechanical reading of two phrases set apart, but rather on a reading of the policy and the Declaration in entirety.

With great respect, I agree with the learned trial judge that the inclusion of the words "upon the giving of such notice, this Agreement shall be cancelled, terminated and at an end" in clause 20 and their omission in clause 23 creates an ambiguity as to whether the distributor's agreement may be terminated pursuant to clause 23 with immediate effect. If a distributorship agreement does not contain a provision for termination without cause it is so terminable only upon giving reasonable notice of termination. A right to terminate a distributorship agreement without cause with immediate effect must be expressly provided for in the agreement . . . The question is whether, having regard to the inclusion of the above words in clause 20 and their omission in clause 23, the words "at any time" in the latter clause nevertheless make it clear and unequivocal that the agreement may be terminated without cause with immediate effect. In my respectful opinion they do not. There is a strong suggestion that where it was intended to provide for termination with immediate effect the concluding words in clause 20 were the ones considered to convey that meaning. The words "at any time" in clause 23 then bear the same relationship to the right to terminate under that provision as the specified events (breach of the agreement, insolvency and change in partnership) bear to the right to terminate in clause 20; they merely indicate that the right to terminate provided by clause 23 may be exercised at any time, but the clause is silent as to when termination may take effect. In the absence of provision for this question, the rule requiring reasonable notice of termination should be applied as an implied term of the contract. The fact that the same requirement would necessarily have to apply to termination for cause pursuant to clause 23 does not in my opinion make this any less a reasonable alternative construction of clause 23. A possible reason for an intended difference between clause 20 and clause 23 with respect to the right to terminate for cause with immediate effect is that clause 20 is for the protection of the manufacturer in the specified events—breach of contract by the distributor, insolvency of the distributor and change in partnership of the distributor—whereas clause 23 gives the distributor as well as the manufacturer the right to terminate for cause. The manufacturer, knowing that it could always terminate for cause with immediate effect pursuant to clause 20, might well have found it acceptable that neither party should have the right to terminate for cause with immediate effect pursuant to clause 23.

Given this ambiguity as to whether the distributor's agreements could be terminated pursuant to clause 23 with immediate effect or whether such termination could take effect only upon reasonable notice, I also agree with Richard J. that it should be resolved against Wynn's and in favour of Hillis by application of the *contra proferentem* rule of construction. It is true that this rule has been most often invoked with reference to the construction of insurance contracts, particularly clauses in such contracts purporting to limit or exclude the insurer's liability. The rule is, however, one of general application whenever, as in the case at bar, there is ambiguity in the meaning of a contract which one of the parties as the author of the document offers to the other, with no opportunity to modify its wording. The rule is stated in its general terms in *Anson's Law of Contract* (25th ed. 1979), at p. 151, as follows:

> The words of written documents are construed more forcibly against the party using them. The rule is based on the principle that a man is responsible for ambiguities in his own expression, and has no right to induce another to contract with him on the supposition that his words mean one thing, while he hopes the Court will adopt a construction by which they would mean another thing, more to his advantage.

The rule is also stated in general terms . . . as follows:

> That principle of interpretation applies to contracts and other documents on the simple theory that any ambiguity in a term of a contract must be resolved against the author if the choice is between him and the other party to the contract who did not participate in its drafting.

For these reasons I am of the opinion that the respondent is liable for breach of contract for its purported termination of the distributor's agreements without giving the appellant reasonable notice of such termination. I would accordingly allow the appeal, set aside the judgment of the Appeal Division and restore the judgment of Richard J. in the Trial Division, with costs in this Court and in the Appeal Division. Costs in the Trial Division should be as awarded by the trial judge.

Source: [1986] 1 S.C.R. 57.

> The contract clearly said it could be terminated at any time, but just as clearly, the court said it could not be. Reading between the lines, what is the real message of the judge toward suppliers who intend to terminate distributorship contracts?

Clearly, the local law of the buyer's jurisdiction must therefore be considered in drafting a distributorship contract. The seller granting the distributorship will almost invariably draft the contract, and in most jurisdictions it should be expected that any ambiguity would be held against that drafter, the seller.

Major Issues in Business and Law Applicable to Distribution Contracts

Whether agents or true distributors conduct international distribution, three major business and legal concerns remain:

- Does the contract for distribution or its terms offend antitrust/competition law, and is it thus illegal?
- If the contract does legally exist, to what extent are its rights and duties exclusive during its life?
- What happens after the contract of distribution is terminated?

These three matters are considered next, and represent issues where international businesspersons should seek detailed assistance from their legal advisors in advance of the contract negotiation process.

Antitrust Legislation

In addition to protection of the distributor, courts and legislatures consider the effect (and potential for abuse) of distributorship agreements on the industry and economy as a whole. Where suppliers and distributors can create contracts that regulate their relationship in their best interest, that interest may not be in accord with the interest in consumers or the public interest in general. In short, governments are concerned that suppliers and distributors do not "gang up" on consumers. As a result, such acts or agreements are prohibited as an abuse of a dominant position, or as generally anticompetitive behavior. In the United States, the law on point is known as antitrust law, embodied in the Sherman Act.[7] It is applicable to all business activity, not just sales and distribution, and we therefore will amplify this discussion in Chapter 12, "Foreign Investment." In Canada and other common law jurisdictions, antitrust law is variously termed as competition law, or laws applicable to combinations in restraint of trade.

Recall from Chapter 7, "Direct Sale of Goods Exports," that U.S. businesses, pursuant to the rules laid out in the Export Trading Company Act of 1982, may engage in direct collaboration to advance export trade that would otherwise be considered anticompetitive or in restraint of trade. Collaboration between U.S. firms therefore may be immune to prosecution in their home jurisdiction, but there is no corresponding foreign immunity from prosecution in jurisdictions abroad that feel the effect of agreements alleged to be anticompetitive or in restraint of trade.

As the European Union is a major market, knowledge of the European antitrust approach is most important for U.S. and other international traders. The European Union deals with its antitrust and competition cases through application of Articles 81 through 86 of the Treaty Establishing the European Community (formerly Articles 85 through 90). The most important article in this context of distribution agreements is Article 81, the general prohibition on anticompetitive behavior by business undertakings.

---

[7]The Sherman Antitrust Act, 15 U.S.C. §§ 1 and 2 provides:

Sec. 1.—Trusts, etc., in restraint of trade illegal; penalty
Every contract, combination in the form of trust or otherwise, or conspiracy, in restraint of trade or commerce among the several States, or with foreign nations, is declared to be illegal. Every person who shall make any contract or engage in any combination or conspiracy hereby declared to be illegal shall be deemed guilty of a felony, and, on conviction thereof, shall be punished by fine not exceeding $10,000,000 if a corporation, or, if any other person, $350,000, or by imprisonment not exceeding three years, or by both said punishments, in the discretion of the court.

Sec. 2.—Monopolizing trade a felony; penalty
Every person who shall monopolize, or attempt to monopolize, or combine or conspire with any other person or persons, to monopolize any part of the trade or commerce among the several States, or with foreign nations, shall be deemed guilty of a felony, and, on conviction thereof, shall be punished by fine not exceeding $10,000,000 if a corporation, or, if any other person, $350,000, or by imprisonment not exceeding three years, or by both said punishments, in the discretion of the court.

Article 81, Treaty Establishing the European Community

Article 81 (ex Article 85)

1. The following shall be prohibited as incompatible with the common market: all agreements between undertakings, decisions by associations of undertakings and concerted practices which may affect trade between Member States and which have as their object or effect the prevention, restriction or distortion of competition within the common market, and in particular those which:

   a. directly or indirectly fix purchase or selling prices or any other trading conditions;

   b. limit or control production, markets, technical development, or investment;

   c. share markets or sources of supply;

   d. apply dissimilar conditions to equivalent transactions with other trading parties, thereby placing them at a competitive disadvantage;

   e. make the conclusion of contracts subject to acceptance by the other parties of supplementary obligations which, by their nature or according to commercial usage, have no connection with the subject of such contracts.

2. Any agreements or decisions prohibited pursuant to this Article shall be automatically void.

3. The provisions of paragraph 1 may, however, be declared inapplicable in the case of:

   —any agreement or category of agreements between undertakings;

   —any decision or category of decisions by associations of undertakings;

   —any concerted practice or category of concerted practices,

   which contributes to improving the production or distribution of goods or to promoting technical or economic progress, while allowing consumers a fair share of the resulting benefit, and which does not:

   a. impose on the undertakings concerned restrictions which are not indispensable to the attainment of these objectives;

   b. afford such undertakings the possibility of eliminating competition in respect of a substantial part of the products in question.

Source: May be viewed at the European Union's website, www.europa.eu.int. Now renumbered as Article 81(1), pursuant to consolidation of the Treaty Establishing the European Community (formerly Article 85, Treaty Establishing the European Economic Community).

The mental process in analyzing EU anticompetitive agreements is that Article 81(1) prohibits certain anticompetitive practices, unless they are exempted through review under Article 81(3), and if not saved, Article 81(2) condemns them as void. Article 82 (formerly Article 86) addresses firms in a dominant market position, and these two articles taken together cover the same substance as the Sherman Antitrust Act in the United States.

As any distribution agreement that affects trade between member states of the European Union is thus within the scope of Article 81, it becomes vital for the parties, including the foreign seller, to determine whether their agreement is in compliance. Where trade between member states is not affected, the national regulation of member states will continue to apply. Note that it is quite easy for a particular distribution arrangement to be considered a matter of trade between member states, particularly when that is the deliberate object of a foreign seller-exporter in setting up a distribution network across Europe.

As a matter of regulatory expedience, block exemptions from application of the Article 81 provisions do exist, in the form of Commission Regulation 2790 of 1999. A *block ex-*

emption recognizes that some agreements between suppliers and distributors that may appear to be caught by the letter of the law are actually good for the parties and the economy, and do not need to be reviewed for compliance by competition authorities. For example, setting up sales territories for individual distributors in a network is reasonable, as is making agreements to that effect. There are conditions attached to this to keep things fair, but the concept is okay in principle; thus, the block exemption. Accordingly, where the parties to an agreement realize that they enjoy the benefit of a block exemption (advised so by their lawyers), they do not need to submit their agreement for approval by government.

In essence, Regulation 2790/99 exempts distribution agreements—which are part of a larger group of relationships known in European law as "vertical arrangements" (agreements in the supply chain running from producer to consumer)—from competition review (antitrust review) where they do not offend European competition principles. In order to take advantage of the block exemption from review, the supplier (foreign or not) must have a market share of no more than 30 percent, and additional (high) revenue ceilings may apply. In such cases where these caps are exceeded, the vertical arrangement cannot escape antitrust review.

Article 4 of Regulation 2790/99 contains the most important limits to this exemption, making it unavailable to the entire agreement between the seller and the distributor where an attempt exists, among other things, to restrict

1. The buyer's ability to determine its sale price, although a maximum sale price or recommended sale price may be permitted.
2. The territory or customers from whom the buyer may passively take unsolicited orders, although active sales outside a given territory or customer group can be prohibited by the contract.
3. Cross-supplies between distributors in a selective distribution system.[8]

Secondary limitations on the availability of the exemption from competition review exist in Article 5 of the same regulation and apply to further individual terms (making the individual terms therefore subject to antitrust review) where the agreement between the seller and the distributor contains:

a. any direct or indirect non-compete obligation, the duration of which is indefinite or exceeds five years. . . ;

b. any direct or indirect obligation causing the buyer, after termination of the agreement, not to manufacture, purchase, sell or resell goods or services, unless such obligation:

—relates to goods or services which compete with the contract goods or services, and

—is limited to the premises and land from which the buyer has operated during the contract period, and

—is indispensable to protect know-how transferred by the supplier to the buyer,

and provided that the duration of such non-compete obligation is limited to a period of one year after termination of the agreement; this obligation is without prejudice to the possibility of imposing a restriction which is unlimited in time on the use and disclosure of know-how which has not entered the public domain;

c. any direct or indirect obligation causing the members of a selective distribution system not to sell the brands of particular competing suppliers.

---

[8]"Selective distribution system" means a distribution system where the supplier undertakes to sell the contract goods or services, either directly or indirectly, only to distributors selected on the basis of specified criteria and where these distributors undertake not to sell such goods or services to unauthorized distributors. Familiar examples as seen in the trade are often advertised as "official outlet for" or "authorized dealer of" a particular brand of wristwatch, jeans, audio equipment, and the like.

Thus significant restraints are placed on what a seller-exporter can contractually impose upon its buyer-distributor in the European Union, and still hope to avoid antitrust investigation and possible sanction. These principles resonate in most jurisdictions of the world, intent on protecting fairness and protecting the final consumer from abusive practices. Accordingly then, as a second hurdle beyond being fair as between the parties, the drafter of the contract will want to consider whether elements of the proposed terms offend local competition law.

Exclusivity in Distributorship Contracts

The road to litigation in many distributorship contracts is paved in many cases with the word *exclusive*. Parties often assume that there is a magic interpretive meaning in this single word and draft appointments such as "The seller appoints the buyer as its exclusive distributor in the territory." Unfortunately, careless use of the word can give rise to many meanings.

Exclusivity can be directed toward a geographic territory, customer groups, and particular products. The distributor will naturally assume that this term is binding on the seller, that the seller is prohibited either from selling on its own account in the foreign territory (or other defining qualifier) or from appointing any other distributor with responsibility to sell in that territory. The seller, on the other hand, may see the term not as binding on it, but as binding on the distributor. The seller may intend that the distributor is not to stray from the assigned territory in its efforts, or that while the seller will not appoint others to distribute, the seller is still free to pursue sales on its own account. It also may interpret the word to mean that the buyer will purchase its supplies only from the seller-exporter, or that the buyer will not carry competing goods from other suppliers. Capping all this is the watchful eye of competition and antitrust authorities, for which the word *exclusive* is a magnet for investigative action.

The seller also may find that it must act as a police officer, attempting to prevent conflicts between its exclusive distributors in different territories. Frequently, each "exclusive" distributor will become aware of sales opportunities in the territory of another and service those opportunities. An immediate complaint to the supplier follows, that one distributor is poaching in the territory of the other. If a seller-exporter-supplier attempts to punish this behavior, perhaps by restricting supply to the "offender," it may find itself acting contrary to a variety of other antitrust provisions.

Assuming that it is even necessary to make distributorships exclusive in the first place (and often it is not commercially necessary), reference must be made to the local law of the jurisdiction where the activity will take place to determine any restrictions on such appointments. Secondly, the contract must be drafted with extreme clarity to avoid any ambiguity as to the effect that use of the word *exclusive* truly intends to create.

Poaching can be addressed in ways that do not require exclusivity between distributors; particularly where any element of product customization is possible. Products with labels, markings, and instruction manuals written in Dutch do not generally sell well in Italy, and from there only imagination is required to slow the leaking of sales from one distinct territory to another. It is a matter only of balancing the added cost of custom production against the headache and cost of contract enforcement. The step that permits this is a careful and detailed definition in contract of the goods (and their custom attributes) that will be supplied to the distributor.

Some goods, however, have universal attributes that cannot be altered, or the customer does not care about the alterations; many of those goods are found in selective distribution systems of authorized dealers: jeans, wristwatches, and perfumes, for example. In such cases, distribution contracts often suffer from the phenomenon of parallel imports: goods shipped to one territory (often sold there at a low price) are reexported to other territories where they may attract a much higher price.

The price differential tends to arise from the fact that the high price of the goods is embodied in their brand name, not as a result of any particularly costly aspect of the production process. Consequently, a seller-exporter can sell to one distributor at a high price and to another at a low price (for that is all the second market can bear), and yet turn a good profit on both sales. The incentive is then quite significant for the second distributor to re-export and sell not in its own market, but in the territory where retail prices are much higher. Both the original seller and the distributor responsible for the higher price territory will be angered by these parallel imports; and often, if the original seller can find the source of the parallel imports, it will terminate its relationship with that offending distributor.

Usually it is markets that are geographically close together with broadly similar social conditions that lead to similar goods being demanded, but with widely disparate economies, that feel the greatest pressures of parallel imports. Thus, parallel imports are not as much of a concern between the United States and Canada, as the last condition is not met; the U.S. and Canadian economies are quite similar, and prices reflect this. The effect is more apparent between Germany and Poland, or Italy and the Former Yugoslavia. Each pair is geographically close (so parallel profits are not consumed in transport costs) and has broadly similar societies with similar demand (both markets demand toothpaste, canned food, and cars), but addressing local economic differences means that suppliers must charge different prices in each market. An instant arbitrage[9] opportunity exists.

As Europe is a region of prosperous markets ringed by others that are less affluent, parallel imports are therefore a frequently encountered issue there, and will be an issue for any foreign supplier who intends to serve the European marketplace while employing differential prices elsewhere. The case below illustrates European regulation of suppliers who attempt to enforce against parallel imports. While technically the case and the treaty require the supplier to the reseller to be based in a member state, this will often enmesh a foreign supplier as well, if the supplier has established a single master distributor in Europe with regional subdistributors. Happily, there is room for supplier protection of its selective distribution systems, but the tests that the European Court of Justice instructs national courts to apply are revealing as to the standards by which distributorship contracts will be judged.

Case C-306/96, *Javico International v. Yves Saint Laurent SA*

Indexed as Case C-306/96, *Javico International v. Yves Saint Laurent Parfums SA (YSLP)*

European Court of Justice, Reference on Interpretation of Article 85(1) of the Treaty[10]

April 28, 1998

REFERENCE to the Court under Article 177 of the EC Treaty by the Cour d'Appel de Versailles (France) for a preliminary ruling in the proceedings pending before that court between Javico International and Javico AG and Yves Saint Laurent Parfums SA (YSLP) on the interpretation of Article 85(1) of the EC Treaty, . . .

---

[9]An opportunity to "buy low" in one market, at the same time that one can "sell high" in another. A profit exists to the extent of the price and cost differential.

[10]Now renumbered as Article 81(1), pursuant to consolidation of the Treaty Establishing the European Community, reproduced earlier in this chapter.

Judgment

1. By judgment of 8 September 1995, received at the Court Registry on 23 September 1996, the Cour d'Appel (Court of Appeal), Versailles, referred to the Court for a preliminary ruling under Article 177 of the EC Treaty two questions on the interpretation of Article 85(1) of the EC Treaty in order to enable it to appraise the validity of a contract containing an obligation to export luxury cosmetics to a non-member country and of a prohibition of reimporting and marketing those products in the Community.

2. The questions have been raised in proceedings brought by Yves Saint Laurent Parfums SA (hereinafter 'YSLP') against Javico International and Javico AG (hereinafter together referred to as 'Javico') for a finding that Javico was in breach of its contractual obligations, that the two contracts between the parties had been properly terminated and that YSLP was entitled to contractual compensation and damages.

3. YSLP enjoys an individual exemption for the selective distribution of its products within the Community (Commission Decision 92/33/EEC of 16 December 1991 relating to a procedure pursuant to Article 85 of the EEC Treaty (IV33.242—Yves Saint Laurent Parfums) (OJ 1992 L 12, p. 24)), the legality of the main provisions of which was upheld by judgment of the Court of First Instance in Case T-19/92 *Leclerc v Commission* [1996] ECR II-1851).

4. On 5 February and 6 May 1992 YSLP concluded with Javico International, whose registered office is in Germany but which does not form part of YSLP's distribution network within the Community, two contracts for the distribution of its products, one covering Russia and Ukraine and the other Slovenia.

5. The distribution contract for Russia and Ukraine provides:

   '1. Our products are intended for sale solely in the territory of the Republics of Russia and Ukraine.

   In no circumstances may they leave the territory of the Republics of Russia and Ukraine.

   2. Your company promises and guarantees that the final destination of the products will be in the territory of the Republics of Russia and Ukraine, and that it will sell the products only to traders situated in the territory of the Republics of Russia and Ukraine. Consequently, your company will provide the addresses of the distribution points of the products in the territory of the Republics of Russia and Ukraine and details of the products by distribution point.'

6. The distribution contract for Slovenia provides:

   'In order to protect the high quality of the distribution of the products in other countries of the world, the distributor agrees not to sell the products outside the territory or to unauthorised dealers in the territory.'

7. Shortly after the conclusion of those contracts, YSLP discovered in the United Kingdom, Belgium and the Netherlands products sold to Javico which should have been distributed in Russia, Ukraine and Slovenia. YSLP therefore terminated the contracts and instituted proceedings before the Tribunal de Commerce, Nanterre, which, by judgment of 21 October 1994, upheld the termination of the two contracts and YSLP's claim for contractual compensation and damages.

8. Javico appealed against that decision to the Cour d'Appel, Versailles, which considered that the validity of the provisions in the distribution contracts at issue had to be appraised in the light of Article 85(1) of the Treaty, the appellants having contended that those contractual provisions were void by virtue of Article 85(2) of the Treaty.

9. In those circumstances, the Cour d'Appel stayed proceedings pending a ruling from the Court of Justice on the following questions:

'1. Where an undertaking (the supplier) situated in a Member State of the European Union by contract entrusts another undertaking (the distributor) situated in another Member State with the distribution of its products in a territory outside the Union, must Article 85(1) of the Treaty establishing the European Economic Community be interpreted as prohibiting provisions in that contract which preclude the distributor from effecting any sales in a territory other than the contractual territory, and hence any sale in the Union, either by direct marketing or by re-exportation from the contractual territory?

2. In the event that the said Article 85(1) prohibits such contractual provisions, must it be interpreted as not being applicable where the supplier otherwise distributes his products on the territory of the Union by means of a selective distribution network which has been the subject of an exemption decision under Article 85(3)?'

The First Question

10. By its first question, the national court asks whether Article 85(1) of the Treaty precludes a supplier established in a Member State from prohibiting a distributor established in another Member State to which it entrusts the distribution of its products in a territory outside the Community from making any sales in a territory other than the contractual territory, including the territory of the Community, either by means of direct sales or by means of re-exportation from the contractual territory.

11. According to settled case-law (see, in particular, Case 56/65 *Minière* and Joined Cases 56/64 and 58/64 *Consten*), agreements between economic operators at different levels of the economic process may be caught by the prohibition contained in Article 85(1) of the Treaty.

12. In order to determine whether agreements such as those concluded by YSLP with Javico fall within the prohibition laid down by that provision it is necessary to consider whether the purpose or effect of the ban on supplies which they entail is to restrict to an appreciable extent competition within the common market and whether the ban may affect trade between Member States.

13. As far as agreements intended to apply within the Community are concerned, the Court has already held that an agreement intended to deprive a reseller of his commercial freedom to choose his customers by requiring him to sell only to customers established in the contractual territory is restrictive of competition within the meaning of Article 85(1) of the Treaty (see, to that effect, Case 86/82 *Hasselblad* and Case C-70/93 *BMW*).

14. Similarly, the Court has held that an agreement which requires a reseller not to resell contractual products outside the contractual territory has as its object the exclusion of parallel imports within the Community and consequently restriction of competition in the common market (see, to that effect, Case C-279/87 *Tipp-Ex*). Such provisions, in contracts for the distribution of products within the Community, therefore constitute by their very nature a restriction of competition (see Case 19/77 *Miller*).

15. However, anti-competitive conduct may not be struck down under Article 85(1) of the Treaty unless it is capable of affecting trade between Member States.

16. If an agreement, decision or practice is to be capable of affecting trade between Member States, it must be possible to foresee with a sufficient degree of probability, on the basis of a set of objective factors of law or of fact, that they may have an influence, direct or indirect, actual or potential, on the pattern of trade between Member States in such a way as to cause concern that they might hinder the attainment of a single market between Member States. Moreover, that effect must not be insignificant (Case 5/69 *Völk*).

17. The effect which an agreement might have on trade between Member States is to be appraised in particular by reference to the position and the importance of the parties

on the market for the products concerned (Case 99/79 *Lancôme*). Thus, even an agreement imposing absolute territorial protection may escape the prohibition laid down in Article 85 if it affects the market only insignificantly, regard being had to the weak position of the persons concerned on the market in the products in question (Joined Cases 100/80 to 103/80 *Musique Diffusion*).

18. It is therefore necessary to determine to what extent the foregoing considerations also apply to agreements, like those at issue in this case, which are intended to apply in a territory outside the Community.

19. In the case of agreements of this kind, stipulations of the type mentioned in the question must be construed not as being intended to exclude parallel imports and marketing of the contractual product within the Community but as being designed to enable the producer to penetrate a market outside the Community by supplying a sufficient quantity of contractual products to that market. That interpretation is supported by the fact that, in the agreements at issue, the prohibition of selling outside the contractual territory also covers all other non-member countries.

20. It follows that an agreement in which the reseller gives to the producer an undertaking that he will sell the contractual products on a market outside the Community cannot be regarded as having the object of appreciably restricting competition within the common market or as being capable of affecting, as such, trade between Member States.

21. Consequently, the agreements at issue, in that they prohibit the reseller Javico from selling the contractual product outside the contractual territory assigned to it, do not constitute agreements which, by their very nature, are prohibited by Article 85(1) of the Treaty. Similarly, the provisions of the agreements in question, in that they prohibit direct sales within the Community and re-exports of the contractual product to the Community, cannot be contrary, by their very nature, to Article 85(1) of the Treaty.

22. Although the contested provisions of those agreements do not, by their very nature, have as their object the prevention, restriction or distortion of competition within the common market within the meaning of Article 85(1), it is, however, for the national court to determine whether they have that effect. Appraisal of the effects of those agreements necessarily implies taking account of their economic and legal context (Case C-393/92 *Almelo*) and, in particular, of the fact that YSLP has established in the Community a selective distribution system enjoying an exemption.

23. In that regard, it is first necessary to determine whether the structure of the Community market in the relevant products is oligopolistic, allowing only limited competition within the Community network for the distribution of those products.

24. It must then be established whether there is an appreciable difference between the prices of the contractual products charged in the Community and those charged outside the Community. Such a difference is not, however, liable to affect competition if it is eroded by the level of customs duties and transport costs resulting from the export of the product to a non-member country followed by its re-import into the Community.

25. If that examination were to disclose that the contested provisions of the agreements concerned had the effect of undermining competition within the meaning of Article 85(1) of the Treaty, it would also be necessary to determine whether, having regard to YSLP's position on the Community market and the extent of its production and its sales in the Member States, the contested provisions designed to prevent direct sales of the contractual products in the Community and re-exports of them to the Community entail any risk of an appreciable effect on the pattern of trade between the Member States such as to undermine attainment of the objectives of the common market.

26. In that regard, intra-Community trade cannot be appreciably affected if the products intended for markets outside the Community account for only a very small percentage of the total market for those products in the territory of the common market.

27. It is for the national court, on the basis of all the information available to it, to determine whether the conditions are in fact fulfilled for the agreements at issue to be caught by the prohibition laid down in Article 85(1) of the Treaty.

28. Accordingly, the answer to the first question must be that Article 85(1) of the Treaty precludes a supplier established in a Member State of the Community from imposing on a distributor established in another Member State to which the supplier entrusts the distribution of his products in a territory outside the Community a prohibition of making any sales in any territory other than the contractual territory, including the territory of the Community, either by direct marketing or by re-exportation from the contractual territory, if that prohibition has the effect of preventing, restricting or distorting competition within the Community and is liable to affect the pattern of trade between Member States. This might be the case where the Community market in the products in question is characterised by an oligopolistic structure or by an appreciable difference between the prices charged for the contractual product within the Community and those charged outside the Community and where, in view of the position occupied by the supplier of the products at issue and the extent of the supplier's production and sales in the Member States, the prohibition entails a risk that it might have an appreciable effect on the pattern of trade between Member States such as to undermine attainment of the objectives of the common market.

The Second Question

[Regarding the second question, the Court concludes] that provisions intended to prevent a distributor from selling directly in the Community and re-exporting to the Community contractual products which the distributor has undertaken to sell in non-member countries do not escape the prohibition laid down in Article 85(1) of the Treaty on the ground that the Community supplier of the products concerned distributes them within the Community through a selective distribution network covered by an exemption decision under Article 85(3) of the Treaty.

Source: May be viewed at the European Court of Justice website, curia.eu.int/en/content/juris/index.html.

Without reading further, ask yourself: Does the court prohibit or allow restrictions against parallel imports imposed by suppliers on distributors? What conditions are attached?

Reduced to the bare minimum, the court is most concerned with whether contract provisions in distributorship agreements have negative effects on the common market. More accurately, the question is whether such restrictions on parallel imports are preventing, restricting, or distorting competition within the Community and are liable to affect the pattern of trade between member states, such as to undermine the attainment of the objectives of the common market. If these negative effects are present, and this will particularly be the case where an oligopoly exists (few sellers and many buyers), then the prohibition will stand. If the volume of parallel imports is very low compared to the total market for those products in the territory of the common market, then the case is a factual matter for the national courts to determine.

Product Liability in Distribution

Liability for defective products and consequential damage is a concern in any sale of goods, whether that be local or international sale, direct sale, or via distributor. In the case of international sales via distributors, the problem is larger as the sale may be subject to two or more sets of laws: the domestic law of the producer-exporter and the local law of the injured party and the local distributor.

The United States

If the injured party brings its action in the United States (recall Chapter 3 generally, civil jurisdiction and forum non conveniens specifically, and *Reyno v. Piper Aircraft* particularly), it has three avenues to approach its claim for damages in product liability: one in contract and two in torts (civil wrongs).

Breach of Contract   In contract law in the United States, supplying a product that is defective and causes damage violates the express or implied warranty of the contract that the goods will be reasonably fit for the use intended. Being in breach of a contract warranty, the manufacturer-seller would be liable for the physical harm and harm to property that were a result of the defect. Such a result can only arise where there is a contract between the injured user and the manufacturer-seller because of the need for privity (a legal relationship between contract parties). If there is an intervening distributor, the injured party's contract is with that distributor, not with the manufacturer, and privity works as a limitation to a suit in contract. If an injured party lacks a contract with the manufacturer-seller, it can frame its action in tort, on the basis of either negligence or strict liability.

Negligence   For a finding of negligence, the injured party must show that the manufacturer-seller owed it a duty of care, that the duty was breached, and that the breach is the proximate cause of its damages, as would be foreseen by a reasonable person. While the obligation on the injured plaintiff to prove duty, breach, and damage cannot be diminished, it is assisted by certain rules of tort, notably statutory duties and the doctrine of *res ispsa loquitor.*[11]

Where a duty of fitness of goods or compliance with a technical standard is prescribed by law (e.g., testing or certification of electrical goods or pharmaceuticals prior to sale), then a failure to meet this requirement represents an automatic finding of both duty and breach of that duty. Where the goods present a defect that would be unreasonable to expect (cars that spontaneously explode, appliances that catch fire) without fault in design or construction by the manufacturer, the injured plaintiff is absolved from showing the defendant's breach. Instead, the onus reverses; now the manufacturer must show that it has *not* been negligent.

Strict Liability   In cases where products are found to be unreasonably dangerous to the user (for example, contaminated foods) and the seller is a commercial seller of such goods, then all its efforts in careful preparation will not save it from liability. It will be held to a standard of strict liability.[12] Neither will it be saved by a lack of contractual privity with the end-user; the public has a right to protection and redress, and negligence need not be shown.

While most nations of the world have not experienced either the frequency or magnitude of U.S. product liability litigation, the concept is an integral part of most legal systems, either in tort, contract, or both.

European Union

In the European Union, Council Directive 85/374/EEC governs product liability, mandating that all producers, importers, and suppliers of goods may be held liable.[13] No exclusionary clause or limitation is effective against an injured person,[14] and the standard for

---

[11]Latin: the thing speaks for itself.

[12]See, for example, *Escola v. Coca-Cola Bottling Co. of Fresno,* 150 P.2d 436 (Cal. 1944).

[13]Council Directive 85/374/EEC, Articles 1 and 3.

[14]Ibid., Article 12.

liability is, quite simply put, that "a product is defective when it does not provide the safety which a person is entitled to expect, taking all circumstances into account."[15]

British Commonwealth

While the United Kingdom now finds its product liability laws governed by the European Union, it was Britain that once again created a Commonwealth legal standard. In the 1930s, fault for defective products required a bridge that would span the absence of any privity of contract between the injured and the producer, and the lack of negligence toward the injured by the distributor. This bridge was found in a Scottish case that has since famously woven its way into the jurisprudence of most common law jurisdictions outside the United States: *M'Alister (or Donoghue) v. Stevenson*. The alternative plaintiff's name is based on the right of a married woman in Scotland to maintain an action in her maiden name. Donoghue became violently ill after drinking a snail that had been present in a bottle of ginger beer. She was remote from the manufacturer in that the bottle had been purchased for her by another person, from a restaurant. Consequently, the UK courts were forced to create their own version of product liability, Lord Atkin saying:

> I would point out that, in the assumed state of the authorities, not only would the consumer have no remedy against the manufacturer, he would have none against any one else, for in the circumstances alleged there would be no evidence of negligence against any one other than the manufacturer; and except in the case of a consumer who was also a purchaser, no contract and no warranty of fitness . . . [16]

Since that time product liability, traceable through distributors to suppliers and manufacturers, has become firmly entrenched in nations of the British Commonwealth. It is, however, not without some limits, as may be seen through the eyes of the Supreme Court of Canada:

> No doubt the courts of this country will continue to search for reasonable and workable limits to the liability of a negligent supplier of manufactured products or services, to the liability of a negligent contractor for contractual undertakings owed to others, and to the liability of persons who negligently make misrepresentations. In this search courts will be vigilant to protect the community from damages suffered by a breach of the "neighbourhood" duty. At the same time, however, the realities of modern life must be reflected by the enunciation of a defined limit on liability capable of practical application, so that social and commercial life can go on unimpeded by a burden outweighing the benefit to the community of the neighbourhood historic principle.[17]

Accommodating Product Liability into the Distribution Contract

International lawsuits on product liability raise just as much concern for the importer-distributor as they should for the manufacturer-exporter. EU law expressly names importers as liable, and in other jurisdictions they will expect to be named in the suit, for they are the "face" of the manufacturer in the foreign market.

As this is likely to happen, suppliers and distributors should provide for it in their contracts. Distributors will, quite fairly, want to be indemnified by the supplier against being found liable in the foreign market (as the "easy target") for defects created by the supplier.

Suppliers also will want to address this issue; recall the section on "Protection" earlier in this chapter. If manufacturer-suppliers are by chance not named in the suit, they will not be able to influence the outcome. Equally, they will want to reserve rights to control litigation strategy in cases that affect their distributors and the right to make or reject offers

[15]Ibid., Article 6.

[16]*M'Alister (or Donoghue) v. Stevenson*, [1932] A.C. 562 (H.L.) at 583.

[17]Estey, J., in *B.D.C. Ltd. v. Hofstrand Farms Limited et al.*, [1986] 1 S.C.R. 228 at 243.

Such suits employ the "shotgun approach": name and sue everybody who could possibly have had a hand in creating the defect and let the judge sort it out.

of settlement. This is because they should be rightfully fearful of allowing precedents to be set that may affect them in other cases where they are named in the suit. For example, where a distributor is sued for selling a defective product, it perhaps cannot afford to defend itself properly and, if the suit is small, it might (incorrectly) say to the court and claimant, "You're right; widgets are defective," just so it can get on with life. This could be disastrous for the manufacturer-supplier, which in other suits now must contend with the fact that someone "from its own side" has gone on record with damaging remarks.

Termination and Post-Termination Events

As can be seen from the materials presented in this chapter, careless termination of a distributorship can result in unintended liability in both civil and common law jurisdictions. When termination occurs simply by expiration of a fixed period of time, suppliers also should ensure that local law provisions do not automatically renew the contract if the business relationship continues in practice after expiration.

Most legal systems provide for recognition of just cause as a reason for early termination, and it is wise that the parties to the agreement lay out (nonexhaustively) what will constitute "just cause" in their relationship. Such provisions must stand the scrutiny of the applicable local law, and its public policy definition of just cause, but having a clear definition between the parties enhances commercial certainty.

Following termination, inventory for which title has not passed usually will revert to the care of the supplier, who presumably will be interested in seeing these goods handed over to a new distributor. Provision should be made in the contract that the former distributor would participate in an orderly transition, as well as a right in the former distributor to assign inventory to which it does have title to the new distributor. Intellectual property such as trademarks and trade dress may be handled in the same manner.

Some general terms of the distributorship contract should be drafted so that they survive the termination of the contract itself and continue on as independent obligations into the future. These include the obligation on the distributor to keep confidential information secret into the future and, to the extent that it is permitted by local competition law, the obligation that the distributor refrain from actively soliciting the customer list that it has turned over to the new distributor of the goods.

Variants of Distribution Agreements

While this chapter has focused on quite traditional distribution relationships ("I make, you sell"), there are a variety of other forms of relationship that have been born as a result of newer developments in business thinking. Most of the principles discussed above will continue to apply, but the nature of these relationships results in contracts that reflect new allocations of rights and responsibilities.

Strategic Alliances

Strategic alliances arise more and more frequently on an international basis. They are founded in contract like a distribution arrangement, but will have added dimensions making them more like traditional partnerships, without going as far (necessarily) as creating a new company subsidiary to the parent firms, or merging the two "allies." In other words, firms with complementary skills agree in contract to work together toward a common goal, much like a joint venture (discussed in Chapter 12). Often, the ultimate goal lies in product distribution, but strategic alliances can cover much wider collaboration between firms. In such cases, the agreement between the firms will have large parts dedicated to the shared responsibilities, the contributions toward expenses, and the control of the direction of the work. The actual coverage of distribution arrangements may form only a minor or secondary part of the agreement. For example, a manufacturer of mobile cellular telephones may enter into a strategic alliance with a major mobile telephone network operator. The network operator will handle distribution of the manufacturer's mobile handsets, and in return, the manufacturer will work to create technologies that make best use of the network facilities, so the operator can offer the most attractive package of services to its customer.

Value-Added Reseller

A variant of the strategic alliance is the value-added reseller. Here, in each step of the distribution chain, the reseller of the product or service is adding value that will hopefully be seen as such by the end-user or consumer. For example, a U.S. aerospace firm may launch and operate a communications satellite and be willing to lease or sell communications bandwidth to others, from the United States, Canada, and Mexico. This is utterly of no use to the residential consumer, unless a reseller of that bandwidth is willing to "add value" by arranging for the transmission of TV programming or Internet download capability on behalf of the residential customer. Even then, other resellers or alliance partners may be required before there can be commercial success for any member of the alliance. Until someone crawls atop the customer's roof and installs a dish receiver, no money from the consumer enters the reselling chain of distribution. Where a communications satellite can blanket a continent, these types of alliances among resellers become international very rapidly.

Systems Integrator

In the case of a systems integrator, a single entrepreneur is acting as the "distributor" for a range of manufacturers, whose complex products must all be adapted or fitted together so they operate in an integrated manner. An example illustrates the point. Litton Industries recently acted as a systems integrator for a major upgrade project for naval destroyers. These older ships required refitting of new communications, sensors, fire-control systems, engines, and environmental systems. As a particular "best choice" existed for each of these components from a variety of different suppliers, someone was obligated to make them work well together, or "integrate" them into a single "system." The distributor in this case is not merely reselling components to the Navy; it is making the overall package work properly, first, by establishing interfaces to be accommodated by the suppliers and, second, performing the project assembly work. Systems integration projects are occurring more often internationally as "best-of-breed" suppliers can now be found almost anywhere, and to overlook international supply solutions results in a less than optimal final product. The legal liability for the fitness of the final product rests with the systems integrator, and the liability of the suppliers of the components is limited to the product specifications provided to them by the systems integrator.

Chapter Summary

A seller-exporter that does not intend to produce its goods abroad, or license its production abroad, quickly encounters others who are willing to represent those products in foreign markets. These new participants usually take the form of either agents (who do not take title to the exported goods) or distributors (who do).

Agents may be appointed who are able to bind the exporting firm in contract, or they may be appointed solely as market makers that bring opportunities to the notice of the exporter. In this latter case, the seller-exporter reserves its powers of contract to itself.

Since true agents stand in the place of the principal, seller-exporters that choose this route must recognize the dangers and potential lack of control associated with agents, and that the principal may well be found responsible for the acts of its agents.

While many control features can be placed in an agency contract, the contract itself may be subject to provisions of local law elsewhere that are intended to protect agents from abuse by their principals. A counterpart to this type of legislation exists in many jurisdictions to protect distributors as well. Both agents and distributors also may benefit from strict common law interpretation of contracts against the seller-exporter that is either their principal or supplier.

In distribution agreements, the chief responsibilities of the distributor are to act in the best interest of the supplier, to maintain inventory and provide service, and to use the trademarks and trade dress of the goods in keeping with the intentions of the supplier.

The chief responsibilities of the supplier are to honor the orders of the distributor and to provide such support as may be required under the contract. This support is aimed at developing the market, often in the form of training and advertising, but also may take the form of assisting and protecting the distributor against the anticompetitive practices of others.

The issue of exclusivity is often important to both suppliers and distributors. Exclusivity is a way of appropriately managing the market for the former, and works as an assurance of the opportunity for success for the latter. As the term is capable of a number of interpretations with widely differing rights and expectations, it is vital that there be a clear understanding by both parties as to what rights and responsibilities are in fact exclusive.

Over and above any rights in local law intended to protect distributors on termination of an agreement, the contract itself must anticipate its eventual end. Accordingly, it must provide for the orderly transition to a new distributor, confidentiality, and the extinguishing of the distributor's rights to sell the product and to use any intellectual property granted to it by the supplier.

Chapter Questions

1. What confusion and liability would be inherent in simply naming a party as the "representative" of a seller-exporter?

2. Explain the rationale by which the European Court of Justice refused to recognize a choice-of-law clause that might otherwise work to the detriment of an agent.

3. In what commercial situations is establishing a relationship with a distributor likely a more appropriate strategic approach to market than using an agent?

4. On what grounds is it justified to say that a sale to a distributor is "something beyond a simple sale contract"? Why and how do some duties carry on after the death of the relationship, and what duties frequently fall into this category?

5. What abusive tactic do suppliers sometimes aim at agents and distributors, and what steps have some legislatures taken to combat this?

6. A German distributor enters into a contract with a U.S. supplier and commits "not to sell the product at a price less than the minimum market price established periodically by the supplier." The distributor is later found to be selling the product at a price only 70 percent of the minimum market price. Who might be attacking the agreement between the supplier and distributor, and on what specific grounds, if the action was heard in European court? What argument might the supplier raise in its defense? What grounds would be used to attack this arrangement if the case was heard in a U.S. court?

7. Explain the phenomenon of parallel imports, why and how they may impinge on a distributor's rights, and why this may become both a business problem and a legal problem for the supplier.

8. Contrast the position in a product liability suit of a distributor in a common law jurisdiction versus the same distributor located in the European Union. Which is exposed to greater liability in principle, and why?

9. Sierra, as supplier, contracts with Delta as "exclusive distributor" of its products in Poland and contracts with Echo as "exclusive distributor" in the neighboring Czech Republic. A short time

later, business troubles brew between Sierra, Delta, and Echo. On these facts alone, what are the most likely causes of conflict and the arguments advanced by each party?

10. In a franchise agreement relating to a hamburger chain, the supplier offering the franchise obligates its distributor (the franchisee) to purchase all decorations, raw materials, foodstuffs, and supplies from companies it controls or has previously approved. Is this a vertical arrangement? Do you think that a European block exemption (or equivalent elsewhere) would be appropriate in the circumstances?

BusinessWeek

Mary Ellen Kitler, an American pharmacologist living in Geneva, Switzerland, has pleaded guilty to filing a false tax return in connection with complex export-diversion schemes that cost such big-name manufacturers as Johnson & Johnson, ICN Pharmaceuticals, Bayer Corp., and Nestle millions of dollars.

In the case, detailed in a Dec. 4, 1995, BW article (see "Exports That Aren't Going Anywhere"), manufacturers sold goods ranging from diabetes-diagnostic strips to Quik chocolate-drink mix at deep discounts to middlemen who claimed that the goods were bound for such spots as Africa, Russia, and the Middle East. In fact, the products were diverted to American distributors and retailers who paid full price, while the middlemen pocketed millions.

Kitler, now 57, was indicted in July, 1995, along with Urs Brunschweiler, an officer of a Geneva-based freight forwarder, and Kotbey M. Kotbey, an Egyptian-born American who also lived in Geneva. Brunschweiler in early 1996 pleaded guilty to a count of conspiracy, specifically for supplying false bills of lading to disguise one of the diversions, and is now awaiting sentencing. Kotbey, who had been awaiting trial, jumped bail last September and is a fugitive, according to Noel L. Hillman, an assistant U.S. attorney in Newark, N.J. Hillman says the trio conspired to fraudulently obtain such goods as diabetes-diagnostic strips from Bayer Group and the LifeScan subsidary of J&J. Kitler allegedly negotiated bargain prices from the companies by claiming that the goods were to be used for charitable purposes in underdeveloped countries. Kotbey's alleged role was to sell the strips into the U.S.

The trio's operations went awry after J&J grew suspicious about Kitler's supposedly charitable front organization, the Anglo-American Foundation. The company alerted prosecutors, who had coincidentally been tracking Kotbey's opera-

tions in Europe. The prosecutors decided to mount a sting to catch the group after Anglo-American Foundation's phone number in Geneva turned out to be Kotbey's.

As part of the sting, J&J offered to sell 3,000 boxes of the diabetes strips to the foundation. It did so, but "salted" those boxes with specially marked coupons, which retail customers could redeem for free strips. When customers, primarily in the New York–New Jersey area, turned in the coupons, the prosecutors could trace them back through retailers and a wholesaler to the trio. With such proof of misrouting in hand, the prosecutors then contacted Brunschweiler, who provided bills of lading that ostensibly showed that the goods had arrived in Moscow, destined for poor people in Azerbaijan.

Kitler was nabbed in mid-1995, when she traveled to a hotel near J&J's headquarters in New Brunswick, N.J., ostensibly to meet company executives. In a plea bargain, Kitler, who also keeps a home in Norristown, Pa., admitted that she failed to disclose in her 1993 tax return that she kept three Swiss bank accounts. In exchange for her Feb. 6 guilty plea to filing a false tax return, the other charges against her have been dropped. She faces up to three years in jail, $250,000 in fines, and the costs of her prosecution when sentenced on May 1.

In all, Kotbey is alleged to have obtained $19 million worth of consumer goods, medical devices, and prescription drugs from the companies by falsely claiming the goods would be exported to impoverished countries. In two schemes, he claimed the goods were destined for poor people. In two others, he claimed they would be routed to military outfits for humanitarian purposes.

Source: Joseph Weber in Philadelphia, edited by Thane Peterson. Copyright 1997, by The McGraw-Hill Companies, Inc. All rights reserved.

11

Intellectual Property and Licensing

Chapter Objectives

Licensing of rights to use intellectual property (including patents, trademarks, and copyright) is an important legal tool that can be used to capitalize on business opportunities in foreign markets. In this chapter we discuss

- The nature of intellectual property and applicable national and international law.
- The risks and rewards in licensing and its place in international business strategy.

- Legal considerations in negotiating the terms and payments in a licensing agreement.

Introduction

In the context of international business transactions, a license is a contractual grant of a right to do or make use of intellectual property by a possessor of that right in one nation in favor of another person or business in another nation.

The intellectual property that is the subject of the transaction may be any combination of patents, trademarks, or copyrights; it may be unprotected secret knowledge, the methodology of a process (secret or otherwise), or the trade dress of the goods themselves. It may be a small technological contribution to an already recognized and widely produced product or it may be the entire package of service and goods delivery, as is frequently the case in franchises.

There are many motivations that lead the owner or other lawful possessor of intellectual property to create a license in favor of a foreign licensee. The grantor of the license (the licensor) is usually attempting to address one or more business concerns and profitable opportunities through a licensee that, for a range of reasons, it cannot or will not address itself.

Patents, Copyright, and Trademarks under National Law

Virtually every nation has some version of national law pertaining to these forms of intellectual property, including those for whom individual property rights mean little in their national commercial fabric. Even the Democratic People's Republic of Korea (North Korea) has a national bureau for intellectual property. Patents for inventions, trademarks for commercial branding, and copyright for artistic and literary works are each a form of monopoly power within a commercial context, and the need to regulate this monopoly power is recognized with similar universality around the world.

In the United States, the regulatory bodies are the U.S. Patent and Trademark Office and the U.S. Copyright Office. They are empowered by and oversee the administration of U.S. Code Titles 35 (Patents), 15 (Trademarks), and 17 (Copyright). Broadly similar offices and legislation operate in most nations, among them the Canadian Intellectual Property Office (all three areas), the UK Patent Office (all three areas), the Instituto Mexicano de la Propiedad Industrial (patents and trademarks), and the European Patent Office (patents only). Note that this is not to suggest that protection for copyright and trademarks is unknown in these latter jurisdictions.

A patent provides its owner with an exclusive right granted by a national government for the protection and exploitation of an invention or other new technical advance, usually for a period of 20 years—the present WTO international standard. The principles of novelty (a new idea), utility (a useful idea), and ingenuity (not an otherwise obvious evolutionary step) must be present for an invention or process to be patentable. Not all nations observe the requirement of all three criteria, but a sufficient number do (the United Kingdom, Japan, Canada, and the United States are examples) to recommend that it is wise for all three elements to be present.

Patent rights prohibit others from making commercial use of the patented invention or technology without the patent owner's consent. This is subject to the real or potential right of a state to compel the licensing of a patent either in the public interest or where the patentee refuses to make commercial use of the patent. If a patent right has otherwise been infringed, an action may lie in a national court, or in opposition, others may challenge the validity of the patentee's right. Through the international conventions discussed below, it is possible to secure patent protection in a number of nations beyond the country of original application.

A copyright protects original works of authorship that have been fixed in a permanent medium—on paper, recordings, pictures, and the like. Copyright works, which are first vested in the author (and may be transferred), may not be reproduced without the consent of the owner for the life of the original author, plus a period of years, usually at least 50 and often 70 years. Works created by corporations or other nonliving juridical persons are given even longer periods in most jurisdictions.

Copyright arises from mere authorship, but as opposed to the high frequency of registered trademarks, registration of copyright in the United States occurs proportionately less often. This is due to the fact that works of U.S. origin only need to be registered in order to commence an infringement action, and this may be done even after the alleged infringement takes place. In most other jurisdictions, registration as a prerequisite to litigation does not exist; indeed, in nations such as Australia and the United Kingdom, no national registration scheme exists. In others, such as Canada, the optional registration process yields a certificate placing the burden of proof of prior ownership on the party in opposition.

Trademarks are used commercially to distinguish goods or services of one business from another, thus aiding both the seller and buyer in preventing confusion. To protect both parties, trademark law seeks to prevent others from intentionally or unintentionally infringing on the goodwill created by the mark. The first user of a trademark is in a position to claim rights to it. The onus is upon any party following in time, if challenged, to defend their use of a similar mark on the basis that their use will not create confusion in the consumer, either through the unrelated nature of the goods or markets or their geographic distance apart. Registration of a trademark establishes notice of the registrant's claim and may establish the local law jurisdiction where any litigation will be heard (federal, in the case of the United States). In some jurisdictions (as is the case in the United States), registration can empower the Customs Service to seize goods intended for import that bear an infringing mark.

The rapid rate at which world markets have come to the doorsteps of consumers has fueled both original conflict and litigation over intellectual property. Infringement of patents can take place anywhere, at often very little cost. Software producers, tracking piracy of software that runs into the hundreds of millions of dollars, have discovered this. For their troubles, they receive a court order authorizing seizure of a near-empty warehouse in a far-off land, and a few sets of CD-burning equipment, the perpetrators gone with their millions and nowhere to be found. Patent litigation is not always so unrewarding, but this scenario is depressingly frequent.

In the case of trademarks, the world and global markets also have become smaller and nearer, but at least they are more populated by firms that intend to do business on commercial terms without resorting to outright piracy. That said, litigation of trademarks, representing enormous amounts in brand value, can become nothing short of a world war, with a battle fought in every jurisdiction to preserve or create rights.

A good example is the long-running battle between Anheuser-Busch, the U.S. brewer of Budweiser beer, and a Czech brewer located in the town of Budejovice. The Czech town is in a Germanic region and was historically known as Budweis; hence, anything from that place, referred to in German, is a Budweiser. It was as a tribute to this city and brewing region that Anheuser-Busch took its name in 1875. Others like it have come into common currency—Hamburger, Frankfurter, and Weiner all are homage in German to their respective cities of origin.

Anheuser-Busch predates its Czech rival by nearly 20 years, and the products did not directly compete in any significant way for almost 100 years. Once they did meet head to head in markets around the world, thanks to advances in preservation, refrigeration, and transportation, the trademark troubles began. The questions follow essentially the same route in every jurisdiction:

1. Should beer that does not come from Budweis be allowed to be called Budweiser?
2. Is a small firm attempting to pass itself off on the name of a giant coopting for free the billions of dollars spent on brand image?
3. Is the customer seeking a taste of the original waters and homeland where it all began, or identifying with a carefully crafted image and lifestyle?
4. Will the customer be genuinely confused?
5. Will bars and retailers who stock both brands care to educate their customers on the potential choice in a request for a "Budweiser"?
6. What of all the other things: colors, bottle shapes, boxes, lettering, the contraction "BUD," and so on?

Outside of their respective countries, Anheuser-Busch has prevailed over the Czech brewer, Budjovicky Budvar, on some or all counts in Argentina, Australia, Brazil, Denmark, Finland, Hungary, Italy, New Zealand, and Spain. Not everything has gone the Anheuser-Busch way, however, particularly where the Czech brewer had an earlier or more established presence. The following English case represents the third round of the battle for beer trademark recognition in the United Kingdom. In the end, neither firm obtains what it truly hoped: complete and exclusive recognition.

Anheuser-Busch v. Budejovicky Budvar N.P.

England and Wales Court of Appeal
February 7, 2000

Lord Justice Peter Gibson:

1. This dispute is the third round of the continuing conflict in the English courts between the American brewer, Anheuser-Busch Incorporated ("AB"), and the Czech brewer, Budejovicky Budvar N.P. ("BB"), over the use and registration of the mark BUD-WEISER and related marks in relation to beer.

6. From 1973, when sales were only worth £4,000, BB's sales here increased steadily. By midsummer 1979 BB had sold in excess of 1,000,000 bottles. From 1974 the retailers, Oddbins, stocked and sold BB's beer, listing it in their published price lists simply as Budweiser.

7. AB made no sales of its Budweiser beer in the United Kingdom otherwise than in the U.S. Embassy and PX stores catering not for the general public but for American service personnel between 1945 and 1973. From 1974 to 1979 there were small sales to the general public not exceeding in total 240,000 cans or bottles. Sales of AB's beer to American servicemen were, however, substantial between 1962 and 1973, varying from 3,600,000 cans to 6,000,000 cans a year. Further, Budweiser as a name associated with AB's beer became well-known to a substantial number of people in the U.K. as a result of visits to the U.S.A. and of advertisements in films and American magazines circulating here.

8. On 1 August 1979 AB commenced proceedings ("the passing off action") against BB, seeking an injunction to prevent BB from selling or dealing in any beer not being AB's beer by the name Budweiser or Bud and from passing off in any other manner. BB counterclaimed for similar relief against AB. Whitford J., in a decision reported under the name *Anheuser-Busch v. Budejovicky Budvar* [1984] F.S.R. 413, dismissed both the claim and the counterclaim. He held that neither AB nor BB was disentitled to use the name Budweiser since in 1979 there was a dual reputation and neither had achieved the reputation improperly and neither was making a misrepresentation. He recognised that some degree of confusion might result, but he said that this was true in the case of marks used in pursuance of registration under s. 12 (2) of the Trade Marks Act 1938 ("the Act"). By that provision, he said, Parliament had recognised that circumstances might arise in which two different persons ought to be entitled to use one and the same mark in respect of the same goods. He regarded Bud as the inevitable abbreviation of the name Budweiser. AB, but not BB, appealed, but this court dismissed the appeal. It accepted that there was substantial evidence of the name Budweiser as associated with AB's beer, and said that there was ample and unchallenged evidence of BB's beer being confused with AB's beer with ample evidence that in the minds of several people the two were in some way connected. This court held that the critical time was when BB first entered the English market in a not negligible way in 1973/4 by which time AB had a reputation with a substantial number of people in this country as the brewer of its Budweiser beer. But it reasoned that because this reputation did not constitute goodwill, there being no sales to the general public and no business in England by then, AB could not succeed in the passing off action. This court confirmed that both AB and BB were entitled to use the name Budweiser in this country.

9. The second round of litigation ("the Bud action") between the parties was triggered by BB applying in 1979 to register BUD as a trade mark in class 32 for beer. This was

opposed under s. 11 of the Act by AB. The Assistant Registrar, Mr. Myall, held that the application was properly registrable under s. 12 (2) and that the opposition failed. On appeal Walton J. agreed (see *BUD Trade Mark* [1988] R.P.C. 535). He referred to the evidence as showing that the use of Bud as a contraction for Budweiser was how drinkers of AB's or BB's beer demanded the beer they wanted. He held that s. 11 did not apply because

> "[w]hat would be the equity in refusing a person registration of a contraction of his proper trade mark, which cannot be complained of at all, which his customers are invariably, as the evidence runs, going to use. Of course precisely and exactly the same applies to AB's Budweiser and the use by their customers of BUD, but I cannot think that if the substantive mark of "Budweiser" in both cases can be fairly used, there can be any question of a court of equity at any time saying: 'But you cannot possibly use the way in which your customers are going to describe it.' The one must, as a matter of equity and justice carry the other."

He therefore agreed with Mr. Myall that the opposition failed and further that s. 12 (2) pointed in the same direction, there being honest concurrent use and the special circumstance that customers for both beers were accustomed to use the same abbreviation as an abbreviation of the real name which both were free to use as against each other. Following that decision, AB registered the same mark for its beer.

30. I come now to s. 12(2). The applicant for registration of a trade mark used by another must bring himself within either "honest concurrent use" or "special circumstances" or both . . .

31. The reason why Rimer J. held that this was a case of honest concurrent use by BB as well as by AB of the trade mark BUDWEISER was that all times since about 1973 BB had used the word Budweiser not just as part of the composite Budweiser Budvar but also on its own. He considered that the thrust of the decision of this court in the passing off action was not that BB was entitled to use the word Budweiser to describe its beer only as part of the composite Budweiser Budvar but that it was entitled to use the word Budweiser in relation to its beer just as was AB. Mr. Hobbs criticised the judge's approach. He said that the decision in the passing off action did not decide the entitlement of BB to use Budweiser's name for trade mark registration purposes, that decision producing a stalemate. He submitted that there had not been honest concurrent use by BB of the trade mark BUDWEISER alone.

32. I own to finding this a difficult point, but I am persuaded by Mr. Kitchin that there has been honest concurrent use by BB of BUDWEISER. Jiri Bocek, a director of BB, in his statutory declaration accurately stated the position when he said:

> "In the UK market for beer, the beer brewed by my company is sold mainly under the trade mark 'BUDWEISER BUDVAR' but the trade mark 'BUDWEISER' is also used and the product is known commonly as Czech BUDWEISER or Czech BUD or BUDWEISER or BUD."

In my judgment in addition to the limited use by BB of BUDWEISER alone in the promotional material to which I have already referred, it is clear that the emphasis in its use of BUDWEISER BUDVAR has in general been on the first word BUDWEISER, which was always likely to be the focus of attention for traders and the public alike. There can be no doubt but that in the passing off action Whitford J. and this court treated BB as using the trade mark BUDWEISER even when the evidence showed it was used in conjunction with BUDVAR. Whitford J. ([1984] F.S.R. at p. 440) described as "the real question" whether AB could stop BB from using the word Budweiser as a trade mark. It is of significance that that judge, with his vast experience in this field, found that in their claims for passing off AB and BB were in a situation analogous to that covered by s. 12(2) (see pp. 441–2), a point also observed by the also very experienced Mr. Myall in his decision in the Bud action (see [1988] R.P.C. at p. 543). As Mr. Myall also said, that was not a view disputed by this court on the appeal in the passing off action. Oliver L.J. said that BB had for some time used the name Budweiser, sometimes as an indication of the geographical origin of its beer "but more recently as a trade name in its own right ([1984 F.S.R. at pp. 448,9). He referred (at p. 468) to BB in 1973 first starting to market in Great Britain under the name Budweiser and he ended his judgment (at p. 471) by agreeing with Whitford J.'s conclusion that both AB and BB were entitled to use the name Budweiser in this country. Dillon L.J. at p. 472 described AB's passing off claim as one to restrain BB from marketing its beer under the name Budweiser and spoke of BB as first starting to market its beer under that name in 1973. He too supported Whitford J.'s conclusion that there was a dual reputation in that name. O'Connor L.J. agreed with both Oliver and Dillon L.JJ.

33. There can be no doubt but that Walton J. thought that this court had decided that both AB and BB were entitled to use the name Budweiser of which both were proprietors. His decision was based on that premise. His conclusion that BB was entitled to obtain registration of the trade mark BUD as a contraction of BUDWEISER, if correct, necessarily entails that BB is also entitled to obtain registration of the unabbreviated trade mark BUDWEISER. There was no appeal by AB from that decision and Mr. Hobbs does not dispute that it is binding on AB.

34. In the light of all the circumstances I accept that there has been concurrent use by BB as well as AB of the trade mark BUDWEISER. Mr. Hobbs has made no suggestion that if there has been such use it was nevertheless not honest. On the facts any such suggestion could not be sustained. Both Whitford J. and this court in the passing off action and Walton J. in the Bud action roundly dismissed the notion that BB had acted dishonestly in such use.

35. Rimer J. also found special circumstances justifying the overriding under s. 12(2) of the s. 11 objection. They consisted of the unusual circumstances of the case, indicating in particular the use by BB's traders and customers of the word Budweiser to refer to its beer.

37. In [sic] follows that despite the excellence of Mr. Hobbs' arguments I would dismiss AB's appeal. Mr. Kitchin accepts that in that event BB's cross-appeal should also be dismissed and it is unnecessary to consider his alternative contention.

Lord Justice Judge:

38. The self indulgence of narrating and commenting on the history of events in the Austro-Hungarian empire and the town known to its German speaking inhabitants as Budweis, or indeed the brewing methods originating in that area which were taken to and adopted in Missouri in the United States of America in the second half of the nineteenth century must be avoided.

39. At that time the limitations of geography, and more restricted methods of business and transport than those available to contemporaries, would have meant that very few individuals familiar with the beer brewed in either Bohemia or Missouri would have had very much idea, or interest, if any, about the beer being brewed abroad. When however the Czech brewery, which I shall describe as BB, sought to expand its sales into the United States in the early part of the last century, battle was joined.

40. The first dispute was compromised in the United States as long ago as 1911. All the relevant history, particularly in relation to the development of both businesses in the United Kingdom after World War II is fully narrated in the earlier judgment of this

court ("the passing off action") brought by the American company, described hereafter as AB and reported at [1984] FSR 413. The second round in the battle (the "Bud" action) was concluded before Walton J in July 1987 ([1988] RPC 535). On his analysis of the Court of Appeal's decision, both BB and AB were entitled to use the name "Budweiser" and neither could prevent the other from doing so. In 1982 Whitford J had observed that the contraction of Budweiser to "Bud" was inevitable, and Walton J concluded that both BB and AB were to be regarded as proprietors of the trademark "Bud", if they wished. This recognised the reality that given the ease with which the word trips off the tongue, evoking, as it does, concepts of warmth and friendship similar to those found in words like "buddy," "mate" and "pal," a customer ordering Budweiser, whether in its American or Czech variety, would be likely to employ the diminutive "Bud." There was no appeal against this decision which, together with that of the Court of Appeal in the passing off action, has had practical consequences for the businesses of both companies. In other words, the decisions of the Court of Appeal and Walton J respectively, have been taken into account and their logical consequences applied by both companies when organising their marketing arrangements in the United Kingdom and their continuing competition with each other.

41. The subsequent history is brought up to date in the judgment of Peter Gibson LJ, and, again, nothing is gained by repetition.

42. The principal issue between AB and BB in the present litigation concerns the entitlement (or otherwise) of BB to register the mark "Budweiser," omitting altogether any reference to "Budvar" which until now, largely but not invariably, has been used by BB in conjunction with Budweiser, while AB has employed Budweiser, by itself, and without any further embellishment or additional words.

43. The relevant statutory provisions are set out in Peter Gibson LJ's judgment. In summary, s. 11 of the Trade Marks Act 1938 prohibits the registration as a trade mark of any matter "the use of which would, by reason of its being likely to deceive or cause confusion or otherwise, be disentitled to protection . . ." Such registration would not be "lawful". S. 12(1) prohibits the registration of any trade mark "in respect of any goods or description of goods that is identical with or nearly resembles a mark belonging to a different proprietor and already on the register . . .".

44. Self evidently, as a trade mark Budweiser Budvar is not identical to Budweiser. If it were, BB would not be seeking to register the word "Budweiser" on its own. Mr Hobbs QC is right when he argues that if AB had thought that some commercial advantage would follow, BB would not have taken kindly to the addition of the word "Budvar" to its product by AB. Further it seems to me likely that there is some continuing confusion between the two products, at any rate in the cases of those individuals who do not appreciate that there are differences between American Budweiser and Czech Budweiser.

45. As a matter of *law* the failure of AB's passing off action was not decisive of the question whether the present application fell within the statutory prohibitions against registration. The issues arising for consideration were not and are not identical. Therefore to the extent that the judge founded his decision on this proposition, and essentially for the reasons given by Peter Gibson LJ and Ferris J, I disagree with him. Therefore I need not analyse the point more closely.

46. S. 12(2) of the 1938 Act provides that in cases of "honest concurrent use, or . . . other special circumstances" it may be proper to permit the registration notwithstanding that marks used by two proprietors are identical, or nearly so. Such registration may be permitted where the specific condition identified in the sub section (honest concurrent use) applies, or in any other circumstance which can properly be described as "special."

47. Guidance about the basis on which this discretion should be exercised is provided by Lord Tomlin in *Pirie's Application* [1933] 50 RPC 147 at p. 159. This decision, and the criteria he identified, do not represent a reworking of the statutory provision, sufficient to cover every case where the court is considering whether to exercise its discretion in favour of registration. Given the nature of the prohibitions in s. 11 and s. 12(1) it seems to me that, normally at any rate, account should be taken of the nature and extent of the risk of confusion or deception, potentially damaging to the public generally, and where the mark has already been registered by another party, damaging to its business, and also whether the party seeking the exercise of the discretion, has, in the context of a serious competitive market, conducted its business on the issues in relation to which registration arises with reasonable integrity. I doubt whether there will be very many circumstances, or combination of circumstances, that are "so special" that the discretion would be exercised in favour of a party whose use of a mark could properly be stigmatised as dishonest. Ultimately the decision depends on all the relevant facts which arise in the individual case and the balanced exercise of the judge's discretion. Save on well known principles this court should not interfere with it.

48. In my judgment the decisive factor in this litigation is that the exercise of the judge's discretion under s. 12(2) cannot be impugned. It focused on the practical realities, at least in part consequent on the sensible application of the previous decisions of the Court of Appeal and Walton J. Customers for either product who genuinely appreciate that there are two products, and that they are different, and who favour the one over the other, are likely to make their orders by specifying or referring to American Bud, or Budweiser, or Czech Bud, or Budweiser. If they are ignorant of the difference, or the difference is immaterial to them, they will ask for Budweiser or Bud and be supplied with whichever product the vendor has in stock. If he happens to stock both, he may ask the customer to specify which, and may then, at any rate if business is slack, become involved in a discussion of the differing qualities of the two beers, and if in expansive mood, with a history lesson. As to the variety he may elect to stock, if he only has room for one, his preference will be for the brew which experience suggests that the majority of his customers prefer. I remain unpersuaded that any consequent problems following the registrations sought by both AB and BB would give rise to confusion or difficulty in the public mind which would be of more than minimal significance and in my judgment it is too late for anything practical now to be done, without simultaneously putting one or other product at a significant and unfair commercial disadvantage as against the other.

49. In view of the way this commercial dispute has developed, and the history already outlined in so many judgments, and the absence of any evidence to justify the conclusion that BB acted dishonestly in respect of its use of Budweiser, or in procuring its customers to use the diminutive "Bud" when ordering its beer, and balancing both the public interest, and the proper preservation of the commercial interests of each of the protagonists, these registrations should be permitted.

50. I agree that the appeals by both AB and BB should be dismissed.

Source: [2000] E.W.J. No. 389

As a result of the judgment, what *can* the parties do? What can the parties *not* do?

Not every firm will face the challenge that these two have, in battling around the world to defend their trademarks. Even so, as markets expand and overlap and products become even more easily transported over greater distances, these types of action will only increase as goods and marks come into conflict. Goods are no longer as territorial as they once were, and the lack of an international system of trademark recognition leaves only the jurisdiction-by-jurisdiction scenario.

Patents, Copyright, and Trademarks under International Conventions

Lying at the heart of intellectual property protection are the laws of states having territorial application. In an effort to drive these rules of application toward greater uniformity, states have subscribed to a variety of international treaties and conventions. An international policy body, the World Intellectual Property Organization (WIPO), based in Switzerland, now also manages many of these treaties and conventions.

At the top of the international hierarchy lies the WTO's Agreement on the Trade Related Aspects of Intellectual Property, or "TRIPS" Agreement, formally known as Annex 1C to the WTO Agreement. It is this Agreement along with the GATS services agreement that greatly extended the reach of the GATT, as the new WTO, to issues beyond trade in goods. The TRIPS Agreement imposes a requirement on all WTO members to extend most-favored-nation status and to provide national treatment in matters related to intellectual property. The intellectual property covered by TRIPS is broadly drawn, including copyright and related rights; trademarks, including service marks; geographical indications; industrial designs; patents; layout designs (topographies) of integrated circuits, and undisclosed information, including trade secrets. The TRIPS Agreement also fixes minimums for levels of protection and enforcement, although nations are free to create greater protection. The TRIPS Agreement is not an optional part of WTO membership, and for many less-well-off member nations, it has represented a major change in economic and development policy.

In the past, nations had considerable liberty to establish whatever rules they saw fit. As less-developed nations tend not to be a source of patentable technologies, but heavy users of patented goods, these nations often provided short or nonexistent patent protection. This approach allowed local firms earlier access to cheaper technology, rather than waiting for the expiration of patents or paying expensive royalties in the interim. In turn, however, this simply caused trade friction, and foreign firms were either quite cautious doing business in these markets or wrote them off entirely. One is left to wonder whether these nations actually benefited in the long run from this type of strategy, but there can be no doubt of the cost to nations associated with increased patent protection and the consequent payment of royalties.

One special point of contention, as an example of the above, is the access of less-developed nations to patented pharmaceuticals. Limited national patent protection allows for the sooner appearance of locally made generic copies, and greater patent protection entails higher costs to these nations and their consumers. Given the sensitive nature of health care issues, and the pressing public need of many nations for affordable drugs, the WTO has suspended the requirement of the establishment of drug patent protection in member nations until 2016.

While special international conventions apply to a few particular economic and technological activities,[1] there are a number of important international agreements securing intellectual property rights or establishing uniformity that have much more general application.

Copyright

Copyright is addressed by the Berne Convention for the Protection of Literary and Artistic Works (1886, and its revisions through 1971). These standards of protection and enforcement of copyright are almost universal,[2] and while the Convention is administered by

---

[1]Examples being the Budapest Treaty on the International Recognition of the Deposit of Microorganisms for the Purposes of Patent Procedure (1977), the Lisbon Agreement for the Protection of Appellations of Origin and their International Registration (1958), or the Brussels Convention Relating to the Distribution of Programme-Carrying Signals Transmitted by Satellite (1974).

[2]150 states as of early 2004, including the United States.

To patent or not to patent; it is not just a question for the examining authorities, but for the applicant as well. A patent entails the publication of the previously undisclosed technical information such that a reasonably skilled tradesperson could replicate the patented item. The potential applicant should therefore ask itself the following questions: Having exchanged all details of my invention and made those details available to the world at large in exchange for near-monopoly rights, am I prepared to travel the world to defend those rights? What would my real financial recovery be in a successful defense? Is it better to keep the information undisclosed, forgo a patent, and keep inventing and improving faster than other people can dissect my technology, and at a rate faster than the natural rate of obsolescence of the technology? A patent is worth nothing if the broadcast of the technology creates hundreds of competitors and death by a thousand cuts.

the WIPO, the WTO TRIPS Agreement mandates compliance of WTO members with the Convention, regardless of whether or not those nations are members of the Berne Convention in their own right. The Berne Convention requires

- National treatment.
- No requirement of notice or registration to obtain copyright protection.
- A minimum protected term of copyright, which is the life of the author plus 50 years.

Patents

The Patent Cooperation Treaty of 1970, or PCT, is also managed by the WIPO and provides for an international system for the filing of patent applications. Membership[3] is open to all those states party to the 1883 Paris Convention for the Protection of Industrial Property.

An international patent as such does not exist, and the regime creates instead a process of filing in one's own country, which on request secures a window of time (now up to 30 months) to file applications in other nations party to the PCT. Ultimately, a patent application will be required in each nation, or in some cases regions (Europe and Africa), where protection is sought. This prevents the situation of a legitimate patent application in one country triggering unscrupulous parties to patent the same item in other countries before the original inventor has had an opportunity to do so.

Trademarks

Latest in time is the Trademark Law Treaty, adopted at Geneva in October 1994. This treaty has attracted over 30 states (including the United States, the United Kingdom, and Japan) and commits state parties to the provisions of the Paris Convention for the Protection of Industrial Property of 1883, as revised and amended, as regards trademarks and service marks. The treaty merely harmonizes basic national standards of registration (10-year renewable periods) but does not create an international register or rights.

Where national filings have been made in a contracting state, the Paris Convention for the Protection of Industrial Property creates a right to priority in filing in other contracting states. The priority period of grace is 12 months for patents and 6 months for industrial designs and trademarks, and the Convention provides as well for national treatment for foreign right holders.

In contrast, the Madrid Agreement Concerning the International Registration of Marks (1891 and as revised and amended through 1979) and the Madrid Protocol of 1989 create an international register, the International Bureau of Intellectual Property, derived from national registration of marks. Eligibility for international registration of a national registra-

---

[3] 120 states as of early 2004, including the United States.

tion is based on the applicant being a national of the contracting state where national registration has taken place, or having a commercial presence in such a state.[4] Thus, while some countries are not contracting states (e.g., the United States), businesses can still avail themselves of the convenience of the agreement where the commercial presence test is met elsewhere.

The effect of the system is to provide the national registrant with automatic trademark rights coverage in all contracting states, with a validity period of 20 years, renewable. Further, the system allows for greater administrative ease, for example, a single point of contact for recording changes in ownership and/or correction of the register.

The European Union also has created a regional system among its member states for the uniform registration and rights associated with trademarks, with renewable registration validity periods of 10 years.[5] This system does not replace national systems, but augments them. As the right to register a mark under the Community system is extended beyond nationals of EU member states to any national of a WTO contracting state, the system is therefore a particularly attractive way to obtain pan-European trademark rights.

The case below gives insight into how trademark rights are dealt with under European directives, and relates to the attempt of a U.S. automaker to quash use of its mark in areas outside autos. Perhaps more importantly, four national governments and the European Commission acted as interveners; the differing positions of these administrative authorities is therefore revealed as well. In addition, the unique European problem of having legislation equally valid in 11 languages creates interpretation problems for the court, as no language is definitive. One can only imagine the situation when membership expands from 15 to a potential 28, with official languages expanding from 11 to 22.

Case C-375/97—*General Motors Corporation*
v. Yplon SA

European Court of Justice

September 14, 1999

Judgment on the interpretation of Article 5(2) of the First Council Directive (89/104/EEC) of 21 December 1988 to approximate the laws of the Member States relating to trade marks (OJ 1989 L 40, p. 1),

[Editor's note: While the case refers to marks of the Benelux Trade Mark Office and Article 5(1) and (2) of the First Council Directive, identical wording is found in Council Regulation (EC) No. 40/94 on the Community trademark, as Article 9. The case will retain its jurisprudential value.]

1. By judgment of 30 October 1997, received at the Court on 3 November 1997, the Tribunal de Commerce (Commercial Court), Tournai, referred to the Court for a preliminary ruling under Article 177 of the EC Treaty (now Article 234 EC) a question on the interpretation of Article 5(2) of the First Council Directive (89/104/EEC) of 21 December 1988 to approximate the laws of the Member States relating to trade marks (OJ 1989 L 40, p. 1, hereinafter 'the Directive').

---

[4]As of early 2004, 71 states have joined in some capacity, 52 to the Madrid Agreement and 57 to the Madrid Protocol, with many having joined both.

[5]See Council Regulation (EC) No. 40/94 of 20 December 1993 on the Community Trademark and Commission Regulation (EC) No. 2868/95 of 13 December 1995 Implementing Council Regulation (EC) No 40/94 on the Community Trademark.

2. The question has been raised in proceedings between General Motors Corporation (hereinafter 'General Motors'), established in Detroit, United States of America, and Yplon SA (hereinafter 'Yplon'), established at Estaimpuis, Belgium, concerning the use of the mark 'Chevy.'

Community Law

3. Article 1 of the Directive, entitled 'Scope,' provides:

    'This Directive shall apply to every trade mark in respect of goods or services which is the subject of registration or of an application in a Member State for registration as an individual trade mark, a collective mark or a guarantee or certification mark, or which is the subject of a registration or an application for registration in the Benelux Trade Mark Office or of an international registration having effect in a Member State.'

4. Article 5(1) and (2), of the Directive, entitled 'Rights conferred by a trade mark,' provides:

    '1. The registered trade mark shall confer on the proprietor exclusive rights therein. The proprietor shall be entitled to prevent all third parties not having his consent from using in the course of trade:

    (a) any sign which is identical with the trade mark in relation to goods or services which are identical with those for which the trade mark is registered;

    (b) any sign where, because of its identity with, or similarity to, the trade mark and the identity or similarity of the goods or services covered by the trade mark and the sign, there exists a likelihood of confusion on the part of the public, which includes the likelihood of association between the sign and the trade mark.

    2. Any Member State may also provide that the proprietor shall be entitled to prevent all third parties not having his consent from using in the course of trade any sign which is identical with, or similar to, the trade mark in relation to goods or services which are not similar to those for which the trade mark is registered, where the latter has a reputation in the Member State and where use of that sign without due cause takes unfair advantage of, or is detrimental to, the distinctive character or the repute of the trade mark.'

The Benelux Legislation

5. Article 13(A)(1)(c) of the Uniform Benelux Law on Trade Marks (hereinafter 'the Uniform Benelux Law'), which transposed into Benelux law Article 5(2) of the Directive, provides:

    'Without prejudice to any application of the ordinary law governing civil liability, the exclusive rights in a trade mark shall entitle the proprietor to oppose:

    . . .

    (c) any use, in the course of trade and without due cause, of a trade mark which has a reputation in the Benelux countries or of a similar sign for goods which are not similar to those for which the trade mark is registered, where use of that sign would take unfair advantage of, or would be detrimental to, the distinctive character or the repute of the trade mark;

    . . . '

6. That provision, which took effect on 1 January 1996, replaced, as from that date, the old Article 13(A)(2) of the Uniform Benelux Law, under which the exclusive rights in the trade mark allowed the proprietor to oppose 'any other use [use other than that de-

scribed in paragraph 1(1), namely use for an identical or similar product] of the trade mark or a similar sign in the course of trade and without due cause which would be liable to be detrimental to the owner of the trade mark.'

The Dispute in the Main Proceedings

7. General Motors is the proprietor of the Benelux trade mark 'Chevy,' which was registered on 18 October 1971 at the Benelux Trade Mark Office for Class 4, 7, 9, 11 and 12 products, and in particular for motor vehicles. That registration asserts the rights acquired under an earlier Belgian registration on 1 September 1961 and earlier use in the Netherlands in 1961 and in Luxembourg in 1962. Nowadays, the mark 'Chevy' is used more specifically in Belgium to designate vans and similar vehicles.

8. Yplon is also the proprietor of the Benelux trade mark 'Chevy,' registered at the Benelux Trade Mark Office on 30 March 1988 for Class 3 products and then on 10 July 1991 for Class 1, 3 and 5 products. It uses those trade marks for detergents and various cleaning products. It is also the proprietor of the trade mark 'Chevy' in other countries, including several Member States.

9. On 28 December 1995 General Motors applied to the Tribunal de Commerce, Tournai, for an injunction restraining Yplon from using the sign 'Chevy' to designate detergents or cleaning products on the ground that such use entails dilution of its own trade mark and thus damages its advertising function. Its action is based, as regards the period prior to 1 January 1996, on the old Article 13(A)(2) of the Uniform Benelux Law and, as from 1 January 1996, on the new Article 13(A)(1)(c) of that Law. It maintains in this regard that its mark 'Chevy' is a trade mark of repute within the meaning of the latter provision.

10. Yplon is defending the action on the ground, in particular, that General Motors has not shown that its trade mark has a 'reputation' in the Benelux countries within the meaning of the new Article 13(A)(1)(c) of the Uniform Benelux Law.

11. The Tribunal de Commerce took the view that determination of the case required clarification of the concept of a trade mark having a reputation and of the question whether the reputation must exist throughout the Benelux countries or whether it is sufficient for it to exist in part of that territory and decided to stay proceedings and refer the following question to the Court for a preliminary ruling:

   'On reading Article 13(A)(1)(c) of the Uniform Benelux Law introduced pursuant to the amending protocol in force since 1 January 1996, what is the proper construction of the term "repute of the trade mark" and may it also be said that such "repute" applies throughout the Benelux countries or to part thereof?'

The Question Referred for a Preliminary Ruling

12. By its question the national court is essentially asking the Court of Justice to explain the meaning of the expression 'has a reputation' which is used, in Article 5(2) of the Directive, to specify the first of the two conditions which a registered trade mark must satisfy in order to enjoy protection extending to non-similar goods or services and to say whether that condition must be satisfied throughout the Benelux countries or whether it is sufficient for it to be satisfied in part of that territory.

13. General Motors contends that, in order to have a reputation within the meaning of Article 5(2) of the Directive, the earlier trade mark must be known by the public concerned, but not to the extent of being 'well-known' within the meaning of Article 6 *bis* of the Paris Convention for the Protection of Industrial Property of 20 March 1883

(hereinafter 'the Paris Convention'), which is a term to which express reference is made, albeit in a different context, in Article 4(2)(d) of the Directive. General Motors further considers that it is sufficient for the trade mark concerned to have a reputation in a substantial part of the territory of a Member State, which may cover a community or a region of that State.

14. Yplon, on the other hand, contends that a trade mark registered in respect of a product or service intended for the public at large has a reputation within the meaning of Article 5(2) of the Directive when it is known by a wide section of that public. The principle of speciality can be departed from only for trade marks which can be associated spontaneously with a particular product or service. The reputation of the trade mark in question should exist throughout the territory of a Member Start [sic] or, in the case of the Benelux countries, throughout one of those countries.

15. The Belgian Government argues that 'trade mark having a reputation' should be construed flexibly and that there is a difference of degree between a mark with a reputation and a well-known mark. The degree to which a trade mark is well known cannot be evaluated in the abstract by, for example, setting a percentage. A reputation in any single one of the three Benelux countries applies throughout the Benelux territory.

16. The French Government submits that the Court should reply that a trade mark's reputation within the meaning of Article 5(2) of the Directive cannot be defined precisely. It is a question of assessing case by case whether the earlier trade mark is known by a wide section of the public concerned by the products covered by the two marks and whether the earlier mark is of sufficient repute that the public associates it with the later contested mark. Once it is established that the earlier mark does have a reputation, the strength of that reputation then determines the extent of the protection afforded by Article 5(2) of the Directive. Territorially, a reputation in a single Benelux country is sufficient.

17. The Netherlands Government submits that it is sufficient for the trade mark to have a reputation with the public at which it is aimed. The degree of knowledge required cannot be indicated in abstract terms. It has to be ascertained whether, in view of all the circumstances, the earlier mark has a reputation which may be harmed if it is used for non-similar products. The mark does not have to be known throughout a Member State or, in the case of Benelux trade marks, throughout the Benelux territory.

18. The United Kingdom Government submits that the decisive question is whether use is made without due cause of the later mark and whether this allows unfair advantage to be taken of, or detriment to be caused to, the distinctive character or the repute of the earlier trade mark. The answer to that question depends on an overall assessment of all the relevant factors and, in particular, of the distinctive character inherent in the mark, the extent of the repute which it has gained, the degree of similarity between the two marks and the extent of the differences between the products or services covered. Protection should be afforded to all trade marks which have acquired a reputation and qualificative criteria should then be applied to limit the protection to marks whose reputation justifies it, protection being granted only where clear evidence of actual harm is adduced. In law, it is not necessary for the reputation to extend throughout the territory of a Member State. However, in practice, proof of actual damage could not be adduced in the case of a trade mark whose reputation is limited to a part of a Member State.

19. In the Commission's submission, 'a trade mark with a reputation' should be understood as meaning a trade mark having a reputation with the public concerned. This is something which is clearly distinguished from a 'well-known' mark referred to in Article 6 *bis* of the Paris Convention. It is sufficient for the mark to have a reputation in a substantial part of the Benelux territory and marks having a reputation in a region merit as much protection as marks having a reputation throughout the Benelux territory.

20. The Court observes that the first condition for the wider protection provided for in Article 5(2) of the Directive is expressed by the words 'er renommeret' in the Danish version of that provision; 'bekannt ist' in the German version; . . . 'goce de renombre' in the Spanish version; 'jouit d'une renommée' in the French version; 'gode di notorietà' in the Italian version; 'bekend is' in the Dutch version; 'goze de prestigio' in the Portuguese version; 'laajalti tunnettu' in the Finnish version; 'är känt' in the Swedish version; and by the words 'has a reputation' in the English version.

21. The German, Dutch and Swedish versions use words signifying that the trade mark must be 'known' without indicating the extent of knowledge required, whereas the other language versions use the term 'reputation' or expressions implying, like that term, at a quantitative level a certain degree of knowledge amongst the public.

22. That nuance, which does not entail any real contradiction, is due to the greater neutrality of the terms used in the German, Dutch and Swedish versions. Despite that nuance, it cannot be denied that, in the context of a uniform interpretation of Community law, a knowledge threshold requirement emerges from a comparison of all the language versions of the Directive.

23. Such a requirement is also indicated by the general scheme and purpose of the Directive. In so far as Article 5(2) of the Directive, unlike Article 5(1), protects trade marks registered for non-similar products or services, its first condition implies a certain degree of knowledge of the earlier trade mark among the public. It is only where there is a sufficient degree of knowledge of that mark that the public, when confronted by the later trade mark, may possibly make an association between the two trade marks, even when used for non-similar products or services, and that the earlier trade mark may consequently be damaged.

24. The public amongst which the earlier trade mark must have acquired a reputation is that concerned by that trade mark, that is to say, depending on the product or service marketed, either the public at large or a more specialised public, for example traders in a specific sector.

25. It cannot be inferred from either the letter or the spirit of Article 5(2) of the Directive that the trade mark must be known by a given percentage of the public so defined.

26. The degree of knowledge required must be considered to be reached when the earlier mark is known by a significant part of the public concerned by the products or services covered by that trade mark.

27. In examining whether this condition is fulfilled, the national court must take into consideration all the relevant facts of the case, in particular the market share held by the trade mark, the intensity, geographical extent and duration of its use, and the size of the investment made by the undertaking in promoting it.

28. Territorially, the condition is fulfilled when, in the terms of Article 5(2) of the Directive, the trade mark has a reputation 'in the Member State.' In the absence of any definition of the Community provision in this respect, a trade mark cannot be required to have a reputation 'throughout' the territory of the Member State. It is sufficient for it to exist in a substantial part of it.

29. As far as trade marks registered at the Benelux Trade Mark Office are concerned, the Benelux territory must be treated like the territory of a Member State, since Article 1 of the Directive regards Benelux trade marks as trade marks registered in a Member State. Article 5(2) must therefore be understood as meaning a reputation acquired 'in' the Benelux territory. For the same reasons as those relating to the condition as to the existence of a reputation in a Member State, a Benelux trade mark cannot therefore be required to have a reputation throughout the Benelux territory. It is sufficient for a Benelux trade mark to have a reputation in a substantial part of the Benelux territory, which part may consist of a part of one of the Benelux countries.

30. If, at the end of its examination, the national court decides that the condition as to the existence of a reputation is fulfilled, as regards both the public concerned and the territory in question, it must then go on to examine the second condition laid down in Article 5(2) of the Directive, which is that the earlier trade mark must be detrimentally affected without due cause. Here it should be observed that the stronger the earlier mark's distinctive character and reputation the easier it will be to accept that detriment has been caused to it.

31. The answer to be given to the question referred must therefore be that Article 5(2) of the Directive is to be interpreted as meaning that, in order to enjoy protection extending to non-similar products or services, a registered trade mark must be known by a significant part of the public concerned by the products or services which it covers. In the Benelux territory, it is sufficient for the registered trade mark to be known by a significant part of the public concerned in a substantial part of that territory, which part may consist of a part of one of the countries composing that territory.

. . .

On those grounds, THE COURT, in answer to the question referred to it by the Tribunal de Commerce, Tournai, by judgment of 30 October 1997, hereby rules:

> Article 5(2) of the First Council Directive (89/104/EEC) of 21 December 1988 to approximate the laws of the Member States relating to trade marks is to be interpreted as meaning that, in order to enjoy protection extending to non-similar products or services, a registered trade mark must be known by a significant part of the public concerned by the products or services which it covers. In the Benelux territory, it is sufficient for the registered trade mark to be known by a significant part of the public concerned in a substantial part of that territory, which part may consist of a part of one of the countries composing that territory.

Source: Indexed as Case C-375/97, *General Motors Corporation v. Yplon SA;* reproduced with permission and may be viewed at http://curia.eu.int/.

General Motors is seeking an injunction at the national court level against use of the word "Chevy" by Yplon. Based on this interpretation of the law by the European Court of Justice, and your knowledge and assumptions about reputation associated with the word and the markets involved, what do you think the outcome will be once this case is returned to the national court for further hearing?

While the above case represents the treatment of intellectual property under an international convention, it is with respect to a region, and the European Directive was negotiated between and applies only to its restrictive club of members. As such, it is not an international convention in the sense that one thinks of the WTO or the WIPO-administered agreements between nations with open rights of accession.

Both the *GM* and *Anheuser-Busch* cases presented above speak directly to the defense of rights by an owner against others; we turn now to the case of an owner who wishes to disseminate its intellectual property to others for its own profit—the creation and operation of licensing agreements.

Business Motivations in Licensing Agreements

The desire to license intellectual property may arise from constraints under the general headings of production, time, money, law, desire, and business focus, which are illustrated below. International businesspersons must understand these business considerations, and should ask their lawyer to be an integral part of the negotiating team that is to establish the license.

An international trader may face a range of problems, including, for example, claims of damaged goods and transportation delays in servicing its overseas clients. Still, the business firm has a good name and reputation overseas, and one that can be profitably exploited. It may be that it is the nature of the goods that contributes to these difficulties (glass, fragility; cement powder and sugar, susceptibility to moisture) and effectively precludes their long distance transportation.

In such cases, licensing allows the domestic manufacturer to offer its process to qualified manufacturers elsewhere, and to offer its brand name as well, in order that the goods may be produced close to the market where they are to be consumed. The domestic manufacturer can then profit through a royalty payment that recognizes the value of the skill, know-how, and branding that it has given to the local producer.

A manufacturer will often discover that it does not have enough production capacity to meet its orders; perhaps it does not have enough money to create that capacity, or not enough time to create it before their orders disappear. This may be the case with a company that designs and makes seasonal items, or has an item that finds a sudden fad following. If this year's fashion happens to be one thing, and after a future date it will be an obsolete product, the company may license production to other firms, again in return for a royalty, in order to capture the temporarily widespread available demand.

Obsolete products in the home market lead to international licensing on other grounds as well. A company with both new and old products in its home market may wish to focus on the new ones over the declining fortunes of its older products; for example, a steel maker producing both disposable razors and old fashioned blades. Given its good reputation and the fact that blades are commonly used elsewhere in the world, it may wish to license away this older product to overseas producers for overseas markets, leaving the firm able to concentrate on its newer products. The same is often done for the production of spare parts for older models. The original manufacturer may discontinue these models and does not wish to be burdened with continued global distribution of now-obsolete spare parts. Smaller firms located overseas will often be happy to produce these spares for their individual markets, on a license basis.

While the domestic producer may have the funds to increase its domestic production capacity, and it would prefer to have a closer connection to the foreign market, it still may not want to, or may not be able to, finance a foreign factory investment. By licensing the production to an overseas firm, it can achieve the overseas production it desires, without requiring investment of its own.

Intellectual property also may be owned by a business that is not a manufacturer at all. This situation arises frequently for movie studios that create on-screen characters that can be turned into toys and games. Movie studios have no desire or experience in the manufacture of toys and games, but own a valuable property that can be turned over to others to exploit in their own sphere of expertise.

The nature of the foreign market also can drive the desire to license. A small foreign market may be so secondary to the objectives of the original producer that it does not want to service it all, but still wants to take advantage of what profit is there. The answer is to let another local firm do this work, and to receive back only a periodic royalty check for the value of the intellectual property provided and a share of the profits it has produced.

The foreign market (and it may have a high profit potential) may have national laws restricting imports of finished goods, and thus it can only be serviced where production takes place inside those borders. This may be a good reason to license production, and additionally if a serious chance of nationalization exists, it is probably preferable to avoid actual and unnecessary investment in the country.

Further, a foreign market may have particular product customization needs that will not fit well with the original manufacturer's production process. For example, a household appliance may operate on an entirely different voltage in a foreign country, and thus it may be better to license production of the customized product abroad rather than risk disruption of longer production runs at home.

Finally, the foreign licensee, when chosen with some care, should have levels of market knowledge and cultural sensitivity that would be nearly impossible for the domestic licensor to match. All other things being equal, the foreign party should be able to design better marketing models, more accurate pricing points, better customer relationships, and greater sales potential than the domestic licensor firm could do itself in that market.

Business Risks Requiring Responses in Contract

With these motivations, there are accompanying risks that must be covered in the licensing contract to the fullest extent possible, while remaining in compliance with the local law applicable to both the licensor and the licensee.

First is the loss of direct control by the licensor of the intellectual property. After the license becomes effective, the licensor will not have the same day-to-day presence to exert a control function over how the intellectual property is employed and presented. In short, the reputation and brand image of the licensor is continually at stake through the acts of the licensee.

Problems happen at a distance, meaning that there must be provision in the agreement for information flow and access to that information. The licensor must maintain a right to inspect the output, premises, and accounts of the licensee. This is for the licensor to remain in a position to ensure that quality controls are being adhered to, that brand image does not suffer, and that the licensor is receiving a correct accounting of its share of the related sales or profits.

The abuse of the intellectual property after the end of the license agreement is often a major concern of the licensor. Frequently, as the foreign manufacturer will act as a distributor as well during the life of the license agreement, a distributorship agreement often forms part of the overall license package. Bearing in mind the elements discussed in Chapter 10 on distributorships, the same considerations of termination and post-termination events will apply to licensing contracts. These will encompass

- Any rights to compensation for termination.
- The desisting from use of the licensed property and its return to the licensor after termination.
- Due regard to noncompete clauses (pursuing the licensor's customers).
- The obligation to maintain confidentiality of trade secrets.
- Any other local law provisions of the foreign country of operations.

Like distributors, licensees will be interested in whether their license will be granted on an exclusive or nonexclusive basis. This should be spelled out in the clearest possible terms, indicating

- Whether such exclusivity, if any, binds the licensor against doing business itself in that market.
- Whether it is a commitment that the licensor will not create any further licensees in that market.
- Whether both restrictions are placed on the licensor.

As local law on licensing goes hand-in-hand with local law on distributorships, provisions will be encountered prohibiting anticompetitive practices in licensing—the U.S. Sherman Act standards and those under Articles 81 and 82 (formerly 85 and 86) of the Treaty Establishing the European Community being examples. Further, many countries require licensing agreements to be registered with their central authorities before the rights contained in them are enforceable in their respective nations, and failure to register also may be an administrative offense. Examples of such nations include Mexico, The Philippines, Guatemala, China, Vietnam, and Saudi Arabia.

Many elements of control that a licensor might wish to exert over its licensees are held to be anticompetitive in most jurisdictions of the world, and for good reason. These include

- Attempts to tie a licensee into fixed supply arrangements from the licensor (with the exception for quality control and bulk purchasing under franchises, discussed below).
- Prohibitions against the licensee obtaining further licenses from the licensor's competitors.
- Price-fixing agreements.
- Quantitative restrictions placed on the licensee's output.
- Control of downstream sales.

At the most restrictive level of generally permissible control over the foreign licensee is the franchise agreement, which is also usually a mix of a distributorship agreement and an intellectual property license. Here, the domestic licensor is giving the foreign local licensee a complete business package, almost on a turnkey basis. With the idea of creating total uniformity in product and presentation, the franchise agreement requires the licensee to follow detailed procedures and practices. Usually it also must source its supplies from the franchisor as a matter of quality control and cost savings available to all licensees through the licensor's aggregate bulk purchases or commissioned manufacturing. In default of the franchisee following procedures and practices to the letter, the franchisor may attempt to withdraw the franchise and its accompanying license.

Franchises given under license usually provide for a choice of forum as that of the franchisor, as it holds most of the bargaining power. From the franchisee's perspective, litigation in a foreign forum also may be the only rapid way of enforcing its rights. This need for speed, rather than the convenience of commencing action in its own jurisdiction and later enforcement abroad, is largely due to the dependency of the local (foreign) franchisee on supply shipments from the (overseas) franchisor.

In the case below, McDonald's Restaurants sought to enforce its right of franchise and license termination under a Master License Agreement (MLA) with its Paris, France, franchisee. Litigation took place in France and was brought back to the United States by the franchisee, which sought to prevent its termination.

Dayan v. McDonald's Corp.

Raymond Dayan et al., Plaintiffs-Appellants, v. McDonald's Corporation, Defendant-Appellee

Appellate Court of Illinois, First District, First Division

April 16, 1984

Opinion by: Buckley

This appeal arises out of a suit brought to enjoin McDonald's Corporation from terminating plaintiff Raymond Dayan's restaurant franchise in Paris, France. Other issues relating to this controversy have been considered twice before by this court . . .

I. Facts

The central issues in this case are factual, involving the propriety of the trial court's findings on Dayan's noncompliance with McDonald's QSC standards and the related finding of McDonald's good-faith termination of the franchise agreement. To the extent necessary, specific trial court findings and the evidentiary basis for those findings have been summarized.

The unique character of the 1971 license agreement was a key factor at trial. The record reveals that the terms of this agreement were the subject of extensive negotiations between McDonald's and Dayan and differed substantially from McDonald's standard licensing agreement. These differences formed the basis for many of the trial court's pivotal evidentiary rulings and findings of fact . . .

Both Barnes and Lubin *(McDonald's International Chairman and Counsel)* testified that they urged Dayan to accept the standard license agreement, but Dayan insisted upon the 1% developmental license. Barnes testified that he told Dayan the 1% license was a mistake and that Dayan would have to spend more than the 2% difference to properly develop the market without McDonald's operational assistance. Lubin testified that he attempted to persuade Dayan to accept the 3% service agreement, stating that the Caribbean franchisees who had similar 1% developmental licenses were having difficulty in complying with QSC standards because they were not requesting that McDonald's provide service under the agreement. Dayan prevailed in his demand for the 1% royalty fee with the limited service provision and the MLA was executed on May 5, 1971.

Article 8.4 provides that Dayan will bear the cost of any service provided.

The necessity of maintaining the QSC standards is explicitly recognized in the MLA. In Article 7.3 of the agreement Dayan acknowledged his familiarity "with the 'McDonald's system,' with McDonald's standards of 'Quality, Service, and Cleanliness,' with the need for the maintenance of McDonald's quality standards and controls." The same article also recites the rationale for maintaining QSC standards—"departure of Restaurants anywhere in the world from these standards impedes the successful operation of Restaurants throughout the world, and injures the value of its [McDonald's] Patents, Trademarks, Tradename, and Property." Under Article 7.3 Dayan agreed to "maintain these standards as they presently existed" and to observe subsequent improvements McDonald's may initiate. Article 7.1 further provides that Dayan will not vary from QSC standards without prior written approval.

The MLA also contains specific default provisions. Article 23.1(a) gives McDonald's the right to terminate if "Dayan shall default in the performance of any term of this agreement and shall fail to remedy such default within sixty (60) days after written notice." Article 13.2 provides "Dayan personally, fully, and unconditionally guarantees the prompt and full performance of all obligations to McDonald's.". . .

Other witnesses called by McDonald's corroborated Barnes' testimony as to the deplorable condition of Dayan's restaurants. In particular, their testimony revealed that Dayan was not using approved products, he refused to delay the opening of his first restaurant even though McDonald's personnel had declared it unfinished and unsuitable for opening, he used no pickles, he charged extra for catsup or mustard, he hid straws and napkins under the counter, he responded to complaints from McDonald's personnel with "If they don't like it, they can buy me out," he refused to take a refresher course at McDonald's "Hamburger University," the stores were filthy and without many items of necessary equipment, the store crews were poorly trained and frequently out of uniform, and customer complaints were numerous . . .

Barnes further testified that in June 1976 he told Dayan that his substandard operation could no longer be tolerated. Barnes informed Dayan that he would be given six months to bring his restaurants up to standard and at the end of this period McDonald's would exercise its right to formal inspection. These inspections were performed eight months later in February 1977 by Sollars and Allin, two McDonald's employees. The trial court characterized these inspections as signaling the "end of five years of indulgence, forbearance, and carte blanche tolerance of Dayan's excuses.". . .

With respect to Dayan's first argument, McDonald's contends that there is no real dispute on the issue of what the QSC standards are. At trial, McDonald's introduced into evidence its operation and training manual and its equipment and maintenance manual, asserting that these manuals and their periodic updates completely set forth all of McDonald's QSC standards. On cross-examination, Dayan testified that he received these manuals and that they "contain" and "set forth the standards of quality, service and cleanliness." He also agreed that a licensee must totally adhere to the standards outlined in McDonald's manuals and updates, that the MLA explicitly provides for maintaining QSC standards, and that quality, service, and cleanliness are paramount and must be maintained at all costs . . .

We have previously examined in detail the standard license agreement which the licensees subject to the offer of proof operated under and the materially different contract Dayan negotiated after rejecting the standard license agreement. The trial court ruled that the offered evidence was not probative of Dayan's contention that McDonald's did not enforce standards and tolerated widespread QSC noncompliance. It found that in consideration for the 3% royalty fee paid by each licensee given in Dayan's offer of proof, McDonald's was obligated to "nurse a substandard operator back to compliance" by marshaling its resources to help the operator. It held that McDonald's failure to terminate the license of an operator subject to the offer of proof was not relevant because McDonald's had a "duty" to work with the substandard operators under their contracts to correct violations before it could default, while Dayan negotiated a "clearly different" contract which did not obligate McDonald's to provide such predefault service . . .

Under the materially different developmental contract negotiated by Dayan, those same service obligations were never incurred by McDonald's and Dayan was therefore not entitled to the same QSC enforcement procedures or predefault assistance. The formal written notice and franchisee payment requirements contained in the service provisions of the Dayan contract effectively preclude a construction that McDonald's was obligated to unilaterally send advisors to Dayan at its own expense as it did in the case of its standard licensees . . .

Next, plaintiff argues that the trial court erred in admitting into evidence the reports of several French court officials that had conducted inspections of his restaurants pursuant to orders by the High Court in Paris issued in connection with McDonald's French lawsuit. Dayan attacks the credibility, competence and admissibility of the testimony and reports of these French court officials.

The record reveals that five huissiers de audiencier, Delatre, Lachkar, Adam, Petit, and Linee, were specifically appointed and ordered by the Paris court to conduct inspections of Dayan's restaurants in April and September of 1978. Under the French legal system, the court determines facts from reports submitted by huissiers and not from oral testimony. All five of these French court officials held the special title of "Huissier de Justice Audiencier," which indicates that they work for the court system and receive their assignments directly from the court. Huissiers that are not "audiencier" receive their assignments from and work at the request of a private party . . .

Here, the trial court made specific findings that the five huissiers were objective, impartial, honest, and worthy of high credibility. The trier of fact had ample opportunity to assess the credibility of these witnesses, since their testimony consumed more than nine full days of trial. The court also listened to weeks of corroborating testimony and received in evidence over 1,000 corroborating photographs. After reviewing the record and the evidence of impeachment called to our attention, we cannot say that conclusions opposite to those reached by the trial court are clearly evident. Plaintiff's attempt to characterize the five huissiers as agents of McDonald's preparing reports for litigation is not borne out by the record. The huissiers were not privately retained by McDonald's but were appointed by the French court to obtain information the court had requested. The fact that McDonald's had petitioned the French court resulted in McDonald's having to bear the cost of the huissier inspections and reports by paying a fee to each huissier for his work. Contrary to plaintiff's assertion, this arrangement does not render the huissiers' testimony or reports incapable of belief . . .

Dayan also argues that the trial court applied an erroneous legal standard in determining whether the franchisor, McDonald's, acted in good faith and proper motive in terminating the franchise agreement. Dayan contends that the trial court confused the distinction between the two separate legal doctrines of good faith and improper motive. In response, McDonald's argues that motive is irrelevant where good cause for termination exists and that it acted in good faith under the most stringent of standards. A resolution of these contentions will necessarily entail an examination of the relationship between good faith and motive and the applicability of these concepts to the case at bar . . .

Concern over franchise abuses has not only been judicial. The legislatures of several States have enacted statutes specifically aimed at the franchise relationship and the protection of the franchisee. (See generally Annot., 67 A.L.R.3d 1299 (1975).) Illinois has adopted the Franchise Disclosure Act (Ill. Rev. Stat. 1981, ch. 121½, par. 701 et seq.), which mandates franchisor disclosure of information described in the Act to prospective franchisees. Subsequent amendments to the act (Pub. Act 81–426, renumbered Pub. Act 81–1509) placed restraints upon the franchisor's right to terminate the relationship. Section 4.3 (Ill. Rev. Stat. 1981, ch. 121½, par. 704.3) prohibits the termination of a franchise agreement by a franchisor except for "good cause" and contains the following definition:

> " 'Good cause' shall include, but not be limited to, the failure of the franchisee or subfranchisor to comply with any lawful provision of the franchise or other agreement and to cure such default after being given notice thereof and a reasonable opportunity to cure such default, which in no event need be more than 30 days." (Ill. Rev. Stat. 1981, ch. 121½, par. 704.3(b).)

. . .

However, plaintiff would have us go further and argues that even if McDonald's had good cause for termination, if it also had an improper motive the termination would be a breach of the implied covenant of good faith. Dayan would attribute to McDonald's a desire to recapture the lucrative Paris market as an impermissible motive. We cannot agree that the doctrine of good faith performance warrants this additional restriction on franchisor discretion.

Initially, we note that no case has been cited nor has our research revealed any case where a franchise termination for good cause was overcome by the presence of an improper motive. As a general proposition of law, it is widely held that where good cause exists, motive is immaterial to a determination of good faith performance. *Corbin on Contracts* states: . . . "Where there is good cause, there is no bad faith." (6 *Corbin on Contracts* sec. 1266, at 368 (Supp. 1982).) . . .

We find no reversible error with respect to the standard applied by the trial court in the case at bar. Our review of the court's memorandum opinion reveals that initially the court applied a test in accord with the holdings stated in the present opinion. After finding good cause for termination existed, the trial court considered plaintiff's improper motive theory and found that McDonald's sole motive for termination was Dayan's failure to maintain QSC standards. If anything, the trial court's scrutiny of this franchise termination exceeded the requirements imposed by our above holding.

IV. Trial Court Findings of Fact

Finally, plaintiff contends that the trial court improperly resolved certain factual issues in favor of McDonald's. Specifically, plaintiff argues that the following findings of fact are contrary to the manifest weight of the evidence: (1) that McDonald's terminated the franchise agreement in good faith; (2) that McDonald's conduct did not amount to a breach of its contractual obligation to provide assistance to the franchisee; (3) that McDonald's did not violate established termination procedures; and (4) that McDonald's did not waive its right to demand strict compliance . . .

Dayan argues that circumstantial evidence presented at trial indicated that McDonald's sole motive in terminating the MLA was a desire to recapture the lucrative Paris market. He takes issue with the trial court's finding that "it is the QSC violations which have actuated the termination mechanism of the MLA and nothing else" and argues that the evidence of McDonald's bad motive rendered a finding of good faith termination clearly erroneous.

Initially, we note that the trial court has unambiguously resolved the bad motive issue in favor of McDonald's. However, any extended discussion of motive is unnecessary in view of our holding on good faith termination of a franchise agreement. If McDonald's had good cause for termination as evidenced by substantial noncompliance with QSC standards, then the termination was made in good faith regardless of what other motives McDonald's may have had. Thus the scope of our inquiry is necessarily reduced to a determination of whether or not the evidence presented at trial warrants a finding of substantial noncompliance with QSC standards.

Our review of the evidence admits of no doubt; the trial court properly resolved this issue in favor of McDonald's. To characterize the condition of Dayan's restaurants as being in substantial noncompliance with McDonald's QSC standards is to engage in profound understatement. Throughout trial the various witnesses struggled to find the appropriate words to describe the ineffably unsanitary conditions observed in these restaurants, as did the trial court in its memorandum opinion . . . The accuracy of these epithets is supported by voluminous, detailed testimonial evidence which consumed many weeks of trial and thousands of pages of transcript and is also corroborated by over 1,000 photographs admitted in evidence at trial . . . We further find plaintiff's limited attempts to discredit this evidence based on a lack of corroborating written reports in the early years to be singularly unavailing. Accordingly, we find no error with respect to the trial court's determination that McDonald's terminated the franchise agreement for good cause and in good faith.

Dayan also argues that McDonald's was obligated to provide him with the operational assistance necessary to enable him to meet the QSC standards. He further contends that McDonald's failed to fulfill his request for assistance and that the trial court's findings to the contrary were against the manifest weight of the evidence.

As we have previously noted, the extent of McDonald's service obligation to Dayan was expressly addressed in Articles 8.3 and 8.4 of the MLA. Dayan was to pay a 1% royalty on gross receipts and receive no service unless he first requested it in writing, McDonald's overseas personnel were available to render service, and Dayan paid for the service . . .

During the first five years of the MLA, Dayan consistently refused to request any operational assistance even though several McDonald's employees testified that they urged him to do so after observing the disgraceful condition of his restaurants. Following the inspections of Allin and Sollars in February 1977 and after being advised by Barnes that McDonald's would no longer tolerate his substandard operation, Dayan verbally asked Sollars for a French-speaking operations person to work in the market for six months. Sollars testified that he told Dayan it would be difficult to find someone with the appropriate background who spoke French but that McDonald's could immediately send him an English-speaking operations man. Sollars further testified that this idea was summarily rejected by Dayan as unworkable even though he had informed Dayan that sending operations personnel who did not speak the language to a foreign country was very common and very successful in McDonald's international system. Nonetheless, Sollars agreed to attempt to locate a qualified person with the requisite language skills for Dayan . . .

We believe this evidence adequately supports the finding of the trial court that Dayan's "severely qualified and isolated request for an operations man rings false." . . .

What Dayan characterizes as "termination procedures" is nothing more than the extensive inspection and instruction given to noncomplying standard licensees under the 3% license agreement in order to assist them in meeting QSC standards. Contrary to plaintiff's contention, the MLA negotiated by him explicitly stated what he had to do if he wished such assistance; he had to request it in writing and pay for it. Accordingly, we reject Dayan's argument that he was entitled to the same operational assistance prior to termination as the standard licensee. The record reveals no such request and, as previously discussed, the limited request for assistance Dayan did make was fulfilled by McDonald's.

Dayan also takes issue with the trial court's finding that McDonald's did not waive its right to demand strict compliance with QSC standards and it should not be estopped from terminating the MLA. However, we note that throughout trial, plaintiff maintained he was in substantial compliance with QSC standards and that McDonald's had manufactured a case against him in order to recapture the Paris market. Consistent with this litigation posture, he failed to properly plead either waiver or estoppel . . . Even if there were evidence to support these affirmative defenses, and here we find very little, it would not overcome plaintiff's pleading omission . . . Accordingly, we find plaintiff has waived these defenses by failing to sufficiently plead them.

In view of the foregoing reasons, the judgment of the trial court denying plaintiff's request for a permanent injunction and finding that McDonald's properly terminated the franchise agreement is affirmed.

Source: 125 Ill. App. 3d 1272.

> Dayan was suggesting that McDonald's had a motive and a tactic that is a familiar concern for distributors. What was Dayan suggesting? Aside from the reality that Dayan did not live up to his QSC obligations, what element of Dayan's strategy in franchise negotiation ultimately proved disastrous in his later litigation?

A licensor also must recognize that the foreign licensee does not work for free. To build a good relationship, one where the licensee will be interested in defending the market and its rights, the licensor must offer decent compensation. As a result, the potential profitability of the licensor under the license will not be as great as if the licensor entered the foreign market as an investor and producer in its own right. That said, the licensor should still be happy with this reduced upside profit potential, because its downside risk for the most part has been reduced as well. The products under license will likely get to market quicker (where the licensee is already established) and there is no financial risk of investment on the shoulders of the licensor.

Consideration must be given to any improvements to the intellectual property during the life of the license agreement. Will improvements be automatically licensed, or will they be the subjects of separate negotiations? What if the licensee makes the improvements? Will they be automatically cross-licensed or licensed back to the original licensor, and will there be a royalty attached to this?

The licensor also must cope with the possibility that it is creating a potential future competitor in the foreign licensee. Although patented, trademarked, or copyright material will revert back to the licensor, general public domain aspects of any technology and know-how will be in the hands of the licensee after the license expires. This, coupled with the fact that the licensee will have been a reasonably dominant force in the foreign market, may mean that it will have established its own name alongside that of the licensed brand. Only a good commercial relationship, a well-drawn noncompete clause (and one not offensive to local law), and a nondisclosure/trade secrets obligation can assist in this regard.

The Old Wolf

Countries are often criticized for their lax approach to protecting intellectual property and their poor enforcement of IP rules. This is off-putting for domestic manufacturers who might otherwise license their IP internationally. This does not have to be the case. Where foreign rules or enforcement is poor, the domestic manufacturer who simply exports to that market is at grave risk of having foreigners "reverse-engineer" its product, and produce and exploit it thereafter. By actually going ahead and licensing overseas production, the domestic firm gets an overseas police officer in its licensee, one who will be interested in its own right in tracking down and litigating anyone who tries to get for free what the licensee must pay for. Even in a lawless place, its nice to have a sheriff in every town. Sometimes the licensor must play the role of the cavalry as backup, but the whole package is better than just exporting and hoping that no one takes advantage of the exporter's long-distance difficulties.

Noncompete clauses or "restrictive covenants" are used to prohibit the former licensee from making use of the knowledge gained under the license for a particular period of time and/or in a geographic area. These are generally acceptable in the majority of trading nations, as long as they are not offensive in the extent of the restriction. No nation will recognize a lifetime ban on the former licensee, prohibiting it from future competition with the licensor everywhere in the world. From there, the willingness of courts to recognize restrictive covenants such as these is a matter of degree in the commercial circumstances, and consultation with a lawyer in the jurisdiction involved will result in a fairly clear picture of what is acceptable. Some nations are less willing, as a matter of public policy, to recognize the validity of such restrictions at all; consequently, their commercial firms receive proportionately less attention from prospective licensors.

In sum, where the licensor fears creating a future competitor and the risk of loss is high, the only other alternative to a well-drafted agreement is not to license the intellectual property in the first place.

Litigation between two firms who were not even parties to the original license is illustrated below. The case fleshes out many of the salient features of license agreements, particularly as they are viewed in common law jurisdictions outside the United States.

FBI Foods v. Cadbury Schweppes Inc.

Indexed as: *Cadbury Schweppes Inc., (Plaintiff/Respondent) v. FBI Foods Ltd., (Defendant/Appellant)*
Supreme Court of Canada
January 28, 1999

Binnie, J.: Clamato juice is a confection of tomato juice and clam broth. By the early 1980s it had developed a market in Canada about 10 times the size of its market in the United States, where it originated. To a significant extent, its success in Canada is attributed to the efforts of the appellants and their predecessors, who manufactured Clamato juice at plants in Vancouver and eastern Ontario under licence from the respondents. The respondents terminated the licence effective April 15, 1983. The courts below concluded that thereafter the appellants misused confidential information related to the Clamato recipe obtained during the licence period to continue to manufacture a rival tomato-based drink, which they called Caesar Cocktail. Liability for breach of confidence is no longer contested. This appeal requires us to consider appropriate remedies for breach of confidence in a commercial context.

The respondents obtained from the British Columbia Court of Appeal a permanent injunction against continued use of the confidential information, or products derived therefrom, plus an award of compensation equivalent to the profits the respondents would have earned had they in fact sold an additional volume of Clamato equivalent to the sales of Caesar Cocktail during the 12-month period following termination of the licence. In this Court the appellants complain that the order of the British Columbia Court of Appeal effectively makes them the insurer of the respondents' profits in the year following the termination, despite the fact it was the respondents who precipitated the termination and thus any market dislocation suffered by Clamato. The appellants want the compensation to be reduced to zero. The respondents, equally indignant, analogize the misused confidential information to a species of property which the appellants have converted to their own use. In their cross-appeal they therefore attack the limitation of their compensation to the profits they would otherwise have earned to a mere 12 months. The respondents say they want the market value of the "pirated" information.

Facts

Duffy-Mott registered in Canada the trademark CLAMATO on October 17, 1969. In the late 1970s, it decided to supply the Canadian market by licensing its trademark and its formula to local juice manufacturers, who undertook "the manufacture, distribution, sale and marketing" of Clamato in an exclusive territory. Caesar Canning Ltd. of British Columbia, now bankrupt, obtained the territory consisting of Ontario and Western Canada for a series of 12-month periods, indefinitely renewable, provided the licensee achieved a minimum volume of sales in each 12-month period. Caesar Canning easily exceeded the minimum volumes in each 12-month period.

By the spring of 1979, Caesar Canning had built up a distribution system and promoted the product with sufficient energy that its territory was extended to include the rest of Canada. Local sources were obtained for the ingredients except the premixed portion of the dry seasonings, which was provided by the licensor, Duffy-Mott. *The Food and Drugs Act,* R.S.C., 1985, c. F-27, and regulations thereunder, and their U.S. equivalent, required disclosure on the product label of all the ingredients in descending order of quantity. However, neither Caesar Canning nor the other appellants ever did discover the precise formula of the respondents' secret "dry mix." Nevertheless, to enable Caesar Canning to produce Clamato, Duffy-Mott communicated related information about its recipe and manufacturing procedures which the trial judge found to be confidential. This finding is no longer attacked.

On May 11, 1981, Caesar Canning entered into a contract with the appellant FBI Foods Ltd. to manufacture Clamato and related products at its Trenton, Ontario plant. The parties called their contract a "Tolling Agreement," and FBI Foods was paid a fixed fee for each case of juice product. The contract was for a period of five years, unless sooner terminated for various reasons, including earlier termination of the underlying Licence Agreement between Duffy-Mott and Caesar Canning. Duffy-Mott consented to, but was not a party to, the Tolling Agreement. To enable it to manufacture Clamato, FBI Foods was given information about the Clamato recipe and methods of manufacture which Duffy-Mott regarded as, and FBI Foods now acknowledges was, confidential.

Termination of the Licence

In 1982, the respondent Cadbury Schweppes acquired the shares of Duffy-Mott and, in a switch of business strategy, decided that Duffy-Mott would take back the production and marketing of Clamato in Canada. To this end, it notified Caesar Canning on April 15, 1982 that the Licence Agreement (and consequently the sub-agreement with FBI Foods) would terminate in 12 months. Caesar Canning was offered an ongoing contract to produce Clamato at a fixed fee per case, which it declined.

It is important to note that the Licence Agreement left Caesar Canning (and therefore FBI Foods) free to compete with the respondent in the juice market after termination. The Licence Agreement provided only that Caesar Canning would no longer have the right to use the trademark CLAMATO and it would not, for a period of five years, manufacture or distribute any product "which includes among its ingredients *clam juice and* tomato juice" (emphasis added).

Armed with 12 months' notice of the termination of its licence, Caesar Canning immediately began work to develop a competing product. Lorne Nicklason, its Manager of Quality Control and Quality Assurance, developed a "reformulated" tomato-based juice over a few months in late 1982, working from the list of ingredients and processing specifications for Clamato, but omitting clams or other seafood. He made sure that the new product was distinguishable chemically from Clamato, with different levels of salt, pH, and soluble solids. However, the trial judge found (93 B.C.L.R. (2d) 318, at p. 325), and it is no longer disputed, that:

> It is beyond doubt that without the formula and process information about Clamato Mr. Nicklason could not have developed Caesar Cocktail personally. He did not have the necessary skills. The evidence is equally persuasive that Caesar Canning could have developed a product as much like Clamato as Caesar Cocktail without using the Clamato recipe by hiring the appropriate skills. It could have done so within the 12-month notice period at modest cost.
>
> . . . Anyone who saw the recipe for Caesar Cocktail would have known that it was derived so entirely from the Clamato formulation as to be a virtual copy without clams. The other variations were very minor.

It must have come as an unpleasant surprise to Duffy-Mott when Caesar Cocktail was able to substantially replicate the look, smell, texture and taste of Clamato juice, and win a significant share of the market without resort to clam broth or other seafood extract.

Caesar Cocktail went on the market immediately after the licensing agreement terminated on April 15, 1983. After being assured that Caesar Canning was not in breach of its contractual covenants with the respondents, FBI Foods agreed to co-pack the new product for eastern Canada. Caesar Cocktail proved to be a success, though its market share trailed a long way behind that of Clamato.

Unbeknownst to the appellants, the respondents had surreptitiously discovered the exact formula of Caesar Cocktail at the end of March 1983 by slipping a technical expert onto the team for the final financial audit of Caesar Canning under the Licence Agreement. Despite this knowledge, the respondents did not take any action to enjoin the manufacture and sale of Caesar Cocktail, or otherwise protest. The respondents mistakenly believed (as did Caesar Canning) that the absence of clam broth in the reformulated recipe would be fatal to their claim.

Caesar Canning did not live long enough to enjoy its new success. It ran into serious financial problems, ceased production on October 23, 1985, and shortly thereafter made an assignment in bankruptcy. The appellant FBI Foods, which by then relied for a significant portion of its business on the production of Caesar Cocktail, purchased the assets of Caesar Canning, including the Caesar Cocktail brand, for $955,000. It decided to carry on this aspect of the business through a wholly owned subsidiary, its co-appellant FBI Brands. The sale of assets was completed on January 10, 1986. Since that time, FBI Brands has produced and sold Caesar Cocktail under various brand names (other than Clamato) throughout Canada.

In 1986, three years after Caesar Cocktail came on the Canadian market, the respondents obtained new and more optimistic legal advice respecting their legal rights, and dispatched a cease and desist letter to FBI Brands. As stated, Caesar Canning, the only entity against which they had a contractual claim, had by that time disappeared into bankruptcy. Eventually, this action was commenced in 1988 against the FBI companies, and the Chief Operating Officer of FBI Foods, Lawrence Kurlender. No claim was ever made for an interlocutory injunction.

Judgments Below

Supreme Court of British Columbia

Though the pleadings outlined several causes of action, Huddart J. found it necessary to deal only with the claim for breach of confidence. She held that the information Duffy-Mott had shared with Caesar Canning and FBI Foods was confidential trade know-how, and that it had been disclosed in confidence to Caesar Canning. She found that, quite apart from any contractual arrangements, express or implied, there is a well-understood obligation of confidentiality in the food industry with respect to such disclosures. . . . [T]he trial judge held that Caesar Canning had wrongfully misused the confidential information in its "reformulation" from Clamato to Caesar Cocktail. Nevertheless, Huddart J. considered that the value of the "confidential information" was both transitory and of marginal importance. The formulation of tomato juice products is well understood in the industry. The absence of clam broth from the juice mixture apparently did not worry consumers. The real marketing edge of "Clamato" was its trademark, which the defendants did not infringe. Although there was conflicting evidence on the point, she accepted evidence of consumer testing by the National Food Laboratory that consumers in a blind taste test could (albeit with some hesitation) detect a difference between Caesar Cocktail and Clamato.

. . .

The trial judge found that the plaintiffs had not established any financial loss. The original Clamato continued to dominate its market niche. However, the trial judge did not send the plaintiffs away empty-handed. She concluded that by misappropriating the confidential information the defendants had wrongfully obtained a 12-month "springboard" into the highly competitive juice market that but for the breach they would not have enjoyed. . . . The registrar later assessed this amount to be $29,761.20.

As to the respondents' claim for a permanent injunction, Huddart J. found that their inactivity since 1983, when they became aware of all pertinent facts, was fatal . . . [S]he questioned the appropriateness of an injunction in a case where much of the "confidential" information was either public or of marginal significance, and any injury could be satisfactorily remedied by financial compensation.

British Columbia Court of Appeal (1996), 23 B.C.L.R. (3d) 325

Cadbury Schweppes fared better in the British Columbia Court of Appeal. Newbury J.A., for the court, accepted the trial judge's findings that there had been a breach of confidence, and that a similar product could have been (but was not) developed independently of the confidential information within 12 months. She found (at p. 345) that:

> . . . the plaintiff cannot ask the Court to restore him to a market monopoly position if in fact that position was vulnerable to attack in the form of legitimate competition from the defendant.

However, Newbury J.A. rejected the "consulting fee" valuation adopted by the trial judge. Pointing out the agreement of the parties that evidence at trial would be limited to liability issues, with an assessment of damages postponed to a later proceeding (if necessary), Newbury J.A. ordered a reference to determine the amount the plaintiffs would have earned if they (instead of the defendants) had in fact sold the volume of Caesar Cocktail marketed by the defendants in the 12-month period following termination. Further, Newbury J.A. concluded (at pp. 351–52) that a permanent injunction was appropriate, because:

. . . the interests of justice require[d] [the] Court to enjoin the continued breach of confidence by the defendants—that is, that it enjoin the defendants from making use in the manufacture of a tomato cocktail, the specifications, technical information, advice, and derivatives thereof, that were disclosed to Caesar Canning Ltd. and/or the defendants or any of them in confidence pursuant to the Licensing and Tolling Agreements, and that are not otherwise generally known.

Analysis

Equity, as a court of conscience, directs itself to the behaviour of the person who has come into possession of information that is in fact confidential, and was accepted on that basis, either expressly or by implication. Equity will pursue the information into the hands of a third party who receives it with the knowledge that it was communicated in breach of confidence (or afterwards acquires notice of that fact even if innocent at the time of acquisition) and impose its remedies. It is worth emphasizing that this is a case of third party liability. The appellants did not receive the confidence from the respondents, but from the now defunct Caesar Canning. The receipt, however, was burdened with the knowledge that its use was to be confined to the purpose for which the information was provided, namely the manufacture of Clamato under licence.

. . .

While the only controversies still alive in this Court turn on the principles on which financial compensation is to be calculated, and whether or not this is a proper case for a permanent injunction, the disagreement among the parties on the remedies reflect[s] their differing views as to the true nature and scope of the cause of action for breach of confidence. This appeal therefore requires us to examine more closely the character of the interest protected in this case, and on that basis to assess the appropriateness of the remedy that was in fact granted by the British Columbia Court of Appeal.

. . .

B. Relationship Between Breach of Confidence and Fiduciary Duty

The respondents at trial pleaded breach of fiduciary duty. The law takes a hard line against faithless fiduciaries. Such a finding, if made, would have assisted the respondents in their claim to what amounts to a remedy that is "proprietary" (i.e., the respondents, in their cross-appeal, claim that the appellants' sales should be treated as belonging to the respondents, by analogy with the principles governing defaulting trustees or patent infringers for the purpose of calculating financial compensation). Thus, while the courts below found that the facts of this case neither fall into one of the established categories of fiduciary relationships (e.g., solicitor and client, principal and agent), nor meet the exceptional criteria for the creation of a fiduciary duty outside those established categories, the respondents seem to think the remedy not only can but should be approached on the same basis as if the fiduciary argument had succeeded.

. . .

In some sense, disclosure of almost any confidential information places the confider in a position of vulnerability to its misuse. Such vulnerability, if exploited by the confidee in a commercial context, can generally be remedied by an action for breach of confidence or breach of a contractual term, express or implied *(Pre-Cam Exploration & Development Ltd. v. McTavish, supra, per* Judson J., at p. 555). In this case, the licensing arrangement expressly contemplated open competition upon termination, subject for a period of five years to avoidance of what came to be recognized as a useless limitation, namely mixing clam broth with tomato juice. While the law will supplement the contractual relationship by importing a duty not to misuse confidential information, there is nothing special in this case to elevate the breached duty to one of a fiduciary character. The respondents' demand to have the appellants' sales treated as an asset "pirated" from the respondents by analogy with a trust estate goes too far.

C. Relevance of the Licence and Tolling Agreements

. . .

Nothing is said expressly in the Licence Agreement or Tolling Agreement about confidentiality. It has already been mentioned that there is no privity of contract between the appellants and the respondents. The only party with whom Duffy-Mott had a contract was Caesar Canning, now bankrupt, who is not and never was a party to these proceedings. The appellant FBI Foods was party to the Tolling Agreement with Caesar Canning, but while Duffy-Mott consented to that agreement, it was not made a party to that contract. However, the appellants contend that the contractual terms limit or circumscribe the equitable duty of confidentiality that would otherwise arise, and restrict the remedy to be granted. In their view, the respondents are entitled to no compensation whatsoever.

. . .

. . . The appellants say the respondents got exactly what they bargained for, namely a competitive post-termination environment in which Clamato could lose market share to a Caesar Canning successor product that met the contractual criteria of being free of clam broth.

This analysis is correct so far as it goes, but it leaves out of consideration the fact the respondents did not bargain for the unfair competition of having their own know-how, imparted in confidence, used against them. The contract cannot reasonably be read as negating the duty of confidence imposed by law . . .

D. Relevance of Respondents' Argument Based on an Alleged "Proprietary" Interest in the Information

. . .

The respondents' characterization of confidential information as property is controversial. Traditionally, courts here and in other common law jurisdictions have been at pains to emphasize that the action is rooted in the relationship of confidence rather than the legal characteristics of the information confided. See, for example, Holmes J. in the United States Supreme Court in *E. I. Du Pont de Nemours Powder Co. v. Masland,* 244 U.S. 100 (1917), at p. 102:

> The word property as applied to . . . trade secrets is an unanalyzed expression of certain secondary consequences of the primary fact that the law makes some rudimentary requirements of good faith. Whether the plaintiffs have any valuable secret or not the defendant knows the facts, whatever they are, through a special confidence that he accepted. The property may be denied but the confidence cannot be. Therefore the starting point for the present matter is not property . . . but that the defendant stood in confidential relations with the plaintiffs, or one of them.

The same point was made in the High Court of Australia, *per* Deane J., in *Moorgate Tobacco Co. v. Philip Morris Ltd.* (1984), 156 C.L.R. 414, at p. 438:

> Like most heads of exclusive equitable jurisdiction, its rational basis does not lie in proprietary right. It lies in the notion of an obligation of conscience arising from the circumstances in or through which the information was communicated or obtained.

. . .

I do not think that the respondents' reliance on intellectual property law is of much assistance here. It ignores "the bargain" that lies at the heart of patent protection. A patent is a statutory monopoly which is given in exchange for a full and complete disclosure by the patentee of his or her invention. The disclosure is the essence of the bargain between the patentee, who obtained at the time a 17-year monopoly on exploiting the invention, and the public, which obtains open access to all of the information necessary to practise the invention. Accordingly, at least one of the policy objectives underlying the statutory remedies available to a patent owner is to make disclosure more attractive, and thus hasten the availability of useful knowledge in the public sphere in the public interest. As pointed out by Hugessen J.A. in *Smith, Kline & French Laboratories Ltd. v. Canada (Attorney General),* [1987] 2 F.C. 359 (C.A.), at p. 366, entrepreneurs in the food industry frequently eschew patent protection in order to avoid disclosure, and thus perhaps perpetuate their competitive advantage beyond the 17-year life span of a patent. We are told that the secrecy of the Coca-Cola recipe has apparently endured for decades. If a court were to award compensation to the respondents on principles analogous to those applicable in a case of patent infringement, the respondents would be obtaining the benefit of patent remedies without establishing that their invention meets the statutory criteria for the issuance of a patent, or paying the price of public disclosure of their secret.

. . .

In the respondents' view their Clamato information is, literally, priceless. They say its continued use must be forever enjoined. It is only past misuse which, being now incurable, will have to be compensated in mere dollars and cents. In the appellants' view, on the other hand, the Court should focus on what the trial judge found was the peripheral importance of the information actually used. Caesar Cocktail, in one formulation or another, would have been on the market. The processing and other details, however confidential, did not add to its market potential. In other words, the appellants' position is that the use of confidential information may have been an actionable wrong but it did not cause any monetary loss to the respondents.

. . .

The law would lose its deterrent effect if defendants could misappropriate confidential information and retain profits thereby generated subject only to the payment of compensation if, as and when they are caught and successfully sued.

I think, however, that one's indignation in this case has to be tempered by an appreciation of the equities between the parties at the date of the trial. Eleven years had passed since Caesar Cocktail went into production, using "nothing very special" information that could promptly have been replaced (had the respondents made a timely fuss) by substitute technology accessible to anyone skilled in the art of juice formulation. At the date of trial, it would have been manifestly unfair to allow information of peripheral importance to control the grant of injunctive relief. The equities in favour of the respondents' claim for an injunction to put Caesar Cocktail off the market rightly yielded to the appellants' equities in continuing a business to whose success the confidential information had so minimally contributed.

. . .

Disposition of the Appeal

The appeal is therefore allowed, with costs, and the Referee is directed to calculate the amount of compensation required to restore to the respondents what the respondents have lost as a result of the appellants' breach of confidence. The period of calculation, for the reasons given, is to be restricted to the 12-month period commencing April 15, 1983. *[With interest, cross-appeal further dismissed.]*

Source: [1999] 1 S.C.R. 142.

Some serious defects existed in the original Duffy-Mott/Caesar Canning licensing agreement that contributed directly to the litigation between Cadbury Schweppes and FBI Foods. What were these defects and how might you have approached them better?

Royalties and Fees

Critical to the commercial success of the licensing agreement will be arrangement between the parties for royalties and fees. If these payments to the licensor in return for its intellectual property and other services are too high, the licensee will have no later interest in working the license as it presents the licensee with no real benefit to do so. Alternatively, if these payments are too low, the licensor will have given away a substantial capital asset and competitive opportunity. No method of royalty and fee calculation can be described as being applicable in all circumstances; too many varying commercial factors are at work in too many widely varying situations. However, there are general principles that can be recognized.

First is the separation of royalties from fees. Royalties are best confined to payments to the licensor arising from activities and undertakings that are within the ability of the licensee to control—that is, revenue from sales of products that embody the intellectual property. This is in contrast to fees, which should be paid in return for goods or services sold or provided by the licensor to the licensee over which the licensee has little or no control. For example, where the licensor provides capital equipment, input supplies, or training and support, the licensee should pay for them directly. Often this does not happen; the licensee is initially short of funds and does not want to make fee payments, or the licensor wants to receive its payments as royalties, which may be taxed more favorably than fee income. Despite this, the separation of royalties from fees is usually more important than it first appears.

Rolling all cash flows into royalty payments produces more negative results than positive. First, it can attract unfavorable attention from tax authorities that object to this inappropriate characterization of the cash flow. Secondly, doing so alters the relationship between the parties. The licensor, who otherwise would be prepared to offer support to its licensee, becomes disinclined to do so, as support becomes a cost that reduces the real return on all future royalty payments. On the other side, the licensee will try to press for ever-greater assistance, rather than develop its own skills and independence, for it can do so without further cost. In the long term, accurate assessments of profitability and cost within the agreement become difficult for both parties.

Not only is it difficult to determine how much of any given royalty payment is compensation for intellectual property and how much is payment for services (perhaps rendered in the distant past), but it also can become a source of resentment. This is particularly true for a licensee who seems to be "paying forever" for services consumed long ago. Memories have a habit of becoming short or long, whichever is more unfavorable. In some situations, an appropriate royalty is a matter of an accepted industry standard, and no amount of bargaining power will move a party away from that rate. In such cases, parties will simply walk away from the deal and give or obtain their license elsewhere or do without. Other approaches are more technical, or at least rooted in some form of rational assessment. At the most basic end of the spectrum, the licensor knows that the licensee will generate a profit out of the use of the intellectual property. The royalty negotiation will cen-

A right to assignment or sublicense will often cause problems, bringing in an existing competitor who may buy the company enjoying the license rights, take up its assets in bankruptcy, solicit a sublicense, or enter into a joint venture with the licensee. A licensor must remember to reserve rights of approval or reversion for any of these events in the original license agreement.

ter on that profit, with the licensor demanding a share—a twentieth, a quarter, a third, or more. This simplistic approach is based on profits and is burdened by the questions of what happens if there are no profits.

The answer to that question, any percentage of zero being zero, is unacceptable to the licensor. This leads licensors rapidly to the conclusion that it is better to calculate royalties on the basis of sales rather than on profits. Doing so makes the licensee responsible for the prudent operation of its selling and administrative operations, and relieves the licensor from being penalized for any poor management on the part of the licensee. Again, the payment of a royalty is most closely tied with aspects of business that the parties can control.

The negotiation of a royalty based on sales will be contractually incorporated into the agreement on the basis of a single figure, say "5 percent of net sales." As negotiations proceed, both the parties themselves and their legal counsel should have an understanding of where such figures are derived, lest the other party consider their bargaining position to be simply irrational.

Assume that a prospective licensee toy manufacturer believes that it must make a $12 million capital investment in order to be in a position to use the intellectual property offered to it under license by a movie studio. This money, for example, would be used to purchase the plant and equipment necessary to manufacture toys with the trademarked image. The licensee (perhaps aided by estimates of the licensor) expects to earn $36 million in sales revenue from the product each year, and assuming proper cost management, expects to net $4 million in profits from these sales. The return (rate of profits) earned by the licensor for each dollar of assets employed in manufacturing is therefore $4 million/$12 million, or 33 percent. The licensee, however, need not invest its money in the intellectual property to make some return, for it could place its $12 million in the stock or bond markets with similar risk and earn, say, a 13 percent investment return, manufacturing nothing. In such a case, the negotiable and divisible return on assets of the intellectual property—that is, that which can be bargained for—is actually 33 percent – 13 percent, or 20 percent. This is the improved return that the intellectual property really offers to the licensee, and a return that it must share with the licensor.

If the parties were of equal bargaining strength, this 20 percent would probably be split evenly. If either party wants the deal badly enough, it may be obliged to accept less than half. Assume that the movie studio is very powerful. It may insist on taking 75 percent of the 20 percent as its share of the available negotiable return (75 percent of the 20 percent being 15 percent) on the licensee's assets, or a 15 percent royalty based on assets. In order to be commercially workable, this 0.15 must be converted into a figure that is based on sales rather than assets, thus

A royalty of $0.15 is expected on each $1 in assets employed	times	$\dfrac{\text{Total assets (\$12 million)}}{\text{Total sales (\$36 million)}}$	equals	Royalty per $1 of sales

which is

$$\frac{0.15}{1} \times \frac{12}{36} = \frac{1.8}{36} = 0.05, \text{ or a 5\% royalty on sales}$$

This approach satisfies all the requirements for a balanced approach to royalties in license agreements. The licensee does not pay royalties based on inflated returns that do not recognize that it could have invested elsewhere without manufacturing at all. The licensor is paid from sales that the intellectual property generates, rather than from profits that are more dependent on the licensee's management skill. Royalty bargaining is focused on the extraordinary returns that the monopoly rights of the intellectual property represent.

Finally, any assistance to the licensee by the licensor should be either free (in recognition that it is also in the licensor's interest to help) or on a cost-recovery or fee-for-service basis. It also should be separate from the royalty, which is limited to a reflection of the value of the intellectual property.

Another method of royalty calculation is appropriate where the licensor merely wishes to dispose of a technology that it has no use for, but remains a saleable item to others. In this case, the licensor will be focused on how much the technology cost it to develop, or how much it would cost the licensee to duplicate the technology itself. Assume that this cost amounted to $1 million. Assume further that it would take the licensee five years to develop it (for undisclosed secrets) on its own, or that patent coverage has another five years to run, or that the intellectual property will be totally obsolete in another five years. If, during those five years, sales of goods containing the technology would amount to $40 million per year, the licensor might seek a royalty of 5 percent of sales, based on $1 million cost recovery divided by $200 million in sales until total obsolescence or loss of the intellectual property rights.

There is no "magic bullet" to dictate appropriate royalty rates, but there is every reason to consider the attitude of courts toward them in infringement actions. First, this is useful as a frame of reference where the commercial realities of a complex licensing agreement are difficult to grasp. Second, in the event of infringement of intellectual property rights (either through abuse of rights by a licensee or by an unrelated party), the owner will be required to establish an appropriate measure of damages acceptable to those same courts.

Among nations where intellectual property rights are highly regarded, the following factors may be worthy of consideration, as laid out by U.S. District Court Judge Tenney in 1970:[6]

> A comprehensive list of evidentiary facts relevant, in general, to the determination of the amount of a reasonable royalty for a patent license may be drawn from a conspectus of the leading cases. The following are some of the factors seemingly more pertinent to the issue herein:
>
> 1. The royalties received by the patentee for the licensing of the patent in suit, proving or tending to prove an established royalty.
> 2. The rates paid by the licensee for the use of other patents comparable to the patent in suit.
> 3. The nature and scope of the license, as exclusive or non-exclusive; or as restricted or non-restricted in terms of territory or with respect to whom the manufactured product may be sold.
> 4. The licensor's established policy and marketing program to maintain his patent monopoly by not licensing others to use the invention or by granting licenses under special conditions designed to preserve that monopoly.
> 5. The commercial relationship between the licensor and licensee, such as, whether they are competitors in the same territory in the same line of business; or whether they are inventor and promotor.

[6]In *Georgia-Pacific Corporation v. United States Plywood Corporation*, 318 F. Supp. 1116 (S.D.N. 4. 1970). While the case was subsequently appealed and damages were reduced, it was done on other grounds not relevant here and the reasoning of Judge Tenney remains sound.

6. The effect of selling the patented specialty in promoting sales of other products of the licensee; the existing value of the invention to the licensor as a generator of sales of his non-patented items; and the extent of such derivative or convoyed sales.

7. The duration of the patent and the term of the license.

8. The established profitability of the product made under the patent; its commercial success; and its current popularity.

9. The utility and advantages of the patent property over the old modes or devices, if any, that had been used for working out similar results.

10. The nature of the patented invention; the character of the commercial embodiment of it as owned and produced by the licensor, and the benefits to those who have used the invention.

11. The extent to which the infringer has made use of the invention; and any evidence probative of the value of that use.

12. The portion of the profit or of the selling price that may be customary in the particular business or in comparable businesses to allow for the use of the invention or analogous inventions.

13. The portion of the realizable profit that should be credited to the invention as distinguished from non-patented elements, the manufacturing process, business risks, or significant features or improvements added by the infringer.

14. The opinion testimony of qualified experts.

15. The amount that a licensor (such as the patentee) and a licensee (such as the infringer) would have agreed upon (at the time the infringement began) if both had been reasonably and voluntarily trying to reach an agreement; that is, the amount which a prudent licensee—who desired, as a business proposition, to obtain a license to manufacture and sell a particular article embodying the patented invention—would have been willing to pay as a royalty and yet be able to make a reasonable profit and which amount would have been acceptable by a prudent patentee who was willing to grant a license.[7]

Beyond patents, there is no reason to think that these principles, appropriately modified, would not enter into consideration of reasonable royalties for the use of copyright and trademarks.

Anatomy of a Licensing Agreement

Having considered the implications of the commercial opportunity, control issues, business risk, and local law regulation, the international businessperson and legal practitioner can place most of these concerns under headings for negotiation. Negotiation often takes place on a clause-by-clause basis, with the royalty rate left for final consideration (and negotiation) based on the scope of the rights conferred and the conditions placed on those rights. The following list is typical but not exhaustive:

1. **Parties.** Accuracy is important for obvious reasons, but additionally because intellectual property is often held in holding companies established in tax-neutral jurisdictions, often therefore bringing a controlled intermediary of either the licensor or licensee into the agreement.

2. **Recitals.** Establishing the intentions of the parties.

3. **Definitions.** As required for ease of negotiation, drafting, and later interpretation.

4. **Date.** Date of agreement and effective date of license, which may be the basis for calculating the duration of the license.

[7]Ibid. at 1120.

5. **Grant.** The specific description of the intellectual property under license, and exclusivity in that grant, as well as terms regarding improvements if not provided separately; often accompanied by annexes of drawings or images and the like.

6. **Acknowledgment of Title.** That the intellectual property belongs to the licensor, that it remains so during and after the license, and that licensee will not attempt to challenge that title.

7. **Territory.** The geographic area, customer groups, or industries in which the licensee may operate.

8. **Restrictions, if any, to the above.**

9. **Exclusivity.** Whether exclusive at all, or binding on licensor not to do business in the territory, or not to create further licensees in that territory, or both.

10. **Term.** Often limited by the expiration of a period of years, or a particular event, or the life of the intellectual property protection.

11. **Most-Favored Treatment.** Whether the licensee has the right to better terms as may be offered and granted to future licensees in other territories.

12. **Renewal.** Whether automatic, whether on certain performance goals being achieved, or whether renewed only in part with renegotiation of specific terms; time limits on renewal negotiations.

13. **Diligence.** The obligation of the licensee to make commercial use of the intellectual property, in any of production, sales, or investment terms, either by meeting specified targets or through its best efforts.

14. **Royalties and Payments.** Lump sums, one-time payments, periodic royalties, minimum royalties, or sliding scales based on performance. Basis for calculation: sales or otherwise; net accounting, exclusive of taxes, duties, freight, returns, or rejected goods.

15. **Accounts and Inspection.** Auditing provisions; access and provision of books of account for licensor's inspections, as well as inspection of premises and production facilities; notice and timing of inspections; financial and operations statements; accounting for sales, profits, and royalties.

16. **Information Sharing.** Obligations regarding market developments, technical developments, or intentions of the licensor to create new licensees, where permitted.

17. **Technical Assistance.** Available support, training, or marketing assistance; for how long, together with provisions on form for requests and fee-based charges to be applied.

18. **Confidentiality.** Limitations on disclosure; requirements for nondisclosure agreements with employees, assigns, or sublicensees, if permitted; time limits for nondisclosure beyond term of license.

19. **Rights to Sublicense.** Whether permitted at all or on approval; whether withheld approval requires reasonable reasons.

20. **Rights to Assignment.** Whether permitted at all or on approval; whether withheld approval requires reasonable reasons.

21. **Rights to Improvements.** Whether licensor obligated to supply licensee with improvements; whether new or increased royalty due or open for negotiation. Where improvements made by licensee: ownership of improvements; whether automatic grant-back of license; whether royalty due; territorial or use limits.

22. **Defense of the Licensed Property.** Carriage and cost of litigation in defense of intellectual property rights; indemnities, sharing of damages; right to settle claims or suits.

23. **Termination.**
    - If by licensor: On notice, on anniversary date, for cause, on bankruptcy or change in control of licensee, or where licensee in breach of a material obligation.
    - If by licensee: On notice, on anniversary date, or on payment of penalty.
    - Effect of termination: Reversion of all rights and property interests to licensor, suspension of rights of licensee; whether an exclusive license may continue as a nonexclusive license; period of any noncompete restrictive covenants.

24. **Choice of Law.** Forum selection; applicable procedural and substantive law.

25. **Arbitration.** Whether available, composition of arbitral panel; applicable rules.

26. **Force Majeure.** Where may be invoked; notice requirements; whether action of governments considered force majeure.

Additionally, with appropriate modifications of the above, franchise agreements will typically include terms relating to

- Acquisition or franchise fees.
- Procedures and standards.
- Approved sources of supply.
- Purchase obligations.
- Capital equipment purchase obligations.
- Inventory maintenance obligations.
- Real estate and site selection criteria.
- Rights of franchisee to additional franchise locations.
- Advertising and support.
- Penalty terms.

Chapter Summary

Licenses are important legal tools to capitalize on otherwise difficult overseas market opportunities, through a contractual grant of a right to do or make use of intellectual property. This may be a combination of patents, trademarks, or copyright; unprotected secret knowledge, or an entire business strategy in the form of a franchise.

Intellectual property is regulated under the local law of nations, with some uniformity and scope of protection created through international conventions. Patents provide exclusive rights for the exploitation of an invention, usually for a period of 20 years, which has become an international standard. Where a patent has been granted, its owner may sue others who infringe upon it, or others may challenge its validity. Copyright protects original works of authorship and vest in that author, subject to transfer, for a period of 50 years or more after the death of the author. Trademarks are used to distinguish goods or services of one business from those of another, and registration is a step toward preventing others from infringing on the goodwill the mark may represent. As the world becomes a smaller place in commercial terms, the potential for conflict between trademarks grows.

Investments in formal registration of intellectual property are only meaningful if the registrant is willing to police its rights. If not, it may be better to operate with as little disclosure as is possible. Litigation can become expensive and worldwide, in order to adequately defend intellectual property rights.

A wide range of business motivations fuel the need for international licensing, usually arising from the potential licensor's constraints of production, time, money, desire, and business focus. Additionally, market attributes or national law may make certain territories more suitable for licensing than others.

The licensing decision has business and legal risks, due to the loss of direct control by the licensor of the intellectual property. This means the image of the licensor is continually at stake; problems happen at a distance, and it can be a challenge for a licensor to remain abreast of what is happening in the overseas market. Abuses of the property can take place, and the licensor may be creating a competitor out of its licensees. At law, licensing shares many of the same concerns as exist with the granting of distributorships, as well as falling under many similar local law provisions and antitrust legislation.

Royalties represent the compensation for a licensor's grant of rights. However, the license must not be simply focused on payment and property; it must foresee and provide for a wide range of future events, to ensure that this valuable asset of the licensor is not misused, or used by unintended persons with unintended consequences.

Chapter Questions

1. What are the primary business motivations for licensing? Provide an example of each, and an explanation of how intellectual property licensing serves each situation.

2. How can a licensee's right to assign the license cause competitive problems for the licensor? What steps can the licensor take to give the licensee the flexibility to bring in other parties, yet retain its own control?

3. Distinguish between patents, trademarks, and copyright, and the type of rights and degree of protection most commonly offered to each under national laws.

4. On what basis are near-identical trademarks permitted to co-exist?

5. "There is no such thing as an international patent." Elaborate on this statement, explaining what does exist in terms of international commitments of states.

6. Contrast the intentions and bargaining position of both a potential licensor and a licensee toward the issues of exclusivity, most-favored treatment, and effect of termination within a license agreement.

7. A licensor may be faced with the fact that its licensee is about to be taken over by a competitor of the licensor, or intends to merge with that competitor. What provisions should appear in the licensing agreement to prevent this circumstance from becoming a disaster for the licensor?

8. Where $16 million of assets produce sales of $40 million and a royalty of 25 percent on assets employed is contemplated, what is an appropriate royalty as a percentage of sales?

9. A license agreement provides for the grant of certain intellectual property from an established manufacturer to a new foreign start-up company, as well as six months of technical assistance provided by an employee of the licensor firm, and the transfer of a machine with a value of $30,000. This is given in return for a royalty of 5 percent of sales resulting from the production of the licensee over the next 10 years. What advice might you offer to the parties as amendments to the terms of their deal?

10. Why might national regulators themselves attack a license agreement between private parties? What legislation is most likely to be brought to bear against private licensing agreements?

BusinessWeek

The U.S. giant is suing Huawei for theft. And the upstart, with its new ally 3Com, faces a rough slog.

It's the shimmering jewel of China's high-tech industry. With its mile-wide campus bordered with palms, Huawei Technologies in the city of Shenzhen is China's answer to Silicon Valley's Cisco Systems (CSCO) Inc. Its 10,000-plus engineers represent the country's best and brightest—and they work for salaries only 20% as high as their counterparts in California. What's more, its state-of-the-art factories, equipped with mammoth robotic parts-picking systems, fill orders for its networking gear with world-class efficiency.

Huawei appears positioned to become a power in the world's networking industry—except for one very large problem. On Jan. 23, after an eight-month investigation, Cisco launched a sweeping lawsuit against Huawei, alleging a host of intellectual-property violations and pushing for an injunction to remove certain Huawei products from the market. Huawei responds that the injunction Cisco seeks is unwarranted, and that it has already addressed Cisco's concerns. Still, the suit has derailed Huawei's expansion into the U.S. market. And it may have led Huawei to seek an alliance to bolster its presence and credibility in networking. A month after the suit, Huawei announced a global joint venture with Cisco's longtime rival, 3Com Corp. (COMS)

The result is the odd couple of networking. It's the much feared newcomer under the cloud of possible scandal and the American has-been, battered for years by Cisco and looking for a muscular ally. On paper, the combination of Huawei and 3Com appears rich with promise. The 51-49 joint venture, with control potentially switching from Huawei to 3Com within two years, could ship products as early as this summer. It provides Huawei with 3Com's global distribution system, along with a strong base in the U.S. And it lets 3Com, which invested $160 million in the venture, fill gaps in its product line and exploit Huawei's low-cost operations. "It is a marriage of convenience," says one Western banker in Hong Kong.

Why would 3Com's CEO Bruce Claflin marry his company to an accused pirate? Claflin says he did so only after 3Com had carried out a detailed investigation of Huawei's source code. Terms of the venture include warranties by Huawei that its products do not infringe intellectual rights. Even if certain Huawei products turn out to have Cisco code, Claflin believes it was not done with management's blessing and has confidence in the company's future offerings.

Cisco begs to differ. Officials say Huawei's infringements are more pervasive. When Huawei and 3Com announced their venture, the reaction at Cisco was, at best, mixed. While Claflin says he had a cordial chat that day with Cisco Chairman John T. Chambers, Cisco Executive Vice-President Charles H. Giancarlo says: "I was so mad I couldn't speak for three days."

Now, China's networking star is back on its heels, and there is little relief in sight. Following Cisco's suit, the company says it's eager to address Cisco's concerns and establish a clean bill of health. But Cisco is keeping the pressure on. It has filed the suit in plaintiff-friendly East Texas, near Huawei's Dallas office. And it's not ruling out suing Huawei in other countries or suing the joint venture. Huawei must also refute charges from U.S. officials that it skirted U.N. sanctions by selling network gear to Saddam Hussein's regime. "It's absolutely untrue," says Huawei's Executive Vice-President Guo Ping.

For Huawei, this is all part of a painful and risky transition. While CEO Ren Zhengfei has brought in top-shelf consultants such as IBM to help build the 15-year-old company, it has benefitted from cheap labor, strong government support, and a relaxed attitude about intellectual rights. That worked as it grew in the Chinese market. But the battle in global markets means hewing to tougher rules. "We want to be judged by the same standards as any world-class company," says Guo.

Even beyond legal concerns, Cisco has reason to keep Huawei on the run. Cisco, with $18.9 billion in 2002 sales, dominates the global market for network gear. Its gross margins are a mouthwatering 70%. That contributed to Cisco's 35% earnings growth, to $987 million, in the quarter ended in April, even while revenue fell 4.2%, to $4.6 billion. Although smaller, Huawei typically undersells Western rivals by 30% or more and is content with lower margins. Even now, weakened by SARS and the Cisco lawsuit, the company is feared. "Huawei is a threat to everyone," says Christine Heckart, vice-president for marketing at rival Juniper Networks (JNPR) Inc. "They bid on everything that moves."

And they've been selling products that look and feel much like Cisco's. For years, even casual observers could see that Huawei's Quidway routers had Cisco-lookalike model numbers and technical specs. Now, Cisco claims that Huawei copied hundreds of pages of Cisco manuals. And Cisco says it found some of its own bugs in Huawei's software. "It's about as likely as two people sitting down to write Hamlet and coming up with exactly the same words," says Michael Howard, principal analyst at Infonetics, a market researcher. Huawei denies that it copied Cisco's products.

3Com's Claflin says he confronted Huawei executives with these issues. In the course of a technical review during the joint venture talks, the companies say they learned that one Huawei engineer admitted using software from a CD he had been given in 1999 that included Cisco code for a little-used networking standard. Last fall, Huawei and 3Com agreed to remove the potentially tainted code from their joint offerings. Claflin's team also urged Huawei to replace its Cisco-like commands, manuals, and packaging with 3Com's. Huawei officials say they agreed to.

In December, before suing, Cisco lined up support in China. Chief Counsel Mark Chandler says he notified the Chinese government of the pending suit and sounded out its reaction. Cisco's leverage: global trade. Having joined the World Trade Organization only in 2001, China is eager to shed its reputation as the world's leading haven for software piracy. As a result, the government appears to be letting Huawei fend for itself. Says an official at China's Ministry of Information Industry: "The government will not give any political help to Huawei."

It looks like a rough slog for the odd couple. True, Cisco sounds a conciliatory note. "Our goal has always been to simply have them stop copying our [intellectual property]," says Chandler. "When there's a verifiable mechanism in place to do that, the litigation ends." But now that Cisco has a fearsome rival on the run, any settlement is likely to be on Cisco's terms.

Source: Peter Burrows in San Mateo, Calif., with Bruce Einhorn in Hong Kong. Copyright 2003, by The McGraw-Hill Companies Inc. All rights reserved.

BusinessWeek

3Com CEO Bruce Claflin defends his outfit's new Chinese partner, deriding charges of intellectual-property theft as "interesting theatrics."

Bruce Claflin, CEO of struggling networking company 3Com Corp., caused a furor in March by announcing a sweeping joint venture with China's Huawei Technologies—just weeks after Huawei had been sued on a range of intellectual-property violations by 3Com's (COMS) Silicon Valley neighbor, Cisco Systems (CSCO). The suit claims that Huawei's products include some of Cisco's carefully guarded source code and that Huawei infringes on copyrights related to Cisco's computer commands and such (see *BW*, 5/19/03, "Cisco: In Hot Pursuit of a Chinese Rival").

A federal judge in East Texas is considering Cisco's motion for a preliminary injunction to prevent Huawei from selling many of its products in the U.S. market. Industry observers predict Cisco may also go after the joint venture once it begins selling products this fall.

Claflin sat down for two extended interviews with *BusinessWeek*'s Computing Editor Peter Burrows in April and early May. The CEO gave his perspective on his company's new partner and the "irrelevant" lawsuit, and he made no secret of his annoyance at how Huawei CEO Ren Zhengfei is portrayed in the U.S. press. Edited excerpts of their conversation follow:

Q: Cisco Executive Vice-President Charlie Giancarlo says he couldn't speak for three days after finding out that 3Com—a longtime respected rival—had done a joint venture with a company Cisco had accused of stealing. Are you surprised to hear that he said that?
A: It's interesting theatrics. They want to portray this as good guys vs. bad guys. But it's not that simple.

Q: You've said that your negotiations with Huawei began in mid-2002, long before Cisco filed suit in January. But even then there were rampant rumors that Cisco might sue Huawei because of the similarities of its routers to Cisco's products. Had you heard these rumors?
A: By that time, Cisco executives were already firing shots across Huawei's bow, making comments in public and such. Huawei knew it would get sued by Cisco and that it would get sued in the U.S.

Q: What were your impressions of Huawei when you first visited the company in August, 2002?
A: They were shrouded in mystery, but it was amazing. There are all these talented engineers, sitting in ample offices with all the latest computers and software. And they have the most advanced robotic [parts warehousing] facility I've ever seen. Let's face it, people have the perception of China as a low-tech, low-cost kind of place. But my first impression was that this was truly a great technology company. It blows your mind when everyone thinks China is all about exploiting low-cost labor.

Q: In the course of reviewing Huawei's products while negotiating the joint venture, were you concerned about some of the similarities to Cisco's products—such as the model numbers, the packaging and such?
A: I asked 3Com's lawyers, and they said [the appearance, names and operating commands] probably didn't infringe [in these areas]. But my judgment was: Why risk it? Why get that close? Huawei agreed to change these things.

Q: What about Cisco's claims that Huawei stole its source code, a much more serious allegation?
A: We looked into Huawei's entire software-development process. We found one case that made us nervous. One engineer said he had seen a CD from a third-party consultant [that seemed to contain Cisco source code related to a little-known networking protocol called EIGRP]. The 3Com side said, let's just ship the [joint-venture] products without EIGRP, since it's not very popular anyway. Huawei agreed to 3Com's proposal.

Q: Why do you think Cisco sued when and where it did? Why the U.S., and not China? And why in Texas rather than in Silicon Valley?
A: Listen, they aren't dummies. I do believe Cisco feels its intellectual property was infringed, but it's not the whole story. There are two courts they care about: the court of law and the court of public opinion. I bet there's not one company out there that doesn't somehow infringe on Cisco in some way. Why did Cisco sue this particular company, at this particular time, in this particular place? I think it's because they view Huawei as a very dangerous competitor. Cisco wanted to do something to get in their way—it wants to cast doubt in the minds of customers.

Q: Huawei and 3Com spent nine months in negotiations leading up to the joint venture. What did you learn about Chinese views on IP in that time?
A: The cultural standard in China's business culture is that IP has to be significant to be worth protecting. They will respect IP if it creates material and has significant impact. Culturally, any Chinese business has difficulty understanding U.S. intellectual-property law. Their idea is that you only protect real innovation.

Q: What do you make of that view? Is that better than our system?

A: Five years ago, I would have said no. But now, I think the U.S. has a problem. We're running around registering patents on innovations that hardly matter.

Q: What did you learn about Ren Zhengfei, Huawei's CEO?

A: If I was to tell you his story and he was an American, we would call it an incredible American success story. Yet instead, all the papers say he's "a former People's Republic of China army official." I find that personally repugnant. Let me be blunt. Mr. Ren, like almost every other able-bodied man of his generation in China, served in the army. My son is a pilot in the U.S. Marine Corps. I'd hate to think that someone years from now would say he's not fit to run a company just because he served his country.

Q: Has anyone questioned your ethics for having done a joint venture with a company that had been accused of crimes by a respected U.S. company?

A: I haven't had anyone question my ethics directly. But one analyst did start attacking Huawei as if they were guilty of the crimes Cisco alleged. I said, "I don't want to be rude, but you have very firmly held opinions on this. Where does that come from? Just because someone tells you something, do you believe it? Is that how you do your research?" His preconceived notion was guilty until proven innocent.

Q: Cisco says it respects 3Com as a rival, and respects 3Com's promise that products sold by the Huawei-3Com joint venture won't infringe Cisco's patents. Still, it's certainly possible that Cisco will sue the joint venture. What would happen then?

A: If Cisco were to sue the joint venture, it's 100% certain that we would countersue. It would be very different than just suing Huawei [which, unlike 3Com, has no U.S. patents with which to negotiate a settlement].

Q: So what's the importance of the lawsuit, from your perspective?

A: The dispute is irrelevant, because we've already addressed all of Cisco's concerns.

Source: Edited by Patricia O'Connell. Copyright 2003, by The McGraw-Hill Companies Inc. All rights reserved.

Chapter

12

Foreign Investment

Chapter Objectives

Foreign investment represents the greatest strategic commitment to foreign markets, and presents the greatest level of risk and reward for international businesspersons.

In this chapter, we discuss

- The business objectives of firms and the social objectives of governments as actors and hosts in foreign investment.
- The risks, rewards, and management challenges in operating branches, subsidiaries, and joint ventures.

- The role and effect of national and international law in governing these operations.
- The private law tactics used in creating and maintaining foreign investments.

Introduction

No greater decision can face a firm engaged in international business than the decision to make foreign investments, particularly in the case of active commercial investment (establishment of operations), but equally so in passive portfolio investment (buying securities issued abroad). The firm must decide whether to commit itself to the foreign market in a manner that involves the highest degree of capital investment and the longest commitment to goal achievement, in a situation often difficult to unravel. This all takes place in an environment that may be susceptible to radical change, with the firm's reduced capability of understanding and adapting to cultural differences. As a result, the commercial potential of such an opportunity should be clear on its face, or capable of explanation in sound and tight commercial terms. If the commercial realities of foreign investment are not well founded, the venture will, at all times, be at serious risk, and no amount of legal creativity will be able to change the situation.

Such an introduction is a brutal one, but "overseas investment" has much in the way of uncharted waters and dangerous rocks that are ready, able, and do sink many ventures. Having said that, the opportunities for commercial gain through foreign investment are there, and can be large, as well as exciting and challenging. Investment abroad may bring new products and processes to new markets, and these new markets may be the source of products and processes unheard of at home. This opportunity to stand with a foot in both territories can represent a major commercial advantage in each territory. As this chapter speaks of foreign investors and local markets, it amounts to the reverse of terminology used elsewhere in the text. The "foreign" aspect now refers to the outside investor acting towards the "local" market where the investment is to be located, unless the context is clear to the contrary.

Business Objectives in Foreign Investment

The business objectives of commercial firms and their legal advisors are as diverse as the markets they serve. If there can be any generality in stating commercial objectives for foreign investment, they usually take one or more of the following forms:

1. Establishment of a physical presence or point of contact.
2. Maintaining control over the supply and distribution chain.
3. A lack of alternatives to providing local service.
4. Local operations required to comply with government requirements or prohibitions.
5. Local operations that comply with consumer and market preferences.
6. Overcoming of transportation challenges.
7. Economies of scale or incentives.
8. Cost advantages in local production or sourcing.

Examples of these are as follows:

1. Presence and contact	A goal in almost all cases, but particularly important for banks.	Citibank, HSBC
2. Systemic (in-house) control	Goods manufacture or distribution	Wal-Mart, IBM
3. No service alternative	Natural resources Restaurants and service firms	Rio Tinto Mines, Shell Oil, McDonald's
4. Government requirements	Where local participation or ownership required	Often in developing nations, or sectorally almost anywhere
5. Consumer preferences	Breweries, dairies	Interbrew, Danone
6. Transportation challenges	Cement, sugar, and perishables	Lafarge, Tate & Lyle
7. Scale economies/incentives	Autos and high technology	Ford, Toyota, Samsung
8. Cost advantages	Where local low-cost labor or materials are available	In developing nations, generally

Where foreign investment is considered, it is usually because the options of merely exporting, distribution, or licensing simply fail to address the commercial realities of the foreign market, either because of its size, local customization needs, or government attitude to these other vehicles. Needless to say, a foreign firm considering investment may have any number of these concerns and constraints acting simultaneously on it.

The foreign firm also may evolve through a series of increasing investment steps from a mere representative office (though some can be quite large) to a wholly owned operating subsidiary or joint venture (though many are quite small). In between these notional extremes are branch operations.

Forms of Foreign Direct Investment

Foreign direct investment refers to overseas investment in productive assets in one country by a firm established in another country. This investment in active business operations separates foreign direct investment (FDI) from portfolio or passive investments in securities.

Passive Investments

Passive minority positions in corporate shareholding (either public or private) are regulated in the first instance by the governing law of business corporations or business associations in the host country. Beyond this, the issuance, ownership, and transfer of corporate shares between passive investors will come within the scope of the host nation's securities regulation laws. This form of foreign investment creates credit risk, currency convertibility/ repatriation, and exchange rate risk, and may trigger special tax rules applicable to dividend and capital flows abroad. Other than to make these general observations, this chapter focuses on active business operation investments, transactions designed to directly engage the foreign investor with the economy of the host nation.

Representative Offices

A representative office acts as an outpost of the foreign firm operating abroad. These tend to be small operations, but in the case of some service industries such as banking, they are small outposts with sometimes heavyweight power in the local economy. In banking, the representative office books the local loan and credit operations with its head office abroad. For industrial and distribution firms, representative offices are used to maintain a presence in the local market, coordinating orders, sales, and service.

The key difference between the representative office and any other form of doing business abroad is the fact that with representative offices, active business operations do not occur in the local market, or the legal fiction is permitted that they do not occur in the local market. This legal fiction is, as above, carrying the local market activity on the account books of the head office as though it was the head office doing the work from a distance. For this reason, the local operation does not generate local market income, and therefore cannot be said to be carrying on business in the local territory. Thus, in a manner acceptable to the local tax authorities, true representative offices and their parent firms abroad are locally tax-exempt. Their revenues and expenses will be recognized for tax purposes in their home jurisdiction.

Tax authorities, however, watch representative offices carefully for any sign that they are becoming active in the local economy. The establishment of repair or warranty services, or setting up the warehousing of goods for distribution, may be sufficient to trigger a tax authority declaration that the foreign firm is actually carrying on business in-country, making it thereafter subject to tax. This concern may be grave, not just because local tax rates may be high. It may be the case that the jurisdiction taxes not only local source income, but also will want to tax the worldwide income of the overseas group, from which the representative office is otherwise indivisible.

The toleration of representative offices by local governments stems from the fact that this local representation is seen to be beneficial for their local economic links to the rest of the world. Secondly, the local government is acting in recognition of the fact that the same privilege is generally extended by other nations of the world to the firms of that local territory. In some cases, particularly in situations such as banking, nations may place limits on foreign investment and participation in key sectors. This may limit the foreign role to representative status only, as full economic licenses are either unavailable or (in the opinion of the foreign investor) have undesirable conditions attached to them.

While financial institutions are frequent users of the representative office form, it should be repeated that many other businesses use this form as well, and further, that many financial institutions go on to become fully functional and locally licensed within their markets abroad.

Branch Operations

The branch operation is one step beyond the representative office in terms of its participation in the local economy. This may include the full range of commercial activity in the local market and submission to local regulation of those activities.

Establishment of a branch, however, does not create a separate legal entity, as the overseas firm contracts in its own name for its real estate, employees, sales, and other operations. As such, a local manager acts as agent for its overseas controlling interests. This results in all the same liabilities that an agent may create, either in tort or contract. Branches will be subject to local taxation on their local source income, and depending on the jurisdiction, this may extend to an attempt to tax the worldwide income of the overseas controlling interest.

Generally, as nonresidents of the local jurisdiction tend to staff senior management positions in branches, and since branch profits flow directly back to nonresidents, branches are ineligible to receive investment and tax incentives otherwise available to foreign investors and local domestic firms.

Assuming decent tax treatment, there are still good reasons for the establishment of branches. First, local foreign investment regulation may not permit actual foreign ownership of a domestic firm, and second, this step may be part of an evolution beyond a representative office on the way to the third form of participation, the foreign subsidiary or joint venture.

Foreign Subsidiaries and Joint Ventures

Establishment of a foreign subsidiary represents the most extensive commitment a foreign firm can make in an overseas jurisdiction. Here, a legal entity will be created in and under the law of the local jurisdiction, or an existing one will be purchased. This new or existing entity may take the form of a corporation or a partnership, may be wholly foreign owned, or may be the product of a joint venture.

While substantial investments can be made in branch operations, subsidiaries tend to involve even greater amounts of capital investment, as well as greater costs associated with their start-up of operations. In addition to cost is time, for often a process of governmental screening takes place prior to the local incorporation of the subsidiary or the purchase of an existing business. After screening and other registration and licensing formalities are complete, the firm is ready to commence operations.

As the subsidiary is a creature of the incorporating jurisdiction, it will be subject to all the laws, regulations, and taxing authority of that jurisdiction. Where foreigners own all or part of the subsidiary, it may be subject also to further special foreign ownership rules. These rules may be beneficial, in the form of investment incentives or concessions: reduced tax rates, for example. Alternatively, and from a completely different mindset, special rules may work a hardship on foreign investors. There may be continued denial of market access to certain sensitive sectors, or there may be caps on their share of ownership if sectoral participation is permitted at all. They also may be denied preferential tax rates that are offered only to locally incorporated firms beneficially owned by local residents. This should immediately give rise to the recognition that no general rule of "national treatment" exists in international law with respect to foreign investment.

All of these drawbacks aside, the foreign investor may conclude that no other alternative to a subsidiary or joint venture can properly and sufficiently address the major commercial opportunities presented by an overseas market. In the case of such joint ventures, the arrangement may be a contractual joint venture (a form of partnership) between the foreign and local party, or it may be an equity joint venture, in which the two sides take shares in one new or existing locally incorporated business.

Foreign Government Policy Objectives

Development and Growth

Among a range of views, governments of the world see a particularly attractive attribute in foreign investment: money for nothing. It is easy to see why: the nation receives this investment from an external source, and the money immediately gets to work creating jobs

Beware of nations offering hefty tax incentives and special concessions for foreign investment. Not all such nations are bad, not even most of them, but why must they offer incentives in the first place? Are they really stable? Incentives and concessions are only as good as the government giving them. With a change of government, policies often change, and promises vanish.

for local people, often bringing with it capital goods, equipment, and technologies. However, viewed from a second perspective, one also held by those same governments, foreign investment necessarily means foreign control of assets, and later resulting cash flows leaving the country. Two words should come to mind from this second observation: *sovereignty* and *taxation.*

No other balancing act goes more directly to the heart of governments anywhere: the forces of economic growth and development versus sovereignty and taxation. This is the double-edged sword of foreign investment, and each nation must establish its economic priorities accordingly.

In nations where foreign investment can greatly add to its potential for economic development, the risk is also the greatest for long-term loss of its wealth, or "national patrimony." If these nations embraced all inbound foreign investment, ultimately there may be nothing left for the local residents to own or do once they are able, as everything worth having or doing will have already been bought or done by foreigners. This dilemma is not confined to developing nations; developed nations habitually place significant restrictions or prohibitions on foreign ownership in banks, media, telecommunications, airlines, power generation, ownership and taxation of land, and arms production.

Nations that are successful in attracting foreign investment do not do so purely because they offer foreigners tax incentives, cheap labor, or raw materials. First and foremost, the best of them are successful because they offer stable and predictable business environments, adequate infrastructure, and dependable legal systems. These are the true preconditions for foreign investment. The remainder are transient at best.

Investment Screening

The majority of nations of the world employ governmental screening processes before permitting foreign direct investment in their territory. Over the past two decades, these screening processes have generally become more liberal. Often there are monetary thresholds before any screening process is invoked, and increasing competition between nations for available foreign investment has served to raise those threshold levels. The 1999 revised rules of the Australian Foreign Investment Review Board may be taken as a case in point, with thresholds quoted in Australian dollars:[1]

> The notification threshold for foreign investment in existing businesses has been increased from $5 million ($3 million for rural businesses) to $50 million. The notification threshold for the acquisition of the Australian assets of an offshore company where it is to be acquired by another offshore company has been increased from $20 million to $50 million. Where properties are not subject to heritage listing, the notification threshold applying to the acquisition of developed non-residential commercial real estate has been increased from $5 million to $50 million. Moreover, the limit for which applications for investment in business and developed non-residential commercial properties are registered, but generally not fully

---

[1] As of early 2004, 1 Australian dollar = approximately 0.77 U.S. dollar.

examined, has been increased from $50 million to $100 million, unless the facts of the proposal raise issues pertaining to the national interest.[2]

Screening at lower thresholds, or mandatory screening in all cases, exists in virtually all of Asia and Africa, whereas some nations such as The Netherlands and Belgium have no screening procedures at all. Consequently, the specific reporting and screening procedures for any nation must be reviewed on a case-by-case basis. Even where broad screening processes do not exist, particular economic sectors may still have foreign ownership limits, and reporting requirements found in securities regulation will be encountered in corporate takeovers.

Competition Policy

Nations are particularly concerned that corporate takeovers may distort competition in their local markets. As a result, major corporate takeovers are reviewed for these distorting effects, regardless of whether they involve foreign investment or not. On the international front, while competition and antitrust review comparable to the U.S. Sherman Act is nothing new, there are recent developments of particular note.

When legislators around the world first began drafting antitrust legislation, none considered that the world would become as economically integrated as it is today. Legislators are now faced with the fact that a merger or takeover between two firms in a distant land may have a dramatic competitive effect in their own markets.

If all nations of the world agreed that a particular merger (a combining of two or more business entities) or a takeover (an investment by one firm in acquiring ownership of another) was an anticompetitive event, then there would be no problem. Such a merger or takeover would be prohibited everywhere. But what of the situation where a merger or takeover is approved in one nation and forbidden by another, on the basis of different competitive effects? The problem created by this situation relates to foreign investment, but not in the traditional sense of the words—it represents a veto of the transaction by one jurisdiction unless the merged business firm decides not to do business in the objecting jurisdiction.

Unfortunately, "just forgoing a jurisdiction" is not likely to be a viable commercial option. To attract the attention of competition and antitrust authorities, the proposed investment/merger/takeover is probably huge in the first place. As it is huge, it probably cannot write off major global markets without serious financial consequences, which places the viability of the original transaction in doubt. When the markets and antitrust authorities in question are those of the United States and the European Union, it is a major problem on both sides of the Atlantic, and for the firms involved.

The first major international case to attract widespread notice was the merger between U.S. aerospace firms Boeing and McDonnell Douglas, which was approved in the United States on July 1, 1997, and only reluctantly so by the European Union on July 24, 1997. This case brought the question of disagreement into focus, and it became a reality in 2001 in the proposed $45 billion takeover/merger of Honeywell International Inc. by the General Electric Company, both U.S. firms. This transaction was approved by the U.S. Department of Justice Anti-Trust Division, subject to minor required concessions by the firms, but was refused as a whole by the Commission of the European Union. In the eyes of the Commission, the transaction failed the EU dominance tests with regard to vertical integration, conglomerate effects, and horizontal overlap.[3] Consequently, the firms called off the transaction, as the exclusion of the merged firm from the EU market made it a com-

---

[2]*Foreign Investment Policy in Australia—A Brief History and Recent Developments,* The Commonwealth Treasury, Australia, 1999, p. 69. May be reviewed at http://www.treasury.gov.au/documents/195/PDF/round5.pdf.

[3]Case No. COMP/M.2220, General Electric/Honeywell, Commission Decision of 03/07/2001, pursuant to Council Regulation 4064/89 on the Control of Concentrations between Undertakings, as amended.

mercial impossibility. Hopefully, the problem is now sufficiently in focus that the EU and the United States will work constructively toward a solution, but it currently seems to be without an effective resolution short of a joint assessment process.

Employee Protection

Widely varying standards of labor and employee protection exist among the nations of the world. Virtually every foreign investor therefore will be engaging employees in nations whose labor standards vary to some extent from more familiar provisions at home.

Firms may find a legitimate competitive advantage in lower wage jurisdictions, but in the fullness of time, this becomes a limited advantage, for increases in local wealth increase both the local standard of living and expected wage rates. A business strategy that is founded on permanently low overseas wages is therefore shortsighted at best and otherwise evil. Thankfully, these exploitative attitudes exist in a relatively tiny minority of foreign investors. One hopes that progress will continue (small as it has been) toward the raising of global labor standards, and that more local law and regulation will be encountered in the future to prevent exploitation.

For its part as a major consumer nation, the United States has enacted 19 U.S.C. § 1307, or Section 307 of the Tariff Act of 1930. This is a statutory prohibition on the importation into the United States (and authorizing Customs seizure) of products made in whole or in part with the use of convict, forced, or indentured labor under penal sanctions, including goods produced through forced or indentured child labor.

Other nations have taken considerable steps in the protection of their own employees. Western Europe has been the leader in effective social protection of workers, and these social attitudes are reflected in the labor laws and employment standards regulation. Eastern Europe can be taken as one philosophical home of worker rights, but the mighty ideals under communist and socialist law achieved mixed results in practice. One can be assured that as Eastern European nations become fully integrated members of the EU, EU standards will be adopted, for this is a condition of membership.[4]

Employment standards regulation is, however, *not* uniform across the EU, and this imposes a due diligence requirement on any foreign investor and their legal advisor considering the establishment of operations. European trade and industrial unions are proportionally more powerful, diverse, and politically active than their North American counterparts, adding a further dimension of research for potential foreign investors.

The German experience can be taken as a case in point, and from Spain to Sweden many of these statutory provisions will be found. In addition to restrictions found in collective agreements, the termination of employees is a sensitive issue at law, and restricts employers in their flexibility.

Germany's "Protection Against Dismissal Act,"[5] or Kündigungsschutzgesetz, applies to firms regularly employing more than five employees and to those employees who have completed six months' continuous employment. While the employer may dismiss workers in this probationary period, thereafter, those qualifying workers may only be dismissed on grounds of incompetence, inappropriate conduct, or redundancy. While the first two forms of dismissal are for cause and are unproblematic (bearing in mind the normal requirements of progressive and documented discipline and notice), redundancy is interpreted much more strictly than might be expected by North Americans.

---

[4]In synopsis, the accession of candidate countries requires each to (1) be a stable democracy, respecting human rights, the rule of law, and the protection of minorities; (2) have a functioning market economy; and (3) adopt the common rules, standards, and policies that make up the body of EU law.

[5]One of a bundle of labor acts found in the German Civil Code, which further includes the Collective Wage Agreements Act, the Act on the Constitution of Business and Industrial Enterprises (the Works Constitution Act), and the Periods of Notice Act.

Decisions on redundancy are the employer's prerogative, but cannot be easily equated to the North American "layoff." The onus is on the employer to show that the job has actually ceased to exist, and the sale of a firm from one owner to a new investor is not a sufficient reason to justify termination of any or all employees in an effort to escape existing employment contracts. Where an employer attempts to justify redundancy on the basis of slow sales or downturn, it will be expected to first eliminate overtime, then reduce work hours for all employees, then apply social criteria for redundancy by selecting those for whom the loss of work will have the smallest impact. This entails selection not purely by seniority, but by evaluating the employee's retraining and job prospects, age, health, length of service, number of dependents, and financial situation.

Another feature not normally found in North America is the operation of works councils, or employee representation on the board of directors of the firm, as set out in the Works Constitution Act. Firms with more than five eligible employees must accommodate works councils, which have rights of codetermination with management in personnel decisions and social affairs and a right to be informed on business operations. At 100 employees, an economic council is added, and at 500 employees, one-third of the supervisory board of either a private or public company must be composed of employee representatives.

Forms of Business Associations

Public companies, private corporations, and general and limited partnerships exist in one form or another in almost all jurisdictions of the world. The names vary in local languages, and their translations into one language sound similar. Unfortunately, the similarity of names is pure deception, for the attributes of one "public company" or "limited liability company" are not consistent from jurisdiction to jurisdiction.

When presented with a choice between foreign business forms, the following dozen principal questions should be foremost in mind:

1. Is a separate legal entity created?
2. Is registration required?
3. Must accounts be made public (audited or otherwise)?
4. Is the ownership interest created through shareholding or membership?
5. Is there a minimum or maximum number of owners required or allowed?
6. Is an owner's interest transferable or not, and if so, on what conditions?
7. Do shares have fixed par values, or are no-par-value shares permitted?
8. Is an owner's liability limited or unlimited?
9. Can debt instruments be issued?
10. Do minimum (share) capital requirements exist?
11. Must an owner's share capital investment be actually subscribed and paid up, or will a promise suffice?
12. Must paid-up contributions be in cash, or are other asset contributions permitted?

If there are broad generalities that can be drawn, most jurisdictions provide for public stock corporations with freely transferable shares and with the corporations subject to public disclosure rules. Private corporations are generally permitted with significant restrictions on ownership and transfer of either shares or membership. Partnerships are founded on either general liability (of all partners) or limited liability (at least one partner with capped liability). Hybrids exist, from the U.S. limited liability partnership (a cross between the limited liability of a corporation and the flow-through finances of a partnership) to a Liechtenstein "Anstalt" or "Stiftung" (commercial establishment or foundation, respectively).

The following table illustrates some of this variety, grouped along relatively common lines frequently encountered in international business and foreign investment. Again, individual business forms will vary in rights, liabilities, and powers, even where the same names are used in each jurisdiction. The form identifiers that usually follow the name of a particular firm are shown in parentheses.

Variants in Corporate and Partnership Form

	France	Germany[7]	Spain	Italy	United Kingdom	Canada	Mexico	Japan
Public "stock" corporation[1]	Société anonyme (SA)	Aktiengesellschaft (AG)	Sociedad anónima (SA)	Società per Azioni (SpA)	Public Limited Company (PLC)	Limited, Ltd, Limitée, Ltée, Incorporated, Corporation, Corp.	Sociedad anónima (SA)	Kabushiki Kaisha (KK)
Private "limited liability" corporation[2]	Société à responsabilité limitée (SARL)	Geschellschaft mit beschränkter Haftung (GmbH)	Sociedad de responsabilidad limitada (SRL or SL)	Società a responsabilità limitata (Srl)	Limited (Ltd)		Sociedad de responsabilidad limitada (SRL)	Yugen Kaisha (YK)
General partnership	Société en nom collectif (SNC)	Offene Handelsgesellschaft (OHG)	Sociedad regular colectiva (SRC)	Società in nome collettivo (SNC)	[4]	[4]	Sociedad en nombre colectivo (SNC)	Gomei Kaisha
Limited partnership	Société en commandite simple (SCS)	Kommanditgesellschaft (KG)	Sociedad en comandita (SC)	Società in accomandita semplice (SAS)	[5]	[5]	Sociedad en comandita (S. en C.)	Goshi Kaisha
Limited partnership with shares[3]	Société en sommandite par actions (SCA)	Kommanditgesellschaft auf Aktien (KgaA)	Sociedad en comandita por acciones (SCA)	Società in accomandita per azioni (SAPA)	[6]	[6]	Sociedad en comandita por acciones (SCA)	[6]

[1]May or may not be listed on a stock exchange.
[2]Not to be confused with a U.S. "limited liability company" (LLC), where flow-through profits or losses are received by owner-members.
[3]Shares held by limited partner are transferable.
[4]No special designation.
[5]No special designation. Limited liability partnerships are designated LLP.
[6]No distinct local equivalent.
[7]These German forms are also found in Austria and Switzerland; Austria uses "Gesmbh" in place of GmbH.

The newest corporate development for international investors is the Societas Europaea (SE), an EU legal provision for the creation of a pan-European company, resulting from the 2001 Statute for a European Company.[6] After October 2004, any investor—European or otherwise—will be in a position to establish a company where a Community cross-border element is present, whose attributes will be recognized across all member states of the EU. This business form will be of significant interest to any investor who had to consider the need and trouble of establishing a number of subsidiaries in different EU states, each under different rules.

An SE will be a public limited liability company with legal personality and share ownership, with minimum capital of €120,000, and must establish its registered office in the EU member state where the central administration of the business takes place.

[6]Council Regulation (EC) No. 2157/2001 of 8 October 2001 on the Statute for a European Company (SE).

To qualify, the SE must be one of the following:

- The result of the merger of two or more existing public limited companies from at least two different EU member states.
- A holding company promoted by public or private limited companies from at least two different member states.
- A subsidiary of companies from at least two different member states.
- A transformation of a public limited company that has, for at least two years, had a subsidiary in another member state.

If this cross-border Community element is not present, the investor will be obligated as a default to establish its business under one of the existing forms available to it under the law of its chosen member state.

The SE will be able to operate on a European-wide basis on a single set of rules and a unified management and reporting system, governed by Community law directly applicable in all member states. The savings in cost, administration, and compliance should be significant in contrast to the difficulties in managing a complex network of subsidiaries. The SE will remain a taxpayer in the different member states where its permanent establishments are located.

The European Company statute has been decades in the making, largely due to the differing approaches taken in member states toward employee participation in management. This has finally been addressed in an accompanying directive on worker involvement, recognizing national differences.[7]

Political Risk

A firm intent on foreign investment will discover that many factors affect its chances of success that are not within its immediate management control, or are at least more removed than would be the case if the investment were made at home. It risks the loss in the overseas market of both its capital and income through external events. The risk of loss of capital arises not through poor management (though that may happen), but through the taking of foreign-owned assets by a host (local) government. The risk of loss of income stems first from the loss of the capital asset, but further from the possibility that its locally generated profits are forbidden from repatriation home, or that the currency in which they are denominated progressively becomes worthless. These capital and income losses result from policy choices of the host nation government, or, in other words, political risk.

Protection from losses such as these can never be adequately provided for to the satisfaction of foreign investors. However, governmental takings are a subject in international law that may give rise to a claim for compensation, and income losses may be mitigated through proper structuring of international investment and business transactions.

The Economic and International Law Dimensions of Political Risk

Political risk exists everywhere there is a government, even in the home jurisdiction of the foreign investor. Foreign investment responds to the level of this political risk, running away from jurisdictions where it is high to places where it is lower.

For investors established in the most politically stable territories, everywhere beyond their borders lie territories of increased risk. Presumably this is compensated by greater returns (such as higher prices or profits, due in part to the scarcity of competitors) or other-

[7]Directive 2001/86/EC.

wise outward foreign investment from stable nations would not take place at all. Persons with capital already located in unstable nations are headed away from them, with their intention of investing abroad representing their desire to find a safe haven for their assets. They are quite willing to accept lower investment returns in exchange for greater safety. The two groups often meet in the middle, or pass each other, based on their relative assessments of political risk.

General political risk stems from the turmoil of a restless population, resentful (rightly or wrongly) of those who govern them and the laws that constrain them. This turmoil can turn into impairment of productivity, markets, and, ultimately, the national economy. Dissent is a healthy part of most societies, but when it threatens all social order, the economic consequences are swift. On the supply side, work is not done or is done poorly, as workers who are preoccupied on social matters (including survival) strike or neglect their jobs. On the demand side, foreign orders dwindle, the demand for the currency of the nation falls, and its value falls in terms of all other currencies. Imports into that nation become proportionately more expensive, then finally out of reach to all but the elite. In a last effort short of martial law, the government blames all its problems on foreigners, an easy target given rising import prices.

General political risk then becomes asset-specific. The government forbids convertibility of the local currency into foreign currencies. This move has four objectives, which in the long run are futile:

1. To halt a decline in its foreign currency reserves (they will never increase again).
2. To prop up the value of the local currency (the world is not so easily fooled).
3. To control what is purchased abroad (thereby creating a black market).
4. To prevent capital and savings from slipping away toward less risky places (foreign currency will be hoarded—unused—and local currency will be rapidly spent in an attempt to convert it to hard goods, fueling inflation and further eroding the value of local currency).

These outcomes drive the government into taking (with or without compensation) the hard assets of foreigners situated in its jurisdiction, again as a measure of hopeful appeasement toward the local citizens. As is usual, therefore, the foreign investor is first to go up against the wall when the revolution comes.

Aside from the outright taking of a foreign investment, host governments exert their power in a number of ways over foreign direct investors. These include repudiating or forcing re-negotiation of contracts, extracting technology disclosures as a price for corporate departure, demanding repayment of loans made to the foreign firm or suspending payments owed to it, and blocking investor funds repatriation as part of its currency control. These are all political risks, and in the most extreme, the foreign direct investor risks actual destruction of assets in riot or civil war.

From the view of the victim-foreigner, this scenario is cast with the host government in the role of villain. However, the roles have often been reversed in the past, and will no doubt be so reversed in the future. The road to foreign investment ruin is littered with astonishing examples of political, economic, cultural, military, and industrial imperialism and colonialism exercised by powerful nations over weaker nations. The result should not be surprising to imperialists and colonialists. Those who would exploit others for their resources and labor must expect that one day the exploited will throw off their bonds and take back what they see as having been taken from them. Such are the lessons of the history of the world.

When colonial and imperial uses and abuses of past centuries came crashing down after the Second World War, dozens of new countries were formed. Their numbers swelled the ranks of the United Nations, each with a desire to affirm their sovereignty and to protect that sovereignty from not only foreign powers but foreign investors as well. This activist group[8] set the policy direction of UNCTAD, created in 1964 as the UN Conference on Trade and Development. After 10 years it achieved agreement on the Charter of Economic Rights and Duties of States, passed by UN General Assembly resolution.

UN Charter of Economic Rights and Duties of States

December 12, 1974

(Excerpt only, emphasis added)

Chapter II Economic Rights and Duties of States

Article 1

Every State has the **sovereign and inalienable** right to choose its economic system as well as its political, social and cultural systems in accordance with the will of its people, **without outside interference,** coercion or threat in any form whatsoever.

Article 2

1. Every State has and shall freely exercise **full permanent sovereignty, including possession,** use and disposal, over **all** its wealth, natural resources and economic activities.
2. Each State has the right:
   a. To regulate and exercise authority over foreign investment within its national jurisdiction **in accordance with its laws and regulations and in conformity with its national objectives** and priorities. No State shall be compelled to grant preferential treatment to foreign investment;
   b. To regulate and supervise the activities of transnational corporations within its national jurisdiction and take measures to ensure that such activities comply with its laws, rules and regulations and conform with its economic and social policies. Transnational corporations shall **not intervene in the internal affairs of a host State.** Every State should, with full regard for its sovereign rights, cooperate with other States in the exercise of the right set forth in this subparagraph;
   c. To nationalize, expropriate or transfer ownership of foreign property, in which case **appropriate** compensation should be paid by the State adopting such measures, taking into account its relevant laws and regulations **and all circumstances that the State considers pertinent.** In any case where the question of compensation gives rise to a controversy, it shall be settled **under the domestic law** of the nationalizing State and by its tribunals, unless it is freely and mutually agreed by all States concerned that other peaceful means be sought on the basis of the sovereign equality of States and in accordance with the principle of free choice of means.

- Among the bolded words, describe the manner in which a nation might use these rights to the disadvantage of foreign investors.

The Charter is drawn broadly, acknowledging expansive sovereign powers and control over foreign investment and economic activity. With this Charter in hand, a government would

[8]The G-77, so-called in 1964 for the number of nations making up their membership. While still referred to as the G-77, the number has grown to over 130 members. It includes most of the over 170 lesser-developed nations and over 40 least-developed nations by UN definition, and shares little in the way of common ground on more contentious aspects of foreign investment with the 30-member Organization for Economic Cooperation and Development (the 30 wealthiest developed nations).

have little trouble convincing itself that a policy taken in the name of the state to confiscate investments and assets of foreigners lies on a plane higher than "mere" international law or equity.

The debate of the degree of right and wrong in a contest between sovereign rights and property rights will continue. As will be seen below, governments in negotiation and tribunals in deliberation struggle with that balance, seeking determination of the limits of legality in expropriation and nationalization.

Expropriation and Nationalization

An expropriation is the taking by government of a privately owned asset through sovereign prerogative. Whether or not prompt, adequate, and effective compensation is given to the affected party is an irrelevancy to the existence of an expropriation. Such compensation only serves to turn an otherwise unacceptable expropriation (illegal or confiscatory) into a more acceptable one (legal) in the eyes of most of the nations of the world engaged in foreign investment. Each case of nationalization is an expropriation, but moreover nationalization is the larger taking of an entire industry or economic sector (e.g., the auto industry or agricultural sector, as opposed to a single firm). At times, expropriation and nationalization are discriminatory in nature, either explicitly so or when the relatively few investments taken from local nationals are eclipsed by much larger takings from foreign investors.

Expropriations are also sometimes described as "creeping," indirect, or de facto. This occurs where the host government enacts unending regulations, administrative requirements, laws, licenses, fees, and taxes, essentially only applicable to foreign investment operations. In time, the foreign-owned firm is strangled, no other foreign investor would buy out the foreign-owned firm, and the firm's only exit strategy is to sell out (if it can) at a low price to either the host government, its nominee, or the firm's local joint venture partner.[9]

As might be expected, foreign investors almost never consider compensation for expropriation to be adequate, sometimes think it is effective, and only rarely judge it to be prompt. "Adequate" speaks to the amount of the compensation, "effective" to its payment in a currency that has value, is convertible, and does not erode the adequacy of the payment. "Prompt" refers to timely delivery of the compensation. It also includes interest, if need be, from the time that the value of the asset is diminished or taken. In cases where all three conditions are fulfilled, it is usually in an expropriation of assets of a firm belonging to a close ally state of the expropriating nation. Even so, one has difficulty in recalling any story of a company delighted at the prospect and untold riches flowing to it from an expropriation.

International law, at least that driven by investing and trading nations, would like to see an additional requirement placed on expropriations, narrowing in particular the broad terms of Article 2(2)(c) of the UN Charter of Economic Rights and Duties of States. This international requirement would obligate expropriations to be for a public purpose, with due process and judicial review and without discrimination on the basis of nationality, all in addition to prompt, adequate, and effective compensation.

Pressing public purposes are not contested grounds for expropriation. All nations must make such decisions in their national interest, be it taking lands for a major road or reserving natural lands as parks, or in a wide range of other similar takings and purposes. What is objectionable is expropriation without a public purpose, or without due process and judicial review, or discrimination on the basis of nationality.

[9]Prime examples, both being arbitration cases done under the auspices of the International Center for Investment Disputes, are Case # ARB/ 77/1 *AGIP v. Democratic People's Republic of Congo*, (1982) 21 ILM 726, (1984) 67 ILR 318; and Case # ARB/77/2 *Benvenuti & Bonfant v. Democratic People's Republic of Congo*, (1982) 21 ILM 740 with correction at 1478, (1984) 67 ILR 345. *Benvenuti & Bonfant* appears later in this chapter.

Most nations recognize this as well, and short of multilateral agreements, the goal must be achieved bilaterally. In the over 40 bilateral investment treaties (BITs) concluded between the nations of North, Central, and South America, including Mercosur and NAFTA, provision is made to recognize these principles, with only a judicial review clause absent in a handful of cases. The Brazil-Venezuela, Ecuador-Paraguay, and Peru-Paraguay bilateral investment treaties do not describe "prompt, adequate, and effective" compensation, but do at least refer to a (more vague) "just compensation" requirement. The following example illustrates a very common format and level of foreign investment protection offered under bilateral investment treaties, seeking to establish an international minimum standard.

Bilateral Investment Treaty USA–Nicaragua

Treaty between the Government of the United States of America and the Government of the Republic of Nicaragua Concerning the Encouragement and Reciprocal Protection of Investment (Extract)

July 1, 1995

Article II

1. With respect to the establishment, acquisition, expansion, management, conduct, operation and sale or other disposition of covered investments, each Party shall accord treatment no less favorable than that it accords, in like situations, to investments in its territory of its own nationals or companies (hereinafter "national treatment") or to investments in its territory of nationals or companies of a third country (hereinafter "most favored nation treatment"), whichever is most favorable (hereinafter "national and most favored nation treatment"). Each Party shall ensure that its state enterprises, in the provision of their goods or services, accord national and most favored nation treatment to covered investments.

2. *a.* A Party may adopt or maintain exceptions to the obligations of paragraph 1 in the sectors or with respect to the matters specified in the Annex to this Treaty. In adopting such an exception, a Party may not require the divestment, in whole or in part, of covered investments existing at the time the exception becomes effective.

   b. The obligations of paragraph 1 do not apply to procedures provided in multilateral agreements concluded under the auspices of the World Intellectual Property Organization relating to the acquisition or maintenance of intellectual property rights.

3. *a.* Each Party shall at all times accord to covered investments fair and equitable treatment and full protection and security, and shall in no case accord treatment less favorable than that required by international law.

   b. Neither Party shall in any way impair by unreasonable and discriminatory measures the management, conduct, operation, and sale or other disposition of covered investments.

4. Each Party shall provide effective means of asserting claims and enforcing rights with respect to covered investments.

5. Each Party shall ensure that its laws, regulations, administrative practices and procedures of general application, and adjudicatory decisions, that pertain to or affect covered investments are promptly published or otherwise made publicly available.

Article III

1. Neither Party shall expropriate or nationalize a covered investment either directly or indirectly through measures tantamount to expropriation or nationalization ("expropriation") except for a public purpose; in a non-discriminatory manner; upon payment of prompt, adequate and effective compensation; and in accordance with due process of law and the general principles of treatment provided for in Article II, paragraph 3.
2. Compensation shall be paid without delay; be equivalent to the fair market value of the expropriated investment immediately before the expropriatory action was taken ("the date of expropriation"); and be fully realizable and freely transferable. The fair market value shall not reflect any change in value occurring because the expropriatory action had become known before the date of expropriation.
3. If the fair market value is denominated in a freely usable currency, the compensation paid shall be no less than the fair market value on the date of expropriation, plus interest at a commercially reasonable rate for that currency, accrued from the date of expropriation until the date of payment.
4. If the fair market value is denominated in a currency that is not freely usable, the compensation paid—converted into the currency of payment at the market rate of exchange prevailing on the date of payment—shall be no less than:
   a. the fair market value on the date of expropriation, converted into a freely usable currency at the market rate of exchange prevailing on that date, plus
   b. interest, at a commercially reasonable rate for that freely usable currency, accrued from the date of expropriation until the date of payment.

Source: Over 40 U.S. bilateral investment treaties exist and are administered by the Department of State. U.S. BITs may be reviewed at http://www.state.gov/e/eb/rls/fs/1139.htm.

- A U.S. investor may in fact receive greater protection than a Nicaraguan investor, should the Nicaraguan government decide to nationalize the assets of both investors. How would this be the case?

The concept of prompt, adequate and effective compensation stems from one of the 20th century's earliest such expropriations after the 1917 Mexican Revolution: the nationalization of U.S. petroleum interests in Mexico. The resulting diplomatic notes between Washington and Mexico City have since become legendary, and insistence on prompt, adequate, and effective compensation has become the American-inspired "international minimum standard" for compensation in expropriation. Widespread acceptance of these principles between these and other nations argues for their existence under the general law among nations, but before such an assertion can be made, one must look at other very important views that refuse to fully fade away.

One concept that still remains in constitutions or the minds of Latin American nations and jurists is the Calvo Doctrine.[10] Carlos Calvo, an Argentinean diplomat and jurist, created this legal mechanism in the late 1800s. It was in response to European and U.S. military moves into the internal affairs of the Americas. While these military expeditions were cloaked with a range of reasons, one intention was to enforce private rights—repayment of financial loans to these states through gunboat diplomacy. The Calvo Doctrine affirmed the equality of sovereign states, in which foreign nationals were not entitled to special rights

---

[10]At one time or another, part of the law of Mexico, Ecuador, Peru, Venezuela, Bolivia, Honduras, El Salvador, Cuba, and embodied in Decision 24 of the Andean Pact (though now loosened by Decision 220 allowing national choice in such matters).

while abroad,[11] and those foreign investors and their investments were subject to local law and tribunals as they found them.

While Calvo could not prevent military action, he could strip away the legal right of private investors to actively seek the protection and assistance of their home states. This was done through what became known as the Calvo clause (inserted into contracts between states and individuals), while the Calvo Doctrine found its way into many regional constitutions.[12]

The most-well-known Calvo clause case is that of North American Dredging, put before the U.S.-Mexico Claims Commission in 1926. Under the Treaty of September 8, 1923, the Claims Commission was a tribunal designed to bring settlement to claims against Mexico resulting from nationalization and related issues conducted by the revolutionary government prior to that date. The U.S. Department of State now considers the Calvo Doctrine to be dead, a notion that is small comfort to an expropriated investor (particularly for those not American), as it will be the investor who will be obligated to contest that fact. The *North American Dredging* case makes clear that while an individual cannot bind its nation from coming to its aid, it can waive the right to seek that aid; moreover, aggrieved investors must be prepared to exhaust their local remedies before seeking shelter elsewhere.

North American Dredging Company of Texas (U.S.A.) v. United Mexican States

U.S.–Mexico Claims Commission, 1926

This case is before this Commission on a motion of the Mexican Agent to dismiss. It is put forward by the United States of America on behalf of North American Dredging Company of Texas, an American corporation, for the recovery of the sum of $233,523.30 with interest thereon, the amount of losses and damages alleged to have been suffered by claimant for breaches of a contract for dredging at the port of Salina Cruz, which contract was entered into between the claimant and the Government of Mexico, November 23, 1912. The contract was signed at Mexico City. The Government of Mexico was a party to it. It had for its subject matter services to be rendered by the claimant in Mexico. Payment therefor was to be made in Mexico. Article 18, incorporated by Mexico as an indispensable provision, not separable from the other provisions of the contract, was subscribed to by the claimant for the purpose of securing the award of the contract. Its translation by the Mexican Agent reads as follows:

> "The contractor and all persons who, as employees or in any other capacity, may be engaged in the execution of the work under this contract either directly or indirectly, shall be considered as Mexicans in all matters, within the Republic of Mexico, concerning the execution of such work and the fulfilment of this contract. They shall not claim, nor shall they have, with regard to the interests and the business connected with this contract, any other rights or means to enforce the same than those granted by the laws of the Republic to Mexicans, nor shall they enjoy any other rights than those established in favor of Mexicans. They are consequently deprived of any rights as aliens, and under no conditions shall the intervention of foreign diplomatic agents be permitted, in any matter related to this contract."

---

[11]A departure from the ancient practice of exempting foreigners from the application of local law, a concept heavily reinforced through the 1800s by colonial powers.

[12]It remains in Chapter 27 of the Mexican Constitution, wholly at odds with, but probably trumped by, the constitutional nature of NAFTA Chapter 11 provisions on dispute settlement.

1. The jurisdiction of the Commission is challenged in this case on the grounds . . . that a contract containing the so-called Calvo clause deprives the party subscribing said clause of the right to submit any claims connected with his contract to an international commission.

The Calvo Clause

4. The Commission does not feel impressed by arguments either in favor of or in opposition to the Calvo clause, in so far as these arguments go to extremes. The Calvo clause is neither upheld by all outstanding international authorities and by the soundest among international awards nor is it universally rejected . . . By merely ignoring world-wide abuses either of the right of national protection or of the right of national jurisdiction no solution compatible with the requirements of modern international law can be reached.

6. The Commission also denies that the rules of international public law apply only to nations and that individuals can not under any circumstances have a personal standing under it . . .

Lawfulness of the Calvo Clause

10. What Mexico has asked of the North American Dredging Company of Texas as a condition for awarding it the contract which it sought is, "If all of the means of enforcing your rights under this contract afforded by Mexican law, even against the Mexican Government itself, are wide open to you, as they are wide open to our own citizens, will you promise not to ignore them and not to call directly upon your own Government to intervene in your behalf in connexion with any controversy, small or large, but seek redress under the laws of Mexico through the authorities and tribunals furnished by Mexico for your protection?" and the claimant, by subscribing to this contract and seeking the benefits which were to accrue to him thereunder, has answered, "I promise."

11. Under the rules of international law may an alien lawfully make such a promise? The Commission holds that he may, but at the same time holds of that he cannot deprive the government of his nation of its undoubted right of applying international remedies to violations of international law committed to his damage. Such government frequently has a larger interest in maintaining the principles of international law than in recovering damage for one of its citizens in a particular case, and manifestly such citizen cannot by contract tie in this respect the hands of his Government. But while any attempt to so bind his Government is void, the Commission has not found any generally recognized rule of positive international law which would give to his Government the right to intervene to strike down a lawful contract, in the terms set forth in the preceding paragraph 10, entered into by its citizen . . .

Interpretation of the Calvo Clause in the Present Contract

15. What, therefore, are the rights which claimant waived and those which he did not waive in subscribing to article 18 of the contract? (a) He waived his right to conduct himself as if no competent authorities existed in Mexico; as if he were engaged in fulfilling a contract in an inferior country subject to a system of capitulations; and as if the only real remedies available to him in the fulfilment, construction, and enforcement of this contract were international remedies. All these he waived and had a right to waive. (b)

He did not waive any right which he possessed as an American citizen as to any matter not connected with the fulfilment, execution, or enforcement of this contract as such. (c) He did not waive his undoubted right as an American citizen to apply to his Government for protection against the violation of international law (internationally illegal acts) whether growing out of this contract or out of other situations. (d) He did not and could not affect the right of his Government to extend to him its protection in general or to extend him its protection against breaches of international law. But he did frankly and unreservedly agree that in consideration of the Government of Mexico awarding him this contract, he did not need and would not invoke or accept the assistance of his Government with respect to the fulfilment and interpretation of his contract and the execution of his work thereunder. The conception that a citizen in doing so impinges upon a sovereign, inalienable, unlimited right of his government belongs to those ages and countries which prohibited the giving up of his citizenship by a citizen or allowed him to relinquish it only with the special permission of his government.

The Calvo Clause and the Claimant

18. If it were necessary to demonstrate how legitimate are the fears of certain nations with respect to abuses of the right of protection and how seriously the sovereignty of those nations within their own boundaries would be impaired if some extreme conceptions of this right were recognized and enforced, the present case would furnish an illuminating example. The claimant, after having solemnly promised in writing that it would not ignore the local laws, remedies, and authorities, behaved from the very beginning as if article 18 of its contract had no existence in fact. It used the article to procure the contract, but this was the extent of its use. It has never sought any redress by application to the local authorities and remedies which article 18 liberally granted it and which, according to Mexican law, are available to it, even against the Government, without restrictions, . . . The record before this Commission strongly suggests that the claimant used article 18 to procure the contract with no intention of ever observing its provisions.

The Calvo Clause and the Claims Convention

19. Claims accruing prior to the signing of the Treaty must, in order to fall within the jurisdiction of this Commission under Article I of the Treaty either have been "presented" before September 8, 1923, by a citizen of one of the Nations parties to the agreement "to [his] Government for its interposition *with the other,*" or, after September 8, 1923, "such claims"—i.e., claims presented for interposition—may be filed by either Government *with this Commission.* Two things are therefore essential, (1) the presentation by the citizen of a claim to his Government and (2) the espousal of such claim by that Government . . .

20. Under article 18 of the contract declared upon the present claimant is precluded from presenting to its Government any claim relative to the interpretation or fulfillment of this contract.—If it had a claim for denial of justice, for delay of justice or gross injustice, or for any other violation of international law committed by Mexico to its damage, it might have presented such a claim to its Government, which in turn could have espoused it and presented it here. Although the claim as presented falls within the first clause of Article I of the Treaty, describing claims coming within this Commission's jurisdiction, it is not a claim that may be rightfully presented by the claimant to its Government for espousal and hence is not cognizable here, pursuant to the latter part of paragraph 1 of the same Article I.

Extent of the Present Interpretation
of the Calvo Clause

23. [E]ach case involving application of a valid clause partaking of the nature of the Calvo clause will be considered and decided on its merits. Where a claim is based on an alleged violation of any rule or principle of international law, the Commission will take jurisdiction notwithstanding the existence of such a clause in a contract subscribed by such claimant. But where a claimant has expressly agreed in writing, attested by his signature, that in all matters pertaining to the execution, fulfillment, and interpretation of the contract he will have resort to local tribunals, remedies, and authorities and then wilfully ignores them by applying in such matters to his Government, he will be held bound by his contract and the Commission will **not** take jurisdiction of such claim.

Decision

25. The Commission decides that the case as presented is not within its jurisdiction and the motion of the Mexican Agent to dismiss it is sustained and the case is hereby dismissed without prejudice to the claimant to pursue his remedies elsewhere or to seek remedies before this Commission for claims arising after the signing of the Treaty of September 8, 1923.

Concurring opinion

Parker, Commissioner:

My fellow Commissioners construe article 18 of the contract before the Commission in this case to mean that with respect to all matters involving the execution, fulfillment, and interpretation of that contract the claimant bound itself to exhaust all remedies afforded under Mexican law by resorting to Mexican tribunals or other duly constituted Mexican authorities before applying to its own Government for diplomatic or other protection, and that this article imposes no other limitation upon any right of claimant.

They further hold that said article 18 was not intended to and does not prevent claimant from requesting its Government to intervene in its behalf diplomatically or otherwise to secure redress for any wrong which it may heretofore have suffered or may hereafter suffer at the hands of the Government of Mexico resulting from a denial of justice, or delay of justice, or any other violation by Mexico of any right which claimant is entitled to enjoy under the rules and principles of international law, whether such violation grows out of this contract or otherwise. I have no hesitation in concurring in their decision that any provision attempting to bind the claimant in the manner mentioned in this paragraph would have been void *ab initio* as repugnant to the rules and principles of international law.

. . .

Accepting as correct my fellow Commissioners' construction of article 18 of the contract, I concur in the disposition made of this case.

Source: (1926) 4 R.I.A.A. 26.

- Assume North American Dredging had gone to a Mexican court seeking damages of $233,523.30 but did not receive a fair hearing. What steps could it have then taken, and how and for what reasons might the Commission decision have been different?

The requirement of exhaustion of local remedies is predicated on the basis that there *are* local remedies available to be exhausted. If due process has been denied, the aggrieved foreign investor will be entitled to not only a minimum standard of compensation, but also a complete indemnity, *restitutio in integrum.*

After the First World War, as part of the Treaty of Versailles and the Geneva Convention, Germany ceded the city of Chorzów[13] and the entire region of Upper Silesia to Poland. The Polish government could further expropriate German **state** assets in this region, but not those of individual German **nationals,** with the value of properly expropriated assets credited to Germany's financial reparations. The Polish government did so, expropriating a factory through a court proceeding that was essentially an administrative fiat, and by merely altering the land registry. The factory—the now-famous (in international law, at least) "Chorzów Factory"—was later determined by the Permanent Court of International Justice to have been, in fact, private property of a German national rather than German state property. The Court drew the following conclusions on the proper degree of compensation in an illegal expropriation where due process was lacking.

Case Concerning the Factory at Chorzów

Judgment No. 13, Claim for Indemnity—The Merits
Permanent Court of International Justice
September 13, 1928

The action of Poland which the Court has judged to be contrary to the Geneva Convention is not an expropriation—to render which lawful only the payment of fair compensation would have been wanting; it is a seizure of property, rights and interests which could not be expropriated even against compensation . . .

It follows that the compensation due to the German Government is not necessarily limited to the value of the undertaking at the moment of dispossession, plus interest to the day of payment. This limitation would only be admissible if the Polish Government had had the right to expropriate, and if its wrongful act consisted merely in not having paid to the two Companies the just price of what was expropriated; in the present case, such a limitation might result in placing Germany and the interests protected by the Geneva Convention, on behalf of which interests the German Government is acting, in a situation more unfavourable than that in which Germany and these interests would have been if Poland had respected the said Convention. Such a consequence would not only be unjust, but also and above all incompatible with the aim of . . . the Convention—that is to say, the prohibition, in principle, of the liquidation of the property, rights and interests of German nationals and of companies controlled by German nationals in Upper Silesia—since it would be tantamount to rendering lawful liquidation and unlawful dispossession indistinguishable in so far as their financial results are concerned.

The essential principle contained in the actual notion of an illegal act—a principle which seems to be established by international practice and in particular by the decisions of arbitral tribunals—is that reparation must, as far as possible, wipe-out all the consequences of the illegal act and re-establish the situation which would, in all probability, have existed if that act had not been committed. Restitution in kind, or, if this is not possible, payment of a sum corresponding to the value which a restitution in kind would bear; the award, if need be, of damages for loss sustained which would not be covered by restitution in kind or payment in place of it—such are the principles which should serve to determine the amount of compensation due for an act contrary to international law.

This conclusion particularly applies as regards the Geneva Convention, the object of which is to provide for the maintenance of economic life in Upper Silesia on the basis of

[13]Pronounced "Kor-zhoff."

respect for the *status quo*. The dispossession of an industrial undertaking—the expropriation of which is prohibited by the Geneva Convention—then involves the obligation to restore the undertaking and, if this be not possible, to pay its value at the time of the indemnification, which value is designed to take the place of restitution which has become impossible. To this obligation, in virtue of the general principles of international law, must be added that of compensating loss sustained as the result of the seizure. The impossibility, on which the Parties are agreed, of restoring the Chorzów factory could therefore have no other effect but that of substituting payment of the value of the undertaking for restitution; it would not be in conformity either with the principles of law or with the wish of the Parties to infer from that agreement that the question of compensation must henceforth be dealt with as though an expropriation properly so called was involved.

Source: P.C.I.J., 1928, Series A, No. 17. Available at http://www.worldcourts.com/pcij/eng/cases/ chorzow2.html.

- The Polish government took a factory. Now it must give back not only the value of the factory, but something more as well. What does this "something more" represent? Why is Poland responsible for repayment of more than it took? Why would it be unacceptable to only order repayment of what was taken?

The Calvo Doctrine is largely abandoned. The existence of due process; nondiscrimination as to nationality; a public purpose; and prompt, adequate, and effective compensation are sufficient to save an expropriation from illegality. Thus, providing it abides by these conditions, a state may use expropriation to give effect to its full permanent sovereignty over all its wealth, natural resources, and economic activities and the activities of foreign investors.

Still, the international community lacks a truly multilateral treaty on the treatment of foreign investment and must rely on its web of bilateral arrangements. The friction between the priorities of the G-77 nations and the OECD seems to ensure that a broad multilateral agreement will remain beyond reach for the foreseeable future. The far-reaching OECD draft Multilateral Agreement on Investment (MAI) died in 1998 as a result of a perceived lack of transparency in its drafting. It suffered from the public's inherent suspicion of an agreement drafted by the wealthy in search of support from the less fortunate, and the simple fact that much of it represented an unacceptable policy commitment for lesser-developed nations.

The future forum for multilateral investment negotiation and the creation of normative rules will be the WTO, as it evolves further in its de facto role as leader in governance of economic relations between states; both UNCTAD and the OECD are unfortunately stamped with the mark of their respective members. There are also strong indications of the direction of these future normative rules, which are found in the nonbinding "soft-law" of the present day. These are the World Bank Guidelines on the Treatment of Foreign Direct Investment. They have an OECD flavor, and because they represent the preferred terms of the World Bank, the Guidelines are a sword over heads of those nations who are most likely to oppose them. Those nations are also those who are in most need of World Bank funding.

Particular note should be given to Part IV of the Guidelines on expropriation, alteration and termination of contracts, and the preferred manner of calculation of prompt, adequate, and effective compensation.

World Bank Guidelines on the Treatment of Foreign Direct Investment

(Preamble omitted)

I. Scope of Application

1. These Guidelines may be applied by members of the World Bank Group institutions to private foreign investment in their respective territories, as a complement to applicable bilateral and multilateral treaties and other international instruments, to the extent that these Guidelines do not conflict with such treaties and binding instruments, and as a possible source on which national legislation governing the treatment of private foreign investment may draw. Reference to the "State" in these Guidelines, unless the context otherwise indicates, includes the State or any constituent subdivision, agency or instrumentality of the State and reference to "nationals" includes natural and juridical persons who enjoy the nationality of the State.

2. The application of these Guidelines extends to existing and new investments established and operating at all times as *bona fide* private foreign investments, in full conformity with the laws and regulations of the host State.

3. These Guidelines are based on the general premise that equal treatment of investors in similar circumstances and free competition among them are prerequisites of a positive investment environment. Nothing in these Guidelines therefore suggests that foreign investors should receive a privileged treatment denied to national investors in similar circumstances.

II. Admission

1. Each State will encourage nationals of other States to invest capital, technology and managerial skill in is territory and, to that end, is expected to admit such investments in accordance with the following provisions.

2. In furtherance of the foregoing principle, each State will:
   a. facilitate the admission and establishment of investments by nationals of other States, and
   b. avoid making unduly cumbersome or complicated procedural regulations for, or imposing unnecessary conditions on, the admission of such investments.

3. Each State maintains the right to make regulations to govern the admission of private foreign investments. In the formulation and application of such regulations, States will note that experience suggests that certain performance requirements introduced as conditions of admission are often counterproductive and that open admission, possibly subject to a restricted list of investments (which are either prohibited or require screening and licensing), is a more effective approach. Such performance requirements often discourage foreign investors from initiating investment in the State concerned or encourage evasion and corruption. Under the restricted list approach, investments in non-listed activities, which proceed without approval, remain subject to the laws and regulations applicable to investments in the State concerned.

4. Without prejudice to the general approach of free admission recommended in Section 3 above, a State may, as an exception, refuse admission to a proposed investment:
   i. which is, in the considered opinion of the State, inconsistent with clearly defined requirements of national security; or
   ii. which belongs to sectors reserved by the law of the State to its nationals on account of the State's economic development objectives or the strict exigencies of its national interest.

5. Restrictions applicable to national investment on account of public policy *(ordre publi-lic)*, public health and the protection of the environment will equally apply to foreign investment.

6. Each State is encouraged to publish, in the form of a handbook or other medium easily accessible to other States and their investors, adequate and regularly updated information about its legislation, regulations and procedures relevant to foreign investment and other information relating to its investment policies including, *inter alia,* an indication of any classes of investment which it regards as falling under Sections 4 and 5 of this Guideline.

III. Treatment

1. For the promotion of international economic cooperation through the medium of private foreign investment, the establishment, operation, management, control, and exercise of rights in such an investment, as well as such other associated activities necessary therefor or incidental thereto, will be consistent with the following standards which are meant to apply simultaneously to all States without prejudice to the provisions of applicable international instruments, and to firmly established rules of customary international law.

2. Each State will extend to investments established in its territory by nationals of any other State fair and equitable treatment according to the standards recommended in these Guidelines.

3. *a.* With respect to the protection and security of their person, property rights and interests, and to the granting of permits, import and export licenses and the authorization to employ, and the issuance of the necessary entry and stay visas to their foreign personnel, and other legal matters relevant to the treatment of foreign investors as described in Section 1 above, such treatment will, subject to the requirement of fair and equitable treatment mentioned above, be as favorable as that accorded by the State to national investors in similar circumstances. In all cases, full protection and security will be accorded to the investor's rights regarding ownership, control and substantial benefits over his property, including intellectual property.

   b. As concerns such other matters as are not relevant to national investors, treatment under the State's legislation and regulations will not discriminate among foreign investors on grounds of nationality.

4. Nothing in this Guideline will automatically entitle nationals of other States to the more favorable standards of treatment accorded to the nationals of certain States under any customs union or free trade area agreement.

5. Without restricting the generality of the foregoing, each State will:

   a. promptly issue such licenses and permits and grant such concessions as may be necessary for the uninterrupted operation of the admitted investment; and

   b. to the extent necessary for the efficient operation of the investment, authorize the employment of foreign personnel. While a State may require the foreign investor to reasonably establish his inability to recruit the required personnel locally, e.g., through local advertisement, before he resorts to the recruitment of foreign personnel, labor market flexibility in this and other areas is recognized as an important element in a positive investment environment. Of particular importance in this respect is the investor's freedom to employ top managers regardless of their nationality.

6. (1) Each State will, with respect to private investment in its territory by nationals of the other States:

   a. freely allow regular periodic transfer of a reasonable part of the salaries and wages of foreign personnel; and, on liquidation of the investment or earlier termination of the employment, allow immediate transfer of all savings from such salaries and wages;

b. freely allow transfer of the net revenues realized from the investment;

c. allow the transfer of such sums as may be necessary for the payment of debts contracted, or the discharge of other contractual obligations incurred in connection with the investment as they fall due;

d. on liquidation or sale of the investment (whether covering the investment as a whole or a part thereof), allow the repatriation and transfer of the net proceeds of such liquidation or sale and all accretions thereto all at once; in the exceptional cases where the State faces foreign exchange stringencies, such transfer may as an exception be made in installments within a period *which* will be as short as possible and will not in any case exceed five years from the date of liquidation or sale, subject to interest as provided for in Section 6 (3) of this Guideline; and

e. allow the transfer of any other amounts to which the investor is entitled such as those which become due under the conditions provided for in Guidelines IV and V.

(2) Such transfer as provided for in Section 6 (1) of this Guideline will be made (a) in the currency brought in by the investor where it remains convertible, in another currency designated as freely usable currency by the International Monetary Fund or in any other currency accepted by the investor, and (b) at the applicable market rate of exchange at the time of the transfer.

(3) In the case of transfers under Section 6 (1) of this Guideline, and without prejudice to Sections 7 and 8 of Guideline IV where they apply, any delay in effecting the transfers to be made through the central bank (or another authorized public authority) of the host State will be subject to interest at the normal rate applicable to the local currency involved in respect of any period intervening between the date on which such local currency has been provided to the central bank (or the other authorized public authority) for transfer and the date on which the transfer is actually effected.

(4) The provisions set forth in this Guideline with regard to the transfer of capital will also apply to the transfer of any compensation for loss due to war, armed conflict, revolution or insurrection to the extent that such compensation may be due to the investor under applicable law.

7. Each State will permit and facilitate the reinvestment in its territory of the profits realized from existing investments and the proceeds of sale or liquidation of such investments.

8. Each State will take appropriate measures for the prevention and control of corrupt business practices and the promotion of accountability and transparency in its dealings with foreign investors, and will cooperate with other States in developing international procedures and mechanisms to ensure the same.

9. Nothing in this Guideline suggests that a State should provide foreign investors with tax exemptions or other fiscal incentives. Where such incentives are deemed to be justified by the State, they may to the extent possible be automatically granted, directly linked to the type of activity to be encouraged and equally extended to national investors in similar circumstances. Competition among States in providing such incentives, especially tax exemptions, is not recommended. Reasonable and stable tax rates are deemed to provide a better incentive than exemptions followed by uncertain or excessive rates.

10. Developed and capital surplus States will not obstruct flows of investment from their territories to developing States and are encouraged to adopt appropriate measures to facilitate such flows, including taxation agreements, investment guarantees, technical assistance and the provision of information. Fiscal incentives provided by

some investors' governments for the purpose of encouraging investment in developing States are recognized in particular as a possibly effective element in promoting such investment.

IV. Expropriation and Unilateral Alterations or Termination of Contracts

1. A State may not expropriate or otherwise take in whole or in part a foreign private investment in its territory, or take measures which have similar effects, except where this is done in accordance with applicable legal procedures, in pursuance in good faith of a public purpose, without discrimination on the basis of nationality and against the payment of appropriate compensation.

2. Compensation for a specific investment taken by the State will, according to the details provided below, be deemed "appropriate" if it is adequate, effective and prompt.

3. Compensation will be deemed "adequate" if it is based on the fair market value of the taken asset as such value is determined immediately before the time at which the taking occurred or the decision to take the asset became publicly known.

4. Determination of the "fair market value" will be acceptable if conducted according to a method agreed by the State and the foreign investor (hereinafter referred to as the parties) or by a tribunal or another body designated by the parties.

5. In the absence of a determination on agreed by, or based on the agreement of, the parties, the fair market value will be acceptable if determined by the State according to reasonable criteria related to the market value of the investment, i.e., in an amount that a willing buyer would normally pay to a willing seller after taking into account the nature of the investment, the circumstances in which it would operate in the future and its specific characteristics, including the period in which it has been in existence, the proportion of tangible assets in the total investment and other relevant factors pertinent to the specific circumstances of each case.

6. Without implying the exclusive validity of a single standard for the fairness by which compensation is to be determined and as an illustration of the reasonable determination by a State of the market value *of* the investment under Section 5 above, such determination will be deemed reasonable if conducted as follows:
   i. for a going concern with a proven record of profitability, on the basis *of* the discounted cash flow value;
   ii. for an enterprise which, not being a proven going concern, demonstrates lack of profitability, on the basis of the liquidation value;
   iii. for other assets, on the basis of (a) the replacement value or (b) the book value in case such value has been recently assessed or has been determined as of the date of the taking and can therefore be deemed to represent a reasonable replacement value.
   For the purpose of this provision:
   —a *"going concern"* means an enterprise consisting of income-producing assets which has been in operation for a sufficient period of time to generate the data required for the calculation of future income and which could have been expected with reasonable certainty, if the taking had not occurred, to continue producing legitimate income over the course of its economic life in the general circumstances following the taking by the State;
   —*"discounted cash flow value"* means the cash receipts realistically expected from the enterprise in each future year of its economic life as reasonably projected minus that year's expected cash expenditure, after discounting this net cash flow for each year by a factor which reflects the time value of money, expected inflation, and the risk associated

with such cash flow under realistic circumstances. Such discount rate may be measured by examining the rate of return available in the same market on alternative investments of comparable risk on the basis of their present value;

—*"liquidation value"* means the amounts at which individual assets comprising the enterprise or the entire assets of the enterprise could be sold under conditions of liquidation to a willing buyer less any liabilities which the enterprise has to meet;

—*"replacement value"* means the cash amount required to replace the individual assets of the enterprise in their actual state as of the date of the taking; and

—*"book value"* means the difference between the enterprise's assets and liabilities as recorded on its financial statements or the amount at which the taken tangible assets appear on the balance sheet of the enterprise, representing their cost after deducting accumulated depreciation in accordance with generally accepted accounting principles.

7. Compensation will be deemed "effective" if it is paid in the currency brought in by the investor where it remains convertible, in another currency designated as freely usable by the International Monetary Fund or in any other currency accepted by the investor.

8. Compensation will be deemed to be "prompt" in normal circumstances if paid without delay. In cases where the State faces exceptional circumstances, as reflected in an arrangement for the use of the resources of the International Monetary Fund or under similar objective circumstances of established foreign exchange stringencies, compensation in the currency designated under Section 7 above may be paid in installments within a period which will be as short as possible and which will not in any case exceed five years from the time of the taking, provided that reasonable, market-related interest applies to the deferred payments in the same currency.

9. Compensation according to the above criteria will not be due, or will be reduced in case the investment is taken by the State as a sanction against an investor who has violated the State's law and regulations which have been in force prior to the taking, as such violation is determined by a court of law. Further disputes regarding claims for compensation in such a case will be settled in accordance with the provisions of Guideline V.

10. In case of comprehensive non-discriminatory nationalizations effected in the process of large scale social reforms under exceptional circumstances of revolution, war and similar exigencies, the compensation may be determined through negotiations between the host State and the investors' home State and failing this, through international arbitration.

11. The provisions of Section I of this Guideline will apply with respect to the conditions under which a State may unilaterally terminate, amend or otherwise disclaim liability under a contract with a foreign private investor for other than commercial reasons, i.e., where the State acts as a sovereign and not as a contracting party. Compensation due to the investor in such cases will be determined in the light of the provisions of Sections 2 to 9 of this Guideline. Liability for repudiation of contract for commercial reasons, i.e., where the State acts as a contracting party, will be determined under the applicable law of the contract.

V. Settlement of Disputes

1. Disputes between private foreign investors and the host State will normally be settled through negotiations between them and failing this, through national courts or through other agreed mechanisms including conciliation and binding independent arbitration.

2. Independent arbitration for the purpose of this Guideline will include any ad hoc or institutional arbitration agreed upon in writing by the State and the investor or be-

tween the State and the investor's home State where the majority of the arbitrators are not solely appointed by one party to the dispute.

3. In case of agreement on independent arbitration, each State is encouraged to accept the settlement of such disputes through arbitration under the Convention establishing the International Centre for Settlement of Investment Disputes (ICSID) if it is a party to the ICSID Convention or through the "ICSID Additional Facility" if it is not a party to the ICSID Convention.

Source: World Bank Report #11415, Legal Framework for Treatment of Foreign Investment, Volume II, Guidelines, September 21, 1992. May be reviewed at http://www-wds.worldbank.org/(advanced search requesting Report 11415).

The World Bank Guidelines expect arbitration to play a major role in foreign investment dispute settlement, which is already the case on both an ad hoc basis and through mechanisms such as the World Bank's own ICSID, the International Centre for Settlement of Investment Disputes, established in 1966.

Arbitration, which is discussed more fully in Chapter 13, provides a means to resolution of conflict that is intended to be binding between the parties, but not having the effect of binding precedent as between others. That said, well-reasoned arbitral awards are highly persuasive, and their power cannot be dismissed.

In 1978, an arbitrator had the opportunity to consider the effect of a stabilization clause in a foreign investment agreement between a private enterprise and a sovereign state. A stabilization clause is a notional reverse of a Calvo cause, in that the sovereign government commits to the maintenance of its national law in status quo, at least as far as the beneficiary of the clause is concerned, for the life of the agreement. Whereas a Calvo clause is the waiver by private enterprise of its right to seek protection, the stabilization clause amounts to a state waiver of its right to wield its sovereignty, either to change the local law or to ignore its own commitment to utilize arbitration in dispute settlement.

In the case, *Texaco Overseas Petroleum et al. v. Libyan Arab Republic,*[14] the arbitrator held that such clauses in "internationalized" contracts (those between states and foreign business entities) were binding upon nations (see also *LIAMCO v. Libya,* discussed in this text in Chapter 2). Not only would minimum standard compensation be due in the event of expropriation or breach, but following the *Chorzów Factory* approach, the breach of the covenant of stability could not be redeemed by simple compensation. A breach of the stability clause was a wrong in and of itself and created liability in the state for full indemnity, including the investor's lost future profits. Bearing in mind that this is an arbitration award and not binding precedent, a foreign party contemplating direct investment with a sovereign government should still consider this as additional protection that it may negotiate for itself.

Profit and Capital Repatriation

The risk association with difficulties in repatriation of funds has been raised previously in this text in Chapter 9, "Trade Payment and Finance." A foreign-owned establishment will undoubtedly use the same strategies as a general trader in protecting the integrity of its locally generated, locally denominated cash flows, but it is also exposed to currency risk associated with its capital (its initial investment), as opposed to simply the income it produces.

The risks bear repeating here, for their effects can be more damaging to a foreign business that has sunk money into physical assets in the host country, particularly whether

1. Total exchange prohibition exists in that nation (funds, particularly foreign currencies, cannot be taken outside that nation for any reason) or

[14](1978) 17 I.L.M. 1.

Even the right to convert is worthless if one is forced to convert currency at the host nation's central bank, which may have no "hard" currency available, or limited or rationed amounts.

2. Partial exchange restriction exists (funds may be removed from a nation only for specified purposes; for example, the repatriation of capital but not profits) or
3. Limits or caps are imposed on withdrawals of foreign currency, either in general or for particular purposes or transactions or
4. Unrealistic government-imposed exchange rates are placed upon funds leaving that nation or
5. Similar requirements of mandatory conversions at unrealistic rates of exchange are imposed on foreign currencies entering that nation or
6. Bank accounts or borrowing in foreign currencies by persons or corporations resident in that nation are forbidden.

The foreign investor has two avenues to negotiate capital protection, which also may be used to obtain income protection, against some of the foreign currency risks associated with operations abroad.

The first may be contained in the foreign investment codes and laws of the host country itself. These may provide that foreign investors have a permanent and general right to convert the local currency into foreign currency, and to export that foreign currency, at least to the extent of the amount of its original investment, regardless of the existing rights of local residents. Note that the possibility of a limitation exists here, in that the privilege may or may not extend to any capital gain that has occurred in the interim between the time of investment and the time of exit. Alternatively, the issue may be provided for in any bilateral investment treaty between the investor's home state and the host government.

The investor's second opportunity to obtain protection, if it has some economic leverage to exert over the host government, occurs at the time of screening or local licensing of the venture. It may be possible at that time to negotiate a venture-specific right of convertibility with the local Department or Ministry of Finance, Taxation, or Foreign Investment.

Note that these represent only rights to convert currency, not a guarantee of the rate that will be obtained. The investor will be in no better position than others, other than it will have the right to convert and the ability to exit with its foreign currency holdings.

Operationally, the foreign investor will have even greater incentive than the goods trader will to find uses for local currency where risk or uncertainty of the value of the local currency is a concern. It also will have more uses for local currency as it has the expense of running its local operations, and should ensure that its payment obligations and contracts call for settlement in local currency—payrolls, supplies, rents and leases, and taxes.

Of course, the firm will hope to ultimately have a local surplus of local currency, if it is to generate a profit. Even in cases where the conversion or export of the local currency is totally blocked, the possibility to conduct countertrade by using this surplus to locally source raw materials for export (for self-use or resale) remains a possibility.[15]

At times, where a host nation places significant restrictions on currency convertibility, there still may be many foreign investors waiting to enter the market. This may be because of the size of that market, and/or the need for early entry to establish a good position, expecting currency convertibility to be just over the horizon. One instantly thinks of China

---

[15]Also described in Chapter 9.

The Old Wolf

The competitive offering of free toys with a kid's meal in U.S. fast-food restaurants emerged about the same time as those restaurants ventured into Asian markets having restrictions on hard currency repatriation of profits. A coincidence or a strategy dictated by local law? The world wonders.

in the late 1980s as an example. In such cases, a foreign investor who is already locally present with a stock of local currency profits it cannot convert may be able to strike a swap contract with the next inbound foreign investor. The contract would provide for the first investor to supply the local investment capital needs of the second investor, in local currency. The second investor would then settle with the first in "hard" convertible currency on an offshore basis, perhaps in the foreign country where their mutual world headquarters are located. The first investor hence disposes of its blocked funds, and the second gets the same (or more) local currency funds it would have had if it had entered the market with hard currency. The swap contract strategy works especially well between related subsidiaries of one firm, and, as per the example given, can be tailored to work between arm's-length companies.

Finally, a range of insurance and guarantee products are available from both the private sector and governmental agencies, which are described in the "Negotiated Investment Protection" section at the end of this chapter.

Wholly Owned Subsidiaries

Where a foreign firm does not need or does not want local participation in its venture, it will usually opt to establish a wholly owned subsidiary. As a result, all the locally generated profits and losses will belong to it and it alone, within a corporate structure that is a creature of the legislation of the host country. As well, a wholly and privately owned subsidiary may be exempt from a range of information reporting requirements, and the foreign investor will obtain and maintain control over its trade secrets and processes. All the previous material covered in this chapter will continue to apply, but there are observations that should be made about wholly owned subsidiaries that are of particular note, and are applicable as well to joint ventures, discussed in the section following.

Despite being locally incorporated, and therefore a technical resident of the incorporating jurisdiction, the fact that the firm is foreign-owned or controlled may trigger the application of other provisions of taxation, or deny it certain benefits that otherwise would be available. The prudent international businessperson and lawyer will verify the application and extent of such tax rules before committing investment to a particular jurisdiction. More happily, the venture will not be burdened with complex management decision making rules and dispute settlement procedures, as are necessary in joint ventures or other instances of local investor participation.

The mechanics of creation of business vehicles in foreign jurisdictions will often differ, as initially discussed above in the section on Forms of Business Associations. As between civil law and common law jurisdictions, civil law sees the involvement of a notary, a private person acting as a professional public servant in the creation and legalization of agreements and documents. Common law notaries perform services that are usually only secondary to the operation of business law in their jurisdictions, but under civil law the role and services of a notary are integral. He or she acts as a neutral third party in drafting binding documents, and acts under authority of law to create business associations such as corporations; these functions are normally performed in common law by adversarial lawyers in the first case, and by government departments in the second.

Asset versus Share Purchases

If the foreign investor chooses to establish a wholly owned new venture through incorporation, it will, by definition, own all the shares of that new corporation. On the other hand, the foreign investor may be attracted to the host nation on the basis of the acquisition opportunities that may be had, and the question then becomes whether to purchase the shares or the assets of a firm that is a going-concern. A share purchase may place the foreign firm in an advantageous position with local financial institutions, as the purchase represents continuation of the existing firm on a going-concern basis. It is not necessary to build up a wholly separate finance relationship from square one, something that is sometimes difficult for lenders and borrowers who have no prior experience with one another.

In the case of share purchases, as is likely the case in the foreign firm's home jurisdiction, it will acquire all rights and responsibilities of the local firm. This is subject to the loss of rights or the gain of additional responsibilities occasioned by a change in control, or a change in control to foreign ownership. Thus, what the buyer sees may not be what the buyer gets as intellectual property held by the local firm under license may be lost under "change of control" termination provisions, or the formerly attractive rate of tax may be unavailable to the foreign owners. It also may receive far more than what it bargains for, in a full host of unseen liabilities. These may include latent environmental or pollution violations, pending lawsuits, and equipment found to be leased rather than owned. Only local due diligence exercised prior to an offer to purchase shares can reveal these dimensions.

The foreign investor may feel therefore that an asset purchase from an existing firm most easily avoids this situation. In this fashion, and assuming a willing seller, the foreign firm can pick and choose between the assets it wants to buy and those it wants to avoid. While this works in principle, caution must be exercised, for host governments may intervene. In some nations, where a new investor intends to buy all or substantially all of the assets of an existing firm, law or regulation requires it to also honor many liabilities as well, such as the employment contracts of existing employees.

Build, Operate, and Transfer (BOT) Projects

The BOT project is a large-scale direct investment (foreign, in the context of international business law) comprising an undertaking to build a particular project in return for an operating concession for a period of years, followed by later transfer of the project to public ownership.

The format is most frequently used where a local government lacks the immediate funds or credit to pay for the project, but the project will be capable of generating its own revenues, such that its construction can be financed, after the fact, from them. Feasible BOT projects all have this built-in capacity to generate funds, typically being airports and seaports, toll bridges and highways, water and oil pipelines, dams and hydroelectric-generation projects, telephone systems, and the like. The future revenues in each case are derived from user fees.

The BOT project is generally, though not necessarily, confined to developing nations and large project engineering and management firms. It reflects a situation where the host government is unable or unwilling to raise the financing necessary for the project, and yet the foreign investor (who must initially finance it) is capable of doing so by its own creditworthiness.

In many jurisdictions, BOT projects are founded on broad statutes that apply to all such projects,[16] or each project may be founded on its own purpose-drafted piece of legislation.

[16]For example, Turkey's Law No. 3996 of 1994, Regarding Engagement in Investments and Services on the Build-Operate-Transfer Model; the Cambodian Anukret on Build-Operate-Transfer (BOT) Contract, Law No. 11/ANK/BK of 1998; Vietnamese Decree on Providing Investment Regulations on BOT, Decree L 62/1998/ND-CP of August 1998 as amended by No. 02/1999/ND-CP of January 1999.

Almost invariably, this legislation exempts the foreign investor from particular forms of taxation, or grants tax holidays, and import duties are waived on a wide range of goods, most often capital equipment to be used in construction. Additional incentives may be subject to individual negotiation, such as low-interest loans for partial financing or grants of land ownership.

Once the project is finished, the foreign investor embarks on a fixed period of operating concession in which it can recoup its costs and profits. The duration of this period may be fixed in governing law as it is in Turkey (49 years) and Cambodia (30 years), or it may be the subject of negotiation in the course of the original agreement, as is done in Vietnam.[17] After the operating concession expires, the foreign investor is obliged to hand over ownership and the right to future profits to the host government.

While the project represents infrastructure construction that is probably essential (and therefore capable of earning money), it is not difficult to foresee the legal problems that may arise from what is still a speculative venture. Most are variations of "who-will-share-in-the-loss." The project may cost more to build than expected, and the ability of an investor to forecast currency exchange rates into the distant future is guesswork at best. The project may be late in commencing operations. It may be unused or surpassed by other airports, other pipelines, or new technologies, torpedoing all sense in its original calculations of cost and profit. In a worst-case scenario for the investor, the host government may cancel the project before it even comes on-line. In the host government's worst-case scenario, the foreign investor may leave before project completion, due to engineering difficulties or corporate bankruptcy. These scenarios illustrate the investor's need to obtain political risk insurance, and the reasons that host governments will demand performance bonds and financial guarantees from the foreign investor.

Variations of the BOT project may result in two other forms of legal relationship, one between the investor and host and the other between a group of investors themselves. In the first, the host government becomes a major equity partner in, or creditor and lender to, the project. This arises in the (common) situation where the foreign investor must draw on its own creditworthiness, but international lenders and guarantee agencies demand to see host government participation in the project before they, in turn, will underwrite the balance of its costs. One cannot fault a third-party lender from wanting to ensure that all parties remain committed to the project. In the second contractual situation, the foreign investor is not alone, and a consortium is formed for construction of complex projects. This consortium may entail the creation of an investment corporation on behalf of all the foreign members, or it may be a partnership, or a contractual arrangement where no new business entity is established.

Joint Ventures

A joint venture, as its name implies, is a joint undertaking, which in the international business law context is between a foreign investor and an investor from the host country. This joint venture (JV) may be either contractual or an equity joint venture. In the first case, no new distinct business is created, and the parties perform their undertakings and share in the profits on a purely contractual basis. In the second situation, a separate partnership or corporation is established and the parties' rights and duties are set out in its founding documents. Commonly, the foreign investor may first establish a subsidiary in its home territory, a low tax jurisdiction, or the host country as its vehicle for representation, to minimize the potential for any flow-back of liability to its parent operation.

[17]Article 47 of the Turkish Law, Article 4 of the Cambodian Anukret, and Article 21 of the Vietnamese Decree, respectively.

Prenegotiation Considerations

The joint venture form may be selected as a result of any one or more of a range of factors. Most often these are

1. Host government limitations placed on corporate equity that may be owned by foreign investors, often 49 percent, thereby mandating local participation.
2. Host government limitations on types of assets that may be foreign owned, thereby mandating local participation.[18]
3. The foreign investor's requirements of embedded local expertise to ensure commercial success in that local market, driving the investor toward what is essentially a partnership.
4. Purpose-driven joint ventures to capture true synergies between the partners, for example, in research and development or manufacturing and distribution.
5. Risk-driven joint ventures where partnership effectively lowers the absolute level of risk borne by any one party.

It is critical that the joint venture have a clear sense of purpose, and one that is shared between the parties. All too often, joint ventures cast the parties into litigation on a range of issues that really boil down to differing views of the strategic direction of the firm. Thus, a lawsuit ostensibly about abuse of the minority shareholder by the majority shareholder is not about abuse at all, but rather the triumph in voting power of one competing strategic view over the other. Had the parties ensured that they had the same strategic mind and purpose in the first place, the courtroom or arbitral conflict would have been avoided.

In the particular context of international joint ventures where restriction on foreign ownership or difficult registration or licensing administration exists, such problems become acute. This particular class of problems often revolves around JV minority partners who are brought in to solve one-time or start-up problems but can be expected to contribute little to the long-run operation of the business. An example might be an international joint venture for the creation of fast-food restaurants. The foreign partner supplies the technology and know-how; the local partner provides food supplies and the land and buildings, and the third partner is the urban municipal government. The presence of this third partner is to ensure that there is deep local administrative commitment to the operation and to ensure the continued availability of water, gas, electricity, and sanitary service. This is fine, until the joint venture decides to expand into another municipality. The principal partners share perhaps 90 percent of the venture and have a continuing concrete offering to make in the expansion of the firm; in contrast, the first municipal government can offer nothing to the expansion, yet will expect to remain a 10 percent shareholder.

Undoubtedly the operational partners would like to take out the first municipal government partner and replace it with the municipal government of the second municipality. They would face a charge of abuse of the minority if they were to do so unilaterally, and their initial investment would suffer; electricity and gas service to their venture in the first municipality might suddenly become spotty.

The only means to avoid this is through proper planning and negotiation at the early stages of creation of the venture. The only long-term partners in the venture should be those who can make a long-term contribution to its success. All other "partners" should be rewarded for their services by being paid (or, in this example, be given a profit share from the operations located in their municipality), such that they do not become a long-term

---

[18]For example, foreign ownership of land may be prohibited, forcing the foreign investor to find a local partner who is in a position to provide land as its share of capital contribution to a new, locally formed corporation (equity joint venture) or as consideration in a contractual joint venture.

Both the international businessperson and his or her lawyer must watch for these potential conflicts and avoid getting boxed in where flexibility will be needed down the road. Always ask yourself before taking on a partner or joint venture party: Do I want and will I need to work forever with this person? If not, how will I get rid of him or her in a way that will not come back to haunt me?

drag on the success of the operation. The contemplation of their exit, with clear triggering events and a transparent process, must be part of the initial plan.

Joint Ventures in Highly Regulated or Controlled Legal Environments

As is suggested above, the joint venture form is often encountered in highly regulated jurisdictions. The jurisdiction with the greatest successful experience in joint ventures is that of the People's Republic of China, and the model that it has developed sets a standard for others to follow, both in theory and in practice. China now allows wholly foreign owned operations in its territory,[19] and as it has liberalized aspects of its regulation to conform to international standards both before and since becoming a member of the WTO, one expects that equity and contractual joint ventures will continue to decline in use in China. The joint venture form will not disappear, however, for the JV still represents an important vehicle for foreign investors to obtain Chinese market sensitivity, capability, and experience.

PRC Law on Sino-Foreign Joint Ventures

Adopted 1979, as amended 1990 and 2001

Article 1

In order to expand international economic co-operation and technological exchange the People's Republic of China shall permit foreign companies, enterprises and other economic entities or individuals (hereinafter referred to as foreign partners) to establish, within the territory of the People's Republic of China, equity joint ventures with Chinese companies, enterprises or other economic entities (hereinafter referred to as partners), in accordance with the principles of equality and mutual benefit that are subjected to the approval by the Chinese government.

Article 2

The Chinese government, pursuant to the provisions of agreements, contracts and articles of association which it has approved, shall protect foreign partners' investment in equity joint ventures, profits due to them and their other legal rights and interests in accordance with the law.

All activities of an equity joint venture shall be governed by the laws and regulations of the People's Republic of China.

[19]Law on Wholly Foreign-Owned Enterprises, adopted April 12, 1986, revised October 31, 2000, at the 18th Meeting of the Standing Committee of the National People's Congress by the Decision on Revision of the "Law of the People's Republic of China Concerning Enterprises with Sole Foreign Investment." The phrase "enterprises with sole foreign investment" is also known and bears the same meaning as "wholly foreign-owned enterprises." An English translation of the law (the Chinese version prevails) may be reviewed at the website of the Chinese Ministry of Commerce (MOFTEC) at http://english.mofcom.gov.cn.

The State shall not subject equity joint ventures to nationalization or expropriation. In special circumstances, however, in order to meet public interest requirements, the State may expropriate an equity joint venture in accordance with the legal procedures, but certain compensation must be paid.

Article 3

Equity joint venture agreements, contracts and articles of association to which the various parties to an equity joint venture are signatories shall be submitted to the state department in charge of foreign economics and trade (hereinafter referred to as an examining and approval authority) for examination and approval. An examining and approval authority shall decide whether or not to grant the approval within three months. Once approved, an equity joint venture shall register with a state administration for industry and commence operations after obtaining a business license.

Article 4

An equity joint venture shall take the form of a limited liability company.

The proportion of investment contributed by a foreign partner as its share of the registered capital of an equity joint venture shall in general be no less than 25 per cent.

Equity joint venture partners shall share profits and bear risks and losses in proportion to their contribution to the registered capital of an equity joint venture.

The transfer of one party's share of the registered capital shall be effected only with the consent of the other parties to the equity joint venture.

Article 5

Each party to an equity joint venture may contribute cash, capital goods, industrial property rights, etc., as its investment in the enterprise.

Technology and equipment contributed as investment by a foreign partner must genuinely be an advanced technology and equipment appropriate to China's needs. If losses occur due to deception resulting from the intentional supply of outdated technology or equipment, compensation shall be paid.

The investment contribution of a Chinese partner may include providing site-use rights for an equity joint venture during its period of operations. If site-use rights are not part of the Chinese partner's investment contribution the equity joint venture shall be required to pay site-use fees to the Chinese government.

The various items of investment mentioned above shall be specified in the equity joint venture contract and articles of association. The value of each item (excluding the site) shall be determined by the equity joint venture partners through joint assessment.

Article 6

An equity joint venture shall establish a board of directors composed of certain number of members determined through consultation by the equity joint venture partners and stipulated in the equity joint venture contract and articles of association. Each equity joint venture partner shall be responsible for the appointment and replacement of its own directors. The chairperson and deputy chairperson shall be selected by the equity joint venture partners through consultation or shall be elected by the board of directors. Where the chairperson is appointed from one party to an equity joint venture, the deputy chairperson shall be appointed from the other party. The board of directors, in accordance with the principles of equality and mutual benefit, shall decide all the important matters of an equity joint venture.

A board of directors is empowered to discuss and take action on, pursuant to the provisions of the articles of association of the equity joint venture, all the important issues concerning the enterprise, namely, enterprise development plans production and operational projects, its income and expenditure budget, profit distribution, labor and wage plans suspension of operations; as well as the appointment or hiring of general manager, deputy general manager, chief engineer, chief accountant and auditor, and determining their functions and powers, remuneration, etc.

The general and deputy general managers (or general and deputy factory heads) shall be appointed separately by each of the joint venture partners.

Matters such as the recruitment, dismissal, remuneration, welfare benefits, labor protection and labor insurance of employees of an equity joint venture shall be stipulated in contracts concluded in accordance with the law.

Article 7

Employees of an equity joint venture may establish a trade union organization according to the law for the promotion of trade union activities and the protection of the legal rights and interests of employees.

An equity joint venture shall provide its enterprise trade union with the necessary facilities for its activities.

Article 8

After payment of equity joint venture income tax on an enterprise's gross profit, pursuant to the tax laws of the People's Republic of China, and after deductions there from as stipulated in its articles of association regarding reserve funds, employee bonus and welfare funds and enterprise development funds, the net profit of an equity joint venture shall be distributed between the equity joint venture partners in proportion to their investment contribution to the enterprise's registered capital.

An equity joint venture may enjoy preferential treatment in the form of tax reductions or exemptions in accordance with the provisions of the relevant state tax laws and administrative regulations.

A foreign partner that reinvests its share of an equity joint venture's net profit within the Chinese territory may apply for a rebate on that portion of income tax already paid.

Article 9

An equity joint venture shall present its business license to a bank or other financial institution authorized by a state exchange control organ to engage in foreign exchange dealings and shall open a foreign exchange account.

An equity joint venture shall conduct its foreign exchange transactions in accordance with the Regulations of the People's Republic of China for Foreign Exchange Control.

An equity joint venture may, in its business operations, obtain funds directly from foreign banks.

The various items of insurance required by an equity joint venture shall be furnished by insurance companies within the Chinese territory.

Article 10

An equity joint venture, within its approved scope of operations and in accordance with the principles of fairness and reasonableness, may purchase raw materials, fuels, and other such materials from both domestic and international markets.

An equity joint venture shall be encouraged to sell its products outside China. It may sell its export products on foreign markets through its own direct channels or its associated agencies or through China's foreign trade establishments. Its products may also be sold on the domestic Chinese market.

If deemed necessary, an equity joint venture may establish branch organizations outside China.

Article 11

Net profit received by a foreign partner after executing obligations prescribed by the relevant laws, agreements and contracts, funds received on the termination or suspension of an equity joint venture's operations and other relevant funds may be remitted abroad in accordance with the exchange control regulations and in the currency specified in the equity joint venture contract.

A foreign partner shall be encouraged to deposit in the Bank of China foreign exchange that it is entitled to remit abroad.

Article 12

Wage income and other legitimate income earned by equity joint venture employees of foreign nationality may be remitted abroad in accordance with the exchange control regulations after payment of individual income tax pursuant to tax laws of the People's Republic of China.

Article 13

The duration of an equity joint venture's term of operations may differ, depending on the line of business and other differing circumstances. The term of operations of some types of equity joint ventures shall be set, while the term of operations of other types of equity joint ventures may be set in some cases, but not set in others. In the case of an equity joint venture which has its term of operations set, the term may be extended subject to the agreement of all equity joint venture partners and the lodging of an application with the examining and approval authority six months before the expiry of the joint venture term. The examining and approval authority shall decide whether to approve or reject an application within one month of its receipt.

Article 14

In the event of an equity joint venture incurring heavy losses, one party failing to execute its obligations as prescribed in the equity joint venture contract or articles of association, or force majeure, etc. the contract may be terminated subject to the negotiation and agreement reached by all parties of an equity joint venture, the approval of examining and approval authority and registration with a state administration for industry and commerce. If a loss is incurred due to a breach of contract, the party that violated the contract provisions shall bear the financial liability for the loss.

Article 15

Any dispute arising between equity joint venture partners that the board of directors is unable to settle through consultation may be resolved through conciliation or arbitration by a Chinese arbitral body or through arbitration conducted by an arbitral body agreed on by all parties of an equity joint venture.

If the parties of an equity joint venture have not stipulated an arbitration clause in their contract or do not reach a written arbitration agreement after a dispute has arisen, they may file a lawsuit in a people's court.

Source: Adopted July 1, 1979, at the 2nd Session of the 5th National People's Congress. Amended April 4, 1990, at the 3rd Session of the 7th National People's Congress in accordance with the Decision to Revise the Law of the People's Republic of China on Sino-Foreign Equity Joint Ventures. Amended March 15, 2001, at the 4th Session of the 9th National People's Congress in accordance with the Decision to Revise the Law of the People's Republic of China on Sino-Foreign Equity Joint Ventures. May be reviewed at China's Ministry of Commerce website at http://english.mofcom.gov.cn.

- Having read this law, what three factors contained in it do you feel have most contributed to the long-term growth and success of the Chinese business environment?

Having a joint venture law or, even where one exists, having a stable political environment where it will be respected is sometimes a luxury. Joint ventures operating under these conditions are risky in the extreme, particularly where the joint venture partner is a government whose priorities and policies can change rapidly for the worse. The following case highlights political risk in the joint venture context. It is an arbitration case with private parties sitting as a tribunal,[20] a common form of dispute settlement mechanism found in joint venture arrangements.

The parties had given jurisdiction to the tribunal to decide "on the merits," akin to using principles of equity and fairness. Some facts had been taken out of debate by the parties in settlement meetings prior to the hearing, and the argument advanced by the Congolese government was largely based on procedural objections and failed to substantiate a counterclaim. As a result, the award raises little in its discussion of law (Congolese, international, or any other), but the case remains important as an illustration of how a foreign investment opportunity can dissolve into a nightmare.

Benvenuti & Bonfant v. The Republic of the Congo

Ad Hoc Arbitration Tribunal (Trolle, Bystricky, and Razafindralambo, Members)
August 15, 1980

[The Tribunal President, Trolle, laid out a description of the preliminary issues and objections, and concluded the Tribunal had jurisdiction to hear the case.]

Towards the end of 1972, Benvenuti and Bonfant (B&B, the Italian corporate claimant) was instructed by the Republic of the Congo (the Government) to examine the feasibility of building and operating in the Congo a factory for the manufacture of plastic bottles.

B&B proposed that the Government should take a share of 40% in a mixed company[21] to be formed. This share was later increased to 60%.

The parties agreed to commission the "Société Italienne d' Engineeering" ("SODISCA") to construct the factory, and SODISCA asked for an advance provision of finance.

B&B undertook to make an advance provision of finance of 22,000,000 CFA[22] (approximately $36,000 US) in a "pro forma of the Preliminary Agreement." This sum was to

---

[20]As judges of a court would in a national legal system.

[21]Editor's note: A joint venture company between public and private parties.

[22]The CFA (Communaute Financiere Africaine, or the African Financial Community) currency, the CFA franc, as of early 2004, trades at approximately 600 to the U.S. dollar. The CFA encompasses Burkina Faso, Senegal, Guinea-Bissau, Côte d'Ivoire, Togo, Benin, Equatorial Guinea, Gabon, Mali, Chad, the Central African Republic, Cameroon, the Congo, and the Comoro Islands. The currency is now tied to the euro at 655.957 CFA per euro.

correspond to B&B's entire share in the capital provided for the formation of the mixed Company. B&B paid the said sum on 6 March 1973.

On 16 April 1973 the parties signed the Agreement which provided for:

a. The creation of a mixed Company with a nominal capital of 55,000,000 CFA, 60% of which was to be owned by the Government and 40% by B&B (Article 1);

b. The right of the Government to repurchase the shares of B&B five years after the formation of the new company, the purchase price to be fixed by common agreement between the parties or in default by arbitration (Article 5);

c. An undertaking by the Government to provide all possible guarantees for the provision of finance which the company might need for the realization of its programme and to grant it a tax status by means of an "establishment agreement" (Article 13); and

d. An undertaking by B&B to guarantee the marketing of the products to the Company to be established (Article 14).

On the date of the Agreement, the Parties also signed the Memorandum and Articles of Association of PLASCO a company which was formed for a duration of 99 years (Article 4) and which was to be run by a Board of Directors of seven members, at least four of whom were to be appointed by the Government (Article 9).

On 21 April 1973, a contract was signed between PLASCO and SODISCA providing for the supply of a plant, ready to operate, for the manufacture of thermoplastic bottles with a production capacity of approximately 8,000,000 units (presumably per year) and of a mineral water bottling factory capable of producing 2,200 bottles an hour. The cost of these two factories was 305,000,000 CFA (approximately $500,000 US). This contract was countersigned by the Minister for Industry on 4 May 1973.

B&B and the Government acted as guarantors for the benefit of SODISCA of the six monthly drafts of PLASCO to a total amount of 250,000,000 CFA, part of the cost of the plants. The drafts were endorsed by the "Caisse Centrale d'Amortissement" of the Congo, and carried interest at 8%.

The Government paid 22,000,000 CFA to SODISCA in March 1973 on behalf of PLASCO, and charged 9,000,000 CFA on the capital of PLASCO representing the value of the site allocated for the construction of these plants. The Government authorized this site to be occupied on 21 August 1973. On the other hand, it failed to make the payment of 2,000,000 CFA which was needed to make up its share.[23]

The first meeting of the Board of Directors of PLASCO took place on 18 October 1973. The minutes of this meeting show that no local bank was prepared to provide PLASCO with working capital and that B&B undertook to guarantee the possible deficit by means of overdraft facilities with the Banque Commerciale Congolaise. It was stressed by the Chairman "that in principal there are to be two meetings a year."

Following a report on the state of PLASCO prepared by Mr. Mombou, Director General at the Ministry of Industry and a Director of PLASCO, the Ministry of Industry called a meeting of the Board of Directors for 4 June 1974. The Agenda included the Government's payment of the last installment of capital of 2,000,000 CFA and the increase of the overdraft facilities from 50 to 100,000,000 CFA.

The Government representatives all failed to attend this meeting. On 17 September 1974 round-table consultation enabled reaching of an agreement for PLASCO to obtain a loan from Banque Centrale so as to alleviate its cash shortage.

[23]Editor's note: 22 million from B&B to SODISCA paid by it on behalf of PLASCO (its total 40 percent contribution to the capital of PLASCO), 22 million from Government to SODISCA paid by it on behalf of PLASCO, plus a 9 million contribution of land to PLASCO makes for a total of 53 million of the 55 million in capital to be contributed by the parties to PLASCO.

B&B secured a meeting of the Board of Directors, to be held in January 1975, fifteen months after the first meeting. According to B&B, the minutes of this meeting acknowledged that B&B had advanced the sum of 43,451,094 CFA so as to meet PLASCO's cash requirements and recorded the Government's promise to repay immediately to B&B the sum of 25,000,000 CFA. At the meeting, the sale prices of the mineral water were fixed taking into account a profit margin of 10% for PLASCO.

In February 1975, the Government acted as guarantor of a loan of 100,000,000 CFA granted by the Banque Commerciale Congolaise to PLASCO.

The bottle-making plant opened in February 1975 and a first batch of 800,000 bottles was delivered almost immediately to SIACONGO which had ordered it. Since this delivery was not paid for, PLASCO made no further deliveries to SIACONGO. This state of affairs, from the beginning, caused outlet problems for PLASCO's products, since the fulfillment of SIACONGO's needs had been one of the major factors in the creation of PLASCO.

When the plant began operating, Mr. Bonfant, the managing Director of PLASCO, and Miss Ingster, formed the "Entrprise de Distribution Congolaise" ("EDICO") so as to meet B&B's obligation to guarantee the commercialisation of the mineral waters processed by PLASCO.

On 3 October 1975, the Government unilaterally fixed by decree the sale prices of the bottles of mineral water at levels lower than those laid down at the meeting of the Board of Directors of PLASCO in January 1975. B&B protested against this measure taken by the Government and stressed that the new prices entailed a loss for PLASCO of 23.86 CFA per bottle of mineral water.

As from November 1975 the Government embarked upon a policy of "radicalisation" which involved, in particular, the creation of government agencies such as the "Management-Party-Union," interference by these agencies in the management of PLASCO and finally the dissolution by decree of 9 November 1975.

After repeated requests by B&B, the Government called a meeting of the Board of Directors which was held on 18 January 1976. At this meeting, new sale prices were fixed for the bottles of mineral water, which would have given PLASCO a profit margin of 10%. In addition a budget for 1976 was approved.

Following an administrative memorandum dated 29 January 1976, Mr. Bonfant was of the opinion that PLASCO had become a State Company without there having been a formal act of expropriation.

Considering that their personal safety was no longer guaranteed and on the advice of Mr. Corradello, Chargé d'Affaires at the Italian Embassy in Brazzaville, according to whom the arrest of Mr. Bonfant was imminent, the latter and most of the Italian personnel of PLASCO hastily left the Congo in February 1976. The registered office of PLASCO was subsequently occupied by the Army. His hasty departure from the Congo prevented Mr. Bonfant from taking with him all the documents of PLASCO and EDICO relating to this case.

The attempts by B&B and the Government to resolve their dispute out of Court were unsuccessful.

B&B claimed damages for

- Nonpayment of its dividends by PLASCO.
- Its lost shareholding in PLASCO.
- Repayment of loans made to benefit PLASCO.
- Repayment of advances to SODISCA and compensation for its dissolution.
- Damages for intangible injury.
- Interest at 15%.

In total, a sum of 657,000,000 CFA (approximately U.S.$1.1 million).

Referring to the 2,000,000 capital contribution that went unpaid, the tribunal concluded that the Government had admitted this was so in correspondence. It concluded further that

- The Government failed to give and deliver "all possible guarantees" in the financing of PLASCO.
- The Government failed to provide special tax status.
- The Government undertook to provide import protection against competing products, but did not.
- SIACONGO's failure to pay its account, as a state-owned company, was a failure of the Government.
- The price-fixing of mineral water caused inevitable damage to PLASCO.
- Dissolution of EDICO and seizure of its assets had no legal justification.
- B&B had no notice of meetings of the PLASCO Board and were frozen out of management, amounting to uncompensated nationalization.
- Appropriate damages based on independent valuations of the firm were in the order of 323,000,000 CFA (approximately U.S.$538,000), at 10 percent interest with U.S.$15,000 in costs.

Source: (1984) 67 I.L.R. 345.

- Unsubstantiated criminal charges were brought against Mr. Bonfant and the army occupied his office. That may be true, but what events prior to the administrative memorandum of January 29, 1976, separate these circumstances as expropriation rather than just a case of a company mismanaged by its principal shareholder and directors, the Government of the Congo? Can you create a statement of your own that marks the boundary between mismanagement and "creeping expropriation"? Is this a case where creeping expropriation can be seen only in hindsight, with the circumstances taken as a whole?

Management and Control Issues

The *Benvenuti & Bonfant* case above illustrates what can happen where management control of a joint venture is lost. The parties to a JV transaction usually deal with issues of formal control by establishing how the board of directors will be composed and imposing voting restrictions as they see fit.

Often, however, composition of the board and voting rights are subject to local law provisions. For example, the Chinese Joint Venture Law in Article 6 spells out a skeleton requirement for the composition of the management of the joint venture. This is a simplification of the law from what it was when originally adopted in 1979. The reason for the simplification is the recognition that no matter how job titles are assigned within a joint venture, the real management power and control rest on the relative and informal ability of the parties to control the economic success or failure of the firm.

In any joint venture, like any other corporation, formal control rests with the party capable of electing a majority of the board of directors. However, more effective control may lie in controlling operational aspects of the firm. Where the firm depends on the continued supply of key raw materials, secret compounds, or employee know-how, or the like, true control lies in the party that controls that supply. The same can be said of a JV manufacturing firm that requires a steady stream of research results from one of its member parties. If management problems in the JV become an issue and the research party refuses to forward new results or refuses to routinely license improvements in its intellectual property, then it is the research party who has control, regardless of the formal composition of the board of the JV. Such scenarios are not pretty; they are threatened or actual breaches of the joint venture agreement, but they are real and they happen.

The Old Wolf

Aside from informal power, how do you paralyze a joint venture? Give it a 50/50 split in voting control between two partners. This ensures deadlock when any contentious issue rises to the board level. Solution: Give a single share to an advisor that both parties trust, to be used as a casting vote when deadlock looms. Consider it to be instant arbitration.

While capital contributions usually dictate the resulting share each joint venture party will receive as its portion of profits or losses (as is the case under the Chinese law, Article 4), voting control need not follow the same split (the Chinese law being silent on this point). As long as the principle of share classes of unequal rights is not offensive to local regulation, this arrangement can be accommodated. The impact of profit or loss sharing based on capital contributions is more acutely felt in non–market economy environments where there is no free market reference for the value of assets contributed by the local party.

It is relatively easy to value the contribution of machinery or equipment, but how can one establish the value of a warehouse or the land under it, absent a local free-market economy? In such cases, usually it is real estate that forms the most important capital contribution of the local party to the joint venture. If the real estate is located in the center of a city near transportation infrastructure, it is worth more; if it is located in the countryside, perhaps it is worth less or is worthless. Not surprisingly in any such cases, the local party always assesses its contribution value as at least 51 percent of the total capital of the venture, and takes the negotiating position that this should be reflected in 51 percent voting control as well.

The same argument can be made with regard to a contribution of intangible property. To give the argument its due, it is not possible to fix a single "true" value on trademarks or secret processes and the like, for they derive their value in the eye of the beholder. However, there is at least a market for intellectual or intangible property to serve as a general frame of reference.

Ancillary Agreements

Almost all joint ventures will have agreements ancillary to the joint venture agreement itself. Most often, these additional agreements are transfers of assets to the joint venture, conditional on the parties' committing themselves in contract to the master joint venture agreement. They are usually incorporated by reference or are attached as appendices to the master joint venture agreement.

The nature of the particular set of ancillary agreements will be unique to the objectives of the joint venture, but the most commonly found are the following:

1. Assignments of leases or transfers of title to real estate.
2. Licensing of use of patents or trademarks.
3. Service agreements, for the provision of administrative support to the venture.
4. Supply agreements, for the provision of raw materials.
5. Assignments of leases or transfers of title to production equipment.
6. Marketing or distribution agreements (for output of the joint venture to be sold in the local market).
7. Purchase agreements relating to output of the joint venture (for output of the joint venture to be bought by the foreign party as a component or raw material in production processes located elsewhere abroad).
8. Financing commitments and agreements, either obtained from local or foreign lenders with the joint venture as beneficiary, or made by the parties themselves.

9. Contracts of employment relating to key employees.

10. Guarantees or indemnities given by the parties, with the joint venture as beneficiary.

Dispute Settlement and Winding Up

A joint venture is well advised to make specific provisions for dispute resolution in its founding documents, as its composition of potentially diverse interests makes it more susceptible to disagreements. Undoubtedly the most important element is the commitment by the parties to work together to find solutions, followed by a mechanism, such as a neutral casting vote where formal voting deadlock is possible. Conciliation, mediation, and arbitration provisions are equally wise steps before resorting to the courts, as per Article 15 of the Chinese JV law above. These procedures are more fully elaborated upon in the next chapter of this text, Chapter 13.

Provisions on winding up the joint venture also should be included in the founding documents, for two reasons. The first is to create a termination mechanism appropriate to ending the venture when it reaches its natural conclusion. If the JV has not been established for a particular limited purpose or time, the parties should approach the question realistically and ask themselves: do we foresee, with reasonable probability, a set of circumstances that would lead to the end of the venture? These may be technical events, such as bankruptcy, change of control, or winding up of either of the venturers, or a change in the commercial priorities of the participating firms, which would create the desire to sell out to the other or otherwise leave. Where such events are foreseen, explicit provision should be made.

The second reason to provide for termination or liquidation is in the event of irreconcilable differences, a form of commercial divorce. This is separate from the recognition of a change in commercial priorities. Instead of one party asking to leave and reaching a friendly settlement with the other, the situation revolves around forcing the issue and ejecting either oneself or the other party from the venture. This may be accomplished through a range of mechanisms. The simplest (and arguably the most dangerous) is to allow either party the right to unilaterally invoke dissolution of the venture. The problem with this method is that it can be triggered when neither party is in a position to make an offer to buy the interest of the other. The result is the winding up of an otherwise fine going-concern at fire sale prices to a new investor team. Everyone loses, except the new owners.

Permitting any party to sell its shares to a third party, on consent of the other principal party, is a second and more viable means of exit. It allows the remaining original joint venture party at least the right to approve its new commercial companion. If it withholds its approval, however, the situation becomes deadlocked, and there is no further means of escape. The potential for increased animosity will become real where one party believes that the other has unreasonably withheld its approval and denied it the chance to leave.

With these concerns in mind, it is customary to provide some form of final failsafe method, either as a last resort or one that the parties can trigger initially. In one form or another, it involves one party requiring the other to purchase (buy out) its interest.

The first formulation is appropriate where one party has a large concern about the chances of the joint venture in achieving a particular goal, milestone, or timeline. Where this is a concern, the concerned party may request a form of escape hatch in the founding documents. Such a provision would force an independent valuation of the venture at such future time or event or default, compelling the subsequent sale of the concerned party's interest to the other, at that valuation price. Of course, if failure to meet the milestone causes both parties to give up hope, then the venture can simply be liquidated and the net proceeds will be shared according to the capital contributions of the parties.

The second formulation is a "shotgun clause," which does not involve independent valuation, but rather the self-assessment by each party of the value of the JV and the value of

The Old Wolf

its interest. Under such a clause, a party who wishes to dissolve the JV has the right to state a value for the joint venture on a per-share basis. With an appropriate provision in the founding documents, this statement of share value forces an obligation upon the party to whom it is made. It may, within a fixed period of time, accept that price as an offer to *buy* its own shares, or to treat (and accept) that price as an offer by the other party to *sell* its shares. For this reason, the "shotgun clause" is also known as a "buy-sell agreement." The mechanism keeps the quotation as close as can be expected to a "true value." If the triggering party quotes a price that is high, it will be accepted as an offer to buy, and the triggering party will have paid a premium price to own all of the firm. If it quotes a price too low, the other party will treat it as an offer to sell, and the triggering party will find it has given away its interest in the venture for very little in return.

Negotiated Investment Protection

There are many instances where the opportunities offered by foreign direct investment are still marginally outweighed by the investor's concerns of political risk associated with the nation in which the particular investment can be made. On a global scale, many such individual decisions can add up to the total rejection of an otherwise viable market for foreign direct investment. In that case, a nation may find its development stalled and the world community will discover a new voice among the others calling out for development aid, grants, and financing. Some commentators would argue that this is a natural result of poor economic and political management on the part of these nations, and that the best cure is to allow events to fall as they may. On the other hand, if the investor concerns are truly questions of perception, it is unfortunate for all concerned that viable opportunities for both profit and development are ignored.

On the basis of this reasoning, the Multilateral Investment Guarantee Agency (MIGA)[24] was established in 1988 as an affiliated but independent and autonomous member of the World Bank Group. Its mandate is to address this sort of situation by offering political risk insurance and guarantees to investors and lenders. In so doing, MIGA helps developing countries attract and retain private investment. The emphasis is squarely on developing nations, and it is prepared to offer this type of insurance where otherwise sound, new, commercial investment opportunities exist that will contribute to the development of the host country.

The insurance and guarantees offered on commercial terms to investors do not relate to the credit risk of the actual venture, but to the legal and regulatory climate that surrounds it. In short, this is compensation for damage stemming from acts or inaction by governments. These may be prohibitions or currency controls on repatriation or transfer of funds, risk of loss through expropriation or other government administrative action, governmental breach of contract or nonperformance where the investor lacks available due process to enforce against the breach, and results of armed conflict and civil unrest.

[24]The MIGA website is at http://www.miga.org.

The fact that the World Bank lies some distance behind MIGA helps prevent or at least discourages the occurrence of the risks that MIGA insures against, and both MIGA and the World Bank provide technical assistance to avoid the macroeconomic conditions that create dampening effects on investor confidence. Nor is this simply a strong-arm tactic, for developing countries are well represented at the policy and operational levels of the institution. Regarding investors, MIGA charges a premium or fee for its insurance and guarantees, with the intention of filling a gap that other insurers refuse to occupy, thus not distorting the global commercial insurance market.

Virtually all developed nations have a parallel national government institution as well. Being of national origin, these insurance and guarantee organizations have the additional policy objective of promoting safety for the investments of their own nationals, and therefore usually a nationality restriction is placed on who may request coverage.

While economic benefits do flow to the host country that is the target of the investment, the organization is also in active pursuit of the foreign policy objectives of the nation that sponsors it, additionally seeking the national benefit that may be achieved through healthy outward investment balances. In the United States, this institution is the Overseas Private Investment Corporation (OPIC),[25] established in 1971 as an independent U.S. government agency and, like MIGA, self-sustaining through its own fees and charges. As is the case with all such national investment protection programs, it is the credit of the nation sponsoring the institution that offers strength and meaning to the guarantees provided.

In Canada, the Export Development Corporation, a Crown (government) corporation, provides this service. It covers the same three heads of loss in convertibility and transfer of funds, expropriation, and political violence, and in addition, offers export payment guarantees for sale of goods transactions. Nearly identical offerings are provided in the United Kingdom, through the UK government's Export Credits Guarantee Department.[26]

Chapter Summary

Foreign investment represents the highest form of commitment and risk that a firm can undertake in pursuing business opportunities abroad. Aside from mere passive portfolio investment, these business operations may start from a relatively modest representative office, or a branch operation, or see the establishment of a subsidiary corporation.

In choosing to make this greater commitment to the market, the foreign investor may choose to go it alone in the form a wholly owned subsidiary, or opt to include a local partner through employment of a joint venture. Joint ventures can take a form more akin to an alliance created through contract, or involve the establishment of a new entity, the equity joint venture.

While the wholly owned subsidiary allows for complete business control in the hands of the foreign investor, the joint venture must accommodate the sometimes-differing objectives of partners. Control mechanisms and dispute settlement protocols will be necessary for smooth operation, as well as a mechanism for the eventual winding up of the firm. This must be designed to fit within the often-strict screening and control that some nations exercise over joint ventures and foreign-owned entities.

Attractive foreign investment destinations also can be exceptionally risky in terms of their political stability, and thus the investor will be concerned with the possibilities of local government action to its detriment. It must consider the possibility of expropriation of its assets, or that its cash flows will be prohibited from leaving the country. The investor may wish to obtain insurance and guarantees from its own government agencies to mitigate this, or from an international body. Stabilization clauses are essentially local guarantees of maintenance of the local legal environment's status quo, but they are only as good a guarantee as the government that gives them.

[25]The OPIC website is at http://www.opic.gov.

[26]The ECGD website is at http://www.ecgd.gov.uk.

International law will apply to this range of events in foreign investment, particularly in the case of expropriation. Established norms have arisen that do away with the age-old exemption of foreigners from host government control, and, in the case of expropriation, the international minimum standard insists on prompt, adequate, and effective compensation for government takings.

Chapter Questions

1. When considering an investment in a business that is already in operation, what business and legal factors would lead a foreign investor toward purchasing all the assets of the target firm rather than all its shares?

2. Explain the reasoning behind a Calvo clause and how it has survived as an antecedent to the UN Charter of Economic Rights and Duties of States.

3. Describe the hallmarks of the creeping expropriation of a private foreign investor's interest in an international joint venture with a government party.

4. Identify five major Chinese policy goals contained within the PRC Law on Sino-Foreign Joint Ventures, and the reasoning that would lie behind them.

5. Why and how would management control by the principal parties be different in equity joint ventures compared to contractual joint ventures?

6. On what grounds would a foreign investor opt for a representative office over a wholly owned subsidiary? If it does so, how may it lose that representative office status and what consequential dangers does it face?

7. What business risks are commonly faced by foreign investors in repatriation of capital and income? What steps could they take to protect the value of these assets and cash flows when exchange controls are threatened?

8. Explain how a government expropriation may result in an indemnity and what the effect of an indemnity is in such an instance. Distinguish the *Chorzów Factory* and *North American Dredging* cases on this basis.

9. How might a foreign investor continue to exert effective control over a joint venture despite not having majority voting control of the firm?

10. Using a simple example, describe the operation of a "shotgun clause."

BusinessWeek

Now that a wrangle with Enron has chilled foreign investors, there are no simple solutions to the subcontinent's shortage of electricity.

It was only a few weeks ago that Kenneth Lay, the tough-talking chairman of Enron, was in India, laying down sales terms for its $2.9 billion, 2,184-megawatt, power-generation plant at Dabhol, near Bombay. Pay up, Lay warned, or he might enlist the help of the U.S. government in helping to rid Enron (ENE) of this white elephant once and for all.

The project remains the largest foreign investment in India by far, but it has been the source of endless controversy. First, the Indian government balked at the prices Enron wanted to charge for energy produced at the plant. Then the Indian government reneged on its contract with Enron, which was terminated in April. Now, Enron wants to sell Dabhol and get all its money back—but the Indian government isn't cooperating. Now, with Enron's stunning buyout by Dynegy (DYN) and Lay out of the chairman's seat in the wake of a scandal involving questionable company transactions, the company has little room for international maneuvering. Small wonder local buyers have descended upon Dabhol: The Tata group, Reliance Industries, ex-Dabhol employees, and even the Indian banks that lent Dabhol money all want those shining steel power towers by the Arabian Sea—but at a discount: 50 cents on the dollar of Enron's asking price of $1.2 billion.

For now, the Indian government has some respite from the pressure of paying for a project on terms many critics say it never should have accepted in the first place. But India's primary problem remains the same: The country doesn't have enough power generation to serve its population. Dabhol was supposed to alleviate that. So was AES's model-power project in the poor, eastern state of Orissa. AES is now battling with the Indian government, citing delinquent payments to its generation business and has wound up its power distribution subsidiary in Orissa. India needs at least 10,000 megawatts more power per year. The country now produces just 60,000.

With private investment on the wane, and India's bedraggled state power boards unable to cope, the talk in New Delhi is once again focused on efforts to strike energy deals with neighbors, from Iran to Myanmar. Given the region's volatile geopolitics, this is no less a minefield for India than negotiating joint ventures with multinational corporations.

Take the ambitious multibillion-dollar gas-pipeline project that was supposed to link Iran with India through Pak-

istan. Backed by all three governments, Unocal and India's Reliance Industries also have shown interest. A grand signing ceremony was set for last August, but then put on hold when India-Pakistan peace talks in Agra collapsed. Now, the war in Afghanistan has shelved the project indefinitely. A pipeline that could have generated $600 million in annual transit fees for Pakistan and maybe brokered peace between India and Pakistan through commercial ties is "virtually dead," according to Indian foreign ministry sources.

A proposed gas pipeline from Bangladesh to India looks like it might meet a similar fate. Since 1996, Unocal has invested $350 million to explore the estimated 60 trillion cubic feet of gas discovered in Bangladesh, which would be sold domestically and to nearby India, the only practical export market for Bangladeshi gas. Development could have major economic implications: In addition to satiating the needs of Bangladesh and power-starved northern India, the project could produce at least $200 million a year for impoverished Bangladesh and reverse that country's trade deficit with India.

Still, the Islamic backlash spawned by the Afghan War hasn't bypassed Bangladesh, a predominantly Muslim country. The new government of Prime Minister Khalida Zia, elected in September, has a 15% representation of fundamentalist Islamic parties which will not tolerate any détente with India, a predominantly Hindu nation. "Bangladesh saw commercial sense, but did not know politically what to do," says former Indian Prime Minister Inder Kumar Gujral, who worked hard at making peace with the country's immediate neighbors.

Not all of the neighbor nations are ambivalent about selling their resources to India. Every year, the tiny Himalayan kingdom of Bhutan exports $800 million worth of hydroelectric power to India, providing a lift to the local economy. Two more export-based hydro power plants that are under way will ensure that, in five years, Bhutan's per-capita income will be the highest in South Asia.

All of these prospects are viable. There's just one problem: The Indian government is short on cash. And given the bickering that shadowed the Dabhol debacle from the beginning, New Delhi is unlikely to find any large international investors to fund construction of such projects. "Even if the Indian government agrees to pay, who will believe them now?" asks Sanjay Bhatnagar, former chief executive of Enron India, who now runs an investment firm in New York and is himself making a bid for the Dabhol project.

In the view of some experts, the lesson from Dabhol is clear: Overseas investors won't come back to India until

New Delhi's politicians quit trying to micromanage the power sector. The government must let the marketplace set the price of energy in India, says Subir Gokarn, chief economist of the National Center of Applied Economic Research. As it stands now, more than 35% of the power produced in India is stolen, and 15% is a free subsidy to rural areas. Privatizing India's vast energy market may well ensure the best commercial and diplomatic deals for India in the subcontinent.

Source: Manjeet Kripalani, India bureau chief for *BusinessWeek.* Edited by Douglas Harbrecht. Copyright 2001, by The McGraw-Hill Companies Inc. All rights reserved.

BusinessWeek

Suzuki money and knowhow make for a better-running Maruti.

Customers like Vikram Shroff don't come around every day. For 15 years, Shroff, his father, and two uncles have driven the same model passenger car, the Maruti 800. The four-door Indian minicar, known for its small but trouble-free engine, retails for just $4,200 and ranks as the world's cheapest auto. Now Shroff, a Bombay garment trader, is especially thrilled. On June 9, he and his family became proud owners of 2,200 shares of the first stock offered by recently privatized Maruti Udyog Ltd. Even though the stock leapt 30% on the first day of trading, to $3.50, Shroff is holding on. "Everyone loves Maruti," he says. "And why not? It has a good product, and now it has good private management."

Maruti will need to maintain that kind of loyalty in the coming years. Because of its former near-monopoly status, the company commands a 54% share of India's annual 700,000-unit passenger-car market. But Maruti struggled after 1995, when its 50-50 joint-venture partners, the Indian government and Japan's Suzuki Motor Corp., began a public fight for control lasting three years. The Industry Ministry refused Suzuki's pleas that Maruti modernize its two factories and offer new models. It also appointed a managing director unacceptable to Suzuki. Paralyzed, Maruti saw its market share drop from 64% to 50% by 1998 as aggressive new rivals such as South Korea's Hyundai Motor Co. swooped in. Maruti's sales and profits for the year ended Mar. 31—$1.55 billion and $31 million—are still below 1998 levels. And liberalized investment rules mean that competition from foreign carmakers is heating up.

Now Maruti is on the counterattack. Last year, the government gave Suzuki clear control by selling it a 4% stake for a premium of $1 billion. Suzuki hiked investment in capacity and distribution and promises a new Maruti model each year. In June, Suzuki got an even freer hand when the government sold 27.5% of its remaining stake in an initial public offering that raised $215 million.

With the auto market now picking up, "all of the positives are coinciding for Maruti," says Managing Director Jagdish Khattar. In the past year, Maruti boosted its market share by four percentage points. Profits for fiscal 2003 were up 40%. Maruti's sales will climb by more than one-quarter, to about $2.1 billion, over the next two years, predicts Bombay's Kotak Securities Ltd.

The force behind Maruti's turnaround, Khattar, is a former Maruti marketing director. After his promotion in 1999, Khattar persuaded 1,100 employees, 20% of the workforce, to take early retirement, and he spent $300 million to more than triple capacity, to 350,000 cars. Maruti has also launched three new Suzuki models. In early July, it introduced a two-door version of its popular compact, the $8,350 Zen.

Clearly, Maruti is on the move. "With Suzuki in charge, the company is more focused," says auto analyst Sachin Kasera of Bombay securities firm Pioneer Intermediaries. By copying quality-control and production methods from a Suzuki plant in Kosai, Japan, Maruti's factory outside New Delhi has boosted output. Marketing Director Kinji Saito, a Suzuki veteran who arrived in India last year, is charged with making Maruti a global export base for Suzuki cars. Under him, Maruti also is upgrading its 159 showrooms into one-stop shops for everything from auto financing and insurance to secondhand-car sales. Average revenues of its dealers jumped 40% in a year. "Our dealers are the interface with our customers, so we have to take care of them," says Saito.

BusinessWeek

In a joint venture, the big U.S. bank breaks into China's financial sector.

It was a first-ever for China's financial sector and a major step forward in banking reform. In a July 8 ceremony on the top floor of the 22-story China Construction Bank (CCB) headquarters in Beijing, financiers drank champagne toasts to a deal that paired Morgan Stanley with CCB, one of China's big four commercial banks, giving Morgan Stanley bragging rights as the first foreign bank to sign a direct joint venture to dispose of the mainland's nonperforming loans.

For Morgan Stanley, the accord represents something more. It keeps the New York firm ahead of the competition as foreign investment banks pour into China looking for a piece of the action. "This is part of a step-by-step development in the opening of China's marketplace," says Stephan F. Newhouse, chairman of Morgan Stanley International. "The direction forward is clear."

Morgan Stanley already had a leg up. The Wall Street bank is part of a nearly nine-year-old experiment in an investment banking joint venture: China International Capital Corp. (CICC). That partnership with CCB made Morgan Stanley the only Western bank privileged to do deals in China until another got permission in April. Over the years, Morgan Stanley has helped market a slew of acquisitions and initial public offerings. In November it advised on a $1.5 billion offering of China Telecom (CHA) Corp. shares. And in January it helped with Anheuser-Busch (BUD) Cos.' $182 million purchase of a larger stake in Tsingtao Beer. It has big plans for investments in stocks and real estate, and wants to do more business in private equity and foreign exchange. "They've got guts," says a rival investment banker in Beijing. "It's a great vision they have for their China business."

But Morgan Stanley's lead in China is by no means assured—and neither are the profits it clearly is hoping for. Over the past 19 months, China has been opening its financial markets to comply with World Trade Organization commitments, and Morgan Stanley's rivals are forging deep links with local partners and pioneering new businesses. CICC is likely to face stiff competition from French investment bank CLSA's recently formed China Euro Securities Ltd., as well as from Hong Kong–based Bank of China International. On July 9, Switzerland's UBS (UBS) got the first chance of any foreign bank to invest in China's domestic "A" share stock markets. It promptly poured in well over $50 million of client funds. (Morgan Stanley plans to sink as much as $300 million of client funds into A shares.) And

Goldman, Sachs & Co., Morgan Stanley's strongest competitor in China, is angling for more IPOs and mergers and acquisitions. "China still holds all the promise," says Richard J. Gnodde, president and managing director of Goldman Sachs (GS) (Asia) LLC. "Every six months we are able to do a deeper and broader range of business."

Beijing's goal in this opening is to create a commercially sound industry that begins to efficiently allocate capital. That is crucial as China undergoes a wrenching restructuring of its state sector and relies more and more on cash-hungry private enterprises to create jobs. But the communist bureaucracy isn't known for its quickness in instituting ground-breaking reforms. For instance, Morgan Stanley's new bad loan deal has yet to be cleared by the bureaucrats at the People's Bank of China, the China Banking Regulatory Commission, or the Ministry of Finance. A chief sticking point is what value will be put on the loans, most of them to state-run companies. "You are still not supposed to sell below book value," says one Western investment banker in China. "How do they get around that?"

Good point. The China Construction Bank is asking the government for "trial permission" to sell the debt at less than par value, says John Langlois, president of Morgan Stanley Properties (China). Assuming that problem is worked out, the venture will be set up as a 70%–30% joint operation, with Morgan Stanley holding the majority stake. It will take on a portfolio of 700 troubled loans to companies with a total book value of $519 million. Instead of liquidating borrowers' assets, the venture plans to help them remake themselves through a combination of debt restructuring, debt forgiveness, and refinancing. But if that doesn't work, it may have to rely on China's untested courts to lay claim to the debtors' assets. "The legal process will be a final option," says Langlois.

So will the foreign investment banks flooding into China make any money? There are a lot of doubters, at least for the near term. But waiting is not a problem for Morgan Stanley's Newhouse. "China is one of the great opportunities anywhere in the world," he says. "It's a place to put one's bets for the next 25 years." He and others are determined to cash in on the vast China financial market, however long it takes.

13

International Alternative Dispute Resolution

Chapter Objectives

Early in this text, we focused on the judicial processes available to both states and international businesspersons in dispute resolution, and the importance of jurisdiction, choice of law, and recognition and enforcement of foreign judgments. We now revisit the question of dispute settlement between international parties without resorting to courts: international alternative dispute resolution.

In this chapter we discuss

- The business reasons and methods available for alternative dispute settlement.

- Arbitration as an alternative to judicial proceedings for international business disputes.

- Recognition and enforcement of arbitration awards as a matter of international and national law.

Introduction

In the United States, differences or disputes frequently arise between the parties in business transactions due to different interpretations or expectations arising out of their contracts or their dealings with each other. This is the case even though the parties usually speak the same language and operate in the same business environments and under the same legal system.

On the international scene, the parties may speak different languages and carry on business in a very different business and legal environment with different cultural and social values that often affect the business expectations of the parties. These factors compound the likelihood of differences or disputes arising between the parties in their business dealings.

In North America, careful businesspersons provide for some form of dispute resolution in their contractual arrangements, or realize that they can, if necessary, resort to the courts to resolve their differences. In international business relationships, a clearly defined dispute resolution process takes on a greater importance, particularly in those cases where a great deal of time and money have been invested in the development of the international business relationship.

Judicial proceedings with an international element are not quick, not easy, and certainly not cheap. While international alternative dispute resolution (ADR) is not instant, effortless, or free, it is certainly a more attractive option on all three counts. ADR is not a new issue facing those who carry on business on an international basis, and over centuries of international trading, businesses have developed effective methods for resolving their differences. For our purposes, these can be categorized as follows:

International Alternative Dispute Resolution

> 1. Negotiation
> 2. Mediation or conciliation
> 3. International commercial arbitration

Negotiation

Negotiation may be an informal or formal dispute resolution process that the parties may use when differences arise in a business relationship. It is a preferred means of resolving disputes where the differences tend to be misunderstandings or the misinterpretation of the terms in a negotiated agreement. Most businesspersons wish to preserve their business relationships, and if the differences are minor or accommodation can be made to correct the differences or expectations of the parties, negotiation of revised terms often will achieve this goal.

Negotiation also may be prescribed as the first step in a more formal dispute resolution procedure set out in a written business agreement or contract of sale. In essence, it is a meeting between the parties to outline their differences and to discuss their positions, and also to explore the possibilities for accommodation or the resolution of their differences. Apart from serious differences or fundamental breaches of an agreement, the negotiation process often will resolve the problems and preserve the business relationship, assuming, of course, that this is an important or desired outcome of the negotiations.

Negotiation is also the preferred process for the resolution of disputes between states that concern business transactions of their respective citizens. These negotiations may be either formal or informal, and are conducted through their appropriate diplomatic services, joint commissions, or high-level government meetings, depending to a large extent on the importance of the issues involved.

Mediation and Conciliation

Mediation and conciliation processes involve the insertion of a neutral, independent, unbiased third party into the dispute resolution process. They represent an effort to resolve the differences between the parties without resorting to formal dispute resolution processes such as the courts or arbitration. Mediation and conciliation are sometimes distinguished by the methodology used by the respective third parties. Both processes are consensual, however, and the parties must mutually agree upon the third party that will act as mediator or conciliator in the dispute. The parties also must agree upon the particular role that the mediator or conciliator will play in the process, and it is here that the two processes may be distinguished. If the third party uses his or her skills to meet with each party on a separate basis and transmit and interpret their respective positions to the other (occasionally suggesting proposals for resolution of the issues), then the third party is acting as a mediator. The process of shuttling back and forth between the parties with proposals and responses would constitute mediation. However, if the third party is not only expected to perform this role, but also to provide a formal written report of the issues and the success or failure of their resolution, the process is usually referred to as conciliation.

The merits of using mediation or conciliation as a part of the dispute resolution process are the fact that a mutually acceptable, unbiased, and independent third party often can identify and prioritize the issues in dispute. He or she can suggest ways in which the parties may overcome the roadblocks that interfere with the resolution of their differences. The processes are most often used where the parties have established a long-term business relationship, and both parties have an incentive to maintain the integrity of the relationship, notwithstanding the apparently serious differences on particular issues that have arisen to affect the relationship.

The International Chamber of Commerce some years ago recognized the desirability of dispute resolution by way of conciliation and established a conciliation process tailored for international disputes. The conciliation process is available on request and is governed by a set of rules for the conduct of conciliation.[1] These provide for the appointment of a sole conciliator by the International Chamber of Commerce if either party makes an application to the Secretariat of the ICC International Court of Arbitration in Paris.

The conciliation process is consensual in nature, and while one party may make the request for conciliation, the other party to the dispute must agree to the conciliation; otherwise, the ICC will treat the matter as a declined request. If both parties agree, the ICC will then proceed to appoint a conciliator (a "neutral"). Once appointed, the conciliator will then contact the parties and advise them of the time limits for each to submit their arguments concerning the dispute.

The procedure under the rules is essentially left with the conciliator, subject to the condition that the conciliator shall be "guided by the principles of fairness and by impartiality and by the wishes of the parties."[2] The rules permit the parties to have legal counsel of their choice to assist them and the conciliator will arrange with the parties for a time and location where the conciliation will take place. The conciliator also has the authority to request additional information at any time from the parties if the information is required for the conciliation process.

The conciliation process is confidential in nature, and all persons associated with the conciliation are expected to maintain the confidentiality of the process.[3]

If the conciliation is successful and an agreement is reached, the agreement is reduced to writing and signed by the parties. The parties will then be bound by the agreement. If no agreement is reached, the conciliator will report to the ICC (without reasons) that the conciliation was unsuccessful, and the process will be deemed to be at an end. If either party should decide to terminate the conciliation at any time during the process, notification of this information to the conciliator also will end the process.

The parties share the costs of the conciliation equally. If the conciliation is unsuccessful, any offers, proposals of the conciliator, and all other information given or received at the conciliation may not be used in any court action or arbitration that may follow the conciliation.[4]

The International Chamber of Commerce is not the only organization to offer conciliation services for the settlement of international disputes. The London Court of International Arbitration, based in London, England, offers a somewhat similar service, and has established its own process for conciliation. It uses the conciliation rules of the United Nations Commission on International Trade Law (UNCITRAL). These rules, which tend to be more detailed than those of the International Chamber of Commerce, are reproduced on page 567.

[1]ICC ADR Rules in force July 1, 2001, ICC Publication No. 809. May be reviewed at http://www. iccwbo.org.
[2]Ibid., Article 5(3).
[3]Ibid., Article 7(1).
[4]Ibid., Article 7.

UNCITRAL Conciliation Rules

General Assembly Resolution 35/52 of December 4, 1980
(Full substantive text, preambles omitted)

Article 1 Application of the Rules

1. These Rules apply to conciliation of disputes arising out of or relating to a contractual or other legal relationship where the parties seeking an amicable settlement of their dispute have agreed that the UNCITRAL Conciliation Rules apply.
2. The parties may agree to exclude or vary any of these Rules at any time.
3. Where any of these Rules is in conflict with a provision of law from which the parties cannot derogate, that provision prevails.

Article 2 Commencement of Conciliation Proceedings

1. The party initiating conciliation sends to the other party a written invitation to conciliate under these Rules, briefly identifying the subject of the dispute.
2. Conciliation proceedings commence when the other party accepts the invitation to conciliate. If the acceptance is made orally, it is advisable that it be confirmed in writing.
3. If the other party rejects the invitation, there will be no conciliation proceedings.
4. If the party initiating conciliation does not receive a reply within thirty days from the date on which he sends the invitation, or within such other period of time as specified in the invitation, he may elect to treat this as a rejection of the invitation to conciliate. If he so elects, he informs the other party accordingly.

Article 3 Number of Conciliators

There shall be one conciliator unless the parties agree that there shall be two or three conciliators. Where there is more than one conciliator, they ought, as a general rule, to act jointly.

Article 4 Appointment of Conciliators

1. *a.* In conciliation proceedings with one conciliator, the parties shall endeavour to reach agreement on the name of a sole conciliator;
   b. In conciliation proceedings with two conciliators, each party appoints one conciliator;
   c. In conciliation proceedings with three conciliators, each party appoints one conciliator. The parties shall endeavour to reach agreement on the name of the third conciliator.
2. Parties may enlist the assistance of an appropriate institution or person in connexion with the appointment of conciliators. In particular,
   a. A party may request such an institution or person to recommend the names of suitable individuals to act as conciliator; or
   b. The parties may agree that the appointment of one or more conciliators be made directly by such an institution or person.

In recommending or appointing individuals to act as conciliator, the institution or person shall have regard to such considerations as are likely to secure the appointment of an independent and impartial conciliator and, with respect to a sole or third conciliator, shall take into account the advisability of appointing a conciliator of a nationality other than the nationalities of the parties.

Article 5 Submission of Statements to Conciliator

1. The conciliator,* upon his appointment, requests each party to submit to him a brief written statement describing the general nature of the dispute and the points at issue. Each party sends a copy of his statement to the other party.

2. The conciliator may request each party to submit to him a further written statement of his position and the facts and grounds in support thereof, supplemented by any documents and other evidence that such party deems appropriate. The party sends a copy of his statement to the other party.

3. At any stage of the conciliation proceedings the conciliator may request a party to submit to him such additional information as he deems appropriate.

Article 6 Representation and Assistance

The parties may be represented or assisted by persons of their choice. The names and addresses of such persons are to be communicated in writing to the other party and to the conciliator; such communication is to specify whether the appointment is made for purposes of representation or of assistance.

Article 7 Role of Conciliator

1. The conciliator assists the parties in an independent and impartial manner in their attempt to reach an amicable settlement of their dispute.

2. The conciliator will be guided by principles of objectivity, fairness and justice, giving consideration to, among other things, the rights and obligations of the parties, the usages of the trade concerned and the circumstances surrounding the dispute, including any previous business practices between the parties.

3. The conciliator may conduct the conciliation proceedings in such a manner as he considers appropriate, taking into account the circumstances of the case, the wishes the parties may express, including any request by a party that the conciliator hear oral statements, and the need for a speedy settlement of the dispute.

4. The conciliator may, at any stage of the conciliation proceedings, make proposals for a settlement of the dispute. Such proposals need not be in writing and need not be accompanied by a statement of the reasons therefor.

Article 8 Administrative Assistance

In order to facilitate the conduct of the conciliation proceedings, the parties, or the conciliator with the consent of the parties, may arrange for administrative assistance by a suitable institution or person.

Article 9 Communication between Conciliator and Parties

1. The conciliator may invite the parties to meet with him or may communicate with them orally or in writing. He may meet or communicate with the parties together or with each of them separately.

---

*In this and all following articles, the term "conciliator" applies to a sole conciliator, two or three conciliators, as the case may be.

2. Unless the parties have agreed upon the place where meetings with the conciliator are to be held, such place will be determined by the conciliator, after consultation with the parties, having regard to the circumstances of the conciliation proceedings.

Article 10 Disclosure of Information

When the conciliator receives factual information concerning the dispute from a party, he discloses the substance of that information to the other party in order that the other party may have the opportunity to present any explanation which he considers appropriate. However, when a party gives any information to the conciliator subject to a specific condition that it be kept confidential, the conciliator does not disclose that information to the other party.

Article 11 Co-operation of Parties with Conciliator

The parties will in good faith co-operate with the conciliator and, in particular, will endeavour to comply with requests by the conciliator to submit written materials, provide evidence and attend meetings.

Article 12 Suggestions by Parties for Settlement of Dispute

Each party may, on his own initiative or at the invitation of the conciliator, submit to the conciliator suggestions for the settlement of the dispute.

Article 13 Settlement Agreement

1. When it appears to the conciliator that there exist elements of a settlement which would be acceptable to the parties, he formulates the terms of a possible settlement and submits them to the parties for their observations. After receiving the observations of the parties, the conciliator may reformulate the terms of a possible settlement in the light of such observations.
2. If the parties reach agreement on a settlement of the dispute, they draw up and sign a written settlement agreement.** If requested by the parties, the conciliator draws up, or assists the parties in drawing up, the settlement agreement.
3. The parties by signing the settlement agreement put an end to the dispute and are bound by the agreement.

Article 14 Confidentiality

The conciliator and the parties must keep confidential all matters relating to the conciliation proceedings. Confidentiality extends also the settlement agreement, except where its disclosure is necessary for purposes of implementation and enforcement.

Article 15 Termination of Conciliation Proceedings

The conciliation proceedings are terminated:

   a. By the signing of the settlement agreement by the parties, on the date of the agreement; or

---

**The parties may wish to consider including in the settlement agreement a clause that any dispute arising out of or relating to the settlement agreement shall be submitted to arbitration.

    b. By a written declaration of the conciliator, after consultation with the parties, to the effect that further efforts at conciliation are no longer justified, on the date of the declaration; or

    c. By a written declaration of the parties addressed to the conciliator to the effect that the conciliation proceedings are terminated, on the date of the declaration; or

    d. By a written declaration of a party to the other party and the conciliator, if appointed, to the effect that the conciliation proceedings are terminated, on the date of the declaration.

Article 16 Resort to Arbitral or Judicial Proceedings

The parties undertake not to initiate, during the conciliation proceedings, any arbitral or judicial proceedings in respect of a dispute that is the subject of the conciliation proceedings, except that a party may initiate arbitral or judicial proceedings where, in his opinion, such proceedings are necessary for preserving his rights.

Article 17 Costs

1. Upon termination of the conciliation proceedings, the conciliator fixes the costs of the conciliation and gives written notice thereof to the parties. The term "costs" includes only:

    a. The fee of the conciliator which shall be reasonable in amount;

    b. The travel and other expenses of the conciliator;

    c. The travel and other expenses of witnesses requested by the conciliator with the consent of the parties;

    d. The cost of any expert advice requested by the conciliator with the consent of the parties;

    e. The cost of any assistance provided pursuant to articles 4, paragraph (2)(b), and 8 of these Rules.

2. The costs, as defined above, are borne equally by the parties unless the settlement agreement provides for a different apportionment. All other expenses incurred by a party are borne by that party.

Article 18 Deposits

1. The conciliator, upon his appointment, may request each party to deposit an equal amount as an advance for the costs referred to in article 17, paragraph (1) which he expects will be incurred.

2. During the course of the conciliation proceedings the conciliator may request supplementary deposits in an equal amount from each party.

3. If the required deposits under paragraphs (1) and (2) of this article are not paid in full by both parties within thirty days, the conciliator may suspend the proceedings or may make a written declaration of termination to the parties, effective on the date of that declaration.

4. Upon termination of the conciliation proceedings, the conciliator renders an accounting to the parties of the deposits received and returns any unexpended balance to the parties.

Article 19 Role of Conciliator in Other Proceedings

The parties and the conciliator undertake that the conciliator will not act as an arbitrator or as a representative or counsel of a party in any arbitral or judicial proceedings in respect of a dispute that is the subject of the conciliation proceedings. The parties also undertake that they will not present the conciliator as a witness in any such proceedings.

Article 20 Admissibility of Evidence in Other Proceedings

The parties undertake not to rely on or introduce as evidence in arbitral or judicial proceedings, whether or not such proceedings relate to the dispute that is the subject of the conciliation proceedings;

   a. Views expressed or suggestions made by the other party in respect of a possible settlement of the dispute;
   b. Admissions made by the other party in the course of the conciliation proceedings;
   c. Proposals made by the conciliator;
   d. The fact that the other party had indicated his willingness to accept a proposal for settlement made by the conciliator.

Model Conciliation Clause

Where, in the event of a dispute arising out of or relating to this contract, the parties wish to seek an amicable settlement of that dispute by conciliation, the conciliation shall take place in accordance with the UNCITRAL Conciliation Rules as at present in force.
   (The parties may agree on other conciliation clauses.)

Source: The UNCITRAL website is at http://www.uncitral.org/en-index.htm.

The "Model Conciliation Clause" is the contractual provision that the parties may use (by including it in their contract) in order to ensure that these rules will in fact be invoked when conciliation is desired.

International Commercial Arbitration

Since medieval times in England, merchants have peacefully taken matters into their own hands to find settlements to their disputes. In many respects, their track record is greatly superior to that of the crowned heads and elected legislatures that have followed them. Medieval trade organizations, the guilds, governed relations between their members. When disputes arose between merchants, the senior members of the merchant guild would be called upon to hear the dispute and render a decision that would be binding upon the disputants. This dispute resolution process, over the centuries, has become what we know today as arbitration.

In essence, the process has changed very little over time. Merchants today, as in the past, usually desire a quick resolution of their differences, and preferably a decision that will not destroy their business relationship. The arbitration process admirably fits these criteria. The process is voluntary, in the sense that the parties agree to resolve their differences in this manner at the time that they enter into a contractual agreement, or later, when a dispute arises. In addition, the selection of the arbitrator is to a large extent in their hands, as well as whether the parties choose to exclude representation by legal counsel.

Part of the attraction of the arbitration process is its simplicity, speed, and relatively low cost compared to the court process, and over the past century, it has become the preeminent method of dispute resolution in international transactions.

**Advantages
of Arbitration**

1.	**Impartial**	Adjudicator is a chosen and agreed neutral individual, often from a third country and perhaps less swayed by politics.
2.	**Final**	Arbitral awards may only be challenged under limited circumstances. No endless appeals.
3.	**Confidential**	In camera proceedings and awards eliminate posturing or negative publicity.
4.	**Expert**	Recognized experts in their field may be chosen as arbitrators, eliminating the need to educate the judge and jury.
5.	**Streamlined**	Arbitration can move more rapidly to the merits.
6.	**Less is more**	Arbitration is less formal, less expensive, less time consuming.
7.	**Less adversarial**	Where desired, the commercial relationship is more likely to survive the dispute.

This has been facilitated as well by the introduction of legislation in most developed countries for the enforcement of international arbitration awards. In the United States, the Federal Arbitration Act[5] applies to international disputes; individual states have enacted their own legislation as well, but the federal act applies to any arbitration clause in a written contract involving interstate commerce. The U.S. act supports and encourages the traditional objectives of arbitration, permitting the arbitration of civil disputes and allowing autonomy in the parties' choice of substantive law, rules, and procedural steps. Further, U.S. courts are prepared to stay court proceedings and compel arbitration where it has been the clear intention of the parties to provide for arbitration. Any interim or final award need only be in writing and signed by the arbitrator(s), and there is no requirement at law for the inclusion of reasons, although this is customary.

Much arbitration is conducted on an ad hoc basis, with the appointment of the arbitrator and the determination of procedure being done privately by the parties. Just as many, however, and most major arbitration cases, are conducted through established international organizations providing arbitration services. Among these are the London Court of International Arbitration,[6] the International Court of Arbitration of the International Chamber of Commerce,[7] and the American Arbitration Association.[8]

These organizations have a long history of providing arbitration services to international businesses. The London Court of International Arbitration is perhaps the oldest arbitration body in the world, dating back to 1892, when it was first established as The London Chamber of Arbitration. The name was changed in 1903. The Secretariat of the London Court is, not surprisingly, located in London, England, but the Court provides its services throughout the world by way of "user councils" operating in all major trading areas.

The International Chamber of Commerce International Court of Arbitration was established in 1923 in Paris, France, but the ICC Court of Arbitration monitors and supervises arbitrators in over 40 countries. The Secretariat of the Court of Arbitration is located within the ICC headquarters in Paris.

The American Arbitration Association, established in 1926, has developed its own range of arbitration rules, with some designed for specific commercial sectors of international business, such as construction, patent, or employment disputes. It maintains international dispute settlement centers in New York and Dublin, Republic of Ireland.

Each of these institutions has established its own set of rules for the conduct of international arbitration, and they are highly similar in effect. The "most international" rules

[5]9 U.S.C. §§1–14.
[6]http://www.lcia-arbitration.com.
[7]http://www.iccwbo.org/index_court.asp.
[8]http://www.adr.org.

In addition to a simple arbitration clause, it is useful to include a reference to the appointing authority (the LCIA, ICC Court of Arbitration, AAA, or a previously chosen arbitrator), the number of arbitrators (one or more, usually an odd number), the place and language of any arbitration, and a choice-of-law clause.

(which can be applied in any case) are those of the UN's UNCITRAL, in use since 1976. These arbitration rules are supported by UNCITRAL's Model Law of 1985, which allows nations to easily adopt their legal systems to accommodate arbitration.

The parties to a commercial relationship are free to choose and make applicable any given set of arbitration rules. Preferably they will make this decision during their original contract negotiations, with an eye to the future, and include an arbitration clause in the form suggested by the rules they intend to invoke.

The Arbitration Process

The arbitration process requires at the outset an agreement by the parties that they will resolve any disputes that arise between them by binding arbitration. This usually takes the form of a clause in the contract or agreement for goods or services (or license or investment agreement) negotiated by the parties. It is important to note that this need not be the only way that parties to an international contract may have recourse to arbitration, as they may agree, for example, to arbitration after a dispute arises between them. The normal approach, however, is to include an arbitration clause in the original agreement, and this is almost always the case where the contract is prepared or reviewed by legal counsel before it is finalized. Both the International Chamber of Commerce and the London Court of International Arbitration offer suitable draft arbitration clauses, as do the UNCITRAL Arbitration Rules.

All of these issues are negotiable, and should be carefully considered by each party in terms of location, convenience, familiarity with the applicable law, and any perceived benefit of naming a member of an arbitration panel if a three-person tribunal is selected.

With respect to the arbitration process itself, the procedure is relatively straightforward. In its simplest form, the parties begin the process by the selection of an arbitrator (or arbitrators). If they have agreed upon a place for the arbitration to take place, the location is decided; otherwise the arbitrator or tribunal may fix the location. The parties then exchange statements of claim and defense and any further statements, including any pleas as to the jurisdiction of the arbitration tribunal. The next step in the process is the hearing itself, where the arbitrator or arbitration tribunal will hear the evidence of the parties, any expert testimony, and final arguments. The arbitrator or arbitration tribunal will then deliberate and issue an award.

The UNCITRAL rules, as noted above, provide greater procedural guidance for the operation of the arbitration process than most other available rule sets. Still, the arbitrator (and the parties) has far greater latitude and flexibility in the conduct of arbitration than would be available to a judge under any national legal system. The UNCITRAL Arbitration Rules are reproduced below. Note particularly the Model Arbitration Clause found in Article 1; the procedural flexibility granted by Articles 15, 24, and 25; the availability of interim measures in Article 26; and the provisions relating to the award itself, contained in Articles 31 and 32.

UNCITRAL Arbitration Rules

General Assembly Resolution 31/98 of December 15, 1976
(Full substantive text, preambles omitted)

Section I. Introductory Rules

Scope of Application
Article 1

1. Where the parties to a contract have agreed in writing* that disputes in relation to that contract shall be referred to arbitration under the UNCITRAL Arbitration Rules, then such disputes shall be settled in accordance with these Rules subject to such modification as the parties may agree in writing.

2. These Rules shall govern the arbitration except that where any of these Rules is in conflict with a provision of the law applicable to the arbitration from which the parties cannot derogate, that provision shall prevail.

Notice, Calculation of Periods of Time
Article 2

1. For the purposes of these Rules, any notice, including a notification, communication or proposal, is deemed to have been received if it is physically delivered to the addressee or if it is delivered at his habitual residence, place of business or mailing address, or, if none of these can be found after making reasonable inquiry, then at the addressee's last-known residence or place of business. Notice shall be deemed to have been received on the day it is so delivered.

2. For the purposes of calculating a period of time under these Rules, such period shall begin to run on the day following the day when a notice, notification, communication or proposal is received. If the last day of such period is an official holiday or a non-business day at the residence or place of business of the addressee, the period is extended until the first business day which follows. Official holidays or non-business days occurring during the running of the period of time are included in calculating the period.

Notice of Arbitration
Article 3

1. The party initiating recourse to arbitration (hereinafter called the "claimant") shall give to the other party (hereinafter called the "respondent") a notice of arbitration.

2. Arbitral proceedings shall be deemed to commence on the date on which the notice of arbitration is received by the respondent.

---

*Model Arbitration Clause

Any dispute, controversy or claim arising out of or relating to this contract, or the breach, termination or invalidity thereof, shall be settled by arbitration in accordance with the UNCITRAL Arbitration Rules as at present in force.

Note—Parties may wish to consider adding:

a. The appointing authority shall be . . . (name of institution or person);
b. The number of arbitrators shall be . . . (one or three);
c. The place of arbitration shall be . . . (town or country);
d. The language(s) to be used in the arbitral proceedings shall be . . .

3. The notice of arbitration shall include the following:
   a. A demand that the dispute be referred to arbitration;
   b. The names and addresses of the parties;
   c. A reference to the arbitration clause or the separate arbitration agreement that is invoked;
   d. A reference to the contract out of or in relation to which the dispute arises;
   e. The general nature of the claim and an indication of the amount involved, if any;
   f. The relief or remedy sought;
   g. A proposal as to the number of arbitrators (i.e. one or three), if the parties have not previously agreed thereon.
4. The notice of arbitration may also include:
   a. The proposals for the appointments of a sole arbitrator and an appointing authority referred to in article 6, paragraph 1;
   b. The notification of the appointment of an arbitrator referred to in article 7;
   c. The statement of claim referred to in article 18.

Representation and Assistance
Article 4

The parties may be represented or assisted by persons of their choice. The names and addresses of such persons must be communicated in writing to the other party; such communication must specify whether the appointment is being made for purposes of representation or assistance.

Section II. Composition of the Arbitral Tribunal

Number of Arbitrators
Article 5

If the parties have not previously agreed on the number of arbitrators (i.e. one or three), and if within fifteen days after the receipt by the respondent of the notice of arbitration the parties have not agreed that there shall be only one arbitrator, three arbitrators shall be appointed.

Appointment of Arbitrators (Articles 6 to 8)
Article 6

1. If a sole arbitrator is to be appointed, either party may propose to the other:
   a. The names of one or more persons, one of whom would serve as the sole arbitrator; and
   b. If no appointing authority has been agreed upon by the parties, the name or names of one or more institutions or persons, one of whom would serve as appointing authority.
2. If within thirty days after receipt by a party of a proposal made in accordance with paragraph 1 the parties have not reached agreement on the choice of a sole arbitrator, the sole arbitrator shall be appointed by the appointing authority agreed upon by the parties. If no appointing authority has been agreed upon by the parties, or if the appointing authority agreed upon refuses to act or fails to appoint the arbitrator within sixty days of the receipt of a party's request therefor, either party may request the Secretary-General of the Permanent Court of Arbitration at The Hague to designate an appointing authority.
3. The appointing authority shall, at the request of one of the parties, appoint the sole arbitrator as promptly as possible. In making the appointment the appointing authority shall use the following list-procedure, unless both parties agree that the list-procedure

should not be used or unless the appointing authority determines in its discretion that the use of the list-procedure is not appropriate for the case:

   a. At the request of one of the parties the appointing authority shall communicate to both parties an identical list containing at least three names;

   b. Within fifteen days after the receipt of this list, each party may return the list to the appointing authority after having deleted the name or names to which he objects and numbered the remaining names on the list in the order of his preference;

   c. After the expiration of the above period of time the appointing authority shall appoint the sole arbitrator from among the names approved on the lists returned to it and in accordance with the order of preference indicated by the parties;

   d. If for any reason the appointment cannot be made according to this procedure, the appointing authority may exercise its discretion in appointing the sole arbitrator.

4. In making the appointment, the appointing authority shall have regard to such considerations as are likely to secure the appointment of an independent and impartial arbitrator and shall take into account as well the advisability of appointing an arbitrator of a nationality other than the nationalities of the parties.

Article 7

1. If three arbitrators are to be appointed, each party shall appoint one arbitrator. The two arbitrators thus appointed shall choose the third arbitrator who will act as the presiding arbitrator of the tribunal.

2. If within thirty days after the receipt of a party's notification of the appointment of an arbitrator the other party has not notified the first party of the arbitrator he has appointed:

   a. The first party may request the appointing authority previously designated by the parties to appoint the second arbitrator; or

   b. If no such authority has been previously designated by the parties, or if the appointing authority previously designated refuses to act or fails to appoint the arbitrator within thirty days after receipt of a party's request therefor, the first party may request the Secretary-General of the Permanent Court of Arbitration at The Hague to designate the appointing authority. The first party may then request the appointing authority so designated to appoint the second arbitrator. In either case, the appointing authority may exercise its discretion in appointing the arbitrator.

3. If within thirty days after the appointment of the second arbitrator the two arbitrators have not agreed on the choice of the presiding arbitrator, the presiding arbitrator shall be appointed by an appointing authority in the same way as a sole arbitrator would be appointed under article 6.

Article 8

1. When an appointing authority is requested to appoint an arbitrator pursuant to article 6 or article 7, the party which makes the request shall send to the appointing authority a copy of the notice of arbitration, a copy of the contract out of or in relation to which the dispute has arisen and a copy of the arbitration agreement if it is not contained in the contract. The appointing authority may require from either party such information as it deems necessary to fulfil its function.

2. Where the names of one or more persons are proposed for appointment as arbitrators, their full names, addresses and nationalities shall be indicated, together with a description of their qualifications.

Challenge of Arbitrators (Articles 9 to 12)

Article 9

A prospective arbitrator shall disclose to those who approach him in connexion with his possible appointment any circumstances likely to give rise to justifiable doubts as to his impartiality or independence. An arbitrator, once appointed or chosen, shall disclose such circumstances to the parties unless they have already been informed by him of these circumstances.

Article 10

1. Any arbitrator may be challenged if circumstances exist that give rise to justifiable doubts as to the arbitrators impartiality or independence.
2. A party may challenge the arbitrator appointed by him only for reasons of which he becomes aware after the appointment has been made.

Article 11

1. A party who intends to challenge an arbitrator shall send notice of his challenge within fifteen days after the appointment of the challenged arbitrator has been notified to the challenging party or within fifteen days after the circumstances mentioned in articles 9 and 10 became known to that party.
2. The challenge shall be notified to the other party, to the arbitrator who is challenged and to the other members of the arbitral tribunal. The notification shall be in writing and shall state the reasons for the challenge.
3. When an arbitrator has been challenged by one party, the other party may agree to the challenge. The arbitrator may also, after the challenge, withdraw from his office. In neither case does this imply acceptance of the validity of the grounds for the challenge. In both cases the procedure provided in article 6 or 7 shall be used in full for the appointment of the substitute arbitrator, even if during the process of appointing the challenged arbitrator a party had failed to exercise his right to appoint or to participate in the appointment.

Article 12

1. If the other party does not agree to the challenge and the challenged arbitrator does not withdraw, the decision on the challenge will be made:
    a. When the initial appointment was made by an appointing authority, by that authority;
    b. When the initial appointment was not made by an appointing authority, but an appointing authority has been previously designated, by that authority;
    c. In all other cases, by the appointing authority to be designated in accordance with the procedure for designating an appointing authority as provided for in article 6.
2. If the appointing authority sustains the challenge, a substitute arbitrator shall be appointed or chosen pursuant to the procedure applicable to the appointment or choice of an arbitrator as provided in articles 6 to 9 except that, when this procedure would call for the designation of an appointing authority, the appointment of the arbitrator shall be made by the appointing authority which decided on the challenge.

Replacement of an Arbitrator

Article 13

1. In the event of the death or resignation of an arbitrator during the course of the arbitral proceedings, a substitute arbitrator shall be appointed or chosen pursuant to the procedure provided for in articles 6 to 9 that was applicable to the appointment or choice of the arbitrator being replaced.
2. In the event that an arbitrator fails to act or in the event of the de jure or de facto impossibility of his performing his functions, the procedure in respect of the challenge and replacement of an arbitrator as provided in the preceding articles shall apply.

Repetition of Hearings in the Event of the Replacement of an Arbitrator

Article 14

If under articles 11 to 13 the sole or presiding arbitrator is replaced, any hearings held previously shall be repeated; if any other arbitrator is replaced, such prior hearings may be repeated at the discretion of the arbitral tribunal.

Section III. Arbitral Proceedings

General Provisions

Article 15

1. Subject to these Rules, the arbitral tribunal may conduct the arbitration in such manner as it considers appropriate, provided that the parties are treated with equality and that at any stage of the proceedings each party is given a full opportunity of presenting his case.

2. If either party so requests at any stage of the proceedings, the arbitral tribunal shall hold hearings for the presentation of evidence by witnesses, including expert witnesses, or for oral argument. In the absence of such a request, the arbitral tribunal shall decide whether to hold such hearings or whether the proceedings shall be conducted on the basis of documents and other materials.

3. All documents or information supplied to the arbitral tribunal by one party shall at the same time be communicated by that party to the other party.

Place of Arbitration

Article 16

1. Unless the parties have agreed upon the place where the arbitration is to be held, such place shall be determined by the arbitral tribunal, having regard to the circumstances of the arbitration.

2. The arbitral tribunal may determine the locale of the arbitration within the country agreed upon by the parties. It may hear witnesses and hold meetings for consultation among its members at any place it deems appropriate, having regard to the circumstances of the arbitration.

3. The arbitral tribunal may meet at any place it deems appropriate for the inspection of goods, other property or documents. The parties shall be given sufficient notice to enable them to be present at such inspection.

4. The award shall be made at the place of arbitration.

Language

Article 17

1. Subject to an agreement by the parties, the arbitral tribunal shall, promptly after its appointment, determine the language or languages to be used in the proceedings. This determination shall apply to the statement of claim, the statement of defence, and any further written statements and, if oral hearings take place, to the language or languages to be used in such hearings.

2. The arbitral tribunal may order that any documents annexed to the statement of claim or statement of defence, and any supplementary documents or exhibits submitted in the course of the proceedings, delivered in their original language, shall be accompanied by a translation into the language or languages agreed upon by the parties or determined by the arbitral tribunal.

Statement of Claim
Article 18

1. Unless the statement of claim was contained in the notice of arbitration, within a period of time to be determined by the arbitral tribunal, the claimant shall communicate his statement of claim in writing to the respondent and to each of the arbitrators. A copy of the contract, and of the arbitration agreement if not contained in the contract, shall be annexed thereto.
2. The statement of claim shall include the following particulars:
   a. The names and addresses of the parties;
   b. A statement of the facts supporting the claim;
   c. The points at issue;
   d. The relief or remedy sought.

The claimant may annex to his statement of claim all documents he deems relevant or may add a reference to the documents or other evidence he will submit.

Statement of Defence
Article 19

1. Within a period of time to be determined by the arbitral tribunal, the respondent shall communicate his statement of defence in writing to the claimant and to each of the arbitrators.
2. The statement of defence shall reply to the particulars (*b*), (*c*) and (*d*) of the statement of claim (article 18, para. 2). The respondent may annex to his statement the documents on which he relies for his defence or may add a reference to the documents or other evidence he will submit.
3. In his statement of defence, or at a later stage in the arbitral proceedings if the arbitral tribunal decides that the delay was justified under the circumstances, the respondent may make a counter-claim arising out of the same contract or rely on a claim arising out of the same contract for the purpose of a set-off.
4. The provisions of article 18, paragraph 2, shall apply to a counter-claim and a claim relied on for the purpose of a set-off.

Amendments to the Claim or Defence
Article 20

During the course of the arbitral proceedings either party may amend or supplement his claim or defence unless the arbitral tribunal considers it inappropriate to allow such amendment having regard to the delay in making it or prejudice to the other party or any other circumstances. However, a claim may not be amended in such a manner that the amended claim falls outside the scope of the arbitration clause or separate arbitration agreement.

Pleas as to the Jurisdiction of the Arbitral Tribunal
Article 21

1. The arbitral tribunal shall have the power to rule on objections that it has no jurisdiction, including any objections with respect to the existence or validity of the arbitration clause or of the separate arbitration agreement.
2. The arbitral tribunal shall have the power to determine the existence or the validity of the contract of which an arbitration clause forms a part. For the purposes of article 21, an arbitration clause which forms part of a contract and which provides for arbitration under these Rules shall be treated as an agreement independent of the other terms of the contract. A decision by the arbitral tribunal that the contract is null and void shall not entail *ipso jure* the invalidity of the arbitration clause.

3. A plea that the arbitral tribunal does not have jurisdiction shall be raised not later than in the statement of defence or, with respect to a counter-claim, in the reply to the counter-claim.

4. In general, the arbitral tribunal should rule on a plea concerning its jurisdiction as a preliminary question. However, the arbitral tribunal may proceed with the arbitration and rule on such a plea in their final award.

Further Written Statements
Article 22

The arbitral tribunal shall decide which further written statements, in addition to the statement of claim and the statement of defence, shall be required from the parties or may be presented by them and shall fix the periods of time for communicating such statements.

Periods of Time
Article 23

The periods of time fixed by the arbitral tribunal for the communication of written statements (including the statement of claim and statement of defence) should not exceed forty-five days. However, the arbitral tribunal may extend the time-limits if it concludes that an extension is justified.

Evidence and Hearings (Articles 24 and 25)
Article 24

1. Each party shall have the burden of proving the facts relied on to support his claim or defence.

2. The arbitral tribunal may, if it considers it appropriate, require a party to deliver to the tribunal and to the other party, within such a period of time as the arbitral tribunal shall decide, a summary of the documents and other evidence which that party intends to present in support of the facts in issue set out in his statement of claim or statement of defence.

3. At any time during the arbitral proceedings the arbitral tribunal may require the parties to produce documents, exhibits or other evidence within such a period of time as the tribunal shall determine.

Article 25

1. In the event of an oral hearing, the arbitral tribunal shall give the parties adequate advance notice of the date, time and place thereof.

2. If witnesses are to be heard, at least fifteen days before the hearing each party shall communicate to the arbitral tribunal and to the other party the names and addresses of the witnesses he intends to present, the subject upon and the languages in which such witnesses will give their testimony.

3. The arbitral tribunal shall make arrangements for the translation of oral statements made at a hearing and for a record of the hearing if either is deemed necessary by the tribunal under the circumstances of the case, or if the parties have agreed thereto and have communicated such agreement to the tribunal at least fifteen days before the hearing.

4. Hearings shall be held *in camera* unless the parties agree otherwise. The arbitral tribunal may require the retirement of any witness or witnesses during the testimony of other witnesses. The arbitral tribunal is free to determine the manner in which witnesses are examined.

5. Evidence of witnesses may also be presented in the form of written statements signed by them.

6. The arbitral tribunal shall determine the admissibility, relevance, materiality and weight of the evidence offered.

Interim Measures of Protection
Article 26

1. At the request of either party, the arbitral tribunal may take any interim measures it deems necessary in respect of the subject-matter of the dispute, including measures for the conservation of the goods forming the subject-matter in dispute, such as ordering their deposit with a third person or the sale of perishable goods.

2. Such interim measures may be established in the form of an interim award. The arbitral tribunal shall be entitled to require security for the costs of such measures.

3. A request for interim measures addressed by any party to a judicial authority shall not be deemed incompatible with the agreement to arbitrate, or as a waiver of that agreement.

Experts
Article 27

1. The arbitral tribunal may appoint one or more experts to report to it, in writing, on specific issues to be determined by the tribunal. A copy of the expert's terms of reference, established by the arbitral tribunal, shall be communicated to the parties.

2. The parties shall give the expert any relevant information or produce for his inspection any relevant documents or goods that he may require of them. Any dispute between a party and such expert as to the relevance of the required information or production shall be referred to the arbitral tribunal for decision.

3. Upon receipt of the expert's report, the arbitral tribunal shall communicate a copy of the report to the parties who shall be given the opportunity to express, in writing, their opinion on the report. A party shall be entitled to examine any document on which the expert has relied in his report.

4. At the request of either party the expert, after delivery of the report, may be heard at a hearing where the parties shall have the opportunity to be present and to interrogate the expert. At this hearing either party may present expert witnesses in order to testify on the points at issue. The provisions of article 25 shall be applicable to such proceedings.

Default
Article 28

1. If, within the period of time fixed by the arbitral tribunal, the claimant has failed to communicate his claim without showing sufficient cause for such failure, the arbitral tribunal shall issue an order for the termination of the arbitral proceedings. If, within the period of time fixed by the arbitral tribunal, the respondent has failed to communicate his statement of defence without showing sufficient cause for such failure, the arbitral tribunal shall order that the proceedings continue.

2. If one of the parties, duly notified under these Rules, fails to appear at a hearing, without showing sufficient cause for such failure, the arbitral tribunal may proceed with the arbitration.

3. If one of the parties, duly invited to produce documentary evidence, fails to do so within the established period of time, without showing sufficient cause for such failure, the arbitral tribunal may make the award on the evidence before it.

Closure of Hearings
Article 29

1. The arbitral tribunal may inquire of the parties if they have any further proof to offer or witnesses to be heard or submissions to make and, if there are none, it may declare the hearings closed.

2. The arbitral tribunal may, if it considers it necessary owing to exceptional circumstances, decide, on its own motion or upon application of a party, to reopen the hearings at any time before the award is made.

Waiver of Rules

Article 30

A party who knows that any provision of, or requirement under, these Rules has not been complied with and yet proceeds with the arbitration without promptly stating his objection to such non-compliance, shall be deemed to have waived his right to object.

Section IV. The Award

Decisions

Article 31

1. When there are three arbitrators, any award or other decision of the arbitral tribunal shall be made by a majority of the arbitrators.

2. In the case of questions of procedure, when there is no majority or when the arbitral tribunal so authorizes, the presiding arbitrator may decide on his own, subject to revision, if any, by the arbitral tribunal.

Form and Effect of the Award

Article 32

1. In addition to making a final award, the arbitral tribunal shall be entitled to make interim, interlocutory, or partial awards.

2. The award shall be made in writing and shall be final and binding on the parties. The parties undertake to carry out the award without delay.

3. The arbitral tribunal shall state the reasons upon which the award is based, unless the parties have agreed that no reasons are to be given.

4. An award shall be signed by the arbitrators and it shall contain the date on which and the place where the award was made. Where there are three arbitrators and one of them fails to sign, the award shall state the reason for the absence of the signature.

5. The award may be made public only with the consent of both parties.

6. Copies of the award signed by the arbitrators shall be communicated to the parties by the arbitral tribunal.

7. If the arbitration law of the country where the award is made requires that the award be filed or registered by the arbitral tribunal, the tribunal shall comply with this requirement within the period of time required by law.

Applicable Law, Amiable Compositeur

Article 33

1. The arbitral tribunal shall apply the law designated by the parties as applicable to the substance of the dispute. Failing such designation by the parties, the arbitral tribunal shall apply the law determined by the conflict of laws rules which it considers applicable.

2. The arbitral tribunal shall decide as *amiable compositeur*[9] or *ex aequo et bono*[10] only if the parties have expressly authorized the arbitral tribunal to do so and if the law applicable to the arbitral procedure permits such arbitration.

[9]Editor's note: *amiable compositeur* (French): a mediator.

[10]Editor's note: *ex aequo et bono* (Latin): "according to what is right and good"; a basis for judgment that may be granted by the parties to the arbitrator.

3. In all cases, the arbitral tribunal shall decide in accordance with the terms of the contract and shall take into account the usages of the trade applicable to the transaction.

Settlement or Other Grounds for Termination
Article 34

1. If, before the award is made, the parties agree on a settlement of the dispute, the arbitral tribunal shall either issue an order for the termination of the arbitral proceedings or, if requested by both parties and accepted by the tribunal, record the settlement in the form of an arbitral award on agreed terms. The arbitral tribunal is not obliged to give reasons for such an award.

2. If, before the award is made, the continuation of the arbitral proceedings becomes unnecessary or impossible for any reason not mentioned in paragraph 1, the arbitral tribunal shall inform the parties of its intention to issue an order for the termination of the proceedings. The arbitral tribunal shall have the power to issue such an order unless a party raises justifiable grounds for objection.

3. Copies of the order for termination of the arbitral proceedings or of the arbitral award on agreed terms, signed by the arbitrators, shall be communicated by the arbitral tribunal to the parties. Where an arbitral award on agreed terms is made, the provisions of article 32, paragraphs 2 and 4 to 7, shall apply.

Interpretation of the Award
Article 35

1. Within thirty days after the receipt of the award, either party, with notice to the other party, may request that the arbitral tribunal give an interpretation of the award.

2. The interpretation shall be given in writing within forty-five days after the receipt of the request. The interpretation shall form part of the award and the provisions of article 32, paragraphs 2 to 7, shall apply.

Correction of the Award
Article 36

1. Within thirty days after the receipt of the award, either party, with notice to the other party, may request the arbitral tribunal to correct in the award any errors in computation, any clerical or typographical errors, or any errors of similar nature. The arbitral tribunal may within thirty days after the communication of the award make such corrections on its own initiative.

2. Such corrections shall be in writing, and the provisions of article 32, paragraphs 2 to 7, shall apply.

Additional Award
Article 37

1. Within thirty days after the receipt of the award, either party, with notice to the other party, may request the arbitral tribunal to make an additional award as to claims presented in the arbitral proceedings but omitted from the award.

2. If the arbitral tribunal considers the request for an additional award to be justified and considers that the omission can be rectified without any further hearings or evidence, it shall complete its award within sixty days after the receipt of the request.

3. When an additional award is made, the provisions of article 32, paragraphs 2 to 7, shall apply.

Costs (Articles 38 to 40)

Article 38

The arbitral tribunal shall fix the costs of arbitration in its award. The term "costs" includes only:

- *a.* The fees of the arbitral tribunal to be stated separately as to each arbitrator and to be fixed by the tribunal itself in accordance with article 39;
- *b.* The travel and other expenses incurred by the arbitrators;
- *c.* The costs of expert advice and of other assistance required by the arbitral tribunal;
- *d.* The travel and other expenses of witnesses to the extent such expenses are approved by the arbitral tribunal;
- *e.* The costs for legal representation and assistance of the successful party if such costs were claimed during the arbitral proceedings, and only to the extent that the arbitral tribunal determines that the amount of such costs is reasonable;
- *f.* Any fees and expenses of the appointing authority as well as the expenses of the Secretary-General of the Permanent Court of Arbitration at The Hague.

Article 39

1. The fees of the arbitral tribunal shall be reasonable in amount, taking into account the amount in dispute, the complexity of the subject-matter, the time spent by the arbitrators and any other relevant circumstances of the case.

2. If an appointing authority has been agreed upon by the parties or designated by the Secretary-General of the Permanent Court of Arbitration at The Hague, and if that authority has issued a schedule of fees for arbitrators in international cases which it administers, the arbitral tribunal in fixing its fees shall take that schedule of fees into account to the extent that it considers appropriate in the circumstances of the case.

3. If such appointing authority has not issued a schedule of fees for arbitrators in international cases, any party may at any time request the appointing authority to furnish a statement setting forth the basis for establishing fees which is customarily followed in international cases in which the authority appoints arbitrators. If the appointing authority consents to provide such a statement, the arbitral tribunal in fixing its fees shall take such information into account to the extent that it considers appropriate in the circumstances of the case.

4. In cases referred to in paragraphs 2 and 3, when a party so requests and the appointing authority consents to perform the function, the arbitral tribunal shall fix its fees only after consultation with the appointing authority which may make any comment it deems appropriate to the arbitral tribunal concerning the fees.

Article 40

1. Except as provided in paragraph 2, the costs of arbitration shall in principle be borne by the unsuccessful party. However, the arbitral tribunal may apportion each of such costs between the parties if it determines that apportionment is reasonable, taking into account the circumstances of the case.

2. With respect to the costs of legal representation and assistance referred to in article 38, paragraph (*e*), the arbitral tribunal, taking into account the circumstances of the case, shall be free to determine which party shall bear such costs or may apportion such costs between the parties if it determines that apportionment is reasonable.

3. When the arbitral tribunal issues an order for the termination of the arbitral proceedings or makes an award on agreed terms, it shall fix the costs of arbitration referred to in article 38 and article 39, paragraph 1, in the text of that order or award.

4. No additional fees may be charged by an arbitral tribunal for interpretation or correction or completion of its award under articles 35 to 37.

Deposit of Costs
Article 41

1. The arbitral tribunal, on its establishment, may request each party to deposit an equal amount as an advance for the costs referred to in article 38, paragraphs (*a*), (*b*) and (*c*).

2. During the course of the arbitral proceedings the arbitral tribunal may request supplementary deposits from the parties.

3. If an appointing authority has been agreed upon by the parties or designated by the Secretary-General of the Permanent Court of Arbitration at The Hague, and when a party so requests and the appointing authority consents to perform the function, the arbitral tribunal shall fix the amounts of any deposits or supplementary deposits only after consultation with the appointing authority which may make any comments to the arbitral tribunal which it deems appropriate concerning the amount of such deposits and supplementary deposits.

4. If the required deposits are not paid in full within thirty days after the receipt of the request, the arbitral tribunal shall so inform the parties in order that one or another of them may make the required payment. If such payment is not made, the arbitral tribunal may order the suspension or termination of the arbitral proceedings.

5. After the award has been made, the arbitral tribunal shall render an accounting to the parties of the deposits received and return any unexpended balance to the parties.

Source: The UNCITRAL website is at http://www.uncitral.org/en-index.htm.

Enforcement of Awards in International Commercial Arbitration

The enforcement of an international commercial arbitration award is obviously of critical importance to the winner in the award, as it is essential that the award is enforceable where the losing party has assets located, or where that party resides. Necessarily, this requires a mechanism by which the award of a private adjudicator becomes enforceable by public authorities—the award must be recognized and enforced by states.

To overcome the problem of recognition of foreign arbitration awards, the United Nations addressed the difficulties by way of its 1958 New York Convention.[11] This convention makes provision that any state ratifying it would either recognize and enforce all foreign arbitration awards or would limit itself to only those states that had also ratified the Convention.[12] The United States made this latter reservation in its ratification in 1970, thereby limiting U.S. enforcement to commercial arbitration awards rendered in a country that is also a party to the Convention. Enforcement of foreign awards in the United States pursuant to the Federal Arbitration Act, must be conducted under either the New York Convention or its regional counterpart, the 17-member Inter-American (or "Panama") Convention.

The effect of ratification of the New York Convention also limits the grounds upon which a state can refuse to recognize a foreign arbitration award to the following circumstances:

---

[11]UN Convention on the Recognition and Enforcement of Foreign Arbitral Awards (the New York Convention), June 10, 1958.

[12]Membership presently includes over 130 nations, representing virtually all major trading nations, including the United States.

Arbitration rules grant arbitrators wide-ranging latitude to make their awards. Where a party to a dispute is bent on defeating recognition and enforcement of an award by a national legal system, it must attack where the award is potentially most vulnerable: the jurisdiction of the arbitrator, point number 4 below. While the other exceptions to recognition and enforcement are powerful, these other technicalities are usually fairly difficult to rationally argue and tend to be difficult for courts to accept.

1. The agreement is invalid under the law. (Article V.1(a)).
2. A party to the agreement suffers from some incapacity. (Article V.1(a)).
3. No proper notice of the arbitration was given. (Article V.1(b)).
4. The award deals with a matter outside the terms of the arbitration. (Article V.1(c)).
5. The arbitration tribunal was not constituted in accordance with the agreement of the parties. (Article V.1(d)).
6. The subject matter of the dispute is not capable of settlement by arbitration in that country. (Article V.1(d)).
7. The award conflicts with the public policy of the state where enforcement is requested. (Article V.2(b)).

On this last ground, public policy, matters such as fraud, corruption, or patent errors of calculation or description open the award to rejection or modification by local courts where recognition and enforcement are sought. Apart from these grounds for refusal, states that have signed the New York Convention are obliged to recognize and thereafter enforce foreign commercial arbitration awards in the same manner as domestic awards. In order to apply for enforcement in a local court, a party need only present the court with an original or certified copy of the award, together with a certified copy of the arbitration agreement. In states that are not signatories of the New York Convention, the arbitration award usually must be converted into a court judgment before it may be recognized and enforced.

Commercial Arbitration between States and Individuals

Frequently, international businesspersons will be conducting transactions where the principal party on the other side is a sovereign state. Nothing prevents a state and an individual from making a provision that arbitration will be used as a means to settlement in the case of a contract dispute between them. An arbitration provision could be applicable to contracts for sale of goods to a state (or a license agreement), but the overwhelming majority of potential disputes will stem from investment contracts.

One can imagine the great range of such disputes. For example, foreign investors may see the nationalization of an oil field after they have completed their exploration work, or the foreign contractor in a build-operate-transfer airport project may have its contract terminated just at the moment of completion.

Such investment contracts have heavy political overtones, as they tend to involve the larger multinational companies, who are almost certain to seek diplomatic intervention of their home state if there is no satisfactory recourse open to them.

Between 1975 and 1977, French professor René-Jean Dupuy had to establish his own jurisdiction, applicable law, and merits in an arbitration in which a state defendant, Libya, refused to attend the proceedings. Rather than make this a neat default judgment, Professor Dupuy took great pains to lay out both his procedural steps and substantive international law analysis. The result is a 132-page award, excerpts of which are reproduced below, which is one of the most important awards in both arbitration and international law.

Texaco v. Libya

Indexed as *Texaco Overseas Petroleum Company and California Asiatic Oil Company v. The Government of the Libyan Arab Republic*

Dupuy, Sole Arbitrator

Award on the Merits, January 19, 1977

1. The present arbitration arises out of 14 Deeds of Concession *[for oil exploration and extraction]* concluded between the competent Libyan authorities (Petroleum Commission or Petroleum Ministry, depending on the date of the contracts) and the above-mentioned companies *[between 1955 and 1966].*

3. . . . The final version of Clause 16 *[of the Deeds of Concession]* . . . reads as follows:

> "The Government of Libya will take all steps necessary to ensure that the Company enjoys all the rights conferred by this Concession. The contractual rights expressly created by this Concession shall not be altered except by mutual consent of the parties.
>
> This Concession shall throughout the period of its validity be construed in accordance with the Petroleum Law and the Regulations in force on the date of execution of the agreement of amendment by which this paragraph (2) was incorporated into this concession agreement. Any amendment to or repeal of such Regulations shall not affect the contractual rights of the Company without its consent."

7. Law No. 11 of 1974 (the Decree of nationalization of 11 February 1974) nationalized the totality of the properties, rights, assets and interests of California Asiatic Oil Company and Texaco Overseas Petroleum Company arising out of the fourteen Deeds of Concession held by those companies . . .

8. The Tribunal should now, on one hand, recall and complete the indications already given in its Preliminary Award of 27 November 1975 relating to the arbitration procedure and, on the other, pronounce on the law applicable to the arbitration of which it has been seized.

9. —by two separate letters dated 2 September 1973, California Asiatic Oil Company and Texaco Overseas Petroleum Company notified the Government of the Libyan Arab Republic that, pursuant to Article 20(1) of the Law on Petroleum of 1955 and to Clause 28 of the Deeds of Concession, they intended to submit to arbitration the dispute between them and the Government and advised the Government that they had appointed as arbitrator a member of the New York Bar, Mr. Fowler Hamilton.

—during the time which was allowed it by Clause 28 of the Deeds of Concession (and which expired on 1 December 1973), the Government of the Libyan Arab Republic did not appoint its arbitrator and, by a circular letter of 8 December 1973, declared that it rejected the request for arbitration;

—the Libyan Government's failure and refusal to appoint an arbitrator led to the companies to use the provision of Clause 28 of the Deeds of Concession which allows the concessionaires to request that the President of the International Court of Justice appoint a Sole Arbitrator . . .

—by letter dated 18 December 1974, the President of the International Court of Justice requested the undersigned, who accepted, to act as Sole Arbitrator to consider the two disputes . . .

—as no date had been proposed by common agreement of the parties to the dispute, the Sole Arbitrator, by cables dated 11 February 1975, confirmed by letters dated 12 February 1975, fixed 24 February 1975 and Geneva as the date and place of the first hearing of the Arbitral tribunal . . .

—on 24 February 1975, the first hearing of the Arbitral Tribunal took place in Geneva at which the Government of the Libyan Arab Republic did not appear. During this hearing the Arbitral Tribunal adopted its Rules of Procedure: the text of these Rules and detailed Minutes of the hearing were sent to the parties to the dispute . . .

[From March 1975 to November 1975, the arbitrator gave repeated opportunities for all parties to make submissions, written memorials, and oral argument.]

—on 27 November 1975, a hearing was held in Geneva at which the Preliminary Award was handed down, the operative part of which stated as follows:

> "The undersigned Sole Arbitrator, having examined the documents of the case indicated hereinbefore, declares himself competent to deal with the merits of the litigation which opposes the Government of the Arab Republic of Libya on the one hand to California Asiatic Oil Company and Texaco Overseas Petroleum Company on the other hand."

[From that date through June 15 and 16, 1976, the arbitrator gave the parties repeated opportunities to present written and oral argument.]

10. It appears from the preceding discussion that from the beginning to the end of the arbitral proceedings the Government of the Libyan Arab Republic has deliberately chosen not to take part in the proceedings and to default: the Tribunal can only say, once again, that it deeply regrets this attitude and recalls that it did everything it could in order that the defendant should be kept constantly and exactly informed of the various stages of the proceedings: the documents of the proceedings *[then listed]* have all been sent, by registered mail, to the defendant. The defendant,—with the sole exception of the letter *[to the president of the PICJ]*—has never appeared . . .

11. The Arbitral Tribunal must now precisely state what law or system of law is applicable to this arbitration, it being understood that the parties themselves are entitled freely to choose the law of procedure applicable to the arbitration and it is only, as is the case here, in the absence of any express agreement between them that the Arbitral Tribunal must determine the law or system of law applicable to the arbitration.

[The arbitrator then dismisses a range of options in turn, on the basis of a carefully reasoned analysis of their faults, concluding that the arbitration must proceed with international law as its governing law.]

16. Therefore, if it is appropriate for the Tribunal to declare that this arbitration, for the reasons stated above, is governed by international law, it is because—the parties wanting to remove the arbitration from any national sovereignty—one cannot accept that the institution of arbitration should escape the reach of all legal systems and be somehow suspended in vacuo . . .

The Merits . . .

18. The tribunal must rule on these submissions *[of the plaintiffs]* by answering the following questions:
    1. Are the Deeds of Concession of a binding nature as regards the parties or not?
    2. In adopting the nationalization measures of 1973 and 1974, has the Libyan Government breached its obligations under these contracts or not? . . .
    3. Is the defendant Government required to perform, and give full effect to, the Deeds of Concession?

4. Should the defendant Government have a time limit and, if so, of what duration, in order to inform the Arbitral Tribunal of the measures it has taken with a view to comply with, and to perform, the award?

[The Arbitrator devotes 12 pages to detailed analysis and review of authorities before concluding . . .]

35. This Tribunal therefore holds that it is established that the Deeds of Concession in dispute are within the domain of international law and that this law empowered the parties to choose the law which was to govern their contractual relations . . .

51. No International jurisdiction whatsoever has ever had the least doubt as to the existence in international law, of the rule *pacta sunt servanda:*[13] it has been affirmed vigorously . . . *[cases cited]* . . . that "it is a fundamental principle of law, which is constantly being proclaimed by international courts, that contractual undertakings must be respected . . . This Tribunal cannot but reaffirm this in turn by stating that the maxim *pacta sunt servanda* should be viewed as a fundamental principle of international law.

52. . . . and enables it to conclude that the Deeds of Concession in dispute have binding force.

53. . . . Three types of reasons could be put forward to justify, or attempt to justify, the behavior of the defendant Government:

[that the contracts were simply administrative, that nationalization was an exercise of sovereignty, and that such rights are preserved under the UN Charter of Rights and Duties of States. The arbitrator devotes 32 pages to this analysis, including a review based on Islamic law, before concluding, absent compensation, a lack of justification exists . . .]

91. . . . to decide otherwise would in fact recognize that all contractual commitments undertaken by a State have been undertaken under a purely permissive condition on its part and are therefore lacking of any legal force and any binding effect. From the point of view of its advisability, such a solution would gravely harm the credibility of States since it would mean that contracts signed by them did not bind them; it would introduce in such contracts a fundamental imbalance because in these contracts only one party—the party contracting with the State—would be bound. In law, such an outcome would go directly against the most elementary principle of good faith and for this reason it cannot be accepted.

[The arbitrator then turns to the measure of compensation, devoting 14 pages to a review of Libyan law, Islamic law, and international law, and international law authorities.]

109. Thus for the general reasons mentioned above, this tribunal must hold that restitutio in integrum is, both under the principles of Libyan law and under the principles of international law, the normal sanction for non-performance of contractual obligations and that it is inapplicable only to the extent that restoration of the status quo ante is impossible . . .

112. . . . Such are the grounds, both generally and in particular, on which this tribunal invites the Libyan Government to perform specifically its own obligations.

114. . . . A time limit of five (5) months *[for specific performance* or restitutio in integrum *to be made],* commencing as from 1 February 1977 and expiring on 30 June 1977, appears, in this respect, to be a desirable solution.

[Further proceedings and costs were reserved pending expiration of the period. In September 1977, a settlement was announced of a 15-month series of deliveries by Libya of $76 million in crude oil to the plaintiffs, who then terminated the proceedings.]

Source: Preliminary award as to jurisdiction at (1979) 53 I.L.R. 389; award on the merits at (1979) 53 I.L.R. 422.

---

[13]Editor's note: Latin, "agreements must be respected."

- Providing more than just a simplistic answer, explain why Libya capitulated and settled in the *Texaco* arbitration case.
- Faced with a lack of cooperation from Libya and its refusal to attend, why did Professor Dupuy, the arbitrator, go to such great lengths to set out the case and law in his award? Why did he not just give a default award to Texaco?

The problems in obtaining relief through arbitration in disputes between states and individuals were the driving force behind the World Bank's[14] Convention on the Settlement of Investment Disputes between States and Nationals of Other States (the ICSID Convention), which entered into force in October 1966.

In an effort to defuse political conflict, over 150 nations[15] have signed (and 139 have ratified[16]) the ICSID Convention and are, in turn, sponsors of the International Center for Settlement of Investment Disputes, which was established pursuant to the Convention.

The ICSID provides facilities for conciliation and arbitration of investment disputes between its contracting states and nationals of other contracting states. Like other arbitral bodies, the ICSID has further created regulations and rules for the conduct of conciliation and arbitration in qualifying disputes.

The principal form of qualifying dispute is one that, in the words of Article 25(1) of the Convention, is a "legal dispute arising directly out of an investment, between a Contracting State (or any constituent subdivision or agency of a Contracting State designated to the Centre by that State) and a national of another Contracting State, which the parties to the dispute consent in writing to submit to the Centre."

Thus, in principle, there is a subject matter, nationality, and consent requirement that must be met. Recognizing these limitations, but desiring an even wider scope for the usefulness of the ICSID, an "additional facility" has been created. The additional facility consists of rules for disputes otherwise falling outside the scope of the ICSID Convention, namely

1. Fact-finding proceedings.
2. Conciliation or arbitration in *investment* disputes where one of the parties is *not* a contracting state or a national of a contracting state.
3. Conciliation and arbitration where at least one of the parties *is* a contracting state or a national of a contracting state where the dispute does *not* arise directly out of an investment, provided that the underlying transaction is not an ordinary commercial transaction.

The following ICSID additional facility case, *Metalclad,* is representative. It illustrates the investment dilemma faced by a U.S. firm that, due to Mexican government action, finds the assets of its wholly owned Mexican subsidiary to be both frozen from operations and worthless if sold. The Metalclad firm has no way forward but to make a claim that it has been treated unfairly and that its investment has, essentially, been taken from it. Thus, the case highlights political risk and expropriation and a dispute settlement tribunal established pursuant to NAFTA provisions and the ICSID additional facility. Of particular note, the president of the tribunal is one of the world's foremost authorities on international law.

---

[14]Properly, the International Bank for Reconstruction and Development.

[15]Again, virtually all nations with an active interest in international business and investment.

[16]As of early 2004.

Metalclad Corporation v. The United Mexican States

International Centre for Settlement of Investment Disputes
(Additional Facility)

Before the Arbitral Tribunal constituted under Chapter Eleven of the North American
Free Trade Agreement

August 30, 2000

Professor Sir Elihu Lauterpacht, CBE, QC:

I. Introduction

1. This dispute arises out of the activities of the Claimant, Metalclad Corporation
   ("Metalclad"), in the Mexican Municipality of Guadalcazar ("Guadalcazar"), lo-
   cated in the Mexican State of San Luis Potosi ("SLP"). Metalclad alleges that Respondent, the United Mexican States ("Mexico"), through its local governments of
   SLP and Guadalcazar, interfered with its development and operation of a hazardous
   waste landfill. Metalclad claims that this interference is a violation of the Chapter
   Eleven investment provisions of the North American Free Trade Agreement
   ("NAFTA"). In particular, Metalclad alleges violations of (i) NAFTA, Article 1105,
   which requires each Party to NAFTA to "accord to investments of investors of another Party treatment in accordance with international law, including fair and equitable treatment and full protection and security"; and (ii) NAFTA, Article 1110,
   which provides that "no Party to NAFTA may directly or indirectly nationalize or expropriate an investment of an investor of another Party in its territory or take a measure tantamount to nationalization or expropriation of such an investment ('expropriation'), except: (a) for a public purpose; (b) on a non-discriminatory basis;
   (c) in accordance with due process of law and Article 1105(1); and (d) on payment
   of compensation in accordance with paragraphs 2 through 6." Mexico denies these
   allegations.

II. The Parties

2. Metalclad is an enterprise of the United States of America, [which, through holding
   companies, is the owner of COTERIN, a Mexican company. In 1993, COTERIN was
   purchased] with a view to the acquisition, development and operation of the latter's
   hazardous waste transfer station and landfill in the valley of La Pedrera, located in
   Guadalcazar. COTERIN is the owner of record of the landfill property as well as the
   permits and licenses which are at the base of this dispute.
3. COTERIN is the "enterprise" on behalf of which Metalclad has, as an "investor of a
   Party," submitted a claim to arbitration under NAFTA, Article 1117.

III. Other Entites

6. The Town Council of Guadalcazar, SLP, is the municipal government of Guadalcazar, the site of the landfill project. While neither Guadalcazar nor SLP are named
   as Respondents, Metalclad alleges that Guadalcazar and SLP took some of the actions claimed to constitute unfair treatment and expropriation violative of NAFTA.

. . .

V. Facts and Allegations

A. The Facilities at Issue

28. In 1990 the federal government of Mexico authorized COTERIN to construct and operate a transfer station for hazardous waste in La Pedrera, a valley located in Guadalcazar in SLP. The site has an area of 814 hectares and lies 100 kilometers northeast of the capital city of SLP, separated from it by the Sierra Guadalcazar mountain range, 70 kilometers from the city of Guadalcazar. Approximately 800 people live within ten kilometers of the site.

29. On January 23, 1993, the National Ecological Institute (hereinafter "INE"), an independent sub-agency of the federal Secretariat of the Mexican Environment, National Resources and Fishing ("SEMARNAP"), granted COTERIN a federal permit to construct a hazardous waste landfill in La Pedrera (hereinafter "the landfill").

B. Metalclad's Purchase of the Site and Its Landfill Permits

30. . . . On April 23, 1993, Metalclad entered into a 6-month option agreement to purchase COTERIN together with its permits, in order to build the hazardous waste landfill.

31. Shortly thereafter, on May 11, 1993, the government of SLP granted COTERIN a state land use permit to construct the landfill. The permit was issued subject to the condition that the project adapt to the specifications and technical requirements indicated by the corresponding authorities, and accompanied by the General Statement that the license did not prejudge the rights or ownership of the applicant and did not authorize works, constructions or the functioning of business or activities.

35. On August 10, 1993, the INE granted COTERIN the federal permit for operation of the landfill. On September 10, 1993, Metalclad exercised its option and purchased COTERIN, the landfill site and the associated permits.

36. Metalclad asserts it would not have exercised its COTERIN purchase option but for the apparent approval and support of the project by federal and state officials.

C. Construction of the Hazardous Waste Landfill

37. Metalclad asserts that shortly after its purchase of COTERIN, the Governor of SLP embarked on a public campaign to denounce and prevent the operation of the landfill.

39. Metalclad further maintains that construction continued openly and without interruption through October 1994. Federal officials and state representatives inspected the construction site during this period, and Metalclad provided federal and state officials with written status reports of its progress.

40. On October 26, 1994, when the Municipality ordered the cessation of all building activities due to the absence of a municipal construction permit, construction was abruptly terminated.

41. Metalclad asserts it was once again told by federal officials that it had all the authority necessary to construct and operate the landfill; that federal officials said it should apply for the municipal construction permit to facilitate an amicable relationship with the Municipality; that federal officials assured it that the Municipality would issue the permit as a matter of course; and that the Municipality lacked any basis for denying the construction permit. Mexico denies that any federal officials represented that a municipal permit was not required, and affirmatively states that a permit was required and that Metalclad knew, or should have known, that the permit was required.

42. On November 15, 1994, Metalclad resumed construction and submitted an application for a municipal construction permit.

44. In February 1995, the Autonomous University of SLP (hereinafter "UASLP") issued a study confirming earlier findings that, although the landfill site raised some concerns, with proper engineering it was geographically suitable for a hazardous waste landfill. In March 1995, the Mexican Federal Attorney's Office for the Protection of the Environment (hereinafter "PROFEPA"), an independent sub-agency of SEMARNAP, conducted an audit of the site and also concluded that, with proper engineering and operation, the landfill site was geographically suitable for a hazardous waste landfill.

D. Metalclad Is Prevented from Operating the Landfill

45. Metalclad completed construction of the landfill in March 1995. On March 10, 1995, Metalclad held an "open house," or "inauguration," of the landfill which was attended by a number of dignitaries from the United States and from Mexico's federal, state and local governments.

46. Demonstrators impeded the "inauguration," blocked the entry and exit of buses carrying guests and workers, and employed tactics of intimidation against Metalclad . . .

50. On December 5, 1995, thirteen months after Metalclad's application for the municipal construction permit was filed, the application was denied. In doing this, the Municipality recalled its decision to deny a construction permit to COTERIN in October 1991 and January 1992 and noted the "impropriety" of Metalclad's construction of the landfill prior to receiving a municipal construction permit.

51. There is no indication that the Municipality gave any consideration to the construction of the landfill and the efforts at operation during the thirteen months during which the application was pending.

52. Metalclad has pointed out that there was no evidence of inadequacy of performance by Metalclad of any legal obligation, nor any showing that Metalclad violated the terms of any federal or state permit; that there was no evidence that the Municipality gave any consideration to the recently completed environmental reports indicating that the site was in fact suitable for a hazardous waste landfill; that there was no evidence that the site, as constructed, failed to meet any specific construction requirements; that there was no evidence that the Municipality ever required or issued a municipal construction permit for any other construction project in Guadalcazar; and that there was no evidence that there was an established administrative process with respect to municipal construction permits in the Municipality of Guadalcazar.

54. Metalclad was not notified of the Town Council meeting where the permit application was discussed and rejected, nor was Metalclad given any opportunity to participate in that process. Metalclad's request for reconsideration of the denial of the permit was rejected.

56. On January 31, 1996, the Municipality filed an *amparo* proceeding in the Mexican courts challenging SEMARNAP's dismissal of its *Convenio* complaint. An injunction was issued and Metalclad was barred from conducting any hazardous waste landfill operations . . .

58. From May 1996 through December 1996, Metalclad and the State of SLP attempted to resolve their issues with respect to the operation of the landfill. These efforts failed and, on January 2, 1997, Metalclad initiated the present arbitral proceedings against the Government of Mexico under Chapter Eleven of the NAFTA.

59. On September 23, 1997, three days before the expiry of his term, the Governor issued an Ecological Decree declaring a Natural Area for the protection of rare cactus.

The Natural Area encompasses the area of the landfill. Metalclad relies in part on this Ecological Decree as an additional element in its claim of expropriation, maintaining that the Decree effectively and permanently precluded the operation of the landfill.

60. Metalclad also alleges, on the basis of reports by the Mexican media, that the Governor of SLP stated, that the Ecological Decree "definitely cancelled any possibility that exists of opening the industrial waste landfill of La Pedrera."

62. The landfill remains dormant. Metalclad has not sold or transferred any portion of it.

. . .

VI. Applicable Law

70. A Tribunal established pursuant to NAFTA Chapter Eleven, Section B must decide the issues in dispute in accordance with NAFTA and applicable rules of international law. *(NAFTA Article 1131(1)).* In addition, NAFTA Article 102(2) provides that the Agreement must be interpreted and applied in the light of its stated objectives and in accordance with applicable rules of international law. These objectives specifically include transparency and the substantial increase in investment opportunities in the territories of the Parties. *(NAFTA Article 102(1)(c)).* The Vienna Convention on the Law of Treaties, Article 31(1) provides that a treaty is to be interpreted in good faith in accordance with the ordinary meaning to be given to the terms of the treaty in their context and in the light of the treaty's object and purpose. The context for the purpose of the interpretation of a treaty shall comprise, in addition to the text, including its preamble and annexes, any agreement relating to the treaty which was made between all the parties in connection with the conclusion of the treaty. *(Id., Article 31(2)(a)).* There shall also be taken into account, together with the context, any relevant rules of international law applicable in the relations between the parties. *(Id., Article 31(3)).* Every treaty in force is binding upon the parties to it and must be performed by them in good faith. *(Id., Article 26).* A State party to a treaty may not invoke the provisions of its internal law as justification for its failure to perform the treaty. *(Id., Article 27).*

71. The Parties to NAFTA specifically agreed to "ENSURE a predictable commercial framework for business planning and investment." *(NAFTA Preamble, para. 6 (emphasis in original)).* NAFTA further requires that "[e]ach Party shall ensure that its laws, regulations, procedures, and administrative rulings of general application respecting any matter covered by this Agreement are promptly published or otherwise made available in such a manner as to enable interested persons and Parties to become acquainted with them." *(Id. Article 1802.1).*

VII. The Tribunal's Decision

72. Metalclad contends that Mexico, through its local governments of SLP and Guadalcazar, interfered with and precluded its operation of the landfill. Metalclad alleges that this interference is a violation of Articles 1105 and 1110 of Chapter Eleven of the investment provisions of NAFTA.

A. Responsibility for the Conduct of State and Local Governments

73. A threshold question is whether Mexico is internationally responsible for the acts of SLP and Guadalcazar . . . "[Mexico] was, and remains, prepared to proceed on the assumption that the normal rule of state responsibility applies; that is, that the Re-

spondent can be internationally responsible for the acts of state organs at all three levels of government" . . .

B. NAFTA Article 1105: Fair and Equitable Treatment

74. NAFTA Article 1105(1) provides that "each Party shall accord to investments of investors of another Party treatment in accordance with international law, including fair and equitable treatment and full protection and security." For the reasons set out below, the Tribunal finds that Metalclad's investment was not accorded fair and equitable treatment in accordance with international law, and that Mexico has violated NAFTA Article 1105(1).

76. . . . Once the authorities of the central government of any Party (whose international responsibility in such matters has been identified in the preceding section) become aware of any scope for misunderstanding or confusion in this connection, it is their duty to ensure that the correct position is promptly determined and clearly stated so that investors can proceed with all appropriate expedition in the confident belief that they are acting in accordance with all relevant laws.

77. Metalclad acquired COTERIN for the sole purpose of developing and operating a hazardous waste landfill in the valley of La Pedrera, in Guadalcazar, SLP.

78. The Government of Mexico issued federal construction and operating permits for the landfill prior to Metalclad's purchase of COTERIN, and the Government of SLP likewise issued a state operating permit which implied its political support for the landfill project.

79. A central point in this case has been whether, in addition to the above-mentioned permits, a municipal permit for the construction of a hazardous waste landfill was required.

80. When Metalclad inquired, prior to its purchase of COTERIN, as to the necessity for municipal permits, federal officials assured it that it had all that was needed to undertake the landfill project . . .

85. Metalclad was led to believe, and did believe, that the federal and state permits allowed for the construction and operation of the landfill . . .

86. Even if Mexico is correct that a municipal construction permit was required, the evidence also shows that, as to hazardous waste evaluations and assessments, the federal authority's jurisdiction was controlling and the authority of the municipality only extended to appropriate construction considerations. Consequently, the denial of the permit by the Municipality by reference to environmental impact considerations in the case of what was basically a hazardous waste disposal landfill, was improper, as was the municipality's denial of the permit for any reason other than those related to the physical construction or defects in the site.

88. In addition, Metalclad asserted that federal officials told it that if it submitted an application for a municipal construction permit, the Municipality would have no legal basis for denying the permit and that it would be issued as a matter of course. The absence of a clear rule as to the requirement or not of a municipal construction permit, as well as the absence of any established practice or procedure as to the manner of handling applications for a municipal construction permit, amounts to a failure on the part of Mexico to ensure the transparency required by NAFTA.

89. Metalclad was entitled to rely on the representations of federal officials and to believe that it was entitled to continue its construction of the landfill . . .

92. The Town Council denied the permit for reasons which included, but may not have been limited to, the opposition of the local population, the fact that construction had

already begun when the application was submitted, the denial of the permit to COTERIN in December 1991 and January 1992, and the ecological concerns regarding the environmental effect and impact on the site and surrounding communities. None of the reasons included a reference to any problems associated with the physical construction of the landfill or to any physical defects therein.

93. The Tribunal therefore finds that the construction permit was denied without any consideration of, or specific reference to, construction aspects or flaws of the physical facility.

99. Mexico failed to ensure a transparent and predictable framework for Metalclad's business planning and investment. The totality of these circumstances demonstrates a lack of orderly process and timely disposition in relation to an investor of a Party acting in the expectation that it would be treated fairly and justly in accordance with the NAFTA.

101. The Tribunal therefore holds that Metalclad was not treated fairly or equitably under the NAFTA and succeeds on its claim under Article 1105.

NAFTA, Article 1110: Expropriation

. . .

103. . . . [E]xpropriation under NAFTA includes not only open, deliberate and acknowledged takings of property, such as outright seizure or formal or obligatory transfer of title in favour of the host State, but also covert or incidental interference with the use of property which has the effect of depriving the owner, in whole or in significant part, of the use or reasonably-to-be-expected economic benefit of property even if not necessarily to the obvious benefit of the host State.

104. By permitting or tolerating the conduct of Guadalcazar in relation to Metalclad which the Tribunal has already held amounts to unfair and inequitable treatment breaching Article 1105 and by thus participating or acquiescing in the denial to Metalclad of the right to operate the landfill, notwithstanding the fact that the project was fully approved and endorsed by the federal government, Mexico must be held to have taken a measure tantamount to expropriation in violation of NAFTA Article 1110(1).

107. These measures, taken together with the representations of the Mexican federal government, on which Metalclad relied, and the absence of a timely, orderly or substantive basis for the denial by the Municipality of the local construction permit, amount to an indirect expropriation.

112. In conclusion, the Tribunal holds that Mexico has indirectly expropriated Metalclad's investment without providing compensation to Metalclad for the expropriation. Mexico has violated Article 1110 of the NAFTA.

VIII. Quantification of Damages or Compensation

A. Basic Elements of Valuation

113. In this instance, the damages arising under NAFTA, Article 1105 and the compensation due under NAFTA, Article 1110 would be the same since both situations involve the complete frustration of the operation of the landfill and negate the possibility of any meaningful return on Metalclad's investment. In other words, Metalclad has completely lost its investment.

114. Metalclad has proposed two alternative methods for calculating damages: the first is to use a discounted cash flow analysis of future profits to establish the fair market value of the investment (approximately $90 million); the second is to value Metalclad's actual investment in the landfill (approximately $20–25 million).

116. Mexico asserts that a discounted cash flow analysis is inappropriate where the expropriated entity is not a going concern. Mexico offers an alternative calculation of fair market value based on COTERIN's "market capitalization." Mexico's "market capitalization" calculations show a loss to Metalclad of $13–15 million.

117. Mexico also suggests a direct investment value approach to damages. Mexico estimates Metalclad's direct investment value, or loss, to be approximately $3–4 million.

118. NAFTA, Article 1135(1)(a), provides for the award of monetary damages and applicable interest where a Party is found to have violated a Chapter Eleven provision. With respect to expropriation, NAFTA, Article 1110(2), specifically requires compensation to be equivalent to the fair market value of the expropriated investment immediately before the expropriation took place. This paragraph further states that "the valuation criteria shall include going concern value, asset value including declared tax value of tangible property, and other criteria, as appropriate, to determine fair market value."

119. Normally, the fair market value of a going concern which has a history of profitable operation may be based on an estimate of future profits subject to a discounted cash flow analysis. *Benvenuti and Bonfant Srl v. The Government of the People's Republic of Congo,* 1 ICSID Reports 330; 21 I.L.M. 758.

120. However, where the enterprise has not operated for a sufficiently long time to establish a performance record or where it has failed to make a profit, future profits cannot be used to determine going concern or fair market value. In *Sola Tiles, Inc. v. Iran (1987)* (14 Iran-U.S.C.T.R. 224, 240–42; 83 I.L.R. 460, 480–81), the Iran-U.S. Claims Tribunal pointed to the importance in relation to a company's value of "its business reputation and the relationship it has established with its suppliers and customers."

121. The Tribunal agrees with Mexico that a discounted cash flow analysis is inappropriate in the present case because the landfill was never operative and any award based on future profits would be wholly speculative.

122. Rather, the Tribunal agrees with the parties that fair market value is best arrived at in this case by reference to Metalclad's actual investment in the project. . . . The award to Metalclad of the cost of its investment in the landfill is consistent with the principles set forth in *Chorzow Factory (Claim for Indemnity) (Merits), Germany v. Poland, P.C.I.J. Series A., No. 17 (1928) at p. 47,* namely, that where the state has acted contrary to its obligations, any award to the claimant should, as far as is possible, wipe out all the consequences of the illegal act and reestablish the situation which would in all probability have existed if that act had not been committed (the *status quo ante).*

123. Metalclad asserts that it invested $20,474,528.00 in the landfill project, basing its value on its United States Federal Income Tax Returns and Auditors' Workpapers of Capitalized Costs for the Landfill reflected in a table marked Schedule A and produced by Metalclad as response 7(a)A in the course of document discovery. The calculations include landfill costs Metalclad claims to have incurred from 1991 through 1996 for expenses categorized as the COTERIN acquisition, personnel, insurance, travel and living, telephone, accounting and legal, consulting, interest, office, property, plant and equipment, including $328,167.00 for "other."

125. The Tribunal agrees, however, with Mexico's position that costs incurred prior to the year in which Metalclad purchased COTERIN are too far removed from the investment for which damages are claimed. The Tribunal will reduce the Award by the amount of the costs claimed for 1991 and 1992.

E. Recipient

129. As required by NAFTA, Article 1135(2)(b), the award of monetary damages and interest shall be payable to the enterprise . . .

X. Award

131. For the reasons stated above, the Tribunal hereby decides that, reflecting the amount of Metalclad's investment in the project, less the disallowance of expenses claimed for 1991 and 1992, less the amount claimed by way of bundling of certain expenses, and less the estimated amount allowed for remediation, plus interest at the rate of 6% compounded annually, the Respondent shall, within 45 days from the date on which this Award is rendered, pay to Metalclad the amount of $16,685,000.00 . . .

Source: Case No. ARB(AF)/97/1, available at http://www.worldbank.org/icsid/cases/mm-award-e.pdf.

- What lessons does the case suggest for businesspersons intent on making investments that depend heavily on land, mining, or other immovable assets?
- Assume the municipality had acted properly, and it did have significant rights of regulation of landfills. Would the outcome of the case be any different? Can investors simply rely on statements by federal officials and cheerfully ignore municipalities?

Chapter Summary

International business poses a number of risks that must be considered by firms both before and after negotiations begin, but of paramount importance is the consideration at the outset of how disputes between the parties may be resolved. Domestic courts of the injured party represent a fall-back position for business disputes, but the courts still may not be a viable source of relief, particularly if the foreign business has no assets outside of its own state (and in the state of the injured party).

Alternatives to consider are negotiation and conciliation, but these are often not solutions, but a means for compromise to rescue a deteriorating business relationship. The most reliable approach to the issue of dispute resolution is by arbitration.

An arbitration clause in a contract for goods or services provides a clear and direct approach to resolving disputes that may arise, and represents a common clause in most international business agreements.

The International Court of Arbitration of the International Chamber of Commerce and the London Court of International Arbitration are two of the best known organizations that have long-established experience in providing arbitration services to international business. The United Nations also has worked to encourage a harmonization of state laws relating to the enforcement of arbitration awards by such treaties as the New York Convention, and has prepared model laws and rules for the conduct of arbitration and conciliation/mediation of disputes.

The International Centre for Settlement of Investment Disputes serves a similar function in the promotion of conciliation and arbitration where qualifying disputes arise between individuals and sovereign states.

Chapter Questions

1. What factors make arbitration preferable to litigation, and which do you see as being the most persuasive in the international context?
2. Create seven examples that would represent valid exceptions under the New York Convention to the recognition and enforcement of an arbitration award.
3. What merits and dangers lie in the parties' grant to their arbitrator of the right of decision *ex aequo et bono*?

4. Where a party is injured in a foreign joint venture relating to an open pit mine abroad, and getting a fair trial in the foreign jurisdiction might be questionable, why might the injured party prefer arbitration over launching a court action in its home jurisdiction?

5. It is common to attack the jurisdiction of the arbitrator in an attempt to avoid recognition and enforcement of an arbitration award. Where does one find a statement of that jurisdiction in order to be able to determine whether it has been exceeded?

6. One of the advantages of arbitration is that it usually provides faster resolution of disputes than litigation. Aside from the simple fact that "time is money," construct two business situations where speedy resolution is in the best interest of both parties.

7. Differentiate between mediation and conciliation, providing examples of disputes where each might be appropriately used.

8. Two business firms that are parties to a contractual joint venture are locked in dispute over their intellectual property rights in a revolutionary new technology developed by the JV. Each party has contributed a measure of cash, its own research and development, certain human resources, and aspects of its own know-how to the development of the new technology. Why would arbitration of this dispute be preferable to litigation, and among the reasons, what do you consider being the most important reason?

9. International agreements for mutual recognition of *anything* are not particularly common. Why then, as early as 1958, were nations willing to grant mutual recognition of *arbitration* awards?

10. Metalclad's Mexican waste disposal site had been completed but was not operating when it was "taken" from Metalclad. Had it been in operation, how would Metalclad's damage award have been affected, and why?

BusinessWeek

Do NAFTA judges have too much authority?

When a Mississippi jury slapped a $500 million judgment on Loewen Group, a Canadian funeral-home chain, in 1995 for breaching a contract with a hometown rival, the company quickly settled the case for $129 million but then decided to appeal. But instead of going to a U.S. court, the Canadians took their case to an obscure three-judge panel that stands distinctly apart from the U.S. legal system. And that panel's decision cannot be appealed.

Thanks to some fine print in the 1994 North American Free Trade Agreement, the case of Loewen Group vs. the U.S. is just one of two dozen wending their way through a little-known and highly secretive process. The panels, using arbitration procedures established by the World Bank, were supposed to ensure that governments in the U.S., Mexico, and Canada would pay compensation to any foreign investor whose property they might seize. U.S. business groups originally demanded the investor-protection mechanism, noting that the Mexican government had a history of nationalizing its oil, electricity, and banking industries, including many U.S. assets.

But even some of NAFTA's strongest supporters say that clever and creative lawyers in all three countries are rapidly expanding the anti-expropriation clause in unanticipated ways. "The question in a lot of these pending cases is, will the panels produce a pattern of decisions that the negotiators never envisioned?" says Charles E. Roh Jr., deputy chief U.S. negotiator for NAFTA, now a partner at Weil, Gotshal & Manges LLC. Some of the early indications, he says, "are troubling."

In one case, a NAFTA panel issued an interpretation of the Mexican Constitution, an authority the NAFTA negotiators hadn't intended to give the panel. In the dispute, a California waste disposal company, Metalclad Corp., was awarded $16.7 million by a NAFTA tribunal after the governor of the state of San Luis Potosi and a town council refused the company a permit to open a toxic waste site. The company had asked for $90 million in damages, insisting that the state and local governments had overstepped their authority.

The majority of the cases are yet to be decided, but the NAFTA panels are controversial nonetheless. For one thing, they are already pitting environmentalists and federal, state, and local government regulators in all three countries against multinationals. The basic disagreement: Business groups want to include NAFTA'S strongest investor-protection provisions in all future free-trade agreements, while many environmentalists would like to scrap the entire procedure as an impediment to government regulatory action. The cases are also complicating efforts to negotiate free-trade agreements with Chile and the hemispheric, 34-nation Free Trade Area of the Americas.

Washington's problem: While such panels may favor U.S. businesses abroad, foreign plaintiffs would enjoy the same such privileges in the U.S. And that could end up giving them protections against regulations far beyond those domestic companies enjoy in their own courts. What's more, states and municipalities have also warned that their ability to govern is being compromised by "a new set of foreign investor rights."

In some cases, the NAFTA suits seek damages for government decisions that are clearly legal but can be questioned under vague notions of international law. For example, a Canadian chemical company, Methanex Corp., bypassed U.S. courts to challenge California's ban on a health-threatening gasoline additive, MTBE, that has been polluting municipal wells and reservoirs. In its $970 million claim, the Canadian company said California Governor Gray Davis had been influenced in his decision by a $150,000 campaign contribution from U.S.-based Archer Daniels Midland Co., the maker of a rival gasoline additive. The campaign contribution was legal, but Methanex' lawyers argued that the Davis decision was "palpably unfair and inequitable" because of ADM's influence. Such an argument wouldn't likely work in a U.S. court.

No laws can be overturned by the panel, but the cost of defending against a NAFTA lawsuit may run so high that it could still deter agencies from imposing strict regulations on foreign companies, critics charge. They point to a decision by Canada not to restrict cigarette marketing after Ottawa was threatened with a NAFTA case by U.S. tobacco companies. In another potentially intimidating move, United Parcel Service Inc. is seeking $160 million in damages from Canada, arguing that the state-owned Canadian postal system, Canada Post, maintains a monopoly on first-class mail and delivers parcels with private Canadian partners.

But right now, the Loewen case is the one in the spotlight. The Mississippi trial was so theatrical that Warner Bros. Inc. and film director Ron Howard have acquired the movie rights, according to attorneys in the case. Canadian funeral chain founder Ray Loewen was vilified as a foreigner, a "gouger of grieving families," an owner of a large yacht, a racist, a customer of foreign banks, and greedy besides, according to the transcript. Yet the State Supreme Court refused to waive the appeal bond, which had been set at $625 million—to be posted in 10 days. (The largest previous verdict in the state had been $18 million.) Loewen filed for bankruptcy protection in 1999 but is hopeful that the imminent NAFTA ruling will revive the company.

Although many of the current cases raise questions, business groups insist that NAFTA-like panels are needed in all trade deals because so many developing nations have poor judicial systems. But they allow that the process may still need some tweaking. "Of course, if I look at the filed cases so far, I could write a pretty scary story," says Scott Miller, a Washington lobbyist for Procter & Gamble Co. And Eric Biehl, a former top Commerce Dept. official, who supports NAFTA, wonders, "how does some mechanism on a trade agreement that no one ever thought much about suddenly get used to open up a whole new appellate process around the U.S. judicial system?" That's a question a lot more people may soon be asking.

Source: Paul Magnusson in Washington. Copyright 2002, by The McGraw-Hill Companies Inc. All rights reserved.

14

Taxation of International Business Transactions

Chapter Objectives

Seemingly, no good deed goes unpunished. A well-thought-out and profitable international business transaction can come apart as a result of its tax consequences. However, many transactions can be saved (and other profitable ones created) with a knowledge of the chief mechanisms of international taxation. Like so much of the law, it is a specialist area, but that is still not a sufficient reason to shy away from the subject, for it has too great an effect on final profitability. International businesspersons and lawyers must have an appreciation of the more timeless tax dimensions in international business, even if specific provisions vary from jurisdiction to jurisdiction and from year to year.

The objectives of this chapter are therefore to provide an understanding of

- The nature, basis, and effect of tax in the international taxation of business transactions.
- The effect and relief of double taxation.

- The process of tax planning and avoidance in structuring international business transactions.

What Is Tax?

Tax is variously described as a compulsory payment mandated by law, of financial resources, from the private sector to a government, without an expectation in the payer of counterperformance owed to it individually by that government.

Thus, tax is not a gift to government. An expropriation is not a tax, or where a government grants a license, the fee paid for it is not a tax. To some purists, an import duty is not a tax, as one of its functions is as a tool for governments to protect their domestic markets. However, import duties would still fit the definition given above.

Other than national defense, no other issue is more closely tied to government than the sovereign right to impose taxation. Therefore, it should come as no surprise that where it has been extremely difficult and time-consuming to achieve worldwide consensus on many international trade issues, getting global consensus on powers of taxation has been impossible and will remain so for the foreseeable future.

Even less charitable definitions of tax are known.

It is this lack of global consensus that creates problems for international businesspersons. There is no "international tax" *per se,* only that the application of domestic tax rules in one jurisdiction can and does conflict (in the eyes of the taxpayer) with the domestic tax rules of another jurisdiction, giving rise to *double taxation.* A network of bilateral tax treaties exists, most crafted along the lines of similar models, and this is the only international law that stands to assist the interests of the taxpayer. The balance of international law is firmly on the side of state interest when it comes to powers of taxation, domestic or extraterritorial.

The different forms of double taxation and bilateral treaty relief will be discussed later in this chapter, but there are a number of fundamental issues that must come first. These are the questions of what is taxed, who is taxed, and how is tax assessed.

Direct versus Indirect Taxation

Economic activity—very broadly defined—is the *what* that governments intend to tax. In international business terms, this is either international investment (doing business *in* another nation) or international trade (doing business *with* another nation).

Direct taxes are those paid to the state by the person who is liable for the tax, so-called, as a direct relationship exists, while indirect taxes are collected by a supplier of goods and services on behalf of a government. As such, direct taxes relate to investments and the income and wealth they produce, while indirect taxes relate to trade in goods and services.

Primary Tax Classifications

Doing business *in* another nation	Investment related	Direct tax	Individual income tax Corporate income tax Capital gains tax Wealth tax
Doing business *with* another nation	Trade related	Indirect tax	Sales tax Excise tax Customs duty

The purpose of all of these taxes is ostensibly good, with the objectives of generating government revenue, social redistribution of wealth, control of consumption, a variety of investment incentives, and general macroeconomic management by government through incentives and disincentives.

Whatever these good domestic purposes of taxation are, the level and type of taxation in any country still has a distorting effect in international trade and investment. First, the general price level of all goods rises, as indirect taxes make both domestic and imported goods more expensive, and direct taxes imposed on producers are passed to consumers (domestic and foreign) in the form of higher prices for domestically produced goods.

The second distortion is between national markets themselves. Taxation differentials make goods and services cheaper in one place than in another, with the result being the diversion of trade flows and, in the extreme, driving them underground. The extent of these distortions is significant. It has troubled governments in their search for inward investment, and foils their desire to promote the goods produced by their exporters.

Indirect taxation (customs duties and sales/excise taxes) has proved to be the field where the most progress in international cooperation has taken place in an attempt to reduce these negative effects. On reflection, one should realize that the vehicle for this cooperation has

Extraterritorial taxation? The fact that some states are party to tax agreements relating to commercial activities in space (satellites, communications, etc.) suggests that governments are willing to be *extraterrestrial* as well.

been the GATT/WTO. The GATT/WTO served to inventory existing import duties (Article X of GATT 47) and freeze them as schedules of commitments (Article II). It then sought to apply them to all imports regardless of origin (most favored nation, Article I) and then to roll them back and down through decades of successive rounds of multilateral trade negotiations. This has largely been successful, though it is incomplete, as import duties have not reached absolute zero across all commodities.

With regard to sales taxes, those that would otherwise be discriminatory (as between imports versus domestic production) are forbidden by the Article III(2) requirement for national treatment. Sales taxes can still have a residual trade-distorting effect, in that they may be applied on an origin versus destination basis.

Where local law requires the collection of sales taxes on an origin basis, all locally manufactured products will be so taxed, but imported goods will not. This is acceptable under WTO rules as nondiscriminatory, because the imported goods receive better treatment than local products.

A destination-type sales tax is collected on the sale of goods inside a jurisdiction regardless of where they are produced, as the destination for consumption is the governing factor. This too is nondiscriminatory, as all goods are treated equally and imports are not disadvantaged.

The difficulty for traders and nations lies where trade occurs between nations using these different methods of sales taxation. The diagram on page 605 illustrates the distortion in trade flows that result from destination, origin, and zero sales taxes.

Thus, while an origin-type sales tax is a valid policy choice, it can only make sense in a world where other nations do the same, and do not opt for either a destination-type sales tax or a zero sales tax.

Countries employing destination-type sales taxes usually also employ a multiple-stage, noncumulative tax, more commonly known as a value-added tax. This is to recognize the reality of sales from a component producer to an assembly producer to a wholesaler to a retailer to the consumer/exporter, and to ensure that the system does not produce a tax-on-tax effect. Each member of the chain receives a tax credit representing the sales tax it has paid, remitting to the government only the difference between the tax it collects on its later sale less the amount of its credits. Since the end-user consumer pays sales tax on a purchase, but neither collects tax from a later sale nor is registered to receive a credit, the local consumer bears the full cost of the sales tax. An exporter who is at the end of a similar chain receives the benefit of the tax credit, but does not include sales tax in its price for foreign sales, recognizing that the foreign end user consumer is not within the jurisdiction of the destination-type sales tax.

Basis for Taxation

Nationals, citizens, and *subjects* are words that appear frequently in domestic tax codes, and are *usually* intended as interchangeable words, but in certain instances their specific meaning may be important. Nationals are those persons or corporations who owe allegiance to, and are entitled to protection by, a particular sovereign state. Citizens are a particular kind of national, in that their allegiance and protection relates to a state in which sovereign power remains in the hands of the people, that is, U.S. nationals are more properly described as U.S. citizens. Subjects are those nationals of a state led by a monarch, again owing allegiance to it, and entitled to protection by it; thus, British nationals are British subjects.

Trade Distortions Resulting from Destination versus Origin Sales Taxes

Country A
10% Destination
sales tax

Country B
10% Origin
sales tax

Sale price of locally
produced goods sold
locally $= 100 \times 1.1 = 110$

Sale price of locally
produced goods sold
locally $= 100 \times 1.1 = 110$

Export price of locally produced
goods $= 100 \times 1.0 = 100$

Export price of locally produced
goods $= 100 \times 1.1 =$ **110**

Local price of imports from Country B =
110 $\times 1.1 = 121$
Local price of imports from Country C =
100 $\times 1.1 = 110$

Local price of imports from Country A =
100 $\times 1.0 = 100$
Local price of imports from Country C =
100 $\times 1.0 = 100$

Local price of imports from Country A =
100 $\times 1.0 = 100$
Local price of exports from Country B =
110 $\times 1.0 = 110$

Export price of locally produced
goods $= 100 \times 1.0 = $ *100*

Price of locally produced
goods sold locally = 100

Cost of production
(before sales tax)
in all nations is 100.

Sales tax diverted
export flows

Country C
No sales tax

Country B cannot export to anyone nor compete in its own market as its goods are never competitively priced.
Its factories will be subsidized by government or will close and move to Country A or Country C.

Country A can compete in its own market and can export to both Country B and Country C, even against
products of a zero-tax jurisdiction.

There is no incentive to smuggle goods into either Country B or Country C as goods may be legally had there
priced at 100.

There is every incentive to smuggle goods into Country A as the cheapest goods found legally there are priced
at 110.

The following sections on citizenship, domicile, and residence as the basis for taxation are as they stand at law in the absence of a bilateral or multilateral treaty; treaties can and do modify the right to tax and make rules for the determination of domicile and residency. Despite the fact that bilateral treaties are very common, the rationale behind treaty provisions is better understood when the kind of problems that can be generated in their absence is also well understood.

Citizenship of Individuals

Very few nations attempt to follow their citizens around the world and consistently tax them on the basis of their worldwide income; the only major nation that does is the United States, regardless of where a U.S. citizen chooses to reside. Foreign earned income of U.S. citizens abroad can be partially excluded, subject to limitations, but even then the U.S. citizen will remain liable for estate tax, even where he or she dies as a nonresident of the United States.

As an exceptionally wealthy nation, and one that also has very substantial fiscal and budget commitments, the United States follows this policy to ensure that wealthy U.S. citizens do not simply establish residency elsewhere. The U.S. government wants to prevent tax exiles from escaping U.S. tax while continuing to enjoy the rights of U.S. citizenship and the right of U.S. entry for visits. For this reason as well, no U.S. bilateral tax treaty concedes or diminishes the U.S. right to tax its citizens on that basis. Of course, non-U.S. citizens (who may or may not be resident in the United States) also generate income from operations in the United States. A nation using the citizenship criteria as a basis for tax therefore also will want to employ a secondary basis for tax—a domestic source basis—to tax income accruing to any person generated from any source within the territorial jurisdiction of that nation.

Domicile and Residence of Individuals

The two terms *domicile* and *residence* are also frequently misused, for their technical definitions are often fused in casual use. Domicile, as it is used internationally, comes from the British common law, where it has two major variants, both meaning an *individual person's* permanent home. The variants are domicile of origin and domicile of choice. All persons in the British view, and where adopted by extension in international law, have at least one domicile. This begins as the domicile of origin, being the permanent home of the individual's father at the time the individual was born, and in later life the individual person may acquire a domicile of choice in another nation by making his or her own permanent home there.

Where a person acquires a domicile of choice, that nation will assert its right to tax that person, perhaps on a worldwide basis. A resort to considering one's domicile of origin only occurs in a dispute over the right to tax when it is impossible (in a complex situation) to determine one's domicile of choice.

One's residency, which is even more widely used by nations as basis to assert the right to tax, again perhaps on a worldwide basis, is different from domicile. One can be a resident of a jurisdiction without that jurisdiction being a permanent home. Residence, under many nations' tax codes, can be triggered simply by being present in the jurisdiction, with a permanent home or not, for a period of 183 days in a tax or calendar year.[1] Since people most frequently have their domicile of choice and their residence in the same place, this gives rise to the unfortunate fusion of the terms.

[1]While 183 days in any one calendar year is the most common formula, the number varies; for example, Panama, Thailand, and Malaysia use 180 days as the trigger for residency; others use lower absolute numbers; still others (much like the United States) use averages together with aggregate visits over the previous two to five years.

Even more technical approaches exist; for example, in the United States, where a non-U.S. citizen not domiciled in the United States will be taxed as a U.S. resident

1. If he or she is a lawful permanent resident of the United States at any time during the calendar year (i.e., in possession of an alien registration card, the "Green Card" test) or
2. Meets the "substantial presence test" of physical presence in the United States for at least 31 days during a current calendar year, and a total of 183 days during a three-year period, which includes the current year and two years preceding, calculated on the basis of the number of days present during the current year, plus one-third of the days present during the first year preceding the current calendar year, plus one-sixth of the days present in the United States during the second year preceding the current calendar year.[2]

This may be subject to a first exception to the substantial presence test, the "closer connection test," where one would otherwise be taxed as a U.S. resident, but that person

1. Was present in the United States for fewer than 183 days during the year,
2. Had a tax home in a foreign country during the year, and
3. Had a closer connection to one foreign country in which that person maintained a tax home,

or subject to a second exception to the substantial presence test, where that test would have otherwise been met, but the person qualifies as a resident of another country under the residency article of a tax treaty between the United States and that other country.

As a result, one can quickly find three jurisdictions attempting to tax a person's worldwide income; for example, where a U.S. citizen adopts a domicile of choice in the United Kingdom and travels to Canada for 183 days or more. Only a resort to applicable tax treaties and the use of credits for foreign tax paid can resolve such tax problems.

Additionally, it should be borne in mind that there are the tax demands of each nation where the person is generating domestic source income. These demands must be paid despite the facts that (a) the person is not a citizen, resident, or domiciliary of that jurisdiction and (b) other jurisdictions are themselves intending to tax that income as part of the person's worldwide income.

Corporate Residence and Domicile

While the United States recognizes that corporations organized under U.S. law are U.S. residents, other nations take a more complex or factual approach.

In the United Kingdom, companies incorporated under local legislation are considered resident,[3] but companies not incorporated under local law (i.e., incorporated elsewhere) are also treated as resident where their central management and control are exercised within the United Kingdom.[4]

The same provision of residency based on incorporation exists in Canada for firms incorporated there after April 26, 1965. In that country, the central management and control test is an important determinant of whether a company is either a factual resident or "carried on business in Canada,"[5] either of which can deem Canadian residency for foreign-incorporated firms or those incorporated in Canada before April 27, 1965.

The following Canadian case, *Birmount Holdings*, examines the common law "central management and control test" as it stood in the United Kingdom (put forward in the *De*

---

[2]*U.S. Tax Guide for Aliens,* IRS Publication 519, may be viewed at http://www.irs.gov/pub/irs-pdf/p519.pdf.

[3]In the United Kingdom, pursuant to the Finance Act, 1988, as amended s. 66.

[4]*De Beers Consolidated Mines Ltd. v. Rae* (1906) A.C. 455.

[5]In Canada, pursuant to the Income Tax Act, R.S.C. 1985, as amended, § 250(4).

Beers case and as it still stands today), confirming it as part of Canadian law. The Greek-owned firm in question was incorporated in Canada prior to the critical 1965 date, escaping the automatic provision that would otherwise deem it to be a Canadian resident. This common law rationale (absent a tax treaty, which will be raised further below) would be applicable to any foreign corporation (e.g. U.S.) doing business in either Canada or the United Kingdom.

Birmount Holdings Ltd. v. Canada

Federal Court of Appeal
April 14, 1978
(extract only)

Heald J.:—This is an appeal from a judgement of the Trial Division dismissing the appeal of the appellant from an income tax assessment for the taxation year 1972, wherein income tax in the sum of some $644,000 was assessed on the gain from the sale of 74.43 acres of land located in Scarborough Township and acquired by the appellant in 1960. The property was held for approximately 11½ years and then sold by the company in 1972.

The issues in the appeal are twofold:

1. Is the profit realized on the sale of subject land income from an adventure or concern in the nature of trade or does it represent the proceeds of an investment resulting in a capital gain?
2. Was the appellant resident in Canada or did it carry on business in Canada at the material time thereby being deemed to be resident here under the provisions of the Income Tax Act?

From the date of appellant's incorporation to the present, the only person beneficially and financially interested in the company was and is Mr. André Mentzelopoulos who is 61 years old and a Greek citizen. Mr. Mentzelopoulos' native language is Greek and his primary working language is French although he spoke in English at the trial. The majority of the evidence given at the trial was given by Mr. Mentzelopoulos. At all times, all of the company's issued stock was held in trust for Mr. Mentzelopoulos, although he was never an Officer or director.

Mr. Mentzelopoulos is a highly successful industrialist of substantial means with investments in Pakistan, Greece, U.S.A., France and Canada. He impressed the learned Trial Judge as ". . . ambitious, mentally very energetic, of great business acumen, shrewd and with nothing about him of the naive."

While he was visiting in Canada, Mr. Mentzelopoulos contacted Mr. Hobson, the General Manager of the Bank of Montreal at Toronto, advising him of his desire to make a permanent investment in Canada, ". . . so my children and grandchildren would find something in a solid country which I considered may be one of the two countries in the world today offering geographical and political security."

Mr. Hobson then introduced Mr. Mentzelopoulos to a Mr. Scott of the Royal Trust Company who suggested to him that he purchase a piece of land about 20 miles away from Toronto consisting of approximately 74 acres. An offer was prepared and delivered to Mr. Mentzelopoulos in Montreal for acceptance and he signed it prior to his departure from Canada. The purchase price of the land was $5,250 per acre for a total of $393,665 . . . The offer to purchase signed by Mr. Mentzelopoulos is dated August 20, 1960.

While Mr. Mentzelopoulos was still in Montreal, either the Bank of Montreal or Royal Trust telephoned him to advise him that he required solicitors to complete subject land purchase, and recommended the firm of Lang, Michener, Cranston, in Toronto whom he retained to handle the matter for him. Mr. Mentzelopoulos spoke to Mr. Robert A. Cranston, Q.C., of that firm by telephone who advised him of the necessary legal arrangements. Mr. Mentzelopoulos informed Mr. Cranston that he wanted to keep this property for his children and consequently Mr. Cranston recommended to him the incorporation of a company since this would enable the shares of the company to be divided among his children upon his death rather than attempting to divide the property.

The company was incorporated on September 16, 1960. The head office is in Toronto. Three common shares in the capital stock of the company were issued to three Toronto directors, namely, Mr. Cranston and two officers of the Royal Trust Company. These directors signed declarations of trust stating that they held all beneficial interest in such shares for Banque La Roche.

Banque La Roche is a bank established and located in Switzerland since 1775. It has had dealings with Mr. Mentzelopoulos' family for the last 75 years. All of Mr. Mentzelopoulos' investments, other than his personal residences, are held for him by Banque La Roche who act as his financial advisors and paying agents. With respect to his various business dealings, Mr. Mentzelopoulos meets with the representatives of Banque La Roche regularly for approximately 2 days of the first week of every second month.

Subject land transaction was completed by deed dated September 26, 1960 . . . the land was unimproved farm land except for a house occupied by a tenant who was grazing cattle on the land and paying a total rental of $50 per month. The tenant vacated on October 6, 1960 . . . Royal Trust re-rented the property for grazing purposes at a reduced rental— in 1962 for $300 and in 1963 and for several years thereafter, for $100 per year.

The Letters Patent state that appellant's sole object is to acquire by purchase subject property in the Township of Scarborough.

Between 1960 and 1972, the period during which the appellant owned subject property, the appellant expended over $148,000 to carry the property including mortgage interest, municipal taxes and administration expenses. By the end of 1970, the rental income from the property had amounted to only $2,000.

The company did not maintain a physical office or a bank account. The financial statements were however prepared in Canada and such income tax returns as were filed, were prepared in this country. Likewise, the seal and books of the company were kept here.

Mr. Mentzelopoulos testified further that since the summer of 1971, an international monetary upheaval was occurring and the American and Canadian dollar were falling in value compared to European currencies such as the Swiss franc. Thus, he said that this currency crisis represented an additional factor which influenced his decision to sell the Scarborough property. It was his view that, accordingly, the property should be sold before the currency devaluation became worse . . . As a result, acting on Mr. Mentzelopulos' instructions, *[the directors]* passed a resolution on January, 31, 1972, accepting *[an offer from a bona fide purchaser]* which offer was in excess of $2,300,000 . . . the net profit on the sale being in excess of $1,700,000.

The learned Trial Judge, after reviewing at some length the evidence before him, both oral and documentary, concluded that subject realty was acquired with the intention of selling it when that could advantageously be done, thus making the transaction one in the nature of trade rather than an investment.

The authorities make it clear that the Court was required to consider the relevant facts as of the time of purchase together with subsequent events together with the statement by Mr. Mentzelopoulos as to the intention of the appellant at the time of acquisition. If, after considering all these matters, the Court concludes that the possibility of turning the property to account for profit in any way which might present itself as convenient or expedient, including resale, was a major motivating factor, or that an investment intention was not the only motivating factor at time of acquisition, then the Court must find any profit ensuing from a resulting sale to be taxable as an adventure in the nature of trade.

A perusal of the Reasons for Judgement satisfies me that the learned Trial Judge did consider the relevant objective facts and circumstances surrounding the transaction and that he also considered carefully the two reasons given by Mr. Mentzelopoulos for selling the property, thereby correctly applying to the facts of the case, the pertinent jurisprudence referred to supra.

[Therefore, the Appeal Court does not disturb the Trial court finding that the transaction was "an adventure or concern in the nature of trade" (and the profit therefore was income), rather than the proceeds of an investment (which would be characterized as a capital gain).]

Turning now to the second issue in this appeal, that is, the question of residence, the governing section of the Income Tax Act, S.C. 1970-71-72, c.63, as amended, is paragraph 250(4)(c), the relevant portions of which read as follows:

> 250. . . . (4) For the purposes of this Act, a corporation shall be deemed to have been resident in Canada throughout a taxation year if
>
> . . . (c) in the case of a corporation incorporated before April 27, 1965 . . . it was incorporated in Canada and, at any time in the taxation year or at any time in any preceding taxation year of the corporation ending after April 26, 1965, it was resident in Canada or carried on business in Canada.

It seems clear from a perusal of the Reasons of the learned Trial Judge, that while he made no finding as to whether or not, in fact, the appellant was resident in Canada, he did find that the appellant's activities in connection with the Scarborough realty constituted carrying on business in Canada, which, by virtue of the provisions of paragraph 250(4)(c), deems the appellant to be a resident of Canada for income tax purposes.

I will deal initially with the question as to whether, on the evidence adduced in this case, the appellant could be said to be resident in Canada in fact. The established rule at common law so far as the residence of a company is concerned was clearly enunciated by Lord Loreburn in the *De Beers* case[6] where he stated that a company resides for income tax purposes where its real business is carried on and the real business is carried on where ". . . the central management and control . . ." actually abides. Lord Loreburn added that the answer is in each case ". . . a pure question of fact to be determined, not according to the construction of this or that regulation or by law, but upon a scrutiny of the course of business and trading." Earlier on, also on page 458 of the report, the learned Lord Chancellor stated: "A company cannot eat or sleep, but it can keep house and do business." We ought, therefore, to see where it really keeps house and does business.

A perusal of the uncontradicted evidence, both oral and documentary, has convinced me that the appellant was, at all relevant times, resident in Canada. I cite the following facts in support of this conclusion:

1. The appellant company was incorporated in Canada, and had Canadian shareholders and directors, from incorporation until the end of January 1972 in the taxation year under review.

2. The appellant company did not have very much business but all the business it did have was in Canada. It purchased land in Canada, it paid taxes on its property in Canada for some 11 years, it paid insurance on the buildings on its property, it leased its Canadian property to Canadian tenants through leases prepared in Canada and executed by its Canadian agents. It had Canadian auditors, Canadian solicitors and a Canadian agent,

---

[6]*De Beers Consolidated Mines Ltd. v. Rae* (1906) A.C. 455 at 458.

The Royal Trust Company, whom it engaged to manage its affairs. Its head office was in Toronto. Its sole incorporating object was to purchase the Scarborough property.

3. Its agent, The Royal Trust in Toronto, maintained a trust account for the appellant. Royal Trust in Toronto, on behalf of the appellant, managed the Scarborough property, paid the taxes, collected the rents, made the mortgage payments, paid the solicitors' fees, made periodic inspections of the property (resulting in recommendations re covering of an old well and that the old farm house on the land be demolished). For these management services, it was paid an annual fee.

4. The Seal and the minute books of the company were kept in Canada.

5. Ontario Corporation Tax Returns were filed by the company's representative in Toronto without consulting Mr. Mentzelopoulos.

6. The appellant filed income tax returns in Canada for the fiscal and calendar years 1968, 1969 and 1970. It filed no income tax returns in any other country.

7. The two directors from the Royal Trust would change from time to time and were changed without reference to Mr. Mentzelopoulos.

8. Mr. Mentzelopoulos relied on his Canadian representatives for advice in dealing with the company's affairs. For example, he informed the Toronto solicitors that he did not wish to see the By-Laws, Resolutions and Minutes of Meetings unless the solicitors felt he should have them.

9. Mr. Mentzelopoulos admitted that ". . . in all my fifteen years of my relationship with Canada I did not over-rule anybody as far as I know. I conversed with them whether something better cannot be done. But I don't think that I over-ruled anybody." He also stated: ". . . I have not the power to over-rule the Royal Trust Company nor to over-rule Lang and Michener."

On the basis of this evidence, I have concluded that the "real business" and the "only business" of the appellant was carried on in Canada and that it "kept house" in Canada during the relevant period and the "central management and control" of the appellant was in Canada.

A decision of the Exchequer court in the case of *Bedford Overseas Freighters Ltd. v. Minister of National Revenue*[7] was remarkably similar on its facts to the case at bar. In that case, the appellant was also incorporated in Canada but largely owned by a non-resident. Its ships were operated and chartered by a non-resident. Although all the directors of the appellant were Canadian, all major decisions were made by the non-resident owner. However, the Canadian directors opened bank accounts, signed cheques and negotiated and signed agreements on behalf of the appellant corporation.

> (Kerr, J. in *Bedford* wrote) "In Bedford's case the management of the business of the company and the controlling power and authority over its affairs were vested in its Canadian directors and they exercised that power and authority in Canada, albeit in large measure to carry out *[the owner's]* instructions and policy decisions made elsewhere by him. In Canada they executed agreements and attended to business and legal affairs of the company which were required in connection with and were essential to the company's business venture of owning and operating the vessels. In my view, the evidence that I have outlined and the facts that have been admitted show that management and control of the company and attention to its interests and affairs were exercised and given to a substantial degree, de jure and de facto, within Canada, by its Canadian directors from the incorporation of the company up to and including its 1964 taxation year."

I adopt the rationale of the above quoted Reasons of the learned Exchequer Court Judge as having equal application to the facts in this case.

[7]70 D.T.C. 6072.

Accordingly, it is my opinion that on the basis of the uncontradicted evidence presented in this case, Canadian residence for the appellant has been established in actual fact, without reference to the deeming provision of section 250(4)(c) which deems residency where business is carried on in Canada.

Source: [1978] F.C.J. No. 302

The court found that the transaction constituted income rather than capital gain and that the appellant was a factual resident of Canada. Thus, the Mentzelopoulos firm would be taxed like any other Canadian in receipt of business income.

- State the test that the Court applies to determine factual residency.
- Had the firm not met this test, what was the second alternative test that would have been applied?

The domicile of European companies within the European Union follows the individual member state legislation, which is primarily civil law, with the common law exceptions of the United Kingdom and Ireland. The civil law preference is much more along the lines of the "central management and control test," expressed in Europe as the place of "central administration or principal place of business," but like the United States, Canada, and the United Kingdom, provision exists to recognize the "statutory seat" (essentially the place of incorporation) as the basis for domicile.

These European phrases may trigger memories from Chapter 5 of European Council Regulation 44/2001, where the same basis is used for establishing jurisdiction for recognition and enforcement of judgments in civil and commercial matters. Note especially that Regulation 44/2001 does not extend to revenue (tax), customs, or administrative matters. While the member nations of the EU may use this basis for determination of domicile for taxation, they are unwilling to raise their commitment and fix it in stone at the multilateral level.

Domestic Source Income of Nonresidents

As discussed in general terms above, nonresidents do not escape from taxation in a jurisdiction simply because they are not residents of that jurisdiction. The taxing authority of that jurisdiction will be equally keen on extracting tax due from operations or investments conducted inside its territory by nonresidents. The concession to nonresidency lies in the fact that the tax authority will usually stop short of taxing the actor's worldwide income, and confine itself to taxing only the locally generated domestic source income.

Domestic source income may stem from investments or assets or it may be active business income. The particular form in which it is generated may give rise to particular tax problems for the nonresident recipient.

Forms of Domestic (Foreign) Source Income from International Business

> 1. Business profits—from a branch
> 2. Dividends—from a subsidiary
> 3. Interest—from a loan
> 4. Capital gains—from sale of an asset
> 5. Royalties—from intellectual property
> 6. Fees—from providing a service

Where international businesspersons operate abroad and receive payment for those activities and have paid foreign tax on those earnings, this most often gives rise to a limited tax credit in their home tax jurisdiction.

Attention must be paid to tax code limitations on the availability and extent of credits for foreign tax paid. Where the foreign jurisdiction imposes tax at a higher rate than the recipient's home jurisdiction, the credit will be limited to the tax that would have been payable had the economic activity taken place in the home jurisdiction.

Similarly, conditions may be placed on the type of home jurisdiction income that may receive the shelter of the foreign tax credit. For example, if an international businessperson pays income tax abroad, it may only be permitted to make use of the corresponding credit to the extent that it has taxable income in its home jurisdiction. This is usually the case with respect to allowable foreign losses as well, which can only be used to offset gains, and not further increase losses, in the home jurisdiction.

Double Taxation

Economic Double Taxation

In the simplest form, which occurs all in one state, a businessperson may encounter economic double taxation. This occurs when the same income flow is taxed twice by one state in the hands of two taxpayers in the same period. For example, where a corporation earns a profit, it will pay tax on it; then from this profit it may choose to distribute dividends to its shareholders/owners. The shareholders will then be liable for tax on those dividends, as the payment is income to the shareholder. In essence, the shareholder/owner is punished for doing through a corporation what would have only been taxed once had the shareholder/owner done the economic activity in his or her own name.

Nations provide a range of responses to this situation, and some do nothing at all, as is the case in the United States, Ireland, and Switzerland. The balance of the countries of the OECD, and most others, attempt to create some form of relief in order to foster a healthy investment climate and to encourage risk-taking through the corporate form.

Relief of Economic Double Taxation

In nations that do take some form of action, five avenues are available. Where the relief given to shareholders is complete and not partial, such systems can be termed as *fully integrated:*

1. The individual taxpayer in receipt of dividends can simply exclude all or part of them from the computation of his or her taxable income (a participation-exemption system).[8]

2. The individual taxpayer in receipt of dividends can employ a much lower rate of tax on those dividends, compared to rates on other income, in the computation of his or her tax payable (a preferred-rate system).[9]

3. The individual taxpayer in receipt of dividends is fully taxed on those dividends, but receives a tax credit for all or some of the corporate tax previously paid (an imputation-credit system).[10]

4. The corporate taxpayer may deduct the amount of the dividends it intends to distribute from its taxable income, thus not paying tax on them (dividend-deduction system), while the individual recipient is fully taxed.[11]

5. The corporate taxpayer can be assessed tax on its profits at two different rates: a higher rate on those profits its intends to retain and a lower rate on those profits it intends to distribute as dividends (a split-rate system).[12]

---

[8]For example, Greece, Luxembourg.

[9]For example, Belgium, the Netherlands.

[10]For example, the United Kingdom and Canada (partial); Mexico and Australia (full credit).

[11]For example, the Czech Republic.

[12]For example, Japan.

International Juridical Double Taxation

Double taxation in international transactions is not confined to just a single taxing authority. The combination of a jurisdiction of a resident taxpayer that desires to tax worldwide income and that taxpayer's generation of income abroad as a nonresident in a jurisdiction that intends to tax domestic source income also gives immediate rise to double taxation. This type of double taxation is known as international juridical double taxation (IJDT), where two states impose comparable taxes on the same person in respect of the same income in the same period. To keep the distinction more clearly in mind, remember that economic double taxation stems from two people taxed in one state, while IJDT arises when two states tax the same person, all on the same income flow in the same period.

An example serves to make the point of the devastating effect that IJDT can have on foreign investment. Assume a corporation resident in Country A (which taxes worldwide income at 50 percent) makes a profit of $100 in Country A and operates a branch in Country B, where it also makes a profit of $100. Country B taxes on the basis of domestic source income, also at a rate of 50 percent. In this case, the branch operation will see its profit of $100 reduced to an after-tax $50, which it may remit home to Country A. At home, the firm faces tax of 50 percent on its worldwide income of $200, or an assessment of $100. The firm has total cash available of $150, being its $100 from domestic operations and its $50 received from abroad. Paying $100 to the Country A tax authority will leave it with group net profit after tax of $150 − $100, or $50.

The significance only arises when one asks what would have happened if the firm had just stuck to its domestic affairs. In that case, a domestic profit of $100 taxed at 50 percent would leave it with a net profit after tax of $50. The amounts, international and domestic, are the same; the obvious question is: in a world of double taxation, why would anyone bother to do business abroad, if at the end of the day there is nothing extra to show for it?

Governments around the world do not like this question, and do not like the equally obvious answer; too many jobs, growth, and development depend on increases in international business activity. The response has been to create mechanisms to fully or partially remove the effect of IJDT; much the same way these were policy responses to economic double taxation.

The example above shows the effect of IJDT where a branch structure was chosen, and, admittedly, foreign branches usually face a heavier tax burden and less access to deductions than do subsidiaries. To their advantage, once branch profits have been taxed in the domestic source country, they may leave that country without further taxation, as they are already in the hands of their owners; recall that branches are indivisible from their overseas controlling interests.

Subsidiaries do, however, customarily face an additional tax, as they are distinct corporations from their foreign owners, and the distribution of a dividend from a subsidiary to its parent will be subject to a withholding tax (usually 5 to 30 percent) levied by the jurisdiction where the subsidiary is located. The rate is usually reduced or run to zero where a tax treaty is in effect between the two nations.

Tax Treaties

One of the main purposes of bilateral tax treaties is to address the negative impact of double taxation, but they also serve to smooth potentially contentious questions of residency and the right to tax, as well as provide for mutual assistance and exchange of information in tax enforcement.

True multilateral treaties are hard to come by in the very sensitive world of taxation. The best that has been achieved is a trio of model conventions: those drafted and used by the United States,[13] the members of the Organization for Economic Cooperation and De-

---

[13]United States Model Income Tax Convention of September 20, 1996, which may be reviewed at http://www.ustreas.gov/offices/tax-policy/library/model996.pdf.

velopment (OECD),[14] and the members of the United Nations.[15] The OECD Model Convention is the most pervasive in number with well over 1,000 bilateral treaties having emerged from it. Its use is no longer confined to the membership of the OECD, for in a globalized trade and investment environment, many other nations have found it appropriate to follow a broadly accepted model.

Whether that is desirable or not for developing countries is another matter, and it was to address exactly that that spurred the UN to prepare its own. The UN was the inheritor of initiatives begun in the time of the League of Nations, but the final result still mirrors the influential OECD/U.S. models, while giving greater latitude for developing states to retain rights of taxation.

It must be well understood that the U.S. and OECD models are not treaties in themselves, but only models upon which actual treaties are negotiated between states. Only then are legal rights affected.

The U.S. and OECD models closely parallel one another, to the point of a majority of common wording and numbering, but the U.S. model further affirms its right to tax on the basis of citizenship. That aside, residency[16] and creation of "permanent establishments"[17] of business operations serve as the basis for individual and business taxation.

The definition of a person under both models includes both individuals and corporate bodies, and both models (where a bilateral treaty is concluded) provide that

1. Where a person is resident in a state (their home state), that state has the right to impose tax on their income.

2. Where a person resident in one state
   - Earns income from immovable property located in another state, the other state may impose tax on that income.
   - Earns business profits in another state, the other state may impose tax on that income to the extent the business profits are attributable to a permanent establishment.
   - Receives dividends from a corporation in another state, the other state may impose tax on those dividends not in excess of the range of 5 to 15 percent of the gross dividend.

[14]OECD Model Convention with Respect to Taxes on Income and on Capital of 28 January 2003, which may be reviewed at http://www.oecd.org/.

[15]United Nations Model Double Taxation Convention between Developed and Developing Countries of 1980, revised 1999, which may be viewed at http://unpan1.un.org/intradoc/groups/public/documents/un/unpan002084.pdf.

[16]Domicile, residence, or place of management is the index for residency, but where on that basis an individual is a resident of both contracting states, then status is determined by where a permanent home is available to that person; if a home exists in both states, then on the basis of that person's closest personal and economic relations; if this cannot be determined, then on the basis of his or her habitual abode; if none, then where he or she is a national; if he or she is a national of both states, then residency is decided by mutual agreement of the taxing authorities. Where a person other than an individual is in question (e.g., a corporation) and is a resident of both contracting states, then it shall be deemed to be a resident only of the state in which its place of effective management is situated (Article 4, OECD and U.S. models).

[17]A lengthy list of "establishments" are defined as "permanent," while others are deliberately excluded. This provision exists in both the U.S. and OECD model conventions, and should be consulted for particulars (Article 5, OECD and U.S. models). A "permanent establishment" is a fixed place of business, including places of management, branches, offices, factories, workshops, mines, wells and quarries, and construction sites with a time horizon greater than 12 months, *but excludes* facilities and inventories of goods solely for storage, display, or delivery; the maintaining of inventories for processing by another enterprise; a purchasing or information office; the carrying on of activities of merely a preparatory or auxiliary character; or any combinations of the excluded activities as long as the overall activity remains only preparatory or auxiliary to the enterprise. Carrying on business through agents and brokers, or controlling a corporation located in another state, also does not create a "permanent establishment."

- Receives interest from a debtor in another state, the other state may impose tax on that interest not in excess of 20 percent of the gross amount (15 percent under the U.S. model).
- Receives royalties from a user in another state, the other state may *not* impose tax on those royalties, unless the recipient has a permanent establishment in the other country, in which case the royalties are treated as business profits.
- Earns employment income in another state, the other state may tax this remuneration, unless the recipient was present in the host state for 183 days or less in any 12 months commencing or ending in that fiscal year, *and* the paying employer is not resident in the host state, *and* the remuneration was not borne by the employer's permanent establishment in the host state. (Note: The U.S. model distinguishes between dependent and independent personal services, giving the other state the right to tax the independent services as business profit where such income is attributable to a "fixed base" located in the other state.)
- Owns capital in another state, the other state may impose tax on that capital.

3. When a host state so taxes a nonresident person as above, the home state of that person must provide relief from international juridical double taxation by either an exemption or a credit for the foreign tax paid. (Note: The U.S. model, reflecting the U.S. preference, adopts the credit approach.)

At a number of points, the U.S. model creates further detail and special rules applicable to Social Security, annuities, child support, exempt persons, real estate investment trusts, beneficial ownership, and limitations of benefits, among others.

The OECD model has been the subject of interpretation of U.S. courts; while the question of a permanent establishment would seem fairly clear when a subsidiary or branch is in issue, the more vague nature of an agency relationship was the subject of the case below. The case turns on legal and economic independence.

Here, a U.S. firm arranges business for Japanese insurance companies, "managing" certain affairs for them inside the United States. The question is whether the Japanese firms therefore have a permanent establishment in the United States or whether the U.S. firm is a true agent. In the first case, the Japanese firms will be subject to tax, in the latter, they will not.

Taisei Fire & Marine Ins. Co. v. Commissioner

Indexed as *The Taisei Fire and Marine Insurance Co., Ltd., et al., v. Commissioner of Internal Revenue*

United States Tax Court
May 2, 1995

Opinion

The principal issue in these consolidated cases is whether, during the years at issue, petitioners had a U.S. permanent establishment by virtue of the activities of a U.S. agent in accepting reinsurance on behalf of each petitioner . . . *[and would thus be liable for tax]*.

Findings of Fact

Each petitioner is a Japanese property and casualty insurance company with its principal place of business in Japan. The stock of each petitioner is publicly traded on a Japanese exchange. There is no stock ownership relationship among petitioners.

Each petitioner has at least one representative office in the United States that provides information on the U.S. market to it and assists its clients in the United States, but which does not have authority to write any form of insurance. Taisei and Fuji do not have U.S. branches and do not have licenses to engage in the insurance business in the United States.

In addition, each petitioner grants authority to two or three different U.S. agents, including Fortress Re, Inc., to underwrite reinsurance on its behalf and to perform certain activities in connection therewith.

The directors of Fortress are Mr. Sabbah, his wife, and Mr. Kornfeld. Mr. Sabbah is the chairman of Fortress, and Mr. Kornfeld is the president and chief underwriter.

Mr. Sabbah handles contacts with insurance companies Fortress represents and has responsibility for reports provided to those companies, in addition to certain administrative responsibilities. Mr. Kornfeld's duties include underwriting the reinsurance entered into on behalf of the companies Fortress represents, establishing retrocession programs with respect to its reinsurance treaties, managing claims with respect to those treaties, and managing the daily affairs of Fortress. Mr. Sabbah and Mr. Kornfeld have total control over the daily operations of Fortress, including the hiring and firing of employees and the assigning of responsibilities to them. Fortress has approximately 20 employees, whose duties include assisting underwriting, handling claims, data processing and computer operations, secretarial support, and accounting services.

Fortress enters into a separate management agreement with each insurance company it represents. The agreements with petitioners are identical except for the net acceptance limit. Since its inception, Fortress has been involved in as many as 10 management agreements in a management year. A management year is defined as the annual period from July 1 to June 30. From inception through June 30, 1989, the management years have been designated as years I through XVI, respectively.

Pursuant to each agreement, Fortress regularly exercises the authority to conclude original reinsurance contracts and to cede reinsurance on behalf of each petitioner.

Each agreement provides Fortress with underwriting authority on a continuous basis until the agreement is terminated. The agreements can be terminated by either party, but only with 6 months' notice, although in practice the notice period has been waived. After termination of an agreement, Fortress continues to have obligations with respect to reinsurance previously underwritten. During the years in issue, Fortress had continuing duties to 13 insurance companies, excluding petitioners, for contracts underwritten in prior management years.

The only material limitation on Fortress' authority under the agreement is a "net acceptance limit," which is the maximum amount of net liability in respect of any one original reinsurance contract that Fortress can accept on behalf of a member. There is no gross acceptance limit in the agreements, so that Fortress can underwrite reinsurance contracts on behalf of a member that are greater than the net acceptance limit, provided that Fortress arranges for retrocessions of the excess over the net acceptance limit. In practice, Fortress sets its own gross acceptance limit, as to which it voluntarily advises petitioners. When approached by Chiyoda with regard to inserting a gross acceptance limit into its agreement, Fortress refused, and Chiyoda dropped its request.

Petitioners utilize the services of Fortress because Fortress has good relationships with reinsurance brokers, has access to good business, and has a profitable business strategy.

Fortress has continued access to good business because it has a reputation for paying its claims promptly and, of immeasurable importance, because its clients are large insurance companies that represent good security. Brokers would not deal with Fortress if its clients were not as financially secure as petitioners. However, there are 21 insurance companies in Japan and hundreds in the world that meet the minimum capital requirements and whom Fortress could have as clients and continue to obtain similar reinsurance business.

For 1986, 1987, and 1988, Fortress earned $1,819,152, $5,023,631, and $20,747,536, respectively, from management fees and profit commissions. Of these amounts, 74 percent, 78 percent, and 62 percent, respectively, were attributable to reinsurance underwritten in management years that ended before the particular calendar years.

Fortress has the authority, under the management agreements . . . to control the investment of funds withheld pursuant to such agreements in its sole discretion. Distributions are made in accordance with the management agreements and are made over a period of years following the management year.

Opinion

Under the Convention Between the United States of America and Japan for the Avoidance of Double Taxation and the Prevention of Fiscal Evasion with Respect to Taxes on Income, Mar. 8, 1971, 23 U.S.T. (Part 1) 969 (hereinafter referred to as the U.S.-Japan convention or convention), the commercial profits of a Japanese resident are exempt from U.S. Federal income tax, unless such profits are attributable to a U.S. permanent establishment. Convention, Art. 8(1). The relevant provisions of the convention whereby a Japanese resident will be deemed to have a U.S. permanent establishment due to the activities of an agent are as follows:

4. A person acting in a Contracting State on behalf of a resident of the other Contracting State, other than an agent of an independent status to whom paragraph (5) of this article applies, shall be deemed to be a permanent establishment in the first-mentioned Contracting State if such person has, and habitually exercises in the first-mentioned Contracting State, an authority to conclude contracts in the name of that resident, unless the exercise of such authority is limited to the purchase of goods or merchandise for that resident.

5. A resident of a Contracting State shall not be deemed to have a permanent establishment in the other Contracting State merely because such resident engages in industrial or commercial activity in that other Contracting State through a broker, general commission agent, or any other agent of an independent status, where such broker or agent is acting in the ordinary course of his business.

[Convention, Art. 9.]

Initially, it is undisputed that Fortress had the authority, which it exercised, to conclude contracts on behalf of petitioners, so that unless Fortress is "a broker, general commission agent, or any other agent of an independent status" within the meaning of Article 9(5), petitioners will be deemed to have U.S. permanent establishments. The parties are in agreement that Fortress was not a "broker" or "general commission agent," and respondent concedes that Fortress was acting in the ordinary course of its business when acting on behalf of petitioners. Thus, the issue before us is whether, during the years at issue, Fortress was an "agent of an independent status" in respect of each petitioner. In this connection, we note that neither petitioners nor respondent has argued that any petitioner should be treated differently from any other petitioner in resolving this issue.

Background

The U.S.-Japan convention itself does not define an "agent of an independent status." In applying a treaty definition, "Our role is limited to giving effect to the intent of the Treaty parties." *Sumitomo Shoji America, Inc. v. Avagliano,* 457 U.S. 176, 185 (1982); see also *Crow v. Commissioner,* 85 T.C. 376, 380 (1985) (quoting *Maximov v. United States,* 299 F.2d 565, 568 (2d Cir. 1962) ("The goal of treaty interpretation is 'to give the specific words a meaning consistent with the genuine shared expectations of the contracting parties.'"), *affd.* 373 U.S. 49 (1963)); *Estate of Burghardt v. Commissioner,* 80 T.C. 705, 708

(1983), *affd. without published opinion* 734 F.2d 3 (3d Cir. 1984). Beyond the literal language, we must examine the treaty's "purpose, history and context." *Crow v. Commissioner,* 85 T.C. at 380.

Our examination shows that the relevant provisions of the convention are not only based upon, but are duplicative of, Article 5, comments 4 and 5, of the 1963 O.E.C.D. Draft [model] Convention (hereinafter referred to as the 1963 model) . . . While the 1963 model itself provides no more definition than the convention, the model is explained in part by a commentary, which states in pertinent part:

> 15. Persons who may be deemed to be permanent establishments must be strictly limited to those who are dependent, both from the legal and economic points of view, upon the enterprise for which they carry on business dealings (Report of the Fiscal Committee of the League of Nations, 1928, page 12). Where an enterprise has business dealings with an independent agent, this cannot be held to mean that the enterprise itself carries on a business in the other State. In such a case, there are two separate enterprises.

> 19. Under paragraph 4 of the Article, only one category of dependent agents, who meet specific conditions, is deemed to be permanent establishments. All independent agents and the remaining dependent ones are not deemed to be permanent establishment. Mention should be made of the fact that the Mexico and London Drafts and a number of Conventions, do not enumerate exhaustively such dependent agents as are deemed to be permanent establishments, but merely give examples. In the interest of preventing differences of interpretation and of furthering international economic relations, it appeared advisable to define, as exhaustively as possible, the cases where agents are deemed to be "permanent establishments."

The substance of Art. 5 was not changed in the 1977 revision, which provides:

> 6. An enterprise shall not be deemed to have a permanent establishment in a Contracting State merely because it carries on business in that State through a broker, general commission agent or any other agent of an independent status, provided that such persons are acting in the ordinary course of their business. [OECD Revised Model Double Taxation Convention on Income and Capital—1977.]

Against the foregoing background, we turn to the determination of Fortress' legal and economic independence.

Legal Independence

The relationship between Fortress and petitioners is defined by the management agreement that Fortress entered into separately with each petitioner. Petitioners have no interest in Fortress, and no representative of any of petitioners is a director, officer, or employee of Fortress. The agreements grant complete discretion to Fortress to conduct the reinsurance business on behalf of petitioners.

Respondent agrees that Fortress had independence with respect to day-to-day operations, but then argues that its actions were restricted by gross acceptance limits and limits on net premium income. However, even if there were such restrictions, they would not necessarily constitute control. The gross acceptance limit and net premium income both relate to the total exposure of petitioners, and even an independent agent only has authority to perform specific duties for the principal. It is freedom in the manner by which the agent performs such duties that distinguishes him as independent.

As to net premium income, there were no limits under the terms of the management agreements. If one of petitioners sought to lower its net premium income from U.S. sources, Fortress' advice was to cede a greater share to Carolina Re, operating in Bermuda. Petitioners could also terminate agreements with their other U.S. agents. Respondent places great weight on the estimates of net premium income Fortress provided to petitioners before each management year, but the estimates are clearly that, and nothing more, and were greatly exceeded for at least one of the years at issue. While Fortress was aware that at times petitioners wanted only to absorb a certain amount of net premium income, Fortress did not change its business to accommodate their concerns.

Respondent further argues that petitioners exercised "comprehensive control" over Fortress by acting as a "pool." However, there is no evidence that petitioners acted in concert to control Fortress. In only rare and isolated instances did petitioners communicate with one another regarding Fortress. Further, there are references to a "pool" throughout the history of Fortress, which period covers relationships with 17 separate U.S. and Japanese insurance companies. The inferences respondent would have us draw from the fact that petitioners are all from Japan and that petitioners are among the participants in regular industry conferences in Japan are simply insufficient to establish the existence of control by a "pool."

Finally, we note that all four petitioners, while not their primary business, did have reinsurance departments. Thus, petitioners had the ability to give detailed instructions to Fortress, yet they did not.

As an agent, Fortress had complete discretion over the details of its work. As an entity, Fortress was subject to no external control. In sum, Fortress was legally independent of petitioners.

Economic Independence

Fortress is owned solely by Mr. Sabbah and his family and Mr. Kornfeld. There was no guarantee of revenue to Fortress, nor was Fortress protected from loss in the event it had been unable to generate sufficient revenue. Fortress has management agreements with four separate clients, whereby any one of them can leave on 6 months' notice. If one of petitioners did end its relationship, Fortress would bear the burden of finding a replacement to subscribe to that client's share of reinsurance contracts.

Respondent argues that Fortress bore no entrepreneurial risk because its operating expenses were covered by a management fee, and because it was guaranteed business due to the creditworthiness of the reinsurers on whose behalf it acted, petitioners.

While the management agreements provided that Fortress earned a percentage of the gross premiums written which effectively covered Fortress' operating expenses, this did not mean that Fortress bore no risk. Fortress had to acquire sufficient business to produce the gross premiums. Further, it appears that this provision of the agreements is normal for an underwriting manager. That respondent's argument on this point misses the mark is illustrated, for example, by a large mutual fund that charges an annual management fee to cover operating expenses. Clearly, the mutual fund company would not be considered dependent on its thousands of investors. Under these circumstances, even with as few as four investors, Fortress cannot be considered dependent on petitioners to pay its operating expenses.

Nor do we agree with respondent's argument that Fortress is able to secure profitable reinsurance contracts only because its clients are petitioners. Although Fortress needs clients with a certain minimum capital to conduct its business, any of hundreds of other insurance companies worldwide would be adequate substitutes. Also, it cannot be denied that Fortress had access to the reinsurance contracts it considered good, in part because of Fortress' relationships and reputation in the industry. In fact, it appears that Fortress' access to profitable reinsurance contracts, as well as its experience and ability to choose profitable reinsurance contracts, attracted petitioners to Fortress, and would attract other insurance companies if Fortress needed another client to take a share of the contracts.

Finally, we think that the amount of Fortress' profits is significant. See Madole, "Agents as Permanent Establishments Under U.S. Income Tax Treaties," 23 *Tax Mgmt. Intl.* 281,

293–294 (1994). For the 3 years in issue, Fortress was paid over $27 million. This is not the kind of sum paid to a subservient company.

Conclusion

In sum, during the years at issue, Fortress was both legally and economically independent of petitioners, thus satisfying the definition of an agent of an independent status under Article 9 of the U.S.-Japan convention. *[The Japanese firms thus do not have a permanent establishment in the United States and are not therefore liable for U.S. tax.]*

Source: 104 T.C. 535 (1995).

- State three factors (business activities) that would likely have been sufficient to tip the balance the other way and lead the Tax Court to conclude that the Japanese insurers did operate a "permanent establishment" in the United States.
- What lesson does this offer to international businesspersons who intend to operate through agents in a country subject to a tax treaty based on the OECD model convention?

Relief of International Juridical Double Taxation

In the best of all possible worlds, a bilateral treaty would allow nations to agree on an allocation of taxing powers for particular forms of cross-border income, as is the case under the OECD/U.S. models with respect to royalties. Presumably the home state is in a better position to assess the allowance of business expense deductions from that gross amount of royalty payment. Nations who are net exporters of intellectual property love this idea, while net importers of intellectual property hate it, because of the obvious consequences of taxing opportunities gained and lost, respectively. Any such exclusive allocation of tax jurisdiction wipes out international juridical double taxation (IJDT). Sadly, this method is not widespread.

Second, a "foreign source exemption" is a unilateral measure that eliminates IJDT, as one jurisdiction eliminates itself, and such an exemption also may arise from bilateral commitments made in the form of Article 23A of the OECD model tax convention. By declaring that income generated abroad will be fully exempt from taxation in the home state of the recipient, the problem of two jurisdictions taxing the same flow is instantly and completely solved. The flow will be taxed in the foreign jurisdiction and that is the end. Such exemptions come in two forms: the full exemption described above and an exemption with progression that allows the home state to consider the income in assessing tax to be imposed on other income (e.g., for purposes of assessing the appropriate tax bracket of the recipient).

The third approach is the "deduction method." In this instance, jurisdiction is not solved because both domestic and foreign jurisdictions still levy tax on the same flow, but the home state of the recipient mitigates the effect of the IJDT to a degree, allowing foreign tax paid to be deducted as a business expense against total income. The deduction of foreign tax paid from total income translates only to a reduction in domestic tax proportional to the prevailing corporate income tax rate in the home jurisdiction, and does not fully offset the foreign tax paid. For example, where foreign withholding tax paid of $150 is allowed as a business expense deduction and the domestic corporate income tax rate is 40 percent, it is equivalent to a tax credit of $60, not a full recompense of the $150 paid abroad.

Finally is the "foreign tax credit" used by the U.S. model and available as an option under Article 23B of the OECD model. Despite the fact that neither the foreign nor domestic tax authority relinquishes its jurisdiction, the foreign tax credit, if fully allowed, does remove the effect of IJDT.

A foreign tax credit does no good to an enterprise that does not have a domestic tax liability to which to apply it! Beware of "ordinary credits," where a deduction is allowed only from that home tax that would be appropriate to the income that was taxed abroad. The home jurisdiction's credit for foreign tax paid on one type of income (e.g., dividends) may be prohibited from application to domestic tax liabilities derived from *other types* of domestic income (e.g., business income). In other words, a home jurisdiction credit for foreign tax paid on dividends might only be available for application against home jurisdiction tax on domestic dividends—and so on for each type of foreign tax paid and domestic income.

Where a foreign income flow, for example, a $100 dividend, attracts a foreign tax (a 15 percent withholding tax, or $15), that underlying gross flow is first included in income and is then taxed a second time in the domestic jurisdiction. In such a case, a full credit of $15 against domestic tax liability removes the effect of the IJDT. This creates a net tax result identical to one that would have occurred if the entire transaction had taken place within the home jurisdiction of the recipient.

Treaty and Double Taxation Implications in Transaction Structuring

In introducing IJDT, the parent–branch example illustrated the impact of international juridical double taxation in effectively wiping out foreign investment. As a precursor to being able to use bilateral tax treaties effectively (and for lawyers to be able to advise clients effectively), both the international businessperson and lawyer must understand the implications of IJDT relief mechanisms as they begin to plan and test the viability of foreign operations transactions. The availability of relief mechanisms stems from either treaty commitment or national tax policy decisions, and will have a large impact on

1. The business choice between establishing a branch operation and establishing a subsidiary.
2. The business choice not to enter a particular market at all.
3. The net cash flows that can be expected after tax in the hands of the overall group of companies or network of branches making up a business interest.

The process of transaction analysis under IJDT and IJDT relief conditions is purely mathematical, seeking to complete the following matrix with the net income after tax related to each option. Even where a treaty presently exists, or only a single IJDT relief mechanism exists, it is important to address all options. One does not know what the future holds in terms of the creation and termination of treaty benefits, or changes to domestic exemption and credit policy, and thus knowing each option allows for early understanding of tax-driven "dealmakers" and "dealbreakers."

Tax Analysis Matrix

	(1) No Measures for IJDT Relief	(2) Foreign Source Exemption	(3) Deduction Method	(4) Foreign Tax Credit
(a) Branch option	Group net income after tax	Group net income after tax	Group net income after tax	Group net income after tax
(b) Subsidiary option	Group net income after tax	Group net income after tax	Group net income after tax	Group net income after tax

The Tax Analysis Matrix follows the formula of

Group net income after tax (GNIAT)	=	Gross group income	–	[Taxes paid in Country B]	–	[Taxes paid in Country A]

The following examples show the matrix in use for the following scenario:

- Income in home Country A: $200
- Income in foreign Country B: $200
- Corporate income tax (CIT) 50 percent on worldwide income, Country A
- Business/corporate income tax (CIT) 50 percent on domestic source income, Country B
- Withholding tax (WT) 20 percent on dividends, royalties, interest, Country B

1. Where no measures exist to mitigate IJDT:
   a. Structured with a foreign branch:

   GNIAT = Gross income – (Tax paid in Country B) – (Tax paid in Country A)
   = 400 – (200 source income in B × 50% CIT) – (400 worldwide income × 50% CIT in A)
   = 400 – 100 – 200
   = **100**

   b. Structured with a foreign subsidiary:

   GNIAT = Gross income – [Tax paid in Country B] – [Tax paid in Country A]
   = 400 – [(200 subsidiary income in B × 50% CIT) + (100 dividends in B × 20% WT)] –
   [(200 domestic income in A + 100 gross foreign dividend income) × 50% CIT]
   = 400 – [100 + 20] – [300 × 50%]
   = 400 – 120 – 150
   = **130**

2. Where a full foreign source exemption exists:
   a. Structured with a foreign branch:

   GNIAT = Gross income – [Tax paid in Country B] – [Tax paid in Country A]
   = 400 – [200 source income in B × 50% CIT] – [200 taxable domestic income × 50% CIT]
   = 400 – 100 – 100
   = **200**

   b. Structured with a foreign subsidiary:

   GNIAT = Gross income – [Tax paid in Country B] – [Tax paid in Country A]
   = 400 – [(200 subsidiary income in B × 50% CIT) + (100 dividends in B × 20% WT)] –
   [200 taxable domestic income × 50% CIT]
   = 400 – [100 + 20] – [100]
   = 400 – 120 – 100
   = **180**

3. Where the deduction method exists:
   a. Structured with a foreign branch:

   GNIAT = Gross income – (Tax paid in Country B) – (Tax paid in Country A)
   = 400 – (200 source income in B × 50% CIT) – ([400 worldwide income –
   100 foreign tax paid deduction] × 50% CIT in A)
   = 400 – 100 – 150
   = **150**

b. Structured with a foreign subsidiary:

GNIAT = Gross income – [Tax paid in Country B] – [Tax paid in Country A]
= 400 – [(200 subsidiary income in B × 50% CIT) + (100 dividends in B × 20% WT)] –
[(200 domestic income in A + 100 gross foreign dividend income – 20 foreign tax paid deduction) × 50% CIT]
= 400 – [100 + 20] – [280 × 50%]
= 400 – 120 – 140
= **140**

4. Where a foreign tax credit exists:
a. Structured with a foreign branch:

GNIAT = Gross income – [Tax paid in Country B] – [Tax paid in Country A]
= 400 – [200 source income in B × 50% CIT] – [(400 worldwide income × 50% CIT) – (100 credit foreign tax paid)]
= 400 – 100 – [200 – 100]
= **200**

b. Structured with a foreign subsidiary:

GNIAT = Gross income – [Tax paid in Country B] – [Tax paid in Country A]
= 400 – [(200 subsidiary income in B × 50% CIT) + (100 dividends in B × 20% WT)] –
[(200 domestic income in A + 100 gross foreign dividend income) × 50% CIT) – (20 credit for foreign withholding tax paid)]
= 400 – [100 + 20] – [150 – 20]
= 400 – 120 – 130
= **150**

The tax analysis matrix displaying group net income after tax becomes

	(1) No Measures for IJDT Relief	(2) Foreign Source Exemption	(3) Deduction Method	(4) Foreign Tax Credit
(a) Branch option	100	200	150	200
(b) Subsidiary option	130	180	140	150

Now the international businessperson and his or her lawyer can consider the results of the matrix. Financially speaking, the branch operation would be the more profitable if either the foreign source exemption or a full foreign tax credit is available. The branch operation is also the least profitable if for any reason IJDT relief is unavailable. It may be such that other commercial realities dictate an entry strategy using a subsidiary (liability issues, demands of investment regulations, etc.), and this choice represents a tax cost of either 20 or 10, depending on IJDT relief available, compared to what might have been under the branch alternative.

Note that even if a branch operation alternative is selected, the firm is not necessarily indifferent between a foreign source exemption (if available) and a foreign tax credit (if available). The two methods in this instance returned the same group net income after tax only because the income tax rates in the two countries were identical. Had the tax rate been higher in Country A than B, an exemption would prove more valuable than a credit as it would exclude funds from being taxed at a higher rate, as opposed to being offset by a smaller credit.

Tax Planning, Avoidance, and Evasion

Good tax planning is the active consideration of all available legal means to make strategic international business decisions with the twin objectives of reducing the overall tax liability of a group of enterprises while attaining the selected international business goals. Anything outside this definition constitutes at least bad tax planning and may constitute an offense under the law. It may be that the planning involves explicitly illegal activity or questionable activity that may be reviewed and be deemed to be illegal, or it may be in error, or it may be a valid tax strategy that minimizes tax but winds up endangering the business goals.

When the analysis and strategy involve only available legal means, the process can be described as tax avoidance. Anything employing less than legal means instantly creates the offense of tax evasion. In the first instance, nations require compliance with the law, meaning that tax declarations must be made, and be made complete in all respects, without misstatement or misrepresentation, such as overreporting of deductible expenses, underreporting of taxable income, or mischaracterization of one type of income as another. Failure to comply can lead to reassessment of tax owing, imposition of further penalty tax, imposition of punitive interest rates on tax and penalty outstanding, administrative sanction in suspension of rights to serve as an officer or director of a corporation, and, ultimately, jail.

Anti-Avoidance Rules

Many tax jurisdictions go beyond this stark legal–illegal distinction and treat elements of tax avoidance as tantamount to tax evasion. In the United States, there exists a judicial willingness to examine the substance of a transaction rather than its form, its business purpose, and whether it is a sham transaction. Additionally, the U.S. Internal Revenue Code is studded with specific anti-avoidance provisions. In Europe, tax authorities may disregard transactions for tax purposes if they are inappropriate to the underlying business objectives (Germany) or abusive of the law (France). In much of the British Commonwealth (Australia, New Zealand, and Canada, for example), particular "general anti-avoidance rules" or "GAAR" exist, which permit the tax authorities to consider the character of a transaction and either disregard it or deem it to be of a different character. Typical of these is Canadian tax authorities' wide-ranging remedial power granted by Canada's Income Tax Act:[18]

> 245(2) General anti-avoidance provision. Where a transaction is an avoidance transaction, the tax consequences to a person shall be determined as is reasonable in the circumstances in order to deny a tax benefit that, but for this section, would result, directly or indirectly, from the transaction or from a series of transactions that includes that transaction.
>
> (5) Determination of tax consequences. Without restricting the generality of subsection (2),
>
> (a) any deduction in computing income, taxable income, taxable income earned in Canada or tax payable or any part thereof may be allowed or disallowed in whole or in part,
>
> (b) any such deduction, any income, loss or other amount or part thereof may be allocated to any person,
>
> (c) the nature of any payment or other amount may be recharacterized, and
>
> (d) the tax effects that would otherwise result from the application of other provisions of this Act may be ignored, in determining the tax consequences to a person as is reasonable in the circumstances in order to deny a tax benefit that would, but for this section, result, directly or indirectly, from an avoidance transaction.

[18]Income Tax Act, R.S.C. 1985, s.245(2) and (5).

Thin Capitalization

Thin capitalization is a condition of a corporate structure that is illegal or may be attacked under the anti-avoidance provisions of most jurisdictions that impose income taxes (bearing in mind that some jurisdictions have no taxes), and particularly in those jurisdictions where interest paid is a deductible corporate expense. It is an effort to recharacterize a corporate dividend, most often improperly or illegally, as a deductible interest expense. In so doing, a foreign investor who wishes to start a company in a high-tax jurisdiction provides a new corporation with a tiny amount of capital (perhaps only a few dollars) and then makes a large loan to the corporation. The corporation undertakes its business, generating revenue, and, as it is saddled with a large loan, makes large interest payments to the investor. This will wipe out all its potential profit, leaving nothing to be taxed in the high-tax jurisdiction, and, of course, no funds for payment of a dividend to the investor. The investor, however, does not care, for all the profits of the corporation are arriving in the investor's hands in the form of an interest payment.

The mischaracterization of this payment as interest stems from the fact that under normal business conditions, the investor would have provided the original funds as paid-up capital in return for shares. There would be no loan and there would be no interest expense. Instead, the corporation would be well-capitalized rather than thinly so, turn a healthy profit, be taxed, and distribute those profits as dividends, subject to further withholding tax to foreign residents. If the foreign investor makes the loan from a low-tax or no-tax jurisdiction, it would also escape tax on the interest payments it receives.

Quite understandably, this is the type of transaction that tax authorities in high-tax jurisdictions wish to prevent, and use a variety of their deeming provisions or substantive tax laws to address.

Abusive Transfer Pricing

Transfer prices are prices set for assets (goods, services, or intangible property) transferred between two entities operating within a non-arm's-length relationship. Nothing is inherently abusive about transfer prices. Notwithstanding a non-arm's length relationship, these transfer prices may still reflect market sale prices. Then again, they might not, simply because no price was set for the transfer at all, or because there is no comparable market price for the asset. Alternatively, the off-market pricing may be an attempt to divert profits from one market to another.

Tax problems in transfer pricing occur in each of these situations. As far as foreign branch operations are concerned, while there is a need for management accounting to maintain control from a financial accounting perspective, there is a lesser concern over transfer prices as the entity is unitary. This is, however, contrary to local taxing authorities, which see a duality of enterprises, one foreign and one domestic. The local tax authority must think in these terms for it wishes to tax income that can be attributed to local operations. The tax problem then becomes one of dissecting the transfer and assigning a price where none existed before.

The variant tax problem occurs in transfers with a price assigned by the actors, but no comparable open-market price exists for the good. This occurs often in the transfer of unique or proprietary goods or intellectual property, or in cost-sharing arrangements in research and development. Taxing authorities will want to review such pricing, and may well extrapolate a figure very different from the actors, because there is room for interpretation of value where no market exists. The internal and international experience of the former Soviet Union in pricing assets and goods serves as a reminder how distorting some of the resulting inaccuracies can be.

Finally, transfer pricing is improperly employed by business actors attempting to divert profits from one jurisdiction to another. With the age-old principle of buy low/sell high in mind, some businesses attempt to maximize profits by generating expenses in high tax jurisdictions and revenues in low-tax jurisdictions. For example, a captive trading house located in a tax haven (a no-tax or low-tax jurisdiction) could, financially speaking, buy raw materials from anywhere at market prices, mark them up astronomically, then sell them to a parent production facility located in a high tax jurisdiction. This would park all the marked-up sale profits in the tax haven, and the parent firm "struggles" along, leaving only a thin or no profit margin to be taxed in the high-tax jurisdiction.

The following example illustrates a no-tax jurisdiction used as a tax sink. In so doing, the company using a trading house converts $40 in after-tax profits into $80 of untaxed profits. The legality of doing so is dependent on the commercial realities associated with the costs and operations of the trading house, and whether doing so violates either the substantive tax provisions or anti-avoidance rules of the jurisdictions involved.

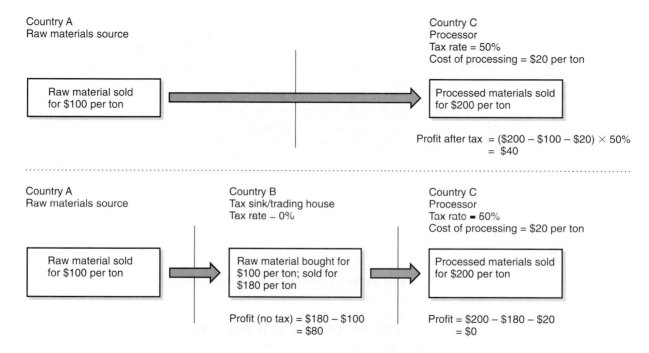

Of course, tax authorities know all about this and many have made abusive transfer prices illegal, or impose anti-avoidance sanctions. Still, reasonable trading profits from transfer prices may be left in tax havens. This may be permitted where the transfer prices between the source of supply, the trading house, and the parent firm are commercially defensible, and the operations in the low- or no-tax jurisdiction are a real operation (not just a fictional office). This commercial reality test must be borne out beyond simply reasons of tax avoidance. Perhaps the corporate group wishes to base its trading house in a location that is physically close to source markets for raw materials or one that advantageously overlaps regional business days by virtue of its location and time zone.

Treaty Shopping

Despite the extensive web of bilateral tax treaties between nations (and in the absence of a broadly accepted multilateral tax treaty), international businesspersons and lawyers will find occasions where no treaty benefit exists. Such situations will result in double taxation between the country of residence of a parent company and the second country where its overseas income is generated.

The response to this situation by many companies is to create a third (and, if necessary, a fourth) company in one (or two) other jurisdictions. Favorable treaty provisions must exist between these jurisdictions so that they can be linked to create a benefit chain between the host country where income is generated and the country of the parent firm's residence. Often these intermediate countries, where one serves as a single conduit or two as a pair of stepping stones, are located in low-tax or no-tax jurisdictions.

In such cases, not only can treaty benefits be taken that were otherwise unavailable directly, but profits also can be stripped away from the highly taxed parent firm, in much the same way as was done with (nonabusive) transfer pricing. The company or companies located in the conduit or stepping-stone countries take legal and beneficial ownership of the operating assets in the host country (taking them from the corporate parent) and become, in turn, owned by the corporate parent. As a result, the profits and initial tax treaty benefits accrue to the holding companies, and the corporate parent is taxed only on funds actually drawn back into its country of residence. Subject to anti-avoidance provisions, treaty benefit limitations, and controlled foreign company legislation, and assuming a right to receive intracompany dividends on a tax-free basis, this final cash flow home may escape taxation in the parent firm's country of residence. The arrangement of conduit and stepping-stone treaty benefits and associated corporate structure is shown in the diagrams on page 629.

Tax Havens

The term *tax havens* has taken on a rather negative connotation in the last 20 years, largely without being particularly deserved in the bigger economic, political, and financial picture. The classical negative image is one of island palm trees shading even shadier tax dodges and potentially criminal funds. There is some truth in that image in particular places, but the centers of financial, banking, insurance, and shipping expertise that have evolved into modern offshore business centers fully eclipse it. The term *tax haven* encompasses low-tax and no-tax jurisdictions, which may or many not offer banking secrecy as well, and includes relatively high-tax jurisdictions that offer either reduced rates or particularly advantageous corporate vehicles for nonresidents.

In the category of the no-tax jurisdiction are Anguilla, Bahamas, Cayman Islands, and Turks and Caicos Islands. Among those with exemptions from tax are Aruba, the British Virgin Islands, Gibraltar, Guernsey, Jersey, and Nevis. Reduced rates of tax are available in Belgium, Ireland, and Switzerland. Holding companies are allowed special rules in the Netherlands and the United Kingdom, and particular nonresident company arrangements can be made in Barbados and Singapore. No one jurisdiction, not even a no-tax jurisdiction, is right for all purposes: some have treaties that others do not, some have corporate vehicles with particular features that others do not. Where a particular transaction is being legally structured, a rather comprehensive search is required to find the right offshore business center to use.

The lists are not exhaustive, for there are many states that fall into each of these categories. Some do so on the basis of the particular type of trade they wish to attract, based

Treaty Shopping through Conduit and Stepping-Stone Jurisdictions

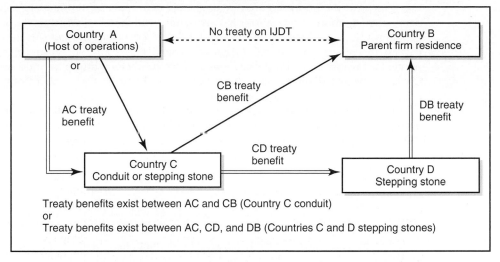

Treaty benefits exist between AC and CB (Country C conduit)
or
Treaty benefits exist between AC, CD, and DB (Countries C and D stepping stones)

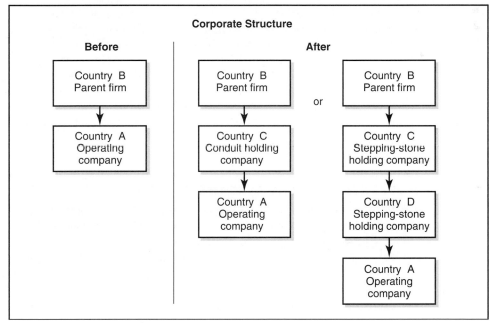

on local financial expertise; for example, shipping and insurance are the specialties of Liberia[19] and Bermuda.[20] Other nations simply have few options. As small islands in some cases, they have no arable land or prospect of using natural resources or industry to build their economies; thus, they have focused on knowledge capital and the ability to use their legal system to their advantage. Alternatively, others such as Switzerland see their role as a banking center tied to their fierce neutrality and their mission is one of a haven of stability and protection in a sometimes unstable and violent world. Lastly, the use of a corporation in a neutral tax haven with no taxes lets a group of investors enjoy the benefit of that neutrality and fiscal transparency. Diverse investors from a score of nations can come

[19]At 52 million gross weight tons, Liberia's ship registry is more than five times larger than that of the United States.

[20]Over 1,600 insurance companies (over 1,000 captive firms) are based there.

The Old Wolf

Tax issues and the use of tax havens are strewn with traps for the unwary, most of them deep, painful, and expensive. This is a specialist area for international tax lawyers and accountants. It is especially important for both international businesspersons and their lawyers to engage professional assistance in one's home jurisdiction and further professionals in the offshore jurisdiction. These advisors know the attitude, latitude, and priorities of their respective domestic tax authority, as well as the particular suitability of the tax planning vehicles they offer. Stick with experience and reputation. Doubtless some of those who offer services over the Internet fall into that category, but finding them among the modern crop of snake-oil dealers may prove difficult.

together in what amounts to a partnership venture, yet still obtain a corporate form, and their profits will flow back to them in equal shares without the distortion of an intermediate tax.

Commonly, tax havens wish to attract incorporators that intend, in fact, to have nothing to do with the jurisdiction that incorporates them. The residence of the owners and their business interests are elsewhere, and the tax haven is perfectly happy with that. The tax haven merely is collecting incorporation and management fees. In policy terms, the tax haven does not wish to be overrun with businesses that will compete with local firms, or will own and develop what few natural resources or industries or tourism opportunities that exist on their territory. As a result, these tax havens generally impose no tax on such non-resident-owned corporations as long as the corporation does not do any business within the tax haven territory. The name of such a corporate form varies in different jurisdictions, but as often as not is referred to as an "International Business Company" (IBC).

Of late, and even more so as terrorist concerns have risen, many offshore business centers have faced pressure from the United States and much of the industrialized world to take greater steps to remove their secrecy and antidisclosure laws that surround their accounts. Some have done so, and this has happened throughout a period where industrialized countries (primarily of the OECD) have seen great pressures on their own economies (recession) and an increasingly competitive international business environment. These latter two facts led to concerted OECD effort to prevent taxation from becoming a competitive weapon (termed as a "race to the bottom") in attracting investment and growth. Recommended measures against tax evasion through policy creation and harmonization became an OECD priority, such as its Report on Harmful Tax Competition (1999), Report on International Tax Avoidance and Evasion (1987), and Report on Thin Capitalization (1987).[21]

Certainly the usefulness of tax havens has been impaired by many of the anti-avoidance provisions found in tax codes around the world and rules on controlled foreign corporations.[22] Controlled foreign corporation (CFC) rules require reporting by and taxation of domestic owners of foreign corporations, particularly targeting foreign personal holding company income and income derived from a base company. Such a legislative approach is an effort to prevent the simple migration of domestic firms toward tax haven bases and the loss of revenue that would result from their departure. As is the case with all things in tax, what should be a clear rule addressing a single policy objective ultimately winds up causing a further range of other problems, requiring governments to endlessly tinker with their tax codes. U.S. CFC legislation dates from the late 1930s, with a major revision in 1962, and remains controversial in its appropriateness today, given that it impairs the competitiveness of U.S. firms operating abroad through foreign corporations.

[21] See http://www.oecd.org.
[22] For example, Subpart F of the U.S. Internal Revenue Code, 26 U.S.C. § 952.

Chapter Summary

Tax is variously described as a compulsory payment mandated by law, of financial resources, from the private sector to a government, without an expectation in the payer of counterperformance owed to it individually by that government.

The sovereign power to tax is closely held by all governments, not lightly given up, and results very rapidly in two jurisdictions intending to tax the same income in the hands of the same taxpayer in the same period: international juridical double taxation. This taxation can take many forms, and, in any case, either as an indirect tax (arising from doing business with another nation, i.e., trade related) or direct tax (arising from doing business in another nation, i.e., investment related). Indirect taxes include sales tax, excise tax, and customs duties, while direct taxes include individual and corporate income tax, capital gains, and wealth tax.

Relative inequalities in taxation levels cause distortions in trade and investment flows, and have proved to be one of the few reasons that bring nations together to solve international tax problems such as questions of residency and international juridical double taxation. Most of these efforts have taken place on a bilateral basis, using fairly widely accepted model conventions, most of which have been inspired through multilateral negotiation in the OECD.

Residency remains as the primary basis for tax, recognizing that, in principle, nations have the right to tax sources of income within their territory. To the extent that this results in double taxation, the provision of a credit or exemption in the second taxing jurisdiction is expected under bilateral treaties to remove the double taxation.

Since these treaties exist, companies attempt to structure their affairs so that they might put them to best fiscal use. As a result, considerable effort goes into transaction planning in search of a structure that will yield the lowest net tax liability to the group of operations under contemplation. Tax authorities are, however, not blind to this, and legislatures have taken pains to develop both specific and general anti-avoidance provisions in their tax codes to combat abuse of such constructs. Thin capitalization, abusive transfer pricing, and treaty shopping are often condemned as illegal, or restricted through a limitation of treaty benefit.

Much to the aggravation of high-tax jurisdictions are those low- or no-tax jurisdictions that offer corporations with particular attributes as tax-planning vehicles to the international business trader and investor. While there are many legitimate uses of such strategies, it is becoming increasingly difficult to access these benefits due to the hard line taken by nations and groups of nations against these offshore business centers. In response, offshore business centers possess strong skill sets in finance, banking, insurance, and shipping, which will keep them in demand as service providers to international business.

Chapter Questions

1. Differentiate between economic double taxation and international juridical double taxation, additionally giving an example of each.
2. How does indirect taxation of the origin and destination type give rise to distortion in the flow of international goods trade?
3. What avenues are open, generally speaking, for nations to offset or eliminate international juridical double taxation? What are the more effective methods in the eyes of persons and corporations subject to IJDT, and why is this so?
4. Explain the consequences attached to being a "permanent establishment" under both the U.S. and OECD model tax conventions, providing two additional concrete examples of what does not constitute a "permanent establishment."
5. Explain the mechanics of thin capitalization and transfer pricing, and on what basis tax authorities would not condemn the latter.

Questions 6 through 10 use the following scenario:

Income in home Country A	$500
Income in foreign Country B	$300

Corporate income tax (CIT)	50% on worldwide income, Country A
Business/corporate income tax (CIT)	50% on domestic source income, Country B
Withholding tax (WT)	20% on dividends, royalties, interest, Country B

6. To maximize group net income after tax where no measures to mitigate IJDT exists, should a branch or subsidiary strategy be employed in Country B? Show your proof.

7. Is a subsidiary preferable to a branch in maximizing group net income after tax where a full foreign source exemption in Country A exists? Show your proof.

8. A branch in Country B is better than a subsidiary in maximizing group net income after tax where the deduction method is employed in Country A. By how much is it better? Show your proof.

9. Is a foreign tax credit in Country A more useful in maximizing group net income after tax when a branch strategy is employed in Country B or when a subsidiary strategy is used?

10. Where some measure of IJDT relief exists, which business strategy is superior in maximizing group net income? If the subsidiary strategy is chosen for business reasons other than tax, which IJDT relief scheme is most advantageous in maximizing group net income after tax?

BusinessWeek

The U.S. international code badly needs fixing. But reforming the system will be bloody.

Tax systems are never pretty. But even by the usual low standards of revenue codes, the way the U.S. taxes exporters and multinationals is especially ugly.

America's system imposes reams of incomprehensible rules on companies and forces them to spend a small fortune on lawyers and accountants. Because of a patchwork of special-interest laws, it generates huge subsidies for some companies yet punishes thousands of others. It encourages massive amounts of sheltering—paper transactions aimed at nothing more than reducing tax bills. And at the end of the day, the Treasury collects stunningly little revenue, perhaps just $5 billion a year. "The U.S. is probably rich enough to get away with stupid taxes," says University of Michigan tax economist James R. Hines Jr. "But it doesn't mean we should have them."

Now, change may be on the way. A World Trade Organization decision to prohibit one big U.S. export subsidy has kicked off a major effort in Washington to rethink the way foreign income is taxed. And the direction reform takes will inevitably create big winners—and big losers—in Corporate America. The billion-dollar question: Will Washington just replace its now-banned subsidies with new corporate tax cuts, or will it reform the way it taxes foreign profits?

With U.S. companies selling more than $150 billion worth of goods overseas each year, and with one-third of all sales of American multinationals coming from their foreign affiliates, the lobbying battle will be fierce. Hanging in the balance will be billions of dollars in profits that escape taxation.

If nothing else, there is broad agreement that the system needs fixing. To avoid taxes, U.S. companies are shifting increasing amounts of assets to low-tax countries. The Cayman Islands, for example, is home to 50 banks, making it the world's fifth-largest banking center. In 1994, the last year of available data, such tax havens accounted for just 3% of the world's gross domestic product but 26% of the assets and 31% of the net profits of U.S. multinationals.

Since then, the problem has gotten worse, despite aggressive efforts by the European Union, the Organization for Economic Cooperation & Development, and the U.N. to curb tax havens. Says Peter Merrill, a partner at accountants PricewaterhouseCoopers LLP: "The mobility of capital is unbelievable. Competitive pressures are going to keep forcing down corporate tax rates."

At the same time, American companies are becoming attractive targets for overseas takeovers—in part because they'll pay lower taxes as foreign-owned businesses. And the rise of the borderless Internet is raising still other questions about the sustainability of an international tax system based on a company's location.

To fight these trends, Washington created a $4 billion-a-year subsidy for exporting corporations. The arrangement allows companies to get a special tax break by creating a Foreign Sales Corporation (FSC), a third-country affiliate through which it can export goods. Most benefits go to a handful of companies. In 2001, for instance, Boeing Corp. (BA) received $222 million in breaks through its FSC.

But the scheme has been declared illegal by the WTO. And U.S. businesses are desperate to replace it with new tax breaks, which, they insist, are essential to staying competitive in the global marketplace. Foreign governments, they note, heavily subsidize their own companies, through tax laws, trade barriers, and direct aid. "Whether we are financing exports or pure financial services, we are essentially competing on price," says Richard D'Avino, a senior vice-president at GE Capital. "A slight difference in cost will determine whether the deal goes to a competitor or to us." And, he adds, taxes can increase GE's costs by 20%.

Critics, however, call the system a giveaway to U.S. companies, largely because multinationals have become so artful at avoiding taxes. They do it two ways: They shift as much income as possible from the U.S. to low-tax nations such as the Caymans or Ireland. And they shuffle tax-deductible expenses from those low-tax countries back to the U.S. The now-infamous practice of reincorporating in Bermuda is "just the tip of the iceberg," says Robert McIntyre, director of Citizens for Tax Justice, a labor-funded tax group. "Bermuda makes it real easy, but it is not the only way to do it."

Although the corporate tax rate in America is 35%, one study found that in 1996 the taxman collected barely 3% on foreign earnings of U.S.-based companies. And tax collections have likely fallen even more as companies get better at shuffling income and costs. Harvard University economist Mihir Desai estimates that big companies slash their taxable income by $84 billion just by reinvesting foreign earnings overseas. Outright sheltering keeps billions more from the tax collector. "We've created a huge amount of complexity, and we collect very little revenue," says Rutgers University economist Rosanne Altshuler.

Some GOP lawmakers, including House Ways & Means Committee Chairman Bill Thomas (R-Calif.), would love to scrap the whole mess. "When people realize how much the U.S. system is out of sync with the rest of the world, we'll have a wholesale reexamination of the tax regime," he says.

Many Democrats, fearful that reform would simply turn into a bigger giveaway, are wary of more than modest changes. Even some business groups worry about getting into a game that will create winners and losers. The National Foreign Trade Council, which represents big multinationals, thinks Congress would be better off repairing the current system rather than replacing it. The tax vice-president at a major U.S.-based bank adds: "Any time you get involved in wholesale changes, you're asking for trouble. The current system is fine for us."

Perhaps, but it is also rife with problems. One reason: The world taxes foreign income two different ways. Much of Europe and the developing world use a territorial system where a country taxes goods and services sold on its soil—no matter where they were produced or where the seller is headquartered.

By contrast, the U.S., along with Britain and Japan, taxes its exporting companies on their worldwide income. To prevent business from being taxed twice, the U.S. gives companies a credit to offset the levies they pay to other countries on the same revenue.

Multinationals get another key benefit. They defer paying taxes on worldwide income until the money is returned to the U.S. Thus, a business can avoid taxes by reinvesting foreign income overseas and manipulating the timing of its decision to return the funds to the U.S.

Less than half of the foreign earnings of U.S. companies are returned to the U.S. parent in any given year. And of profits generated in low-tax countries, just 7% comes back to the U.S.

Companies have also invented creative ways to shift income to low-tax countries. One practice, known as earnings stripping, lets them shuffle patents and other intellectual property to, say, Ireland. The U.S. parent will pay as much as possible in royalties to its Irish subsidiary and deduct those costs against its U.S. taxes. Or a U.S. parent can borrow from a Caribbean affiliate, taking big interest deductions at home. The Internal Revenue Service tries to prevent companies from abusing these practices by limiting the deductions. But companies just find ways around them.

The most lucrative practice is known as transfer pricing. An American manufacturer buys parts from a subsidiary in, say, Singapore. To reduce its U.S. taxes, the company pays the highest possible prices to its overseas affiliates, thus maximizing deductions here and paying relatively low taxes there.

Sometimes, companies get even more aggressive. The most extreme recent example is the Bermuda shuffle, where companies move their paper headquarters to Bermuda—which has no business income tax—even though management remains in the U.S. The new company can not only shelter foreign income but also cut taxes on U.S. revenues. In recent years, companies such as Tyco International, Ingersoll-Rand, and the consulting firm Accenture have set up headquarters in Bermuda.

But these tax savings come at a price. Companies are diverted from the business of selling products and instead focus time and money on cutting taxes. University of Michigan tax economist Joel B. Slemrod estimates that the nation's 500 biggest companies spend more than $1 billion a year complying with the tax laws. And perhaps half of that cost is linked to international tax rules.

The effort to trim can also be disastrous for a company's image. New Britain (Conn.) toolmaker Stanley Works tried the Bermuda shift earlier this year. But following a firestorm of criticism from Congress, shareholders, and unions, Stanley dropped the effort.

Why did Stanley do it? Said CEO John Trani at the time: "Tax rates in other countries are much lower. It's not a choice. If you don't deal with [it], you get extinguished."

Stanley is a straightforward outfit that sells hammers and other tools. But think of the coming struggle over how companies that sell downloadable software or music will be taxed. Sorting out where such products are made and who taxes them will be a nightmare.

Already, the European Union is demanding the right to tax Internet transactions, most of which are generated by U.S. companies. America is trying to persuade other nations to go slow—with little success so far. "The [Europeans] are taking a very hard line," says University of Chicago economist Austan Goolsbee, an Internet tax expert. "They are going to try to impose taxes not just on physical goods but on digitally delivered goods."

Is there a solution to this mess? One possibility is for the U.S. to adopt a variation of the European-style territorial system. Called a dividend exemption regime, it would allow companies to avoid tax on all foreign income—except for passive investments. But it would also bar them from loading up on artificially inflated deductions generated by their foreign subsidiaries.

Today's U.S. system is so inefficient, say economists John Mutti and Harry Grubert, that exempting overseas income from taxes would actually generate $7 billion more for the Treasury than the current regime, which is supposed to be taxing it.

Here's another solution: Limit businesses' ability to defer the taxes they pay on foreign sales. Companies would pay tax on those revenues in the year they are earned, rather than when they repatriate the money back to the U.S. In return, they would get a tax-rate reduction. The plan would end a lot of gaming of the system, simplify the rules, and help investors figure out how much tax companies really pay. But it would also be a cash-flow nightmare for businesses.

A third alternative: Scrap the income tax and replace it with a consumption levy, such as a flat tax. That may seem extreme, but many economists are convinced that today's tax code is breaking down. Says PwC's Merrill: "You're really going to have a difficult time maintaining the income tax in a competitive, fluid, capital market."

In the short run, Congress is likely to go for a much more modest fix. It will drop the now-illegal FSC subsidy and in return, give U.S. business $4 billion in new tax breaks—some aimed at exporters, others aimed at all companies.

But such a solution will only buy time. In the end, Washington is going to have to find a way to modernize its tax code. Or else it can expect to see more and more U.S. companies shipping out.

Subject Index

Case Index